14 - 170 - 836

This Is My Best

America's 85 Greatest Living Authors Present

THIS IS MY BEST

IN THE THIRD QUARTER OF THE CENTURY

Edited by Whit Burnett

PS536
B79

DOUBLEDAY & COMPANY, INC., GARDEN CITY, NEW YORK

Grateful acknowledgment is made to the following for permission to reprint their copyrighted material:

ATHENEUM PUBLISHERS

For "Box," a play by Edward Albee, which appears in the book *Box and Quotations From Chairman Mao-Tse-Tung.* Copyright © 1968, 1969 by Edward Albee. Reprinted by permission. Caution: Professionals and amateurs are hereby warned that "Box," being fully protected under the Copyright Laws of the United States of America, The British Empire, including the Dominion of Canada, and all other countries of the Berne and Universal Copyright Conventions, are subject to royalty. All rights, including professional, amateur, motion picture, recitation, lecturing, public reading, radio and television broadcasting, and the rights of translation into foreign languages, are strictly reserved. Particular emphasis is laid on the question of readings, permission for which must be secured from the author's agent in writing. All inquiries should be addressed to the William Morris Agency, 1350 Avenue of the Americas, New York, N.Y.; "Prologue" to *Caesar at the Rubicon,* a play about politics by Theodore H. White. Copyright © 1968 by Theodore H. White. Reprinted by permission of the author and Atheneum Publishers.

KAY BOYLE

For "The Wild Horses," which appeared in *The Saturday Evening Post.* Copyright © 1966 by Kay Boyle. Reprinted by permission.

GEORGE BRAZILLER, INC.

For "Thee," by Conrad Aiken. Copyright © 1967 by Conrad Aiken. Reprinted by permission.

CITY LIGHTS BOOKS

For "Wales Visitation," from *Planet News* (1961–67). Copyright © 1968 by Allen Ginsberg. Reprinted by permission.

COLUMBIA UNIVERSITY PRESS

For "Art and the Symbol," from *Art and Technics,* by Lewis Mumford (pp. 30–32). Reprinted by permission.

Contents

VI   STORYTELLERS

VII   FIGURES IN THE ROUND

VIII   THE HUMAN ORDEAL

IX   THE COLLOID AND THE CRYSTAL

X   ART AND THE SYMBOL

Foreword

(*From a letter to 6,000 balloters*)

". . . Since both the publishers and I feel that the nominating of authors for this new volume will be a major evaluating project and one beyond the scope of one editor and his associates, we are frankly turning to you and other especially selected authors, editors, librarians, critics, and discerning readers to ask: Will you help select these greatest living American authors?

In the balloting a quarter of a century ago it was no great problem nominating Eugene O'Neill, Ernest Hemingway, H. L. Mencken, Carl Sandburg, Theodore Dreiser, Maxwell Anderson, Edna St. Vincent Millay, Robert Frost, Willa Cather, Sinclair Lewis, Stephen Vincent Benét, Van Wyck Brooks, Dorothy Parker, Langston Hughes, William Faulkner, Elmer Rice, Robinson Jeffers, Carl Van Doren, James Thurber, John Dewey, Richard Wright, and many others.

But in today's changed literary scene, who will replace such authors in *This Is My Best* (in the Third Quarter of the Century) as the greatest living American authors today? . . . authors who, after being chosen will be asked (as in 1942) to make their own selection from their lifetime output and to comment on why they consider it their best.

More than 500 authors have been listed on the ballot. (In 1942 the listed authors numbered 430.)

Many of those in the original *This Is My Best* are still going strong, and their names, of course—John Gunther, Marianne Moore, Edmund Wilson, Erskine Caldwell, Katherine Anne Porter, John Dos Passos, Thornton Wilder, William Saroyan, Archibald MacLeish, Lillian Hellman, S. J. Perelman, Ogden Nash and others—are included on the ballot.

But what about the ones who have risen since the balloting in 1941-42? How do you rate Edward Albee, Truman Capote, Tennessee Williams, Arthur Miller, Eudora Welty, John Hersey, James Dickey, William Alfred, Gore Vidal, Norman Mailer, Jack Kerouac, Louis Auchincloss, James Jones, Bernard Malamud, Henry Miller, J. D. Salinger, William Styron, John Updike, John Ciardi, Robert Lowell, Richard Wilbur, Paddy Chayefsky, Mary McCarthy, George F. Kennan, Elizabeth Hardwick and many more?"

The answers to the questions (asked above in 1968 and 1969) are in this book. And if the wait of almost two years was a long one, it should, we think, be worth it. *This Is My Best In the Third Quarter of the Century,* or the Last Third of the Century, if you prefer, is a cross-section of America and of American writing by eighty-five American authors brought together in this book because their contemporary readers, critics, fellow authors and others decided they should be in it.

The idea of such a community-of-effort is not a new one. *This Is My Best* was originated by this editor at the beginning of the 'forties in the publication of a volume of ninety-three authors, chosen by equally selective balloting. And, as a first of its kind, it was a successful enough venture. One test, I suppose, of the book's quasi-permanent value may be that in spite of its many editions, for twenty-eight years it has been almost impossible for the editor himself to buy a secondhand copy. People who read the authors of those days treasured them—they were famous; they were great; and they said things of importance.

But such is mortality, that, since 1942, more than sixty of the ninety-three writers in that volume are no longer living. Of the thirty surviving authors, however, twenty-two[1] will be found illuminating this volume twenty-eight years later, and six of these, John Steinbeck, Thornton Wilder, Archibald MacLeish, Katherine Anne Porter, Marianne Moore and John Dos Passos, were among the current top twenty-four vote-getters. "With two exceptions (Galbraith and Lippmann)[2]," David Dempsey, of the *Saturday Review,* observed of the balloting, "the leaders were 'creative' writers, a pleasant reversal of the current publishing emphasis on nonfiction."

If there were giants in the old days, it takes time to make giants. And time cuts down giants, too. In 1942 America had three living winners of the Nobel Prize for Literature, Sinclair Lewis, first in 1930, Eugene O'Neill, in 1936, and Pearl Buck, 1938, all included in the *Best* of that period. *This Is My Best* today may well contain future candidates, since among the ninety-three authors in the 1942 collection three did not receive that recognition until much later: William Faulkner did not receive the Nobel Prize until 1948, Ernest Hemingway until 1954, and John Steinbeck until 1962. Writers who were not in the earlier collection and who have made their reputations since 1942, some since 1960, constitute three quarters of the authors in *This Is My Best* today.

[1] Authors who were in the 1942 volume and who, with different selections, are also represented in this are: Conrad Aiken, Kay Boyle, Pearl Buck, Erskine Caldwell, John Dos Passos, James T. Farrell, John Gunther, Joseph Wood Krutch, Archibald MacLeish, Marianne Moore, Lewis Mumford, Ogden Nash, Allan Nevins, S. J. Perelman, Katherine Anne Porter, William Saroyan, William L. Shirer, Cornelia Otis Skinner, John Steinbeck, Jesse Stuart, Mark Van Doren and E. B. White. The "new" authors are in the contents.

[2] See combined list of ballots in the Appendix.

Given the premise that these are not the personal choices of an editor or a publisher but an attempt to assay quality and stature through the opinions (mostly signed) of a dozen or so categories of literary-minded people throughout the country, some rather special in their fields, *This Is My Best* is more a repository of values than an avant-garde experiment in their dissolution. It is not a book of young discoveries, but of more full-fledged writers, or as Dempsey put it, more seasoned timber than young sprouts. It is a book, in short, composed by writers of many books, writers who use words and not pictures, film, pigments, bronze or tomato cans to express themselves. And all of it was written prior to man's first step on the moon—even Dr. Asimov's piece about the planets—and thus is not in competition with some other expressions of modernity that could be faddish and ephemeral. Its energy is less kinetic, mechanical, pop or electronic than human, an area where artistic standards are relevant in the struggle for permanence.

Tennessee Williams, who has enjoyed perhaps the greatest success of any playwright of his generation, was, as the record shows, No. 1 author in the combined votes of all categories of voters. John Steinbeck, who died after his selection was made, came second; the Americanized English poet, W. H. Auden, was third; a short story writer and novelist, J. D. Salinger was fourth most-voted-for-inclusion; and next in order came three more playwrights, Edward Albee, Thornton Wilder, a novelist, of course, too, and Arthur Miller; with Russian-born Vladimir Nabokov (naturalized in 1945) eighth; Walter Lippmann, the journalist, ninth; and Archibald Mac-Leish, poet, playwright and critic, tenth.

In what order the various groups voted for their authors will be found in the Appendix. For a person holding this book, what is perhaps more important is whether *This Is My Best* is an interesting, readable, significant and enjoyable appraisal of contemporary writing worth the labor it took to assemble. We think it is.

Specifically, of the eighty-five authors, thirty write novels or short stories, nineteen are poets, fifteen are historians, biographers or journalists, five are dramatists, and sixteen are essayists covering everything from natural history and human behavior to theories of space. Frequently the work is quite intimate, as in the *Portraits,* where, for instance, Nabokov's "best" is a short, lyrical portrait of his mother gathering mushrooms in a long-vanished Russia, a scene he regards with more retrospective delight, we must surmise, than his novels like *Lolita* or perhaps even *Ada.* Or is it that death and distance deepen involvement for an author, and such finality gives a special aura to things which makes an author prefer such a work to other of his fictions? I think of Capote's little girl in the South, dressing like a fine lady, and killed by the car; Alfred Kazin's intimate family portrait of the Aunt in the household of his youth and childhood; the two appraisals of John F. Kennedy, after his death, by James Reston and Arthur M. Schlesinger, Jr.

There is only one piece in *This Is My Best* that was chosen before by its author and chosen again this generation later. The author is Marianne Moore, who, in the year of her 81st birthday when she got a gold medal from highly appreciative circles, wrote of her original selection twenty-eight years before: "Bach plays back Bach . . ." Thus a generation later, an indomitable spirit was still asking her poetic question, "What Are Years?"

The book is not divided into Best Biographers, Best Dramatists, Best Novelists, et cetera. Writers cross boundaries these days as soundlessly as technicians move in space. A playwright may be a novelist and a poet, and sometimes, like Williams, something of a poet in the play form. And another, Norman Mailer, who did, after all, settle on a segment from a novel, seems to be almost anything protean he sets his mind to, except perhaps the elected mayor of a metropolis. The seeming paucity of literary criticism in this volume may be because some critics when asked for their best came back with poetry. On the other hand, we found no poet selecting as his best anything but poems.

The ten rather loosely unified sections are: (1) *The American Scene,* opening with John Updike's Pennsylvania home place in an essay-like story of many facets, and closing with *Where's a Poet From?* by the Illinois-born good gray Conway, Massachusetter, Archibald MacLeish; (11) in *The Old History and the New,* Allan Nevins sets the tone, Barbara Tuchman, John Kenneth Galbraith, Bruce Catton, Norman Cousins and Henry Steele Commager particularize; John Hersey ventures into China for his story, Harrison Salisbury's best reviews the myth of Stalinism, and Will and Ariel Durant range the whole field of history from the Greeks to us; (111) *A Gallery of Portraits* is what it says it is, as nostalgic as Phyllis McGinley's *Girl with Comic Book* and as naturalistic as Philip Roth's *O, This Father!* (IV) *Nobody Knows My Name* is black and white, from Styron's Virginia of 1831 through Cass Mastern's South of a generation later, to the present day of Ralph Ellison, James Baldwin and Gwendolyn Brooks, with an aside from Robert Lowell; (v) in *Thanksgiving for a Habitat,* the poets find a home, or seek one; (VI) *Storytellers* tell their stories; (VII) *Figures in the Round* considers Caesar, Michaelangelo, Thomas Wolfe, and the Kennedy of Schlesinger and Reston; (VIII) *The Human Ordeal* is man a little short on dignity, from E. B. White's man and pig and Buchwald's answers to the young, to Henry Miller's metaphysical lostness in the world, and Joseph Heller's *Lieutenant Scheisskopf,* with related predicaments from Cornelia Otis Skinner, John Barth, Ogden Nash, James T. Farrell, Tom Wolfe, the reporter in depth, and S. J. Perelman with his moths; (IX) *The Colloid and the Crystal* takes its title from Joseph Wood Krutch's studied essay on forms in nature, a nature as a *Boundless Deep* for Michener and the oceanic origins of Hawaii, and something else again for Steinbeck; the vastness of the Sahara for John Gunther, a matrix of Utopias for Margaret Mead, and infinite space (and communication problems) for Dr. Asimov; (X) *Art and the Symbol* concludes the book with, among others, Mary McCarthy, who settles the Colonel's hash; William F. Buckley, Jr. at odds with his Church over the things done to the Latin Mass; Thornton Wilder, dramatizing the Fates; Allen Tate, the critic, a poet here with *Seasons of the Soul;* Erich Fromm, analyzing *Hope, Faith and Fortitude;* Edward Albee abstracting humanity in his one-act *Box;* Pearl Buck coming home to a strange, emotional, fleeting, psychic experience; and Conrad Aiken with a metaphysical poem, *Thee.*

So, such seasoned folk of letters have produced in their lifetimes that combination of quality and bulk which Thomas Mann once said was essential to greatness in the artist.

A few words on omissions. Humorists, for example, are very scarce these days. They are scarce everywhere, according to Representative S. J. Perelman (Erwinna, Pennsylvania). "Humor that's destined for print," he told a *New York Times* reporter in 1969, "has almost entirely disappeared because of the growth of communications. What passes for humor on TV doesn't deserve the name." And with fewer humorists (and philosophers whom readers know and recognize) writers of the old familiar essay are also in short supply, as Clifton Fadiman recently bemoaned. "They are victims," he says, "of a literary taste that runs to the spontaneous, the wild and dynamic. The familiar essay does not attempt to surprise the reader, overwhelm, defy or attack him," he told the journalist John Leo. "Rather it offers him a civilized, often humorous view of human life. The tone is intimate. It assumes an audience of fairly intelligent, educated people. For all these reasons, it's very unpopular now."

We regret some name-authors are not in this book through no fault of the editor. There is no way to force or bribe a writer to tell you what he considers his own best work. Some would rather name their worst, avoiding perhaps any show of *hubris.* Walter Lippmann was "most flattered," he wrote, "but I do not feel that I am a competent judge of my own work and therefore am unable to participate." And of his journalist friends, who have read him since "The Scholar in a Troubled World," his Phi Beta Kappa address at Harvard which stands up today as well as when he wrote it in 1932, none would take it on himself to choose for Mr. Lippmann. Edmund Wilson, the novelist, essayist, and a critic of almost everything including the Internal Revenue Service, chose to be a dropout because, he said, in 1942 a very long selection of his in *This Is My Best* was trimmed by the publisher (unbeknownst to the editor) and while we were willing to offer to print it again in toto if it was his selection, Mr. Wilson did more than demur, he enumerated gratuitously twenty-one other things he regretted he "finds it impossible for him to do," including (for history) autographing books for strangers and donating copies of his books to libraries.

Several significant authors of our time have died, among them Upton Sinclair, Conrad Richter, and Max Eastman. Some were just too busy with their work, like Catherine Drinker Bowen. Lillian Hellman, for the same reason, begged off "until next time." Since, for this editor, a book like this comes only once a generation and, at most, twice a lifetime, next time, all things considered, may be a little late for both of us.

Samuel Eliot Morison, who ranked high with our advisers, should be here with the signing of the Peace Treaty with Japan, but the Admiral, on a trip around the world, did not care to excerpt from the fourteenth (and last) volume of his distinguished nineteen-year work, *The History of the United States Naval Operations in World War II*. And James Gould Cozzens wrote that he could not decide upon his best. The problem of choice produced an extraordinary aversion in the case of John Cheever, who so dislikes to go back to anything once its published he'd rather be out than in. He never keeps a book of his own in his house more than a few weeks after it has appeared, he says, never reads over his past work and has no opinions about it.

For this editor who had Salinger in his writing class at Columbia University and published his first four short stories in *Story,* it is not easy to admit that Jerry is not in this collection. Actually he is in practically nobody's collection, and if he were anywhere he would be here. But that's his way now; even as fourth man on the list of 517 authors voted upon, he is skittish of selecting anything for anyone. "Sorry, Whit, but that's hardly news to you. Friendly regards, otherwise."

Dr. Reinhold Niebuhr might well have been among our few living philosopher-theologians, for he was in *This Is My Philosophy* some years ago, but he wrote he did not have the "strength or inclination to make a judgment and supply an introduction."

In this assembly, eight-five distinguished American authors, whose distinction and integrity are outstanding, have affirmed their confidence in their art, their judgment and this undertaking, ten more than were promised in the project, all uniformly sharing in its work, its possible increment, and whatever of critical appreciation or disfavor may be. And if there is not here a "God's plenty," to paraphrase John Dryden's comment on Chaucer's *Canterbury Tales,* then here is America's plenty from a plentiful country, with many of its values, implied or explicit, from its creative workers, recording, in one way or another, themselves and their times.

When he chose his *America Was Promises* in 1942, Archibald MacLeish wrote: "It is a poem about America. But more about ourselves . . . and it tells us . . . that unless the people of a country, the whole people of a country, make the promises come true for the sake of the people, others will make them come true. And not for the sake of the people. For the sake of others." . . . That year another poet, William Carlos Williams, the physician, commented: "The life of my day has breathed into these poems whatever value they have." Oddly, many of that day's greats were not at all averse to naming their "best," and some, like Hemingway, Mencken, and Dreiser, were quite casual. Sinclair Lewis, who, like Cheever, never opened his books "after the pleasant first five minutes when they come new from the publisher," passed the buck to Carl Van Doren, who chose *Dinner with the Babbitts,* to the complete approval of Mr. Lewis, which permitted him, he wrote, "to reserve my perusal of the opera of Mr. Sinclair Lewis for my old age, just after I shall have finished Dante and Sir Hall Caine and a manual of the wild flowers." e. e. cummings wrote: "please honour my contribution by surrounding it with a little silence. Silence is lively; and deathful is doubletalk, eg la guerre."

The new comments in *This Is My Best* speak for themselves. Today MacLeish, for instance, turns from his plays in verse and poems-to-the-nation—or to the moon—preferring a few quiet, highly personal poems, about a dead Hemingway, a good wife, Sandburg gone, boulders in a New England pasture "praising the world by being in it, praising the earth by being stone . . ." and, like the old friend Robert Frost he quotes, hopes only " 'to leave a few poems it will be hard to get rid of.' "

"There are those who say that literature is on the way out," Alan Pryce-Jones, the critic, wrote recently in the New York *Post.* "It seems to me more than likely that it is temporarily being suffocated by talent." A hundred years ago, there was little talent, he avers, but "some genius," and such great ones were writing then as Dickens, Whitman, Dostoyevsky, Hugo, Nietzsche, Arnold, Manzoni and Perez Galdos, "with greatness in varying degrees spread over many countries."

Literature, alas (especially the novel and, of course, the drama) is often viewed as a departing shade, wasted of its former grandeur. Perhaps the greatness of the dead always overshadows the stature of the living. Faulkner, once a talent, was not always recognized for genius. Perhaps, as readers, the better part of profit is to take what the passing decade sifts out, and then enjoy what stands up for the quarter, and leave the century to the critics, academies and revivals.

For, essentially, the people in this book are living with us now.

It has been a privilege in one lifetime of editing to have had dealings with the authors in these two large, related books[3], *This Is My Best,* 1942, and *This Is My Best,* 1970, among whose pages were many greats and some good personal friends. These books cover a good part of the writing century, from Agnes Replier, the essayist, born in 1858, and George Ade, the humorist, born ten years later (and Booth Tarkington, Upton Sinclair, Joseph Hergesheimer, John Dewey, Carl Van Doren, and eighty-six others) to Philip Roth, Tom Wolfe, Allen Ginsberg, and Henry Miller today. If the first contained those authors risen to fame in the first forty-two years of the 1900s, this new volume contains most of the survivors of the first book and a preponderant representation of the new growth in American letters since the 'forties. In the year 2000, perhaps some other editor will bring out a final volume, with living comments also, to complete a century of the written word in American.

For a two-generation-spanning experience, I join my publishers in thanking all who helped in this project, the voters, advisers (who shall be specified in the Appendix), the publishers, editors, agents, Ken McCormick and Sally Arteseros at Doubleday and my perennial consultant, Hallie Burnett in Connecticut, and, above all, the authors in this book for each his special art and individuality, for the time and effort and correspondence and patience that combined to launch and finish a joint effort in bright, particular words in a great variety of form and substance at a period when the form and substance of writing and many things else are under wide and deepening scrutiny.

WHIT BURNETT

[3] Three, really, if you have a copy of the 103 greatest contemporary authors in *The World's Best,* (1950).

I
The American Scene

John Updike

PACKED DIRT, CHURCHGOING, A DYING CAT, A TRADED CAR

Dear Mr. Burnett:

Your 1942 anthology was one of the treasured books in our house, so I think I am acquainted with the format; of course I am delighted to be included. I would nominate, as my contribution, the short story *Packed Dirt*, etc., from the collection *Pigeon Feathers*.

This would be my comment:

Each of my efforts is the best I can do at that time, on that project. For a reader, the "best" would be the one that works best, contains the most truth, for him. I am often surprised—pleasantly—by the moments of my *oeuvre* especially treasured by a correspondent or a critic. For of course I do have my lurking suspicions, my lurking favorites. The short story lengthily titled "Packed Dirt, Churchgoing, A Dying Cat, A Traded Car" was written, as I remember, in the spring of 1961, at a time when my wits seemed sunk in a bog of anxiety and my customary doubts that I could write another word appeared unusually well justified. Slowly I had begun to piece together a montage of aborted ideas eventually published as "The Blessed Man of Boston, My Grand-mother's Thimble, and Fanning Island" and in the same slow motion, that paralyzed Spring, I continued with the story I suggest you reprint. If the story is dense, it is because there was a pressure of memory and worry upon it; as these farflung images collected at my typewriter, a bigger better kind of music felt to be arising out of compression. Staleness and dread evidently wanted to sing. I seemed to understand at last Proust's remark about the essence of the writer's task being the perception of con-

nections between unlike things. The themes here interwoven—
and there is a good deal of conscious art in this farraginous narrative, and more fiction than may meet the eye—had long been
present to me: paternity and death, earth and faith and cars. But
I had not seized them so directly before. It was to be the last of
my stories about Pennsylvania, and foreshadows, in the incident
precipitating the hero's plunge into terror, the sexual themes that
have unaccountably concerned me since. But the heart of the
story, toward which all tends, is of course the father, his generous and comical manner of dying. As might as well be said of
the subsequent novel, my favorite, *The Centaur:* it is a good
story because it has a good man in it.

Best wishes,
John Updike

Cumberland Terrace,
London

Different things move us. I, David Kern, am always affected—reassured,
nostalgically pleased, even, as a member of my animal species, made proud
—by the sight of bare earth that has been smoothed and packed firm by
the passage of human feet. Such spots abound in small towns: the furtive
break in the playground fence dignified into a thoroughfare, the trough of
dust underneath each swing, the blurred path worn across a wedge of
grass, the anonymous little mound or embankment polished by play and
strewn with pebbles like the confetti aftermath of a wedding. Such unconsciously humanized intervals of clay, too humble and common even to
have a name, remind me of my childhood, when one communes with dirt
down among the legs, as it were, of presiding fatherly presences. The earth
is our playmate then, and the call to supper has a piercingly sweet escha-
tological ring.

The corner where I now live was recently widened so that the cars
going back and forth to the summer colony on the Point would not be
troubled to slow down. My neighbor's house was sold to the town and

wrecked and picked clean by salvagers and finally burned in a great bonfire of old notched beams and splintered clapboards that leaped tree-high throughout one whole winter day's cold drizzle. Then bulldozers, huge and yellow and loud, appeared on the street and began to gnaw, it seemed, at the corner of our house. My third child, a boy not yet two, came running from the window in tearful panic. After I tried to soothe him with an explanation, he followed me through the house sobbing and wailing " 'Sheen! 'Sheen!" while the machines made our rooms shake with the curses of their labor. They mashed my neighbor's foundation stones into the earth and trimmed the levelled lot just as my grandmother used to trim the excess dough from the edge of the pieplate. They brought the curve of the road right to the corner of my property, and the beaten path that does for a sidewalk in front of my home was sheared diagonally by a foot-high cliff.

Last night I was coming back from across the street, fresh from an impromptu civic lamentation with a neighbor at how unsightly, now that the snow was melted, the awkward-shaped vacant lot the bulldozers had left looked, with its high raw embankment gouged by rivulets and littered with old chimney bricks. And soon, we concluded, now that spring was here, it would be bristling with weeds. Crossing from this conversation, I noticed that where my path had been lopped the cliff no longer existed; feet—children's feet, mostly, for mostly children walk in our town—had worn the sharpness away and molded a little ramp by which ascent was easier.

This small modification, this modest work of human erosion, seemed precious to me not only because it recalled, in the slope and set of the dirt, a part of the path that long ago had led down from my parents' back yard to the high-school softball field. It seemed precious because it had been achieved accidentally, and had about it that repose of grace that is beyond willing. We in America have from the beginning been cleaving and baring the earth, attacking, reforming the enormity of nature we were given, which we took to be hostile. We have explored, on behalf of all mankind, this paradox: the more matter is outwardly mastered, the more it overwhelms us in our hearts. Evidence—gaping right-of-ways, acres mercilessly scraped, bleeding mountains of muddy fill—surrounds us of a war that is incapable of ceasing, and it is good to know that now there are enough of us to exert a counter-force. If craters were to appear in our landscape tomorrow, the next day there would be usable paths threading down the blasted sides. As our sense of God's forested legacy to us dwindles, there grows, in these worn, rubbed, and patted patches, a sense of human legacy

—like those feet of statues of saints which have lost their toes to centuries
of kisses. One thinks of John Dewey's definition of God as the union of
the actual and the ideal.

There was a time when I wondered why more people did not go to
church. Taken purely as a human recreation, what could be more delightful,
more unexpected than to enter a venerable and lavishly scaled building
kept warm and clean for use one or two hours a week and to sit and
stand in unison and sing and recite creeds and petitions that are like paths
worn smooth in the raw terrain of our hearts? To listen, or not listen, as
a poorly paid but resplendently robed man strives to console us with scraps
of ancient epistles and halting accounts, hopelessly compromised by words,
of those intimations of divine joy that are like pain in that, their instant
gone, the mind cannot remember or believe them; to witness the windows
donated by departed patrons and the altar flowers arranged by withdrawn
hands and the whole considered spectacle lustrous beneath its patina of
inheritance; to pay, for all this, no more than we are moved to give—
surely in all democracy there is nothing like it. Indeed, it is the most
available democratic experience. We vote less than once a year. Only in
church and at the polls are we actually given our supposed value, the soul-
unit of one, with its noumenal arithmetic of equality: one equals one
equals one.

My preaching fouls the words and corrupts me. Belief builds itself
unconsciously and in consciousness is spent. Throughout my childhood I
felt nothing in church but boredom and an oppressive futility. For reasons
my father never explained, he was a dutiful churchman; my mother, who
could use her senses, who had read Santayana and Wells, stayed home
Sunday mornings, and I was all on her side, on the side of phenomena,
in those years, though I went, with the other children, to Sunday school.
It was not until we moved from the town and joined a country church
that I, an adolescent of fifteen, my head a hotbed of girls and literature,
felt a pleasant emotion in church. During Lent—that dull season, those
forty suspended days during which Spring is gathering the mineral energy
to make the resurrection that the church calendar seizes upon as conven-
iently emblematic—I ushered with my father at the Wednesday-night
services. We would arrive in our old car—I think it was the Chevrolet then
—on those raw March nights and it pleasantly surprised me to find the
building warm, the stoked furnace already humming its devotions in the
basement. The nave was dimly lit, the congregation small, the sermon
short, and the wind howled a nihilistic counterpoint beyond the black win-

dows blotted with garbled apostles; the empty pews, making the minister seem remote and small and emblematic, intensified our sensation of huddling. There was a strong sepia flavor of early Christianity: a minority flock furtively gathered within the hostile enormity of a dying, sobbing empire. From the rear, the broad back and baked neck of the occasional dutiful son loomed bullishly above the black straw hats of the mischievous-looking old ladies, gnarled by farmwork, who sat in their rows like withered apples on the shelves of a sweet-smelling cellar. My father would cross and uncross and recross his legs and stare at his thoughts, which seemed distant. It was pleasant to sit beside him in the rear pew. He was not much of a man for sitting still. When my parents and I went to the movies, he insisted on having the aisle seat, supposedly to give his legs room. After about twenty minutes he would leap up and spend the rest of the show walking around in the back of the theatre drinking water and talking to the manager while my mother and I, abandoned, consoled ourselves with the flickering giants of make-believe. He had nothing of the passive in him; a church always became, for him, something he helped run. It was pleasant, and even momentous, when the moment for action came, to walk by his side up the aisle, the thump of our feet the only sound in the church, and to take the wooden, felt-floored plates from a shy blur of white robes and to administer the submission of alms. Coins and envelopes sought to cover the felt. I condescended, stooping gallantly into each pew. The congregation seemed The Others, reaching, with quarters glittering in their crippled fingers, toward mysteries in which I was snugly involved. Even to usher at a church mixes us with the angels, and is a dangerous thing.

The churches of the Village had this Second Century quality. In Manhattan, Christianity is so feeble its future seems before it. One walks to church past clattering cafeterias and ravaged newsies in winter weather that is always a shade of Lent, on pavements spangled with last night's vomit. The expectantly hushed shelter of the church is like one of those spots worn bare by a softball game in a weed-filled vacant lot. The presence of the city beats like wind at the glowing windows. One hastens home afterward, head down, hurrying to assume the disguise—sweaters and suntans—of a non-churchgoer. I tried not to go, but it was not in me not to go. I never attended the same church two Sundays in succession, for fear I would become known, and be expected. To be known by face and name and financial weight robs us of our unitary soul, enrolls us against those Others. Devil's work. We are the others. It is of the essence to be a stranger in church.

On the island the very color of my skin made me strange. This Caribbean island had been abandoned to the descendants of its slaves. Their church was on a hill; it has since been demolished, I have learned from letters, by a hurricane. To reach it one climbed a steep path made treacherous by the loose rubble of coral rock, jagged gray clinkers that bore no visible relation to the pastel branches that could be plucked, still pliant, from the shallows by Maid's Beach. Dull-colored goats were tethered along the path; their forelegs were tangled in their ropes so tightly that whenever they nodded the bush anchoring them nodded in answer. For windows the church possessed tall arched apertures filled not with stained glass but with air and outward vision; one could see the goats stirring the low foliage and the brightly dressed little girls who had escaped the service playing on the packed dirt around the church. The service was fatiguingly long. There were exhaustive petitionary prayers (for the Queen, the Prime Minister, Parliament) and many eight-versed hymns sung with a penetrating, lingering joy and accompanied by a hand-pumped organ. The organ breathed in and out, loud and soft, and the congregation, largely female, followed its ebb and flow at a brief but noticeable distance; their lips moved behind the singing, so I seemed immersed in an imperfectly synchronized movie. Musical stress, the British accent, and Negro elision worked upon the words a triple harmony of distortion. "Lait eth's waadsa *cull* raio-ind . . ." Vainly seeking my place in the hymn—for without a visual key I was lost—I felt lifted within a sweet, soughing milk, an aspiring chant as patient as the nodding of the goats.

Throughout the service, restless deacons slipped in and out of the windows. Bored myself—for we grow sated even with consolation—I discovered that without moving from my pew I too could escape through those tall portals built to admit the breeze. I rested my eyes on earth's wide circle round. From this height the horizon of the sea was lifted halfway up the sky. The Caribbean seemed a steeply tilted blue plane to which the few fishing boats in the bay below had been attached like magnetized toys. God made the world, Aquinas says, in play.

Matter has its radiance and its darkness; it lifts and it buries. Things compete; a life demands a life. On another English island, in Oxford—it is a strange fact about Americans, that we tend to receive our supernatural mail on foreign soil—I helped a cat die. The incident had the signature: decisive but illegible. For six years I did not tell my wife about it, for fear it would frighten her. Some hours before, I had left her at the hospital in the early stages of labor. Wearing a sterilized gown and mask, I had visited her in a white-tiled room along whose walls gleaming gutters stood ready to drain torrents of blood. Her face, scrubbed and polished, was fervent like a child's, and she seemed, lying there swathed in white, ready for nothing so much as a graduation ceremony. She would break off talking, and listen as if to the distant voice of a schoolmistress, and her face would grow rapt, and when the contraction had passed she would sigh and say, "That was a good one," and chatter some more to me of how I would feed myself alone and who I would send the telegrams to.

Shooed from the room, stripped of my mask, I tried to wait, and was told, the comical husband of the American cartoons, to run on home; it would be a time. I went outside and took a bus home. It was the last day of March. I had been born in March, and I had looked forward to welcoming my child to the month; but she was late. We lived on Iffley Road, and around midnight, for some reason—I think to mail a letter, but what letter could have been that important?—I was out walking a few blocks from our flat. The night was cold enough for gloves. The sensations of turning into a father—or, rather, the lack of sensations; the failure of sympathetic pain, the hesitation of dread, the postponement of pride—made the street seem insubstantial. There was not that swishing company of headlights that along an American road throws us into repeated relief. The brick homes, save for an occasional introverted glow in an upstairs window, were dark in the vehement shadows of privacy behind the dry hedges and spiked walls. The streetlamps—wintry, reserved—drain color from everything. Myself a shadow, I noticed another in the center of the road. A puddle of black, as I watched, it curled on itself; its ends lifted from the macadam and seemed to stretch in a yawn. Then it became inert again. I was horrified; the shape was about the size of a baby. When it curled the second time, I went to it, my footsteps the only sound in the street.

It was a cat that had been struck by a car. Struck but not quite killed: a testament to the modest speed and sensible size of English automobiles. By the impersonal witness of the lamps burning in the trees I couldn't be sure what color its fur was—it seemed orange-yellow, tabbied with stripes of dark ginger. The cat was plump and wore a collar. Someone had loved it. Blackness from one ear obscured one side of its head and when I touched her it was like a cup. For the third time, the cat stretched, the tips of its hind feet quivering luxuriously in that way cats have. With a great spastic effort it flipped over onto its other side, but made no cry. The only sound between us was my crooning as I carried it to the side of the street and laid it behind the nearest hedge.

A sallow upstairs light in this home was glowing. I wondered if the cat was theirs. Was it their love invested in my hands? Were they watching as I pushed, crouching, with my burden through their hedge? I wondered if I would be taken for a trespasser, a "poacher"; as an American, I was nervous of English tabus. In my own brutal country it was a not uncommon insult to kill a cat and throw the body into an enemy's yard, and I was afraid that this would be taken that way. I thought of writing a note to explain everything, but I had no paper and pen. I explained to the cat, how I was taking her (I felt it was female) out of the street so no more cars would hit her, how I would put her here in the nice safe dirt behind the hedge, where she could rest and get well. I did not believe she would get well; I think she was dead already. Her weight had felt dead in my hands and when I laid her down she did not stretch or twitch again.

Back in my flat, I discovered that one glove was smeared with blood. Most of the palm and three of the fingers were dyed wine-brown. I hadn't realized there was so much blood. I took off my gloves and carefully wrote a note, explaining that I had found this cat in the middle of the street, still alive, and that I had put it behind this hedge to be safe. If, as I thought, the cat was dead, I hoped that the finders would bury it. After some deliberation, I signed my name and address. I walked back and tucked the note under the cat's body, which seemed at home behind the hedge; it suffered my intrusion a trifle stiffly. It suggested I was making too much fuss, and seemed to say to me, *Run on home.*

Back is my flat once more, I felt abruptly tired, though my heart was pounding hugely. I went to bed and set the alarm for three and read a book. I remember the title, it was Chesterton's *The Everlasting Man.* I turned off the light and prayed for my wife and, though I did not believe myself capable of it, fell asleep. The alarm at three came crashing into some innocent walk of a dream and my frail head felt like a hollow cup. I dressed and went out to the public phone booth a block away and called the hospital. A chirping voice, after some rummaging in the records, told me that several hours ago, in the first hour of April (in the United States it was still March), a perfect female infant had been born. To me.

The next morning, after all the telegrams had been managed, I went back to the hedge, and the cat and my note were gone. Though I had left my address, I never received a letter.

When we returned from England, we bought a car. We had ordered it through my parents from folders they had sent us, and, though its shade of blue was more naïve, more like a robin's egg, than we had expected, this '55 Ford proved an excellent buy. Whether being shuffled from side to side of West Eighty-fifth Street every morning or being rammed in second gear up a washed-out mountain road in Vermont, it never complained. In New York, hot tar from a roof-patching job rained onto its innocent paint, and in Vermont its muffler was racked and rent on a shelf of rock, and in Massachusetts it wallowed, its hot clutch stinking, up from repeated graves of snow. Not only sand and candy wrappers accumulate in a car's interior, but heroisms and instants of communion. We in America make love in our cars, and listen to ball games, and plot our wooing of the dollar: small wonder the landscape is sacrificed to these dreaming vehicles of our ideal and onrushing manhood.

In the beginning, my wife and I would lovingly lave with soap and warm water the unflecked skin of the hood as if it were the thorax of a broad blue baby, and toward the end we let the gallant old heap rust where it would. Its eggshell finish grew grizzled with the stains of dropped maple seeds. Its doors balked at closing; its windows refused to roll down. But I somehow never believed we would ever trade it in, though the little girl born across the ocean in the ominous turning of April, now a vocal and status-conscious democrat of nearly six, applied more and more petulant pressure. The deal was consummated while my soul had its face turned, and Detroit the merciless mother contracted to devour her child. But before the new car arrived, there was a month's grace, and in this grace I enjoyed a final fling with my car, my first, my only—for all the others will be substitutes. It happened this way:

Dancing at a party with a woman not my wife, it seemed opportune to turn her hand in mine and kiss her palm. For some time her thighs had been slithering against mine, and, between dances, she developed a nervous clumsy trick of lurching against me, on tiptoe, and rubbing her breasts against my forearm, which was braced across my chest as I held a cigarette. My first thought was that I might burn her; my second, that Nature in her gruff maternal way had arranged one of her opportunities—as my mother, when I was a child, would unpredictably determine to give me a birthday or Hallowe'en party. Obediently I bowed my head and kissed my friend's moist palm. As it withdrew from the advance, her fingertips caressed my chin in the absent-minded manner of one fingering the muzzle of an importunate dog. The exchange transposed us into a higher key; I could hardly hear my own voice, and our dancing lost all connection with the music, and my hand explored her spine from a great aerial distance. Her back seemed mysteriously taut and hard; the body of a strange woman retains more of its mineral content, not being transmuted, through familiarity, into pure emotion. In a sheltered corner of the room we stopped dancing altogether and talked, and what I distinctly remember is how her hands, beneath the steady and opaque appraisal of her eyes, in nervous slurred agitation blindly sought mine and seized and softly gripped, with infantile instinct, my thumbs. Just my thumbs she held, and as we talked she moved them this way and that as if she were steering me. When I closed my eyes, the red darkness inside my lids was trembling, and when I rejoined my wife, and held her to dance, she asked, "Why are you panting?"

After we got home, and surveyed our four children, and in bed read a few pages made unbearably brilliant by their patina of martinis, and turned out the light, she surprised me by not turning her back. Alcohol, with its loosening effect, touches women more deeply than men in this respect; or perhaps, like a matched pair of tuning forks, I had set her vibrating. Irritated by whatever illicit stimulations, we took it out on each other.

To my regret, I survived the natural bliss of satiety—when each muscle is like a petal snugly curved in a corolla of benediction—and was projected onto the wrinkled, azoic territory of insomnia. That feathery anxious embrace of my erect thumbs tormented me in twenty postures. My stomach turned in love of that woman; I feared I would be physically sick and lay on my back gingerly and tried to soothe myself with the caress of headlights as they evolved from bright slits on the wall into parabolically accelerating fans on the ceiling that then vanished: this phenomenon, with its intimations of a life beyond me, had comforted wakeful nights in my earliest childhood. In Sunday school I had been struck by the passage in which Jesus says that to lust after a woman in thought is the same as committing adultery. Now I found myself helplessly containing the conviction that souls, not deeds, are judged. To feel a sin was to commit it; to touch the brink was to be on the floor of the chasm. The universe that so easily permitted me to commit adultery became, by logical steps each one of which went more steeply down than the one above it, a universe that would easily permit me to die. The enormities of cosmic space, the maddening distension of time, history's forgotten slaughters, the child smothered in the dumped icebox, the recent breakdown of the molecular life-spiral, the proven physiological roots of the mind, the presence in our midst of idiots, Eichmanns, animals, and bacteria—all this evidence piled on, and I seemed already eternally forgotten. The dark vibrating air of my bedroom seemed the dust of my grave; the dust went up and up and I prayed upward into it, prayed, prayed for a sign, any glimmer at all, any microscopic loophole or chink in the chain of evidence, and saw none. I remembered a movie I had seen as a child in which a young criminal, moaning insanely, is dragged on rubber legs down the long corridor to the electric chair. I became that criminal. My brain in its calcium vault shouted about injustice, thundered accusations into the lustreless and tranquil homogeneity of the air. Each second my agony went unanswered justified it more certainly: the God who permitted me this fear was unworthy of existence. Each instant my horror was extended amplified God's non-existence, so, as the graph of certain equations fluctuates more and more widely as it moves along the lateral coördinate, or as the magnetic motive-power in atom-smashers accelerates itself, I was caught in a gathering vortex whose unbearably shrill pitch moved me at last to drop my weight on my wife's body and beg, "Wake up. Elaine. I'm so frightened."

I told her of the centuries coming when our names would be forgotten, of the millennia when our nation would be a myth and our continent an ocean, of the aeons when our earth would be vanished and the stars themselves diffused into a uniform and irreversible tepidity. As, an hour before, I had transferred my lust to her, so now I tried to pass my fear into her. It seemed to offend her sense of good taste that I was jealous of future aeons and frantic because I couldn't live through them; she asked me if I had never been so sick I gave up caring whether I lived or died. This contemptible answer—the decrepit Stoic response—acquired a curious corroboration: eventually, just as I had during the strenuous birth of my fatherhood, I fell asleep, and dreamt of innocent and charming scenes.

The next day, a Saturday, was my birthday. It passed like any day except that underneath the camouflage of furniture and voices and habitual actions I felt death like a wide army invisibly advancing. The newspaper told of nothing but atrocities. My children, wounded and appalled in their competition, came to me to be comforted and I was dismayed to see myself, a gutted shell, appearing to them as the embodiment and pledge of a safe universe. Friends visited, and for the first time truly in my life I realized that each face is suppressing knowledge of an immense catastrophe; our faces are dams that wrinkle under the strain. Around six the telephone rang. It was my mother calling from Pennsylvania; I assumed she had called because of my birthday, so I chattered humorously about the discomforts of growing old for a minute before she could tell me, her voice growing faint, the news. My father was in the hospital. He had been walking around with chest pains for two weeks and suffered shortness of breath at night. She had finally seduced him into a doctor's office; the doctor had taken a cardiogram and driven him to the hospital. He was a seriously sick man.

Instantly I was relieved. The weight on me rolled away. All day death had been advancing under cover and now it had struck, declared its position. My father had engaged the enemy and it would be defeated.

I was restored to crisp health in the play-world of action. That night we had a few friends in for my birthday party and the next day I took the two older children to Sunday school and went myself to church. The faintly lavender lozenge-panes of the white-mullioned windows glowed and dimmed fitfully. It was a spottily overcast day, spitting a little snow. While I was at church my wife had cooked a lamb dinner and as I drank the coffee it became clear that I must drive to Pennsylvania. My mother and I had agreed I would fly down and visit him in a few days; I would have to see about renting a car at the Philadelphia end. This was potentially awkward because, self-employed, I had no credit card. The awkwardness suddenly seemed easy to surmount. I would drive. The car would be traded in a few days, it had just been greased; I had a vision of escaping our foul New England spring by driving south. In half an hour my bag was packed and in my churchgoing suit I abandoned my family. *Run on home.*

Along Route 128 I picked up a young sailor who rode with me all the way to New York and, for two hours through Connecticut, drove my car. I trusted him. He had the full body, the frank and fleshy blue-eyed face of the docile Titans—guileless, competent, mildly earnest—that we have fattened, an ocean removed from the slimming Latin passions and Nordic anxieties of Europe, on our unprecedented abundance of milk and honey, vitamins and protein. He had that instinctive optimism of the young animal that in America is the only generatrix of hope we have allowed ourselves; until recently, it seemed enough. He was incongruously—and somehow reassuringly—tanned. He had got the tan in Key West, where he had spent twenty-four hours, hitching the rides to and from on Navy jets. He had spent the twenty-four hours sleeping on the beach and selecting souvenirs to send back to his parents and girl friend. His parents lived in Salem, his girl friend in Peabody. He wanted to marry her, but his parents had old-fashioned ideas, they thought he was too young. And a lot of these guys in the service say, Don't get married, don't ever get married. But she was a nice girl, not so pretty or anything, but really nice: he really wanted to marry her.

I asked him how old he was. He was twenty-two, and was being trained as an airplane mechanic. He wanted at the end of his hitch to come back to Salem and live. He figured an airplane mechanic could find some sort of job. I told him, with a paternal firmness that amazed my ears, to marry her; absolutely; his parents would get used to it. The thing about parents, I told him, was that secretly, no matter what you did, they liked you anyway. I told him I had married at the age of twenty-one and had never for a minute been sorry.

He asked me, "What do you do? Teach?"

This impressed me. My grandfather had been a teacher, and my father was a teacher, and from my childhood up it had been assumed by the people of our neighborhood that I in turn would become a teacher. "No," I said. "I'm a writer."

He seemed less offended than puzzled. "What do you write?"

"Oh—whatever comes into my head."

"What's the point?"

"I don't know," I told him. "I wish I did."

We talked less freely after that. At his request I left him off in wet twilight at a Texaco station near the entrance of the New Jersey Turnpike. He hoped to get a ride from there all the way to Washington. Other sailors were clustered out of the rain in the doorways of the station. They hailed him as if they had been waiting for him, and as he went to them he became, from the back, just one more sailor, anonymous, at sea. He did not turn and wave goodbye. I felt I had frightened him, which I regretted, because he had driven for me very well and I wanted him to marry his girl. In the dark I drove down the pike alone. In the first years of my car, when we lived in Manhattan, it would ease up to seventy-five on this wide black stretch without our noticing; now the needle found its natural level at sixty. The windshield wipers beat, and the wonderland lights of the Newark refineries were swollen and broken like bubbles by the raindrops on the side windows. For a dozen seconds a solemn cross of colored stars was suspended stiffly in the upper part of the windshield: an airplane above me was coming in to land.

I did not eat until I was on Pennsylvania soil. The Howard Johnsons in Pennsylvania are cleaner, less crowded, more homelike in their furnishings. The decorative plants seem to be honestly growing, and the waitresses have just a day ago removed the Mennonite cap from their hair, which is still pulled into a smooth bun flattering to their pallid, sly faces. They served me with that swift grace that comes in a country where food is still one of the pleasures. The familiar and subtle irony of their smiles wakened in me that old sense, of Pennsylvania knowingness—of knowing, that is, that the truth is good. They were the innkeeper's daughters, God had given us crops, and my wagon was hitched outside.

When I returned to the car, the music on the radio had changed color. The ersatz hiccup and gravel of Atlantic Seaboard hillbilly had turned, inland, backwards into something younger. As I passed the Valley Forge intersection the radio relived a Benny Goodman quintet that used to make my scalp freeze in high school. The speedometer went up to seventy without effort.

I left the toll road for our local highway and, turning into our dirt road, I was nearly rammed from behind by a pair of headlights that had been pushing, Pennsylvania style, six feet behind me. I parked beside my father's car in front of the barn. My mother came unseen into the yard, and, two voices calling in the opaque drizzle, while the dogs yapped deliriously in their pen, we debated whether I should move my car further off the road. "Out of harm's way," my grandfather would have said. Complaining, I obeyed her. My mother turned as I carried my suitcase down the path of sandstone steppingstones, and led me to the back door as if I would not know the way. So it was not until we were inside the house that I could kiss her in greeting. She poured us two glasses of wine. Wine had a ceremonial significance in our family; we drank it seldom. My mother seemed cheerful, even silly, and it took an hour for the willed impetus of gaiety to ebb away. She turned her head and looked delicately at the rug and the side of her neck blushed as she told me, "Daddy says he's lost all his faith."

Since I had also lost mine, I could find nothing to say. I remembered, in the silence, a conversation I had had with my father during a vacation from college. With the habitual simplicity of his eagerness to know, he had asked me, "Have you ever had any doubts of the existence of a Divine Being?"

"Sure," I had answered.

"I never have," he said. "It's beyond my ability to imagine it. The divinity of Jesus, yes; but the existence of a Divine Being, never." He stated this not as an attempt to influence me, but as a moderately curious fact he had that moment discovered about himself.

"He never was much one for faith," my mother added, hurt by my failure to speak. "He was strictly a works man."

I slept badly; I missed my wife's body, that weight of pure emotion, beside me. I was enough of a father to feel lost out of my nest of little rustling souls. I kept looking out of the windows. The three red lights of the chimneys of the plant that had been built some miles away, to mine low-grade iron ore, seemed to be advancing over our neighbor's ridged field toward our farm. My mother had mistaken me for a stoic like my father and had not put enough blankets on the bed. I found an old overcoat of his and arranged it over me; its collar scratched my chin. I tipped into sleep and awoke. The morning was sharply sunny; sheep hustled, heads toppling, through the gauzy blue sky. It was authentic spring in Pennsylvania. Some of the grass in the lawn had already grown shiny and lank. A yellow crocus had popped up beside the BEWARE OF THE DOG sign my father had had a child at school make for him.

I insisted we drive to Alton in my car, and then was sorry, for it seemed to insult their own. Just a few months ago my father had traded in on yet one more second-hand car: now he owned a '53 Plymouth. But while growing up I had been ambushed by so many mishaps in my father's cars that I insisted we take the car I could trust. Or perhaps it was that I did not wish to take my father's place behind the wheel of his car. My father's place was between me and Heaven; I was afraid of being placed adjacent to that far sky. First we visited his doctor. Our old doctor, a man who believed that people simply "wore out" and nothing could be done about it, had several years ago himself worn out and died. The new doctor's office, in the center of the city, was furnished with a certain raw sophistication. Rippling music leaked from the walls, which were hung with semi-professional oils. He himself was a wiry and firm-tongued young man not much older than myself but venerable with competence and witnessed pain. Such are the brisk shepherds who hop us over the final stile. He brought down from the top of a filing cabinet a plaster model of the human heart. "Your own heart," he told me, "is nice and thin like this; but your dad's heart is enlarged. We believe the obstruction is here, in one of these little vessels on the outside, luckily for your dad."

Outside, in the streets of Alton, my own heart felt enlarged. A white sun warmed the neat façades of painted brick; chimneys like peony shoots thrust through budding treetops. Having grown accustomed to the cramped improvised cities of New England, I was patriotically thrilled by Alton's straight broad streets and superb equipment of institutions. While my mother went off to buy my daughter a birthday present, I returned a book she had borrowed to the Alton Public Library. I had forgotten the deep aroma of that place, mixed of dust and cleaning fluid and binder's glue and sweet pastry baking in the shop next door. I revisited the shelf of P. G. Wodehouse that in one summer I had read straight through. I took down *Mulliner Nights* and looked in the back for the stamped date, in '47 or '48, that would be me. I never thought to look for the section of the shelves where my own few books would be placed. They were not me. They were my children, mysterious and self-willed.

In driving to the hospital on Alton's outskirts, we passed the museum grounds, where every tree and flower-bed wore a name-tag and black swans drifted through flotillas of crumbled bread. As a child I had believed literally that bread cast upon the waters came back doubled. I remembered that within the museum there were mummies with astonished shattered faces; a tiny gilt chair for a baby Pharaoh; an elephant tusk carved into thousands of tiny Chinamen and pagodas and squat leafy trees; miniature Eskimo villages that you lit up with a switch and peeped into like an Easter egg; cases of arrowheads; rooms of stuffed birds; and, upstairs, wooden chests decorated with hearts and pelicans and tulips by the pious "plain people" and iridescent glassware from the kilns of Baron von Steigel and slashing paintings of Pennsylvania woodland by the Shearers and bronze statuettes of wrestling Indians that stirred my first erotic dreams and, in the round skylit room at the head of the marble stairs, a black-rimmed pool in whose center a naked green lady held to her pursed lips a shell whose lucent contents forever spilled from the other side, filling this whole vast upstairs—from whose Palladian windows the swans in their bready pond could be seen trailing fan-shaped wakes —with the music and chill romance of falling water. The world then seemed an intricate wonder displayed for my delight with no price asked. Above the trees across the pond one saw rose glints of the hospital, an orderly multitude of tall brick rectangles set among levelled and lovingly tended grounds, an ideal city of the ill.

I had forgotten how grand the Alton hospital was. I had not seen its stately entrance, approached down a grassy mall bright with the first flush of green, since, at the age of seven, I had left the hospital unburdened of my tonsils. Then, too, it had been spring, and my mother was with me. I recalled it to her, and she said, "I felt so guilty. You were so sick."

"Really? I remember it as so pleasant." They had put a cup of pink rubber over my nose and there had been a thunderous flood of the smell of cotton candy and I opened my eyes and my mother was reading a magazine beside my bed.

"You were such a hopeful boy," my mother said, and I did not look at her face for fear of seeing her crying.

I wondered aloud if a certain girl in my high school class were still a nurse here.

"Oh, dear," my mother said. "Here I thought you came all this way to see your poor old father and all you care about is seeing—" And she used the girl's maiden name, though the girl had been married as long as I had.

Within the hospital, she surprised me by knowing the way. Usually, wherever we went, it was my father or I who knew the way. As I followed her through the linoleum maze, my mother's shoulders seemed already to have received the responsible shawl of widowhood. Like the halls of a palace, the hospital corridors were lined with patient petitioners. Negro girls electrically dramatic in their starched white uniforms folded bales of cotton sheets; gray men pushed wrung mops. We went through an Exit sign, down a stairway, into a realm where gaunt convalescents in bathrobes shuffled in and out of doorways. I saw my father diagonally through a doorway before we entered his room. He was sitting up in bed, supported sultanlike by a wealth of pillows and clad in red-striped pajamas.

I had never seen him in pajamas before; a great man for the shortest distance between two points, he slept in his underclothes. But, having been at last captured in pajamas, like a big-hearted lion he did not try to minimize his humiliation, but lay fully exposed, without a sheet covering even his feet. Bare, they looked pale, gentle, and oddly unused.

Except for a sullen lymphatic glow under his cheeks, his face was totally familiar. I had been afraid that his loss of faith would show, like the altered shape of his mouth after he had had all his teeth pulled. With grins we exchanged the shy handshake that my going off to college had forced upon us. I sat on the window sill by his bed, my mother took the chair at the foot of the bed, and my father's roommate, a tanned and fortyish man flat on his back with a crushed vertebra, sighed and blew smoke toward the ceiling and tried, I suppose, not to hear us. Our conversation, though things were radically changed, followed old patterns. Quite quickly the talk shifted from him to me. "I don't know how you do it, David," he said. "I couldn't do what you're doing if you paid me a million dollars a day." Embarrassed and flattered, as usual, I tried to shush him, and he disobediently turned to his roommate and called loudly, "I don't know where the kid gets his ideas. Not from his old man, I know that. I never gave that poor kid an idea in my life."

"Sure you did," I said softly, trying to take pressure off the man with the painful back. "You taught me two things. Always butter bread toward the edges because enough gets in the middle anyway, and No matter what happens to you, it'll be a new experience."

To my dismay, this seemed to make him melancholy. "That's right, David," he said. "No matter what happens to you, it'll be a new experience. The only thing that worries me is that *she*"—he pointed at my mother—"will crack up the car. I don't want anything to happen to your mother."

"The car, you mean," my mother said, and to me she added, "It's a sin, the way he worships that car."

My father didn't deny it. "Jesus I love that car," he said. "It's the first car I've ever owned that didn't go bad on me. Remember all those heaps we used to ride back and forth in?"

The old Chevy was always getting dirt in the fuel pump and refusing to start at awkward hours. Once, going down Fire Hill, the left front wheel had broken off the axle; my father wrestled with the steering wheel while the tires screamed and the white posts of the guard fence floated calmly toward my eyes. When the car slid sideways to a stop just short of the embankment my father's face was stunned and the corners of his mouth dribbled saliva. I was surprised; it had not occurred to me to be frightened. The '36 Buick had drunk oil, a quart every fifty miles, and loved to have flat tires after midnight, when I would be gliding home with a scrubbed brain and the smell of lipstick in my nose. Once, when we had both gone into town and I had dropped him off and taken the car, I had absent-mindedly driven home alone. I came in the door and my mother said, "Why, where's your father?"

My stomach sank. "My Lord," I said, "I forgot I had him!"

As, smiling, I took in breath and prepared to dip with him into reminiscence of these adventures, my father, staring stonily into the air above his pale and motionless toes, said, "I love this place. There are a lot of wonderful gentlemen in here. The only thing that worries me is that mother will crack up the car."

To my horror I saw that my mother, leaning forward red-faced in the chair at the foot of the bed, was silently crying. He glanced at her and said to me, "It's a funny feeling. The night before we went to see the doctor I woke up and couldn't get my breath and realized I wasn't ready to die. I had always thought I would be. It's a funny feeling."

"Luckily for your dad," "all his faith," "wonderful gentlemen": these phrases were borne in on me with a dreadful weight and my tongue seemed pressed flat on the floor of its grave. The pajama stripes under my eyes stirred and streamed, real blood. I wanted to speak, to say how I needed him and to beg him not to leave me, but there were no words, no form of words available in our tradition. A pillar of smoke poured upward from the sighing man in the other bed.

Into this pit hesitantly walked a plain, painfully clean girl with a pad and pencil. She had yellow hair, thick lips, and, behind pink-rimmed glasses, large eyes that looked as if they had been corrected from being crossed. They flicked across our faces and focussed straight ahead in that tunnel-vision gaze of those who know perfectly well they are figures of fun. The Jehovah's Witnesses who come to the door wear that funnelled expression. She approached the bed where my father lay barefoot and, suppressing a stammer, explained that she was from Lutheran Home Missions and that they kept accounts of all hospitalized Lutherans and notified the appropriate pastors to make visitations. Clearly she had measured my father for a rebuff; perhaps her eyes, more practiced in this respect than mine, spotted the external sign of loss of faith that I had missed. At any rate my father was a Lutheran by adoption; he had been born and raised a Presbyterian and still looked like one.

"That's *aw*fully nice of you," he told the girl. "I don't see how you people do it on the little money we give you."

Puzzled, she dimpled and moved ahead with her routine. "Your church is—?"

He told her, pronouncing every syllable meticulously and consulting my mother and me as to whether the word "Evangelical" figured in the official title.

"That would make your pastor Reverend—"

"Yeah. He'll be in, don't worry about it. Wild horses couldn't keep him away. Nothing he likes better than to get out of the sticks and drive into Alton. I didn't mean to confuse you a minute ago; what I meant was, just last week in church council we were talking about you people. We couldn't figure out how you do anything on the little money we give you. After we've got done feeding the furnace and converting the benighted Hindoo there isn't anything left over for you people that are trying to help the poor devils in our own back yard."

The grinning girl was lost in this onslaught of praise and clung to the shreds of her routine. "In the meantime," she recited, "here is a pamphlet you might like to read."

My father took it from her with a swooping gesture so expansive

I got down from the window sill to restrain him physically, if necessary. That he must lie still was my one lever, my one certainty about his situation. "That's awfully nice of you," he told the girl. "I don't know where the hell you get the money to print these things."

"We hope your stay in the hospital is pleasant and would like to wish you a speedy recovery to full health."

"Thank you; I know you're sincere when you say it. As I was telling my son David here, if I can do what the doctors tell me I'll be all right. First time in my life I've ever tried to do what anybody ever told me to do. The kid was just telling me, 'No matter what happens to you, Pop, it'll be a new experience.'"

"Now if you will excuse me I have other calls to pay."

"Of course. You go right ahead, sick Lutherans are a dime a dozen. You're a wonderful woman to be doing what you're doing."

And she left the room transformed into just that. As a star shines in our heaven though it has vanished from the universe, so my father continued to shed faith upon others. For the remainder of my visit with him his simple presence so reassured me, filled me with such a buoyant humor, that my mother surprised me, when we had left the hospital, by remarking that we had tired him.

"I hadn't noticed," I said.

"And it worries me," she went on, "the way he talks about the movies all the time. You know he never liked them." When I had offered to stay another night so I could visit him again, he had said, "No, instead of that why don't you take your mother to the movies?" Rather than do that, I said, I would drive home. It took him a moment, it seemed, to realize that by my home I meant a far place, where I had a wife and children; though at the time I was impatient to have his consent, it has since occurred to me and grieved me that during that instant his face was blank he was swallowing the realization that he was no longer the center of even his son's universe. Having swallowed, he told me how good I had been to come all this way to see him. He told me I was a good son and a good father; he clasped my hand. I felt I would ascend straight north from his touch.

I drove my mother back to her farm and got my bag and said goodbye on the lawn. The little sandstone house was pink in the declining sunlight; the lawn was a tinkling clutter of shy rivulets. Standing beside the BEWARE OF THE DOG sign with its companion of a crocus, she smiled and said, "This is like when you were born. Your father drove through a snowstorm all the way from Wheeling in our old

Ford." He had been working with the telephone company then; the story of his all-night ride was the first myth in which I was a character. Darkness did not fall until New Jersey. The hour of countryside I saw from the Pennsylvania Turnpike looked enchanted—the branches of the trees underpainted with budding russet, the meadows nubbled like new carpets, the bronze sun slanting on Valley Forge and Levittown alike. I do not know what it is that is so welcome to me in the Pennsylvania landscape, but it is the same quality—perhaps of reposing in the certainty that the truth is good—that is in Pennsylvania faces. It seemed to me for this sunset hour that the world is our bride, given to us to love, and the terror and joy of the marriage is that we bring to it a nature not our bride's.

There was no sailor to help me drive the nine hours back. New Jersey began in twilight and ended in darkness, and Manhattan made its gossamer splash at its favorite hour, eight o'clock. The rest of the trip was more and more steeply uphill. The Merritt Turnpike seemed meaninglessly coquettish, the light-controlled stretch below Hartford maddeningly obstinate, and the hour above that frighteningly empty. Distance grew thicker and thicker; the intricate and effortful mechanics of the engine, the stellar infinity of explosive sparks needed to drive it, passed into my body, and wearied me. Repeatedly I stopped for coffee and the hallucinatory comfort of human faces, and after every stop, my waiting car, companion and warm home and willing steed, responded to my pressure. It began to seem a miracle that the car could gather speed from my numb foot; the very music on the radio seemed a drag on our effort, and I turned it off, obliterating time. We climbed through a space fretted by scattered brilliance and bathed in a monotonous wind. I had been driving forever; furniture, earth, churches, women, were all things I had innocently dreamed. And through those aeons my car, beginning as a mechanical spiral of molecules, evolved into something soft and organic and consciously brave. I lost, first, heart, then head, and finally any sense of my body. In the last hour of the trip I ceased to care or feel or in any real sense see, but the car, though its soul the driver had died, maintained steady forward motion, and completed the endless journey safely. Above my back yard the stars were frozen in place, and the shapes of my neighbors' houses wore the wonder that children induce by whirling.

Any day now we will trade it in; we are just waiting for the phone to ring. I know how it will be. My father traded in many cars. It happens so cleanly, before you expect it. He would drive off in the

old car up the dirt road exactly as usual and when he returned the
car would be new, and the old was gone, gone, utterly dissolved back
into the mineral world from which it was conjured, dismissed without
a blessing, a kiss, a testament, or any ceremony of farewell. We in
America need ceremonies, is I suppose, sailor, the point of what I have
written.

John Ciardi

THE RIVER

Dear Mr. Burnett:

I choose it because I like it as a poem and because I feel it opens a new range for me. It's a new sort of thing for me and I think perhaps a new (if small) step in contemporary poetry. In this series (an autobiographical series now in progress and I choose "The River" as a good example) I am trying to take back into poetry the kind of "fictional" detail long since surrendered to novelists and short story writers. The obvious danger of the method is that the detail might drown the poetry; the challenge is to manage the detail and still keep the tension of poetry. Whether or not I have met the challenge will have to rest with the reader's decision. I can only say I find myself excited by the method and mean to expand it into a substantial autobiographical series, of which I now have about ten parts in final or near-final form.

John Ciardi

By easy stations where time crossed and left
the banks ahead untouched, the river slipped
seven looped miles from springs to a salt mouth,
brackish a good five miles back from flood tide
but rock-fresh all its length into an ebb.

A cumulus of elm- and maple-green
was every summer, the heaven of it pierced
by a white slatted Congregational spire
four-sided, with a clock for every wind.
And every wind and clock a story told.

A stone-fenced tidy Zion of thrift and God
the Congregational saints began there once,
their housefronts white on the hills yet, where I heard
the bells to Concord. In the clattering hour
history most chooses, midnight spurred its horse,
and Paul Revere came pounding at the doors
scarred by his knuckles yet—so I was told,
though only the pure-in-heart, the well invested,
and eagle scouts dead in the line of duty
can see the scars, not always.
                                    Seen, unseen,
the saints rode west and northwest all one night
cross country from green to green of the elm squares

leaving behind bad sculptures and good law,
enough to fill a countryside of causes.

Every nineteenth of April, though now by day
and with refreshments by the American Legion,
he rides again past children waving flags,
and beats on one door of one house still standing
as it was then, though it's a funeral parlor
these new days, though this day, the half day
it takes to fill the windows with DARs
in ribboned bonnets and tricorned gentlemen,
the corpse in residence must be wheeled away
and down the elevator to the cold room
till that year's rider clatters round the corner
where the horse van that dropped him at South and Main
waits at High and Winthrop to take him on
to the next house of the next town on his way,
already forgotten by the hoodlum young
storming the Armory for free ice cream
and bottles of what Boston still calls "tonic."

This is what I remember from a first.
A half day taken from the mailman's wake
to let a rider by, and a costumed clatter
over the dead man's interrupted state.
Locked in his cellar, he forecast forever
under whose stairs he would lie long the same
while hats and bonnets changed. That afternoon—
whichever year it was—I did my duty
beside his box in the light they brought him back to
before they wheeled him off again forever.

But, first, a hoodlum with my hoodlum pack,
my flag and hand out screaming with the rest,
I stormed the Armory for the Legion's handout.
And ducked out on him fast among his roses.
He was a good round chuckle everyday
he hauled his bag, and every week he left
one more $10 piece of Pa in the slot,
and that was food and drink, and a quick Lord's Prayer

as Ma had ordered, and I could have the river
and he his promises:
                          The rafts and cockles
and leaky tubs I drifted summer through
touched every bank. Water rats quizzed my statue
at holes I knew. Dragonflies hummed me dry.
And alewife ran the flickering of their instinct
under my awe. I scooped them in their seizure
and sat seized in my shell, their slate blue tremble
a mystery like quicksilver at my barefeet
in the constant inch of water beyond bailing.

Then, like the corpse put by for history's party,
or an undelivered mail, sender unknown,
they came one year and tasted their first water
and turned up the white mushrooms of their bellies
bloated like easy death and scummed with oil
in clots and rafts that stank back to the sea
and came up on the tide, and came and went
a week, ten days, till nothing came again
but a few eels too ugly not to live.

Is there a longer death than rivers die
out of the sainted valleys of their first,
following the mist blown tribes and their dim totems,
and the congregation of saints beside the water
that came and went, and still came and still went
where black stumps of the rotted shipyards stubbed
the sewer-slimed edges of the rotted river?
Where, through the same green cumulus, the spire
the saints appointed as their arm to God
lifted its four clocks to the rose of winds
that took the Captains out past God,

                                         down river,
clearing Hull point, aslant to Provincetown,
and on to the Azores and Canaries.
Until the Trades grew wicked with their south,
the cargo was still God and Medford Rum,
with barter as it came.

                              But before landfall
on the Gold Coast, God's corpse went into the hold
and chain and shackles rigged them out as slavers
triangling to Jamaica in their stink
to trade what flesh had not gone to the sharks
for kegs of black molasses, and then home,
the hold scrubbed out with soda, God broken out
like a new flag to fly above the Square
where God's distillery waited for the syrup
to start a new firewater its three ways
from God, past God, to God again one Sunday.

Their portraits climb the stairs yet, or look down
from rows of deacons and from the bank's walls—
Nathaniels, Ebenezers, Jonathans.
Burnsided, muttonchopped, full-beavered, shaved,
bone-leathered, paunched, frill-collared, or homespun,
all crossed with a gold chain from which time hangs
to take out or put back as the trade turns.

Back to the Sundays when the sloops and barks
wove lines above the chimney tops, the wharves
silent, the gray dray horses out to pasture
not hearing how the bells poured down from God
to call the Captain's carriage from the hill,
its two spang chestnuts, polished like new boots,
clopping between the pickets, and his Priscilla
bonneted prim but shawled in Indian silk—
a trophy from her trophy home to God
from mysteries of his untold own, but home,
a proper man and propertied and a deacon
with the white house still growing on the hill,
sprouting a new farm after every voyage.

God took them in. His minister at the door
came forward to honor him home, such blessings
he brings us once again from the main deep
to the good farms of the righteous. As one by one,
from offstage in themselves, squires with their ladies
passed, tipping their toppers, and God took them in

through the arched door, His portrait rayed above,
fingering the great gold chain from which time hangs.

And cleared his throat—a peel of organ sound—
when all but the tired horses swishing flies
had gone in from the Square and shut the door
on the concluded world with its beasts left over.

Sun in the morning. The river's grenades of light
blinding the ripples. Cock's matins sung. The crows'
black souls, like monks from a grimoire,
scudding back to their hills of warlock oaks.
A lamb bleating its last lawn before Easter—

When I left the river I could walk all day
inside one Captain's name. The miles of farms
and tangled woodland his. Ebenezer Hutchens—
master at twenty, owner at twenty-four,
banker at twenty-seven. He died white
and dry as a peeled oak in his blind eighties
whose bark and beard of youth had known the crows
from more hells than the congregation counted,
but owned the valley on both sides of the river
west of the Square and spire, and the crows' hills
north to the town line through the granite knobs
with black ponds, grubbed with leeches, in their shadows
seeping to fern and deadfall where a day
blushed Indian pipes, white trillium, lady's-slippers
from bark- and moss-rot of cool bottoms,
the scrub untouched there from the first of saints
into that country.

              Sun in the morning
to a pine wood dusk over blueberry clearings,
I walked that one name, rounding its farms like pounds
in the wood shadow. At the Seven Hills,
its white cliff in the last light on the highest,
the Captain's House looked down on the toy spire
that was his boundary stake in the spread valley.

The ships were gone. The river dead. The wharf,
a coalyard drab with barges. The distillery,
blue-lawed to virtue once the trade had ended.
Molasses came from Boston.

                    A smoke from Sumter
signaled the Hutchenses, Bradfords, Woollseys
to the hot running Gettysburgs of the righteous.
Even without trade, courage is a cause
and spills its blue boys long to the larks of God.

Old men of the GAR came out to march,
battle flags clearing the way for Paul Revere
every nineteenth of April. But on the hill
in 'forty-seven, Captain Ebenezer,
hunched at his desk of Honduran iron wood,
could tell a future. When abolitionist ladies
called in hymn-singing virtue to petition
against The Trade, and, thinking still as housewives,
complained that slave-ships stank—as if bad odor
were the offense of evil—Ebenezer
unhunched an instant, raised a Captain's head
out of his ruin and answered to first causes:
"Yes, ladies, slavers stink, but money don't."

And was dead himself before one son changed odor
under McClellan's nose, though well downwind
in the smallpox ghettos of the Potomac. Still
one son stormed Mobile and came home with contacts
that were no harm no trade. And another jingled
high Washington among desks that lost nothing
when money was to be made in the Sutlers' Peace.

The Armory took his name beside the river.
An outlet from its boilers steamed all winter
just at the water line to let me dream
I knew a secret hot spring to the center
and walked on caverns hung with diamond darks.
While in the Armory's groins the Hutchens Light Guard
rattled the rifle range, shouted its numbers,
or changed to West Point uniforms on Ball nights

and danced with lady-shadows past the windows
of the upper vault, my eyes glued to the light
that danced away and came and danced and came.

It was my country and a mystery sung
by bird, by brook, by squirrels chattering,
and shadows through the trees and old lies told
and histories tipping truths. The stone-farmed hills
hand-labored to their falling pasture walls
let fall a stone a season from their ruin.
The town was the invader. Dying barns
backed half the houses to a picket fence
and apple trees. Great bones of hand-chipped granite
trimmed off the squires' lawns, topped with iron fences.
Cellar walls three feet thick, with every block
of field stone a day's labor for two men
bore oak-pegged beams, like ark work, or found money,
building its city firm. But still the cows
roamed to the edge of pavement, and the weeds
poked through a cellar hole that blotched half the Square,
where the first inn and first stage out from Boston
had rambled till its fire. And still the river
slipped easy as its first from the drowned boys
of summer at their play in sight of farms,
the clay pit, and the old wharf peppered black
where once molasses leaked a bait for flies
in the droning summer from the first, not long.

Then like a traffic's roar Boston spilled out,
first Irish, then Italian. A field at a time
the land went out. The Captain's house came down,
steam shovels ate his lawns, grazed his hills flat
for diagrams of two-by-fours drawn up
a day at a time and hammered shut, roofed, boarded,
given their doors, and left to find a name
with twenty years to pay at six per cent.
The Captain's bones flowered open to his grandsons
in vaults of promised paper with such names
as the valley had not spelled in all its time,
but still could add

payable to the order
of the Estate of Ebenezer Hutchens
a Bond and Mortgage convenanted with
Sean Flaherty and said estate to wit:
Aram Perunian and said estate to wit:
Carminantonio Ciardi and said estate
revised to Concetta Ciardi, widow, to wit:
that the lands and bounds and premises hereinafter
together with etc. heretofore
of the Estate of Ebenezer Hutchens
—pay off their life time or return to wit,
whose name, come off the land, returns to it.

A life. And better traded than for molasses.
My father traded his for four hundred weeks
of the $10 checks from Metropolitan.
Two mailmen died before his mail stopped coming.
I think my mother thought they were pall-bearers
the government kept sending in his honor.
She liked wakes, and held one for every check
before she sputtered her slant name on the back
and wept it out for food. She knew some wrong
was being done her but was not sure which
and stayed suspicious on principle. Were we wronged?
our piece of a slaver's acre black with blood?
The tales I knew were old and wonderful.
Old and therefore wonderful. Old and dying.

And I was young and happier than her tears
could change me from. The filthy river slipped
smooth as its first. And all one prowling summer
when Will Howe got a job. I had day jobs
on his canoe, a leakless Indian legend
so tremblingly beyond my hammered sticks
that I could stroke the two miles to the Lakes
and prowl the pinefringe sure of mocassin tracks
under the bracken, or cut straight across
the mile-wide water further than the world,
unwronged by any day, in my own country,
whose dead I haunted and whose dead I am.

MacKinlay Kantor

SIL WAGGONER (CHAPTER XXIII)
from SPIRIT LAKE

Dear Mr. Burnett:

Andersonville was selected by the Book-of-the-Month Club. *Spirit Lake* wasn't.

Andersonville received approval from the *Reader's Digest* Condensed Books in having a portion of the novel chosen for publication therein. *Spirit Lake* was turned down.

Andersonville roosted on the best seller lists for over a year. *Spirit Lake* didn't.

Andersonville, in translation, was a Book-of-the-Month in West Germany. Not so *Spirit Lake.*

Andersonville, in translation, was a Book-of-the-Month in Spain. *Spirit Lake? Nunca.* Never.

Other nations in which best-selling translations of *Andersonville* were circulated include France, Italy, Denmark, Yugoslavia, Poland—

Well, they'll get around to *Spirit Lake* one of these days.

I knew that *Spirit Lake* would be my best work to date— knew it during the wearying but exciting years of its composition —knew it when the book was published in 1961— Know it now.

Ah yes a few daring reviewers bucked the negative reaction of *Time, Newsweek, The New Yorker* and others of that clan. "If the Great American Novel can be written, this is it," said the New Orleans *Times-Picayune.* "This IS the American frontier of the 1850's," said the Columbus *Dispatch.* And Mr. John Barkham, in *Saturday Review* Syndicate, declared, "Mr. Kantor has written a ringing, declamatory prose which, in its climactic moments, attains an almost bardic fervor. The prose sings, exults, laughs, weeps and wonders."

It was difficult for me to make a choice of which modest portion of a half-million-word novel to include in the present anthology. There are hundreds of characters, including more than a score of principals.

I decided on Sil Waggoner because he appears but once. He is one stout weed growing in an ocean of prairie grass, one pebble of sleet in a prairie blizzard, one scrap of flame in a prairie fire. Yet he is complete in this brief episode. His life—past, present and future—can be measured and understood. And appreciated, I trust.

A woman named Lulu and her common-law husband, an itinerant whiskey-seller, are left stranded in southern Minnesota when outlaw Indians steal their team. The man lies unconscious and besotted in his plundered wagon. The scrawny trull (so worn and ugly that even the depraved Inkpaduta and his sons do not desire to rape her) crouches without food, shelter or hope. It is winter, and bitter cold and snow and winds come howling closer. . . .

I read this portion aloud to my wife the afternoon when I wrote it. Irene was still mourning about Lulu, as we prepared to go out for dinner.

"You mean we'll never see her again?"

"No."

"But what will happen to her in that blizzard which you said was on the way?"

"I suppose she'll be frozen to death."

Irene wailed, "I can't *stand* it. Please, please have her *rescued!*"

"Impossible. Nobody around to do it."

But I kept thinking about it while I shaved and took my shower. Returning to our bedroom, I told Irene, "Just for your own satisfaction, here's what *might* have happened—" and in synopsis related the ensuing episode.

She said, "You must put that in the book. Please do, if only for my sake."

So I did.

MacKinlay Kantor

W hen that thing come screeching, and I listened to the howl of it, I thought: I'm better off in here than out there, or my name ain't Sil Waggoner. Old Bill Dog he thought the same. He didn't have much tail —somebody'd whacked it off when he was a pup, fore I acquired him or he acquired me, or whatever— Didn't have much tail, but what he did have he'd plant right tight over his bunghole, and try to press it between his hind legs, every time I opened the door. Like to say, Gracious, Mr.! Don't put me out in that plaguèd wind and snow—don't make me go! And I'd say to him, Hain't you lucky? How'd you like to be out there, hey? And twas like he said he didn't want to be, no way.

So I stretched front the fire and congratulated myself. I was setting neat and I knew it. Kept laughing as I thought of my logrolling. There hain't a white neighbor within thirty mile, not that I know of; but mine's a timber claim in part, and twas easy to cut enough to make a Ten-by-Twelve, eight foot high on the walls. (Slim logs, naturally, for a double wall to be banked solid with sod in between. Snugness was what I craved.) Had them logs stacked for drying in no time at all. Been a fur man and even mountain man in my time, and timber man as well. In such pursuits you learn to use an axe, or else you ain't going to be no kind of man for long. But, working sole alone, I couldn't get them twelve-foot logs up to the top, even slender as they was. So I figured like this: I'd got the logs cut, I'd let them weather—even choose some good chunks of long-grain which would split for shingles, and thus rive out my shakes— Have all the pieces, so to speak, to be put together. If folks come round that might help with the raising of the house, fine enough. If they didn't come, I'd just set tight until they *did*. Built myself a neat little soddy in two three days, and Bill Dog and I was cozy in that. Dug her in, deep enough and high enough so's I could use her for a stable if I was ever fortunate to get that cabin up. Well. Chance come along in the shape of a three-striper and four army privates. They'd rode down from Ridgely looking for some Indin horse thieves, but the Indins had skun out; though I guess the soldiers did recover three stolen horses and deliver them back to the rightful owners. They was on their way returning to the fort when they seen my smoke and come to learn what was what. When I seen who was nearing, I went to meet them with a bottle. We had a nip or two, and then I says: Gentlemen, I got a jug as well. (Didn't tell them that I had more'n one jug buried,) to last me through the winter if twas bad, and sure as shooting she looked like she was going to be.) Gentlemen, I tell you: let's raise up my house, and when it's up I'll then produce my jug and a quarter-eagle apiece. You can't earn money that fast in the Army. Or leastways I couldn't when I was youthful and served under Colonel Henry Dodge in the old First Dragoons! We had this house up so fast twould make your head spin; and then our heads really did spin a little, count of the jug. They took their sore heads on to Ridgely next morning, and here I was a-chuckling beside my new mansion, with only the fireplace to go.

Time of the storm, though, in December: you've heard folks say twas cold as a witch's teat, but that cold would of froze the teats clean off any witch *I* ever see. How the wind did blow and the snow did pile! Clean to my ridgepole at that there side the cabin! Man congratulates himself if he's snug amid such matters, and Bill Dog and I was snug enough. Had pemmican, jerked venison in plenty; smoked fish by the quintal, or so it seemed; two kegs fat salt pork I'd freighted in behind my critters and hadn't even touched; barrel of flour, nother of meal; plenty salt, sorghum, vinegar, sugar, and such fixings. Didn't need no candles—Bill Dog and I went to bed with the prairie birds and rose in the same good company. Pine knots around if we had to make a glim.

For recreation I owned a Bible that belonged to my dead mother. I'd treasured that little Book my whole life through, though strayed from many of its teachings. I'd lain with many's the woman, but I stayed away from bats and cows, and didn't go around breaking the legs of any pure young girls. I'd had two wives within my time, but both of them was tawny—one Arapaho and one Pawnee—and both was long since departed. . . . Still I liked to read my mother's Book, times. Reading mighty slow, howsomever—we didn't catch much schooling down in the Femme Osage where I was born. I'd busted the Third, Fourth, Sixth, and Seventh

Commandments wide open. Kind of preened myself that I'd been able to keep the First, Second, Eighth, Ninth, and Tenth. Fifth always bewildered me. Man I knew up the Missouri had committed what he called the Shorter Catechism when he was a younger— Oh, I don't know how much he'd committed but he'd committed a great share. And he said it like this: *Fifth Commandment requireth the preserving the honor of, and performing the duties belonging to, every one in their several places and relations, as superiors, inferiors, or equals.* Again and again I'd wheedle him into saying it out loud, and all I earned was bewilderment. How was a man to know whether he'd broke the Fifth or not? Wasn't no way I could savvy it, so I just give up.

Well. Bible was all I had for reading matter, cept a raggy *New-York Daily Times,* date of September first. Some mover give it to me, passing in October. I could trick my eyesight any time I figured twas worth it, and that was seldom. *Kansas is realizing all the horrors of anarchy and civil war. . . . Murder of eight pro-Slavery men on Pottowatomie Creek, by a party of Free State men. The victims were most horribly mutilated. In some instances, after their throats had been cut, their legs and arms had been chopped off and their eyes gouged out. All the pro-Slavery families at Hickory Point were driven off at the point of the bayonet, and their horses and provisions stolen by the Free State men.* Says I to Bill Dog, Hain't you glad that you and me's settled down to spend a comfortable old age in Minnesota Territory where there ain't things like that a-happening? And Bill he lowed he was glad. And don't, he says, read me no more of them ass-in-*ine* bulletins bout such doings, or bout Newport that also it tolt in the same paper. *The Great Ball At Newport. . . . It has given to the Bellevue an* éclat *which no other house in Newport can boast of, and will be closely followed up by a series of hops, charades, concerts, masquerades, tableaux, and other social amusements, that will end the season in a most brilliant manner.* Says I to Bill Dog, And hain't you pleasured that you got no necessity for putting on white tar-le-ton and crimson bro-cade and flounces of black lace, and going peer-oh-etting like Mrs. Woodville from Baltimore or Miss Schaumberg from Philadelphia or Mrs. Morgan Livingston from New-York, with a white lace mantill-a and blue feathers in your hair? And Bill he lowed he didn't want no part of it.

He who runs may read, like the fellow says. But truly I didn't need to read no way. Just set happied with a notion of our blessings: everything from saleratus to dried peaches and back again. Potatoes down in the potato hole to keep them far below frost; turnips also; onions; name it, Mr., and we'll feed! Whole big keg of prairie hens that I put down in salt, out in the solid lean-to that I tacked against the cabin's end, to say nothing of four fresh deer a-hanging inside there, and now they'd be froze solid for the season, and thus preserved.

Lean-to chinked and rocked right tight: couldn't ary a rat get inside, let alone a larger varmint. Bear might come, try to rip off the door, but I've met bears afore this—and bigger ones than they got here, and grayer, by gad. That's how come these pink wads on the side of my head, and my left ear tore half off. Grizzly. But he's laying out, up past Fort Benton somewheres, and *he* ain't hearing nothing out of *either* ear. Long ago, that was. . . .

One kind of varmints was around here, howsomever, but they made tracks and I reckon are still making them. Twas maybe a fortnight fore the storm began. I'd seen elk sign; went to some distance to follow it up, but fortune didn't smile. Bill Dog was minding the manse, and minding it loudly as I thought, for I could hear him when I topped that rise of prairie out yonder. Two varmints they were, both bent on making solution of the big brass padlock and heavy chain I'd tinkered to the slab door of that lean-to. I've learnt, the mean way, that twas wise to lock up when there was movers going through the country, and every once in awhile some movers did come through. But these varmints wasn't movers—not for the moment, anyways. I had my double-barreled Kaintuck, and put the first ball into the logs smack betwixt their heads. No, no, I had no call to kill!— didn't want to have a bunch of yellowbellies waiting for me in the weeds every time I stepped outside to make my water. Tis kind of like a boys' game with Indins: they like to steal, but if you tag an ordinary Indin at it, he just thinks he's tagged, and then he laughs, and maybe starts right in to beg instead. They wasn't none from hereabouts. I hadn't seen their like afore; and all the local Wapakoots had left me strictly minding my own business, for I wouldn't even yield a nipperkin of whiskey; they knew it well. . . . I turned up the second barrel, and locked it, and let drive again; but by this time the bastards was halfway to the crick and going hard. I creased that ball acrost, maybe two foot or so above them; oh, yes, Mr.—they heard it make its music, and it was like putting a fresh charge in a can of powder tied behind a cat (if folks are mean enough). They fairly soared! I was loaded up again, by the time they stopped to make a few insulting signs. They didn't know my old Kaintuck would take six fingers in a load—thought that they was well beyond my range. So I put another ball above their heads—twas right down by that little draw, behint that single cottonwood. You ought to seen the tracks they made, with one more ball a-singing on its way, and me a-whooping and a-hollering like I was gone demented, and Bill Dog a-trying to tear down the house door to join in. . . . No, no, they hain't been here again, and I don't reckon that they'll come. I figure there's one old white-shock-headed turkey cock that they ain't going to wherrit any more, whether I affix that padlock or I don't.

So here come some of the poisonest weather that a man could meet. I wouldn't have give a mouse-pelt for ary soul that was caught in it. Twas blue cold. That's the worst: the air truly turns to blue, and there is a kind of whining sound like a gang of fiddlers was standing back yonder somewheres, all drawing their long bows acrost their strings, keeping steady, drawing on and on, but always playing that same note. And if you try to face it, you think it's bees or yellow jackets that have got around you in a mass; but actually tis only pebbles of the snow, driving like salt-and-pepper from a shotgun that's fired square in your face, and stinging all the while. You can't breathe, you can't see, the air's solid with it, you can't hear nothing but that screech of mighty unseen fiddlers and the wild strings that they're a-playing on; and it all pours like angry needle tips a-jabbing at your hide, and itching up your nose until the snot flows out and freezes so you got twin icicles a-hanging . . . and forcing through your lids against your eyeballs, till you think your eyes are bloodied and the blood is freezing there as well; but still it all looks dark and blue!

I'd planned my wood and thought I planned it well. Two stacks on either side the door, starting in as high as I could reach, and stretching out a couple rods on either side. No matter now which quarter marked the storm, I'd have the shelter of one pile or tother. Thus I made it my business to see that I started taking wood from off *the furthest end away;* and thus there'd always be some fuel for evil days, right next the door. But, pshaw! The going to the stable—that was something else. I had my critters there in the old soddy; two yoke was all I had—I'd sold the rest —but they was all I'd need for any future hauling. . . . Pshaw!—when I stepped out from shelter of that woodpile I liked to choke to death. Worse than that, I couldn't see a blame thing. Well, shit and soap and sulphur!—they'd abide right where they was, those oxen. They'd had plenty hay the last time I seen to 'em, and the snow was bound to blow inside, and they'd eat that— You couldn't teach an ox that he should build a fire, melt the snow, boil the water, and then drink *that,* rather than munch snow firsthand. They'd suffer slightly if the snow kept up, but only slightly; and I never seen an ox that wasn't built for suffering.

So now my problem was to find my house again. Would you believe

it? I hadn't gone a rod beyond the woodpiles' end—I'd swear to that—
and yet my house was *gone*. Yes, sir, clean gone. I ducked my head
against my chest, and lifted up my fists to half protect my face, and
started back through all that rush of sand and fleas and pepper, salt, and
emptiness, and lack of breath— Why, certainly, my house *was there*. But
twasn't.

Now, this will be a caution (what I says) if I fall down to die right
here in my front yard!

But Bill Dog saved the day. He didn't like to be alone, and so he made
protest gainst the whole idee. I heard him bark, just faint, but I heard him;
and twas quite the other way around; seemed like my gol damn house
had moved around the compass; but there he was, a-barking in the wrong
direction, so I started working toward him. Next thing I knew I stumbled
fair against my woodpile; and I fought my way along that jagged pile.
But I was on the wrong side—had to climb back to the other end, and
round the corner of it—and there I was, quite sheltered, but my mouth
was open wide and I was crying tears of ice. Hadn't been for that blame
dog, I'd ended up down by the crick somewheres; and someone *might*
have found me when it thawed again, if ever it *did* thaw. . . . We had a
little nip on that; leastways I did.

And then a-setting through those hours, with one window darkened
steady as the snow went mounting, until finally it blotted out; there
wasn't even paleness in the window any more. But Bill and I were contented as two ticks in a fox's ear, pleased and fat. I had corn biscuits with
a splash of sorghum; fried a plate of pork and onions; my Bill Dog he had
a piece of venison complete with bone, and he licked the last fried onion
off my tin. Spread myself on robes before the fire, old Bill a-laying close.
I tried to read my mother's Bible, but I couldn't spell it out to suit—the
print is mighty small, the flames and light was jumpy, and I went to sleep
on *Better is a dinner of herbs where love is* . . . and so I dreamt about it.
Dreamt about another fire in the Femme Osage of Old Mizzoo, some forty
years agone. Dreamt about an old man talking, telling tales; and that old
man he wasn't me, his name was Daniel Boone. We called him Colonel.
And he'd let the neighbor kids come in and listen whilst he yarned. He
set there with white-braided locks, and he told of being took by Indins
years before, when he was hunting on the Green (that's in Kentucky).
The women, Colonel Boone was saying in his quiet elder voice, *they fell
a-searching of my hunting-shirt, to see what I was toting.* . . .

Then I waked again—not Daniel Boone, but me, Silvanus Waggoner
—and there I was alone in Minnesota Territory; and I was getting long in

years. Once in awhile I couldn't help but brood. Now, take Bill Dog: I reckoned him as five or six, in age, and how much longer would he be with me? Five year, if I was lucky. And then I'd be alone (tis sad that dogs are always older, faster, than the men they're wedded to). And Little-Woman-Never-Cries was buried under rocks so long before (she died in trying to bear the only son I ever might have had) and Pretty-Gopher-Running, she was gone nigh onto fifteen years, of the consump. Oh, after that I batched it strictly, seeking females only when I felt the need. But there was more to lonesomeness than seeking females, or forgetting them. There was the times I'd look down at that brindled dog and want to scream at him: Gol damn it, *talk!* Why can't you *talk?* . . . For I'd gone talking to myself, and answering as well; twas quite a habit, growing steadily; and that's the way a lone man gets a name for lunacy so frequent. And more than that: the wish to have another form within those walls; the times when you were weary, wearier than any slave that ever worked, because you'd drove yourself so hard; and all you wished to do was rid yourself of boots, extend your feet, just set and stare into that fire . . . wouldn't it be a wonder if you dozed, and then awakened smart, with smells of cooking all around?—and heard a kindly light-formed laugh, a woman's laugh, with pride and all appreciation flowing in her tone— And heard her say: Pull up now, Sil. I got the meal well-cooked; and here's the hot-bread fresh . . . I want that you should taste this wild grape jam I made whilst you was hunting!

Well. Nothing in the Bible matches that for lonesomeness (the feel within you, worse than any words). And then you'd mutter: Aw, tarnation . . . and pick up them softened fuzzy scraps of *New-York Daily Times* again, and try to fix your smoky eyes upon the lines of print, and try to spell it out again.

The disease was undoubtedly introduced on Yellow Hook and along shore from infected vessels anchored for awhile in the Channel between Fort Hamilton and Staten Island.

Disease, disease. You didn't care how many people died of it.

And reach around and twist the banjo from the peg where it was hung, push back the rawhide loop to get it clear, and feel the fingers tightening and loosening, and hear the strings make little clinks and jinks; then start a-whacking soft and slow . . . not knowing what to sing, trying to sing something lately popular that I'd heard sung on a steamboat when I come up the Mississip some months before.

I'm dreaming of sweet Hallie . . . listen to that mockingbird, listen to that mockingbird . . . but twas a new song, and I didn't know the words, and wasn't certain of the tune.

*Home to me his trumpets peal, and at my side he'll softly kneel, with
a gold distaff and a golden reel. Ko-mell-a-lolla-boo, shy-doo-rah.*
. . . Now, Bill Dog, why you fretting?
. . . Don't you like my music?
*Frog went a-wooing, he did ride! Kemo, kimo, kay-ro! Sword and a
pistol by his side! Kemo, kimo, kay-ro!*
. . . By gol, you don't pay me grace nor heed.
. . . Naw, you don't want to go out. Listen to that wind!
*Kemo, kimo, kay-ay-row! Strim, stram, flom-a-diddle, lolly-bolly-rig-dam!
Mule met a kimo!*
. . . Now, look here, sir! When I was last out for wood, you went along.
Stood about two foot from the door, and sprayed them logs; and then
you hiked it for the fireside. You sure don't need to go again.
*So he led us down to cypress swamp; the ground was low and mucky.
There stood John Bull in martial pomp, and here was old Kentucky!
O Kentucky . . . ye hunters of Kentucky! O Kentucky. . . .*
. . . Howling, are you? By dad, that's adding insult! Don't need to
howl because it's coming night, and storming still—twon't do no good to
howl. This crazy wind and sleet and God alone knows what depth of snow
by now— It ain't a-going to stop just cause you whine and moan.
. . . By dad, I'll give you one to howl about!
*What become of your bloodhounds, Lord Ronald, my son? What be-
come of your bloodhounds, my pretty one? Oh, they puffed and they
died . . . mother, make my bed soon, for I'm wearied of hunting, and fain
would lie doon.*
By God. That damn dog.
Couldn't be anyone out there.
He's plumb crazy!
Just scairt of the storm, I reckon. Can't blame him.
*Oh, I fear you are poisoned, Lord Ronald, my son! Oh, I fear you are
poisoned, my pretty one! . . . Oh, yes, I am poisoned—*
Well, that's enough for me! *Couldn't* be anybody out there. But—

After I'd carried her inside she kept mumbling: *Light . . . light . . .*
through her frozen lips; which I took to mean that she'd glimpsed a
little bit of firelight that kind of skittered crost the drifts. Oh, yes, that's
what she must of seen, although she couldn't see it fur.
This looked like quite a chore, and right at first I never thought to
save her. But I had one tub and one big bucket, so I started in. Tried
to prop her on a mound of robes, propped high on her side, with both
arms hanging off into the bucket of icy water, and both limbs pushed

down into the tub. I pulped up a bunch of onions and spread the wet sauce over her face and ears—she hadn't looked like much to start with, poor old thing, and didn't look like nothing human or female now, with all that onion mess a-pasted over her and fairly in her hair. But still she owned gumption, and she'd try to talk. Kept saying weakly: *Light* . . . and after while she says, *My man* . . . *went down in it* . . . *back there somewheres. Drunk* . . . and I says, Lady, if your man's out there, and drunk, he *ain't*, that's all, he *ain't!* He's down in hell this minute, and will be the drunkest that he's ever been fore he gets out of hell! I says, part way to answer all her mumblings, and part way to give me comfort whilst I toiled, a-rubbing them poor limbs of her'n with ice, one at a time— I says: If he's out there somewheres behint where you was laying, there couldn't *fifty* Bill Dogs locate him. I'll dig him out sometime next spring. Just get yourself all customed up to widowhood! . . . I might have added also: And customed up to life without two hands and without any feet!—but couldn't bring myself to even say the words, and hated much to think them. But in another hour I could take a little heart; I watched the solid ice a-coming out, and forming on her limbs. If you had ever see the like, you'd ne'er forget. Just solid casings, solid ice, a-rising through the raw skin where I'd rubbed and worn it red with rubbing—solid blocks of ice around both feet— And solid gloves—ice, you know—around both hands—

She'd moan like a sick cat at times, and other hours she would be so silent that I thought her dead. And helpless as a baby wren; I had to tend her every way. I stowed her in the bed, she got it wet right off; and finally I had sense enough to employ a wide flat pan I'd bought when I was fitting out: twas meant for cooking maple sap, but it would serve. I'd put my hands within her armpits, hoist her up in bed, and set her on the pan—

She wasn't conscious much until the second day that followed. And now I turn away from recollecting all the agonizing that she had, when blood was flowing once again into them blackened swolled-up members of her body. But still I nursed and tussled, whilst she raved or whilst she mumbled . . . Indins . . . ah, they'd took the team her husband drove . . . took a led horse that her husband bought from movers that he met . . . vinegar, she talked about, and whiskey too . . . and gut-aches that her husband sobbed of . . . and just the way I'd thought her dead, she thought that she was dead herself. And who was I, if that befell? If she was dead— Who was I? Angel, devil, spook? She didn't know.

And for some reason Bill Dog liked to lay beside her bed. He wouldn't move for hours: just lay quiet, beating tail against puncheons of the floor,

like he was saying she belonged to him. He was the one who'd sensed that
she was in the snow.

Feel better, lady?

Yes.

Limbs still a-hurting pretty bad, I reckon.

Yes . . . it hurts so much.

Now, don't you cry again, lady. Twon't do no good.

I'm . . . crying . . . cause my limbs . . . they'll have to cut them off
. . . now, won't they?

Nope.

You mean— I won't be crippled?

Oh, kind of, for awhile. But I've seen frosted limbs as bad or worse
than your'n, and seen the people get the use of them again. Your hands
and feet are better by the hour.

Where is this?

What say?

I mean—where am I? Is this—in a town?

Hell no, madam. Hain't another shack in thirty mile. We're nigh the
South Fork of the Watonwan. But not too nigh.

What's—your name?

Sil Waggoner. Silvanus, if I want to sound important.

Is—there—anybody else—?

Nobody else. I'm wifeless, childless. But I ain't Bill Dog-less. That's him,
laying there beside you.

I can't—see—

Don't you bother. Your face is all swolled up. Just try and catch a
snooze. . . .

. . . Oh!

There, there, sister. Everything's all right.

I guess I was . . . asleep again.

Three hours, more or less. Now, how'd you like a little broth?

Oh, yes . . . please . . .

That taste right good?

Oh, yes. What is it?

Well, if I was one kind of Indin, I'd say *hupa*. If I was another kind
I'd say *wahanpi*. And thus twould go. But I ain't any kind of Indin, so
we'll just call it any kind of soup you want to say. . . . What's that? Oh,
it's got deermeat, bones, and onions, prairie hen, a smidge of turnip and
potato— Right good, ain't it? Bill Dog likes it too.

Where is he?

Bill Dog? Right beside you. See?

Oh, yes. I think . . . I'm seeing better now.

So you are. Ain't so fat-faced as before. You know, twas Bill that found you.

Yes. I member when you tolt me . . . seems so long ago. But he couldn't find Pay, could he? Could he? Pay Lorimer . . . my husband?

No, I tolt you that as well. Reckon your man Pay is gone to the Good Place in a chariot of snow!

No, no, he couldn't— Couldn't go! Not there. Just to—the Bad Place. Cause he's . . . bad . . . like me. That's where I'll go.

Where?

The Bad Place.

I don't think you're going nowhere right away. But why the Bad Place?

Cause I was bad. My whole life long. I guess . . . times when you're at death's door . . . a body thinks about such things. My whole life long, I said! My *whole life*— Mr., you know what I was, through all my younger years? A whore. That's what I was. You hear me. Just a whore.

Gol damn it, lady, who's to judge? And what's the difference? Who's the worst—the whores, or men who use 'em? I've used plenty in my time. And I don't feel so *bad,* right now!

That's cause you're good.

Well, some would laugh at that! Now I want—

Mr.?

My name is Sil.

Mr. Sil. What you been—your whole life long?

Oh, this and that and tother. I was in the Army one time—First Dragoons. Went way up the Muddy, worked for the American Fur, worked for the Choteaus, beat around some mean country along of Jim Bridger and such. Been a sutler too. Hunted hides. Farmer, storekeep, factor, lumberman. This and that and tother, like I said. But this is my place now. I'm getting old, I aim to set. Also, old lady, I aim to put you back to sleep again, if I have to whop you on the head! Ahh—you want to use your fancy pot again, afore you go to sleep?

No . . . I don't . . . need to.

. . . Oh.

Well, that sounds better! First time you hain't woke a-yelling.

What day is—today?

Tis Thursday.

Is it storming still?

Kind of quitting now. But mighty deep—the drifts. And all-plumb-festered *cold.*

Why, Mr. Sil, my eyes is *so* much better! I can really see.

Oh, your whole face is better. And your feet's much better, too. I took a good look at them, while ago. Flesh is lightening. But they're still all swolled up terrible.

And they do hurt awful. But—I kind of hate to say it—I'm right hungry—

Well, we'll tend to *that,* immediate.

. . . Mr. Sil.

You was quiet, for so long, I thought you'd drapped asleep again.

I was watching, whilst you cooked. Mr. Sil—your ear. I—I was watching—

My left ear? Gol damn grizzly. Long ago. Me and Jim Bridger—

Yes. But— You—ever been in New Orleans? Long ago, I mean?—

Nope.

You ever been—in St. Louis? Long ago?—

Was in St. Louis just eight months agone. Fore I come up to St. Paul and—

But— In St. Louis, many years since?

A hundred times, I reckon.

Did you ever go to Essart's Pleasure Parlors?

Ha, ha! Did I? When I was younger. Don't mind telling you—since —ah—you tolt me how you spent *your* years— I used to rip it off five times a night!

With me.

What say? What say? How's *that?*

You member Lulu?

Why—I— *Lulu!* She was—

I'm her.

I—I don't know what to say—

Course, I don't look the same no more. I'm old, and all used up.

You hain't *storying?*

Course not. I knew I'd seen that ear before. And heard—about the grizzly bear—

Lulu. . . . I'm. . . . Gol damn, my hands are shaking!

Hain't it queer?

If anybody'd . . . tolt me. . . .

Hain't it queer?

Lionel Trilling

HUCKLEBERRY FINN

Dear Mr. Burnett:

I am probably not exceptional among writers in not wanting
to be invidious to the rest of my work by choosing one piece as
"the best". But of my essays, the one on *Huckleberry Finn* has
my special affection. For one thing, it allowed itself to be written
with no trouble at all. For another, it has made more money for
me than any other of my essays—it was written as the introduction to a college edition of the novel on a royalty arrangement and
for a good many years it brought me substantial semi-annual
checks. Yet another reason for my affection is that it was written
out of feelings and perceptions I first had in my boyhood, when
I read *Huckleberry Finn* every few months. And then the essay
has for me a curious interest in that what I say in it about the ending of the novel generated a swarm of critical essays taking issue
with my view.

Yours sincerely,
Lionel Trilling

In 1876 Mark Twain published *The Adventures of Tom Sawyer* and in the same year he began what he called "another boys' book." He set little store by the new venture and said that he had undertaken it "more to be at work than anything else." His heart was not in it—"I like it only tolerably well as far as I have got," he said, "and may possibly pigeonhole or burn the MS when it is done." He pigeonholed it long before it was done and for as much as four years. In 1880 he took it out and carried it forward a little, only to abandon it again. He had a theory of unconscious composition and believed that a book must write itself; the book which he referred to as "Huck Finn's Autobiography" refused to do the job of its own creation and he would not coerce it.

But then in the summer of 1881 Mark Twain was possessed by a charge of literary energy which, as he wrote to a friend, was more intense than any he had experienced for many years. He worked all day and every day, and periodically he so fatigued himself that he had to recruit his strength by a day or two of smoking and reading in bed. It is impossible not to suppose that this great creative drive was connected with—was perhaps the direct result of—the visit to the Mississippi he had made earlier in the year, the trip which forms the matter of the second part of *Life on the Mississippi*. His boyhood and youth on the river he so profoundly loved had been at once the happiest and most significant part of Mark Twain's life; his return to it in middle age stirred vital memories which revived and refreshed the idea of *Huckleberry Finn*. Now at last the book was not only ready but eager to write itself. But it was not to receive much conscious help from its author. He was always full of second-rate literary schemes and now, in the early weeks of the summer, with *Huckleberry Finn* waiting to complete itself, he turned his hot energy upon several of these sorry projects, the completion of which gave him as much sense of satisfying productivity as did his eventual absorption in *Huckleberry Finn.*

When at last *Huckleberry Finn* was completed and published and widely loved, Mark Twain became somewhat aware of what he had accomplished with this book that had been begun as journeywork and depreciated, postponed, threatened with destruction. It is his master-piece, and perhaps he learned to know that. But he could scarcely have estimated it for what it is, one of the world's great books and one of the central documents of American culture.

2

Wherein does its greatness lie? Primarily in its power of telling the truth. An awareness of this quality as it exists in *Tom Sawyer* once led Mark Twain to say of the earlier work that "it is *not* a boys' book at all. It will be read only by adults. It is written only for adults." But this was only a manner of speaking, Mark Twain's way of asserting, with a dis-cernible touch of irritation, the degree of truth he had achieved. It does not represent his usual view either of boys' books or of boys. No one, as he well knew, sets a higher value on truth than a boy. Truth is the whole of a boy's conscious demand upon the world of adults. He is likely to believe that the adult world is in a conspiracy to lie to him, and it is this belief, by no means unfounded, that arouses Tom and Huck and all boys to their moral sensitivity, their everlasting concern with justice, which they call fairness. At the same time it often makes them skillful and profound liars in their own defense, yet they do not tell the ultimate lie of adults: they do not lie to themselves. That is why Mark Twain felt that it was impossible to carry Tom Sawyer beyond boyhood—in ma-turity "he would lie just like all the other one-horse men of literature and the reader would conceive a hearty contempt for him."

Certainly one element in the greatness of *Huckleberry Finn*—as also in the lesser greatness of *Tom Sawyer*—is that it succeeds first as a boys' book. One can read it at ten and then annually ever after, and each year find that it is as fresh as the year before, that it has changed only in be-

coming somewhat larger. To read it young is like planting a tree young
—each year adds a new growth-ring of meaning, and the book is as
little likely as the tree to become dull. So, we may imagine, an Athenian
boy grew up together with the *Odyssey*. There are few other books which
we can know so young and love so long.

The truth of *Huckleberry Finn* is of a different kind from that of *Tom
Sawyer*. It is a more intense truth, fiercer and more complex. *Tom
Sawyer* has the truth of honesty—what it says about things and feelings
is never false and always both adequate and beautiful. *Huckleberry Finn*
has this kind of truth, too, but it has also the truth of moral passion;
it deals directly with the virtue and depravity of man's heart.

Perhaps the best clue to the greatness of *Huckleberry Finn* has been
given to us by a writer who is as different from Mark Twain as it is
possible for one Missourian to be from another. T. S. Eliot's poem, "The
Dry Salvages," the third of his *Four Quartets,* begins with a meditation
on the Mississippi, which Mr. Eliot knew in his St. Louis boyhood. These
are the opening lines:

> I do not know much about gods; but I think that the river
> Is a strong brown god . . .

And the meditation goes on to speak of the god as

> almost forgotten
> By the dwellers in cities—ever, however, implacable,
> Keeping his seasons and rages, destroyer, reminder of
> What men choose to forget. Unhonoured, unpropitiated
> By worshippers of the machine, but waiting, watching and
> waiting.[1]

Huckleberry Finn is a great book because it is about a god—about, that
is, a power which seems to have a mind and will of its own, and which,
to men of moral imagination, appears to embody a great moral idea.

Huck himself is the servant of the river-god, and he comes very close
to being aware of the divine nature of the being he serves. The world
he inhabits is perfectly equipped to accommodate a deity, for it is full
of presences and meanings which it conveys by natural signs and also by
preternatural omens and taboos: to look at the moon over the left shoulder,
to shake the tablecloth after sundown, to handle a snakeskin, are ways
of offending the obscure and prevalent spirits. Huck is at odds, on moral
and aesthetic grounds, with the only form of Christianity he knows, and

[1] Copyright, 1943, by T. S. Eliot, reprinted by permission of Harcourt, Brace and
Company.

his very intense moral life may be said to derive from his love of the river. He lives in a perpetual adoration of the Mississippi's power and charm. Huck, of course, always expresses himself better than he can know, but nothing draws upon his gift of speech like his response to his deity. After every sally into the social life of the shore, he returns to the river with relief and thanksgiving; and at each return, regular and explicit as a chorus in a Greek tragedy, there is a hymn of praise to the god's beauty, mystery, and strength, and to his noble grandeur in contrast with the pettiness of men.

Generally the god is benign, a being of long sunny days and spacious nights. But, like any god, he is also dangerous and deceptive. He generates fogs which bewilder, and he contrives echoes and false distances which confuse. His sandbars can ground and his hidden snags can mortally wound a great steamboat. He can cut away the solid earth from under a man's feet and take his house with it. The sense of the danger of the river is what saves the book from any touch of the sentimentality and moral ineptitude of most works of the imagination which contrast the life of nature with the life of society.

The river itself is only divine; it is not ethical and good. But its nature seems to foster the goodness of those who love it and try to fit themselves to its ways. And we must observe that we cannot make—that Mark Twain does not make—an absolute opposition between the river and human society. To Huck much of the charm of the river life is human: it is the raft and the wigwam and Jim. He has not run away from Miss Watson and the Widow Douglas and his brutal father to a completely individualistic liberty, for in Jim he finds his true father, very much as Stephen Dedalus in James Joyce's *Ulysses* finds his true father in Leopold Bloom.[2] The boy and the Negro slave form a family, a primitive community—and it is a community of saints.

Huck's intense and even complex moral quality may possibly not appear on a first reading, for one may be caught and convinced by his own estimate of himself, by his brags about his lazy hedonism, his avowed preference for being alone, his dislike of civilization. The fact is, of course that he is involved in civilization up to his ears. His escape from society is but his way of reaching what society ideally dreams of for itself. Responsibility is the very essence of his character, and it is perhaps to the point that the original of Huck, a boyhood companion of Mark Twain's

---

[2] In Joyce's *Finnegan's Wake* both Mark Twain and Huckleberry Finn appear frequently. The theme of rivers is, of course, dominant in the book; and Huck's name suits Joyce's purpose, as so many names do, for Finn is one of the many names of his hero. Mark Twain's love of and gift for the spoken language makes another reason for Joyce's interest in him.

named Tom Blenkenship, did, like Huck, "light out for the Territory," only to become a justice of the peace in Montana, "a good citizen and greatly respected."

Huck does indeed have all the capacities for simple happiness he says he has, but circumstances and his own moral nature make him the least carefree of boys—he is always "in a sweat" over the predicament of someone else. He has a great sense of the sadness of human life, and although he likes to be alone, the words "lonely" and "loneliness" are frequent with him. The note of his special sensibility is struck early in the story: "Well, when Tom and me got to the edge of the hilltop we looked away down into the village and could see three or four lights twinkling where there were sick folks, maybe; and the stars over us was sparkling ever so fine; and down by the village was the river, a whole mile broad, and awful still and grand." The identification of those three or four lonely lights as the lamps of sick-watches defines Huck's character.

His sympathy is quick and immediate. When the circus audience laughs at the supposedly drunken man who tries to ride the horse, Huck is only miserable: "It wasn't funny to me . . . ; I was all of a tremble to see his danger." When he imprisons the intending murderers on the wrecked steamboat, his first thought is of how to get someone to rescue them, for he considers "how dreadful it was, even for murderers, to be in such a fix. I says to myself, there ain't no telling but I might come to be a murderer myself yet, and then how would I like it." But his sympathy is never sentimental. When at last he knows that the murderers are beyond help, he has no inclination to false pathos. "I felt a little bit heavy-hearted about the gang, but not much, for I reckoned that if they could stand it I could." His will is genuinely good and therefore he has no need to torture himself with guilty second thoughts.

Not the least remarkable thing about Huck's feeling for people is that his tenderness goes along with the assumption that his fellow men are likely to be dangerous and wicked. He travels incognito, never telling the truth about himself and never twice telling the same lie, for he trusts no one and the lie comforts him even when it is not necessary. He instinctively knows that the best way to keep a party of men away from Jim on the raft is to beg them to come aboard to help his family stricken with smallpox. And if he had not already had the knowledge of human weakness and stupidity and cowardice, he would soon have acquired it, for all his encounters forcibly teach it to him—the insensate feud of the Graingerfords and Shepherdsons, the invasion of the raft by the Duke and the King, the murder of Boggs, the lynching party, and the speech of

Colonel Sherburn. Yet his profound and bitter knowledge of human depravity never prevents him from being a friend to man.

No personal pride interferes with his well-doing. He knows what status is and on the whole he respects it—he is really a very *respectable* person and inclines to like "quality folks"—but he himself is unaffected by it. He himself has never had status, he has always been the lowest of the low, and the considerable fortune he had acquired in *The Adventures of Tom Sawyer* is never real to him. When the Duke suggests that Huck and Jim render him the personal service that accords with his rank, Huck's only comment is, "Well, that was easy so we done it." He is injured in every possible way by the Duke and the King, used and exploited and manipulated, yet when he hears that they are in danger from a mob, his natural impulse is to warn them. And when he fails of his purpose and the two men are tarred and feathered and ridden on a rail, his only thought is, "Well, it made me sick to see it; and I was sorry for them poor pitiful rascals, it seemed like I couldn't ever feel any hardness against them any more in the world."

And if Huck and Jim on the raft do indeed make a community of saints, it is because they do not have an ounce of pride between them. Yet this is not perfectly true, for the one disagreement they ever have is over a matter of pride. It is on the occasion when Jim and Huck have been separated by the fog. Jim has mourned Huck as dead, and then, exhausted, has fallen asleep. When he awakes and finds that Huck has returned, he is overjoyed; but Huck convinces him that he has only dreamed the incident, that there has been no fog, no separation, no chase, no reunion, and then allows him to make an elaborate "interpretation" of the dream he now believes he has had. Then the joke is sprung, and in the growing light of the dawn Huck points to the debris of leaves on the raft and the broken oar.

Jim looked at the trash, and then looked at me, and back at the trash again. He had got the dream fixed so strong in his head that he couldn't seem to shake it loose and get the facts back into its place again right away. But when he did get the thing straightened around he looked at me steady without ever smiling, and says:

"What do dey stan' for? I'se gwyne to tell you. When I got all wore out wid work, en wid de callin' for you, en went to sleep, my heart wuz mos' broke bekase you wuz los', en I didn' k'yer no mo' what became er me en de raf'. En when I wake up en fine you back agin, all safe en soun', de tears come, en I could a got down on my knees en kiss yo' foot, I's so thankful. En all you wuz thinkin' 'bout wuz how you could make a fool uv ole Jim wid a lie. Dat truck dah is *trash;* en trash is what people is dat puts dirt on de head er dey fren's en makes 'em ashamed."

Then he got up slow and walked to the wigwam, and went in there without saying anything but that.

The pride of human affection has been touched, one of the few prides that has any true dignity. And at its utterance, Huck's one last dim vestige of pride of status, his sense of his position as a white man, wholly vanishes: "It was fifteen minutes before I could work myself up to go and humble myself to a nigger; but I done it, and I warn't sorry for it afterwards either."

This incident is the beginning of the moral testing and development which a character so morally sensitive as Huck's must inevitably undergo. And it becomes an heroic character when, on the urging of affection, Huck discards the moral code he has always taken for granted and resolves to help Jim in his escape from slavery. The intensity of his struggle over the act suggests how deeply he is involved in the society which he rejects. The satiric brilliance of the episode lies, of course, in Huck's solving his problem not by doing "right" but by doing "wrong." He has only to consult his conscience, the conscience of a Southern boy in the middle of the last century, to know that he ought to return Jim to slavery. And as soon as he makes the decision according to conscience and decides to inform on Jim, he has all the warmly gratifying emotions of conscious virtue. "Why, it was astonishing, the way I felt as light as a feather right straight off, and my troubles all gone . . . I felt good and all washed clean of sin for the first time I had ever felt so in my life, and I knowed I could pray now." And when at last he finds that he cannot endure his decision but must change it and help Jim in his escape, it is not because he has acquired any new ideas about slavery—he believes that he detests Abolitionists; he himself answers when he is asked if the explosion of a steamboat boiler had hurt anyone, "No'm, killed a nigger," and of course he finds nothing wrong in the responsive comment, "Well, it's lucky because sometimes people do get hurt." Ideas and ideals can be of no help to him in his moral crisis. He no more condemns slavery than Tristram and Lancelot condemn marriage; he is as consciously *wicked* as any illicit lover of romance and he consents to be damned for a personal devotion, never questioning the justice of the punishment he has incurred.

Huckleberry Finn was once barred from certain libraries and schools for its alleged subversion of morality. The authorities had in mind the book's endemic lying, the petty thefts, the denigrations of respectability and religion, the bad language and the bad grammar. We smile at that excessive care, yet in point of fact *Huckleberry Finn* is indeed a subversive book—no one who reads thoughtfully the dialectic of Huck's great moral crisis will ever again be wholly able to accept without some question and some irony the assumptions of the respectable morality by which he lives, nor will ever again be certain that what he considers the clear dictates of moral reason are not merely the engrained customary beliefs of his time and place.

3

We are not likely to miss in *Huckleberry Finn* the subtle, implicit moral meaning of the great river. But we are likely to understand these moral implications as having to do only with personal and individual conduct. And since the sum of individual pettiness is on the whole pretty constant, we are likely to think of the book as applicable to mankind in general and at all times and in all places, and we praise it by calling it "universal." And so it is; but like many books to which that large adjective applies, it is also local and particular. It has a particular moral reference to the United States in the period after the Civil War. It was then when, in Mr. Eliot's phrase, the river was forgotten, and precisely by the "dwellers in cities," by the "worshippers of the machine."

The Civil War and the development of the railroads ended the great days when the river was the central artery of the nation. No contrast could be more moving than that between the hot, turbulent energy of the river life of the first part of *Life on the Mississippi* and the melancholy reminiscence of the second part. And the war that brought the end of the rich Mississippi days also marked a change in the quality of life in America which, to many men, consisted of a deterioration of American moral values. It is of course a human habit to look back on the past and to find it a better and more innocent time than the present. Yet in this instance there seems to be an objective basis for the judgment. We cannot disregard the testimony of men so diverse as Henry Adams, Walt Whitman, William Dean Howells, and Mark Twain himself, to mention but a few of the many who were in agreement on this point. All spoke of something that had gone out of American life after the war, some simplicity, some innocence, some peace. None of them was under any illusion about the amount of ordinary human wickedness that existed in the old days, and Mark Twain certainly was not. The difference was in the public attitude, in the things that were now accepted and made respectable in the national ideal. It was, they all felt, connected with new emotions about money. As Mark Twain said, where formerly "the people had desired money," now they "fall down and worship it." The new gospel was, "Get money. Get it quickly. Get it in abundance. Get it in prodigious abundance. Get it dishonestly if you can, honestly if you must."[3]

With the end of the Civil War capitalism had established itself. The relaxing influence of the frontier was coming to an end. Americans increasingly became "dwellers in cities" and "worshippers of the machine." Mark Twain himself became a notable part of this new dispensation. No one worshipped the machine more than he did, or thought he did —he ruined himself by his devotion to the Paige typesetting machine by which he hoped to make a fortune even greater than he had made by his writing, and he sang the praises of the machine age in *A Connecticut Yankee in King Arthur's Court.* He associated intimately with the dominant figures of American business enterprise. Yet at the same time he hated the new way of life and kept bitter memoranda of his scorn, commenting on the low morality or the bad taste or the smugness and dullness of the men who were shaping the national ideal and directing the destiny of the nation.

Mark Twain said of *Tom Sawyer* that it "is simply a hymn, put into prose form to give it a worldly air." He might have said the same, and with even more reason, of *Huckleberry Finn,* which is a hymn to an older America forever gone, an America which had its great national faults, which was full of violence and even of cruelty, but which still maintained its sense of reality, for it was not yet enthralled by money, the father of ultimate illusion and lies. Against the money-god stands the river-god, whose comments are silent—sunlight, space, uncrowded time, stillness and danger. It was quickly forgotten once its practical usefulness had passed, but, as Mr. Eliot's poem says, "The river is within us. . . ."

4

In form and style *Huckleberry Finn* is an almost perfect work. Only one mistake has ever been charged against it, that it concludes with Tom Sawyer's elaborate, too elaborate, game of Jim's escape. Certainly

[3] *Mark Twain in Eruption,* edited by Bernard De Voto, p. 77.

this episode is too long—in the original draft it was much longer—
and certainly it is a falling-off, as almost anything would have to be,
from the incidents of the river. Yet it has a certain formal aptness—
like, say, that of the Turkish initiation which brings Molière's *Le
Bourgeois Gentilhomme* to its close. It is a rather mechanical development of an idea, and yet some device is needed to permit Huck to return to his anonymity, to give up the role of hero, to fall into the
background which he prefers, for he is modest in all things and could
not well endure the attention and glamour which attend a hero at a
book's end. For this purpose nothing could serve better than the
mind of Tom Sawyer with its literary furnishings, its conscious romantic
desire for experience and the hero's part, and its ingenious schematiza-
tion of life to achieve that aim.

The form of the book is based on the simplest of all novel-forms,
the so-called picaresque novel, or novel of the road, which strings its
incidents on the line of the hero's travels. But, as Pascal says, "rivers
are roads that move," and the movement of the road in its own mysterious life transmutes the primitive simplicity of the form: the road
itself is the greatest character in this novel of the road, and the hero's
departures from the river and his returns to it compose a subtle and
significant pattern. The linear simplicity of the picaresque novel is
further modified by the story's having a clear dramatic organization: it
has a beginning, a middle and an end, and a mounting suspense of
interest.

As for the style of the book, it is not less than definitive in American literature. The prose of *Huckleberry Finn* established for written
prose the virtues of American colloquial speech. This has nothing to
do with pronunciation or grammar. It has something to do with ease
and freedom in the use of language. Most of all it has to do with
the structure of the sentence, which is simple, direct, and fluent, maintaining the rhythm of the word-groups of speech and the intonations
of the speaking voice.

In the matter of language, American literature had a special problem.
The young nation was inclined to think that the mark of the truly
literary product was a grandiosity and elegance not to be found in
the common speech. It therefore encouraged a greater breach between its
vernacular and its literary language than, say, English literature of the
same period ever allowed. This accounts for the hollow ring one now
and then hears even in the work of our best writers in the first half
of the last century. English writers of equal stature would never have

made the lapses into rhetorical excess that are common in Cooper and Poe and that are to be found even in Melville and Hawthorne.

Yet at the same time that the language of ambitious literature was high and thus always in danger of falseness, the American reader was keenly interested in the actualities of daily speech. No literature, indeed, was ever so taken up with matters of speech as ours was. "Dialect," which attracted even our serious writers, was the accepted common ground of our popular humorous writing. Nothing in social life seemed so remarkable as the different forms which speech could take—the brogue of the immigrant Irish or the mispronunciation of the German, the "affectation" of the English, the reputed precision of the Bostonian, the legendary twang of the Yankee farmer, and the drawl of the Pike County man. Mark Twain, of course, was in the tradition of humor that exploited this interest, and no one could play with it nearly so well. Although today the carefully spelled-out dialects of nineteenth-century American humor are likely to seem dull enough, the subtle variations of speech of *Huckleberry Finn,* of which Mark Twain was justly proud, are still part of the liveliness and flavor of the book.

Out of his knowledge of the actual speech of America Mark Twain forged a classic prose. The adjective may seem a strange one, yet it is apt. Forget the misspellings and the faults of grammar, and the prose will be seen to move with the greatest simplicity, directness, lucidity, and grace. These qualities are by no means accidental. Mark Twain, who read widely, was passionately interested in the problems of style; the mark of the strictest literary sensibility is everywhere to be found in the prose of *Huckleberry Finn.*

It is this prose that Ernest Hemingway had chiefly in mind when he said that "all modern American literature comes from one book by Mark Twain called *Huckleberry Finn.*" Hemingway's own prose stems from it directly and consciously; so does the prose of the two modern writers who most influenced Hemingway's early style, Gertrude Stein and Sherwood Anderson (although neither of them could maintain the robust purity of their model); so, too, does the best of William Faulkner's prose, which, like Mark Twain's own, reinforces the colloquial tradition with the literary tradition. Indeed, it may be said that almost every contemporary writer who deals conscientiously with the problems and possibility of prose must feel, directly or indirectly, the influence of Mark Twain. He is the master of the style that escapes the fixity of the printed page, that sounds in our ears with the immediacy of the heard voice, the very voice of unpretentious truth.

John Dos Passos

EPILOGUE
to the DISTRICT OF COLUMBIA TRILOGY

Dear Mr. Burnett:

I picked out this piece—you'll have to decide for yourself whether it is free verse or cadenced prose—which I wrote in great agony of mind in 1952, when it became obvious that nothing would be done to curb the excesses of New Deal institutions afflicted with giantism, or to remedy sufficiently the mistakes in international policy that turned our short term victory in World War II into a long term defeat, because it seems to me somehow to fit the mood of today.

John Dos Passos

Spence's Point
Thanksgiving Day

We learned; but not enough; there is more to learn.
The American People
entered our years of defeat with so little preparation
we have not yet learned how deep the disaster. We had leaders but
like Moses they led us into the wilderness and like Moses
died;
and I am left leaderless
in wild darkness and the terror of death. (Death is not terrible;
but the misgiving of our light, the little light that gave hope's inkling
flicker to the toilsome piecing of torn deceits into a fresh, hazardous,
already perhaps threadbare, so sought for
phrase that may perhaps with luck hold true;
the fear
that our drudgery, the urging of mind and muscle to hard work,
laughter and the sick surprise of pain, our common comfort
in the sayings of our fathers said,
in the grimy comicalness of everyday,
might not,
as I believed,
be the beating out of a link, however flawed, however badly made, in
the chain of lives, linked by danger and miseries and splendor and crime
through suffering generations, proceeding, blunderingly and ill-advised, to
some better, though hardly explainable, destination;
that fear is very terrible.)

As an American I believe:

always in the beginning long ago way down, beneath my father's doubts and the fears his father felt,

there was belief that stood them in good stead:

in the anguish of departure and the queasy ships,

in the quick heartbeat of arrival in sight of the low gray land afloat on bays and inlets, the lowering forests inland, (everpresent the threat of fires, the smoke-pall over the jerrybuilt settlement); there was belief that flared against fear under the bright sky,

the newworld wind northwest;

in the sight of fish in unimaginable millions churning the estuaries in their spring rush upriver to spawn, in the green corn's quick sprouting, and the abundance of peaches; and in the pack of furs the trapper brings in on his back

promise of independence:—the hut of sods

will next year be a cabin, the muddaubed log house will next year be tight clapboard or a mansion of brick; exultation

in the windy freedom of a continent, the singing birds, plentiful shots along the woods' edge at game for the pot:—

in the jostle of immigrants in the seaport slums,

busy to forget the old world, to learn the new, to make

money make money, to turn an honest dollar, busy to cheat,

to be cheated, to invest, to get plenty for nothing, busy to

enjoy opportunity, to exercise independence,

always in the beginning long ago,

way down, there was belief that next year:

'Me I'm not much but my boy:

he'll go to school and learn American.'

In our years of defeat

in our century of power we have forgotten

our American:

the harangue delivered from a stump at the edge of town, the affirmation penned by candlelight in a Spencerian hand, the protests of delegates in convention assembled, the congregations sitting silent with furrowed brows searching for the light within, the blankfaced obstinacy of townmeeting, the brawling, hot with torchlight and whiskey, of mobs for independence, the battering down of obstacles, the opening of waggonroads, canals along the rivers;

the fury of secession; the Union made irrevocable

in massacre and in sorrow and in murder
and by the sacrifice of righteous men; the founding of states out among
the sagehens on the prairie, railroads advancing rail by rail with clamor
of hammers through the West. My father knew
that language; those things his father learned; but there is more to
learn. Shall I sicken for the lack of will
to blazen in words my belief
against the driving sky that rains disaster? Our century of
power to ruin has wrought no answering power to build,
to establish, to plant securely on foundations.

Do we lack the penmanship to declare again the independence that lived
in the flourish of my father's signature, in Mother's homilies:—'An American is as good as any man, he must behave better,' to a naughty small
boy made to stand in the corner; in the needlepoint (the careful jams and
jellies, the meticulous rinsing of china, the affirmation of old prints, The
Peaceable Kingdom stored in dust in the attic, pride of ancestry in the
notes in the family bible, shade trees planted with posterity in the mind),
of Grandmother's domestic economy?

It was how they behaved: my father's goodhumor with darkskinned
diggers of ditches, the enquiry after the health of the waiter, his daily
joshing with the officer fresh from County Cork full of sweat under his
high blue helmet at the Avenue crossing, the way his deference brings
out the innate gentle manners of the bushy old barefoot man
who shows us the spring on the mountainside
who can't read and write but no matter in a land where there is plenty
of freedom
a man's worth his weight; a man free from hate or suspicion or envy
will recognize kinship in other men for no other reason than that they
are men; a free man has a splendor about him,
moving easily joshingly courteously among a variety of equal citizens,
varying in antecedents, in ancestry, in honesty, in schooling, in attainments,
each smirched with the common (in which I share by inheritance, by
education, by preference) degradation of the shoddy mean,
but sharing an infinitesimal, always near extinction but never extinguish-
able, inkling of splendor.

My father, my grandfathers living out their lives, in some things fortunate, in some things unfortunate, Americans varying in antecedents,

assumed without thinking, taking it for granted, often denying it,

their belief in the precarious splendor a man's life assumes when he is for a moment free

from tyranny and taskmasters and the cramping cage of enslaving institutions. The words

are tired and old: 'democratic', 'republican', a coinage worn senseless in the market's transactions, the birthright's daily sale, but they ring. (There is so much evil in the life of man that a tiny good, a moment's opportunity, a breath of independence, produces us immediately abundance of lesser goods so readily mortgaged and sold that we forget

the price our fathers paid. That is why God's temple is always full of moneychangers, because of the riches it offers.) The words are slurred with too much saying but they ring

as loud as the meanings we endow them with.

The republic's foundations are not in the sound of words,

they are in the shape of our lives, fellowcitizens.

They trace the outlines of a grand design. To achieve

greatness a people must have a design before them

too great for accomplishment. Some things we have learned, but not enough; there is more to learn. Today

we must learn

to found again

in freedom

our republic.

James Dickey

MAY DAY SERMON TO THE WOMEN OF GILMER COUNTY, GEORGIA, BY A WOMAN PREACHER LEAVING THE BAPTIST CHURCH

Dear Mr. Burnett:

It is a pleasure to hear that I have been chosen for *This Is My Best;* I remember your last edition, which I read while in the service, so long ago.

. . . As for a prefatory statement, I've chosen "May Day Sermon" because it appears to me to embody more of the kind of subject matter I have wished to work with up to this point than any of the rest of my poems, and because the mode of treating this subject matter—which encompasses animals, religion, natural scenery and sex-as-action—is as near as I have been able to get to the kind of lengthy intensity I have hoped for.

James Dickey

Lake Katherine
Columbia, S.C.

E ach year at this time I shall be telling you of the Lord
—Fog, gamecock, snake, and neighbor—giving men all the help they need
To drag their daughters into barns. Children, I shall be showing you
The fox-hide stretched on the door   like a flying-squirrel   fly
Open   to show you the dark where the one pole of light is paid out
In spring by the loft, and in it the croker sacks sprawling and shuttling
Themselves into place as it comes   comes   through spiders dead
Drunk on their threads   the hogs' fat bristling   the milk
Snake in the rafters unbending through gnats to touch the last place
Alive on the sun with his tongue   I shall be flickering from my mouth
Oil   grease-cans   lard-cans   nubbins   cobs   night
Coming   floating   each May with night coming I cannot help
Telling you how he hauls her to the centerpole   how the tractor moves
Over as he sets his feet and hauls   hauls   ravels her arms and hair
In stump-chains: Telling: telling of Jehovah come and gone
Down on His belly   descending   creek-curving   blowing His legs

Like candles, out   putting North Georgia copper on His head
To crawl in under the door in dust red enough to breathe
The breath of Adam into: Children, be brought where she screams and
   begs
To the sacks of corn and coal   to nails   to the swelling ticks
On the near side of mules, for the Lord's own man has found the limp
Rubber that lies in the gulley   the penis-skin like a serpent
Under the weaving willow.

                    Listen: often a girl in the country,
Mostly sweating   mostly in spring, deep enough in the holy Bible
Belt, will feel her hair rise up   arms rise, and this not any wish

Of hers, and clothes like lint shredding off her   abominations
In the sight of the Lord: will hear the Book speak like a father
Gone mad: each year at this time will hear the utmost sound
Of herself, as her lungs cut, one after one, every long track
Spiders have coaxed from their guts   stunned spiders fall
Into Pandemonium   fall   fall   and begin to dance like a girl
On the red clay floor of Hell   she screaming   her father screaming
Scripture   CHAPter and verse   beating it into her with a weeping
Willow branch   the animals stomping   she prancing and climbing
Her hair   beasts shifting from foot to foot about the stormed
Steel of the anvil   the tractor gaslessly straining   believing
It must pull up a stump   pull   pull down the walls of the barn
Like Dagon's temple   set the Ark of the Lord in its place   change all
Things for good, by pain. Each year at this time you will be looking up
Gnats in the air   they boil   recombine   go mad with striving
To form the face of her lover, as when he lay at Nickajack Creek
With her by his motorcycle   looming   face trembling with exhaust
Fumes   humming insanely—each May you hear her father scream like
    God
And King James as he flails   cuds richen   bulls chew themselves white-
    faced
Deeper into their feed bags, and he cries something the Lord   cries
Words! Words! Ah, when they leap   when they are let out of the Bible's
Black box   they whistle   they grab the nearest girl and do her hair up
For her lover in root-breaking chains   and she knows she was born to
    hang
In the middle of Gilmer County   to dance, on May Day, with holy
Words all around her   with beasts with insects   O children NOW
In five bags of chicken-feed the torsos of prophets form   writhe
Die out as her freckled flesh   as flesh and the Devil twist and turn
Her body to love   cram her mouth with defiance   give her words
To battle with the Bible's in the air: she shrieks sweet Jesus and God

I'm glad   O my God-darling   O lover   O angel-stud   dear heart
Of life put it in me   *give*   you're killing   KILLING: each
Night each year at this time I shall be telling you of the snake-

doctor drifting from the loft, a dragonfly, where she is wringing
Out the tractor's muddy chains   where her cotton socks prance,
Where her shoes as though one ankle were broken, stand with night
Coming and creatures drawn by the stars, out of their high holes
By moon-hunger driven   part the leaves   crawl out of Grimes Nose
And Brasstown Bald: on this night only I can tell how the weasel pauses
Each year in the middle of the road   looks up at the evening blue
Star to hear her say again   O again   YOU CAN BEAT ME TO
   DEATH
And I'll still be glad:
                             Sisters, it is time to show you rust
Smashing the lard-cans more in   spring after spring   bullbats
Swifts barn swallows   mule-bits clashing on walls   mist turning
Up white out of warm creeks: all over, fog taking the soul from the body
Of water   gaining   rising up trees   sifting up through smoking green
Frenzied levels of gamecocks sleeping from the roots   stream-curves
Of mist: wherever on God's land is water, roads rise up the shape of rivers
Of no return: O sisters, it is time   you cannot sleep with Jehovah

Searching for what to be, on ground that has called Him from His Book:
Shall He be the pain in the willow, or the copperhead's kingly riding
In kudzu, growing with vines toward the cows   or the wild face working
   over
A virgin, swarming like gnats or the grass of the west field, bending
East, to sweep into bags and turn brown   or shall He rise, white on white,
From Nickajack Creek as a road?   The barn creaks like an Ark   beasts
Smell everywhere the streams drawn out by their souls the flood-
sigh of grass in the spring   they shall be saved   they know as she screams
Of sin as the weasel stares   the hog strains toward the woods
That hold its primeval powers:
                             Often a girl in the country will find
                             herself
Dancing with God in a mule's eye, twilight drifting in straws from the
   dark
Overhead of hay   cows working their sprained jaws sideways at the hour
Of night all things are called: when gnats in their own midst and fury
Of swarming-time, crowd into the barn   their sixty-year day consumed
In this sunset die in a great face of light that swarms and screams
Of love.
             Each May you will crouch like a sawhorse to make yourself
More here you will be cow-chips   chickens croaking for her hands

That shook the corn over the ground   bouncing   kicked this way
And that, by the many beaks   and every last one of you will groan
Like nails barely holding   and your hair be full of the gray
Glints of stump-chains. Children, each year at this time you will have
Back-pain, but also heaven   but also   also this lovely other life-
pain between the thighs: woman-child or woman in bed in Gilmer
County   smiling in sleep like blood-beast and Venus together
Dancing the road as I speak, get up   up in your socks and take
The pain you were born for: that rose through her body straight
Up from the earth like a plant, like the process that raised overhead
The limbs of the uninjured willow.
                              Children, it is true
That the kudzu advances, its copperheads drunk and tremendous
With hiding, toward the cows   and wild fences cannot hold the string
Beans as they overshoot their fields: that in May the weasel loves love
As much as blood   that in the dusk bottoms young deer stand half
In existence, munching cornshucks   true that when the wind blows
Right   Nickajack releases its mist   the willow leaves stiffen once
More   altogether   you can hear   each year at this time you can hear
No   Now, no   Now   Yes   Again   More   O   O my God
I love it   love you   don't leave   don't   don't stop O GLORY
Be:
     More dark   more coming   fox-fire crawls over the okra-
patch   as through it a real fox creeps to claim his father's fur
Flying on doornails   the quartermoon on the outhouse begins to shine
With the quartermoonlight of this night   as she falls and rises,
Chained to a sapling like a tractor   WHIPPED for the wind in the
     willow
Tree   WHIPPED for Bathsheba and David   WHIPPED for the woman
     taken
Anywhere   anytime   WHIPPED for the virgin sighing   bleeding
From her body   for the sap and green of the year   for her own good
And evil:
               Sisters, who is your lover? Has he done nothing but come
And go? Has your father nailed his cast skin to the wall as evidence
Of sin? Is it flying like a fox in the darkness   dripping pure radiant
     venom
Of manhood?
                    Yes, but *he* is unreeling in hills between his long legs
The concrete of the highway   his face in the moon beginning
To burn   twitch   dance like an overhead swarm   he feels a nail

Beat through his loins far away   he rises in pain and delight, as spirit
Enters his sex   sways   forms   rises with the forced, choked red
Blood of her red-headed image, in the red-dust, Adam-colored clay
Whirling and leaping   creating   calling: O on the dim,   gray   man-
track of cement flowing into his mouth   each year he turns the moon
  back
Around on his handlebars   her image going all over him like the wind
Blasting up his sleeves. He turns off the highway, and

                                                        Ah, children,
There is now something else to hear: there is now this madness of engine
Noise in the bushes   past reason   ungodly   squealing   reverting
Like a hog turned loose in the woods   Yes, as he passes the first
Trees of God's land   game-hens overhead   and the farm is ON
Him   everything is more   *more*   MORE as he enters the black
Bible's white swirling ground   O daughters   his heartbeat great
With trees   some blue leaves coming   NOW   and right away fire
In the right eye   Lord   more   MORE   O Glory   land
Of Glory: ground-branches hard to get through   coops where fryers
  huddle
To death, as the star-beast dances and scratches at their home-boards,
His rubber stiffens on its nails: Sisters, understand about men and sheaths:

About nakedness: understand how butterflies, amazed, pass out
Of their natal silks   how the tight snake takes a great breath   bursts
Through himself and leaves himself behind   how a man casts finally
Off everything that shields him from another   beholds his loins
Shine with his children forever   burn with the very juice
Of resurrection: such shining is how the spring creek comes
Forth from its sunken rocks   it is how the trout foams and turns on
Himself   heads upstream, breathing mist like water, for the cold
Mountain of his birth   flowing   sliding in and through the ego-
maniacal sleep of gamecocks   shooting past a man with one new blind
Side   who feels his skinned penis rise like a fish through the dark
Woods, in a strange lifted-loving form   a snake about to burst
Through itself on May Day   and leave behind on the ground   still
Still   the shape of a fooled thing's body:

                                                he comes on   comes
Through the laurel, wiped out on his right by an eye-twig   now he
Is crossing the cow track   his hat in his hand going on before
His face   then up   slowly over   over like the Carolina moon

Coming into Georgia feels the farm close its Bible and ground-
fog over him his dark side blazing something whipping
By, beyond sight: each year at this time I shall be letting you

Know when she cannot stand when the chains fall back on
To the tractor when you should get up when neither she nor the pole
Has any more sap and her striped arms and red hair must keep her
From falling when she feels God's willow laid on her, at last,
With no more pressure than hay, and she has finished crying to her lover's
Shifting face and his hand when he gave it placed it, unconsumed,
In her young burning bush. Each year by dark she has learned

That home is to hang in home is where your father cuts the baby
Fat from your flanks for the Lord, as you scream for the viny foreskin
Of the motorcycle rider. Children, by dark by now, when he drops
The dying branch and lets her down when the red clay flats
Of her feet hit the earth all things have heard—fog, gamecock
Snake, and lover—and we listen: Listen children, for the fog to lift
The form of sluggish creeks into the air: each spring, each creek
On the Lord's land flows in two O sisters, lovers, flows in two
Places: where it was, and in the low branches of pines where chickens
Sleep in mist and that is where you will find roads floating free
Of the earth winding leading unbrokenly out of the farm of God
The father:
                     Each year at this time she is coming from the barn she
Falls once, hair hurting her back stumbles walking naked
With dignity walks with no help to the house lies face-down
In her room, burning tuning in hearing in the spun rust-
groan of bedsprings, his engine root and thunder like a pig,
Knowing who it is must be knowing that the face of gnats will wake,
In the woods, as a man: there is nothing else this time of night
But her dream of having wheels between her legs: tires, man,
Everything she can hold, pulsing together her father walking
Reading intoning calling his legs blown out by the ground-
fogging creeks of his land: Listen listen like females each year
In May O glory to the sound the sound of your man gone wild
With love in the woods let your nipples rise and leave your feet
To hear: This is when moths flutter in from the open, and Hell
Fire of the oil lamp shrivels them and it is said
To her: said like the Lord's voice trying to find a way

Outside the Bible O sisters O women and children who will be
Women of Gilmer County you farm girls and Ellijay cotton mill
Girls, get up each May Day up in your socks it is the father
Sound going on about God making, a hundred feet down,
The well beat its bucket like a gong: she goes to the kitchen,
Stands with the inside grain of pinewood whirling on her like a cloud
Of wire picks up a useful object two they are not themselves
Tonight each hones itself as the moon does new by phases
Of fog floating unchanged into the house coming atom
By atom sheepswool different smokes breathed like the Word
Of nothing, round her seated father. Often a girl in the country,
Mostly in spring mostly bleeding deep enough in the holy Bible
Belt will feel her arms rise up up and this not any wish
Of hers will stand, waiting for word. O daughters, he is rambling
In Obadiah the pride of thine heart hath deceived thee, thou
That dwelleth in the clefts of the rock, whose habitation is high
That saith in his heart O daughters who shall bring me down
To the ground? And she comes down putting her back into
The hatchet often often he is brought down laid out
Lashing smoking sucking wind: Children, each year at this time
A girl will tend to take an ice pick in both hands a lone pine
Needle will hover hover: Children, each year at this time
Things happen quickly and it is easy for a needle to pass
Through the eye of a man bound for Heaven she leaves it naked goes
Without further sin through the house floating in and out of all
Four rooms comes onto the porch on cloud-feet steps down and out
And around to the barn pain changing her old screams hanging
By the hair around her: Children, in May, often a girl in the country
Will find herself lifting wood her arms like hair rising up
To undo locks raise latches set gates aside turn all things
Loose shoo them out shove pull O hogs are leaping ten
Million years back through fog cows walking worriedly passing out
Of the Ark from stalls where God's voice cursed and mumbled
At milking-time moving moving disappearing drifting
In cloud cows in the alders already lowing far off no one
Can find them each year: she comes back to the house and grabs double
Handfuls of clothes
                              and her lover, with his one eye of amazing grace
Of sight, sees her coming as she was born swirling developing
Toward him she hears him grunt she hears him creaking

His saddle   dead-engined   she conjures one foot whole from the ground-
fog to climb him behind   he stands up   stomps   catches   roars
Blasts the leaves from a blinding twig   wheels   they blaze up
Together   she breathing to match him   her hands on his warm belly
His hard blood renewing like a snake   O now   now as he twists
His wrist, and takes off with their bodies:

                                         each May you will hear it
Said that the sun came as always   the sun of next day burned
Them off with the mist: that when the river fell back on its bed
Of water   they fell from life   from limbs   they went with it
To Hell   three-eyed   in love, their legs around an engine, her arms
Around him. But now, except for each year at this time, their sound
Has died: except when the creek-bed thicks its mist   gives up
The white of its flow to the air   comes off   lifts into the pine-poles
Of May Day   comes back as you come awake in your socks and crotch-
    hair
On new-mooned nights of spring   I speak   you listen and the pines fill
With motorcycle sound as they rise, stoned out of their minds on the
    white
Lightning of fog   singing   the saddle bags full of her clothes
Flying   snagging   shoes hurling away   stockings grabbed-off
Unwinding and furling on twigs: all we know   all we could follow
Them by was her underwear   was stocking after stocking where it tore
Away, and a long slip stretched on a thorn   all these few gave
Out. Children, you know it: that place was where they took
Off into the air   died   disappeared   entered my mouth   your mind
Each year   each pale, curved breath   each year as she holds him
Closer wherever he hurtles   taking her   taking her   she going forever
Where he goes   with the highways of rivers   through one-eyed
Twigs   through clouds of chickens   and grass with them bends
Double   the animals lift their heads   peanuts and beans exchange
Shells in joy   joy like the speed of the body and rock-bottom
Joy: joy by which the creek-bed appeared to bear them out of the Bible
's farm   through pine-clouds of gamecocks where no earthly track
Is, but those risen out of warm currents   streams born to hang
In the pines of Nickajack Creek: tonight her hands are under
His crackling jacket   the pain in her back enough to go through
Them both   her buttocks blazing in the sheepskin saddle: tell those

Who look for them   who follow by rayon stockings   who look on
    human

Highways   on tracks of cement and gravel   black weeping roads
Of tar: tell them that she and her rider have taken no dirt
Nor any paved road   no path for cattle   no county trunk or trail
Or any track upon earth, but have roared like a hog on May Day
Through pines and willows: that when he met the insane vine
Of the scuppernong   he tilted his handlebars back and took
The road that rises in the cold mountain spring from warm creeks:
O women in your rayon from Lindale, I shall be telling you to go
To Hell   by cloud   down where the chicken-walk is running
To weeds   and anyone can show you where the tire-marks gave out
And her last stocking was cast   and you stand as still as a weasel
Under Venus   before you dance   dance yourself blue with blood-
joy looking into the limbs   looking up into where they rode
Through cocks tightening roots with their sleep-claws. Children,
They are gone: gone as the owl rises, when God takes the stone
Blind sun off its eyes, and it sees   sees hurtle in the utter dark
Gold of its sight, a boy and a girl buried deep in the cloud
Of their speed   drunk, children   drunk with pain and the throttle
Wide open, in love   with a mindless sound   with her red hair
In the wind streaming gladly for them both   more than gladly
As the barn settles under the weight of its pain   the stalls fill once
More with trampling like Exodus   the snake-doctor gone the rats begin-
        ning
On the last beans   and all the chicks she fed, each year at this time
Burst from their eggs as she passes:
                                        Children, it is true that mice
No longer bunch on the rafters, but wade the fields like the moon,
Shifting in patches   ravenous   the horse floats, smoking with flies,
To the water-trough   coming back less often   learning to make
Do with the flowing drink of deer   the mountain standing   cold
Flowing into his mouth   grass underfoot   dew   horse or what
ever he is now   moves back into trees where the bull walks
With a male light spread between his horns   some say screams like a girl
And her father yelling together:
                                        Ah, this night in the dark laurel
Green of the quartermoon I shall be telling you that the creek's last
Ascension is the same   is made of water and air   heat and cold
This year as before: telling you not to believe every scream you hear
Is the Bible's: it may be you or me   it may be her sinful barn-
howling for the serpent, as her father whips her, using the tried

And true rhythms of the Lord. Sisters, an old man at times like this
Moon, is always being found   yes found with an ice pick on his mind,
A willow limb in his hand. By now, the night-moths have come
Have taken his Bible and read it   have flown, dissolved, having found
Nothing in it for them. I shall be telling you each moon   each
Year at this time, Venus rises   the weasel goes mad at the death
In the egg, of the chicks she fed for him by hand: mad in the middle
Of human space he dances   blue-eyed   dances with Venus rising
Like blood-lust over the road   O tell your daughters   tell them
That the creek's ghost can still   O still can carry double
Weight of true lovers   any time   any night as the wild turkeys claw
Into the old pines of gamecocks, and with a cow's tongue, the Bible calls
For its own, and is not heard   and even God's unsettled great white father
head with its ear to the ground, cannot hear   know   cannot pick
Up where they are   where her red hair is streaming through the white
Hairs of His centerless breast: with the moon   He cries with the cow all
Its life penned up with Noah in the barn   talk of original
Sin as the milk spurts   talk of women   talk of judgment and flood
And the promised land:
                    Telling on May Day, children: telling
That the animals are saved without rain   that they are long gone
From here   gone with the sun   gone with the woman taken
In speed   gone with the one-eyed mechanic   that the barn falls in
Like Jericho at the bull's voice   at the weasel's dance   at the hog's
Primeval squeal   the uncut hay walks when the wind prophesies in the
    west
Pasture   the animals move   roam, with kudzu creating all the earth
East of the hayfield: Listen: each year at this time the county speaks
With its beasts and sinners   with its blood   the county speaks of nothing
Else each year at this time: speaks as beasts speak to themselves
Of holiness learned in the barn: Listen   O daughters   turn   turn
In your sleep   rise with your backs on fire   in spring   in your socks
Into the arms of your lovers: every last one of you, listen one-eyed
With your man   in hiding   in fog where the animals walk through
The white breast of the Lord   muttering   walk with nothing
To do but be   in the spring laurel in the mist and self-sharpened
Moon   walk through the resurrected creeks   through the Lord
At their own pace   the cow shuts its mouth and the Bible is still
Still open at anything   we are gone   the barn wanders over the earth.

Gore Vidal

EX-SENATOR

To my mind, this fragment from *Washington DC* is a successful rendering of a most difficult and (for that reason?) unfashionable genre: the deliberate mingling of actual and invented people and events in order to create a work which is neither traditional novel nor plain history, but a celebrating of time as the imagination conceives it and the memory recalls it.

Gore Vidal

The false-hearty voices and over-affectionate gestures of embarrassed men made painful Burden's now infrequent visits to the Senate cloak-room. To his colleagues as well as to himself, he was already on the outside, his place in the world usurped by a younger man.

For thirty-six years Burden had watched men come to the Senate and go, and if the going was involuntary, it was always unbearably sad. As he had been to others, they were now to him: affectionate but clumsy and altogether inadequate in the presence of the common nightmare, a career's end. Once he had given up all hope of the Presidency, he had taken it for granted that he would remain in the Senate until his death, a touching tableau which would take place on a leather sofa in the cloakroom, surrounded by friends to whom he would address a few final remarks, for the *Record*. But unless he were to die before January, this dream was ended, too. He was finished; he would never return, and everyone knew it. They also knew that he had somehow been forced out of the race by Clay. Fortunately, none suspected the truth, and he could at least depart with honor intact.

The cloakroom was crowded, and for the first time in weeks, Burden was no longer the sole object of pity. The day before had been the first Tuesday after the first Monday in November, and during that day the sovereign people had voted.

"It's hair-raising," said one Senator. "Never seen anything like it." He pulled Burden into the group. "You're lucky, getting out, still un-defeated champion."

With awe, they spoke of Senator McCarthy. Until now, The Club had not taken him seriously, regarding his publicity as a kind of theatre. Now they realized to what extent they had underestimated him. He had campaigned against his Senate enemies, and he had been victorious. Even the majority leader of the Senate had gone down in defeat.

"The dirtiest campaign in the history of politics," declaimed an elderly Senator, famed for the savagery of his tongue.

"The people are nuts on this Communism thing. Calling Tydings a Communist!" Heads shook at the thought.

"Perhaps," said Burden, "the time has come to take a stand." But the time, apparently, was not yet at hand. If Tydings could be defeated, no Senator was safe. The people were in an irresponsible mood and the wise man did his best to soothe and humor them by seeming to agree that the war in Korea was going badly because of traitors at home. It was a somber time in the country's history, and Burden was delighted. If he must fall, why not the Republic, too? Broken marble where the Capitol was, scorched skulls among the tangled grass of uncut lawns. Glorious vision!

Momberger entered the cloakroom from the Senate floor. He signaled Burden.

"Lousy news." That was the apparent consensus. With some passion the two colleagues denounced the electorate. Neither really blamed McCarthy. When the people went mad, there would always be someone to incite them to greater follies. McCarthy could not be held responsible; the beast was simply true to itself, and could not be otherwise.

"But it was a near thing for Clay." Momberger gave Burden a sheet of figures. "Final figures, county by county."

Burden studied the list of counties, *his* counties; he knew each one as if it was his own child, knew how it had voted for forty years, knew why, could judge with some accuracy how it would vote. The numbers on the page represented not just an abstract electorate but friends and allies, enemies and detractors. He took some satisfaction in the narrowness of Clay's victory: a plurality of twenty-two hundred and four votes out of more than a million cast.

"We damned near lost the state." Momberger looked grim; in two years' time he himself would have to face the same voters.

Burden was soothing. "There's nothing here to worry you. In two years McCarthy will be gone."

"I'm not so sure. And just look what he did to Tydings and Benton and Lucas. Why, he chewed 'em blood raw." Momberger's frontier phrases had been acquired, Burden knew, not on the frontier but from a thousand Western novels read during a Pawtucket, Rhode Island, childhood. Now of course Jesse was so venerable that people assumed that he had indeed traveled with Davy Crockett, known Pat Garrett, and dealt as an equal with the brothers James. Of the Senators, Burden alone knew Momberger's secret.

"You would have made a better race, you old fool! Why in hell didn't you run?" Momberger looked at him narrowly, head slightly cocked, eyes half shut against the desert's glare.

"Oh, Jesse . . ." Burden sighed. He had given out so many stories now that he had forgotten which one he had confided to Momberger. Officially, of course, he was leaving the Senate because he felt that the time had come for him to cease to be an actor and join the audience. Unfortunately, the suspicious probings of others had encouraged him to elaborate. There were, he intimated, books to be written, universities to be taught at, a Federal judgeship to be filled, and of course money to be made for the first time in his life. In the last few months he had hinted at everything from a fatal illness to a lifelong desire to be Ambassador to Ireland (this madness he had confided to an intimate of the Secretary of State, and he writhed at the thought of what that worthy must think of his pretensions, for he was not loved by the Administration).

"Thirty-six years is long enough in this place," he said to Momberger, who replied, "Like hell it is!"

A page approached Burden. "Your office just called, Senator. They said Mr. Sanford's arrived."

Momberger looked at Burden, somewhat puzzled. "Now what are you up to with Blaise Sanford? You're not fixin' to be one of those lousy columnists, are you?"

"Not Blaise, his son."

"That rich little Commie . . ."

"A friend of Diana, remember?"

"You don't have much luck with sons-in-law, do you?"

In the corridor outside the Senate Chamber, Irene Bloch embraced him. *"Cher ami!"* The voice rang out. Tourists paused to stare.

"What an election!" She held him by his wrists, as though he might, like St. Theresa, levitate.

"Cicero said that life is like a place in the theatre . . ." But Burden was not allowed to finish.

"So many dear friends defeated! Poor Senator Lucas, a saint, gone!"

"We all must go, Irene. I'm late for an appointment."

"But *you* will never go. I mean you'll stay on in Washington, won't you?"

"What else? Where else can I earn a living?" But the attempt at pathos failed, too. She was not listening.

"To know that you are still here makes it all so much better. Now where is Senator Taft?"

Burden said that he had not the slightest idea.

"According to his office, he is on the floor. You've seen the poll of course?" She stared past him, searching for Taft.

Burden shook his head. Stealthily he got one wrist free of her.

"Taft is the practically unanimous choice of the Republican leaders, which means he's absolutely certain to be nominated."

She frowned as Senator McCarthy, squat and smiling, crossed the hall, attended by Irish.

"What about General Eisenhower?"

"Not a chance." Irene was flat. "They don't like him and neither do I. Did you see what Harold Griffiths wrote about him yesterday? Even *he* has given up on Eisenhower, and you know his passion for the military."

"Peter Sanford is waiting for me." Burden got the other wrist free.

"Comme il est méchant!" But she said it gaily. "You must come and have tea with me soon, *à deux.*" She smiled significantly and tapped his face with an elegant claw. "After January, anyway; I'm booked until then."

Peter sat alone in the outer office, reading a paperback book which he thrust guiltily in his pocket but not before Burden had seen that it was *The Federalist Papers.* Burden had noticed that since the war interest in the American past had waned, at least outside the academic world. For the majority, history began with the New Deal, and any contemplation of the old Republic was downright antipathetic to those who wanted reform in the present and perfection in the future, a category to which Peter so notoriously belonged.

"Where's Mrs. Blaine?"

"Gone out for lunch, she said."

"I am deserted. You see me among the ruins of Carthage. Ponder my fate and count no day happy unless it be your last."

"You are in melancholy form!" Peter laughed appreciatively and followed Burden into the inner office. In the center of the room stood a large packing case, half filled with books.

"But you are still here for another three months . . ."

"Even so . . ." Burden stretched out on the leather sofa. "I want to depart stealthily, a bit at a time, unobserved. So that by the time my term ends, I shall have vanished without anyone noticing it."

"You fear pity?"

"Who does not?"

"Women do not. Some men." Peter showed Burden a newspaper folded open to an inside page. "There he is, being told about the election."

Burden gazed at the photograph without emotion. In the uniform of a colonel, Clay shook the hand of General MacArthur, who was gravely "congratulating the Senator-elect. Since his nomination in June, Colonel Overbury has been on active duty in Korea. As a front line officer with the U. S. First Cavalry Division, Colonel Overbury refused to campaign for public office, saying, 'The people of my state know by now what I stand for. As a fighting soldier, I am not at liberty to say anything except that this dirty business has got to be done, and I am doing what I can, in my small way.'"

Burden let the paper drop. "He's won!" That seemed the least as well as the most that could be said.

Peter nodded; his wide body barely fitted into the rocking chair. "It was genius, going back in the Army."

"It would be ironic if now he were to become a true hero just to disprove your story." Burden found himself, perversely, wanting to attack Peter, to support Clay.

"Luckily he hasn't gone that far. He's been at headquarters most of the time, but who will ever know that? Particularly after all those photographs of him in action. Apparently he plans to stay in Korea until January. Then he'll return in glory to take his seat in the Senate."

"He'll make a good Senator." Burden almost meant what he said.

"Good?" Peter's expression of disbelief annoyed Burden.

"Yes, good. He is ambitious, therefore he must be good."

"Or at least not be notoriously bad."

"He will certainly be diligent . . ."

"Or give the impression."

"*That* takes diligence." Burden chuckled, despite his own agony. "You must be compassionate. There's nothing more difficult for the modern politician with his eye on the White House than to seem to

be busy without actually doing anything for which he might later be
held accountable. He'll work hard, don't worry."

"For himself."

"He would be unnatural if he did not."

"Then I want unnatural men to govern us."

"To *govern?* No one governs in this house!" Burden exploded.
Truth at last. "The thing's too big. When I came here, a Senator
who wanted to do something could often accomplish it, if he cared
sufficiently. But now? We say 'Yea' or 'Nay' and our yesses and noes
are usually perfectly calculable in advance. Yet, believe it or not, there
was actually a time when legislation originated in the Congress. I
myself, in early days, once wrote a law which became the law of the
land. Now of course we receive our legislation already prepared for us,
the work of a thousand lawyers in a hundred bureaus, and nobody
here bothers to read a fraction of those bills we approve or disapprove."

"It is too big."

"It is too big."

But Peter would not accept Burden's dark view. "Individual Senators
still have power in some things. Clay will have power."

Burden shook his head. "Not in the Senate, he won't. He'll be just
another yes or no and the whips will know in advance just how he'll
vote."

"Perhaps one should abandon the whole system."

"We have abandoned it," said Burden. "We now live under a Presidential dictatorship, with periodic referendums which allow us to change
the dictator but not the dictatorship."

"Perhaps that is the only way this sort of society can be governed."

"It would be a shame to think so. But then I am reactionary, a
normal state at my age."

"We all react to the hateful present, even though there was nothing
better in the past." Peter was bleak. "I'm confident of that."

"Of course there were better times." Burden rose to the challenge,
thought of Shiloh, tried to speak of Lee and Lincoln, but Peter would
have none of it.

He drowned out Burden. "The apes have always governed us, and
our complaints are simply monkey chatter . . ."

"No!" Burden surprised himself by his own passion. "We had our
golden age." He indicated the portrait of Jefferson above the mantel-
piece. "I admit it was brief and that like all things human it went
wrong, which was no one's fault. Things do with us, and neither

your monkeys nor the apes can be held responsible. The good is rare, that's all, and not easy for most of us to live with."

Peter was stubborn. "There was never a golden age. There will never be a golden age and it is sheer romance to think we can ever be other than what we are now." He was radiant in his despair.

Burden sighed, knowing the mood too well. "Well, if that is so, then let us say that there was a time in our history when a few men of influence wanted things to be better than they are, unlike today when all that matters is money . . ." He stopped, and smiled. "But no matter how things are or were or will be, you go on as I do—or used to—trying to make things better. After all, if you were really so pessimistic you wouldn't publish *The American Idea* or be concerned with anything but pleasure in the moment."

"Pleasure in the moment varies from person to person," Peter was cryptic. For a long moment both men were silent while Peter rocked back and forth and Burden contemplated the painting of Jefferson. Then Peter said, "Why do you think that what I wrote about Clay had so little effect? It was the truth, and it was devastating."

"Apparently not. In any case the public is impressed only by winners."

"But winners have become losers. They've even gone to jail."

"But to say that Clay was a false hero . . ."

"And I proved that he was . . ."

". . . only confuses people who have already accepted him as what they think he is, a genuine hero, the subject of an extraordinary amount of publicity. That's all that matters, the large first impression. You cannot change it, short of a public trial."

Peter gave a sigh which became a groan. The rocking chair creaked beneath his weight. "I suppose I am naive."

"Optimistic is a better word. You think to be right is enough. It never is. Though I must say if it hadn't been for the war in Korea, I think you would have defeated Clay. Why do you hate him?" Burden was curious to hear the answer.

"Why do you?"

"But I don't." Burden told the truth.

"But he forced you out. You should hate him."

Burden sat back in the chair, suddenly alert, aware of danger. "How do you know that?"

But Peter seemed not to have heard him. "Diana thinks it's because my father prefers Clay to me. But that's too simple. I've never much liked my father, which means I should be glad he's got himself involved with Clay because it will end badly."

"All things do. You say he forced me out . . . ?"

"It's really Enid." Peter stopped his rocking and clutched his huge knees; he seemed carved from stone. "Clay killed her, you know."

"Ah . . ." Burden gestured to show how impossible it was for him to comment upon the private affairs of a family not his own.

"Oh, I know she might not have survived anyway, but they did edge her out."

"Now you would like to edge out Clay."

"It would be satisfying."

"The way you think he edged me out?" Burden put the question directly.

"Yes." Peter looked Burden full in the face. "It was that old business about the Indian land sale. Rather than be exposed by Clay, you quit the race."

On Burden's desk a brass ruler lay diagonally across a copy of the *Congressional Record*. Not liking the angle, he readjusted the ruler so that it neatly bisected the document at the center. "How," he asked, "do you happen to know this?"

"I have a friend at the *Tribune* who occasionally lets me see things in advance. Harold Griffiths has written a column describing the whole business. It's already set in type."

"Why is Harold Griffiths writing this now, when I am no longer in politics?"

"He thinks you had something to do with what I wrote. Since he can't attack me because of Father . . ."

Unable to contain himself, Burden asked the question that ought not to be asked. "Do *you* believe I took a bribe?"

"Why shouldn't you?" Peter got to his feet, his voice suddenly loud. "Considering what the others are, why should you be different?"

"One must be." But Burden's voice was inaudible.

Peter spoke through him. "There is no virtue in any of us, Senator. We are savages and don't say it was better when he was alive." Peter struck the painted face of Jefferson. "He lied and cheated and wrote lovely prose and collected recipes and wanted to lord it over this foolish land and did and died and that was the end of him. And don't say that it matters what opinion the future holds of you, for the human race will stop one day, not a moment too soon, and then it will not have mattered one single damn who was an ape and who was a monkey in this filthy cage."

Peter was at the door; he paused in his tirade and stared briefly at the framed text from Plato. Then he turned back to Burden, his voice normal. "If I were you, I'd appeal to Blaise. He likes you, as much as he can like anyone outside of Clay, and that's not really liking but what the Greeks called the 'unfortunate passion,' and speaking of Greek, your Plato's wrong." He pointed to the text on the wall: " 'Each of us is not born for himself alone.' It's a forgery. Plato never wrote that letter. Perhaps he should have written it, but he didn't. What can I do to help you?"

They crossed Chain Bridge and turned left on the road toward Great Falls. It had been years since Burden had made this journey, and he found the countryside sadly altered. Wooden frameworks of new houses stood, their pale wood raw against dark trees while billboards advertised entire new communities where life could be lived on easy terms with every modern appliance, a mere twenty minutes from downtown Washington. Burden liked nothing that he saw. But he refused to be distressed by anything today. He would think of nothing but the cool woods that smelled of mushrooms and decay.

"That's the turnoff there, at the gas station."

"O.K.," said the chauffeur, a young Negro found for him by Henry who had gone to work for the government with Burden's reluctant blessing. To lose the somber Henry was like losing a brother but he could not refuse him the chance to become available for a government pension. Solemnly Henry had departed that summer, promising to reappear every Sunday to tend the roses, and in fact he did make an occasional appearance at the house to discuss politics with the Senator and spray a rose or two. He also spoke privately and at length with his replacement but so far had yet to convince the young man that his employer should be addressed as "Sir." Passively, Burden disliked the new driver but the effort to find another was beyond him.

Nor was Kitty any help. She had no interests now except the birds, for whom she was currently building an elaborate sanctuary. In their twittering company her days were spent. Wearing a bathrobe and slippers, hair all undone, she seldom spoke to anyone, which was just as well, for with age her mind had filled with fantasies and instead of blurting out embarrassing truths she now revealed eccentric dreams that astonished and repelled even those who knew her best. But she

was happy among her birds, and Burden envied her for having so completely escaped the human. There would be no pain for Kitty ever again,
other than brief sorrow at a bird's fall, made instantly pleasurable by
a burial service witnessed by trees. Now that he needed her, she was
gone, which was fair enough, for in the days when she had needed
him he had taken her for granted, had left her behind while he pursued
the Presidency, year after year, back and forth across the continent.
Now there would be no more journeys; he was home again but the
girl he had married half a century before had ceased to exist and in
her place an old woman with thin hair crumbled stale bread to feed
birds.

"Where do I go now?" The voice combined hostility and petulance.
Burden looked out the window. They were on an unfamiliar road
with new houses to left and right, each with its high television antenna
drawing from the air crude pictures and lying words. Oh, detestable
age! he thought, hating all.

"It's straight ahead. Just keep on." He had recognized the patch of
woods where Henry usually parked. At least the pine trees were unchanged, unspoiled.

"I want you to wait," said Burden coldly; then turned and walked
toward the woods where North and South had met in deadly battle
and, that day at least, the South, his South, had won.

Burrs stuck to his trousers as he made his way slowly through tall
grass, but he did not pause to pick them off. He was intent on finding
his hill. Everything depended on that now. Once he had achieved it,
all would be well. He would be safe from attack, protected by that
Southern victory, redolent of virtue, courage, honor. Like burrs the
words stuck to his mind. And though he reminded himself that words
meant only what one wanted them to mean, he also knew that, once
invested with meaning, words became magic, and could destroy as well
as sustain.

The field was the same. But upon the hill where he used to sit,
trees had been cleared, a cellar dug, and in orderly piles cement block
was stacked. The bullet would long since have been dug up by the
bulldozer which had scooped out the cellar of the house-to-be.

"What're you doing here?" The voice belonged to a sad-faced man
in blue jeans and windbreaker.

"I'm sorry." Burden was gracious. "I am Senator Day."

"I didn't ask who you were. I asked what are you doing here. This
is private property."

Stung, Burden stepped back, away from the profaned hill. "I'm sorry. I didn't know anyone lived here. I used to visit . . ."

"I've got signs posted. I'm sure you can read."

"Yes. Very well. Thank you." In a rage, Burden turned his back on the man. He had said who he was and yet the man had persisted in his rudeness. So a world of honor ends.

Burden made his way back through the woods to the car, aware that the man in the field continued to watch him as if he might suddenly set the woods afire or in some other way diminish the value of the property.

Burden's driver had turned on the radio full volume. He was listening raptly, thick lips ajar, to the thunder of a lover's lament.

"Turn that damned thing off!" A long slow look as the young man absorbed the command. Then he switched off the radio and, slowly, opened the car door for Burden.

"Take the river road. I'll tell you when to stop." As the car started, Burden realized that he was shivering. He held his hands together and with all his strength forced each hand to steady the other. But tremors still went through his body. Obviously a delayed reaction to what Peter had told him. By deliberately refusing to address his mind to his own ruin, the body had been forced to absorb the shock the mind disowned.

He tried to imagine what the next few days would be like. The story would break on Thursday. He could anticipate the sneering tone. Lately Harold had taken to writing exposés of small (never great) corruptions in the Congress. Padded payrolls and illegal campaign contributions were the usual crimes, momentarily embarrassing to the legislator involved but seldom causing much damage. Americans had always believed that their representatives were corrupt since, given the same opportunity, they would be, too. As it was, the common folk daily cheated one another, misrepresenting the goods they sold and otherwise conducting themselves like their governors. If Clay Overbury was able to present himself as a war hero and be elected, why, then, they reckoned, more power to him. After all, he was no different from the used-car dealer who makes a profit on a car he knows will not run properly. Of course, "If you can't be good, be careful" was the national wisdom, and it was hardly wise to be caught. Yet Burden was by no means convinced that Clay, for one, would have been defeated even if he had not had a war to hide in. The people seemed genuinely uninterested in moral matters. What mattered was winning, and Clay had won. For that matter if he himself had become President in 1940, the taking of Nillson's money would have been regarded in retrospect as a brilliant necessity which in a sense it had been. Even now he regretted not so much the selling of his vote as the abandoning of his responsibility to the Indians.

Sweat clouded his face while cold arms and legs twitched as though they were on strings, manipulated by someone not himself. He must regain control. He recalled a visit recently made him by one of the Indians whose land was sold to Nillson. "Best thing ever happened to us, selling off that land. No damn oil in it anyway, and if we had stayed there we'd gone right on the way we was, ignorant as all hell. Now I got my own business and . . ." Success story: a bad action with good results.

But Burden refused himself this easy comfort. He had all his life believed that one should behave in a certain way despite the example of others, and for most of his life he had been honest. Even as he sounded most royally all the depths and shoals of honor, he had made few compromises with his own sense of virtue. That others did not share his scrupulous niceness merely made him all the more pleased with himself. Now all that was at an end and he would be revealed as what he was, worse than the others because they at least never for a moment believed that it was better to be honest than dishonest, noble than ignoble, good than bad; no sophistry as to what was *truly* good could save him from himself, not to mention from the world's contempt once Harold's column had been printed. And to be truthful, it was the thought of what others would say that gave him the most pain. To know that they would laugh at him for being found out, take delight in the end of his career and then, easily, forget that he had ever existed, since what, after all, was he, but just another crooked politician who had had his day?

"Stop here."

The driver put on the brakes too quickly. Burden's bad shoulder struck against the side of the car. He cursed softly. Then before the fool could ask what he was supposed to do next, Burden told him that he was to wait. "I'm going to take a walk. You can play the radio if you like."

Trees without leaves descended a steep slope to the Potomac, whose brown waters swirled about sharp rocks that broke the river's flow, like so many stepping-stones set out for a giant's use.

A narrow path zigzagged among trees to which he clung as he

hurried, like a boy, toward the river, nothing in his mind but a desire to escape entirely the present and the human.

Abruptly the path turned to reveal a ruined cabin with roof half gone, door sprung and windows broken in. He stopped and looked inside. The floor was strewn with yellow newspapers and ashes from old fires. He thought of the soul's dark cottage which, battered and decayed, let in new light, but only to reveal, on closer inspection, empty beer bottles, used contraceptives, and a man's shoe. He continued his descent through the cool woods, the roar of water upon rocks growing louder with each step.

The path ended at a narrow rocky beach. Between tall boulders worn smooth by the last glacier, his father stood, wearing a torn Confederate uniform and holding a rifle, just as he had that day in the field at Manassas when his son had failed to recognize him. But there was no mistaking him now. The blazing eyes of the furious boy he had never known were those of the man who had been his life's tormentor.

Burden spoke first. "You were right," he said. "It has all gone wrong. You should be pleased." He took a tentative step toward the Confederate corporal, who took a step back, revealing as he did the torn cloth of his tunic, bright with a new wound's blood.

"You're bleeding still!" The triumphant shout caused the boy to hold his rifle in such a way as to bar Burden's approach to him. But in his passion Burden was not to be put off by mere death. All life was now concentrated in that single gaping wound and all that needed doing in the world was the staunching of the blood.

With stiff fingers Burden removed a handkerchief from his pocket. Then he walked toward the wounded soldier, half expecting him to run away. But this was no ordinary youth; it was his father honorably struck by an enemy's bullet in the field of battle. The Confederate corporal did not flinch even when at last they were face to face.

For a long moment Burden stared into the blue eyes that perfectly reflected empty sky. Then slowly he extended the hand which held the handkerchief. Now only the rifle barred his way. He waited patiently until at last, marvelously, the rifle was lowered. With a cry he flung himself upon the youth who was his father, plunged the handkerchief into the wound, lost his balance, fell against the beloved, was taken into those long-dead arms, and like impatient lovers, they embraced and together fell.

Richard Eberhart

THE IDES OF MARCH
and other poems

Dear Whit:

In selecting something for *This Is My Best:*

I want to say what I want to say in poetry. The compulsion to write the poem, enacting its truth in words, is stronger than regard for the reception of the poem in the world. I write what I am compelled to write, not what I think the reader wants to hear, not to the style of a year or a decade, not to a group or to a group manifesto or program. I write as individualist.

About the value of an audience, we know, for instance, that Hopkins' poetry had little to do with an audience, for he had none (except a few friends, "for a poet is a public in himself") and, having none to ruin him or to praise him, he could be passionately devoted to the truth, and address his poems to it.

The truth about poetry is complex. In some letters Hopkins regretted an audience and fame, "the being known." He got his audience long after his death.

Do not think that I do not like or want an audience. The problem in our open, dynamic, and shifting society is whether we can have a unified audience, whether there can be a cultural situation in which a large, articulate, intelligent and sensitive audience would know, love and promote the best poetry of a time. Or must a democracy produce millions who maintain a newspaper taste in poetry, in ignorance of the best, while a relatively few conduct and use the higher poetry mainly in universities and colleges? Can this dichotomy be resolved in this country? Do the best poets in fact close this gap? Although it took Whitman decades to be known posthumously as the poet of the people, of all

America, do what I call persons with a newspaper sensibility in poetry even now read him? Is his chief audience this late still the university, the educated sensibility?

The use of poetry is its good. If it is not used it is useless, to say the obvious.

If poetry is subjective to me, I realize that its reception is part of the objective reality of the world. It would thus seem reasonable, in reviewing my own forty years of writing poetry, to name poems (to represent a core of one's work) which have been used repeatedly in anthologies, textbooks, or elsewhere.

However, I would like to reverse direction from the objective to the subjective, and arbitrarily choose four new poems from *Shifts of Being,* published in 1968, The Ides of March, Outwitting the Trees, Evil, and Marrakech; and two new poems, not yet published in book form, John Ledyard, and Will.

Richard Eberhart

THE IDES OF MARCH

As I was riding through New England
Along about the Ides of March
I passed by an ancient graveyard
And looked hard at the stones:

It was the deepest look I ever gave,
It was a look I had given long ago,
The most intimate and the most personal,
For I wondered what I signified.

I could not see my next connection,
Nor any of the loves I have in life
As divorced from that immaculate glimpse
Of the permanent end of human being.

The car bore on through the countryside,
Plunging in meshes of society,
We were going to meet our friends in the world,
In the next connection of belief and delight.

We were going to meet the world incarnate
Without reference to the rigors or Ides of March;
As we slid through the freshening Springtide
We faintly apprehended the fatal glance.

It is that glance of the eternal judgment
Of the silence of the manifold gravestones
Frightens me as we seize in love and belief
The love not to ask what is our ultimate end.

As I was riding through New England
Along about the Ides of March
I was the essence of the questioner,
Only the glance of the gravestones answered me.

OUTWITTING THE TREES

I do not think there is any way to outwit the trees.
They have a nature of a hundred years at the least
And stand eighty feet in the air from the bank of the river.
Sometimes the rains darken their trunks; sometimes the snows
Burden their branches; sometimes the wind crepitates them
Knocking a huge branch to earth; sometimes they are quiet
Under full moonlight in the stealthy take of Autumn.
They move more than you would think in empathy with nature.

We change. They seem to say, I am standing still
But I will give and bend and move as I am urged,
Come any season. Only catastrophe will see me horizontal.
They know the sap rising, the ice cracking, know the signs
Of a changing season, mean to be imperturbable.
How lovely they give pine scent to the winds' upliftings,
With what subtleties they live through the days and the years.
How they are inspiritors of a lofty attitude.

To them Plato and Aristotle are nothing.
They do not care about Shakespeare or Christ.
The political upheavals of one century or another
Are of no concern, and if a young man dies
In some replete war in the twentieth century
They could not care less. Their ancestors stood over
The earth in centuries long before the twentieth.
They blazon their truth fixed beyond the human.

We have to import into them our longings
For a permanence we do not have, theirs relative
Only, for who knows the future of vegetation or man,
It is their angelic statelihood we admire,
They cannot kill, maim, demean, despise, or cheat,
All day they express the perfection that we feel
But cannot create or enact. They are not critical.
There is no way to outwit the trees, nor would I wish to.

EVIL

When I entertained evil
I played upon him as if he were good.
At my red banquet table
I set before him peppery food.

I thought he was king of the world.
His elegance, his subtlety
Were without question in my mind.
His sensibility was exquisite.

He seemed like a devil incarnate
But so much like my friends, myself,
That I recognized a hidden truth.
At a banquet table nothing offends.

We talked of the affairs of state.
Should one turn the other cheek?
The idea was that to lose face
Was a shame in being weak.

None thought to kill was bad.
The pictures of the lacerated Vietnamese
Were somehow not to be mentioned.
None thought that any here was obese.

There is a certain delicacy
In what to say at a dinner party.
The idea is to accept man as he is
And rejoice at eating hearty.

Now I opened a bottle of Rosé.
It was a symbol of relaxation.
We were all feeling well
And I offered a toast to the nation.

I said, let us drink to freedom.
This seemed brightly reasonable
As everyone around the table arose
In our state of hedonism.

We drank to the glory of our state,
None thinking this uncouth.
We drank to individual aims,
And to the complexity of truth.

Our guest, a ruler of the world,
Was delightful, polite. I saw his bloat.
He said that evil was the greatest good,
My imaginary bullet through his throat.

MARRAKECH

The dance begins with the sun descending
Beyond the Koutubia in Marrakech so ancient
And so fable present: the old tell fables
As the Moroccans listen in eyed attention
In the marketplace of vitality and veiled women.
But the dancers, O the dancers, priests of devotion

From the high Atlas mountains, perhaps twelve,
A boy of ten, shining men under thirty,
Their feet bare and hard on the bare, hard earth,
Begin to dance to two taut goatskin drums,
Beaten with hard crooked sticks, thin in the diameter,
The one fiercely antiphonal to the other,
Together beating compelling rhythm to action,
Action in the flow of the loose, ancient garments
Of the men as they strike in both hands
Double metal castanets in the dry, high air of late day.
One would come forth, loosening his devotion,
Gyrating and flashing in compelling immediacy,
Total in ecstasy, overwhelming the senses,
And fall back, and another would step forth lightly,
Deftly begin his interpretive energy, total
Devotion to sound, rhythm, style of the dance,
And fall back, and his fellow come out before
To outdo the predecessor, turn and leap and gyrate
In ochre ambience, and the drums' insistence
Proclaiming efficient animal action,
The passion of primitive man exultant,
And each came forward, each leaped taller,
Flashed lower, turned subtler, rose higher
Prolonging intensity of animal strategy,
A rapture of magnitude pervaded the air,
Sound and sense reached to magical ability,
One drummer on his knees, the drum head vertical,
Beat out the passion of ancient centuries,
Appeared the thronging nature of tribal power,
And the laughing gods fell to the earth, spent,
And the high heart bent down with them to the earth,
And the heart was raised up to the Atlas mountains,
In the superabundant, delirious air of sundown,
And the laughing gods fell to the earth, spent,
And the heart bent down with them to the earth,
Cleansed in the nature of rhythm and rite,
The dance was a thing in itself triumphant,
Music and dance the perfection of the free,
And before one could think of the meaning

The driven passion of the drums begins again,
O ancient Africa, O tribal ecstasy!
A dance of six hundred years on the same spot,
They come out again instantaneous and eternal,
And leap and turn, passionately leap and fall,
And all are made whole again under the red sky
And all is made whole in the heart and time.

JOHN LEDYARD

Only death remains
To tell us
How great we were

Great with life,
The stone entablature
By the river

Tells us
Of a youth who made a canoe
From a cedar,

Descended the Connecticut,
Discovered far places,
Died the great voyager

Far from home,
Lost in Africa,
Youthful, valiant, destroyed.

That was in another century.
The incised bronze fades,
His name only remembered

By insignificant lovers in the Spring
Who read his story
And clasp each other,

Amazed at intrepidity
For all they want is themselves,
His valiancy hallucinatory,

His trial of the world incredible,
Their heroes themselves,
They only want to clasp each other.

Only death remains
To tell us
How great we were

Speaks the voice of the voyager
From fading bronze letters,
Great with desire.

WILL

What is will but the advent of the free?
Is the sailor who sails on the sea, whose vessel
Descends from Eagle Light to shoal Duck Harbor on Ile au Haut,
Casting anchor near the weir, and remaining overnight,
Voyaging outward in the morning, out to the open ocean
Turning east to the bull music of Roaring Bull Ledge,
Going thence northeast before a following southwester
To the Light of Swans Island, thence to Frenchboro
And up the chart to Placentia, west across Blue Hill Bay,
Across Jericho, and into Eggemoggin Reach and through it,
Back to mooring near Weir Cove on Cape Rosier,

Nearer to reality than a man of land sitting on the shore,
Immovable so he seems, despite changes of tide, of wind,
Impervious to fog rolling in or lifting, the light's decline,
Or its rise to scintillant brilliance in a forenoon of glass,
Is this man nearer to reality being without action,
Willing imagination in his snug bone case,
Containing within his skull voyages past and future?

He wills to sit still and listen to the secret music
Of sidereal roarings beyond the reach of human hearing,
It is the play of imagination without danger of drowning
Where the will is free to assume the freedom of its desire.

The contemplation of heaven has to be this side of death.
The contemplation of the minute particulars of tragedy
Speaks in superior oracles to the pain and ordeal of the real,
A voyage of endless nuances and considerations
Giving the illusion of reality beyond the grasp of the actual.
To sink in thought is less possible than to sink in wood,
So it seems, for the dogged persistence of the mind exists,
Its raptures incalculable, its blazons searching the deeps,
Its dream equal to the effects and douse of Ulysses,
Its structure of the possible greater than the actual.

Yet in plethoric instances of imagined reality
Where mischance is the limit of the breathing tone
Man's concern is with reality itself
And he shall imagine beyond the vastness of the universe
His brace against, bout with Roaring Bull Ledge,
Dreaming of the truths beyond the seas
Because he stood to the compass on the waves of chance,
Ironist who dared the danger of the open ocean,
Pulled down by fate in willing the control of action,
Enigmatic helmsman of the real, man of imagination.

Norman Mailer

DEBORAH
from AN AMERICAN DREAM

Dear Whit:

Sometimes it seems to me useful to think of two kinds of novels—novels of manners, and modern explosive surrealistic novels in which the very notion of society, let alone manners, is bulldozed away in order to see which strange skeletons of fish and what buried treasure comes steaming up in the ore. Out of my own work I suppose *Why Are We In Vietnam?* would most satisfy the latter category, and *An American Dream* might prove for some to be my most substantial attack on the problem of writing a novel of manners. They are hard novels to do well. Now that we are approaching the end of the seventh decade of the twentieth century they are becoming novels which are almost impossible to do well. The old totemistic force of manners, the old totemistic belief that breaching a manner inspired a curse has been all but lost in the avalanche of social deterioration which characterizes our era. Yet what can appear more attractive and sinister to us than a tea ceremony at the edge of a cliff. So I often think *An American Dream* is my best book. I tried for more in this novel than anywhere else and hence was living for a while with themes not easily accessible to literary criticism, not even to examination. The passage I now choose is not obligatorily the best few thousand words in the work, but comes at least from the latter part of the first chapter and therefore offers few discomforts of orientation to the reader, and no demand on me for a synopsis of preceding events. Perhaps it may also serve to illumine the fine nerve of dread back of every good manner. Manner is the mandarin of mood, and in the shattering of every mood is an existential breath—does laughter or the murderous next ensue?

Yours,
Norman Mailer

Walking the street just this cold night in March, the horrors were beginning. On these occasions when I had to see her, my instinct gave the warning that if I waited another half hour, even another ten minutes, I might lose her forever. It made no sense, I was almost always wrong in my anticipation of her mood, I was too rattled these months ever to divine what her mood might be, and yet I knew that the way I would probably lose her in the end was by waiting too long on some exceptional night when she might be hoping I would call. For once a certain moment was passed, once Deborah ever said to herself, "I am rid of him, I am rid of him now finally and forever," then it would all be gone. She was nothing if not final, she took forever to form her mind, but come the moment and she would not look back.

So I went into an outdoor booth, and shivering in the trapped cold air, I phoned her apartment. She was home—there were agonies on those nights I phoned and she was out—but she was home this night, and she was cordial. Which was a very bad sign.

"*Darling*," she said, "where have you been? You must rush over." She was a handsome woman, Deborah, she was big. With high heels she stood at least an inch over me. She had a huge mass of black hair and striking green eyes sufficiently arrogant and upon occasion sufficiently amused to belong to a queen. She had a large Irish nose and a wide mouth which took many shapes, but her complexion was her claim to beauty, for the skin was cream-white and her cheeks were colored with a fine rose, centuries of Irish mist had produced that complexion. It was her voice however which seduced one first. Her face was large and all-but-honest; her voice was a masterwork of treachery. Clear as a bell, yet slithery with innuendo, it leaped like a deer, slipped like a snake. She could not utter a sentence for giving a tinkle of value to some innocent word. It may have been the voice of a woman you would not trust for an instant, but I did not know if I could forget it.

"I'll be right over," I said.

"Run. You must *run.*"

When we separated, she was the one who had moved out. Our marriage had been a war, a good eighteenth-century war, fought by many rules, most of them broken if the prize to be gained was bright enough, but we had developed the cheerful respect of one enemy general for another. So I had been able to admire the strategic splendor of leaving me in our apartment. It *stifled* her, she explained to me, it was a source of much misery. If we were to separate, there was small logic for her to remain behind in an apartment she did not like, no, it was better for her to leave me there, I was fond of the apartment after all. I was not, I had never been, but I had pretended to be fond. Therefore I inherited her misery. Now the apartment, the empty stadium of our marriage, stifled *me,* but I had not the pluck, the time, nor the clean desperation to move. I used it as a place to drop my dirty shirts. Meanwhile, she hopped from one fine suite to another; there was always a friend leaving for Europe, and no one was ready to remind Deborah she was very behind on the rent. (What cowards were her friends!) I would get the bill finally, it would be a knockout, $2700 for three months rent—I would hold it, no question of paying. Part of the attrition on my military reserves had been the expenses. Deborah got four hundred dollars a week—it was senseless to give her less, she would merely run up her bills, and I had been scuffling and humping, taking three hundred dollars for a spot appearance on a television show, and seven hundred fifty for a spiced-up lecture to some Ladies Auxiliary in Long Island—"The Existential Approach to Sex." Yes, debt was grinding me bad, I was something like $16,000 in the hole already and probably worse—I did not care to count.

The apartment she had now was a small duplex suspended some hundred or more feet above the East River Drive, and every vertical surface within was covered with flock, which must have gone for twenty-five dollars a yard; a hot-house of flat velvet flowers, royal, sinister, cultivated in their twinings, breathed at one from all four walls, upstairs and down. It had the specific density of a jungle conceived by Rousseau, and Deborah liked it the best of her purloined pads. "I feel warm in here," she would say, "nice and *warm.*"

The maid let me in. "Madame is upstairs in the bedroom," she said with a smile. She was a young German maid who must have had an interesting life in the ruins of Berlin from the age of five, for nothing missed her attention. She had taken lately to smiling at me with a droll mocking compassionate and very wound-up spite which promised portfolios of detail if I were ever rich enough to turn her tongue just once. I was sometimes tempted to start, to grab her in the hall and take her spiced mouth, lay my tongue on hers and rustle up with a stroke those overtones of malicious music she could sing. What Madame did with me she knew too well because I might still spend a night with Deborah from time to time, but what Madame did with others . . . that would have to be bought.

I ascended the stairway, a padded perfumed aisle up a wall of flowers. Deborah was in bed. Her body was not only large but lazy and she hopped into bed whenever she did not know what else to do.

"My God," she said, "you look awful." Her mouth turned fond at the corners. She never disliked me so much as when I came to see her looking my best. "You really are a contemptible-looking creature this evening."

Did she know about the balcony? Sometimes I was convinced I was mad, because it seemed not at all exceptional to me that Deborah had been in touch with the moon and now had the word. She had powers, my Deborah, she was psychic to the worst degree, and she had the power to lay a curse. Once after a fight with her, I had been given traffic tickets three times in fifteen minutes, once for going down a one-way street, once for jumping a red light, and once because the policeman in the last car did not like my eye and decided I was drunk. That had been all in the form of a warning from Deborah, I was certain of that. I could see her waiting alone in bed, waving her long fingers languidly to spark the obedient diabolisms and traffic officers at her command.

"It was a bad party," I said.

"How is Philippe?"

"Looking well."

"He's a *very* attractive man. Don't you think so?" said Deborah.

"Everyone we know is attractive," I said to annoy her.

"Except you, pet. You look as if you've used up your liver for keeps this time."

"I'm not very happy," I said.

"Well, come *here* and live. There's no reason why you can't move back with me."

Her invitation was open. She wanted me to dispose of my apartment, sell our furniture, move in with her. After a month she would move out again, leaving me with the velvet flock.

"If you'd come this afternoon," she went on, "you could have seen Deirdre. Now she's off to school. You are a swine not to have seen her." Deirdre was her daughter, my step-daughter. Deborah's first husband had been a French count. He had died of a lingering illness after a year of marriage, and Deirdre, so far as I knew, had been the child of that marriage, a delicate haunted girl with eyes which contained a promise she would learn everything about you if she looked too long, and so chose not to look. I adored her, I had realized for years that being step-father to Deirdre was the most agreeable part of our marriage; for that reason I tried to see her as little as possible now.

"Is she pleased at going back to school this trip?"

"She would have been more pleased if you had come by." Deborah's complexion was mottling with red. When she became angry a red flush, raw as a rash, spotted her neck. "You pretended to love that child for so long, and now you give her no attention."

"It's too painful," I said.

"God, you're a whimperer," said Deborah. "Sometimes I lie here and wonder how you ever became a hero. You're such a bloody whimperer. I suppose the Germans were whimpering even worse than you. It must have been quite a sight. You whimpering and they whimpering, and you going pop pop pop with your little gun."

Never had she gone quite so far before. "How do you tell that story these days?" Deborah went on.

"I don't tell it."

"Except when you're too drunk to remember."

"I'm never too drunk to remember."

"I can't get over the way you look," Deborah exclaimed. "I mean you really look like some poor peddler from the Lower East Side."

"I'm descended from peddlers."

"Don't I know it, honey-one," said Deborah. "All those poor materialistic grabby little people."

"Well, they never hurt anyone particularly." This was a reference to her father.

"No, they didn't, and they didn't have the guts to do anything else either. Except to make your father brainy enough to make your mother and then make you." She said this with such a stir of fury that I moved uneasily. Deborah was violent. I had a bad scar on my ear. People thought it came from the ring, but the truth was less presentable—Deborah had once bitten it half-through in a fight.

"Go easy," I said.

"You're fragile tonight, aren't you?" She nodded, her face almost gentle, almost attentive, as if she were listening to the echo of an event. "I know something happened to you."

"I don't want to talk about it." Which was in effect a counter-attack. Deborah could not bear not to know.

"I thought you were dead," said Deborah. "Isn't that funny. I was certain you were dead."

"Were you sorry?"

"Oh, I felt a great woe." She smiled. "I thought you were dead and you'd left a will that you wished to be cremated. I was going to keep your ashes in an urn. There—right by the window table. Each morning I was going to take a handful of your dust and drop it on the East River Drive. In time, who knows, you might have been *strewn* all over New York."

"I would have done my best to haunt you."

"Can't, pet. Not when you're cremated. That atomizes the soul. Didn't you know?" Her green eyes had a particularly bad light. "Come here, darling, and give a kiss."

"I'd rather not."

"Tell me why not."

"Because I threw up a while ago and my breath is foul."

"Bad smells never bother me."

"Well, they bother me. And you've been drinking rum. You smell Godawful." It was true. When she drank too much, a stench of sweet rot lifted from her. "The Irish were never meant to go near rum," I said, "it brings out the odor of their fat."

"Do you talk this way to all your little girls?"

She did not know what I did with the days and weeks I spent away from her. This was forever agitating her rage. Once, years ago, she uncovered an affair I had been keeping in a corner. It had been with a rather ordinary young lady who (for compensation, no doubt) had been a burning wizard in bed. Otherwise, the girl was undeniably plain. Somehow, Deborah learned about her. The subsequent details are vicious, private detectives, so forth, but the indigestible issue was that Deborah had gone with the private detective to a restaurant where the girl always had lunch and studied her through a meal, all through a long meal the poor girl ate by herself. What a scene followed!

"I don't think I've been quite so marooned in all my beloved life," Deborah had said. "I mean, *figure-toi*, pet, I had to keep up a conversation with the detective, a *horrible* man, and he was laughing at me. All that money spent on fees, and for what, a poor wet little mouse. She was even afraid of the *waitresses*, and this was a *tea*-room. What a big boy you must be to take up with a sparrow."

The real part of her fury was that no intrigue had ensued; if the affair had been with one of her friends, or with some other woman of parts, then Deborah could have gone to war and fought one of her grand campaigns, hook and eye, tooth and talon, a series of parties with exquisite confrontations; but I had merely been piddling and that was the unforgivable sin. Since that time Deborah spoke only of my *little girls*.

"What do you say to them, pet?" asked Deborah now, "do you say, 'Please stop drinking so much because you smell like a piece of fat,' or do you say, 'Oh God, darling, I love your stink?'"

The mottling had spread in ugly smears and patches upon her neck, her shoulders, and what I could see of her breast. They radiated a detestation so palpable that my body began to race as if a foreign element, a poison altogether suffocating, were beginning to seep through me. Did you ever feel the malignity which rises from a swamp? It is real, I could swear it, and some whisper of ominous calm, that heavy air one breathes in the hours before a hurricane, now came to rest between us. I was afraid of her. She was not incapable of murdering me. There are killers one is ready to welcome, I suppose. They offer a clean death and free passage to one's soul. The moon had spoken to me as just such an assassin. But Deborah promised bad burial. One would go down in one's death, and muck would wash over the last of one's wind. She did not wish to tear the body, she was out to spoil the light, and in an epidemic of fear, as if her face—that wide mouth, full-fleshed nose, and pointed green eyes, pointed as arrows—would be my first view of eternity, as if she were ministering angel (ministering devil) I knelt beside her and tried to take her hand. It was soft as a jellyfish, and almost as repugnant—the touch shot my palm with a thousand needles which stung into my arm exactly as if I had been swimming at night and lashed onto a Portuguese man o' war.

"Your hand feels nice," she said in a sudden turn of mood.

There was a period when we held hands often. She had become pregnant after three years of marriage, a ticklish pregnancy to conserve, for there had been something malformed about her uterus—she was never explicit—and her ducts had suffered from a chronic inflammation since Deirdre had been born. But we had succeeded, we wanted a child, there was genius between us we believed, and we held hands for the first six months. Then we crashed. After a black night of drink and a quarrel beyond dimension, she lost the baby, it came brokenly to birth, in terror, I always thought, of the womb which was shaping it, came out and went back in again to death, tearing by this miscarriage the hope of any other child for Deborah. What it left behind was a heartland of revenge. Now, cohabiting with Deborah was like sitting to dinner in an empty castle with no more for host than a butler and his curse. Yes, I knelt in fear and my skin lived on thin wire, this side of a profound shudder. All the while she stroked my hand.

But compassion, the trapped bird of compassion, struggled up from my chest and flew to my throat. "Deborah, I love you," I said. I did not know at that instant if I meant it truly, or was some monster of deception, hiding myself from myself. And having said it, knew the mistake. For all feeling departed from her hand, even that tingling so evil to my flesh, and left instead a cool empty touch. I could have been holding a tiny casket in my palm.

"Do you love me, pet?" she asked.

"Yes."

"It must be awful. Because you know I don't love you any more at all."

She said it so quietly, with such a nice finality, that I thought again of the moon and the promise of extinction which had descended on me. I had opened a void—I was now without center. Can you understand? I did not belong to myself any longer. Deborah had occupied my center.

"Yes, you're looking awful again," said Deborah. "You began to look all right for a little while, but now you look awful again."

"You don't love me."

"Oh, not in the least."

"Do you know what it's like to look at someone you love and see no love come back?"

"It must be awful," said Deborah.

"It's unendurable," I said. Yes, the center was gone. In another minute I would begin to grovel.

"It is unendurable," she said.

"You do know?"

"Yes, I do."

"You have felt it?"

"There was a man I loved very much," she said, "and he didn't love me."

"You never told me that before."

"No, I didn't."

Before we married, she told me everything. She confessed every last lover—it had been her heritage from the convent: she had done more than tell me, she had gone to detail—we would giggle in the dark while she tapped my shoulder with one cultivated and very learned finger, giving me a sense of the roll and snap and lurch and grace (or lack of it) in each of her lovers, she had even given me a sense of what was good in the best of them, and I had loved her for it, painful as the news had sometimes been, for I had known at least what I was up against, and how many husbands could ever say that? It was the warrant of our love; whatever our marriage had been, that was our covenant, that had been her way of saying I was more valuable than the others.

And now she was inside me, fused at my center, ready to blow the rails.

"You don't mean it," I said.

"I do. There was one man I never told you about. I never told anyone about him. Although once, somebody guessed."

"Who was the man?"

"He was a bullfighter. Marvelous ripe man."

"You're lying."

"Have it your way."

"It wasn't a bullfighter."

"No, it wasn't. It was someone far better than a bullfighter, far greater." Her face had turned plump with malice, and the red mottling had begun to fade. "As a matter of fact, it was the finest and most extraordinary man I ever knew. Delicious. Just a marvelous wild feast of things. I tried to make him jealous once and lost him."

"Who could it be?" I asked.

"Don't bother to hop on one foot and then the other like a three-year-old who's got to go to the Lou. I'm not going to tell you." She took a sip of her rum, and jiggled the tumbler not indelicately, as if the tender circles of the liquor might transmit a message to some distant force, or—better—receive one. "It's going to be a bore not having you here once in a while."

"You want a divorce," I said.

"I think so."

"Like that."

"Not like *that,* darling. *After* all that." She yawned prettily and looked for the moment like a fifteen-year-old Irish maid. "When you didn't come by today to say goodbye to Deirdre . . ."

"I didn't know she was leaving."

"Of course you didn't know. How could you know? You haven't called in two weeks. You've been nuzzling and nipping with your little girls." She did not know that at the moment I had no girl.

"They're not so little any more." A fire had begun to spread in me. It was burning now in my stomach and my lungs were dry as old leaves, my heart had a herded pressure which gave promise to explode. "Give us a bit of the rum," I said.

She handed over the bottle. "Well, they may not be so little any more, but I doubt that, pet. Besides I don't care. Because I made a vow this afternoon. I said to myself that I would never . . ." and then she did not speak the rest of the sentence, but she was talking about something she had done with me and never with anyone else. "No," said Deborah, "I thought: There's no need for that any more. Never again. Not with Steve."

I had taught it to her, but she had developed a pronounced royal taste of her own for that little act. Likely it had become the first of her pleasures.

"Not ever again?" I asked.

"Never. The thought—at least in relation to you, dear sweet—makes me brush my gums with peroxide."

"Well, goodbye to all that. You don't do it so famously if the truth be told."

"Not so famously as your little girls?"

"Not nearly as well as five I could name."

The mottling came back to her neck and shoulders. A powerful odor of rot and musk and something much more violent came from her. It was like the scent of the carnivore in a zoo. This last odor was fearful —it had the breath of burning rubber.

"Isn't that odd?" asked Deborah. "I haven't heard a word of complaint from any new beau."

From the day of our separation she had admitted to no lover. Not until this moment. A sharp sad pain, almost pleasurable, thrust into me. It was replaced immediately by a fine horror.

"How many do you have?" I asked.

"At the moment, pet, just three."

"And you . . ." But I couldn't ask it.

"Yes, darling. Every last little thing. I can't tell you how shocked they were when I began. One of them said: 'Where did you ever learn to root about like that? Didn't know such things went on outside a Mexican whorehouse.'"

"Shut your fucking mouth," I said.

"Lately I've had the most famous practice."

I struck her open-handed across the face. I had meant—some last calm intention of my mind had meant—to make it no more than a slap, but my body was speaking faster than my brain, and the blow caught her on the side of the ear and knocked her half out of bed. She was up like a bull and like a bull she charged. Her head struck me in the stomach (setting off a flash in that forest of nerves) amd then she drove one powerful knee at my groin (she fought like a prep-school bully) and missing that, she reached with both hands, tried to find my root and mangle me.

That blew it out. I struck her a blow on the back of the neck, a dead cold chop which dropped her to a knee, and then hooked an arm about her head and put a pressure on her throat. She was strong, I had always known she was strong, but now her strength was huge. For a moment I did not know if I could hold her down, she had almost the strength to force herself up to her feet and lift me in the air, which in that position is exceptional strength even for a wrestler. For ten or twenty seconds she strained in balance, and then her strength began to pass, it passed over to me, and I felt my arm tightening about her neck. My eyes were closed. I had the mental image I was pushing with my shoulder against an enormous door which would give inch by inch to the effort.

One of her hands fluttered up to my shoulder and tapped it gently. Like a gladiator admitting defeat. I released the pressure on her throat, and the door I had been opening began to close. But I had had a view of what was on the other side of the door, and heaven was there, some quiver of jeweled cities shining in the glow of a tropical dusk, and I thrust against the door once more and hardly felt her hand leave my shoulder, I was driving now with force against that door: spasms began to open in me, and my mind cried out then, "Hold back! you're going too far, hold back!" I could feel a series of orders whip like tracers of light from my head to my arm, I was ready to obey, I was trying to stop, but pulse packed behind pulse in a pressure up to thunderhead; some black-biled lust, some desire to go ahead not unlike the instant one comes in a woman against her cry that she is without protection came bursting with rage from out of me and my mind exploded in a fireworks of rockets, stars, and hurtling embers, the arm about her neck leaped against the whisper I could still feel murmuring in her throat, and *crack* I choked her harder, and *crack* I choked her again, and *crack* I gave her payment —never halt now—and *crack* the door flew open and the wire tore in her throat, and I was through the door, hatred passing from me in wave after wave, illness as well, rot and pestilence, nausea, a bleak string of salts. I was floating. I was as far into myself as I had ever been and universes wheeled in a dream. To my closed eyes Deborah's face seemed to float off from her body and stare at me in darkness. She gave one malevolent look which said: "There are dimensions to evil which reach beyond the light," and then she smiled like a milkmaid and floated away and was gone. And in the midst of that Oriental splendor of landscape, I felt the lost touch of her finger on my shoulder, radiating some faint but ineradicable pulse of detestation into the new grace. I opened my eyes. I was weary with a most honorable fatigue, and my flesh seemed new. I had not felt so nice since I was twelve. It seemed inconceivable at this instant that anything in life could fail to please. But there was Deborah, dead beside me on the flowered carpet of the floor, and there was no question of that. She was dead, indeed she was dead.

Archibald Macleish

WHERE'S A POET FROM?

W.B.:

I have twice before contributed notes to selections of poems of mine in this enterprise and each time I have found it more difficult. I don't like the word "best," which is at best invidious, and I feel self-conscious, not to say silly, applying it to work of my own. All any man can decently hope is that *something*—a line, a few lines, maybe an entire poem—will turn out to be *good*. And it is not for him to decide which, if any. Frost put it as well as it can be put at the Amherst dinner on his eightieth birthday: ". . . to leave a few poems it will be hard to get rid of." Hard, that is, for *others* to get rid of. This is not modesty—certainly not false modesty—it is common sense. A poem, if it *is* one (and not all are) has a life of its own and will make its own way in the world, through eclipse and neglect and rediscovery and fame and all the phases. When you think about the whole of your work, as you must on receipt of a letter from the editor of this anthology, you think in these terms. And, if you name a particular piece, you are naming it with this hope in mind: that it will prove to have such a life. At least it is with this hope in mind that I name a few poems from a book I published last year, *The Wild Old Wicked Man*.

faithfully
Archibald MacLeish

WHERE'S A POET FROM?

Where he's born?
Settles? Where the papers claim him?
Carl Sandburg, born in Illinois,
died in Flat Rock, Carolina, in Chicago famous—

where was Sandburg from? Chicago?
People knew where Frost was from
in spite of San Francisco—from New England.
What town or what proud country knew this other coming?

He lived around: he lived in Kansas,
Chicago on the Old West Side,
Michigan, Nebraska—in Wisconsin.
Where was Carl from in the Carolinas when he died?

His tongue might tell: he talked "Peoria"—
O as in Oh or Low, the way
the railroad trainmen on the Illinois
called it in those cool reverberating stations.

His sound might say: he said "Missouri"—
a stumbled M and an S and an OO
long as a night freight off across the prairie
asking the moon for answers and the sound goes through and through.

Where was Sandburg from, old poet,
dead in Carolina in his great repute?
"Peoria," he said, "Missouri," the neglected names
that now, because his mouth has spoken them, are beautiful.

MARK'S SHEEP

Mark's sheep, I said, but they were only
stones, boulders in the uncropped grass,
granite shoulders weathered to the bone
and old as that first morning where God was.

And yet they looked like sheep—so like
you half expected them to startle,
bolt in a leap because some tyke
had barked, because a bluejay darted—

dart of shadow under blue of jay—
or someone shouted by the water trough,
slammed a car-door, drove away,
or squirrels quarreled, or a gun went off,

or just because they must: that terrified
impulse to be somewhere else
browsers and ruminators seem to share
as though they knew, they only, the sky falls

and *here* is dangerous (as of course it is).
But Mark's sheep never startled from the grass.
They knew their place, their boulders' business:
to let the nights go over, the days pass,

let years go, summer, autumn, winter,
each by itself, each motionless, alone,
praising the world by being in it,
praising the earth by being stone.

SURVIVOR

On an oak in autumn
there'll always be
one leaf left at the top of the tree
that won't let go with the rest and rot—
won't cast loose and skitter and sail
and end in a puddle of rain in a swale
and fatten the earth and be fruitful . . .
                                        No,

it won't and it won't and it won't let go.
It rattles a kind of a jig tattoo,
a telegrapher's tattle that *will* get through
like an SOS from a struggling ship
over and over, a dash and a skip.

You cover your head with your quilt and still
that telegrapher's key on Conway hill
calls to Polaris.

              I can spell:
I know what it says . . . I know too well.
I pull my pillow over my ear
but I hear.

THE BOATMEN OF SANTORIN

The boatmen on the bay of Santorin
where the world blew up about the time of Minos
sit with their hands on their oars inviting the tourists.

Visit the myth! Visit the fable!
Visit the drowned volcano where the world
blew up about the time of Minos!

The sea sings. The sun shines.
Visit the end of the world! they shout to you.

And all at once on the bright blue
tourist sea, suds of pumice,
floating shoals of grey decaying stone,
grate at the wooden oars.

                    We float here
feathering death at our oar-blades.

HEMINGWAY

"In some inexplicable way an accident."
            —Mary Hemingway

Oh, not inexplicable. Death explains,
that kind of death: rewinds remembrance
backward like a film track till the laughing man
among the lilacs, peeling the green stem,
waits for the gunshot where the play began;

rewinds those Africas and Idahos and Spains
to find the table at the Closerie des Lilas,
sticky with syrup, where the flash of joy
flamed into blackness like that flash of steel.

The gun between the teeth explains.
The shattered mouth foretells the singing boy.

LATE ABED

Ah, but a good wife!
To lie late in a warm bed
(warm where she was) with your life
suspended like a music in the head,
hearing her foot in the house, her broom
on the pine floor of the down-stairs room,
hearing the window toward the sun go up,
the tap turned on, the tap turned off,
the saucer clatter to the coffee cup . . .

To lie late in the odor of coffee
thinking of nothing at all, listening . . .

and she moves here, she moves there,
and your mouth hurts still where last she kissed you:
you think how she looked as she left, the bare
thigh, and went to her adorning . . .

You lie there listening and she moves—
prepares her house to hold another morning,
prepares another day to hold her loves . . .

You lie there
thinking of nothing
watching the sky . . .

"THE WILD OLD WICKED MAN"

Too old for love and still to love!—
Yeats's predicament and mine—all men's:
the aging Adam who must strut and shove
and caper his obscene pretense . . .

And yet, within the dry thorn grove,
singer to singer in the dusk, there cries
(Listen! Ah, listen, the wood dove!)
something conclusion never satisfies;

and still when day ends and the wind goes down
and not a tree stirs, not a leaf,
some passion in the sea beats on
and on . . .
                    (Oh, listen, the sea reef!)

Too old for love and still to long . . .
for what? For one more flattering proof
the flesh lives and the beast is strong?—
once more upon the pulse that hammering hoof?

Or is there something the persistent dove,
the ceaseless surges and the old man's lust
all know and cannot say? Is love

what nothing concludes, nothing must,
pure certainty?

                    And does the passionate man
most nearly know it when no passion can?
Is this the old man's triumph, to pursue
impossibility—and take it too?

II

The Old History and the New

Allan Nevins

THE OLD HISTORY AND THE NEW

Dear Mr. Burnett:

  My selection, delivered first as a brief speech in the Library of Congress, was chosen because of my earnest belief that history must be made vital by ever-new ideas, and durable by felicity of expression. It grows as civilization grows.

Sincerely yours,
Allan Nevins

It is recorded that when the British Empire went to war in 1914 one of its outlying dependencies astonished the Cabinet, sitting anxiously in Downing Street, with a crisp message. It read: "Barbados is behind you!" I am here in a humbler role than Barbados held in 1914. If I seem to have come to assure the august muse Clio that I am behind History, its writing, its reading, and its future growth, actually I appear only to raise a question; and for this even the least of us may sometimes be heard. When James Ford Rhodes delivered the presidential address to the American Historical Association in Boston in 1899, he remarked that he would be vain indeed if he thought he could say anything new about historical pursuits. Perhaps I may echo the deprecatory sentence that he added: "Yet to a sympathetic audience, to people who love history, there is always the chance that a fresh treatment may present the commonplaces in some different combination, and augment for the moment an interest which is perennial." Particularly is there reason to speak when history is in such a troubled position as it holds today.

Like everything else, the writing of history is always in a state of change. If slow, the change is evolutionary; if abrupt and drastic, it is revolutionary; and today I think it is plainly revolutionary. In the wake of two wars, and in the midst of the vast scientific innovations inaugurated by the unlocking of nuclear power, nearly every department of thought has been subjected to revolutionary stresses. Written history, as all have agreed from Thucydides to Mommsen, is largely an effort to chart lines of force. The entire outlook of his-

tory has been disturbed by the two global wars. As the French Revolution brought the common man for the first time under the lens
of history, so the politicoeconomic upheavals of the last half century
have brought a large number of neglected peoples and societies under
continuous historical examination. At the same time, as Newtonian
and Darwinian advances in science once changed the outlook of all
students of history, so the advances of the age of Einstein have again
sweepingly altered our interpretations of the past. Relativity reigns not
in physics and astronomy alone, but in writings upon the development of society.

We will be unable to comprehend fully the present revolutionary
changes for some time to come. Nevertheless, we can confidently affirm that our view of the history of Alabama is being perceptibly
altered by the recent transformation of Africa. The facts of the past
do not change, but our view of them does. Similarly, our view of
the history of national states and regional alignments is being jarred
into new angles of vision by the recent strides in communication and
transportation that give mankind enlarged capacities for interaction.
Some of them are beneficent; some are not. But they do bring us
nearer the one world of which Wendell Willkie spoke. When Britain
and France went to war in the eighteenth century, wrote Macaulay,
red men scalped each other on the Great Lakes, and black men
clubbed each other to death on the Niger. Still, the slaughter was
then limited. But if the United States and Russia threaten each other
with nuclear weapons today, all continents, all countries, all cities not
only *feel* endangered but *are* endangered; and this fact gives us a
compulsive new outlook upon the past as well as the future.

History becomes a more formidable subject every year. Once its
tools were simple, the most important being diligence and accuracy
in research, judgment in interpretation, and force in style. Once it
concerned itself with themes that might be called majestic, but which
were plain and understandable. These subjects, for the English-speaking
peoples, were primarily political, constitutional, and religious. History
was regarded as largely a training for lawyers, legislators, administrators,
and the clergy. Political order and constitutional regularity were counted
the two proudest contributions of the British and American peoples
to society. They were lofty historical themes in themselves, and still
loftier if viewed as tributary to the history of freedom, our proudest
word, or of freedom and equality, our proudest phrase. The word
sociology had not then been invented by Herbert Spencer, and econom-

ics in pre-Marxian days—or in England before R. H. Tawney and
in America before Thorstein Veblen—was not discussed as the historical determinant that many later concluded it to be.

Henry Adams, one of the ablest figures in the old historical tradition, believed that the grand central theme in studying the past
ought to be national character, its sources, its growth, and its results. That is, he believed this before he became fascinated by the
Gallery of Machines in the Paris Exposition of 1900 and the 40-foot
dynamos humming there; before, as he writes, his "historical neck
[was] broken by the sudden irruption of forces totally new." He
had written his nine-volume history of the administrations of Jefferson
and Madison, he tells us, to delineate the character of the young
Republic, although only six chapters in the first volume and four
in the ninth dealt directly with the subject. His basic idea was better
than George Bancroft's conviction that history is the will of God
working through events, or John Fiske's that it is the will of God
working through events and Social Darwinism. Most later historians,
however, have pronounced Adams' theme at once too broad and too
narrow: too broad, in the sense that it was too vaguely subjective,
for anything can be read into the national character; and too narrow, in that character, however defined, is only one strand in the
complex web of human development. The modern historian insists
upon studying society as a whole, in its entirety and its constant
flux.

His attitudes and tools have therefore become nearly as complex
as society itself. He wishes to know as many facts about social structure as Sidney and Beatrice Webb mastered in England, or John R.
Commons on this side of the Atlantic, and more. He would like to
know more about psychology in relation to historical change than
William James knew. He hopes to learn as much as R. H. Tawney
learned about the way in which political doctrines, religious beliefs,
and economic interests are all knit together by a thousand threads,
and to display his knowledge as lucidly as Tawney did in *Religion
and the Rise of Capitalism*. The modern historian wishes also to be
as alert to new implements as the graduate students who are declaring today in scores of American and European universities that
much as they would value a working command of another language,
they would prize still more a full knowledge of computers. That is,
they would prize an understanding of the way in which the most
expert numerical techniques, the mastery of statistics, and the ability

to frame complex problems for computer solution can cast new light upon a hundred subjects from poverty in Calcutta to voting patterns in Chicago.

In brief, the modern student of history feels that he must know something of a broad array of new conceptual tools—economic, sociological, anthropological, numerical, psychological—in analyzing the development of society as a totality. This he calls the "conceptualization" of history. He believes that we move forward in our mastery of the past not alone by old-fashioned factfinding and factual analysis, but by the use of quite new bodies of knowledge and new interpretations based mainly in the new social studies. (They are not really social *sciences,* though often miscalled that.) The rise of these studies, antedating and paralleling the changes just mentioned as stemming from two global wars and new scientific discoveries, has added to their revolutionary force. What may be called a new history seems to many to be emerging. When James Ford Rhodes delivered his presidential address of 1899, which *The Atlantic Monthly* published in February 1900, its laudation of Herodotus, Thucydides, and Tacitus carried a distinctly old-fashioned air. Its concepts were few and simple. The modern student would say that we have passed beyond them.

Rhodes, for example, clearly had no idea that a great new historical study called demography was already being born. He had little realization that a new connection between psychology and history was appearing, tinged by the ideas of Freud and Jung, which would in time enable young American scholars to explain the personalities of the slave and the slaveowner—men in whom James Ford Rhodes was deeply interested—in more acute and complete terms.

Rhodes could not foresee, any more than you and I could only a quarter century ago, that numerical studies of society—that is, numerical analyses of population at different age levels, of epidemics and mortality, of food production and the incidence of malnutrition, and other subjects—would soon become important. Two years ago we had Peter Laslett of Cambridge University with us in the Huntington Library. He first opened my eyes to the extent to which the whole thought and outlook of a society in which the average lifespan of its members covered only 30 years, as in Elizabethan days, was unescapably quite different from the thought and outlook of a society in which the average lifespan reached 60 years, as it had by the time of Elizabeth II. This is one of the most interesting facets of demography. When I read Mr. Laslett's book, *The World We Have Lost,* a broader study of the social structure of preindustrial Britain, he opened my eyes again.

As for social anthropology and cultural anthropology, they were alike unknown, in their present-day meaning, when James Ford Rhodes wrote. For example, the blood feud as it was known in the old antebellum South, and was pictured in Mark Twain's tragic chronicle of the battles of the Shepherdson and Grangerford clans in *Huckleberry Finn,* cried in vain for an analysis by the cultural anthropologist. Mark Twain tells us that Baldy Shepherdson, like his enemy Colonel Grangerford, was a patrician and in his own eyes a gentleman. He could nevertheless shoot down a defenseless 14-year-old boy in cold blood and feel happily proud of the feat, a fact that only the social anthropologist and the psychologist could properly explain.

All advanced historians rejoiced when one social anthropologist, Mrs. Ruth Benedict, just after the last great war, produced her historical study of the Japanese character entitled *The Chrysanthemum and the Sword.* Her title emphasized the evident contradictions in the national character: the contradictions displayed by the Japanese, who are, as she wrote, "to the highest degree, both aggressive and unaggressive, both militaristic and aesthetic, both insolent and polite, rigid and adaptable, submissive and resentful of being pushed around, loyal and treacherous, brave and timid, conservative and hospitable to new ways." So eminent a historian of Japan as the late Sir George Sansom, the best historian any oriental nation has had, tells us that he had often felt impatient and confused because of his failure to grasp the national character; that he had almost concluded that only the creative artist could do the job. Sansom thought perhaps such an artist could illuminate the problem by flashes of insight, as Somerset Maugham seemed to him to have illuminated the Spanish temperament in his novel *Don Fernando.* But when Sansom read *The Chrysanthemum and the Sword* he took heart. He saw how well anthropological insights could serve history.

"It is a valuable book," he writes, "for not only does it give in very clear language an accurate picture of certain dominant features of Japanese life, but also it encourages one to believe that, in skilled hands, the technique of the social anthropologist may presently be applied with success to the study of other great societies." And we know how high a valuation General MacArthur, approaching the book from another point of view, set upon it.

As the new tools are applied, and as fresh conceptual analyses of old historical problems are developed out of constant advances in all the social disciplines, we catch at least glimmerings of a broader outlook upon history. The new tools do not themselves guarantee breadth. We might search for that particular quality in vain in the work of such a revolutionary experimenter with fresh techniques as Sir Lewis Namier. Unquestionably Namier was an expert in political behaviorism and in what is called "career-line analysis." Yet for all his ingenuity and penetration in the exploration of British political history, Sir Lewis achieved a singularly small popular following in Great Britain, and none at all in the United States. Although he founded a distinct historical school, he never showed enough breadth, vision, or stylistic distinction to capture the public mind or be read outside the universities. While Tawney had breadth, as did Mrs. Benedict, most specialists in social-study interpretations are too specialized to cultivate it, and too narrow to garner its fruits. They are all too often just monograph writers.

It is a fact that in the United States the three historians who have made the deepest impression in recent times have done so through provocative new ideas broadly—not narrowly—related to the social studies. The three are Frederick Jackson Turner, who demonstrated the significance of the frontier as an evolutionary molder of the American people; Vernon L. Parrington, who in treating the history of our literature chose to follow what he called "the broad path of our political, economic, and social development, rather than the narrower belletristic" path; and Charles A. Beard, who in his *Economic Origins of Jeffersonian Democracy,* which is a better book than his *Economic Interpretation of the Constitution,* demonstrated that after the Constitution was ratified it still had to be filled in and given life, that this had to be done by an active, well-organized party, and that under Hamilton's leadership this party acted on economic lines for purposes mainly economic. All three historians provoked acrimonious controversies. And all three would have subscribed to an aphorism I once heard uttered by Hugh Trevor-Roper: "All historical developments, including religious developments, are meaningless except in their social framework."

This aphorism requires an illustration, which can be picked up anywhere. One is found in Robert Heilbroner's recent book on *The Limits of American Capitalism.* How, he asks, can we explain why in the early decades of the industrial revolution the British aristocracy, so proud, exclusive, and conservative, formed strong alliances with the rising leaders of manufacturing and trade, while the French aristocracy placed itself in disastrous antagonism to them? One part of the complex explanation doubtless lies in the role of the British younger sons. But the story takes meaning only in the whole social framework.

Yes, a comprehension of the possibilities of the new studies ought to give history greater versatility and breadth. In this broader outlook, with a social orientation and a constant use of such disciplines as economics, anthropology, and psychology, some of the old controversies that have troubled historical work will tend to disappear. The hoary disputation over the place of the hero in history, for example, may grow dim. More attention will be paid to the psychology of the masses, to the drift of the age, and to great formative movements; less attention to individuals who are supposed to have towering stature and to play cataclysmic parts in history. That such cataclysmic personages do appear from time to time nobody can deny. The greatest religious leaders—Buddha, Jesus, Mohammed; the greatest scientists—Copernicus, Darwin, Einstein; the greatest political leaders—Caesar, Napoleon, Churchill—will always hold their places as men who have deepened the flow of history.

It is surely a clear truth in advanced Western countries that while superficial aspects of society change rapidly, its fundamental character alters but slowly and gradually and changes more often through mass action than by individual leverage. Tocqueville declared that this was true of the United States, and it is true of other nations as well. It is another important fact, although discovered only in the last century, that in advanced Western societies ideas more often percolate upward than downward. This was not at all the belief of Froude, Carlyle, or Francis Parkman. It has been very much the belief of the best later historians of culture like George Macaulay Trevelyan and of sociologists like Pareto. In this realization by the newer school, also, some old controversies will tend to fade. And the maxim that history is past politics, a statement that Johns Hopkins University once inscribed on its walls, can no longer be accepted if we throw emphasis upon the history of integrated society.

A quite false idea of history is inculcated by such misleading labels as the Jacksonian Era, or the Age of Theodore Roosevelt, whether we think of men or parties. Leaders of great force of character like Jackson, or of great ability combined with force like Roosevelt, do in certain circumstances become the captains who head important movements. But are they truly the creators of an era? Seldom is this the fact. They may take charge of impulses that had their roots far back in the past and were growing powerful when they seized the helm, as Jackson did. Or they may become catalysts of vaguely defined bodies of opinion to which they give clear shape and direction, as T.R. did. They often fill an important third role in becoming centers of legend. Myths accumulate about them, and the myths invented by partisan followers, heightening their stature, become powerful in themselves. Any student of Jefferson has to distinguish between the real and the legendary Jefferson, a task that Henry Adams found difficult. Still more, a student has to distinguish between the actual Lincoln and the Lincoln that Carl Sandburg, among others, turned into so appealing a mixture of poetry, fable, and solid worth. Economics, sociology, and psychology do history a service in helping shake us free of these old misconceptions.

Thus far I have spoken respectfully and appreciatively of the new approaches to history and the new tools available in writing it. The new history is introducing fresh winds into a stuffy room, and these breezes should be welcomed. We need a spirit of cooperation. No true scholar should be a partisan of the new history, treated as one of the social studies, as something hostile to the old history, treated as one of the humanities; or a partisan of the old literary history as something hostile to the new scientific history. Properly viewed, they are not antagonistic to each other; they are complementary. Our task is to set proper metes and bounds to each and find just how they can be mutually helpful. This is the question I said I came to raise.

What disturbs me most is the tendency of many workers in the social studies to arrogate too large a field to themselves, to overrate their expertness, and to forget the towering achievements of their elders and contemporaries in the humanities. As Arthur M. Schlesinger, Jr., remarked, some men think that "social science" methods are not one of several paths to social wisdom, but the central and infallible path. They fling out challenges upon the necessity of using something called "integrated theory construction" as if this invalidated all previous writing. When they speak of history it is in condescending terms. C. Wright Mills, for example, in suggesting a genetic approach to sociological problems, warned students against "that dull pudding called sketching in the historical background." They plainly wish to see history become so specialized and scientific that it will lose all relation to literature. It will possess so few of the age-old attractions we have associated with the arts of narration, description, and personal portraiture or characterization, that few people will deem it worth reading.

This attitude, if given full rein, would destroy history as art—for it is an art. It would eliminate all the color and drama we have associated with history as *story*—for it is fundamentally a dramatic story. It would reduce historical writing to a narrow set of topics seldom related to any broad framework of meaning. Many of the subjects presented by sociology to the historian are highly interesting within fixed limits: a study of the mobility of population at a given time and place, for example; a study of mass religion; a study of working hours and leisure employments. To treat them expertly, however, requires complicated new principles that are hard to explain to readers and a new vocabulary that easily degenerates into an alien lingo, while they must be digested into a general narrative or they will mean little. The economist has *his* principles and poses the same problem of digestion into a larger whole; so does the psychologist; and what historian can master *every* such specialty?

This danger of losing touch with the intelligent reader, the inquisitive general public, and everybody else but one or two fellow specialists is recognized by champions of the new approaches. One of them, Keith Thomas, the author of the opening article in the issue which the *Times Literary Supplement* devoted to the new history last April, indicates that it will be hard to swallow the new fare, but that the dose must be taken. "Sociological thinking," he writes, and he might have added anthropological thinking, psychological thinking, and the rest, "has usually been pioneered by rootless intellectuals, foreign observers and immigrants. It does not come easily to the English academic, who has always been more closely involved with the established social order. It involves cooperative scholarship and organized research, a world of seminars, workshops and graduate programmes, which is alien to the individualist, prima donna tradition in which most English historians have been reared. It brings with it the risk of jargon and obscurity, whereas history has always been regarded as a subject which should be intelligible and attractive to the layman. In the age of the historical factory some nostalgia is inevitably felt for the simpler days of the domestic system. But it is misguided to resist . . . professionalism." This champion of what we may call multispecialized history implies that "the coming revolution," the overthrow of history as written in the past, must and will be accepted.

All this would be highly alarming if we did not realize that the mainstream of history will sweep on in the old channels. History has always been written primarily on a humanistic basis, is today so written, and by every index we can measure will continue to be thus written. What are the histories of recent years that we keep on a convenient shelf? Are they books memorable for social-science expertness? Or are they histories that Mr. Thomas may hold in contempt because they are written by "individualist, prima donna" writers in a manner "intelligible and attractive to the layman"? As I read a list of ten American books the question answers itself:

James Truslow Adams, *The Epic of America*
Carl Becker, *The Heavenly City of the Eighteenth-Century Philosophers*
Van Wyck Brooks, *The Flowering of New England*
Bruce Catton, *A Stillness at Appomattox*
Margaret Leech, *Reveille in Washington*
Garrett Mattingly, *The Armada*
Samuel Eliot Morison, *The Maritime History of Massachusetts*
Barbara W. Tuchman, *The Guns of August*
Carl Van Doren, *Secret History of the American Revolution*
Edmund Wilson, *Patriotic Gore*

The *Times Literary Supplement* essayist was good enough to tell us that even when possession is taken of the historical field by its new masters, a place will be found for writers of the old school. They can find employment as popularizers of the invaluable stores of new knowledge brought them by the social-science experts. "If history is to maintain a deserving place in the affections of the reading public," he states, "it is essential that those with a gift for popular exposition should master the new techniques, so that, even if they do not themselves contribute to knowledge, they may at least be able to evaluate the contribution of others." That is, men of literary attainments and traditional attitudes will never be able to write books that have any originality or add anything to the world's libraries. But they can use their "gift for popular exposition" to make the really valuable histories by the specialists palatable to the masses. They can "evaluate the contribution" of the real writers and tell people what to think of them. Such condescension, such magnanimity! In this adjustment the old-fashioned historians will get a place— a footstool seat. They will be given a little piece of pie—humble pie.

Such a statement does grave injustice to the great majority of economists, anthropologists, and sociologists, who feel, just like the great majority of historians, that we are all partners in the search for an enlarged truth; that we can adjust our pretensions amicably; that no true worker looks down on another; and that least of all does he look down upon an august, rich, and continuously vital tradition. One of my old-time students, Dr. Edward Saveth, recently edited an illuminating volume entitled *American History and the Social Sciences*. Largely made up of essays by men learned in the social disciplines, it is instructive in content and refreshing in temper. Dr. Saveth dedicated the book to me as a *narrative* (he meant a *humanistic*) *historian*, not because he saw that in my ignorance I badly needed to read it, but because he knew I would like its outlook.

One reason why specialists in the social studies seek a proper definition of their place in our partnership lies in their realization that for vast areas of historical study their skills have little or no value. They do not aim at the effects of a Clarendon in character study, or an Acton in the dissection of events, or a Lecky in painting social canvases. They know they cannot. One contributor stated frankly that while certain areas are amenable to social-science concepts—community studies, entrepreneurship, political leadership—many are not. Another writer admitted that many social concepts, like status, class, and image, are vaguely defined. Even Turner never satisfactorily defined "frontier"; 17 different definitions of "power" have been listed. Various critics have noted that although Carl Becker said a great deal about the importance of the social-science approach to history, when he wrote his *Heavenly City* he scarcely touched upon one of the really central aspects of the eighteenth century, namely, its social science. Arthur Schlesinger, pointing out that Namier dismissed a whole range of historical issues because they were not susceptible of quantification, commented: "I am bound to reply that almost all important questions are important precisely because they are *not* susceptible to quantitative answers."

The social scientists who count are for various reasons as humble-minded as the historians who count. They know that their ideas and methods must be pooled in history with other ideas and methods, and they cannot be too dogmatic. They know that much of their material is likely to be so dull to lay readers that active minds will balk at it. Above all, if they have been properly educated, they have a reverence for the greatest humanists. They know that the writing of a sound piece of history possessing literary distinction demands high talent and sometimes calls forth touches of genius. There are plenty of substitutes for the opaque prose that the social scientist can furnish; there is little substitute for high literary talent, and none at all for genius.

Why and how are the best historical works written? They are planned because the author has a vision, or an approach to one. The subject takes hold of him, inspires him, and lifts him to a plane where he sees as in a golden dream the volume he intends to write. He sees also that it must be written in a particular way: in precisely *his* way and no other, with *his* selection of facts and *his* points of view.

To take one example in many, why did Lytton Strachey write *Elizabeth and Essex,* a masterpiece of compressed and highly dramatic narrative history? The chances are ten to one that Strachey wrote it because, after prolonged reading and reflection, he suddenly said to himself, "What a superb subject is embedded in that particular stretch of English history! What histrionic qualities the boastful, impetuous Essex, the sly Francis Bacon, the enigmatic, cautious Elizabeth revealed!" Or why did George Macaulay Trevelyan write *Garibaldi and the Thousand?* Again, no doubt, because after travel and long study Trevelyan said to himself: "I can make this one of the most enthralling tales of daring, fortitude, and patriotic devotion to be told in our time." These men did not write their books because they saw an opportunity to make unprecedented explorations into the field of psychological analysis or the sociology of rebellion.

The quality which good historical writing most demands, wrote James Anthony Froude, is—what? Social awareness? economic expertise? No, he replied, "Imagination." To my mind, Froude was absolutely right. Imagination is essential to re-creation of the past, and it is re-creation at which the historical artist aims. The imagination here invoked is not invention: it is the imagination that enabled Livy to *hear* the clash and jingle of the peck of rings, stripped from Roman knights on the bloody field of Cannae, that a Carthaginian emissary poured out on the senate floor in Africa after Hannibal's victory; the imagination that enabled Francis Parkman to *feel* the warmth of the turbid Mississippi off its Arkansas shore as La Salle, drifting downstream, plunged his arm over the side of the canoe. Other historians might give a different answer from Froude to the query as to what quality is most needed by the historian, but they would name some intellectual gift or trait, not some department of learning.

When Kipling wrote that there are a hundred different ways of writing tribal lays, and every single one of them is right, he stated a primary truth about history. A good historian sees how a certain subject can be shaped to make the most of the particular materials he possesses, the talents and experience he has accumulated, or the legitimate demands of public taste—demands that change sharply from time to time. This is right and proper. Especially is it right and proper for a writer to shape his book according to his talents. If he has great gifts, as my friend Bruce Catton, for example, had in approaching the Civil War, he does this by intuition and an inner compulsion. If he alters his design to make room for economic factors, or anthropological factors, that do not come naturally to him, he spoils it.

Ah, says the social scientist, but look at such a famous piece of literary history as Carlyle's *French Revolution*. How can you defend its manifest historical inadequacies? It should be studied by classes in English literature. But who would recommend it for study by earnest and informed students of French history? It contains nothing about the financial crisis that set the Revolution in motion. The economic specialist would throw it out of his library for that deficiency. It says almost nothing about the social changes that accompanied the Revolution, and nothing about the new civil institutions that grew out of it. Sociologists and governmental specialists would condemn it for that. What does it say about patterns of voting behavior, or mob psychology? Is it more than a fossil remnant in history?

The true historian catches up this challenge at once. What *does* Carlyle's *French Revolution* offer? he asks. Little that the social-science specialist values, everything that the humanist values. Are not historians humanists? It has passages of as tremendous moral force as were ever written, reminding us that Goethe told Eckermann that young Carlyle would produce masterpieces of moral insight. It has passages of superb pictorial vividness, reminding us of Lecky's comment that Carlyle saw the French Revolution as by lightning flashes. It has a burning intensity few writers can match, a fervent sincerity bursting from a hot heart and a sleepless brain, so that, as Carlyle himself put it, his writings rushed up "like rockets druv by their own burning." On the strictly historical side, it has a perception that the best French authorities have admired; for Carlyle, as François Aulard writes, perceived that the common people of France were the true heroes of the epic struggle. It has a command of the psychology of both individuals and masses that possesses almost unique value. As J. Holland Rose states, Carlyle "shows us the workings of the human heart as no other historian of institutions and no microscopic analyst, like Taine, has ever done or ever will do." It is for the social-science specialist to annotate Carlyle, as they have done, not for modern Carlyles—if we are fortunate enough to produce one—to annotate or popularize the books of the specialists.

One of the greatest attractions of history as a study lies in its endless variety, a variety that time cannot wither nor custom stale. The true historian does more than tolerate its versatilities; he admires its protean richness. The intolerance of a few social scientists, whose specialization too often gives them a mole-like vision, seems to me a sin that can do grievous harm to historical writing. Carl Becker, at whose side I taught for a year in Cornell University, was a historian I warmly admired. He had a wide-ranging love of historical reading; I used to see him move slowly across the sleet-swept campus above Lake Cayuga, with a great armload of books he was carrying from the university library to his home. He wrote one of the best books on our craft in *Everyman His Own Historian*. Yet, under the influence of Frederick Jackson Turner, Becker once yielded to a spirit of intolerance. He declared that Turner might well boast of the fact that his contributions to history and the social sciences had been set forth only in monographic studies, essays, and occasional addresses, that his collected works did not fill much space, that he had never yielded to the demand of his disciples and publishers for a "great work."

"Seven volumes at the very least they seem to demand," wrote Becker, "in stately leather-backed tomes for preference, something they may point to with pride as an achievement, a life work, one of those 'comprehensive' and 'definitive' histories no doubt which posterity may be expected to label 'standard,' and straightway shelve with Gibbon and Grote behind glass doors, rarely opened."

In this statement it is not the commendation of Turner for restricting his best work to short monographs that jars upon us. That eminent historian had every right to shape his work according to his own talents and vision, and it is because he did just this that *The Fontier in American History* is one of our assured classics. The jarring note is in Carl Becker's intolerant reference to Gibbon and Grote. These writers do not reside behind glass doors seldom opened. I doubt if any historian in any country is more frequently reached down from the shelves than Gibbon, or, even after nearly 200 years, read with more profit. I doubt if a survey would not show that every day some thousands of people in the United States and Great Britain, in Canada and Australasia, in South Africa, India, and the isles of the sea, can be found looking into *The Decline and Fall*. Grote holds a lesser place. But if Carl Becker could have read the admiring essay on Grote just written by the Italian historian Arnaldo Momigliano, dedicated to his friends of the Hebrew University of Jerusalem, and published in England and America, he would have done more justice to the continued vitality of a writer as well known in French, German, and Italian translations as in English. There is a place for the writer of a multivolume set as well as for the monograph writer; a place for Mommsen and Prescott, McMaster, Francis

Parkman, and A. T. Mahan, as well as for the best authority on econometrics.

The first requirement of the true lover of history is that he shall delight in its endless varieties—that he shall be tolerant of all themes, all approaches, and all styles, so long as the work under examination meets two tests. First, it must be written in a patient search for truth about some phase or segment of the past. Imagination must go ino this search, imagination as a literary as well as a historical tool. In the second place, its presentation of truth must be designed to give moral and intellectual nutriment to the spirit of man, just as our most ambitious poetry, fiction, and philosophy should be so designed. This is essentially a literary design. Why did Thucydides describe so graphically the terrible plague which shook the Peloponnesian army and paint so faithfully the public attributes of Pericles? For precisely the same reason, I take it, that Aeschylus wrote the great drama of *Agamemnon,* and Euripides, the drama of *Medea.* They wished to prove spiritual and moral situations in a search for truth, and they intended to provide moral and intellectual nutriment for the spirit of man.

Or to take a modern instance, why did our own Henry Charles Lea write in such richly documented form his *History of the Inquisition of the Middle Ages,* probably the most important contribution any American has made to European history? Why did he present all the horrors of the Inquisition with calm, judicial pen? Because he felt that the truth would carry sweeping moral lessons. When far back in college days I read those three volumes, I had a teacher at hand, Guy Stanton Ford, who could tell me how controversial they were. Lord Acton, a Catholic, took some different views of the Inquisition. Happily, I did not linger over the adverse criticism. I pressed on to devour what is to me the most memorable of Lea's works, his depressing and yet exalting book on *The Moriscos of Spain, Their Conversion and Expulsion,* which finds its climax in the forcible exile of the Hispanic Moors who had built so richly attractive a civilization. This masterly study of the brutalities of political and ecclesiastical intolerance, and the ensuing material and moral losses that crippled the Spanish nation for generations, was but a faraway, awesome story to the sophomore in the University of Illinois. Later it did not seem so far away. When the Nazi persecution of the Jews repeated the story with terrible additions, I was writing a great deal for the press. The fierce truthfulness of Lea's history and its profound moral and material lessons could then be remembered in that full force which had made his book a work of literature.

The list of works that meet the test I have named—tests of literature as well as history—is long and slowly but steadily grows longer. Something could easily be said of a third test, the test of style. The nature of style, however, is often misconceived. Style is the man; that is, style is most important when it reflects the rich, full personality of a writer of intellectual power and fully developed character, and, through this writer, something of the temper and outlook of an era. So it was with Gibbon and Parkman, with Macaulay and Prescott. Their style was not impressive because of cadenced phrases, ingenious tropes, and well-climaxed chapters. It was memorable because the full personality of the author, and the spirit of the age, shone through. Certainly prose style is never given striking distinction by anything that the apparatus of the social scientist can impart to it; indeed, such scientists are likely to corrupt and debase it. William Makepeace Thackeray once wrote a piece of history, *The Four Georges,* of surpassing stylistic merit. Experts in economics, sociology, and anthropology could perhaps add a good deal to the content of those historical essays—but at the cost of depriving a classic work of all its vitality.

If anyone doubts that the spirit of an age counts nearly as much in the production of a distinctive style as the mind and character of the author, let him ask whether the outlook and attitudes of an exuberantly romantic and optimistic young America do not appear in the spirited, highly colored narratives of William Hickling Prescott, John Lothrop Motley, and Francis Parkman. Or let him consider what Maynard Keynes writes, in his essay on Malthus, about the British tradition of humane science, the spirit of a long age. Keynes speaks of "that tradition of Scotch and English thought, in which there has been, I think, an extraordinary continuity of *feeling,* if I may so express it, from the eighteenth century to the present time—the tradition which is suggested by the names of Locke, Hume, Adam Smith, Paley, Bentham, Darwin, and Mill, a tradition marked by a love of truth and a most noble lucidity, by a prosaic sanity free from sentiment or metaphysic, and by an immense disinterestedness and public spirit. There is a continuity in these writings, not only of feeling, but of actual matter." If this could be said of the thinkers of a long scientific age, could not a parallel statement, with an equally impressive list of names, be made about the historians?

If any social scientist will look with candid eye at the world's great treasury of historical writing and consider how much of the best of this writing is narrative, descriptive, and expository, and how little of it is analytical, he will rise from this examination with chastened temper. If he will further consider how well the best narrative and descriptive histories have endured the tooth of time, and how rapidly once-famous pieces of analytic history have become dated and empty, he will have further food for thought. A humble temper befits all historians, and the social scientists will do well to cultivate it. No one will deny that they can give us valuable new patterns of thought, useful new insights, and large bodies of original new facts. They can stimulate our mind, widen our vision, and whet our appetite for deeper truths. Like every study, history needs constantly to face new fronts and absorb novel ideas and techniques; as today we have a new painting, a new music, and a new poetry, we unquestionably need in some fields a new history.

These fields, however, are limited. Look at the important historical works of our time, and ask how many of them would have been improved by specialized elements drawn from the social sciences. Could Van Wyck Brooks' half dozen volumes on American cultural history, beginning with *The Flowering of New England,* have been so improved? Could Samuel Eliot Morison's series on naval history, beginning with his *Maritime History of Massachusetts* and ending with his record of the Pacific war, have been so improved? Or could Walter Prescott Webb's book on the application of the industrial revolution to the conquest and settlement of the trans-Mississippi country, *The Great Plains,* published a generation ago (1931), be made more interesting to the general reader, or more essential to the student, by application of the newer concepts? Not in any significant degree.

We have come a long way since Bancroft could write about God working by examples, and Motley could intimate that a complicated century in European history should be viewed primarily as an 80 years' war for liberty. The old theological and political prepossessions have largely vanished. They have given way to our scientific age. Experts in the social sciences can help us gather more of the fruits of this age. Frederick Jackson Turner was right when he declared that data from "studies of politics, economics, sociology, psychology, biology, and physiography, all must be used." Nevertheless, the grand outlines and vital principles of history as it has been written down the ages still stand. The newer studies have no application whatever to wide areas of history and, when they do apply, should usually be regarded as adventitious and subordinate. Let the social scientists, in presenting their discoveries, remember that history, ever since Herodotus settled down in his native Halicarnassus to write chapters based mainly on his personal observation and reflection, has been greatest when it is viewed not as a branch of science but as a department of literature. Let them remember the truth that Henry David Thoreau put into a pregnant sentence: "It is not worth the while to go round the world to count the cats in Zanzibar."

John Hersey

THE PATH

Dear Whit Burnett:

The passage I have selected for your anthology is from *A Single Pebble* . . . which I would be in favor of giving the title "The Path," which is the title of the section of the novel from which this passage comes. By way of introduction:

How can I assert that this passage from *A Single Pebble* will be seen as my best work? I imagine, like any other writer, that my best work is yet to come—probably tomorrow morning I shall write it. Yes, tomorrow morning. Wait and see! For now I have chosen these pages because I like them and they happen to tip the peak of a novel into something like the space the editor has suggested.

The book is a tale of a trip taken up the river called by the Chinese "the Great," the Yangtze, by a young American engineer on an errand for his firm to see whether it would make sense for the company to try to sell the Chinese government a vast power project in the river's famous and dangerous gorges. The junk carries a cargo of bales of cotton. All the way through the gorges it is hauled against strong currents by a ragged gang of trackers who creep along the shore, harnessed to a towline, led by a head tracker nicknamed Old Pebble, who sings chanteys punctuated by rhythmic shouts of pain and patience from the others as they take step after step, "Ayah! . . . Ayah! . . ." The engineer is impatient to find the best site for his dam. The owner's wife, Su-ling, tells him stories of the river's past. The head tracker, who seems at first a simple, good man—"I pull the towline. . . . I have very little. . . . In spare time ashore I drink wine. I never

fight. . . . I have no home; my body is my home. . . ."—
later appears more difficult to fathom, as the engineer begins to
see Old Pebble's deep ties to the river, to its myths and history
and inexorable power which seem never to have changed and
which gradually unsettle the engineer's confident dream of a
dam.

This scene takes place in the last of the gorges, called Wind-Box
Gorge. The great spring run-off has begun; the river has risen
thirty feet in three days and is approaching the point of danger at
which all gorge traffic must be shut down until the waters subside.
As the junk moves into the upper throat of the gorge, the engineer, sitting forward on a coil of bamboo hawser watching the
trackers, hears the bumping of the sampan against the hull of the
junk. "This bumping, along with the junk's heartbeat, voiced by
the drum, and the tinkling of the masthead bells, and the
trackers' sob-like shouts, and the cook's penetrating humming,
and the creaking of tons of twisting cypress beneath us, and the
hard occasional crack of the owner's raging voice, and Su-ling's
soft words, and the insistent swish of the river, and above all
Old Pebble's burning songs—all were mixed together in the
seashell of my inner ear into a rhythmic rushing sound that
came and went, a kind of panting of excitement, terror, and
wonder."

Best wishes to the book,
John Hersey

The trackers climbed high across a hip of shingle and entered the
beginning of a path routed by hand from the face of one of the cliffs.
This seemed to me the most terrible place on the whole river.

Men working with chisels had cut out of the steep cliff a running
rectangle of rock to make this path. It was scooped out of the flat face
of the mountain, which was too perpendicular to permit an ordinary ledge
being formed. The path had a ceiling, an inner wall, and a floor of solid
rock; all it had for outer wall was peril. It ran more or less, but not

exactly, on a horizontal plane; wherever possible, it followed strata of rock, presumably along the softer faults in the limestone.

I can still see vividly in my mind's eye Old Pebble entering the dangerous place.

I remember that in the gorge itself, that day, the sight gave me a sickening feeling, and now, these many years later, the memory of it still faintly does.

The cliff was sheer, rising at an angle, I would say, of more than eighty degrees; I have a distinct impression that in some places in Wind-Box Gorge parts of the mighty precipices actually overhang the river. Where it began, the path was about thirty feet above the surface of the water, so that from the deck of the junk we looked up at it, more than half the height of our mast. Su-ling told me that in winter, at low water, at what the rivermen call "zero," the path would be more than sixty feet above the surface, while late in the spring, perhaps a month after we were there, it would be nearly as much, or more, under the surface. When the melted snows of many mountains of Tibet course toward the sea, and when, riding the crests of those thaws, the run-off of spring rains that have fallen on half a million square miles of Chinese hills flow too down the Great River, its power becomes unimaginable, even to a hopeful young hydraulic engineer.

These were the very cliffs against which, in its record year, the river had climbed in a short time two hundred and seventy-five feet.

What giddied me then, and still does now, about this awful path was not just its hazardous appearance: I was most intensely disturbed by the sense it gave me of the gap between the Chinese on the junk and myself, between Su-ling and myself, between the head tracker singing his beautiful chanteys and myself, between those to whom I was supposed to provide modern wonders of engineering and myself, a putative agent of provision. To begin with, the path was more than a thousand years old, so Su-ling said: T'ang dynasty, she said, and perhaps earlier. Chinese rivermen had been satisfied for a millennium—for more than five times the whole age of my native country—to use this awful way of getting through Wind-Box Gorge. How could I, in the momentary years of my youth, have a part in persuading these people to tolerate the building of a great modern dam that would take the waters of Tibet and inner China, with their age-old furies, on its back, there to grow lax and benign? How could I span a gap of a thousand years—a millennium in a day? These people on the junk could be said to be living in the era between Charlemagne and William the Conqueror, in the time of serfs and villeins, before the Crusades, before Western printing and gunpowder, long, long before Chaucer and Giotto and Thomas Aquinas and Dante. And they were satisfied (or so I thought) to exist in Dark Ages, while I lived in a time of enlightenment and was not satisfied.

The sight of that path made me wonder whether a dam was the right thing with which to start closing the gap.

There was something else about the path: I could not help feeling the incredible patience that had gone into its making. Surely only one man at a time could have worked there, hammering and chiseling out fragments of stone and dropping the pieces into the river below. How many years did these miles of jeopardous corridor take to cut? What patience! What all-enduring patience! And what a chasm between such patience and my hasty world! I was a young man who grew easily bored; more than a few weeks at any one engineering problem gave me a feeling of stagnation, and of wasting the magic of my youth. Suppose I had been called upon to cut stone on a path like this for fifty years of my life, to be relieved then by my son? What if I had been called upon to haul a junk through this path all my life? Old Pebble had this patience. The cook had been right to compare him to a tree; he endured his Sisyphus life with the same patience as a tree its growth.

Worst of all was this: The one-sided corridor cut from the cliffs was just high enough for trackers leaning forward on their halters, towing heavy weights, creeping almost; a man could not stand straight on his two feet in that space. In ten centuries this corridor had never been enlarged, but had been left the same height—a proper height for straining trackers, it seemed, not for men walking erect, proud and unharnessed. I thought of debased men I had read about, but I could not imagine any more enslaved, more doomed, than the trackers who traversed that tight path, with a mountain of stone pressing on their shoulderblades and death off the edge to the left. Yet what a broad grin Old Pebble had used to wear at night, who had trudged through that horrible path a hundred times; what devils of happiness in his eyes sometimes!

The strain of Old Pebble's towing was great. He leaned so far forward that his hands groped and clawed along the ground. His body was leashed, but his head was free, and it moved all around, and I could see his wild excited eyes darting here and there and everywhere, searching, searching. . . .

Sometimes the hollow of the cut-out path acted as a baffle, and the trackers' shouts—"Ayah! . . . Ayah! . . ."—came down to us queerly overblown; at other times the cries were muffled, as if the sounds had fallen right into the swallowing water.

Some of the men were obviously fear-bound by the place they were in, for they cringed against the inner wall as they towed, scraping shoulders and arms along the already flesh-smoothed rock, as far from the edge as could be. I saw the eyes of some of them, gazing down on the dangerous gutter with the moody stare that sometimes covers man's terror, while the eyes of others wore no such curtains but glanced out in frank awful fear. Still others could not even dare look outward, but kept their faces turned to the beloved limestone that supported them.

Old Pebble's face showed no fear. I saw it, now and then, and it was contorted by an expression of eagerness, of yearning, of passion. His eyes restlessly roved the gorge, from mountaintop to churning flood, searching. . . .

Suddenly the wild look on Old Pebble's face made me feel a rush of anxiety, and I felt sick at my stomach.

Could this river be dammed before such as he were ready to have it dammed?

I went aft. I kneeled by the game board, fighting my nausea. I put my hand on my watch pocket and wanted my stolen watch to be there.

Su-ling and the owner, with the sandalwood board between them, were calmly moving the wooden pips, trying with sweet mutual patience to outflank, capture, annihilate. Su-ling said to me, "Tonight we anchor at Kwei-fu. It will be dark when we get there. In the morning you will see the salt boileries. They say the place has the smell of the sea, and when we get there I want to ask you if that is true."

I was wonderfully calmed by her assurance of our arrival at a new anchorage. "Have you never been to the sea?" I asked her.

"I have been to Ichang," she said, as if she knew not where the sea might be, "and I have been to Chungking. Once I walked north from the Great River seventy-five li to visit my maternal grandmother, but when I reached her village they said she was dead. . . . Tell me: What does the sea smell like?"

"Some other time," I said, and getting unsteadily to my feet I went forward again, for though I still felt ill, I had to watch.

Again I settled on the coil of bamboo rope.

I saw that Old Pebble's eyes were sweeping a cliff on the opposite side of the river, across from the tracking path. His excited gaze climbed from the water level to the very top of the cliff.

I turned toward the far side of the river. There, in a zigzag pattern up a perpendicular rock seven hundred feet high, ran a series of square holes, six inches across, I would say, and a foot or so deep. Su-ling had told me downriver about these holes, and sitting on the foredeck earlier in the day I had been looking for them. They marked the ladder of Mêng Liang, the general of the Eastern Kingdom, in the Sung dynasty, whose ships had been shut into Wind-Box Gorge and were trapped there by great chains across the river, while the army of the Western Kingdom camped in smug security on top of the mountain above; but soldiers of Mêng Liang, starting from the bottom, cut these holes with hammer and chisel, inserted beam ends in them, then, squatting on the beams that stuck straight out from the cliff, cut higher holes, until they had made a ladderway enough for a seventy-storey building, and at last a whole army climbed up the terrible exposed stairway and defeated its surprised enemy. And what had given Mêng Liang's men the patience and courage to do all this? I felt sure they had simply looked at the trackers' path cut from the stone across the way, and perhaps thought of trackers hauling junks along it; exactly as Old Pebble and his ragged companions were hauling ours these hundreds of years later.

What patience! What everlasting endurance! This patience was not simply a matter of resignation, for it had in it a large measure of determination, even of aspiration. . . .

I looked back up at Old Pebble again in the scooped-out path. He was still gazing across at the ladder holes, and there was the same look on his face of ecstasy-in-work as he had worn at the rapids of Hsintan. Perhaps he felt for a moment a tug of the aspiration I had seen in those zigzag marks on the cliff. Or perhaps the holes up the wall of the gorge, so old, so familiar, gave him a feeling of certainty that the Great River would never change.

Suddenly he broke off the chantey he had been singing, a harsh lament of a scholar who had won honors at court but had lost a love at home. For three whole groan-shouts by the others there was no song at all.

Then Old Pebble broke into the most amazing song I had ever heard from him; a whirling, spiraling, soaring sound of pure joy. It seemed to me to be wordless. He was pulling now with all his strengh; he held one arm reaching forward, as if that would hurry him. Still he looked across at the marks of the reddish cliff.

His song now was like a miracle—as wonderful as the first crying of a newborn child.

The junk was tending out into the stream as it fetched around a projecting bluff, at the upper side of which the big creaking boat was suddenly taken into a nasty race of swirling water, full of froth and splashes. We were coming near the upper gate of the gorge. The water was horrible. It looked like the rushing, sucking billowing wake of the ocean liner on which I had crossed the Pacific.

Old Pebble still stared across the river. His face had a look of great happiness or great pain—much like faces of people caught in photographs of terrible disasters, their mouths drawn by agony into seeming smiles. His song was thrilling. He strained wildly at his harness.

"Ayah! . . . Ayah! . . ."

I watched him very closely, for I wanted to try to guess what was in his mind.

Just then, at the very crest of a climbing line of wordless song, he lost his footing.

I saw him go down. He had been pulling so hard on the towline that a slight slip of one foot was enough to throw him flat. I stood up on the pitching deck, and I believe I uttered a cry. The head tracker seemed at first not to be trying to rise. I remembered his agility in bounding over ten thousand rocks coming up the river, yet now he lay at first inert, like a man either dead or dreaming. The other trackers still strained at their ropes and still called out their slow time-beating shouts, and the cook hummed. The trackers moved forward, and the junk moved forward, inch by inch.

Suddenly the head tracker began to writhe on the stone pathway. Was he hurt?

The hands of the almost creeping second tracker had come up to the prostrate man's feet. I saw the hands grasp the leader's ankles and move them to one side, toward the river.

Old Pebble rolled and doubled up and give out his first shriek, a terrible piercing salute to his fate, which he recognized, I guess, long before I did.

I glanced at the river. My thoughts were selfish. What would the men up there do to us? They could not slacken their efforts! I grew dizzy for a moment as I remembered the reeling of the junk that time in much easier water in Witches' Mountain Gorge when the farmer boy had caught his foot and the head tracker had knocked two other trackers off the rope; I steadied myself, grasping the mat cowling of the main cabin.

Again I looked up at the path. There was a kind of struggle going on.

The head tracker seemed to be trying to slip his sennit off the towline so he could get out of the way of the trackers. They were moving forward. They were practically on him. Apparently the sennit would not relax its grip on the hawser.

Then the head tracker fell off the edge of the path, screaming as he fell. His towing harness brought him up short, and he swung there against the rock wall, some ten feet below the path and perhaps twice that much above the surface of the water.

With one more agonized unison groan, the trackers halted. The first two men huddled against the inner wall of the pathway, bearing the weight of the head tracker and also their share of the pull of the boat.

There are many things about those few moments of which I am not sure, and which puzzle me. For one thing, I do not know whether the head tracker had fallen of his own choice or had been turned off the ledge by the trackers who followed him. He had been in their way; he had seemed unable to get free. I had seen the second man push aside the head tracker's legs—toward the river—in order that the second tracker and the others might keep towing, keep moving. I do not know exactly what had happened. The head tracker had been an admired and necessary man, and perhaps one who was loved, certainly not one to be, as it were, thrown away; yet his stumbling had imperiled the junk and all its crew, and all the other trackers. Who had made the choice?

In my confused reaction there was another part, too. This had to do with the owner. A few moments after the head tracker's first scream, just after his fall from the path, the owner came running forward to see what the matter was. I caught as in a camera, and still can produce from my mind's file a fogged print of it, the expression of his face when he saw what had happened: an expression of satisfaction. His haggard, money-worn face was clearly satisfied in the first instant of seeing the head tracker hanging there. Then at once the threat to his property, to the junk and its cargo, and to himself, must have struck the owner, and anxiety rushed in to jostle the first reflex aside. Close behind the owner came his wife, young and lantern-bright, and her face, too, I saw. Her first response was far from that of her husband: she was crushed by what she saw. Her sorrow must have been deep, deep; its frozen weight must have held it down; only a small part of it showed on the surface. Her response was the one I would have expected also from him, for I had thought the head tracker was a kind of helping son to him; thus the owner's reflex troubled and puzzled me.

Another factor: the cook's phlegmatic reaction. At the moment of the head tracker's first shriek, the cook had been squatting on his heels not far from me on the foredeck over the fourth cargo compartment of the junk near his open-air galley brazier; he had been peeling turnips, as I have said, and had been humming along with Old Pebble's songs. After the first cry, when I heard the Old Big rushing noisily forward to investigate and turned my head to watch him come (and perhaps, I dare say, to look for Su-ling, who was sure to be close behind him), my gaze brushed across the cook, who was still squatting, still peeling, and even still humming, though now he was, with the same precise little tune-stitches, basting not the tracker's silken music but the coarse sacking of others' screams and worried shouts. His face was placid. His eyes were on his work. Later I looked at him again, and he had still not lifted his face to the scene on the wall of the gorge. I had seen that he was friendly with the head tracker; many evenings on the river those two had entertained us all. Could the cook not bear to watch what was happening? Or was he simply not interested? Had it something to do with "enough" on the Great River? Or with grief? That humming!

Most puzzling of all: What had been in Old Pebble's mind at the moment of his fall? Had something about Mêng Liang's ladder made him think suddenly about my dam which would mean the end of all trackers? I did not know; I do not know.

I looked up at the cliff. No one seemed to have any idea what to do. The great craft shook and yawed. The bells chirped. I was afraid. The bow steersman walked calmly back to the cook's brazier and poured himself some tea. The men on the bow sweep stood silent, with hooded eyes. The cook hummed. The sampan pounded the hull.

The owner began to jump up and down on the foredeck, screaming to whichever trackers carried knives (against this very contingency, among others, I suppose) to cut the braided bamboo rope on which the head tracker was suspended and let him drown, and then tow away. I can see now that there was probably no alternative to this. The effort of hoisting Old Pebble back up the towpath might have been enough, when subtracted from the effort of towing, or merely of holding the heavy junk where it was, to have allowed the current to wrest the boat from the control of the remaining trackers and carry it, without steerageway and therefore helpless, onto well-known perils downstream; and in any case, the rock towpath cut from the cliff would not have given room for leverage on the part of enough men to hoist the head tracker up again.

Thus, his drowning had been determined by his first misstep. Dimly I think I realized this certainty at the time, though I had certainly not been prepared for it beforehand.

The owner literally danced on the foredeck, leaping up and down and flapping his black cotton gown, like a huge, earthbound, logy, death-excited buzzard, and he called out in rattling accents to the trackers to cut the fallen man away and start up again. The head tracker swinging on the rope against the rocks protested in harsh echoing cries. Su-ling began to whimper in tones as soft as her usual laughter. The swift water made a rushing sound on every hand.

At first the trackers did nothing. I was amazed at their steadiness, holding all that wood against all that water. For what reward? With what in their minds during that minute? They leaned and pulled and did not move, though the owner screamed for action.

It was at last the third man who, straining forward all the time, slowly pulled from his cotton bellyband a short dirk, honed on one side of the blade, and with what seemed feeble pecking and tapping motions began to fret the thick towing hawser at the place where it hung over the edge of the path. He could not reach the head tracker's sennit, which was over the side of the cliff. His efforts seemed weak because he could spare so little from his share of the work of braking the junk. And could one doubt that he was reluctant? The man who had been second on the hawser huddled against the cliff, helping to hold the junk and bearing Old Pebble's weight. He must have been wonderfully strong.

I will never forget that scene in those few moments—the boiling gutter of Wind-Box Gorge between fantastic vertical limestone masses nearly a thousand feet high; the head tracker hanging twenty feet above the freshet in the white cotton loop of his towing harness, screaming not so much for rescue, which he must have known to be impossible, as in protest against his certain mortality, while the forty-odd other trackers, leaderless, leaned frozen against their towing halters, straining with turgid thighs and started veins simply to hold the eighty-ton junk against the springtime river, in a slanting, rigid, silent tableau, like that of some frieze of long-ago times; the junk trembling under our feet and yawing in the flood; the owner flapping his gown and his thin beard, shouting his half of a fateful duet, ordering the others to hurry and cut away the head tracker and get on with hauling the junk out of the whispering race of the Yangtze to the town beyond; the impasse of reluctance and horror; my incredulity. . . .

I stood on the deck shocked. The cook hummed on. The owner urged speed, and Su-ling moaned with a subdued grief which seemed impersonal, timeless—the endless grief of suffering poor people in the face of disaster. I could hear the bow steersman slurping in his teacup. I was nearly struck down by a rush of agony and anger, and of pity for the head tracker, and suddenly forgetting all my doubts about him I thought him what he had said he was, a simple good man, and I thought his fate unfair, and his companions' indifference to it seemed to me unspeakably savage, and I felt a desperate love of life, of my own life, and I watched the slow gnawing of the bamboo hawser up there. If that was a minute, it was a very long one. It made me come close to sensing the meaning of the most awesome concepts: paralysis, burial, infinity.

By the time I was able to move, it was already much too late. But even had I been able to act sooner, I doubt that I could have changed anything.

I ran to the Old Big and pushed him in the chest with my fists, and shouted to him to stop what was happening.

He kept right on shrieking over my shoulder, commanding the man with the knife to hurry.

I pushed and protested; he dodged and urged. I guess we did a sort of dance of death on the slapping planks of the foredeck.

Thus it happened that my back was turned when the head tracker fell into the river. I heard the brief final scream of complaint and prayer, and then there was nothing but water-sound, boat-sound, and bell-sound, and even they seemed hushed.

I spun around. I saw in the water a flash of white shoulder band. A blue-clad rump rolled over; a hand reached for the rungless sky. For a moment the strong struggling man got his head above water, but at once he was dragged frightfully under again.

"Ayah!" the remaining trackers shouted in their changeless tone. They had taken a step upriver, while the thrashing body was not yet even opposite us.

I heard the owner grunt, "Ayah!" echoing the trackers and seeming to want to add to their strength the push of his lungs, but their word was an expression in his throat of despair and weariness.

There were sounds of such strange feelings in this utterance that I could not help tearing my eyes from the rolling man in the water, now abreast of us, to the face of the owner beside me. Its deep lines were contorted; its half-veiled eyes and beard-fringed lips were terribly bitter.

What *had* gone through the mind of the Old Big, to write such changes on the crumpled parchment he wore for a face? Delight, fear, murderousness, bitterness. I shall never know; I know only that those changes hit me full and hard, and had their part in making that day one that has haunted my whole life.

As I watched, the expression of bitterness was quickly changing, firming, as when new ice spreads its brooding feathers over a lake on a wintry night.

Then this tight-stretched, rope-muscled man leapt into a surprising action—an action of utmost charity.

He ran with springy steps across the deck, and cast off the painter of the sampan from the tholepins where it had been cleated, and in his wide-sleeved black gown jumped like a side-slipping crow from the deck of the junk onto the floorboards of the small boat, which heaved and skidded away from the junk with the crash of his weight. The boat whirled quickly away from us, with the Old Big miraculously standing up in it. Su-ling gasped once and was silent thereafter.

I heard the owner shout the head tracker's name in a hoarse desperate cackle.

"Ayah! . . . Ayah! . . ." The junk was moving forward now.

I saw the owner bend down and pick up a sculling oar and straighten up, waving the T-handled blade to help keep his balance. The cup of a boat shook and dipped and spun in the mad waters, and now the owner's face was toward us, howling the name of his head tracker, and now we saw his back as he fought, still standing, to keep his balance, making me think of the mock-drunk ropewalkers I had seen in the circuses of my boyhood.

He actually managed from time to time to dip the oar blade in the water, in a surely futile effort to speed his would-be merciful voyage. He went away from us very fast. From a distance, in that haste-spoiled water, we could not see whether the head tracker was getting his head out any more. The owner disappeared around a bend in the river, flapping and chopping in a regular semaphore of his amazing balance, a tiny black staggering figure in the huge water-cut from the rock mountain, a tiny human being way off there, erect, incredibly brave, crying out in the echoing gorge to his needed companion and support, whom he would save if he could.

"Ayah! . . . Ayah! . . ."

The cook, whose humming had stopped with the fall, and who afterwards had been standing on the deck watching with the rest of us, gave a quiet order to the drummer, suggesting a signal for a slightly faster pace, and reminding the drummer that the drum alone would set the trackers' rate of progress now. In this way the cook paid tribute to the absence of the head tracker's haunting chanteys, and also took command of the junk.

"Ayah! . . . Ayah! . . . Ayah! . . . Ayah! . . ."

I barely noticed how we got through the upper mouth of the gorge, for I was full of what I had seen, dazed by it, and sad.

The negotiation of that final half-mile or so—that was all, but how much!—must have called for something like a miracle from the trackers, something above heart and sinew. The men were without leadership, and they had to go through the worst stretch of the river we had yet seen. I really believe that more was required of our forty-odd men as we passed the upper limits of Wind-Box Gorge than had been asked of the three hundred fifty hired-on rag bags at the New Rapids, who leaned there on the lines but did not extend themselves, and certainly did not drain the very lees of their spirits, as our trackers must have done at the mouth of the gorge, stretching their strength beyond belief.

Yet our going through safely was not a miracle. It was a triumph of unremarkable men, a triumph of their patience and of the astounding love for each other of poverty-stricken brothers in pain and trouble.

They had eaten nothing all day. They had suffered the loss of a friend at their very feet. They had lost, too, their accustomed master, and though they may have hated the owner, and though probably none of them had seen with his eyes the Old Big's going, they must have heard his piercing cries of remorse and helpless, tottering need as the sampan rushed away from us, and they must have heard the name he called and must have known the meaning of those shouts. Now there were no more beautiful songs. Now only the hollow drum hummed to them from the junk.

Yet somehow they hauled us through.

As I say, I hardly saw any of this happen. I sat on the coil of rope thinking of Old Pebble.

I wondered again what he had been thinking about in those last moments, and whether his fall had been sheer accident or if he had been felled, as it were, by an idea, by some realization. Had he thought of the dam?

That possibility, crossing my mind for the second time, made me shudder.

Then I felt a strange revulsion and doubt. Had Old Pebble really been singing as beautifully as I had thought—or had the burning intensity of those last few minutes before his fall been in *my* mind only? Was it possible that he had been singing exactly as he had always sung, and that fear and excitement and aspiration, which I had felt on seeing the holes of Mêng Liang's ladder, had sharpened *my* senses?

What did I feel? As yet I scarcely knew. I was tired and puzzled.

Old Pebble was dead. He had been a nobody, a ragged faceless tracker among thousands of ragged faceless trackers on the Great River. His death changed nothing; there would be no obituaries. Even his closest friend, the cook, had scarcely seemed to notice his death. His body was in the river, but that did not change the river. Could the river be changed? Was Su-ling right—could *nothing* change the Great River?

Gradually, as if waking from a dream, I began to think more coherent thoughts. Of course the river could be changed. I was an engineer. I dealt with facts. Dams were made of steel and concrete. The holes in Mêng Liang's ladder were cut into hard stone. The water above a dam would one day cover many of those holes. An engineer dealt with objective facts. There was no place in my life for shadowy thoughts about faceless nobodies. Old Pebble was dead.

Yet I could not help remembering what the head tracker had told me he wanted of life: to pull on the towline, a little wine when he went ashore, a hoard of friendship. That was all. A dam was not among the things he listed. Had there been a dam he would not have died. Would he have wanted a dam if he had known that?

I am not at all sure. He wanted to haul junks, drink wine, and have friends.

I had been in a great hurry to survey this river. What did I think now about my dam—about skimming a millennium in a day?

Barbara W. Tuchman

"GIVE ME COMBAT"

The title of the chapter from which the following selection is chosen is taken from Romain Rolland as quoted in a part of the chapter not reprinted below. After the opening night of his play *Les Loups* which was both a comment about, and incident in the Dreyfus Affair and caused a near riot in Paris, he wrote in his diary, "I would rather have this life of combat than the mortal calm and mournful stupor of these last years. God give me struggle, enemies, howling crowds, all the combat of which I am capable."

To select a passage from all one's writing as definitively the "best" is impossible. I have chosen a section from *The Proud Tower* because that is the one of my books, I think, that tells us the most about ourselves. This after all is the function of all history. The particular passage chosen is not necessarily the "best" in the book but it is, I think, a good example of the elements of historical writing: action, ideas, synthesis and significance.

Barbara W. Tuchman

FRANCE: 1894–99

"The permanent glamour of France" was a phrase used by an English-man of the nineties, Sir Almeric Fitzroy, secretary to the Duke of Devonshire. He felt that every child of Western civilization owed a debt to the country from which "came the impulse that dissolved the old world in agony and gave life and passion to the present." For two years, from the summer of 1897 to the summer of 1899, the agony of that old dissolution returned. Rent by a moral passion that reopened past wounds, broke apart society and consumed thought, energy and honor, France plunged into one of the great commotions of history.

During those "two interminable years" of struggle to secure the retrial of a single individual unjustly convicted, "life was as if sus-pended," wrote Léon Blum, a future premier, then in his twenties. It was as if, in those "years of tumult, of veritable civil war . . . everything converged upon a single question and in the most intimate feelings and personal relationships everything was interrupted, turned upside down, reclassified. . . . The Dreyfus Affair was a human crisis, less extended and less prolonged in time but no less violent than the French Revolution."

It "would have divided the angels themselves," wrote the Vicomte de Vogüé, on the opposite side from Blum. "Above the base motives and animal passions, the finest souls in France flung themselves at each other with an equal nobility of sentiments exasperated by their fearful conflict."

The protagonists felt a grandeur in the storm that battered them. Decadence was exorcised in the violence of their feelings and they felt conscious again of "high principles and inexhaustible energies." Hate, evil and fear encompassed them as well as courage and sacrifice. Their combat was epic and its issue was the life of the Republic. Each side fought for an idea, its idea of France: one the France of Counter-Revolution, the other the France of 1789; one for its last chance to arrest progressive social tendencies and restore the old values; the other to cleanse the honor of the Republic and preserve it from the clutches of reaction. The Revisionists, who fought for retrial, saw France as the fount of liberty, the country of light, the teacher of reason, the codifier of law, and to them the knowledge that she could have perpetrated a wrong and connived at a miscarriage of justice was insufferable. They fought for Justice. Those on the other side claimed to fight in the name of *Patrie* for the preservation of the Army as the shield and protector of the nation and of the Church as the guide and instructor of its soul. They assembled under the name of Nationalists and in their ranks sincere men were partners of demagogues and succumbed to methods that were reckless and brutal and terms that were foul, so that the world watched in wonder and scorn and the name of France suffered. Locked in mutual ferocity and final commitment the contenders could not disengage, although their struggle was splitting the country and fostering opportunity for the enemy at their frontiers, which every day the enemy measured.

The *casus belli* was condemnation of a Jewish army officer for treason in behalf of Germany; the object of the battle was on the one hand to prevent, on the other to obtain, a reopening of the case.

The arrest, trial, conviction and sentencing of Captain Alfred Dreyfus, an artillery officer assigned to the General Staff, which took place in the months October to December, 1894, was not a deliberate plot to frame an innocent man. It was the outcome of a reasonable suspicion acted on by dislike, some circumstantial evidence and instinctive prejudice. Evidence indicated betrayal of military secrets to Germany by some artillery officer on the General Staff. Dreyfus, besides fitting the requirements, was a Jew, the eternal alien: a natural suspect to absorb the stain of treason. As a person he was not liked by his brother officers. Stiff, silent, cold and almost unnaturally correct, he was without friends, opinions or visible feelings, and his officiousness on duty had already attracted unfavorable attention. These characteristics appeared sinister as soon as he came under suspicion. His appearance, the reverse of flamboyant, seemed the perfect cover for a spy. Of medium height and weight, medium brown hair, and medium age, thirty-six, he had a tone-less voice, and unremarkable features distinguished only by rimless pince-nez, the fashionable form of eyeglasses in his milieu. His guilt was im-mediately presumed. When motive and material proof could not be found, the officers who were charged with the inquiry, especially Major Henry and Colonel du Paty de Clam, made up for it by helpful construction and fabrication. Certain that they were dealing with a vile traitor who had sold secrets of military defence to the traditional enemy, they felt justified in supplying whatever was needed to convict him. The dossier they assembled, later to be known as the "Secret File," was persuasive enough to cause the General Staff chiefs sincerely to believe Dreyfus guilty, but it lacked legal proof. Knowing this, and dealing in a case particularly sensitive because of the involvement of Germany, and fearing the blackmail of the press, the then Minister of War, General Mercier, ordered, and the Government of which he was a member permitted, Captain Dreyfus' court-martial to be held *in camera*. When the questions of the five military judges indicated their doubts, the Secret File was submitted to them and withheld from the defence. Convinced by these documents, the judges reached a unanimous verdict of guilty. The death penalty for political crimes having been abolished in 1848, the sentence was life imprisonment. On the prisoner's refusal to confess and persist-ence in maintaining his innocence, he was ordered confined to Devil's Island, one of three prison islands off the coast of South America used for desperate criminals. A barren rock two miles long and five hundred yards wide, it was cleared of all but guards to accommodate Dreyfus alone, in a stone hut under perpetual surveillance. The unanimity of the military court seemed confirmed by a published rumor that Dreyfus had confessed, which, as it passed from journal to journal, acquired the force of an official statement and satisfied the public.

The next three years were marked by the long, painful struggle for judicial review, in which both sides exerted the most intense efforts on the one hand to uncover, on the other hand to conceal the truth. . . .

Once Dreyfus had been convicted on false evidence, any reopening of the case would reveal the Ministry of War, the General Staff and General Mercier as dishonored; in short, as a colleague said, if in a retrial "Captain Dreyfus is acquitted, it is General Mercier who becomes the traitor." Through every reinvestigation and taking of testimony, the trial of Esterhazy, the trial of Zola, the inquiry of the Court of Appeals, the final trial at Rennes, Mercier beat back the forces of Revision and held the citadel of the false verdict. Angular, haughty, icy-faced, never wavering in self-control even when the whole structure he had built was tottering, he reminded an observer of the character in Dante's Inferno who looked around him with disdain, "as if he held Hell in great contempt."

All the strength, except truth, was on his side. Each time the Dreyfusards brought forward new evidence which they were certain this time must force a retrial, it was quashed, suppressed, thrown out or matched with new fabrications by the Army, supported by the Government, by all the *bien-pensants* or right-thinking communicants of the Church, and by the screams and thunders of four-fifths of the press.

[The body of the chapter covers the tumultuous events of the battle for Revision. We re-enter the Affair in February 1899.]

Suddenly and strangely on top of all the excitement, the President of France, Félix Faure, died. The public sensed something unexplained and the truth in fact was too embarrassing to be told. Proud of his amatory prowess, President Faure died in the performance thereof in a ground-floor room of the Elysée. An aura of something hushed up was added to the atmosphere already charged with aggression and suspicion.

In the election of a new president, held in the midst of hysterical battle over jurisdiction of the Court, Emile Loubet, President of the Senate, a steady, simple Republican and product of peasant stock, won over the Conservative Méline. As Premier at the time of the Panama scandal, Loubet was despised by the Nationalists. They called his election an "insult to France," a "challenge to the Army," a "victory for Jewish treason." Their hired mobs sent to hoot his progress from the Gare St-Lazare to the Elysée raised such a clamor that even the band playing the "Marseillaise" could not be heard. "The Republic will not founder in my hands," said Loubet calmly. "They know it and it maddens them."

The Right in a state of ungovernable excitement was prepared to make it founder. "In a week we will have driven Loubet from the Presidency," boasted Jules Lemaître. The state funeral of Faure was fixed on as the occasion for a coup d'état. The Army must be persuaded to save the country. The "Leaguers" thought they could do it by a cry, a gesture, an occasion, and did not concern themselves with serious organization. Their plan was to intercept the military escort of the cortege while it was returning from the cemetery to its barracks in the Place de la Nation, and lead it to seize the Elysée. Déroulède joined by Guérin led a band of two hundred patriots in the streets, caught hold of the bridle of General Roget, commander of the escort, shouting, "To the Elysée, General! Follow us, General, follow us! To the Place Bastille! To the Hotel de Ville! To the Elysée! Friends await us. I beg you, General, save France, establish a Republic of the people, kick out the *parlementaires!*" The General kept his head and kept moving, the crowd, ignorant but willing, shouted, "Save France! *Vive l'Arméel*", the troops sweeping Déroulède and his followers with them, marched on to the barracks and entered. Déroulède, throwing open his coat to reveal his deputy's scarf, emblem of parliamentary immunity, was nevertheless carted off to the police station to be indicted for insurrection and provide at his trial one more cause for combative passions. The fiasco did nothing to daunt the expectations of the Right. In the following month the Anti-Semitic League received 56,000 francs from the Duc d'Orléans and 100,000 from Boni de Castellane.

Hardly had breath been drawn when the verdict that all France was awaiting was announced by the Cour de Cassation. Forty-six judges in scarlet and ermine declared for Revision. A cruiser was sent to bring Dreyfus back from Devil's Island for retrial. Zola returned from England with an article which *l'Aurore* headlined in the now familiar type, JUSTICE! He saw all factional and party lines now dissipated in one great division separating France into two camps: the forces of reaction and the past against the forces of justice and the future. This was the logical order of battle to complete the task of 1789. With the unquenchable optimism of their age the Dreyfusards hailed the Court's decision as the herald of social justice for the century about to be born. A great burden of shame seemed lifted and replaced by pride in France. "What other country," wrote a correspondent of *Le Temps* at The Hague where the Peace Conference was assembled, "has had the privilege of making the world's heart beat faster as we have for the last three years?" Revision meant not only the triumph of justice but of "the liberty of mankind." Others beside Frenchmen felt this universality. William James, traveling in Europe, wrote as he saw daylight breaking through the Affair, "It may be one of those moral crises that become starting points and high water marks and leave traditions and rallying cries and new faces behind them."

The Nationalists were flung into paroxysms of wrath. Caran d'Ache drew a cartoon showing Dreyfus with a smirk and Reinach with a whip ordering, "Come here, Marianne." On the facing page he drew

Zola emerging from a toilet bowl holding a toy Dreyfus, with the caption, "Truth Rising from Its Well."

Fury at the Court's decision was vented the next day on the head of President Loubet when he attended the races at Auteuil. It was the Sunday of *le Grand Steeple,* the most fashionable event of the season. When the President's carriage drove up to the grandstand, groups of well-dressed gentlemen wearing in their buttonholes the white carnation of the royalists and the blue cornflower of the anti-Semites, and brandishing their canes, shouted in pounding rhythm, *"Dé-mis-sion!* [resign] *Pa-na-ma! Dé-mis-sion! Pa-na-ma!"* Through the howls and threats Loubet took his seat. Suddenly a tall man with a blond moustache, wearing a white carnation and white cravat, later identified as the Baron Fernand de Christiani, detached himself from the group, dashed up the steps two at a time and struck the President on the head with a heavy cane. Ladies screamed. A sudden silence of general stupor followed, then an uproar as the assailant's companions rushed to rescue him from the guards. As some were arrested others converged on the police in yelling groups, striking with their canes. The scene was *"un charivari infernal."* General Zurlinden, Governor of Paris, telephoned for reinforcements of three cavalry detachments. Loubet, though shaken, apologized for the disturbance to Countess Tornelli, the Italian Ambassadress, in the seat beside him. "It was a place of honor," she replied.

In Loubet's top hat the Republic itself had been assaulted and the public was startled and indignant. Telegrams from committees and municipal councils all over France poured in expressing a loyalty deeper than might have been supposed from the experience of the last years. Loubet announced that as an invited guest he intended to appear at next Sunday's races at Longchamps. Forewarned, the leagues and newspapers of both sides called for demonstrations and assembled their battalions. The Government took extraordinary precautions. Thirty squadrons of cavalry and a brigade of infantry in battle dress were lined up along the route from the Elysée to Longchamps, while at the racecourse itself dragoons of the *Garde Républicaine* armed with rifles were stationed at every ten yards around the course and at every betting window. Mounted police guarded the lawn. More than 100,000 people turned out along the route and at the racecourse, many wearing the red rose boutonniere of the Left. Again the threat of the Right brought out the workers, less, perhaps, to defend the bourgeois state than to defy the representatives of the ruling class. The presence of more than six thousand guardians of the law prevented a major outbreak, but throughout the day demonstrators clashed, private riots and melees erupted, cries and counter-cries resounded, hundreds were arrested, reporters and police as well as demonstrators were injured. As the crowds flowed back to Paris in the evening the turbulence swept through the cafés; *"Vive la République!"* met *"Vive l'Armée!"* Bottles and glasses, carafes and trays were hurled, tables and chairs became weapons, police charged; anger, broken heads and national animosities mounted. Even outside Paris, in a pension in Brest where officers and professors boarded, "these young men equally animated by love of France" could no longer talk to or understand each other without coming to the point of a duel. It was time, urged *Le Temps,* for a "truce of God."

But it was not to be had. When again the Government fell in the week after Longchamps, the fears and difficulties to be faced in office were now so great that for eight days no one could form a Government. In the vacuum the man who came forward with intent to "liquidate" the Affair was able to impose conditions that would otherwise have been unacceptable. He was René Waldeck-Rousseau, fifty-three, the leading lawyer of Paris and a polished orator, known as the "Pericles of the Republic." A Catholic from Britanny, wealthy and wellborn, he was impressive in manner and British in appearance, with cropped hair and moustache, a taste for hunting and fishing, a talent for watercolors and impeccable clothes. Rochefort called him *Waldeck le pommadé* because he was so well groomed. Admired by the Radicals and approved by the Center, he represented the *juste milieu.*

With the retrial of Dreyfus ahead, the Affair was moving toward climax. To retain office under the terrible buffeting he could expect, Waldeck deliberately chose to form a Government which, by being equally obnoxious to both sides, would cancel the blows of either. He selected a Socialist, Millerand, as Minister of Commerce and a military hero, the Marquis de Galliffet, "butcher" of the Commune, as Minister of War. The tumult in press and parliament that greeted this remarkable expedient was unequalled. "Pure madness . . . absolute lunacy . . . monstrous . . . infamous!" came from both sides. The appointment of Millerand not only infuriated the Right; his acceptance created a scandal and a schism in his own party and in the Socialist International of major proportions and historic significance. Acceptance of office in a capitalist Government was a betrayal comparable to that of Judas. Profoundly saddened, Jaurès begged Millerand to shun the offer, but Waldeck had knowingly selected a man to whom the lure of office was strong. The Socialists now had to face the choice whether or not to support the Waldeck Government when it came to the Chamber for a vote of confidence. If the Government lost, the prospect was chaos. Jaurès was persuaded by Lucien Herr's argument: "What a triumph for Socialism that the Republic cannot be saved without calling on the party of the proletariat!" The Guesde faction, however, clung to the class struggle. Socialists, stated Guesde, "enter Parliament as though we were in an enemy State only in order to fight the enemy class." Jaurès warned that if Socialism persisted in this attitude it would sink to the level of "sterile and intransigent anarchism," but he did not prevail. The Union Socialiste broke apart; twenty-five of the parliamentary members agreed to support the Government; seventeen refused. Guesde enchanted his group with the exciting suggestion that it should greet the new Government's appearance in the Chamber with cries of *"Vive la Commune!"* but, so as not to find themselves allied with the Right, abstain when it came to a vote.

For ten minutes next day they stood hurling *"Vive la Commune! A bas les fusilleurs! A bas l'assassin!"* at the new ministers. The object of it all, General the Marquis de Galliffet, Prince de Martigues, nearly seventy, with red-bronze face and bright eyes, looked mockingly on the scene, half-gratified, half-disgusted. He had fought in the Crimea, Italy, Mexico, Algeria and at Sedan, where he had led his regiment into the last cavalry charge with the reply to his commanding officer, "As often as you like, Sir, as long as one of us is left." Impressed by the great Gambetta's patriotism and fighting spirit, Galliffet became and remained a loyal Republican and openly despised Boulanger. The eyes in his highly colored face were sunk on either side of a nose like the beak of a bird of prey, but his figure was vigorous and young and he still wore "the same air that had made his fortune, as of a bandit chief who feared nothing or a *grand seigneur* who cared for nothing." Despite a silver-plated stomach and a limp from old wounds, he played tennis in the Tuileries Gardens and his love affairs, recounted with sparkle and ribaldry, were the delight of the Bixio. He told how Mme de Castiglione showed him her nude portrait by Baudry, and when he asked if she was really as beautiful as that, she disrobed and posed on the sofa. "The picture was better," Galliffet concluded. He was called the *sabreur de la parole* because he told stories "as if he were charging at the head of his squadron." Devoted to the fighting efficiency of the Army and to Picquart who had served under his command, he had become a Revisionist. For this sin he was cut at the Jockey, and after he became a Minister, resigned from the Cercle de l'Union, less because of his own opinions than because of "imbecile" members who got themselves arrested at Auteuil; as he said, "It's not possible to belong to a club if one has to arrest the members; it's not sociable." Caustic and eccentric, proud of having nothing to live on but his pension after having once been rich, he possessed "courage, effrontery, intelligence, contempt for death and thirst for life."

He needed all these to become Minister of War at the peak of the Affair. Confronting the taunts of the Guesde extremists in the Chamber, he suddenly stood up and barked, *"L'assassin, présent!"* The din became general. Nationalists, Radicals, Center, were shouting insults and shaking fists. Millerand, a lawyer like Waldeck, with gray hair *en brosse,* a lorgnon, a neat black moustache and a precise, aggressive manner, was wilting. His moustache trembled and he looked "like a huge cat caught in a downpour." Galliffet was observed taking down names and explained later, "I thought I'd better invite those chaps to dinner." Waldeck, trying to speak, stood at the tribune for an hour without being heard for more than ten minutes. He fought desperately and succeeded in establishing the Government by a majority of twenty-six.

Galliffet joined it "without illusions," he wrote to Princess Radziwill, because of its promise to pacify France, "if that is still possible. The Rightist papers beg me to do another Boulanger and those of the Left want me to cut off the heads of all the Generals who displease them. The public is an idiot. If I touch a guilty general I am accused of massacring the Army; if I abstain I am accused of treason. What a dilemma. Pity me." Actually, although he found Loubet "too bourgeois," he was pleased to be a Minister and was very "gay and amusing" at the next meeting of the Bixio. He told a lively story of a rather large but lovely lady of forty-five who visited him at his office to propose a little deal involving 20,000 horses to be bought for the Army. There would be a million in it for him. "A million," he said to her. "That's not much considering the twenty-five million I got from the Syndicate as everyone knows. Go to see Waldeck. He is jealous of me because he only got seventeen million."

Six weeks later, on August 8, 1899, the retrial of Dreyfus by a new court-martial was schedule to open in the garrison town of Rennes, a Catholic and aristocratic corner of traditionally Counter-Revolutionary Brittany. France quivered in expectation; as each week passed bringing the moment closer, the tension grew. The world's eyes were turned

on Rennes. All the important foreign newspapers sent their star correspondents. Lord Russell of Killowen, the Lord Chief Justice of England,
came as an observer. All the leading figures in the Affair, hundreds
of French journalists and important political, social and literary figures
crammed the town. The Secret File was brought from Paris in an
iron box on an artillery caisson. No one anywhere talked of anything
but the coming verdict. Acquittal would mean for the Dreyfusards
vindication at last; for the Nationalists it would be lethal; an unimaginable blow not to be permitted. As if on order they returned to the
theme of the first blackmail: Dreyfus or the Army. "A choice is to
be made," wrote Barrès in the *Journal;* Rennes, he said, was the Rubicon.
"If Dreyfus is innocent then seven Ministers of War are guilty and the
last more than the first," echoed Meyer in *Le Gaulois.* General Mercier,
leaving for Rennes to appear as a witness, issued his Order of the Day:
"Dreyfus will be condemned once more. For in this affair someone is
certainly guilty and the guilty one is either him or me. As it is certainly
not me, it is Dreyfus. . . . Dreyfus is a traitor and I shall prove it."

At six o'clock on the morning of August 8 the Court convened
with an audience of six hundred persons in the hall of the *lycée,* the
only room in Rennes large enough to accommodate them. In the front
row, next to former President Casimir-Périer, sat Mercier, his yellow
lined face as expressionless as ever, and nearby, the widow of Colonel
Henry in her long black mourning veil. Dignitaries, officers in uniform,
ladies in light summer dresses and more than four hundred journalists
filled the rows behind. Colonel Jouaust, presiding officer of the seven
military judges, called out in a voice hoarse under the pressure of the
moment, "Bring in the accused."

At once every chattering voice was stilled, every mouth closed,
people seemed to hold their breath as with one movement every head
in the audience turned toward a small door in the wall on the right.
Every gaze fastened on it with a kind of shrinking awe as if fearful
to look upon a ghost. For the accused was a ghost, whom no one in
the room had laid eyes on for almost five years, whom no one there
beyond his family, lawyers and original accusers had ever seen at all.
For five years he had been present in all their minds, not as a man
but as an idea; now he was going to walk through the door and they
would look on Lazarus. A minute passed, then another while the waiting
people were gripped in silence, an agonized silence, "such a silence as
never before could have overtaken a crowd."

The door opened, two guards were seen; between them came forward a thin, worn, desiccated figure, a strange shred of humanity, seeming neither young nor old, with a shrunken face and dried-out skin, and a body looking almost hollowed out but holding itself erect as if not to falter in the last few yards between the door and the witness box. Only the pince-nez familiar from the pictures had not suffered. A movement of "horror and pity" passed through the watchers, and the look bent on him by Picquart whose life he had changed beyond repair was so intense it could be felt by the people in between. Others present whose careers he had changed or broken—Clemenceau, Cavaignac—saw him for the first time.

For four and a half years Dreyfus had hardly spoken or heard a spoken word. Illness, fever, tropical sun, periods of chains and brutality when the frenzy in France was reflected by his gaolers, had enfeebled him. He could barely speak and only slowly understand what was spoken to him. Mounting the three steps to the tribune he staggered momentarily, straightened himself, saluted with impenetrable face, raised his gloved hand to take the oath, removed his hat, revealed the hair turned prematurely white. He remained a statue. He knew nothing of the Affair, the battle of the press, the duels and petitions, riots, street mobs, Leagues, trials, libel suits, appeals, coups d'état; nothing of Scheurer-Kestner, Reinach, the arrest of Picquart, the trial of Zola, the court-martial of Esterhazy, the suicide of Colonel Henry, the attack on the person of the President of France. During the trial, the impression he made on many was unfavorable. Rigidly determined to allow nothing to show that would appeal to pity, he antagonized many who came prepared to pity. G. A. Henty who came like most of the English, believing him to have been framed, left voicing doubts. "The man looked and spoke like a spy . . . and if he isn't a spy I'll be damned if he oughtn't to be one." Henty spoke for the last romantics who expected abstract concepts like Justice to be unequivocal and people who behaved oddly to be spies.

In the end it was not the impression Dreyfus made that determined the outcome any more than it was he who made the Affair: it was the dilemma Mercier had formulated long ago and it was General Mercier among the hundreds of witnesses who dominated the trial. Cold in authority, haughty in self-assurance, he took full responsibility for the original order withholding the Secret File from the defence, which he said was a "moral" decision. When on the witness stand he refused to answer questions he did not like; when not on the stand he intervened without being asked. When the Secret File was under examination he ordered the public excluded and the Court obeyed him. When questioned on the Army's suppression of evidence, the cynicism of his answers, Reinach confessed, "was almost admirable, . . . as if crime might be the source of a kind of beauty." Mercier "has become hallucinated," wrote Galliffet. "He thinks France is incarnated in his person . . . but all the same he is an honorable man."

As the weeks of examination and testimony dragged on with the succession of witnesses personally and passionately involved, the contention of lawyers, the disputes of journalists and observers, the heated feelings of the town, suspense as to the verdict became almost insupportable. In Paris rumors of another coup d'état planned for the day Mercier was to testify caused the Government to raid the homes of a hundred suspects and arrest sixty-five in their beds, including Déroulède but missing Guérin, who got away, barricaded himself in a house in the Rue Chabrol with a cache of munitions and fourteen companions, where he held out against a somewhat lackluster police siege for six weeks. "I don't budge from my office from 7 A.M. to 7 P.M. seven days a week, in order to be prepared for anything," wrote Galliffet.

On August 14 the too eloquent and aggressive Maître Labori, who "looked like Hercules and pleaded like a boxer," was shot outside the court, but not killed, by a young man with red hair who ran away shouting, "I've just killed the Dreyfus! I've just killed the Dreyfus!" The name again had become an abstraction. The attack raised the temperature to the level of madness. Since the assailant had run away with Labori's briefcase and had not been caught, it seemed to the Dreyfusards a deliberate plot and one more proof that the Nationalists would stop at nothing. They denounced their opponents as "murderers," a "General Staff of criminals" and swore that "for every one of ours we shall kill one of theirs—Mercier, Cavaignac, Boisdeffre, Barrès." Wrote Princess Radziwill to Galliffet, "My God, what an end to the century!"

The end of the trial came on September 9 and all the world gasped at the unbelievable verdict. By a vote of 5–2 Dreyfus was condemned again with "extenuating circumstances" which permitted a sentence of five years, already served, instead of a mandatory life sentence. Since there could obviously be nothing extenuating about treason, the rider was provocative to both sides. It had been devised by the prosecution, which realized that it would be easier to obtain a verdict of guilty if the judges did not have on their consciences the prospect of sending Dreyfus back to Devil's Island.

The effect of the verdict was as of some awful disaster. People were stunned. Queen Victoria telegraphed Lord Russell, "The Queen has learned with stupefaction the frightful verdict and hopes the poor martyr will appeal it to the highest judges." "Iniquitous, cynical, odious, barbarous," wrote *The Times* correspondent, bereft of sentence structure. Like an angry Isaiah, Clemenceau demanded, "What remains of the historic tradition that once made us champions of justice for the whole of the earth? A cry will ring out over the world: Where is France? What became of France?" World opinion suddenly became an issue, more acutely because of the coming International Exposition of 1900. At Evian on Lake Geneva, where many of the *gratin* spent their summer holidays, Proust found the Comtesse de Noailles weeping and crying, "How could they do it? What will the foreigners think of us now?" In the Nationalist camp the same thought was cause for rejoicing. "Since 1870 it is our first victory over the foreigner," exulted *Le Gaulois*.

Strength of feeling everywhere was made plain; the whole world cared. Excitement in Odessa was "simply extraordinary"; there was intense indignation in Berlin, "disgust and horror" in far-off Melbourne, protest meetings in Chicago and suggestions from all quarters for boycott of the Exposition. In Liverpool copies of *The Times* were bought out in minutes and soon sold at a premium. From Norway the composer Grieg wrote refusing an invitation to conduct his music at the Théâtre Chatelet because of his "indignation at the contempt for justice shown in your country." The English, riding at the time a wave of anti-French feeling because of Fashoda, were most indignant of all. Hyde Park rang with protest meetings, newspapers denounced the "insult to civilization," industrial firms and cultural societies urged boycott of the Exposition as a means of bringing pressure on the French Government, travelers were urged to cancel proposed visits, a hotelkeeper in the Lake District evicted a honeymooning French couple and one writer to the editor asserted that even the question of the Transvaal "pales into insignificance before the larger questions of truth and justice." *The Times,* however, reminded readers that many Frenchmen had risked "more than life itself" to prevent the defeat of justice and could not be expected to abandon the struggle to redress the wrong of Rennes.

The fight did in fact go on, but public opinion was worn out. The Affair was one of those situations for which there was no good solution. Waldeck-Rousseau offered Dreyfus a pardon which, despite the fierce objections of Clemenceau, was accepted on grounds of humanity—since Dreyfus could go through no more—and with the proviso that it would not terminate the effort to clear his name. Galliffet issued to the Army an Order of the Day: "The incident is closed. . . . Forget the past so that you may think only of the future." Waldeck introduced an Amnesty Bill annulling all pending legal actions connected with the case and angering both sides: the Right because Déroulède was excluded; the Dreyfusards because Picquart, Reinach and others who had suffered injustice or had been sued could not clear themselves. Waldeck was adamant. "The amnesty does not judge, it does not accuse, it does not acquit; it ignores." Debate nevertheless continued furious and lasted for a year before the bill became law. Animosities did not close over. Positions taken during the Affair hardened and crystallized. Lemaître, who had entered it more for sensation than from conviction, became a rabid royalist; Anatole France moved far to the left. . . .

Persistent and unrelenting efforts by Mathieu Dreyfus, Reinach and Jaurès succeeded against all obstacles in achieving a final Revision and a "breaking" of the Rennes verdict by the Cour de Cassation. On July 13, 1906, the eve of Bastille Day, almost twelve years after Dreyfus' arrest and seven years after Rennes, a bill restoring Dreyfus and Picquart to the Army was carried in the Chamber by 442–32, with de Mun still among the negatives. Dreyfus, decorated with the Legion d'Honneur, was promoted to Major and Picquart to General, the ranks they would have reached by the normal course of events. . . .

Rennes was the climax. After Rennes neither the fight for Justice nor the struggle of the Right against the Republic was over, but the Affair was. While it lasted, France exhibited, as in the Revolution, political man at his most combative. It was a time of excess. Men plunged in up to the hilt of their capacities and beliefs. They held nothing back. On the eve of the new century the Affair revealed what energies and ferocity were at hand to greet it.

John Kenneth Galbraith

HOW KEYNES CAME TO AMERICA

Dear Mr. Burnett:
    You are persuasive. . . . I suppose the enclosed piece on
Keynes would be my selection. I am honored to be included.

Yours faithfully,
John Kenneth Galbraith

Harvard University

"I believe myself to be writing a book on economic theory which will largely revolutionize—not, I suppose, at once but in the course of the next ten years—the way the world thinks about economic problems."
Letter from J. M. Keynes to George Bernard Shaw, New Year's Day, 1935.

The most influential book on economic and social policy so far in this century, *The General Theory of Employment, Interest, and Money,* by John Maynard Keynes, was published twenty-nine years ago last February in Britain and a few weeks later in the United States. A paper-back edition is now available in the United States for the first time, and quite a few people who take advantage of this bargain will be puzzled at the reason for the book's influence. Though comfortably aware of their own intelligence, they will be unable to read it. They will wonder, accordingly, how it persuaded so many other people— not all of whom, certainly were more penetrating or diligent. This was only one of the remarkable things about this book and the revolution it precipitated.

By common, if not yet quite universal agreement, the Keynesian revolution was one of the great modern accomplishments in social design. It brought Marxism in the advanced countries to a total halt. It led to a level of economic performance that now inspires bitter-end conservatives to panegyrics of unexampled banality. Yet those responsible have had no honors and some opprobrium. For a long while, to be known as an active Keynesian was to invite the wrath of those who equate social advance with subversion. Those concerned developed a habit of reticence. As a further consequence, the history of the revolution is, perhaps, the worst told story of our era.

It is time that we knew better this part of our history and those who made it, and this is a little of the story. Much of it turns on the almost unique unreadability of "The General Theory" and hence the need for people to translate and propagate its ideas to government officials, students and the public at large. As Messiahs go, Keynes was deeply dependent on his prophets.

"The General Theory" appeared in the sixth year of the Great Depression and the fifty-third of Keynes's life. At the time Keynes, like his great contemporary Churchill, was regarded as too clear-headed and candid to be trusted. Public officials are not always admiring of men who say what the right policy should be. Their frequent need, especially in matters of foreign policy, is for men who will find persuasive reasons for the wrong policy. Keynes had foreseen grave difficulty from the reparations clauses of the Versailles Treaty and had voiced them in "The Economic Consequences of the Peace," a brilliantly polemical volume, which may well have overstated his case and which certainly was unjust to Woodrow Wilson.

Later in the twenties, in another book, he was equally untactful toward those who invited massive unemployment in Britain in order to return sterling to the gold standard at its pre-war parity with the dollar. The man immediately responsible for this effort, a highly orthodox voice in economic matters at the time, was the then Chancellor of the Exchequer, Winston Churchill, and that book was called "The Economic Consequences of Mr. Churchill."

From 1920 to 1940 Keynes was sought out by students and intellectuals in Cambridge and London; was well known in London theater and artistic circles; directed an insurance company; made, and on occasion lost, quite a bit of money; and was an influential journalist. But he wasn't really trusted on public questions. The great public trade union which identifies trustworthiness with conformity kept him outside. Then came the Depression. There was much unemployment, much suffering. Even respectable men went broke. It was necessary, however unpleasant, to listen to the candid men who had something to say. This is the terrible punishment the gods reserve for fair weather statesmen.

It is a measure of how far the Keynesian revolution has proceeded that the central thesis of "The General Theory" now sounds rather commonplace. Until it appeared, economists, in the classical (or non-socialist) tradition, had assumed that the economy, if left to itself, would find its equilibrium at full employment. Increases or decreases in wages and in interest rates would occur as necessary to bring about this pleasant result. If men were unemployed, their wages would fall in relation to prices. With lower wages and wider margins, it would be profitable to employ those from whose toil an adequate return could not previously have been made. It followed that steps to keep wages at artificially high levels, such as might result from the ill-considered efforts by unions, would cause unemployment. Such efforts were deemed to be the principal cause of unemployment.

Movements in interest rates played a complimentary role by insuring that all income would ultimately be spent. Thus, were people to decide for some reason to increase their savings, the interest rates on the now more abundant supply of loanable funds would fall. This, in turn, would lead to increased investment. The added outlays for investment goods would offset the diminished outlays by the more frugal consumers. In this fashion, changes in consumer spending or in investment decisions were kept from causing any change in total spending that would lead to unemployment.

Keynes argued that neither wage movements nor changes in the rate of interest had, necessarily, any such agreeable effect. He focused attention on the total of purchasing power in the economy—what freshmen are now taught to call aggregate demand. Wage reductions might not increase employment; in conjunction with other changes, they might merely reduce this aggregate demand. And he held that interest was not the price that was paid to people to save but the price they got for exchanging holdings of cash, or its equivalent, their normal preference in assets, for less liquid forms of investment. And it was difficult to reduce interest beyond a certain level. Accordingly, if people sought to save more, this wouldn't necessarily mean lower interest rates and a resulting increase in investment. Instead, the total demand for goods might fall, along with employment and also investment, until savings were brought back into line with investment by the pressure of hardship which had reduced saving in favor of consumption. The economy would find its equilibrium not at full employment but with an unspecified amount of unemployment.

Out of this diagnosis came the remedy. It was to bring aggregate demand back up to the level where all willing workers were employed, and this could be accomplished by supplementing private expenditure with public expenditure. This should be the policy wherever intentions to save exceeded intentions to invest. Since public spending would not perform this offsetting role if there were compensating taxation (which is a form of saving), the public spending should be financed by borrowing—by incurring a deficit. So far as Keynes can be condensed into a few paragraphs, this is it. "The General Theory" is more difficult. There are nearly 400 pages, some of them of fascinating obscurity.

Before the publication of "The General Theory," Keynes had urged his ideas directly on President Roosevelt, most notably in a famous letter to *The New York Times* on December 31, 1933: "I lay overwhelming emphasis on the increase of national purchasing power resulting from government expenditure which is financed by loans." And he visited F.D.R. in the summer of 1934 to press his case, although the session was no great success; each, during the meeting, seems to have developed some doubts about the general good sense of the other.

In the meantime, two key Washington officials, Marriner Eccles, the exceptionally able Utah banker who was to become head of the Federal Reserve Board, and Lauchlin Currie, a former Harvard instructor who was director of research and later an economic aide to Roosevelt (and later still a prominent victim of McCarthyite persecution), had on their own account reached conclusions similar to those of Keynes as to the proper course of fiscal policy. When "The General Theory" arrived, they took it as confirmation of the course they had previously been urging. Currie, a highly qualified economist and teacher, was also a skilled and influential interpreter of the ideas in the Washington community. Not often have important new ideas on economics entered a goverment by way of its central bank. Nor should conservatives worry. There is not the slightest indication that it will ever happen again.

Paralleling the work of Keynes in the thirties and rivaling it in importance, though not in fame, was that of Simon Kuznets and a group of young economists and statisticians at the University of Pennsylvania, the National Bureau of Economic Research and the United States Department of Commerce. They developed the now familiar concepts of National Income and Gross National Product and their components and made estimates of their amount. Included among the components of

National Income and Gross National Product was the saving, investment, aggregate of disposable income and the other magnitudes of which Keynes was talking. As a result, those who were translating his ideas into action knew not only what needed to be done but how much. And many who would never have been persuaded by the Keynesian abstractions were compelled to belief by the concrete figures from Kuznets and his inventive colleagues.

However, the trumpet—if the metaphor is permissible for this particular book—that was sounded in Cambridge, England, was heard most clearly in Cambridge, Massachusetts. Harvard was the principal avenue by which Keynes's ideas passed to the United States. Conservatives worry about universities being centers of disquieting innovation. Their worries are surely exaggerated—but it has occurred.

In the late thirties, Harvard had a large community of young economists, most of them held there by the shortage of jobs that Keynes sought to cure. They had the normal confidence of their years in their ability to remake the world and, unlike less fortunate generations, the opportunity. They also had occupational indication of the need. Massive unemployment persisted year after year. It was degrading to have to continue telling the young that this was merely a temporary departure from the full employment norm, and that one need only obtain the needed wage reductions.

Paul Samuelson of M.I.T., who, almost from the outset, was the acknowledged leader of the younger Keynesian community, has compared the excitement of the young economists, on the arrival of Keynes's book, to that of Keats on first looking into Chapman's Homer. Some will wonder if economists are capable of such refined emotion, but the effect was certainly great. Here was a remedy for the despair that could be seen just beyond the Yard. It did not overthrow the system but saved it. To the non-revolutionary, it seemed too good to be true. To the occasional revolutionary, it was. The old economics was still taught by day. But in the evening, and almost every evening from 1936 on, almost everyone discussed Keynes.

This might, conceivably, have remained a rather academic discussion. As with the Bible and Marx, obscurity stimulated abstract debate. But in 1938, the practical instincts that economists sometimes suppress with success were catalyzed by the arrival at Harvard from Minnesota of Alvin H. Hansen. He was then about fifty, an effective teacher and a popular colleague. But most of all he was a man for whom economic ideas had no standing apart from their use.

The economists of established reputation had not taken to Keynes. Faced with the choice between changing one's mind and proving that there is no need to do so, almost everyone opts for the latter. So it was then. Hansen had an established reputation, and he did change his mind. Though he had been an effective critic of some central propositions in Keynes's "Treatise on Money," an immediately preceding work, and was initially rather cool to "The General Theory," he soon became strongly persuaded of its importance.

He proceeded to expound the ideas in books, articles and lectures and to apply them to the American scene. He persuaded his students and younger colleagues that they should not only understand the ideas but win understanding in others and then go on to get action. Without ever seeking to do so or being quite aware of the fact, he became the leader of a crusade. In the late thirties Hansen's seminar in the new Graduate School of Public Administration was regularly visited by the Washington policymakers. Often the students overflowed into the hall. One felt that it was the most important thing currently happening in the country and this could have been the case.

The officials took Hansen's ideas, and perhaps even more his sense of conviction, back to Washington. In time there was also a strong migration of his younger colleagues and students to the capital. Among numerous others were Richard Gilbert, now a principal architect of Pakistan's economic development, who was a confidant of Harry Hopkins; Richard Musgrave, now of Princeton, who applied Keynes's and Hansen's ideas to the tax system; Alan Sweezy, now of California Institute of Technology, who went to the Federal Reserve and the W.P.A.; George Jaszi, who went to the Department of Commerce; Griffiths Johnson, who served at the Treasury, National Resources Planning Board and the White House; and Walter Salant, now of the Brookings Institution, who served in several Federal agencies. Keynes himself once wrote admiringly of this group of young Washington disciples.

The discussions that had begun in Cambridge continued through the war years in Washington. One of the leaders, a close friend of Hansen's but not otherwise connected with the Harvard group, was Gerhard Colm of the Bureau of the Budget. Colm, a German refugee who made the transition from a position of influence in Germany to one of influence in the United States in a matter of some five years, played a major role in reducing the Keynesian proposals to workable estimates of costs and quantities. Keynesian policies became central to what was called postwar planning and designs for preventing the re-emergence of massive unemployment.

Meanwhile, others were concerning themselves with a wider audience. Seymour Harris, another of Hansen's colleagues and an early convert to Keynes, became the most prolific exponent of the ideas in the course of becoming one of the most prolific scholars of modern times. He published half a dozen books on Keynes and outlined the ideas in hundreds of letters, speeches, memoranda, Congressional appearances and articles. Professor Samuelson, mentioned above, put the Keynesian ideas into what became (and remains) the most influential textbook on economics since the last great exposition of the classical system by Alfred Marshall. Lloyd Metzler, now of the University of Chicago, applied the Keynesian system to international trade. Lloyd G. Reynolds, at a later stage, gathered a talented group of younger economists at Yale and made that university a major center of discussion of the new trends.

Nor was the Harvard influence confined to the United States. At almost the same time that "The General Theory" arrived in Cambridge, Massachusetts, a young Canadian graduate student named Robert Bryce arrived from Cambridge, England. He had been in Keynes's seminar and had, as a result, a special licence to explain what Keynes meant in his more obscure passages. With two or three other Canadian graduate students, Bryce went on to Ottawa and to a succession of senior posts culminating in his present one as Deputy Minister of Finance. Canada was perhaps the first country to commit itself to a firmly Keynesian economic policy.

Meanwhile, with the help of the academic Keynesians, a few businessmen were becoming interested. Two New England industrialists, Henry S. Dennison of the Dennison Manufacturing Company in Framingham and Ralph Flanders of the Jones and Lamson Company of Springfield, Vermont (and later United States Senator from Vermont) hired members of the Harvard group to tutor them in the ideas. Before the war they had endorsed them in a book, in which Lincoln Filene of Boston and Morris E. Leeds of Philadelphia had joined, called "Toward Full Employment." It was only slightly more readable than Keynes. In the later war years, the Committee for Economic Development, led in these matters by Flanders and the late Beardsley Ruml, and again with the help of the academic Keynesians, began explaining the ideas to businessmen.

In Washington during the war years the National Planning Association had been a center for academic discussion of the Keynesian ideas.

At the end of the war Hans Christian Sonne, the imaginative and liberal New York banker, began underwriting both N.P.A., and the Keynesian ideas. With the C.E.D., in which Sonne was also influential, N.P.A. became another important instrument for explaining the policy to the larger public. (In the autumn of 1949, in an exercise of unparalleled diplomacy, Sonne gathered a dozen economists of strongly varying views at Princeton and persuaded them to sign a specific endorsement of Keynesian fiscal policies. The agreement was later reported to the Congress in well-publicized hearings by Arthur Smithies of Harvard and Simeon Leland of Northwestern University.)

In 1964, ten years after the publication of "The General Theory," the Employment Act of that year gave the Keynesian system the qualified but still quite explicit support of law. It recognized, as Keynes had urged, that unemployment and insufficient output would respond to positive policies. Not much was said about the specific policies but the responsibility of the Federal Government to act in some fashion was clearly affirmed. The Council of Economic Advisers became, in turn, a platform for expounding the Keynesian view of the economy and it was brought promptly into use. Leon Keyserling, as an original member and later chairman, was a tireless exponent of the ideas. And he saw at an early stage the importance of enlarging them to embrace not only the prevention of depression but the maintenance of an adequate rate of economic expansion. Thus in a decade had the revolution spread.

Those who nurture thoughts of conspiracy and clandestine plots will be saddened to know that this was a revolution without organization. All who participated felt a deep sense of personal responsibility for the ideas; there was a varying but deep urge to persuade. But no one ever responded to plans, orders, instructions, or any force apart from his own convictions. That perhaps was the most interesting single feature of the Keynesian revolution.

Something more was, however, suspected. And there was some effort at counter-revolution. Nobody could say that he preferred massive un-employment to Keynes. And even men of conservative mood, when they understood what was involved, opted for the policy—some asking only that it be called by some other name. The Committee for Economic Development, coached by Ruml on semantics, never advocated deficits. Rather it spoke well of a budget that was balanced only under conditions of high employment. Those who objected to Keynes were also invariably handicapped by the fact that they hadn't (and couldn't) read the book.

It was like attacking the original Kama Sutra for obscenity without being able to read Sanskrit. Still, where social change is involved, there are men who can surmount any handicap.

Appropriately Harvard, not Washington, was the principal object of attention. In the fifties, a group of graduates of mature years banded together in an organization called the Veritas Foundation and produced a volume called "Keynes at Harvard." It found that "Harvard was the launching pad for the Keynesian rocket in America." But then it damaged this not implausible proposition by identifying Keynesianism with socialism, Fabian socialism, Marxism, Communism, Fascism and also literary incest, meaning that one Keynesian always reviewed the works of another Keynesian. More encouragingly, the authors also reported that "Galbraith is being groomed as the new crown prince of Keynesism (sic)." Like so many others in similar situations, the authors sacrificed their chance for credibility by writing not for the public but for those who were paying the bill. The university was unperturbed, the larger public sadly indifferent. The book evidently continues to have some circulation on the more thoughtful fringes of the John Birch Society.

As a somewhat less trivial matter, another and more influential group of graduates pressed for an investigation of the Department of Economics, employing as their instrument the visiting committee that annually reviews the work of the department on behalf of the Governing Boards. The Keynesian revolution belongs to our history; so accordingly does this investigation.

It was conducted by Clarence Randall, then the exceptionally articulate head of the Inland Steel Company, with the support of Sinclair Weeks, a manufacturer, former Senator and tetrarch of the right wing of the Republican Party in Massachusetts. In due course, the committee found that Keynes was, indeed, exerting a baneful influence on the Harvard economic mind and that the department was unbalanced in his favor. As always, there was the handicap that the investigators, with one or two possible exceptions, had not read the book and were otherwise uncertain as to what they attacked. The department, including the members most skeptical of Keynes's analysis—no one accepted all of it and some very little—unanimously rejected the committee's finding. So, as one of his last official acts before becoming High Commissioner to Germany, did President James Bryant Conant. There was much bad blood.

In ensuing years there was further discussion of the role of Keynes at Harvard and of related issues. But it became increasingly amicable, for the original investigators had been caught up in one of those fascinating and paradoxical developments with which the history of the Keynesian (and doubtless all other) revolutions is replete. Shortly after the committee reached its disturbing conclusion, the Eisenhower Administration came to power.

Mr. Randall became a Presidential assistant and adviser. Mr. Weeks became Secretary of Commerce and almost immediately was preoccupied with the firing of the head of the Bureau of Standards over the question of the efficacy of Glauber's salts as a battery additive. Having staked his public reputation against the nation's scientists and engineers on the issue (as the late Bernard De Voto put it) that a battery could be improved by giving it a laxative, Mr. Weeks could hardly be expected to keep open another front against the economists. But much worse, both he and Mr. Randall were acquiring a heavy contingent liability for the policies of the Eisenhower Administration. And these, it soon developed, had almost as strong a Keynesian coloration as the department at Harvard.

President Eisenhower's first Chairman of the Council of Economic Advisers was Arthur F. Burns of Columbia University and the National Bureau of Economic Research. Mr. Burns had credentials as a critic of Keynes. In his introduction to the 1946 annual report of the National Bureau, called "Economic Research and the Keynesian Thinking of Our Times," he had criticized a version of the Keynesian underemployment equilibrium and concluded a little heavily that "the imposing schemes for governmental action that are being bottomed on Keynes's equilibrium theory must be viewed with skepticism." Alvin Hansen had replied rather sharply.

But Burns was (and is) an able economist. If he regarded Keynes with skepticism, he viewed recessions (including ones for which he might be held responsible) with positive antipathy. In his 1955 Economic Report, he said, "Budget policies can help promote the objective of maximum production by wisely allocating resources *first between private and public uses;* second, among various government programs." (Italics added.) Keynes, reading these words carefully, would have strongly applauded. And, indeed, a spokesman for the N.A.M. told the Joint Economic Committee that they pointed "directly toward the planned and eventually the socialized economy."

After the departure of Burns, the Eisenhower Administration incurred a deficit of no less than $9.4 billions in the national income accounts in the course of overcoming the recession of 1958. This was by far the largest deficit ever incurred by an American Government in peacetime; it exceeded the *total* peacetime expenditure by F.D.R. in any year up to 1940. No administration before or since has given the economy such a massive dose of Keynesian medicine. With a Republican Administration, guided by men like Mr. Randall and Mr. Weeks, following such policies, the academic Keynesians were no longer vulnerable. Keynes ceased to be a wholly tactful topic of conversation with such critics.

Presidents Kennedy and Johnson have continued what is now commonplace policy. Advised by Walter Heller, a remarkably skillful exponent of Keynes's ideas, they added the new device of the deliberate tax reduction to sustain aggregate demand. And they abandoned, at long last, the doubletalk by which advocates of Keynesian policies combined advocacy of measures to promote full employment and economic growth with promises of a promptly balanced budget. "We have recognized as self-defeating the effort to balance our budget too quickly in an economy operating well below its potential," President Johnson said in his 1965 report.

Now, as noted, Keynesian policies are the new orthodoxy. Economists are everywhere to be seen enjoying their new and pleasantly uncontroversial role. Like their predecessors who averted their eyes from unemployment, many are now able to ignore—often with some slight note of scholarly righteousness—the new problem, which is an atrocious allocation of resources between private wants and public needs, especially those of our cities. (In a sense, the Keynesian success has brought back an older problem of economics, that of resource allocation, in a new form.) And there is the dangerously high dependence on military spending. But these are other matters.

We have yet to pay proper respect to those who pioneered the Keynesian revolution. Everyone now takes pride in the resulting performance of the economy. We should take a little pride in the men who brought it about. It is hardly fitting that they should have been celebrated only by the reactionaries. The debt to the courage and intelligence of Alvin Hansen is especially great. Next only to Keynes, his is the credit for saving what even conservatives still call capitalism.

Bruce Catton

HANDWRITING ON THE WALL

On January 17, 1961, just before he finished his second term as President, Dwight D. Eisenhower issued a farewell address expressing his concern about the possible effect on American liberties of the enormous size of the national defense effort. President Eisenhower was not arguing that we should get along with a smaller effort; he was simply warning that "the potential for the disastrous rise of misplaced power exists and will persist," and in his book, *Waging Peace,* he asserted that this struck him as "the most challenging message I could leave with the people of this country."

In a few sentences his message made the warning explicit:
"In the councils of government we must guard against the acquisition of unwarranted influence, whether sought or unsought, by the military-industrial complex. . . . We must never let the weight of this combination endanger our liberties or democratic processes. We should take nothing for granted. Only an alert and knowledgeable citizenry can compel the proper meshing of the huge industrial and military machinery of defense with our peaceful methods and goals, so that security and liberty may prosper together."

The military-industrial complex the President was talking about came to its first flowering during the Second World War, when nothing seemed to matter but total victory in an all-out struggle. Decisions on purely domestic policies, some of them of profound long-range importance, came more and more from the leaders of this complex. To a profound extent, the direction in which

America would be headed once the war ended was up to the men who bought, sold or produced the military hardware.

In comparatively minor positions—first on the staff of the National Defense Advisory Commission, and later with the War Production Board—I got a long firsthand view of the way the military-industrial complex grew and operated. In 1948 I tried to tell something about it in a book, *The War Lords of Washington,* and I have chosen the first chapter of that book for inclusion here.

Whether this is "my best" I simply do not know. Authors are notoriously poor judges of the comparative merits, or otherwise, of their own books. I do feel that a glimpse at the complex at the time of its birth may be of some interest. In addition, I still feel a grim fascination with the way in which an outspoken ex-newspaperman, Robert Horton, bluntly told the Secretary of the Navy, three days before Pearl Harbor, that the Navy did not seem to be entirely prepared for what might soon happen to it.

In any case, here it is.

                                                    Bruce Catton

They were often admitted to be the ablest men in the nation and they were very high up in the Defense Effort, and the best was none too good for them. If, collectively, they were neither as beautiful nor as terrible as an army with banners, individually they were very impressive. Their faces had that indefinable but unmistakable gloss which comes to faces that are photographed a great deal (good food, right living, and the proper kind of publicity can do much for a man) and if the North Lounge of the Carlton had been set aside for the party it was only fitting and proper.

For this was a rather special evening. Mr. Donald Nelson was giving a dinner in honor of the Vice-President, and of all the people in Washington only some two dozen had been invited. It was a little strange, when you stopped to think about it; this particular group of two dozen people,

no more and no less, had never been segregated like this before and never
would be again, and to bring them together—to make precisely these
men and no others the select, obvious, inescapably chosen twenty-four—
had taken signs and portents in the sky and a compelling breath on the
face of the waters. Something momentous had had to happen, to the
world at large and to the republic in particular, to bring this about.
It had happened, and no one present knew quite what it was, but even
the dullest knew vaguely that it had not yet stopped happening. It was the
evening of Thursday, December 4, 1941.

On that particular evening there was nothing much to show that the
calendar was moving on to one of those crucial, turning-point dates
which say: Hereafter, nothing is ever going to be quite the same again.
It was just a Thursday evening, and if the situation had grown a bit
tense, why, then, it had been tense for a year and more and no one's
appetite had been spoiled thereby. The paneled walls were lost in a haze
of dim lights and cigar smoke before they reached the high ceiling, and
any shadow which a Coming Event might be casting was effectively lost
in the expensive dusk. It touched the high spirits and good nature
of none of the assembled guests.

Except, perhaps, for Frank Knox. The Secretary of the Navy was
grave as he joined the others at the bar before dinner, preoccupied
with his own thoughts as he took his place at the dinner table on the
left hand of his host. As a life-long Republican he had joined an objec-
tionably Democratic cabinet because he felt that a time of emergency
had arrived, and he had lately been confirmed in this opinion by confidential reports from the far side of the Pacific. He was no better fitted
than the next man to appraise and interpret the shape of things to come,
but he did know physical trouble when he saw it, and he saw it
coming now quite clearly. Also, as a simple man who had been one of
Teddy Roosevelt's Rough Riders, he knew a responsibility when he saw
one, and the weight of the responsibility which he, as Secretary of the
Navy, was carrying around right now was oppressive. The buzz and
chatter of two dozen men enjoying the before-dinner cocktail eddied
around him without quite touching him.

Then, too, there was the Vice-President, Mr. Henry Wallace. He was
fitted to see what was coming; fitted to understand it, even to go out
and meet it head-on, if people would only let him. But he had been
touched, somehow, with a kind of Cassandra curse, so that any warning he
uttered was apt to go unheeded. Tonight he stood in the group by
the bar, nursing a soft drink which he did not especially want, and made

small talk with men who—as no one knew better than himself—were unalterably opposed to that shifting one-tenth of him which they were able to see and understand. The heir-apparent to the New Deal dynasty was mingling socially with blue-chip industrialists tonight, and nobody felt quite natural about it.

Nobody, of course, except Nelson. Nelson felt natural anywhere. He was big, jovial, and self-possessed, and his round red face beamed through the cigar smoke like a harvest moon through the September haze. This dinner party might look like a shotgun wedding between industry and the administration—indeed, in a sense Nelson was the man holding the shotgun—but all the decencies were being observed, and in any case it had seemed to Nelson that some such meeting as this was necessary. The defense program was in a bad way. It had brought together, out on the open stage of public life in Washington, all of the unsolved contradictions, the unhealed antagonisms, and the poorly formulated aspirations of a country which had just been through a very hard and perplexing decade, and nothing was working quite right. Nelson clung firmly to a simple faith: that the country's groups and parties were not really divided by anything deep and fundamental, and that men of diverse backgrounds and viewpoints could work together admirably if they just sat down with each other, got thoroughly acquainted, and recognized their agreement on a common objective. This dinner party was a step toward that end: to make big business and Henry Wallace mutually familiar, leading each to see that the other did not have cloven hoofs. It would be a good trick if it worked, and Nelson was going to make it work if there was any virtue in relaxation, good food and drink, and the social graces.

He was courteously deferential to his guest of honor, the Vice-President, and to Mr. William Knudsen, the head man of the Office of Production Management. It was part of Nelson's genius that he could understand, and like, both of these utterly dissimilar men: Wallace, who could talk on any subject so long as it was strictly of an intellectual cast, and Knudsen, who could talk on any subject so long as it was purely mechanical. Between Nelson and Knudsen there was a faint sense of strain. Their stars had come into collision, somewhere. Washington is a city whose very air is flavored by the subtle shiftings of the beliefs, the hopes, and the desires of men who undertake to forecast and to analyze trends and coming events; and it was beginning to be the conclusion of such men that Nelson and Knudsen could not long go on as coequals in the defense program. This conclusion was not a private matter. It got into men's relationships and affected men's plans. Knudsen and Nelson were both conscious of it. One of the two, said the word in the air, was Wrong. Sooner or later things would come to a head. A latter-day Viking minus his helmet, Knudsen stood immobile among the others, a glass cupped in his heavy hand, small eyes twinkling out of a florid, impassive face. Physically, he was about the only man present who matched Nelson.

But if everyone relaxed and made friendly talk, there was a queer feeling of tension in the air. This particular grouping of men was incongruous. The lion was lying down with the lamb, and both parties were quite aware that the time wasn't really ripe for it. A centrifugal force had been balanced by a force from the outside, but the balance was temporary and unstable and everybody concerned was keeping his eyes open and his fingers crossed. A dozen hostilities had been buried but burial had not been the sequel to death. After years of struggle, oddly matched rivals had made a truce, but it was only a truce and not a treaty of enduring peace. This was the century of progress and it was likewise the century of the common man, but what the common man and his progress were going to look like when the dust finally settled had not yet been disclosed. In unstable equilibrium a carefully contrived edifice had been set up, a house of irrational and wishful dreams, built on the shifting sands; for better or for worse they were going to try to make it endure through whatever howling storm the gods might be sending.

In any case, it was a fine evening and a fine party. After a time the men got around the long table for dinner. Dim light on the high walls, ruddy faces over white shirt fronts, deft waiters serving from silver dishes, a sharp-visaged *maître* hovering unobtrusively in the background, a hum of talk dotted with occasional bursts of masculine laughter; this is as it was in the beginning, is now and forever shall be, Washington without end, and the Carlton is a very fine hotel indeed. We are insulated, here. There is a war going on but it is a long way off, and nothing is going to happen that will really force us to grapple with the fundamentals. . . .

And finally the plates were taken away and the cigars were lighted, and Nelson got up to enfold the diners in the soft arms of after-dinner talk. On the surface, Nelson sounded just like a Rotarian: There is no difference among us as to aims, just differences over methods, which are unimportant. We are men of good will and we are working together, and behold there is no clash or disharmony that good fellowship and understanding will not cure. I have known our Vice-President and I have found him to be a great man and a regular fellow, who has contributed much to the defense effort; Mr. Knudsen is a great man and a regular fellow, likewise, and his contributions also have been immense. I have the utmost confidence in and so forth. . . . But underneath, nearly inaudible beneath the pat good-fellow phrases and the beaming smile, there was a note of almost desperate pleading and anxiety: This government and private industry *can* make a go of it; we *can* sink our differences of opinion; there is *not* any basic, soul-compelling conflict here except the one that is coming on us from the outside, and for God's sake let's forget our doubts and mistrusts and realize what we're really up against and do something about it, because this is our last chance. . . . And so, after a while, Nelson presented the Vice-President, and sat down.

Now picture Henry Wallace, standing at the head of a long table looking down at a double row of faces, a double row of masks, groping for the thing to say that would bridge the gap between himself, and what he stood for, and the dominant majority. He stood there, his untidy hair straying down over one eye, head bent forward a little, smiling an uncertain smile, and he reached for the right word and did not find it. His long suit was to be himself—tenacious, uncompromising, building after the pattern that had been shown him on the mount— and this was not the night for it. He was capable of many things, but to adopt the Nelson touch and move lightly over things that could not be said—that, of all conceivable gambits, just was not in him, not on this night and before this audience. He was an alien in this room, and everybody knew it. Most of the men present felt toward him a mixture of condescension and resentment. He had nothing to say to them, nothing that they could understand, nothing that he could put into their kind of talk. So he was reminded of a story, and he told it. It was just a story, neither very good nor very bad, and it drew a round of polite laughter. The Vice-President sat down, to the relief of himself and his listeners.

Then Knudsen. He stood up, solid, honest, peering out from under his blond eyebrows, massive shoulders slightly stooped, talking in the quaint, stage-dialect Scandinavian brogue that never quite left him. He was at home here, and he talked on a level that his audinece could understand. . . . We've had a big job to do here, and it has been tough, but all things considered it is being done pretty well. And this war overseas is simply a neighborhood disturbance of the peace on a big scale. We, the peace-loving people, had been trying to go our own way and mind our own business; now, because of this brawl, we have had to forget our ordinary work and take steps to restore order. We are the neighbors, getting together to stop an intolerably noisy gin party in the corner apartment. Pretty soon we'll have it squelched, and then we'll all go home and pick up exactly where we left off.

Thus Knudsen, and the world revolution as he saw it.

Then rose to his feet Edward R. Stettinius, Jr., incredibly handsome, with florid, youthful face under silvery hair, faultlessly groomed, giving out the easy, smiling good fellowship of a Y.M.C.A. secretary. It was this good man's misfortune that unofficial Washington knew him, from first to last, under the irreverent nickname of Junior. Just Junior. He carried with him the aura of a noble past; son of a Morgan partner, chairman of the board of U. S. Steel, amiable host at a vast estate in the horse country of Virginia, he had been one of the first great names of the business world to be brought into the rearmament program. Striking failures had occurred, in the defense effort, and the record trailed at his heels; a record, when all was said and done, of trusting that everything would come out all right if only people could be induced to believe that it would. Like Knudsen, he was a handsome ornament in the New Deal's collection of eminent reputations; also like Knudsen, he had suffered because the reputation had been given prolonged exposure to very foul weather. . . . Tonight, he said, he had good tidings of great joy for the assembled guests.

"I've just heard from Harry," he said, in the manner of one who refers to the best-loved of all the well-loved intimates of his friends. "Harry is better—lots better. He'll be able to leave the hospital soon, and he'll be back with us before long."

Now this was all very fine, except that the Harry of these remarks was Harry Hopkins, recently hospitalized with the stomach ulcers that were his constant torment. Things had come, then, thus far: a chairman-in-absentia of the board of U. S. Steel, standing in a roomful of his peers, could refer to Hopkins' impending recovery and to his return to a seat at the right hand of the President as to a bit of good news at which all present would rejoice. Harry Hopkins: we'll tax and tax and spend and spend, and look at all those men leaning on their shovels; and here is U. S. Steel, in silvery-haired person, welcoming him to our bosom. Unquestionably, every valley shall be exalted. Mr. Stettinius sat down, all aglow, and the guests patted their palms together politely, and there were no snide remarks.

Upon invitation of the host, Frank Knox stood up. The Secretary of the Navy was in no mood for light banter. Not for him were the funny stories of the Vice-President, the quizzical parables of Knudsen, or the soft good fellowship of Stettinius. Knox performed his social duty by paying his respects to his host, remarking that he thought this kind of get-together was a good idea, and mentioning that he was glad to be present. Then, darkly serious, he looked down the long table for a moment in silence.

"I feel that I can speak very frankly, within these four walls," he said. "I want you to know that our situation tonight is very serious—more serious, probably, than most of us realize. We are very close to war. War may begin in the Pacific at any moment. Literally, at any moment. It may even be beginning tonight, while we're sitting here, for all we know. We are that close to it."

He paused, and the silence was impressive. Then he went on, his voice rising confidently.

"But I want you all to know that no matter what happens, the United States Navy is ready! Every man is at his post, every ship is at its station. The Navy is ready. Whatever happens, the Navy is not going to be caught napping."

He sat down, and there was a hum of comment. Nelson leaned over toward him.

"Are things really as bad as that, Frank?" he asked quietly.

"Every bit as bad," said Knox, nodding vigorously. "It can start at any minute."

Nelson meditated for a moment.

"You know," he said, "if we do have to fight the Japs, I can't see that there'd be much for our Army to do. Won't it be pretty much a Navy show?"

Knox nodded again.

"Oh, yes, of course. We're all ready for them, you know. We've had our plans worked out for twenty years. Once it starts, our submarines will go in to blockade them, and sooner or later our battle fleet will be able to force an action. It won't take too long. Say about a six months' war."

But there is always somebody around to spoil a good effect. Belshazzar gave a big dinner in Babylon once, and right at the height of the festivities a mysterious hand appeared and traced some words upon the wall, the general purport being that the dam had busted and that good men should take to the hills. Tonight the spoil-sport, or moving finger, was a black-haired, bullet-headed man named Robert Wyman Horton, who rejoiced in the cumbersome title of Director of Information in the Office for Emergency Management of the Executive Office of the President.

Horton was a misfit at this party. He was the official mouthpiece, so to speak, for the defense program—for OPM, SPAB, and all the rest of it—and he had watched the entire process at close range ever since the formation of the original Defense Commission at the time of the fall of France, and he was not impressed by what he had seen. He was a Vermonter, exemplifying to a marked degree every characteristic of that rugged state; at all times and places he believed in saying exactly what he thought, and what he thought was usually rather acrid. He had thoughts, now, for which he craved utterance, and he passed up to Nelson a note which said, in effect, "How about calling on me for a few remarks next?"

Fortified by the all-is-well assurances of the Secretary of the Navy, Nelson glanced at the note, rose to his feet, and remarked that they would now hear from Mr. Horton, the Director of Information. He sat down, not without a faint misgiving or two about what might be coming next, and Horton got up. It was not long before Nelson realized that his faint misgiving was amply justified.

"I have been very interested," said Horton, "in the little talk which the Secretary of the Navy has just made. It has been very encouraging to be assured that the Navy is ready for whatever may happen. But somehow, some of the things I've seen recently make me wonder if the Secretary of the Navy may not be mistaken."

He fixed his cold blue eyes on Knox's face and went on.

"The other afternoon," he said, "I had to go over to the Navy Department to attend a conference. It was a little before four o'clock when I got over there. I was almost trampled underfoot in the lobby by captains and admirals, rushing out with golf bags over their shoulders. It seemed to me that the high-ranking people in the Department were knocking off work rather early, if we're so close to a war."

(Knox leaned over to Nelson and whispered savagely, behind his hand: "Who *is* this son of a bitch?")

"But the thing that really bothers me," Horton went on, "is something that happened last week. I had occasion to take a little trip down Chesapeake Bay on a little Coast Guard patrol boat. We were down around Norfolk, and late in the day the skipper of the boat—a chief petty officer—decided it might be interesting to cruise up to the navy yard and see what we could see. So up we went. We not only cruised up to the yard, but we cruised all through it. Nobody challenged us, nobody stopped us, nobody did anything to find out if we were really in a Coast Guard boat or just in a cabin cruiser painted gray.

"Now I've heard a lot about Navy security measures lately. Some of the news we've tried to get out, over at OPM, has been held up because the Navy objected that it would violate security. Okay; if we're close to war we have to be careful about giving away military information. But as I understand it, one of the top military secrets right now is the fact that the British aircraft carrier *Illustrious* is in the yard at Norfolk for repairs. Well, we cruised right by her dock. There she was, standing up like a ten-story building, with an enormous Union Jack flying over her. If we could cruise in like that and see her, I should think any German agent who wanted to could do the same.

"Anyhow, we left the yard after a while and went out through Hampton Roads, and pretty soon it got dark and we wanted to tie up somewhere and make a phone call. So we headed into the nearest place, which happened to be one of those big new navy installations— I think it was a mine base. We came in, after dark, and tied up at a pier where there were three or four minesweepers tied up. Nobody challenged us. Nobody tried to find out whether we were really in a Coast Guard boat, or whether we had any business in there. Nobody paid any attention to us at all. We got off the boat and walked along the pier, looking for some place where we could find a telephone. We didn't find any, so we walked on to dry land and pretty soon we came to a guard house or sentry box of some kind. We hammered on the door, and by and by a sailor stuck his head out, and we asked him where there was a public telephone. He pointed vaguely up the road and said it was about half a mile. So we walked up there. The guard didn't pay any attention to us. He didn't know who we were, but he didn't ask for a pass and he didn't want to see any credentials. For all he knew we might have been Hitler's grandsons.

"Sure, the CPO I was with had a uniform on. But there are at least thirty places in Norfolk where you can walk in and buy a CPO's uniform. All it takes is a little money. We could have been spies, saboteurs, anything—but the Navy, which is so touchy about the press releases that come out of OPM, let us wander all over that base, after dark, for upwards of half an hour, without once bothering to find out who we were or what our business was. We could have blown the whole place to pieces, for all the obstacles the Navy put in our way."

Horton paused, and looked coldly at Knox, who by now was painfully close to apoplexy.

"Mister Secretary," he said, "I don't think your Navy *is* ready."

This was the night of December 4, 1941.

Norman Cousins

MODERN MAN IS OBSOLETE

Some ideas come to a man whole—not because they suddenly appear out of nowhere but because they have been taking shape slowly in his mind over a period of time, requiring only a jolt for them to emerge full size. This *Saturday Review* editorial was written the same day the bomb was dropped, August 6, 1945, but I had been living with the central ideas in the editorial for at least ten years. Even before the bombing of Hiroshima, I had been thinking in a fairly sustained way about the implications of war in an age of advanced science and technology.

In the years since the editorial appeared, some observers have been generous enough to comment that it anticipated many of the major issues growing out of the development of nuclear energy. To the extent that this is true, it is the result not of any insights but of sustained concern.

One more note. *Modern Man Is Obsolete* is as much a statement of personal philosophy as it is an attempt to perceive the implications of an historic event.

Norman Cousins

Whatever elation there is in the world today because of final victory in the war is severely tempered by fear. It is a primitive fear, the fear of the unknown, the fear of forces man can neither channel nor comprehend. This fear is not new; in its classical form it is the fear of irrational death. But overnight it has become intensified, magnified. It has burst out of the subconscious and into the conscious, filling the mind with primordial apprehensions. It is thus that man stumbles fitfully into a new age of atomic energy for which he is as ill equipped to accept its potential blessings as he is to counteract or control its present dangers.

Where man can find no answer, he will find fear. While the dust was still settling over Hiroshima, he was asking himself questions and finding no answers. The biggest question of these concerns the nature of man. Is war in the nature of man? If so, how much time has he left before he employs the means he has already devised for the ultimate in self-destruction—extinction? And now that the science of warfare has reached the point where it threatens the planet itself, is it possible that man is destined to return the earth to its aboriginal incandescent mass blazing at fifty million degrees? If not—that is, if war is not in the nature of man—then how is he to interpret his own experience, which tells him that in all of recorded history there have been only 300 years in the aggregate during which he has been free of war?

Closely following upon these are other questions, flowing out endlessly from his fears and without prospect of definitive answer. Even assuming that he could hold destructive science in check, what changes would the new age bring or demand in his everyday life? What changes would it bring or demand in his culture, his education, his philosophy, his religion, his relationships with other human beings?

In speculating upon these questions, it should not be necessary to prove that on August 6, 1945, a new age was born. When on that day a parachute containing a small object floated to earth over Japan, it marked the violent death of one stage in man's history and the beginning of another. Nor should it be necessary to prove the saturating effect of the new age, permeating every aspect of man's activities, from machines to morals, from physics to philosophy, from politics to poetry; in sum, it is an effect creating a blanket of obsolescence not only over the methods and the products of man but over man himself.

It is a curious phenomenon of nature that only two species practise the art of war—men and ants, both of which, ironically, maintain complex social organizations. This does not mean that only men and ants engage in the murder of their own kind. Many animals of the same species kill each other, but only men and ants have practised the science of organized destruction, employing their massed numbers in violent combat and relying on strategy and tactics to meet developing situations or to capitalize on the weaknesses in the strategy and tactics of the other side. The longest continuous war ever fought between men lasted thirty years. The longest ant war ever recorded lasted six-and-a-half weeks, or whatever the corresponding units would be in ant reckoning.

It is encouraging to note that while all entomologists are agreed that war is instinctive with ants, not all anthropologists and biologists are agreed that war is instinctive with men. The strict empiricists, of course, find everything in man's history to indicate that war is locked up with his nature. But a broader and more generous, certainly more philosophical, view is held by those scientists who claim that the evidence to date is incomplete and misleading, and that man *does* have within him the power of abolishing war. Prominent among these is Julian Huxley, who draws a sharp distinction between human nature and the *expression* of human nature. Thus war is not a reflection but an expression of his nature. Moreover, the expression may change, as the factors which lead to war may change. "In man, as in ants, war in any serious sense is bound up with the existence of accumulations of property to fight about. . . . As for human nature, it contains no specific war instinct, as does the nature of harvester ants. There is in man's makeup a general aggressive tendency, but this, like all other human urges, is not a specific and unvarying instinct; it can be molded into the most varied forms."

But even if this gives us a reassuring answer to the question—is war inevitable because of man's nature?—it still leaves unanswered the question concerning the causes leading up to war. The expression of man's nature will continue to be warlike if the same conditions are continued that have provoked warlike expressions in him in the past. And since man's survival on earth is now absolutely dependent on his ability to avoid a new war, he is faced with the so-far insoluble problem of eliminating those causes.

In the most primitive sense, war in man is an expression of his competitive impulses. Like everything else in nature, he has had to fight for existence; but the battle against other animals, once won, gave way in his evolution to battle against his own kind. Darwin called it the survival of the fittest, and its most overstretched interpretation is to be found in "Mein Kampf," with its naked glorification of brute force and the complete worship of might makes right. In the political and national sense, it has been the attempt of the "have-nots" to take from the "haves," or the attempt of the "haves" to add further to their lot at the expense of the "have-nots." Not always was property at stake; comparative advantages were measured of terms of power, and in terms of tribal or national superiority. The good luck of one nation became the hard luck of another. The good fortune of the Western powers in obtaining "concessions" in China at the turn of the century was the ill fortune of the Chinese. The power that Germany stripped from Austria, Czechoslovakia, Poland, and France at the beginning of World War II she added to her own.

What does it matter, then, if war is not in the nature of man so long as man continues through the expression of his nature to be a viciously competitive animal? The effect is the same, and therefore the result must be as conclusive—war being the effect, and complete obliteration of the human species being the result.

If this reasoning is correct, then modern man is obsolete, a self-made anachronism becoming more incongruous by the minute. He has exalted change in everything but himself. He has leaped centuries ahead in inventing a new world to live in, but he knows little or nothing about his own part in that world. He has surrounded and confounded himself with gaps—gaps between revolutionary science and evolutionary anthropology, between cosmic gadgets and human wisdom, between intellect and conscience. The struggle between science and morals that Henry Thomas Buckle foresaw a century ago has been all but won by science. Given time, man might be expected to bridge those gaps normally; but by his own hand, he is destroying even time. Communication, transportation, war no longer wait on time. Decision and execution in the modern world are becoming virtually synchronous. Thus, whatever bridges man has to build and cross he shall have to build and cross immediately.

This involves both biology and will. If he lacks the actual and potential biological equipment to build those bridges, then the birth certificate of the atomic age is in reality a *memento mori*. But even if he possesses the necessary biological equipment, he must still make the decision which says that he is to apply himself to the challenge. Capability without decision is inaction and inconsequence.

Man is left, then, with a crisis in decision. The main test before him involves his will to change rather than his ability to change. That he is capable of change is certain. For there is no more mutable or adaptable animal in the world. We have seen him migrate from one extreme clime to another. We have seen him step out of backward societies and join advanced groups. We have seen, within the space of a single generation, tribes of headhunters spurn their acephalous pastimes and rituals and become purveyors of the Western arts. This is not to imply that the change was necessarily for the better; only that change was possible. Changeability with the headhunters proceeded from external pressure and fear of punishment, true, and was only secondarily a matter of voluntary decision. But the stimulus was there; and mankind today need look no further for stimulus than its own desire to stay alive. The critical power of change, says Spengler, is directly linked to the survival drive. Once the instinct for survival is stimulated, the basic condition for change can be met.

That is why the quintessence of destruction as potentially represented by modern science must be dramatized and kept in the forefront of public opinion. The full dimensions of the peril must be seen and recognized. Then and only then will man realize that the first order of business is the question of continued existence. Then and only then will he be prepared to make the decisions necessary to assure that survival.

In making these decisions, there are two principal courses that are open to him. Both will keep him alive for an indefinite or at least a reasonably long period. These courses, however, are directly contradictory and represent polar extremes of approach.

The first course is the positive approach. It begins with a careful survey and appraisal of the obsolescences which constitute the afterbirth of the new age. The survey must begin with man himself. "The proper study of Mankind is Man," said Pope. No amount of tinkering with his institutions will be sufficient to insure his survival unless he can make the necessary adjustments in his own relationship to the world and to society.

The first adjustment or mutation needed in the expression of his nature, to use Huxley's words, is his savagely competitive impulses. In the pre-Atomic Age, those impulses were natural and occasionally justifiable, though they often led to war. But the rise of materialistic man had reasons behind it and must be viewed against its natural setting. Lyell, Spencer, Darwin, Lamarck, Malthus, and others have concerned themselves with various aspects of this natural setting, but its dominant feature was an insufficiency of the goods and the needs of life. From Biblical history right up through the present, there was never time when starvation and economic suffering were not acute somewhere in the world.

This is only part of the story, of course, for it is dangerous to apply an economic interpretation indiscriminately to all history. Politics, religion, force for force's sake, jealousy, ambition, love of conquest, love of reform—all these and others have figured in the equations of history and war. But the economic factor was seldom if ever absent, even when it was not the prime mover. Populations frequently increased more rapidly than available land, goods, or wealth. Malthus believed that they increased so rapidly at times that war or plague became nature's safety valve. This interpretation has undergone some revision, but it is not the interpretation but the circumstances that raises the problem.

Yet all this has been—or can be—changed by the new age. Man now has it within his grasp to emancipate himself economically. If he wills it, he is in a position to refine his competitive impulse; he can take the step from competitive man to coöperative man. He has at last unlocked enough of the earth's secrets to provide for his needs on a world scale. The same atomic and electrical energy that can destroy a city can also usher in an age of economic sufficiency. It need no longer be a question as to which peoples shall prosper and which shall be deprived. There is power enough and resources enough for all.

It is here that man's survey of himself needs the severest scrutiny, for he is his own greatest obstacle to the achievement of those attainable and necessary goals. While he is willing to mobilize all his scientific and intellectual energies for purposes of death, he is unwilling to undertake any comparable mobilization for purposes of life. He has shattered the atom and harnessed its fabulous power to a bomb, but he balks—or allows himself to be balked—when it comes to harnessing that power for human progress. Already, many representatives of industry have counseled words of synthetic caution, informing a puzzled public that we shall not see the practical application of atomic energy for general use in our lifetime. If it works out this way, it will not be because of any lack of knowledge or skill, but only because of the fear in certain quarters that atomic energy will mean a complete revamping of the economic structure, with the probability that it would be operated as a government utility or public service.

This is not a matter of urging a change away from the present economic structure just for the sake of change; it is recognition of a hard new fact of life that has made that economic structure obsolete in an Atomic Age just as it has made practically all our other institutions obsolete.

The cry is certain to go up against further government experimentation with atomic energy for peacetime purposes, and industry will demand that government withdraw and give it the right to carry on its own experiments. These experiments, however, would most likely be no more consequential than the atomic bomb would have been if left to decentralized chance. Moreover, it takes enthusiasm to fertilize invention, and there is as yet little discernible enthusiasm for atomic energy in those quarters which are asking for the right to sponsor its peace-time uses. However understandable this lack of enthusiasm may be, it should not blind public opinion to the critical importance of having research for practical use carried on with the same urgency, the same fulness, the same scope and intensity as it has been for war ends thus far.

The size of the opportunity is exceeded only by the size of the promise. But even as man stands on the threshold of a new age, he is being pulled back by his coattails and told to look the other way, told that he must not allow his imagination to get out of hand—all this at a time when he should know almost instinctively that if he can put the same courage, daring, imagination, ingenuity, and skill that he demonstrated in winning the war into meeting the problems of the new age, he can win the peace as well.

He must believe, too, that mobilization of science and knowledge in peace should not be confined to cosmic forces, but must be extended to his other needs, principally health. What a fantastic irony that organized science knows the secret of the atom but as yet knows not a fig about the common cold! Who can tell what advances in medical knowledge might accrue to the welfare of mankind if as much mobilized effort were put into the study of man as there has been of matter! Cancer, heart disease, nephritis, leukemia, encephalitis, poliomyelitis, arteriosclerosis, aplastic anemia—all these are anomalies in the modern world; there is no reason why mobilized research should not be directed at their causes and cure. Nor is there any reason why even old age should not be regarded as a disease to be attacked by science in the same intensive fashion.

Surveying other adjustments he will have to make if he chooses the positive course, man must consider himself in relation to his individual development. He can have the limitless opportunities that can come with time to think. The trend during the last fifty years towards shorter work weeks and shorter hours will not only be continued but sharply accelerated. Not more than half of each week will be spent earning a living. But a revolution is needed in his leisure-time activities —which so far have come to be associated almost entirely with the commodities of vended amusement. Once before, the world knew a Golden Age where the development of the individual—his mind and his body—was considered the first law of life. In Greece, it took the form of the revolution of awareness, the emancipation of the intellect from the limitations of corroding ignorance and prejudice.

Once again, if man wills it, he can be in a position to restore that first law of life. But he will have to effect a radical transformation in his approach to and philosophy of education, which must prepare him for the opportunities and responsibilities not only of his chosen work but for the business of living itself. The primary aim should be the development of a critical intelligence. The futile war now going on between specialization and general study must be stopped. There need no longer be any conflict between the two. The individual will need both—specialization for the requirements of research, general knowledge for the requirements of living. As for the problem of time in which to accomplish these dual objectives, formalized education until the twenty-fifth or thirtieth year is doubtless indicated; but it should not abruptly end there. Education, like the capacity of the mind itself, has no rigid boundaries. Unlimited exploration should be the first imperative of any educational program.

We have saved for last the most crucial aspect of this general survey relating to the first course: the transformation or adjustment from national man to world man. Already he has become a world warrior; it is but one additional step—though a long one—for him to develop a world conscience. This is not vaporous idealism, but sheer driving necessity. It bears directly on the prospects of his own survival. He will have to recognize the flat truth that the greatest obsolescence of all in the Atomic Age is national sovereignty. Even back in the old-fashioned rocket age before August 6, 1945, strict national sovereignty was an anomalous and preposterous hold-over from the tribal instinct in nations. If it was anomalous then, it is the quintessence of anomaly now. The world is a geographic entity. This is not only the basic requisite for world government but the basic reason behind the need. A common ground of destiny is not too large a site for the founding of any community.

Reject all other arguments for *real* world government—reject the economic, the ideological, the sociological, the humanitarian arguments, valid though they may be. Consider only the towering problem of policing the atom—the problem of keeping the smallest particle of matter from destroying all matter. We are building on soapbubbles if we expect this problem to be automatically solved by having America, Britain, and Canada keep the secret to themselves. That is not only highly improbable, but would in itself stimulate the other nations to undertake whatever additional research might be necessary over their present experimentation to yield the desired results. In all history, there is not a single instance of a new weapon being kept exclusively by any power or powers; sooner or later either the basic principles become generally known or parallel devices are invented. Before long, the atomic bomb will follow the jet plane, the rocket bomb, radar, and the flame thrower into general circulation. We must not forget that we were not the only horse in the atomic derby; we just happened to finish first. The others will be along in due time.

Nor can we rely on destructive atomic energy to take care of itself. Already there is the tempting but dangerous notion to the effect that the atomic bomb is so horrible and the terror of retaliation so great that we may have seen the last of war. This is quasilogical, but war is no respecter of logic, relative or absolute. And if history teaches us anything, it is that the possibility of war increases in direct proportion to the effectiveness of the instruments of war.

Far from banishing war, the atomic bomb will in itself constitute a cause of war. In the absence of world control as part of world government, it will create universal fear and suspicion. Each nation will live nervously from one moment to the next, not knowing whether the designs or ambitions of other nations might prompt them to attempt a lightning blow of obliteration. The ordinary, the inevitable differences among nations which might in themselves be susceptible of solution might now become the signals for direct action, lest the other nation get in the first and decisive blow. Since the science of warfare will no longer be dependent upon armies but will be waged by push-buttons, releasing radio-controlled rocket planes carrying cargoes of atomic explosives, the slightest suspicion may start all the push-buttons going.

There is the argument, of course, that each nation will realize this; that is, that the first button might lead to universal catastrophe as all the other nations rush to their switchboards of annihilation. Here, too, there is the unwarranted presupposition of reason. In an atmosphere of high tension and suspicion, reason is an easy victim. Moreover, there will always be the feeling that one nation can escape though all the others may go down. What a temptation for the blitzkriegers!

No; there is no comfort to be derived from the war-is-now-too-horrible theory. There is one way and only one to achieve effective control of destructive atomic energy and that is through centralized world government. Not loose, informal organization. Not even through an international pool, or through an international policing agreement. A police force is no better than its laws, and there can be no laws without government. Finally, the potency of the weapon must dictate the potency of its control.

There is no need to discuss the historical reasons pointing to and arguing for world government. There is no need to talk of the difficulties in the way of world government. There is need only to ask whether we can afford to do without it. All other considerations become either secondary or inconsequential.

It would be comforting to know that the world had several generations in which it might be able to evolve naturally and progressively into a single governmental unit. In fact, even as late as August 5, 1945, it seemed that the Charter of the United Nations had made an adequate beginning in that direction, providing the machinery for revision which might lead within fifteen or twenty years to a real world structure. But the time factor has been shattered. We no longer have a leeway of fifteen or twenty years; whatever must be done must be done with an immediacy which is in keeping with the urgency. Once the basic peace settlements are arranged, the United Nations must convene again for an Atomic Age inventory, undertaking an overall examination of the revolutionary changes in the world since its conference in San Francisco in the long-ago spring of 1945.

If all this sounds like headlong argument, posing methods or solutions which seem above the reach of mortal man, the answer must be that mortal man's reach was long enough apparently to push science and invention ahead by at least five hundred years during five years of experimentation on atomic energy. His ability to do this not only indicates that he can extend or over-extend himself when pressed, but emphasizes the need to do the same with government.

In meeting this need, man need not be frightened by the enormity of the differences which shall have to be accommodated within the world structure. We can agree with Macneile Dixon in "The Human Situation," that "Many are the races and many the temperaments. There are vehement and hot-headed men, selfless and conciliatory men. They display, varying as they do in appearance, talents, behavior, every type of unpredictable reaction to their surroundings. There are sybarites and ascetics, dreamers and bustling active men of affairs, clever and stupid, worldly and religious, mockers and mystics, pugnacious, loyal, cunning, treacherous, cheerful and melancholy men. There are eagles among them, tigers, doves, and serpents. 'He was a comedian on the stage,' said the wife of a celebrated funny man, 'but a tragedian in the home.'" All these differences are in addition to those of ideology, politics, and geography.

And yet, it is not in spite of these variations but because of them that man is now in need of a general amalgam. If those variations did not exist, if man's actions were uniform and uniformly predictable, then man would be as free of war as the vegetable kingdom. The differences point up the problem; not the problem the differences.

The important question is not how great an obstacle the differences may be to the setting up of a closely knit world structure, but whether man will be in a better position to reconcile those differences within world government than without it.

Man must decide, moreover, what is more important—his differences or his similarities. If he chooses the former, he embarks on a path that will, paradoxically, destroy the differences and himself as well. If he chooses the latter, he shows a willingness to meet the responsibilities that go with maturity and conscience. Though heterogeneity is the basic manifestation of nature, as Spencer observed, a still greater manifestation is the ability of nature to create larger areas of homogeneity which act as a sort of rim to the spokes of the human wheel.

True, in making the jump to world government, man is taking a big chance. Not only does he have to create the first world authority, but he shall have to make sure that this authority is wisely used. The world institution must be compatible with—indeed, must promote—free institutions. This challenge is not less important than the challenge to establish world government itself, for all through history there has been too great a contradiction between ideals and institutions and the forces which have taken over those ideals and institutions. Another way of saying this is that we have too often allowed the best ideas to fall into the hands of the worst men. There has not been a great ideal or idea which has not been perverted or exploited at one time or another by those who were looking for means to an end—the end being seldom compatible with the idea itself. The greatest idea ever to be taken up by the mind of man—Christianity—was for centuries violated and corrupted by its very administrators. Alexander's vision of a brotherhood of man fell victim to its own force—force based on might makes right. Mohammed dreamed of a universal religion based on the noblest of ethics, and taught that conversion by the sword was no conversion at all; yet his followers built an empire largely at the point of the sword. Passing from religion to politics, we have only to consider the immediate past. It was in the name of socialism and social progress that Fascism came to Italy and Nazism to Germany.

That is the double nature of the challenge: to bring about world government and to keep it pure. It is a large order, perhaps the largest order man has had to meet in his 50,000-odd years on earth, but he himself has set up the conditions which have made the order necessary.

All these are the various mutations and adjustments needed in the expression of man's nature, in his way of life, his thinking, his economics, his education, his conditioning and orientation, and his concept of government in an Atomic Age. But if he rejects this, the first course, there is yet another way, an alternative to world government. This is the second course. Preposterous as this second course may seem, we describe it in all seriousness, for it is possible that through it man may find a way to stay alive—which is the central problem under consideration in this paper.

The second course is relatively simple. It requires that man destroy, carefully and completely, everything relating to science and civilization. Let him destroy all machines and the knowledge which can build or operate those machines. Let him raze his cities, smash his laboratories, dismantle his factories, tear down his universities and schools, burn his libraries, rip apart his art. Let him murder his scientists, his doctors, his teachers, his lawmakers, his mechanics, his merchants, and anyone who has anything to do with the machinery of knowledge or progress. Let him punish literacy by death. Let him abolish nations and set up the tribe as sovereign. In short, let him revert to his condition in society in 10,000 B.C. Thus emancipated from science, from progress, from government, from knowledge, from thought, he can be reasonably certain of safeguarding his existence on this planet.

This is the alternative to world government—if modern man wishes an alternative.

Harrison E. Salisbury

THE WORLD AS A PRISON

Dear Whit:

I have been writing about Russia for twenty-five years, but it took Alexander Solzhenitsyn's *The First Circle* to bring many of my feelings into sharp focus. For this reason I think my review of Solzhenitsyn epitomizes better than any other single piece of my writing what I think of Stalin's Russia and that of his heirs.

With every good wish,
Harrison Salisbury

The New York Times
New York

The concept of the world as a prison comes naturally to a Russian
—his world *is* a prison. So it was under the Czars. So it quickly became
again in the flabby white hands of the paranoid Josef Stalin. A penal
society throws into dramatic relief the basic human condition: the trivial
becomes tragic; the absurd becomes profound; weakness becomes strength
and unreasoned faith gives life its only logic.

This is the subject of Aleksandr Solzhenitsyn's "The First Circle,"
and it is this which gives the work an epic quality. But it is Solzhenitsyn's camera eye, his absolute sense of pitch, his Tolstoyan power of
characterization, his deep humaneness, his almost military discipline and
Greek feeling for the unities which (let us say it at once) make his
work a classic.

Solzhenitsyn sets his story in a few fleeting hours—a little less than
five days from Dec. 24 to Dec. 28, 1949. The scene is a special prison
"institute" in Moscow. The characters are the prisoners, their guards,
the directors of the Institute, the high officials of the Police Ministry,
Stalin himself in an unforgettable portrait, three or four magnificent
Russian women, a few simple peasants, several pallid bureaucrats.

The plot is almost unimportant (although the story of the Institute's
crash program to invent a voice scrambler and voice-identification technique is filled with dramatic suspense), because we know as soon as
we begin to read that all are doomed—the brilliant mathematician
(who seals his fate by destroying the work which would have given
him freedom); the police "Institute Director" who knows instinctively

that he will soon be placed behind his own bars; the pathetic young woman who finds her only love with a brash youngster whose braggadoccio assures his death; the dilettante diplomat who fears (correctly) that his only act of decency has condemned him to destruction; and, of course, Stalin, beset with fear, premonitions of treachery and death, alone, morbid, weary, beginning his descent into the final years of madness.

The young Russian poet, Yevgeny Yevtushenko said last summer of Solzhenitsyn: "He is our only living classic." Yevtushenko was right. When comparisons of Solzhenitsyn are made with Tolstoy, Dostoevsky and Turgenev this is not hyperbole. He is, curiously, a major 19th-century novelist suddenly appearing in the last half of the 20th century. No *nouvelle vague* tendencies here; no sign of blurred technique, soft focus, existentialist philosophy. Just hard-edged prose, honed Toledo-sharp, a sureness of colloquial language and an implicit accuracy of scene which has its links with Hugo, Dickens, Thackeray, Balzac, Zola.

If the question arises, as inevitably it does, as to how we must compare Pasternak and Solzhenitsyn, the answer is simple. Pasternak was a great poet, perhaps Russia's greatest in this century. "Doctor Zhivago" was a poet's complex, image-ridden fantasy of his country under the rule of the Bolsheviks. Solzhenitsyn is no fantasist. He tells it like it is. The penal society of which he writes *is Russia,* not some Orwellian concept. It is Russia, here and now; as it was yesterday and last month and for a hundred years before that.

The problem of presenting Solzhenitsyn to the American audience (as it was of Pasternak before him) is to distinguish between Solzhenitsyn the literary genius and Solzhenitsyn the center of politico-literary controversy, the target of repression and censorship, hero of the fight against a return to Stalinism.

And the problem of discussing "The First Circle" is to disentangle the journalistic from the literary. Like his earlier and more slender work, "One Day in the Life of Ivan Denisovich," "The First Circle" is an astounding piece of political journalism as well as a literary work of art. It is the modern counterpart of Dostoevsky's memoirs from "The House of the Dead." Dostoevsky's work was written after five years in Czarist prisons and five more years in Siberian exile. It brought to the Russia of his day the first sensitive report of the world-within-a-world which was the Czarist penal system. No literate Russian could forget after reading "The House of the Dead" that, as Dostoevsky said: "The very best of men may be coarsened and hardened into a brute by habits. Blood and power intoxicate;

coarseness and depravity are developed. The man and the citizen is lost forever in the tyrant."

But it is a lesson which Russia, and we along with the Russians, must learn over and over again. In the Soviet period we have had an endless succession of prison camp revelations. The horrors have been stated and restated almost to ennui.

Now, however, the towering figure of Solzhenitsyn appears. He, like Dostoevsky, is a survivor. He, too, spent years in prison and exile; and when he writes of that society-within-a-society it is as though we had never before experienced it. In his work, terror is so workaday, brutality so banal, that we know every line he writes is true; we know that each of the dozens of stories he weaves together like the bright strands of a Bokhara rug is a real story; that each man and each woman are real men and women—indeed, in Moscow, amazing as it may seem, not a few of Solzhenitsyn's characters are alive today, survivors like him of "The First Circle" of hell.

The spirits who inhabited Dante's First Circle had committed no sins and this, in essence, is true of those who inhabit Solzhenitsyn's First Circle. As in Dante, this Circle stands on the edge of the eternal abyss, and descent is easy, frequent and almost inevitable. But Solzhenitsyn deals not with the spirits of the past. His men and women are flesh and blood; they love; they hate; they laugh; they cry; they gossip; they dream. All of their dreams are impossible.

And suddenly we understand that prison, terror, corruptibility, and sadism refine and purify the human ethos. It is not in the end the prisoners who are destroyed, even though they may lose their lives. It is the jailers, the army of jailers which Stalin created and which flourished until, quite literally, one-third or one-half of Russia became a prison enterprise, run by prison engineers, directed by police generals, inhabited by police victims. The problem of finding new cadres of prisoners to meet the inexorable needs of the "Industrial Department" of the Police system was tremendous. In the end, of course, the system devoured its creators.

You know on reading "The First Circle" that the spirit of a man like Gleb Nerzhin, the brilliant prisoner-mathematician, cannot be destroyed. You know that Lev Rubin, a Communist and a philosopher, cannot be crushed no matter how his body is tortured. Serafina Vitalyevna is a waif-like girl, but the spark of love kindled in her heart will not be extinguished by all of Stalin's policemen.

It is the oppressors who are doomed. Stalin is doomed. Beria is doomed.

His lieutenant, Abakumov, is doomed. The prison chief, Lieutenant Colonel Klimentiev, is doomed. The system is Moloch. It devours. No one co-opted by Stalin can survive.

A word about the setting of Solzhenitsyn's story. He describes not the Siberian prison camp whose barbed wire, wooden palisade and watch-towers became such a familiar feature of Stalin's Russia—and was the scene of "One Day in the Life of Ivan Denisovich." He describes the Mavrino Special Prison, a scientific institute located on the outskirts of Moscow, manned almost entirely by prisoner-scientists and prisoner-tech-nicians with a small admixture of "free" employes who worked for the police administration. This institution and scores like it were a fungus-like excrescence of the Stalin penal system. Here men and women of special skills and special talents were assembled to solve great scientific, military or engineering problems. The atomic bomb, at least in part, was developed in such institutions. Many of Russia's leading aeronautics specialists worked for years in prison institutes, especially before World War II.

This kind of institution was called in prisoner jargon a "sharashka." As is noted by Thomas P. Whitney—to whom we are indebted for a vivid and idiomatic translation of Solzhenitsyn's robust prose—this word means "an operation based on bluff or deceit." Its derivation is unclear but it was almost certainly brought into the language by the Stalin era, perhaps originally in the late 1920's when for the first time Stalin's prison wardens began to organize skilled engineers and technicians into what was called a "sharashkaya fabrika," or a "factory of black deeds."

Before Stalin finished, he managed to organize his whole country on that principle. But it did not work. He was not able to stifle the human spirit. This is the optimistic message of Solzhenitsyn. Tyrants have been trying to crush the Russian dedication to humane ideals for so many years that it is hard to know when the effort first began. They have not succeeded. Solzhenitsyn is testimony to their failure. At a time when dark clouds lie on the horizon and strident forces clash over America's future, this is a lesson to give us heart.

Solzhenitsyn—man and work—has been controversial since he first emerged on the Soviet literary scene in the late 1950's, after eight years in a labor camp and three years in exile. (He was arrested in 1945 for making rude remarks about Stalin in letters to a friend.)

His first novel, "One Day in the Life of Ivan Denisovich," appeared in the Soviet literary magazine Novy Mir in Nov., 1962, only at the personal intervention of Nikita Khrushchev. It has yet to come out in book form in Russia. Its wide publication abroad—four separate paperback editions in the United States alone—aroused his critics. When Khrushchev fell from power, Solzhenitsyn lost his patron and his publisher. His next two novels, "The Cancer Ward" and "The First Circle," have yet to appear in either magazine or book form at home, although an estimated 5,000 typewritten and carbon copies of the manuscripts are said to be circulating by hand. By his own testimony, hostile propagandists have spread stories calling him everything from a conscious tool of the West to a collaborator with the Germans and a defector to Egypt.

In May, 1967, Solzhenitsyn formally complained to the Soviet Union of Writers that the secret police had seized his manuscripts and other personal papers, and that unauthorized copies of his works were being distributed against his will in Moscow. He warned that it was likely that copies of the manuscripts would cross the frontier and be published abroad. He demanded protection against this eventuality, pointing out that Russia's failure to ratify the international copyright agreement left her authors helpless to control foreign publication.

A long wrangle followed in Moscow, culminating with an informal hearing by his Writers' Union colleagues on Sept. 22, 1967. Solzhenitsyn asked that his books be published; his critics demanded he draft a public letter denouncing the "exploitation" of his work in the West and repudiating "the role that has been ascribed to you in the West" as a "leader of the political opposition." He refused.

Because no formal objection was made to publication of "The Cancer Ward," Novy Mir set it up in type, galleys were corrected by the author, and it was scheduled to appear in the Jan., 1968, issue. It did not— reportedly as the result of a personal decision by Leonid Brezhnev, ratified by the Politburo.

Galleys of "The Cancer Ward" almost immediately appeared in western Europe, and arrangements were made for publication. Manuscript copies of "The First Circle" followed. How did they—and the steadily increasing number of Russian works still unpublished in the Soviet Union—reach the West?

There are a number of routes. In the 1920's and early 1930's, Russian writers were encouraged to publish their works in Berlin, site of several Russian publishing houses and a large émigré colony. Copyright was thus established, even when the published work was banned in Moscow.

In the purge period, however, writers who published in Berlin were brought to trial on charges of deliberately seeking to evade Soviet censorship.

Today, an author may permit a copy of his manuscript to fall into hands which he can disavow, while knowing those hands will bear it abroad. (Solzhenitsyn has declared that any publication of his work abroad is without his permission and without his collaboration. It is an important point: Andrei Sinyavsky and Yuli M. Daniel, among others, are presently serving sentences in labor camps because they helped send their manuscripts out of the country.)

Or, like Pasternak's "Doctor Zhivago," a manuscript may be scheduled for publication in Novy Mir and submitted thereafter to Western publishing houses. The Italian house, Feltrinelli, was in possession of the "Zhivago" manuscript when the Soviet party line changed, and Novy Mir's publication of "Zhivago" was cancelled; Feltrinelli refused to return the manuscript, and "Zhivago" was brought to the world.

When Svetlana Stalin went abroad, and publication of her "Twenty Letters to a Friend" was announced, Soviet secret police (K.G.B.) rifled her Moscow apartment, seized a copy of her manuscript and her personal photograph album. These materials were given to a police sales agent, Moscow journalist Victor Lewis, who peddled them to Western publishers in an effort to disrupt the regular publication plans. One of the many ironies of this enterprise was the fact that the K.G.B., in their anxiety to get their version of the Svetlana manuscript published in the West, entered into dealings with at least one western European publisher known to be subsidized by the C.I.A.

Intramural skirmishes between C.I.A. and K.G.B. agents over manuscripts have come to light more than once. A leading anti-Soviet organization in West Germany, N.T.S., is known to receive C.I.A. subsidies, and is known also to be infiltrated by K.G.B. agents. N.T.S. has served as a two way underground railroad—for manuscripts smuggled out of Moscow to the West, and then smuggled back in again. Evidence is overwhelming that, in this operation, the C.I.A. and K.G.B. take in each other's wash.

In the particular instance of Solzhenitsyn, versions of "The Cancer Ward" and "The First Circle" probably reached the West through Czech sources. Solzhenitsyn short stories and excerpts from "The Cancer Ward" have appeared in Czech and Slovak publications, and the Czechs strongly supported him in his demands for freedom to publish, an end to Soviet censorship, and ratification of the international copyright agreement. But so long as Soviet censorship prevents any substantial body of Russian literature to appear at home, and so long as Moscow refuses to adhere to the copyright convention, the flow of unauthorized, semi-authorized and/or openly purloined manuscripts from Russia to the West is certain to continue.

Henry Steele Commager

1918-1968: IS THE WORLD SAFE FOR ANYTHING?

Dear Mr. Burnett:

The trouble with a selection of this kind is that "my best" is not really suitable for the kind of volume you project. I am tempted, e.g., to let you reprint my essay on Joseph Story, but I doubt that it would be received with joy by your readers; it is a bit too technical for that. So too with my essay on John Fiske—that requires a knowledge of American historical writing that cannot be assumed in most readers. I am very tempted to direct you to the section on William James in *The American Mind* and perhaps I should give you it as one alternative.

The alternative—which I am sending herewith—is an easier one: one of my recent articles in the *Saturday Review*. It seems about the right length . . . and it is reasonably timely without being journalistic.

Henry Commager

Amherst College,
Amherst, Massachusetts

"The anniversary of Armistice Day should stir us to great exaltation of spirit because of the proud recollection that it was our day, a day above those early days of that never-to-be-forgotten November which lifted the world to the high levels of vision and achievement upon which the great war for democracy and right was fought and won." So wrote the dying Woodrow Wilson on the fifth anniversary of that day which had concluded the war to end war and to make the world safe for democracy.

Surely the world had a right to exult when this greatest and most terrible of wars dragged to its weary end. Militarism had been crushed, aggression frustrated, tyranny ended, injustice rectified, democracy vindicated, and peace assured; for now, after centuries of yearning and striving, men of good will had set up a league to preserve peace. No more wars, no more tyranny—mankind had at last sailed into the safe harbors of peace.

Rarely in history have such high hopes been dashed so low, and Wilson added to his tribute the bitter lamentation that the glory of Armistice Day was tarnished by the recollection that "we withdrew into a sullen and selfish isolation which is deeply ignoble . . . cowardly and dishonorable." So we did, but we were not alone in selfishness or dishonor. Even before the guns fell silent over the stricken battlefields of Europe, the great coalition that had won victory had come apart. Russia, defeated and desperate, had plunged into Communism; and the other partners, each with its own fears and ambitions, glared at each other over the conferences tables; while Germany, embittered by defeat, plotted vengeance; and the most ancient of empires fell apart. "Authority was dispersed," wrote Winston Churchill, "the world unshackled, the weak became the strong, the sheltered became the aggressive, and a vast fatigue dominated collective action."

Nineteen-eighteen did not usher in the millennium, it ushered in a half century of conflict—turbulence, war, revolution, desolation, and ruin on a scale never before seen or even imagined. It was a half century that leveled more cities, ravaged more countries, subverted more societies, obliterated more of the past, endangered more of the future, cost more lives, and uncovered more savagery than any time since the barbarians swarmed over Western Europe. Ancient nations were overthrown, empires fragmented, principles of law subverted, and traditional standards of morality repudiated. The era which was to have seen the end of war ushered in instead the most terrible of wars, which rose to a climacteric in the most terrible of weapons; the era which was to have seen the triumph of democracy saw instead the triumph of tyranny; the era which was to have witnessed the triumph of science over inveterate ills heard instead the hoofbeats of the Four Horsemen of the Apocalypse.

Once again the blood-dimmed tide was loosed, and the world was sucked into war. Once again the "freedom-loving" nations triumphed; once again men of good will came together to set up a league that would preserve peace; once again major powers were excluded from the new organization—China, Japan, Germany—while those who controlled it used it as a stage on which to indulge their rivalries and voice their grievances. The great powers glared at each other with ceaseless animosity. Soon the hottest of wars was succeeded by the coldest, and we had Robert Frost to remind us that "for destruction ice is also great and would suffice." During the whole quarter century after the fall of Italy, Germany, and Japan, war and violence were continuous: in India and Pakistan, in Israel and the Arab lands, in Greece and Turkey, in Algiers and Tunisia, Hungary and Berlin, Cuba and Haiti, Argentina and Bolivia, the Congo and Nigeria, Laos and Indonesia. If the great powers did not grapple with each other in global wars, they consoled themselves, as it were, with local wars in Korea and Vietnam, and with arming themselves for Armageddon.

How can we explain this long succession of blunders and tragedies almost without parallel in history? How could men whose resolution and courage had triumphed over mortal peril, whose skills and resourcefulness had enabled them to master nature, fail so greatly? They could control the great globe itself, but not themselves; solve infinite problems, but not finite; penetrate to the stars, but neglect the earth on which they stood. Noble in reason they doubtless were, infinite in faculty, like a god in apprehension, but in action more like a dinosaur unable to adapt to an unfamiliar environment than like an angel. The contrast between intellectual talents and social accomplishments seemed to make a mockery of free will; the contrast between expectations and realities threw doubt on the theory of progress.

There were, no doubt, particular and immediate causes for the collapse of order after the first war. That war had bled victors and vanquished to exhaustion; it had killed off potential leaders of the new generation; it had left a heritage of confusion for victors and bitterness for defeated; it had launched Communism in Russia and revolution elsewhere; it had fatally weakened Britain's hold on her empire; it had left Americans baffled and disillusioned and prepared to embrace isolationism.

The Second World War had wasted even more human material, and moral resources than the First, and had shattered, even more violently, the existing pattern of political life. But these are excuses rather than explanations. After all, Europe had been afflicted by previous wars, but had recovered and returned to her traditional position. And after all, the United States had been exempted from the wrath of both the great wars and had emerged from both with her resources unimpaired, yet she too suffered the malaise that afflicted the Old World. We must seek deeper causes for a change in the currents of history so great that it resembles rather a change in the tides of Nature herself. Nor are these hard to find.

First, and most fundamental, among the causes of our malaise is one that we stubbornly refuse to recognize: the emergence of the forgotten, the neglected, the disparaged, the impoverished, the exploited, and the desperate; one-half of the human race came out of the long dusk that hid it from our view and into the bright light of history. Here is not only the greatest revolution of our time but, by almost any test, the greatest revolution since the discovery of America and the shift in the center of gravity from the Mediterranean to the Atlantic and beyond. "The peoples of Europe," said Woodrow Wilson at the close of the first war, "are in a revolutionary state of mind. They do not believe in the things that have been practiced upon them in the past, and they mean to have new things practiced." That proved to be true of Russia—a truth even Wilson failed to recognize—and it proved even more true of the vast, heaving, turbulent peoples of Asia and Africa.

Stirred by the Wilsonian principle of self-determination after the First World War, and released by the breakup of the great empires and colonial systems after the Second, these peoples threw off their ancient bondage and struck for equality. Now they are determined to close, in a single generation, that gap of centuries which separated them from the peoples of the West—to close it peacefully if that is possible, otherwise through revolution and violence. They are determined to wipe out the century-long inferiority, the exploitation, the bondage which the West imposed upon them; to conquer poverty, ignorance, disease that afflict them disproportionately; and to take their equal place among the nations of the world. No wonder the whole globe is convulsed by this prodigious upheaval. The failure of the West, and particularly of the United States, to understand and co-operate with this revolution is a greater blunder, by far, than the earlier failure of Europe to understand the significance of the American Revolution, or of the West, including the United States, to understand the significance of the Russian Revolution. It is a failure of global dimensions.

This was a revolution of two large continents—three if South America is included—against two smaller. No less ominous, it was a revolution of the colored races against the white. The exploitation, the inferiority, the bondage which the West had imposed upon Asia and Africa was racial as well as geographical. The subjugation of colored peoples by white had gone on for centuries until Europeans, in Old and New Worlds, came to assume that it was part of the cosmic order of things. White Europeans committed genocide against the native races of the Americas in the sixteenth and seventeenth centuries, destroying ancient civilizations, wiping out, by war and disease, perhaps ten millions of Indians—one of the great holocausts of history. White Europeans filled the ranks of labor in the New World by enslaving millions of Africans—a business in which all the civilized nations of Europe engaged. White Europeans invaded Asia, imposed their will on old and proud peoples, and ruled over them with arrogance and violence. Nor was racial exploitation confined to Asia and Africa: It was carried to the New World and flourished for two centuries as slavery and for another as social and economic subjugation.

Here, then, is the second great cause of our current malaise: the racial revolution—a revolution which takes protean form in different countries and continents but has, almost everywhere, two common denominators: the refusal of all colored peoples to wear any longer the badge of inferiority which whites have fastened on them, and the inability of most whites, in America and in Europe, to acknowledge their responsibility and their guilt or to realize that this long chapter of history is coming to an end.

One of the great paradoxes of history is that the revolt of the non-Western world against the West is being carried on with tools and principles fashioned by the West. The tools are science and technology; the principles are those of modern nationalism. Here is a third fundamental explanation of the crisis of our time: the ravages of nationalism. For ours is, indubitably, the great age of nationalism: Within the past quarter century, some sixty nations have been "brought forth" while older nationalism has been given a new lease on life.

In its earlier manifestations—in the eighteenth and early nineteenth centuries—nationalism tended to consolidate, to centralize, to mitigate particularism and parochialism, and to encourage administrative efficiency and cultural unity, especially in the United States, Italy, and Germany. But almost from the beginning—in the Old World and in Spanish America—nationalism stimulated fragmentation along racial, linguistic, and religious lines; almost from the beginning it exacerbated chauvinism, imperialism, and militarism. Whether in the long run the advantages of political efficiency and cultural self-consciousness will outweigh the disadvantages of national antipathies and cultural chauvinism still remains to be decided. But it is difficult to avoid the conclusion that the nationalism of our own time is profoundly dangerous.

Alas, the new nations that have emerged from the disruption of empires have imitated, or adopted, all the worst features of the old. Small, they yearn to be large; weak, they pile up armaments; vulnerable, they seek alliances; insecure, they develop into police states; without political traditions, they hover constantly on the brink of civil war or anarchy; without viable economies, they are dependent on richer neighbors; without cultural unity, they manufacture an artificial culture and impose it by force; striving convulsively to be independent, they become increasingly dependent and threaten the peace of their neighbors and of the world. How many recent crises have been precipitated by their ambitions and quarrels—quarrels exploited, all too often, by the great powers: the crisis of Berlin and East Germany, the recurring crises of Arab-Israeli relations, the crises of Cyprus, of the Congo, Algiers, Nigeria, Rhodesia, the crisis of India and Pakistan, of North and South Korea, of Indonesia and Laos and Vietnam.

These new countries, it will be said, are but following the bad example of the older nations of the West. This is true enough, but with two fateful differences: first, the new nations are committed to ideologies that involve them with fellow believers everywhere and engage them in larger quarrels; and, second, that they are operating in a world shadowed by nuclear clouds.

For the triumph of malevolent over benevolent nationalism, the great powers—and most of all the United States and Russia—bear a heavy responsibility. Far from curbing competitive nationalism, they have abetted it. To the new nations of Asia and Africa they provided lavish military aid—the largest portion of American aid after the war, for example, was military. They interfered high-handedly in the internal affairs of these new nations. They built up networks of alliances designed to bring small nations into the orbit of large; they tried to divide the world into two armed camps with no room for neutralists. Nor did they for a moment curb their own chauvinism, their own commitment to military solutions of world problems, their own traditional nationalism and traditional sovereignty.

Closely related to the revolutionary upsurge of underprivileged peoples and the equally revolutionary impact of the new nationalism was the revolution precipitated by science and technology, and the rising expectations which it nourished. For the first time in history, science and technology seemed to bring the good life within the reach of men and women everywhere—the end of hunger, the wiping out of contagious diseases, the prolongation of life, security from the elements, the preservation and development of natural resources, the pleasures of learning and of the arts. In the twentieth century, it was at least reasonable to hope that the burdens which had for so long afflicted mankind would be lifted.

Once again, expectations were to be disappointed. The gap between what men imagined and what they enjoyed had aways been deep; now the gap between what men were taught to expect and what they actually received seemed intolerable. The machinery of life grew ever more elaborate, but the products of that machinery became less and less gratifying. At the end of a generation of unparalleled advance in science and technology, mankind found hunger more widespread, violence more ruthless, and life more insecure than at any time in the century.

Nor was this disappointment confined to the backward peoples of the globe: Even in America, which boasted almost limitless resources and the most advanced technology, poverty was familiar in millions of households, white as well as black; cities decayed, the countryside despoiled, air and streams polluted; lawlessness, official and private, was contagious; and war and the threat of war filled the minds of men with hatred and fear.

The symbol—more than the symbol—of this failure of science to bring expected rewards was the discovery and exploitation of nuclear energy. To release the energy of the atom was assuredly one of the greatest achievements in the history of science, and one that held out possibilities almost limitlessly benign. Instead, the United States and, after her, competing powers, concentrated their scientific talents on harnessing atomic energy for war. As Churchill wrote prophetically in 1929: "Without having improved appreciably in virtue or enjoying wiser guidance, mankind has got into its hands for the first time the tools by which it can unfailingly accomplish its own extermination. That is the point in human destinies to which all the glories and toils of men have at last led them." Nor was there any assurance that those who stood at the levers of control would refuse to use these weapons of infinite destruction if they thought their own survival was at stake. After all, Americans had used them in 1945; after all Americans, Russians, Chinese, and Frenchmen were carrying on continuous experiments to achieve even greater destructive power. And after all, prominent statesmen, not least those in the United States, did not hesitate to shake the raw head and bloody bones of nuclear destruction at intransigent opponents elsewhere on the globe. And if it could be said that only madmen would actually carry out such threats, the inevitable reply was that two madmen, Hitler and Stalin, had fought their way to power in the recent past, and that as yet the resourcefuness of mankind had not devised any way of preventing a repetition of this monstrous situation.

Finally, consider one of the great paradoxes of our day: at the time of the triumph of the experimental method in science, we should abandon it in the realm of politics. Clearly, one of the causes—and one of the manifestations, too—of our malaise is the rejection of the practical, the relative, the organic view of society and politics, and the embrace of the doctrinaire, the absolute, and the static. The substitution of ideological for realistic policies is the hallmark of much of modern political philosophy, but it has not heretofore been characteristic of the American. In the name of doctrinaire notions of Aryan superiority, Hitler was prepared to bring down a Götterdämmerung upon his own country and the world; in the name of doctrinaire Marxism, the Soviet was prepared to subvert all other governments; and in the name of "containment," the United States seems prepared to bustle about the globe putting down subversion and revolution. Our commitment, to be sure, has not been wholehearted; and the almost instinctive distaste of the American people for ideological principles has inspired widespread protest against the new departure. But even as the bankruptcy of the ideological approach to the great convulsive problems of the world becomes clearer, we seem to adopt the same approach to the issues of domestic politics.

There is nothing more implacable than ideological enmities or crusades —witness the religious wars of the sixteenth and seventeenth centuries —and one explanation of the peculiar ferocity of so many of our modern wars, even the American, is the ideological or quasi-religious character. Ordinary rivalries and conflicts involve interests and issues that can be settled by negotiation and compromise. But ideological conflicts are moral, and honorable men find it difficult to compromise on principles or negotiate about morals. Woodrow Wilson had a more doctrinaire mind than Franklin Roosevelt, but Wilson could call for "peace without victory" while Roosevelt insisted on "unconditional surrender."

The three great powers that glare ceaselessly upon each other, and whose conflicts shake the globe, are all committed to ideological positions which they find difficult to compromise. The leaders of all three nations know—as religious fanatics of the seventeenth century knew—that they are the pure of heart, that their cause is just, that they stand at Armageddon and battle for the Cause. Naturally, all three attempt to rally the smaller nations to their side, to enlist them in their crusades; and all are inclined to believe that those who are not with them are against them. None can tolerate deviation from the true faith. The Russians put down Hungarians and Czechs who transgress the scriptures; the Chinese punish dissenters even at the cost of civil war; the Americans will tolerate deviation in Guatemala or Santo Domingo and in Cuba only because they have succeeded in isolating it.

The ideological approach took over even in the American domestic arena—in politics, race relations, education, and elsewhere. It stigmatized the crusade of Joseph McCarthy against subversives, real or imagined; it sustains the ceaseless zeal of the House Un-American Activities Committee through the years in its search for Communists in government or in the universities; it provides moral fervor to George Wallace's arguments for white supremacy and logic to opponents of open-housing who proclaim that God is white. It characterizes, alike, students who think that the universities are all corrupt and fit only to be burned because they do not instantly involve themselves in current affairs, a Vice Presidential candidate who thinks all demonstrations are pernicious, and Senators who are prepared to subvert the Constitution because Supreme Court judges do not automatically respond to obscenity with moral fervor.

The symptom of ideology is impatience, and its offspring is violence. Those who see the great turbulent issues of politics or law or society in simple terms of right and wrong are impatient with compromise or concession and even with reason. Impatience characterizes much of American life in the second half of the twentieth century: impatience of the young with the old, and of the old with the young; impatience with due process of law; impatience with old ideas rooted in tradition, and with new ideas that lack the authority of tradition; impatience with those who are neutral, and those who are independent; impatience with the machinery of adjudication and arbitration; impatience with any solutions short of utopian.

And with impatience goes violence. This is natural enough: When men no longer believe in reason, when they no longer have confidence in the potentialities of history, they naturally turn to violence for the solution —or the liquidation—of their problems. Russia resorted to violence to get rid of the embarrassment of independence in Czechoslovakia; South Africa resorted to violence to dispose of the awkward fact of a predominantly Negro population; the Arabs have no communications with the Israelis except by acts of violence; the United States elevates aimless violence against Vietnam to a philosophy. The connection between violence and ideology is not fortuitous but consequential.

In all of the great changes and developments that have characterized the last half century and condemned it to disorder, the United States has played a prominent part. It shared the failure to appreciate and support the great revolution of the underprivileged peoples; it shared —and indeed exemplified—the subordination of colored peoples to white; it stimulated and supported self-determination after the first war, and the breakup of ancient empires after the second; and did nothing to mitigate the ravages of chauvinistic nationalism. It devoted a major part of its scientific energies to war and the preparation for war, and exalted the role and the power of the military. It embraced an ideological approach to the great problems of international politics and sought to imprison in ideological straitjacket the turbulent tides of history. In most of this, Americans departed from their own traditions and betrayed their own character. Is it too much to hope that we will return to our traditions and rediscover our true character?

Will and Ariel Durant

THE LESSONS OF HISTORY

Dear Mr. Burnett:

Thank you for your invitation to ballot for our literary giants. I'm too ignorant about contemporary American literature to have any right to participate; but I rejoice to see how many authors are flourishing in this supposedly decadent land and age.

Sincerely,
Will Durant

The authors' comment is taken from Chapter One of The Lessons of History, *by Will and Ariel Durant, as follows:*

". . . Obviously historiography cannot be a science. It can only be an industry, an art, and a philosophy—an industry by ferreting out the facts, an art by establishing a meaningful order in the chaos of materials, a philosophy by seeking perspective and enlightenment. 'The present is the past rolled up for action, and the past is the present unrolled for understanding'[1])—or so we believe and hope. In philosophy we try to see the part in the light of the whole; in the 'philosophy of history' we try to see this moment in the light of the past. We know that in both cases this is a counsel of perfection; total perspective is an optical illusion. We do not know the whole of man's history; there were probably many civilizations before the Sumerian or the Egyptian; we have just begun to dig! We must operate with

[1] *The Reformation*, New York, 1957.

partial knowledge, and be provisionally content with probabili-
ties; in history, as in science and politics, relativity rules, and all
formulas should be suspect. 'History smiles at all attempts to
force its flow into theoretical patterns or logical grooves; it
plays havoc with our generalizations, breaks all our rules; history
is baroque.'[2] Perhaps, within these limits, we can learn enough
from history to bear reality patiently, and to respect one another's delusions."

Will and Ariel Durant

GROWTH AND DECAY

We have defined civilization as "social order promoting cultural creation." It is political order secured through custom, morals, and law,
and economic order secured through a continuity of production and
exchange; it is cultural creation through freedom and facilities for the
origination, expression, testing, and fruition of ideas, letters, manners, and
arts. It is an intricate and precarious web of human relationships, laboriously built and readily destroyed.

Why is it that history is littered with the ruins of civilizations, and
seems to tell us, like Shelley's "Ozymandias," that death is the destiny
of all? Are there any regularities, in this process of growth and decay,
which may enable us to predict, from the course of past civilizations,
the future of our own?

Certain imaginative spirits have thought so, even to predicting the
future in detail. In his Fourth Eclogue Virgil announced that some
day, the ingenuity of change having been exhausted, the whole universe,
by design or accident, will fall into a condition precisely the same as in
some forgotten antiquity, and will then repeat, by deterministic fatality
and in every particular, all those events that had followed that condition
before.

[2] *The Age of Reason Begins,* Will and Ariel Durant, N.Y. 1961.

Alter erit tum Tiphys, et altera quae vehat Argo
delectos heroas; erunt etiam altera bella,
atque iterum ad Troiam magnus mittetur Achilles—

"there will then be another [prophet] Tiphys, and another Argo will
carry [Jason and other] beloved heroes; there will also be other wars,
and great Achilles will again be sent to Troy." Friedrich Nietzsche
went insane with this vision of "eternal recurrence." There is nothing so
foolish but it can be found in the philosophers.

History repeats itself, but only in outline and in the large. We may
reasonably expect that in the future, as in the past, some new states
will rise, some old states will subside; that new civilizations will begin
with pasture and agriculture, expand into commerce and industry, and
luxuriate with finance; that thought (as Vico and Comte argued) will
pass, by and large, from supernatural to legendary to naturalistic explanations; that new theories, inventions, discoveries, and errors will
agitate the intellectual currents; that new generations will rebel against
the old and pass from rebellion to conformity and reaction; that experiments in morals will loosen tradition and frighten its beneficiaries;
and that the excitement of innovation will be forgotten in the unconcern
of time. History repeats itself in the large because human nature changes
with geological leisureliness, and man is equipped to respond in stereotyped ways to frequently occurring situations and stimuli like hunger,
danger, and sex. But in a developed and complex civilization individuals
are more differentiated and unique than in a primitive society, and many
situations contain novel circumstances requiring modifications of instinctive response; custom recedes, reasoning spreads; the results are less
predictable. There is no certainty that the future will repeat the past.
Every year is an adventure.

Some masterminds have sought to constrain the loose regularities of
history into majestic paradigms. The founder of French socialism, Claude-
Henri de Rouvroy, Comte de Saint-Simon (1760–1825), divided the past
and the future into an alternation of "organic" and "critical" periods:

> The law of human development . . . reveals two distinct and al-
> ternative states of society: one, the organic, in which all human actions
> are classed, foreseen, and regulated by a general theory, and the purpose
> of social activity is clearly defined; the other, the critical, in which all
> community of thought, all communal action, all coordination have ceased,
> and the society is only an agglomeration of separate individuals in conflict
> with one another.

Each of these states or conditions has occupied two periods of history.

One organic period preceded that Greek era which we call the age of philosophy, but which we shall more justly call the age of criticism. Later a new doctrine arose, ran through different phases of elaboration and completion, and finally established its political power over Western civilization. The constitution of the Church began a new organic epoch, which ended in the fifteenth century, when the Reformers sounded the arrival of that age of criticism which has continued to our time. . . .

In the organic ages all basic problems [theological, political, economic, moral] have received at least provisional solutions. But soon the progress achieved by the help of these solutions, and under the protection of the institutions realized through them, rendered them inadequate, and evoked novelties. Critical epochs—periods of debate, protest, . . . and transition, replaced the old mood with doubt, individualism, and indifference to the great problems. . . . In organic periods men are busy building: in critical periods they are busy destroying.

Saint-Simon believed that the establishment of socialism would begin a new organic age of unified belief, organization, co-operation, and stability. If Communism should prove to be the triumphant new order of life Saint-Simon's analysis and prediction would be justified.

Oswald Spengler (1880–1936) varied Saint-Simon's scheme by dividing history into separate civilizations, each with an independent life span and trajectory composed of four seasons but essentially two periods: one of centripetal organization unifying a culture in all its phases into a unique, coherent, and artistic form; the other a period of centrifugal disorganization in which creed and culture decompose in division and criticism, and end in a chaos of individualism, skepticism, and artistic aberrations. Whereas Saint-Simon looked forward to socialism as the new synthesis, Spengler (like Talleyrand) looked backward to aristocracy as the age in which life and thought were consistent and orderly and constituted a work of living art.

For Western existence the distinction lies about the year 1800—on one side of that frontier, life in fullness and sureness of itself, formed by growth from within, in one great, uninterrupted evolution from Gothic childhood to Goethe and Napoleon; and on the other the autumnal, artificial, rootless life of our great cities, under forms fashioned by the intellect. . . . He who does not understand that this outcome is obligatory and insusceptible of modification must forgo all desire to comprehend history.

On one point all are agreed: civilizations begin, flourish, decline, and disappear—or linger on as stagnant pools left by once life-giving streams. What are the causes of development, and what are the causes of decay?

No student takes seriously the seventeenth-century notion that states arose out of a "social contract" among individuals or between the people and a ruler. Probably most states (i.e., societies politically organized) took form through the conquest of one group by another, and the establishment of a continuing force over the conquered by the conqueror; his decrees were their first laws; and these, added to the customs of the people, created a new social order. Some states of Latin America obviously began in this way. When the masters organized the work of their subjects to take advantage of some physical boon (like the rivers of Egypt or Asia), economic prevision and provision constituted another basis for civilization. A dangerous tension between rulers and ruled might raise intellectual and emotional activity above the daily drift of primitive tribes. Further stimulation to growth could come from any challenging change in the surroundings, such as external invasion or a continuing shortage of rain—challenges that might be met by military improvements or the construction of irrigation canals.

If we put the problem further back, and ask what determines whether a challenge will or will not be met, the answer is that this depends upon the presence or absence of initiative and of creative individuals with clarity of mind and energy of will (which is almost a definition of genius), capable of effective responses to new situations (which is almost a definition of intelligence). If we ask what makes a creative individual, we are thrown back from history to psychology and biology —to the influence of environment and the gamble and secret of the chromosomes. In any case a challenge successfully met (as by the United States in 1917, 1933, and 1941), if it does not exhaust the victor (like England in 1945), raises the temper and level of a nation, and makes it abler to meet further challenges.

If these are the sources of growth, what are the causes of decay? Shall we suppose, with Spengler and many others, that each civilization is an organism, naturally and yet mysteriously endowed with the power of development and the fatality of death? It is tempting to explain the behavior of groups through analogy with physiology or physics, and to ascribe the deterioration of a society to some inherent limit in its loan and tenure of life, or some irreparable running down of internal force. Such analogies may offer provisional illumination, as when we compare the association of individuals with an aggregation of cells, or the circulation of money from banker back to banker with the systole and diastole of the heart. But a group is no organism physically added to its constituent individuals; it has no brain or stomach of its own; it must think or feel with the brains or nerves of its members. When the group or a civilization declines, it is through no mystic limitation of a corporate life, but through the failure of its political or intellectual leaders to meet the challenges of change.

The challenges may come from a dozen sources, and may by repetition or combination rise to a destructive intensity. Rainfall or oases may fail and leave the earth parched to sterility. The soil may be exhausted by incompetent husbandry or improvident usage. The replacement of free with slave labor may reduce the incentives to production, leaving lands untilled and cities unfed. A change in the instruments or routes of trade —as by the conquest of the ocean or the air—may leave old centers of civilization becalmed and decadent, like Pisa or Venice after 1492. Taxes may mount to the point of discouraging capital investment and productive stimulus. Foreign markets and materials may be lost to more enterprising competition; excess of imports over exports may drain precious metal from domestic reserves. The concentration of wealth may disrupt the nation in class or race war. The concentration of population and poverty in great cities may compel a government to choose between enfeebling the economy with a dole and running the risk of riot and revolution.

Since inequality grows in an expanding economy, a society may find itself divided between a cultured minority and a majority of men and women too unfortunate by nature or circumstance to inherit or develop standards of excellence and taste. As this majority grows it acts as a cultural drag upon the minority; its ways of speech, dress, recreation, feeling, judgment, and thought spread upward, and internal barbarization by the majority is part of the price that the minority pays for its control of educational and economic opportunity.

As education spreads, theologies lose credence, and receive an external conformity without influence upon conduct or hope. Life and ideas become increasingly secular, ignoring supernatural explanations and fears. The moral code loses aura and force as its human origin is revealed, and as divine surveillance and sanctions are removed. In ancient Greece the philosophers destroyed the old faith among the educated classes; in many nations of modern Europe the philosophers achieved similar results. Protagoras becomes Voltaire, Diogenes Rousseau, Democritus Hobbes, Plato Kant, Thrasymachus Nietzsche, Aristotle Spencer, Epicurus Diderot. In antiquity and modernity alike, analytical thought dissolved the religion that had buttressed the moral code. New religions came, but they were divorced from the ruling classes, and gave no service to the state. An age of weary skepticism and epicureanism followed the triumph of rationalism over mythology in the last century before Christianity, and follows a similar victory today in the first century after Christianity.

Caught in the relaxing interval between one moral code and the next, an unmoored generation surrenders itself to luxury, corruption, and a restless disorder of family and morals, in all but a remnant clinging desperately to old restraints and ways. Few souls feel any longer that "it is beautiful and honorable to die for one's country." A failure of leadership may allow a state to weaken itself with internal strife. At the end of the process a decisive defeat in war may bring a final blow, or barbarian invasion from without may combine with barbarism welling up from within to bring the civilization to a close.

Is this a depressing picture? Not quite. Life has no inherent claim to eternity, whether in individuals or in states. Death is natural, and if it comes in due time it is forgivable and useful, and the mature mind will take no offense from its coming. But do civilizations die? Again, not quite. Greek civilization is not really dead; only its frame is gone and its habitat has changed and spread; it survives in the memory of the race, and in such abundance that no one life, however full and long, could absorb it all. Homer has more readers now than in his own day and land. The Greek poets and philosophers are in every library and college; at this moment Plato is being studied by a hundred thousand discoverers of the "dear delight" of philosophy overspreading life with understanding thought. This selective survival of creative minds is the most real and beneficent of immortalities.

Nations die. Old regions grow arid, or suffer other change. Resilient man picks up his tools and his arts, and moves on, taking his memories with him. If education has deepened and broadened those memories, civilization migrates with him, and builds somewhere another home. In the new land he need not begin entirely anew, nor make his way without friendly aid; communication and transport bind him, as in a nourishing placenta, with his mother country. Rome imported Greek civilization and transmitted it to Western Europe; America profited from European civilization and prepares to pass it on, with a technique of transmission never equaled before.

Civilizations are the generations of the racial soul. As life overrides death with reproduction, so an aging culture hands its patrimony down to its heirs across the years and the seas. Even as these lines are being written, commerce and print, wires and waves and invisible Mercuries of the air are binding nations and civilizations together, preserving for all what each has given to the heritage of mankind.

IS PROGRESS REAL?

Against this panorama of nations, morals, and religious rising and falling, the idea of progress finds itself in dubious shape. Is it only the vain and traditional boast of each "modern" generation? Since we have admitted no substantial change in man's nature during historic times, all technological advances will have to be written off as merely new means of achieving old ends—the acquisition of goods, the pursuit of one sex by the other (or by the same), the overcoming of competition, the fighting of wars. One of the discouraging discoveries of our disillusioning century is that science is neutral: it will kill for us as readily as it will heal, and will destroy for us more readily than it can build. How inadequate now seems the proud motto of Francis Bacon, "Knowedge is power"! Sometimes we feel that the Middle Ages and the Renaissance, which stressed mythology and art rather than science and power, may have been wiser than we, who repeatedly enlarge our instrumentalities without improving our purposes.

Our progress in science and technique has involved some tincture of evil with good. Our comforts and conveniences may have weakened our physical stamina and our moral fiber. We have immensely developed our means of locomotion, but some of us use them to facilitate crime and to kill our fellow men or ourselves. We double, triple, centuple our speed, but we shatter our nerves in the process, and are the same trousered apes at two thousand miles an hour as when we had legs. We applaud the cures and incisions of modern medicine if they bring no side effects worse than the malady; we appreciate the assiduity of our physicians in their mad race with the resilience of microbes and the inventiveness of disease; we are grateful for the added years that medical science gives us if they are not a burdensome prolongation of illness, disability, and gloom. We have multiplied a hundred times our ability to learn and report the events of the day and the planet, but at times we envy our ancestors, whose peace was only gently disturbed by the news of their village. We have laudably bettered the conditions of life for skilled workingmen and the middle class, but we have allowed our cities to fester with dark ghettos and slimy slums.

We frolic in our emancipation from theology, but have we developed a natural ethic—a moral code independent of religion—strong enough to keep our instincts of acquisition, pugnacity, and sex from debasing our civilization into a mire of greed, crime, and promiscuity? Have we really outgrown intolerance, or merely transferred it from religious to national, ideological, or racial hostilities? Are our manners better than before, or worse? "Manners," said a nineteenth-century traveler, "get regularly worse as you go from the East to the West; it is bad in Asia, not so good in Europe, and altogether bad in the western states of America"; and now the East imitates the West. Have our laws offered the criminal too much protection against society and the state? Have we given ourselves more freedom than our intelligence can digest? Or are we nearing such moral and social disorder that frightened parents will run back to Mother Church and beg her to discipline their children, at whatever cost to intellectual liberty? Has all the progress of philosophy since Descartes been a mistake through its failure to recognize the role of myth in the consolation and control of man? "He that increaseth knowledge increaseth sorrow, and in much wisdom is much grief."

Has there been any progress at all in philosophy since Confucius? Or in literature since Aeschylus? Are we sure that our music, with its complex forms and powerful orchestras, is more profound than Palestrina, or more musical and inspiring than the monodic airs that medieval Arabs sang to the strumming of their simple instruments? (Edward Lane said of the Cairo musicians, "I have been more charmed with their songs . . . than with any other music that I had ever enjoyed.") How does our contemporary architecture—bold, original, and impressive as it is—compare with the temples of ancient Egypt or Greece, or our sculpture with the statues of Chephren and Hermes, or our bas-reliefs with those of Persepolis or the Parthenon, or our paintings with those of the van Eycks or Holbein? If "the replacement of chaos with order is the essence of art and civilization," is contemporary painting in America and Western Europe the replacement of order with chaos, and a vivid symbol of our civilization's relapse into confused and structureless decay?

History is so indifferently rich that a case for almost any conclusion from it can be made by a selection of instances. Choosing our evidence with a brighter bias, we might evolve some more comforting reflections. But perhaps we should first define what progress means to us. If it means increase in happiness its case is lost almost at first sight. Our capacity for fretting is endless, and no matter how many difficulties we surmount, how many ideals we realize, we shall always find an excuse for being magnificently miserable; there is a stealthy pleasure in rejecting mankind or the universe as unworthy of our approval. It seems silly to define progress in terms that would make the average child a higher, more advanced product of life than the adult or the sage—for certainly the child is the happiest of the three. Is a more objective definition possible? We shall here define progress as the increasing control of the environment by life. It is a test that may hold for the lowliest organism as well as for man.

We must not demand of progress that it should be continuous or universal. Obviously there are retrogressions, just as there are periods of failure, fatigue, and rest in a developing individual; if the present stage is an advance in control of the environment, progress is real. We may presume that at almost any time in history some nations were progressing and some were declining, as Russia progresses and England loses ground today. The same nation may be progressing in one field of human activity and retrogressing in another, as America is now progressing in technology and receding in the graphic arts. If we find that the type of genius prevalent in young countries like America and Australia tends to the practical, inventive, scientific, executive kinds rather than to the painter of pictures or poems, the carver of statues or words, we must understand that each age and place needs and elicits some types of ability rather than others in its pursuit of environmental control. We should not compare the work of one land and time with the winnowed best of all the collected past. Our problem is whether the average man has increased his ability to control the conditions of his life.

If we take a long-range view and compare our modern existence, precarious, chaotic, and murderous as it is, with the ignorance, superstition, violence, and diseases of primitive peoples, we do not come off quite forlorn. The lowliest strata in civilized states may still differ only slightly from barbarians, but above those levels thousands, millions have reached mental and moral levels rarely found among primitive men. Under the complex strains of city life we sometimes take imaginative refuge in the supposed simplicity of pre-civilized ways; but in our less romantic moments we know that this is a flight reaction from our actual tasks, and that the idolizing of savages, like many other young moods, is an impatient expression of adolescent maladaptation, of conscious ability not yet matured and comfortably placed. The "friendly and flowing savage" would be delightful but for his scalpel, his insects, and his dirt. A study of surviving primitive tribes reveals their high rate of infantile mortality, their short tenure of life, their lesser stamina and speed, their greater susceptibility to disease. If the prolongation of life indicates better control of the environment, then the tables of mortality proclaim the advance of man, for longevity in European and American whites has tripled in the last three centuries. Some time ago a convention of morticians discussed the danger threatening their industry from the increasing tardiness of men in keeping their rendezvous with death. But if undertakers are miserable progress is real.

In the debate between ancients and moderns it is not at all clear that the ancients carry off the prize. Shall we count it a trivial achievement that famine has been eliminated in modern states, and that one country can now grow enough food to overfeed itself and yet send hundreds of millions of bushels of wheat to nations in need? Are we ready to scuttle the science that has so diminished superstition, obscurantism, and religious intolerance, or the technology that has spread food, home ownership, comfort, education, and leisure beyond any precedent? Would we really prefer the Athenian agora or the Roman comitia to the British Parliament or the United States Congress, or be content under a narrow franchise like Attica's, or the selection of rulers by a praetorian guard? Would we rather have lived under the laws of the Athenian Republic or the Roman Empire than under constitutions that give us habeas corpus, trial by jury, religious and intellectual freedom, and the emancipation of women? Are our morals, lax though they are, worse than those of the ambisexual Alcibiades, or has any American President imitated Pericles, who lived with a learned courtesan? Are we ashamed of our great universities, our many publishing houses, our bountiful public libraries? There were great dramatists in Athens, but was any greater than Shakespeare, and was Aristophanes as profound and humane as Molière? Was the oratory of Demosthenes, Isocrates, and Aeschines superior to that of Chatham, Burke, and Sheridan? Shall we place Gibbon below Herodotus or Thucydides? Is there anything in ancient prose fiction comparable to the scope and depth of the modern novel? We may grant the superiority of the ancients in art, though some of us might still prefer Notre Dame de Paris to the Parthenon. If the Founding Fathers of the United States could return to America, or Fox and Bentham to England, or Voltaire and Diderot to France, would they not reproach us as ingrates for our blindness to our good fortune in living today and not yesterday—not even under Pericles or Augustus?

We should not be greatly disturbed by the probability that our civilization will die like any other. As Frederick asked his retreating troops at Kolin, "Would you live forever?" Perhaps it is desirable that life should take fresh forms, that new civilizations and centers should have their turn.

Meanwhile the effort to meet the challenge of the rising East may reinvigorate the West.

We have said that a great civilization does not entirely die—*non omnis moritur*. Some precious achievements have survived all the vicissitudes of rising and falling states: the making of fire and light, of the wheel and other basic tools; language, writing, art, and song; agriculture, the family, and parental care; social organization, morality, and charity; and the use of teaching to transmit the lore of the family and the race. These are the elements of civilization, and they have been tenaciously maintained through the perilous passage from one civilization to the next. They are the connective tissue of human history.

If education is the transmission of civilization, we are unquestionably progressing. Civilization is not inherited; it has to be learned and earned by each generation anew; if the transmission should be interrupted for one century, civilization would die, and we should be savages again. So our finest contemporary achievement is our unprecedented expenditure of wealth and toil in the provision of higher education for all. Once colleges were luxuries, designed for the male half of the leisure class; today universities are so numerous that he who runs may become a Ph.D. We may not have excelled the selected geniuses of antiquity, but we have raised the level and average of knowledge beyond any age in history.

None but a child will complain that our teachers have not yet eradicated the errors and superstitions of ten thousand years. The great experiment has just begun, and it may yet be defeated by the high birth rate of unwilling or indoctrinated ignorance. But what would be the full fruitage of instruction if every child should be schooled till at least his twentieth year, and should find free access to the universities, libraries, and museums that harbor and offer the intellectual and artistic treasures of the race? Consider education not as the painful accumulation of facts and dates and reigns, nor merely the necessary preparation of the individual to earn his keep in the world, but as the transmission of our mental, moral, technical, and aesthetic heritage as fully as possible to as many as possible, for the enlargement of man's understanding, control, embellishment, and enjoyment of life.

The heritage that we can now more fully transmit is richer than ever before. It is richer than that of Pericles, for it includes all the Greek flowering that followed him; richer than Leonardo's, for it includes him and the Italian Renaissance; richer than Voltaire's, for it embraces all the French Enlightenment and its ecumenical dissemination. If progress is real despite our whining, it is not because we are born any healthier, better, or wiser than infants were in the past, but because we are born to a richer heritage, born on a higher level of that pedestal which the accumulation of knowledge and art raises as the ground and support of our being. The heritage rises, and man rises in proportion as he receives it.

History is, above all else, the creation and recording of that heritage; progress is its increasing abundance, preservation, transmission, and use. To those of us who study history not merely as a warning reminder of man's follies and crimes, but also as an encouraging remembrance of generative souls, the past ceases to be a depressing chamber of horrors; it becomes a celestial city, a spacious country of the mind, wherein a thousand saints, statesmen, inventors, scientists, poets, artists, musicians, lovers, and philosophers still live and speak, teach and carve and sing. The historian will not mourn because he can see no meaning in human existence except that which man puts into it; let it be our pride that we ourselves may put meaning into our lives, and sometimes a significance that transcends death. If a man is fortunate he will, before he dies, gather up as much as he can of his civilized heritage and transmit it to his children. And to his final breath he will be grateful for this inexhaustible legacy, knowing that it is our nourishing mother and our lasting life.

III

A Gallery of Portraits

Vladimir Nabokov

PORTRAIT OF MY MOTHER

Dear Mr. Burnett,

My husband asks me to answer your letter. He regrets he cannot undertake to furnish a prefatory comment. He can only say that he has a special fondness for the fragment he has chosen.

Mrs. Vladimir Nabokov

Montreux, Switzerland

To love with all one's soul and leave the rest to fate, was the simple rule she heeded. *"Vot zapomni* [now remember]," she would say in conspiratorial tones as she drew my attention to this or that loved thing in Vyra—a lark ascending the curds-and-whey sky of a dull spring day, heat lightning taking pictures of a distant line of trees in the night, the palette of maple leaves on brown sand, a small bird's cuneate footprints on new snow. As if feeling that in a few years the tangible part of her world would perish, she cultivated an extraordinary consciousness of the various time marks distributed throughout our country place. She cherished her own past with the same retrospective fervor that I now do her image and my past. Thus, in a way, I inherited an exquisite simulacrum—the beauty of intangible property, unreal estate—and this proved a splendid training for the endurance of later losses. Her special tags and imprints became as dear and as sacred to me as they were to her. There was the room which in the past had been reserved for her mother's pet hobby, a chemical laboratory; there was the linden tree marking the spot, by the side of the road that sloped up toward the village of Gryazno (accented on the ultima), at the steepest bit where one preferred to take one's "bike by the horns" (*bika za roga*) as my father, a dedicated cyclist, liked to say, and where he had proposed; and there was, in the so-called "old" park, the obsolete tennis court, now a region of moss, mole-heaps, and mushrooms, which had been the scene of gay rallies in the eighties and nineties (even her grim father would shed his coat and give the heaviest racket an appraisive shake) but which, by the time I was ten, nature had effaced with the thoroughness of a felt eraser wiping out a geometrical problem.

By then, an excellent modern court had been built at the end of the "new" part of the park by skilled workmen imported from Poland for that purpose. The wire mesh of an ample enclosure separated it from the flowery meadow that framed its clay. After a damp night the surface acquired a brownish gloss and the white lines would be repainted with liquid chalk from a green pail by Dmitri, the smallest and oldest of our gardeners, a meek, black-booted, red-shirted dwarf slowly retreating, all hunched up, as his paintbrush went down the line. A pea-tree hedge (the "yellow acacia" of northern Russia), with a midway opening, corresponding to the court's screen door, ran parallel to the enclosure and to a path dubbed *tropinka Sfinksov* ("path of the Sphingids") because of the hawkmoths visiting at dusk the fluffy lilacs along the border that faced the hedge and likewise broke in the middle. This path formed the bar of a great T whose vertical was the alley of slender oaks, my mother's coevals, that traversed (as already said) the new park through its entire length. Looking down that avenue from the base of the T near the drive one could make out quite distinctly the bright little gap five hundred yards away—or fifty years away from where I am now. Our current tutor or my father, when he stayed with us in the country, invariably had my brother for partner in our temperamental family doubles. "Play!" my mother would cry in the old manner as she put her little foot forward and bent her white-hatted head to ladle out an assiduous but feeble serve. I got easily cross with her, and she, with the ballboys, two barefooted peasant lads (Dmitri's pug-nosed grandson and the twin brother of pretty Polenka, the head coachman's daughter). The northern summer became tropical around harvest time. Scarlet Sergey would stick his racket between his knees and laboriously wipe his glasses. I see my butterfly net propped against the enclosure— just in case. Wallis Myers' book on lawn tennis lies open on a bench, and after every exchange my father (a first-rate player, with a cannonball service of the Frank Riseley type and a beautiful "lifting drive") pedantically inquires of my brother and me whether the "follow-through," that state of grace, had descended upon us. And sometimes a prodigious cloudburst would cause us to huddle under a shelter at the corner of the court while old Dmitri would be sent to fetch umbrellas and raincoats from the house. A quarter of an hour later he would reappear under a mountain of clothing in the

vista of the long avenue which as he advanced would regain its leop-
ard spots with the sun blazing anew and his huge burden unneeded.

She loved all games of skill and gambling. Under her expert hands,
the thousand bits of a jigsaw puzzle gradually formed an English
hunting scene; what had seemed to be the limb of a horse would
turn out to belong to an elm and the hitherto unplaceable piece would
snugly fill up a gap in the mottled background, affording one the
delicate thrill of an abstract and yet tactile satisfaction. At one time,
she was very fond of poker, which had reached St. Petersburg society
via diplomatic circles, so that some of the combinations came with
pretty French names—*brelan* for "three of a kind," *couleur* for "flush,"
and so on. The game in use was the regular "draw poker," with,
occasionally, the additional tingle of jackpots and an omnivicarious
joker. In town, she often played poker at the houses of friends until
three in the morning, a society recreation in the last years before
World War One; and later, in exile, she used to imagine (with the
same wonder and dismay with which she recalled old Dmitri) the
chauffeur Pirogov who still seemed to be waiting for her in the relentless frost of an unending night, although, in his case, rum-laced
tea in a hospitable kitchen must have gone a long way to assuage
those vigils.

One of her greatest pleasures in summer was the very Russian sport
of *hodit' po gribï* (looking for mushrooms). Fried in butter and
thickened with sour cream, her delicious finds appeared regularly on
the dinner table. Not that the gustatory moment mattered much. Her
main delight was in the quest, and this quest had its rules. Thus,
no agarics were taken; all she picked were species belonging to the
edible section of the genus *Boletus* (tawny *edulis,* brown *scaber,* red
aurantiacus, and a few close allies), called "tube mushrooms" by some
and coldly defined by mycologists as "terrestrial, fleshy, putrescent, cen-
trally stipitate fungi." Their compact pilei—tight-fitting in infant plants,
robust and appetizingly domed in ripe ones—have a smooth (not lamel-
late) under-surface and a neat, strong stem. In classical simplicity of
form, boletes differ considerably from the "true mushroom," with its
preposterous gills and effete stipal ring. It is, however, to the latter,
to the lowly and ugly agarics, that nations with timorous taste buds
limit their knowledge and appetite, so that to the Anglo-American
lay mind the aristocratic boletes are, at best, reformed toadstools.

Rainy weather would bring out these beautiful plants in profusion
under the firs, birches and aspens in our park, especially in its older

part, east of the carriage road that divided the park in two. Its shady recesses would then harbor that special boletic reek which makes a Russian's nostrils dilate—a dark, dank, satisfying blend of damp moss, rich earth, rotting leaves. But one had to poke and peer for a goodish while among the wet underwood before something really nice, such as a family of bonneted baby *edulis* or the marbled variety of *scaber,* could be discovered and carefully teased out of the soil.

On overcast afternoons, all alone in the drizzle, my mother, carrying a basket (stained blue on the inside by somebody's whortleberries), would set out on a long collecting tour. Toward dinnertime, she could be seen emerging from the nebulous depths of a park alley, her small figure cloaked and hooded in greenish-brown wool, on which countless droplets of moisture made a kind of mist all around her. As she came nearer from under the dripping trees and caught sight of me, her face would show an odd, cheerless expression, which might have spelled poor luck, but which I knew was the tense, jealously contained beatitude of the successful hunter. Just before reaching me, with an abrupt, drooping movement of the arm and shoulder and a "Pouf!" of magnified exhaustion, she would let her basket sag, in order to stress its weight, its fabulous fullness.

Near a white garden bench, on a round garden table of iron, she would lay out her boletes in concentric circles to count and sort them. Old ones, with spongy, dingy flesh, would be eliminated, leaving the young and the crisp. For a moment, before they were bundled away by a servant to a place she knew nothing about, to a doom that did not interest her, she would stand there admiring them, in a glow of quiet contentment. As often happened at the end of a rainy day, the sun might cast a lurid gleam just before setting, and there, on the damp round table, her mushrooms would lie, very colorful, some bearing traces of extraneous vegetation—a grass blade sticking to a viscid fawn cap, or moss still clothing the bulbous base of a dark-stippled stem. And a tiny looper caterpillar would be there, too, measuring, like a child's finger and thumb, the rim of the table, and every now and then stretching upward to grope, in vain, for the shrub from which it had been dislodged.

Arthur Miller

GIRL IN THE PARK
from AFTER THE FALL

Dear Mr. Burnett:

    I have no idea which piece of writing is "my best" but I liked this scene when I wrote it and still do. I hope this answers all questions.

Arthur Miller

[*After a fruitless knockdown fight with his wife which has led them both to an impasse, Quentin finds himself strolling aimlessly along Central Park. A bench is nearby, and the sound of traffic. A young Negro hurries past, neat, wearing sunglasses, on the lookout, halts to flick dust off his shined shoes, goes on. An old woman in shapeless dress carries a shopping bag and a parrot in a cage across, limping. Quentin strolls on and sits on the bench, briefcase on his lap.*]

QUENTIN – How few the days are that hold the mind in place; like a tapestry hanging on four or five hooks. Especially the day you stop becoming; the day you merely are. I suppose it's when the principles dissolve, and instead of the general gray of what ought to be you begin to see what is. Even the bench by the park seems alive, having held so many actual men. The word "Now" is like a bomb through the window, and it ticks.

[*The old woman recrosses with the parrot.*]

Now a woman takes a parrot for a walk. What will happen to it when she's gone? Everything suddenly has consequences.

[*A plain girl in tweeds passes, reading a paperback.*]

And how bravely a homely woman has to be! How disciplined of her, not to set fire to the Museum of Art.

[*A Negro appears in pantomime asking for a light, which Quentin gives him.*]

And how does he keep so neat, and the bathroom on another floor? He must be furious when he shaves.

[*The Negro hurries off, seeing his girl.*]

[*Alone*] And whatever made me think that at the end of the day I absolutely had to go home?

[*Maggie appears, looking about for someone, as Quentin sits on "park bench."*]

Now there's a truth; symmetrical, lovely skin, undeniable.

MAGGIE – 'Scuse me, did you see a man with a big dog?

QUENTIN – No. But I saw a woman with a little bird.

MAGGIE – No, that's not him. Is this the bus stop?

QUENTIN – Ya, the sign says—

MAGGIE [*sitting beside him*] I was standing over there and a man came with this big dog and just put the leash in my hand and walked away. So I started to go after him but the dog wouldn't move. And then this other man came and took the leash and went away. But I don't think it's really his dog. I think it's the first man's dog.

QUENTIN – But he obviously doesn't want it.

MAGGIE – But maybe he wanted for me to have it. I think the other man just saw it happening and figured he could get a free dog.

QUENTIN – Well, you want the dog?

MAGGIE – How could I keep a dog? I don't even think they allow dogs where I live. What bus is this?

QUENTIN – Fifth Avenue. This is the downtown side. Where do you want to go?

MAGGIE [*after thinking*] Well, I could go there.

QUENTIN – Where?

MAGGIE – Downtown.

QUENTIN – Lot of funny things go on, don't they?

MAGGIE – Well, he probably figured I would like a dog. Whereas I would if I had a way to keep it, but I don't even have a refrigerator.

QUENTIN—Yes. That must be it. I guess he thought you had a refrigerator.

[*She shrugs. Pause. He looks at her as she watches for the bus. He has no more to say.*]

LOUISE [*appearing*] You don't talk to any woman—not like a *woman!* You think reading your brief is *talking* to me?

[*She exits. In tension Quentin leans forward, arms resting on his knees. He looks at Maggie again.*]

QUENTIN [*with an effort*] What do you do?

MAGGIE [*as though he should know*] On the switchboard. [*Laughs.*] Don't you remember me?

QUENTIN [*surprised*] Me?

MAGGIE—I always sort of nod to you every morning through the window.

QUENTIN [*after an instant*] Oh. In the reception room!

MAGGIE—Sure! Maggie! [*Points to herself.*]

QUENTIN—Of course! You get my numbers sometimes.

MAGGIE—Did you think I just came up and started talking to you?

QUENTIN—I had no idea.

MAGGIE [*laughs*] Well, what must you have thought! I guess it's that you never saw me altogether. I mean just my head through that little window.

QUENTIN—Well, it's nice to meet all of you, finally.

MAGGIE [*laughs*] You go back to work again tonight?

QUENTIN—No, I'm just resting for a few minutes.

MAGGIE [*with a sense of his loneliness*] Oh. That's nice to do that. [*She looks idly about. He glances down her body as she rises.*] Is that my bus down there?

QUENTIN—I'm not really sure where you want to go. . . .

[*A man appears, eyes her, glances up toward the bus, back to her, staring.*]

MAGGIE—I wanted to find one of those discount stores; I just bought a phonograph but I only have one record. I'll see you! [*She is half backing off toward the man.*]

MAN—There's one on Twenty-seventh and Sixth Avenue.

MAGGIE [*turning, surprised*] Oh, thanks!

QUENTIN [*standing*] There's a record store around the corner, you know.

MAGGIE—But is it discount?

QUENTIN—Well, they all discount—

MAN [*slipping his hand under her arm*] What, ten per cent? Come on, honey, I'll get you an easy fifty per cent off.

MAGGIE [*to the man, starting to move off with him*] Really? But a Perry Sullivan . . . ?

MAN—Look, I'll give it to you—I'll give you two Perry Sullivans. Come on!

MAGGIE [*she halts, suddenly aware, disengages her arm, backs*] 'Scuse me, I—I—forgot something.

MAN [*reaching toward her*] Look, I'll give you ten records. [*Calls off*] Hold that door! [*Grabs her.*] Come on!

QUENTIN [*moving toward him*] Hey!

MAN [*letting her go, to Quentin*] Ah, get lost! [*He rushes off*] Hold it, hold the door!

> [*Quentin watches the "bus" go by, then turns to her. She is absorbed in arranging her hair—but with a strangely doughy expression, removed.*]

QUENTIN—I'm sorry. I thought you knew him.

MAGGIE—No. I never saw him.

QUENTIN—Well—what were you going with him for?

MAGGIE—He said he knew a store. Where's the one you're talking about?

QUENTIN—I'll have to think a minute. Let's see . . .

MAGGIE—Could I sit with you? While you're thinking?

QUENTIN—Sure!

> [*They return to the bench. He waits till she is seated; she is aware of the politeness, glances at him as he sits. Then she looks at him fully, for some reason amazed.*]

That happen to you very often?

MAGGIE [*factually*] Pretty often.

QUENTIN—It's because you talk to them.

MAGGIE—But they talk to me, so I have to answer.

QUENTIN—Not if they're rude. Just turn your back.

MAGGIE [*she thinks about that, and indecisively*] Oh, okay. [*As though remotely aware of another world, his world*] Thanks, though—for stopping it.

QUENTIN—Well, anybody would.

MAGGIE—No, they laugh. I'm a joke to them. You—going to rest here very long?

QUENTIN—Just a few minutes. I'm on my way home—I never did this before.

MAGGIE—Oh! You look like you always did. Like you could sit for hours under these trees, just thinking.

QUENTIN—No. I usually go right home. [*Grinning*] I've always gone right home.

MAGGIE—See, I'm still paying for the phonograph, whereas they don't sell records on time, you know.

QUENTIN—They're afraid they'll wear out, I guess.

MAGGIE—Oh, that must be it! I always wondered. 'Cause you *can* get phonographs. How'd you know that?

QUENTIN—I'm just guessing.

MAGGIE [*laughing*] I can never guess those things! I don't know why they do anything half the time! [*She laughs more deeply. He does.*] I had about ten or twenty records in Washington, but my friend got sick, and I had to leave. [*Pause. Thinks.*] His family lived right over there on Park Avenue.

QUENTIN—Oh. Is he better?

MAGGIE—He died. [*Tears come into her eyes quite suddenly.*]

QUENTIN [*entirely perplexed*] When was this?

MAGGIE—Friday. Remember they closed the office for the day?

QUENTIN—You mean [*Astounded*] Judge Cruse?

MAGGIE—Ya.

QUENTIN—Oh, I didn't know that you—

MAGGIE—Yeah.

QUENTIN—He was a great lawyer. And a great judge too.

MAGGIE [*rubbing tears away*] He was very nice to me.

QUENTIN—I was at the funeral; I didn't see you, though.

MAGGIE [*with difficulty against her tears*] His wife wouldn't let me come. I got into the hospital before he died. But the family pushed me out and—I could hear him calling, "Maggie . . . Maggie!" [*Pause.*] They kept trying to offer me a thousand dollars. But I didn't want anything, I just wanted to say good-by to him! [*She opens her purse, takes out an office envelope, opens it.*] I have a little of the dirt. See? That's from his grave. His chauffeur drove me out—Alexander.

QUENTIN – Did you love him very much?

MAGGIE – No. In fact, a couple of times I really left him.

QUENTIN – Why didn't you altogether?

MAGGIE – He didn't want me to.

QUENTIN – Oh. [*Pause.*] So what are you going to do now?

MAGGIE – I'd love to get that record if I knew where they had a discount—

QUENTIN – No, I mean in general.

MAGGIE – Why, they going to fire me now?

QUENTIN – Oh, I wouldn't know about that.

MAGGIE – Although I'm not worried. Whereas I can always go back to hair.

QUENTIN – To where?

MAGGIE – I used to demonstrate hair preparations. [*Laughs, squirts her hair with an imaginary bottle.*] You know, in department stores? I was almost on TV once. [*Tilting her head under his chin*] It's because I have very thick hair, you see? I have my mother's hair. And it's not broken. You notice I have no broken hair? Most women's hair is broken. Here, feel it, feel how [*She has lifted his hand to her head and suddenly lets go of it.*] Oh, 'scuse me!

QUENTIN – That's all right!

MAGGIE – I just thought you might want to feel it.

QUENTIN – Sure.

MAGGIE – Go ahead. I mean if you want to. [*She leans her head to him again. He touches the top of her head.*]

QUENTIN – It is, ya! Very soft.

MAGGIE [*proudly*] I once went from a page boy to a bouffant in less than ten minutes.

QUENTIN – What made you quit?

[*A student sitting nearby looks at her.*]

MAGGIE – They start sending me to conventions and all. You're supposed to entertain, you see.

QUENTIN – Oh yes.

MAGGIE – There were parts of it I didn't like—any more. [*She looks at the student, who turns away in embarrassment.*] Aren't they sweet when they look up from their books!

[*The student walks off, mortified. She turns with a laugh to*

Quentin. He looks at her warmly, smiling. A clock strikes eight in a distant tower.]

QUENTIN – Well, I've got to go now.

MAGGIE – 'Scuse me I put your hand on my head.

QUENTIN – Oh, that's all right. I'm not *that* bad. [*He laughs softly, embarrassed.*]

MAGGIE – It's not bad to be shy.

[*Pause. They look at each other.*]

QUENTIN – You're very beautiful, Maggie.

[*She smiles, straightens as though his words had entered her.*]

And I wish you knew how to take care of yourself.

MAGGIE – Oh . . . [*Holding a ripped seam in her dress*] I got this torn on the bus this morning. I'm going to sew it home.

QUENTIN – I don't mean that.

[*She meets his eyes again—she looks chastised.*]

Not that I'm criticizing you. I'm not at all. You understand?

[*She nods, absorbed in his face.*]

MAGGIE – I understand. I think I'll take a walk in the park.

QUENTIN – You shouldn't. It's getting dark.

MAGGIE – But it's beautiful at night. I slept there one night when it was hot in my room.

QUENTIN – God, you don't want to do that. [*Glancing at the park loungers*] Most of the animals around here are not in the zoo.

MAGGIE – Okay. I'll get a record, then. 'Scuse me about my hair if I embarrassed you.

QUENTIN [*laughing*] You didn't.

MAGGIE [*touching the top of her head as she backs away*] It's just that it's not broken. [*He nods.*] I'm going to sew this home. [*He nods. She indicates the park, upstage.*] I didn't *mean* to sleep. I just fell asleep.

[*Several young men now rise, watching her.*]

QUENTIN – I understand.

MAGGIE – Well . . . see you! [*Laughs.*] If they don't fire me!

QUENTIN – 'By.

[*She passes two men who walk step for step behind her, whispering in her ear together. She doesn't turn or answer. Now a group of men is beginning to surround her. Quentin, in anguish, goes and draws her away from them.*]

Maggie! [*He takes a bill from his pocket, moving across stage.*] Here, why don't you take a cab? It's on me. Go ahead, there's one right there! [*Points and whistles upstage and right.*] Go on, grab it!

MAGGIE—Where—where will I tell him to go but?

QUENTIN—Just cruise in the Forties—you've got enough there.

MAGGIE—Okay, 'by! [*Backing out*] You . . . you just going to rest more?

QUENTIN—I don't know.

MAGGIE [*wondrously*] Golly, that's nice!

[*She hurries off. He stands staring after her. Likewise, the men watch the "cab" going by, then walk off.*]

Louis Auchincloss

CHARLEY STRONG'S MANUSCRIPT
(1921)

Dear Mr. Burnett:

My novel, *The Rector of Justin,* tells the story of Dr. Francis
Prescott, the veteran headmaster of a New England boys' school,
Justin Martyr, who occupies a unique position in the annals of
private education, worshipped by generations of graduates. But he
is also detested by many, and in 1946, the year of his death, there
is a growing body of opinion that he may have done quite as
much harm as good. Nobody, however, denies that he is a man
of passionate sincerity and (despite periods of deep depression
and doubt) of vibrant faith. The favorite of all his graduates, one
Charley Strong, his "golden boy," is the victim of shrapnel in
World War I and stays on in Paris, a condemned, idle and disillusioned man. There he takes up with Dr. Prescott's daughter,
Cordelia. They cannot marry, as Cordelia's husband, a Catholic,
refuses her a divorce, but they live together in open defiance of
the old man on the other side of the Atlantic, whose brooding dis-
approval, however, is with them every day. Charley Strong starts
to write a novel of which only one chapter is completed by 1921,
the year in which he dies. This chapter he gives to Dr. Prescott,
who comes to Paris to look after him at the end, sending Cordelia away to travel with her mother. This excerpt from the novel
is that chapter.

Louis Auchincloss

New York, N.Y.

It happened in Southampton in the summer after my fifth form year. Claude is a cousin of Mummy's, halfway between our ages, a giddy, discontented old maid who is always trying to put her hands on me and stares in provoking, smiling silence during family meals. When she asked me to come to her bedroom to tell me a "secret," I went, to find her naked and still smiling. She was shameless and shrill, and the white puffy flesh on her buttocks gave way under my groping fingers as if it had been cotton on sticks. I took it for granted that she would be pregnant and that I would get syphilis. Neither event occurred, but when the war came, and mud, they seemed a natural consequence.

There is very little purity in Paris, and yet the air is pure. There is very little cleanliness about the French, and yet their minds are clean. How the visiting Sunday preachers at Justin dwelt on purity: clean young men and clean young women offering each other unstained bodies in a marriage of true sacrament! Harry Nolan tells me that he and Libby wake up sometimes at night and find themselves consummating the act. I think that in the greenish light of the chapel I must have visualized the wedding night like that. A love that transcends embarrassment, an orgasm that explodes as the Grail is raised to the altar, a naked odorless copulation, passionate but unsweating, before a white surpliced choir, witnessing without concupiscence and bursting into song. Is it not thus that Henry Esmond would copulate? And Prince Albert and the Chevalier Bayard? And even the preachers themselves, old as they are, if they still do it, and my Latin master, Mr. Van Wormser, sitting in the back with his big bony wife in the little straw hat with the silly peonies? Imagine how much of it there is and how blessed!

People always think me innocent, naïve, good. They whisper things they think I shouldn't hear. Oh, Charley, sweetie, no, she's not for you, I'm not for you, you need a nice girl. I am cream chicken and green peas at a children's party; I am spun sugar and ice cream; I am the peck of a kiss after a subscription dance at the Plaza on a spring vacation. I am confusion and hot, slow tears after a wet dream. Little do they know, giggling by the shoe lockers in the cellar of Lowell House or hiding under the beds while the old women clean the cubicles to look under their skirts, that Charley, who blushes at their stories, Charley whom they delight to shock, pretending to be doing things that even *they* wouldn't really do in the showers, Charley who falls asleep at lights and dreams of sports and Mother, this same Charley has no bottom to his voluptuousness. Nay, your wives, your daughters, your matrons and your maids could not fill up the cistern of my lust.

Hope for redemption can lie only in casting myself at the feet of him whom I have betrayed. For it is he, I know, who made me senior prefect; the upper school's election is merely advisory, and it is by no means clear that I had a majority. I enjoy the transient popularity of looks and football prowess, and I have no avowed enemies. But I am deemed too much a Christer to be a real leader, and when he told me of my appointment, I trembled and wept at such an act of trust. He it was who baptized and confirmed me, he who talked to me of my doubts and miseries, he who gave me a love that made the shallow, prattling love of shallow, prattling parents seem like the spray on one's face in a speedboat at sea.

Yes, hope is only in him. Redemption is only in him. He prefers Saint Augustine to Saint Francis, the Magdalene to Saint Cecilia. He knows that purity is not to be confused with inexperience. Those also are saved who flee from Alexandria to the desert and raise long grey El Greco arms and roll wide white El Greco eyes to a God who glares fiercely over their heads at the flickering light of the about-to-be consumed city revels which they have shrewdly abandoned. I must go to the Cape and leave Southampton; I must abandon Father, Mother and Cousin Claude; I must flee to the Cape to confess and kiss his feet, wash his feet, sit at his feet.

Daddy cannot understand my leaving in the middle of the season. When I tell him that the Rugby fifth esteemed it the greatest of honors to be asked to Dr. Arnold's in the summer holidays, he says it is nonsense. Daddy thinks everything is nonsense. There is something eternal about people who think this, and I find it hard to believe when I visualize the gay striped summer waistcoat over the round little belly, the shivering pince-nez, the coughs as he taps his egg at breakfast, a Dickensian Yankee, that Daddy is as dead as ever I shall be, that Mother is a widow on the Riviera and that my sister Alice is an older maid than Claude.

Daddy concedes that Dr. Prescott may be a great headmaster, but doubts that he is quite a gentleman. Old Boston family? What has that to do with it? King Edward is not a gentleman. The Kaiser is not a gentleman. Very few royalties, indeed, are gentlemen. But Delancey Parker *is* a gentleman; so is Emlen Rutherfurd. It takes Harvard on top of Justin to make a gentleman. A club on top of God. Never forget that, my boy.

At Lola's last week on the Rue de Peur, under a window through which I could see at dawn the flèche of the Sainte-Chapelle, two young men in red silk shirts huddled side by side, arms about each other's necks. Lola, in one of her moods, had gone to an inner room with a Russian who had parked his taxi below, and outside the door Leo, cigarette dangling, dispassionately waited. These are the innocents. What do they know of the flickering sky over El Greco's deserts? What do they know of damnation? They were not taught by a master.

"I am sorry, Charley, for what transpired, particularly that it should have happened in your home, but I suspect there was an element of seduction. Stay up here, my boy, until your cousin has left Southampton. And do not think that life is over because of this. *I* was not pure when I married. You see how I honor you with my confidence. You could make a good tale of this next term, but you won't. No, boy, don't weep. Get up and go out. Walk down the beach and breathe in the Atlantic. Recite *Dover Beach* if you must. It will go well with your present sentiments. But don't be late for dinner. Mr. Depew is coming, and I want my senior prefect to entertain him."

Had I fornicated only that I might be forgiven?

When Madame de Genlis returned to Paris after an exile that had lasted a quarter of a century, a period which had encompassed the revolution, the directorate, the consulate and the empire, what struck her most was that ladies who received their callers on the chaise-longue no longer covered their ankles. The *couvre-pied* had fled with democracy; France had wanted neither one nor the other, and are there grades of importance in the junk pile? Seduction by Claude, forgiveness for seduction by Claude, the love of Prescott and shrapnel in the Argonne.

Sixth form year! With the sixth behind him Dr. Arnold wouldn't have traded his job for any in England. I see the blond senior prefect standing on the dais with eye on wristwatch and finger pressing the assembly bell; I see him dashing down the football field, one arm stiffly out, for an eighty-yard gain; I see him singing loudest in the song fest, laughing loudest at the headmaster's reading of Leacock. He keeps exhorting the lower forms to a greater showing of school spirit and the upper to a greater cooperation with the prefects, until at last he fades through innumerable examples of example giving into a kind of cinema poster of Tom Brown, a puppet to jig about the stage and prattle in a disguised voice, manipulated by five strong fingers behind the curtain, a Faust who has sold his soul to God.

In the whole process of non-living it is the least lived year, waiting for the emerald green of June with the creamy white parchment and prize books rebound in morocco leather, thinking of graduation first as a day to be dreaded, then as a release and finally as an extinction, not because there is no life after school (though that may be) but because school has sucked out one's life, and the holy vampire with the arching eyebrows who loves to read Lucretius and Epictetus has taken one's blood and bones for the cause (as of course one had begged him to!) and spread upon his green, green campus a fragment of one's translucent skin, a lock of yellow damp hair.

That was the life one made love to, was it not; that was the sacrifice one sought, to let the middle-aged god return to his earth and his boys in the guise of one of them, to rejuvenate and redeem his school through the medium of a captive senior prefect? What does it matter that there is nothing left of one when the great spirit moves out of one's body? Is the process not ecstasy? Or as near it as one would ever come?

When I think of early communion I always think of it as being in the spring, and I feel the sweet sad tug of a pointless melancholy and the light, exhilarating caress of a warm zephyr against my cheeks as I cross an empty campus to what I hope will be an almost empty chapel. And then I remember the sting of the sour cheap wine on its passage to my empty stomach and the wonderful rumble of the comfortable words. How he could say that word "comfortable"! It seemed to have more syllables than four and to be filled with the biggest of pillows; it suggested a great dark cool leathery gentlemen's club with discreet silent attendants, visible only because of their white raiment, passing between the half-sleeping members with delectables. And I would close my eyes, kneeling at the altar rail, so tightly that I would see explosions of light and spots of blue, and when the service was over I would go back, faithful hound, to help him with his disrobing and listen mutely to the flow of the day's instruction.

"I have noticed, Charley, that Mr. Taylor's dormitory is habitually late for morning roll call. I have noticed that there are more books overdue in the library, that the back row in the schoolroom was giggling last night at prayers, that there was a fight with tin basins in Mr. Dugdale's lavatory, that shoes are not always shined, that tongues are not always clean, that minds are spotted and flesh is vile (at least as second formers may conceive it), that virtue has departed from the campus and the great veil in the temple is rent in twain. Do you know who rent it?"

How could I think I would survive being his boy, his son, his victim? My formmates keep their respectful distance; the faculty step gingerly by me. The Rector's hound is safe only when the Rector is present, to allay with a finger's touch the bristling hair on his neck. But if I give him youth, he gives me redemption. I enter into him and become but a pulse of a mighty being. With what dawdling sentiment do I see myself as an aide-de-camp standing on a hilltop over the battle, absorbed in my general's tactics and mindless of the shells and bullets over my head! But there will be other battles in which such things may receive their due consideration.

The war has been a godsend for people who like to blame things on things. My virgin sister Alice and my virgin-in-heart mother at Cannes, on terrace after terrace, nibbling macaroons under a macaroon sun, tell of me and my vices in subdued tones that throb with pride. A total wreck, so much promise, such a tragedy, such a loss. Oh, yes, it might have been better had he been killed outright. There are worse things than death, far worse, and it is I, his mother, who tell you that. I hope when I go, I go quickly, like dear Mr. Popley, at eighty-eight, on his tennis court at Hyères last Sunday. I should never wish to survive my faculties or live to be a burden to Alice. I want to live just so long as I'm useful, not a minute longer. Well, it's kind of you to say so, but if I *do* look young for my years, it's because I try to take an interest in what the young people do and say. After all, the future depends on them. And that's what I mind about Charley. He doesn't seem to care what's happening in the world today outside of that woman (I won't mention her name!) and her trashy crowd. Well, of course, I can't imagine *what* Dr. Prescott thinks about it! When Alice was last in Paris, she ran into her right smack in the Rue de la Paix. Naturally, she cut her. Oh, yes, she cut her dead. Alice is one of the few of her generation who remembers how to do that. It's another of the arts that was lost in the war.

I can hear the rumble of Dr. Prescott's laugh in the rustle of autumn leaves on the Champs Elysées as I sip my cointreau. I can hear it in taxi horns. I heard it in the exchange of artillery in the Argonne; I heard it in the slush of boots through the oozing mud of the terrible spring of 1918. He was always bigger or smaller than life, louder or softer than any sound. At times he was as silly as a letter from Mother; at times he seemed to bear as little relation to my present as the memory of one of Alice's big marquise dolls. And at times he loomed over the war-lit battlefield like a leering caricature of the Kaiser, exulting in Armageddon, or exulting that he had predicted it, flitting back and forth across the beam streaked firmament with Cardinal Richelieu in a grotesque game of tag, now the pursued, now the pursuer, like a dog and cat in a jerky animated cartoon.

Ridiculous? The only faith of Marlowe and Webster was that the grinning skull was less ridiculous than the jeweled crown that it wore askew. But can naught be funnier than zero?

Alfred Kazin

COUSIN SOPHIE

Dear Mr. Burnett:

I chose "Cousin Sophie" because, of all my different writings, "Sophie" touched the deepest vein of personal feeling and elegiac remembrance. It is an elegy to a woman whose life in many ways was a failure, who always felt herself odd and unloved, but who left so deep an impression on the youngster who grew up near her, constantly having her in his sight, that the writing felt like the purest love-offering. All my senses came into play when I wrote this.

Alfred Kazin

Our cousin Sophie was a difficult case. Because she had always lived with us, and had often taken care of me as a child when my mother was ill, I could have thought of her as my other mother, but she always seemed too young, restless, tormented. Although she was certainly not pretty—her long face usually looked sad or bitter, and when she was gay, wildly and almost desperately gay—she radiated, as if it were warmth from her body, a passionate and angry vividness. All my life I had seen her, with the long black hair which had never been cut, her embroidered Russian blouses and velvet skirts, against the background of a tiny rectangle room scented with musk, with patchouli, while above the bed covered with a tickly India spread there hung, side by side, two pictures. One (I learned their names only much later) was Sir George Frederic Watts's *Hope*—a blindfolded young lady with bare feet sat on a globe earnestly listening for the vibration of the single string on her harp; the other was Pierre-Auguste Cot's *The Storm*. As the lovers raced before the storm, their heads were apprehensively yet exultantly turned back; and the cloak that the godlike lover was tenderly holding over the woman's shoulders, so light and flimsy that it barely covered her nakedness, seemed woven in its lightness and transparency of "love" itself, so that the gauze veil which together they held over their heads, though too flimsy to shield them from the storm, carried some deeper knowledge of desire that explained the shyness of the woman and the confident and protective smile of the man. As they ran together, just ahead of the storm, they seemed to be running not only under the same veil, but with the same feet.

I had looked at Sophie under those two pictures all my life, just as I had looked at her blouses, her skirts and her petticoats—there was no closet—or could smell from her warm and fragrant flesh, as soon as she came near me, the musk and sandalwood, or could feel her presence again whenever I touched her velvet skirts on the hangers and the stiff crinkly surface of the India spread on her bed. She was never easy with anyone, never tender; there was something about her long sweeping hair and the ungraspable scent of her body that was like the resistance of velvet, which retreats back into itself, in soft and recessive lines, after you have touched it. As a child I had often watched her, while she sat doing her hair in front of the mirror, suddenly in despair let the great mane fall over her face; or else she would sit coldly coiling her hair, doubling and then binding with long black hairpins each sheaf she caught up in her hand. Her moods were always extreme. The whole long day for her was like a sundial, either washed in sunlight or cold-gray in shadow; the moody, somber Sophie, in whose face one saw the control of her despair, alternated with a Sophie reckless, agonized, violently gay, who as she threw her great hair back, or bent over the mandolin with the little black pick in her hand, or coldly stared at some possible suitor stiffly seated at our dinner table whom my mother had hopefully brought in, impressed herself all through my boyhood with that proud and flashing loneliness that I was to recognize immediately when I first saw *Carmen*.

Sophie was not just the unmarried cousin who had always lived with us; her unmarriedness, her need of a husband, of some attachment, was our constant charge and preoccupation. To this my mother gave as much thought as she did to us, and at the center of our household, whether she was off in her room under the picture of the two lovers fleeing from the storm, or in the kitchen with her friends from "the shop," drinking tea, eating fruit, or playing at the mandolin, one always saw or felt the vividly resentful figure of Sophie—Sophie beating at the strings of that yellow-shining, deep-bosomed, narrow-waisted mandolin, Sophie standing in front of the great mirror in the kitchen combing up her black black hair. As I watched with amazement, she kept one plait of hair suspended in her hand and then unceasingly and rhythmically, with the curved comb glistening in rhinestones, drew it with her long bony fingers through her hair, back and forth, until, when she had sifted and coiled and piled it up again, she would gather out the last straggle-thin threads in her hand as if it were a claw, and with a last sidelong look, manage with one gesture to throw a little ball of hair away and to give herself one last approving glance in the mirror. How natural it had always been to stand behind Sophie and to watch her combing her hair; or to steal into her room to smell the musk, the patchouli, the stingingly sweet face powder, the velvet skirts whose creases seemed still to mark the pressure of her body, the slips whose straps seemed just to have slipped off her shoulder. In the sepia dusk of the old prints, the lovers still ran rapturously before the storm, *Hope* held up her harp, and the bony gnarled wicker bookstand was filled with romantic English novels like *The Sheik* and Russian novels in stippled blue bindings which Sophie and Sophie alone could have brought into the house. And as if the difference had not already been made sufficiently clear between a mother who always seemed old to me and Sophie forever sultry and vivid, it was brought closer by the fact that my mother was at home all day and that Sophie appeared only in the evenings; when she was home, she was often elaborately sick in bed, with a bed jacket, while my mother brought her softboiled eggs and toast. The difference in their status was established by the way my mother worked, and waited on her, and told us to be quiet when Sophie was ill; we knew from my mother's constant expression of anxiety over her, from her anguished sulky looks of demanding love, that Sophie lacked something that everyone else in the world possessed.

It was my mother who had impressed all this upon me with an attentiveness, an unremitting anxiety and concern, which from our earliest days had impressed my sister and me with Sophie's special need, with Sophie's unhappiness. For Sophie was unmarried, Sophie needed love: that was what I understood so early about her—so early, when did I not know this about her? When was it not made clear that we were to watch out for Sophie, to look after her, to see to it, somehow, that Sophie's deepest wish might yet be granted, that her life would find its appointed center at last in a husband? When did I not know this, and whenever did we not feel, my sister and I, like juvenile marriage brokers? Although Sophie lived as far as possible from the kitchen, enclosed in her scent, her exotic pictures and books, although she was lodged like a guest deep in the corner room where she would be least likely to be bothered, there was always, behind our tense and tremulous family life, the obligation to look out for her, to be mindful of her special need, to remember that she had some agonizing lack that others did not have, that certainly my mother, by being married, no longer had. Because of this we were always to look out, even on a walk, for someone, for *the* someone, who would give Sophie what she needed, and so take her away. For Sophie was a great sufferer, Sophie was an acute case; she was a woman who needed love, who throbbed with a special need of love, whose need burned in her, giving her a sultry and splendid fire. This made her figure in my mind as the priestess of some cult which she alone represented. Her need of love went to depths that were her secret, though we were all continually engaged with this need. Loneliness had become her profession. It glowered in her like a passion and was her passion, so that by contrast with her friends from the shop, unmarried like herself, she seemed quicksilver, menacingly alive, radiating heat, a sullen fire, out of the lifelong feeling that she had been deserted.

She was a great sufferer; life had let her down. You could see it in the long pendulous face, stretched into a tense mask of resentful grief, in the bulging eyes constantly trained on you with a look reproachful, flirtatious or demanding. Every encounter with her was personal and intense; even a little boy could feel that it was a love affair to live so near her, for every look that Sophie gave and every look at Sophie herself, as sometimes she lay fully dressed on the India print, staring moodily at the window, had its loverlike strain, its tone and color of feeling, its arousement, its brooding air of possible rapture but present sorrow. All that a man would experience in loving women —the moodiness, the dark excitement, the constant sense of being stretched to new possibilities of feeling—I first guessed at from being near to Sophie. The best of what I ever knew as a child I got from this nearness to Sophie, lay in this brooding, dark, sultry arousement, this sudden brushing of wings, when I felt that it was Sophie, in her insistence on love, in the fierce sullenness with which an immigrant dressmaker no longer young lived for love, that made up the living contrast to my mother's brooding carefulness and distrust.

With my mother every morsel of life was paid for in fear. You calculated the price of everything before you bought it, and even if you bought it, you could not enjoy it for thinking how much it had cost you. The mark of my mother's character was not caution, which denotes a lack of imagination, but an unrelenting remembrance of our powerlessness, of every hurt, betrayal and sorrow, unquestioning obedience to the dark god, a fearful pledge of grim solidarity with all the forces that had ever molded her and all the people she had ever met. If, at any given hour of the night, my mother happened to wake in pain, her first concern was not with this pain itself, but with pain as the center of a universe all of whose numbers were somehow related to her and for whom she bore distinct responsibility. She could never let go of anything—of no one she had ever known, of no experience. This quality, which anyone could easily have confused with unselfishness, and which made my mother honestly think of herself as a humble sufferer, entirely devoted to others, made her extraordinary in the tension with which she gripped every piece of experience to herself and then imposed it on your consciousness. If, at any hour of the day or night—it did not matter whether she was feeding her children or had been awakened from a deep sleep—someone should mention a Mrs. Bernstein whom she had not seen since the steerage twenty years before, and of whom she knew nothing, not even her first name, my mother would immediately, like a spider, work back and forth on the few threads that connected her with Mrs. Bernstein—she would brood and brood on her, and absorb into the texture of her present sorrow the life story of someone she had not thought of in years.

In my mother's world no one ever shrugged her shoulders; no one was ever bored or lazy; no one was ever cynical; no one ever laughed. She was an indentured servant of the emotions, and always a slave to other people. This crushing sense of responsibility operated on everyone near her, so that I could never look at a woman well-dressed, proud, sensuous, without instinctively sharing my mother's condemnation of her as frivolous and unkind. My mother was bent, arthritic, and always walked as if she were controlling pain. I seemed always to see her bent to someone's service. Her whole being expressed so momentously her awareness of the grimness of life that one felt that she had taken a solemn oath never to forget it. So deep within her that no actual occurrence could ever modify it, this faithfulness to pain stored in her unrelenting heart every incident, every new occasion of pain, until it, too, became an interior event, an episode in the life of thought.

Later, in the years after Sophie had gone from us, when my mother's anxiety about her became even more acute, I began to see that what held my mother was not her dread merely but the grip of thought on every event, so that life was steeped in care and postponed with infinite considerations. It was from this brooding inner life of my mother's, which in its suffering stubbornness seemed to incorporate the history of the Jews, and was so pledged to permanence that it became her idea of the Eternal, it was from the dread that constantly pressed on her, that I, already stamped with so many of my mother's apprehensions, blindly sought relief through Sophie. She was not only a woman, but a woman who openly and passionately demanded things for herself—who even seemed to be nothing but a demanding self.

If there was one quality about my mother which dominated her, it was her refusal ever to enjoy openly or even to admit that she craved enjoyment. She never ate with us, but waited on us like a servant, handing in dishes from the stove, and after the others had finished, sat at one corner of the table chewing at the leftovers. Yet any day at six Sophie would arrive from the "shop," sulky and complaining of a headache, as if she had spent the afternoon shopping instead of sitting over a sewing machine high above Seventh Avenue, and having been served by my mother, would lie on her bed moodily watching the lights from the great delicatessen sign across the street flashing on her wall while she waited for her friends to come in. They were dressmakers from the "shop" and all unmarried "girls" like herself, who night after night gathered around Sophie in our apartment, made her home their home and always seemed part of our family, for they boarded around the neighborhood. I loved to see them come in any night, for they were gay and careless and affectionate, rich and warm. Whenever they came in the place would sparkle, and even my mother looked pleased as she ran about handing out glasses of tea. Sophie would get positively drunk with excitement. Flushed with joy as she sat at the center of the table surrounded by her friends, her head bobbing up and down like a swimmer racing through the water, her eyes glittering, she bent over the mandolin and flashed the shiny black pick back and forth across the tight steel strings while the polished and ornamented wood of the mandolin reflected the lights hung in the ceiling. In the flashing of her thumb across the strings, in the red faces of her friends sitting too near the stove, and in the songs we sang, I saw that abandonment, that thirst, with which she would give herself, some day, to the ideal loved one.

Surely it was for this look, this possibility, even for her desperateness, that I loved Sophie—for something that said the world is made to be risked, for some sense that our fate is not always to be deliberated. With all the emptiness in our cousin's life, she stood up for herself, she launched herself again and again on those terrible seas—while my mother crept about, silently suffering her bruised and wounded shoulder, eating in her corner after mealtimes like a dog, working every minute of the day as if her life were nothing, as if it consisted in serving others with that same suffering care. Sophie knew that the world owed her something—love, a home, a husband, and from the edge of her bed she waited fiercely, her arms implacably crossed, her bulging eyes mad with rage and expectancy, waiting for *him* to come, for her life to reach its consummation. And while she waited, my mother waited on her, nursed her when she was ill, coaxed her back to life when she was depressed, and all day long, whatever else she was doing, always kept between her tasks the pressing thought to find Sophie a husband, to relieve Sophie of the shame of her unmarried state. I could positively see into my mother's mind as she went about the streets doing her marketing, or buying material for her dressmaking—I could just see her inspecting every likely-looking man who came along, setting traps for every unmarried man between thirty and fifty (so long as he was a Jew and able to make "a nice living") who should happen to pass between Rockaway Avenue and Junius Street on a given day. How many candidates she brought news of before she would even dare bring them back for direct inspection—Sophie listening all the while to my mother's report with a look on her face scornful and disbelieving, like a princess impatiently being fitted for a gown who cannot make the dressmakers, down on their knees with pins in their mouths, understand how trying they are. And how many were the candidates she actually brought home whom Sophie would stare down at dinner because of some minor awkwardness, like eating too noisily, of which the *chaimyankel,* the poor wretch, had no notion whatsoever as he innocently slurped away at his *borscht,* not knowing that with each spoonful he was digging his grave. And how sad it always seemed to me that though there were a few candidates of whom she could actually approve, and who in turn did feel something for her, the affair always stopped short, even of friendship. Long after Doctor Sheshtov, that pleasantly mustached and philosophic dentist who in his sweet and sage way had allowed her to hope, had proved to us—all of whom had followed the affair breathlessly, and who had tried to hurry up the courtship by going to him, only to him, to have our teeth fixed— long after he had plainly shown that he was not the marrying kind after all, it was impossible for his name to come up without such a look of bitterness on Sophie's face that I could no longer pass even his street without feeling guilty. My mother grimly set her teeth and openly wished him *six feet underground for what he had done to our Sophie.*

We were all in it with *our Sophie.* Not an evening ever passed that Sophie was away at a movie or at a union benefit with her friends that my mother did not break down at the kitchen table, and throwing out her arms half in despair, half in entreaty to God, ask *what is going to happen to our Sophie?* Not a week ever passed that I was not made to feel by my mother that the sadness and the loneliness of life were proved by the fate of *our Sophie,* who, as my mother put it, drifted about in life aimlessly, to and fro—because she was not married. Our cousin's life had no *character* to it, no clear-cut destiny. Let down, let down by life, let down by so many men who could have married her, who should have married her, who had promised to marry her, who had acted as if they would marry her! Our Sophie, our poor abandoned Sophie, our charge, our weary child, our lonely lonely Sophie! This was how my mother spoke of Sophie's unmarried state: always in terms of need, of the great one who would take loneliness away, of the long loneliness that would be ended by one human being. This was what my own parents had sought in marriage, for as my handsome father had been an orphan from earliest childhood and my mother regarded herself as ugly and unwanted, they had settled on each other in disbelief that anyone else would love them. My mother once told me how she and my father had made their alliance: they had met in an East Side boarding-house, they were from neighboring provinces in the old country, they married. And on the Saturday night they married, knowing hardly anyone, my mother had gone out to bring some food back to their room and found my father sobbing. Long before I knew anything else, it seems to me, I knew that people were married because they were lonely, that people had a *right* to get married because they were lonely, that loneliness could be relieved only by marriage, and that without marriage you were condemned to your original and catastrophic loneliness. Lonely you were born and lonely you would die—you were lonely as a Jew and lonely in a strange land, lonely, always lonely even in the midst of people, for my family communicated with each other from loneliness to loneliness, in thought, as I could guess my mother's mind no matter how far away she was. In the end, from my mother's insistence on Sophie's *need* and Sophie's *fate,* I carried away the picture of a woman or man as an abject soul wandering about the world looking for the other—seeking a cloak against the onrushing black sky that one saw in the picture of the two lovers who fled before the storm, running under the same cover, almost with the same feet.

Katherine Anne Porter

THE DOCTOR AND THE CONDESA

Miss Porter's first selection, "The Cracked Looking Glass,"* brought with it her comment: "I do not know if this story is my best, it is only one of my favorites." In *This Is My Best* in 1942 she chose her well-known story set in Obregon's Mexico, "Flowering Judas." The selection from her long novel, *Ship of Fools,* on which she worked for many years, she said she preferred to leave to the editor. "No writer knows his 'best,'" she wrote from her home in Washington, D.C. "He only has favorites." The fragment, with its alternating play between age and youth, evokes much of the relationship between Schumann and women, youth and life, and is a favorite passage of more than one reader.

The Editor

* (too long for inclusion)

Frau Otto Schmitt still feeling somewhat intimidated by her recent encounters with a world of male unaccountability which she found dismaying in her new and tender state of widowhood. She was beginning to realize with astonishment that she had never really known any man but her husband; no women except wives of her husband's friends, or old maid teachers as remote from her womanly confidences as if they belonged to another species. For years she had hardly seen anyone, outside of her classrooms of younger students, except in the company of her husband: indeed, she had lived her married life almost literally in his presence. His state of health after the war had made it seem at times almost as if he were her child; in better times, a kind sympathetic brother; yet always her husband, after all. And oh, what a poor preparation for her life without him he had given her! Where could she turn, to whom could she speak, sure of a gentle human response?

Almost she took it as an answer to prayer when Dr. Schumann appeared alone at the head of the deck and stood at the rail. She approached him as nearly as she might without, she hoped, appearing to ambush him, but she longed to be near him if only for a moment, for he soothed and reassured her sense of all that was right, good, and appropriate in every way.

The left side of his face was turned towards her, and she could have worshipped that noble *Mensur* scar. Her husband's scar, quite as impressive as the Doctor's, had been her life's pride. It reminded her of salutary facts: that his family had been superior to her own, that his university dueling had further enhanced him socially; that altogether he could have made an advantageous marriage, a rich one. But no, he had chosen her, with her tiny dowry, and her brothers who had never touched a foil; and had never, he told her, regretted it for a moment; for which she never ceased to be grateful to him. The Doctor's scar was as perfectly placed as could be: for if a student flinched, turned his head or lowered his chin, he was apt to be slashed even on the forehead, or the cheekbone—she had seen too many such scars—and it was a disgrace to him, unless it could be blamed on the awkward swordsmanship of the other—and how does one go about explaining *that,* all one's life? Frau Schmitt had grown a little tired of hearing Frau Rittersdorf boast that her husband was a bold dueler, always the challenger, always the victor, with four scars on his left cheek, every one a beauty, a split to the teeth, and not a quarter-inch apart! Well, she suspected Frau Rittersdorf of exaggeration, at times. Besides, one good scar well placed was enough—what was it for, after all? A token in the living flesh, another kind of medal bestowed for proved courage. Having achieved it, a gentleman might then go about his other concerns and occupations.

In her shy adoring mood she almost crept towards the Doctor, who turned and gave her that serious smile she admired in him, and seemed about to speak, when the raucous chorus of *"Cucaracha"* broke upon the evening air. La Condesa, in a flowing white dress and green sandals, sailed out of the salon in her swarm of grotesque courtiers, riffled her fingers and smiled charmingly at the Doctor, and walked on swiftly, her skirts flying, the students howling their song and keeping time in a rumba step. One of them, a stringy boy in purple tweed Oxford bags, like tucked-up skirts, lolloped in the rear a safe distance, mimicking her frail complaining voice: "Ah, youth, beautiful youth, she's not having any, thank you."

He even had the impudence to wink outright at Frau Schmitt, who scarcely believed her eyes. She turned in dismay to Dr. Schumann, and could only gasp, "Well! . . . but did you ever?"

Dr. Schumann moved nearer, and they stood together watching the students—their convulsed gait, their apelike grimacing, the flying impudent gestures of their hands, in the graceful wake of La Condesa. How could she, who seemed so acutely aware of herself and all around her, tolerate for a moment such effrontery? He suppressed a huge sigh, turned back to the sea, and said to Frau Schmitt, in a melancholy voice: "It is hardly to be believed, the malignance of the young. We hear a great deal, do we not? spoken against the middle-aged, and too much of it is true—about our growing faults of sloth, of selfishness, of complacency, of despair—"

"I hope not despair, dear Dr. Schumann," said Frau Schmitt, uneasily.

"Above all, despair," said the Doctor firmly. "But the real wicked-ness," he said, "is in youth. We sin, we older ones, and we know we sin; some of us try hard to repent, to make reparation. But they—" he inclined his head towards the students—"they sin and they do not even know it; or they know it and they glory in it. They are shameless, cruel, and proud . . . they love themselves with a passion unknown to age—perhaps exhausted," he added, with some sudden touch of humor, "in age . . . but still, they sin all day long against all that exists, from the human heart to the Holy Ghost, and when they are tired of sinning they lie down and sleep like newly washed lambs. All that ignorant scorn and mockery," said the Doctor, "all that senseless cruel jeering against a lady who is suffering, and who has never harmed them!"

Frau Schmitt said, with naïve, gentle wonder: "But Doctor! This is the first time I ever heard you speak harshly!"

"I mean to be harsh," said the Doctor, calmly. "I am the voice of rebuke itself lifted in the wilderness, or over the waste of waters! I wish my words were stones that I might throw them to crack the heads of those savages."

"Or their hearts," said Frau Schmitt.

"No, they have no hearts," said the Doctor.

Frau Schmitt was silent, feeling that she had been drawn beyond her depths, and yet, such depths as she longed to be drawn to. Ruefully she watched his gaze as it followed the figure of La Condesa disap-pearing around the stern; saw what she saw, read it in her own way, thought her own simple thoughts. What a pity such a good man should fall in love with such a woman. And at his age too, and mar-ried, and all! Oh, it was frightening, and it happened all too often. Her faith in the Doctor wavered, sank, recovered somewhat, but never in its former glory. She felt newly wounded, left out of things again, life was going to pass her by. She wished only to say her rosary and place herself in God's hands, and go to sleep and forget. There was never again to be anything pleasant or good in this world for her. After a stricken moment, she murmured a little formal phrase proper to leave-taking, and went on her way.

Dr. Schumann wondered at himself, reflected somewhat on his words, and regretted them as immoderate: that is, spoken out of place, with undue emphasis, at the wrong moment, and to the wrong person—indeed, they should never have been spoken at all, he concluded, the feeling which inspired them being itself suspect. He made a little Act of Contrition in the depths of his mind, stretched himself in the nearest deck chair, and closed his eyes. The deck was dimly lighted and deserted for the moment, all silence except for the lulling sound of the waves. Dr. Schumann, who before had been playing with the notion of signing up for another voyage, then and there in a flash of insight knew that this voyage was to be his last. In his relief at being given a glimpse of the certain end of a journey that was proving to be, mysteriously, a surprisingly trying time for him, the Doctor fell into a gentle sleep.

When he opened his eyes, La Condesa was stretched beside him in the neighboring chair to his right, quite at her ease, wide awake, pensively beautiful, regarding the darkened sea as if she were waiting for a curtain to rise. He was so amazed he almost stammered:

"W-what have you done with those terrible young men?"

"They can be a little dull at times, that's true," she told him calmly. "They got tired of playing the monkey, and said they were going to play dice. You were sleeping enviably. How do you do it?"

Dr. Schumann sat up, feeling refreshed and restored to his center. He said almost merrily, "A clear conscience, of course!"

"Of course," said La Condesa. "I can see that you are a man who could not live without a clear conscience."

"There are worse things to have," said the Doctor, sturdily, being by now well aware that he must begin to take a firmer hand with this erratic lady who was after all his patient. "Tell me, have you nothing to reproach your own conscience with just now?"

"I know nothing about a conscience," said La Condesa. "I have instead just the faintest sense of honor which does almost as well . . . intermittently! But as to my promise to you, I have kept it until now—can you not *see*? But it does not make me happy; no, it causes me actue anguish, I have cactus in my veins, and why do I do it? For you, as I told you; why do you ask more?"

"I did not even ask that," said Dr. Schumann, "that least of all. Indeed, I never would have made so bold as to dream of such a thing."

"I know," said La Condesa, almost with tenderness. "I need badly something to help me sleep. I cannot endure any longer."

"Try just a little longer to do without," said the Doctor, "and I promise to help you when the time comes."

"I detest martyrdom in all its forms," said La Condesa. "So unbecoming to me. I cannot be heroic—I detest that even more. Yet, see—here I am promising to be both because you think it may be good for me—good for what, my soul?"

"Your soul as well, no doubt," said the Doctor, amiably.

"Do you expect some great change in me because of this strange voyage, so unexpected, so unlike anything I have ever known?" asked La Condesa. "A miracle of some kind?"

The Doctor began to speak, and at that point they both noticed the rather comic pair, the scrawny Lizzi and the little fat Herr Rieber, ascending to the boat deck, followed rather furtively at a little distance by Ric and Rac, the twins. Neither La Condesa nor the Doctor mentioned these apparitions, or hardly noticed them, and went on with their conversation, pleasantly.

Ric and Rac, after skulking about the boat deck, keeping well out of sight of the objects of their attentions, whose habits and designs they knew well, heard at last a confusion of most promising sounds coming from behind the second great funnel, a fairly dark and private place: a light scuffling, slipping boot heels, frantic smothered feminine yaps and hisses, a male voice gleefully gurgling and crowing. Ric and Rac could not understand the words, but they knew in their bones the lingua franca of gallantry. Discreetly as little foxes they approached, holding each other back, for fear the other would get the first glimpse, exchanging shrewd glances, the whites of their eyes gleaming, their pointed red tongues running round their open mouths. The wind whistled past their ears and whipped their hair against their cheeks; their stringy garments flattened against their meager frames as they leaned upon the funnel and slid round towards the enticing noises.

In greedy silence and stillness they observed the expected scene. Lizzi and Herr Rieber were huddled together on the deck, backs to the funnel, fighting, laughing, wrestling. He was trying to play with her knees, and she was pulling down her skirts with one hand and pushing feebly at him with the other. Ric and Rac waited for something more interesting, but the bony girl broke away and shoved the fat man almost over on his back. The front of her blouse was open almost to the belt and the children remarked with distaste that there was really nothing to see. Tossing her head about, squealing, the girl's wild eyes pointed suddenly at Ric and Rac. She gave a shrill, new kind of scream, "Oh, look, oh look, oh—" waving her long arms at them.

Herr Rieber sobered at once, and as Lizzi sprang upright in an instantaneous unfolding movement like a jackknife, he got to his feet by squatting first, then supporting himself on a coil of rope and at last heaving himself up with a laborious groan. Ric and Rac merely took a step backward around the funnel, still gazing, balanced for flight if necessary.

"*What* are you doing here, you shameless creatures?" asked Herr Rieber, taking a somewhat choked but severely paternal tone.

"Watching you," said Rac, pertly, putting out her tongue; and Ric joined in, "Go on, don't stop. We'll tell you if anybody's coming."

Herr Rieber, honestly shocked by such early cynicism, rushed at them snarling, with ready hands, but they leaped out of his reach.

"Out of here!" bawled Herr Rieber, almost beside himself. Ric and Rac danced, actually clapping their hands for pure glee, as Herr Rieber bounded here and there after them, aiming blows which landed in air and turned him right about. Ric and Rac pranced savagely around him, shouting, "A peso, a peso, or we'll tell—a peso or we'll tell—a peso—"

"Monsters!" cried Lizzi hoarsely. "You horrible little—"

"A peso, a peso!" chanted Ric and Rac, still sliding around Herr Rieber and avoiding his blows with perfect ease. Herr Rieber stopped, panting, head down like an exhausted bull in the ring. He reached in his pocket. A peso rang on the deck and rolled. Ric put his foot on it. "One for her too," he said, "one for her." His face was sharp and cool and wary. Herr Rieber cast away another peso. Ric snatched them both and clutching them in one hand he motioned to Rac, who followed him instantly.

Running, they collided somewhere at the head of the steps, and both of them saw the same thing at once and had the same notion about it. The canvas covering of one of the lifeboats was partly unfastened, it hung loose and could easily be opened further. They tried the fastenings, which gave way surprisingly; they raised the flap and wriggled into the boat, Rac first, Ric following, without a word.

The boat was very much deeper than they had thought. With a good deal of scrambling about, they managed to bring their faces up to the opening in the flap, where they listened attentively, faces touching, for some moments. Then the fat man and the scrawny girl passed by them, she buttoning her blouse and both of them very angry-looking. Ric lost his balance and made a scrabbling noise; the girl turned her head and peered toward them without seeing; then she stumbled on the steps and the fat man took her arm. "Careful, my beautiful," he said softly.

"Stop that," she said, bitterly, snatching away from him.

Ric and Rac fell back into the boat, all tangled up giggling in the darkness. "Give me my peso," said Rac fiercely, clutching Ric in the ribs and digging her nails in. "Give me my peso or I'll tear your eyes out."

"Take it," said Ric, in the same tone, clenching his fist over the money. "Go on, take it, just try!"

Locked in what seemed to be a death grapple, they rolled to the bottom of the boat and fought furiously, knees in ribs, claws in hair; the pain they inflicted on each other had a strong undertow of pleasure. Little by little they fell quiet and then began to giggle again. A young officer passing stopped to listen, his face very thoughtful. Stepping forward, he snatched back the canvas, and whatever he saw there appeared to turn him to stone for a second. Then, throwing himself over the side and bending down nearly head first, he seized them and dragged them both over the side of the boat. They were as light as if their bones were hollow, and they came out limp and dangling as broken dolls.

La Condesa and Dr. Schumann remained at ease in their long chairs, watching the ship's lights dance in the darkened sea, and the Doctor was saying: "One has no new weaknesses, no new strengths, but only developments, accentuations, diminishments, or perversions of original potentialities. These may at times be so abrupt and powerful they give the illusion of radical change, but it is only illusion, I am afraid. As one grows older, one is more conscious of the shifting, unstable elements in one's temperament. One attempts to keep accounts, to assume control, you might say. One realizes at last, simply and perhaps with some dismay, that what one was told in childhood is after all true—one is immortal certainly, but not in this flesh. One . . ." He paused.

"One, one—one," said La Condesa lightly. "Who is this *One* you are always talking about? Let's talk about us—you and me, precisely."

"Myself, I have a very ordinary weakness of the heart; so I ship as doctor for a voyage or two, following the prescription I have so often given others, hoping for a little repose, imagine. Now if only I can live long enough once more to see my wife chasing the chickens out of our country kitchen with a broom, and scolding steadily, I shall ask no more of this world. How much that dear woman has scolded me, and everybody and everything, all her married life, at least, with such good reasons always, and for everybody's good, for truly she is nearly always right—and what has it come to?"

"Well," said La Condesa gaily, "for you at least, it has come to an end for a little while."

Dr. Schumann chose to smile only a little at this and looked away over the rail to the waters. "Imagine me, a doctor, after all these years in quiet Heidelberg thinking I should find repose from the world on a ship. I am astonished at myself for thinking, now maybe I shall learn something new about myself or the people I live with; but no such thing. I have seen all this before, over and over, only never until now did I see it on a ship. These people I have seen them all before, only in other places, under different names. I know their diseases almost by looking at them, and if you know what sickness is in a man you very often can tell what form his vices and his virtues have taken."

"Now talk about me," said La Condesa, clasping her long hands lightly about her knee and bending forward from the leg rest of her chair.

There appeared at the upper end of the deck an unusual group in a state of violent action. A young officer with his cap knocked crooked was struggling with those dreadful Spanish twins. Yet in spite of all, the officer continued to advance firmly and managed a kind of ragged progress toward Dr. Schumann and La Condesa, hauling his captives, who were trying to bite his hands.

"More mischief," said Dr. Schumann, his serenity fading away. "I have yet to see those children in a situation where they are not making trouble for somebody." He called out to the young officer, "What is happening?"

The young officer blushed at the question. He planted himself before the Doctor and renewed his grip on Ric and Rac, who suddenly gave up struggling and stood stock-still, sullen eyes gazing at nothing. The young officer began: "Sir, these children, these unspeakable—"

Ric and Rac made a concerted bolt for freedom in opposite directions so that his arms flew wide but he did not lose hold of them. His blush deepened until his ears seemed about to burst into flames. He turned his head from side to side, mouth opening and closing in silence, appealing to them both wordlessly that in the presence of a lady he could not continue.

"I am a mother," said La Condesa encouragingly, giving him a most unmaternal smile; her bright red mouth rounded and softened, her eyebrows went up. "I can guess the very worst and truly I must say I do not find it so bad. What do you think, Doctor?"

"I agree that no matter what they did, they are little monsters," said Dr. Schumann, bending his head to observe them without hope, "and entirely outside any usual mode of discipline."

"They were in a lifeboat," said the young officer, stuttering slightly. "They had unfastened the edge of the canvas top and had crawled in—"

"And were amusing themselves?" asked La Condesa. "Well, *il faut passer la jeunesse* . . . infancy is a great bore, I find, one's own first, and then other peoples' . . . my poor children were not in the least monstrous, on the contrary almost disconcertingly normal—but they were quite simply bores until they were eighteen years old. Then they became charming young men to whom one could talk. I do not know how this miracle occurs. And so," she added, "we must wait and have patience with such phenomena as these," and she smiled enchantingly at the children, who stared back with utter malignance.

"Nothing of the sort will happen with these," said Dr. Schumann. "Their evil is in the egg of their souls." And then to the young officer: "Can't you just hand them over to their parents?"

"Their parents, my God!" said the young officer, in a spurt of contempt and despair. "Have you not seen them, sir?"

"Then," said La Condesa, "I see nothing for it but to let them go —or," and she looked tenderly into the burning eyes of the two little criminals, "perhaps we should save time and trouble for everybody if we threw them overboard?"

"Yes, Madame, a good idea," said the young officer, bitterly, "and a pity it cannot be carried out."

"Oh, you take everything too seriously," she said. "They're only children."

"Devil-possessed, though," said Dr. Schumann. La Condesa studied his friendly benevolent face now overcast with an almost military severity. "What an old-fashioned sort of man you are," she said, admiringly.

The Doctor's eyelids flinched once. "Yes, I know—a little dull, no doubt."

"But charming!" she said, and reached for his hand.

The young officer, whose moral sense was in a particularly tender, inflamed state, was almost as shocked by this gesture as he had been by the sight of Ric and Rac in the boat. So all the rumors he had heard about La Condesa were true! He saw himself abandoned to his dilemma with Ric and Rac—very well, they were no worse than their elders. Let them do as they pleased. He loosed them as if he were throwing off vipers; they broke instantly into their long, shambling run up the deck. He then bowed with a courtesy as false as he dared to show to La Condesa and the Doctor, straightened his cap and moved on.

La Condesa glanced after him and laughed, in a fresh, joyous tone, her eyes glistening. "Poor, nice young man," she said, "he's still too young—too young to remember his own childhood. Dear Doctor, I have never understood the dogma of Original Sin. Children are only perfectly natural little animals before they are brought under the whip —why be shocked at them?"

"There is nothing discoverable of good in these," said the Doctor. "Never these. Why deceive ourselves with hope? They will come to no good end."

"They are not in such a good state now," said La Condesa. She leaned back and drew a long breath. "What kind of childhood had you?"

"An innocent one," said Dr. Schumann, in perfect good temper again, "or so I like to think."

"Ah, so you like to think and maybe it is true," cried La Condesa. "But can't you remember anything interesting at all? Did nothing gay ever happen to you?"

Dr. Schumann meditated in silence for a few moments, began to smile rather reluctantly, then decided to make a clean breast of it.

"Innocence," he began, "our highly debatable innocence . . ."

"So you do have some amusing memories," said La Condesa, laying her silky hand over his, the blue veins standing up branched like a little tree. "Well, truth—to encourage you—I was never innocent, never. I had not the opportunity, for one thing, surrounded as I was by attractive cousins, boys of the most adventurous temperament, like mine. I had no aptitude for it, above all, never the wish. I could never endure to think that any secret or any pleasure was being kept from me. I surmised without help, everything, very early. From there to experience, it was only a step; from experience to habit a matter of moments. I cannot be sorry for anything except that I did not always make the most of my chances!"

"I *was* innocent," said Dr. Schumann, "as a calf; full of hopes and animal spirits, a simple soul without a care, believing everything I was taught, an obedient loving child . . . I could be kissed into anything," he said. "But still, it is true that at the age of five I seduced my little girl cousin aged three, and at six I was in turn seduced by a little girl playmate aged nine. In our ignorance, we did preposterous things— not even parodies," he said. "Both of my playmates were very nice, charming, virtuous girls who turned out well, married happily, and spanked their own children thoroughly for the least thing. Yet I say, the impulses that drove us were grounded in Original Sin, in which I believe as I do the Real Presence. . . ."

"I believe in neither," said La Condesa, without emphasis.

"Still you must allow me my beliefs," said the Doctor, gently. "As for innocence, does anyone know what it is? For I remember guilt and pleasure, always associated, yet never seeming to touch that part of my life and those acts founded on the moral law and which seemed real to me and not a fable, or a mere daydream, and which I do believe were innocent."

"I shall not try to follow this," said La Condesa. "Are we not talking for pleasure? Theological discussion fills me with gloom. I had all the joys of sinning as you call it, without guilt," she said, with a certain complacency. "But you must have been a most charming little person. I should have adored you, even then. Some of my crimes were of a base, unimaginative order, I am sorry to say. When I was four I persuaded my little brother to drink lye-water used for cleaning drains, telling him it was milk. He took a mouthful, spat it out, ran shrieking. He was rescued at once, his mouth scrubbed out; I was punished, beaten black and blue; otherwise nothing came of it. And indeed, I meant no harm—I was only curious to see whether it would kill him. But older people do not understand these things."

"Ah, childhood," said Dr. Schumann, "time of the tender bud, the unfolding leaf." They both laughed pleasantly and sat back in their long chairs.

"Truth is, it was not so bad," said La Condesa. She lifted the Doctor's hand and slipped her fingers between his, knitting them together.

"I love you," she said, gently and unexpectedly. "Not so much you, perhaps, though you are very nice, but I love what you are. I like gravity and seriousness and strong principles in a man. There is nothing more repellent to me than a frivolous, timid, vacillating man, who does not know his own mind and his own heart. And why? Because then he cannot ever know the mind and heart of a woman. Were you ever unfaithful to your wife?"

"Well!" exclaimed Dr. Schumann. "What a question!"

"Oh yes, I know, you have to be surprised and even a little shocked. It is quite proper, you are always right. But think a moment. It is not just curiosity and impertinence in me. Partly that, of course, but there is something more besides, and it is that something more I want you to believe—"

Dr. Schumann untangled his fingers from hers, took her hand in his, and then slipped his fingers to her pulse.

"How does it do?" she asked. "Is it settling down?"

"Very well," he said, "perhaps better than mine just now. But then I have told you," he said, and yet could not help mentioning again his unsteady heart. "At any moment," he told her, and laid her hand down again.

"I think it is enviable to know how you will die," she said, "and that it will be sudden and not ugly. I wish I knew, because I am afraid of long suffering and disfigurement. I don't want to leave a hideous body behind me—"

"You are just hopelessly vain," said Dr. Schumann, and it sounded as if he were praising her. "I know that nothing is more precious than beauty to the one who has it. And it is hard to come into the world in beauty and to go out in ugliness. And it is like any other gift or quality in the least worth having, you must be born with it, you cannot acquire it, and you should treat it as it deserves."

"But you find me beautiful now?"

"Of course," said the Doctor. After a short pause he said, "I will answer your question truthfully. I was never unfaithful to my wife."

"How charming of you," said La Condesa, sympathetically. "It must have been dull at times."

Dr. Schumann, who had always viewed himself as the soul of reserve, found himself possessed by a demon of frankness. "It was," he answered simply, amazed at himself, "but she was faithful to me, and that could have been a little dull for her, too, at times."

"Were you really so very good because you wished to be, or was it your weak heart?"

"My heart was sound until about two years ago," said Dr. Schumann with a faint trace of resentment, feeling that his confidence was being abused, and that perhaps he deserved it.

"But you love me just a little, don't you?"

"No," said Dr. Schumann, "not at all. Not at all if I know in the least what love is. I know what I should say, I know that is not very gallant, but I am not a man who can afford to say what he does not mean; and would you wish to hear it? There is perhaps not time for that sort of thing."

La Condesa took his chin between thumb and fingers and kissed him on the forehead twice. Her round mouth left two shiny red smears on his face. Dr. Schumann looked very pleased but quite calm.

"You are delicious," she told him. "You are exactly right. I love you." She added, "Let me wipe your dirty face." She touched her wet tongue to her small lace-bordered handkerchief and scrubbed away the red spots and said, "If anyone saw us now, they would think we were the most devoted married pair."

"Someone has already seen us," said Dr. Schumann, "the very one of all people who would enjoy it most."

They sat in silence, hands folded, heads inclined towards the sea, faces tranquil, as Frau Rittersdorf strolled by alone. "Such divine weather for sitting out," she informed them in a high clear voice, full of the most intimate sympathy and comprehension. She paused, shivered a little, and wrapped her thin scarf about her bare arms. "Perhaps one should be careful of the night air, especially at sea," she said, smiling gaily. She bent over and peered into their faces with the most ravenous inquiry. They gazed back calmly. A second's hesitation and Frau Rittersdorf moved on slowly, tossing back over her shoulder, "After all, rheumatism and arthritis lurk in night air and we're only young once."

"What a museum piece," said La Condesa, also in a high, clear sweet voice, aimed at Frau Rittersdorf's undulating shoulder blades.

"Oh come now," said Dr. Schumann mildly, "do leave that sort of thing to her," and he seemed ruffled and uncomfortable.

La Condesa gave a little saw-edged trill of laughter. Then she fell silent again for a moment, and her face was grieved and weary.

"I loathe women," she said, in a tone of flat, commonplace sincerity such as the Doctor had never heard in her voice. "I hate being one. It is a shameful condition. I cannot be reconciled to it."

"That is a pity," said Dr. Schumann, who in his heart knew that he quite agreed with her. But he did his manly duty of reassuring her. "And you are quite wrong. It may be a misfortune to be a woman, so many of you seem to think so, but there is nothing shameful in it— it is a destiny to be faced, like any other. Truth is," he told her earnestly, "you are a more than ordinarily perverse sort of being, and a change of sex would do nothing for you. There are many men of your temperament and of your habits; if you were a man, you would still be a mischief-maker, a taker of drugs, a seducer."

La Condesa rose lightly as a cloud, opened her arms wide as if to embrace him, leaned over him smiling and exhilarated. "Naturally!" she said with delight, "but think with what freedom, and more opportunity, and no scolding from mossy old souls like you!"

Dr. Schumann rose deliberately and stepped back from her hands that were about to rest on his shoulders. "I am not scolding," he said, in pure forthright anger, "and you are talking like any foolish woman!"

"And you sound like a husband," cried La Condesa over his shoulder, for he had turned and was leaving her, "like *any* foolish man!" and her terrible peals and trills of laughter followed him, blowing like a cold rain down his collar as she ran after him, came abreast, slipped her arm around his elbow, folded her hand in his. "You are adorable and you *can't* shake me off," for Dr. Schumann was trying to reclaim his arm without losing at least the appearance of dignity.

She loosed him then and stepped before him, and he saw that her eyes were wild and inhuman as a monkey's. "Stop," she said, her laughter threatening to slide into tears. She held his hands and laid her head on his shoulder lightly for an instant. "Oh, can't you see? I am tired, I am crazy, I must sleep or die . . . You must give me a *piqûre,* a huge one that will make me sleep for days . . . Oh, don't leave me, you can't —you shan't, I won't let you go! . . . Oh, quiet me—put me to sleep!"

Dr. Schumann gripped her hands and held her off, searching her face shrewdly, hoping to be able to refuse her, but what he saw decided him at once. "Yes," he said, "yes."

She turned at once, dropping her hands at her side, and they walked together through the ship towards her cabin. "Ah," she said, and raised to him under the mottled light of the passage a ravaged and desolate face, unbelievably changed, "ah, you are so good. Oh, never believe I am not grateful . . . and now I can keep my promise not to take any more ether!"

"Ether," said the Doctor, on a rising note of diciplinary severity. "You still have ether? You did keep back a flask, then?"

"Of course," she said, responding instantly to his tone of voice with a faintly contemptuous impatience. "When will you learn not to trust me in anything?"

Dr. Schumann stopped short and turned to face her. "Even now?" he asked.

"Even now," she said boldly. Before the expression in his face as he studied hers for the space of a breath, she lowered her eyelids and glanced aside.

"Well," he said at last, in a dry distant voice, "you shall have your *piqûre* just the same. Go on by yourself," he said, turning off towards his own cabin. "I will join you in a few minutes. You may trust me, as you know well enough," he said, and was amazed at his own bitterness. She turned and went her way as if she had already forgotten him, as if his given word could be so taken for granted she could treat it lightly—which was true, he admitted to himself with a wry little grimace of humor, or had been true until now. As he was selecting and arranging the ampules for the *piqûre,* the Doctor began to think fairly clearly and in a more or less straight line, with the reasonable, cooler part of his mind. He had not failed, he thought, in his responsibility to her as her physician. Yet he could not deny that his personal feelings for her had intervened and helped to create a situation very unbecoming to him—to her, also, he admitted with reluctance. But all these shocks and upsets—her constant turning of every meeting between them into scenes which left them both prostrated; the constant danger of his having another heart attack; her reckless disregard for appearances, which could so easily make the kind of scandal the Doctor shuddered even to think about—ah, well, it all must end. He called upon not only the reserves of his authority as ship's physician, but, if she resisted, upon the Captain's final word, and resolved that this unruly relationship should be put in order at once. She must be treated like a hysterical woman with no control over her own acts. She could have been the death of him with her silly melodramas. Nonsense, and there was to be no more of it. Yet, he intended to be merciful and consign her to a narcotic limbo, which was, after all, her notion of Paradise.

"Oh," said La Condesa, sitting up at sight of him, her face shining with relief from anxiety, "I am so happy to see you again! I was so afraid you would not come!"

"What?" said Dr. Schumann, amazed. "When I had just assured you that I would not fail you?"

"Ah," she said, "it is just then one should begin to doubt! The eternal vow—ah, that is the one that is always broken!"

"I did not make any such vow, remember," said Dr. Schumann, "it was only a little promise for this very evening." He resisted the slow ripple of apprehension that ruffled his own nervous system and disturbed the marrow of his bones; here at any moment, if he did not act with speed and decision, was the beginning of another scene.

"I am keeping here and now the promise I made you," he told her, "and the only one I did make." As he approached the side of her bed, needle poised, she dropped back on her pillows and gave him a melting glance of confidence. They smiled at each other lovingly as he took hold of her upper arm.

Phyllis McGinley

PORTRAIT OF GIRL WITH COMIC BOOK

Dear Whit:

I chose "Portrait of Girl with Comic Book" because it seems to me one of the more original of my poems. Many poets have written about youth and childhood. I think I am one of the few who has tried defining that strange, forlorn time of life when the child is painfully emerging into adolescence but has not yet reached a tangible shore. And I like to believe the effort comes off—that the verse is, as nearly as possible, a genuine interior portrait of a thirteen-year-old girl. The other two poems belong to the same mood, even if the latter two refer to the end of adolescence rather than the beginning.

Phyllis McGinley

PORTRAIT OF GIRL WITH COMIC BOOK

Thirteen's no age at all. Thirteen is nothing.
It is not wit, or powder on the face,
Or Wednesday matinées, or misses' clothing,
Or intellect, or grace.
Twelve has its tribal customs. But thirteen
Is neither boys in battered cars nor dolls,
Not *Sara Crewe,* or movie magazine,
Or pennants on the walls.

Thirteen keeps diaries and tropical fish
(A month, at most); scorns jumpropes in the spring;
Could not, would fortune grant it, name its wish;
Wants nothing, everything;
Has secrets from itself, friends it despises;
Admits none to the terrors that it feels;
Owns half a hundred masks but no disguises;
And walks upon its heels.

Thirteen's anomalous—not that, not this:
Not folded bud, or wave that laps a shore,
Or moth proverbial from the chrysalis.
Is the one age defeats the metaphor.
Is not a town, like childhood, strongly walled
But easily surrounded; is no city.
Nor, quitted once, can it be quite recalled—
Not even with pity.

THE DOLL HOUSE

After the children left it, after it stood
For a while in the attic,
Along with the badminton set, and the skis too good
To be given away, and the Peerless Automatic
Popcorn Machine that used to fly into rages,
And the Dr. Dolittle books, and the hamsters' cages,
She brought it down once more
To a bedroom, empty now, on the second floor
And put the furniture in.
                              There was nothing much
That couldn't be used again with a bit of repair.
It was all there,
Perfect and little and inviolate.
So, with the delicate touch
A jeweler learns, she mended the rocking chair,
Meticulously laundered
The gossamer parlor curtains, dusted the grate,
Glued the glazed turkey to the flowered plate,
And polished the Lilliput writing desk.
                                        She squandered
One bold October day and half the night
Binding the carpets round with a ribbon border;
Till, to her grave delight
(With the kettle upon the stove, the mirror's face
Scoured, the formal sofa set in its place),
She saw the dwelling decorous and in order.

It was a good house. It had been artfully built
By an idle carpenter once, when the times were duller.
The windows opened and closed. The knocker was gilt.
And every room was painted a suitable color
Or papered to scale
For the sake of the miniature Adam and Chippendale.
And there were proper hallways,
Closets, lights, and a staircase. (What had always

Pleased her most
Was the tiny, exact, mahogany newel post.)
And always, too, wryly she thought to herself,
Absently pinning
A drapery's pleat, smoothing a cupboard shelf—
Always, from the beginning,
This outcome had been clear. Ah! She had known
Since the first clapboard was fitted, first rafter hung
(Yet not till now had known that she had known),
This was no daughters' fortune but her own—
Something cautiously lent to the careless young
To dazzle their cronies with for a handful of years
Till the season came
When their toys diminished to programs and souvenirs,
To tousled orchids, diaries well in arrears,
Anonymous snapshots stuck round a mirror frame,
Or letters locked away.
                        Now seed of the past
Had fearfully flowered. Wholly her gift at last,
Here was her private estate, a peculiar treasure
Cut to her fancy's measure.
Now there was none to trespass, no one to mock
The extravagance of her sewing or her spending
(The tablecloth stitched out of lace, the grandfather's clock,
Stately upon the landing,
With its hands eternally pointing to ten past five).

Now all would thrive.

Over this house, most tranquil and complete,
Where no storm ever beat,
Whose innocent stair
No messenger ever climbed on quickened feet
With tidings either of rapture or of despair,
She was sole mistress. Through the panes she was able
To peer at her world reduced to the size of dream
But pure and unaltering.
                        There stood the dinner table,
Invincibly agleam
With the undisheveled candles, the flowers that bloomed

Forever and forever,
The wine that never
Spilled on the cloth or sickened or was consumed.

The *Times* lay at the doorsill, but it told
Daily the same unstirring report. The fire
Painted upon the hearth would not turn cold,
Or the constant hour change, or the heart tire
Of what it must pursue,
Or the guest depart, or anything here be old.

"Nor ever," she whispered, "bid the spring adieu."

And caught into this web of quietness
Where there was neither After nor Before,
She reached her hand to stroke the unwithering grasses
Beside the small and incorruptible door.

BALLADE OF LOST OBJECTS

Where are the ribbons I tie my hair with?
    Where is my lipstick? Where are my hose—
The sheer ones hoarded these weeks to wear with
    Frocks the closets do not disclose?
Perfumes, petticoats, sports chapeaux,
    The blouse Parisian, the earring Spanish—
Everything suddenly ups and goes.
    And where in the world did the children vanish?

This is the house I used to share with
    Girls in pinafores, shier than does.
I can recall how they climbed my stair with
    Gales of giggles, on their tiptoes.
Last seen wearing both braids and bows
    (But looking rather Raggedy-Annish),
When they departed nobody knows—
    Where in the world did the children vanish?

Two tall strangers, now I must bear with,
  Decked in my personal furbelows,
Raiding the larder, rending the air with
  Gossip and terrible radios.
Neither my friends nor quite my foes,
  Alien, beautiful, stern, and clannish,
Here they dwell, while the wonder grows:
  Where in the world did the children vanish?

Prince, I warn you, under the rose,
  Time is the thief you cannot banish.
These are my daughters, I suppose.
  But where in the world did the children vanish?

Herman Wouk

THE AUTHOR AND HIS BOOK

Having no favorites among my published books, I asked my editor, Le Baron Barker, Jr., to select a scene from *Youngblood Hawke,* my longest work.

Youngblood Hawke is a tragic love triangle. On that frame is stretched a panoramic American tale of conflict between innocence and corruption. I like the book because it is serious in theme, broad in canvas and (these are *The New Yorker*'s words) "continuously entertaining." That is my idea of what one kind of good novel should be.

Arthur Youngblood Hawke comes to New York from Kentucky to get his first novel published. At a Christmas party he encounters a rich, seductive older New York woman, Frieda Winter, who is active in the arts. He visits her at home, and there they have a sudden, dazing sexual encounter. She goes off to Europe. When she returns, he does not hear from her for months. He is too inexperienced, proud, and self-conscious to communicate with her again, until this scene.

Jeanne Green, referred to in this excerpt, is the heroine of the story, and I think the best realized—so far—of the women I have created.

Herman Wouk

I

No man can know what it is like to be a woman taking her firstborn in her arms for the first time; but a writer who holds a freshly printed copy of his first book must have a fair idea of what the woman feels. It lies rectangular and spotless in his hands, with his name on the jacket. It is his pass to the company of the great. Fielding, Stendhal, Melville, Tolstoy wrote books. Now he has written one. It does not matter that the dust lies brown and thick on millions of books in libraries everywhere, it does not matter that most new books fall dead, it does not matter that of the thousands of books published each year only a half dozen will survive the season. All that may be. Meantime he has written a book! The exaltation does not last. It cannot. It is too piercing. It is gone before he has drawn twenty breaths. But in those twenty breaths he has smelled the sweetest of all savors, the savor of total fulfillment. After that, no matter what success he may achieve, he is just another writer, with a writer's trials and pleasures. That joy never comes again in all its first purity.

Hawke's first copy of *Alms for Oblivion* arrived in the mail on a morning in June, a few weeks before publication day. The volume seemed to fill his hot squalid loft room with light. He sat at his desk, staring and staring at it, enjoying his once-in-a-lifetime thrill. Then the question arose, what to do with the book? Hovey morality called on him to send it to his mother. Rationally, the person entitled to the book was Jeanne Green. She had been of the greatest help in preparing the manuscript for the press. Now she was working steadily on the chapters of *Chain of Command* as they came from his pen.

He and Jeanne had become warm comrades. He was in love with her, or he thought he was. He found her magnetically appealing. Yet he never tried to make love to her. The best reason he could discern for this was his knowledge that she would yield, and he would find himself a married man; married to a clever, lovely, but somewhat forbidding young woman. Jeanne's strictness seemed less a matter of conventional morality than of her own nature. She allowed no fooling around in her work, she tolerated nothing loose or second-rate in his manuscripts, and in the same way, he knew, she would require that he be a faithful husband. He was willing to be a faithful husband—indeed a faithful husband to Jeanne Green, he believed; only not quite yet!

The real trouble was that the incredible Christmas Day episode with Mrs. Winter haunted him. He had not heard from her again. He knew from the gossip columns that she had returned to New York months ago. She had made no effort to track him down. At first he had told himself that she was being discreet, that in due course a letter or a wire would come to his telephoneless lair. None came. His pride became irked. He could not bring himself to call her, yet he felt balked of an exciting experience. How could a woman make love to him once in that wild way, and then ignore his existence? He was determined that somehow or other she would acknowledge his existence again, and that the suspense in his mind would be resolved, even if it took only one more innocuous meeting.

So when the volume of *Alms for Oblivion* came to his hand, what he did in the end was to send it to Mrs. Winter. He wasted half a day writing and rewriting a letter to go with it: a letter that defied his efforts to edit out an injured, high-flown note. He knew he was doing an ill-considered thing; and because of Jeanne, an unjust thing; and perhaps for that reason he could not get the letter to sound right. Also, there was the problem that her husband might read it! Finally he typed it up and mailed it off with his precious volume.

Mrs. Winter had quite definite ideas about what she wanted in life, and about how things should be done for her. For instance, she loved to be awakened about ten in the morning, and no earlier. At ten her husband was gone to his Broad Street office; at ten the chauffeur had taken the two girls off to their private school, and little Paul to his school; at ten the mail had arrived; and at ten the sun had risen far enough over the midtown towers of New York, even in the dead of winter, to dapple the treetops of the park, which she could see when she sat propped in bed. At ten, moreover, fresh flowers had come from the florist, so that the maid would bring them in with the newspapers, the mail, and the tea. Mrs. Winter had an acute sense of the sweetness of life and the preciousness of the passing moment. Her existence was ordered so that each moment, day by day, was as pleasant as possible. Fresh flowers in one's bedroom in the morning was a slight pleasure, but an easy and unfailing one.

It was early in June, so the flowers were lilacs, huge fragrant bunches. The day was sunny. The mail was heavy and looked interesting. She had had a good weekend of tennis and talk at her home in Connecticut. Last night the opening of the play she had attended had been a failure; a special treat, since the producer was a woman she disliked, a mannish bore who tended to wax theological about the drama. She had had her semi-annual physical checkup a few days ago, and the doctor—who, old as he was, treated her with a debonair goatishness that she rather liked— had said that she was in the best shape ever, a real wonder. That too, was not randomly achieved. Mrs. Winter worked at staying healthy. People who dissipated, who burned the candle at both ends, she considered fools. The candle was invaluable, it was one's single sure possession. Properly trimmed and cared for it gave plenty of charming light from one end, for a long long time.

The package that came from Youngblood Hawke did not catch her attention at first. The shape was a familiar one, a cardboard book carton. Publishers were always sending new books to Mrs. Winter. She knew most of them, and she was a free member of the inner circle of New York celebrities whose talk could get a book started like nothing else. As usual, she telephoned her office while she drank her first cup of tea. The wistful, soft, bald young bachelor who had been her secretary for half a dozen years had only one bit of news; *The Doctor's Dilemma* had played the night before to a house of twenty-three hundred dollars. She knew without checking that this was a fall-off of two hundred odd dollars from the previous Monday. The show was slipping, and at this rate would not break even, unless the actors' contracts were renegotiated. "Call Jock Maas. Keep calling him till you get him. You know how he is in the morning. Tell him that I want him to meet me at four at the office," she said.

She opened the newspapers to the theatrical pages and glanced at the first and last paragraphs of the reviews, to be sure that the play had failed. (It had, most satisfyingly.) Then she noticed that the book package was addressed by hand. That was unusual. She picked it off the blue silk quilt and held it close to her nearsighted eyes: *From A. Youngblood Hawke, 345 W. 28th St*. She opened it quickly, pulled out the book, and a folded letter fell on the quilt.

Dear Mrs. Winter:

I send you herewith the first copy off the press of my first novel, *Alms for Oblivion*. I could make this letter one long string of apologies: for the crudity of my book, for my presumption in sending it to you, for certain things which you may or may not remember. I am not even sure you remember me! You were kind enough to make your library available to me on Christmas Day last year. Unlike you, I remember our encounter well. I am half in the business of remembering. And I recall that you said to me, on two different occasions, "Never, never apologize." So I won't.

Why do I select you for the doubtful honor of receiving this book, which means so much in my life, and can mean so little in yours? Why do I burden you with a favor which to you may be no favor, but an embarrassment and a bore? Because you were once kind to a young man alone in New York, and because kindness is not an outstanding trait of the people in the city.

I came to the city as so many young men have done before me, in order to make my way. You called me a determined young man, and I think I am one. I wish I could believe that, with this book, I have broken into the identity that I believe will be mine some day. But looking at it now, at the first copy off the press, a month or so before the critics will pass judgment, I find my work not up to the mark. It is no use listing my mistakes; a woman of taste like yourself will see them all too clearly. But I will say this. As long as I live I do not think I will be ashamed of *Alms for Oblivion* as a first effort. So I send you this gift, faulty as it is, with a good conscience.

I am not seeking to renew our acquaintance, or to force myself on you. That would be a paltry use of a volume which may be meaningless to anyone else, but which looked to me, when I first drew it out of the box it came in, like the Holy Grail. You live in a world to which I will always be a stranger. In time I think I will be a welcome and respected stranger, an Othello in your Venice. Until your world seeks me out, whether to reward me for this young and botched first novel, or to acknowledge my gifts when I have made a better demonstration of them—as I shall—I am content to drudge along in obscurity. I have not even moved from the room without a telephone, though I have little money now.

So please accept this tribute, dear Mrs. Winter, in the spirit in which I send it. And as for this stilted and inarticulate letter, understand it for what it is. I allow myself two luxuries that I have not yet earned—Havana cigars, and the excessive pride of an artist.

I cannot forget the breakfast you gave me, out of your kindness, on Christmas Day in your grand home on Fifth Avenue. I have been a little delayed in thanking you properly. Now here is *Alms for Oblivion.*

Sincerely yours,
Arthur Hawke

It is not given to many women to get such a letter. Mrs. Winter did not even glance at the book until she had picked up the telephone and fired off a telegram to Youngblood Hawke. Then she did examine it curiously, especially the picture of the young man on the back of the jacket, a broad-shouldered fellow who needed a haircut, scowling ferociously into the camera, his chin resting on a clenched fist. A small smile came and went on Mrs. Winter's face.

2

When he caught his first glimpse of her, coming toward him through the warm-weather strollers in the zoo—the old ladies, the nurses with baby carriages, the college boys and girls holding hands in snatched lunch-hour idylls—he was disappointed. There was nothing very feminine in her walk, it was a swingy no-nonsense stride, purse tucked under one arm and the other arm pumping back and forth. And she was so obviously an older woman! There wasn't a trace of girlishness in the blue-gray suit, the severe blue hat, the big plain blue leather purse. He was lounging against the rail before the lion's cage, where they had agreed to meet, when he noticed her. She saw him almost at the same instant. Her free hand shot up in a characteristic movement, a bend at the elbow and a brief sharp wriggle of her blue-gloved fingers. "Hello!" She shook hands firmly. "Gad, you're not half as tall as I remembered you. That's good. I thought of you as a sort of man mountain."

She was looking up at him with the nearsighted peer out of large gray eyes, with the downward tilt of the head, as though somehow she could see better out of the top part of her pupils. He had never felt so awkward, so empty of words. "We picked a nice day for it," he said, stammering on *picked.*

"Yes, didn't we? One of the few days of the year when the town isn't smelling like the inside of an old garage. . . . Good heavens, what's that, and why?" He had taken the florist's box from behind his back, where he had been holding it like a high school boy. She accepted the box and opened it at once. "Well! God knows how many years it's been since somebody gave me a flower! I mean when I wasn't chairlady of a committee or something—a white camellia! Bless your heart, I'm putting it on this minute. I should be giving you a flower, or some kind of a present anyway, for sending me that book." She pinned the camellia deftly to the lapel of her suit. "You're overwhelming me. There. How's that? Where shall we go?"

She was so completely at her ease, he thought; but he found himself cutting off every sentence that came to his tongue because it seemed to have a double meaning. He was looking silently at her, a big helpless yokel. She took his hand and pressed it, smiling. "Shall we just walk? Have you had your look at your *larn?*" When he had telephoned her, in response to her wire, and had suggested this meeting place, she had made a great joke of the way he said "lion." "He's not much to look at now, poor sleepy *larn.*" The lion was curled in a corner of the cage. "I know where there are trees in bloom. Come! Then we'll go to the Margrave for lunch, okay? I eat there all the time. It's good."

"Any place is all right, Mrs. Winter."

As they strolled uptown through the park she said, "You're very thoughtful, aren't you? I looked in my library this morning and found you'd returned the book while I was in Europe. I hadn't forgotten you, Mr. Hawke, but I'd forgotten the books."

He could not find his tongue. What was the matter with him? "They were useful," he forced himself to say. "I was a little taken aback when I learned you'd gone to Europe."

"Well, you recall, I said I'd try to get some English actors for that Shakespeare festival. Which is coming along beautifully, by the way. It's no good writing to actors, they give the letters to their agents. No fine actor really gives a damn about business. They want heaps of money, sure, but mostly they want a part, and they want to be told they'll be marvellous in it. You have to talk to an actor. So there was nothing to do but get on the boat. . . . I've heard wonderful things about your book. Roberto Luzzatto bought it for Anne Karen, didn't he?"

"Yes. Luzzatto wanted me to write the screenplay, too, but I thought I'd better write another book. I'm more than halfway through."

"Another book already? My, you're a fast worker," she said.

At that moment he was looking down at her, and her eyes met his. It seemed they both thought at once of the double meaning. An uncertain embarrassed smile flickered on her face. Then they both broke into laughter, rollicking laughter, laughter that filled him with excitement, it acknowledged so much and promised so much. The intervening months dissolved; the spell of Mrs. Winter blazed up as it had on that amazing afternoon, and she looked as desirable, all at once, as she had in his fantasies. She was older than he, and that was beautiful; see the college girl sitting on the bench they were walking past, the lumpy adolescent with the unlined pretty face, the inexpert paint, holding hands with an empty-faced boy! This woman was his equal, free and strong as a man, yet radiant with allure. Her stride in the daylight was purposeful, head-long, and that was lovely; where was the charm in the languishing daw-dling steps of a girl? There were no eyes in the world like Frieda Winter's, gray, huge, sometimes merry and sometimes sharply alert, but always disturbing as they peered up under the very high arch of her dark brows. As for Jeanne—well, he was having an adventure, why the hell not? He was only twenty-seven, and he was free.

It was delicious to walk with Frieda Winter along a lane of flowering trees. He told her that Luzzatto was after him again to do the screen-play, because Anne Karen had rejected a scenario prepared by a Hollywood writer; but that he intended to decline. "Why? Are you afraid Holly-wood will corrupt you?" she said with amused irony.

"Not at all. It's a question of time. My feeling is that if I work every day as though I were being shot at sunrise tomorrow, I may barely get my main jobs done in twenty or thirty years. There's no room in the scheme for writing movies."

"There's the question of money."

"My needs are few."

"But an artist shouldn't live like a hermit or a beggar. I don't believe in that. It's cramping. And it cuts you off from the experiences you ought to have."

"I won't always live this way. I have an investment program that will slowly but surely make me independent."

Mrs. Winter looked up at him keenly, then laughed. "I see. Very fine, very fine!"

He was more at ease in elegant restaurants now. Often he took Jeanne to the places he read about in the columns, and now and then he went himself, and read a book, ignoring the waiters' stares, while he ate complicated and exquisite French dishes alone. He thought he gave a fair account of himself ordering the food and wine, though the deference of the captain was aimed at Mrs. Winter. The captain had greeted her by name, with a more than routine bow.

She said, "Tell me about this investment program of yours. That sounds decidedly long-headed for a young writer."

When he began describing Scotty Hoag she wrinkled her nose, very much like his mother. "Real estate is not for somebody like you."

"Well, all I can tell you is, I invested ten thousand dollars with him in January. In the middle of May he sold the property, before it was even completed, and returned twenty-two thousand dollars to me."

"You were lucky. What did you do with that money?"

"I invested half of it in another project of Scotty's, a housing development that has Federal support. I wanted to put all the money into it, but he insisted that I salt away half in government bonds."

"Did you?"

Hawke toyed with the stem of his martini glass, and looked at her with a sidewise grin. "No. I told him I did, but I bought some stocks, and some commodity futures." He laughed as she shook her head. "I knew you wouldn't like that. All the same I've made eleven hundred dollars on onions and lard contracts, if you'll believe me, in a few weeks of fooling around. Before I made a move I studied up on the subject. I made theoretical purchases and sales for a few months. If you watch yourself you go in and out fast and you can't really get hurt. It's interesting. What's more, it's fun."

"But why should you put your mind to that kind of thing? Onions and lard, indeed."

"Mrs. Winter, I sold the movie rights in *Alms for Oblivion* for thirty thousand dollars. When all the bites came out—agent, publisher, taxes—I was left with about eight or so. Eight thousand instead of thirty is quite a cut! If I'm to achieve independence by my own efforts—without living like a hermit which, I agree with you, is not for me—I'm going to have to manage my money."

Frieda Winter said with a few quick raps of her cigarette lighter, "Look here, if you want your money managed there are people who do that too, reliable people who make it their business."

"Sure. You come to them with half a million dollars and they'll do all kinds of smart things with it. They're not going to build eight thousand back up to thirty."

"My husband is as good an investment manager as any in the business. He's really good. He's written a book, and all that, and he's done pretty well for a couple of musicians and writers I've sent to him over the years. He won't put you in commodity futures, but whatever money you make and give to him you'll have, and it'll yield you something too."

Hawke said, sitting up, "Wait, is he the Winter of Willis and Winter? *Rational Investing?*"

"Yes."

"Why, I've read that book. It's very good. Aside from everything else, he can write, and he has a sense of humor. And he's your husband! Why didn't that occur to me?"

Mrs. Winter's smile was strange, a mere wrinkling of her mouth. "Paul is quite a person. You'll have to meet him. I think he could help you, and keep you out of a lot of trouble."

"Well, right now nearly all my surplus money is with Scotty Hoag, Mrs. Winter."

"Why don't you call me Frieda? I shouldn't be Mrs. Winter to you, should I?"

They were looking in each other's eyes, and her business-like glance changed into quite another look. Hawke cleared his throat. "I suppose not, Frieda."

"Now what will I call you? It seems to me I had a name for you, a pretty good one."

Hawke said, with considerable embarrassment, "I remember, if you don't. Bloody."

Frieda Winter laughed, a low quiet laugh, and glanced mechanically around at the other tables. "Well that sounds like the Christmas spirit, doesn't it? Sausages and corn fritters in a shut-up house and all that. No, it won't do for an ordinary weekday, will it? What shall it be? Not Youngblood."

"No, only strangers trying to get friendly in a hurry call me that. And Hollywood people. For some reason they love it. My name is Arthur, Frieda."

"Then Arthur it is. Now tell me, this man Hoag down in Kentucky— why is he bothering to manage your money for you?"

"I think it flatters his vanity to be associated with a live novelist. He's an old college classmate of mine. I think too he enjoys patronizing me with his superior wisdom about real estate. Besides, on however small a scale, I'm supplying him with venture capital."

Frieda spun her lighter swiftly. "By and large people like that are out for themselves. It might not be a bad thing, somewhere along the line, if Paul looked into your Mr. Hoag. There are painless and effective ways of checking on business men."

Hawke didn't like the idea, but he realized the prudence of it. "That would be very kind of him."

The food came: cold poached salmon for both of them, garnished with garden vegetables. The captain poured a sip of white wine into Hawke's glass, gravely keeping up the New York fiction that an American can tell one wine from another. Hawke just as gravely sipped, and nodded. He had simply ordered the most expensive number in the white Burgundies, and its taste was excellent.

Frieda said, "Well, what do we drink to? Shall we say to literature, and to hell with onions, lard, and real estate?"

"To money, so long as it's honestly earned," Hawke said.

"Nothing doing. I won't drink to money, and I'm damned if you will. Here's to your book, Arthur, and here's to my book—for which I'm more grateful than I can say."

"The book, then," Hawke said, and they drank.

For a few minutes they ate eagerly, laughing at each other.

"Now, a couple of questions," Frieda said. "You lost me, cutting thirty thousand dollars down to eight. Where did all that money go, again?"

"For one thing Prince House took half."

"Half!"

"Jay maintains stoutly that it's standard for a first novel."

"Arthur, Jay Prince drives hard bargains, everybody knows that. But that's robbery."

"He gave me a printed form contract and I signed it. What's more I tied up two more books on that formula."

"Christ! Didn't you have an agent or a lawyer?"

"No. Being fresh down out of the hills, still full of my last meal of fried squirrels, as you might say, I naturally was playing the suave man of the world. I've had two arguments with Jay about that contract since. One last Christmas, right after Ferdie Lax told me something about movie percentages. Jay put me off with that heavy joviality of his—we wouldn't have any trouble, men of good will could always get together, let's get the book published and then we'll see —that kind of thing. Then three days ago, when they sent me that first book off the press, I went down and talked to him again. I lost that argument too. You see he's so damned *pleasant* about it. So I'm pleasant and nothing gets changed, nothing on paper. Just cheerful chatter about the future. Meantime he's collected my thirteen-plus thousand dollars. I owed it to him, and I was honor bound to give it to him. In return I got vague talk of a new contract, and maybe a refund if the book is a hit. It's more than he advanced me on all three books. And the contract says I owe him half the movie rights of two more books."

Frieda's arched brows contracted in a fierce way, emphasizing the slant of her eyes. She looked almost Chinese. "You'll have to get ugly with Jay."

"I'm becoming aware of that."

"Get an agent to do your arguing for you. Their business is getting ugly when necessary. I can recommend several."

"Well, I thought maybe I'd get hold of Ferdie Lax."

Frieda ate in silence for a little while. "That's all right. Ferdie can be as jovial a thug as Jay and then some. Of course you need an Eastern agent for magazine rights and that kind of thing, but Ferdie can arrange that. You'll have to give him ten percent of everything you earn."

"I know."

"And Ferdie is no Mahatma Gandhi, you understand. All he wants is money. He makes money by being on your side. Ferdie Lax is okay, Arthur."

The captain was filling her glass. "Everything all right, Mrs. Winter?"

"Fine. Fred, this young man is a new and important novelist, Youngblood Hawke."

The captain, with a sidewise dip of the head, and a small bow, said "Yes, sair, Mr. Hawke," and refilled his glass too. When he left Frieda said, "It helps when they know your name. Sometimes you want a reservation at the last minute."

"Seems to me all I'd have to say is I'm a friend of Mrs. Winter?"

"Oh well. This is around the corner from home. I use it a lot for lunch." She drank wine and laughed. "I must say I've fallen into quite a different vein than I intended. Sitting here in my old business corner and all. We haven't talked about anything but money, have we?"

"No. It's been all onions and lard, so far."

"You might as well be having lunch with Paul. Let's beat it. I want my coffee, and then I want to see where you work. The room without a telephone."

"Frieda, it's a hole, it's almost stagey it's so squalid. It's hot and it smells and I left it in a disgusting mess. I wouldn't take a dog up there, let alone Frieda Winter of Fifth Avenue."

"Oh, damn that Frieda Winter of Fifth Avenue, will you? I won't be patronized just because you don't have money, you're goddamn anxious for money, yourself, Bloody my boy." She was glaring at him from under her brows like an offended cat, the gray eyes wide and menacing. It was a droll, delightful effect.

Grinning, he said, "So I'm Bloody again."

Her anger, real or assumed, dissolved into amusement. What a face this woman had! She said, "It just came out. I guess because you were being a bloody bore. We'll have our coffee and then we're going to look at young Balzac's garret, do you hear?"

"Yes, Mrs. Winter," Hawke said.

She put her fingers for a moment on his clasped hands on the table. "Okay," she said. "That's settled."

When the captain brought the check he laid it unhesitatingly beside Frieda. She started to sign, but Hawke whisked the check from under her pen, saying, "Are you out of your mind?"

She said, "Look, Bloody, I'm not going to play snatch-the-check with you. But don't be a fool. I run an account here. It's all expenses for me. I eat on the government and I'm damn well entitled to do so with the taxes I pay. Give me the check."

"Where I come from men still pay if they take a lady to lunch."

"Oh, look, this is a business lunch, I exploit every writer I know, one way or another, and all I'm really after is the dramatic rights to your next novel. Don't you know that? Please give me the check and stop being a bully."

He gave her the check; it seemed the least ridiculous thing to do, though the little incident was not pleasant. At bottom he was enough of a Hovey boy still to be relieved at saving twenty-seven dollars, the price he had seen scrawled on the back of the check. "So much for the honor of Southern manhood," he muttered.

She signed the check cheerfully. "The Civil War didn't kill it, but the income tax did," she said. "Let's get on to your garret."

Tom Wolfe

THE FUGITIVE

Dear Mr. Burnett:

I wrote my first magazine article six years ago, and right away one thing began to fascinate me. Namely, how—in non-fiction— to get inside of scenes and characters with at least as much cortical voltage as the best novels and short stories . . . and preferably more, since fiction seems to be dying of terminal acne . . . I found I could use certain techniques easily enough if I did intensive reporting: scene-by-scene construction, "telling details," extended dialogue, and so-on. I found I could even do some very fancy things with point of view. But the fiction writer's most potent device—the interior monologue—seemed closed to the non-fiction writer . . . unless he were writing a memoir, like DeQuincey's *Confessions of an English Opium Eater* or Claude Brown's *Manchild in the Promised Land* . . . In non-fiction it is one thing to give the reader a bus tour of your own mind—and quite another to try to get inside of somebody else's.

But in *The Electric Kool-Aid Acid Test* I suddenly found myself with a clear shot at this particular feat. The people in the book had already done most of the work, the reporting, for me. The book's protagonist, Ken Kesey, and his psychedelic band, the Merry Pranksters, were continually recording their own adventures, on the spot, in every conceivable way, with movies, tapes, even videotapes, photographs, letters, diaries. For example, during his fugitive days in Mexico, following the second of two arrests for possession of marijuana, Kesey wrote a series of letters to his friend Larry McMurtry, describing not only what had happened but what was going through his mind. He made several tapes on the spot in jungle hideouts. I also interviewed him many times about this whole experience. I interviewed Black Maria, Zonker and other Merry Pranksters involved in it. By the time I had accumulated all this material, I saw I was in a position to go all the way with the interior monologue. This sort of experiment is probably the most sensitive area of all in the current controversy over the "new non-fiction" or "new journalism." But I don't see why . . . all it takes, when you get right down to it, is the usual . . . information and technique. . . .

Tom Wolfe

Haul ass, Kesey. Move. *Scram. Split flee hide vanish disintegrate.* Like *run.*

Rrrrrrrrrrrrrrrrrrrevrevrevrevrevrevrevrevrev or are we gonna have just a late late Mexican re-run of the scene on the rooftop in San Francisco and sit here with the motor spinning and watch with fascination while the cops they climb up once again to *come git you*—

They just opened the door down below, Rotor Rooter, so you have maybe 45 seconds assuming they be slow and sneaky and sure about it

Kesey sits in a little upper room in the last house down the beach, $80 a month, on paradise-blue Bandarias Bay, in Puerto Vallarta, on the west coast of Mexico, state of Jalisco, one step from the floppy green fronds of the jungle, wherein flourish lush steamy baboon lusts of paranoia—Kesey sits in this little rickety upper room with his elbow on a table and his forearm standing up perpendicular and in the palm of his hand a little mirror, so that his forearm and the mirror are like a big rear-view mirror stanchion on the side of a truck and thus he can look out the window and see them but they can't see him—

COME ON, MAN, DO YOU NEED A COPY OF THE SCRIPT TO SEE HOW
THIS MOVIE GOES? YOU HAVE MAYBE 40 SECONDS LEFT BEFORE THEY
COME GET YOU
—a Volkswagen has been cruising up and down the street for no
earthly reason at all, except that they are obviously working with
the fake telephone linesmen outside the window who whistle—
THERE THEY GO AGAIN
—whistle in the slow-brain brown Mexican huarache day-laborer way,
for no earthly reason except that they are obviously synched in, finked
in, with the Volkswagen. Now a tan sedan comes along the street,
minus a license plate but plus a stenciled white number—*exactly like
a prison stencil*—police and two coatless guys inside, both in white
shirts so they're *not* prisoners—
ONE TURNED LOOKED BACK!
IF YOU WERE WATCHING ALL THIS ON A MOVIE SCREEN YOU KNOW
WHAT YOUR REACTION WOULD BE THROUGH A MOUTHFUL OF POPCORN
FROM THE THIRD ROW: "WHAT MORE DO YOU NEED, YOU DOLT! SCRAM
OUTTA THERE . . .
—But he has just hooked down five dexedrines and the old motor
is spinning and rushing most nice and euphorically in fascination and
a man can't depart this nice $80-a-month snug harbor on paradise-
blue Bandarias Bay just yet with a cool creek of speed rush in his
veins. It is such a tiny little fink scene as he sees it in the hand
mirror. He can tilt it and see his own face entropied with the strain
and then tilt it—a sign!—a sparrow, fat and sleek, dives through
the dwindling sun into a hole in one of the lampposts; home.
MORE TELEFONO TRUCKS! TWO LOUD WHISTLES THIS TIME—FOR NO
EARTHLY REASON EXCEPT TO COME GIT YOU. YOU HAVE MAYBE 35
SECONDS LEFT
—Kesey has Cornel Wilde Running Jacket ready hanging on the wall,
a jungle-jim corduroy jacket stashed with fishing line, a knife, money,
DDT, tablet, ball-points, flashlight, and grass. Has it timed by test
runs that he can be out the window, down through a hole in the
roof below, down a drain pipe, over a wall and into thickest jungle in 45 seconds—well, only 35 seconds left, but head start is all
that's needed, with the element of surprise. Besides, it's so fascinating
to be here in subastral projection with the cool rushing dex, synched
into *their* minds and his own, in all its surges and tributaries and
convolutions, turning it this way and that and rationalizing the situation for the 100th time in split seconds, such as: If they have that

many men already here, the phony telephone men, the cops in the
tan car, the cops in the Volkswagen, what are they waiting for?
why haven't they crashed right in through the rotten doors of this
Rat building— But he gets the signal even before he finishes the question:

WAITING! THEY KNOW THEY'VE GOT YOU, FOOL, HAVE KNOWN FOR
WEEKS. BUT THEY'RE CERTAIN YOU'RE CONNECTED WITH ALL THE LSD
BEING SMUGGLED UP FROM MEXICO AND THEY WANT TO TAKE IN AS BIG A
HAUL AS POSSIBLE WHEN THEY FINALLY SLAM IT. LIKE LEARY; THEY
MUST HAVE BEEN WATCHING A DREADFUL LONG TIME BEFORE THEY WERE
CONTENT THEY HAD HIM ON SOMETHING WORTH HIS SIZE. THIRTY YEARS.
FOR A HARVARD DOCTOR WITH GRASS. THAT'S HOW BAD THEY WANTED
THE WHOLE BUSINESS LOCKED AWAY. THAT'S HOW DANGEROUS THEY
CONSIDER THE WHOLE BUSINESS. AND THEY WERE COMPLETELY CORRECT—
IF NOT IN THEIR FANTASY, THEN AT LEAST IN THEIR EVALUATION OF THE
PRESENT AND EVER-GROWING PSYCHEDELIC THREAT

A NOISE DOWN BELOW.

THEM?

30 SEGUNDOS LEFT?

—maybe it's Black Maria, come back with good things for eating
and stuff for the new disguise, Steve Lamb, mild-mannered reporter
and all-around creep—

RUN, FOOL!

—Shhhhhhhhhhhhhhhhh. Such a quiet secret muffled smile will be on
Black Maria's face.

Rrrrrrrrrrrrrrrrrrrrrevrevrevrevrevrevrevrevrevrev It could have been
all so quiet, just him and Zonker and the smoldering Black Maria in
this $80-a-month paradise-blue Bandarias Bay in Puerto Vallarta. If the
suicide ruse and the rest of the main Fugitive fantasy had but worked.

The trip into Mexico was easy, because everything with Boise was
easy. Boise always *knew*. They picked up Zonker in L.A., and then
Jim Fish, and they coasted on over the line at Tijuana. No hassle
to cross over into Mexico. The border at Tijuana is like a huge
superhighway toll station, a huge concrete apron and ten or fifteen
customs booths in a row for all the cars pouring over into Tijuana
from San Diego and points north, all plastic green and concrete like
part of suburban superhighway America. So they rolled on over the
line with Kesey hidden in the back of Boise's old panel truck and
heart don't even thump too bad. Spirits up, a little of the Prankster
élan back in the cosmos. In true Prankster fashion they spent one

third their money stash on a Madman Muntz autostereo rig to go along with all the over valuables, like tape recorders and many tapes.

The next likely hassle is visas, because this shapes up as a long stay. Might be hot to try to get Kesey one in Tijuana, because Tijuana is just a California annex, really, the slums of San Diego, and they just might very well know about the case.

"We'll do it in Sonoita, man," says Boise. "They don't give a shit there. Put down a couple of bucks and they can't see anything else."

Sonoita is almost due east of Tijuana, just south of the Arizona border. Kesey uses his good shuck I D there and all is jake in Sonoita. Fugitive!—real-life and for sure now.

Then south down so-called Route 2 and so-called Route 15, bouncing and grinding along through the brown dust and scrawny chickens and animal dung brown dust fumes of western Mexico, towns of Coyote, Caborca, Santa Ana, Querobabi, Cornelio, El Oasis, hee, Hermosillo, hah, Pocitos Casas, Cieneguito, Guaymas, Camaxtli, Mixcoatl, Tlazolteotl, Quetzalcoatl, Huitzilopochtli, Tezcatlipoca haunting the Dairy Queen Rat Queen crossroads in the guise of a Rat, a Popoluactli-screeing rat, Tetzcotl, Yaotl, Titlacahuan he whose slaves we are, Ochpaniiztl priestly Angel-freaked out in a motorcycle made from the vaseline skin of Gang Bang Girl Meets White Trash . . . a confetti of skulls and death in western Mexico, the Rat lands. Not one inch of it is picturesque burros and shawls or nova Zapata hats or color-TV pink chunks of watermelon or water lilies or gold feathers or long eyelashes or high combs or tortillas and tacos and chili powder or fluty camote vendors or muletas or toreros or olés or mariachi bands or water lilies or blood of the dahlia or tinny cantinas or serapes or movie black marias with shiny black hair and steaming little high round pubescent bottoms. None of the old Mexico we know and love on the 21-day excursion fare. Just the boogering brown dust and bloated rat corpses by the road, goats, cows, chickens with all four feet up in the air at the Tezcatlipocan skull rot crossroads of Mexico.

To Kesey it was a hopeless flea-bitten desert he was fleeing into. But Boise made it bearable. Boise always *knew*. Boise was wizened and thin-faced and he had the awfulest New England high flat whine, and he didn't belong anywhere near here, but he was *here, now,* and he *knew*. The truck breaks down for the fourteenth time—

"No hassle, man. We just back it up on a rock, man . . . Then we just take the tire off and fix it."

More flat, Rat country, mosquito and flea, into total nothing, like the lines of perspective in a surrealist painting, but Boise makes you realize it is all the same, here as anywhere. Boise lecherously scanning the streets as they bounce through the dead chicken towns just like it was only Saturday night on Broadway in North Beach, spotting a good-looking gringa muchacha padding along the side of the road with honest calves,

25 SECONDS LEFT, FOOL!

and he says, "Shall we get her over and *ball* her, man?" all in the same New England whine, as if he were saying, Wanna Coke, or not? Kesey looks at Boise's lined face and his thin lips, looks ancient, only a glitter comes out of the eyes, nice and lecherous, dead certain and crazy alive at the same time. And Boise in that moment is in the tiny knot of Perfect Pranksters, the inner circle, ascending into the *sangha* for good.

In Guaymas, on the gulf, Jim Fish wants out. *An early attack of paranoia, Jim Fish?* and catches a bus back to the U.S., leaving Kesey, Boise and Zonker and the equipment. But was it not ever so? You're either on the bus or off the bus. Kesey's spirits were picking up. Boise was pulling everything together::: this crazy New Englander is *here* in these Rat lands.

"Hey, man . . ." Boise points at a construction scene they're going by. ". . . see *that?*" as if to say, There's the whole thing, right there.

A whole gang of workmen are trying to put the stucco on the ceiling of a building they're finishing up. One fat man is mixing up the stucco in a washtub. One skinny one is scooping the stucco up out of the tub with a little trowel and pitching it up underhanded at the ceiling. A little of it sticks—and three or four guys stand on a plank scaffolding taking stabs at smoothing it out—but most of it falls down on the floor and three or four more are hunkered down there scraping it up off the floor and shoveling it back in the tub and the skinny guy skinnies up another little gob with his skinny trowel and they all stare again to see what happens. They are all hunkering around in huaraches, worthless flat Rat woven sandals, up on the scaffolding, down on the floor, waiting to see what happens, how fate brings it off with this little gob of nothing pitched up at the Rat expanse . . .

And it's all there—the whole Mexico Trip—

"They have a saying, 'Hay tiemp—'" Boise hooks the steering wheel to get around an ice-cream vendor in the middle of the road "—o,' 'There is time.' "

20 SECONDS, IDIOT!

Huaraches, which are *the* Rat shoe. It all synchs. Mexico is the Rat paradise. But of course! It is not worthless—it is perfection. It is as if all the Rat things of all the Rat lands of America, all the drive-ins, mobile-home parks, Dairy Queens, superettes, Sunset Strips, auto-accessory stores, septic-tank developments, souvenir shops, snack bars, lay-away furniture stores, Daveniter living rooms, hot-plate hotels, bus-station paperback racks, luncheonette in-the-booth jukebox slots, raw-concrete service-station toilets with a head of urine in the bowl, Grey-hound bus toilettes with paper towels and vomit hanging over the hockey-puckblack rim, Army-Navy stores with Bikini Kodpiece Briefs for men, Super Giant racks with matching green twill shirts and balloon-bottom pants for honest toilers, $8,000 bungalows with plastic accordion-folding partitions and the baby asleep in there in a fold-away crib of plastic net, picnic tables with the benches built onto them used in the dining room, Jonni-Trot Bar-B-Q sandwiches with a carbonated fruit drink, aluminum slat awnings, aluminum sidings, lukewarm coffee-"with" in a china mug with a pale brown pool in the saucer and a few ashes, a spade counter chef scraping a short-order grill with a chalky Kitchy-Brik and he won't take your order till he's through, a first-come-first-serve doctor's waiting room with modest charwomen with their dresses stuck on the seats of shiny vinyl chairs and they won't move to get loose for fear you'll look up their dress, plaid car coats from Sears and a canvas cap with a bill, synthetic dresses for waitresses looking like milky cellophane, Rat cones, Rat sodas, Rat meat-salad sandwiches, Rat cheezies, Ratburg-ers—it is as if all the Rat things of all the Rat lands of America had been looking for their country, their Canaan, their Is-ra-el, and they found it in Mexico. It has its own Rat aesthetics. It's hulking beautiful . . .

Then they reached Mazatlan, the first full-fledged resort you reach on the west coast of Mexico, coming down from the States. Every-body's trip was fishing in Mazatlan. Along the old Avenida del Mar and the Paseo Claussen, white walls with nice artistic Rat fishing scenes and hotel archways with great shiny blue marlins hanging inside the arches and gringos with duckbill caps here to catch me some mar-lin. Mariachi music at last, with the trumpets always breaking and dropping off the note and then struggling up again. Zonker has the bright idea of going to O'Brien's Bar, on the beach front, place he

got beat up out back of once by thirteen Mexican fags. Zonker enjoys revisiting scenes of previous debacles. *Like also spends hours on
the beach telling them how his true and fiercest fear is of being
attacked by a shark while swimming . . . as he picks flea-bite scabs
until his legs stream blood to the luscious world . . . then goes
swimming.*

O'Brien's brings on the paranoia right away. It is a break in the
Rat movie. It is dark and a Mexican band plays—signaling to the
Rat sensibility that it will cost too much. Rat souls everywhere fear
dark, picturesque restaurant, knowing instinctively they will pay dearly
for the bullshit ambiance, dollar a drink probably. O'Brien's was crowded,
and then through the cocktail gloom: *heads.* A bunch of kids with
the jesuschrist hair, the temple bells and donkey beads, serape vests,
mandalas; in short, American heads. Zonker recognizes them immediately. They're not only American heads, but from San Jose, and some
had been to the Acid Tests. *Just what the Fugitive needs to blow
the whole suicide ruse. Guess who I saw in Mexico . . ."* Naturally,
Zonk, with his zest for debacle, hails them over. Kesey is introduced
as "Joe," and nobody pays him much mind except for one dark
little girl, Mexican-looking, with long black hair.

"When were you born?" she says to Kesey. She doesn't sound Mexican. *She sounds like Lauren Bacall speaking through a tube.*

"I'm a Virgo." *No sense hitting a ball three hits you can see
coming if you can cut across the fourth.*

"I thought so. I'm a Scorpio."

"Beautiful."

The black Scorpio obviously knows Zonk best. She knows him when.
But Zonk belongs to the ages and it comes to pass that Zonk or
no Zonk, she and Kesey relax out in the open air on the pier one
night down by a Mazatlan Rat beach, all dirt and scrabble, but the
waves and the wind and the harbor lights do it up right and the
moon hits some kind of concrete shaft there, putting her in the dark,
in the shadow, and him in the light, lit up by the moon, as if
some designer drew a line precisely between their bodies. *Black Maria,*
he decides.

So Black Maria joins the Fugitive band and they go off to Puerto
Vallarta. Puerto Vallarta is out of the Rat lands. All picture-book
Mexico. Paradise-blue Bandarias Bay and a pure white beach and white
latino cottages right up against the jungle, which is a deep raw green,
and clean. Fat green fronds lapping up against the back of the houses

on the beach. Macaw sounds, or very near it. Secret poisonous orchid and orange pops and petals winking out when the foliage moves.
A nice romantic Gothic jungle. Zonker hassles with an oily little
real-estate man and gets the last house on the edge of town for $80
a month. The rent is low because the jungle is too close for the
tourists, the jungle and too many Mexican kids and chickens and the
rural dung dust. Boise heads back to the U.S. and Kesey, Zonker
and Black Maria move in. They have the upper half of the house,
one floor and a spiral staircase up to the roof. Up on the roof is
a kind of thatched hut, the highest perch around, a perfect lookout
post and a snug harbor. Kesey decides to risk a phone call to the
States to let Faye and everybody know he's O.K. He goes into
town and calls Peter Demma in the Hip Pocket Book Store in Santa
Cruz. A little metallic clanking about by the telefonista señoritas down
at central. And then,

"Peter?"

From many Rat miles away: "Ken!" Very surprised, naturally . . .

So Kesey whiled the time sitting in the snug hacienda on the
edge of Puerto Vallarta sipping beer and smoking many joints and
writing in a notebook occasionally. He wanted to get a little of all
this down and send it to Larry McMurtry.

"Larry:

"Phone calls to the states 8 bucks apiece besides was ever a good
board to bound my favorite ball of bullshit prose offen, it was
you . . ."

Like all about Black Maria. In many ways she is so great. She
is quiet and has a kind of broody beauty. She cooks. She looks
Mex and speaks Mex. She can even hassle Mex. She sounds out the
Mayor of Puerto Vallarta as to how safe Kesey will be here in town.
Hay tiempo, he says. The extradition takes forever. Very nice to
know . . .

And yet Black Maria is not completely a Prankster. She wants to
be a part of all this, she wants to do this thing, but *she does it
without belief.* It is like the Mexican part of her Black Maria thing.
She has all the trappings of Mexican—she looks it, she speaks it,
her grandfather was even Mexican—but she is not Mexican. She is
Carolyn Hannah of San Jose, California, under everything else, even
the blood. He wrote in the notebook:: *Moving the dark Indian*

  10 SECONDS LEFT, YOU FREAKING EE-JOT!!!!
body out of the Indian land weakened the Indian blood with chicken

soup and matzoh balls. So much of the fire concealed by the dark
and broody beauty lies just that deep. Because she does it without
belief. And yet it is very nice up here in this thatched perch atop
the last house. A car heads up the street—Zonker and Black Maria
coming back to the house. He peers over the edge at the car kicking up the dusk, then writes in the notebook, it is a perfect lookout, *allowing me to see them, without them seeing me.* Many things
. . . synch.

Zonker and Black Maria drove down the road, scattering up the
kids and the chickens and the dust, and Black Maria pointed up
to the top of the house and said to Zonker:

"Look, there's Kesey." Then she looked out the window and stared
at the jungle. "I bet he thinks we can't see him."

THE JIG IS UP. Zonker brings a telegram from Paul Robertson back
in San Jose and it is a bear. It is not even a warning, it
    5 SECONDS—5 SECONDS LEFT—YOU REALLY JES GON' SIT THERE FOR
THE SQUASH?
is final. THE JIG IS UP, it says. Meaning, it turned out, that the
suicide ruse had been exposed and the cops knew he was in Puerto
Vallarta. *Exposed?*—hell, the suicide prank had turned into a goddamn comic opera. For a start, Dee had pulled a sort of Dee-out, as
Mountain Girl feared. Dee had driven up looking for a cliff near Humboldt Bay, about 250 miles north of San Francisco, up near Eureka,
California, not far from the Oregon border in redwoods country. He got
up to the last hill going up there and the panel truck wouldn't pull the
hill. So he called into town for a tow truck and the garage man and the
tow truck pulled the suicide vehicle up the last mile. Hired and paid for
and thanks a lot. Always nice to hire some help to commit suicide. Next
Dee dropped Kesey's distinctive sky-blue boots down to the shore below
—but they hit the water instead and sank without a bubble. Next the goddamned romantic suicide desolate foaming cliff was so goddamned
desolate, nobody noticed the truck for about two weeks, despite the Ira
Sandperl for President sign on the rear bumper. Apparently people figured
the old heap had been abandoned. The Humboldt county police finally
checked it out on February 11. Next, the suicide note, which seemed so
ineluctably convincing as Kesey and Mountain Girl smoked a few joints
and soared into passages of Shelleyan *Weltschmerz*—it gave off a giddy
scent of put-on, even to the straight cops of the Humboldt. There were

certain inconsistencies. Like the part about the truck smashing into a red-wood. Well—even in a Dee-out, Dee couldn't exactly ask the tow-truck man, Well, now that you've towed it up here, how about jamming it into a tree for me. Next, the late, happy call to Peter Demma in Santa Cruz. Demma had really been bowled over to hear from Kesey. A lot of people, a lot of people who liked him, had really been worried that he was dead. And now here was Kesey calling him—*alive*—with a message for Faye and the whole thing. That was Saturday. The next night, Sunday, February 13, Demma dropped into Manuel's Mexican Restaurant in Santa Cruz, and there was his old friend Bob Levy. By way of making conversation, Levy says,

"What have you heard from Ken?"

"I just got a *call* from him!" says Demma. "From Puerto Vallarta!"

That's interesting.

Levy happened to be a reporter for the Watsonville *Register-Pajaronian,* Watsonville being a town near Santa Cruz. The next afternoon, Monday, the lead story in the Watsonville *Register-Pajaronian* carried a five-column headline reading:

MISSING NOVELIST TURNS UP IN MEXICO

The next day, Tuesday, the San Jose *Mercury* picked up the story and put a little more spin on it with a story headlined:

KESEY'S CORPSE HAVING A BALL IN PUERTO VALLARTA

2 SECONDS, OH CORPSE OF MINE!
THAT'S NO BLACK MARIA SHHHHHHHHUFFLING UP THE STAIRS OUTSIDE
THE DOOR, DOLT, IT'S A COP CLUMP UP THE STAIRS NO EARTHLY
SOUND LIKE IT
SHARP WHISTLE FROM THE TELEFONISTAS
VW BACKING DOWN THE STREET
THIS IS TRULY IT, TRULY IT
GRAB THE CORNEL WILDE RUNNING JACKET, FOOL! MAKE THE BRAIN
CATCH HOLD! RRRRRRRRRRRRRRREVREVREVREV SPINNING AND IN THE GIANT
PYRAMIDAL CELLS OF BETZ OF PRECENTRAL CEREBRAL CORTEX RISE AND
HEAVE AND SLIP GANGLIONIC LAYER SHUDDERS AND GIGGLES SYNAPSES LIGHT
LIKE RANDOM BEATLE FLASHBULBS KHEEWWW BLASTING OUT SILLY FROM
MOTOR HOMUNCULUS YOU MISSED YR FLASH OH MIGHTY MASTICATOR,
SALIVATOR, VOCALIZER, SWALLOWER, LICKER, BITER SUCKER BROW-KNITTER

LOOKER BLINKER RUBBERNECKER THUMBER PRODDER UPYOURS FINGERER RINGWEARER NOSEPICKER WAVER DRINKER ARMLIFTER BODYBENDER HIP-SWIVELER KNEER SPRINGER RUNNER

ZERO::::::::ooooooooo:::::::::RUN!

Sonbitch! The gears catch at last, he springs up, grab Cornel Wilde jacket, leaps through the back window, down through the hole, down the drainpipe—now vault the wall, you mother, into the jungle floppy—

AWWRRRRRAMMMMANNNNNNN

WHAZZAT?

His head is down but he can see it

WHAZZAT!

Up there in the window he just jumped out of

BROWN!

He can feel it. There is a vibration on the parasympathetic efferent fibres behind the eyeballs and it hums

HRRRRRRRRRAMANNNNNNNNNNN

Two of them one brown dumpy Mex with gold-handle butt gun one crewcut American FBI body-snatcher watching him flying like a monkey over the wall into the jungle the brown Mex holds gold gun but the brain behind that face too brown moldering Mex earth to worry about couldn't hit a peeing dog

PLUNGE

into the lapping P.V. fronds bursting orchid and orange the motor homunculus working perfect now powerful gallop into the picturebook jungles of Mexico—

A moment later Black Maria walked into the apartment. She found Kesey gone and the Cornel Wilde jungle running jacket gone. That trip again. Well, he'll come back when he's ready to, worn out, and things will be cool for a while. Kesey had gotten paranoid as hell, but that wasn't the only thing. He *liked* this Fugitive game.

Philip Roth

OH, THIS FATHER!

I like this passage from *Portnoy's Complaint*—a novel in the form of a monologue by a psychoanalytic patient—for the way it *moves:* the way it announces its subject—"Oh, this father!" —and then proceeds to explore the ambiguities of feeling and the recollected experiences that call forth these three opening words and their exclamation point. In that the passage describes the range of a father's appeal and deficiencies, it charts the range of a young son's filial attachment, a crucial matter in this book, where the wildly polar feelings that the little boy Portnoy has toward his parents seem to the big boy, patient Portnoy, to continue to shape the life of his affections, and thus to pervert his every attempt to be, for good or bad, his own kind of man. I like the graphic and, I think, economical way the passage records the birth of Portnoy's ambivalence, and the way it reveals the little boy's focus upon sexuality and the sexual parts: the birth, that is, of Portnoy's Oedipus Complex. Of course I was not interested here in making a case for Freud's great illuminating idea about sons and their parents, nor, in any primary way, was I using it to aid or stimulate my imagination. To me, the success of this passage lies ultimately in *the breaking down of that idea;* not destroying its general validity with an aberrant example either, *but restoring it to its sources in experience*. The intellectual formulation is beautiful in its magnitude, its sweep. But that is only a kind of beauty, a kind of vision. There is also the beauty of the imagined instance, with its fleshy specificity, its authenticity of detail, mood, and feeling. I admit to finding some beauty of this last sort here.

Philip Roth

Oh, this father! this kindly, anxious, uncomprehending, constipated father! Doomed to be obstructed by this Holy Protestant Empire! The self-confidence and the cunning, the imperiousness and the contacts, all that enabled the blond and blue-eyed of his generation to lead, to inspire, to command, if need be to oppress—he could not summon a hundredth part of it. How could he oppress?—he *was* the oppressed. How could he wield power?—he *was* the powerless. How could he enjoy triumph, when he so despised the triumphant—and probably the very idea. "They worship a Jew, do you know that, Alex? Their whole big-deal religion is based on worshiping someone who was an established Jew at that time. Now how do you like that for stupidity? How do you like that for pulling the wool over the eyes of the public? Jesus Christ, who they go around telling everybody was God, was actually a Jew! And this fact, that absolutely kills me when I have to think about it, *nobody else pays any attention to.* That he was a Jew, like you and me, and that they took a Jew and turned him into some kind of God after he is already dead, and then—and this is what can make you absolutely crazy—then the dirty bastards turn around afterwards, and who is the first one on their list to persecute? who haven't they left their hands off of to murder and to hate for two thousand years? The Jews! who gave them their beloved Jesus to begin with! I assure you, Alex, you are never going to hear such a *mishegoss* of mixed-up crap and disgusting nonsense as the Christian religion in your entire life. And that's what these big shots, so-called, believe!"

Unfortunately, on the home front contempt for the powerful enemy was not so readily available as a defensive strategy—for as time went on, the enemy was more and more *his* own beloved son. Indeed, during that extended period of rage that goes by the name of my adolescence, what terrified me most about my father was not the violence I expected him momentarily to unleash upon me, but the violence I wished every night at the dinner table to commit upon his ignorant, barbaric carcass. How I wanted to send him howling from the land of the living when he ate from the serving bowl with his own fork, or sucked the soup from his spoon instead of politely waiting for it to cool, or attempted, God forbid, to express an opinion on any subject whatsoever . . . And what was especially terrifying about the murderous wish was this: if I tried, chances were I'd succeed! *Chances were he would help me along!* I would have only to leap across the dinner dishes, my fingers aimed at his windpipe, for him instantaneously to sink down beneath the table with his tongue hanging out. Shout he could shout, squabble he could squabble, and oh *nudjh,* could he *nudjh!* But defend himself? against *me?* "Alex, keep this back talk up," my mother warns, as I depart from the roaring kitchen like Attila the Hun, run screaming from yet another half-eaten dinner, "continue with this disrespect and you will give that man a heart attack!" "Good!" I cry, slamming in her face the door to my room. "Fine!" I scream, extracting from my closet the zylon jacket I wear only with my collar up (a style she abhors as much as the filthy garment itself). "Wonderful!" I shout, and with streaming eyes run to the corner to vent my fury on the pinball machine.

Christ, in the face of my defiance—if my father had only been my mother! and my mother my father! But what a mix-up of the sexes in our house! Who should by rights be advancing on me, retreating—and who should be retreating, advancing! Who should be scolding, collapsing in helplessness, enfeebled totally by a tender heart! And who should be collapsing, instead scolding, correcting, reproving, criticizing, faultfinding without end! Filling the patriarchal vacuum! Oh, thank God! thank God! at least *he* had the cock and the balls! Pregnable (putting it mildly) as his masculinity was in this world of *goyim* with golden hair and silver tongues, between his legs (God bless my father!) he was constructed like a man of consequence, two big healthy balls such as a king would be proud to put on display, and a *shlong* of magisterial length and girth. And they were *his:* yes, of this I am absolutely certain, they hung down off of, they were connected on to, they could not be taken away from, *him!*

Of course, around the house I saw less of his sexual apparatus than I did of her erogenous zones. And once I saw her menstrual blood . . . saw it shining darkly up at me from the worn linoleum in front of the kitchen sink. Just two red drops over a quarter of a century ago, but they glow still in that icon of her that hangs, perpetually illuminated, in my Modern Museum of Gripes and Grievances (along with the box of Kotex and the nylon stockings, which I want to come to in a moment). Also in this icon is an endless dripping of blood down through a drainboard into a dishpan. It is the blood she is draining from the meat so as to make it kosher and fit for consumption. Probably I am confusing things—I sound like a son of the House of Atreus with all this talk of blood—but I see her standing at the sink salting the meat so as to rid it of its blood, when the attack of "woman's troubles" sends her, with a most alarming moan, rushing off to her bedroom. I was no more than four or five, and yet those two drops of blood that I beheld on the floor of her kitchen are visible to me still . . . as is the box of Kotex . . . as are the stockings sliding up her legs . . . as is—need I even say it?—the bread knife with which my own blood would be threatened when I refuse to eat my dinner. That knife! *That knife!* What gets me is that she herself did not even consider the use of it anything to be ashamed of, or particularly reticent about. From my bed I hear her babbling about her problems to the women around the mah-jongg game: *My Alex is suddenly such a bad eater I have to stand over him with a knife.* And none of them apparently finds this tactic of hers at all excessive. I have to stand over him with a knife! And not one of those women gets up from the mah-jongg table and walks out of her house! Because in their world, that is the way it is with bad eaters—you have to stand over them *with a knife!*

It was years later that she called from the bathroom, Run to the drugstore! bring a box of Kotex! immediately! And the panic in her voice. Did I run! And then at home again, breathlessly handed the box to the white fingers that extended themselves at me through a narrow crack in the bathroom door . . . Though her menstrual troubles eventually had to be resolved by surgery, it is difficult nevertheless to forgive her for having sent me on that mission of mercy. Better she should have bled herself out on our cold bathroom floor, better *that,* than to have sent an eleven-year-old boy in hot pursuit of sanitary napkins! Where was my sister, for Christ's sake? Where was her own emergency supply? Why was this woman so grossly insensitive to the vulnerability of her own little boy—on the one hand so insensitive to my shame, and yet on the other, so attuned to my deepest desires!

. . . I am so small I hardly know what sex I am, or so you would imagine. It is early in the afternoon, spring of the year Four. Flowers are standing up in purple stalks in the patch of dirt outside our building. With the windows flung open the air in the apartment is fragrant, soft with the season—and yet electric too with my mother's vitality: she has finished the week's wash and hung it on the line; she has baked a marble cake for our dessert tonight, beautifully bleeding—there's that blood again! there's that knife again!—anyway expertly bleeding the chocolate in and out of the vanilla, an accomplishment that seems to me as much of a miracle as getting those peaches to hang there sus- pended in the shimmering mold of jello. She has done the laundry and baked the cake; she has scrubbed the kitchen and bathroom floors and laid them with newspapers; she has of course dusted; needless to say, she has vacuumed; she has cleared and washed our luncheon dishes and (with my cute little assistance) returned them to their place in the *milchiks* cabinet in the pantry—and whistling like a canary all the morning through, a tuneless melody of health and joy, of heedlessness and self- sufficiency. While I crayon a picture for her, she showers—and now in the sunshine of her bedroom, she is dressing to take me downtown. She sits on the edge of the bed in her padded bra and her girdle, rolling on her stockings and chattering away. Who is Mommy's good little boy? Who is the best little boy a mommy ever had? Who does Mommy love more than anything in the whole wide world? I am absolutely punchy with delight, and meanwhile follow in their tight, slow, agonizingly delicious journey up her legs the transparent stockings that give her flesh a hue of stirring dimensions. I sidle close enough to smell the bath powder on her throat—also to appreciate better the elastic intricacies of the dangling straps to which the stockings will presently be hooked (undoubtedly with a flourish of trumpets). I smell the oil with which she has polished the four gleaming posts of the mahogany bedstead, where she sleeps with a man who lives with us at night and on Sunday afternoons. My father they say he is. On my fingertips, even though she has washed each one of those little piggies with a warm wet cloth, I smell my lunch, my tuna fish salad. Ah, it might be cunt I'm sniffing. Maybe it is! Oh, I want to growl with pleasure. Four years old, and yet I sense in my blood—uh-huh, again with the blood—how rich with passion is the moment, how dense with possibility. This fat person with the long hair whom they call my sister is away at school. This man, my father, is off somewhere making money, as best he is able. These two are gone, and who knows, maybe I'll be lucky, maybe they'll never come back . . . In the meantime, it is afternoon, it is spring, and for me and me alone a woman is rolling on her stockings and singing a song of love. Who is going to stay with Mommy forever and ever? *Me.* Who is it who goes with Mommy wherever in the whole wide world Mommy goes? *Why me, of course. What a silly question—but don't get me wrong, I'll play the game!* Who had a nice lunch with Mommy, who goes downtown like a good boy on the bus with Mommy, who goes into the big store with Mommy . . . and on and on and on . . . so that only a week or so ago, upon my safe return from Europe, Mommy had this to say—

"Feel."

"What?"—even as she takes my hand in hers and draws it toward her body—"Mother—"

"I haven't gained five pounds," she says, "since you were born. Feel," she says, and holds my stiff fingers against the swell of her hips, which aren't bad . . .

And the stockings. More than twenty-five years have passed (the game is supposed to be over!), but Mommy still hitches up the stockings in front of her little boy. Now, however, he takes it upon himself to look the other way when the flag goes fluttering up the pole—and out of concern not just for his own mental health. That's the truth, I look away not for me but for the sake of that poor man, my father! Yet what preference does Father really have? If there in the living room their grown-up little boy were to tumble all at once onto the rug with his mommy, what would Daddy do? Pour a bucket of boiling water on the raging, maddened couple? Would he draw *his* knife—or would he go off to the other room and watch television until they were finished? "What are you looking away—?" asks my mother, amused in the midst of straightening her seams. "You'd think I was a twenty-one-year-old girl; you'd think I hadn't wiped your backside and kissed your little tushy for you all those years. Look at him"—this to my father, in case he hasn't been giving a hundred percent of his attention to the little floor show now being performed—"look, acting like his own mother is some sixty-year-old beauty queen."

Once a month my father took me with him down to the *shvitz* bath, there to endeavor to demolish—with the steam, and a rubdown, and a long deep sleep—the pyramid of aggravation he has built himself into during the previous weeks of work. Our street clothes we lock away in the dormitory on the top floor. On rows of iron cots running horizontal to the lockers, the men who have already been through the ringer down below are flung out beneath white sheets like the fatalities of a violent catastrophe. If it were not for the abrupt thunderclap of a fart, or the snores sporadically shooting up around me like machine-gun fire, I would believe we were in a morgue, and for some strange reason undressing in front of the dead. I do not look at the bodies, but like a mouse hop frantically about on my toes, trying to clear my feet of my undershorts before anybody can peek inside, where, to my chagrin, to my bafflement, to my mortification, I always discover in the bottommost seam a pale and wispy brush-stroke of my shit. Oh, Doctor, I wipe and I wipe and I wipe, I spend as much time wiping as I do crapping, maybe even more. I use toilet paper like it grew on trees—so says my envious father—I wipe until that little orifice of mine is red as a raspberry; but still, much as I would like to please my mother by dropping into her laundry hamper at the end of each day jockey shorts such as might have encased the asshole of an angel, I deliver forth instead (deliberately, Herr Doctor? —or just inevitably?) the fetid little drawers of a boy.

But here in a Turkish bath, why am I dancing around? There are no women here. No women—and no *goyim*. Can it be? There is nothing to worry about!

Following the folds at the base of his white buttocks, I proceed out of the dormitory and down the metal stairs to that purgatory wherein the agonies that come of being an insurance agent, a family man, and a Jew will be steamed and beaten from my father's body. At the bottom landing we sidestep a pile of white sheets and a mound of sopping towels, my father pushes a shoulder against a heavy windowless door, and we enter a dark quiet region redolent of wintergreen. The sounds are of a tiny, unenthusiastic audience applauding the death scene in some tragedy: it is the two masseurs walloping and potching at the flesh of their victims, men half-clad in sheets and stretched out across marble slabs. They smack them and knead them and push them around, they slowly twist their limbs as though to remove them in a piece from their sockets —I am hypnotized, but continue to follow after my father as we pass alongside the pool, a small green cube of heart-stopping ice water, and come at last to the steam room.

The moment he pushes open the door the place speaks to me of prehistoric times, earlier even than the era of the cavemen and lake dwellers that I have studied in school, a time when above the oozing bog that was the earth, swirling white gasses choked out the sunlight, and aeons passed while the planet was drained for Man. I lose touch instantaneously with that ass-licking little boy who runs home after school with his A's in his hand, the little overearnest innocent endlessly in search of the key to that unfathomable mystery, his mother's approbation, and am back in some sloppy watery time, before there were families such as we know them, before there were toilets and tragedies such as we know them, a time of amphibious creatures, plunging brainless hulking things, with wet meaty flanks and steaming torsos. It is as though all the Jewish men ducking beneath the cold dribble of shower off in the corner of the steam room, them lumbering back for more of the thick dense suffocating vapors, it is as though they have ridden the time-machine back to an age when they existed as some herd of Jewish animals, whose only utterance is *oy, oy* . . . for this is the sound they make as they drag themselves from the shower into the heavy gush of fumes. They appear, at long last, my father and his fellow sufferers, to have returned to the habitat in which they can be natural. A place without *goyim* and women.

I stand at attention between his legs as he coats me from head to toe with a thick lather of soap—and eye with admiration the baggy substantiality of what overhangs the marble bench upon which he is seated. His scrotum is like the long wrinkled face of some old man with an egg tucked into each of his sagging jowls—while mine might hang from the wrist of some little girl's dolly like a teeny pink purse. And as for his *shlong,* to me, with that fingertip of a prick that my mother likes to refer to in public (once, okay, but that once will last a lifetime) as my "little thing," his *shlong* brings to mind the fire hoses coiled along the corridors at school. *Shlong:* the word somehow catches exactly the brutishness, the *meatishness,* that I admire so, the sheer mindless, weighty, and unselfconscious dangle of that living piece of hose through which he passes streams of water as thick and strong as rope—while I deliver forth slender yellow threads that my euphemistic mother calls "a sis." A sis, I think, is undoubtedly what my sister makes, little yellow threads that you can sew with . . . "Do you want to make a nice sis?" she asks me—when I want to make a torrent, I want to make a flood: I want like he does to shift the tides of the toilet bowl! "Jack," my mother calls to him, "would you close that door, please? Some example you're setting for you know who." But if only that had been so, Mother! If only you-know-who could have found some inspiration in what's-his-name's coarseness! If only I could have nourished myself upon the depths of his vulgarity, instead of that too becoming a source of shame. Shame and shame and shame and shame—every place I turn something else to be ashamed of.

Saul Bellow

MOSBY'S MEMOIRS

Dear Mr. Burnett:

I wrote *Mosby's Memoirs* on six successive mornings in the
Mexican town of Oaxaca without the aid of tequila. I seemed
to need no stimulants. I was in a state of all but intolerable excitement, or was, as the young now say, "turned on." A young
and charming friend typed the manuscript for me. Reading it I
found little to change. The words had come readily. I felt as they
went into the story that I was striking them with a mallet. I
seldom question what I have written in such a state. I simply feel
gratitude and let it go at that.

Sincerely,
Saul Bellow

The birds chirped away. Fweet, Fweet, Bootchee-Fweet. Doing all the things naturalists say they do. Expressing abysmal depths of aggression, which only Man—Stupid Man—heard as innocence. We feel everything is so innocent—because our wickedness is so fearful. Oh, very fearful!

Mr. Willis Mosby, after his siesta, gazing down-mountain at the town of Oaxaca where all were snoozing still—mouths, rumps, long black Indian hair, the antique beauty photographically celebrated by Eisenstein in *Thunder over Mexico.* Mr. Mosby—Dr. Mosby really; erudite, maybe even profound; thought much, accomplished much—had made some of the most interesting mistakes a man could make in the twentieth century. He was in Oaxaca now to write his memoirs. He had a grant for the purpose, from the Guggenheim Foundation. And why not?

Bougainvillaea poured down the hillside, and the hummingbirds were spinning. Mosby felt ill with all this whirling, these colors, fragrances, ready to topple on him. Liveliness, beauty, seemed very dangerous. Mortal danger. Maybe he had drunk too much mescal at lunch (beer, also). Behind the green and red of Nature, dull black seemed to be thickly laid like mirror backing.

Mosby did not feel quite well; his teeth, gripped tight, made the muscles stand out in his handsome, elderly tanned jaws. He had fine blue eyes, light-pained, direct, intelligent, disbelieving; hair still thick, parted in the middle; and strong vertical grooves between the brows, beneath the nostrils, and at the back of the neck.

The time had come to put some humor into the memoirs. So far it

had been: Fundamentalist family in Missouri—Father the successful
builder—Early schooling—The State University—Rhodes Scholarship—
Intellectual friendships—What I learned from Professor Collingwood—
Empire and the mental vigor of Britain—My unorthodox interpretation
of John Locke—I work for William Randolph Hearst in Spain—The
personality of General Franco—Radical friendships in New York—
Wartime service with the O.S.S.—The limited vision of Franklin D.
Roosevelt—Comte, Proudhon, and Marx revisited—De Tocqueville once
again.

Nothing very funny here. And yet thousands of students and others
would tell you, "Mosby had a great sense of humor." Would tell their
children, "This Mosby in the O.S.S.," or "Willis Mosby, who was in
Toledo with me when the Alcázar fell, made me die laughing." "I shall
never forget Mosby's observations on Harold Laski." "On packing the
Supreme Court." "On the Russian purge trials." "On Hitler."

So it was certainly high time to do something. He had given it some
consideration. He would say, when they sent down his ice from the hotel
bar (he was in a cottage below the main building, flowers heaped upon
it; envying a little the unencumbered mountains of the Sierra Madre)
and when he had chilled his mescal—warm, it tasted rotten—he would
write that in 1947, when he was living in Paris, he knew any number
of singular people. He knew the Comte de la Mine-Crevée, who sheltered
Gary Davis the World Citizen after the World Citizen had burnt his
passport publicly. He knew Mr. Julian Huxley at UNESCO. He discussed social theory with Mr. Lévi-Straus but was not invited to dinner
—they ate at the Musée de l'Homme. Sartre refused to meet with him;
he thought all Americans, Negroes excepted, were secret agents. Mosby
for his part suspected all Russians abroad of working for the G.P.U.
Mosby knew French well; extremely fluent in Spanish; quite good in
German. But the French cannot identify originality in foreigners. That
is the curse of an old civilization. It is a heavier planet. Its best minds
must double their horsepower to overcome the gravitational field of
tradition. Only a few will ever fly. To fly away from Descartes. To fly
away from the political anachronisms of left, center, and right persisting
since 1789. Mosby found these French exceedingly banal. These French
found him lean and tight. In well-tailored clothes, elegant and dry, his
good Western skin, pale eyes, strong nose, handsome mouth, and virile
creases. *Un type sec.*

Both sides—Mosby and the French, that is—with highly developed
attitudes. Both, he was lately beginning to concede, quite wrong. Possibly

equidistant from the truth, but lying in different sectors of error. The French were worse off because their errors were collective. Mine, Mosby believed, were at least peculiar. The French were furious over the collapse in 1940 of *La France Pourrie,* their lack of military will, the extensive collaboration, the massive deportations unopposed (the Danes, even the *Bulgarians* resisted Jewish deportations), and, finally, over the humiliation of liberation by the Allies. Mosby, in the O.S.S., had information to support such views. Within the State Department, too, he had university colleagues —former students and old acquaintances. He had expected a high post-war appointment, for which, as director of counter-espionage in Latin America, he was ideally qualified. But Dean Acheson personally disliked him. Nor did Dulles approve. Mosby, a fanatic about *ideas,* displeased the institutional gentry. He had said that the Foreign Service was staffed by rejects of the power structure. Young gentlemen from good Eastern colleges who couldn't make it as Wall Street lawyers were allowed to interpret the alleged interests of their class in the State Department bureaucracy. In foreign consulates they could be rude to D.P.s and indulge their country-club anti-Semitism, which was dying out even in the country clubs. Besides, Mosby had sympathized with the Burnham position on managerialism, declaring, during the war, that the Nazis were winning because they had made their managerial revolution first. No Allied combination could conquer, with its obsolete indus-trialism, a nation which had reached a new state of history and tapped the power of the inevitable, etc. And then Mosby, holding forth in Washington, among the elite Scotch drinkers, stated absolutely that however deplorable the concentration camps had been, they showed at least the rationality of German political ideas. The Americans had no such ideas. They didn't know what they were doing. No design existed. The British were not much better. The Hamburg fire-bombing, he argued in his clipped style, in full declarative phrases, betrayed the idiotic emptiness and planlessness of Western leadership. Finally, he said that when Acheson blew his nose there were maggots in his handkerchief.

Among the defeated French, Mosby admitted that he had a galled spirit. (His jokes were not too bad.) And of course he drank a lot. He worked on Marx and Tocqueville, and he drank. He would not cease from mental strife. The Comte de la Mine-Crevée (Mosby's own im-provisation on a noble and ancient name) kept him in PX booze and exchanged his money on the black market for him. He described his swindles and was very entertaining.

Mosby now wished to say, in the vein of Sir Harold Nicolson or

Santayana or Bertrand Russell, writers for whose memoirs he had the
greatest admiration, that Paris in 1947, like half a Noah's Ark, was waiting
for the second of each kind to arrive. There was one of everything.
Something of this sort. Especially among Americans. The city was very
bitter, grim; the Seine looked and smelled like medicine. At an American
party, a former student of French from Minnesota, now running a shady
enterprise, an agency which specialized in bribery, private undercover
investigations, and procuring broads for V.I.P.s, said something highly
emotional about the City of Man, about the meaning of Europe for Americans, the American failure to preserve human scale. Not omitting to
work in Man the Measure. And every other tag he could bring back
from Randall's *Making of the Modern Mind* or *Readings in the Intellectual
History of Europe*. "I was tempted," Mosby meant to say (the ice arrived
in a glass jar with tongs; the natives no longer wore the dirty white
drawers of the past). "Tempted . . ." He rubbed his forehead, which
projected like the back of an observation car. "To tell this sententious
little drunkard and gyp artist, formerly a pacifist and vegetarian, follower
of Gandhi at the University of Minnesota, now drivng a very handsome
Bentley to the Tour d'Argent to eat duck *à l'orange*. Tempted to say,
'Yes, but we come here across the Atlantic to relax a bit in the past.
To recall what Ezra Pound had once said. That we would make another Venice, just for the hell of it, in the Jersey marshes any time we
liked. Toying. To divert ourselves in the time of colossal mastery to
come. Reproducing anything, for fun. Baboons trained to row will bring
us in gondolas to discussions of astrophysics. Where folks burn garbage
now, and fatten pigs and junk their old machines, we will debark to hear
a concert.' "

Mosby the thinker, like other busy men, never had time for music.
Poetry was not his cup of tea. Members of Congress, Cabinet officers,
Organization Men, Pentagon planners, Party leaders, Presidents had no
such interest. They could not be what they were and read Eliot, hear
Vivaldi, Cimarosa. But they planned that others might enjoy these things
and benefit by their power. Mosby perhaps had more in common with
political leaders and Joint Chiefs and Presidents. At least, they were in
his thoughts more often than Cimarosa and Eliot. With hate, he pondered
their mistakes, their shallowness. Lectured on Locke to show them up.
Except by the will of the majority, unambiguously expressed, there was
no legitimate power. The only absolute democrat in America (perhaps in
the world—although who can know what there is in the world, among
so many billions of minds and souls) was Willis Mosby. Norwithstanding

his terse, dry, intolerant style of conversation (more precisely, examination), his lank dignity of person, his aristocratic bones. Dark long nostrils hinting at the afflictions that needed the strength you could see in his jaws. And, finally, the light-pained eyes.

A most peculiar, ingenious, hungry, aspiring, and heartbroken animal, who, by calling himself Man, thinks he can escape being what he really is. Not a matter of his definition, in the last analysis, but of his being. Let him say what he likes.

> Kingdoms are clay: our dungy earth alike
> Feeds beast as man; the nobleness of life
> Is to do thus.

Thus being love. Or any other sublime option. (Mosby knew his Shakespeare anyway. *There* was a difference from the President. And of the Vice-President he said, "I wouldn't trust him to make me a pill. A has-been druggist!")

With sober lips he sipped the mescal, the servant in the coarse orange shirt enriched by metal buttons reminding him that the car was coming at four o'clock to take him to Mitla, to visit the ruins.

"Yo mismo soy una ruina," Mosby joked.

The stout Indian, giving only so much of a smile—no more—withdrew with quiet courtesy. Perhaps I was fishing, Mosby considered. Wanted him to say I was *not* a ruin. But how could he? Seeing that for him I *am* one.

Perhaps Mosby did not have a light touch. Still, he thought he did have an eye for certain kinds of comedy. And he *must* find a way to relieve the rigor of this account of his mental wars. Besides, he could really remember that in Paris at that time people, one after another, revealed themselves in a comic light. He was then seeing things that way. Rue Jacob, Rue Bonaparte, Rue du Bac, Rue de Verneuil, Hôtel de l'Université —filled with funny people.

He began by setting down a name: Lustgarten. Yes, there was the man he wanted. Hymen Lustgarten, a Marxist, or former Marxist, from New Jersey. From Newark, I think. He had been a shoe salesman, and belonged to any number of heretical, fanatical, bolshevistic groups. He had been a Leninist, a Trotskyist, then a follower of Hugo Oehler, then of Thomas Stamm, and finally of an Italian named Salemme who gave up politics to become a painter, an abstractionist. Lustgarten also gave up politics. He wanted now to be successful in business—rich. Believing that the nights he had spent poring over *Das Kapital* and Lenin's *State and Revolution* would give him an edge in business dealings. We were staying in the same hotel. I couldn't at first make out what he and his wife were doing. Presently I understood. The black market. This was not then reprehensible. Postwar Europe was like that. Refugees, adventurers, G.I.s. Even the Comte de la M.-C. Europe still shuddering from the blows it had received. Governments new, uncertain, infirm. No reason to respect their authority. American soldiers led the way. Flamboyant business schemes. Machines, whole factories, stolen, treasures shipped home. An American colonel in the lumber business started to saw up the Black Forest and send it to Wisconsin. And, of course, Nazis concealing their concentration-camp loot. Jewels sunk in Austrian lakes. Art works hidden. Gold extracted from teeth in extermination camps, melted into ingots and mortared like bricks into the walls of houses. Incredibly huge fortunes to be made, and Lustgarten intended to make one of them. Unfortunately, he was incompetent.

You could see at once that there was no harm in him. Despite the bold revolutionary associations, and fierceness of doctrine. Theoretical willingness to slay class enemies. But Lustgarten could not even hold his own with pushy people in a *pissoir*. Strangely meek, stout, swarthy, kindly, grinning with mulberry lips, a groggy, curving mouth which produced wrinkles like gills between the ears and the grin. And perhaps, Mosby thought, he comes to mind in Mexico because of his Toltec, Mixtec, Zapotec look, squat and black-haired, the tip of his nose turned downward and the black nostrils shyly widening when his friendly smile was accepted. And a bit sick with the wickedness, the awfulness of life but, respectfully persistent, bound to get his share. Efficiency was his style— action, determination, but a traitorous incompetence trembled within. Wrong calling. Wrong choice. A bad mistake. But he was persistent.

His conversation amused me, in the dining room. He was proud of his revolutionary activities, which had consisted mainly of cranking the mimeograph machine. Internal Bulletins. Thousands of pages of recondite examination of fine points of doctrine for the membership. Whether the American working class should give *material* aid to the Loyalist Government of Spain, controlled as that was by Stalinists and other class enemies and traitors. You had to fight Franco, and you had to fight Stalin as well. There was, of course, no material aid to give. But *had* there been any, *should* it have been given? This purely theoretical problem caused splits and expulsions. I always kept myself informed of these curious agonies of sectarianism, Mosby wrote. The single effort made by Spanish Republicans to purchase arms in the United States was thwarted by that friend of liberty Franklin Delano Roosevelt, who allowed one ship, the *Mar Cantábrico,* to be loaded but set the Coast Guard after it to turn it back to port. It was, I believe, that *genius* of diplomacy, Mr. Cordell Hull, who was responsible, but the decision, of course, was referred to F.D.R., whom Huey Long amusingly called Franklin de la *No!* But perhaps the most refined of these internal discussions left of left, the documents for which were turned out on the machine by that Jimmy Higgins, the tubby devoted party-worker Mr. Lustgarten, had to do with the Finnish War. Here the painful point of doctrine to be resolved was whether a Worker's State like the Soviet Union, even if it was a *degenerate* Workers' State, a product of the Thermidorian Reaction following the glorious Proletarian Revolution of 1917, could wage an Imperialistic War. For only the *bourgeoisie* could be Imperialistic. Technically, Stalinism could not be Imperialism. By definition. What then should a Revolutionary Party say to the Finns? Should they resist Russia or not? The Russians were monsters but they would expropriate the Mannerheim White-Guardist landowners and move, painful though it might be, in the correct historical direction. This, as a sect-watcher, I greatly relished. But it was too foreign a subtlety for many of the sectarians. Who were, after all, Americans. Pragmatists at heart. It was *too* far out for Lustgarten. He decided, after the war, to become (it shouldn't be hard) a rich man. Took his savings and, I believe his wife said, his mother's savings, and went abroad to build a fortune.

Within a year he had lost it all. He was cheated. By a German partner, in particular. But also he was caught smuggling by Belgian authorities.

When Mosby met him (Mosby speaking of himself in the third person as Henry Adams had done in *The Education of Henry Adams*)—when Mosby met him, Lustgarten was working for the American Army, employed by Graves Registration. Something to do with the procurement of crosses. Or with supervision of the lawns. Official employment gave Lustgarten PX privileges. He was rebuilding his financial foundations by the illegal sale of cigarettes. He dealt also in gas-ration coupons which the French Government, anxious to obtain dollars, would give you if you exchanged your money at the legal rate. The gas coupons were sold on the black market. The Lustgartens, husband and wife, persuaded Mosby to do this once. For them, he cashed his dollars at the bank, not with la Mine-Crevée. The occasion seemed important. Mosby gathered that Lustgarten had to drive at once to Munich. He had gone into the dental-supply business there with a German dentist who now denied that they had ever been partners.

Many consultations between Lustgarten (in his international intriguer's trenchcoat, ill-fitting; head, neck, and shoulders sloping backward in a froggy curve) and his wife, a young woman in an eyelet-lace blouse and black velveteen skirt, a velveteen ribbon tied on her round healthy neck. Lustgarten, on the circular floor of the bank, explaining as they stood apart. And sweating blood; being reasonable with Trudy, detail by tortuous detail. It grated away poor Lustgarten's patience. Hands feebly remonstrating. For she asked female questions or raised objections which gave him agonies of patient rationality. Only there was nothing rational to begin with. That is, he had had no legal right to go into business with the German. All such arrangements had to be licensed by Military Government. It was a black-market partnership and when it began to show a profit, the German threw Lustgarten out. With what they call impunity. Germany as a whole having discerned the limits of all civilized systems of punishment as compared with the unbounded possibilities of crime. The bank in Paris, where these explanations between Lustgarten and Trudy were taking place, had an interior of some sort of red porphyry. Like raw meat. A color which bourgeois France seemed to have vested with ideas of potency, mettle, and grandeur. In the Invalides also, Napoleon's sarcophagus was of polished red stone, a great, swooping, polished cradle containing the little green corpse. (We have the testimony of M. Rideau, the Bonpartist historian, as to the color.) As for the living Bonaparte, Mosby felt, with Auguste Comte, that he had been an anachronism. The Revolution was historically necessary. It was socially justified. Politically, economically, it was a move toward industrial democracy. But the Napoleonic drama itself beonged to an archaic category of personal ambitions, feudal ideas of war. Older than feudalism. Older than Rome. The commander at the head of armies— nothing rational to recommend it. Society, increasingly rational in its organization, did not need it. But humankind evidently desired it. War is a luxurious pleasure. Grant the first premise of hedonism and you must accept the rest also. Rational foundations of modernity are cunningly accepted by man as the launching platform of ever wilder irrationalities.

Mosby, noting these reflections in a blue-green color of ink which might have been extracted from the landscape. As his liquor had been extracted from the green spikes of the mescal, the curious sharp, dark-green fleshy limbs of the plant covering the fields.

The dollars, the francs, the gas rations, the bank like the beefsteak mine in which W. C. Fields invested, and shrinking but persistent dark Lustgarten getting into his little car on the sodden Parisian street. There were few cars then in Paris. Plenty of parking space. And the streets were so yellow, gray, wrinkled, dismal. But the French were even then ferociously telling the world that they had the *savoir-vivre,* the *gai savoir.* Especially Americans, haunted by their Protestant Ethic, had to hear this. My God—sit down, sip wine, taste cheese, break bread, hear music, know love, stop running, and learn ancient life-wisdom from Europe. At any rate, Lustgarten buckled up his trenchcoat, pulled down his big hoodlum's fedora. He was bunched up in the seat. Small brown hands holding the steering wheel of the Simca Huit, and the grinning despair with which he waved.

"*Bon voyage,* Lustgarten."

His Zapotec nose, his teeth like white pomegranate seeds. With a sob of the gears he took off for devastated Germany.

Reconstruction is big business. You demolish a society, you decrease the population, and off you go again. New fortunes. Lustgarten may have felt, *qua* Jew, that he had a right to grow rich in the German boom. That all Jews had natural claims beyond the Rhine. On land enriched by Jewish ashes. And you never could be sure, seated on a sofa, that it was not stuffed or upholstered with Jewish hair. And he would not use German soap. He washed his hands, Trudy told Mosby, with Life-buoy from the PX.

Trudy, a graduate of Montclair Teachers' College in New Jersey, knew French, studied composition, had hoped to work with someone like Nadia Boulanger, but was obliged to settle for less. From the bank, as Lustgarten drove away in a kind of doomed, latently tearful daring in the rain-drenched street, Trudy invited Mosby to the Salle Pleyel, to hear a Czech pianist performing Schönberg. This man, with muscular baldness, worked very hard upon the keys. The difficulty of his enter-prise alone came through—the labor of culture, the trouble it took to preserve art in tragic Europe, the devoted drill. Trudy had a nice face for concerts. Her odor was agreeable. She shone. In the left half of her countenance, one eye kept wandering. Stone-hearted Mosby, making fun of flesh and blood, of these little humanities with their short inventories of bad and good. The poor Czech in his blazer with chased buttons and the muscles of his forehead rising in protest against *tabula rasa*— the bare skull.

Mosby could abstract himself on such occasions. Shut out the piano. Continue thinking about Comte. Begone, old priests and feudal soldiers! Go, with Theology and Metaphysics! And in the Positive Epoch En-lightened Woman would begin to play her part, vigilant, preventing the managers of the new society from abusing their powers. Over Labor, the supreme good.

Embroidering the trees, the birds of Mexico, looking at Mosby, and the hummingbird, so neat in its lust, vibrating tinily, and the lizard on the soil drinking heat with its belly. To bless small creatures is supposed to be real good.

Yes, this Lustgarten was a funny man. Cheated in Germany, licked by the partner, and impatient with his slow progress in Graves Registration, he decided to import a Cadillac. Among the new postwar millionaires of Europe there was a big demand for Cadillacs. The French Government, moving slowly, had not yet taken measures against such imports for rapid resale. In 1947, no tax prevented such transactions. Lustgarten got his family in Newark to ship a new Cadillac. Something like four thousand dollars was raised by his brother, his mother, his mother's brother for the purpose. The car was sent. The customer was waiting. A down payment had already been given. A double profit was expected. Only, on the day the car was unloaded at Le Havre new regulations went into effect. The Cadillac could not be sold. Lustgarten was stuck with it. He couldn't even afford to buy gas. The Lustgartens were seen one day moving out of the hotel, into the car. Mrs. Lustgarten went to live with musical friends. Mosby offered Lustgarten the use of his sink for washing and shaving. Weary Lustgarten, defeated, depressed, frightened at last by his own plunging, scraped at his bristles, mornings, with a modest cricket noise, while sighing. All that money—mother's savings, brother's pension. No wonder his eyelids turned blue. And his smile, like a spinster's sachet, the last fragrance ebbed out long ago in the trousseau never used. But the long batrachian lips continued smiling.

Mosby realized that compassion should be felt. But passing in the night the locked, gleaming car, and seeing huddled Lustgarten, sleeping, covered with two coats, on the majestic seat, like Jonah inside Leviathan, Mosby could not say in candor that what he experienced was sympathy. Rather he reflected that this shoe salesman, in America attached to foreign doctrines, who could not relinquish Europe in the New World, was now, in Paris, sleeping in the Cadillac, encased in this gorgeous Fisher Body from Detroit. At home exotic, in Europe a Yankee. His timing was off. He recognized this himself. But believed, in general, that he was too early. A pioneer. For instance, he said, in a voice that creaked with shy assertiveness, the French were only now beginning to be Marxians. He had gone through it all years ago. What did these people know! Ask

them about the Shakhty Engineers! About Lenin's Democratic Central-
ism! About the Moscow Trials! About "Social Fascism"! They were
ignorant. The Revolution having been totally betrayed, these Europeans
suddenly discovered Marx and Lenin. "Eureka!" he said in a high voice.
And it was the Cold War, beneath it all. For should America lose, the
French intellectuals were preparing to collaborate with Russia. And should
America win they could still be free, defiant radicals under American protection.

"You sound like a patriot," said Mosby.

"Well, in a way I am," said Lustgarten. "But I am getting to be
objective. Sometimes I say to myself, 'If you were outside the world, if
you, Lustgarten, didn't exist as a man, what would your opinion be of
this or that?'"

"Disembodied truth."

"I guess that's what it is."

"And what are you going to do about the Cadillac?" said Mosby.

"I'm sending it to Spain. We can sell it in Barcelona."

"But you have to get it there."

"Through Andorra. It's all arranged. Klonsky is driving it."

Klonsky was a Polish Belgian in the hotel. One of Lustgarten's associates,
congenitally dishonest, Mosby thought. Kinky hair, wrinkled eyes like
Greek olives, and a cat nose and cat lips. He wore Russian boots.

But no sooner had Klonsky departed for Andorra, than Lustgarten
received a marvelous offer for the car. A capitalist in Utrecht wanted
it at once and would take care of all excise problems. He had all the
necessary *tuyaux*, unlimited drag. Lustgarten wired Klonsky in Andorra
to stop. He raced down on the night train, recovered the Cadillac, and
started driving back at once. There was no time to lose. But after sitting
up all night on the *rapide*, Lustgarten was drowsy in the warmth of the
Pyrenees and fell asleep at the wheel. He was lucky, he later said, for the
car went down a mountainside and might have missed the stone wall that
stopped it. He was only a foot or two from death when he was awakened
by the crash. The car was destroyed. It was not insured.

Still faintly smiling, Lustgarten, with his sling and cane, came to
Mosby's café table on the Boulevard Saint-Germain. Sat down. Removed
his hat from dazzling black hair. Asked permission to rest his injured
foot on a chair. "Is this a private conversation?" he said.

Mosby had been chatting with Alfred Ruskin, an American poet.
Ruskin, though some of his front teeth were missing, spoke very clearly
and swiftly. A perfectly charming man. Inveterately theoretical. He had

been saying, for instance, that France had shot its collaborationist poets. America, which had no poets to spare, put Ezra Pound in Saint Elizabeth's. He then went on to say, barely acknowledging Lustgarten, that America had had no history, was not a historical society. His proof was from Hegel. According to Hegel, history was the history of wars and revolutions. The United States had had only one revolution and very few wars. Therefore it was historically empty. Practically a vacuum.

Ruskin also used Mosby's conveniences at the hotel, being too fastidious for his own latrine in the Algerian back-streets of the Left Bank. And when he emerged from the bathroom he invariably had a topic sentence.

"I have discovered the main defect of Kierkegaard."

Or, "Pascal was terrified by universal emptiness, but Valéry says the difference between empty space and space in a bottle is only quantitative, and there is nothing intrinsically terrifying about quantity. What is your view?"

We do not live in bottles—Mosby's reply.

Lustgarten said when Ruskin left us, "Who is that fellow? He mooched you for the coffee."

"Ruskin," said Mosby.

"*That* is Ruskin?"

"Yes, why?"

"I hear my wife was going out with Ruskin while I was in the hospital."

"Oh, I wouldn't believe such rumors," said Mosby. "A cup of coffee, an apéritif together, maybe."

"When a man is down on his luck," said Lustgarten, "it's the rare woman who won't give him hell in addition."

"Sorry to hear it," Mosby replied.

And then, as Mosby in Oaxaca recalled, shifting his seat from the sun—for he was already far too red, and his face, bones, eyes, seemed curiously thirsty—Lustgarten had said, "It's been a terrible experience."

"Undoubtedly so, Lustgarten. It must have been frightening."

"What crashed was my last stake. It involved family. Too bad in a way that I wasn't killed. My insurance would at least have covered my kid brother's loss. And my mother and uncle."

Mosby had no wish to see a man in tears. He did not care to sit through these moments of suffering. Such unmastered emotion was abhorrent. Though perhaps the violence of this abomination might have told Mosby something about his own moral constitution. Perhaps Lustgarten did not want his face to be working. Or tried to subdue his agitation, seeing from Mosby's austere, though not unkind, silence that this was not his way. Mosby was by taste a Senecan. At least he admired Spanish masculinity—the *varonil* of Lorca. The *clavel varonil,* the manly red carnation, the clear classic hardness of honorable control.

"You sold the wreck for junk, I assume?"

"Klonsky took care of it. Now look, Mosby. I'm through with that. I was reading, thinking in the hospital. I came over to make a pile. Like the gold rush. I really don't know what got into me. Trudy and I were just sitting around during the war. I was too old for the draft. And we both wanted action. She in music. Or life. Excitement. You know, dreaming at Montclair Teachers' College of the Big Time. I wanted to make it possible for her. Keep up with the world, or something. But really—in my hospital bed I realized—I was right the first time. I am a Socialist. A natural idealist. Reading about Attlee, I felt at home again. It became clear that I am still a political animal."

Mosby wished to say, "No, Lustgarten. You're a dandler of swarthy little babies. You're a piggyback man—a giddyap horsie. You're a sweet old Jewish Daddy." But he said nothing.

"And I also read," said Lustgarten, "about Tito. Maybe the Tito alternative is the real one. Perhaps there is hope for Socialism somewhere between the Labour Party and the Yugoslav type of leadership. I feel it my duty," Lustgarten told Mosby, "to investigate. I'm thinking of going to Belgrade."

"As what?"

"As a matter of fact, that's where you could come in," said Lustgarten. "If you would be so kind. You're not *just* a scholar. You wrote a book on Plato, I've been told."

"On the *Laws.*"

"And other books. But in addition you know the Movement. Lots of people. More connections than a switchboard. . . ."

The slang of the forties.

"You know people at the *New Leader?*"

"Not my type of paper," said Mosby. "I'm actually a political conservative. Not what you would call a Rotten Liberal but an out-and-out conservative. I shook Franco's hand, you know."

"Did you?"

"This very hand shook the hand of the Caudillo. Would you like to touch it for yourself?"

"Why should I?"

"Go on," said Mosby. "It may mean something. Shake the hand that shook the hand."

Very strangely, then, Lustgarten extended padded, swarthy fingers. He looked partly subtle, partly ill. Grinning, he said, "Now I've made contact with real politics at last. But I'm serious about the *New Leader*. You probably know Bohn. I need credentials for Yugoslavia."

"Have you ever written for the papers?"

"For the *Militant*."

"What did you write?"

Guilty Lustgarten did not lie well. It was heartless of Mosby to amuse himself in this way.

"I have a scrapbook somewhere," said Lustgarten.

But it was not necessary to write to the *New Leader*. Lustgarten, encountered two days later on the Boulevard, near the pork butcher, had taken off the sling and scarcely needed the cane. He said, "I'm going to Yugoslavia. I've been invited."

"By whom?"

"Tito. The Government. They're asking interested people to come as guests to tour the country and see how they're building Socialism. Oh, I know," he quickly said, anticipating standard doctrinal objection, "you don't build Socialism in one country, but it's no longer the same situation. And I really believe Tito may redeem Marxism by actually transforming the dictatorship of the proletariat. This brings me back to my first love—the radical movement. I was never meant to be an entrepreneur."

"Probably not."

"I feel some hope," Lustgarten shyly said. "And then also, it's getting to be spring." He was wearing his heavy moose-colored bristling hat, and bore many other signs of interminable winter. A candidate for resurrection. An opportunity for the grace of life to reveal itself. But perhaps, Mosby thought, a man like Lustgarten would never, except with supernatural aid, exist in a suitable form.

"Also," said Lustgarten touchingly, "this will give Trudy time to reconsider."

"Is that the way things are with you two? I'm sorry."

"I wish I could take her with me, but I can't swing that with the Yugoslavs. It's sort of a V.I.P. deal. I guess they want to affect foreign radicals. There'll be seminars in dialectics, and so on. I love it. But it's not Trudy's dish."

Steady-handed, Mosby on his patio took ice with tongs, and poured more mescal flavored with *gusano de maguey*—a worm or slug of delicate flavor. These notes on Lustgarten pleased him. It was essential, at this

point in his memoirs, to disclose new depths. The preceding chapters
had been heavy. Many unconventional things were said about the state
of political theory. The weakness of conservative doctrine, the lack, in
America, of conservative alternatives, of resistance to the prevailing
liberalism. As one who had personally tried to create a more rigorous
environment for slovenly intellectuals, to force them to do their homework,
to harden the categories of political thought, he was aware that on the
Right as on the Left the results were barren. Absurdly, the college-bred
dunces of America had longed for a true Left Wing movement on the
European model. They still dreamed of it. No less absurd were the Right
Wing idiots. You cannot grow a rose in a coal mine. Mosby's own Right
Wing graduate students had disappointed him. Just a lot of television
actors. Bad guys for the Susskind interview programs. They had transformed the master's manner of acid elegance, logical tightness, factual
punctiliousness, and merciless laceration in debate into a sort of shallow
Noël Coward style. The real, the original Mosby approach brought
Mosby hatred, got Mosby fired. Princeton University had offered Mosby
a lump sum to retire seven years early. One hundred and forty thousand
dollars. Because his mode of discourse was so upsetting to the academic
community. Mosby was invited to no television programs. He was like
the Guerrilla Mosby of the Civil War. When he galloped in, all were
slaughtered.

Most carefully, Mosby had studied the memoirs of Santayana, Malraux,
Sartre, Lord Russell, and others. Unfortunately, no one was reliably or
consistently great. Men whose lives had been devoted to thought, who had
tried mightily to govern the disorder of public life, to put it under some
sort of intellectual authority, to get ideas to save mankind or to offer it
mental aid in saving itself, would suddenly turn into gruesome idiots.
Wanting to kill everyone. For instance, Sartre calling for the Russians
to drop A-bombs on American bases in the Pacific because America
was now presumably monstrous. And exhorting the Blacks to butcher
the Whites. This moral philosopher! Or Russell, the Pacifist of World
War I, urging the West to annihilate Russia after World War II. And
sometimes, in his memoirs—perhaps he was gaga—strangely illogical.
When, over London, a Zeppelin was shot down, the bodies of Germans
were seen to fall, and the brutal men in the street horribly cheered,
Russell wept, and had there not been a beautiful woman to console
him in bed that night, this heartlessness of mankind would have broken
him utterly. What was omitted was the fact that these same Germans

who fell from the Zeppelin had come to bomb the city. They were going to blow up the brutes in the street, explode the lovers. This Mosby saw.

It was earnestly to be hoped—this was the mescal attempting to invade his language—that Mosby would avoid the common fate of intellectuals. The Lustgarten digression should help. The correction of pride by laughter.

There were twenty minutes yet before the chauffeur came to take the party to Mitla, to the ruins. Mosby had time to continue. To say that in September the Lustgarten who reappeared looked frightful. He had lost no less than fifty pounds. Sun-blackened, creased, in a filthy stained suit, his eyes infected. He said he had had diarrhea all summer.

"What did they feed their foreign V.I.P.s?"

And Lustgarten shyly bitter—the lean face and inflamed eyes materializing from a spiritual region very different from any heretofore associated with Lustgarten by Mosby—said, "It was just a chain gang. It was hard labor. I didn't understand the deal. I thought we were invited, as I told you. But we turned out to be foreign volunteers of construction. A labor brigade. And up in the mountains. Never saw the Dalmatian coast. Hardly even shelter for the night. We slept on the ground and ate shit fried in rancid oil."

"Why didn't you run away?" asked Mosby.

"How? Where?"

"Back to Belgrade. To the American Embassy at least?"

"How could I? I was a guest. Came at their expense. They held the return ticket."

"And no money?"

"Are you kidding? Dead broke. In Macedonia. Near Skoplje. Bug-stung, starved, and running to the latrine all night. Laboring on the roads all day, with pus in my eyes, too."

"No first aid?"

"They may have had the first, but they didn't have the second."

Mosby thought it best to say nothing of Trudy. She had divorced him. Commiseration, of course.

Mosby shaking his head.

Lustgarten with a certain skinny dignity walking away. He himself seemed amused by his encounters with Capitalism and Socialism.

The end? Not quite. There was a coda: The thing had quite good form.

Lustgarten and Mosby met again. Five years later. Mosby enters an elevator in New York. Express to the forty-seventh floor, the executive dining room of the Rangeley Foundation. There is one other passenger, and it is Lustgarten. Grinning. He is himself again, filled out once more.

"Lustgarten!"

"Willis Mosby!"

"How are you, Lustgarten?"

"I'm great. Things are completely different. I'm happy. Successful. Married. Children."

"In New York?"

"Wouldn't live in the U.S. again. It's godawful. Inhuman. I'm visiting."

Without a blink in its brilliancy, without a hitch in its smooth, regulated power, the elevator containing only the two of us was going up. The same Lustgarten. Strong words, vocal insufficiency, the Zapotec nose, and under it the frog smile, the kindly gills.

"Where are you going now?"

"Up to *Fortune*," said Lustgarten. "I want to sell them a story."

He was on the wrong elevator. This one was not going to *Fortune*. I told him so. Perhaps I had not changed either. A voice which for many years had informed people of their errors said, "You'll have to go down again. The other bank of elevators."

At the forty-seventh floor we emerged together.

"Where are you settled now?"

"In Algiers," said Lustgarten. "We have a Laundromat there."

"We?"

"Klonsky and I. You remember Klonsky?"

They had gone legitimate. They were washing burnooses. He was married to Klonsky's sister. I saw her picture. The image of Klonsky, a cat-faced woman, head ferociously encased in kinky hair, Picasso eyes at different levels, sharp teeth. If fish, dozing in the reefs, had nightmares, they would be of such teeth. The children also were young Klonskys. Lustgarten had the snapshots in his wallet of North African leather. As he beamed, Mosby recognized that pride in his success was Lustgarten's opiate, his artificial paradise.

"I thought," said Lustgarten, "that *Fortune* might like a piece on how we made it in North Africa."

We then shook hands again. Mine the hand that had shaken Franco's hand—his that had slept on the wheel of the Cadillac. The lighted case opened for him. He entered in. It shut.

Thereafter, of course, the Algerians threw out the French, expelled the Jews. And Jewish-Daddy-Lustgarten must have moved on. Passionate fatherhood. He loved those children. For Plato this childbreeding is the lowest level of creativity.

Still, Mosby thought, under the influence of mescal, my parents begot me like a committee of two.

From a feeling of remotion, though he realized that the car for Mitla had arrived, a shining conveyance waited, he noted the following as he gazed at the afternoon mountains:

> Until he was some years old
> People took care of him
> Cooled his soup, sang, chirked,
> Drew on his long stockings,
> Carried him upstairs sleeping.
> He recalls at the green lakeside
> His father's solemn navel,
> Nipples like dog's eyes in the hair
> Mother's thigh with wisteria of blue veins.
>
> After they retired to death,
> He conducted his own business
> Not too modestly, not too well.
> But here he is, smoking in Mexico
> Considering the brown mountains
> Whose fat laps are rolling
> On the skulls of whole families.

Two Welsh women were his companions. One was very ancient, lank. The Wellington of lady travelers. Or like C. Aubrey Smith, the actor who used to command Gurkha regiments in movies about India. A great nose, a gaunt jaw, a pleated lip, a considerable mustache. The other was younger. She had a small dewlap, but her cheeks were round and dark eyes witty. A very satisfactory pair. Decent was the word. English traits. Like many Americans, Mosby desired such traits for himself. Yes, he was pleased with the Welsh ladies. Though the guide was unsuitable. Overweening. His fat cheeks a red pottery color. And he drove too fast.

The first stop was at Tule. They got out to inspect the celebrated Tule tree in the churchyard. This monument of vegetation, intricately and densely convolved, a green cypress, more than two thousand years old, roots in a vanished lake bottom, older than the religion of this little heap of white and gloom, this charming peasant church. In the comfortable dust, a dog slept. Disrespectful. But unconscious. The old lady, quietly dauntless, tied on a scarf and entered the church. Her stiff genuflection had real quality. She must be Christian. Mosby looked into the depths of the Tule. A world in itself! It could contain communities. In fact, if he recalled his Gerald Heard, there was supposed to be a primal tree occupied by early ancestors, the human horde housed in such appealing, dappled, commodious, altogether beautiful organisms. The facts seemed not to support this golden myth of an encompassing paradise. Earliest man probably ran about on the ground, horribly violent, killing everything. Still, this dream of gentleness, this aspiration for arboreal peace was no small achievement for the descendants of so many killers. For his religion, this tree would do, thought Mosby. No church for him.

He was sorry to go. *He* could have lived up there. On top, of course. The excrements would drop on you below. But the Welsh ladies were already in the car, and the bossy guide began to toot the horn. Waiting was hot.

The road to Mitla was empty. The heat made the landscape beautifully crooked. The driver knew geology, archaeology. He was quite ugly with his information. The Water Table, the Caverns, the Triassic Period. Inform me no further! Vex not my soul with more detail. I cannot use what I have! And now Mitla appeared. The right fork continued to Tehuantepec. The left brought you to the Town of Souls. Old Mrs. Parsons (Elsie Clews Parsons, as Mosby's mental retrieval system told him) had done ethnography here, studied the Indians in these baked streets of adobe and fruit garbage. In the shade, a dark urinous tang. A long-legged pig struggling on a tether. A sow. From behind, observant Mosby identified its pink small female opening. The dungy earth feeding beast as man.

But here were the fascinating temples, almost intact. This place the Spanish priests had not destroyed. All others they had razed, building churches on the same sites, using the same stones.

A tourist market. Coarse cotton dresses, Indian embroidery, hung under flour-white tarpaulins, the dust settling on the pottery of the region, black saxophones, black trays of glazed clay.

Following the British travelers and the guide, Mosby was going once more through an odd and complex fantasy. It was that he was dead. He had died. He continued, however, to live. His doom was to live life to the end as Mosby. In the fantasy, he considered this his purgatory. And when had death occurred? In a collision years ago. He had thought it a near thing then. The cars were demolished. The actual Mosby was killed. But another Mosby was pulled from the car. A trooper asked, "You okay?"

Yes, he was okay. Walked away from the wreck. But he still had the whole thing to do, step by step, moment by moment. And now he heard a parrot babbling, and children panhandled him and women made their pitch, and he was getting his shoes covered with dust. He had been working at his memoirs and had provided a diverting recollection of a funny man—Lustgarten. In the manner of Sir Harold Nicolson. Much less polished, admittedly, but in accordance with a certain protocol, the language of diplomacy, of mandarin irony. However certain facts had been omitted. Mosby had arranged, for instance, that Trudy should be seen with Alfred Ruskin. For when Lustgarten was crossing the Rhine, Mosby was embracing Trudy in bed. Unlike Lord Russell's beautiful friend, she did not comfort Mosby for the disasters he had (by intellectual commitment) to confront. But Mosby had not advised her about leaving Lustgarten. He did not mean to interfere. However, his vision of Lustgarten as a funny man was transmitted to Trudy. She could not be the wife of such a funny man. But he *was,* he *was* a funny man! He was, like Napoleon in the eyes of Comte, an anachronism. Inept, he wished to be a colossus, something of a Napoleon himself, make millions, conquer Europe, retrieve from Hitler's fall a colossal fortune. Poorly imagined, unoriginal, the rerun of old ideas, and so inefficient. Lustgarten didn't have to happen. And so he *was* funny. Trudy too was funny, however. What a large belly she had. Since individuals are sometimes born from a twin impregnation, the organism carrying the undeveloped brother or sister in vestigial form—at times no more than an extra organ, a rudimentary eye buried in the leg, or a kidney or the beginnings of an ear somewhere in the back—Mosby often thought that Trudy had a little sister inside her. And to him she was a clown. This need not mean contempt. No, he liked her. The eye seemed to wander in one hemisphere. She did not know how to use perfume. Her atonal compositions were foolish.

At this time, Mosby had been making fun of people.

"Why?"

"Because he had needed to."

"Why?"

"Because!"

The guide explained that the buildings were raised without mortar. The mathematical calculations of the priests had been perfect. The precision of the cut stone was absolute. After centuries you could not find a chink, you could not insert a razor blade anywhere. These geometrical masses were balanced by their own weight. Here the priests lived. The walls had been dyed. The cochineal or cactus louse provided the dye. Here were the altars. Spectators sat where you are standing. The priests used obsidian knives. The beautiful youths played on flutes. Then the flutes were broken. The bloody knife was wiped on the head of the executioner. Hair must have been clotted. And here, the tombs of the nobles. Stairs leading down. The Zapotecs, late in the day, had practiced this form of sacrifice, under Aztec influence.

How game this Welsh crone was. She was beautiful. Getting in and out of these pits, she required no assistance.

Of course you cannot make yourself an agreeable, desirable person. You can't will yourself into it without regard to the things to be done. Imperative tasks. Imperative comprehensions, monstrous compulsions of duty which deform. Men will grow ugly under such necessities. This one a director of espionage. That one a killer.

Mosby had evoked, to lighten the dense texture of his memoirs, a Lustgarten whose doom was this gaping comedy. A Lustgarten who didn't have to happen. But himself, Mosby, also a separate creation, a finished product, standing under the sun on large blocks of stone, on the stairs descending into this pit, he was complete. He had completed himself in this cogitating, unlaughing, stone, iron, nonsensical form.

Having disposed of all things human, he should have encountered God.

Would this occur?

But having so disposed, what God was there to encounter?

But they had now been led below, into the tomb. There was a heavy grille, the gate. The stones were huge. The vault was close. He was oppressed. He was afraid. It was very damp. On the elaborately zigzag-carved walls were thin, thin pipings of fluorescent light. Flat boxes of ground lime were here to absorb moisture. His heart was paralyzed. His lungs would not draw. Jesus! I cannot catch my breath! To be shut in here! To be dead here! Suppose one were! Not as in accidents which ended, but did not quite end, existence. *Dead*-dead. Stooping, he looked for daylight. Yes, it was there. The light was there. The grace of life still there. Or, if not grace, air. Go while you can.

"I must get out," he told the guide. "Ladies, I find it very hard to breathe."

James Jones

THE DIVERS

To ask a writer to select from his own work one short piece about which he can say "This Is My Best" is to present him with an almost impossible task. He will find he likes one thing for one reason, and something else for another. A great many of my own favorite bits in my writing, I find, require on the part of the reader a great deal of information, emotional and character development which have already been imparted to him in the book, in order for him to appreciate the piece itself. Others, which I might think excellent in themselves, will not stand alone outside of the ambiance of the book they were written for. The piece which appears below seems to avoid these pitfalls, and seems to me to be an interesting character study as well as to project emotionally a somewhat dangerous adventure.

James Jones

Paris

The silence was enormous. Only by taking a breath from his regulator could Grant reassure himself he still could hear. He had expected that; but only by thinking about it most seriously could he be sure which way was up and which way down. His only contact with the entire world really, was the thick chain to which he clung thirty feet down. It disappeared ten feet below him, and ten feet above him. And from it some gentle—terrifyingly gentle—omnipotent, ubiquitous force tried perpetually to pull him.

Looking around itself, his mind tried desperately to relate this to some experience he and it might have had together in the past, and failed. Physically, it was a little like being blind, or half-blind. Or, because of the "No Up And No Down," like being an eyeless embryo floating in the womb maybe. Once as a child, to test his eyes, the doctor had put drops in them which dilated the pupils and when he tried to see with them everything was hazy and blurry and would not focus. This was like that. When he put his depth gauge against his facemask, he could by straining his eyes just barely read the luminous numbers. When he moved one hand away to full arm's length, it all but disappeared into invisibility as a shadow. When he wiggled his fingers his eyes could not be sure they moved.

But emotionally, it made him think of something quite else. When he was five years old his father had tried to teach him to swim in a swimming pool by putting a float on his back and pulling him out into the water. He was all right as long as he could stand on the step, or hold onto the ledge on the side, but the moment that his arms and legs, moving in the water, seeking, could find no solid material to support him, he began to scream, literally scream, with rage and fear. It was sheer blind animal-cowardice and panic. No amount of explanation or aid by his father could change it. That was the way he felt now, and he tried hard to swallow it, put it down, down there somewhere in the region of his belly, of his trained abdominal muscles, where he might possibly control it. What in the name of God, really, was he doing here? Lucky was right.

It had all begun auspiciously enough. Heroically, even picturesquely. The bridge here crossed a complex of shallow mangrove swamps, then just as it hit the deeper river channel bent left in a long sweeping curve inland and along the shore to cross the river—a curve the car had failed to make. The big mobile crane, with its huge additional truck of extra equipment and weights, could only be utilized by positioning it on the bridge itself, and it took up a good three feet more than half the roadway. This automatically required a cordon of local police Constables to stop highway traffic a good distance off from the work area and then filter the cars one at a time through the narrow space remaining. That already made the whole affair something of an occasion, a lark. Many of the cars preferred to pull off the long bridge, park, walk back and watch. Many other cars, knowing beforehand of the big flap coming, had driven out from town to watch. So there was quite a considerable crowd hanging over the bridge balustrade or milling around.

Before this audience Bonham directed the positioning of the big crane, after calculating as best he could from the hole in the balustrade the arc of fall the car had taken. A diving dinghy for them to dress out in and dive from, was stationed out in the stream, attached by two hawsers to bridge supports to keep it in position. From it a heavy anchorline would be dropped to where Bonham thought the car was. A Jamaican boatman tended the boat. Orloffski would tend for the divers. Bonham's authority in all of this was immense, formidable. Even police Inspectors took orders from him. Then they two were dressing out in rubber wet-suits because of the chill river water, and then the rest of the gear, under the eyes of the goggling crowd up above.

They had ridden out with their gear in the Constabulary's largest police van with the Chief Inspector in charge of the job. The five of them: himself, Bonham, Orloffski, Doug and Wanda Lou. Lucky and Letta Bonham had chosen to stay at home. On the way Bonham had hauled out a bottle of gin under the eyes of the Chief Inspector, helped himself to a large belt of it, and handed it to Grant. "And we're gonna need at least one more of these snorts before we're done with *this*," he said grimly with his stormcloud smile; "make sure it's in the boat." Everybody drank, including Wanda Lou who was giggling and grinning like a kid on a picnic, the only one abstaining being the colored, rather prim Chief Inspector. But he made no comment. And it was like that with all the rest of it. Whatever they might all think of Bonham, publicly or privately, they needed him now. And he knew it. He was the only one who could do the work that must be done. And he could do it cheaper than any old-fashioned hardhat diver from Kingston that they would have to fly up with his air hoses and compressors and special tender.

In the boat, after the anchorline had been placed to his satisfaction and they were dressed out, Bonham told Grant to go first. In the bow, pointed up stream, the water made a smooth heavy little curl against the forepeak, Grant noted. Bonham handed him a coil of light manila line with a heavy metal clip spliced expertly into one end, a loop of the rope spliced into itself at the other. "The water will be moving you. Look for the anchorline. If you miss it, don't worry. Swim up to the surface to orient yourself in this muck, and swim back upstream to the stern to catch it. Go down it thirty feet and wait for me. I'll be right behind you."

Grant nodded. (He was afraid to speak.) He made a back entry and rolled over to look down, exhaling to make himself sink a little, and saw what he could only describe as a sea of gray skim milk, in which he appeared to be immersed. Then almost immediately on his right, so fast it surprised him, the anchorchain moved slowly past him in a stately way, a shadowline which he grabbed for and caught. The catch brought him up short, like a running man grabbing a tree branch overhead. The line descended below him into nothingness, and when he looked up it ascended above him into nothingness. There was some light in the skim milk, but it did not seem to come from any particular direction and instead was omnipresent. That was when he first got scared. Only his bubbles mounting gave him a sense of direction. It took every ounce of will he possessed, each time, to haul himself another arm's length down the chain in this cold soup. At thirty feet he stopped and waited, and that was where he still was. Where the hell was Bonham?! Peering at the luminous bezel on his diving watch, he read that he had been down here a minute and four seconds. The luminosity of his watch bezel was as warm to him and as sane and as safe as a roaring fire in a fire-place. Where the *fuck* was Bonham?! What the *fuck* was he doing here?!

He remembered Lucky had told him practically the same thing about herself, last night as they were getting ready for bed, after they had gone to bed. They had both by now learned automatically to speak in whispers before the thin walls of the miserable little room. "I don't know what the hell I'm doing here! I really don't! You don't want me! You don't want a woman! You want some kind of a moveable beast, that you can hop on and fuck, after you've spent the day killing fish, and playing with sharks, and then nights getting drunk with your boy friends! Then you want to come home and get laid! I don't like killing, and I don't like dangerous games, or men who like danger, or sportsmen! And I don't like you! I like people who are sensitive, and intelligent, and—and *sensitive!* . . . And *you* don't want *me!* You want a Wanda Lou! That's what you need!" He had lain, cold and silent, and heard her out. He wasn't angry. He was miserable. Did she think he wanted to make this dive? Finally she had said: "All right, you go! Go ahead! But I don't have to! And I'm not going to! I'm not going out there and sit on some boat and suffer agonies! I'm going to stay at Bonham's!—I'm going to stay at Bonham's, and get drunk, by myself!" In the morning she had found she had an ally in Letta Bonham, who didn't want to go either. For the same reasons.

Beside him a shadow appeared in the skim milk soup, and as it came closer—to half an arm's length—he recognized it as Bonham. The big man came close to him, putting his mask almost against Grant's, and studied his face. Grant pointed to his watch and grimaced inside his mask, and made a questioning gesture with his head toward the surface. Bonham frowned inside his own and made an irritable shrug. Some or other damn thing had detained him. Then motioning Grant to follow, he passed him, his coil of manila line over one arm, and started on down hand over hand on the chain. Grant followed, keeping him in sight just inside the circle of visibility, which here seemed to diminish to six or eight feet. It seemed to shrink some as they descended. From below Bonham stopped and glanced up at him once questioningly, a dim apparition, the mask appearing to be one huge Cyclopean eye in the middle of his great head. Grant had seen blind newts, eyeless, in caves in Kentucky. It must have been like this for their remote ancestors, when they began to lose their unneeded sight. The pervasive current had by now become such a part of his existence that his body automatically allowed for it in its movements, a sort of horizontal gravity along which at any moment he could fall.

Bonham wasted no time at all. On the bottom where the heavy anchor rested on what appeared to be mud-silted rock, he clipped his manila line onto a line of the anchorchain ten feet up, motioning Grant to watch. The other end with the loop he made a slipknot out of by pulling the rope back through the loop, and snugged this up tight over his right arm in his right armpit. Then motioning Grant to stay where he was, he took the coil of line in his left hand, let go of the chain and began paying the coil out with his right. Motionless except for his hands, his head toward Grant, he began to move away from Grant backwards, carried downstream by the current. Once, at just about the outer limit of Grant's visibility, he stopped and swam off to his left, then back and off to his right, for all the world like a huge pendulum of some strange horizontal clock swinging in a horizontal gravity. Then he disappeared into the world of skim milk.

Grant watched the rope, hanging onto the chain with one arm, feeling very helpless, very much the neophyte. Twice more it did its pendulous arcing search, then Bonham reappeared in the murk, calmly recoiling the rope as he pulled himself back to the chain. By his gestures he communicated that the car was too far away to work on, that they would have to move the dinghy and anchorchain. Then, almost as an afterthought, he tapped Grant and motioned a question: did Grant want to go and do what he had done. Numbly, Grant nodded.

It was ridiculously easy. Lying relaxed in the water, he payed out on his line and watched Bonham and the anchorline fade from sight. He did not have to arc-search, since Bonham had indicated the wrecked car was at the very end of the manila line, and off to the left toward the bridge supports. When he reached the end of his line, with the slipknot tugging securely at his right armpit he swam thirty, thirty-five feet off to his left, and sure enough there it was, about six feet below him. It seemed sort of unbelievable. It had nosed down some into the layer of silt, but otherwise was sitting upright on its wheels on the slight slope. Two bright spiderwebs on the safety glass of the windshield showed where the people's heads had struck. Staring at it, Grant stopped swimming; and immediately the current began to carry him away from it back to the center of his arc. When he swam a little, he stayed stationary; when he swam a lot, he moved back toward it. He could see what Bonham had meant about the impossibility of working from here. He stopped swimming and let himself be carried. Then he started coiling his line into his left hand. Soon Bonham and the anchorline appeared in the murk. When he was back onto the chain, Bonham motioned that they should go up. Using Bonham's knowledge and techniques he had moved, blind, sixty feet downstream and back, thirty-five feet sideways and back, seen the car, and had expended very little energy. He was beginning to get cold.

Back on top in the boat Bonham gave instructions and then sat and relaxed, breathing deeply, while the boatman and two men on the bridge supports set about moving the boat to where he wanted it. Orloffski changed their tanks for them. They were using the large-size single tanks for this operation, because it was so shallow, but Bonham had brought along a lot of them. "No use having to worry about air too, while you're working."

In the sun-heated air and sunshine the wet-suits very soon began to get uncomfortably warm. After splashing over the side to cool off and opening the zippers of the shirts, they climbed back into the boat and Bonham hauled out his gin bottle. "Well, what do you think of it? The dive?" he grinned. "Like it?"

"I can't say I really like it," Grant said cautiously, "with those people in there. Or even without them. But it seems ridiculously easy, the way you do it."

"Experience, kid," Bonham said and winked. He seemed very pleased with himself, very satisfied with his work, despite the tragic reason for it. "We're in luck, actually," he said. "The way it's sitting I don't think I'll have to use a cutting torch on it. Some of them get so smashed up they look like accordions." He paused and frowned strangely. "But I haven't decided whether we ought to get the bodies out first, or not. Well, we'll have a look first. Hey!" he called to the boatman. "That's about it! Right there! Let off easy now with that anchor!"

Up on the bridge the crowd appeared to have grown, when Grant looked. He waved up at Doug and Wanda Lou, who waggled a bottle back at him. "She set, boss," the boatman said. —"Well?" Bonham said. "Shall we go?"

It would have been possible to say with some truthfulness that it was easier for Ron going down the second time, but it would not have been all the truth. He was prepared for certain things. He knew more about, and how to manipulate, the clip-on lines. He was prepared for the limited skim-milk visibility, ready to grab for the slow, stately moving anchorchain as it passed him. But the truth was, when Bonham said "Well? Shall we go?" like that, he didn't want to go down again. He had been down there, he had done it, he had seen the car. He wanted to rest on his laurels, and stay up here and not go back. But he could find no unabject way of stating this to Bonham, so silently and idiotically, he went.

This time the heavy anchor rested about twelve or fifteen feet from the car. They could just make out its bulk dimly through the murk as they hung on the chain. Bonham had judged well in his moving of the anchor. Also, it was almost directly upsteam from the car now, thus reducing enormously the swimming arc necessary to move around at the ends of the clip lines. Side by side they calmly and easily drifted down on the car as they payed out on the lines. This time Bonham had clipped his line on much closer to the actual bottom, so that as they came alongside one on either side, drifting backward and peering over their shoulders, they were just level with the windows of the car.

The window on Grant's side was closed. Peering in, he could see quite clearly the man and the girl, both black Jamaicans. Both had their heads thrown back and their mouths open with a look of sort of wondering stupefaction on their faces, but the man had slipped and slid down a little toward the girl while the girl had slid closer to her window. Grant could look straight down into her face. Her eyes were wide open; but he could not tell, further away, about the man. The girl's long hair drifted slowly to and fro around her head as the water within the car moved to some rhythm of its own. And drifting in unison with it about a foot above the man's head was an object which after several seconds Grant was able to make out as a pair of women's panties. This struck him, in the words of some asshole poet or other, as "passing strange." It was the only phrase for it. It was also somehow very sad. Looking down, he saw that the woman's dress was clear up around her waist, and that from the waist down she was nude. He could see her navel and the black spiky hair on her vagina. Whether she had been like that before, or whether the crash and then the water rushing in had hiked it up, was impossible to tell.

It could not have been more than a few seconds that he stared at her through his facemask, breathing slowly to the sing of his regulator, but it seemed a long time. She certainly was dead. So was the man. A little fish of some kind darted out from somewhere as if anticipating an easy meal here, then as if sensing the presence of larger life than himself close by, darted away. Then Bonham, who had taken all this in from the other side, came swimming up over the top of the car on the end of his clip line. He had decided, he gestured, to take the bodies out of the car first, and he motioned Grant to go and get the hoisting-

and signal-line which they had brought down with them this time and Bonham had clipped to the chain. Grant made a motion as of breaking the window on his side with something, but Bonham shook his head and held up a finger. The window on his side was already open, he informed Grant by pointing and making a cranking motion. And again he motioned for Grant to go get the line.

Grant swam away, pulling himself in on his line and coiling it as he moved upcurrent. He unclipped the extra line at the anchor. From here in this gray gloomy water the car was almost invisible. Bonham was completely so. Grant felt a pang of loneliness, and suddenly realized he was cold. He recalled that, had he not come along, Bonham would have done this job alone, had done others like it alone. Tugging three times which was the signal for more slack, he took a turn of the line over his arm and let himself drift back down, his admiration for Bonham growing.

Bonham had managed to get the door open on the driver's side and to insert himself far enough to get his hands on the body of the man. But he was having trouble with the door. Grant watched fascinated for a moment, then hurried to help. Just as would a high strong wind, or gravity if the car were hanging by its front bumper on a chain, the current kept gently but persistently pushing the door shut against Bonham. In order to back out with the man he had to keep patiently pushing the door partway open again, then inch himself backward a bit before it pressed him again. Why hadn't he waited on Grant? Grant didn't know. In any case, with him to help it was easier. Paying out a few feet of his line till he could grasp the door, he hauled back in on the line until he held the door standing wide open in the current. Nodding vigorously at him, and holding up one hand in the thumb and forefinger circle salute for: Good! Okay! Bonham went on backing out with the man.

Once outside, holding the body firmly in a sort of lifeguard's cross-chest carry so as not to lose it to the current, he motioned for the extra line, wrapped it around him under the arms and knotted it in a perfect bowline. Then he tugged four times, and the dead Jamaican, his arms splayed outward from the rope and looking ridiculously helpless, went sailing off upward at a flat angle into the current, for all the world like some dead soul rising to some skim-milk heaven. Ten feet above them he grew dim, then disappeared in the murk.

One down, Grant thought. He was glad he had not had to touch him. And one to go. But then Bonham did an incomprehensible thing. Worming his way back into the front seat of the car—which was certainly dangerous enough in any case, pressed against the wheel like that—instead of trying to get hold of her and work his way back out, he began meticulously and carefully with his sausage fingers to put the panties back on the body of the dead Jamaican girl. All of him now, except from his heels to the tips of his long professional flippers, which projected beyond the nearly closed car door, was cramped longitudinally into the car's front seat.

Grant had noted, while holding the door for him to get the man out, that the panties had disappeared from the former position where they floated a foot or so above the man's head. And later, when he let go the door to pass Bonham the hauling-line, he had noticed that they were stuck into Bonham's weight belt. They were white and showed up noticeably. But in the stress of working and of even being down there, he had not thought anything of that one way or the other. Probably Bonham was going to keep them as some kind of a gruesome souvenir of the job? But now he could hardly believe what his eyes were showing him, as he peered in through the door. Hauling in a little on his line, he swam around to the front and peered in through the windshield between the spiderwebby cracked spots. What in the name of God could he be doing it for?

Bonham was not having any easy time of it, either. His big behind was jammed in between the wheel and the seat, and his great shoulders pressed down between the dashboard and the belly of the girl. His chin and facemask pushed practically right down into her spiky crotch. He could not move anything at all except his arms. And with these he was doggedly trying to get her slippery right foot that was down on the floor through the right leg-hole of the panties.

Grant watched from outside as success kept eluding him. Finally Bonham shrugged his whole tightly pressed body to try and get into a better position. Grant felt a suffocating faintness of terror at the thought of being in that position himself, of what would happen if the big diver should bump his mouthpiece against something and lose it. He would never get out. He would simply have to lay squeezed in there and drown. Even with Grant's help he could not get out fast enough to do any good.

What in the name of *God* was he *doing* it for!

Again the big man shrugged his entire body irritably, and Grant could feel the car shake a little under his hand. Bonham had apparently succeeded with the right foot and was now turning his attention to the left.

But this proved to be an even more obstinate obstacle than the right.

Partially this was because his weight pressed down on her in this position he was in and would not allow her legs to come together. To Grant's eye beyond the windshield it appeared grotesquely that even in death this girl was determined to keep her legs apart, a defiant unruly gesture to the, perhaps, whole of humanity.

Suddenly, furiously, as if driven beyond normal expectation, Bonham shook his whole body from top to foot rather the way a dog will shake himself from head to tail in separate sections. The result of that was to pop his body up out of the combined pressures squeezing it, and his tank rang alarmingly against the car roof. From outside Grant could only float at the end of his clip-line helplessly and watch. The girl had now slipped down in the seat, her two legs in the air in a position of copulation. From above her, floating against the car roof, Bonham, bending the left leg in from the knee, could slip the left foot through its panty-hole. But more than that he could not do. Carefully he worked the panties up her legs to above her knees, but having no leverage with which to lift her body, he could get them no further. He had made a herculean effort. Looking up furiously and ferociously at the windshield, he motioned Grant violently to get the door open.

Grant, who had just looked at his watch wondering about air, nodded vigorously and then just as he turned to swim back to the door saw Bonham reach back with his left hand and pull his reserve wire! Grant felt no need to pull his own. But Bonham, having expended a great deal more energy, especially in this latest effort with the panties, had also used a great deal more air.

So time was getting important. In spite of that, once he had her outside, which took at least a minute and a half of worming and snaking backward while pulling her, Bonham handed her to Grant.

Grant, hanging in the water at the end of his own rope in the current, and now holding the girl too under the arms so that his two hands pressed her lush firm breasts in their bra, felt distinctly peculiar. He had seen her around town a few times, he remembered now, usually in bars. She had been peculiarly attractive sexually. The bare skin of her arms was very slippery when the backs of his hands touched it, and being so limp she was hard to hold. He did not get any sensation of corpse-coldness from her in the chill water.

The current of course had immediately carried her dress down to its full length at her knees. Bonham was forced to push it irritably back up. He motioned for Grant to hold it. Then slowly and carefully he went about putting her panties properly back in place. He was breathing very slowly now, holding each breath a long time, to conserve his air.

During Bonham's struggle in the car the extra hauling-line had drifted back down toward them in the current, and Grant had swum up for it and attached it to the car bumper. Now Bonham got it and tied the girl to it, tugged four times, and they watched her ascend into skim-milk heaven as the man had done. Bonham immediately tapped his mouthpiece and heaved his shoulders in the signal that he was almost out of air. He took off swimming on a rising angle toward the anchor-line. His air of course would come easier as they rose and as it expanded in the tank under the lessening pressure. Then slowly they came up the anchorline side by side, Bonham shaking his head disgustedly. When their heads popped out into that always-surprising, always-strange-looking world of sun and free air, he dropped his mouthpiece and pushed his mask up on his forehead, and the first thing he said was: "If I'd known it was gonna be that hard, I wouldn'a done it."

"But why . . ." Grant began, dropping his own mouthpiece and pushing up his own mask. He got no further because Bonham motioned him to silence, jerking his head toward Orloffski and the boatman in the boat above them.

Another small boat was just taking off the girl's body, as they climbed in. Up above on the bridge the crowd watched in silence. The men in the other boat had immediately wrapped the body in a blanket as if they didn't want to look at it, as if to do so would be obscene. Their gesture made Grant immediately think of his own act of holding the dead girl, her two breasts in his hands, the feel of her slippery wet skin. What would those guys have done in his position? "I'll tell you all about it later," Bonham said shortly, and stretched his arms out along the gunwale.

When they did talk about it later, the great panty-replacing episode, Grant learned that Bonham—quite erroneously, obviously—had hoped to do it quickly enough and unobtrusively enough so that Grant simply would not notice it. "Besides, I was afraid of losing them in the current, if I took her outside." —"Them? The panties?" Grant asked. —"*Yeah,* damn it! *And* her! *And/or* her!" Bonham said irritably, and then added: "But I didn't know it was going to be that hard to do!" But basically, he would have preferred that nobody know anything about it except for himself. And the main reason he had decided to do it: and here a simpleminded fatuous look of smug sexual propriety came over his big face: was because of the guy's poor wife and four kids back home in

GaBay, who would have to live all this down. It was true that: and
here a schoolboy leer fleeted across his face, shredding momentarily the
look of sexual decorum: he had taken Anna Rachel out a few times
himself, sneaked her out on the sly so to speak, and she was a good kid.
But mainly: and here the sweet decorum settled back in place heavily,
and stayed: he was thinking of the guy's poor wife and four kids. No
gossipy scandal like that ever helped anybody.

All of this conversation took place some time later of course, at The
Neptune Bar in fact, that evening, where the whole gang of them sat
drinking innumerable gin-tonics. Bonham had taken Grant to another,
empty table to make his explanation privately. But by that time Grant
had already learned something else about Bonham that forced him to re-
evaluate his conception of the man, something Lucky had found out
during her long day of beer-drinking with Letta Bonham.

The upshot of it was that Bonham could not get it up with his wife.
Letta Bonham had told this to Lucky.

As Lucky was so fond of saying: "Sometimes I think the whole of the
United States is totally and completely sexually sick, sick to danger
point." Well, it had been one of Grant's main themes all his life, in
all his work. And now here was good old simple, uncomplicated Al
Bonham in it too, up to his balls, so to speak.

"I suppose there'll be a lot of gossip about it anyway, hunh?" Grant
said finally after they had discussed it all.

"Sure, but at least this way they won't know, will they?" Bonham
said.

"Well, I guess from all I've heard about Anna Rachel, they'll still be
able to guess pretty close. Won't they?"

"But they won't have *proof*," Bonham said. "Anyway I think I did
the right thing, don't you?"

"Even at the risk of your life?"

Bonham made a throw-away gesture. "It wasn't that dangerous."

"It could have been."

"Well, it wasn't. And I figure I owed her that. Don't you think I
did the right thing?" he said again.

"I guess you did, Al," Grant said, and then saw that that was simply
not enough for Bonham. He pretended to think. "Yes. Yes, I'm sure
you did the right thing, Al," he added.

IV
Nobody Knows My Name

William Styron

VIRGINIA: 1831*

from THE CONFESSIONS OF NAT TURNER

Dear Mr. Burnett:

You may preface my choice by saying I think it is among my best because it is as successful a fusion as I have as yet achieved of character portrayal, narrative momentum, and a sense of environment—a combination which I believe to be an ideal in the creation of meaningful or worthwhile fiction.

Sincerely yours,
William Styron

Roxbury, Connecticut

* As titled when excerpted by *The Paris Review*.

Hark always declared that he could distinguish between good white people and bad white people—and even white people who lay between good and bad—by their smell alone. He was very solemn about all this; over the years he had worked out many subtleties and refinements upon his original philosophy, and he could talk endlessly as we worked alongside each other—advising me at the top of his voice, assigning exact, marvelous odors to white people like Moses handing down the law. About much of this he was deadly serious, and as he jabbered away his broad, bold face would become furrowed in the most worrisome thought; but Hark's nature was basically humorous, outward-going, beneficent, serene, and he could not long sustain a somber mood, even though many horrible things had happened to him.

Finally something connected with a white person and a certain smell would tickle some interior nerve: against all restraint the giggles would begin to well up from his belly and in an instant he would have broken down, clutching himself in helpless, wheezing, rich, delirious laughter. "Now, Nat, maybe it jes' *me,*" he would begin seriously, "but dis yere nose of mine she jes' get better ev'y day. Like I was comin' roun' de side of de barn yestiddy evenin' and dere's ole Miss Maria a-feedin' the chickens. She seed me afore I could take off. 'Hark!' say she. 'Hark! Come right yere!' So I come, an' awready my nose begin twitchin' like a mushrat pokin' up out'n de swamp. 'Hark!' say she. 'Whar de corn?' 'Why, what corn, Miss Maria?' say I, de ole smell gittin' strong now. 'De corn in de shed for de chickens!' de ole bitch say.

'You suppose' to have a couple bushels shelled fo' my chickens and dere ain't a cupful lef'! Dis de fo'th time in a month! You a shiftless black nigger scoundrel and I pray to see de day my brother sells you off to Mississippi! *Git* dat corn shelled right now, you shiftless nigger!' Jesus jumpin' Judas, de smell, Nat, comin' out dat woman, if it water 'twould have drown' me in my shoes. What it like? 'Twas like an ole catfish somebody lef' three days up on a stump in July." And he would begin to giggle softly, already clutching at his midriff. "Stink! Even de buzzards fly away from ole pussy like dat!" And glorious laughter.

But not all of them had smells like this, according to Hark. Mr. Joseph Travis, our master, had "a right honest stench about him," said Hark, "like a good horse what worked him up a sweat." Joel Westbrook, the boy whom Travis employed as an apprentice, was an uncertain, gawky lad, given to temper fits but amiable, even generous when in the mood; hence to Hark his smell had a changing, fitful quality; "Sometime dat boy smell right pretty, like hay or somethin', other time he smell up a storm." This offensive Miss Maria Pope was to Hark, however, in every way consistent in her smell. She was Travis's half sister, who had come down from Petersburg to live with Travis and his family after her mother's death. A bony, angular woman, she suffered from blocked sinuses which caused her to breathe through her mouth; as a result her lips were always peeling to the quick and sometimes bled, which necessitated a poultice of lard, and this gave her ever-parted mouth a blanched appearance altogether ghostly and strange. Her eyes wandered distantly, and she was given to stroking her wrists. She hated us Negroes, who were at her beck and call, with a kind of profound and pointless hatred which was all the more burdensome to us because she was not really of the family, and therefore her attitude had a harsh, remote, despotic quality. On summer nights, from the windows of the upstairs room where she slept, I could hear her sobbing hysterically and crying out for her departed mother. She was about forty, I suspect a virgin, and she read aloud from the Bible incessantly with a kind of hollow-eyed, mesmeric urgency, her favorite passages being John 13, which deals with humility and charity, and the sixth chapter of I Timothy, beginning: *Let as many servants as are under the yoke count their own masters worthy of all honour, that the name of God and his doctrine be not blasphemed.* Indeed, according to Hark, she once flattened him up against the porch wall and made him repeat this homily until he had committed it to memory. I have no doubt that she was more than a little cracked, but this did not diminish my intense dislike of Miss Maria Pope, though occasionally I felt myself feeling sorry for her against my better judgment.

But Miss Maria is, in a manner of speaking, only incidental to a man I am trying to get at in a roundabout fashion—namely, Mr. Jeremiah Cobb, the judge who was about to sentence me to death, and into whose earlier acquaintance I was led by a complicated series of transactions which I must here try briefly to describe.

As I told Mr. Gray, I was born the property of Benjamin Turner, about whom I remember only a little. Upon his abrupt death when I was around eight or nine (a miller and dealer in timber, he was killed while felling a cypress tree, having turned his back on the monster at an improvident moment), I passed by bequest into the possession of his brother, Samuel Turner, whose property I remained for ten or eleven years. These years, and those preceding them, I shall return to in due course. Eventually Samuel Turner's fortunes declined, and there were other problems; at any one, he was unable to continue to operate the sawmill he inherited, along with me, from his brother, and so for the first time I was sold, to Mr. Thomas Moore—a sale which a weakness for irony impels me to remark was effected at the moment I reached my manhood, during my twenty-first year. I was the property of Mr. Moore, who was a small farmer, for nine years until his death (another bizarre misadventure; Moore broke his skull while presiding at the birth of a calf. It had been a balky delivery, and he had wrapped a cord around the calf's protruding hooves in order to yank it out; as he sweated and tugged and as the calf mused at him soulfully from the damp membranes of its afterbirth, the cord snapped, catapulting him backward and fatally against a gatepost. I had very little use for Moore, and my grief was meager, yet at the time I could not but help begin to wonder if ownership of me did not presage a diminution of fortune, as does the possession, I am told, of a certain kind of elephant in India), and upon Mr. Moore's demise I became the property of his son, Putnam, who was then fifteen. The following year (that is to say, last year) Mr. Moore's widow, Miss Sarah, married Joseph Travis, a childless widower of fifty-five desirous of offspring, who lived in this same country region of Cross Keys, an expert wheelwright by trade and the last person so luckless as to enjoy me in the pride of ownership. For although under law I was Putnam's by title, I belonged also to Travis, who had the right to exercise full control over me until Putnam reached his majority. Thus when Miss Sarah wed Joseph Travis and became domiciled beneath his roof, I turned into a kind of twofold property—not an unheard-of arrangement but additionally unsatisfying to property already half deranged at being owned even once.

Travis was moderately prosperous, which is to say that like a few of the other inhabitants of this backwater, he managed to eke out slightly more than a living. Unlike the hapless Moore, he was adept at that which the Lord had him cut out to do, and it was a great relief for me to be able to help him at his trade after the long years at Moore's and the monotony of toting his water and sopping his feverish, languishing pigs and alternately baking and freezing in his cornfield and his cotton patch. In fact, because of the circumstances of my new employment—which was to act as a general handyman around the wheel shop—I had a sense of well-being, physical at least, such as I had not felt since leaving Samuel Turner's nearly ten years before. Like most of the other property owners of the region, Travis was also a small farmer, with fifteen acres or so in corn, cotton, and hay, plus an apple grove whose principal function it was to produce cider and brandy. Since the relative success of the wheel shop, however, Travis had cut back on his farm holdings, leasing out his acreage to others, and retaining just the apple orchard, and a small produce garden and patch of cotton for his own use. Besides myself, Travis owned only two Negroes—a number, however, not unusual in its smallness, inasmuch as few white people in the region could any longer afford to support more than five or six slaves, and it was rare indeed to find a citizen prosperous enough to own as many as a dozen. Travis himself had recently owned seven or eight, not counting several unserviceable children, but as his acreage diminished and his solitary craft flourished, he had no need for this obstreperous pack, indeed found so many fat mouths to feed a burden on his capital, and thus, three years before, with great moral misgivings (or so I heard) sold off the whole lot—all but one—to a trader specializing in labor for the Mississippi delta. The one left was Hark, who was my age lacking a year. Born on a vast tobacco plantation in Sussex County, he had been sold to Travis at the age of fifteen after the tobacco sucked the soil dry and the land went to rack and ruin. I had known him for years and had come to love him like a brother. The other Negro, acquired subsequent to the Mississippi sale, was Moses, a husky, tar-black, wild-eyed boy of twelve or thereabouts whom Travis, finding himself belatedly short-handed, had bought at the Richmond market several months before my arrival. He was strong and strapping for his age, and bright enough, I think; but he never quite got over the separation from his mammy; it left him bereft, stuporous, and he cried a lot and peed in his pants, sometimes even when he was at work, and all in all was a nuisance, becoming a great trial to Hark especially, who had a mother's soul in the body of a bull, and felt compelled to soothe and nurse the foundling.

This then was the population of our household at the time when I first encountered Jeremiah Cobb, almost one year to the day before he sentenced me to death: three Negroes—Hark, Moses, myself—six white people—Mr. and Mrs. Travis and Putnam, Miss Maria Pope, and two more besides. The last were the previously mentioned Joel Westbrook, fifteen years old, a budding wheelwright whom Travis had apprenticed to himself; and Travis's child by Miss Sarah, an infant boy of two months born with a purple blemish spreading across the center of his tiny face like the single shriveling petal of a blighted gentian. The white people, of course, lived in the main house, a modest, plain but comfortable two-storied structure of six rooms which Travis had built twenty years before. He had hewn the beams himself, planed the timbers, made it all weather-tight with pine gum and mortar, and had been wise enough to leave standing round it several enormous beech trees which offered shade from any angle against the summer sun. Adjacent to the house, separated from it only by the pigpen and a short path through the vegetable garden, was the wheel shop, converted from a one-time barn: here was the center of activity on the farm, here were the stores of oak and ashwood and iron, the forge and anvils, the bending frames, the modeling hammers and tongs and vises and the rows of chisels and punches and all the other equipment which Travis employed in his demanding craft. Doubt-less at least in part because of my repute (decent albeit somewhat ambiguous and suspect in a way I will soon explain) as a kind of harmless, runabout, comic nigger minister of the gospel, I was later made custodian of the shop; in fact, prompted by Miss Sarah's avowal of my integrity, Travis gave into my keeping one of two sets of keys. I had plenty enough to do, but I cannot honestly say that my work here was toilsome; unlike Moore, Travis was no taskmaster, being by nature unable, I think, to drive his servants unreasonably and already having been well provided with willing help in the person of his stepson and the Westbrook boy, who was an eager apprentice if there ever was one.

Thus my duties, compared to what I had been used to, were light and fairly free of strain: I kept the place clean and added my shoulder to a job when extra strength was needed, such as bending a wheel rim, and frequently I spelled Hark as he pumped at the bellows of the forge, but generally speaking (and for the first time in years) the tasks

I encountered were those calculated to tax not my muscles but my ingenuity. (For instance, the loft of the shop since its conversion from the status of a barn had still been infested by bats, tolerable enough when the place was the abode of cattle but an insufferable plague of drizzling bat shit to humans laboring daily below. Travis had tried half a dozen futile measures to rid himself of the pests, including fire and smoke, which nearly burned the place down; whereupon at this point I went out into the woods to a certain nest I knew of and plucked a blacksnake out of hibernation, wrenching it from the tail-end of its winter's sleep and installing it in the eaves. When spring came a week later the bats quickly vanished, and the blacksnake continued in friendly, satisfied residence, slithering benevolently around the circumference of the shop as it gobbled up rats and field mice, its presence earning me, I know, quiet admiration in Travis's regard.) So, all things being equal, from the beginning of my stay with Travis, I was in as palmy and benign a state as I could remember in many years. Miss Maria's demands were annoying, but she was a small thorn. Instead of the nigger food I was accustomed to at Moore's, fat pork and corn pone, I got house food like the white people—a lot of lean bacon and red meat, occasionally even the leavings from a roast of beef, and often white bread made of wheat—and the lean-to shed adjoining the wheel shop where Hark and I shared housekeeping was roomy enough, with the first bed elevated above the ground that I had slept on since the old days with Samuel Turner; and I constructed, with my owner's blessing, an ingenious wooden vent leading through the wall from the forge, which was always banked with charcoal: the vent could be shut off in the summer, but in the winter its constant warmth made Hark and me (the poor boy Moses slept in the house, in a damp kitchen closet, where he could be available for errands night and day) as snug as two grubs beneath a log. Above all, I had quite a bit of time on my hands. I could fish and trap and do considerable Scriptural reading. I had for going on to several years now considered the necessity of exterminating all the white people in Southampton County and as far beyond as destiny carried me, and there was thus available to me more time than I had ever had before to ponder the Bible and its exhortations, and to think over the complexities of the bloody mission that was set out before me.

The particular November day I met Jeremiah Cobb is clear in my memory: an afternoon of low gray clouds scudding eastward on a gusty wind, cornfields brown and sere stretching toward the distant woods, and the kind of stillness which comes with that time of autumn, the buzz and hum of insects having flickered out, the songbirds flown south, leaving the fields and woods to dwell in a vast gray globe of silence; nothing stirs, minutes pass in utter quiet, then through the smoky light comes the sound of crows cawing over some far-off cornfield, a faint raucous hullabaloo which swiftly dwindles off in the distance, and silence again, broken only by the scratching and scrabble of dead wind-blown leaves. That afternoon I heard dogs yapping in the north, as if they were coming down the road. It was a Saturday, Travis and Joel Westbrook had driven that morning to Jerusalem on an errand, and only Putnam was at work in the shop. I was outside at the corner of my shed cleaning some rabbits from my trapline, when in the midst of this deep and brooding silence I heard the dogs yapping up the road. They were foxhounds, but not enough of them for a hunt, and I recall being puzzled, my puzzlement vanishing just as I rose and looked up the road and saw a whirlwind of dust: out of the whirlwind came a tall white man in a pale beaver hat and gray cloak, perched on the seat of a dogcart drawn by a frisky jet-black mare. Behind and below the seat were the dogs, three flop-eared hounds yapping at one of Travis's yellow cur dogs who was trying to get at them through the spokes of the wheels. It was, I think, the first time I ever saw a dogcart with dogs. From where I stood I saw the dogcart draw up to a halt in front of the house, then saw the man dismount; I thought he came down clumsily, seeming for an instant to falter or to stumble as if weak in the knees, but then, instantly regaining control of himself, he muttered something half aloud and at the same time aimed a kick at the yellow dog, missed wildly, his booted foot fetching up against the side of the carriage with a clatter.

It was comical to watch—a white man's discomfiture, observed on the sly, has always been a Negro's richest delight—but even as I felt the laughter gurgling up inside me the man turned and my laughter ceased. I was now able to observe him for the first time straight on: the face I beheld was one of the most unhappy faces I had ever seen. It was blighted, ravaged by sorrow, as if grief had laid actual hands on the face, wrenching and twisting it into an attitude of ineradicable pain. Now too I could see that the man was a little drunk. He stared somberly at the dog howling at him from the dust of the road, then raised his hollow eyes briefly to the gray clouds scudding across the heavens. I thought I heard a groan pass his lips; a spasm of coughing seized him. Then with an abrupt, clumsy gesture he drew the cloak about his gaunt and bony frame and proceeded with fumbling gloved hands to fasten the

mare to the tethering post. Just then I heard Miss Sarah call from
the porch. "Judge Cobb!" I heard her cry. "Sakes alive! What are you
doin' down this way?" He shouted something back to her, the cadence
of his words obscure, muffled against the gusty wind. The leaves whirled
around him, all the dogs kept yapping and howling, the pretty little mare
chafed and tossed her mane and stamped. I managed to make out the
words: a hunt in Drewrysville, he was taking his dogs there, a grinding
noise in the spindle box of his wheel. He thought the axle broke, split,
something; being nearby he had come here for repairs. Was Mr. Joe
to home? Downwind came Miss Sarah's voice from the porch, loud,
buxom, cheerful: "Mr. Joe's done gone to Jerusalem! My boy Putnam's
here, though! He'll fix that wheel for you, Judge Cobb, straightaway!
Won't you come in and set a spell!" Thank you no ma'am, Cobb
hollered back; he was in a rush, he'd get that axle fixed and be on his
way. "Well, I 'spect you know where the cider press is," Miss Sarah
called. "Right next to the shop. They's some brandy too! Just help yourself and drink your fill!"

I went back to the corner of the shed, attending to my rabbits, and
paid no more mind to Cobb for the moment. Travis had allowed me to
have the trapline, and in fact encouraged me in the enterprise since by
arrangement he was to get two out of every three rabbits I caught.
Such an agreement was satisfactory to me, inasmuch as this game was
plentiful in the countryside and the two or three rabbits a week left
for Hark and me were as much as we cared to eat, and more; nor did it
matter to me that Travis sold most of the rabbits in Jerusalem and
retained the money, which was clear profit, since if he was to earn
interest on the capital which, body and brain, I represented anyway, I
was glad to be capitalized upon in one small way which I myself took
pleasure in. For after all of the dull drudgery at Moore's, it was the
greatest delight to me to be able to make use of some actual indwelling
talent, to fashion the traps myself—box traps which I made out of scrap
pine from the shop, sawing and planing the wood with my own hands,
carving the pegs and the notched pins which tripped the doors, and
uniting one after another of the neat miniature coffins into a single
smoothly operating, silent, lethal assembly. But this was not all. As much
as manufacturing the traps I enjoyed walking the trapline at daybreak
in the silence of the countryside, when frost crackled on the ground and
the hollows overflowed as if with milk in the morning mists. It was a
three-mile hike through the woods along a familiar pine-needled path,
and I devised a sort of cloth pouch to take along with me, in which

I carried my Bible and my breakfast—two apples and a piece of streak-of-lean pork already cooked the night before. On my return, the Bible shared the pouch with a couple of rabbits, which I brained bloodlessly with a hickory club. A multitude of squirrels preceded me on these walks, in rippling stop-and-go motion; with some of them I became quite familiar and I bestowed names upon them, prophetic Hebrew names like Ezra and Amos, and I numbered them among God's blest since unlike rabbits they could not by nature be easily trapped and could not by law be shot (at least by me, Negroes being denied the use of guns). It was a silent, gentle, pristine time of day, and as the sun shone pale through the dews and the mists and the woods hovered round me gray and still in the autumnal birdless quiet, it was like the morn of Genesis with the breath of creation fresh upon it.

Near the end of my trapline there was a little knoll, surrounded on three sides by a thicket of scrub oak trees, and here I would make my breakfast. From this knoll (though hardly taller than a small tree, it was the highest point of land for miles) I could obtain a clear and secret view of the countryside, including several of the farmhouses which it had already become my purpose eventually to invade and pillage. Thus these morning trapping expeditions also served to allow me to reconnoiter and to lay plans for the great event which I knew was in the offing. For at such times it seemed that the spirit of God hovered very close to me, advising me in this fashion: *Son of man, prophesy, and say, Thus saith the Lord; Say, a sword, a sword is sharpened, and also furbished: it is sharpened to make a sore slaughter* . . . Of all the Prophets it was Ezekiel with his divine fury to whom I felt closest by kinship, and as I sat there these mornings, the pork and apples devoured, the bag of brained cottontails at my side, I would for a long time ponder Ezekiel's words because it was through his words that the wishes of the Lord concerning my destiny (even more so than through the words of the other Prophets) seemed most clearly to be revealed: *Go through the midst of Jerusalem, and set a mark upon the foreheads of the men that sigh and that cry for all the abominations that be done in the midst thereof* . . . *Slay utterly old and young, both maids and little children, and women: but come not near any man upon whom is the mark* . . . Often as I brooded over these lines, I wondered why God should wish to spare the well-meaning and slay the helpless; nonetheless, it was His word. Great mornings, filled with hints, auguries, portents! I find it hard to describe the exaltation which seized me at such times when, crouched upon my secret knoll in gray momentous dawns, I saw in the unfolding future—fixed there as immutably as Saul or Gideon—myself, black as the blackest vengeance, the illimitable, devastating instrument of God's wrath. For on these mornings as I looked down upon the gray and somber and shriveling landscape it seemed as if His will and my mission could not be more plain and intelligible: to free my people I must one day only commence with the slumbering, mist-shrouded dwellings below, destroying all therein, then set forth eastward across the swamps and fields, where lay Jerusalem.

But to get back to Cobb, rather meanderingly I'm afraid, and again by way of Hark. Hark had a flair for the odd, the off-center: had he been able to read and write, been white, free, living in some Elysian time when he was anything but negotiable property worth six hundred dollars in a depressed market, he might have been a lawyer; to my disappointment, Christian teachings (my own mainly) had made only the shallowest imprint upon his spirit, so that being free of spiritual rules and restraints he responded to the mad side of life and could laugh with abandon, thrilling to each day's new absurdity. In short, he had a feeling for the crazy, the unexpected; all in all, this caused me mild envy. There was for instance the time when our shed behind the wheel shop was still uncompleted, and our master paid us a visit during a roaring thunderstorm, gazing skyward at the water cascading through the roof. "It's leaking in here," he said, to which Hark replied: "Nawsuh, Marse Joe, hit leakin' outside. Hit *rainin'* in here." Likewise, it was Hark who gave expression to that certain inward sense—an essence of being which is almost impossible to put into words—that every Negro possesses when, dating from the age of twelve or ten or even earlier, he becomes aware that he is only merchandise, goods, in the eyes of all white people devoid of character or moral sense or soul. This feeling Hark called "black-assed," and it comes as close to summing up the numbness and dread which dwells in every Negro's heart as any word I have ever known. "Don' matter who dey is, Nat, good or bad, even ol' Marse Joe, dey white folks dey gwine make you feel *black-assed*. Never seed a white man smile at me yet 'thout I didn' feel just about twice as black-assed as I was befo'. How come dat 'plies, Nat? Figger a white man treat you right you gwine feel *white-assed*. Naw *suh!* Young massah, old massah sweet-talk me, I jes' feel *black-assed* th'ough an' th'ough. Figger when I gets to heaven like you says I is, de good Lord hisself even *He* gwine make old Hark feel black-assed, standin' befo' de golden throne. Dere He is, white as snow, givin' me a lot of sweet talk and me feelin' like a *black-assed* angel. 'Cause pretty soon I know His line, yas *suh!* Yas *suh,* pretty soon I can hear Him holler out: 'Hark! You dere, boy! Need some spick and span roun' de throne room. Hop to, you *black-assed* scoundrel! Hop to wid de mop and de broom!'"

It is impossible to exaggerate the extent to which white people dominate the conversation of Negroes, and it is with certainty I can record that these were the words that Hark (who had come out of the shed to help me dress and clean the rabbits) had been speaking on this gray November day when, like the most vaguely discernible shadow, we felt simultaneously a presence at our crouched backs and again, half startled, looked upward to see the distressed and ravaged face of Jeremiah Cobb. I don't know whether he overheard Hark's words, it would hardly have mattered if he had. Both Hark and I were taken unawares by the man's magisterial, sudden, lofty figure looming above us, swaying slightly against the smoky sky; so abruptly and silently had he come upon us that it was a long instant before the face of him actually registered, and before we were able to let slip from our hands the bloody rabbits and begin to move erect into that posture of respect or deference it is wise for any Negro to assume whenever a strange white man—always a bundle of obscure motives—enters upon the scene. But now, even before we had gotten up, he spoke. "Go on," he said, "go on, go on," in a curiously rough and raspy voice—and with a motion of his hands he bade us to continue at our work, which we did, easing back slowly on our haunches yet still gazing up into the unsmiling, bleak, tormented face. Suddenly a hiccup escaped his lips, a sound incongruous and unseemly and even faintly comical emanating from that stern face, and there was a long moment of silence all around; he hiccuped again, and this time I was sure I sensed Hark's huge body beginning to shudder with—with what? Laughter? Embarrassment? Fear? But then Cobb said: "Boys, where's the press?"

"Yondah, massah," Hark said. He pointed to the shed several yards away, directly at the side of the shop, where the cider barrels lay in a moist and dusty rank in the shadows past the open door. "Red bar'l, massah. Dat's de bar'l fo' a gennleman, massah." When the desire to play the obsequious coon came over him, Hark's voice became so plump and sweet that it was downright unctuous. "Marse Joe, he save dat red bar'l for de *fines'* gennlemens."

"Bother the cider," Cobb said, "where's the brandy?"

"Brandy in de bottles on de shelf," said Hark. He began to scramble to his feet. "I fix de brandy fo' you, massah." But again Cobb motioned him back with a brisk wave of his hand. "Go on, go on," he said. The voice was not pleasant, neither was it unkindly; it had rather a distant, abstracted quality, yet somehow it remained tinged with pain as if the mind which controlled it struggled with a preoccupying disquiet. He was abrupt, aloof, but there was nothing one might call arrogant about him. Nonetheless, something about the man offended me, filled me with the sharpest displeasure, and it wasn't until he limped unsteadily past us through the crackling brown patch of weeds toward the cider press, saying not another word, that I realized that it wasn't the man himself who annoyed me so much as it was Hark's manner in his presence—the unspeakable bootlicking Sambo, all giggles and smirks and oily, sniveling servility. Hark had slit open a rabbit. The body was still warm (on Saturdays I often collected my game in the afternoon), and Hark was holding it aloft by the ears to catch the blood, which we saved to bind stews. I can recall my sudden fury as we crouched there, as I looked up at Hark, at the bland, serene glistening black face with its wide brow and the grave, beautiful prominences of its cheekbones. With dumb absorption he was gazing at the stream of crimson blood flowing into the pan he held below. He had the face one might imagine to be the face of an African chieftain—soldierly, fearless, scary, and resplendent in its bold symmetry—yet there was something wrong with the eyes, and the eyes, or at least the expression they often took on, as now, reduced the face to a kind of harmless, dull, malleable docility. They were the eyes of a child, trustful and dependent, soft doe's eyes mossed over with a kind of furtive, fearful glaze, and as I looked at them now—the womanish eyes in the massive, sovereign face mooning dumbly at the rabbit's blood— I was seized by rage. I heard Cobb fumbling around in the cider press, clinking and clattering. We were out of earshot. "Black toadeater," I said. "Snivelin' black toadeatin' white man's bootlickin' scum! You, Hark! Black *scum!*"

Hark's soft eyes rolled toward me, trusting yet fearful. "How come—" he began in an abrupt startled voice.

"Hush your face, man!" I said. I was furious. I wanted to let him have the back of my hand flush in the mouth. "Just hush, man!" I began to mimic him, hoarsely, beneath my breath. "Red bar'l, massah! Dat's de bar'l wid de *gennlemen's* cidah! I fix de brandy fo' you, massah!' How come you make with that kind of talk, bootlickin' nigger suckup? It was enough to make me plain ordinary *sick!*"

Hark's expression grew hurt, downcast; he moped disconsolately at the ground, saying nothing but moving his lips in a moist, muttering, abstracted way as if filled with hopeless self-recrimination. "Can't you see, miserable nigger?" I persisted, boring in hard. "Can't you see the *difference*? The difference betwixt plain politeness and bootlickin'? He didn't even say, 'Get me a drink.' He said just, 'Where the press?' A *question,* that's all. And there *you* is, already: scramblin' and scroungin' like a bitch pup, massah this and massah that! You enough to make a man chuck up his dinner!" *Be not hasty in thy spirit to be angry: for anger resteth in the bosom of fools.* Ashamed suddenly, I calmed myself. Hark was a vision of dejection. More gently I said: "You just got to *learn,* man. You got to learn the difference. I don't mean you got to risk a beatin'. I don't mean you got to be uppity and smart. But they is some kind of limit. And you ain't a *man* when you act like that. You ain't a man, you is a fool! And you do this all the time, over and over again, with Travis and Miss Maria and Lord help you even with them two *ķids.* You don't learn nothin'. You a fool! *As a dog returneth to his vomit, so a fool returneth to his folly.* You a *fool,* Hark. How'm I goin' to teach you?"

Hark made no reply, only crouched there muttering in his hurt and dejection. I was seldom angry at Hark, but my anger when it came had the power to grieve him. Loving him as I did, I often reproved myself for my outbursts and for the misery they caused him, but in certain ways he was like a splendid dog, a young, beautiful, heedless, spirited dog who had, nonetheless, to be trained to behave with dignity. Although I had not yet told him of my great plans, it was my purpose that when the day came to obliterate the white people, Hark would be my right arm, my sword and shield; for this he was well endowed, being quick-witted and resourceful and as strong as a bear. Yet the very sight of white skin cowed him, humbled him, diminished him to his most fawning and servile abasement; and I knew that before placing my ultimate trust in him I must somehow eliminate from his character this weakling trait which I had seen before in Negroes who, like Hark, had spent most of their early lives on big plantations. Certainly it would not do to have a chief lieutenant who was at heart only an abject nigger, full of cheap grins and comic shufflings, unable to gut a white man and gut him without a blink or qualm. In short, Hark was for me a necessary and crucial experiment. Though it is a painful fact that most Negroes are hopelessly docile, many of them are filled with fury, and the unctuous coating of flattery which surrounds and encases that fury is but a form of self-preservation. With Hark, I knew I must strip away and destroy that repulsive outer guise, meanwhile encouraging him to nurture the murderous fury which lay beneath. Yet somehow I did not think it would take too much time.

"I don' know, Nat," Hark said finally. "I tries and tries. But hit seem I cain't git over dat black-assed feelin'. I tries, though." He paused, ruminating, nodding his head ever so slightly over the bloody carcass in his hands. "'Sides, dat man he look so sad an' mou'nful. Never seed such a sad an' mou'nful man. Kind of felt sorry fo' de man. What you reckon made him so sad-lookin' anyways?"

I heard Cobb returning from the press through the weeds, unsteadily, stumbling slightly, with a brittle crackling sound of underbrush being trampled underfoot. "Feel sorry for a white man and you wastin' your sorrow," I said in a low voice. Then even as I spoke I made a sudden connection in my mind, remembering how a few months before I had overheard Travis speaking to Miss Sarah about this man Cobb, and the terrors which had beset him grisly and Job-like within the space of a single year: a merchant and banker of property and means, chief magistrate of the county, master of the Southampton Hounds, he lost his wife and two grown daughters to typhoid fever on the coast of Carolina, whither, ironically, he had sent his ladies to recuperate from winter attacks of the bronchial ailments to which all three were prone. Shortly afterward his stable, a brand-new structure on the outskirts of Jerusalem, burned to the ground in one horrid and almost instantaneous holocaust, incinerating all therein including two or three prize Morgan hunters and many valuable English saddles and harnesses, not to mention a young Negro groom. Subsequently, the unfortunate man, having taken heavily to the bottle to ease his affliction, fell down some stairs and broke his leg; the limb failed to mend properly, and although ambulatory, he was plagued by a hectic, mild, irresistible fever and by unceasing pain. When I first heard of all this adversity I could not help but feel a spasm of satisfaction (do not consider me altogether heartless—I am not, as you shall surely see; but the contentment a Negro takes in a white man's misery, existing like a delicious tidbit among bleak and scanty rations, can hardly be overestimated), and I must confess that now as I heard Cobb behind me toiling back through the noisy weeds I experienced anew the same sense of gratification. (*For the thing which I greatly feared is come upon me, and that which I was afraid of is come unto me. I was not in safety, neither had I rest, neither was I quiet; yet trouble came . . .*) A small thrill of pleasure coursed through my flesh.

I thought he was going to walk past us to the shop or perhaps the house. Certainly I was taken by surprise when, instead, Cobb halted next to us with his boots practically atop one of the skinned rabbits. Again Hark and I started to rise, again he motioned for us to continue work. "Go on, go on," he repeated, taking a huge gulp from the bottle. I heard the brandy vanish with a froglike croak in the back of his gullet, then the long aspirated gasp of breath, the final wet smacking of lips. "Ambrosia," he said. Above us the voice was self-confident, sturdy, stentorian; it had an unmistakable vigor and force, even though the tired undertone of sorrow remained, and I felt the residue of an emotion, ever so faint, which I must confess was only the fear I was born and brought up with. "*Am-ba-ro-sia,*" he said. My fear receded. The yellow cur dog came snuffling up and I hurled into his face a slippery blue handful of rabbits' guts, which he made off with into the cotton patch, groaning with pleasure. "A Greek word," Cobb went on. "From *ambrotos,* that is to say, immortal. For surely the gods were conferring upon us poor humans a kind of immortality, no matter how brief and illusory, when they tendered us this voluptuous gift, made of the humble and omnipresent apple. Comforter to the lonely and outcast, an anodyne for pain, a shelter against the chill wind of remorseless, oncoming death—surely such an elixir must be touched by the hand of something or someone divine!" Another hiccup—it was like a species of shriek, really prodigious—racked his frame, and again I heard him take a swig from the bottle. Intent upon my rabbits, I had not as yet looked up, but I had caught a glimpse of Hark: transfixed, with bloody glistening hands outstretched, he was gazing open-mouthed at Cobb with a look of absolute attention, a kind of ignorant and paralyzed awe affecting to behold; straining to understand, he moved his lips silently in unison with Cobb's, chewing upon the gorgeous syllables as if upon air; droplets of sweat had burst forth from his black brow like a spray of quicksilver, and for an instant I could almost have sworn that he had ceased breathing. "Aaa-h," Cobb sighed, smacking his lips. "Pure delight. And is it not remarkable that to his already estimable endowments—the finest wheelwright in the Southside of Virginia— your master Mr. Joseph Travis should add another supreme talent, that of being the most skillful distiller of this ineffable potion within the span of a hundred miles? Do you not find that truly remarkable? Do you *not* now." He was silent. Then he said again, ambiguously, in a voice which seemed—to me at least—touched with threat: "Do you *not* now?"

I had begun to feel uncomfortable, disturbed. Perhaps I was over-sensitive (as always) to the peculiar shading of a white man's tone; nonetheless, there seemed to be something pointed, oppressive, sardonic about this question, alarming me. It has been my usual experience that when a strange white man adopts this florid, familiar manner, and when his listener is black, the white man is out to have a little fun at the black man's expense. And such had been my developing mood of tension during the recent months that I felt I must avoid at all costs (and no matter how harmless the by-play) even the faintest premonition of a *situation*. Now the man's wretched question had deposited me squarely upon a dilemma. The trouble is: a Negro, in much the same way as a dog, has constantly to interpret the *tone* of what is being said. If, as was certainly possible, the question was merely drunken-rhetorical, then I could remain humbly and decently mute and scrape away at my rabbit. This (my mind all the while spinning and whirling away like a water mill) was the eventuality I preferred—dumb nigger silence, perhaps a little scratching of the old woolly skull, and an illiterate pink-lipped grin, reflecting total incomprehension of so many beautiful Latin-isms. If on the other hand, as seemed more likely from the man's ex-pectant silence, the question was drunken-surly-sarcastic and demanding of an answer, I would be forced to mutter the customary Yassuh—Nawsuh being impermissible in view of the simple-minded nature of the question. What was so disturbing about this moment was my fear (and these fears, one may be assured, are neither vagrant nor inconse-quential) that the Yassuh might very well be followed by something like this: "Ah, you do now. You *do* find it remarkable? Am I to understand then that you consider your master a dummox? That be-cause he can make wheels he can't make brandy? You darkies don't have much regard for your owners these days, do you? Well, I want to tell you something, Pompey, or whatever your ludicrous name is, that . . ." et cetera. The changes on this situation are endless, and do not think me overly cautious: motiveless nigger-needling is a common sport. But at this point it was not the possibility of humiliation I wanted to avoid so much as the possibility that having recently vowed that humiliation would never again be a constraint upon me, or a repression, I would be forced to surmount it by beating the man's brains out, thus completely wrecking all my great designs for the future.

I had begun to shake, and I felt a stirring, a kind of watery weakness in my bowels; just then, however, came a fortunate distraction: nearby in the woods there arose the sound of a crashing in the undergrowth, and we all three turned to see a tawny mud-streaked wild sow lumber out of a thicket, snorting and grunting, trailed by her squealing brood; now as quickly as they appeared pig and piglets seemed to dissolve back into the sere and withered forest, the space of sky above silent and gray and desolate with low-hanging, tattered, wind-driven clouds like smudged cotton through which faint sunlight seeped yellowish and wan. Distracted, our eyes lingered on the scene for a moment, and then came a slamming noise, very close, as the door of the shop opened suddenly, and caught by the wind, hurled itself on screaming hinges backward against the wall. "Hark!" a voice called. It was my boy owner, Putnam. "Where you, Hark?" The child was in a foul mood; I could tell this from the blotches on his pale white face: they grew prominent and rosy whenever he became exercised or harassed. I should add that Putnam had more or less had it in for Hark ever since the preceding year when, out hunting hickory nuts on a balmy afternoon, Hark had innocently but clumsily ambushed Putnam and Joel West-brook in some tangled carnal union by the swimming pond, both of the boys naked as catfish on the muddy bank, writhing about and skylarking with each other in the most oblivious way. "Never seed such foolishness," Hark had said to me, "But 'twarn't like I was gwine pay it no never mind. Nigger don' care 'bout no white boys' foolish-ness. Now dat daggone Putnam he so mad, you'd think it was *me* dat *dey* caught jackin' off de ole bird." I sympathized with Hark but in the end I couldn't take it too seriously, as it simply typified an uncorrectable condition: white people really see nothing of a Negro in his private activity, while a Negro, who must walk miles out of his path to avoid seeing everything white people do, has often to suffer for even the most guileless part of his ubiquitous presence by being called a spy and a snooping black scoundrel.

"Hark!" the boy called again. "Get in here straight away! What do you think you're doin' out there, you no-account nigger! Fire's gone plumb out! Get in here, God durn you lazy wretch!" The boy wore a leather apron; he had a coarse-featured, sullen, pouty-mouthed face with flowing dark hair and long side whiskers: as he shouted at Hark, I felt a brief, fleeting spasm of rage and I longed for the day to arrive when I might get my hands on him. Hark scrambled to his feet and made off for the shop as Putnam called out again, this time to Cobb: "I think you have someways broke a axle, Judge, sir! My stepdad will fix it! He should be here afore too long!"

"Very well," Cobb called back. Then so abruptly that for an instant I thought he was still talking to the boy, he said: *"As a dog returneth to his vomit, so a fool returneth to his folly.* That of course is most familiar, but for the life of me I am unable to place it within the Scriptures. I suspect however that it is one of the Proverbs of King Solomon, whose delight it was to rail at fools, and to castigate human folly . . ." As he went on talking, a queasy sensation crept over me: the customary positions were reversed, the white man this time had caught the nigger at *his* gossip. How did I know that my own black blabbermouth would betray me, and that he would overhear every word I had said? Humiliated, ashamed of my humiliation, I let the sticky wet rabbit corpse fall from my fingers and braced my spirit, preparing for the worst. "Was it not Solomon who said the fool shall be the servant to the wise? Was it not he too who said a fool despiseth his father's instruction? And is not the instruction of the father, through Paul the Jew of Tarsus, manifest even to the fools of this great dominion, to wit: *Stand fast therefore in the liberty wherewith Christ hath made us free, and be not entangled again with the yoke of bondage!*" As he continued to speak I slowly stood erect, but even at my full height he towered over me, sickly, pale, and sweating, his nose, leaking slightly in the cold, like a great scimitar protruding from the stormy and an-guished face, the brandy bottle clutched in one huge mottled hand against his breast as he stood there in a limping posture, swaying and perspiring, speaking not so much to me as through and past me toward the scudding clouds. "Yes, and to this comes the reply, to this mighty and manifest truth we hear the response"—he paused for an in-stant, hiccuping, and then his voice rose in tones of mockery—"to this irresistible and binding edict we hear the Pharisee cry out of that great institution the College of William & Mary, out of Richmond, from the learned mountebanks abroad like locusts in the Commonwealth: 'Theology must answer theology. Speak you of liberty? Speak you of the yoke of bondage? How then, country magistrate, do you answer this? Ephe-sians Six, Five: *Servants, be obedient to them that are your masters according to the flesh, with fear and trembling, in singleness of your heart, as unto Christ.* Or this, my hayseed colleague, how answer you to this? One Peter, Two, Eighteen: *Servants, be subject to your masters with all fear; not only to the good and gentle, but also to the froward.* There, friend—*there*—is not that divine sanction for the bondage of which you rave and prattle? Merciful God in heaven, will such casuistry never end! Is not the handwriting on the wall?" For the first time he seemed to look at me, fixing me for a moment with his feverish eyes before upending the bottle, thrusting its neck deep into his throat, where the brandy gulped and gurgled. *"Howl ye,"* he resumed, *"Howl ye: for the day of the Lord is at hand: it shall come as a destruction from the Almighty.* You're the preacher they call Nat, are you not? Tell me then, preacher, am I not right? Is not Isaiah only a witness to the truth when he says *howl ye?* When he says the day of the Lord is at hand, and it shall come as a destruction from the Almighty? Tell me in the honesty of truth, preacher: is not the handwriting on the wall for this beloved and foolish and tragic Old Dominion?"

"Praise God, mastah," I said, "that sure is true." My words were evasively meek and humble, with a touch of ministerial sanctimony, but I uttered them mainly to cover up my sudden alarm. For now I was truly afraid that he had identified me; the fact that this strange and drunken white man knew who I was smote me like a blow between the eyes. A Negro's most cherished possession is the drab, neutral cloak of anonymity he can manage to gather around himself, allowing him to merge faceless and nameless with the common swarm: impudence and misbehavior are, for obvious reasons, unwise, but equally so is the display of an uncommon distinction, for if the former attributes can get you starved, whipped, chained, the latter may subject you to such curiosity and hostile suspicion as to ruinously impair the minute amount of freedom you possess. As for the rest, his words had spilled from his lips so rapidly and wildly that I was as yet unable to get the exact drift of his thought, which seemed nonetheless mighty precarious for a white man; and I still could not get over the sensation that he was trying to bait me, or lead me into some kind of trap. To conceal my dismay and confusion, again I mumbled, "That sure is true," and I chuckled idiotically, gazing toward the ground while I slowly wagged my head—as if to indicate that this poor darky understood precious little if indeed he understood anything.

But now, bending down slightly, his face drifted nearer to me, the skin close up not flushed and whiskey-pink as I had imagined but pale as lard, utterly bloodless and seeming to grow even whiter as I forced myself to return his gaze. "Don't play dumb with me," he said. There was no hostility in his voice, its sound was more request than command. "Your mistress pointed you out to me just now. Even so, I would have known, I could have distinguished between you two. The other Negro, what's his name?"

"Hark," I said. "That's Hark, mastah."

"Yes, I would have known you. I would have known even had I

not overheard you. 'Feel sorry for a white man and the sorrow is wasted.' Is that not what you said?"

A shiver of fear, old and habitual and humiliating, passed through me, and despite myself I averted my eyes and blurted: "I'm sorry I said that, mastah. I'm dreadful sorry. I didn't mean it, mastah."

"Poppycock!" he exclaimed. "Sorry that you said you're *not* sorry for a white man? Come, come, preacher, you don't mean that. You don't mean that, do you?" He paused, waiting for an answer, but by now my distress and embarrassment had so unsettled me that I couldn't even force a reply. Worse, I had begun to despise and curse myself for my own slow-witted inability to deal with the situation. I stood there licking my lips as I gazed out toward the woods, feeling suddenly like the most squalid type of cornfield coon.

"Now don't play dumb with me," he repeated, the voice edged with a tone almost gentle, curiously ingratiating. "Your reputation precedes you, as it were. For several years now there has come to my attention wondrous bruit of a remarkable slave, owned at different times by various masters here in the vicinity of Cross Keys, who had so surpassed the paltry condition into which he had been cast by destiny that— *mirabile dictu*—he could swiftly read, if called upon to demonstrate, from a difficult and abstract work in natural philosophy, and in a fair hand inscribe page after page of random dictation, and had mastered his numbers as far as a comprehension of simple algebra, and had so attained an understanding of Holy Scripture that such of those few adepts in the science of divinity as had examined his knowledge of the Bible came away shaking their heads in wonder at the splendor of his erudition." He paused and belched. My eyes moved back again toward his, and I saw him wipe his mouth with his sleeve. "Rumor!" he resumed quickly. Now his voice had risen to a kind of impassioned runaway sing-song, his eyes were wild and obsessed. "Astounding rumor to emerge from the backwoods of Old Virginny! Astounding as those rumors which in olden times came back from the depths of Asia— that at the source of the River Indus, I believe it was, dwelt a species of mammoth rat, six feet long, which could dance a lively jig while accompanying itself on a tambourine, and when approached would sprout heretofore invisible wings and fly to the topmost branch of the nearest palm tree. Rumor almost impossible to entertain! For to believe that from this downtrodden race, the very laws governing which bind it to an ignorance more benighted and final than death, there could arise one single specimen capable of spelling *cat* is asking rational

intelligence to believe that balmy King George the Third was not a
dastardly tyrant or that the moon is made of clabber cheese!" He
had begun to jab his finger at me as he spoke, a long bony finger
with hairy joints, sending it forth into my face in quick thrusts like a
snake's darting neck. "But beyond this, mind you, beyond this—to
imagine this . . . this prodigy, this *paragon,* a Negro *slave*—oh, perish
the vile word!—who had acquired the lineaments not just of literacy
but of knowledge, who it was rumored could almost speak in the
accents of a white man of breeding and cultivation; who, in short,
while still one of this doomed empire's most wretched minions, had
transcended his sorry state and had become not a thing but a *person*—
all this is beyond the realm of one's wildest imagination. No. No! The
mind boggles, refuses to accept such a grotesque image! Tell me,
preacher, how do you spell *cat?* Come now, prove to me the reality
of this hoax, this canard!" He kept jabbing his finger at me, the voice
cajoling, amiable, the eyes still wintry-wild and obsessed. The smell of
applejack was around him like a sweet vapor. "Cat!" he said. "Spell
cat. Cat!"

I had begun to feel surely that he was not being sarcastic, that he
was somehow trying to express mad, hulking, terrifying feelings beyond
anyone's surmise. I felt blood pounding at my temples and the cold
sweat of fear and anxiety clammy beneath my arms. "Don't mock me,
mastah, I pray you," I breathed in a whisper. "Kindly please, mastah.
Don't mock me." Time crept past and we were both silent, gazing at
each other, and the November wind boomed behind us in the forest,
crashing like giant, diminishing footfalls across the graying waste of
cedar and cypress and pine; for a moment my compliant lips trembled
on a broken wisp of air, faltering—"Ca-, Ca-"—and a grief-haunted
sense of futility, childish, lifelong, nigger-black, welled up in me like
a sigh of pain. I stood there sweating in the blustery wind, thinking:
So this is the way it is. Even when they care, even when they are
somehow on your side they cannot help but taunt and torment you.
The palms of my hands slimy, and my mind roaring, thinking: I do
not want to, but now, now if he forces me to spell the word I will
have to try to kill him. I lowered my eyes again, saying more distinctly:
"Don't mock me, mastah, please."

Yet now Cobb, adrift in his brandy haze, seemed to have forgotten
what he had said to me and turned away, staring madly toward the
forest where the wind still thrashed and flayed the distant treetops.
He clutched the bottle as if with desperation at a lopsided angle against

his chest, and a trickle of brandy oozed out against his cloak. With his other hand he began to massage his thigh, holding the leg so tightly that above the knuckles the flesh grew bone-white. "Almighty God," he groaned, "this everlasting mortal ache! *If a man live many years and rejoice in them all, yet let him remember the days of darkness, for they shall be many*. God, God, my poor Virginia, blighted domain! The soil wrecked and ravaged on every hand, turned to useless dust by that abominable weed. Tobacco we cannot any longer raise, nor cotton ever, save for a meager crop in these few southern counties, nor oats nor barley nor wheat. A wasteland! A plump and virginal principality, a cornucopia of riches the like of which the world has never seen, transformed within the space of a century to a withering, defeated hag! And all to satisfy the demand of ten million Englishmen for a pipeful of Virginia leaf! Now even that is gone, and all we can raise is horses! Horses!" he cried as if to himself now, stroking and kneading his thigh. "Horses and what else, *what else?* Horses and pickaninnies! *Pickaninnies!* Little black infants by the score, the hundreds, the thousands, the tens of thousands! The fairest state of them all, this tranquil and beloved domain—what has it now become? A *nursery* for Mississippi, Alabama, Arkansas. A monstrous breeding farm to supply the sinew to gratify the maw of Eli Whitney's infernal machine, cursed be that blackguard's name! In such a way is our human decency brought down, when we pander all that is in us noble and just to the false god which goes by the vile name of *Capital!* Oh, Virginia, woe betide thee! Woe, thrice woe, and ever damned in memory be the day when poor black men in chains first trod upon thy sacred strand!"

Groaning in pain now, fiercely stroking his thigh with one hand while with the other he elevated the bottle to his lips and drained it to the dregs, Cobb seemed, for once, oblivious of me, and I recall thinking that wisdom dictated my stealing out of his presence, if only I could find a decent way to do it. In scattered, disordered riot, all manner of emotions had run through me as he had spoken; not in years having heard a white man talk in this crazy fashion, I would not be honest if I did not admit that what he said (or the drunken gist of it, stealing in upon my consciousness like some unreal ghostly light) caused me to feel a shiver of awe and something else, dim and remote, which might have been a thrill of hope. But for some reason I cannot explain, both awe and hope swiftly retreated in my mind, dwindled, died, and even as I looked at Cobb, I could only smell the musky scent of danger—flagrant, imminent danger—and feel a sense of suspicion and mistrust such as I had rarely ever known. Why? It is perhaps impossible to explain save by God, who knows all things. Yet I will say this, without which you cannot understand the central madness of nigger existence: beat a nigger, starve him, leave him wallowing in his own shit, and he will be yours for life. Awe him by some unforeseen hint of philanthropy, tickle him with the idea of hope, and he will want to slice your throat.

Yet now before I could make any kind of move, a cracking noise sounded behind us as once again the shop door opened, swung wide, and drove itself with windy force against the wall. And as we turned then, Hark emerged with shirttail flying, scrambling away from the shop, plunging in panicky headlong flight toward the fields and the woods beyond. Legs churning, his great black body moved at a furious gallop; his eyes rolled white with alarm. Scant yards behind him now came Putnam, his leather apron flapping as he brandished a stick of lightwood, bawling at the top of his voice. "You, Hark, come back here! Come back here, you dad-dratted no-good an'mal! I'll get hold of you at last, black bastard!" Fleet as a deer, Hark scampered across the open lot, bare black feet sowing puffs of dust, the barnyard cat fleeing his approach, goose and gander too, cumbersomely flapping their flightless wings, emitting dismal honking sounds as they waddled from his path. On he came past us, looking neither left nor right, eyes round and white as eggshells, and we could hear the voice panting *ah-ah-ah* as he sprinted for the woods, moving now with such nimble-footed speed that he seemed whisked forward like a sail on the wind. Far beyond, losing ground each second, came the pimpled boy, still howling. "Stop! You, Hark! Black wretch! Stop!" But Hark's great legs were churning as if propelled by steam; vaulting the pump trough, he soared through the air in a gigantic leap like something suspended by wire or wings, struck the earth with a thumping sound, and without breaking stride, bounded on toward the distant forest, the inside of his bare soles flashing splendidly pink. Then all of a sudden it was as if he had been felled by a cannon ball: his head snapped back, and the rest of him including his pinwheeling legs sailed out and forward, and he came down flat on his back with a bladdery, sacklike thud, directly beneath the clothesline which, at gullet level, had intercepted his flight. But as Cobb and I stood watching, watched him shake his head and try to rise up on his elbows, we saw now not one but two forces, though equally sinister and somber, converging on Hark from opposite directions: Putnam, still waving his lightwood stick, and Miss Maria

Pope, who had appeared as if from nowhere like some augury of frustrate bitchery and vengeance, bearing down upon Hark with a hobbled spinster's gait amid black snapping yards of funereal gingham. Blown back on the wind, her voice already was hysteric with shrill malevolence. "It's up the tree for you, nigger!" she screeched. "Up the tree!"

"Now," I heard Cobb murmur, "now we are about to witness a ritual diversion indigenous to this Southern clime. We are about to witness two human beings whipping another."

"No, mastah," I said. "Marse Joe don't 'low his niggers to be beaten. But there's ways around that, as you will surely see. You about to witness something else, mastah."

"Not a speck of charcoal in the shop!" Putnam was shouting in a kind of wail.

"And not a drop of water in the kitchen pail!" Miss Maria shrilled. As if vying with each other to be the chiefest victim of Hark's enormity, they surrounded him, encompassed the prostrate form, squawking like birds. Hark staggered to his feet, shaking his head with the slow, stunned, dizzy bewilderment of an about-to-be-slaughtered ox that has received a faulty glancing blow. "It's up the tree with him this time, impudent black scoundrel!" Miss Maria cackled. "Putnam, get the ladder!"

"Hark's most dreadful feared of heights," I found myself explaining to Cobb. "This for him is worse than a hundred beatings."

"A fantastic specimen!" Cobb breathed. "A regular *gladiator,* a veritable black Apollo. And swift as a race horse! Where did your master get him?"

"From up Sussex way," I said, "about ten, eleven years ago, mastah, when they broke up one of the old plantations." I paused for a moment, half wondering to myself why I was proffering all this information. "Hark's all forlorn now," I went on, "heartsick and forlorn. On the outside he's very cheery, but inside he's just all torn up. He can't keep his mind on anything. That's how come he forgets his chores, and how come he gets punished. Poor old Hark . . ."

"Why is that, preacher?" said Cobb. Putnam had fetched a ladder now from the barn, and we watched the procession as it made its way across the windswept lot, bleak and gray in the fading autumnal light— Miss Maria in the lead, grim, hands clenched, her back stiff and straight as a poker, Putnam behind with the ladder, and between them Hark in his dusty gray denim, shuffling along with his head bent in total dejection, looming over the two of them like some huge Goliath, a giant towering above a pair of vengeful, hurrying dwarfs. In Indian file, straight as an arrow, they made their way toward an ancient and enormous maple whose lowermost branch, leafless now, stretched across the pale sky like a naked arm twenty feet above the earth. I could hear Hark's bare feet scuffing across the ground, scuffing like the feet of a reluctant child. "Why is that?" Cobb said again.

"Well, mastah, I'll tell you," I said. "Couple years ago, afore I became Marse Joe's property, Marse Joe had to sell off most all of his niggers. Sell them off down to Mississippi, where you know they are planting considerable cotton. Hark told me Marse Joe was in a misery about this, but he just couldn't do anything else. Well, amongst these niggers was Hark's wife and Hark's child—little boy about three or four years old he was then. Hark cared for that little boy almost more than anything."

"Yah, yah, yah," I could hear Cobb murmur, making little clucking sounds beneath his breath.

"So when that little boy was gone, Hark near about went mad with grief, couldn't think about anything else."

"Yah, yah, yah, yah."

"He wanted to run away and follow them all the way down to Mississippi, but I talked him out of it. See, he'd already run off once years ago and hadn't gotten anywhere. Besides, it's always been my idea that a nigger should follow all the rules and regulations so far as he was able."

"Yah, yah, yah."

"Anyway," I went on. "Hark ain't been quite right ever since then. You might say he's just been distracted. That's why he does things— or doesn't do things—that get him punished. And I'll be quite truthful with you, mastah, he *doesn't* do his chores, but I tell you he just can't help it."

"Yah, yah," Cobb muttered, "yah, great God, the logical outcome . . . *the ultimate horror!*" He had begun to hiccup again and the sound came forth in intermittent gasps, almost like sobs. He started to say something else, thought better of it, turned away, whispering over and over again: "*God, God, God, God, God.*"

"Now about this here," I explained. "Like I say, Hark's most dreadful feared of high places. Last spring the roof leaked and Marse Joe sent Hark and me up to fix it. But Hark got halfway up and he just froze there. Begun to whimper and mumble to hisself and wouldn't go an inch further. So I had to fix that roof myself. Anyway, Marse

Putnam and Miss Maria caught ahold of this fear of Hark's—you might say they found out his weak spot. Like I said, Marse Joe won't tolerate anyone to mistreat his niggers, to beat them or anything like that. So whenever Marse Joe's away, and Marse Putnam and Miss Maria figger they can get away with it, why, they run old Hark up a tree."

Which is what they were doing even as I spoke, their voices muffled, remote, indistinct now on the blustery wind. Putnam propping the long ladder against the tree trunk, then jerking his arm furiously upward as he bade Hark to climb. And Hark began climbing, reluctantly, at the third rung turning his frightened face imploringly back as if to see whether they might not have had a change of heart, but this time Miss Maria's arms jerked upward—*up, nigger, up*—and again Hark continued his climb, knees quaking beneath his trousers. At last arrived at the lowermost branch, Hark swung himself off the ladder, clutching the tree so tightly that I could see even from this distance the veins standing out against the muscles of his arms, then with a sort of scrounging, sliding motion of his rump, deposited himself in the crotch formed by trunk and branch, and sat there embracing the tree with his eyes squeezed shut—dizzy, windy yards above the earth. Then Putnam removed the ladder and laid it flat on the ground beneath the tree.

"Five, ten minutes will go by, mastah," I said to Cobb, "and then old Hark will commence crying and moaning. Just wait and see. Then pretty soon he'll start swaying. Crying and moaning and swaying there on that branch like he's about to fall off. Then Marse Putnam and Miss Maria'll set that ladder up against the tree and Hark'll climb down. I reckon they get scared Hark will fall off and break his neck and they wouldn't want that to happen. No, they just want to give old Hark a poor time for a while."

"Yah, yah, yah," Cobb murmured, distantly now.

"And that for Hark is a poor time indeed," I said.

"Yah, yah, yah," he replied. I don't know whether he was listening to me or not. "Great God! Sometimes I think . . . sometimes . . . *it is like living in a dream!*"

Then suddenly, without another word, Cobb was gone, limping in gaunt strides toward the house, the empty brandy flask still clutched in his hand, cloak flapping, shoulders hunched against the wind. I crouched down again above my rabbits, watching Cobb limp and sway across the lot and up to the front porch, his voice faint and weary as he called out: "Hallo, Miz Travis, think I'll come in and set a spell after all!" And Miss Sarah's voice way off within, high and full of cheer, and the sound of the door slamming as Cobb vanished inside the house. I stripped the white translucent inner skin from a rabbit, separating it from the pinkish flesh, and plunged the corpse into the cool water, feeling the guts squirming wet and slimy beneath my fingers. Blood mingled with the water, turning it a muddy crimson. Gusts of wind swept through the cotton patch, whistling; an army of dead withered leaves marched along the edge of the barn, rolled with a husky scrabbling noise across the vacant yard. I gazed down into the bloody water, thinking of Cobb. *Go through the midst of Jerusalem, and set a mark upon the foreheads of the men that sigh and that cry for all the abominations, that be done in the midst thereof . . . Slay utterly old and young, both maids and little children, and women: but come not near any man upon whom is the mark . . .*

Suddenly I found myself thinking: It is plain, yes, plain, plain. When I succeed in my great mission, and Jerusalem is destroyed, this man Cobb will be among those few spared the sword . . .

Across the roof of the woods the wind rushed in hissing, majestic swoop and cadence, echoing in far-off hollows with the thudding sound of footfalls. Gray and streaked, boiling, in ponderous haste, the clouds fled eastward across the lowering heavens, growing darker now in the early dusk. After a bit I heard Hark begin to moan, a soft disconsolate wordless wail, filled with dread. For long minutes he moaned, swaying high in his tree. Then I heard the *tap-tap-tapping* of the ladder as they set it against the tree trunk and let him down.

Robert Penn Warren

CASS MASTERN

The narrator of *All the King's Men,* Jack Burden, a cousin, two two generations later, of Cass Mastern comes into possession of Cass's diary, and as a candidate for the Ph.D. in history attempts to use it, and other family documents, as the basis for his dissertion. But Burden, who is trying to justify himself in a world which he conceives to be merely mechanistic and amoral, cannot face the story of that distant kinsman who found in a moral issue his final reality.

The story of Cass needs a word of background. He was born and spent his childhood in a cabin in the red hills of Georgia, in dire poverty. His older brother, Gilbert, had fled that poverty, gone to Mississippi, and had found, mysteriously, perhaps criminally, his start in life. By the 1850s Gilbert reappears at the cabin, now a "cotton snob," a gentleman in black broadcloth, with baronial estates. Now he would take Cass back to "Valhalla," his plantation, to educate him as a gentleman, put him in politics, and make him great—"great" as an adjunct of the power of Gilbert Mastern.

After a Spartan regime of tutoring at Valhalla, Cass is sent to Lexington, Kentucky, to Transylvania University, where he is taken up by Duncan Trice, a rich, fashionable, and somewhat dissipated friend of his brother. The selection below opens with the first meeting of Cass and Arabella Trice, the young wife of Duncan.

Robert Penn Warren

...He had remarked how, when she first came in, into the shadowy room, her eyes had seemed black. But he had been mistaken, he was to discover, and that discovery was the first step toward his undoing. After the greeting ("she greeted me with great simplicity and courtesy and bade me again take my seat"), she remarked on how dark the room was and how the autumn always came to take one unawares. Then she touched a bellpull and a Negro boy entered. "She commanded him to bring light and to mend the fire, which was sunk to ash, or near so. He came back presently with a seven-branched candlestick which he put upon the table back of the couch on which I sat. He struck a lucifer but she said, 'Let me light the candles.' I remember it as if it were only yesterday when I sat on that couch. I had turned my head idly to watch her light the candles. The little table was between us. She leaned over the candles and applied the lucifer to the wicks, one after another. She was leaning over, and I saw how the corset lifted her breasts together, but because she was leaning the eyelids shaded her eyes from my sight. Then she raised her head a little and looked straight at me over the new candle flames, and I saw all at once that her eyes were not black. They were blue, but a blue so deep that I can only compare it to the color of the night sky in autumn when the weather is clear and there is no moon and the stars have just well come out. And I had not known how large they were. I remember saying that to myself with perfect clearness, 'I had not known how large they were,' several times, slowly, like a man marvelling. Then

I knew that I was blushing and I felt my tongue dry like ashes in my mouth and I was in the manly state.

"I can see perfectly clearly the expression on her face even now, but I cannot interpret it. Sometimes I have thought of it as having a smiling hidden in it, but I cannot be sure. (I am only sure of this: that man is never safe and damnation is ever at hand, O God and my Redeemer!) I sat there, one hand clenched upon my knee and the other holding an empty glass, and I felt that I could not breathe. Then she said to her husband, who stood in the room behind me, 'Duncan, do you see that Mr. Mastern is in need of refreshment?'"

The year passed. Cass, who was a good deal younger than Duncan Trice, and as a matter of fact several years younger than Annabelle Trice, became a close companion of Duncan Trice and learned much from him, for Duncan Trice was rich, fashionable, clever, and high-spirited ("much given to laughter and full-blooded"). Duncan Trice led Cass to the bottle, the gaming table and the racecourse, but not to the "illicit sweetness of the flesh." Duncan Trice was passionately and single-mindedly devoted to his wife. ("When she came into a room, his eyes would fix upon her without shame, and I have seen her avert her face and blush for the boldness of his glance when company was present. But I think that it was done by him unawares, his partiality for her was so great.") No, the other young men, members of the Trice circle, led Cass first to the "illicit sweetness." But despite the new interests and gratifications, Cass could work at his books. There was even time for that, for he had great strength and endurance.

So the year passed. He had been much in the Trice house, but no word beyond the "words of merriment and civility" had passed between him and Annabelle Trice. In June, there was a dancing party at the house of some friend of Duncan Trice. Duncan Trice, his wife, and Cass happened to stroll at some moment into the garden and to sit in a little arbor, which was covered with a jasmine vine. Duncan Trice returned to the house to get punch for the three of them, leaving Annabelle and Cass seated side by side in the arbor. Cass commented on the sweetness of the scent of jasmine. All at once, she burst out ("her voice low-pitched and with its huskiness, but in a vehemence which astonished me"), "Yes, yes, it is too sweet. It is suffocating. I shall suffocate." And she laid her right hand, with the fingers spread, across the bare swell of her bosom above the pressure of the corset.

"Thinking her taken by some sudden illness," Cass recorded in the journal, "I asked if she were faint. She said, No, in a very low, husky voice. Nevertheless I rose, with the expressed intention of getting a glass of water for her. Suddenly she said, quite harshly and to my amazement, because of her excellent courtesy, 'Sit down, sit down, I don't want water!' So somewhat distressed in mind that unwittingly I might have offended, I sat down. I looked across the garden where in the light of the moon several couples promenaded down the paths between the low hedges. I could hear the sound of her breathing beside me. It was disturbed and irregular. All at once she said, 'How old are you, Mr. Mastern?' I said twenty-two. Then she said, 'I am twenty-nine.' I stammered something, in my surprise. She laughed as though at my confusion, and said, 'Yes, I am seven years older than you, Mr. Mastern. Does that surprise you, Mr. Mastern?' I replied in the affirmative. Then she said, 'Seven years is a long time. Seven years ago you were a child, Mr. Mastern.' Then she laughed, with a sudden sharpness, but quickly stopped herself to add, 'But I wasn't a child. Not seven years ago, Mr. Mastern.' I did not answer her, for there was no thought clear in my head. I sat there in confusion, but in the middle of my confusion I was trying to see what she would have looked like as a child. I could call up no image. Then her husband returned from the house."

A few days later Cass went back to Mississippi to devote some months to his plantation, and, under the guidance of Gilbert, to go once to Jackson, the capital, and once to Vicksburg. It was a busy summer. Now Cass could see clearly what Gilbert intended: to make him rich and to put him into politics. It was a flattering and glittering prospect, and one not beyond reasonable expectation for a young man whose brother was Gilbert Mastern. ("My brother is a man of great taciturnity and strong mind, and when he speaks, though he practices no graces and ingratiations, all men, especially those of the sober sort who have responsibility and power, weigh his words with respect.") So the summer passed, under the strong hand and cold eye of Gilbert. But toward the end of the season, when already Cass was beginning to give thought to his return to Transylvania, an envelope came addressed to him from Lexington, in an unfamiliar script. When Cass unfolded the single sheet of paper a small pressed blossom, or what he discovered to be such, slipped out. For a moment he could not think what it was, or why it was in his hand. Then he put it to his nostrils. The odor, now faint and dusty, was the odor of jasmine.

The sheet of paper had been folded twice, to make four equal sections.

In one section, in a clean, strong, not large script, he read: "Oh, Cass!" That was all.

It was enough.

One drizzly autumn afternoon, just after his return to Lexington, Cass called at the Trice house to pay his respects. Duncan Trice was not there, having sent word that he had been urgently detained in the town and would be home for a late dinner. Of that afternoon, Cass wrote: "I found myself in the room alone with her. There were shadows, as there had been that afternoon, almost a year before, when I first saw her in that room, and when I had thought that her eyes were black. She greeted me, civilly, and I replied and stepped back after having shaken her hand. Then I realized that she was looking at me fixedly, as I at her. Suddenly, her lips parted slightly and gave a short exhalation, like a sigh or suppressed moan. As of one accord, we moved toward each other and embraced. No words passed between us as we stood there. We stood there for a long time, or so it seemed. I held her body close to me in a strong embrace, but we did not exchange a kiss, which upon recollection has since seemed strange. But was it strange? Was it strange that some remnant of shame should forbid us to look each other in the face? I felt and heard my heart racing within my bosom, with a loose feeling as though it were un-moored and were leaping at random in a great cavity within me, but at the same time I scarcely accepted the fact of my situation. I was somehow possessed by incredulity, even as to my identity, as I stood there and my nostrils were filled with the fragrance of her hair. It was not to be believed that I was Cass Mastern, who stood thus in the house of a friend and benefactor. There was no remorse or horror at the turpitude of the act, but only the incredulity which I have referred to. (One feels incredulity at the first breaking of a habit, but horror at the violation of a principle. Therefore what virtue and honor I had known in the past had been an accident of habit and not the fruit of will. Or can virtue be the fruit of human will? The thought is pride.)

"As I have said, we stood there for a long time in a strong embrace, but with her face lowered against my chest, and my own eyes staring across the room and out a window into the deepening obscurity of the evening. When she finally raised her face, I saw that she had been silently weeping. Why was she weeping? I have asked myself that question. Was it because even on the verge of committing an irremediable wrong she could weep at the consequence of an act which she felt powerless to avoid? Was it because the man who held her was much younger than she and his embrace gave her the reproach of youth and seven years? Was it because he had come seven years too late and could not come in innocence? It does not matter what the cause. If it was the first, then the tears can only prove that sentiment is no substitute for obligation, if the second, then they only prove that pity of the self is no substitute for wisdom. But she shed the tears and finally lifted her face to mine with those tears bright in her large eyes, and even now, though those tears were my ruin, I cannot wish them unshed, for they testify to the warmth of her heart and prove that whatever her sin (and mine) she did not step to it with a gay foot and with the eyes hard with lust and fleshly cupidity.

"The tears were my ruin, for when she lifted her face to me some streak of tenderness was mixed into my feelings, and my heart seemed to flood itself into my bosom to fill that great cavity wherein it had been leaping. She said, 'Cass'—the first time she had ever addressed me by my Christian name. 'Yes,' I replied. 'Kiss me,' she said very simply, 'you can do it now.' So I kissed her. And thereupon in the blindness of our mortal blood and in the appetite of our hearts we performed the act. There in that very room with the servants walking with soft feet somewhere in the house and with the door to the room open and with her husband expected, and not yet in the room the darkness of evening. But we were secure in our very recklessness, as though the lustful heart could give forth a cloud of darkness in which we were shrouded, even as Venus once shrouded Aeneas in a cloud so that he passed unspied among men to approach the city of Dido. In such cases as ours the very recklessness gives security as the strength of the desire seems to give the sanction of justice and righteousness.

"Though she had wept and had seemed to perform the act in a sadness and desperation, immediately afterward she spoke cheerfully to me. She stood in the middle of the room pressing her hair into place, and I stumblingly ventured some remark about our future, a remark very vague for my being was still confused, but she responded, 'Oh, let us not think about it now,' as though I had broached a subject of no consequence. She promptly summoned a servant and asked for lights. They were brought and thereupon I inspected her face to find it fresh and unmarked. When her husband came, she greeted him familiarly and affectionately, and as I witnessed it my own heart was wrenched, but not, I must confess, with compunction. Rather with a violent jealousy. When he spoke to me and took my hand, so great was my disturbance that I was sure that my face could not but betray it."

So began the second phase of the story of Cass Mastern. All that year, as before, he was often in the house of Duncan Trice, and as before he was often with him in field sports, gambling, drinking, and racegoing. He learned, he says, to "wear his brow unwrinkled," to accept the condition of things. As for Annabelle Trice, he says that sometimes looking back, he could scarcely persuade himself that "she had shed tears." She was, he says, "of a warm nature, reckless and passionate of disposition, hating all mention of the future (she would never let me mention times to come), agile, resourceful, and cheerful in devising to gratify our appetites, but with a womanly tenderness such as any man might prize at a sanctified hearthside." She must indeed have been agile and resourceful, for to carry on such a liaison undetected in that age and place must have been a problem. There was a kind of summerhouse at the foot of the Trice garden, which one could enter unobserved from an alley. Some of their meetings occurred there. A half-sister of Annabelle Trice, who lived in Lexington, apparently assisted the lovers or winked at their relationship, but, it seems, only after some pressure by Annabelle, for Cass mentions "a stormy scene." So some of the meetings were there. But now and then Duncan Trice had to be out of town on business, and on these occasions Cass would be admitted, late at night, to the house, even during a period when Annabelle's mother and father were staying there; so he actually lay in the very bed belonging to Duncan Trice.

There were, however, other meetings, unplanned and unpredictable moments snatched when they found themselves left alone together. "Scarce a corner, cranny, or protected nook or angle of my friend's trusting house did we not at one time or another defile, and that even in the full and shameless light of day," Cass wrote in the journal, and when Jack Burden, the student of history, went to Lexington and went to see the old Trice house he remembered the sentence. The town had grown up around the house, and the gardens, except for a patch of lawn, were gone. But the house was well maintained (some people named Miller lived there and by and large respected the place) and Jack Burden was permitted to inspect the premises. He wandered about the room where the first meeting had taken place and she had raised her eyes to Cass Mastern above the newly lighted candles and where, a year later, she had uttered the sigh, or suppressed moan, and stepped to his arms; and out into the hall, which was finely proportioned and

with a graceful stair, and into a small, shadowy library; and to a kind
of back hall, which was a well "protected nook or angle" and had,
as a matter of fact, furniture adequate to the occasion. Jack Burden
stood in the main hall, which was cool and dim, with dully glittering
floors, and, in the silence of the house, recalled that period, some
seventy years before, of the covert glances, the guarded whispers, the
abrupt rustling of silk in the silence (the costume of the period certainly
had not been designed to encourage casual vice), the sharp breath,
the reckless sighs. Well, all of that had been a long time before, and
Annabelle Trice and Cass Mastern were long since deader than mackerel,
and Mrs. Miller, who came down to give Jack Burden a cup of tea
(she was flattered by the "historical" interest in her house, though
she didn't guess the exact nature of the case), certainly was not "agile"
and didn't look "resourceful" and probably had used up all her energy
in the Ladies Altar Guild of St. Luke's Episcopal Church and in the
D.A.R.

The period of the intrigue, the second phase of the story of Cass
Mastern, lasted all of one academic year, part of the summer (for Cass
was compelled to go back to Mississippi for his plantation affairs and
to attend the wedding of his sister Lavinia, who married a well-con-
nected young man named Willis Burden), and well through the next
winter, when Cass was back in Lexington. Then, on March 19, 1854,
Duncan Trice died, in his library (which was a "protected nook or
angle" of his house), with a lead slug nearly the size of a man's thumb
in his chest. It was quite obviously an accident.

The widow sat in church, upright and immobile. When she once
raised her veil to touch at her eyes with a handkerchief, Cass Mastern
saw that the cheek was "pale as marble but for a single flushed spot,
like the flush of fever." But even when the veil was lowered he detected
the fixed, bright eyes glittering "within that artificial shadow."

Cass Mastern, with five other young men of Lexington, cronies and
boon companions of the dead man, carried the coffin. "The coffin which
I carried seemed to have no weight, although my friend had been of
large frame and had inclined to stoutness. As we proceeded with it,
I marvelled at the fact of its lightness, and once the fancy flitted into
my mind that he was not in the coffin at all, that it was empty,
and that all the affair was a masquerade or mock show carried to ludicrous and blasphemous length, for no purpose, as in a dream. Or to
deceive me, the fancy came. I was the object of the deception, and all
the other people were in league and conspiracy against me. But when

that thought came, I suddenly felt a sense of great cunning and a wild exhilaration. I had been too sharp to be caught so. I had penetrated the deception. I had the impulse to hurl the coffin to the ground and see its emptiness burst open and to laugh in triumph. But I did not, and I saw the coffin sink beneath the level of the earth on which we stood and receive the first clods upon it.

"As soon as the sound of the first clods striking the coffin came to me, I felt a great relief, and then a most overmastering desire. I looked toward her. She was kneeling at the foot of the grave, with what thoughts I could not know. Her head was inclined slightly and the veil was over her face. The bright sun poured over her black-clad figure. I could not take my eyes from the sight. The posture seemed to accentuate the charms of her person and to suggest to my inflamed senses the suppleness of her members. Even the funereal tint of her costume seemed to add to the provocation. The sunshine was hot upon my neck and could be felt through the stuff of my coat upon my shoulders. It was preternaturally bright so that I was blinded by it and my eyes were blinded and my senses swam. But all the while I could hear, as from a great distance, the scraping of the spades upon the piled earth and the muffled sound of earth falling into the excavation."

That evening Cass went to the summerhouse in the garden. It was not by appointment, simply on impulse. He waited there a long time, but she finally appeared, dressed in black "which was scarce darker than the night." He did not speak, or make any sign as she approached, "gliding like a shadow among shadows," but remained standing where he had been, in the deepest obscurity of the summerhouse. Even when she entered, he did not betray his presence. "I cannot be certain that any premeditation was in my silence. It was prompted by an overpowering impulse which gripped me and sealed my throat and froze my limbs. Before that moment, and afterwards, I knew that it is dishonorable to spy upon another, but at the moment no such considerations presented themselves. I had to keep my eyes fixed upon her as she stood there thinking herself alone in the darkness of the structure. I had the fancy that since she thought herself alone I might penetrate into her being, that I might learn what change, what effect, had been wrought by the death of her husband. The passion which had seized me to the very extent of paroxysm that afternoon at the brink of my friend's grave was gone. I was perfectly cold now. But I had to know, to try to know. It was as though I might know myself by knowing her. (It is human defect—to try to know oneself by the self of another. One can only know oneself in God and in His great eye.)

"She entered the summerhouse and sank upon one of the benches, not more than a few feet from my own location. For a long time I stood there, peering at her. She sat perfectly upright and rigid. At last I whispered her name, as low as might be. If she heard it, she gave no sign. So I repeated her name, in the same fashion, and again. Upon the third utterance, she whispered, 'Yes,' but she did not change her posture or turn her head. Then I spoke more loudly, again uttering her name, and instantly, with a motion of wild alarm she rose, with a strangled cry and her hands lifted toward her face. She reeled, and it seemed that she would collapse to the floor, but she gained control of herself and stood there staring at me. Stammeringly, I made my apology, saying that I had not wanted to startle her, that I had understood her to answer yes to my whisper before I spoke, and I asked her, 'Did you not answer to my whisper?'

"She replied that she had.

" 'Then why were you distressed when I spoke again?' " I asked her.

" 'Because I did not know that you were here,' she said.

" 'But,' I said, 'you say that you had just heard my whisper and had answered to it, and now you say that you did not know I was here."

" 'I did not know that you were here,' she repeated, in a low voice, and the import of what she was saying dawned upon me.

" 'Listen,' I said, 'when you heard the whisper—did you recognize it as my voice?'

"She stared at me, not answering.

" 'Answer me,' I demanded, for I had to know.

"She continued to stare, and finally replied hesitantly, 'I do not know.'

" 'You thought it was—' I began, but before I could utter the words she had flung herself upon me, clasping me in desperation like a person frantic with drowning, and ejaculating. 'No, no, it does not matter what I thought, you are here, you are here!' And she drew my face down and pressed her lips against mine to stop my words. Her lips were cold, but they hung upon mine.

"I too was perfectly cold, as of a mortal chill. And the coldness was the final horror of the act which we performed, as though two dolls should parody the shame and filth of man to make it doubly shameful.

"After, she said to me, 'Had I not found you here tonight, it could never have been between us again.'

" 'Why?' I demanded.

" 'It was a sign,' she said.

" 'A sign?' I demanded.

" 'A sign that we cannot escape, that we—' and she interrupted herself, to resume, whispering fiercely in the dark—'I do not want to escape—it is a sign—whatever I have done is done.' She grew quiet for a moment, then she said, 'Give me your hand.'

"I gave her my right hand. She grasped it, dropped it, and said, 'The other, the other hand.'

"I held it out, across my own body, for I was sitting on her left. She seized it with her own left hand, bringing her hand upward from below to press my hand flat against her bosom. Then, fumblingly, she slipped a ring upon my finger, the finger next to the smallest.

" 'What is that?' I asked.

" 'A ring,' she answered, paused, and added, 'It is his ring.'

"Then I recalled that he, my friend, had always worn a wedding ring, and I felt the metal cold upon my flesh. 'Did you take it off of his finger?' I asked, and the thought shook me.

" 'No,' she said.

" 'No?' I questioned.

" 'No,' she said, 'he took it off. It was the only time he ever took it off.'

"I sat beside her, waiting for what, I did not know, while she held my hand pressed against her bosom. I could feel it rise and fall. I could say nothing.

"Then she said, 'Do you want to know how—how he took it off?'

" 'Yes,' I said in the dark, and waiting for her to speak, I moved my tongue out upon my dry lips.

" 'Listen,' she commanded me in an imperious whisper, 'that evening after—after it happened—after the house was quiet again, I sat in my room, in the little chair by the dressing table, where I always sit for Phebe to let down my hair. I had sat there out of habit, I suppose, for I was numb all over, I watched Phebe preparing the bed for the night.' (Phebe was her waiting maid, a comely yellow wench somewhat given to the fits and sulks.) 'I saw Phebe remove the bolster and then look down at a spot where the bolster had lain, on my side of the bed. She picked something up and came toward me. She stared at me—and her eyes, they are yellow, you look into them and you can't see what is in them—she stared at me—a long time—and then she held out her hand, clenched shut and she watched me—and then—slow, so slow—she opened up the fingers—and there lay the ring on the palm of her hand—and I knew it was his ring but all I thought was, it is gold and it is lying in a gold hand. For Phebe's hand was gold—I had never noticed how her hand is the color of pure gold. Then I looked up and she was still staring at me, and her eyes were gold, too, and bright and hard like gold. And I knew that she knew.'

"'Knew?' I echoed, like a question, but I knew, too, now. My friend had learned the truth—from the coldness of his wife, from the gossip of servants—and had drawn the gold ring from his finger and carried it to the bed where he had lain with her and had put it beneath her pillow and had gone down and shot himself but under such circumstances that no one save his wife would ever guess it to be more than an accident. But he had made one fault of calculation. The yellow wench had found the ring.

"'She knows,' she whispered, pressing my hand hard against her bosom, which heaved and palpitated with a new wildness. 'She knows—and she looks at me—she will always look at me.' Then suddenly her voice dropped, and a wailing intonation came into it: 'She will tell. All of them will know. All of them in the house will look at me and know—when they hand me the dish—when they come into the room—and their feet don't make any noise!' She rose abruptly, dropping my hand. I remained seated, and she stood there beside me, her back toward me, the whiteness of her face and hands no longer visible, and to my sight the blackness of her costume faded into the shadow, even in such proximity. Suddenly, in a voice which I did not recognize for its hardness, she said in the darkness above me, 'I will not abide it, I will not abide it!' Then she turned, and with a swooping motion leaned to kiss me upon the mouth. Then she was gone from my side and I heard her feet running up the gravel of the path. I sat there in the darkness for a time longer, turning the ring upon my finger."

After that meeting in the summerhouse, Cass did not see Annabelle Trice for some days. He learned that she had gone to Louisville, where, he recalled, she had close friends. She had, as was natural, taken Phebe with her. Then he heard that she had returned, and that night, late, went to the summerhouse in the garden. She was there, sitting in the dark. She greeted him. She seemed, he wrote later, peculiarly cut off, remote, and vague in manner, like a somnambulist or a person drugged. He asked about her trip to Louisville, and she replied briefly that she had been down the river to Paducah. He remarked that he had not known that she had friends in Paducah, and she said that she had none there. Then, all at once, she turned on him, the vagueness changing to violence, and burst out, "You are prying—you are prying into my affairs—and I will not tolerate it." Cass stammered out some excuse before she cut in to say, "But if you must know, I'll tell you. I took her there."

For a moment Cass was genuinely confused.

"Her?" he questioned.

"Phebe," she replied, "I took her to Paducah, and she's gone."

"Gone—gone where?"

"Down the river," she answered, repeated, "down the river," and laughed abruptly, and added, "and she won't look at me any more like that."

"You sold her?"

"Yes, I sold her. In Paducah, to a man who was making up a coffle of Negroes for New Orleans. And nobody knows me in Paducah, nobody knew I was there, nobody knows I sold her, for I shall say she ran away into Illinois. But I sold her. For thirteen hundred dollars."

"You got a good price," Cass said, "even for a yellow girl as sprightly as Phebe." And, as he reports in the journal, he laughed with some "bitterness and rudeness," though he does not say why.

"Yes," she replied, "I got a good price. I made him pay every penny she was worth. And then do you know what I did with the money, do you?"

"No."

"When I came off the boat at Louisville, there was an old man, a nigger, sitting on the landing stage, and he was blind and picking on a guitar and singing 'Old Dan Tucker.' I took the money out of my bag and walked to him and laid it in his old hat."

"If you were going to give the money away—if you felt the money was defiled—why didn't you free her?" Cass asked.

"She'd stay right here, she wouldn't go away, she would stay right here and look at me. Oh, no, she wouldn't go away, for she's the wife of a man the Motley's have, their coachman. Oh, she'd stay right here and look at me and tell, tell what she knows, and I'll not abide it!"

Then Cass said, "If you had spoken to me I would have bought the man from Mr. Motley and set him free, too."

"He wouldn't have sold," she said, "the Motleys won't sell a servant."

"Even to be freed?" Cass continued, but she cut in, "I tell you I won't have you interfering with my affairs, do you understand that?" And she rose from his side and stood in the middle of the summerhouse, and he saw the glimmer of her face in the shadow and heard her agitated breathing. "I thought you were fond of her," Cass said.

"I was," she said, "until—until she looked at me like that."

"You know why you got that price for her?" Cass asked, and without waiting for an answer, went on, "Because she's yellow and comely and well-made. Oh, the drovers wouldn't take her down chained in a coffle. They wouldn't wear her down. They'll take her down the river soft. And you know why?"

"Yes, I know why," she said, "and what is it to you? Are you so charmed by her?"

"That is unfair," Cass said.

"Oh, I see, Mr. Mastern," she said, "oh, I see, you are concerned for the honor of a black coachman. It is a very delicate sentiment, Mr. Mastern. Why—" and she came to stand above him as he still sat on the bench—"why did you not show some such delicate concern for the honor of your friend? Who is now dead."

According to the journal, there was, at this moment, "a tempest of feeling" in his breast. He wrote: "Thus I heard put into words for the first time the accusation which has ever in all climes been that most calculated to make wince a man of proper nurture or natural rectitude. What the hardened man can bear to hear from the still small voice within, may yet be when spoken by any external tongue an accusation dire enough to drain his very cheeks of blood. But it was not only that accusation in itself, for in very truth I had supped full of that horror and made it my long familiar. It was not merely the betrayal of my friend. It was not merely the death of my friend, at whose breast I had levelled the weapon. I could have managed somehow to live with those facts. But I suddenly felt that the world outside of me was shifting and the substance of things, and that the process had only begun of a general disintegration of which I was the center. At that moment of perturbation, when the cold sweat broke on my brow, I did not frame any sentence distinctly to my mind. But I have looked back and wrestled to know the truth. It was not the fact that a slave woman was being sold away from the house where she had had protection and kindness and away from the arms of her husband into debauchery. I knew that such things had happened in fact, and I was no child for after my arrival in Lexington and my acquaintance with the looser sort of companions, the sportsmen and the followers of the races,

I had myself enjoyed such diversions. It was not only the fact that the woman for whom I had sacrificed my friend's life and my honor could, in her own suffering, turn on me with a cold rage and the language of insult so that I did not recognize her. It was, instead, the fact that all of these things—the death of my friend, the betrayal of Phebe, the suffering and rage and great change of the woman I had loved—all had come from my single act of sin and perfidy, as the boughs from the bole and the leaves from the bough. Or to figure the matter differently, it was as though the vibration set up in the whole fabric of the world by my act had spread infinitely and with ever increasing power and no man could know the end. I did not put it into words in such fashion, but I stood there shaken by a tempest of feeling."

When Cass had somewhat controlled his agitation, he said, "To whom did you sell the girl?"

"What's it to you?" she answered.

"To whom did you sell the girl?" he repeated.

"I'll not tell you," she said.

"I will find out," he said. "I will go to Paducah and find out."

She grasped him by the arm, driving her fingers deep into the flesh, "like talons," and demanded, "Why—why are you going?"

"To find her," he said. "To find her and buy her and set her free." He had not premeditated this. He heard the words, he wrote in the journal, and knew that that was his intention. "To find her and buy her and set her free," he said, and felt the grasp on his arm released and then in the dark suddenly felt the rake of her nails down his cheek, and heard her voice in a kind of "wild sibilance" saying, "If you do— if you do—oh, I'll not abide it—I will not!"

She flung herself from his side and to the bench. He heard her gasp and sob, "a hard dry sob like a man's." He did not move. Then he heard her voice, "If you do—if you do—she looked at me that way, and I'll not abide it—if you do—" Then after a pause, very quietly, "If you do, I shall never see you again."

He made no reply. He stood there for some minutes, he did not know how long, then left the summerhouse, where she still sat, and walked down the alley.

The next morning he left for Paducah. He learned the name of the trader, but he also learned that the trader had sold Phebe (a yellow wench who answered to Phebe's description) to a "private party" who happened to be in Paducah at the time but who had gone on down-river. His name was unknown in Paducah. The trader had presumably sold Phebe so that he would be free to accompany his coffle when it had been made up. He had now headed, it was said, into South Kentucky, with a few bucks and wenches, to pick up more. As Cass had predicted, he had not wanted to wear Phebe down by taking her in the coffle. So getting a good figure of profit in Paducah, he had sold her there. Cass went south as far as Bowling Green, but lost track of his man there. So rather hopelessly, he wrote a letter to the trader, in care of the market at New Orleans, asking for the name of the purchaser and any information about him. Then he swung back north to Lexington.

At Lexington he went down to West Short Street, to the Lewis C. Robards barracoon, which Mr. Robards had converted from the old Lexington Theatre a few years earlier. He had a notion that Mr. Robards, the leading trader of the section, might be able, through his downriver connections, to locate Phebe, if enough of a commission was in sight. At the barracoon there was no one in the office except a boy, who said that Mr. Robards was downriver but that Mr. Simms was "holding things down" and was over at the "house" at an "inspection." So Cass went next door to the house. (When Jack Burden was in Lexington investigating the life of Cass Mastern, he saw the "house" still standing, a two-story brick building of the traditional residential type, roof running lengthwise, door in center of front, window on each side, chimney at each end, lean-to in back. Robards had kept his "choice stock" there and not in the coops, to wait for "inspection.")

Cass found the main door unlocked at the house, entered the hall, saw no one, but heard laughter from above. He mounted the stairs and discovered, at the end of the hall, a small group of men gathered at an open door. He recognized a couple of them, young hangers-on he had seen about town and at the track. He approached and asked if Mr. Simms was about. "Inside," one of the men said, "showing." Over the heads, Cass could see into the room. First he saw a short, strongly made man, a varnished-looking man, with black hair, black neck-cloth, large bright black eyes, and black coat, with a crop in his hand. Cass knew immediately that he was a French "speculator," who was buying "fancies" for Louisiana. The Frenchman was staring at something beyond Cass's range of vision. Cass moved farther and could see within.

There he saw the man whom he took to be Mr. Simms, a nonde-script fellow in a plug hat, and beyond him the figure of a woman. She was a very young woman, some twenty years old perhaps, rather slender, with skin slightly darker than ivory, probably an octaroon, and hair crisp rather than kinky, and deep dark liquid eyes, slightly bloodshot, which stared at a spot above and beyond the Frenchman. She did not wear the ordinary plaid Osnaburg and kerchief of the female slave for sale, but a white, loosely cut dress, with elbow-length sleeves, and skirts to the floor and no kerchief, only a band to her hair. Beyond her, in the neatly furnished room ("quite genteel," the journal called it, while noting the barred windows), Cass saw a rocking chair and little table, and on the table a sewing basket with a piece of fancy needlework lying there with the needle stuck in it, "as though some respectable young lady or householder had dropped it casually aside upon rising to greet a guest." Cass recorded that somehow he found himself staring at the needlework.

"Yeah," Mr. Simms was saying, "yeah." And grasped the girl by the shoulder to swing her slowly around for a complete view. Then he seized one of her wrists and lifted the arm to shoulder level and worked it back and forth a couple of times to show the supple articulation, saying, "Yeah." That done, he drew the arm forward, holding it toward the Frenchman, the hand hanging limply from the wrist which he held. (The hand was, according to the journal, "well moulded, and the fingers tapered.") "Yeah," Mr. Simms said, "look at that-air hand. Ain't no lady got a littler, teensier hand. And round and soft, yeah?"

"Ain't she got nuthen else round and soft?" one of the men at the door called, and the others laughed.

"Yeah," Mr. Simms said, and leaned to take the hem of her dress, which with a delicate flirting motion he lifted higher than her waist, while he reached out with his other hand to wad the cloth and draw it into a kind of "awkward girdle" about her waist. Still holding the wad of cloth he walked around her, forcing her to turn (she turned "without resistance and as though in a trance") with his motion until her small buttocks were toward the door. "Round and soft, boys," Mr. Simms said, and gave her a good whack on the near buttock to make the flesh tremble. "Ever git yore hand on anything rounder ner softer, boys?" he demanded. "Hit's a cushion, I declare. And shake like sweet jelly."

"God-a-Mighty and got on stockings," one of the men said.

While the other men laughed, the Frenchman stepped to the side of the girl, reached out to lay the tip of his riding crop at the little depression just above the beginning of the swell of the buttocks. He held the tip delicately there for a moment, then flattened the crop across the back and moved it down slowly, evenly across each buttock, to trace the fullness of the curve. "Turn her," he said in his foreign voice.

Mr. Simms obediently carried the wad around, and the body followed in the half revolution. One of the men at the door whistled. The Frenchman laid his crop across the woman's belly as though he were a "carpenter measuring something or as to demonstrate its flatness," and moved it down as before, tracing the structure, until it came to rest across the thighs, below the triangle. Then he let his hand fall to his side, with the crop. "Open your mouth," he said to the girl.

She did so, and he peered earnestly at her teeth. Then he leaned and whiffed her breath. "It is a good breath," he admitted, as though grudgingly.

"Yeah," Mr. Simms said, "yeah, you ain't a-finden no better breath."

"Have you any others?" the Frenchman demanded. "On hand?"

"We got 'em," Mr. Simms said.

"Let me see," the Frenchman said, and moved toward the door with, apparently, the "insolent expectation" that the group there would dissolve before him. He went out into the hall, Mr. Simms following. While Mr. Simms locked the door, Cass said to him, "I wish to speak to you, if you are Mr. Simms."

"Huh?" Mr. Simms said ("grunted" according to the journal), but looking at Cass became suddenly civil for he could know from dress and bearing that Cass was not one of the casual hangers-on. So Mr. Simms admitted the Frenchman to the next room to inspect its occupant, and returned to Cass. Cass remarked in the journal that trouble might have been avoided if he had been more careful to speak in private, but he wrote that at the time the matter was so much upon his mind that the men who stood about were as shadows to him.

He explained his wish to Mr. Simms, described Phebe as well as possible, gave the name of the trader in Paducah, and offered a liberal commission. Mr. Simms seemed dubious, promised to do what he could, and then said, "But nine outa ten you won't git her, Mister. And we got sumthen here better. You done seen Delphy, and she's nigh white as airy woman, and a sight more juicy, and that gal you talk about is nuthen but yaller. Now Delphy—"

"But the young gemmun got a hankeren fer yaller," one of the hangers-on said, and laughed, and the others laughed too.

Cass struck him across the mouth. "I struck him with the side of my fist," Cass wrote, "to bring blood. I struck him without thought, and

I recollect the surprise which visited me when I saw the blood on his chin and saw him draw a bowie from his shirt front. I attempted to avoid his first blow, but received it upon my left shoulder. Before he could withdraw, I had grasped his wrist in my right hand, forced it down so that I could also use my left hand, which still had some strength left at that moment, and with a turning motion of my body I broke his arm across my right hip, and then knocked him to the floor. I recovered the bowie from the floor, and with it faced the man who seemed to be the friend of the man who was now prostrate. He had a knife in his hand, but he seemed disinclined to pursue the discussion."

Cass declined the assistance of Mr. Simms, pressed a handkerchief over his wound, walked out of the building and toward his lodgings, and collapsed on West Short Street. He was carried home. The next day he was better. He learned that Mrs. Trice had left the city, presumably for Washington. A couple of days later his wound infected, and for some time he lay in delirium between life and death. His recovery was slow, presumably retarded by what he termed in the journal his "will toward darkness." But his constitution was stronger than his will, and he recovered, to know himself as the "chief of sinners and a plague spot on the body of the human world." He would have committed suicide except for the fear of damnation for that act, for though "hopeless of Grace I yet clung to the hope of Grace." But sometimes the very fact of damnation because of suicide seemed to be the very reason for suicide: he had brought his friend to suicide and the friend, by that act, was eternally damned; therefore he, Cass Mastern, should, in justice, insure his own damnation by the same act. "But the Lord preserve me from self-slaughter for ends which are His and beyond my knowledge."

Mrs. Trice did not come back to Lexington.

He returned to Mississippi. For two years he operated his plantation, read the Bible, prayed, and, strangely enough, prospered greatly, almost as though against his will. In the end he repaid Gilbert his debt, and set free his slaves. He had some notion of operating the plantation with the same force on a wage basis. "You fool," Gilbert said to him, "be a private fool if you must, but in God's name don't be a public one. Do you think you can work them and them free? One day work, one day loaf. Do you think you can have a passel of free niggers next door to a plantation with slaves? If you did have to set them free, you don't have to spend the rest of your natural life nursing them. Get them out of this country, and take up law or medicine. Or preach the Gospel and at least make a living out of all this praying." Cass tried for more than a year to operate the plantation with his free Negroes, but was compelled to confess that the project was a failure. "Get them out of the country," Gilbert said to him. "And why don't you go with them. Why don't you go North?"

"I belong here," Cass replied.

"Well, why don't you preach Abolition right here?" Gilbert demanded. "Do something, do anything, but stop making a fool of yourself trying to raise cotton with free niggers."

"Perhaps I shall preach Abolition," Cass said, "some day. Even here. But not now. I am not worthy to instruct others. Not now. But meanwhile there is my example. If it is good, it is not lost. Nothing is ever lost."

"Except your mind," Gilbert said, and flung heavily from the room.

There was a sense of trouble in the air. Only Gilbert's great wealth and prestige and scarcely concealed humorous contempt for Cass saved Cass from ostracism, or worse. ("His contempt for me is a shield," Cass wrote. "He treats me like a wayward and silly child who may learn better and who does not have to be taken seriously. Therefore my neighbors do not take me seriously.") But trouble did come. One of Cass's Negroes had a broad-wife on a plantation near by. After she had had some minor trouble with the overseer, the husband stole her from the plantation and ran away. Toward the Tennessee border the pair were taken. The man, resisting officers, was shot; the woman was brought back. "See," Gilbert said, "all you have managed to do is get one nigger killed and one nigger whipped. I offer my congratulations." So Cass put his free Negroes on a boat bound upriver, and never heard of them again.

"I saw the boat head out into the channel, and watched the wheels churn against the strong current, and my spirit was troubled. I knew that the Negroes were passing from one misery to another, and that the hopes they now carried would be blighted. They had kissed my hands and wept for joy, but I could take no part in their rejoicing. I had not flattered myself that I had done anything for them. What I had done I had done for myself, to relieve my spirit of a burden, the burden of their misery and their eyes upon me. The wife of my dead friend had found the eyes of the girl Phebe upon her and had gone wild and had ceased to be herself and had sold the girl into misery. I had found their eyes upon me and had freed them into misery, lest I should do worse. For many cannot bear their eyes upon them, and enter into evil and cruel ways in their desperation. There was in Lexington a decade and more before my stay in that city, a wealthy lawyer named Fielding L. Turner, who had married a lady of position from Boston. This lady Caroline Turner, who had never had blacks around her and who had been nurtured in sentiments opposed to the institution of human servitude, quickly became notorious for her abominable cruelties performed in her fits of passion. All persons of the community reprehended her floggings, which she performed with her own hands, uttering meanwhile little cries in her throat, according to report. Once while she was engaged in flogging a servant in an apartment on the second floor of her palatial home, a small Negro boy entered the room and began to whimper. She seized him and bodily hurled him through the window of the apartment so that he fell upon stone below and broke his back to become a cripple for his days. To protect her from the process of law and the wrath of the community, Judge Turner committed her to a lunatic asylum. But later the physicians said her to be of sound mind and released her. Her husband in his will left her no slaves, for to do so would, the will said, be to doom them to misery in life and speedy death. But she procured slaves, among them a yellow coachman named Richard, mild of manner, sensible, and of plausible disposition. One day she had him chained and proceeded to flog him. But he tore himself from the chains that held him to the wall and seized the woman by the throat and strangled her. Later he was captured and hanged for murder, though many wished that his escape had been contrived. This story was told me in Lexington. One lady said to me, 'Mrs. Turner did not understand Negroes.' And another, 'Mrs. Turner did it because she was from Boston where the Abolitionists are.' But I did not understand. Then, much later, I began to understand. I understood that Mrs. Turner flogged her Negroes for the same reason that the wife of my friend sold Phebe down the river: she could not bear their eyes upon her. I understand, for I can no longer bear their eyes upon me. Perhaps only a man like my brother Gilbert can in the midst of evil retain enough of innocence and strength to bear their eyes upon him and to do a little justice in the terms of the great injustice."

So Cass, who had a plantation with no one to work it, went to Jackson, the capital of the state, and applied himself to the law. Before he left, Gilbert came to him and offered to take over the plantation and work it with a force of his people from his own great place on a share basis. Apparently he was still trying to make Cass rich. But Cass declined, and Gilbert said, "You object to my working it with slaves, is that it? Well, let me tell you, if you sell it, it will be worked with slaves. It is black land and will be watered with black sweat. Does it make any difference then, which black sweat falls on it?" And Cass replied that he was not going to sell the plantation. Then Gilbert, in an apoplectic rage, bellowed, "My God, man, it is land, don't you understand, it is land, and land cries out for man's hand!" But Cass did not sell. He installed a caretaker in the house, and rented a little land to a neighbor for pasture.

He went to Jackson, sat late with his books, and watched trouble gathering over the land. For it was the autumn of 1858 when he went to Jackson. On January 9, 1861, Mississippi passed the ordinance of secession. Gilbert had opposed secession, writing to Cass: "The fools, there is not a factory for arms in the state. Fools not to have prepared themselves if they have foreseen the trouble. Fools, if they have not foreseen it, to act thus in the face of facts. Fools not to temporize now and, if they must, prepare themselves to strike a blow. I have told responsible men to prepare. All fools." To which Cass replied: "I pray much for peace." But later, he wrote: "I have talked with Mr. French, who is, as you know, the Chief of Ordnance, and he says that they have only old muskets for troops, and those but flintlocks. The agents have scraped the state for shotguns, at the behest of Governor Pettus. Shotguns, Mr. French said, and curled his lips. And what shotguns, he added, and then told me of a weapon contributed to the cause, an old musket barrel strapped with metal to a piece of cypress rail crooked at one end. An old slave gave his treasure to the cause, and does one laugh or weep?" After Jefferson Davis had come back to Mississippi, having resigned from the Senate, and had accepted the command of the troops of Mississippi with the rank of Major General, Cass called upon him, at the request of Gilbert. He wrote to Gilbert: "The General says that they have given him 10,000 men, but not a stand of modern rifles. But the General also said, they have given me a very fine coat with fourteen brass buttons in front and a black velvet collar. Perhaps we can use the buttons in our shotguns, he said, and smiled."

Cass saw Mr. Davis once more, for he was with Gilbert on the steamboat *Natchez* which carried the new President of the Confederacy on the first stage of his journey from his plantation, Brierfield, to Montgomery. "We were on old Mr. Tom Leather's boat," Cass wrote in the journal, "which had been supposed to pick up the President at a landing a few miles below Brierfield. But Mr. Davis was delayed in leaving his house and was rowed out to us. I leaned on the rail and saw the little black skiff proceeding toward us over the red water. A man waved from the skiff to us. The captain of the *Natchez* observed the signal, and gave a great blast of his boat's whistle which made our ears tingle and shivered out over the expanse of waters. The boat stopped and the skiff approached.

Mr. Davis was received on board. As the steamboat moved on, Mr. Davis looked back and lifted his hand in salute to the Negro servant (Isaiah Montgomery, whom I had known at Brierfield) who stood in the skiff, which rocked in the wash of the steamboat, and waved his farewell. Later, as we proceeded upriver toward the bluffs of Vicksburg, he approached my brother, with whom I was standing on the deck. We had previously greeted him. My brother again, and more intimately, congratulated Mr. Davis, who replied that he could take no pleasure in the honor. 'I have,' he said, 'always looked upon the Union with a superstitious reverence and have freely risked my life for its dear flag on more than one battle-field, and you, gentlemen, can conceive the sentiment now in me that the object of my attachment for many years has been withdrawn from me.' and he continued, 'I have in the present moment only the melancholy pleasure of an easy conscience.' Then he smiled, as he did rarely. There-upon he took his leave of us and retired within. I had observed how worn to emaciation was his face by illness and care, and how thin the skin lay over the bone. I remarked to my brother that Mr. Davis did not look well. He replied, 'A sick man, it is a fine how-de-do to have a sick man for a president.' I responded that there might be no war, that Mr. Davis hoped for peace. But my brother said, 'Make no mistake, the Yankees will fight and they will fight well and Mr. Davis is a fool to hope for peace.' I replied, 'All good men hope for peace.' At this my brother uttered an indistinguishable exclamation, and said, 'What we want now they've got into this is not a good man but a man who can win, and I am not interested in the luxury of Mr. Davis's conscience.' Then my brother and I continued our promenade in silence, and I reflected that Mr. Davis was a good man. But the world is full of good men, I now reflect as I write these lines down, and yet the world drives hard into darkness and the blindness of blood, even as now late at night I sit in this hotel room in Vicksburg, and I am moved to ask the mean-ing of our virtue. May God hear our prayer!"

Gilbert received a commission as colonel in a cavalry regiment. Cass enlisted as a private in the Mississippi Rifles. "You could be a captain," Gilbert said, "or a major. You've got brains enough for that. And," he added, "damned few of them have." Cass replied that he preferred to be a private soldier, "marching with other men." But he could not tell his brother why, or tell his brother that, though he would march with other men and would carry a weapon in his hand, he would never take the life of an enemy. "I must march with these men who march," he wrote in the journal, "for they are my people and I must partake with them of all bitterness, and that more fully. But I cannot take the life of another man. How can I who have taken the life of my friend, take the life of an enemy, for I have used up my right to blood." So Cass marched away to war, carrying the musket which was, for him, but a meaningless burden, and wearing on a string, against the flesh of his chest, beneath the fabric of the gray jacket, the ring which had once been Duncan Trice's wedding ring and which Annabelle Trice, that night in her summerhouse, had slipped onto his finger as his hand lay on her bosom.

Cass marched to Shiloh, between the fresh fields, for it was early April, and then into the woods that screened the river. (Dogwood and redbud would have been out then.) He marched into the woods, heard the lead whistle by his head, saw the dead men on the ground, and the next day came out of the woods and moved in the sullen withdrawal toward Corinth. He had been sure that he would not survive the battle. But he had survived, and moved down the crowded road "as in a dream." And he wrote: "And I felt that henceforward I should live in that dream." The dream took him into Tennessee again—Chickamauga, Knoxville, Chattanooga, and the nameless skirmishes, and the bullet for which he waited did not find him. At Chickamauga, when his company wavered in the enemy fire and seemed about to break in its attack, he moved steadily up the slope and could not understand his own inviolability. And the men regrouped, and followed. "It seemed strange to me," he wrote, "that I who in God's will sought death and could not find it, should in my seeking lead men to it who did not seek." When Colonel Hickman congratulated him, he could "find no words" for answer.

But if he had put on the gray jacket in anguish of spirit and in hope of expiation, he came to wear it in pride, for it was a jacket like those worn by the men with whom he marched. "I have seen men do brave things," he wrote, "and they ask for nothing." And he added, "It is not hard to love men for the things they endure and for the words they do not speak." More and more, too, there crept into the journal the comments of the professional soldier, between the prayers and the scruples— criticism of command (of Bragg after Chickamauga), satisfaction and an impersonal pride in maneuver or gunnery ("the practice of Marlowe's battery excellent"), and finally the admiration for the feints and delays executed by Johnston's virtuosity on the approaches to Atlanta, at Buzzard's Roost, Snake Creek Gap, New Hope Church, Kenesaw Mountain ("there is always a kind of glory, however stained or obscured, in whatever man's hand does well, and General Johnston does well").

Then, outside Atlanta, the bullet found him. He lay in the hospital and rotted slowly to death. But even before the infection set in, when the wound in the leg seemed scarcely serious, he knew that he would die. "I shall die," he wrote in the journal, "and shall be spared the end and the last bitterness of war. I have lived to do no man good, and have seen others suffer for my sin. I do not question the Justice of God, that others have suffered for my sin, for it may be that only by the suffering of the innocent does God affirm that men are brothers, and brothers in His Holy Name. And in this room with me now, men suffer for sins not theirs, as for their own. It is a comfort to know that I suffer only for my own." He knew not only that he was to die, but that the war was over. "It is over. It is all over but the dying, which will yet go on. Though the boil has come to a head and has burst, yet must the pus flow. Men shall come together yet and die in the common guilt of man and in the guilt that sent them hither from far places and distant firesides. But God in His Mercy has spared me the end. Blessed be His Name."

There was no more in the journal. There was only the letter to Gilbert, written in the strange hand, dictated by Cass after he had grown too weak to write. "Remember me, but without grief. If one of us is lucky, it is I . . ."

Ralph Ellison

LAMENT FOR TOD CLIFTON

I have chosen this section from *Invisible Man* because it seems to represent the moment in the plot wherein the narrator becomes aware of the basic irony of his political role and begins to move painfully from a state of illusionment to a sense of reality. Up to now he has played naïvely at the role of political leader, has sustained his removal from Harlem for threatening to become authentic, and with no loss of faith in the Brotherhood and its vision. Now, coincident with the slaying of Clifton, he has been ordered back to Harlem and by way of recouping the Brotherhood's loss of influence in the district—and by way of giving expression to the wide-spread grief attending the slaying— he improvises a public spectacle through which he hopes to politicalize the violent injustice of the young leader's death. In- volved here as personal motive is his own need to redeem the memory of Clifton from the "guilt" of having left the Brother- hood and becoming in his bitterness the purveyor of anti-Negro stereotypes—an act which threatens the narrator's own sense of security and integrity. And well it should, for Clifton's act fore- shadows the narrator's own loss of faith and the death of his iden- tity as political leader.

His decision is most portentous, for the moment the people gather and the corpse begins to wind through the streets to the beat of drums the narrator is plunged into an underground of memory and music, ritual and rhetoric; and I suppose I'm drawn to this section because of the way it makes this process visual. I like, too, the manner in which its various elements are combined to dramatic effect: the funeral march, the group singing, the slow ritual ascension of the "mountain" and the ceremonial manner in which the body of the slain leader is borne upward to receive the last words of the narrator. Yes, and I like the reverse-English rhetoric of the "sermon" itself.

Since this scene is really a *peripetia* announcing a major turn in the plot, I am especially pleased that here once again, and with a not too obvious maintenance of the tension established between the narrator's character and his way with public events, this act also flows in the opposite direction of that he intended. For in the process of organizing a mass political gesture he stumbles to a depth of human experience which renders both the superficiality of the Brotherhood's program and the duplicity of its leaders inescapable. Indeed, he plunges into that realm beneath the level of the merely rational where men, aroused by the sight and smell of blood and knowing themselves to be in the presence of (and the possible victims of) violent and unjust death, are moved to an awareness of the necessity for human fraternity which overrides all considerations of race, class, creed or color.

What is involved here is, for the narrator (and I hope for the reader), a process of ironic perception: By attempting to dignify and politicalize Tod Clifton's slaying he discovers that the Brotherhood which has sought to teach men how to live possesses no ceremonial forms for dealing with death. Thus he is forced willy-nilly back upon himself and upon that which he shares most irrevocably with the people of Harlem i.e., to those ritual and ceremonial forms taken from the Protestant tradition which Negro Americans had begun to structure to their own religious and cultural needs as far back as the early days of enslavement, and which recently were to be observed most movingly during the funeral ceremony for Martin Luther King. Throughout the plot the narrator had struggled to put his past behind him and now it is through blending elements from the old ritual for the dead with political motives that he discovers the true source of a life-enhancing and politically effective leadership for Harlem. These elements are also a source of strength for the writer and I found pleasure—and some pain—in using them to tell my tale. . . .

Ralph Ellison

The funeral was arranged to attract the largest number. Instead of holding it in a church or chapel, we selected Mount Morris Park, and an appeal went out for all former members to join the funeral march.

It took place on a Saturday, in the heat of the afternoon. There was a thin overcast of clouds, and hundreds of people formed for the procession. I went around giving orders and encouragement in a feverish daze, and yet seeming to observe it all from off to one side. Brothers and sisters turned up whom I hadn't seen since my return. And members from downtown and outlying districts. I watched them with surprise as they gathered and wondered at the depths of their sorrow as the lines began to form.

There were half-draped flags and black banners. There were black-bordered signs that read:

BROTHER TOD CLIFTON

OUR HOPE SHOT DOWN

There was a hired drum corps with crape-draped drums. There was a band of thirty pieces. There were no cars and very few flowers.

It was a slow procession and the band played sad, romantic, military marches. And when the band was silent the drum corps beat the time on drums with muffled heads. It was hot and explosive, and delivery men avoided the district and the police details were increased in number. And up and down the streets people looked out of their apartment windows and men and boys stood on the roofs in the thin-veiled sun.

I marched at the head with the old community leaders. It was a slow march and as I looked back from time to time I could see young zoot-suiters, hep cats, and men in overalls and pool-hall gamblers stepping into the procession. Men came out of barber shops with lathered faces, their neckcloths hanging, to watch and comment in hushed voices. And I wondered, Are they all Clifton's friends, or is it just for the spectacle, the slow-paced music? A hot wind blew from behind me, bringing the sick sweetish odor, like the smell of some female dogs in season.

I looked back. The sun shone down on a mass of unbared heads, and above flags and banners and shining horns I could see the cheap gray coffin moving high upon the shoulders of Clifton's tallest companions, who from time to time shifted it smoothly on to others. They bore him proudly and there was an angry sadness in their eyes. The coffin floated like a heavily loaded ship in a channel, winding its way slowly above the bowed and submerged heads. I could hear the steady rolling of the drums with muffled snares, and all other sounds were suspended in silence. Behind, the tramp of feet; ahead, the crowds lining the curbs for blocks. There were tears and muffled sobs and many hard, red eyes. We moved ahead.

We wound through the poorest streets at first, a black image of sorrow, then turned into Seventh Avenue and down and over to Lenox. Then I hurried with the leading brothers to the park in a cab. A brother in the Park Department had opened the lookout tower, and a crude platform of planks and ranked saw horses had been erected beneath the black iron bell, and when the procession started into the park we were standing high above, waiting. At our signal he struck the bell, and I could feel my eardrums throbbing with the old, hollow, gut-vibrant Doom-Dong-Doom.

Looking down, I could see them winding upward in a mass to the muffled sound of the drums. Children stopped their playing on the grass to stare, and nurses at the nearby hospital came out on the roof to watch, their white uniforms glowing in the now unveiled sun like lilies. And crowds approached the park from all directions. The muffled drums now beating, now steadily rolling, spread a dead silence upon the air, a prayer for the unknown soldier. And looking down I felt a lostness. Why were they here? Why had they found us? Because they knew Clifton? Or for the occasion his death gave them to express their protestations, a time and place to come together, to stand touching and sweating and breathing and looking in a common direction? Was either explanation adequate in itself? Did it signify love or politicized hate? And could politics ever be an expression of love?

Over the park the silence spread from the slow muffled rolling of the drums, the crunching of footsteps on the walks. Then somewhere in the procession an old, plaintive, masculine voice arose in a song, wavering, stumbling in the silence at first alone, until in the band a euphonium horn fumbled for the key and took up the air, one catching and rising above the other and the other pursuing, two black pigeons rising above a skull-white barn to tumble and rise through still, blue air. And for a few bars the pure sweet tone of the horn and the old man's husky baritone sang a duet in the hot heavy silence. "There's Many a Thousand Gone." And standing high up over the park something fought in my throat. It was a song from the past, the past of the campus and the still earlier past of home. And now some of the older ones in the mass were joining in. I hadn't thought of it as a march before, but now they were marching to its slow-paced rhythm, up the hill. I looked for the euphonium player and saw a slender black man with his face turned toward the sun, singing through the upturned bells of the horn. And several yards behind, marching beside the young men floating the coffin upward, I looked into the face of the old man who had aroused the song and felt a twinge of envy. It was a worn, old, yellow face and his eyes were closed and I could see a knife welt around his upturned neck as his throat threw out the song. He sang with his whole body, phrasing each verse as naturally as he walked, his voice rising above all the others, blending with that of the lucid horn. I watched him now, wet-eyed, the sun hot upon my head, and I felt a wonder at the singing mass. It was as though the song had been there all the time and he knew it and aroused it; and I knew that I had known it too and had failed to release it out of a vague, nameless shame or fear. But he had known and aroused it. Even white brothers and sisters were joining in. I looked into that face, trying to plumb its secret, but it told me nothing. I looked at the coffin and the marchers, listening to them, and yet realizing that I was listening to something within myself, and for a second I heard the shattering stroke of my heart. Something deep had shaken the crowd, and the old man and the man with the horn had done it. They had touched upon something deeper than protest, or religion; though now images of all the church meetings of my life welled up within me with much suppressed and forgotten anger. But that was past, and too many of those now reaching the top of the mountain and spreading massed together had never shared it, and some had been born in other lands.

And yet all were touched; the song had aroused us all. It was not the words, for they were all the same old slave-borne words; it was as though he'd changed the emotion beneath the words while yet the old longing, resigned, transcendent emotion still sounded above, now deepened by that something for which the theory of Brotherhood had given me no name. I stood there trying to contain it as they brought Tod Clifton's coffin into the tower and slowly up the spiral stairs. They set it down upon the platform and I looked at the shape of the cheap gray coffin and all I could remember was the sound of his name.

The song had ended. Now the top of the little mountain bristled with banners, horns and uplifted faces. I could look straight down Fifth Avenue to 125th Street, where policemen were lined behind an array of hot-dog wagons and Good Humor carts; and among the carts I saw a peanut vendor standing beneath a street lamp upon which pigeons were gathered, and now I saw him stretch out his arms with his palms turned upward, and suddenly he was covered, head, shoulders and out-flung arms, with fluttering, feasting birds.

Someone nudged me and I started. It was time for final words. But I had no words and I'd never been to a Brotherhood funeral and had no idea of a ritual. But they were waiting. I stood there alone; there was no microphone to support me, only the coffin before me upon the backs of its wobbly carpenter's horses.

I looked down into their sun-swept faces, digging for the words, and feeling a futility about it all and an anger. For this they gathered by thousands. What were they waiting to hear? Why had they come? For what reason that was different from that which had made the red-cheeked boy thrill at Clifton's falling to the earth? What did they want and what could they do? Why hadn't they come when they could have stopped it all?

"What are you waiting for me to tell you?" I shouted suddenly, my voice strangely crisp on the windless air. "What good will it do? What if I say that this isn't a funeral, that it's a holiday celebration, that if you stick around the band will end up playing 'Damit-the-Hell the Fun's All Over'? Or do you expect to see some magic, the dead rise up and walk again? Go home, he's as dead as he'll ever die. That's the end in the beginning and there's no encore. There'll be no miracles and there's no one here to preach a sermon. Go home, forget him. He's inside this box, newly dead. Go home and don't think about him. He's dead and you've got all you can do to think about you." I paused. They were whispering and looking upward.

"I've told you to go home," I shouted, "but you keep standing there. Don't you know it's hot out here in the sun? So what if you wait for what little I can tell you? Can I say in twenty minutes what was building twenty-one years and ended in twenty seconds? What are you waiting for, when all I can tell you is his name? And when I tell you, what will you know that you didn't know already, except perhaps, his name?"

They were listening intently, and as though looking not at me, but at the pattern of my voice upon the air.

"All right, you do the listening in the sun and I'll try to tell you in the sun. Then you go home and forget it. Forget it. His name was Clifton and they shot him down. His name was Clifton and he was tall and some folks thought him handsome. And though he didn't believe it, I think he was. His name was Clifton and his face was black and his hair was thick with tight-rolled curls—or call them naps or kinks. He's dead, uninterested, and, except to a few young girls, it doesn't matter . . . Have you got it? Can you see him? Think of your brother or your cousin John. His lips were thick with an upward curve at the corners. He often smiled. He had good eyes and a pair of fast hands, and he had a heart. He thought about things and he felt deeply. I won't call him noble because what's such a word to do with one of us? His name was Clifton, Tod Clifton, and, like any man, he was born of woman to live awhile and fall and die. So that's his tale to the minute. His name was Clifton and for a while he lived among us and aroused a few hopes in the young manhood of man, and we who knew him loved him and he died. So why are you waiting? You've heard it all. Why wait for more, when all I can do is repeat it?"

They stood; they listened. They gave no sign.

"Very well, so I'll tell you. His name was Clifton and he was young and he was a leader and when he fell there was a hole in the heel of his sock and when he stretched forward he seemed not as tall as when he stood. So he died; and we who loved him are gathered here to mourn him. It's as simple as that and as short as that. His name was Clifton and he was black and they shot him. Isn't that enough to tell? Isn't it all you need to know? Isn't that enough to appease your thirst for drama and send you home to sleep it off? Go take a drink and forget it. Or read it in *The Daily News*. His name was Clifton and they shot him, and I was there to see him fall. So I know it as I know it.

"Here are the facts. He was standing and he fell. He fell and he kneeled. He kneeled and he bled. He bled and he died. He fell in a heap like any man and his blood spilled out like any blood; *red* as any blood, wet as any blood and reflecting the sky and the buildings and birds and trees, or your face if you'd looked into its dulling mirror—and it dried in the sun as blood dries. That's all. They spilled his blood and he bled. They cut him down and he died; the blood flowed on the walk in a pool, gleamed a while, and, after awhile, became dull then dusty, then dried. That's the story and that's how it ended. It's an old story and there's been too much blood to excite you. Besides, it's only important when it fills the veins of a living man. Aren't you tired of such stories? Aren't you sick of the blood? Then why listen, why don't you go? It's hot out here. There's the odor of embalming fluid. The beer is cold in the taverns, the saxophones will be mellow at the Savoy; plenty good-laughing-lies will be told in the barber shops and beauty parlors; and there'll be sermons in two hundred churches in the cool of the evening, and plenty of laughs at the movies. Go listen to 'Amos and Andy' and forget it. Here you have only the same old story. There's not even a young wife up here in red to mourn him. There's nothing here to pity, no one to break down and shout. Nothing to give you that good old frightened feeling. The story's too short and too simple. His name was Clifton, Tod Clifton, he was unarmed and his death was as senseless as his life was futile. He had struggled for Brotherhood on a hundred street corners and he thought it would make him more human, but he died like any dog in a road.

"All right, all right," I called out, feeling desperate. It wasn't the way I wanted it to go, it wasn't political. Brother Jack probably wouldn't approve of it at all, but I had to keep going as I could go.

"Listen to me standing up on this so-called mountain!" I shouted. "Let me tell it as it truly was! His name was Tod Clifton and he was full of illusions. He thought he was a man when he was only Tod Clifton. He was shot for a simple mistake of judgment and he bled and his blood dried and shortly the crowd trampled out the stains. It was a normal mistake of which many are guilty. He thought he was a man and that men were not meant to be pushed around. But it was hot downtown and he forgot his history, he forgot the time and the place. He lost his hold on reality. There was a cop and a waiting audience but he was Tod Clifton and cops are everywhere. The cop? What about him? He was a cop. A good citizen. But this cop had an itching finger and eager ear for a word that rhymed with 'trigger,' and when Clifton fell he had found it. The Police Special spoke its lines and the rhyme was completed. Just look around you. Look at what he made, look inside you and feel his awful power. It was perfectly natural. The blood ran like blood in a comic-book

killing, on a comic-book street in a comic-book town on a comic-book
day in a comic-book world.

"Tod Clifton's one with the ages. But what's that to do with you in this
heat under this veiled sun? Now he's part of history, and he has received
his true feeedom. Didn't they scribble his name on a standardized pad?
His Race: colored! Religion: unknown, probably born Baptist. Place of
birth: U. S. Some southern town. Next of kin: unknown. Address: unknown. Occupation: unemployed. Cause of death (be specific): resisting
reality in the form of a .38 caliber revolver in the hands of the arresting
officer, on Forty-second between the library and the subway in the heat of
the afternoon, of gunshot wounds received from three bullets, fired at
three paces, one bullet entering the right ventricle of the heart, and
lodging there, the other severing the spinal ganglia traveling downward
to lodge in the pelvis, the other breaking through the back and traveling
God knows where.

"Such was the short bitter life of Brother Tod Clifton. Now he's in
this box with the bolts tightened down. He's in the box and we're in
there with him, and when I've told you this you can go. It's dark in
this box and it's crowded. It has a cracked ceiling and a clogged-up
toilet in the hall. It has rats and roaches, and it's far, far too expensive
a dwelling. The air is bad and it'll be cold this winter. Tod Clifton is
crowded and he needs the room. 'Tell them to get out of the box,'
that's what he would say if you could hear him. 'Tell them to get out
of the box and go teach the cops to forget that rhyme. Tell them to
teach them that when they call you *nigger* to make a rhyme with *trigger*
it makes the gun backfire.'

"So there you have it. In a few hours Tod Clifton will be cold bones
in the ground. And don't be fooled, for these bones shall not rise again.
You and I will still be in the box. I don't know if Tod Clifton had a
soul. I only know the ache that I feel in my heart, my sense of loss.
I don't know if *you* have a soul. I only know you are men of flesh and
blood; and that blood will spill and flesh grow cold. I do not know if
all cops are poets, but I know that all cops carry guns with triggers.
And I know too how we are labeled. So in the name of Brother Clifton
beware of the triggers; go home, keep cool, stay safe away from the sun.
Forget him. When he was alive he was our hope, but why worry over a
hope that's dead? So there's only one thing left to tell and I've already
told it. His name was Tod Clifton, he believed in Brotherhood, he
aroused our hopes and he died."

I couldn't go on. Below, they were waiting, hands and handkerchiefs shading their eyes. A preacher stepped up and read something out of his Bible, and I stood looking at the crowd with a sense of failure. I had let it get away from me, had been unable to bring in the political issues. And they stood there sun-beaten and sweat-bathed, listening to me repeat what was known. Now the preacher had finished, and someone signaled the bandmaster and there was solemn music as the pallbearers carried the coffin down the spiraling stairs. The crowd stood still as we walked slowly through. I could feel the bigness of it and the unknownness of it and a pent-up tension—whether of tears or anger, I couldn't tell. But as we walked through and down the hill to the hearse, I could feel it. The crowd sweated and throbbed, and though it was silent, there were many things directed toward me through its eyes. At the curb were the hearse and a few cars, and in a few minutes they were loaded and the crowd was still standing, looking on as we carried Tod Clifton away. And as I took one last look I saw not a crowd but the set faces of individual men and women.

We drove away and when the cars stopped moving there was a grave and we placed him in it. The gravediggers sweated heavily and knew their business and their brogue was Irish. They filled the grave quickly and we left. Tod Clifton was underground.

I returned through the streets as tired as though I'd dug the grave myself alone. I felt confused and listless moving through the crowds that seemed to boil along in a kind of mist, as though the thin humid clouds had thickened and settled directly above our heads. I wanted to go somewhere, to some cool place to rest without thinking, but there was still too much to be done; plans had to be made; the crowd's emotion had to be organized. I crept along, walking a southern walk in southern weather, closing my eyes from time to time against the dazzling reds, yellows and greens of cheap sport shirts and summer dresses. The crowd boiled, sweated, heaved; women with shopping bags, men with highly polished shoes. Even down South they'd always shined their shoes. "Shined shoes, shoed shines," it rang in my head. On Eighth Avenue, the market carts were parked hub to hub along the curb, improvised canopies shading the withering fruits and vegetables. I could smell the stench of decaying cabbage. A watermelon huckster stood in the shade beside his truck, holding up a long slice of orange-meated melon, crying his wares with hoarse appeals to nostalgia, memories of childhood, green shade and summer coolness. Oranges, cocoanuts and alligator pears lay in neat piles on little tables. I passed, winding my way through the slowly moving crowd. Stale and wilted flowers, rejected downtown, blazed

feverishly on a cart, like glamorous rags festering beneath a futile spray
from a punctured fruit juice can. The crowd were boiling figures seen
through steaming glass from inside a washing machine; and in the streets
the mounted police detail stood looking on, their eyes noncommittal
beneath the short polished visors of their caps, their bodies slanting
forward, reins slackly alert, men and horses of flesh imitating men and
horses of stone. Tod Clifton's *Tod,* I thought. The hucksters cried
above the traffic sounds and I seemed to hear them from a distance, unsure
of what they said. In a side street children with warped tricycles were
parading along the walk carrying one of the signs, BROTHER TOD CLIFTON,
OUR HOPE SHOT DOWN.

And through the haze I again felt the tension. There was no denying
it; it was there and something had to be done before it simmered away
in the heat.

James Baldwin

NOBODY KNOWS MY NAME:

A Letter from the South

"Sonny's Blues," a story precluded from inclusion because of its length—the story was Mr. Baldwin's first choice as his best piece of work—is here replaced by the famous essay of the author's, "Nobody Knows My Name." And since it speaks directly to the reader, Mr. Baldwin has abstained from any further comment.

The Editor

I walked down the street, didn't have on no hat,
Asking everybody I meet,
Where's my man at?

                                                          —Ma Rainey

Negroes in the North are right when they refer to the South as the Old Country. A Negro born in the North who finds himself in the South is in a position similar to that of the son of the Italian emigrant who finds himself in Italy, near the village where his father first saw the light of day. Both are in countries they have never seen, but which they cannot fail to recognize. The landscape has always been familiar; the speech is archaic, but it rings a bell; and so do the ways of the people, though their ways are not his ways. Everywhere he turns, the revenant finds himself reflected. He sees himself as he was before he was born, perhaps; or as the man he would have become, had he actually been born in this place. He sees the world, from an angle odd indeed, in which his fathers awaited his arrival, perhaps in the very house in which he narrowly avoided being born. He sees, in effect, his ancestors, who, in everything they do and are, proclaim his inescapable identity. And the Northern Negro in the South sees, whatever he or anyone else may wish to believe, that his ancestors are both white and black. The white men, flesh of his flesh, hate him for that very reason. On the other hand, there is scarcely any way for him to join the black community in the South: for both he and this community are in the grip of the immense illusion that their state is more miserable than his own.

This illusion owes everything to the great American illusion that our state is a state to be envied by other people: we are powerful, and we are rich. But our power makes us uncomfortable and we handle it very ineptly. The principal effect of our material well-being has been to set the children's teeth on edge. If we ourselves were not so fond of this illusion, we might understand ourselves and other peoples better than we do, and be enabled to help them understand us. I am very often tempted to believe that this illusion is all that is left of the great dream that was to have become America; whether this is so or not, this illusion certainly prevents us from making America what we say we want it to be.

But let us put aside, for the moment, these subversive speculations. In the fall of last year, my plane hovered over the rust-red earth of Georgia. I was past thirty, and I had never seen this land before. I pressed my face against the window, watching the earth come closer; soon we were just above the tops of trees. I could not suppress the thought that this earth had acquired its color from the blood that had dripped down from these trees. My mind was filled with the image of a black man, younger than I, perhaps, or my own age, hanging from a tree, while white men watched him and cut his sex from him with a knife.

My father must have seen such sights—he was very old when he died—or heard of them, or had this danger touch him. The Negro poet I talked to in Washington, much younger than my father, perhaps twenty years older than myself, remembered such things very vividly, had a long tale to tell, and counseled me to think back on those days as a means of steadying the soul. I was to remember that time, whatever else it had failed to do, nevertheless had passed, that the situation, whether or not it was better, was certainly no longer the same. I was to remember that Southern Negroes had endured things I could not imagine; but this did not really place me at such a great disadvantage, since they clearly had been unable to imagine what awaited them in Harlem. I remembered the Scottsboro case, which I had followed as a child. I remembered Angelo Herndon and wondered, again, whatever had become of him. I remembered the soldier in uniform blinded by an enraged white man, just after the Second World War. There had been many such incidents after the First War, which was one of the reasons I had been born in Harlem. I remembered Willie McGhee, Emmett Till, and the others. My younger brother had visited Atlanta some years before. I remembered what they had told me about it. One of my brothers, in uniform, had had his front teeth kicked out by a white officer. I remembered my mother telling us how she had wept and prayed and tried to kiss the venom out of her suicidally embittered son. (She managed to do it, too; heaven only knows what she herself was feeling, whose father and brothers had lived and died down here.) I remembered myself as a very small boy, already so bitter about the pledge of allegiance that I could scarcely bring myself to say it, and never, never believed it.

I was, in short, but one generation removed from the South, which was now undergoing a new convulsion over whether black children had the same rights, or capacities, for education as did the children of white people. This is a criminally frivolous dispute, absolutely unworthy of this nation; and it is being carried on, in complete bad faith, by completely uneducated people. (We do not trust educated people and rarely, alas, produce them, for we do not trust the independence of mind which alone makes a genuine education possible.) Educated people, of any color, are so extremely rare that it is unquestionably one of the first tasks of a nation to open all of its schools to all of its citizens. But the dispute has actually nothing to do with education, as some among the eminently uneducated know. It has to do with political power and it has to do with sex. And this is a nation which, most unluckily, knows very little about either.

The city of Atlanta, according to my notes, is "big, wholly segregated, sprawling; population variously given as six hundred thousand or one million, depending on whether one goes beyond or remains within the city limits. Negroes 25 to 30 per cent of the population. Racial relations, on the record, can be described as fair, considering that this is the state of Georgia. Growing industrial town. Racial relations manipulated by the mayor and a fairly strong Negro middle class. This works mainly in the areas of compromise and concession and has very little effect on the bulk of the Negro population and none whatever on the rest of the state. No integration, pending or actual." Also, it seemed to me that the Negroes in Atlanta were "very vividly *city* Negroes"—they seemed less patient than their rural brethren, more dangerous, or at least more unpredictable. And: "Have seen one wealthy Negro section, very pretty, but with an unpaved road. . . . The section in which I am living is composed of frame houses in various stages of disrepair and neglect, in which two and three families live, often sharing a single toilet. This is the other side of the tracks; literally, I mean. It is located, as I am told is the case in many Southern cities, just beyond the underpass." Atlanta contains a high proportion of Negroes who own their own homes and exist, visibly anyway, independently of the white world. Southern towns distrust this class and do everything in their power to prevent its appearance. But it is a class which has a certain usefulness in Southern cities. There is an incipient war, in fact, between Southern cities and Southern towns—between the city, that is, and the state—which we will discuss later. Little Rock is an ominous example of this and it is likely—indeed, it is certain—that we will see many more such examples before the present crisis is over.

Before arriving in Atlanta I had spent several days in Charlotte, North Carolina. This is a bourgeois town, Presbyterian, pretty—if you like towns—and socially so hermetic that it contains scarcely a single decent restaurant. I was told that Negroes there are not even licensed to become electricians or plumbers. I was also told, several times, by white people, that "race relations" there were excellent. I failed to find a single Negro who agreed with this, which is the usual story of "race relations" in this country. Charlotte, a town of 165,000, was in a ferment when I was there because, of its 50,000 Negroes, four had been assigned to previously all-white schools, one to each school. In fact, by the time I got there, there were only three. Dorothy Counts, the daughter of a Presbyterian minister, after several days of being stoned and spat on by the mob—"spit," a woman told me, "was hanging from the hem of Dorothy's dress"—had withdrawn from Harding High. Several white students, I was told, had called—not called *on*—Miss Counts, to beg her to stick it out. Harry Golden, editor of *The Carolina Israelite,* suggested that the "hoodlum element" might not so have shamed the town and the nation if several of the town's leading businessmen had personally escorted Miss Counts to school.

I saw the Negro schools in Charlotte, saw, on street corners, several of their alumnae, and read about others who had been sentenced to the chain gang. This solved the mystery of just what made Negro parents send their children out to face mobs. White people do not understand this because they do not know, and do not want to know, that the alternative to this ordeal is nothing less than a lifelong ordeal. Those Negro parents who spend their days trembling for their children and the rest of their time praying that their children have not been too badly damaged inside, are not doing this out of "ideals" or "convictions" or because they are in the grip of a perverse desire to send their children where "they are not wanted." They are doing it because they want the child to receive the education which will allow him to defeat, possibly escape, and not impossibly help one day abolish the stifling environment in which they see, daily, so many children perish.

This is certainly not the purpose, still less the effect, of most Negro schools. It is hard enough, God knows, under the best of circumstances, to get an education in this country. White children are graduated yearly who can neither read, write, nor think, and who are in a state of the most abysmal ignorance concerning the world around them. But at least they are white. They are under the illusion—which, since they are so badly educated, sometimes has a fatal tenacity—that they can do whatever they want to do. Perhaps that is exactly what they *are* doing, in which case we had best all go down in prayer.

The level of Negro education, obviously, is even lower than the general level. The general level is low because, as I have said, Americans have so little respect for genuine intellectual effort. The Negro level is low because the education of Negroes occurs in, and is designed to perpetuate, a segregated society. This, in the first place, and no matter how much money the South boasts of spending on Negro schools, is utterly demoralizing. It creates a situation in which the Negro teacher is soon as powerless as his students. (There are exceptions among the teachers as there are among the students, but, in this country surely, schools have not been built for the exceptional. And, though white people often seem to expect Negroes to produce nothing but exceptions, the fact is that Negroes are really just like everybody else. Some of them are exceptional and most of them are not.)

The teachers are answerable to the Negro principal, whose power over the teachers is absolute but whose power with the school board is slight. As for this principal, he has arrived at the summit of his career; rarely indeed can he go any higher. He has his pension to look forward to, and he consoles himself, meanwhile, with his status among the "better class of Negroes." This class includes few, if any, of his students and by no means all of his teachers. The teachers, as long as they remain in this school system, and they certainly do not have much choice, can only aspire to become the principal one day. Since not all of them will make it, a great deal of the energy which ought to go into their vocation goes into the usual bitter, purposeless rivalry. They are underpaid and ill treated by the white world and rubbed raw by it every day; and it is altogether understandable that they, very shortly, cannot bear the sight of their students. The children know this; it is hard to fool young people. They also know why they are going to an overcrowded, outmoded plant, in classes so large that even the most strictly attentive student, the most gifted teacher cannot but feel himself slowly drowning in the sea of general helplessness.

It is not to be wondered at, therefore, that the violent distractions of puberty, occurring in such a cage, annually take their toll, sending female children into maternity wards and male children into the streets. It is not to be wondered at that a boy, one day, decides that if all this studying is going to prepare him only to be a porter or an elevator boy—or his teacher—well, then, the hell with it. And there they go, with an overwhelming bitterness which they will dissemble all their lives, an unceasing effort which completes their ruin. They become the menial or the criminal or the shiftless, the Negroes whom segregation has produced and whom the South uses to prove that segregation is right.

In Charlotte, too, I received some notion of what the South means by "time to adjust." The NAACP there had been trying for six years before Black Monday to make the city fathers honor the "separate but equal" statute and do something about the situation in Negro schools. Nothing whatever was done. After Black Monday, Charlotte begged for "time": and what she did with this time was work out legal stratagems designed to get the least possible integration over the longest possible period. In August of 1955, Governor Hodges, a moderate, went on the air with the suggestion that Negroes segregate themselves voluntarily—for the good, as he put it, of both races. Negroes seeming to be unmoved by this moderate proposal, the Klan reappeared in the counties and was still active there when I left. So, no doubt, are the boys on the chain gang.

But "Charlotte," I was told, "is not the South." I was told, "You haven't seen the South yet." Charlotte seemed quite Southern enough for me, but, in fact, the people in Charlotte were right. One of the reasons for this is that the South is not the monolithic structure which, from the North, it appears to be, but a most various and divided region. It clings to the myth of its past but it is being inexorably changed, meanwhile, by an entirely unmythical present: its habits and its self-interest are at war. Everyone in the South feels this and this is why there is such panic on the bottom and such impotence on the top.

It must also be said that the racial setup in the South is not, for a Negro, very different from the racial setup in the North. It is the etiquette which is baffling, not the spirit. Segregation is unofficial in the North and official in the South, a crucial difference that does nothing, nevertheless, to alleviate the lot of most Northern Negroes. But we will return to this question when we discuss the relationship between the Southern cities and states.

Atlanta, however, *is* the South. It is the South in this respect, that it has a very bitter interracial history. This is written in the faces of the people and one feels it in the air. It was on the outskirts of Atlanta that I first felt how the Southern landscape—the trees, the silence, the liquid heat, and the fact that one always seems to be traveling great distances—seems designed for violence, seems, almost, to demand it. What passions cannot be unleashed on a dark road in a Southern night! Everything seems so sensual, so languid, and so private. Desire can be acted out here; over this fence, behind that tree, in the darkness, there; and no one will see, no one will ever know. Only the night is watching and the night was made for desire. Protestantism is the wrong religion for people in such climates; America is perhaps the last nation in which such a climate belongs. In the Southern night everything seems possible, the most private, unspeakable longings; but then arrives the Southern day, as hard and brazen as the night was soft and dark. It brings what was done in the dark to light. It must have seemed something like this for those people who made the region what it is today. It must have caused them great pain. Perhaps the master who had coupled with his slave saw his guilt in his wife's pale eyes in the morning. And the wife saw his children in the slave quarters, saw the way his concubine, the sensual-looking black girl, looked at her—a woman, after all, and scarcely less sensual, but white. The youth, nursed and raised by the black Mammy whose arms had then held all that there was of warmth and love and desire, and still confounded by the dreadful taboos set up between himself and her progeny, must have wondered, after his first experiment with black flesh, where, under the blazing heavens, he could hide. And the white man must have seen his guilt written somewhere else, seen it all the time, even if his sin was merely lust, even if his sin lay in nothing but his power: in the eyes of the black man. He may not have stolen his woman, but he had certainly stolen his freedom—this black man, who had a body like his, and passions like his, and a ruder, more erotic beauty. How many times has the Southern day come up to find that black man, sexless, hanging from a tree!

It was an old black man in Atlanta who looked into my eyes and directed me into my first segregated bus. I have spent a long time thinking about that man. I never saw him again. I cannot describe the look which passed between us, as I asked him for directions, but it made me think, at once, of Shakespeare's "the oldest have borne most." It made me think of the blues: *Now, when a woman gets the blues, Lord, she hangs her head and cries. But when a man gets the blues, Lord, he grabs a train and rides.* It was borne in on me, suddenly, just why these men had so often been grabbing freight trains as the evening sun went down. And it was, perhaps, because I was getting on a segregated bus, and wondering how Negroes had borne this and other indignities for so long, that this man so struck me. He seemed to know what I was feeling. His eyes seemed to say that what I was feeling he had been feeling, at much higher pressure, all his life. But my eyes would never see the hell his eyes had seen. And this hell was, simply, that he had never in his life owned anything, not his wife, not his house, not his child, which could not, at any instant, be taken from him by the power of white people. This is what paternalism means. And for the rest of the time that I was in the South I watched the eyes of old black men.

Atlanta's well-to-do Negroes never takes buses, for they all have cars. The section in which they live is quite far away from the poor Negro section. They own, or at least are paying for, their own homes. They drive to work and back, and have cocktails and dinner with each other. They see very little of the white world; but they are cut off from the black world, too.

Now, of course, this last statement is not literally true. The teachers teach Negroes, the lawyers defend them. The ministers preach to them and bury them, and others insure their lives, pull their teeth, and cure their ailments. Some of the lawyers work with the NAACP and help push test cases through the courts. (If anything, by the way, disproves the charge of "extremism" which has so often been made against this organization, it is the fantastic care and patience such legal efforts demand.) Many of the teachers work very hard to bolster the morale of their students and prepare them for their new responsibilities; nor did those I met fool themselves about the hideous system under which they work. So when I say that they are cut off from the black world, I am not sneering, which, indeed, I scarcely have any right to do. I am talking about their position as a class—*if* they are a class—and their role in a very complex and shaky social structure.

The wealthier Negroes are, at the moment, very useful for the administration of the city of Atlanta, for they represent there the potential, at least, of interracial communication. That this phrase is a euphemism, in Atlanta as elsewhere, becomes clear when one considers how astonishingly little has been communicated in all these generations. What the phrase almost always has reference to is the fact that, in a given time and place, the Negro vote is of sufficient value to force politicians to bargain for it. What interracial communication also refers to is that Atlanta is really growing and thriving, and because it wants to make even more money, it would like to prevent incidents that disturb the peace, discourage investments, and permit test cases, which the city of Atlanta would certainly lose, to come to the courts. Once this happens, as it certainly will one day, the state of Georgia will be up in arms and the present administration of the city will be out of power. I did not meet a soul in Atlanta (I naturally did not meet any members of the White Citizen's Council, not, anyway, to talk to) who did not pray that the present mayor would be re-elected. Not that they loved him particularly, but it is his administration which holds off the holocaust.

Now this places Atlanta's wealthy Negroes in a really quite sinister position. Though both they and the mayor are devoted to keeping the peace, their aims and his are not, and cannot be, the same. Many of those lawyers are working day and night on test cases which the mayor is doing his best to keep out of court. The teachers spend their working day attempting to destroy in their students—and it is not too much to say, in themselves—those habits of inferiority which form one of the principal cornerstones of segregation as it is practiced in the South. Many of the parents listen to speeches by people like Senator Russell and find themselves unable to sleep at night. They are in the extraordinary position of being compelled to work for the destruction of all they have bought so dearly—their homes, their comfort, the safety of their children. But the safety of their children is merely comparative; it is all that their comparative strength as a class has bought them so far; and they are not safe, really, as long as the bulk of Atlanta's Negroes live in such darkness. On any night, in that other part of town, a policeman may beat up one Negro too many, or some Negro or some white man may simply go berserk. This is all it takes to drive so delicately balanced a city mad. And the island on which these Negroes have built their handsome houses will simply disappear.

This is not at all in the interests of Atlanta, and almost everyone there knows it. Left to itself, the city might grudgingly work out compromises designed to reduce the tension and raise the level of Negro life. But it is not left to itself; it belongs to the state of Georgia. The Negro vote has no power in the state, and the governor of Georgia—that "third-rate man," Atlantans call him—makes great political capital out of keeping the Negroes in their place. When six Negro ministers attempted to create a test case by ignoring the segregation ordinance on the buses, the governor was ready to declare martial law and hold the ministers incommunicado. It was the mayor who prevented this, who somehow squashed all publicity, treated the ministers with every outward sign of respect, and it is his office which is preventing the case from coming into court. And remember that it was the governor of Arkansas, in an insane bid for political power, who created the present crisis in Little Rock—against the will of most of its citizens and against the will of the mayor.

This war between the Southern cities and states is of the utmost importance, not only for the South, but for the nation. The Southern states are still very largely governed by people whose political lives, insofar, at least, as they are able to conceive of life or politics, are dependent on the people in the rural regions. It might, indeed, be more honorable to try to guide these people out of their pain and ignorance instead of locking them within it, and battening on it; but it is, admittedly, a difficult task to try to tell people the truth and it is clear that most Southern politicians have no intention of attempting it. The attitude of these people can only have the effect of stiffening the already implacable Negro resistance, and this attitude is absolutely certain, sooner or later, to create great trouble in the cities. When a race riot occurs in Atlanta, it will not spread merely to Birmingham, for example. (Birmingham is a doomed city.) The trouble will spread to every metropolitan center in the nation which has a significant Negro population. And this is not only because the ties between Northern and Southern Negroes are still very close. It is because the nation, the entire nation, has spent a hundred years avoiding the question of the place of the black man in it.

That this has done terrible things to black men is not even a question. "Integration," said a very light Negro to me in Alabama,

"has always worked very well in the South, after the sun goes down."
"It's not miscegenation," said another Negro to me, "unless a black
man's involved." Now, I talked to many Southern liberals who were
doing their best to bring integration about in the South, but met
scarcely a single Southerner who did not weep for the passing of
the old order. They were perfectly sincere, too, and, within their
limits, they were right. They pointed out how Negroes and whites
in the South had loved each other, they recounted to me tales of
devotion and heroism which the old order had produced, and which,
now, would never come again. But the old black men I looked at
down there—those same black men that the Southern liberal had loved;
for whom, until now, the Southern liberal—and not only the liberal
—has been willing to undergo great inconvenience and danger—they
were not weeping. Men do not like to be protected, it emasculates
them. This is what black men know, it is the reality they have
lived with; it is what white men do not want to know. It is not
a pretty thing to be a father and be ultimately dependent on the
power and kindness of some other man for the well-being of your
house.

But what this evasion of the Negro's humanity has done to the
nation is not so well known. The really striking thing, for me, in
the South was this dreadful paradox, that the black men were stronger
than the white. I do not know how they did it, but it certainly
has something to do with that as yet unwritten history of the Negro
woman. What it comes to, finally, is that the nation has spent a
large part of its time and energy looking away from one of the
principal facts of its life. This failure to look reality in the face
diminishes a nation as it diminishes a person, and it can only be
described as unmanly. And in exactly the same way that the South
imagines that it "knows" the Negro, the North imagines that it has
set him free. Both camps are deluded. Human freedom is a complex, difficult—and private—thing. If we can liken life, for a moment,
to a furnace, then freedom is the fire which burns away illusion.
Any honest examination of the national life proves how far we are
from the standard of human freedom with which we began. The
recovery of this standard demands of everyone who loves this country a hard look at himself, for the greatest achievements must begin somewhere, and they always begin with the person. If we are
not capable of this examination, we may yet become one of the most
distinguished and monumental failures in the history of nations.

Robert Lowell

FOR THE UNION DEAD

If anyone knew his best poem, I think he would be too elated to reveal the secret; like some powerful chemical formula, this certainty should be guarded and sipped by stealth. Anyway I have no idea. Each poem was meant to be alive and new, and many were once ambitious. I chose "For the Union Dead" partly because of its length, neither overmodest nor hoggishly long for this collection. All one winter I cut, added and tinkered. Some of my better lines came to me a few days before I read the poem at the Boston Garden Festival.

> He rejoices in man's lovely,
> peculiar power to choose life and die.

I have written nothing else for an occasion, and feel no desire to try again. Here the demands helped and even inspired me to pull three incoherent sketches together. One was about an aquarium, one about a parking lot, one about a Boston club. I do not regard persuasive interpretations of his own poems as one of the poet's most useful chores. I wished to write something natural on the brazen and overworked subject of Colonel Shaw. I wished to give my own structure to the free verse I had learned from my friend, William Carlos Williams. My poem may be about a child maturing into courage and terror. My lines are on the dry and angry side, but the fish and steamshovels are Tahitian. In 1959 I had a message. Since then the blacks have perhaps found their "break," but the landscape remains.

Robert Lowell

"Relinguunt Omnia Servare Rem Publicam."

The old South Boston Aquarium stands
in a Sahara of snow now. Its broken windows are boarded.
The bronze weathervane cod has lost half its scales.
The airy tanks are dry.

Once my nose crawled like a snail on the glass;
my hand tingled
to burst the bubbles
drifting from the noses of the cowed, compliant fish.

My hand draws back. I often sigh still
for the dark downward and vegetating kingdom
of the fish and reptile. One morning last March,
I pressed against the new barbed and galvanized

fence on the Boston Common. Behind their cage,
yellow dinosaur steamshovels were grunting
as they cropped up tons of mush and grass
to gouge their underworld garage.

Parking spaces luxuriate like civic
sandpiles in the heart of Boston.
A girdle of orange, Puritan-pumpkin colored girders
braces the tingling Statehouse,

shaking over the excavations, as it faces Colonel Shaw
and his bell-cheeked Negro infantry
on St. Gaudens' shaking Civil War relief,
propped by a plank splint against the garage's earthquake.

Two months after marching through Boston,
half the regiment was dead;
at the dedication,
William James could almost hear the bronze Negroes breathe.

Their monument sticks like a fishbone
in the city's throat.
Its Colonel is as lean
as a compass-needle.

He has an angry wrenlike vigilance,
a greyhound's gentle tautness;
he seems to wince at pleasure,
and suffocate for privacy.

He is out of bounds now. He rejoices in man's lovely,
peculiar power to choose life and die—
when he leads his black soldiers to death,
he cannot bend his back.

On a thousand small town New England greens,
the old white churches hold their air
of sparse, sincere rebellion; frayed flags
quilt the graveyards of the Grand Army of the Republic.

The stone statues of the abstract Union Soldier
grow slimmer and younger each year—
wasp-wasted, they doze over muskets
and muse through their sideburns . . .

Shaw's father wanted no monument
except the ditch,
where his son's body was thrown
and lost with his "niggers."

The ditch is nearer.
There are no statues for the last war here;
on Boyleston Street, a commercial photograph
shows Hiroshima boiling

over a Mosler Safe, the "Rock of Ages"
that survived the blast. Space is nearer.
When I crouch to my television set,
the drained faces of Negro school-children rise like balloons.

Colonel Shaw
is riding on his bubble,
he waits
for the blesséd break.

The Aquarium is gone. Everywhere,
giant finned cars nose forward like fish;
a savage servility
slides by on grease.

Gwendolyn Brooks

THE LOVERS OF THE POOR

The poetry I have chosen issues from the guts of black life.
That is why I have chosen it.

Gwendolyn Brooks

THE MOTHER

Abortions will not let you forget.
You remember the children you got that you did not get,
The damp small pulps with a little or with no hair,
The singers and workers that never handled the air.
You will never neglect or beat
Them, or silence or buy with a sweet.
You will never wind up the sucking-thumb
Or scuttle off ghosts that come.
You will never leave them, controlling your luscious sigh,
Return for a snack of them, with gobbling mother-eye.

I have heard in the voices of the wind the voices of my dim killed
    children.
I have contracted. I have eased
My dim dears at the breasts they could never suck.
I have said, Sweets, if I sinned, if I seized
Your luck
And your lives from your unfinished reach,
If I stole your births and your names,
Your straight baby tears and your games,
Your stilted or lovely loves, your tumults, your marriages, aches, and your
    deaths,
If I poisoned the beginnings of your breaths,
Believe that even in my deliberateness I was not deliberate.

Though why should I whine,
Whine that the crime was other than mine?—
Since anyhow you are dead.
Or rather, or instead,
You were never made.
But that too, I am afraid,
Is faulty: oh, what shall I say, how is the truth to be said?
You were born, you had body, you died.
It is just that you never giggled or planned or cried.

Believe me, I loved you all.
Believe me, I knew you, though faintly, and I loved, I loved you
All.

WE REAL COOL

THE POOL PLAYERS.
SEVEN AT THE GOLDEN SHOVEL.

We real cool. We
Left school. We

Lurk late. We
Strike straight. We

Sing sin. We
Thin gin. We

Jazz June. We
Die soon.

THE LOVERS OF THE POOR

ARRIVE. THE LADIES FROM THE LADIES'
BETTERMENT LEAGUE

Arrive in the afternoon, the late light slanting
In diluted gold bars across the boulevard brag
Of proud, seamed faces with mercy and murder hinting
Here, there, interrupting, all deep and debonair,
The pink paint on the innocence of fear;
Walk in a gingerly manner up the hall.
Cutting with knives served by their softest care,
Served by their love, so barbarously fair.
Whose mothers taught: You'd better not be cruel!
You had better not throw stones upon the wrens!
Herein they kiss and coddle and assault
Anew and dearly in the innocence
With which they baffle nature. Who are full,
Sleek, tender-clad, fit, fiftyish, a-glow, all
Sweetly abortive, hinting at fat fruit,
Judge it high time that fiftyish fingers felt
Beneath the lovelier planes of enterprise.
To resurrect. To moisten with milky chill.
To be a random hitching-post or plush.
To be, for wet eyes, random and handy hem.
          Their guild is giving money to the poor.
The worthy poor. The very very worthy
And beautiful poor. Perhaps just not too swarthy?
Perhaps just not too dirty nor too dim
Nor—passionate. In truth, what they could wish
Is—something less than derelict or dull.
Not staunch enough to stab, though, gaze for gaze!
God shield them sharply from the beggar-bold!
The noxious needy ones whose battle's bald
Nonetheless for being voiceless, hits one down.

But it's all so bad! and entirely too much for them.
The stench; the urine, cabbage, and dead beans,
Dead porridges of assorted dusty grains,
The old smoke, *heavy* diapers, and, they're told,
Something called chitterlings. The darkness. Drawn
Darkness, or dirty light. The soil that stirs.
The soil that looks the soil of centuries.
And for that matter the *general* oldness. Old
Wood. Old marble. Old tile. Old old old.
Not homekind Oldness! Not Lake Forest, Glencoe.
Nothing is sturdy, nothing is majestic,
There is no quiet drama, no rubbed glaze, no
Unkillable infirmity of such
A tasteful turn as lately they have left,
Glencoe, Lake Forest, and to which their cars
Must presently restore them. When they're done
With dullards and distortions of this fistic
Patience of the poor and put-upon.
        They've never seen such a make-do-ness as
Newspaper rugs before! In this, this "flat,"
Their hostess is gathering up the oozed, the rich
Rugs of the morning (tattered! the bespattered. . . .)
Readies to spread clean rugs for afternoon.
Here is a scene for you. The Ladies look,
In horror, behind a substantial citizenness
Whose trains clank out across her swollen heart.
Who, arms akimbo, almost fills a door.
All tumbling children, quilts dragged to the floor
And tortured thereover, potato peelings, soft-
Eyed kitten, hunched-up, haggard, to-be-hurt.
        Their League is allotting largesse to the Lost.
But to put their clean, their pretty money, to put
Their money collected from delicate rose-fingers
Tipped with their hundred flawless rose-nails seems . . .
        They own Spode, Lowestoft, candelabra,
Mantels, and hostess gowns, and sunburst clocks,
Turtle soup, Chippendale, red satin "hangings,"
Aubussons and Hattie Carnegie. They Winter
In Palm Beach; cross the Water in June; attend,
When suitable, the nice Art Institute;

Buy the right books in the best bindings; saunter
On Michigan, Easter mornings, in sun or wind.
Oh Squalor! This sick four-story hulk, this fibre
With fissures everywhere! Why, what are bringings
Of loathe-love largesse? What shall peril hungers
So old old, what shall flatter the desolate?
Tin can, blocked fire escape and chitterling
And swaggering seeking youth and the puzzled wreckage
Of the middle passage, and urine and stale shames
And, again, the porridges of the underslung
And children children children. Heavens! That
Was a rat, surely, off there, in the shadows? Long
And long-tailed? Gray? The Ladies from the Ladies'
Betterment League agree it will be better
To achieve the outer air that rights and steadies,
To hie to a house that does not holler, to ring
Bells elsetime, better presently to cater
To no more Possibilities, to get
Away. Perhaps the money can be posted.
Perhaps they two may choose another Slum!
Some serious sooty half-unhappy home!—
Where loathe-love likelier may be invested.

        Keeping their scented bodies in the center
Of the hall as they walk down the hysterical hall,
They allow their lovely skirts to graze no wall,
Are off at what they manage of a canter,
And, resuming all the clues of what they were,
Try to avoid inhaling the laden air.

THE BLACKSTONE RANGERS

I

AS SEEN BY DISCIPLINES

There they are.
Thirty at the corner.
Black, raw, ready.
Sores in the city
that do not want to heal.

II

THE LEADERS

Jeff. Gene. Geronimo. And Bop.
They cancel, cure and curry.
Hardly the dupes of the downtown thing
the cold bonbon,
the rhinestone thing. And hardly
in a hurry.
Hardly Belafonte, King,
Black Jesus, Stokely, Malcolm X or Rap.
Bungled trophies.
Their country is a Nation on no map.

Jeff, Gene, Geronimo and Bop
in the passionate noon,
in bewitching night
are the detailed men, the copious men.
They curry, cure,
they cancel, cancelled images whose Concerts
are not divine, vivacious; the different tins
are intense last entries; pagan argument;
translations of the night.

The Blackstone bitter bureaus
(bureaucracy is footloose) edit, fuse
unfashionable damnations and descent;
and exulting, monstrous hand on monstrous hand,
construct, strangely, a monstrous pearl or grace.

III

GANG GIRLS

A Rangerette

Gang Girls are sweet exotics.
Mary Ann
uses the nutrients of her orient,
but sometimes sighs for Cities of blue and jewel
beyond her Ranger rim of Cottage Grove.
(Bowery Boys, Disciples, Whip-Birds will
dissolve no margins, stop no savory sanctities.)

Mary is
a rose in a whiskey glass.

Mary's
Februaries shudder and are gone. Aprils
fret frankly, lilac hurries on.
Summer is a hard irregular ridge.
October looks away.
And that's the Year!
            Save for her bugle-love.
Save for the bleat of not-obese devotion.
Save for Somebody Terribly Dying, under
the philanthropy of robins. Save for her Ranger
bringing
an amount of rainbow in a string-drawn bag.
"Where did you get the diamond?" Do not ask:
but swallow, straight, the spirals of his flask
and assist him at your zipper; pet his lips
and help him clutch you.

Love's another departure.
Will there be any arrivals, confirmations?
Will there be gleaning?

Mary, the Shakedancer's child
from the rooming-flat, pants carefully, peers at
her laboring lover. . . .
          Mary! Mary Ann!
Settle for sandwiches! settle for stocking caps!
for sudden blood, aborted carnival,
the props and niceties of non-loneliness—
the rhymes of Leaning.

V
Thanksgiving for a Habitat

V

Thanksgiving for a Habitat

Karl Shapiro

ADAM AND EVE

Dear Whit Burnett:

I have never thought of any of my poems as "best" because I write in many *genres* and cannot mount a proper competition among my works. Many of what I think of as my favorite poems are unique and are therefore automatically best. For example a recent poem, "Aubade," is certainly one of the most successful poems I have ever written—in my opinion as its author and critic—but it is the sole example of that kind of poem in my repertoire. I debated between my "Aubade" and the "Adam and Eve" sequence.

"Adam and Eve" is the only narrative poem I have written. I am very moved when I read it to audiences, and so are they. Usually I read it last in a recital, for that reason. I love to *move* audiences.

In one of my books I published a note about the poem. The note gives a little of the etiology of the poem and I will repeat it:

These poems were originally printed under the title *Eden Retold*. The poems in this series are not symbolic but literal interpretations. That is, I wrote them according to my own interpretation of the lines in Genesis, where they are first presented. Rilke says that Adam was *determined* to leave the Garden. My argument in the poem is that God determined him to leave it. Much of the imagery of the poems is drawn from the imagery of the *Zohar* or central work of the cabala, some from the renegade Freudian, Wilhelm Reich. The viewpoint of the sequence, that man is for the world, not for the afterworld, is Jewish.

It is my belief and not simply a poetic notion that Genesis describes the transition from pre-sexuality to sexuality. In a sense, this is the most obvious statement one can make; and, in a sense, it is the most obscure. Consequently, I used the most sensual imagery I could find to describe the seduction of Eve by the thought of the penis, and the seduction of Adam by his wife.

Only a few weeks ago I (or rather my wife) solved a problem of an obscurity in the poem and in the myth itself by changing the wording of a line. In future editions of the poem in poem IV, The Tree of Guilt, stanza four, line 6, the line will read, "Again the snake was seized and from its lip." Explicators can see why. Formerly this line read, "Again he seized the snake and from its lip." The revision makes the poem perfect, in my opinion, though I had to wait more than fifteen years for the final touch.

Sincerely,
Karl Shapiro

I

THE SICKNESS OF ADAM

In the beginning, at every step, he turned
As if by instinct to the East to praise
The nature of things. Now every path was learned
He lost the lifted, almost flower-like gaze

Of a temple dancer. He began to walk
Slowly, like one accustomed to be alone.
He found himself lost in the field of talk;
Thinking became a garden of its own.

In it were new things: words he had never said,
Beasts he had never seen and knew were not
In the true garden, terrors, and tears shed
Under a tree by him, for some new thought.

And the first anger. Once he flung a staff
At softly coupling sheep and struck the ram.
It broke away. And God heard Adam laugh
And for his laughter made the creature lame.

And wanderlust. He stood upon the Wall
To search the unfinished countries lying wide
And waste, where not a living thing could crawl,
And yet he would descend, as if to hide.

His thought drew down the guardian at the gate,
To whom man said, 'What danger am I in?'
And the angel, hurt in spirit, seemed to hate
The wingless thing that worried after sin,

For it said nothing but marvelously unfurled
Its wings and arched them shimmering overhead,
Which must have been the signal from the world
That the first season of our life was dead.

Adam fell down with labor in his bones,
And God approached him in the cool of day
And said, 'This sickness in your skeleton
Is longing. I will remove it from your clay.'

He said also, 'I made you strike the sheep.'
It began to rain and God sat down beside
The sinking man. When he was fast asleep
He wet his right hand deep in Adam's side

And drew the graceful rib out of his breast.
Far off, the latent streams began to flow
And birds flew out of Paradise to nest
On earth. Sadly the angel watched them go.

II
THE RECOGNITION OF EVE

Whatever it was she had so fiercely fought
Had fled back to the sky, but still she lay
With arms outspread, awaiting its assault,
Staring up through the branches of the tree,
The fig tree. Then she drew a shuddering breath
And turned her head instinctively his way.
She had fought birth as dying men fight death.

Her sigh awakened him. He turned and saw
A body swollen, as though formed of fruits,
White as the flesh of fishes, soft and raw.
He hoped she was another of the brutes
So he crawled over and looked into her eyes,
The human wells that pool all absolutes.
It was like looking into double skies.

And when she spoke the first word (it was *thou*)
He was terror-stricken, but she raised her hand
And touched his wound where it was fading now,
For he must feel the place to understand.
Then he recalled the longing that had torn
His side, and while he watched it whitely mend,
He felt it stab him suddenly like a thorn.

He thought the woman had hurt him. Was it she
Or the same sickness seeking to return;
Or was there any difference, the pain set free
And she who seized him now as hard as iron?
Her fingers bit his body. She looked old
And involuted, like the newly-born.
He let her hurt him till she loosed her hold.

Then she forgot him and she wearily stood
And went in search of water through the grove.

Adam could see her wandering through the wood,
Studying her footsteps as her body wove
In light and out of light. She found a pool
And there he followed shyly to observe.
She was already turning beautiful.

III
THE KISS

The first kiss was with stumbling fingertips.
Their bodies grazed each other as if by chance
And touched and untouched in a kind of dance.
Second, they found out touching with their lips.

Some obscure angel, pausing on his course,
Shed such a brightness on the face of Eve
That Adam in grief was ready to believe
He had lost her love. The third kiss was by force.

Their lips formed foreign, unimagined oaths
When speaking of the Tree of Guilt. So wide
Their mouths, they drank each other from inside.
A gland of honey burst within their throats.

But something rustling hideously overhead,
They jumped up from the fourth caress and hid.

IV
THE TREE OF GUILT

Why, on her way to the oracle of Love,
Did she not even glance up at the Tree
Of Life, that giant with the whitish cast
And glinting leaves and berries of dull gray,
As though covered with mold? But who would taste
The medicine of immortality,
And who would 'be as God'? And in what way?

So she came breathless to the lowlier one
And like a priestess of the cult she knelt,
Holding her breasts in token for a sign,
And prayed the spirit of the burdened bough
That the great power of the tree be seen
And lift itself out of the Tree of Guilt
Where it had hidden in the leaves till now.

Or did she know already? Had the peacock
Rattling its quills, glancing its thousand eyes
At her, the iridescence of the dove,
Stench of the he-goat, everything that joins
Told her the mystery? It was not enough,
So from the tree the snake began to rise
And dropt its head and pointed at her loins.

She fell and hid her face and still she saw
The spirit of the tree emerge and slip
Into the open sky until it stood
Straight as a standing-stone, and spilled its seed.
And all the seed were serpents of the good.
Again he seized the snake and from its lip
It spat the venomous evil of the deed.

And it was over. But the woman lay
Stricken with what she knew, ripe in her thought
Like a fresh apple fallen from the limb
And rotten, like a fruit that lies too long.
This way she rose, ripe-rotten in her prime
And spurned the cold thing coiled against her foot
And called her husband, in a kind of song.

v

THE CONFESSION

As on the first day her first word was *thou*.
He waited while she said, 'Thou art the tree.'
And while she said, almost accusingly,
Looking at nothing, 'Thou art the fruit I took.'
She seemed smaller by inches as she spoke,
And Adam wondering touched her hair and shook,
Half understanding. He answered softly, 'How?'

And for the third time, in the third way, Eve:
'The tree that rises from the middle part
Of the garden.' And almost tenderly, 'Thou art
The garden. *We*.' Then she was overcome,
And Adam coldly, lest he should succumb
To pity, standing at the edge of doom,
Comforted her like one about to leave.

She sensed departure and she stood aside
Smiling and bitter. But he asked again,
'How did you eat? With what thing did you sin?'
And Eve with body slackened and uncouth,
'Under the tree I took the fruit of truth
From an angel. I ate it with my other mouth.'
And saying so, she did not know she lied.

It was the man who suddenly released
From doubt, wept in the woman's heavy arms,
Those double serpents, subtly winding forms
That climb and drop about the manly boughs;
And dry with weeping, fiery and aroused,
Fell on her face to slake his terrible thirst
And bore her body earthward like a beast.

VI
SHAME

The hard blood falls back in the manly fount,
The soft door closes under Venus' mount,
The ovoid moon moves to the Garden's side
And dawn comes, but the lovers have not died.
They have not died but they have fallen apart
In sleep, like equal halves of the same heart.

How to teach shame? How to teach nakedness
To the already naked? How to express
Nudity? How to open innocent eyes
And separate the innocent from the wise?
And how to re-establish the guilty tree
In infinite gardens of humanity?

By marring the image, by the black device
Of the goat-god, by the clown of Paradise,
By fruits of cloth and by the navel's bud,
By itching tendrils and by strings of blood,
By ugliness, by the shadow of our fear,
By ridicule, by the fig-leaf patch of hair.

Whiter than tombs, whiter than whitest clay,
Exposed beneath the whitening eye of day,
They awoke and saw the covering that reveals.
They thought they were changing into animals.
Like animals they bellowed terrible cries
And clutched each other, hiding each other's eyes.

VII

EXILE

The one who gave the warning with his wings,
Still doubting them, held out the sword of flame
Against the Tree of Whiteness as they came
Angrily, slowly by, like exiled kings,

And watched them at the broken-open gate
Stare in the distance long and overlong,
And then, like peasants, pitiful and strong,
Take the first step toward earth and hesitate.

For Adam raised his head and called aloud,
'My Father, who has made the garden pall,
Giving me all things and then taking all,
Who with your opposite nature has endowed

Woman, give us your hand for our descent.
Needing us greatly, even in our disgrace,
Guide us, for gladly do we leave this place
For our own land and wished-for banishment.'

But woman prayed, 'Guide us to Paradise.'
Around them slunk the uneasy animals,
Strangely excited, uttering coughs and growls,
And bounded down into the wild abyss.

And overhead the last migrating birds,
Then empty sky. And when the two had gone
A slow half-dozen steps across the stone,
The angel came and stood among the shards

And called them, as though joyously, by name.
They turned in dark amazement and beheld
Eden ablaze with fires of red and gold,
The garden dressed for dying in cold flame,

And it was autumn, and the present world.

Mark Van Doren

DUNCE SONGS

Dear Whit:
    Here is my reason for the selection of "Dunce Songs": *Because the writing of them gave me so much pleasure.*
    Short and sweet, and it's all I have or (I think) need to say.

Sincerely,
Mark Van Doren

1

Where is the bell, the horn,
I hear as I go by,
Go by the invisible wall
That holds up half the sky,
The sky whose other half
Falls down like gold wheat chaff
And sprinkles all the air,
And powders my dull hair?
So people cry and cry:
Who wears that glittery crown,
That crown? And I say I.
Oh, what a falling down
As I go by, go by.

2

If rain rose,
And leaves fell upward—
Oh, me, oh, them
Sky-high together.

That is my house.
Here I am homesick.
Bright, oh, bright,
Forever, ever.

Raindrops, leaves
Round me like mica.
Snow whirls
In a ball of water.

Give it a shake.
That's me in the middle.
White, oh, white—
See now? I am laughing.

3

Some day,
When the great clock
Of dawn strikes, and keeps on striking—
What's gone wrong, the president will shout, why doesn't somebody,
Somebody stop it?—

That day,
When the music starts
That no man ever heard before—
Bong, bong, the bells up there, whish, whish,
The windy singing—

That time
Will be my time:
No minutes, years, no coming, going—
Night, poor night, laid out in white—oh, my soul,
The death of darkness—

Whee, whee,
The waking birds.
(Yet I do pity them a little—
Come close, I'm whispering—yes, I too will miss their brave
Songs at sunset.)

4

Then I'll be four-footed,
And modest with fur.
All over, all under,
Seemly and still.

Then I'll be patient:
A part of the ground.
I will go slowly,
And lowly—oh, sweet,

Then I'll be one of them
He that made all
Looks after the longest,
And tenderest loves.

Then I'll be quiet—
You can be quick—
And lie down all summer,
All winter, and sleep.

5

I have no enemy.
If I did,
I would wait for him, in the black dark, and thwack him—
Ha! on the head.

Or else I would grow
A green worm in my heart
And feed it all day till the strength of its poison
Was death to the world.

Yes, but I have none.
All are my lovers—
Harry, and Jack, and even the great ones,
That cause the long wars,

All are my little
Sweet friends that I wait for,
In the warm sun, and stroke them, stroke them—
Ha, my poor head!

6

Her hand in my hand,
Soft as the south wind,
Soft as a colt's nose,
Soft as forgetting;

Her cheek to my cheek,
Red as the cranberry,
Red as a mitten,
Red as remembering—

Here we go round like raindrops,
Raindrops,
Here we go round
So snug together,

Oh, but I wonder,
Oh, but I know,
Who comforts like raisins,
Who kisses like snow.

7

If I had a wife
I would love her as kings
Loved queens in the old days, or as princes
Maidens,
Met in the dew, by a stile, of a morning—
"How do you do, my pretty?"
And all of that.

If I had a wife
I would come home sometimes
Dressed like a stranger, and when she stared,
"Lady,"
I'd say, and woo her in wonder—
"How can there be such shining?"
And all of that.

If I had a wife
I would never be done
With remembering how it is now when, oh,
I am lonesome,
And no one is here but my dog and my cat—
"Well, old boys! Hungry?"
And all of that.

8

Pepper and salt
And summer savory—
Those are for luckier tables and tongues
Than my old woman
And I have.

The sun and the wind,
Those are our seasoning;
With maybe nine drops of rain on a Thursday—
Yes, my old woman's
A smart one.

She holds up her bonnet
Just when He is looking—
Oh, the love in His eyes, oh, the millions of tears.
Even my old woman
Is weeping.

9

Love me little, love me long,
Then we neither can be wrong:
You in giving, I in taking;
There is not a heart breaking
But remembers one touch,
Or maybe seven, of too much.

Love me more than halfway, though.
Let me think, then let me know.
And I promise you the same:
A little wild, a little tame;
Lest it ever seem long:
Tick, tock, ding, dong.

W. H. Auden

THANKSGIVING FOR A HABITAT

Dear Mr. Burnett:

Although I have selected three poems for *This Is My Best* I find it very difficult to comment on my own work. It's simply not my business. Will you excuse me?

W. H. Auden

II
THANKSGIVING FOR A HABITAT

For Geoffrey Gorer

Nobody I know would like to be buried
    with a silver cocktail shaker,
a transistor radio and a strangled
    daily help, or keep his word because

of a great-great-grandmother who got laid
    by a sacred beast. Only a press lord
could have built San Simeon: no unearned income
    can buy us back the gait and gestures

to manage a baroque staircase, or the art
    of believing footmen don't hear
human speech. (In adulterine castles
    our half-strong might hang their jackets

while mending their lethal bicycle chains:
    luckily, there are not enough
crags to go round.) Still, Hetty Pegler's Tump
    is worth a visit, so is Schönbrunn,

to look at someone's idea of the body
    that should have been his, as the flesh
Mum formulated shouldn't: that whatever
    he does or feels in the mood for,

stocktaking, horseplay, worship, making love,
    he stays the same shape, disgraces
a Royal I. To be overadmired is not
    good enough: although a fine figure

is rare in either sex, others like it
    have existed before. One may
be a Proustian snob or a sound Jacksonian
    democrat, but which of us wants

to be touched inadvertently, even
    by his beloved? We know all about graphs
and Darwin, enormous rooms no longer
    superhumanize, but earnest

city planners are mistaken: a pen
    for a rational animal
is no fitting habitat for Adam's
    sovereign clone. I, a transplant

from overseas, at last am dominant
    over three acres and a blooming
conurbation of country lives, few of whom
    I shall ever meet, and with fewer

converse. Linnaeus recoiled from the Amphibia
    as a naked gruesome rabble,
Arachnids give me the shudders, but fools
    who deface their emblem of guilt

are germane to Hitler: the race of spiders
    shall be allowed their webs. I should like
to be to my water-brethren as a spell
    of fine weather: Many are stupid,

and some, maybe, are heartless, but who is not
    vulnerable, easy to scare,
and jealous of his privacy? (I am glad
    the blackbird, for instance, cannot

tell if I'm talking English, German or
   just typewriting: that what he utters
I may enjoy as an alien rigmarole.) I ought
   to outlast the limber dragonflies

as the muscle-bound firs are certainly
   going to outlast me: I shall not end
down any esophagus, though I may succumb
   to a filter-passing predator,

shall, anyhow, stop eating, surrender my smidge
   of nitrogen to the World Fund
with a drawn-out *Oh* (unless at the nod
   of some jittery commander

I be translated in a nano-second
   to a c.c. of poisonous nothing
in a giga-death). Should conventional
   blunderbuss war and its routiers

invest my bailiwick, I shall of course
   assume the submissive posture:
but men are not wolves and it probably
   won't help. Territory, status,

and love, sing all the birds, are what matter:
   what I dared not hope or fight for
is, in my fifties, mine, a toft-and-croft
   where I needn't, ever, be at home *to*

those I am not at home *with,* not a cradle,
   a magic Eden without clocks,
and not a windowless grave, but a place
   I may go both in and out of.

III

THE CAVE OF MAKING

In Memoriam Louis MacNeice

For this and for all enclosures like it the archetype
    is Weland's Stithy, an antre
more private than a bedroom even, for neither lovers nor
    maids are welcome, but without a
bedroom's secrets: from the Olivetti portable,
    the dictionaries (the very
best money can buy), the heaps of paper, it is evident
    what must go on. Devoid of
flowers and family photographs, all is subordinate
    here to a function, designed to
discourage daydreams—hence windows averted from plausible
    videnda but admitting a light one
could mend a watch by—and to sharpen hearing: reached by an
    outside staircase, domestic
noises and odors, the vast background of natural
    life are shut off. Here silence
is turned into objects.
                            I wish, Louis, I could have shown it you
    while you were still in public,
and the house and garden: lover of women and Donegal,
    from your perspective you'd notice
sights I overlook, and in turn take a scholar's interest
    in facts I could tell you (for instance,
four miles to our east, at a wood palisade, Carolingian
    Bavaria stopped, beyond it
unknowable nomads). Friends we became by personal
    choice, but fate had already
made us neighbors. For Grammar we both inherited
    good mongrel barbarian English

which never completely succumbed to the Roman rhetoric
    or the Roman gravity, that nonsense
which stood none. Though neither of our dads, like Horace's
    wiped his nose on his forearm,
neither was porphyry-born, and our ancestors probably
    were among those plentiful subjects
it cost less money to murder. Born so, both of us
    became self-conscious at a moment
when locomotives were named after knights in Malory,
    Science to schoolboys was known as
Stinks, and the Manor still was politically numinous:
    both watched with mixed feelings
the sack of Silence, the churches empty, the cavalry
    go, the Cosmic Model
become German, and any faith if we had it, in immanent
    virtue died. More than ever
life-out-there is goodly, miraculous, lovable,
    but we shan't, not since Stalin and Hitler,
trust ourselves ever again: we know that, subjectively,
    all is possible.
                To you, though,
ever since, last Fall, you quietly slipped out of Granusion,
    our moist garden, into
the Country of Unconcern, no possibility
    matters. I wish you hadn't
caught that cold, but the dead we miss are easier
    to talk to: with those no longer
tensed by problems one cannot feel shy and, anyway,
    when playing cards or drinking
or pulling faces are out of the question, what else is there
    to do but talk to the voices
of conscience they have become? From now on, as a visitor
    who needn't be met at the station,
your influence is welcome at any hour in my ubity,
    especially here, where titles
from *Poems* to *The Burning Perch* offer proof positive
    of the maker you were, with whom I
once collaborated, once at a weird Symposium
    exchanged winks as a juggins
went on about Alienation.

                                    Who would, for preference,
      be a bard in an oral culture,
obliged at drunken feasts to improvise a eulogy
      of some beefy illiterate burner,
giver of rings, or depend for bread on the moods of a
      Baroque Prince, expected,
like his dwarf, to amuse? After all, it's rather a privilege
      amid the affluent traffic
to serve this unpopular art which cannot be turned into
      background noise for study
or hung as a status trophy by rising executives,
      cannot be "done" like Venice
or abridged like Tolstoy, but stubbornly still insists upon
      being read or ignored: our handful
of clients at least can rune. (It's heartless to forget about
      the underdeveloped countries,
but a starving ear is as deaf as a suburban optimist's:
      to stomachs only the Hindu
integers truthfully speak.) Our forerunners might envy us
      our remnant still able to listen:
as Nietzsche said they would, the *plebs* have got steadily
      denser, the *optimates,*
quicker still on the uptake. (Today, even Talleyrand
      might seem a naïf: he had so
little to cope with.) I should like to become, if possible,
      a minor atlantic Goethe,
with his passion for weather and stones but without his silliness
      re the Cross: at times a bore, but,
while knowing Speech can at best, a shadow echoing
      the silent light, bear witness
to the Truth it is not, he wished it were, as the Francophile
      gaggle of pure songsters
are too vain to. We're not musicians: to stink of Poetry
      is unbecoming, and never
to be dull shows a lack of taste. Even a limerick
      ought to be something a man of
honor, awaiting death from cancer or a firing squad,
      could read without contempt: (at
that frontier I wouldn't dare speak to anyone

in either a prophet's bellow
or a diplomat's whisper).
                              Seeing you know our mystery
   from the inside and therefore
how much, in our lonely dens, we need the companionship
   of our good dead, to give us
comfort on dowly days when the self is a nonentity
   dumped on a mound of nothing,
to break the spell of our self-enchantment when lip-smacking
   imps of mawk and hooey
write with us what they will, you won't think me imposing if
   I ask you to stay at my elbow
until cocktail time: dear Shade, for your elegy
   I should have been able to manage
something more like you than this egocentric monologue,
   but accept it for friendship's sake.

POSTSCRIPT

   Timeless fictional worlds
   Of self-evident meaning
   Would not delight,

   Were not our own
   A temporal one where nothing
   Is what it seems.

   A poem—a tall story:
   But any good one
   Makes us want to know.

   Only tuneless birds,
   Inarticulate warriors,
   Need bright plumage.

   In a brothel, both
   The ladies and gentlemen
   Have nicknames only.

Speechless Evil
Borrowed the language of Good
And reduced it to noise.

A dry sad day.
What pirate falsehood
Has beheaded your stream of Truth?

At lucky moments we seem on the brink
Of really saying what we think we think:
But, even then, an honest eye should wink.

Nature, consistent and august,
Can't teach us what to write or do:
With Her the real is always true,
And what is true is also just.

Time has taught you
                        how much inspiration
your vices brought you,
                        what imagination
can owe temptation
                    yielded to,
that many a fine
                    expressive line
would not have existed,
                        had you resisted:
as a poet, you
                know this is true,
and though in Kirk
                    you sometimes pray
to feel contrite,
                    it doesn't work.
Felix Culpa, you say:
                        perhaps you're right.

You hope, yes,
                your books will excuse you,
save you from hell:
                    nevertheless,

without looking sad,
                    without in any way
seeming to blame
                    (He doesn't need to,
knowing well
                    what a lover of art
like yourself pays heed to),
                                        God may reduce you
on Judgment Day
                    to tears of shame,
reciting by heart
                    the poems you would
have written, had
                    your life been good.

XII

THE COMMON LIFE

For Chester Kallman

A living room, the catholic area you
   (Thou, rather) and I may enter
without knocking, leave without a bow, confronts
   each visitor with a style,

a secular faith: he compares its dogmas
   with his, and decides whether
he would like to see more of us. (Spotless rooms
   where nothing's left lying about

chill me, so do cups used for ashtrays or smeared
   with lipstick: the homes I warm to,
though seldom wealthy, always convey a feeling
   of bills being promptly settled

with checks that don't bounce.) There's no *We* at an instant,
   only *Thou* and *I,* two regions
of protestant being which nowhere overlap:
   a room is too small, therefore,

if its occupants cannot forget at will
   that they are not alone, too big
if it gives them any excuse in a quarrel
   for raising their voices. What,

quizzing ours, would Sherlock Holmes infer? Plainly,
   ours is a sitting culture
in a generation which prefers comfort
   (or is forced to prefer it)

to command, would rather incline its buttocks
   on a well-upholstered chair
than the burly back of a slave: a quick glance
   at book titles would tell him

that we belong to the clerisy and spend much
   on our food. But could he read
what our prayers and jokes are about, what creatures
   frighten us most, or what names

head our roll call of persons we would least like
   to go to bed with? What draws
singular lives together in the first place,
   loneliness, lust, ambition,

or mere convenience, is obvious, why they drop
   or murder one another
clear enough: how they create, though, a common world
   between them, like Bombelli's

impossible yet useful numbers, no one
   has yet explained. Still, they do
manage to forgive impossible behavior,
   to endure by some miracle

conversational tics and larval habits
   without wincing (were you to die,
I should miss yours). It's a wonder that neither
   has been butchered by accident,

or, as lots have, silently vanished into
   History's criminal noise
unmourned for, but that, after twenty-four years,
   we should sit here in Austria

as cater-cousins, under the glassy look
   of a Naples Bambino,
the portrayed regards of Strauss and Stravinsky,
   doing British crossword puzzles,

is very odd indeed. I'm glad the builder gave
   our common-room small windows
through which no observed outsider can observe us:
   every home should be a fortress,

equipped with all the very latest engines
   for keeping Nature at bay,
versed in all ancient magic, the arts of quelling
   the Dark Lord and his hungry

animivorous chimeras. (Any brute
   can buy a machine in a shop,
but the sacred spells are secret to the kind,
   and if power is what we wish

they won't work.) *The ogre will come in any case:*
   so Joyce has warned us. Howbeit,
fasting or feasting, we both know this: without
   the Spirit we die, but life

without the letter is in the worst of taste,
   and always, though truth and love
can never really differ, when they seem to,
   the subaltern should be truth.

Ezra Pound

THE CONFUCIUS CANTO AND THE USURA CANTO, XIII and XLV

The state of his health has not permitted Ezra Pound to supply a commentary on his choice, "Canto XIII" and "Canto XLV," but it is clear from the selection he made two years ago for a *Selections from the Cantos* paperback that they are high among his favorite passages from the long poem, his masterwork, to which he has devoted so many years. The choice is appropriate because these two Cantos give us the essence of two of the major and recurrent themes in the *Cantos,* Confucianism— "Canto XIII" is the "Kung" (Confucius) Canto—and Economics-as-history—"Canto XLV" being the famous "Usura" Canto.

The paperback *Selections from the Cantos* was, at the time of this selection, in progress of production at New Directions through James Laughlin, long Mr. Pound's publisher and friend.

The Editor

CANTO XIII

Kung walked
            by the dynastic temple
        And into the cedar grove,
                and then out by the lower river,
And with him Khieu, Tchi
        and Tian the low speaking
And "we are unknown," said Kung,
"You will take up charioteering?
        Then you will become known,
"Or perhaps I should take up charioteering, or archery?
"Or the practice of public speaking?"
And Tseu-lou said, "I would put the defences in order,"
And Khieu said, "If I were lord of a province
I would put it in better order than this is."
And Tchi said, "I would prefer a small mountain temple,
"With order in the observances,
            with a suitable performance of the ritual,"
And Tian said, with his hand on the strings of his lute
The low sounds continuing
        after his hand left the strings,
And the sound went up like smoke, under the leaves,
And he looked after the sound:
        "The old swimming hole,
"And the boys flopping off the planks,

"Or sitting in the underbrush playing mandolins."
         And Kung smiled upon all of them equally.
And Thseng-sie desired to know:
         "Which had answered correctly?"
And Kung said, "They have all answered correctly,
"That is to say, each in his nature."
And Kung raised his cane against Yuan Jang,
         Yuan Jang being his elder.
For Yuan Jang sat by the roadside pretending to
         be receiving wisdom.
And Kung said
         "You old fool, come out of it,
Get up and do something useful."
         And Kung said
"Respect a child's faculties
From the moment it inhales the clear air,
But a man of fifty who knows nothing
         Is worthy of no respect."
And "When the prince has gathered about him
All the savants and artists, his riches will be fully employed."
And Kung said, and wrote on the bo leaves:
         If a man have not order within him
He cannot spread order about him;
And if a man have not order within him
His family will not act with due order;
         And if the prince have not order within him
He cannot put order in his dominions.
And Kung gave the words "order"
and "brotherly deference"
And said nothing of the "life after death."
And he said
         "Anyone can run to excesses,
It is easy to shoot past the mark,
It is hard to stand firm in the middle."
And they said: If a man commit murder
         Should his father protect him, and hide him?
And Kung said:
         He should hide him.
And Kung gave his daughter to Kong-Tch'ang
         Although Kong-Tch'ang was in prison.

And he gave his niece to Nan-Young
       although Nan-Young was out of office.
And Kung said "Wan ruled with moderation,
       In his day the State was well kept,
And even I can remember
A day when the historians left blanks in their writings,
I mean for things they didn't know,
But that time seems to be passing."
A day when the historians left blanks in their writings,
But that time seems to be passing."
And Kung said, "Without character you will
       be unable to play on that instrument
Or to execute the music fit for the Odes.
The blossoms of the apricot
       blow from the east to the west,
And I have tried to keep them from falling."

CANTO XLV

WITH *Usura*

With usura hath no man a house of good stone
each block cut smooth and well fitting
that design might cover their face,
with usura
hath no man a painted paradise on his church wall
harpes et luz
or where virgin receiveth message
and halo projects from incision,
with usura
seeth no man Gonzaga his heirs and his concubines
no picture is made to endure nor to live with
but it is made to sell and sell quickly
with usura, sin against nature,
is thy bread ever more of stale rags
is thy bread dry as paper,
with no mountain wheat, no strong flour
with usura the line grows thick

with usura is no clear demarcation
and no man can find site for his dwelling.
Stone-cutter is kept from his stone
weaver is kept from his loom
WITH USURA
wool comes not to market
sheep bringeth no gain with usura
Usura is a murrain, usura
blunteth the needle in the maid's hand
and stoppeth the spinner's cunning. Pietro Lombardo
came not by usura
Duccio came not by usura
nor Pier della Francesca; Zuan Bellin' not by usura
nor was La Calunnia painted.
Came not by usura Angelico; came not Ambrogio Praedis,
Came no church of cut stone signed: *Adamo me fecit.*
Not by usura St Trophime
Not by usura Saint Hilaire,
Usura rusteth the chisel
It rusteth the craft and the craftsman
It gnaweth the thread in the loom
None learneth to weave gold in her pattern;
Azure hath a canker by usura; cramoisi is unbroidered
Emerald findeth no Memling
Usura slayeth the child in the womb
It stayeth the young man's courting
It hath brought palsey to bed, lyeth
between the young bride and her bridegroom
                    CONTRA NATURAM
They have brought whores for Eleusis
Corpses are set to banquet
at behest of usura.

Richard Wilbur

WALKING TO SLEEP

It occurred to me, a few years back, to write a poem out of the idea that a man's approach to sleep is an index of his approach to life. The poem was long meditated, and took a good while to set down. I like the result because, though a long, wild and somewhat dense poem, "Walking to Sleep" does not mislay its simple drift and point. In other words, my taste is Baroque. Another thing I like about "Walking to Sleep" is my memory of its composition. There are times when a writer does not so much change his mind as give in to a mutiny of his subject-matter. I had intended this poem to confine itself to an increasingly contemptible recommendation of avoidance and anaesthesis; the poem, however, insisted on closing with a counter-movement, with the proposal of "another tack and footing." The poem was right.

Richard Wilbur

As a queen sits down, knowing that a chair will be there,
Or a general raises his hand and is given the field-glasses,
Step off assuredly into the blank of your mind.
Something will come to you. Although at first
You nod through nothing like a fogbound prow,
Gravel will breed in the margins of your gaze,
Perhaps with tussocks or a dusty flower,
And, humped like dolphins playing in the bow-wave,
Hills will suggest themselves. All such suggestions
Are yours to take or leave, but hear this warning:
Let them not be too velvet green, the fields
Which the deft needle of your eye appoints,
Nor the old farm past which you make your way
Too shady-linteled, too instinct with home.
It is precisely from Potemkin barns
With their fresh-painted hex signs on the gables,
Their sparkling gloom within, their stanchion-rattle
And sweet breath of silage, that there comes
The trotting cat whose head is but a skull.
Try to remember this: what you project
Is what you will perceive; what you perceive
With any passion, be it love or terror,
May take on whims and powers of its own.
Therefore a numb and grudging circumspection

Will serve you best, unless you overdo it,
Watching your step too narrowly, refusing
To specify a world, shrinking your purview
To a tight vision of your inching shoes
Which may, as soon you come to think, be crossing
An unseen gorge upon a rotten trestle.
What you must manage is to bring to mind
A landscape not worth looking at, some bleak
Champaign at dead November's end, its grass
As dry as lichen, and its lichens grey,
Such glumly simple country that a glance
Of flat indifference from time to time
Will stabilize it. Lifeless thus, and leafless,
The view should set at rest all thoughts of ambush.
Nevertheless, permit no roadside thickets
Which, as you pass, might shake with worse than wind;
Revoke all trees and other cover; blast
The upstart boulder which a flicking shape
Has stepped behind; above all, put a stop
To the known stranger up ahead, whose face
Half turns to mark you with a creased expression.
Here let me interject that steady trudging
Can make you drowsy, so that without transition,
As when an old film jumps in the projector,
You will be wading a dun hallway, rounding
A newel post, and starting up the stairs.
Should that occur, adjust to circumstances
And carry on, taking these few precautions:
Detach some portion of your thought to guard
The outside of the building; as you wind
From room to room, leave nothing at your back,
But slough all memories at every threshold;
Nor must you dream of opening any door
Until you have foreseen what lies beyond it.
Regardless of its seeming size, or what
May first impress you as its style or function,
The abrupt structure which involves you now
Will improvise like vapor. Groping down
The gritty cellar steps and past the fuse-box,
Brushing through sheeted lawn-chairs, you emerge

In some cathedral's pillared crypt, and thence,
Your brow alight with carbide, pick your way
To the main shaft through drifts and rubbly tunnels.
Promptly the hoist, ascending toward the pit-head,
Rolls downward past your gaze a dinted rock-face
Peppered with hacks and drill-holes, which acquire
Insensibly the look of hieroglyphics.
Whether to surface now within the vast
Stone tent where Cheops lay secure, or take
The proffered shed of corrugated iron
Which gives at once upon a vacant barracks,
Is up to you. Need I, at this point, tell you
What to avoid? Avoid the pleasant room
Where someone, smiling to herself, has placed
A bowl of yellow freesias. Do not let
The thought of her in yellow, lithe and sleek
As lemonwood, mislead you where the curtains,
Romping like spinnakers which taste the wind,
Bellying out and lifting till the sill
Has shipped a drench of sunlight, then subsiding,
Both warm and cool the love-bed. Your concern
Is not to be detained by dread, or by
Such dear acceptances as would entail it,
But to pursue an ever-dimming course
Of pure transition, treading as in water
Past crumbling tufa, down cloacal halls
Of boarded-up hotels, through attics full
Of glassy taxidermy, moping on
Like a drugged fire-inspector. What you hope for
Is that at some point of the pointless journey,
Indoors or out, and when you least expect it,
Right in the middle of your stride, like that,
So nearly that you never feel a thing,
The kind assassin Sleep will draw a bead
And blow your brains out.
                                    What, are you still awake?
Then you must risk another tack and footing.
Forget what I have said. Open your eyes
To the good blackness not of your room alone

But of the sky you trust is over it,
Whose stars, though foundering in the time to come,
Bequeath us constantly a jetsam beauty.
Now with your knuckles rub your eyelids, seeing
The phosphenes caper like St. Elmo's fire,
And let your head heel over on the pillow
Like a flung skiff on wild Gennesaret.
Let all things storm your thought with the moiled flocking
Of startled rookeries, or flak in air,
Or blossom-fall, and out of that come striding
In the strong dream by which you have been chosen.
Are you upon the roads again? If so,
Be led past honeyed meadows which might tempt
A wolf to graze, and groves which are not you
But answer to your suppler self, that nature
Able to bear the thrush's quirky glee
In stands of chuted light, yet praise as well,
All leaves aside, the barren bark of winter.
When, as you may, you find yourself approaching
A crossroads and its laden gallows tree,
Do not with hooded eyes allow the shadow
Of a man moored in air to bruise your forehead,
But lift your gaze and stare your brother down,
Though the swart crows have pecked his sockets hollow.
As for what turn your travels then will take,
I cannot guess. Long errantry perhaps
Will arm you to be gentle, or the claws
Of nightmare flap you pathless God knows where,
As the crow flies, to meet your dearest horror.
Still, if you are in luck, you may be granted,
As, inland, one can sometimes smell the sea,
A moment's perfect carelessness, in which
To stumble a few steps and sink to sleep
In the same clearing where, in the old story,
A holy man discovered Vishnu sleeping,
Wrapped in his maya, dreaming by a pool
On whose calm face all images whatever
Lay clear, unfathomed, taken as they came.

John Berryman

from DREAM SONGS

Dear Mr. Burnett:

. . . Maybe my best work so far is in "Homage to Mistress Bradstreet," but that's too long for you. Of "The Dream Songs," you might use 1, 29, 77, 89, 382, 384, 385, as representing not the least interesting moments of a poem of nearly 400 pp.*

Yours sincerely,
John Berryman

* The first three poems are from "77 Dream Songs," 1964, awarded the Pulitzer Prize for Poetry in 1965; the other four are from "His Toy, His Dream, His Rest," 1968, which won the National Book Award for Poetry in 1969. Together, these two books come to 399 pages. Speaking of "The Dream Songs" as a whole, Mr. Berryman wrote: "Whatever its wide cast of characters, the poem is essentially about an imaginary character (not the poet, not me) named Henry, a white American in early middle age sometimes in blackface, who has suffered an irreversible loss and talks about himself in the first person, sometimes in the third, sometimes even in the second; he has a friend, never named, who addresses him as Mr. Bones and variants thereof. Requiescant in pace." (The Editor.)

1

Huffy Henry hid the day,
unappeasable Henry sulked.
I see his point,—a trying to put things over.
It was the thought that they thought
they could *do* it made Henry wicked & away.
But he should have come out and talked.

All the world like a woolen lover
once did seem on Henry's side.
Then came a departure.
Thereafter nothing fell out as it might or ought.
I don't see how Henry, pried
open for all the world to see, survived.

What he has now to say is a long
wonder the world can bear & be.
Once in a sycamore I was glad
all at the top, and I sang.
Hard on the land wears the strong sea
and empty grows every bed.

29

There sat down, once, a thing on Henry's heart
só heavy, if he had a hundred years
& more, & weeping, sleepless, in all them time
Henry could not make good.
Starts again always in Henry's ears
the little cough somewhere, an odour, a chime.

And there is another thing he has in mind
like a grave Sienese face a thousand years
would fail to blur the still profiled reproach of. Ghastly,
with open eyes, he attends, blind.
All the bells say: too late. This is not for tears;
thinking.

But never did Henry, as he thought he did,
end anyone and hacks her body up
and hide the pieces, where they may be found.
He knows: he went over everyone, & nobody's missing.
Often he reckons, in the dawn, them up.
Nobody is ever missing.

77

Seedy Henry rose up shy in de world
& shaved & swung his barbells, duded Henry up
and p.a.'d poor thousands of persons on topics of grand
moment to Henry, ah to those less & none.
Wif a book of his in either hand
he is stript down to move on.

—Come away, Mr Bones.

—Henry is tired of the winter,
& haircuts, & a squeamish comfy ruin-prone proud national mind,
   & Spring (in the city so called).
Henry likes Fall.
Hé would be prepared to líve in a world of Fáll
for ever, impenitent Henry.
But the snows and summers grieve & dream;

thése fierce & airy occupations, and love,
raved away so many of Henry's years
it is a wonder that, with in each hand
one of his own mad books and all,
ancient fires for eyes, his head full
& his heart full, he's making ready to move on.

89

Op. posth. no. 12

In a blue series towards his sleepy eyes
they slid like wonder, women tall & small,
of every shape & size,
in many languages to lisp 'We do'
to Henry almost waking. What is the night at all,
his closed eyes beckon you.

In the Marriage of the Dead, a new routine,
he gasped his crowded vows past lids shut tight
and a-many rings fumbled on.
His coffin like Grand Central to the brim
filled up & emptied with the lapse of light.
Which one will waken him?

O she must startle like a fallen gown,
content with speech like an old sacrament
in deaf ears lying down,

blazing through darkness till he feels the cold
& blindness of his hopeless tenement
while his black arms unfold.

382

At Henry's bier let some thing fall out well:
enter there none who somewhat has to sell,
the music ancient & gradual,
the voices solemn but the grief subdued,
no hairy jokes but everybody's mood
subdued, subdued,

until the Dancer comes, in a short short dress
hair black & long & loose, dark dark glasses,
uptilted face,
pallor & strangeness, the music changes
to 'Give!' & 'Ow!' and how! the music changes,
she kicks a backward limb

on tiptoe, pirouettes, & she is free
to the knocking music, sails, dips, & suddenly
returns to the terrible gay
occasion hopeless & mad, she weaves, it's hell,
she flings to her head a leg, bobs, all is well,
she dances Henry away.

384

The marker slants, flowerless, day's almost done,
I stand above my father's grave with rage,
often, often before
I've made this awful pilgrimage to one
who cannot visit me, who tore his page
out: I come back for more.

I spit upon this dreadful banker's grave
who shot his heart out in a Florida dawn
O ho alas alas
When will indifference come. I moan & rave
I'd like to scrabble till I got right down
away down under the grass

and ax the casket open ha to see
just how he's taking it, which he sought so hard
we'll tear apart
the mouldering grave clothes ha & then Henry
will heft the ax once more, his final card,
and fell it on the start.

385

My daughter's heavier. Light leaves are flying.
Everywhere in enormous numbers turkeys will be dying
and other birds, all their wings.
They never greatly flew. Did they wish to?
I should know. Off away somewhere once I knew
such things.

Or good Ralph Hodgson back then did, or does.
The man is dead whom Eliot praised. My praise
follows and flows too late.
Fall is grievy, brisk. Tears behind the eyes
almost fall. Fall comes to us as a prize
to rouse us toward our fate.

My house is made of wood and it's made well,
unlike us. My house is older than Henry;
that's fairly old.
If there were a middle ground between things and the soul
or if the sky resembled more the sea,
I wouldn't have to scold   my heavy daughter.

Allen Ginsberg

WALES VISITATION

Dear Mr. Burnett:

I choose "Wales Visitation" for this volume of transient preferences inasmuch as it combines Personal Visionary Nature Pantheist Traditions with equally old shamanistic tradition of trance-drug altered consciousness prophecy.

As terminal note indicates I was looking thru LSD eyes at the English landscape seen before me by Blake and Wordsworth who had articulated coherent intimations of immortality in previous human centuries. In time their contemporarily cranky perceptions were recognized as old harmonious nature.

I had hoped since 1948 to be able to inscribe poetry during a consciously heightened state of mind. There had been some doubt that language was possible in this "moment" since Eliot seemed to proscribe speech during ecstasy, and most Wisdom texts agree.

Allen Ginsberg

White fog lifting & falling on mountain-brow
        Trees moving in rivers of wind
                                    The clouds arise
    as on a wave, gigantic eddy lifting mist
        above teeming ferns exquisitely swayed
                                        along a green crag
        glimpsed thru mullioned glass in valley raine—

Bardic, O Self, Visitacione, tell naught
    but what seen by one man in a vale in Albion,
            of the folk, whose physical sciences end in Ecology,
                        the wisdom of earthly relations,
            of mouths & eyes interknit ten centuries visible
                    orchards of mind language manifest human,
    of the satanic thistle that raises its horned symmetry
        flowering above sister grass-daisies' pink tiny
                        bloomlets angelic as lightbulbs—

Remember 160 miles from London's symmetrical, thorned tower
            & network of TV pictures flashing bearded your Self
    the lambs on the tree-nooked hillside this day bleating
    heard in Blake's old ear, & the silent thought of Wordsworth
                                    in eld Stillness
    clouds passing through skeleton arches of Tintern Abbey—
                    Bard Nameless as the Vast, babble to Vastness!

All the Valley quivered, one extended motion, wind
                    undulating on mossy hills
        a giant wash that sank white fog delicately down red runnels
                                on the mountainside
        whose leaf-branch tendrils moved asway
                                in granitic undertow down—
and lifted the floating Nebulous upward, and lifted the arms of the
                                                                    trees

            and lifted the grasses an instant in balance
            and lifted the lambs to hold still
        and lifted the green of the hill, in one solemn wave

A solid mass of Heaven, mist-infused, ebbs thru the vale,
        a wavelet of Immensity, lapping gigantic through Llanthony Valley,
        the length of all England, valley upon valley under Heaven's ocean
                                tonned with cloud-hang,
                    Heaven balanced on a grassblade—
Roar of the mountain wind slow, sigh of the body,
            One Being on the mountainside stirring gently
                    Exquisite scales trembling everywhere in balance,
one motion thru the cloudy sky-floor shifting on the million feet of daisies,
one Majesty the motion that stirred wet grass quivering
            to the farthest tendril of white fog poured down
                        through shivering flowers on the mountain's
                                                                    head—

No imperfection in the budded mountain,
            Valleys breathe, heaven and earth move together,
        daisies push inches of yellow air, vegetables tremble,
                    green atoms shimmer in grassy mandalas,
sheep speckle the mountainside, revolving their jaws with empty eyes,
                    horses dance in the warm rain,
        tree-lined canals network through live farmland,
                    blueberries fringe stone walls
            on hill breasts nippled with hawthorn,
        pheasants croak up meadow-bellies haired with fern—

Out, out on the hillside, into the ocean sound, into delicate
                                    gusts of wet air,
Fall on the ground, O great Wetness, O Mother, No harm on thy body!
Stare close, no imperfection in the grass,
                    each flower Buddha-eye, repeating the story,
                                the myriad-formed soul
Kneel before the foxglove raising green buds, mauve bells drooped
        doubled down the stem trembling antennae,
    & look in the eyes of the branded lambs that stare
        breathing stockstill under dripping hawthorn—
I lay down mixing my beard with the wet hair of the mountainside,
        smelling the brown vagina-moist ground, harmless,
                tasting the violet thistle-hair, sweetness—
One being so balanced, so vast, that its softest breath
            moves every floweret in the stillness on the valley floor,
        trembles lamb-hair hung gossamer rain-beaded in the grass,
lifts trees on their roots, birds in the great draught
            hiding their strength in the rain, bearing same weight,

Groan thru breast and neck, a great Oh! to earth heart
                            Calling our Presence together
            The great secret is no secret
                    Senses fit the winds,
                        Visible is visible,
        rain-mist curtains wave through the bearded vale,
            grey atoms wet the wind's Kaballah

Crosslegged on a rock in dusk rain,
            rubber booted in soft grass, mind moveless,
        breath trembles in white daisies by the roadside,
                    Heaven breath and my own symmetric
            Airs wavering thru antlered green fern
drawn in my navel, same breath as breathes thru Capel-Y-Ffn,
            Sounds of Aleph and Aum
                        through forests of gristle,
        my skull and Lord Hereford's Knob equal,
                            All Albion one.

What did I notice? Particulars! The
                    vision of the great One is myriad—
          smoke curls upward from ash tray,
                         house fire burned low,
The night, still wet & moody black heaven
                                  starless
          upward in motion with wet wind.

July 29, 1967 (LSD)—August 3, 1967 (London)

VI
Storytellers

Bernard Malamud

THE JEWBIRD

Dear Mr. Burnett:

"The Jewbird" was inspired by Howard Nemerov's "Digressions Around a Crow" in the Spring 1962 *Carleton Miscellany*. It was about a talking bird, and I said to myself, thinking of a jewfish, suppose the bird had been Jewish. At that point the story came to life.

Sincerely yours,
Bernard Malamud

The window was open so the skinny bird flew in. Flappity-flap with
its frazzled black wings. That's how it goes. It's open, you're in.
Closed, you're out and that's your fate. The bird wearily flapped through
the open kitchen window of Harry Cohen's top-floor apartment on First
Avenue near the lower East River. On a rod on the wall hung an escaped
canary cage, its door wide open, but this black-type longbeaked bird—
its ruffled head and small dull eyes, crossed a little, making it look like a
dissipated crow—landed if not smack on Cohen's thick lamb chop, at
least on the table, close by. The frozen foods salesman was sitting at
supper with his wife and young son on a hot August evening a year
ago. Cohen, a heavy man with hairy chest and beefy shorts; Edie, in
skinny yellow shorts and red halter; and their ten-year-old Morris (after
her father)—Maurie, they called him, a nice kid though not overly
bright—were all in the city after two weeks out, because Cohen's mother
was dying. They had been enjoying Kingston, New York, but drove back
when Mama got sick in her flat in the Bronx.

"Right on the table," said Cohen, putting down his beer glass and
swatting at the bird. "Son of a bitch."

"Harry, take care with your language," Edie said, looking at Maurie,
who watched every move.

The bird cawed hoarsely and with a flap of its bedraggled wings—
feathers tufted this way and that—rose heavily to the top of the open
kitchen door, where it perched staring down.

"Gevalt, a pogrom!"

"It's a talking bird," said Edie in astonishment.

"In Jewish," said Maurie.

"Wise guy," muttered Cohen. He gnawed on his chop, then put down the bone. "So if you can talk, say what's your business. What do you want here?"

"If you can't spare a lamb chop," said the bird, "I'll settle for a piece of herring with a crust of bread. You can't live on your nerve forever."

"This ain't a restaurant," Cohen replied. "All I'm asking is what brings you to this address?"

"The window was open," the bird sighed; adding after a moment, "I'm running. I'm flying but I'm also running."

"From whom?" asked Edie with interest.

"Anti-Semeets."

"Anti-Semites?" they all said.

"That's from who."

"What kind of anti-Semites bother a bird?" Edie asked.

"Any kind," said the bird, "also including eagles, vultures, and hawks. And once in a while some crows will take your eyes out."

"But aren't you a crow?"

"Me? I'm a Jewbird."

Cohen laughed heartily. "What do you mean by that?"

The bird began dovening. He prayed without Book or tallith, but with passion. Edie bowed her head though not Cohen. And Maurie rocked back and forth with the prayer, looking up with one wide-open eye.

When the prayer was done Cohen remarked, "No hat, no phylacteries?"

"I'm an old radical."

"You're sure you're not some kind of a ghost or dybbuk?"

"Not a dybbuk," answered the bird, "though one of my relatives had such an experience once. It's all over now, thanks God. They freed her from a former lover, a crazy jealous man. She's now the mother of two wonderful children."

"Birds?" Cohen asked slyly.

"Why not?"

"What kind of birds?"

"Like me. Jewbirds."

Cohen tipped back in his chair and guffawed. "That's a big laugh. I've heard of a Jewfish but not a Jewbird."

"We're once removed." The bird rested on one skinny leg, then on the other. "Please, could you spare maybe a piece of herring with a small crust of bread?"

Edie got up from the table.

"What are you doing?" Cohen asked her.

"I'll clear the dishes."

Cohen turned to the bird. "So what's your name, if you don't mind saying?"

"Call me Schwartz."

"He might be an old Jew changed into a bird by somebody," said Edie, removing a plate.

"Are you?" asked Harry, lighting a cigar.

"Who knows?" answered Schwartz. "Does God tell us everything?"

Maurie got up on his chair. "What kind of herring?" he asked the bird in excitement.

"Get down, Maurie, or you'll fall," ordered Cohen.

"If you haven't got matjes, I'll take schmaltz," said Schwartz.

"All we have is marinated, with slices of onion—in a jar," said Edie.

"If you'll open for me the jar I'll eat marinated. Do you have also, if you don't mind, a piece of rye bread—the spitz?"

Edie thought she had.

"Feed him out on the balcony," Cohen said. He spoke to the bird. "After that take off."

Schwartz closed both bird eyes. "I'm tired and it's a long way."

"Which direction are you headed, north or south?"

Schwartz, barely lifting his wings, shrugged.

"You don't know where you're going?"

"Where there's charity I'll go."

"Let him stay, papa," said Maurie. "He's only a bird."

"So stay the night," Cohen said, "but no longer."

In the morning Cohen ordered the bird out of the house but Maurie cried, so Schwartz stayed for a while. Maurie was still on vacation from school and his friends were away. He was lonely and Edie enjoyed the fun he had, playing with the bird.

"He's no trouble at all," she told Cohen, "and besides his appetite is very small."

"What'll you do when he makes dirty?"

"He flies across the street in a tree when he makes dirty, and if nobody passes below, who notices?"

"So all right," said Cohen, "but I'm dead set against it. I warn you he ain't gonna stay here long."

"What have you got against the poor bird?"

"Poor bird, my ass. He's a foxy bastard. He thinks he's a Jew."

"What difference does it make what he thinks?"

"A Jewbird, what a chuzpah. One false move and he's out on his drumsticks."

At Cohen's insistence Schwartz lived out on the balcony in a new wooden birdhouse Edie had bought him.

"With many thanks," said Schwartz, "though I would rather have a human roof over my head. You know how it is at my age. I like the warm, the windows, the smell of cooking. I would also be glad to see once in a while the *Jewish Morning Journal* and have now and then a schnapps because it helps my breathing, thanks God. But whatever you give me, you won't hear complaints."

However, when Cohen brought home a bird feeder full of dried corn, Schwartz said, "Impossible."

Cohen was annoyed. "What's the matter, crosseyes, is your life getting too good for you? Are you forgetting what it means to be migratory? I'll bet a helluva lot of crows you happen to be acquainted with, Jews or otherwise, would give their eyeteeth to eat this corn."

Schwartz did not answer. What can you say to a grubber yung?

"Not for my digestion," he later explained to Edie. "Cramps. Herring is better even if it makes you thirsty. At least rainwater don't cost anything." He laughed sadly in breathy caws.

And herring, thanks to Edie, who knew where to shop, was what Schwartz got, with an occasional piece of potato pancake, and even a bit of soupmeat when Cohen wasn't looking.

When school began in September, before Cohen would once again suggest giving the bird the boot, Edie prevailed on him to wait a little while until Maurie adjusted.

"To deprive him right now might hurt his school work, and you know what trouble we had last year."

"So okay, but sooner or later the bird goes. That I promise you."

Schwartz, though nobody had asked him, took on full responsibility for Maurie's performance in school. In return for favors granted, when he was let in for an hour or two at night, he spent most of his time overseeing the boy's lessons. He sat on top of the dresser near Maurie's desk as he laboriously wrote out his homework. Maurie was a restless type and Schwartz gently kept him to his studies. He also listened to him practice his screechy violin, taking a few minutes off now and then to rest his ears in the bathroom. And they afterwards played dominoes. The boy was an indifferent checker player and it was impossible to teach him chess. When he was sick, Schwartz read him comic books though he personally disliked them. But Maurie's work improved in school and even his violin teacher admitted his playing was better. Edie gave Schwartz credit for these improvements though the bird pooh-poohed them.

Yet he was proud there was nothing lower than C minuses on Maurie's report card, and on Edie's insistence celebrated with a little schnapps.

"If he keeps up like this," Cohen said, "I'll get him in an Ivy League college for sure."

"Oh I hope so," sighed Edie.

But Schwartz shook his head. "He's a good boy—you don't have to worry. He won't be a shicker or a wifebeater, God forbid, but a scholar he'll never be, if you know what I mean, although maybe a good mechanic. It's no disgrace in these times."

"If I were you," Cohen said, angered, "I'd keep my big snoot out of other people's private business."

"Harry, please," said Edie.

"My goddamn patience is wearing out. That crosseyes butts into everything."

Though he wasn't exactly a welcome guest in the house, Schwartz gained a few ounces although he did not improve in appearance. He looked bedraggled as ever, his feathers unkempt, as though he had just flown out of a snowstorm. He spent, he admitted, little time taking care of himself. Too much to think about. "Also outside plumbing," he told Edie. Still there was more glow to his eyes so that though Cohen went on calling him crosseyes he said it less emphatically.

Liking his situation, Schwartz tried tactfully to stay out of Cohen's way, but one night when Edie was at the movies and Maurie was taking a hot shower, the frozen foods salesman began a quarrel with the bird.

"For Christ sake, why don't you wash yourself sometimes? Why must you always stink like a dead fish?"

"Mr. Cohen, if you'll pardon me, if somebody eats garlic he will smell from garlic. I eat herring three times a day. Feed me flowers and I will smell like flowers."

"Who's obligated to feed you anything at all? You're lucky to get herring."

"Excuse me, I'm not complaining," said the bird. "You're complaining."

"What's more," said Cohen, "even from out on the balcony I can hear you snoring away like a pig. It keeps me awake at night."

"Snoring," said Schwartz, "isn't a crime, thanks God."

"All in all you are a goddamn pest and free loader. Next thing you'll want to sleep in bed next to my wife."

"Mr. Cohen," said Schwartz, "on this rest assured. A bird is a bird."

"So you say, but how do I know you're a bird and not some kind of a goddamn devil?"

"If I was a devil you would know already. And I don't mean because your son's good marks."

"Shut up, you bastard bird," shouted Cohen.

"Grubber yung," cawed Schwartz, rising to the tips of his talons, his long wings outstretched.

Cohen was about to lunge for the bird's scrawny neck but Maurie came out of the bathroom, and for the rest of the evening until Schwartz's bedtime on the balcony, there was pretended peace.

But the quarrel had deeply disturbed Schwartz and he slept badly. His snoring woke him, and awake, he was fearful of what would become of him. Wanting to stay out of Cohen's way, he kept to the birdhouse as much as possible. Cramped by it, he paced back and forth on the balcony ledge, or sat on the birdhouse roof, staring into space. In the evenings, while overseeing Maurie's lessons, he often fell asleep. Awakening, he nervously hopped around exploring the four corners of the room. He spent much time in Maurie's closet, and carefully examined his bureau drawers when they were left open. And once when he found a large paper bag on the floor, Schwartz poked his way into it to investigate what the possibilities were. The boy was amused to see the bird in the paper bag.

"He wants to build a nest," he said to his mother.

Edie, sensing Schwartz's unhappiness, spoke to him quietly.

"Maybe if you did some of the things my husband wants you, you would get along better with him."

"Give me a for instance," Schwartz said.

"Like take a bath, for instance."

"I'm too old for baths," said the bird. "My feathers fall out without baths."

"He says you have a bad smell."

"Everybody smells. Some people smell because of their thoughts or because who they are. My bad smell comes from the food I eat. What does his come from?"

"I better not ask him or it might make him mad," said Edie.

In late November Schwartz froze on the balcony in the fog and cold, and especially on rainy days he woke with stiff joints and could barely move his wings. Already he felt twinges of rheumatism. He would have liked to spend more time in the warm house, particularly when Maurie was in school and Cohen at work. But though Edie was good-hearted and might have sneaked him in in the morning, just to thaw out, he was afraid to ask her. In the meantime Cohen, who had been reading articles about the migration of birds, came out on the balcony one night after work when Edie was in the kitchen preparing pot roast, and peeking into the birdhouse, warned Schwartz to be on his way soon if he knew what was good for him. "Time to hit the flyways."

"Mr. Cohen, why do you hate me so much?" asked the bird. "What did I do to you?"

"Because you're an A-number-one trouble maker, that's why. What's more, whoever heard of a Jewbird? Now scat or it's open war."

But Schwartz stubbornly refused to depart so Cohen embarked on a campaign of harassing him, meanwhile hiding it from Edie and Maurie. Maurie hated violence and Cohen didn't want to leave a bad impression. He thought maybe if he played dirty tricks on the bird he would fly off without being physically kicked out. The vacation was over, let him make his easy living off the fat of somebody else's land. Cohen worried about the effect of the bird's departure on Maurie's schooling but decided to take the chance, first, because the boy now seemed to have the knack of studying—give the black bird-bastard credit—and second, because Schwartz was driving him bats by being there always, even in his dreams.

The frozen foods salesman began his campaign against the bird by mixing watery cat food with the herring slices in Schwartz's dish. He also blew up and popped numerous paper bags outside the birdhouse as the bird slept, and when he had got Schwartz good and nervous, though not enough to leave, he brought a full-grown cat into the house, supposedly a gift for little Maurie, who had always wanted a pussy. The cat never stopped springing up at Schwartz whenever he saw him, one day managing to claw out several of his tailfeathers. And even at lesson time, when the cat was usually excluded from Maurie's room, though somehow or other he quickly found his way in at the end of the lesson, Schwartz was desperately fearful of his life and flew from pinnacle to pinnacle—light fixture to clothes-tree to door-top—in order to elude the beast's wet jaws.

Once when the bird complained to Edie how hazardous his existence was, she said, "Be patient, Mr. Schwartz. When the cat gets to know you better he won't try to catch you any more."

"When he stops trying we will both be in Paradise," Schwartz answered. "Do me a favor and get rid of him. He makes my whole life worry. I'm losing feathers like a tree loses leaves."

"I'm awfully sorry but Maurie likes the pussy and sleeps with it."

What could Schwartz do? He worried but came to no decision, being afraid to leave. So he ate the herring garnished with cat food, tried hard not to hear the paper bags bursting like fire crackers outside the birdhouse at night, and lived terror-stricken closer to the ceiling than to the floor, as the cat, his tail flicking, endlessly watched him.

Weeks went by. Then on the day after Cohen's mother had died in her flat in the Bronx, when Maurie came home with a zero on an arithmetic test, Cohen, enraged, waited until Edie had taken the boy to his violin lesson, then openly attacked the bird. He chased him with a broom on the balcony and Schwartz frantically flew back and forth, finally escaping into his birdhouse. Cohen triumphantly reached in, and grabbing both skinny legs, dragged the bird out, cawing loudly, his wings wildly beating. He whirled the bird around and around his head. But Schwartz, as he moved in circles, managed to swoop down and catch Cohen's nose in his beak, and hung on for dear life. Cohen cried out in great pain, punched the bird with his fist, and tugging at its legs with all his might, pulled his nose free. Again he swung the yawking Schwartz around until the bird grew dizzy, then with a furious heave, flung him into the night. Schwartz sank like stone into the street. Cohen then tossed the birdhouse and feeder after him, listening at the ledge until they crashed on the sidewalk below. For a full hour, broom in hand, his heart palpitating and nose throbbing with pain, Cohen waited for Schwartz to return but the broken-hearted bird didn't.

That's the end of that dirty bastard, the salesman thought and went in. Edie and Maurie had come home.

"Look," said Cohen, pointing to his bloody nose swollen three times its normal size, "what that sonofabitchy bird did. It's a permanent scar."

"Where is he now?" Edie asked, frightened.

"I threw him out and he flew away. Good riddance."

Nobody said no, though Edie touched a handkerchief to her eyes and Maurie rapidly tried the nine times table and found he knew approximately half.

In the spring when the winter's snow had melted, the boy, moved by a memory, wandered in the neighborhood, looking for Schwartz. He found a dead black bird in a small lot near the river, his two wings broken, neck twisted, and both bird-eyes plucked clean.

"Who did it to you, Mr. Schwartz?" Maurie wept.

"Anti-Semeets," Edie said later.

Truman Capote

CHILDREN ON THEIR BIRTHDAYS

> Does any writer really know what his "best work" is? As a
> matter of fact, I'm quite certain I haven't *written* any yet. Mean-
> while, I nominate *Children on Their Birthdays,* an autobiographi-
> cal story that has for me the deepest personal significance.
>
> Truman Capote

This Story is for Andrew Lyndon

Yesterday afternoon the six-o'clock bus ran over Miss Bobbit. I'm not sure what there is to be said about it; after all, she was only ten years old, still I know no one of us in this town will forget her. For one thing, nothing she ever did was ordinary, not from the first time that we saw her, and that was a year ago. Miss Bobbit and her mother, they arrived on that same six-o'clock bus, the one that comes through from Mobile. It happened to be my cousin Billy Bob's birthday, and so most of the children in town were here at our house. We were sprawled on the front porch having tutti-frutti and devil cake when the bus stormed around Deadman's curve. It was the summer that never rained; rusted dryness coated everything; sometimes when a car passed on the road, raised dust would hang in the still air an hour or more. Aunt El said if they didn't pave the highway soon she was going to move down to the seacoast; but she'd said that for such a long time. Anyway, we were sitting on the porch, tutti-frutti melting on our plates, when suddenly, just as we were wishing that something would happen, something did; for out of the red road dust appeared Miss Bobbit. A wiry little girl in a starched, lemon-colored party dress, she sassed along with a grown-up mince, one hand on her hip, the other supporting a spinsterish umbrella. Her mother, lugging two cardboard valises and a wind-up victrola, trailed in the background. She was a gaunt shaggy woman with silent eyes and a hungry smile.

All the children on the porch had grown so still that when a cone of wasps started humming the girls did not set up their usual holler. Their attention was too fixed upon the approach of Miss Bobbit and her mother, who had by now reached the gate. "Begging your pardon," called Miss Bobbit in a voice that was at once silky and childlike, like a pretty piece of ribbon, and immaculately exact, like a movie-star or a school-marm, "but might we speak with the grown-up persons of the house?" This, of course, meant Aunt El; and, at least to some degree, myself. But Billy Bob and all the other boys, no one of whom was over thirteen, followed down to the gate after us. From their faces you would have thought they'd never seen a girl before. Certainly not like Miss Bobbit. As Aunt El said, whoever heard tell of a child wearing makeup? Tangee gave her lips an orange glow, her hair, rather like a costume wig, was a mass of rosy curls, and her eyes had a knowing, penciled tilt; even so, she had a skinny dignity, she was a lady, and, what is more, she looked you in the eye with manlike directness. "I'm Miss Lily Jane Bobbit, Miss Bobbit from Memphis, Tennessee," she said solemnly. The boys looked down at their toes, and, on the porch, Cora McCall, who Billy Bob was courting at the time, led the girls into a fanfare of giggles. "*Country* children," said Miss Bobbit with an understanding smile, and gave her parasol a saucy whirl. "My mother," and this homely woman allowed an abrupt nod to acknowledge herself, "my mother and I have taken rooms here. Would you be so kind as to point out the house? It belongs to a Mrs. Sawyer." Why, sure, said Aunt El, that's Mrs. Sawyer's, right there across the street. The only boarding house around here, it is an old tall dark place with about two dozen lightning rods scattered on the roof: Mrs. Sawyer is scared to death in a thunderstorm.

Coloring like an apple, Billy Bob said, please ma'am, it being such a hot day and all, wouldn't they rest a spell and have some tutti-frutti? and Aunt El said yes, by all means, but Miss Bobbit shook her head. "Very fattening, tutti-frutti; but *merci* you kindly," and they started across the road, the mother half-dragging her parcels in the dust. Then, and with an earnest expression, Miss Bobbit turned back; the sunflower yellow of her eyes darkened, and she rolled them slightly sideways, as if trying to remember a poem. "My mother has a disorder of the tongue, so it is necessary that I speak for her," she announced rapidly and heaved a sigh. "My mother is a very fine seamstress; she has made dresses for the society of many cities and towns, including Memphis and Tallahassee. No doubt you have noticed and admired the dress I am wearing. Every stitch of it was handsewn by my mother. My mother can copy any pattern, and just recently she won a twenty-five dollar prize from the *Ladies' Home Journal*. My mother can also crochet, knit and embroider.

If you want any kind of sewing done, please come to my mother. Please advise your friends and family. Thank you." And then, with a rustle and a swish, she was gone.

Cora McCall and the girls pulled their hair-ribbons nervously, suspiciously, and looked very put out and prune-faced. I'm *Miss* Bobbit, said Cora, twisting her face into an evil imitation, and I'm Princess Elizabeth, that's who I am, ha, ha, ha. Furthermore, said Cora, that dress was just as tacky as could be; personally, Cora said, all my clothes come from Atlanta; plus a pair of shoes from New York, which is not even to mention my silver turquoise ring all the way from Mexico City, Mexico. Aunt El said they ought not to behave that way about a fellow child, a stranger in the town, but the girls went on like a huddle of witches, and certain boys, the sillier ones that liked to be with the girls, joined in and said things that made Aunt El go red and declare she was going to send them all home and tell their daddies, to boot. But before she could carry forward this threat Miss Bobbit herself intervened by traipsing across the Sawyer porch, costumed in a new and startling manner.

The older boys, like Billy Bob and Preacher Star, who had sat quiet while the girls razzed Miss Bobbit, and who had watched the house into which she disappeared with misty, ambitious faces, they now straightened up and ambled down to the gate. Cora McCall sniffed and poked out her lower lip, but the rest of us went and sat on the steps. Miss Bobbit paid us no mind whatever. The Sawyer yard is dark with mulberry trees and it is planted with grass and sweet shrub. Sometimes after a rain you can smell the sweet shrub all the way into our house; and in the center of this yard there is a sundial which Mrs. Sawyer installed in 1912 as a memorial to her Boston bull, Sunny, who died after having lapped up a bucket of paint. Miss Bobbit pranced into the yard toting the victrola, which she put on the sundial; she wound it up, and started a record playing, and it played the Court of Luxemborg. By now it was almost nightfall, a firefly hour, blue as milkglass; and birds like arrows swooped together and swept into the folds of trees. Before storms, leaves and flowers appear to burn with a private light, color, and Miss Bobbit, got up in a little white skirt like a powderpuff and with strips of gold-glittering tinsel ribboning her hair, seemed, set against the darkening all around, to contain this illuminated quality. She held her arms arched over her head, her hands lily-limp, and stood straight up on the tips of her toes. She stood that way for a good long while, and Aunt El said it was right smart of her. Then she began to waltz around and around, and around and around she went until Aunt El said, why, she was plain dizzy from the sight. She stopped only when it was time to rewind the victrola; and when the moon came rolling down the ridge, and the last supper bell had sounded, and all the children had gone home, and the night iris was beginning to bloom, Miss Bobbit was still there in the dark turning like a top.

We did not see her again for some time. Preacher Star came every morning to our house and stayed straight through to supper. Preacher is a rail-thin boy with a bushy shock of red hair; he has eleven brothers and sisters, and even they are afraid of him, for he has a terrible temper, and is famous in these parts for his green-eyed meanness: last Fourth of July he whipped Ollie Overton so bad that Ollie's family had to send him to the hospital in Pensacola; and there was another time he bit off half a mule's ear, chewed it and spit it on the ground. Before Billy Bob got his growth, Preacher played the devil with him, too. He used to drop cockleburrs down his collar, and rub pepper in his eyes, and tear up his homework. But now they are the biggest friends in town: talk alike, walk alike; and occasionally they disappear together for whole days, Lord knows where to. But during these days when Miss Bobbit did not appear they stayed close to the house. They would stand around in the yard trying to slingshot sparrows off telephone poles; or sometimes Billy Bob would play his ukulele, and they would sing so loud Uncle Billy Bob, who is Judge for this county, claimed he could hear them all the way to the courthouse: *send me a letter, send it by mail, send it in care of the Birming-ham jail.* Miss Bobbit did not hear them; at least she never poked her head out the door. Then one day Mrs. Sawyer, coming over to borrow a cup of sugar, rattled on a good deal about her new boarders. You know, she said, squinting her chicken-bright eyes, the husband was a crook, uh huh, the child told me herself. Hasn't an ounce of shame, not a mite. Said her daddy was the dearest and the sweetest daddy and the sweetest singing man in the whole of Tennessee. . . . And I said, honey, where is he? and just as off-hand as you please she says, Oh, he's in the penitentiary and we don't hear from him no more. Say, now, does that make your blood run cold? Uh huh, and I been thinking, her mama, I been thinking she's some kinda foreigner: never says a word, and sometimes it looks like she don't understand what nobody says to her. And you know, they eat everything *raw*. *Raw* eggs, *raw* turnips, carrots—no meat whatsoever. For reasons of health, the child says, but ho! she's been straight out on the bed running a fever since last Tuesday.

That same afternoon Aunt El went out to water her roses, only to discover them gone. These were special roses, ones she'd planned to send to the flower show in Mobile, and so naturally she got a little hysterical. She rang up the Sheriff, and said, Listen here, Sheriff, you come over here right fast. I mean somebody's got off with all my Lady Anne's that I've devoted myself to heart and soul since early spring. When the Sheriff's car pulled up outside our house, all the neighbors along the street came out on their porches, and Mrs. Sawyer, layers of cold cream whitening her face, trotted across the road. Oh shoot, she said, very disappointed to find no one had been murdered, oh shoot, she said, nobody's stole them roses. Your Billy Bob brought them roses over and left them for little Bobbit. Aunt El did not say one word. She just marched over to the peach tree, and cut herself a switch. Ohhh, Billy Bob, she stalked along the street calling his name, and then she found him down at Speedy's garage where he and Preacher were watching Speedy take a motor apart. She simply lifted him by the hair and, switching blueblazes, towed him home. But she couldn't make him say he was sorry and she couldn't make him cry. And when she was finished with him he ran into the backyard and climbed high into the tower of a pecan tree and swore he wasn't ever going to come down. Then his daddy stood at the window and called to him: Son, we aren't mad with you, so come down and eat your supper. But Billy Bob wouldn't budge. Aunt El went and leaned against the tree. She spoke in a voice soft as the gathering light. I'm sorry, son, she said, I didn't mean whipping you so hard like that. I've fixed a nice supper, son, potato salad and boiled ham and deviled eggs. Go away, said Billy Bob, I don't want no supper, and I hate you like all-fire. His daddy said he ought not to talk like that to his mother, and she began to cry. She stood there under the tree and cried, raising the hem of her skirt to dab at her eyes. I don't hate you, son. . . . If I didn't love you I wouldn't whip you. The pecan leaves began to rattle; Billy Bob slid slowly to the ground, and Aunt El, rushing her fingers through his hair, pulled him against her. Aw, Ma, he said, Aw, Ma.

After supper Billy Bob came and flung himself on the foot of my bed. He smelled all sour and sweet, the way boys do, and I felt very sorry for him, especially because he looked so worried. His eyes were almost shut with worry. You're s'posed to send sick folks flowers, he said righteously. About this time we heard the victrola, a lilting faraway sound, and a night moth flew through the window, drifting in the air delicate as the music. But it was dark now, and we couldn't tell if

Miss Bobbit was dancing. Billy Bob, as though he were in pain, doubled up on the bed like a jackknife; but his face was suddenly clear, his grubby boy-eyes twitching like candles. She's so cute, he whispered, she's the cutest dickens I ever saw, gee, to hell with it, I don't care, I'd pick all the roses in China.

Preacher would have picked all the roses in China, too. He was as crazy about her as Billy Bob. But Miss Bobbit did not notice them. The sole communication we had with her was a note to Aunt El thanking her for the flowers. Day after day she sat on her porch, always dressed to beat the band, and doing a piece of embroidery, or combing curls in her hair, or reading a Webster's dictionary—formal, but friendly enough; if you said good-day to her she said good-day to you. Even so, the boys never could seem to get up the nerve to go over and talk with her, and most of the time she simply looked through them, even when they tomcatted up and down the street trying to get her eye. They wrestled, played Tarzan, did foolheaded bicycle tricks. It was a sorry business. A great many girls in town strolled by the Sawyer house two and three times within an hour just on the chance of getting a look. Some of the girls who did this were: Cora McCall, Mary Murphy Jones, Janice Ackerman. Miss Bobbit did not show any interest in them either. Cora would not speak to Billy Bob any more. The same was true with Janice and Preacher. As a matter of fact, Janice wrote Preacher a letter in red ink on lace-trimmed paper in which she told him he was vile beyond all human beings and words, that she considered their engagement broken, that he could have back the stuffed squirrel he'd given her. Preacher, saying he wanted to act nice, stopped her the next time she passed our house, and said, well, hell, she could keep that old squirrel if she wanted to. Afterwards, he couldn't understand why Janice ran away bawling the way she did.

Then one day the boys were being crazier than usual; Billy Bob was sagging around in his daddy's World War khakis, and Preacher, stripped to the waist, had a naked woman drawn on his chest with one of Aunt El's old lipsticks. They looked like perfect fools, but Miss Bobbit reclining in a swing, merely yawned. It was noon, and there was no one passing in the street, except a colored girl, baby-fat and sugar-plum shaped, who hummed along carrying a pail of blackberries. But the boys, teasing at her like gnats, joined hands and wouldn't let her go by, not until she paid a tariff. I ain't studyin' no tariff, she said, what kinda tariff you talkin' about, mister? A party in the barn, said Preacher, between clenched teeth, mighty nice party in the barn. And she, with a sulky shrug, said, huh, she intended studyin' no barn parties. Whereupon Billy Bob capsized her berry pail, and when she, with despairing, piglike shrieks, bent down in futile gestures of rescue, Preacher, who can be mean as the devil, give her behind a kick which sent her sprawling jellylike among the blackberries and the dust. Miss Bobbit came tearing across the road, her finger wagging like a metronome; like a schoolteacher she clapped her hands, stamped her foot, said: "It is a well-known fact that gentlemen are put on the face of this earth for the protection of ladies. Do you suppose boys behave this way in towns like Memphis, New York, London, Hollywood or Paris?" The boys hung back, and shoved their hands in their pockets. Miss Bobbit helped the colored girl to her feet; she dusted her off, dried her eyes, held out a handkerchief and told her to blow. "A pretty pass," she said, "a fine situation when a lady can't walk safely in the public daylight."

Then the two of them went back and sat on Mrs. Sawyer's porch; and for the next year they were never far apart, Miss Bobbit and this baby elephant, whose name was Rosalba Cat. At first, Mrs. Sawyer raised a fuss about Rosalba being so much at her house. She told Aunt El that it went against the grain to have a nigger lolling smack there in plain sight on her front porch. But Miss Bobbit had a certain magic, whatever she did she did it with completeness, and so directly, so solemnly that there was nothing to do but accept it. For instance, the tradespeople in town used to snicker when they called her *Miss* Bobbit; but by and by she was Miss Bobbit, and they gave her stiff little bows as she whirled by spinning her parasol. Miss Bobbit told everyone that Rosalba was her sister, which caused a good many jokes; but like most of her ideas, it gradually seemed natural, and when we would overhear them calling each other Sister Rosalba and Sister Bobbit none of us cracked a smile. But Sister Rosalba and Sister Bobbit did some queer things. There was the business about the dogs. Now there are a great many dogs in this town, rat terriers, bird dogs, bloodhounds; they trail along the forlorn noon-hot streets in sleepy herds of six to a dozen, all waiting only for dark and the moon, when straight through the lonesome hours you can hear them howling: someone is dying, someone is dead. Miss Bobbit complained to the Sheriff; she said that certain of the dogs always planted themselves under her window, and that she was a light sleeper to begin with; what is more, and as Sister Rosalba said, she did not believe they were dogs at all, but some kind of devil. Naturally the Sheriff did nothing; and so she took the matter into her own hands. One morning, after an especially loud night, she was seen stalking through the town with Rosalba at her side, Rosalba carrying a flower basket filled with rocks; whenever they saw a dog they paused while Miss Bobbit scrutinized him. Sometimes she would shake her head, but more often she said, "Yes, that's one of them. Sister Rosalba," and Sister Rosalba, with ferocious aim, would take a rock from her basket and crack the dog between the eyes.

Another thing that happened concerns Mr. Henderson. Mr. Henderson has a back room in the Sawyer house; a tough runt of a man who formerly was a wildcat oil prospector in Oklahoma, he is about seventy years old and, like a lot of old men, obsessed by functions of the body. Also, he is a terrible drunk. One time he had been drunk for two weeks; whenever he heard Miss Bobbit and Sister Rosalba moving around the house, he would charge to the top of the stairs and bellow down to Mrs. Sawyer that there were midgets in the walls trying to get at his supply of toilet paper. They've already stolen fifteen cents' worth, he said. One evening, when the two girls were sitting under a tree in the yard, Mr. Henderson, sporting nothing more than a nightshirt, stamped out after them. Steal all my toilet paper, will you? he hollered, I'll show you midgets. . . . Somebody come help me, else these midget bitches are liable to make off with every sheet in town. It was Billy Bob and Preacher who caught Mr. Henderson and held him until some grown men arrived and began to tie him up. Miss Bobbit, who had behaved with admirable calm, told the men they did not know how to tie a proper knot, and undertook to do so herself. She did such a good job that all the circulation stopped in Mr. Henderson's hands and feet and it was a month before he could walk again.

It was shortly afterwards that Miss Bobbit paid us a call. She came on Sunday and I was there alone, the family having gone to church. "The odors of a church are so offensive," she said, leaning forward and with her hands folded primly before her. "I don't want you to think I'm a heathen, Mr. C.; I've had enough experience to know that there is a God and that there is a Devil. But the way to tame the Devil is not to go down there to church and listen to what a sinful mean fool he is. No, love the Devil like you love Jesus: because he is a powerful man, and will do you a good turn if he knows you trust him. He has frequently done me good turns, like at dancing school in Memphis. . . . I always called in the Devil to help me get the biggest part in our annual show. That is common sense; you see, I knew Jesus wouldn't have any truck with dancing. Now, as a matter of fact, I have called in the Devil just recently. He is the only one who can help me get out of this town. Not that I live here, not exactly. I think always about somewhere else, somewhere else where everything is dancing, like people dancing in the streets, and everything is pretty, like children on their birthdays. My precious papa said I live in the sky, but if he'd lived more in the sky he'd be rich like he wanted to be. The trouble with my papa was he did not love the Devil, he let the Devil love him. But I am very smart in that respect; I know the next best thing is very often the best. It was the next best thing for us to move to this town; and since I can't pursue my career here, the next best thing for me is to start a little business on the side. Which is what I have done. I am sole subscription agent in this county for an impressive list of magazines, including *Reader's Digest, Popular Mechanics, Dime Detective* and *Child's Life*. To be sure, Mr. C., I'm not here to sell you anything. But I have a thought in mind. I was thinking those two boys that are always hanging around here, it occurred to me that they are men, after all. Do you suppose they would make a pair of likely assistants?"

Billy Bob and Preacher worked hard for Miss Bobbit and for Sister Rosalba, too. Sister Rosalba carried a line of cosmetics called Dewdrop, and it was part of the boys' job to deliver purchases to her customers. Billy Bob used to be so tired in the evening he could hardly chew his supper. Aunt El said it was a shame and a pity, and finally one day when Billy Bob came down with a touch of sunstroke she said, all right, that settled it, Billy Bob would just have to quit Miss Bobbit. But Billy Bob cussed her out until his daddy had to lock him in his room; whereupon he said he was going to kill himself. Some cook we'd had told him once that if you ate a mess of collards all slopped over with molasses it would kill you sure as shooting; and so that is what he did. I'm dying, he said, rolling back and forth on his bed, I'm dying and nobody cares.

Miss Bobbit came over and told him to hush up. "There's nothing wrong with you, boy," she said. "All you've got is a stomach ache." Then she did something that shocked Aunt El very much: she stripped the covers off Billy Bob and rubbed him down with alcohol from head to toe. When Aunt El told her she did not think that was a nice thing for a little girl to do, Miss Bobbit replied: "I don't know whether it's nice or not, but it's certainly very refreshing." After which Aunt El did all she could to keep Billy Bob from going back to work for her, but his daddy said to leave him alone, they would have to let the boy lead his own life.

Miss Bobbit was very honest about money. She paid Billy Bob and Preacher their exact commission, and she would never let them treat her, as they often tried to do, at the drugstore or to the picture show. "You'd better save your money," she told them. "That is, if you want to go to college. Because neither one of you has got the brains to win a scholarship, not even a football scholarship." But it was over money that Billy Bob and Preacher had a big falling out; that was not the real reason, of course: the real reason was that they had grown cross-eyed jealous over Miss Bobbit. So one day, and he had the gall to do this right in front of Billy Bob, Preacher said to Miss Bobbit that she'd better check her accounts carefully because he had more than a suspicion that Billy Bob wasn't turning over to her *all* the money he collected. That's a damned lie, said Billy Bob, and with a clean left hook he knocked Preacher off the Sawyer porch and jumped after him into a bed of nasturtiums. But once Preacher got a hold on him, Billy Bob didn't stand a chance. Preacher even rubbed dirt in his eyes. During all this, Mrs. Sawyer, leaning out an upper story window, screamed like an eagle, and Sister Rosalba, fatly cheerful, ambiguously shouted, Kill him! Kill him! Kill him! Only Miss Bobbit seemed to know what she was doing. She plugged in the lawn hose, and gave the boys a close-up blinding bath. Gasping, Preacher staggered to his feet. Oh honey, he said, shaking himself like a wet dog, honey, you've got to decide. "Decide *what?*" said Miss Bobbit, right away in a huff. Oh, honey, wheezed Preacher, you don't want us boys killing each other. You got to decide who is your real true sweetheart. "Sweetheart, my eye," said Miss Bobbit. "I should've known better than to get myself involved with a lot of country children. What sort of businessman are you going to make? Now, you listen here, Preacher Star: I don't want a sweetheart, and if I did, it wouldn't be you. As a matter of fact, you don't even get up when a lady enters the room."

Preacher spit on the ground and swaggered over to Billy Bob. Come on, he said, just as though nothing had happened, she's a hard one, she is, she don't want nothing but to make trouble between two good friends. For a moment it looked as if Billy Bob was going to join him in a peaceful togetherness; but suddenly, coming to his senses, he drew back and made a gesture. The boys regarded each other a full minute, all the closeness between them turning an ugly color: you can't hate so much unless you love, too. And Preacher's face showed all of this. But there was nothing for him to do except to go away. Oh, yes, Preacher, you looked so lost that day that for the first time I really liked you, so skinny and mean and lost going down the road all by yourself.

They did not make it up, Preacher and Billy Bob; and it was not because they didn't want to, it was only that there did not seem to be any straight way for their friendship to happen again. But they couldn't get rid of this friendship: each was always aware of what the other was up to; and when Preacher found himself a new buddy, Billy Bob moped around for days, picking things up, dropping them again, or doing sudden wild things, like purposely poking his finger in the electric fan. Sometimes in the evenings Preacher would pause by the gate and talk with Aunt El. It was only to torment Billy Bob I suppose, but he stayed friendly with all of us, and at Christmas time he gave us a huge box of shelled peanuts. He left a present for Billy Bob, too. It turned out to be a book of Sherlock Holmes; and on the fly-leaf there was scribbled, "Friends Like Ivy On the Wall Must Fall." That's the corniest thing I ever saw, Billy Bob said. Jesus, what a dope he is! But then, and though it was a cold winter day, he went in the backyard and climbed up into the pecan tree, crouching there all afternoon in the blue December branches.

But most of the time he was happy, because Miss Bobbit was there, and she was always sweet to him now. She and Sister Rosalba treated him like a man; that is to say, they allowed him to do everything for them. On the other hand, they let him win at three-handed bridge, they never questioned his lies, nor discouraged his ambitions. It was a happy while. However, trouble started again when school began. Miss Bobbit refused to go. "It's ridiculous," she said, when one day the principal, Mr. Copland, came around to investigate, "really ridiculous; I can read and write and there are *some* people in this town who have every reason to know that I can count money. No, Mr. Copland, consider for a moment and you will see neither of us has the time nor energy. After all, it would only be a matter of whose spirit broke first, yours or mine. And besides, what is there for you to teach me? Now, if you knew anything about dancing, that would be another matter; but under the circumstances, yes, Mr. Copland, under the circumstances, I suggest we forget the whole thing." Mr. Copland was perfectly willing to. But the rest of the town thought she ought to be whipped. Horace Deasley wrote a piece in the paper which was titled "A Tragic Situation." It was, in his opinion, a tragic situation when a small girl could defy what he, for some reason, termed the Constitution of the United States. The article ended with a question: *Can she get away with it?* She did; and so did Sister Rosalba. Only she was colored, so no one cared. Billy Bob was not so lucky. It was school for him all right; but he might as well have stayed home for the good it did him. On his first report card he got three F's, a record of some sort. But he is a smart boy, I guess he just couldn't live through those hours without Miss Bobbit; away from her he always seemed half-asleep. He was always in a fight, too; either his eye was black, or his lip was split, or his walk had a limp. He never talked about these fights, but Miss Bobbit was shrewd enough to guess the reason why. "You are a dear, I know, I know. And I appreciate you, Billy Bob. Only don't fight with people because of me. Of course they say mean things about me. But do you know why that is, Billy Bob? It's a compliment, kind of. Because deep down they think I'm absolutely wonderful."

And she was right: if you are not admired no one will take the trouble to disapprove. But actually we had no idea of how wonderful she was until there appeared the man known as Manny Fox. This happened late in February. The first news we had of Manny Fox was a series of jovial placards posted up in the stores around town: Manny Fox Presents the Fan Dancer Without the Fan; then, in smaller print: Also, Sensational Amateur Program Featuring Your Own Neighbors—First Prize, A Genuine Hollywood Screen Test. All this was to take place the following Thursday. The tickets were priced at one dollar each, which around here is a lot of money; but it is not often that we get any kind of flesh entertainment, so everybody shelled out their money and made a great todo over the whole thing. The drugstore cowboys talked dirty all week, mostly about the fan dancer without the fan, who turned out to be Mrs. Manny Fox. They stayed down the highway at the Chucklewood Tourist Camp; but they were in town all day, driving around in an old Packard which had Manny Fox's full name stenciled on all four doors. His wife was a dead-pan pimento-tongued redhead with wet lips and moist eyelids; she was quite large actually, but compared to Manny Fox she seemed rather frail, for he was a fat cigar of a man.

They made the pool hall their headquarters, and every afternoon you could find them there, drinking beer and joking with the town loafs. As it developed, Manny Fox's business affairs were not restricted to theatrics. He also ran a kind of employment bureau: slowly he let it be known that for a fee of $150 he could get for any adventurous boys in the county high-class jobs working on fruit ships sailing from New Orleans to South America. The chance of a lifetime, he called it. There are not two boys around here who readily lay their hands on so much as five dollars; nevertheless, a good dozen managed to raise the money. Ada Willingham took all she'd saved to buy an angel tombstone for her husband and gave it to her son, and Acey Trump's papa sold an option on his cotton crop.

But the night of the show! That was a night when all was forgotten: mortgages, and the dishes in the kitchen sink. Aunt El said you'd think we were going to the opera, everybody so dressed up, so pink and sweet-smelling. The Odeon had not been so full since the night they gave away the matched set of sterling silver. Practically everybody had a relative in the show, so there was a lot of nervousness to contend with. Miss Bobbit was the only contestant we knew real well. Billy Bob couldn't sit still; he kept telling us over and over that we mustn't applaud for anybody but Miss Bobbit; Aunt El said that would be very rude, which sent Billy Bob off into a state again; and when his father bought us all bags of popcorn he wouldn't touch his because it would make his hands greasy, and please, another thing, we mustn't be noisy and eat ours while Miss Bobbit was performing. That she was to be a contestant had come as a last-minute surprise. It was logical enough, and there were signs that should've told us; the fact, for instance, that she had not set foot outside the Sawyer house in how many days? And the victrola going half the night, her shadow whirling on the window shade, and the secret, stuffed look on Sister Rosalba's face whenever asked after Sister Bobbit's health. So there was her name on the program listed second in fact, though she did not appear for a long while. First came Manny Fox, greased and leering, who told a lot of peculiar jokes, clapping his hands, ha, ha. Aunt El said if he told another joke like that she was going to walk straight out: he did, and she didn't. Before Miss Bobbit came on there were eleven contestants, including Eustacia Bernstein, who imitated movie stars so that they all sound like Eustacia, and there was an extraordinary Mr. Buster Riley, a jug-eared old wool-hat from way in the back country who played "Waltzing Matilda" on a saw. Up to that point, he was the hit of the show; not that there was any marked difference in the various receptions, for everybody applauded generously, everybody, that is, except Preacher Star. He was sitting two rows ahead of us, greeting each act with a donkey-loud boo. Aunt El said she was never going to speak to him again. The only person he ever applauded was Miss Bobbit. No doubt the Devil was on her side, but she deserved it. Out she came, tossing her hips, her curls, rolling her eyes. You could tell right away it wasn't going to be one of her classical numbers. She tapped across the stage, daintily holding up the sides of a cloud-blue skirt. That's the cutest thing I ever saw, said Billy Bob, smacking his thigh, and Aunt El had to agree that Miss Bobbit looked real sweet. When she started to twirl the whole audience broke into spontaneous applause; so she did it all over again, hissing, "Faster, faster," at poor Miss Adelaide, who was at the piano doing her Sunday-school best. "I was born in China, and raised in Jay-pan . . ." We had never heard her sing before, and she had a rowdy sandpaper voice. ". . . if you don't like my peaches, stay away from my can, o-ho o-ho!" Aunt El gasped; she gasped again when Miss Bobbit, with a bump, up-ended her skirt to display blue-lace underwear, thereby collecting most of the whistles the boys had been saving for the fan dancer without the fan, which was just as well, as it later turned out, for that lady, to the tune of "An Apple for the Teacher" and cries of gyp gyp, did her routine attired in a bathing suit. But showing off her bottom was not Miss Bobbit's final triumph. Miss Adelaide commenced an ominous thundering in the darker keys, at which point Sister Rosalba, carrying a lighted Roman candle, rushed onstage and handed it to Miss Bobbit, who was in the midst of a full split; she made it, too, and just as she did the Roman candle burst into fiery balls of red, white and blue, and we all had to stand up because she was singing "The Star Spangled Banner" at the top of her lungs. Aunt El said afterwards that it was one of the most gorgeous things she'd ever seen on the American stage.

Well, she surely did deserve a Hollywood screen test and, inasmuch as she won the contest, it looked as though she were going to get it. Manny Fox said she was: Honey, he said, you're real star stuff. Only he skipped town the next day, leaving nothing but hearty promises. Watch the mails, my friends, you'll all be hearing from me. That is what he said to the boys whose money he'd taken, and that is what he said to Miss Bobbit. There are three deliveries daily, and this sizable group gathered at the post office for all of them, a jolly crowd growing gradually joyless. How their hands trembled when a letter slid into their mailbox. A terrible hush came over them as the days passed. They all knew what the other was thinking, but no one could bring himself to say it, not even Miss Bobbit. Postmistress Patterson said it plainly, however: The man's a crook, I knew he was a crook to begin with, and if I have to look at your faces one more day I'll shoot myself.

Finally, at the end of two weeks, it was Miss Bobbit who broke the spell. Her eyes had grown more vacant than anyone had ever supposed they might, but one day, after the last mail was up, all her old sizzle came back. "O.K., boys, it's lynch law now," she said, and proceeded to herd the whole troupe home with her. This was the first meeting of the Manny Fox Hangman's Club, an organization which, in a more social form, endures to this day, though Manny Fox has long since been caught and, so to say, hung. Credit for this went quite properly to Miss Bobbit. Within a week she'd written over three hundred descriptions of Manny Fox and dispatched them to Sheriffs throughout the South; she also wrote letters to papers in the larger cities, and these attracted wide attention. As a result, four of the robbed boys were offered good-paying jobs by the United Fruit Company, and late this spring, when Manny Fox was arrested in Uphigh, Arkansas, where he was pulling the same old dodge, Miss Bobbit was presented with a Good Deed Merit award from the Sunbeam Girls of America. For some reason, she made a point of letting the world know that this did not exactly thrill her. "I do not approve of the organization," she said. "All that rowdy bugle blowing. It's neither good-hearted nor truly feminine. And anyway, what is a good deed? Don't let anybody fool you, a good deed is something you do because you want something in return." It would be reassuring to report she was wrong, and that her just reward, when at last it came, was given out of kindness and love. However, this is not the case. About a week ago the boys involved in the swindle all received from Manny Fox checks covering their losses, and Miss Bobbit, with clodhopping determination, stalked into a meeting of the Hangman's Club, which is now an excuse for drinking beer and playing poker every Thursday night. "Look, boys," she said, laying it on the line, "none of you ever thought to see that money again, but now that you have, you ought to invest it in something practical—like me." The proposition was that they should pool their money and finance her trip to Hollywood; in return, they would get ten percent of her life's earnings which, after she was a star, and that would not be very long, would make them all rich men. "At least," as she said, "in this part of the country." Not one of the boys wanted to do it: but when Miss Bobbit looked at you, what was there to say?

Since Monday, it has been raining buoyant summer rain shot through with sun, but dark at night and full of sound, full of dripping leaves, watery chimings, sleepless scuttlings. Billy Bob is wide-awake, dry-eyed, though everything he does is a little frozen and his tongue

is as stiff as a bell tongue. It has not been easy for him, Miss
Bobbit's going. Because she'd meant more than that. Than what? Than
being thirteen years old and crazy in love. She was the queer things
in him, like the pecan tree and liking books and caring enough about
people to let them hurt him. She was the things he was afraid to
show anyone else. And in the dark the music trickled through the
rain: won't there be nights when we will hear it just as though it
were really there? And afternoons when the shadows will be all at
once confused, and she will pass before us, unfurling across the lawn
like a pretty piece of ribbon? She laughed to Billy Bob; she held
his hand, she even kissed him. "I'm not going to die," she said.
"You'll come out there, and we'll climb a mountain, and we'll all
live there together, you and me and Sister Rosalba." But Billy Bob
knew it would never happen that way, and so when the music came
through the dark he would stuff the pillow over his head.

Only there was a strange smile about yesterday, and that was the
day she was leaving. Around noon the sun came out, bringing with
it into the air all the sweetness of wisteria. Aunt El's yellow Lady
Anne's were blooming again, and she did something wonderful, she
told Billy Bob he could pick them and give them to Miss Bobbit
for good-bye. All afternoon Miss Bobbit sat on the porch surrounded
by people who stopped by to wish her well. She looked as though
she were going to Communion, dressed in white and with a white
parasol. Sister Rosalba had given her a handkerchief, but she had
to borrow it back because she couldn't stop blubbering. Another little
girl brought a baked chicken, presumably to be eaten on the bus; the
only trouble was she'd forgotten to take out the insides before cooking
it. Miss Bobbit's mother said that was all right by her, chicken was
chicken; which is memorable because it is the single opinion she ever
voiced. There was only one sour note. For hours Preacher Star had
been hanging around down at the corner, sometimes standing at the curb
tossing a coin, and sometimes hiding behind a tree, as if he didn't want
anyone to see him. It made everybody nervous. About twenty minutes
before bus time he sauntered up and leaned against our gate. Billy Bob
was still in the garden picking roses; by now he had enough for a bonfire,
and their smell was as heavy as wind. Preacher stared at him until he
lifted his head. As they looked at each other the rain began again,
falling fine as sea spray and colored by a rainbow. Without a word,
Preacher went over and started helping Billy Bob separate the roses
into two giant bouquets: together they carried them to the curb.

Across the street there were bumblebees of talk, but when Miss Bobbit saw them, two boys whose flower-masked faces were like yellow moons, she rushed down the steps, her arms outstretched. You could see what was going to happen; and we called out, our voices like lightning in the rain, but Miss Bobbit, running toward those moons of roses, did not seem to hear. That is when the six-o'clock bus ran over her.

Eudora Welty

A WORN PATH

The pleasure this story gave me in the writing came in the naturally occurring closeness of the narrative with the meaning. The journey to help another is a worn path—it remains indelible even with the frailty of the body and in the mind clouded with age, and even for a cause of little hope. I've been asked so often by students if the child is not really dead that I suppose their teachers must tell them this would make the story mean more. But I think it would make it mean less, for then the dramatic quality and the feeling and the meaning of the story—all of which belong to the living—would be diminished. While it may certainly suggest that the old lady would probably keep going her path to the end of her days if the child died before her and she didn't realize it, for the duration of the story the child is alive and needs help and the old lady is going to get it for him, and the path is worn.

Eudora Welty

It was December—a bright frozen day in the early morning. Far out in the country there was an old Negro woman with her head tied in a red rag, coming along a path through the pinewoods. Her name was Phoenix Jackson. She was very old and small and she walked slowly in the dark pine shadows, moving a little from side to side in her steps, with the balanced heaviness and lightness of a pendulum in a grand-father clock. She carried a thin, small cane made from an umbrella, and with this she kept tapping the frozen earth in front of her. This made a grave and persistent noise in the still air, that seemed meditative like the chirping of a solitary little bird.

She wore a dark striped dress reaching down to her shoe tops, and an equally long apron of bleached sugar sacks, with a full pocket: all neat and tidy, but every time she took a step she might have fallen over her shoelaces, which dragged from her unlaced shoes. She looked straight ahead. Her eyes were blue with age. Her skin had a pattern all its own of numberless branching wrinkles and as though a whole little tree stood in the middle of her forehead, but a golden color ran underneath, and the two knobs of her cheeks were illumined by a yellow burning under the dark. Under the red rag her hair came down on her neck in the frailest of ringlets, still black, and with an odor like copper.

Now and then there was a quivering in the thicket. Old Phoenix said, "Out of my way, all you foxes, owls, beetles, jack rabbits, coons and wild animals! . . . Keep out from under these feet, little bob-whites. . . . Keep the big wild hogs out of my path. Don't let none of those come running my direction. I got a long way." Under her small black-freckled hand her cane, limber as a buggy whip, would switch at the brush as if to rouse up any hiding things.

On she went. The woods were deep and still. The sun made the pine needles almost too bright to look at, up where the wind rocked. The cones dropped as light as feathers. Down in the hollow was the mourning dove—it was not too late for him.

The path ran up a hill. "Seem like there is chains about my feet, time I get this far," she said, in the voice of argument old people keep to use with themselves. "Something always take a hold of me on this hill—pleads I should stay."

After she got to the top she turned and gave a full, severe look behind her where she had come. "Up through pines," she said at length. "Now down through oaks."

Her eyes opened their widest, and she started down gently. But before she got to the bottom of the hill a bush caught her dress.

Her fingers were busy and intent, but her skirts were full and long, so that before she could pull them free in one place they were caught in another. It was not possible to allow the dress to tear. "I in the thorny bush," she said. "Thorns, you doing your appointed work. Never want to let folks pass, no sir. Old eyes thought you was a pretty little *green* bush."

Finally, trembling all over, she stood free, and after a moment dared to stoop for her cane.

"Sun so high!" she cried, leaning back and looking, while the thick tears went over her eyes. "The time getting all gone here."

At the foot of this hill was a place where a log was laid across the creek.

"Now comes the trial," said Phoenix.

Putting her right foot out, she mounted the log and shut her eyes. Lifting her skirt, leveling her cane fiercely before her, like a festival figure in some parade, she began to march across. Then she opened her eyes and she was safe on the other side.

"I wasn't as old as I thought," she said.

But she sat down to rest. She spread her skirts on the bank around her and folded her hands over her knees. Up above her was a tree in a pearly cloud of mistletoe. She did not dare to close her eyes, and when a little boy brought her a plate with a slice of marble-cake on it she spoke to him. "That would be acceptable," she said.

But when she went to take it there was just her own hand in the air.

So she left that tree, and had to go through a barbed-wire fence. There she had to creep and crawl, spreading her knees and stretching her fingers like a baby trying to climb the steps. But she talked loudly to herself: she could not let her dress be torn now, so late in the day, and she could not pay for having her arm or her leg sawed off if she got caught fast where she was.

At last she was safe through the fence and risen up out in the clearing. Big dead trees, like black men with one arm, were standing in the purple stalks of the withered cotton field. There sat a buzzard.

"Who you watching?"

In the furrow she made her way along.

"Glad this not the season for bulls," she said, looking sideways, "and the good Lord made his snakes to curl up and sleep in the winter. A pleasure I don't see no two-headed snake coming around that tree, where it come once. It took a while to get by him, back in the summer."

She passed through the old cotton and went into a field of dead corn. It whispered and shook and was taller than her head. "Through the maze now," she said, for there was no path.

Then there was something tall, black, and skinny there, moving before her.

At first she took it for a man. It could have been a man dancing in the field. But she stood still and listened, and it did not make a sound. It was as silent as a ghost.

"Ghost," she said sharply, "who be you the ghost of? For I have heard of nary death close by."

But there was no answer—only the ragged dancing in the wind.

She shut her eyes, reached out her hand, and touched a sleeve. She found a coat and inside that an emptiness, cold as ice.

"You scarecrow," she said. Her face lighted. "I ought to be shut up for good," she said with laughter. "My senses is gone. I too old. I the oldest people I ever know. Dance, old scarecrow," she said, "while I dancing with you."

She kicked her foot over the furrow, and with mouth drawn down, shook her head once or twice in a little strutting way. Some husks blew down and whirled in streamers about her skirts.

Then she went on, parting her way from side to side with the cane, through the whispering field. At last she came to the end, to a wagon track where the silver grass blew between the red ruts. The quail were walking around like pullets, seeming all dainty and unseen.

"Walk pretty," she said. "This the easy place. This the easy going."

She followed the track, swaying through the quiet bare fields, through the little strings of trees silver in their dead leaves, past cabins silver from weather, with doors and windows boarded shut, all like old women under a spell sitting there. "I walking in their sleep," she said, nodding her head vigorously.

In a ravine she went where a spring was silently flowing through a hollow log. Old Phoenix bent and drank. "Sweet-gum makes the water sweet," she said, and drank more. "Nobody know who made this well, for it was here when I was born."

The track crossed a swampy part where the moss hung as white as lace from every limb. "Sleep on, alligators, and blow your bubbles." Then the track went into the road.

Deep, deep the road went down between the high green-colored banks. Overhead the live-oaks met, and it was as dark as a cave.

A black dog with a lolling tongue came up out of the weeds by the ditch. She was meditating, and not ready, and when he came at her she only hit him a little with her cane. Over she went in the ditch, like a little puff of milkweed.

Down there, her senses drifted away. A dream visited her, and she reached her hand up, but nothing reached down and gave her a pull. So she lay there and presently went to talking. "Old woman," she said to herself, "that black dog come up out of the weeds to stall you off, and now there he sitting on his fine tail, smiling at you."

A white man finally came along and found her—a hunter, a young man, with his dog on a chain.

"Well, Granny!" he laughed. "What are you doing there?"

"Lying on my back like a June-bug waiting to be turned over, mister," she said, reaching up her hand.

He lifted her up, gave her a swing in the air, and set her down. "Anything broken, Granny?"

"No sir, them old dead weeds is springy enough," said Phoenix, when she had got her breath. "I thank you for your trouble."

"Where do you live, Granny?" he asked, while the two dogs were growling at each other.

"Away back yonder, sir, behind the ridge. You can't even see it from here."

"On your way home?"

"No sir, I going to town."

"Why, that's too far! That's as far as I walk when I come out myself, and I get something for my trouble." He patted the stuffed bag he carried, and there hung down a little closed claw. It was one of the bob-whites, with its beak hooked bitterly to show it was dead. "Now you go on home, Granny!"

"I bound to go to town, mister," said Phoenix. "The time come around."

He gave another laugh, filling the whole landscape. "I know you old colored people! Wouldn't miss going to town to see Santa Claus!"

But something held old Phoenix very still. The deep lines in her face went into a fierce and different radiation. Without warning, she had seen with her own eyes a flashing nickel fall out of the man's pocket onto the ground.

"How old are you, Granny?" he was saying.

"There is no telling, mister," she said, "no telling."

Then she gave a little cry and clapped her hands and said, "Git on away from here, dog! Look! Look at that dog!" She laughed as if in admiration. "He ain't scared of nobody. He a big black dog." She whispered, "Sic him!"

"Watch me get rid of that cur," said the man. "Sic him, Pete! Sic him!"

Phoenix heard the dogs fighting, and heard the man running and throwing sticks. She even heard a gunshot. But she was slowly bending forward by that time, further and further forward, the lids stretched down over her eyes, as if she were doing this in her sleep. Her chin was lowered almost to her knees. The yellow palm of her hand came out from the fold of her apron. Her fingers slid down and along the ground under the piece of money with the grace and care they would have in lifting an egg from under a setting hen. Then she slowly straightened up, she stood erect, and the nickel was in her apron pocket. A bird flew by. Her lips moved. "God watching me the whole time. I come to stealing."

The man came back, and his own dog panted about them. "Well, I scared him off that time," he said, and then he laughed and lifted his gun and pointed it at Phoenix.

She stood straight and faced him.

"Doesn't the gun scare you?" he said, still pointing it.

"No, sir, I seen plenty go off closer by, in my day, and for less than what I done," she said, holding utterly still.

He smiled, and shouldered the gun. "Well, Granny," he said, "you must be a hundred years old, and scared of nothing. I'd give you a dime if I had any money with me. But you take my advice and stay home, and nothing will happen to you."

"I bound to go on my way, mister," said Phoenix. She inclined her head in the red rag. Then they went in different directions, but she could hear the gun shooting again and again over the hill.

She walked on. The shadows hung from the oak trees to the road like curtains. Then she smelled wood-smoke, and smelled the river, and she saw a steeple and the cabins on their steep steps. Dozens of little black children whirled around her. There ahead was Natchez shining. Bells were ringing. She walked on.

In the paved city it was Christmas time. There were red and green electric lights strung and crisscrossed everywhere, and all turned on in the daytime. Old Phoenix would have been lost if she had not distrusted her eyesight and depended on her feet to know where to take her.

She paused quietly on the sidewalk where people were passing by. A lady came along in the crowd, carrying an armful of red-, green- and silver-wrapped presents; she gave off perfume like the red roses in hot summer, and Phoenix stopped her.

"Please, missy, will you lace up my shoe?" She held up her foot.

"What do you want, Grandma?"

"See my shoe," said Phoenix. "Do all right for out in the country, but wouldn't look right to go in a big building."

"Stand still then, Grandma," said the lady. She put her packages down on the sidewalk beside her and laced and tied both shoes tightly.

"Can't lace 'em with a cane," said Phoenix. "Thank you, missy. I doesn't mind asking a nice lady to tie up my shoe, when I gets out on the street."

Moving slowly and from side to side, she went into the big building, and into a tower of steps, where she walked up and around and around until her feet knew to stop.

She entered a door, and there she saw nailed up on the wall the document that had been stamped with the gold seal and framed in the gold frame, which matched the dream that was hung up in her head.

"Here I be," she said. There was a fixed and ceremonial stiffness over her body.

"A charity case, I suppose," said an attendant who sat at the desk before her.

But Phoenix only looked above her head. There was sweat on her face, the wrinkles in her skin shone like a bright net.

"Speak up, Grandma," the woman said. "What's your name? We must have your history, you know. Have you been here before? What seems to be the trouble with you?"

Old Phoenix only gave a twitch to her face as if a fly were bothering her.

"Are you deaf?" cried the attendant.

But then the nurse came in.

"Oh, that's just old Aunt Phoenix," she said. "She doesn't come for herself—she has a little grandson. She makes these trips just as regular as clockwork. She lives away back off the Old Natchez Trace." She bent down. "Well, Aunt Phoenix, why don't you just take a seat? We won't keep you standing after your long trip." She pointed.

The old woman sat down, bolt upright in the chair.

"Now, how is the boy?" asked the nurse.

Old Phoenix did not speak.

"I said, how is the boy?"

But Phoenix only waited and stared straight ahead, her face very solemn and withdrawn into rigidity.

"Is his throat any better?" asked the nurse. "Aunt Phoenix, don't you hear me? Is your grandson's throat any better since the last time you came for the medicine?"

With her hands on her knees, the old woman waited, silent, erect and motionless, just as if she were in armor.

"You mustn't take up our time this way, Aunt Phoenix," the nurse said. "Tell us quickly about your grandson, and get it over. He isn't dead, is he?"

At last there came a flicker and then a flame of comprehension across her face, and she spoke.

"My grandson. It was my memory had left me. There I sat and forgot why I made my long trip."

"Forgot?" The nurse frowned. "After you came so far?"

Then Phoenix was like an old woman begging a dignified forgiveness for waking up frightened in the night. "I never did go to school, I was too old at the Surrender," she said in a soft voice. "I'm an old woman without an education. It was my memory fail me. My little grandson, he is just the same, and I forgot it in the coming."

"Throat never heals, does it?" said the nurse, speaking in a loud, sure voice to old Phoenix. By now she had a card with something written on it, a little list. "Yes. Swallowed lye. When was it?—January—two-three years ago—"

Phoenix spoke unasked now. "No, missy, he not dead, he just the same. Every little while his throat begin to close up again, and he not able to swallow. He not get his breath. He not able to help himself. So the time come around, and I go on another trip for the soothing medicine."

"All right. The doctor said as long as you came to get it, you could have it," said the nurse. "But it's an obstinate case."

"My little grandson, he sit up there in the house all wrapped up, waiting by himself," Phoenix went on. "We is the only two left in the world. He suffer and it don't seem to put him back at all. He got a sweet look. He going to last. He wear a little patch quilt and peep out holding his mouth open like a little bird. I remembers so plain now. I not going to forget him again, no, the whole enduring time. I could tell him from all the others in creation."

"All right." The nurse was trying to hush her now. She brought her a bottle of medicine. "Charity," she said, making a check mark in a book.

Old Phoenix held the bottle close to her eyes, and then carefully put it into her pocket.

"I thank you," she said.

"It's Christmas time, Grandma," said the attendant. "Could I give you a few pennies out of my purse?"

"Five pennies is a nickel," said Phoenix stiffly.

"Here's a nickel," said the attendant.

Phoenix rose carefully and held out her hand. She received the nickel and then fished the other nickel out of her pocket and laid it beside the new one. She stared at her palm closely, with her head on one side.

Then she gave a tap with her cane on the floor.

"This is what come to me to do," she said. "I going to the store and buy my child a little windmill they sells, made out of paper. He going to find it hard to believe there such a thing in the world. I'll march myself back where he waiting, holding it straight up in this hand."

She lifted her free hand, gave a little nod, turned around, and walked out of the doctor's office. Then her slow step began on the stairs, going down.

Erskine Caldwell

WARM RIVER

The writing of a short story can be a dangerous adventure. What makes it dangerous may be the misguided belief of a writer that he is obligated to tell a story. And, when this design is followed, the structure is sure to be a contrived plot garishly colored with the gaudy crayons of the topical and sensational.

But the short story can be more than this. It can be the explicit expression of a casual feeling or a deep emotion when, in conflict or with sympathy, two or more persons act in response to the desires and motivations of the mind and heart. Although it is evasive and not aways successfully attained, this is the essence of fiction that writers of durable reading seek to implant in their works.

Readers of the present short story, "Warm River," will find that it is an adventure without beginning or end, and consequently it is completely devoid of plot or conscious structure. But perhaps it does convey some human feeling, and, if so, "Warm River" is not without its implications.

Erskine Caldwell

Dunedin, Florida

The driver stopped at the suspended footbridge and pointed out to me the house across the river. I paid him the quarter fare for the ride from the station two miles away and stepped from the car. After he had gone I was alone with the chill night and the star-pointed lights twinkling in the valley and the broad green river flowing warm below me. All around me the mountains rose like black clouds in the night, and only by looking straight heavenward could I see anything of the dim afterglow of sunset.

The creaking footbridge swayed with the rhythm of my stride and the momentum of its swing soon overcame my pace. Only by walking faster and faster could I cling to the pendulum as it swung in its wide arc over the river. When at last I could see the other side, where the mountain came down abruptly and slid under the warm water, I gripped my handbag tighter and ran with all my might.

Even then, even after my feet had crunched upon the gravel path, I was afraid. I knew that by day I might walk the bridge without fear; but at night, in a strange country, with dark mountains towering all around me and a broad green river flowing beneath me, I could not keep my hands from trembling and my heart from pounding against my chest.

I found the house easily, and laughed at myself for having run from the river. The house was the first one to come upon after leaving the footbridge, and even if I should have missed it, Gretchen would have called me. She was there on the steps of the porch waiting for me.

When I heard her familiar voice calling my name, I was ashamed of myself for having been frightened by the mountains and the broad river flowing below.

She ran down the gravel path to meet me.

"Did the footbridge frighten you, Richard?" she asked excitedly, holding my arm with both of her hands and guiding me up the path to the house.

"I think it did, Gretchen," I said, "but I hope I outran it."

"Everyone tries to do that at first, but after going over it once, it's like walking a tightrope. I used to walk tightropes when I was small—didn't you do that, too, Richard? We had a rope stretched across the floor of our barn to practice on."

"I did, too, but it's been so long ago I've forgotten how to do it now."

We reached the steps and went up to the porch. Gretchen took me to the door. Someone inside the house was bringing a lamp into the hall, and with the coming of the light I saw Gretchen's two sisters standing just inside the open door.

"This is my little sister, Anne," Gretchen said. "And this is Mary."

I spoke to them in the semidarkness, and we went on into the hall. Gretchen's father was standing beside a table holding the lamp a little to one side so that he could see my face. I had not met him before.

"This is my father," Gretchen said. "He was afraid you wouldn't be able to find our house in the dark."

"I wanted to bring a light down to the bridge and meet you, but Gretchen said you would get here without any trouble. Did you get lost? I could have brought a lantern down with no trouble at all."

I shook hands with him and told him how easily I had found the place.

"The hack driver pointed out to me the house from the other side of the river, and I never once took my eyes from the light. If I had lost sight of the light, I'd probably be stumbling around somewhere now in the dark down there getting ready to fall into the water."

He laughed at me for being afraid of the river.

"You wouldn't have minded it. The river is warm. Even in winter, when there is ice and snow underfoot, the river is as warm as a comfortable room. All of us here love the water down there."

"No, Richard, you wouldn't have fallen in," Gretchen said, laying her hand in mine. "I saw you the moment you got out of the hack, and if you had gone a step in the wrong direction, I was ready to run to you."

I wished to thank Gretchen for saying that, but already she was going to the stairs to the floor above, and calling me. I went with her, lifting my handbag in front of me. There was a shaded lamp, lighted but turned low, on the table at the end of the upper hall, and she picked it up and went ahead into one of the front rooms.

We stood for a moment looking at each other, and silent.

"There is fresh water in the pitcher, Richard. If there is anything else you would like to have, please tell me. I tried not to overlook anything."

"Don't worry, Gretchen," I told her. "I couldn't wish for anything more. It's enough just to be here with you, anyway. There's nothing else I care for."

She looked at me quickly, and then she lowered her eyes. We stood silently for several minutes, while neither of us could think of anything to say. I wanted to tell her how glad I was to be with her, even if it was only for one night, but I knew I could say that to her later. Gretchen knew why I had come.

"I'll leave the lamp for you, Richard, and I'll wait downstairs for you on the porch. Come as soon as you are ready."

She had left before I could offer to carry the light to the stairhead for her to see the way down. By the time I had picked up the lamp, she was out of sight down the stairs.

I walked back into the room and closed the door and bathed my face and hands, scrubbing the train dust with brush and soap. There was a row of hand-embroidered towels on the rack, and I took one and dried my face and hands. After that I combed my hair, and found a fresh handkerchief in the handbag. Then I opened the door and went downstairs to find Gretchen.

Her father was on the porch with her. When I walked through the doorway, he got up and gave me a chair between them. Gretchen pulled her chair closer to mine, touching my arm with her hand.

"Is this the first time you have been up here in the mountains, Richard?" her father asked me, turning in his chair towards me.

"I've never been within a hundred miles of here before, sir. It's a different country up here, but I suppose you would think the same about the coast, wouldn't you?"

"Oh, but Father used to live in Norfolk," Gretchen said. "Didn't you, Father?"

"I lived there for nearly three years."

There was something else he would say, and both of us waited for him to continue.

"Father is a master mechanic," Gretchen whispered to me. "He works in the railroad shops."

"Yes," he said after a while, "I've lived in many places, but here is where I wish to stay."

My first thought was to ask him why he preferred the mountains to other sections, but suddenly I was aware that both he and Gretchen were strangely silent. Between them, I sat wondering about it.

After a while he spoke again, not to me and not to Gretchen, but as though he were speaking to someone else on the porch, a fourth person whom I had failed to see in the darkness. I waited, tense and excited, for him to continue.

Gretchen moved her chair a few inches closer to mine, her motions gentle and without sound. The warmth of the river came up and covered us like a blanket on a chill night.

"After Gretchen and the other two girls lost their mother," he said, almost inaudibly, bending forward over his knees and gazing out across the broad green river, "after we lost their mother, I came back to the mountains to live. I couldn't stay in Norfolk, and I couldn't stand it in Baltimore. This was the only place on earth where I could find peace. Gretchen remembers her mother, but neither of you can yet understand how it is with me. Her mother and I were born here in the mountains, and we lived here together for almost twenty years. Then after she left us, I moved away, foolishly believing that I could forget. But I was wrong. Of course I was wrong. A man can't forget the mother of his children, even though he knows he will never see her again."

Gretchen leaned closer to me, and I could not keep my eyes from her darkly framed profile beside me. The river below us made no sound; but the warmth of its vapor would not let me forget that it was still there.

Her father had bent farther forward in his chair until his arms were resting on his knees, and he seemed to be trying to see someone on the other side of the river, high on the mountain top above it. His eyes strained, and the shaft of light that came through the open doorway fell upon them and glistened there. Tears fell from his face like fragments of stars, burning into his quivering hands until they were out of sight.

Presently, still in silence, he got up and moved through the doorway. His huge shadow fell upon Gretchen and me as he stood there momentarily before going inside. I turned and looked towards him but, even though he was passing from sight, I could not keep my eyes upon him.

Gretchen leaned closer against me, squeezing her fingers into the hollow of my hand and touching my shoulder with her cheeks as though she were trying to wipe something from them. Her father's footsteps grew fainter, and at last we could no longer hear him.

Somewhere below us, along the bank of the river, an express train crashed down the valley, creaking and screaming through the night. Occasionally its lights flashed through the openings in the darkness, dancing on the broad green river like polar lights in the north, and the metallic echo of its steel rumbled against the high walls of the mountains.

Gretchen clasped her hands tightly over my hand, trembling to her fingertips.

"Richard, why did you come to see me?"

Her voice was mingled with the screaming metallic echo of the train that now seemed far off.

I had expected to find her looking up into my face, but when I turned to her, I saw that she was gazing far down into the valley, down into the warm waters of the river. She knew why I had come, but she did not wish to hear me say why I had.

I do not know why I had come to see her, now. I had liked Gretchen, and I had desired her above anyone else I knew. But I could not tell her that I loved her, after having heard her father speak of love. I was sorry I had come, now after having heard him speak of Gretchen's mother as he did. I knew Gretchen would give herself to me, because she loved me; but I had nothing to give her in return. She was beautiful, very beautiful, and I had desired her. That was before. Now, I knew that I could never again think of her as I had come prepared.

"Why did you come, Richard?"

"Why?"

"Yes, Richard; why?"

My eyes closed, and what I felt was the memory of the star-pointed lights twinkling down in the valley and the warmth of the river flowing below and the caress of her fingers as she touched my arm.

"Richard, please tell me why you came."

"I don't know why I came, Gretchen."

"If you only loved me as I love you, Richard, you would know why."

Her fingers trembled in my hand. I knew she loved me. There had been no doubt in my mind from the first. Gretchen loved me.

"Perhaps I should not have come," I said. "I made a mistake, Gretchen. I should have stayed away."

"But you will be here only for tonight, Richard. You are leaving early in the morning. You aren't sorry that you came for just this short time, are you, Richard?"

"I'm not sorry that I am here, Gretchen, but I should not have come. I didn't know what I was doing. I haven't any right to come here. People who love each other are the only ones—"

"But you do love me just a little, don't you, Richard? You couldn't possibly love me nearly so much as I love you, but can't you tell me that you do love me just a little? I'll feel much happier after you have gone, Richard."

"I don't know," I said, trembling.

"Richard, please—"

With her hands in mine I held her tightly. Suddenly I felt something coming over me, a thing that stabbed my body with its quickness. It was as if the words her father had uttered were becoming clear to me. I had not realized before that there was such a love as he had spoken of. I had believed that men never loved women in the same way that a woman loved a man, but now I knew there could be no difference.

We sat silently, holding each other's hands for a long time. It was long past midnight, because the lights in the valley below were being turned out; but time did not matter.

Gretchen clung softly to me, looking up into my face and laying her cheek against my shoulder. She was as much mine as a woman ever belongs to a man, but I knew then that I could never force myself to take advantage of her love, and to go away knowing that I had not loved her as she loved me. I had not believed any such thing when I came. I had traveled all that distance to hold her in my arms for a few hours, and then to forget her, perhaps forever.

When it was time for us to go into the house, I got up and put my arms around her. She trembled when I touched her, but she clung to me as tightly as I held her, and the hammering of her heart drove into me, stroke after stroke, like an expanding wedge, the spears of her breasts.

"Richard, kiss me before you go," she said.

She ran to the door, holding it open for me. She picked up the lamp from the table and walked ahead up the stairs to the floor above.

At my door she waited until I could light her lamp, and then she handed me mine.

"Good night, Gretchen," I said.

"Good night, Richard."

I turned down the wick of her lamp to keep it from smoking, and then she went across the hall towards her room.

"I'll call you in the morning in time for you to catch your train, Richard."

"All right, Gretchen. Don't let me oversleep, because it leaves the station at seven-thirty."

"I'll wake you in plenty of time, Richard," she said.

The door was closed after her, and I turned and went into my room. I shut the door and slowly began to undress. After I had blown out the lamp and had got into bed, I lay tensely awake. I knew I could never go to sleep, and I sat up in bed and smoked cigarette after cigarette, blowing the smoke through the screen at the window. The house was quiet. Occasionally, I thought I heard the sounds of muffled movements in Gretchen's room across the hall, but I was not certain.

I could not determine how long a time I had sat there on the edge of the bed, stiff and erect, thinking of Gretchen, when suddenly I found myself jumping to my feet. I opened the door and ran across the hall. Gretchen's door was closed, but I knew it would not be locked, and I turned the knob noiselessly. A slender shaft of light broke through the opening I had made. It was not necessary to open the door wider, because I saw Gretchen only a few steps away, almost within arm's reach of me. I closed my eyes tightly for a moment, thinking of her as I had all during the day's ride up from the coast.

Gretchen had not heard me open her door, and she did not know I was there. Her lamp was burning brightly on the table.

I had not expected to find her awake, and I had thought surely she would be in bed. She knelt on the rug beside her bed, her head bowed over her arms and her body shaken with sobs.

Gretchen's hair was lying over her shoulders, tied over the top of her head with a pale blue ribbon. Her nightgown was white silk, hemmed with a delicate lace, and around her neck the collar of lace was thrown open.

I knew how beautiful she was when I saw her then, even though I had always thought her lovely. I had never seen a girl so beautiful as Gretchen.

She had not heard me at her door, and she still did not know I was there. She knelt beside her bed, her hands clenched before her, crying.

When I had first opened the door, I did not know what I was about to do; but now that I had seen her in her room, kneeling in prayer beside her bed, unaware that I was looking upon her and hearing her words and sobs, I was certain that I could never care for anyone else as I did for her. I had not known until then, but in the revelation of a few seconds I knew that I did love her.

I closed the door softly and went back to my room. There I found a chair and placed it beside the window to wait for the coming of day. At the window I sat and looked down into the bottom of the valley where the warm river lay. As my eyes grew more accustomed to the darkness, I felt as if I were coming closer and closer to it, so close that I might have reached out and touched the warm water with my hands.

Later in the night, towards morning, I thought I heard someone in Gretchen's room moving softly over the floor as one who would go from window to window. Once I was certain I heard someone in the hall, close to my door.

When the sun rose over the top of the mountain, I got up and dressed. Later, I heard Gretchen leave her room and go downstairs. I knew she was hurrying to prepare breakfast for me before I left to get on the train. I waited awhile, and after a quarter of an hour I heard her coming back up the stairs. She knocked softly on my door, calling my name several times.

I jerked open the door and faced her. She was so surprised at seeing me there, when she had expected to find me still asleep, that she could not say anything for a moment.

"Gretchen," I said, grasping her hands, "don't hurry to get me off —I'm not going back this morning—I don't know what was the matter with me last night—I know now that I love you—"

"But, Richard—last night you said—"

"I did say last night that I was going back early this morning, Gretchen, but I didn't know what I was talking about. I'm not going back now until you go with me. I'll tell you what I mean as soon as breakfast is over. But first of all I wish you would show me how to get down to the river. I have got to go down there right away and feel the water with my hands."

William Saroyan

LETTERS TO THE ARMENIANS
1. Calouste Gulbenkian
2. Yeghishe Charentz

Dear Whit:

About the letters to Calouste Gulbenkian and Yeghishe Charentz, from the book *Letters From 74 Rue Taitbout:* I was obliged to write the blurb for the book after the publisher sent me a home-made blurb that I refused to believe had been wrought by human mind. In the blurb I wrote there is the phrase, "the unwritten letter." Well, is there such a thing? Yes, I believe every human being is continuously sending such a letter to those few other human beings who are in his life and meaning. Well, are these two letters of that order? That is, "unwritten?" Yes, they are, but because I am a writer by nature and profession, with many years of experience, and a rather heightened skill at both producing the raw material of art, and at removing from the raw material all non-essentials, these "unwritten" letters are now, as I have said in the blurb, at last written. Thirty-one miscellaneous letters to various people, written one a day in Paris during August 1967, are about 1000th of the number I have written and am still writing. But do we mean *written*? Well yes, since I'm a writer, but also no, since the point about them is that they are "happening" to everybody all the time—they are certainly always of the *equivalent* of written—argued, grumbled, mumbled, groaned, shouted, prayed, or cursed. There is unquestionably a continuous artless reply in every man about everything that enters into his experience. The world itself is probably made out of these replies. I have selected these two letters because they demonstrate what I mean and at the same time inform me, if nobody else, how limitless the variations of writing can be.

William Saroyan

I

Calouste Gulbenkian:

When I arrived at the Avis Hotel in Lisbon, in May of 1949 I was surprised to learn that you occupied all of the mezzanine floor.

"Gulbenkian?" I said to the manager of the hotel. "Do you mean the man who is rich?"

"The richest man in the world," the manager of the hotel said. "He is Armenian, as I believe you are."

I was forty-one years old at the time, and in a bad way, having just left my wife, small son, and smaller daughter, for reasons that were grave enough to make my leaving imperative.

I was in a state of spiritual shock. I missed something. I could say it was my wife, my son, and my daughter, but I'm afraid it was something else—I missed the truth. I was suddenly without home, continuity, and meaning. I was without myself, my own ghost. I was not only lost, I was cut down. I was in fact dead. But I *seemed* to be alive. If anything, more alive than ever, from not knowing what to do next, or where to go, in order to start being alive in the truth again.

You were almost twice my age, and in vigorous good health. You mentioned during lunch that your father had lived to be ninety-eight and that you believed you would live at least that long, too. The money that came to you daily from oil leases which you had negotiated on behalf of countries having the oil and countries wanting to buy it did not stop four years later when you did, however. Money flows in secret rivers in many different places, from somewhere to somebody, and the river that had flowed to you for so long continued to flow, after your death at eighty-four, to the Foundation you established in Lisbon.

At that time Russia was putting pressure on Iran and Irak, and there appeared to be a chance that these countries would be taken into the Soviet Socialistic body of nations, whereupon the flow of the rivers would be diverted from you to the Soviet government or to the people of Iran and Irak.

I tend to ask anybody I am with simple questions, not in rudeness but in the interest of truth, and so I asked if such a condition would come to you as a blow, or a sorrow, and you replied, "Oh no, if it happens, I shall not mind at all. It will be all right, not so much because in any event I am not a poor man, but rather because change of one sort or another is always happening and unavoidable, and there is no reason for me to regret any change that affects my interests. It may even be a good thing—for me, even. I might find time to concern myself more with art—I love great paintings, for instance. And the money involved might be put to better use than I might ever manage, although I have great numbers of skilled people working on the problem of how best to put to work the money that has come to me."

The richest man in the world, or at any rate one of the richest men in the world, speaking to me in this manner, in the Armenian language as well as now and then in English, pleased me, for I have always believed that money ought not to go to a few lucky people in the world as long as there is poverty of any kind among the majority of the people. In short, you were speaking both truthfully and honorably about your good luck in having had the skill of negotiation which had started the making of your great fortune.

Because of my own particular astonishment and anxiety at that time I listened carefully to everything you said. You had no idea how things were with me, although you may have suspected that something was wrong. I know I do when I am in the company of somebody in some kind of trouble. On the one hand, it really didn't matter that you happened to be an Armenian, and on the other, it pleased me deeply that you were, for I needed to see somebody in the family, so to put it. I needed to talk to somebody who might very well be almost a relative, and while I didn't think of you as a father, or somebody who was something like a father, I did feel that there was a real connection between us. We had almost nothing in common, and yet we were instantly related: it happened when you surprised and pleased me by speaking a dialect of Armenian that was no trouble at all for me to understand, and I was delighted to notice that you instantly understood my replies in the dialect of Bitlis.

In a sense, we were both homeless, we had no geographical country of our own as we had once had and as we had ever since *wanted* to have, excepting the very small portion of what was once our country, which had become a part of Soviet Russia in 1921.

By nature, neither of us could make a life there, if in fact we would *want* to, even had we had our own independent nation. You had made your way in Istanbul, in Tehran, in Mosul, in Baghdad, in London, in Paris, in Lisbon, and in many of the other cities of the world. And in a sense I was making my way in much the same manner, starting in California, moving on to New York, and from there to Europe, and to Soviet Armenia in 1935.

We simply did not belong to a geographical and political country that was our own. We lived and worked here and there, but it was known that you were Armenian and that I was Armenian, and at lunch we acknowledged to each other instantly that we were. We spoke our language, and enjoyed doing so.

I was pleased when you said, "The waiters who are paid to pass along things I say in English, French, Portuguese, and other languages shall be very puzzled today. Very few people in the world make a point of learning the Armenian language. In a moment you will observe the headwaiter as he comes to this table to move a fork or pour wine, but actually to listen to our speech, and to wonder what language it is. I speak Turkish and Arabic as well, of course, and he has heard me do so, but he has never heard me speak Armenian. I shall enjoy his bewilderment."

And sure enough, the headwaiter did in fact come to our table and very slowly pour wine, as you said in Armenian, "Let us please keep talking, I want him to hear the Armenian language being spoken."

And simply to comply with your request I said, "But he knows you are Armenian, and he will presume that we are speaking that language, won't he?" And you said, "Well, it is one thing to know we are speaking the Armenian language, but another to know what we are saying. He is paid to pass along information about anything I happen to say that he hears and understands, but what information can he sell this time?"

I said, "He can certainly say an Armenian from America had lunch with you today, but no business of any kind was discussed or transacted —they just ate and drank and spoke Armenian."

And then the waiter was obliged to go back to his watchful place, and you said, "I am glad you have come to Lisbon, but how did you happen to come to this hotel? People reserve rooms a year in advance, and there are very few rooms to be had."

"At the airport I asked the taxi driver to take me to the best hotel in Lisbon," I said. "And the taxi driver said in Portuguese, which I neither speak nor understand but nevertheless understood when he spoke it: 'Well, the best is the Avis, but it is very expensive.' And so I came here. Ribeira, the manager, at first told me there was no room, but after a glance at my passport, he asked me to wait five or ten minutes. And then he said, 'Room 404,' and I must say I like the room very much, especially the tile floor and walls and halls, tile everywhere."

We had lunch the following day, too, and dinner several times, and you began to suspect that something was the matter, for I was hungover every day, and went by taxi every afternoon and again every evening to the casino at Estoril and gambled—winning and losing, and losing, and winning, and drinking all the time, and of course there were pretty women there to be taken somewhere, so that between the gambling, drinking, and women I decided it didn't matter any more; it was all right, I really didn't care that I was dead, homeless, lost, and forty-one years old. I don't know how you found out, but one day at lunch you said, "In all the years I have been in Lisbon, I have never set foot in the casino at Estoril. If it happens that you need money, please let me know." I must say I was dumbfounded, both that you knew I was spending so much time at the casino and that you nevertheless wanted to help me—even with money. But I am the Saroyan I am. I pay my own way. I make mistakes and pay for them. I am not permitted to accept money from others for any purpose or reason. I said, "Thank you very much, I am all right. I have everything." But that very night my luck (if there is in fact such a thing when a man is drowning) was incredible, both when it was good and when it was bad, so that in the end I didn't even have money enough to leave the casino with one of the women there. And almost nothing in Room 404, only a few dollars, and one gold coin worth about fifty dollars, and there was still the hotel bill to pay. The next day at the casino I exchanged the gold coin for enough chips to at least begin to play carefully, but sooner or later I cannot do anything carefully, and I began to bet everything I had in one play, and to win, too. And so it went for the next two or three hours. And then I had enough money both for the hotel and to take a train to Biarritz. I didn't want to fly, I wanted to sit in a train and try to think.

I won't say anything about gambling, except that it has been a part of my life from the beginning. In money I have been a winner many times, but in money I am a heavy loser over the years. In other things, happening at the same time as the gambling, I have been a winner, including writing. During our meetings at lunch and dinner we talked about many things, a hundred times more than the few things I have here remembered, and during our last lunch we touched upon the future, knowing I was taking a train the following morning and we might not meet again for a long time, if ever. Again you said, "If you need anything, anything at all, please tell me." And again I thanked you and said I was just fine.

At Biarritz I gambled again, but the rampage was over and if I won, it was money of the kind that one counts and puts against things one can pay for as one goes along, and if I lost, it was only a small part of what I had, so I knew the worst was over.

I didn't like Biarritz, but I didn't dislike it, either. It was not at all like Lisbon and Estoril, both of which I loved. I may say I instantly liked the Portuguese people, who are mainly poor, but stand and walk with a kind of elegance and pride that I was deeply moved by, children, men, women, and even very old men and women. And they had faces upon which were engraved the lines of deep sorrow, gentility, honor, and courtesy. For instance, when the taxi arrived at the Avis, not knowing the value of the Portuguese money, I made a guess and put quite a variety of coins into the hand of the taxi driver. He protested, or at any rate (having lately come from Rome) I imagined that he had protested and I began to bring out more money, but his protest had been that I had put *too much* money into his hand. He picked out a number of the more valuable coins and handed them back to me. I was deeply moved, for in Rome, no matter how much I gave a taxi driver, he immediately cried that he could not live unless people were more generous, he had a wife and many children, and so on and so forth. And of course I found myself frequently at Machado's for food and drink, and to listen to the men and women who sang fado, which so suited my own condition at the time.

In Biarritz it was another story entirely: the casino was a boring place, the players were cautious and pompous, and there didn't seem to be any women I cared to look at twice.

I went on to Paris and stopped at the Scribe. One of the reasons I did so was that Scribe to me means "to write," and I felt my best chance of getting myself back together again was to write, and I went there because during my first visit to Paris, in 1935, I had gone into the hotel just to have a look at it, and finally in 1945, when I had been in the American Army, the Scribe had been a popular hangout for foreign correspondents, photographers, and writers. Almost every night at the Scribe there had been a poker game in which I took a seat, finally losing three thousand dollars to my friend Robert Capa.

I had an outside room, and it seemed to me to be just right for going to work—a top-floor room with a sloping ceiling, like an attic.

I hoped to do a novel, for I needed money—not immediately, but in the future: a divorce coming up, two small kids to support, and so on and so forth. I didn't wait, I brought out the portable typewriter, I put paper beside it, a sheet of paper upon the rubber roller, and I began to write, simultaneously glad that I was at least *trying* to get back together and *disbelieving* in the possibility of it, even. (What could I write?) The going was rough, but I kept at it, and then after five or six days I stopped, I had had enough.

What I had written was not a novel, but it was a long short story, and it was about you, and it was about me, and the name of it was "The Assyrian."

My mother's kid brother had a son who was living in Paris at that time with his bride, and he had read in the *Herald* that I had come to town and was stopping at the Scribe, so one afternoon he came up to the room to talk. I had known him from the time of his birth, when I had been ten or eleven years old. I was glad to see him again, to hear about his adventures during four years in the Navy.

And then he said, "How come you're traveling alone?"

I told him I had left my wife and kids, and then he said, "Tell me all about it, will you?"

But I couldn't, and then he said, "What do you think of *my* marriage?" I didn't understand, and told him so.

He then said, "I mean, I'm here in Paris with my wife, I'm trying to write, and she's trying to write, too."

I told him that that sounded all right to me.

We went down to the street and walked to where he was living in an attic somewhere on the Left Bank, and I sat and chatted with his wife.

And then the three of us went to dinner nearby, and after dinner he brought a manuscript out of his back pocket, a rather thick manuscript, folded as if for slipping into an envelope and mailing, and he said,

"Will you read this, please, right now, right here, and tell me honestly if I can write, if I ought to go on, or if I ought to forget it?"

Well, it was a kind of short novel, but it wasn't easy to read because he hadn't cleaned the type on his machine, and all of the vowels looked alike. All the same, I read the story very carefully, and although it was badly written, it *was* a story—of confusion, sorrow, ignorance, doubt, and the state of being lost. As I read I tried to think how I would speak to him about what he had written, and he smoked one cigarette after another, compelling me to say, "I read very slowly, please be patient, I don't want to miss any of it," and then at last I came to the last word, and he very nearly leaped at me, saying, "Tell me, tell me the truth, don't tell me any lies."

I don't think I told him any lies when I said, "Well, the writing *does* lack skill, it has no real style, but that's all right, don't worry about that, skill and style will come if you write enough, the important thing is that the story is a very good one, a very important one, but don't write it again, study it, revise it carefully, perhaps salvage it, but at the same time move on to a new work."

"Am I a writer?" he said, and of course the proper answer to that question would be, "If you can ask such a question, you are not a writer," but I didn't say that. I said, "I think you are. I would like to ask you to find it in yourself to believe you are, because if you don't believe that, your writing will show it."

We walked about a mile to a vaudeville theater and went in, and after the show we sat at a sidewalk table and drank whiskey and smoked cigarettes and talked.

Now, the point about my cousin is this: his story had things in it that were also in the story I had just finished writing, "The Assyrian," about yourself and myself, and at the same time about other people, and other things, so that I was impelled to think, "My cousin's in trouble, too, he's in a lot of trouble. What's eating *him*?"

After having lived in Paris with his wife for two years, they returned to the United States, because she was pregnant and she wanted the child to be born in California. One day when I ran into him in Fresno, he said, "I just read your new book, *The Assyrian and Other Stories,* and the best thing in it is the title story, but why did you call Gulbenkian an Assyrian? Why didn't you call the story 'The Armenian'?"

I said, "It comes to the same thing. The Assyrians have always been close to us, and lately almost the same thing."

"I don't understand," he said. "Everything in the story is so true, and then it turns out the writer has made the two main characters Assyrian, and they're not Assyrian, they're Armenian."

But he was saying something else, only I wasn't sure I knew what it was. But I knew he was in trouble, *still* in trouble, his son was two years old, and his wife had just given birth to a daughter, and these things didn't seem to have done anything for him that all of us, Armenians, Assyrians, and everybody else, have always believed would do *everything* for us.

"It's one of your best stories," he said. "Maybe it's the best one you've ever written or ever will write, why call them Assyrians?"

"Well, all right," I said at last. "I guess I goofed. I won't do it again."

He roared with laughter, shouting, "No, no, that's not what I mean, God damn it, I'm not giving you a lecture, I just wish you had called them what they are, that's all." But he didn't say anything about his own writing, and I had heard he had tried operating a vineyard but hadn't liked it and had gotten out of it, and then had taken a kind of unbelievable job for a while in a big department store, selling shoes. But he had given that up, too.

Well, what's he got to do with us? This. He was, he is, he always will be, one of us. Shall I say homeless? No, the hell with that. Lost? No, he was no more lost than anybody else in the world. I really don't know what I should say, except that he was in so much trouble that for ten years he kept going to places for all kinds of treatments— shock and pills and whatever else the confused doctors and psychiatrists happened to believe in at the time—and finally he started trying another way out, and then at last he made it, the hard way: divorced by that time, his kids out of sight for years by that time, the car that he was forever washing and waxing and rubbing until it looked like a little blue jewel fell slowly over a small cliff near Piedra upon an abandoned railroad track in gasoline flames, himself a jumping and running torch. And then lying upon thick grass, asking for water, saying with annoyance to the girl who had seen his car go over the cliff, "What are these people here for?" And then to the highway patrol cop who pushed his way through the people, "Are you going to kill me?" And hours later at the Veterans Hospital, when he was no longer anything anybody ought to look at, he kept saying, "I'm not going to die, am I?" And early in the morning he did, he died, forty-four years old, God have mercy on his soul.

I probably goofed saying we were Assyrians, but not really, because in a sense everybody in the world is an Assyrian, a remnant of a once-mighty race, now all but extinct.

2

Yeghishe Charentz:

We met at your hotel, the Metropole on Red Square, in Moscow, in June of the year 1935, when I was not yet twenty-seven years old, and you were perhaps thirty-seven, a small wiry man with a great hawk nose, dark restless eyes that nevertheless had patience and humor, and a deep warm voice, the greatest poet of Armenia.

Well, now, it's thirty-two years later.

In 1960 I heard that you were imprisoned in Erivan in 1937, two years after our meeting. The cocaine you had for so long lived by had been withdrawn, and for that reason and for surely other reasons not known to other people, or if known not broadcast, you ended your life, supposedly by ramming your head upon the stone wall of your prison cell. This is a kind of suicide that seems impossible to achieve, but that does not mean that it *is* impossible, or that you died in some other manner. I don't know. In Erivan in 1960 I was told you had managed the matter in the manner I have described.

Charentz, my friend, what's the matter with us? Not poets, not writers. What's the matter with Armenians? Or is that whole thing a fantasy of some kind, and Armenians are not Armenians, each of them is only who he is and that's the end of it? Is it possible we have gone through all that history in ignorance, not about ourselves alone, but about everybody, about all nationalities, all peoples, all tribes—ethnic, as everybody keeps saying in America these days, geographical, political, religious, economic, industrial, philosophical, and so on and so forth endlessly—telling ourselves and everybody else, "We are Armenians and don't ever forget it."

And somebody else puts forward his message, "We are Abkhazes, and don't ever forget it." How could I forget it? I didn't know there *was* such a people until I met a writer in Moscow in 1960 who told me he was an Abkhaz. You couldn't have wanted to meet a nicer guy. What's more, he looked like a member of my own family. But that's not all. In Erivan I met some Kurdish writers, and they were all decent, sincere, courteous, and more often than not isolated and lonely. In Turkey I met Turkish writers, and it was the same with them. All decent men, good men, not especially good writers perhaps, but let the critics or time concern itself with that, it's none of my business. In Israel I met Israeli writers, all kinds of decent men writing in the Hebrew language. In America I met writers who were Jews from Russia and Poland, Hungary and Brooklyn, and they were all writing in English, and they were not only decent but also funny, and like members of my own immediate family.

You wrote a poem when you were a very young man, "My Armenia," which Armenians all over the world read and weep, and recite and weep, and teach their kids to read and weep. I have heard it recited two or three dozen times and have scarcely been able not to weep, not so much from having met you, from having stood in your presence, from having spoken with you, and from having noticed your isolation, loneliness, comedy, and despair, but from the simple majesty of your usage of the Armenian language, from the love in your usage of the language of the rocky land, from the anger about our small place being in the middle of the highway of history, and the refusal of all of us to be dislodged.

What did you mean by *your* Armenia? The words are clear enough that you meant *that* place and *those* people, but what did you really mean? Most Armenians, like most other people—Abkhazes, Kurds, Turks, Israelis, American Jews, Italians, Germans, English, Scots, Irish, French, Greeks, Spanish—are terrible bores, crooks, connivers, conspirators, cheaters, liars, opportunists, and all-around sons of bitches. I have them in my own family, and they amaze me. My mouth falls open in confusion and speechlessness, but I still insist on trying at least to understand them even after it is no longer possible to respect them. Every piece of land on the face of the earth is beautiful, not just the land which is Armenia. So what did you mean? Were you actually talking about something else? Is it not possible that your Armenian might have the same meaning to another man? Might he not be anybody, of any family? And what you said of Armenia, might it not have been said, might it not now be said, of any place on earth?

What's the cocaine for, Charentz? What's the ramming of the head on the stone wall for?

Listen, I have not forgotten what you said when my appointment to visit Maxim Gorky with you was canceled because of what I had written at the request of a number of Russians in Moscow, about my impressions of Armenia, of Russia, but more particularly about people, about human life under Communism. They asked for it, and I wrote it. I wrote it free of charge and they even kept the manuscript. I never make carbon copies, so they have the only copy, or they destroyed it, or lost it. I don't have it, and therefore am unable to study the absurdity of my trying with all my heart to write honestly.

You said, "My boy, you must try to be a little more clever than that. Say yes, and spit in their eye."

In other words, "Avoid trouble, keep the truth to yourself. This is not the time or place for it."

And instantly I felt how right you were.

Well, then, Charentz, why didn't *you* say yes, and spit in their eye? The truth is coming out now little by little, and it isn't hurting Communism, or Russia, or Armenia, or people, or anything else—it's *helping*. Why aren't you here to notice this for yourself?

Charentz, my boy, in Moscow you were my father, but now it's different, and I am old, older than I once believed I would ever be, but I am also still young, and as you see still writing, so listen again:

Your little daughter in your room in Moscow in 1935, to whom you were feeding expensive pastry at a time when bread was hard to come by, because you were a great writer and entitled to the best of everything, feeding the beautiful little girl food as wrong for her as cocaine was for you—I saw her in Erivan in 1960, and in her arms was her little son, also named Yeghishe Charentz.

I saw them both, my dear friend and countryman, and they were beautiful.

There you were again in your mother's arms. And there was your Armenia, and your Armenian people.

"My sun-flavored Armenia," you said in your poem, which is impossible to put into English, or for that matter into any other language.

Why didn't *you* say yes?

I'll tell you why, Charentz.

Because you are more than an Armenian, more even than only another member of the human race. You are a poet, so shocked by the treachery of all men seeking to save their skins at any cost that only with the help of cocaine could you stay among them and pretend to be one of them.

God love them, as every poet is obliged to say, not with contempt but with charity. They all did, they are all doing, only what you advised me to do, which I have never done, which you never did.

Kay Boyle

THE WILD HORSES

The title "The Wild Horses," was given this story by *The Saturday Evening Post* at the time that magazine published it. My title had been "Seven Say You Can Hear Corn Grow," which, however grave its drawbacks, at least had the virtue of referring to something in the story. I myself have never been able to find more than one horse in "The Wild Horses." Having said this, I would like to add that I chose this story for the present collection because it is essentially about young people and about the terribly critical problems disturbing and destroying young people who are alive today. Year after college year, I become more deeply involved with young men and young women who seek to follow the various signs and stars and tides and winds which will guide them to all they wish to be. This story is no more than a brief entry in the vast recording of the eager and desperate (and all too often despairing) search the young have undertaken; but it has as well another meaning for me. In its earliest shape and form, I read it aloud to the graduate students in one of my night workshops at San Francisco College. This was something I had never done before. The suggestions the students made were many, and discussion among them about certain points in the story became very heated. If Dan Minos and the lost girl live for a moment, it is because my students helped to give them life.

Kay Boyle

Dan Minos was a boy who collected all kinds of odd information from the newspapers he read—bits and pieces of things that had already taken place, or were still taking place, here and there in the world—such as the report that an octopus in Berlin, Germany, was devouring itself at the rate of a half inch of tentacle per day. One of the aquarium officials had stated that the octopus was suffering from some emotional upset, and if the situation continued, it would certainly be dead by the end of the month. The boy read this and looked at his own gnawed fingernails, and then looked quickly at something else.

Once he read about how scientists are trying to dilute the venom in the stings of jellyfish that drift along the eastern seaboard like fringed umbrellas (as the paper put it), pulsing in and out among the bathers, with limp, curved handles hanging under them, while the tide, or some unseen hand, opens and closes them continuously. This poison, went the story, is stored in cups along the umbrella handles, and it acts in the same way as the stuff South American Indians tip their arrowheads with, causing paralysis, failure of the respiratory organs, and death in the case of small sea animals. Another time there was a half-page report on the remarkable navigating abilities of the green turtle, saying that the U. S. Navy was financing a study of how this large seafarer finds the pin-point island of its birth.

When Dan's mother came back to their Brooklyn apartment at night, she would bring some newspaper or other with her that a customer had left behind on a table in the restaurant where she worked. Some nights it might be the *Herald Tribune* or maybe *The New York Times* that she carried with her handbag into the kitchen; other nights it might be the *Journal-American* or the *Daily News*. But whatever paper it was, Dan would go through the pages of it in his room before he went to sleep, not noticing the name of the paper or the date, but, reading the columns eagerly, as if in search of some final communiqué that would tell him how either beast or man had coped with the predicament of circumstances; as if seeking in the silent doom of animals without knowing precisely what he sought, some indication of what his own vocabulary might one day be.

If you have come to the conclusion that Dan Minos speculated on these things he read because the world of newsprint was the only world he functioned in, you are wrong; for he had as well the daily world of high school, and he had major-league baseball to follow, and television to present to him as reality the myths of power by which America lives. It was more that he carried the news items he read like a kind of shield between himself and others, a shield that was never emblazoned with any likeness of himself, but with that of aquarium official, or of scientist isolating the sting of jellyfish, or naval experimenter tagging green turtles at Ascension Island. Once it was the likeness of a German priest he carried, a priest who had been sitting in the front row of the circus when the lion tamer clutched at his heart and fell to the floor of the enclosed arena. The wild beasts had slunk down from their perches, the newspaper item said, and moved stealthily toward the fallen lion tamer while the spectators watched with bated breath for what was absolutely certain to take place. And then the priest had run forward, pulled open the door of the cage, warded off the lions with a chair, and dragged the stricken man to safety. (Whether or not the lion tamer died of his heart attack, the newspaper did not say.)

It was only the story of the harness-racing horse that went berserk in an airfreighter eight thousand feet above the ocean that Dan couldn't put to any immediate use.

"Sometimes I've thought of being a pilot, a commercial pilot," Dan said to his mother that evening when she came home, "but then I read this thing about the horse in the airplane and maybe I don't feel the same about pilots any more."

"If my opinion was to be asked," his mother said, "I'd say go ahead and be a commercial pilot, and forget about the horse." She worked as a waitress, and she never gave him any real trouble except when he came in so late at night that, for hours, she'd have been walking her high heels sideways up and down the street outside. Sometimes it was three o'clock when he'd come home, and she'd be walking back and forth on the Brooklyn street without so much as a Kleenex to stop her crying, complaining about him to anyone passing by. "He doesn't know five o'clock in the afternoon from midnight," she'd say to anyone at all. "I don't know how he gets along. He can't tell good from bad." Or she'd give a description of him, in case someone had seen him, saying, "He's nearly six foot tall, and his shoulders are broad, and he's nicely built, the way his father was. He'd be good-looking if he went and got his hair cut every now and then."

She got up now from the kitchen table and crossed the room and took a can of beer out of the refrigerator, and she swore under her breath as the new-type, built-in-the-can opener tore a piece out of her nail. "But my opinion isn't worth anything to anybody, living or dead," she said.

Dan looked at her dark orange hair and her face bleached white as a china cup, with the various features painted carefully on it. "There were six horses in the plane," he said, thinking of this thing that had taken place yesterday or maybe the day before, "and this one, this champion, he panicked. He'd been winning harness races everywhere—Australia, New Zealand, all over—the paper said. He was worth seventy-five thousand dollars, and he was kicking and rearing like at a rodeo."

"All they had to do was turn around," the mother said, drinking exquisitely from the can. "Planes can always turn around and go back, the way cars can't. You get yourself on a thruway in a car, and if you're heading west you have to go to Chicago whether you want to go there or not."

"This plane was going to Montreal," Dan said. "They couldn't go back."

"What's so special about Montreal?" the mother asked, her small cherry, upper lip moustached with foam.

"The handler, he said they'd tried cutting the sling around the horse's ribs so they could get him to lie down," the boy said. "There were three of them trying to quiet him, but he threw them off, and his front legs were hanging out over the side of the stall. He was smashing against the cockpit, like trying to get to the controls. The other five horses had started acting up, so that's when the pilot told them what to do."

"I don't want to hear what they did," the mother said, taking another swig of beer.

"You can't change it by not listening," Dan said. "It happened. You can't make things different by just looking the other way."

"If you drank a can of beer every now and then, things would look different to you, whether they were or not," his mother said. "It would relax you. It would do you good."

"The pilot of the airfreighter said the horse had to be destroyed," Dan said, perhaps not even having heard her speak. "That's the word he used," he explained. "But they didn't have a gun."

"They could have pushed the horse out the hatch," the mother said. She got up from her chair and carried the empty beer can across the kitchen to where it had to go. "For a horse worth seventy-five thousand dollars, they could have afforded a parachute," she said, daintily pressing her foot, in a bedroom slipper trimmed with gilded feathers, on the pedal of the garbage pail. When the white lid gaped open, she dropped the beer can inside. "Can't you see that horse parachuting out of the plane, pulling the rip cord and everything?" she said, and she gave a little scream of laughter. Then she took another can of beer from the refrigerator and walked carefully back to the table in her wedge-soled slippers and sat down. "So this time maybe you'll open it for me," she said to him as she had said it on so many other evenings.

Dan took the can in his narrow fingers and twisted the flat metal tongue from its misted top. "I bought another pair of eyelashes today. Better quality," she went on. "Real dark long ones, with a new kind of stickum on them. If I go to the show tomorrow night, maybe you'll help me put them on."

"So when the flight engineer got the word from the pilot about what to do, he grabbed a fire ax," Dan said. He was seeing it exactly as it must have been.

"Stop it!" his mother cried out with sudden ferocity. "I don't have to hear it! I have a hard enough time working myself to death on my feet all day!"

"You have to hear it," Dan said. He looked at her small, bright, trembling mouth and her quivering chin, but he did not seem to see her. "If you don't know whether you're on the side of the horse they killed or on the side of the pilot, there's no sense trying to work out your life. You have to decide that first," he said.

"On the side of the horse or the side of the pilot? You're crazy!" she cried out in fury, her hand too agitated now to lift the can of beer.

And then, two nights later, on Christopher Street, in Greenwich Village, Dan made the acquaintance of the girl. It could have been any month and any Saturday, with no extremes of any kind in the bluish New York air. It had not yet begun to go dark when Dan saw the old man lying across the curb near the corner of Seventh Avenue, lying flat on his thin back with his legs sticking out into the street, so that the passing traffic had to swing around them. His ancient trousers were slashed as if by a knife, and his shoes were split by the bunions and corns he had carried around with him for a half century or more. His small head, economically crowned with a crew cut of the purest white, lay in a semblance of ease and comfort on the sidewalk paving. The same white bristled without hostility along his jaws, and his cheekbones were bright as apples on either side of his short, scarlet nose. Beside him, in a black sweater and slacks, the girl squatted, her face masked by a swinging curtain of long, straight, almost tinsel-colored hair. She was trying to raise the old man by his shoulders, and she was trying to push her bracelets and the black sweater sleeves back on her forearms, to get these encumbrances out of the way. "Repeatedly striking with force between the horse's eyes"—the newspaper line kept going, for no good reason, through Dan's mind as he stooped down—"the flight engineer brought the frenzied pacer to its knees, and the ordeal of terror for man and beast was over."

"He looks as though he's been here a week," the girl said.

"I'll get his shoulders," Dan said, and the girl shifted out of his way, on the heels of her loafers.

The mottled-tweed jacket the man wore was soft and expensive to the touch; but however good it had once been, and whatever tall and elegant stranger had worn it once with grace, frayed wool now hung like feathers from the cuffs and from the jaunty lapels. As Dan drew him up onto the sidewalk, the girl moved on her heels beside them, her knees in the tight black slacks almost touching her chin, her bracelets ringing musically when she placed her palms beneath the old man's head. The three of them might have been quite alone in the crowded street. No one slackened his pace, no one turned to look in their direction, perhaps because of the sad, sharp odor of grieving dreams and rotted teeth that lay in an aura around the sleeping man. Dan knew that aura well. It was there winter and summer, in snow or in rain, in the gutters and alleyways of the city streets he wandered. It lay in stupor under the park benches in the early mornings when drunks sobbed aloud to grass and stone the furious accusations of their pain.

"You'd better get that pint out of his hip pocket," Dan said to the silky lengths of the girl's hair, knowing, too, the exact size and shape the flask would be. "Sometimes when they fall, it cuts them up right through their clothes."

"You're sharp, aren't you, kid?" the girl said. For the first time now she looked up at him, and he saw that her eyes were wide and dark and stormy, and her brows and lashes were smudged like charcoal across her face. "I happen to live in this city," she said. "I happen to live right on this street."

Dan still held the little man under the armpits, and as he looked down at the girl he thought of the things that might be of interest to say. He might tell her that in Japan a drunk is called *otora-san,* which means "Honorable Mr. Tiger," and that there are over a hundred and fifty sobering-up stations over there called "Tiger Boxes." He could even give her the statistics, saying that just last year one hundred and twenty-eight thousand and ninety-seven drunks had been taken by the police to "Tiger Boxes" to sleep it off. But he had got the little old man in a sitting position, with his neat head fallen forward on his breast, and it did not seem the moment to speak.

The girl reached into the little man's back pocket and took out the gold-and-red-lettered bottle that had clung so perilously to his hip. "Two houses up, there's an alley where he can lie down, where the fuzz won't see him," she said. She slipped the half-empty flask into the depths of her black shoulder bag, her bracelets ringing like sleigh bells as she moved.

They were walking now, the little old man held upright between them and Dan thought of the Potawatomi Indians on Michigan's Upper Peninsula drinking for solace, as one newspaper had said. The professor who made the report had been drinking for two years with them, and he said that alcohol now substituted for the tribal customs and rituals that had disappeared from their lives. Alcohol, the professor stated to the press, had given them the illusion that their ancestral rights had restored to them the high status that Potawatomi men had held until the white man had come upon the scene. "This professor said drinking was a way for them of asking for pity," Dan wanted to say to the girl, but he didn't say it. Nor did he tell her that in Brazil the police let sleeping drunks lie as long as they didn't block the sidewalk. With the little man propelled between them, they had come to the alleyway, and there seemed no reason to speak of things that were taking place so far away.

"Get him to the end, back there behind the garbage cans," the girl said, and the pigeons who had been pecking at the paving stones hurried aside to let them pass.

The girl lowered her half of the little man to the ground, and Dan could not see the back of her neck because of the window shade of hair drawn down across her shoulders. But he saw her slender waist and her narrow hips and the long, slim, tapering legs in the black slacks, and he could not look away.

"I'll put my jacket under his head," he said, once the little man lay flat on his back in comfort.

The girl waited until he had folded it under the neat head, and then she drew the old man's right hand free of the elegant frayed sleeve and laid it, palm down, on his breast.

"Give me the other one," she said to Dan. It lay as if cast off, as if forgotten, on the alley stone, and Dan lifted it while she took the whiskey flask out of her bag. Then she bent the old man's will-less arm so that his two hands lay upon his heart, and she closed his fingers around the flask so that he—this ancient, malodorous infant in his asphalt crib —would find it there in solace when he awakened. "Regulations," the girl said. "Orders from the top."

She stood up now, and Dan saw that she was not tall, and that her hair was parted in the middle, and that she had no lipstick on her mouth. "This is my job. I get paid for it," she was saying, and a look of singular shrewdness was in her stormy eyes. "I've got quite an important position. I get paid by the city," she said.

"If they're hiring people, I'd be free to work every night," Dan said. They walked down the alley together, past the last of the pigeons hastening back and forth in the beginning of dusk, their eyes cocked sharply in their smooth, gray-feathered skulls. And every word that he and the girl exchanged seemed as reasonable to him as the story of that other, foreign pigeon who had hopped a hundred and sixty miles across Denmark with its wings bound. The newspaper had said that it crossed two rivers, nobody knew how, to get back to where it came from. "I'd like a job like that," he said.

"You have to be twenty to work for the city," the girl said. "You look too young." As they entered Christopher Street again, the street lights came on in the early evening and she shifted her black bag higher on her shoulder, walking now with that sort of frenzied dedication that takes people across deserts and prairies, not caring about food or drink or sleep, driven toward some final destination that has no geography or name. "You have to know Spanish and French and Puerto Rican, and a lot about history," she said.

"I know about things like that," Dan said, keeping step beside her.

"I read a lot." He thought of the green turtles' knowledge of the currents of the sea and the beaches they came back to, not every year but whenever they could make it, sometimes navigating more than a thousand miles to reach the hot white sands where they had been born. "The green turtles' lives are something like history," he said. "Anyway, Columbus left written records about them. I read about how they come swimming in to these beaches and dig their holes and lay their eggs. Columbus and the other explorers, like Leif Ericson and everyone, they used to eat the eggs."

"Did they eat them fried or boiled?" the girl asked sternly. "These are the things you have to know."

"That wasn't in the paper," Dan said, and his voice was troubled. They had come to the corner of Seventh Avenue, and the girl turned left without any hesitation, and Dan followed where she led. "They have something like a compass inside them—the turtles," he went on saying.

The girl and he were moving through the electric blue and yellow and red of the café lights, and through the spaces of city dark, and his head was turned to watch the side of her face changing as the lights and the diluted darkness changed. "I think I have something like that, too," Dan said. "I bet I could find New York wherever I was. I could come straight back across the country without needing maps or roads or anything like that."

"What country?" the girl asked, with the sharp edge of something different in her voice. "What country are you talking about?"

"Well, this country. The United States. I mean, America," Dan said, as if not quite certain of the name.

"You're pretty weak on geography," the girl said. She was stepping down from the curb, over rotting orange peels, over onion tops that had once been green, and over flattened grapefruit rinds. "We haven't got a country. Wise up, kid. We've got New York," she said.

They crossed this street as they had crossed the others, moving through the altering sections of dark and light. Wherever the girl was taking him was of no importance, and the impatience of the words she spoke was transformed to gentleness by the sight of the curve of her cheekbone, and the delicacy of her temple and brow when she swung back her hair. They were entering warehouse territory now, and high above the traffic hung the letters of a sign not written in neon, but only faintly alight with the dying glow of bulbs set in its frame. VOLUNTEERS OF AMERICA, the sign read, and Dan knew that a queue of men would be standing beneath it, standing night or day, crippled or upright, sober or drunk, and no matter what time of year it was, waiting to pass through the double doors.

"They're waiting for something to eat," Dan said.

The girl did not take the trouble to turn her head and look at him. But she said, "They're waiting for me. I make a report on them every night. I'm the only one in the field the city trusts." And even this Dan did not question, believing as he did that everything she said was true.

Just this side of the slowly moving queue of men she slipped, without warning, into the shadows of a warehouse doorway, and flattened her shoulders and her narrow hips against the wall. "Don't let them see you," she whispered, and Dan stepped in beside her. "If they start running after me, don't move. Stay out of sight. Some of them are still very strong, even though they're old. If they once get hold of you, they squeeze you terribly in their arms," she said, her voice still hushed, "and they push their chins into your face."

"About us not having a country," Dan said. He was standing so close to her in the darkness that he could hear the breath running in and out of her mouth. "Did you read that in the paper, that we only have New York?"

"Oh, the paper!" she said in irritation.

"Sometimes there are interesting things in the paper," he said. "Last night I read about the artichoke war they're having in France."

"Do you speak French?" the girl asked quickly. "Sometimes I need it. Some nights there're Frenchmen standing in line, sailors who jumped their ships and haven't any place to go. I have to get their names. I have to make an official report on them."

Dan waited a moment, thinking of this, and then he said, "Do you report back on these men? Is that the kind of work you do?"

"You're very handsome," the girl said softly, her breath running gently in the darkness, her voice turned tender and low. "I like your hair and the way you talk, and everything, but you don't seem to understand things very well. I'm paid by the city to call them back from where they are. I'm the only one that can do it."

And this might have been the whispered password, the valid signal given that would cause the sentries to lower their guns and let the trusted through, for now the girl stepped out of the doorway, and her bracelets rang as she made a megaphone of her hands. "Oh, Daddy, Daddy, Daddy!" she cried out in almost unbearable and strident despair, and some in the slowly advancing queue turned their heads, as if aroused from sleep, and some did not. "Oh, Pa*pa,* Pa*pa,* Pa*pa!*" she cried as a daughter from a foreign country might have cried out from the sucking undertow before the final music from the drowning played. "Oh, Daddy, Daddy, Daddy, help me!" she cried. "Oh, Popio, Popio, here I am! I'm here!" And now that she had summoned them four times, a wail of anguish rose from the throats of those who had broken from the line and stumbled back through the darkness to where she was.

Brenda, Shirley, Mary, Barbara were the names they called out as they tried to run in other men's cast-off shoes, in the outsized bags of other men's trousers, and could not. Jean, Amy, Pat, Ann, the muffled voices sobbed like foghorns, and the men in whose throats the hoarse names rose fumbled their way past light poles and fire hydrants, felt their way like blind men along the warehouse walls toward the sound and the flesh of all they had mislaid in the desert of their lives.

"We'd better get going," the girl said to Dan. She was standing beside him again in the shelter of the doorway, her breath coming fast. "Just run, just run," she whispered, and she pulled him out onto the sidewalk, her fingers tight around his hand.

They did not stop until they had reached the flight of subway steps, and there she let Dan's hand drop. As she threw back her head to look up at him in the wash of the street light, she shook her bracelets savagely.

"You were faster than any of them," Dan said. Without warning, the vision of the racing horse gone berserk plunged through his thoughts again. As it reared in terror, hammering the cockpit of the airfreighter with its frantic hoofs, Dan touched the girl's silver hair with uncertain fingers, saying, "But you'll have to stop running soon, before you get too tired."

"No, no!" the girl said, whispering it quickly. She stood close to him, looking up at him with her wild, stormy eyes. "You have to get somewhere, don't you?" she said. And then she put her arms in the black sweater sleeves tightly, tightly, around Dan's hips, tightly, as if forever, with her head pressed fiercely against the beating of his heart.

It was only for a minute, and then she was gone, running like crazy across Seventh Avenue. The green light turned to red as Dan got to the curb, and the beams of headlights poured between them, and he waited, understanding now with singular clarity the urgency of the choice to be made between horse and pilot, man and man. He could see the white of the harness pacer's eye, and the features of the airfreighter pilot's face, and he knew what should have been done in that interval when the election of either life or death hung in the balance eight thousand feet above the sea. He could not hear the pilot's voice saying *quiet, quiet* to the stampeding terror. He could not hear it naming the destination to which they were—man and horse—committed, as the course of turtle and pigeon-with-its-wings-bound named it louder and clearer than catastrophe. Instead, the pilot's voice, not only heard but visible, as are the words contained in comic-strip balloons, pronounced *destroy,* thus summoning death as witness to his fear. *We are not turning back. We shall complete this flight as scheduled,* he might have said, but he did not say it; and, standing waiting at the curb, Dan felt the failure of all men in the pilot's failure, and he whispered, "Quiet, now, quiet," to the horse or the girl or the traffic passing by. When the light changed again and the cars halted, he crossed, running, in the direction the girl had fled.

But she was not in the alley off Christopher Street. The little old man was gone, and only his empty flask and the garbage pails were there. At the VOLUNTEERS OF AMERICA, the sign had gone dark, and for once the street was empty. There was no queue of derelict men waiting at the door. It was growing cold, but Dan did not think of this as he walked up one street and down another, searching among the faces that passed in twos or threes through the lights from the cafés, and searching among the solitary others that lingered in the intervals of dark. If he did not find her tonight, still it would not be the end, he kept saying to himself, for he could come back every night, whatever the weather, and on one of the streets, around one of the corners, he would hear her bracelets ringing or see her tinsel hair. If it was not tonight, it would be the night after, or maybe three nights later, or else at the end of the week; and after they had put the drunks to sleep, they would sit down on a curbstone together, and he would say, or try to say, "Don't call the lost men back from where they are. Don't make them remember. Just let them go." He would tell her about things that were taking place in other parts of America, beyond New York; about the Middle West, for instance, where seven university professors had made a tape recording proving that you can hear corn grow.

It was four o'clock in the morning when he got back to Brooklyn. His mother was walking up and down outside, complaining loudly enough about him for any neighbors who were awake to hear.

"Your jacket!" she cried out when she saw him coming up the street. "You had your good jacket on when you left the house! Oh, God, oh, God!" she wept.

Above them, as they went into the apartment house together, the morning star was fading from the sky.

Jesse Stuart

LOVE IN THE SPRING

"Love in the Spring" is out of my world, which is a part of the hill and mountain country of Eastern Kentucky, which is a part of Appalachia, which is an important segment of America, the only one which has a definite culture of its own. My outlying area is larger than England, Scotland, Wales, the South and North Irelands combined—but with a population comparable to the City of London.

If "Love in the Spring" and other episodes of mine woven from the fabric of words and dreams are durable enough to last, it is because my world is real. This world, real and created, is my very own into which trespassers enter but never take over. One has to be born into it, live in it, really to know it.

My world has become much larger than the physical world of W-Hollow into which I was born. A spring world of green, deep, narrow-gauged valleys where wild flowers bloom in profusion, where streams cascade down after a torrential rain; with patches of corn, tobacco growing in summer in the valleys and on upland slopes; with autumns of ripening grain and colored leaves where winds sing; with dark winters, where trees are stripped by cold rains and icy winds, leave hills dark, austere and forlorn.

The four seasons are balanced and diversified in my world—descriptions are always exciting for this writer, a son of this piece of American earth. But the original humanity here is more exciting than the physical aspects, seasonal beauty and winter's depressive moods. Each man and woman is one or more stories, poems and novels—too many for one writer to write. Out of this comes this episode, "Love in the Spring," a short story created by the characters. All I had to do was record and with help select it for you.

W-Hollow is the center of my world, and I still live a mile from where I was born. At the age of six or seven I began writing of this world—and I have never stopped. I have written of my friends and relatives (I have no enemies, for I am one of them), in poems, stories and novels. I have written of three generations where my characters are all akin to each other and to me.

My world has now become so large that my green and dark hills of W-Hollow can no longer hold my friends and relatives. They have gone out to all America and to countries in the world where I haven't been. (I've been in 74.)

"Love in the Spring," I believe, is a light, humorous leaf from the Family Tree.

Jesse Stuart

It was last April when I met Effie. It was over at the Put-Off Ford at the Baptis foot-washing. Effie is a Slab Baptis. She was there having her feet washed. And I can't forget that day in April. It is always work in the spring. Fence to fix. Plowing to do. Cattle to tend to. Seems like everything is to do in the spring on the place. Planting crops is the big job. We don't have no place to go only to church and we don't feel like going there only on Sunday. That is the day we have off and we don't have that day off until we've milked seven cows and slopped the hogs and got in wood and got up water for the day. I can't forget that Sunday in last spring when I met Effie. I just packed in the last load of wood and Mom says to me: "Elster, you are going to fall for a woman sometime so hard that it's going to hurt you. Run around and talk about Mort Anderson being in love and how silly he is. Wait till you fall in love once. The love bug is going to bite you right over the heart."

I went to the baptizing with a clean white starched shirt on and a blue necktie and blue serge pants and black slippers. I looked

about as good in them as I can look. I felt good just to get off
to the foot-washing. I remember that row of elms along Little Sandy
River had just started to leaf out. The rest of the hills just had a
few sycamores and poplars down along the creeks that had leafed
a little. It was a pretty morning. And down by the ford I never
saw as many people in my life gathered at that one place. And
I've seen a lot of baptizings there. Horses hitched to the trees with
ropes and bridle reins. Wagons here and there with washing-tubs of
grub in them and chears where whole families rid miles in them
to the foot-washing. And horses eating yaller corn out'n the wagon
beds of a lot of the wagons. I just walked down where they's singing "Where the Healing Waters Flow." It was soft music and I
wished I was a child of the Lord's then. Good people—the Baptis
is—we live neighbors to them. Ain't no better people to help you
out in a time of sickness or weedy crops in the spring. Come right
in and help you out. Now on this bank and washing feet. I walked
down along the edge of the river where the horseweeds had been
tromped down. I just wanted to look the crowd over. A whole row
up and a whole row down. The row standing up was a-washing the
feet of them on the ground. Just setting there on the ground as
unconcerned and washing feet. Then they would sing another verse
of "Where the Healing Waters Flow."

I looked up in front of me. I couldn't believe my eyes. I saw
the prettiest woman I ever saw in my life. She was prettier than a
speckled pup. Honest I never saw anything like her. Eyes that just
looked at you and melted like yellow butter on hot corn bread—
blue kind of eyes—and a face that was smooth as silk and cheeks
the color of the peeling on a roman beauty apple in September. Her
hair was the color of golden corn silks in August hanging from the
shooting corn. Hair pretty and curly waving in the wind. I never
saw a woman so pretty in my life. Her hands didn't look to me
like no hands that had held to the hoe handle like my mother's
hands and my sisters'. Her hands were pretty and soft. Her teeth
were white as a bubble of foam in the Sandy River. She was an
angel among the sinners trying to come clean. My heart beat faster
when I saw her. Some man had his back to me. He was washing
her foot. He had an old chipped washpan and a big towel and a
bar of home-made soap made from oaktree ashes. He'd put it on
her foot like he was putting axle grease on a wagon hub. Then he
would smear it with his hands and rub. Then he would take the

towel and dry her foot till it would look pink as a wild crab-ap-
ple blossom. I just stood there and looked at her. She looked at
me. He saw her looking and he looked around. Of all the big ugly
devils I ever saw in my life it was this fellow, Jonas Pratt's boy,
Tawa Pratt. Lived down on Little Sandy on that big farm in the
bend by the grove of cedars. When he turned around and saw me
looking he said: "Ain't you a Baptis?"

And I said: "No I ain't no Slab Baptis. I'm a Methodist and I
go to Plum Grove to church."

"Go on about your business then," he said, "and leave us Baptis
alone. This ain't no side show. We are here worshiping the Lord."

I could see he just didn't want me to see the girl. He didn't
like me. I didn't like him. I don't care if he was worshiping the
Lord. And I says to him: "If that's the way you feel about it, all
right. But I want to know the name of the girl here with you and
where she lives."

That burnt him up. His lips just spread out and he showed them
big yaller horse-teeth in front. I just thinks to myself: "What woman
could kiss that awful mouth behind them big horse-teeth?" He looked
at me with them black polecat eyes and his hair was right down over
his eyes. He was a sorry-looking devil.

The girl says to me: "I'm Effie Long. I live up on Duck Puddle." I never said a word. I'd go to Duck Puddle. That's just down
on Little Sandy four miles and up a hollow that comes into Little
Sandy not far from the riffles. I knowed right then and there I'd
see that woman again. I said to myself as I walked back from the
riverbank over through horseweeds: "That's my wife if I can get
her. Pretty as a angel right out of Heaven."

I thought of what Mom told me. I would fall for a skirt. I
did like the looks of that woman. I went home. I remember it like
it was just one hour ago. The daisies looked good to me. First
time flowers ever did look good to me. I pulled off the top of a
sweet William and smelt it. It smelt sweet as sugar.

"The love bug's got me right over the heart," I said to Mom
soon as I got in at the door. "I saw my wife at the foot-washing
—over there among the Baptis today at the Put-Off Ford."

And Mom she says: "Elster, you ain't fell for no Slab Baptis, have
you? No Slab Baptis woman can ever come under this Methodist
roof until she's been converted into the Methodist faith. That bunch

all running around and drinking licker. Won't see no licker in heaven nor no spittoons for that old terbacker."

That's how women are. Right half of the time. When a man is in love, what does he care for spittoons in heaven and bad licker or good licker? What does he care who a Methodist is or a Slab Baptis is? He wants his woman. That's the way I felt. Mom married Pop fifty years ago and she don't know what it is to be young and be in love. I just never said a word.

A week hadn't passed till I heard about church down on Duck Puddle. Slab Baptis holding a pertracted meeting down there. I put on a white starched shirt, a blue necktie and blue serge pants and my black slippers and I went down there. It was a awful walk through the brush and over them ridges. But I followed the fox hunters' paths for more than two miles across through the brush. I walked across the rocks at the riffle and hit the big wagon road up to the church. Meeting was a-going on when I got there. I had to stop and ask four or five times before I found the place. A pretty place after a body gets there but a devil of a time getting to it. I never went inside the house till I peeped in at the winders and looked over the house to see if I could see Effie. I looked and looked. And one time when I looked with my eyes up agin the winderpanes the Slab Baptis preacher said: "A lot of pilferers on the outside of the house tonight. The devil in sheep's clothing is out there. Methodists are snooping around." When I heard this I slipped back in the dark. I'm a Methodist and couldn't be nothing else. Methodist church is good enough for Pa and Mom and Grandpa and Grandma and it's good enough for me. Even if they don't want me, for I bet on chicken fights and play cards once in a while.

I slipped back to the winder. I had looked every place but the amen corner. I looked up there and saw the angel I had seen over at the ford. She was in a mighty good place to be. Me a Methodist and out in the dark. I picked up courage and just walked up and bolted in at the door. I found a empty seat and I saw Effie start looking at me. I started looking at her. And I looked up there and saw old Tawa too. He was in the amen corner. He started showing them teeth soon as he saw me. And I thinks to myself: "Old boy, one of these days I'm going to get me a rock and knock them ugly teeth down your throat. Running around here with a set of horse-teeth in your mouth."

The crowd looked at me. A lot of them had seen me at the

Methodist church. A lot of them had seen me at the foot-washing. They all knowed I was a Methodist. They know the Harkreaders are all Methodist—every last devil of them!

I just waited till church was out. I was going to take Effie home. And I had my mind made up. If that horse-toothed thing of a Tawa should come around me and started anything, it would just be too bad. I was going to use my fists long as they would stand it. I got bad bones in my little fingers. And after my fists I was going to knife it with him and after that if he whopped me I was going to use the balance of power. I carried it right in my pocket. The prettiest little .22 you ever saw in your life—could put five balls between your eyes before you could say "Jack Robinson." I don't go into no strange territory unless I go prepared for the worst. That's the way we got to do here. I don't care if we are Baptis and Methodist.

The preacher was saying: "Men and women, since you got to work in your crops tomorrow and I got to work in mine, we'll call the meeting till tomorrow night at seven. All of you be here and bring your songbooks. Sing 'Almost Persuaded,' folks, and all who wants to come up and jine us just come right on." I never saw so many people fall at the altar.

Church was out and the people already saved—the young people went home and the old people stayed to pray with the people at the "mourner's bench." They was just a-going on something awful. A lot of them were sheep that had left the Methodist flock too. A bunch that wanted to stay in our church and drink licker and play cards and we just wouldn't have it in Plum Grove. Effie come right down the aisle and I said: "Honey, how about seeing you home tonight?" I know my face got red when she said: "All right." Here was old Tawa right behind her with that crazy grin showing that big set of yellow horse-teeth. I thought if he wanted anything he could get it on this night. I didn't speak to him. No use to hide it. He didn't like me and I didn't like him.

I got Effie by the arm, and I held it like a leech. We didn't speak. We just walked out of the house and past a bunch of boys at the door waiting for their girls and the other fellow's girl. People just looked at us. Boys lit up their cigarettes and pipes and the old men started spitting their ambeer. A lot of the women lit up their pipes too—old long-stemmed clay pipes. Something you don't see around our church at Plum Grove among them already saved. If they done it they went home or out behind the brush.

I hadn't got out from under the oak trees by the church house till I had Effie by the hand. And I said: "Honey, I can't eat, drink, work, nor sleep for thinking about you." And I reached down and got her by the little soft hand, and she looked up at me and said: "Ain't it funny? I feel the same way about you. I have felt that way ever since I saw you at the foot-washing. I can't forget you. I keep thinking about you. When I saw you tonight I was thinking about you." I just squeezed her hand a little harder and I said: "Was you, Honey?" Then we went on out the path without speaking.

We went out past the Duck Puddle graveyard. White tombstones gleaming there in the moonlight. Lord, it was a sad thing to think about. I wondered what had become of old Tawa. It was a little dark even if the moon was shining. I didn't care though. I had Effie. I didn't blame him for loving her, but I just didn't want him to get her.

I guess we went through twenty pairs of drawbars before we come to Effie's place. It was a little log house upon the side of the bank, pretty with flowers in the yard. I'd always thought flowers was for the womenfolks. I told Effie I'd never liked flowers till I met her. I told her everything like that. We just went up to her door. I said a lot about the crops. Before I started to leave we was standing out at the well-gum. The moon come down upon her old log house there among all them roses and flowers. It was a mighty pretty place. Effie said: "Guess I'd better get in the house and get to bed. Got to work tomorrow." And I said: "Where, Honey?" "In the terbacker field," she said. And then I said: "W'y, you don't work in no terbacker and stay as white as you are." She said: "That's all you know about it, Elster. I use stocking legs on my arms and a sunbonnet." And I says: "Honey, I love you. I want to marry you." I just pulled her up to me and kissed her there in the moonlight. Soon I left her there and run over the hill like a dog. Tears come into my eyes. Just to think about that. I used to laugh at such stuff. Now, I had six or seven miles to walk home and blue Monday and the plow before me the next day. But seeing Effie was worth a dozen trips like this. When a man is in love he just don't care.

I went to bed that night—must have been morning. It was after the roosters crowed for midnight. Lord, but I was tired. I just could see Effie. I could pull her up to me and kiss her. I could see her eyes, I could see her teeth. I could see her log house in the moonlight. I just couldn't forget it all.

I got up and et my breakfast. Drunk two cups of black coffee and went out to milk the cows. I'd just stop at the barn and look off into the wind. Pa come up to me and he said: "Elster, what in the devil and Tom Walker's got into you here lately—just go around with your head up in the air dreaming. W'y, you even stop when you are shaving your face. If I didn't see you the other day shave half of your face and put the razor up I'm a liar." I never said anything, for it was the truth. I just couldn't help it for thinking about Effie.

I went out to plow corn. I took the mule and the double-shovel plow and went down the path by the barn. I didn't pay any attention but I started the plow on the wrong side of the field and was plowing up the corn. I couldn't think about anything but Effie and how I run away and left that night with my eyes filled with tears. Then I thought: "W'y, I must be crazy to act like this. I'm forgetting everything. I'm not happy as I was. I can't laugh like I did. She didn't say she would marry me. That's it. That's what's the matter." I just couldn't get back to see Effie that week. I had too much to do. Too much corn to plow and seven cows to milk.

Well, I went out to work Tuesday morning. I couldn't work. I thought I'd go up and see Uncle Tid Porter. He lives right on the bank above us. He gives us boys a lot of advice. Uncle Tid was in the woodyard whacking off a few sticks of stovewood. I walked up and I said: "Uncle Tid, I'm in love with a girl. I can't sleep. I can't work. I can't do anything. I'm going crazy."

You ought to have seen Uncle Tid sling his ax agin the ground and laugh. You know Uncle Tid is a pretty good doctor when we can't get one from town. He uses the yarb remedies and he does pretty well. Used to be the only doctor in this section. Now, he gives us advice along with spring tonics of slipper-elm bark, shoemake bark and ginsang and snakeroot. "Well," said Uncle Tid, shaking his long thin chin whiskers stained with a little terbacker juice— his blue-walled eye squinted a little—"when did you meet this girl and where is she from?"

"I met her last month at the Slab Baptis foot-washing at the Put-Off Ford. She's from Duck Puddle. She's a beauty, too, Uncle Tid.

W'y, Uncle Tid, to tell you the truth, I never loved a flower till I met her. Now I notice them. See the wild rose in bloom in the woods. I noticed them this morning. She is with me everywhere I go. I can't sleep. I can't eat."

"It's love in the spring," said Uncle Tid. "Love in the spring is so uncertain I wouldn't trust it. Don't be too sure of yourself and jump in and try to marry. Wait a while. Just go out and watch life in the spring. Go to the house and put the mule in the pasture. Take the afternoon off and go to the pond and watch the frogs. Go find some black snakes in love and watch them. Watch the terrapins and the turtles. Everything is in love now. Listen to the songs of the birds. Listen how they sing to each other. It is time to be in love. All the earth is in love now. And love is so uncertain in the spring."

I just got on the mule and went back home. I took the harness off old Barnie and put it on the stall in the barn and I slapped him with the bridle and made him skiddoo to the pasture. I laid up the drawbars and I made for the pond. There's a lot of bull-grass there and about a foot of water. It's a regular frog and water-snake hangout. Lord, of all the noise! I slipped up by the pond. They all hushed. I never heard another noise only I heard some plump-plumps into the water. I saw that I'd scared them. So I laid down on my belly behind a bunch of bull-grass out of sight from the frogs. It wasn't two minutes before they all started singing. The old frogs didn't do much singing. They'd been in love and out again or they'd just took on some other kind of love after so many springs. The little frogs made up for lost time. They'd get up on a log and jump off and chase each other. I crawled up to the edge of the pond and watched them. If you don't believe young frogs love in the spring when they are doing all of that hollering you just go around the pond and see for yourself.

When I got up to leave there, I heard the birds singing. They sung their love songs to each other and it seemed like I could understand some of the words. But the prettiest thing I saw was two snakes entwined upon the bank in the sun. They were black snakes and very much in love. If it had been before I met Effie I would have picked me up a rock and killed them because Pa says they kill all the birds and young rabbits. I saw two turtles out in the pond on a log. They were bathing in the sun. I just watched them a while. No wonder I fell in love with Effie, pretty a girl as she is. No wonder I dream of her at night and plan a house to take her to. My mother's bread don't taste as good to me as it used to taste. My bed at home don't look as good as it used to look and home and Mom and Pa don't seem the same. I just can't help feeling that way. I dream of the way Effie is going to bake my bread and fix my bed and clean my shirts and patch my pants. Life is great; and to be in love, love is so much greater. It's about one of the greatest things in the world—to be in love till you can cry. I just went to bed thinking about the house here where we live. Just to see Effie with a blue dress and a little white apron on, lifting big white fluffy biscuits out of the pan—white biscuits with brown tops—and good hot gravy made out of milk—and butter yaller as a daisy eye—and steam off my coffee hot as hell and strong as love!

I just thought: "Well, I'm going to tell Pa and Ma that I am leaving them. That I am going to marry that little Slab Baptis and hunt me a home and help to replenish the earth with a good stock. A body can look at her and tell that she is of good stock and I ain't of such bad stock."

I went to the house. I never got the mule back out of the pasture. I was through. Of course I knowed Pa would hate to see me go and it would break Mom's heart when I told her. Mom is a shouting Methodist and it would kill her to see me marry one of them Slab Baptis that drink licker and bet on chicken fights and play cards. But no use to lie to Mom about it. I would go today and fix everything up. Frogs could fall in love and the birds and snakes and terrapins and lizards—well, why didn't I have the same right? And if Pa put his jib in I would tell him to stay out of my love affair and Uncle Tid Porter too. It may be love in the spring but I loved in the spring.

I'll never forget going into the house. Mom was making biscuit dough. I heard Pa telling her I put the mule up and knocked off for half day. Pa didn't like it and he was worried. "Well," I says to Mom, "I got news for you." And Mom says: "What kind of news, Elster?" And I says: "I am going to leave you. Going to get married."

"Who are you going to marry?" says Pa—his neck and face red as a hen's comb in the spring.

"I am going to marry Effie Long—that little girl I met over at the foot-washing last month," I said to Pa.

"One of them Slab Baptis?" said Pa.

"Yes, one of them Slab Baptis," I said.

"And you been raised under a roof like this one," Mom said, "under a Methodist roof—and then go and marry a Slab Baptis—one that has a religion that believes in drinking and playing poker and betting on rooster fights and spitting at cracks in the crib floor. Then you going to marry one of them kind. Remember Elster, if you get burnt you got to set on the blister. You are brought up to believe a certain way it is hard to break away from. Elster, your people have been Methodist for nearly a hunderd years. And you go marry that infidel. Don't you ever let her darken my door. You can come back when you want to but you be sure you keep her away."

The tears come from Mom's eyes. Pa put his hands up over his eyes. And I said to Mom: "Home here ain't the same any more since I met Effie. Life ain't the same, I tell you. My bed ain't the same upstairs and the good biscuits ain't the same."

"Your Ma's bread is the same. Good as it was twenty years ago. Best cook in the country. Then you talk about the bread and even your bed upstairs. Son, I'm not going to stand for anything like that. You can get out of this house if that is the way you feel about things around here. Get your clothes and go." Pa said it and his voice kinda quivered.

I went upstairs and got my clothes. It didn't take me long, for I don't have many. Lord, it burned me up to think about the whole thing. Life with Effie and I'd never come home to see the boys and Mom and Pa. I'd stay away till they would be glad to see me. That's what I'd do. They'd have to send to Duck Puddle to get me.

I put my clothes into the newspaper and got my work clothes —my heavy shoes and my Sunday shoes and my .22 pistol. I thought it might come in handy about a home of my own. I went down through the front room. Mom was crying. "Ain't you going to eat a bite before you leave?" Mom said. And I said: "Nope, I don't believe I care for anything to eat."

"Take a piece of hot corn bread and butter it and eat a piece of smoked ham as you go."

I took it. Lord, but it tasted good. I had et Mom's cooking for eighteen years and it was good. But I went out of the house. I wasn't going to wait till fall. Couldn't plant any ground that late. I was going to marry early enough to rent some ground and get out a late crop and pray for a late fall so they would ripen. I could make it all right.

I walked out into the sunlight. It was a pretty day in May. I never felt so good in all my life. Had my clothes under my arm and going to get my sweet Effie—sweeter than the wild red rose. I went down past the barn and I said farewell to the milk cows, Boss, Fern, Star, Daisy, Little Bitty, Roan and Blacky. I waved my hands to them and to Pete and Barnie in the pasture—mules I'd worked many a day. Barnie nickered at me. He walked along the pasture fence far as he could follow me. I'd been his master ever since he was a colt. Now he would get another master. I said good-by to the trees, the barn, to everything. I was going to a new country.

Sky was pretty above me. The birds never sung any sweeter for me. The wind had music in it. Flowers bloomed so pretty by the road, whole hillsides covered with wild roses. Well, when I got to the riffles the sun was getting pretty low on tother hill. I knowed it would soon be time for them to come from the fields. I'd just get in there a little after suppertime. Lord, but I was hungry. I got across the rocks at the riffle all right, and I went right up the creek till I come to the church house. I was moving fast to get there before dark. A little moon in the sky already.

I crossed the ditch by the church and took out toward the first pair of bars. If I ever go over a road once I never forget it. I soon came to the second pair of bars. The moon was a little bigger in the sky. One of them quarter moons. And a dry moon at that. One edge kinda turned up. Darkness had come at last but here was the house. Light in the front room. So I goes up and looks in. There was old Tawa. He was setting on the couch beside of my Effie. I knocked on the door. Effie come to the door. I said: "How are you, Honey?" and I just closed her in my arms. Old Tawa showed them big horse-teeth with that funny grin—them polecat eyes just a-snapping.

"Come here, Mart Long," Tawa hollered.

"Come where?" said a voice from upstairs. I heard him getting out of the bed. Sounded like the whole loft was coming in. Must 'a' been a big feller. "What are you coming here for?" said Tawa.

"If it's any your business," I said, "I'm coming here to marry Effie. That's why I've come."

"You ain't getting Effie," said Tawa. "She belongs to me. I'm one of her kind. I am a Slab Baptis. I ain't no damned infidental."

I thought I'd take my .22 out and blow his lights out. Calling me a infidental. I never did like the Methodists so much as I did now. And I said: "Who in the hell are you calling a infidental? You polecat you. I'll clean this floor with you." I started to turn Effie loose and get him. Just then in stepped Sourwood Long, Effie's pap.

"There's that infidental Methodist," said Tawa to Sourwood.

And Sourwood said: "W'y, he just looks like the rest of us. Got eyes like us and a mouth and talks. W'y, he's like the rest of us only I don't want Effie marrying you until you repent and get into our church."

"I have come after Effie right now," I said. "Besides, I am a Methodist. I don't intend to repent neither. Why can't she get into the Methodist church? What's wrong with us?"

"And what's wrong with us?" said Sourwood. Black beard covering his face. His arms were big as fence posts and hairy as a brier thicket around a old fence row. He kept them folded upon his big hairy chest. He didn't have many teeth. Had a lot of snags in his mouth—a big nose and he was dark as a wet piece of chestnut bark.

"Nothing ain't wrong with us," said Tawa. "We are the only people right. You know we got a lot of them Methodists in our church when the pertracted meeting was going on. Left your church for ours."

"You got a lot that couldn't stay in our church," I said. I was ready to fight. I still had Effie in my arms. I hadn't turned her loose yet.

"You ain't going to marry Effie. I wouldn't have one of you fellers in my house for dinner let alone in my family to put up with you a lifetime. Get out of here right now."

Another voice from upstairs. "Sourwood, what's going on down there?"

"Malinda, what are you doing up there? A Methodist has come to get Effie. Come on down here."

"Better let a Methodist have her than that thing down there. That Tawa. Get 'em both out of here. Get 'em out quick."

I never saw Effie's mother. I don't know how it was done. It was done so quick. Old Tawa must 'a' come around the back side of the house and upon the front porch and hit me over the head with something. I remember I waked up out in the yard. My clothes were under my head for a piller. The moon was in the sky. It just seemed like I'd been asleep and had slept a little too long. Seemed like a dream. Lights all out of the house just like nothing had ever happened. They's all in bed, I guess. Don't know what ever become of Tawa. Have never seen him from that day to this. I can hardly tell you how I got home. I was about half crazy from that lick. I remember I was so hungry. I remember, too, the chickens were crowing for the daylight. I didn't have my .22 on me. It was gone.

Mom was getting breakfast. I went in and I said: "Mom, your biscuits are all right. Lord, I can eat twenty-two this morning. I'm so hungry."

"Where's your wife?" Mom said.

"I took another notion," I said. "I remembered what you said. I didn't want one of them infidentals after we've been Methodists so long. I thought it over and changed my mind."

"I thought you would," said Mom. "A boy with your raising and get into a mix-up like that. Couldn't bring her home. You'll do better marrying one of your own kind. I'm making you some good strong coffee."

"Good strong coffee is what I need. Strong as love but not love in the spring. Love in the fall. Coffee hot as hell too."

Lord, but Mom did look good to me in that apron. She just looked the best I ever saw her. And her biscuits tasted right too. "Mom, you are the best girl I've ever had," I said and I kinda give Mom a bear hug and she says to this day I cracked a couple of her ribs. She says she can hardly get her breath at times ever since I hugged her.

This has been a day in September. Uncle Tid Porter was down today. He said to me: "Now is the kind of weather to fall in love—now while the chill winds blow and the leaves fly—now while the frost has come. The spring is the time to marry and go on a gay carousal like the frog. Like the snakes and the flowers and all living things. Spring is the time to marry—not the time to fall in love. Love in the spring is fickle as the wind."

"I have often wondered what has become of Tawa," I said to Uncle Tid, "the fellow that loved the girl I loved last spring—w'y, he's the ugliest human being I ever saw for to love as pretty a woman as Effie—"

"She's married him, I guess," said Uncle Tid. "That's the way of a woman. They do the unexpected thing—not knowing which way the wind will blow and if there will be snow or rain tomorrow. That's what a man likes—he likes the unexpected thing."

The wind blows outside. The wind is cool. Pa is out at the barn putting a roof over the fattening hog pen. Mom is still complaining of her ribs: "I never heard of that but once before in my life. A teacher come to this deestrict to teach school and he hugged one of Mort Giggin's girls—it was Ester, I believe—and he broke three of her ribs. I tell you he never got another school in this deestrict."

Jean Stafford

THE LIBERATION

Dear Whit:

I'd be glad enough to have you use one of my stories—"The Liberation," I think, if you want one with a Western setting. But I can't write about my own work, so I doubt if I would qualify.

Yours,
Jean Stafford

(In her Author's Note to The Collected Stories of Jean Stafford, *published in 1969, Miss Stafford did say, however: "I could not wait to quit my tamed-down native grounds . . . but my roots remain in the semi-fictitious town of Adams, Colorado, although the rest of me may abide in the South or the Midwest or New England or New York. Most of the people in my stories are away from home, too, and while they are probably homesick, they won't go back . . .")*

The Editor.

On the day Polly Bay decided to tell her Uncle Francis and his sister, her Aunt Jane, that in a week's time she was leaving their house and was going East to be married and to live in Boston, she walked very slowly home from Nevilles College, where she taught, dreading the startled look in their eyes and the woe and the indignation with which they would take her news. Hating any derangement of the status quo, her uncle, once a judge, was bound to cross-examine her intensively, and Aunt Jane, his perfect complement, would bolster him and baffle her. It was going to be an emotional and argumentative scene; her hands, which now were damp, would presently be dripping. She shivered with apprehension, fearing her aunt's asthma and her uncle's polemic, and she shook with rebellion, knowing how they would succeed in making her feel a traitor to her family, to the town, and to Colorado, and, obscurely, to her country.

Uncle Francis and Aunt Jane, like their dead kinsmen, Polly's father and her grandfather and her great-grandmother, had a vehement family and regional pride, and they counted it virtue in themselves that they had never been east of the Mississippi. They had looked on the departures of Polly's sisters and her cousins as acts of betrayal and even of disobedience. They had been distressed particularly by removals to the East, which were, they felt, iconoclastic and, worse, rude; how, they marveled, could this new generation be so ungrateful to those intrepid early Bays who in the forties had toiled in such peril and with such fortitude across the plains in a covered wagon and who with such perseverance had put down the roots for their traditions in this town that they had virtually made? Uncle Francis and Aunt Jane had done all in their power—through threats and sudden illnesses and cries of "Shame!"—to prevent these desertions, but, nevertheless, one by one, the members of the scapegrace generation had managed to fly, cut off without a penny, scolded to death, and spoken of thereafter as if they were unredeemed, treasonous, and debauched. Polly was the last, and her position, therefore, was the most uncomfortable of all; she and her aunt and uncle were the only Bays left in Adams, and she knew that because she was nearly thirty they had long ago stopped fearing that she, too, might go. As they frequently told her, in their candid way, they felt she had reached "a sensible age" —it was a struggle for them not to use the word "spinster" when they paid her this devious and crushing compliment. She knew perfectly well, because this, too, they spoke of, that they imagined she would still be teaching *Immensee* in German I years after they were dead, and would return each evening to the big, drafty house where they were born, and from which they expected to be carried in coffins ordered for them by Polly from Leonard Harper, the undertaker, whose mealy mouth and shifty eye they often talked about with detestation as they rocked and rocked through their long afternoons.

Polly had been engaged to Robert Fair for five months now and had kept his pretty ring in the desk in her office at college; she had not breathed a word to a soul. If she had spoken out when she came back from the Christmas holidays in her sister's Boston house, her uncle and aunt, with a margin of so much time for their forensic pleas before the college year was over, might have driven her to desperate measures; she might have had to flee, without baggage, in the middle of the night on a bus. Not wanting to begin her new life so haphazardly, she had guarded her secret, and had felt a hypocrite.

But she could not keep silent any longer; she had to tell them and start to pack her bags. She did not know how to present her announcement—whether to disarm them with joy or to stun them with a voice of adamant intention. Resenting the predicament, which so occupied her that her love was brusquely pushed aside, and feeling years younger than she was—an irritable adolescent, nerve-racked by growing pains—she now snatched leaves from the springtime bushes and tore them into shreds. It was late May and the purple lilacs were densely in blossom, offering their virtuous fragrance on the wind; the sun was tender on the yellow willow trees; the mountain range was blue and fair and free of haze. But Polly's senses were not at liberty today to take in these demure delights; she could not respond today at all to the flattering fortune that was to make her a June bride; she could not remember of her fiancé anything beyond his name, and, a little ruefully and a little cynically, she wondered if it was love of him or boredom with freshmen and with her aunt and uncle that had caused her to get engaged to him.

Although she loitered like a school child, she had at last to confront the house behind whose drawn blinds her aunt and uncle awaited her return, innocent of the scare they were presently to get and anticipating the modest academic news she brought each day to serve them with their tea. She was so unwilling that when she came in sight of the house she sat down on a bench at a trolley stop, under the dragging branches of a spruce tree, and opened the book her uncle had asked her to bring from the library. It was *The Heart of Midlothian*. She read with distaste; her uncle's pleasures were different from her own.

Neither the book, though, nor the green needles could hide from her interior eye that house where she had lived for seven years, since her father had died; her mother had been dead for many years and her sisters had long been gone—Fanny to Washington and Mary to Boston —but she had stayed on, quiet and unquestioning. Polly was an undemanding girl and she liked to teach and she had not been inspired to escape; she had had, until now, no reason to go elsewhere although, to be sure, these years had not been exclusively agreeable. For a short time, she had lived happily in an apartment by herself, waking each morning to the charming novelty of being her own mistress. But Uncle Francis and Aunt Jane, both widowed and both bereft of their heartless children, had cajoled her and played tricks upon her will until she had consented to go and live with them. It was not so much because she was weak as it was because they were so extremely strong that she had at last capitulated out of fatigue and had brought her things in a van to unpack them, sighing, in two wallpapered rooms at the top of the stout brown house. This odious house, her grandfather's, was covered with broad, unkempt shingles; it had a turret, and two bow windows within which begonia and heliotrope fed on the powerful mountain sun. Its rooms were huge, but since they were gorged with furniture and with garnishments and clumps and hoards of artifacts of Bays, you had no sense of space in them and, on the contrary, felt cornered and nudged and threatened by hanging lamps with dangerous dependencies and by the dark, bucolic pictures of Polly's forebears that leaned forward from the walls in their insculptured brassy frames.

The house stood at the corner of Oxford Street and Pine, and at the opposite end of the block, at the corner of Pine and Plato (the college had sponsored the brainy place names), there was another one exactly like it. It had been built as a wedding present for Uncle Francis by Polly's grandfather, and here Uncle Francis and his wife, Aunt Lacy, had reared an unnatural daughter and two unnatural sons, who had flown the coop, as he crossly said, the moment they legally could; there was in his tone the implication that if they had gone before they had come of age, he would have haled them back, calling on the police if they offered to resist. Uncle Francis had been born litigious; he had been predestined to arraign and complain, to sue and sentence.

Aunt Jane and Uncle Richard had lived in Grandpa's house, and their two cowed, effeminate sons had likewise vanished when they reached the age of franchise. When both Uncle Richard and Aunt Lacy had been sealed into the Bay plot, Uncle Francis had moved down the street to be with his sister for the sake of economy and company, taking with him his legal library, which, to this day, was still in boxes in the back hall, in spite of the protests of Mildred, their truculent housekeeper. Uncle Francis had then, at little cost, converted his own house into four inconvenient apartments, from which he derived a shockingly high income. A sign over the front door read, "The Bay Arms."

Polly's parents' red brick house, across the street from Uncle Francis's —not built but bought for them, also as a wedding present—had been torn down. And behind the trolley bench on which she sat there was the biggest and oldest family house of all, the original Bay residence, a vast grotesquerie of native stone, and in it, in the beginning of Polly's life, Great-grandmother had imperiously lived, with huge, sharp diamonds on her fichus and her velvet, talking without pause, of red Indians and storms on the plains, because she could remember nothing else. The house was now a historical museum; it was called, not surprisingly, the Bay. Polly never looked at it without immediately remembering the intricate smell of the parlor, which had in it moss, must, belladonna, dry leaves, wet dust, oil of peppermint, and something that bound them all together —a smell of tribal history, perhaps, or the smell of a house where lived a half-cracked and haughty old woman who had come to the end of the line.

In those early days, there had been no other houses in this block, and the Bay children had had no playmates except each other. Four generations sat down to Sunday midday dinner every week at Great-grandmother's enormous table; the Presbyterian grace was half as long as a sermon; the fried rabbit was dry. On Christmas Eve, beneath a towering tree in Grandpa's house, sheepish Uncle Richard, as Santa Claus, handed round the presents while Grandpa sat in a central chair like a king on a throne and stroked his proud goatee. They ate turkey on Thanksgiving with Uncle Francis and Aunt Lacy, shot rockets and pinwheels off on the Fourth of July in Polly's family's back yard. Even now, though one of the houses was gone and another was given over to the display of minerals and wagon wheels, and though pressed-brick bungalows had sprung up all along the block, Polly never entered the street without the feeling that she came into a zone restricted for the use of her blood kin, for there lingered in it some energy, some air, some admonition that this was the territory of Bays and that Bays and ghosts of Bays were, and forever would be, in residence. It was easy for her to vest the wind in the spruce tree with her great-grandmother's voice and to hear it say, "Not a one of you knows the sensation of having a red Indian arrow whiz by your sunbonnet with wind enough to make the ribbons wave." On reflection, she understood the claustrophobia that had sent her sisters and cousins all but screaming out of town; horrified, she felt that her own life had been like a dream of smothering.

She was only pretending to read Walter Scott and the sun was setting and she was growing cold. She could not postpone any longer the discharge of the thunderbolt, and at last she weakly rose and crossed the street, feeling a convulsion of panic grind in her throat like a hard sob. Besides the panic, there was a heavy depression, an ebbing away of self-respect, a regret for the waste of so many years. Generations should not be mingled for daily fare, she thought; they are really contemptuous of one another, and the strong individuals, whether they belong to the older or the younger, impose on the meek their creeds and opinions, and if they are strong enough, brook no dissent. Nothing can more totally subdue the passions than familial piety. Now Polly saw, appalled and miserably ashamed of herself, that she had never once insisted on her own identity in this house. She had dishonestly, supinely (thinking, however, that she was only being polite), allowed her aunt and uncle to believe that she was contented in their house, in sympathy with them, and keenly interested in the minutiae that preoccupied them: their ossifying arteries and their weakening eyes, their dizzy spells and migrant pains, their thrice-daily eucharist of pills and drops, the twinges in their old, uncovered bones. She had never disagreed with them, so how could they know that she did not, as they did, hate the weather? They assumed that she was as scandalized as they by Uncle Francis's tenants' dogs and children. They had no way of knowing that she was bored nearly to frenzy by their vicious quarrels with Mildred over the way she cooked their food.

In the tenebrous hall lined with closed doors, she took off her gloves and coat, and, squinting through the shadows, saw in the mirror that her wretchedness was plain in her drooping lips and her frowning forehead; certainly there was no sign at all upon her face that she was in love. She fixed her mouth into a bogus smile of courage, she straightened out her brow; with the faintest heart in the world she entered the dark front parlor, where the windows were always closed and the shades drawn nearly to the sill. A coal fire on this mild May day burned hot and blue in the grate.

They sat opposite each other at a round, splayfooted table under a dim lamp with a beaded fringe. On the table, amid the tea things, there was a little mahogany casket containing the props with which, each day, they documented their reminiscences of murders, fires, marriages, bankruptcies, and of the triumphs and the rewards of the departed Bays. It was open, showing cracked photographs, letters sallow-inked with age, flaccid and furry newspaper clippings, souvenir spoons flecked with venomous green, little white boxes holding petrified morsels of wedding cake. As Polly came into the room, Aunt Jane reached out her hand and, as if she were pulling a chance from a hat, she picked a newspaper clipping out of the box and said, "I don't think you have ever told Polly the story of the time you were in that train accident in the Royal Gorge. It's such a yarn."

Her uncle heard Polly then and chivalrously half rose from his chair; tall and white-haired, he was distinguished, in a dour way, and dapper in his stiff collar and his waistcoat piped with white. He said, "At last our strayed lamb is back in the fold." The figure made Polly shiver.

"How late you are!" cried Aunt Jane, thrilled at this small deviation from routine. "A department meeting?" If there had been a department meeting, the wreck in the Royal Gorge might be saved for another day.

But they did not wait for her answer. They were impelled, egocentrically and at length, to tell their own news, to explain why it was that they had not waited for her but had begun their tea. Uncle Francis had been hungry, not having felt quite himself earlier in the day and having, therefore, eaten next to nothing at lunch, although the soufflé that Mildred had made was far more edible than customary. He had several new symptoms and was going to the doctor tomorrow; he spoke with infinite peace of mind. Painstakingly then, between themselves, they discussed the advisability of Aunt Jane's making an appointment at the beauty parlor for the same hour Uncle Francis was seeing Dr. Wilder; they could in this way share a taxi. And what was the name of that fellow who drove the Town Taxi whom they both found so cautious and well-mannered? Bradley, was it? They might have him drive them up a little way into the mountains for the view; but, no, Francis might have got a bad report and Jane might be tired after her baking under the dryer. It would be better if they came straight home. Sometimes they went on in this way for hours.

Polly poured herself a cup of tea, and Aunt Jane said, as she had said probably three thousand times in the past seven years, "You may say what you like, there is simply nothing to take the place of a cup of tea at the end of the day."

Uncle Francis reached across the table and took the newspaper clipping from under his sister's hand. He adjusted his glasses and glanced at the headlines, smiling. "There was a great deal of comedy in that tragedy," he said.

"Tell Polly about it," said Aunt Jane. Polly knew the details of this story by heart—the number of the locomotive and the name of the engineer and the passengers' injuries, particularly her uncle's, which, though minor, had been multitudinous.

Amazing herself, Polly said, "Don't!" And, amazed by her, they stared.

"Why, Polly, what an odd thing to say!" exclaimed Aunt Jane. "My dear, is something wrong?"

She decided to take them aback without preamble—it was the only way—and so she said, "Nothing's wrong. Everything's right at last. I am going to be married ten days from today to a teacher at Harvard and I am going to Boston to live."

They behaved like people on a stage; Aunt Jane put her teacup down, rattling her spoon, and began to wring her hands; Uncle Francis, holding his butter knife as it were a gavel, glared.

"What are you talking about, darling?" he cried. "Married? What do you mean?"

Aunt Jane wheezed, signaling her useful asthma, which, however, did not oblige her. "Boston!" she gasped. "What ever for?"

Polly returned her uncle's magisterial look, but she did so obliquely, and she spoke to her cuffs when she said, "I mean 'married,' the way you were married to Aunt Lacy and the way Aunt Jane was married to Uncle Richard. I am in love with a man named Robert Fair and *he* is with *me* and we're going to be married."

"How lovely," said Aunt Jane, who, sight unseen, hated Robert Fair.

"Lovely perhaps," said Uncle Francis the magistrate, "and perhaps not. You might, if you please, do us the honor of enlightening us as to the qualifications of Mr. Fair to marry and export you. To the best of my knowledge, I have never heard of him."

"I'm quite sure we don't know him," said Aunt Jane; she coughed experimentally, but her asthma was still in hiding.

"No, you don't know him," Polly said. "He has never been in the West." She wished she could serenely drink her tea while she talked, but she did not trust her hand. Fixing her eyes on the maidenhair fern in a brass jardiniere on the floor, she told them how she had first met Robert Fair at her sister Mary's cottage in Edgartown the summer before.

"You never told us," said Uncle Francis reprovingly. "I thought you said the summer had been a mistake. Too expensive. Too hot. I thought you agreed with Jane and me that summer in the East was hard on the constitution." (She had; out of habit she had let them deprecate the East, which she had loved at first sight, had allowed them to tell her that she had had a poor time when, in truth, she had never been so happy.)

Shocked by her duplicity, Aunt Jane said, "We ought to have suspected something when you went back to Boston for Christmas with Mary instead of resting here beside your own hearth fire."

Ignoring this sanctimonious accusation, Polly continued, and told them as much of Robert Fair as she thought they deserved to know, eliding some of his history—for there was a divorce in it—but as she spoke, she could not conjure his voice or his face, and he remained as hypothetical to her as to them, a circumstance that alarmed her and one that her astute uncle sensed.

"You don't seem head over heels about this Boston fellow," he said.

"I'm nearly thirty," replied his niece. "I'm not sixteen. Wouldn't it be unbecoming at my age if I *were* lovesick?" She was by no means convinced of her argument, for her uncle had that effect on her; he could make her doubt anything—the testimony of her own eyes, the judgments of her own intellect. Again, and in vain, she called on Robert Fair to materialize in this room that was so hostile to him and, through his affection, bring a persuasive color to her cheeks. She did not question the power of love nor did she question, specifically, the steadfastness of her own love, but she did observe, with some dismay, that, far from conquering all, love lazily sidestepped practical problems; it was no help in this interview; it seemed not to cease but to be temporarily at a standstill.

Her uncle said, "Sixteen, thirty, sixty, it makes no difference. It's true I wouldn't like it if you were wearing your heart on your sleeve, but, my Lord, dear, I don't see the semblance of a light in your eye. You look quite sad. Doesn't Polly strike you as looking downright blue, Jane? If Mr. Fair makes you so doleful, it seems to me you're better off with us."

"It's not a laughing matter," snapped Aunt Jane, for Uncle Francis, maddeningly, had chuckled. It was a way he had in disputation; it was intended to enrage and thereby rattle his adversary. He kept his smile, but for a moment he held his tongue while his sister tried a different tack. "What I don't see is why you have to go to Boston, Polly," she said. "Couldn't he teach Italian at Nevilles just as well as at Harvard?"

Their chauvinism was really staggering. When Roddy, Uncle Francis's son went off to take a glittering job in Brazil, Aunt Jane and his father had nearly reduced this stalwart boy to kicks and tears by reiterating that if there had been anything of worth or virtue in South America, the grandparent Bays would have settled there instead of in the Rocky Mountains.

"I don't think Robert would like it here," said Polly.

"What wouldn't he like about it?" Aunt Jane bridled. "I thought our college had a distinguished reputation. Your great-grandfather, one of the leading founders of it, was a man of culture, and unless I am sadly misinformed, his humanistic spirit is still felt on the campus. Did you know that his critical study of Isocrates is *highly* esteemed among classical scholars?"

"I mean I don't think he would like the West," said Polly, rash in her frustration.

She could have bitten her tongue out for the indiscretion, because her jingoistic uncle reddened instantly and menacingly, and he banged on the table and shouted, "How does he know he doesn't like the West? You've just told us he's never been farther west than Ohio. How does he dare to presume to damn what he doesn't know?"

"I didn't say he damned the West. I didn't even say he didn't like it. I said *I* thought he wouldn't."

"Then *you* are presuming," he scolded. "I am impatient with Easterners who look down their noses at the West and call us crude and barbaric. But Westerners who renounce and denounce and derogate their native ground are worse."

"Far worse," agreed Aunt Jane. "What can have come over you to turn the man you intend to marry against the land of your forebears?"

Polly had heard it all before. She wanted to clutch her head in her hands and groan with helplessness; even more, she wished that this were the middle of next week.

"We three are the last left of the Bays in Adams," pursued Aunt Jane, insinuating a quaver into her firm, stern voice. "And Francis and I will not last long. You'll only be burdened and bored with us a little while longer."

"We have meant to reward you liberally for your loyalty," said her uncle. "The houses will be yours when we join our ancestors."

In the dark parlor, they leaned toward her over their cups of cold tea, so tireless in their fusillade that she had no chance to deny them or to defend herself. Was there to be, they mourned, at last not one Bay left to lend his name and presence to municipal celebrations, to the laying of cornerstones and the opening of fairs, Polly thought they were probably already fretting over who would see that the grass between the family graves was mown.

Panicked, she tried to recall how other members of her family had extricated themselves from these webs of casuistry. Now she wished that she had more fully explained her circumstances to Robert Fair and had told him to come and fetch her away, for he, uninvolved, could afford to pay the ransom more easily than she. But she had wanted to spare him such a scene as this; they would not have been any more reticent with him; they would have, with this same arrogance—and this under-handedness—used their advanced age and family honor to twist the argument away from its premise.

Darkness had shrunk the room to the small circle where they sat in the thin light of the lamp; it seemed to her that their reproaches and their jeremiads took hours before they recommenced the bargaining Aunt Jane had started.

Reasonably, in a judicious voice, Uncle Francis said, "There is no reason at all, if Mr. Fair's attainments are as you describe, that he can't be got an appointment to our Romance Language Department. What is the good of my being a trustee if I can't render such a service once in a way?"

As if this were a perfectly wonderful and perfectly surprising solution, Aunt Jane enthusiastically cried, "But of course you can! That would settle everything. Polly can eat her cake and have it, too. Wouldn't you give them your house, Francis?"

"I'd propose an even better arrangement. Alone here, Jane, you and I would rattle. Perhaps we would move into one of my apartments and the Robert Fairs could have this house. Would that suit you?"

"It would, indeed it would," said Aunt Jane. "I have been noticing the drafts here more and more."

"I don't ask you to agree today, Polly," said Uncle Francis. "But think it over. Write your boy a letter tonight and tell him what your aunt and I are willing to do for him. The gift of a house, as big a house as this, is not to be scoffed at by young people just starting out."

Her "boy," Robert, had a tall son who in the autumn would enter Harvard. "Robert has a house," said Polly, and she thought of its dark-green front door with the brilliant brass trimmings; on Brimmer Street, at the foot of Beacon Hill, its garden faced the Charles. Nothing made her feel more safe and more mature than the image of that old and handsome house.

"He could sell it," said her indomitable aunt.

"He could rent it," said her practical uncle. "That would give you additional revenue."

The air was close; it was like the dead of night in a sealed room and Polly wanted to cry for help. She had not hated the West till now, she had not hated her relatives till now; indeed, till now she had had no experience of hate at all. Surprising as the emotion was—for it came swiftly and authoritatively—it nevertheless cleared her mind and, outraged, she got up and flicked the master switch to light up the chandelier. Her aunt and uncle blinked. She did not sit down again but stood in the doorway to deliver her valediction. "I don't want Robert to come here because I don't want to live here any longer. I want to live my own life."

"Being married is hardly living one's own life," said Aunt Jane.

At the end of her tether now, Polly all but screamed at them, "We *won't* live here and that's that! You talk of my presuming, but how can *you* presume to boss not only me but a man you've never even seen? I don't want your houses! I hate these houses! It's true—I hate, I despise, I abominate the West!"

So new to the articulation of anger, she did it badly and, ashamed to death, began to cry. Though they were hurt, they were forgiving, and both of them rose and came across the room, and Aunt Jane, taking her in a spidery embrace, said, "There. You go upstairs and have a bath and rest and we'll discuss it later. Couldn't we have some sherry, Francis? It seems to me that all our nerves are unstrung."

Polly's breath toiled against her sobs, but all the same she took her life in her hands and she said, "There's nothing further to discuss. I am leaving. I am not coming back."

Now, for the first time, the old brother and sister exchanged a look of real anxiety; they seemed, at last, to take her seriously; each waited for the other to speak. It was Aunt Jane who hit upon the new gambit. "I mean, dear, that we will discuss the wedding. You have given us very short notice but I daresay we can manage."

"There is to be no wedding," said Polly. "We are just going to be married at Mary's house. Fanny is coming up to Boston."

"Fanny has known all along?" Aunt Jane was insulted. "And all this time you've lived under our roof and sat at our table and never told *us* but told your sisters, who abandoned you?"

"Abandoned me? For God's sake, Aunt Jane, they had their lives to lead!"

"Don't use that sort of language in this house, young lady," said Uncle Francis.

"I apologize. I'm sorry. I am just so sick and tired of—"

"Of course you're sick and tired," said the adroit old woman. "You've had a heavy schedule this semester. No wonder you're all nerves and tears."

"Oh, it isn't that! Oh, leave me alone."

And, unable to withstand a fresh onslaught of tears, she rushed to the door. When she had closed it upon them, she heard her aunt say, "I simply can't believe it. There must be some way out. Why, Francis, we would be left altogether *alone,*" and there was real terror in her voice.

Polly locked the door to her bedroom and dried her eyes and bathed their lids with witch hazel, the odor of which made her think of her Aunt Lacy, who, poor simple creature, had had to die to escape this family. Polly remembered that every autumn Aunt Lacy had petitioned Uncle Francis to let her take her children home for a visit to her native Vermont, but she had never been allowed to go. Grandpa, roaring, thumping his stick, Uncle Francis bombarding her with rhetoric and using the word "duty" repeatedly, Polly's father scathing her with sarcasm, Aunt Jane slyly confusing her with red herrings had kept her an exhausted prisoner. Her children, as a result, had scorned their passive mother and had wounded her, and once they finally escaped, they had not come back—not for so much as a visit. Aunt Lacy had died not having seen any of her grandchildren; in the last years of her life she did nothing but cry. Polly's heart ached for the plight of that gentle, frightened woman. How lucky *she* was that the means of escape had come to her before it was too late! In her sister's Boston drawing room, in a snowy twilight, Robert Fair's proposal of marriage had seemed to release in her an inexhaustible wellspring of life; until that moment she had not known that she was dying, that she was being killed—by inches, but surely killed—by her aunt and uncle and by the green yearlings in her German classes and by the dogmatic monotony of the town's provincialism. She shuddered to think of her narrow escape from wasting away in these arid foothills, never knowing the cause or the name of her disease.

Quiet, herself again, Polly sat beside the window and looked out at the early stars and the crescent moon. Now that she had finally taken her stand, she was invulnerable, even though she knew that the brown sherry was being put ceremoniously on a tray, together with ancestral Waterford glasses, and though she knew that her aunt and uncle had not given up—that they had, on the contrary, just begun. And though she knew that for the last seven days of her life in this house she would be bludgeoned with the most splenetic and most defacing of emotions, she knew that the worst was over; she knew that she would survive, as her sisters and her cousins had survived. In the end, her aunt and uncle only *seemed* to survive; dead on their feet for most of their lives, they had no personal history; their genesis had not been individual—it had only been a part of a dull and factual plan. And they had been too busy honoring their family to love it, too busy defending the West even to look at it. For all their pride in their surroundings, they had never contemplated them at all but had sat with the shades drawn, huddled under the steel engravings. They and her father had lived their whole lives on the laurels of their grandparents; their goal had already been reached long before their birth.

The mountains had never looked so superb to her. She imagined a time, after Uncle Francis and Aunt Jane were dead, when the young Bays and their wives and husbands might come back, free at last to admire the landscape, free to go swiftly through the town in the foothills without so much as a glance at the family memorials and to gain the high passes and the peaks and the glaciers. They would breathe in the thin, lovely air of summits, and in their mouths there would not be a trace of the dust of the prairies where, as on a treadmill, Great-grandfather Bay's oxen plodded on and on into eternity.

The next days were for Polly at once harrowing and delightful. She suffered at the twilight hour (the brown sherry had become a daily custom, and she wondered if her aunt and uncle naïvely considered getting her drunk and, in this condition, persuading her to sign an unconditional indenture) and all through dinner as, by turns self-pitying and contentious, they sought to make her change her mind. Or, as they put it, "come to her senses." At no time did they accept the fact that she was going. They wrangled over summer plans in which she was included; they plotted anniversary speeches in the Bay museum; one afternoon Aunt Jane even started making a list of miners' families among whom Polly was to distribute Christmas baskets.

But when they were out of her sight and their nagging voices were out of her hearing, they were out of her mind, and in it instead, was Robert Fair, in his rightful place. She graded examination papers tolerantly, through a haze; she packed her new clothes into her new suitcases and emptied her writing desk completely. On these starry, handsome nights, her dreams were charming, although, to be sure, she sometimes woke from them to hear the shuffle of carpet slippers on the floor below her as her insomniac aunt or uncle paced. But before sadness or rue could overtake her, she burrowed into the memory of her late dream.

The strain of her euphoria and her aunt's and uncle's antipodean gloom began at last to make her edgy, and she commenced to mark the days off on her calendar and even to reckon the hours. On the day she met her classes for the last time and told her colleagues goodbye and quit the campus forever, she did not stop on the first floor of the house but went directly to her room, only pausing at the parlor door to tell Aunt Jane and Uncle Francis that she had a letter to get off. Fraudulently humble, sighing, they begged her to join them later on for sherry. "The days are growing longer," said Aunt Jane plaintively, "but they are growing fewer."

Polly had no letter to write. She had a letter from Robert Fair to read, and although she knew it by heart already, she read it again several times. He shared her impatience; his students bored him, too; he said he had tried to envision her uncle's house, so that he could imagine her in a specific place, but he had not been able to succeed, even with the help of her sister. He wrote, "The house your malicious sister Mary describes could not exist. Does Aunt Jane *really* read Ouida?"

She laughed aloud. She felt light and purged, as if she had finished a fever. She went to her dressing table and began to brush her hair and to gaze, comforted, upon her young and loving face. She was so lost in her relief that she was pretty, and that she was going to be married and was going away, that she heard neither the telephone nor

Mildred's feet upon the stairs, and the housekeeper was in the room before Polly had turned from her pool.

"It's your sister calling you from Boston," said Mildred with ice-cold contempt; she mirrored her employers. "I heard those operators back East giving themselves *some* airs with their la-di-da ways of talking."

Clumsy with surprise and confusion (Mary's calls to her were rare and never frivolous), and sorry that exigency and not calm plan took her downstairs again, she reeled into that smothering front hall where hat trees and cane stands stood like people. The door to the parlor was closed, but she knew that behind it Aunt Jane and Uncle Francis were listening.

When Mary's far-off, mourning voice broke to Polly the awful, the impossible, the unbelievable news that Robert Fair had died that morning of the heart disease from which he had intermittently suffered for some years, Polly, wordless and dry-eyed, contracted into a nonsensical, contorted position and gripped the telephone as if this alone could keep her from drowning in the savage flood that had come from no-where.

"Are you there, Polly? Can you hear me, darling?" Mary's anxious voice came louder and faster. "Do you want me to come out to you? Or can you come on here now?"

"I can't come now," said Polly. "There's nothing you can do for me." There had always been rapport between these sisters, and it had been deeper in the months since Robert Fair had appeared upon the scene to rescue and reward the younger woman. But it was shattered; the bearer of ill tidings is seldom thanked. "How can you help me?" Polly demanded, shocked and furious. "You can't bring him back to life."

"I can help bring you back to life," her sister said. "You must get out of *there,* Polly. It's more important now than ever."

"Do you think that was why I was going to marry him? Just to escape this house and this town?"

"No, no! Control yourself! We'd better not try to talk any more now—you call me when you can."

The parlor door opened, revealing Uncle Francis with a glass of sherry in his hand.

"Wait, Mary! Don't hang up!" Polly cried. There was a facetious air about her uncle; there was something smug. "I'll get the sleeper from Denver tonight," she said.

When she hung up, her uncle opened the door wider to welcome her to bad brown sherry; they had not turned on the lights, and Aunt Jane, in the twilight, sat in her accustomed place.

"Poor angel," said Uncle Francis.

"I am so sorry, so very sorry," said Aunt Jane.

When Polly said nothing but simply stared at their impassive faces, Uncle Francis said, "I think I'd better call up Wilder. You ought to have a sedative and go straight to bed."

"I'm going straight to Boston," said Polly.

"But why?" said Aunt Jane.

"Because he's there. I love him and he's there."

They tried to detain her; they tried to force the sherry down her throat; they told her she must be calm and they asked her to remember that at times like this one needed the love and the support of one's blood kin.

"I am going straight to Boston," she repeated, and turned and went quickly up the stairs. They stood at the bottom, calling to her: "You haven't settled your affairs. What about the bank?" "Polly, get hold of yourself! It's terrible, I'm heartbroken for you, but it's not the end of the world."

She packed nothing: she wanted nothing here—not even the new clothes she had bought in which to be a bride. She put on a coat and a hat and gloves and a scarf and put all the money she had in her purse and went downstairs again. Stricken but diehard, they were beside the front door.

"Don't go!" implored Aunt Jane.

"You need us now more than ever!" her uncle cried.

"And we need you. Does that make no impression on you, Polly? Is your heart that cold?"

She paid no attention to them at all and pushed them aside and left the house. She ran to the station to get the last train to Denver, and once she had boarded it, she allowed her grief to overwhelm her. She felt chewed and mauled by the niggling hypochondriacs she had left behind, who had fussily tried to appropriate even her own tragedy. She felt sullied by their disrespect and greed.

How lonely I have been, she thought. And then, not fully knowing what she meant by it but believing in it faithfully, she said half aloud, "I am not lonely now."

VII

Figures in the Round

Theodore H. White

PROLOGUE to
CAESAR AT THE RUBICON

No one knows what his best work is. But there are moments when one enjoys writing. Generally, for the past thirty years, I have worked at describing the events of our times, at home and abroad, their wars and politics. In 1966 I indulged myself with a year of flight from the twentieth century to explore the Rome of Caesar, his times and its kinship with our own. From that came a play about politics called *Caesar at the Rubicon*. The introduction to that play came rather quickly and with much pleasure to me.

Theodore H. White

Who he was, or what he was, or what manner of man he was—
no one knows for sure. Every age has carved its own Caesar, dressing
him with its own passions and fears, tonguing him with the wit and
wisdom of its passing moment. So we know of Caesar the tyrant and
Caesar the merciful; of Caesar the killer and Caesar the lawmaker; of
Caesar the wise and Caesar the lover; and of Caesar the Deified.

Two episodes of ripping violence have gripped the imagination of
all men who have tried to recall Caesar—the Act at the Rubicon and
the Act of Assassination. But old history makes both these acts too
simple. Caesar was so big, he has been seen generally only in outline.
Before his time the world of Rome was set in one direction, and
because of him that world turned about. No other single individual—
except the Christ—caused so great a change in Western man's thinking. Legends sprang from him; he had a power, a force, a genius that
crowded everything but his personality out of the thinking of Rome
in his own time and for centuries thereafter.

Yet, beneath all legends was a man: born Gaius Julius Caesar, probably in 102 B.C. And I, in this study, have been trying to explore not
what history says he did, but how he may have felt while doing it.
Of this complicated man we know much that we have for millennia
either misunderstood or been trying to forget; but today, as history
swings through an echoing cycle, he appears once again fresh—perhaps
more a man of our time than of any other time but his own.

Barbarian, primitive, savage though Caesar's Rome may have been, men tormented themselves and each other in that city and time with the same problems of freedom, of law, of order, of discipline, of empire that torment us today. Mobs rioted in Rome's streets in a tempo of ferocity that surpassed by far the civil violence of our time. Wars on distant frontiers lured the legions on and on to adventures no stay-at-home could comprehend. Romans indulged themselves, in Caesar's time, with the same carnal pleasures of flesh, of drink, of revel that lately have become our way of life, too.

A pagan cruelty totally alien to us was, however, commonplace. Death and killing in public places was a matter of games and entertainment; murder was political tactic; and extermination was foreign policy. The great historic challenge to man's casual inhumanity was not to come for another two generations when the Christ spoke for mercy; but already, in Caesar, one finds a first serious questioning of the limits of force; for he, who understood killing better than any other man of his time, came to recognize that force and cruelty alone could not create the order which he sought; thus, in him one sees the first tentative exploration of mercy as a policy of government. If, in the end, in his barbarian world, he reached the limit of reason and stepped across the borderline to madness—this, too, is not unfamiliar in our age of paranoiac dictators.

The problem in writing of Caesar is that he was, at once, so naturally barbarian—and so thoroughly, relevantly, modern, too. The facts can be read either way.

There are, to be sure, fragments of fact on which all scholars, romantics, mythmakers do agree:

The man himself, of course: tall, gaunt, thin of lip, long of neck (with ugly, wrinkled neck folds), pale of skin, black of eyes, balding. Handsome he must have been as a youth. But we can see him only in profile in the coins he approved as self-portraits at the end of his days as Dictator—the unflattering image of an ugly, yet attractive, rogue, the faintest trace of some sardonic smile on his lips.

Much more vivid is the outline he draws of himself in his writing: the silhouette of the horseman in scarlet cape, the cape flaring back against the wind, the horse always galloping. Through the writing surges always a furious impatience—a slow, calculated waiting, and then the controlled speed of his action when it bursts. What remains to us of his writings is almost entirely of war, and thus the pace of his action is exaggerated. He chooses clear targets, then instantly strikes, his men moving at forced march by day and night, faster than any other troops of antiquity, advancing at the dog-trot, opening combat always on the dash.

Yet over and over again, in these writings, these stark accountings of action, his rhythm breaks, and there come those characteristic Caesarian passages of curiosity and wonderment. He crosses the Channel to scourge the savage Britons—and diverts himself and the reader with reflection on the mystery of the Druids; again, diverts attention to a mechanical examination of how men build coracles of skin; suspends his bloody story of the Gallic conquest to entertain himself and Romans with an anthropologist's study of the customs of the Gauls; halts the flow of action to invite the reader with a description of the flow of a river; and, again and again, pauses in storytelling to muse on panic, courage, leadership, infection of rumor, as men clash with men in stress.

It is in these strange, subordinate reflections that one has the most authentic echo of the Caesar of politics—the furious, perplexed, yet thoughtful man who mystified a generation that could not even dimly guess his ultimate purpose.

For he *was* a mystery to his time.

Romans had watched him grow: offspring of a once-great patrician family, now decayed; orphaned in a time of trouble; and pledged by the doting women who brought him up to be a priest—a *flamen dialis* (had he become a *flamen dialis,* the world would never have known history's Caesar; those servants of Jupiter's Temple were forbidden to gaze upon a dead body, view an army in array of war, mount a horse or spend more than a day away from Rome). Politics prevented his induction as a temple priest, and so he graduated, a teen-ager, to the education normal for a boy of his time—tactics of war and rhetoric for the Forum. He dabbled in poetry as a youth (later, when he became Dictator, it is said that he caused all his poetry to be burned, a mark of editorial good taste that few other dictators have even fleetingly considered), then became a fashionable young man with a gift for politics. As a politician he was a "traitor to his class," the nobility —for he was of the party of *"populares,"* those who claimed to speak for the masses and learned to organize their votes. As a politician-organizer, he became a master, climbing steadily through elective offices up the ladder of honors—quaestor, aedile, praetor, consul; briber, grafter, vote manipulator, boss, speechmaker. A sportsman of the bed (after the death of his first wife), he apparently couched with every Roman matron he could reach, specializing in the wives and sisters of enemies, friends and partners (old rumor has it that he seduced the wives of both partners in his first triumvirate); tasted the women, young and old, of every age and country; kept a stable of gladiators as men now keep a stable of horses—but beyond that an ascetic who rarely drank and had no particular craving for fine food.

Romans watched his early career, not quite understanding—he fostered a law to let the High Priesthood (Pontifex Maximus) be chosen by popular vote, and then got himself elected. Engineered deals, politics, arrangements for older, more stupid men until in 59 B.C. he himself emerged at the political summit as consul. Whereupon he threw all Rome into turmoil with his laws and reforms.

Thus, Rome was glad to be rid of him when he asked, out of what ambition his enemies could not fathom, that he be given command of the bloody northern front, the war against the Gauls and Germans.

And when, after nine years, he came back from that war, there was no Gaul any longer and the Germans cowered in fright. But the Caesar who came back was even more mysterious than the one who had left.

For, as in any great man, there were many Caesars.

The Caesar who came back was the Dictator-to-be, and this was the Caesar they killed on the Ides of March, 44 B.C. This Caesar, the Dictator, is the man who cramps our memories still. There is the echo of this Caesar in all that we do today; in our calendar, which counts twelve months, beginning in January, reaching midsummer in July (named for himself) as he ordained it; this is the Caesar whose name is an epithet or adjective of common use in every language of the Western world; this is the Caesar whose name or title cloaked every Kaiser, Tsar, Imperator or Emperor who has aspired to world dominion since.

Of this Caesar—his laws, his victories, his decrees, his sunset affair with Cleopatra, his death—we have been told over and over again since men began to write history. It is this Caesar who has fascinated almost as many great writers as the Christ himself; yet all have seen him at the end of life. Shakespeare, drawing him from Plutarch, made him the moody tyrant, creature of fate. Shaw made him the witty, detached adventurer, toying with life and empire as a game; Mommsen made him the brooding genius, shaper of the future. In our time, Thornton Wilder has made him the urbane and cynical phrasemaker, world-weary, soul-tired, helplessly awaiting his end, yet amused as the end approaches.

But there was another earlier Caesar, a Caesar all too often forgotten and far more kin to us than to the people of his time.

This other Caesar was oddly modern and romantic. A youth of eighteen, married to the young Cornelia whom he loved, ordered by Sulla, the cruelest Dictator of the age, to divorce her—this Caesar refused to divorce his wife, and fled with her to the hills because he loved her. (While Pompey, later his great rival, then a young man, too, divorced his pregnant wife because the Dictator told him to do so.) This early Caesar was the man who all alone in the Roman Senate stood to insist that the co-conspirators of Catiline be given fair and open trial as the law required before being put to death; and risked his life to make the point that all free men must have fair trial before the passage of judgment. This was the Caesar who (some scholars insist) shocked every decent senator by inventing the world's first newspaper—the Acta Diurna, posted on the walls of Rome during his first consulate, an open account of the proceedings (hitherto secret) of the Senate so that the people might read and know the talk and debate of their leaders.

Above all, this early Caesar was a man of politics. Rome was a Republic; the people were sovereign; their votes made power. To sway those votes was to sway power itself, and thus he invented, or developed, many of those techniques and devices so familiar to us in our manipulation of popular votes today. This horrified his aristocratic colleagues, who expected to decide among themselves who should lead, and then receive from the people simple, uncomplicated assent to what they proposed. Caesar changed all this, for, as a *"popularis,"* a man of the people's party, he taught the people all too well how great was their power and turned them against what he called the *"factio paucorum,"* the "clique of the few," the Establishment of the day.

Between the two Caesars, the early Caesar of the *populares* and the later Caesar, Dictator, a transformation of personality so great intervenes that it cries for understanding. This exercise in melodrama is an attempt to catch the episode of transformation.

The name of the episode is the Rubicon.

Every schoolboy in the Western world knows that Caesar crossed the Rubicon—even though no one today can distinguish which of the three little gullies that fall off the shoulder of Sant' Arcangelo, just north of Rimini, is actually Caesar's Rubicon.

The Rubicon is more than an event, more even than a watershed. It was tragedy, one of the half-dozen great tragedies of human civilization. With the crossing of the Rubicon in 49 B.C., five hundred years of experiment in self-government failed.

Only a century before, Polybius, the Greek historian, had described Rome to the world as the supreme triumph of republican achievement, the solid proof that not only could citizens rule themselves, but that no other way of government had ever been more successful. Each year the people elected two leaders, twin consuls, to direct the state. An august Senate, its members all former magistrates elected over the years by the people, consulted with each other and the consuls, who then offered proposals of new law to the citizens. Once the citizens, assembled in voting files, had approved these laws, the whole became one: SPQR—*Senatus Populusque Romanus*—the Roman state united in arms and faith to challenge all. Judges and juries meted out even-handed justice to all who held citizenship and *"fiat justitia, ruat caelum"* ("let justice be done though the heavens fall"). The Senate approved treaties, proposed commands and generals; and once the people in Assembly approved, armies marched forth and the world trembled.

Polybius wrote only a generation before it all began to dissolve, at the apogee of the Republic, with Carthage and Greece both defeated. Roman women in those days spun wool, educated their children, shunned games, theaters and public appearances; ceremonies were observed; distinguished citizens worked their own fields; it was an honor to serve as soldier, and only property-owning citizens qualified to bear arms. But the very success of the Republic undermined it. Even as Polybius wrote, wealth of conquest was pouring in; mobs in the street were soon demanding their share; leaders and senators grew rich; generals began to sense the power of their arms and raise their own troops; amusement, luxury and fornication changed the image of the Roman woman from Cornelia, mother of the Gracchi, to Clodia, the aristocratic harlot of the Tiber.

All this had been happening for sixty years (from the time of the Gracchi) before Caesar left for Gaul as a political soldier. In Rome there were only two noble occupations—war and politics; but an accelerating squalor and greed divorced them from the older selflessness and patriotism of which Polybius wrote. Caesar went north, snatching his combat command as political spoils, his authority won from the Assembly and Senate, as British guards officers once won their commission, by favor in high place and ready cash on the table.

The man who left Rome was seen by the Roman establishment and its world of fashion as a deft and stubtle politician, a master of words, rhetoric and demagoguery. But little more than that. In gossip he was—as Catullus, that marvelous poet, describes him—the "white cockpigeon" bouncing through every bed of Rome. Of him, the most they could hope for was that he might guard the Alpine passes; and many hoped that in those Alpine passes or on their gloomy western slopes he would lose his life.

The military problem before him was the problem that had haunted Romans for four hundred years: the barbarians beyond the Alpine wall. For centuries, Gauls and Germans had come raiding, wheeling, killing, howling up to the foothills of the passes to harass and burn the frontier, to threaten the great Po valley, the fairest land in all Italy.

To this problem Caesar brought not only new tactics—his triple-line formation, his new-type javelin, novel engineering and logistic inventions —but also his élan and ability to inspire infantry.

All these he used in a simple strategy: His enemy were tribesmen who fought by no accepted rules in what, today, we might call total guerrilla war. There is only one way to crush guerrilla warfare—it is to go for the cities, the homes, the shelters. It is to kill women, children, old people, innocents, all alike, as one forces the enemy to protect his dear ones. You erase the base in which irregular warfare breeds, you purge it. Caesar purged Gaul. In nine years he branded it, seared it, scorched it.

The dark and gloomy cliffs of the Alps were transformed by Caesar from a military barrier to a simple geographical feature on Europe's wrinkled surface. He crossed the Rhine and struck terror into the Germans; he crossed the Channel and bloodied the Britons. When he was through with his work, the barbarian wars were over—in Gaul forever, in Germany for generations. And all done by a handful of foot-soldiers—never more than fifty thousand men put an end to the civilization of fifteen million Gauls. At any moment, all might have been lost; a single misjudgment, a single siege gone wrong, a single rashness, and he would have been swallowed by the forests and by history.

Yet he was not. He triumphed.

The man who returned, thus, after nine years of war in Gaul at the end of 50 B.C. to claim triumphal honors, as was the ancient custom, was entirely different from the master politician who had left, the ladies'-man of gossip. The man returning was Caesar Imperator.

To both sides it must have seemed absurd.

To those in Rome it must have seemed absurd that they should take their leadership, guidance and strategy from a poor poet, a bad priest, a skillful Forum politician, a man whose victories—they were sure—had come by luck and chance. Gaul was now the richest of all conquered lands and, by tradition, it was the Senate's right to share the spoils among the nobles. Should the white cockpigeon alone make this decision? For he had announced that he would be consul again—and if they let him run, they knew, from his first term in office, that he would make his decisions alone.

To Caesar it was even more absurd. He had brought back peace and victory. To make this peace secure, he now required that the Roman state show mercy: to conquered Gauls, to new citizens, to those who had suffered. He required that Rome show gratitude: to his veterans, to his allies. He required, above all, that Rome change; thus, he proposed to run again for the consulship. It could not be, he felt, that these aging, rotted senators, dominated by a faction of a few ancient families, should dispose of a world, for loot and greed, that he had won by risk of life and troops—and which he *knew* he understood better than they. Nor could he accept that the mobs in the Forum, those present in Assembly under the Capitoline Hill, should be the only ones allowed to vote the laws while his soldiers and the farmer families who bred them, equally Roman citizens, who could not afford the trip to Rome, were deprived of the right to vote.

He held at his command the greatest army in the world; no force ever known to war except, perhaps, that of Alexander the Great could until his time equal it; none could match its victories. And yet in Rome, where gratitude should be, was envy. In Rome, where the law bobbed and danced between the roaring of the crowd and the intrigues of the Senate, there was no order except what blade and muscle imposed. In Rome his enemies cited laws by which they might summon him to lay down command and return to face trial before packed juries for indictments yet unframed. And where old laws left loopholes, they now passed laws that reached back years in time to snare him.

There is a magic to the law. One reads Caesar and there is instinct reverence for the law in every line that he writes. But which laws should he accept, and which repudiate? One set of laws gave him every right to run for consul, present or absent; another denied that right.

And what if the old laws were wrong? What then?

What if laws require one to face trial, then, perhaps, die, and one knows the law is being used not as law but as voodoo—and that if one snaps one's finger to set the troops on march, the law is done with?

That was Caesar's problem at the Rubicon.

Insanity, I think, is best defined as a situation where an individual loses contact with reality. It makes no difference what the reality is. If the reality is in itself absurd, if reality is mad, and the individual, judged by normal standards, is sane, then, nonetheless, the individual must be judged mad for rejecting absurd reality.

The political transformation of Caesar *popularis* to Caesar *dictator* happened, I think, at the Rubicon. But to the man personally, more than that probably happened. We have lived and still live in an age when dictators, risen through the people, are carried away to think of themselves as divine, the expression of God's will, or Gods themselves.

Some such transformation of personality under pressure must have happened to Caesar in the few weeks he paused at Ravenna, by the Rubicon, en route home from victory to the expected ceremony of triumph. He returned to his base camp in northern Italy late in 50 B.C. —expecting honor. He found the law prepared against him, and trial impending which might, if he obeyed the summons, bring him shameful exile at the best, death at the worst. He pleaded. He negotiated with those who held the power back in Rome. The last line in his history of the Gallic wars (written by his companion Hirtius) tells of his effort to reach some sort of settlement with the Senate of Rome within the law. The book ends:

"*. . . tamen Caesar omnia patienda esse statuit, quoad sibi spes aliqua relinqueretur iure potius disceptandi quam belli gerendi*" ("Nonetheless, Caesar decided to endure all in patience so long as any hope was left to him of settling matters by law, rather than by making war").

But it was not to be. They forced the issue to arms—or perhaps it was he who did so. Students of ancient jurisprudence argue whose guilt it was with as much emotion, today, as men did in 50 B.C.

Whichever way it was, I have done my best to imagine how it may have been in Caesar's mind as he, finally, came to reject both reality and law. The datings, episodes, programs, negotiations embedded in the essay-melodrama that follows are as close to accurate as modern scholarship will allow me to be. Yet it must be noted that though classical scholars have worked on this turbulent six-week period of decision with enormous insight and diligence, they have never come to any unanimity on fact, or motivations, or law, or justice.

The words, talk and action of the episode that follows I have drawn from imagination, skipping as best I could between the facts on which scholars are agreed.

Irving Stone

THE HUMAN BODY

Michelangelo Buonarotti was born at an unfortunate time in Tuscan history: all of the great Florentine marble carvers had either died or moved to Rome. He had been wet-nursed by a family of Settignano stonecutters; he wanted to do nothing in or with his life except sculpt marble. But there was no remaining master to whom he could be apprenticed. In 1489, at thirteen, his father permitted him to be apprenticed to Ghirlandaio, who was doing the murals in Santa Maria Novella. Michelangelo was later to tell Pope Julius II, "Painting is not my trade"; yet in the months he spent in Ghirlandaio's studio he learned enough about the technique of mural painting to complete the forty-year task of covering the Sistine vault in an epochal four years.

In 1488, Lorenzo de Medici converted his wife's garden into a sculpture garden, and brought Bertoldo, a master sculptor, to train a new generation of marble carvers. Michelangelo got himself admitted, earned Il Magnifico's admiration, was taken into the Medici Palace as a son. Here he was educated, here he learned his craft. Three years later Lorenzo died, the Florentines drove his family out of the palace. Michelangelo purchased a large piece of marble. He would sculpt a memorial to Lorenzo.

Dissection was punishable by death in Florence. When the young Michelangelo (he was then sixteen) asked his close friend, Prior Bichiellini, head of Santa Spirito, if he could work on the corpses in the dead room, the Prior ejected him from the monastery library. A few weeks later when the Prior was showing Michelangelo some illustrated manuscripts, he left behind him a certain large key.

Mrs. Stone and I moved to Italy in September of 1956, living and working there for several years, in Florence, Carrara, Sienna, Bologna. This particular chapter from *The Agony and the Ecstasy* was written in Rome, where we had the good fortune to become friends with several brilliant young Italian doctors . . .

Irving Stone

Now he knew the answer. It had been buried within him for a long time. He came to grips with its necessity. There was no escape. He could never become any part of the sculptor he planned to be until he had trained himself through dissection; until he knew the workings of every last component within the human body, precisely what function it served and how it accomplished its end; the interrelation of all the parts, bone, blood, brain, muscle, tendon, skin, guts. Figures in the round had to be complete, seen from every angle. A sculptor could not create movement without perceiving what caused the propulsion; could not portray tension, conflict, drama, strain, force unless he saw every fiber and substance at work within the body that was shaping the power and drive; unless he knew what a movement in front did to the corresponding muscles behind; until he grasped the whole of the human body itself.

Learn anatomy he must!

It was not until the fourth or fifth session that Michelangelo began to notice the key, of and by itself. The prior used it not only to keep books open but as a place marker when he closed a volume, a pointer when he was underscoring lines.

Always the key. Always the same key. But never when he was in the study with others, either monks or lay friends.

Why?

He went back a dozen times in the following weeks. If he set about his drawing for an hour or two the prior would come through the church, greet him cheerily, invite him into the study. And invariably the big bronze key came out of the desk.

At night Michelangelo lay awake, seeing the key before him. During the day he went for long walks in the fall rain up to the Maiano quarry, holding dialogues with himself.

"It must mean something. But what? What are keys for? Obviously to open doors. How many doors are there in which I am interested? Only one. The dead-room door."

He would have to take a gamble. If the prior meant for him to have it, well and good; if he did not, then he would simply carry it off by accident, forgetfully, and return it the next day. During the night he would let himself in through the rear garden gate of the monastery, make his way to the dead room. If the key fitted the door, then his assumption would be correct. If it did not . . .

It was midnight when he reached the monastery, having slipped out of his house noiselessly so as to waken no one, and taken a circuitous route to the hospital from Santa Croce across the Ponte Vecchio, past the Pitti palace, through a maze of side streets. In this way he missed the night guards who followed a prescribed route with their lanterns and could be seen a piazza away.

He hugged the walls of the infirmary on the Via Sant'Agostino, turned into the Via Maffia to the little gate in the center of the block above which the fresco of Our Lady with the Child by Agnolo Gaddi gleamed softly in the darkness. All Santo Spirito keys opened this gate; he admitted himself, slipped past the stables on his left, avoided the main walk because the next building was the dormitory for lay brothers, skirted the walls of the dark kitchen, his breath coming a little faster now, made an angular dart to the inner wall of the infirmary.

He found the open, central arch, slipped into the corridor admitting to the cells for patients, the doors of which were closed, and turned toward the dead room. An oil lamp stood in a niche. He took a candle out of the green canvas bag he carried, lighted the wick, shielded it under his cape.

His only serious danger was from the chief of the infirmary; but since the monk was also encharged with the administration of the properties of the order, working from dawn to dark supplying the needs of the infirmary, guesthouse and monastery, he was not likely to venture out of his cell on nocturnal inspections. Once the five o'clock supper was served, the patients were made ready for sleep and the doors of their cells closed.

There was no resident doctor; the patients were not expected to grow sicker or ask for help during the night. They docilely did what was expected of them.

He stood for a moment rigid, before the door of the dead room. He inserted the big key, made a slow movement to the right, then left, felt the lock slip. In an instant he had opened the door, darted into the room, closed and locked the door behind him. And at this moment of commitment he did not know whether he dared face the task ahead.

The dead room was small, about eight feet by ten, windowless. The stone walls were whitewashed, the floor of rough blocks. In the center of the room, on narrow planks mounted on two wooden horses, and wrapped from head to foot in a burial sheet, was a corpse.

He stood leaning against the door, breathing hard, the candle shaking in his hand like trees in a *tramontana*. It was the first time he had been alone in a room with death, let alone locked in, and on a sacrilegious errand. His flesh felt as though it were creeping along his bones; he was more frightened than he had ever been in his life.

Who lay wrapped in that sheet? What would he find when he unrolled the body and dropped the winding cloth to the floor? What had this unfortunate creature done that he should now, without his knowledge or consent, be mutilated?

"What kind of nonsense is this?" he demanded of himself. "What difference could it make to a man already dead? His body does not get into the kingdom of heaven, only his soul. I have no intention of dissecting this poor fellow's soul, even if I should stumble across it."

Reassured by his own grim humor, he put down his bag and looked for a place to set his candle, of importance to him not only for light but as a clock as well: for he had to be safely out of here before three in the morning when the monks who operated the large bakehouse on the corner of the Via Sant'Agostino and Piazza Santo Spirito rose to make the day's bread for the monastery, the deserving poor and the relatives of all who lived here. It had taken much experimenting to ascertain with accuracy how long each type of candle would burn. This one, for which he was now searching for a resting place, was the three-hour variety; when it began its first sputtering he would have to leave. He must also exercise care that no drippings could be discovered the next morning.

He emptied his bag of its scissors and kitchen knife, flattened it on the floor, held the candle upside down for a moment, then secured it in the soft wax. He took off his cape, for he was already sweating in the cold room, laid it in a corner, uttered a jumbled prayer which sounded like, "Lord forgive me, for I know not what I do," and approached the corpse.

First he would have to unroll it from its winding sheet. The trestle bench was narrow. He had not known that he could be so clumsy. Slowly he wrestled the stiff body, first raising the legs until the sheet pulled out from under the lower half, then lifting it from the waist and holding it in his left arm, against his chest, until he could maneuver the cloth from around the torso and head. The winding sheet was long, he had to go through the tortuous process five times before he finally divested the cadaver of its protective wrapping.

He picked up his candle from the floor, held it aloft in his left hand to study the body. His first feeling was one of pity for this dead man. His second was one of fear:

"This is how I shall end up!"

Suddenly all the differences between life and death became apparent.

The face was expressionless; the mouth semi-open, the skin green from gangrene. The man had been strongly built and was in mid-life when apparently he had received a stab wound in the chest. The cadaver had been here long enough to sink to the temperature of this freezing room.

His nostrils picked up an odor, something like very old flowers dying in water. It was not strong, it fell away when he backed to the wall to get a moment of relief; but it came to him again as he approached the cadaver, and from that point remained in his nostrils inescapably.

Where to begin? He raised the arm on the side closest to him and felt a cold such as he had never felt before. Not colder than anything else, but different. It was a cold filled with emotional content, a hard cold, not the skin, but the muscle under it. The skin was soft, like velvet. He felt disgust, as though an iron hand were squeezing his stomach. All his memories of warm arms and shoulders recurred to him. He withdrew.

It was a considerable time before he could pick up the knife from the floor, recall what he had read about the human body, the few illustrations he had seen. He poised over the cadaver, frozen himself, swallowing hard. Then he brought the knife down and made his first incision: from the chestbone down to the groin. But he had not exerted enough pressure. The skin was surprisingly tough.

He started over. Now applying strength behind the knife, he found the substance under the skin quite soft. The skin opened about two inches. He asked himself, "Where is the blood?" for it did not flow. This increased his impression of cold and death. Then he saw the fat, a soft, deep yellow. He knew what it was, for he had seen fat cut from animals in the markets. He made a deeper cut to reach the muscle, which was different in color from the skin and the fat, and harder to cut. He studied the dark red columns of fibers. He cut again and saw the bowel.

The smell was growing heavier. A nausea started within him. At the first cut he had summoned all his strength to proceed; now all sensations came together: the cold, fear, smell, reaction to death. He was repulsed by the slippery feeling of the tissue, the fat fluidifying on his fingers like oil. He wanted to put his hands in hot water and wash them.

"What do I do now?"

He trembled, hearing his voice echo off the stone walls. He was in little danger of being heard, for he was bound at his back by the solid wall beyond which lay the garden, to his side by the chapel reserved for the death services, on the infirmary side by stone through which no sound could penetrate.

It was dark inside the cavity. He picked up the candle, secured the canvas bag under the foot of the cadaver, placed his candle at body height.

All of his senses were heightened. The intestines that he now began to handle were cold, slippery, moving. A pain ricocheted through his own bowels. He took one side of the flap in one of his hands, the other side in the other, held them apart to have a careful look. He saw a pale gray transparent snake, long, going round and round in coils. It had a superficial aspect of mother-of-pearl, shining because humidified, filled up with something that moved and emptied when he touched it.

His initial emotion of disgust was overcome by excitement. He picked up his knife and started to cut upwards from the bottom of the rib cage. The knife was not strong enough. He tried his scissors but had to angle along the ribs, one at a time. The rib bones were hard; it was like cutting wire.

Suddenly the candle began to splutter. Three hours already! He could not believe it. Yet he did not dare ignore the warning. He set his green bag and candle on the floor, picked up the winding sheet from the corner. The wrapping process was a thousandfold more difficult than the unwrapping because he could no longer turn the corpse on its side or the whole of its guts would spill out onto the floor.

The perspiration ran down into his eyes, his heart pounded so loud he thought it would wake the monastery as he used the last vestige of his strength to lift the corpse from the table with one arm while he pulled the winding sheet under and around the necessary five times. He barely had a moment to make sure that the corpse was stretched out upon the planks as he had found it, to check the floor for possible stains or wax, before the candle gave its last flickering sputter and went out.

He had enough control to take a wandering route home, stopping a dozen times to retch against the corners of buildings and in the darkness of open ground. The smell of the corpse was in his nostrils with every breath he took. When he reached home he was afraid to boil water on Lucrezia's glowing embers for fear the noise would wake the family; yet he could not live without getting the feel of that fat off his fingers. He hunted quietly for some harsh lye soap to use in the cold water.

His body, as he got into bed, was icy. He huddled against his brother, but not even Buonarroto's warmth could help him. Several times he had to rise and retch into a pail. He heard Lucrezia get out of bed, dress and make her way through the kitchen and down the circular stairway to the street as the faintest tinge of pearl gray touched his window overlooking the stables on the Via dei Bentaccordi.

He had chills and fever all day. Lucrezia made him a chicken broth, but he could not hold it down. The family came one by one into the bedroom to find out what was the matter with him. He lay there feeling as clammy as the corpse. Nothing was able to remove the smell of death from his nostrils. After he had assured Lucrezia that it was not her supper which had upset him, she returned to the kitchen to boil up an herb bouquet to cure him. Monna Alessandra examined him for spots. By late afternoon he was able to retain a little of the herb tea, for which he thanked Lucrezia most gratefully.

About eleven o'clock he rose, slipped into his shoes, *calze,* warm shirt and cloak, and with his legs rickety beneath him, made his way to Santo Spirito.

There was no corpse in the dead room. Neither was there one on the following night. The two days gave him a chance to recover. On the third night he again found a body in its winding sheet on the planked table.

The second cadaver was older, with white beard patches on a big red face, the skin tight, the fluid under the skin marbleized. This time he used his knife with more authority, opening the abdomen with a clean cut, then using his left hand to pry apart the rib cage, which made a noise like crackling wood. It remained attached at the collarbone.

He picked up his candle and held the light close to the innards, for this was his first complete view. He saw something pale red, netlike in design, and of solid tissue, which he deduced was the lungs. This network had a black covering, something that he had heard happened to wool workers.

Experimentally, he pressed the lung; a hissing noise came out of the mouth of the corpse. He dropped the candle in fright. Fortunately it did not go out. When he regained his calm and had picked up the candle, he realized that in touching the lung he had forced out the residual air; and for the first time he understood what breathing was, because he could see and feel and hear the communication between the lungs and the mouth, realized what it did to the whole figure.

After he had moved aside the lung he noticed a dark red mass; this must be the heart. It was covered by a shining membrane. Probing, he found that all of the tissue was connected to a form shaped something like an apple, almost free in the chest, attached only at the top of the pyramid.

"Shall I take it out?"

He hesitated a moment, then picked up his scissors, cut across the pyramidal membrane. Substituting his knife, he peeled away the membrane as though he were opening a banana. Now he had the heart in his two hands. Unexpectedly, he was hit by an emotional impact as strong as Hercules' club. If the soul and heart were one, what happened to this unfortunate cadaver's soul now that he had cut out its heart?

As quickly as it had come, the fear departed. In its place came a sense of triumph. He was holding a human heart in his hands! He felt the happiness that arises out of knowledge, for now he knew about the most vital organ of the body, what it looked like, how it felt. He opened the heart with his knife, was shocked to find that there was nothing inside. He replaced it in its cavity, put back the chest's rib structure, which artists had observed so well from the lean Tuscans around them. But now he knew precisely where the heart beat beneath it.

He did not have the faintest idea of how to start work on the snake of the intestine. He picked up a piece, pulled. It came easily for a time, about five feet of it; the bowels were attached loosely to the posterior wall, and came away. Then he began to feel resistance. The upper part was enlarged, a sort of bag was attached, which he deduced was the stomach. He had to use his knife to cut it loose.

He freed some twenty-five feet of bowel, fingered it, feeling the differences of size and content. Some places had fluid in them, some solid;
he learned that it was a continuous channel, with no opening from the
beginning to the end. To get a concept of its interior aspect he cut
into it with his knife at several points. The lower bowel contained stools.
The smell was terrible.

Tonight he had a four-hour candle, but already it began to splutter.
He bundled the viscera back into the abdominal cavity, and with great
difficulty got the corpse rewrapped.

He ran to the fountain in the Piazza Santo Spirito and scrubbed
his hands, but he could not get the feeling of dirt off his fingers. He
stuck his head into the icy water to wash away the sense of guilt,
standing for a moment with his hair and face dripping water; then ran
all the way home, shaking as though with ague.

He was emotionally exhausted.

He awoke to find his father standing over him, a displeased look on his
face.

"Michelangelo, get up. It's noon. Lucrezia is putting food on the
table. What kind of new nonsense is this, that you sleep until dinner?
Where were you last night?"

Michelangelo lay staring up at Lodovico.

"I'm sorry, Father. I'm not feeling well."

He washed carefully, combed his hair, put on fresh clothing and
went to the table. He thought he was going to be all right. When
Lucrezia brought in a bowl of beef stew, he rushed back into his bedroom
and retched into the chamber pot until his insides were sore.

But that night he was back in the dead room.

Before he had the door locked behind him he was drenched in the
smell of putrefaction. He unwound the sheet, saw that the left leg of the
corpse was of a brown color with a green secretion coming out from
under the skin, the leg swollen half again its size. The rest of the body
was ash gray, the face completely sunken.

He began to work where he had left off the night before, cutting
directly to the bowel, and unraveled it piece by piece. He placed it on the
floor and raised his candle close to the cavity. There were a number of
the organs he had been searching for: the spleen on the left side, the
liver on the right. He recognized the liver from the beeves and lambs
cut up in the markets; bilaterally, just aside of the bone column, were
the kidneys.

He picked them up carefully and perceived that they were connected with the bladder by small tubes, like wires. He went on to where the liver was attached, posteriorly; cut the ligaments with his scissors and removed it from the cavity. He studied the shape in his hands, examining the small bladder attached to its lower side, opened it with his knife. A dark green fluid came out.

He moved his candle closer, saw something that he had missed before: the abdominal cavity was separated from the chest cavity by a dome-shaped muscle. In the center of this dome were two holes through which passed tubes connecting the stomach with the mouth. The second big channel, alongside the backbone, went up into the chest. He now realized that from the chest to the abodomen there were only two means of communication, one bringing food and liquids. The other baffled him. He lifted the bone structure of the chest but could not determine what the second channel was used for. The candle spluttered.

As he crept silently up the stairs of his house he found his father waiting for him.

"Where have you been? What is that horrible odor about you? You smell like death."

Michelangelo mumbled an excuse with eyes cast down, brushed past Lodovico to the security of his bedroom.

He could not sleep.

"Will I never get used to this?" he groaned.

The next night there was no corpse in the dead room. He had an uneasy feeling of impending danger as he noticed that the section of floor where he had allowed the bowels to rest had been scrubbed, and was brighter than the stones around it. A bit of wax from his candle had been left untouched at the foot of the plank table. Yet even if his activities had been noticed, he was protected by the vow of silence in the monastery.

The following night he found a boy of about fifteen who showed no external evidence of disease. The pale skin, almost completely white, was soft to the touch. The eyes were blue when he raised the lids, deep in color, contrasting with the pale white of the eyelids. Even in death he was attractive.

"Surely he will wake up," he murmured.

He saw that the boy was still without hair on his chest, and felt a pity deeper than he had known since he had viewed his first corpse.

He turned away; he'd wait until another night. Then, facing the corner of the whitewashed walls, he stopped. By the next morning this lad would be buried under four feet of earth in the Santo Spirito cemetery.

He touched the boy, found him as cold as winter; beautiful, but as dead as all the others.

He made his incisions expertly now, put his hand under the chestbone. It came away easily. Up toward the neck he felt a tubelike appendage, about an inch in diameter, that gave the impression of a series of hard rings; among these rings he found a soft membranous tube that came down from the neck. He could not find where the tube ended and the lung began, but when he pulled on it the boy's neck and mouth moved. He took his hand out swiftly and shuddered away from the table.

A moment later he cut the tube blindly, not being able to see it, then lifted the lungs out separately. They were light in weight and when he squeezed them he found that the sensation was rather like squeezing snow. He tried to cut the lung open with his knife, put it on the table and, with a hard surface under him, found that it was like cutting through dry sponge. In one of the lungs he found a pale yellow-white mucus which kept the lung moist, in the other a pink-red mucus. He wanted to get his hand down the boy's mouth in order to search out the throat and neck, but the feel of the teeth and tongue repelled him.

Suddenly he felt as though someone were in the room with him, though he knew it was impossible because he had locked the door from the inside. Tonight was just too difficult.

He wrapped up the corpse easily, for it weighed so little, put it back on the table, and let himself out.

He could not risk his father's again detecting the odor of death, so he walked the streets until he found a wineshop in the workmen's quarter that was open. He drank a little of the Chianti. When the proprietor turned his back, he sprinkled the rest of the wine over his shirt.

Lodovico was outraged when he smelled the strong wine.

"It is not enough that you wander the streets all night doing God alone knows what, associating with what manner of loose women, but now you come home smelling like a cheap tavern. I can't understand you. What is driving you to these evil ways?"

The only protection he could give his family was to keep them in ignorance. It was best for his father to believe that he was carousing, about which Lodovico was learning a great deal from Giovansimone, who frequently came in with his face bloodied and clothes torn. But as the days passed, and Michelangelo stumbled into the house every morning toward dawn, the family rose in arms. Each was outraged for his own special reason. Lucrezia because he was not eating, his uncle Francesco because he was afraid Michelangelo would run into debt, his aunt Cassandra on moral grounds. Only Buonarroto brought a smile to his brother's lips.

"I know you are not carousing," he said.

"How could you know that?"

"Simple: you haven't asked me for a scudo since you bought those candles. Without money you do not buy women in Florence."

He realized that he would have to find somewhere else for his daily rest. The Topolinos would never ask questions, he could stay there, but Settignano was so far away; he would lose valuable hours coming and going. In the morning he went to the Duomo workshop and mounted the stool before his drawing table. Beppe came over to greet him, a puzzled expression on his homely old face.

"My young friend, you look like a cadaver. What have you been making with yourself?"

Michelangelo looked up sharply.

"I've been . . . working, Beppe."

Beppe cackled toothlessly.

"Ah, that I were young enough for that kind of work! Well, do not try to raise Hercules' club every night. Remember, what you put into the ladies at night you don't have left to spend on marble in the morning."

That night he came across his first ugly corpse, one that made him shiver as he observed what could happen to God's handiwork. The man was about forty, with a big dark red face, swollen near the neck. The mouth was open, the lips blue, the whites of the eyes full of red spots. Through the yellow teeth he could see the dark red tongue, swollen, filling almost the whole mouth.

He put his hand on the man's face. The cheeks felt like uncooked dough. Now seemed a good time to get at the structure of the human face. He picked up the smaller of his knives and cut from the hairline to the bridge of the nose. He tried to peel the skin off the forehead but he could not, it was too closely attached to the bone. He cut on top of each eyebrow to the edge of the eye, stripped the skin from the corner of the eye outward, continued from the eye to the ear, then down along the cheekbone.

The effect of this mutilation was so ghastly that he could not work on it. He picked up the winding sheet from the corner, covered the man's head, and turned his attention to the hipbone, to the fibered muscles of the heavy thigh.

A couple of nights later when there was a new corpse, he cut lightly into the skin of the face, peeling it off with his scissors. Under the thin yellow tissue of fat he discovered a large membrane of red muscular tissue which went continuously from the ear around the lips to the other ear. Now he had his first understanding of how these muscles could move the face to laughter, smiles, tears, grief.

Under it was a thicker tissue extending from the corner of the jaw to the base of the skull. Putting his finger under this second layer, he pushed the tissue a little and saw the jaw move. He worked it up and down to simulate the chewing movement, then searched for the muscle that would move the eyelid. He had to see inside the cavity of the eye to know what made it move. Trying to push his finger inside, he exerted too much pressure. The eye globe broke. A white mucus poured out over his fingers, leaving the cavity empty.

He turned away terror-stricken, walked to a corner of the white-washed wall and crushed his forehead against its coldness, fighting desperately the desire to retch. When he had regained control of himself he went back to the corpse, cut the tissue from around the second eye, found where it was attached at the bottom of the cavity. Then putting his finger in above the eye and moving it slowly inside, he plucked it out. He turned it around and around in his hand, trying to find out how it moved. He held his candle close, peered into the empty cavity. On the bottom he could perceive a hole through which gray soft tissuelike wires went up into the skull. Until he could remove the top of the skull and expose the brain, he could learn nothing about how an eye sees.

His candle had only a bit of tallow. He cut the flesh away from the bridge of the nose, saw clearly what had happened to his own under Torrigiani's fist.

The candle spluttered.

Where to go? He dragged himself away from Santo Spirito. His body ached with tiredness, his eyes smarted, his stomach and spirits were in a state of revulsion. He could not face Lodovico, who would surely be waiting for him at the top of the stairs, screaming that he was going straight to the Stinche.

He made his way to the workshop of the Duomo. It was easy to throw his bag over the gate, then hoist himself over. In the moonlight the blocks of white marble glistened with white luminosity, the chips around the semi-finished columns were like snow, clean and refreshing. The cold air settled his stomach. He went toward his workbench, cleared a place under it, stretched out, covered himself with a heavy piece of canvas and fell asleep.

He woke a few hours later; the sun had risen. In the piazza he could hear the noise of the *contadini* setting up their stalls. He walked to the fountain, washed, bought himself a slice of *parmigiano,* two thick-crusted *panini,* and returned to the workyard.

He tried to cut marble around the edges of the Hercules block, thinking that the feel of the iron instruments would bring him enjoyment. He soon set them down, climbed up on his stool and began to draw: the arm, muscles and joints, the jaw, the heart, the head. When Beppe arrived, came close to give him a *buon giorno,* he spread a concealing hand over the sheet before him. Beppe stopped short; but not before he got a look at an empty eye socket and exposed viscera. He shook his head grimly, turned and walked away.

At noon Michelangelo went home to dinner, to allay Lodovico's fears about his absence.

It took him several days to work up the courage to return to the dead room and crack a man's skull. Once there he began working rapidly with hammer and chisel, cutting backward from the bridge of the nose. It was a nerve-racking experience, for the head moved each time he made a stroke. Nor did he know how much force to exert to break the bone. He could not get the skull open. He covered the head, turned the man over, spent the rest of the night studying the structure of the spinal column.

With the next cadaver he did not make the mistake of cutting backward on the skull, but instead cut around the head, from the tip of the left ear along the hairline, taking three or four hard blows of the hammer to penetrate the half inch of bone. There was now room enough to keep his scalpel under the skull and cut all the way around. A white-yellow cream escaped; the fissure opened wider. When he had cut the bone more than halfway, he used his scalpel as a lever and ripped. The skull lifted off in his hands.

It was like dry wood. He was so shaken he barely prevented its dropping onto the floor. He shifted his eyes from the skull to the corpse. He was horrified, for with the top of the head off, the face was absolutely destroyed.

Again he was overcome by a sense of guilt; but with the skull lifted off he had his first look at a human brain. As an artist he had been fascinated by what created expression; what was it in the brain that enabled the face to convey emotion? Holding his candle close to the brainpan, he saw that the mass inside was yellow-white, with red-blue lines on the surface, the arteries and veins going in all directions. He could see that the mass of the brain was divided in the middle, exactly corresponding to the divided line of the skull. He could detect no odor, but to his first touch it was wet, very soft and even, like the skin of a soft fish.

He put the skull back on top of the head, wrapping the sheet tightly at the top to hold it in place. He was neither ill nor distressed as he had been on most other nights, but could hardly wait to get back to his next corpse and open the brain itself.

When he took off his next skull he was astonished to think that men could be so different when their brains looked and felt so much alike. From this he deduced that there must be a physical substance inside the brain which differed with each man. Using his index finger, he moved around the base of the skull, learned that the brain was completely detached and free from the bone. Putting his fingers on both sides, he tried to take it out whole. It would not lift.

Where his fingers came together the mass was attached by something like a series of wires to the bottom of the skull basin. He cut the wires, pulled out the mass. It was so soft, and at the same time so slippery, he had to concentrate tremendously just to hold it together. He looked at it in wonderment and admiration: from this relatively small substance, which could weigh no more than a couple of pounds, emerged all the greatness of the human race: art, science, philosophy, government, all that men had become for good as well as evil.

When he cut the brain down the line of division it was similar to cutting very soft cheese; there was no noise, no spoilage, no odor. The two halves were exactly alike. No matter where he cut, it was all the same, gray in color, a little yellowish. He pushed the corpse over on the table to make enough space to lay the brain out on the wooden plank, and was amazed to see that in and by itself it had no structure, that it slowly collapsed over the wooden boards.

The holes in the skull he found filled with the same wirelike substance he had had to break in order to detach the brain. Following these strands down through the neck, he surmised that this substance was the sole connection between the brain and the body. The front holes he discerned were between the brain and the eyes; the other two holes corresponded to the ears. He pushed through the inch-and-a-half hole at the back base of the skull, connecting to the vertebrae; this was the connection between the brain and the back.

He was exhausted now, for he had worked for five hours and was glad when his candle burned out.

He sat on the edge of the fountain in the Piazza Santo Spirito throwing cold water at his face and asking himself:

"Am I obsessed to be doing these things? Have I the right to do this just because I say it is for sculpture? What price might I have to pay for this precious knowledge?"

Spring arrived, the air warmed. Beppe told him of some sculpture that needed doing for the new vault of the vestibule of Santo Spirito: carved capitals and a number of worked stones to decorate the vault and the doors.

Malcolm Cowley

THOMAS WOLFE:
THE PROFESSIONAL DEFORMATION

Who is Malcolm Cowley to say what is the best of Malcolm Cowley? Perhaps there isn't any. But I like this essay first published in *Atlantic Monthly* in 1958 because it offers a key that unlocks two doors: one to the extraordinary character of Thomas Wolfe, the other to his work as a novelist. I said of him in another connection that he was a tragic hero not so much of the literary art as of the pure act of writing.

Malcolm Cowley

During his early days in New York, Wolfe used to write in bound ledgers opened on top of the icebox, so that he stood at his work like a factory hand. Later he wrote at a table, using ordinary sheets of manuscript paper, but more of them than anyone else with good eyesight, for ninety of his penciled words filled a sheet. He wrote at top speed, never hesitating for a word, as though he were taking dictation. The moment a sheet was finished, he would push it aside without stopping to read it over or even to number it. In the course of filling thousands of sheets with millions of words, he developed a wart on the middle finger of his right hand "almost as large and hard," he said in a letter, "but not as valuable, as a gambler's diamond."

He was not so much an author of books as a member of that much less familiar species, the writing man, *homo scribens*. His life was spent in conjugating a single verb in various tenses—*scribam, scripsi, scriptum est*—with the result that his working habits and problems are even more interesting to study than the works themselves. Indeed, they reveal the works in a rather unexpected light and help to explain why their real virtues were achieved at an inevitable cost to the writing man and his readers.

The first of his problems was how to maintain a steady flow of words from the vast reservoir of his conscious memories to the moving tip of his pencil. Before the flow could be established he would go through weeks or months of self-torture, walking the streets of Brooklyn at night, fleeing to Europe, staying drunk for days on end. Once the flow started, it might continue for months, during which his pencil sprayed out words like water from a hose. "You forget to eat, to shave, to put on a clean shirt when you have one," says Wolfe's autobiographical hero George Webber in *You Can't Go Home Again.* "You almost forget to sleep, and when you do try to you can't—because the avalanche has started and it keeps going night and day. . . . You can't stop yourself—and even if you could you'd be afraid to because there'd be all that hell to go through getting started up again."

Revision formed part of his system too, but not the usual sort of revision that consists in making interlinear changes, then having the draft retyped. "When he was dissatisfied with a scene or character," says his friend Edward C. Aswell, who had watched him working, ". . . he would put it aside, and rewrite it some different way from start to finish." In other words, he had to start the flow over again and continue until he had reached the end of an episode. He would remember new details and incidents the second time, so that his rewritten manuscripts were longer—often several times longer—than the first drafts. After being copied by a typist, they were tied in a bundle and put away in the big pine packing box that stood in the middle of his parlor. Then, in the same frenzy of production, he might go to work on another episode, often one remembered from a different period of his life.

His friends wondered how it was that he could reach into the packing box and, after a little fumbling, produce the desired episode, even if it had been written months or years before. I think the answer must be that he had his own filing system, chronological by subject matter. If the episode belonged to his boyhood, it would go below the episodes relating to his studies at Harvard, which in turn went below his years of teaching at Washington Square College and his love affair with Aileen Bernstein, which went below his struggles to write a second novel. All were parts of "the book" into which he planned to transcribe all his life, his world and time, in a continuous flow of memories. His ambition, announced by George Webber, was "To use myself to the top of my bent. To use everything I have. To milk the udder dry, squeeze out the last drop, until there is nothing left."

Unfortunately the book of his life was too big to be published or even to be written. His memories would have to be divided into separate books, or novels, and each of these would have to be something more than a chronological series of events; it would also have to possess its own structure and controlling theme. That was the problem of changing flow into form, which always puzzled him and for which he found a solution only in his first novel, as if without trying.

Look Homeward, Angel had a natural unity because, as Wolfe said in a letter to Mrs. Margaret Roberts, his English teacher in Asheville, it was "the story of a powerful creative element"—that is, Eugene Grant, or the author as a boy—"trying to work its way toward an essential isolation; a creative solitude; a secret life—its fierce struggles to wall this part of its life away from birth, first against the public and savage glare of an unbalanced, nervous, brawling family group, later against school, society, all the barbarous invasions of the world." As always it was a book of memories, but they were shaped and controlled by a theme close to the author's heart, the familiar theme of the young artist in a hostile environment. It had a natural beginning, which was the artist's birth, and a natural end, which was his escape from the environment.

But what could he do after writing *Look Homeward, Angel?* "I've got too much material," George Webber tells his friend Randy Shepperton. "It keeps backing up on me . . . until sometimes I wonder what in the name of God I'm going to do with it—how I'm going to find a frame for it, a channel, a way to make it flow. . . . Sometimes it actually occurs to me that a man may be able to write no more because he gets drowned in his own secretions." Then after a pause George says, "I'm looking for a way. I think it may be something like what people vaguely mean when they speak of fiction. A kind of legend, perhaps."

In 1930, the year after the publication of *Look Homeward, Angel,* Wolfe was looking for a legend into which he could fit everything he had felt and seen after leaving Asheville. Since he was in Europe at the time, and since his strongest emotion, outside of the passionate desire to write another book, was longing for the home he had lost—irretrievably, so he thought, for Asheville people had threatened to lynch him if he came back—he fixed upon the Antaeus legend of the giant born from the marriage of earth and water. He gave the legend a special turn, however, to fit his circumstances. In a letter to Maxwell Perkins, his editor at Scribner's, he explained that the argument of the new book would be:

> . . . of the Lybyan giant, the brother of Polyphemus, the one-eyed, and the son of Gaea and Poseidon, whom he hath never seen, and through his father, the grandson of Cronos and Rhea, whom he remembereth. He contendeth with all who seek to pass him by, he searcheth alway for his

father, he crieth out: "Art thou my father? Is it thou?" and he wrestleth with that man, and he riseth up from each fall with strength redoubled, for his strength cometh up out of the earth, which is his mother. Then cometh against him Heracles, who contendeth with him, who discovereth the secret of his strength, who lifteth him from the earth whence his might ariseth, and subdueth him. But from afar now, in his agony, he heareth the sound of his father's foot: he will be saved for his father cometh!

Of course the giant born of earth was Eugene Gant again, or Wolfe in person. His brother Polyphemus was intended to stand for the sterility that hates life; probably he was to be represented by Francis Starwick, the homosexual dramatist who appears in *Of Time and the River*. Gaea or Earth was to be introduced in the same novel as Mrs. Esther Jack, but the manuscript chapters about her were omitted from the published book and filed away; later they would figure in *The Web and the Rock*. Heracles the antagonist was to be the city of New York. As for the father, Wolfe's plan was that he should never be seen. But in a final chapter called "Pacific End"—later Wolfe thought of it as a final complete book, though he never got round to writing it—Antaeus was to hear "the thunder of horses on a beach (Poseidon and his horses); the moon dives out of clouds; he sees a print of a foot that can belong only to his father, since it is like his own; the sea surges across the beach and erases the print; he cries out 'Father' and from the sea far out, and faint upon the wind, a great voice answers 'My Son!' "

It was a magnificent conception, if slightly overblown; the trouble was that Wolfe was psychologically unable to carry it through. Like Eugene Gant he was gripped by an obsessive desire to say everything, with the result that "all ordered plans, designs, coherent projects for the work he had set out to do . . . were burned up in a quenchless passion, like a handful of dry straw." Soon the Antaeus legend got mixed with others, and the hero—without ceasing to be Thomas Wolfe—was called upon to play the successive parts of Orestes, Faustus the student, Telemachus, Jason, and Faustus in love. The more he worked on the book, the farther he seemed from its "Pacific End." By the beginning of the fourth year after the publication of *Look Homeward, Angel*, he had written a million new words, on his own estimate, and the great conception was not so much burned up as buried like Herculaneum under a flow of lava. It was Perkins who saved him, by suggesting how he might make a novel out of one segment of the material, saving the rest for other books. Even then almost half the segment had to be pared away before *Of Time and the River* was published in 912 pages.

The plan he evolved for a third novel was less Wagnerian. As he described the book in a letter to Aswell, who had become his editor after Wolfe left Scribner's, "It is about one man's discovery of life and the world, and in this sense it is a book of apprenticeship." The hero's name would be changed from Eugene Gant to George Webber, and his height would shrink from six feet five to five feet nine; Wolfe was looking for a protagonist whose angle of vision didn't quite duplicate the author's, so that his world could be treated more objectively. Webber would be the eternal innocent on his painful way to knowledge—another Candide or Wilhelm Meister—and the lessons he learned in a succession of adventures would be summed up in the title, *You Can't Go Home Again.*

It was a conception better suited to Wolfe's writing habits than that of his second novel had been, for it was loose enough so that one episode after another could be fitted into the scheme. But already, as he worked on it, the episodes had proliferated and some of them had grown almost to the length of separate books. His immense store of memories was imposing its pattern on the narrative, or its lack of pattern. The bandy-legged figure of George Webber was being presented less and less objectively until it became indistinguishable from the author's figure; George seemed to grow taller as one looked at him. By the spring of 1938 Wolfe had once again written more than a million words, which he turned over to Aswell before leaving for the West. Most of the words—too many of them—were published in three volumes after his death. No one can say how Wolfe himself would have finished the novel, or group of novels, or in how much time, or how and whether, if he had lived, he could have brought himself to relinquish all that private wealth of words.

But although he was incapable of solving the larger problem of form, he did solve a lesser problem in a way that is often overlooked. Wolfe's unit of construction was the episode, not the scene or chapter or novel. He always had trouble connecting the episodes, many of which were complete and strikingly effective in themselves. Two of the best are "The Web of Earth" and "A Portrait of Bascom Hawke," both of which were printed in *Scribner's Magazine,* although the "Portrait" was afterward taken apart and fitted into *Of Time and the River.* Other fine episodes are the long passages about the death of Old Gant, written for inclusion in the same novel while Wolfe and Perkins were revising it; the account of the students in Professor Hatcher's (or Baker's) famous course in the drama; the disintegration of Francis Starwick; the story of Nebraska Crane (partly in *The Web and the Rock* and partly in *You Can't Go Home Again*); and the visit to Nazi Germany called "I Have a Thing to Tell You." If these had been published separately, from the text of the original manuscripts—as *The Story of a Novel* was published—Wolfe might have gained a different reputation, not as an epic poet in prose, but as the author of short novels and portraits, little masterpieces of sympathy and penetration. But with his mania for bigness, one can't be sure that he would have enjoyed that other kind of fame.

Most of Wolfe's faults as a writer were closely and fraternally connected with his virtues; both resulted from his method of composition. Take for example the fault most frequently and justifiably urged against him: that he was unable to criticize his own work, that he couldn't distinguish what was good in it from what was absurd or pretentious, and that he wouldn't take criticism from others. Wolfe acknowledged the fault even when he was a very young man; at twenty-two he said in a letter to George Pierce Baker, "I admit the virtue of being able to stand criticism. Unfortunately it is a virtue I do not happen to possess." It wasn't that he was lacking either in humility or in critical talent. One couldn't talk with him about books for ten minutes without finding that he was perceptive and discriminating about other people's work, if he had read it. He didn't apply that sort of discrimination to his own work not through inability to do so, as he sometimes said, but chiefly as a matter of policy.

In a sense he chose to be only half of an author. The usual author is two persons or personalities working in partnership. One of them says the words to himself, then writes them down; the other listens to the words, or reads them, and then silently exclaims. "This is good, this is what you wanted to say, but *this!* Can't you say it again and say it better?" A result of the dialogue between the writer and the reader within is that the usual manuscript moves ahead spasmodically—a sentence or two, a pause while another sentence is phrased and rejected and rephrased, then a rapidly written paragraph, then another pause while reader and writer argue silently (or even aloud) about what has been said, then the sound of a page crumpled and dropped into the wastebasket, then a day's interval, perhaps, then another page that goes better. . . .

With time always pressing him, Wolfe couldn't afford to stumble ahead by a process of inner dialectic. There had to be that uninterrupted flow of memories from mind to paper; if he once questioned the value of the memories or changed the words that came to him, the flow halted for the day or night or perhaps for weeks. The solution he found instinctively, but later supported with arguments, was to suppress the critical side of his nature, or at least to keep it silent until an episode was finished; then if the inner critic objected to what he had written, he would do it over from the beginning, again without allowing the critic to interrupt. It was an effective system for producing words—very often accurate and truly inspired words—but it involved a great deal of wasted effort for the writer and wasted time for the reader of his published work.

Another fault urged against him is his use of formulas, including stock phrases, paired nouns or verbs where only one is needed ("grief and anguish," "sneered at and derided"), as well as the inevitable and therefore useless epithet. Here again the fault results from his system of writing and is closely connected with virtues that it helped him to achieve. Wolfe composed his novels, or rather the episodes that went into his novels, much as ancient bards, standing before a company of warriors, composed their epic poems. Like them, if for different reasons, he had to maintain an unbroken flow of words, with the result that there had to be moments when his pencil moved automatically while his mind was preparing the next powerful effect.

I couldn't help thinking of Wolfe when reading a passage in Moses Finley's illuminating book, *The World of Odysseus:*

> The repeated formula [Finley says] is indispensable in heroic poetry. The bard composes directly before his audience; he does not recite memorized lines. In 1934, at the request of Professor Milman Parry, a sixty-year-old Serbian bard who could neither read nor write recited for him a poem of the length of the *Odyssey,* making it up as he went along, yet retaining meter and form and building a complicated narrative. The performance took two weeks, with a week in between, the bard chanting for two hours each morning and two more in the afternoon.
>
> Such a feat makes enormous demands in concentration on both the bard and his audience. That it can be done at all is attributable to the fact that the poet, a professional with long years of apprenticeship behind him, has at his disposal the necessary raw materials: masses of incidents and masses of formulas, the accumulation of generations of minstrels who came before him.

Wolfe was perhaps the only American author of this century who could have duplicated the feat of the Serbian bard. That was because he had the same sort of equipment: partly an enormous store of characters and incidents (drawn from his own experience, not from the traditions of the race), and partly a supply of epithets, metaphors, and synonyms (remembered from his early reading) that could be applied to any human situation. His writing was a sort of chant, like the declamation of a Homeric bard.

Poetry of a traditional sort can be written faster than prose, and Wolfe kept falling into traditional poetry. His books, especially *Of Time and the River*, are full of lines in Elizabethan blank verse.

Were not their howls far broken by the wind?

huge limbs that stiffly creak in the remote
demented howlings of the burlywind,

and something creaking in the wind at night.

Page after page falls into an iambic pattern, usually a mixture of pentameters and hexameters. Other passages—in fact there is a whole book of them called *A Stone, A Leaf, A Door,* selected from Wolfe's writing by John S. Barnes—are a rather simple kind of cadenced verse:

Naked and alone we came into exile.
In her dark womb
We did not know our mother's face.

Often there are internal rhymes and half-rhymes: "October is the season for *returning:* the bowels of youth are *yearning* with lost love. Their mouths are *dry* and bitter with *desire:* their hearts are *torn* with the *thorns* of spring." Again there are phrases almost meaningless in themselves, but used as musical themes that are stated and restated with variations, sometimes through a whole novel. "A stone, a leaf, a door" is one of the phrases; others are "O lost" and "naked and alone" in *Look Homeward, Angel,* and "of wandering forever and the earth again," repeated perhaps a hundred times in *Of Time and the River.* All these patterns or devices—cadence, meter, rhyme, assonance, refrains—are those into which the language naturally falls when one is trying to speak or write it passionately and torrentially. They are not the marks of good prose—on the contrary—and yet in Wolfe's case, as in that of a few other natural writers, they are the means of achieving some admirable effects, including an epic movement with its surge and thunder. They also help Wolfe to strike and maintain a *tone,* one that gives his work a unity lacking in its structure, a declamatory tone that he needs for his effort to dignify a new race of heroes and demigods, to suffuse a new countryside with legend, and to bring new subjects into the charmed circle of those considered worthy to be treated in epic poems.

His persistent immaturity—still another fault that is often urged against him—was not so much a weakness of character as it was a feature of his literary policy. He had to play the part of an innocent in the great world. He had to have illusions, then lose them painfully, then replace them with others, because that repeated process was the story he wanted to tell. He had to be naïve about his emotions in order to feel them more intensely and in order to convey the impression—as he does in his best work—that something as commonplace as boarding a train or writing a book is being experienced not only for the first time in the author's life but for the first time in history. If he had learned from the experience of others, he would have destroyed that sense of uniqueness. If he had said to himself with the wisdom of middle age, "There must be a catch somewhere," in his exultation, or, "You'll feel better about it tomorrow," in his bottomless despair, he would have blunted the edge of both feelings and made them less usable as memories.

God said in the proverb, "Take what you want and pay for it." That might have been the motto and moral of Wolfe's collected works and of his private life as well. Determined as he was to find words for every experience, he denied himself many of the richest experiences because they might have interfered with his writing, or simply because he had no time for them. He never had a real home after he was seven years old; he never owned so much as a square foot of the earth he loved (even his grave is in a family plot); he never planted a tree or a garden, never married, never fathered a child. Much as he loved good company, he spent most of his time alone in dingy lodgings or roaming the streets at night. He played no games, took part in no sports, displayed no social accomplishments. Indeed, he had few amusements: eating and drinking were the first two, and afterward came travel, making love, and conversation, in about that order of importance. He didn't enjoy music, or much enjoy art (except the paintings of Breughel and Cranach); he stopped going to the theatre after his quarrel with Mrs. Bernstein; and though he liked to talk about books, I suspect that he did comparatively little reading after he left Harvard. His real avocation was the physical act of writing; his one preoccupation was preparing for the act. He said in a letter to Mrs. Roberts, written a few months before his death:

> . . . there is no rest, once the worm gets in and begins to feed upon the heart—there can never after that be rest, forgetfulness, or quiet sleep again. . . . After this happens, a man becomes a prisoner; there are times when he almost breaks free, but there is one link in the chain that always holds; there are times when he almost forgets, when he is with his friends, when he is reading a great book or poem, when he is at the theatre, or on a ship, or with a girl—but there is one tiny cell that still keeps working; even when he is asleep, one lamp that will not go out. . . .
>
> As far as I am concerned, there is no life without work—at least, looking back over my own, everything I can remember of any value is somehow tied up with work.

The price Wolfe paid in his life was not the price of his debauches, which were intense while they lasted, like all his other activities—once he landed in jail and another time in a German hospital with a broken head, richly deserved—but which were occasional or intermittent. He paid more for his one great virtue than for all his vices. He paid for his hours of steady writing, for his sleepless nights, for his efforts to remember and interpret everything that happened, to find a key to it all, to give form to his memories. The price was partly in terms of health, for he was drawing sight drafts against his constitution without stopping to ask whether there was still a credit balance.

But there was also a price in mental health that most of his critics have been too considerate to mention, even long after his death. His alternating moods of exuberance and despair became more extreme; especially the periods of despair were longer and deeper. Many physicians would say that in his last years he was a victim of manic-depressive psychosis.

He also developed paranoid symptoms, as manic-depressives often do. There were ideas of reference and delusions of persecution and grandeur. At times he thought the whole literary world was leagued in a conspiracy to keep him from working. "As for that powerful and magnificent talent I had two years ago," he wrote to Perkins in January, 1937, "—in the name of God is that to be lost entirely, destroyed under the repeated assaults and criminalities of this blackmail society under which we live? *Now* I know what happens to the artist in America." His farewell letter to Perkins was a magnificent piece of sustained eloquence—130 of his manuscript pages—but in places it was a crazy man's letter. One fine sentence is often quoted: "And I shall wreak out my vision of this life, this way, this world and this America, to the top of my bent, to the height of my ability, but with an unswerving devotion, integrity and purity of purpose that shall not be menaced, altered or weakened by any one." But the following sentences, which reveal his state of mind, are usually slurred over:

> I will go to jail because of this book if I have to. I will lose my friends because of it, if I will have to. I will be libeled, slandered, blackmailed, threatened, menaced, sneered at, derided and assailed by every parasite, every ape, every blackmailer, every scandalmonger, every little Saturday Reviewer of the venomous and corrupt respectabilities. I will be exiled from my country because of it, if I have to. . . . But no matter what happens I am going to write this book.

That is impressive as eloquence, but not as a statement of the facts. Wolfe was planning to write a book that might have hurt a few persons, notably Mrs. Bernstein and some of the staff at Scribner's, but not so much as some of his neighbors in Asheville had been hurt by *Look Homeward, Angel.* Nobody was trying to keep him from writing it. For the author it would involve absolutely no danger of prison, blackmail, ostracism, or exile. "I am a righteous man," he said in the letter, with an undertone of menace, "and few people know it because there are few righteous people in the world." There are many with delusions of righteousness, which they use as an excuse for being unjust to others. Wolfe was becoming one of them, as he must have realized in part of his mind—the Dr. Jekyll part, as he sometimes called it. At this point, as at some others, he was losing touch with reality.

It had better be made clear that his fits of despair were not the "down" phase of a manic-depressive cycle. There was no loss of appetite or vigor, no moping in silence; on the contrary there were quarrels, broken furniture, and a torrent of spoken and written words. The fits did not recur at regular intervals and they were not induced by mere pretexts; on the contrary they had understandable causes, usually connected with his work. As Wolfe said to Alfred S. Dashiell of *Scribner's Magazine* in one of his many letters of apology:

> The effort of writing or creating something seems to start up a strange and bewildering conflict in the man who does it, and this conflict at times almost takes on physical proportions so that he feels he is struggling not only with his own work but also with the whole world around him, and he is so beset with demons, nightmares, delusions and bewilderments that he lashes out at everyone and everything, not only people he dislikes and mistrusts, but sorrowfully enough, even against the people that he knows in his heart are his friends.
>
> I cannot tell you how completely and deeply conscious I have been of this thing and how much bloody anguish I have sweat and suffered when I have exorcised these monstrous phantoms and seen clearly into what kind of folly and madness they have led me.

It had all started so boyishly and admirably with his gift for feeling joys and sorrows more deeply than others. He chose to cultivate the gift because it helped him in his writing, and gradually it had transformed his character. At first he was proud, if in a rather sheepish fashion, of sometimes losing control of himself. He wrote to his sister Mabel in May, 1929, "Don't be afraid of going crazy—I've been there several times and it's not at all bad." It was indeed an almost normal state for a romantic artist forcing himself, provoking himself, beyond the natural limit of his emotions. Soon he began to feel the sort of dismay he expressed in the letter to Dashiell, but it was becoming too late to change his professional habits. There were always occasions in the literary life for those fits of manic exultation and, increasingly, of despair—the sense of loss on publishing a book, the insults of a few reviewers (notably Bernard DeVoto), the strain of getting started again, the fatigue that followed months of steady writing, the disappointment when Perkins felt that his latest work wasn't quite his best, the injustice of a suit against him for libel—and all these hurts became more painful as he brooded over them in solitude or drank to forget them, until at last he couldn't help interpreting them as signs that his talent was threatened by a vast conspiracy. His psychosis, if we call it that, was not organic or toxic, nor was it functional in the usual sense of being an illness due to unsolved emotional conflicts. Like the oversized wart on the middle finger of his right hand, it was a scar he had earned in combat, a professional deformation.

Tennessee Williams

THE DEPARTURE OF LORD BYRON

Dear Whit:

I am best at monologues and they fall somewhere between rhetoric and poetry, sometimes more toward the one and sometimes more toward the other. I think (I hope) that Lord Byron's monologue in *Camino Real* falls more toward poetry.

Yours,
Tennessee Williams

[*There is the sound of loud desert wind and a flamenco cry
followed by a dramatic phrase of music.*

*A flickering diamond blue radiance floods the hotel entrance.
The crouching, grimacing Hunchback shakes his hoop of bells
which is the convention for the appearance of each legendary
figure.*

*Lord Byron appears in the doorway readied for departure.
Gutman raises his hand for silence.*]

GUTMAN – You're leaving us, Lord Byron?

BYRON – Yes, I'm leaving you, Mr. Gutman.

GUTMAN – What a pity! But this is a port of entry and departure.
There are no permanent guests. Possibly you are getting a little restless?

BYRON – The luxuries of this place have made me soft. The metal
point's gone from my pen, there's nothing left but the feather.

GUTMAN – That may be true. But what can you do about it?

BYRON – Make a departure!

GUTMAN – From yourself?

BYRON – From my present self to myself as I used to be!

GUTMAN – *That's* the *furthest* departure a man could make. I guess
you're sailing to Athens? There's another war there and like all wars
since the beginning of time it can be interpreted as a—struggle for
what?

BYRON—For *freedom!* You may laugh at it, but it still means something to *me!*

GUTMAN—Of course it does! I'm not laughing a bit, I'm beaming with admiration.

BYRON—I've allowed myself many distractions.

GUTMAN—Yes, indeed!

BYRON—But I've never altogether forgotten my old devotion to the—

GUTMAN—To the *what,* Lord Byron?

[*Byron passes nervous fingers through his hair.*]

You can't remember the object of your one-time devotion?

[*There is a pause. Byron limps away from the terrace and goes toward the fountain.*]

BYRON—When Shelley's corpse was recovered from the sea . . .

[*Gutman beckons the Dreamer who approaches and accompanies Byron's speech.*]

—It was burned on the beach at Viareggio.—I watched the spectacle from my carriage because the stench was revolting . . . Then it—fascinated me! I got out of my carriage. Went nearer, holding a handkerchief to my nostrils!—I saw that the front of the skull had broken away in the flames, and there—

[*He advances out upon the stage apron, followed by Abdullah with the pine torch or lantern.*]

And there was the brain of Shelley, indistinguishable from a cooking stew!—*boiling, bubbling, hissing!*—in the *blackening—cracked—pot—* of his skull!

[*Marguerite rises abruptly. Jacques supports her.*]

—Trelawney, his friend, Trelawney, threw salt and oil and frankincense in the flames and finally the almost intolerable stench—

[*Abdullah giggles. Gutman slaps him.*]

—was *gone* and the burning was *pure!*—as a man's burning should be . . .

A man's burning *ought* to be pure!—*not* like mine—(a crepe suzette —burned in brandy . . .)

Shelley's burning was finally very *pure!*
But the body, the corpse, split open like a grilled pig!

[*Abdullah giggles irrepressibly again. Gutman grips the back of his neck and he stands up stiff and assumes an expression of exaggerated solemnity.*]

—And then Trelawney—as the ribs of the corpse unlocked—reached into them as a baker reaches quickly into an oven!

[*Abdullah almost goes into another convulsion.*]

—And snatched out—as a baker would a biscuit!—the *heart* of Shelley! Snatched the heart of Shelley out of the blistering corpse!— Out of the purifying—blue-flame . . .

[*Marguerite resumes her seat; Jacques his.*]

—And it was *over!*—I thought—

[*He turns slightly from the audience and crosses upstage from the apron. He faces Jacques and Marguerite.*]

—I thought it was a disgusting thing to do, to snatch a man's heart from his body! What can one man do with another man's heart?

[*Jacques rises and strikes the stage with his cane.*]

JACQUES [*passionately*] He can do this with it!

[*He seizes a loaf of bread on his table, and descends from the terrace.*]

He can twist it like this!

[*He twists the loaf.*]

He can tear it like this!

[*He tears the loaf in two.*]

He can crush it under his foot!

[*He drops the bread and stamps on it.*]

—*And kick it away—like this!*

[*He kicks the bread off the terrace. Lord Byron turns away from him and limps again out upon the stage apron and speaks to the audience.*]

BYRON – That's very true, Señor. But a poet's vocation, which used to be my vocation, is to influence the heart in a gentler fashion than you have made your mark on that loaf of bread. He ought to purify it and lift it above its ordinary level. For what is the heart but a sort of—

[*He makes a high, groping gesture in the air.*]

—A sort of—*instrument!*—that translates *noise* into *music,* chaos into —*order* . . .

[*Abdullah ducks almost to the earth in an effort to stifle his mirth, Gutman coughs to cover his own amusement.*]

—*a mysterious order!*

[*He raises his voice till it fills the plaza.*]

—That was my vocation once upon a time, before it was obscured by vulgar plaudits!—Little by little it was lost among gondolas and palazzos!—masked balls, glittering salons, huge shadowy courts and torch-lit entrances!—Baroque façades, canopies and carpets, candelabra and gold plate among snowy damask, ladies with throats as slender as flower-stems, bending and breathing toward me their fragrant breath—
—Exposing their breasts to me!
Whispering, half-smiling!—And everywhere marble, the visible grandeur of marble, pink and gray marble, veined and tinted as flayed corrupting flesh,—all these provided agreeable distractions from the rather frightening solitude of a poet. Oh, I wrote many cantos in Venice and Constantinople and in Ravenna and Rome, on all of those Latin and Levantine excursions that my twisted foot led me into—but I wonder about them a little. They seem to improve as the wine in the bottle—dwindles . . . *There is a passion for declivity in this world!* And lately I've found myself listening to hired musicians behind a row of artificial palm trees—instead of the single—pure-stringed instrument of my heart . . .
Well, then, it's time to leave here!

[*He turns back to the stage.*]

—There is a time for departure even when there's no certain place to go!

I'm going to look for one, now. I'm sailing to Athens. At least I can look up at the Acropolis, I can stand at the foot of it and look up at broken columns on the crest of a hill—if not purity, at least its recollection . . .

I can sit quietly looking for a long, long time in absolute silence, and possibly, yes, *still* possibly—

The old pure music will come to me again. Of course on the other hand I may hear only the little noise of insects in the grass . . .

But I am sailing to Athens! *Make voyages!—Attempt them!*—there's nothing else . . .

MARGUERITE [*excitedly*] *Watch where he goes!*

> [*Lord Byron limps across the plaza with his head bowed, making slight, apologetic gestures to the wheedling Beggars who shuffle about him. There is music. He crosses toward the steep Alleyway Out. The following is played with a quiet intensity so it will be in a lower key than the later Fugitivo Scene.*]

Watch him, watch him, see which way he goes. Maybe he knows of a way that we haven't found out.

JACQUES—Yes, I'm watching him, Cara.

> [*Lord and Lady Mulligan half rise, staring anxiously through monocle and lorgnon.*]

MARGUERITE—Oh, my God, I believe he's going up that alley.

JACQUES—Yes, he is. He has.

LORD and LADY MULLIGAN—Oh, the fool, the idiot, he's going under the arch!

MARGUERITE—Jacques, run after him, warn him, tell him about the desert he has to cross.

JACQUES—I think he knows what he's doing.

MARGUERITE—I can't look!

> [*She turns to the audience, throwing back her head and closing her eyes. The desert wind sings loudly as Byron climbs to the top of the steps.*]

BYRON [*to several porters carrying luggage—which is mainly caged birds*] THIS WAY!

[*He exits.*]

[*Kilroy starts to follow. He stops at the steps, cringing and looking at Gutman. Gutman motions him to go ahead. Kilroy rushes up the stairs. He looks out, loses his nerve and sits—blinking his nose. Gutman laughs as he announces—*]

GUTMAN – Block Nine on the Camino Real!

[*He goes into the hotel.*]

William L. Shirer

THE DEATH OF HITLER
and
THE END OF THE THIRD REICH

These two selections form the concluding pages of *The Rise and Fall of the Third Reich,* depicting the *Goetterdaemmerung* of the short-lived barbarian empire that Adolf Hitler, with the enthusiastic support of the German people, built.

For most of the world and especially for Europe, by that time in shambles from the devastation of nearly six years of war, which Hitler had launched on September 1, 1939, the fall of Nazi Germany came as a great deliverance. To me it was that too but also a little more. It was the end of a long assignment that had begun in the late 1920's when I had first gone to Germany, then under the expiring Weimar Republic. From September, 1934, until December, 1940, I had spent most of my time in Berlin covering the rise of the Third Reich, watching at first hand, with increasing fascination and horror, Hitler consolidate his power as dictator of this great but baffling nation, and then lead it off to war and conquest.

In June of 1941, I published my impressions of that time in *Berlin Diary.* Exactly a year before the idea for the bigger book had begun to take root. Back in Berlin after watching the Germans crush France I began to brood over the future. It was a bleak summer for me. Germany, having conquered Poland, Norway and Denmark, the low countries and France, was the master of Europe. Hitler had not yet committed the folly of attacking Russia and declaring war on the United States. He was planning to conquer Britain in the fall. Somehow, against all the evidence, against the opinion of almost everyone, I did not believe that he would succeed. I never lost hope, as my dispatches and diary show, that in the end he would be brought down, his savage empire destroyed, and some semblance of decency restored in the world.

If so, I thought I would try some day to get down in a book how it was that Europe came to the brink of the abyss and how it happened that a great and cultured people, the Germans, succumbed in the twentieth century to such a mindless and murderous barbarism. Perhaps after that I could do another volume on how the French, the most civilized of the Europeans and with a glittering history of achievement behind them, fell to pieces so quickly that spring and early summer of 1940.

I doubt, though, if in the end I would ever have attempted the monumental task of getting to the bottom of the German story had not the secret archives of the Third Reich fallen into the hands of the Allies at the end of the war. Personal experience, though valuable, would not have been enough without the documentation. But with both on hand I eventually set to work. The excerpts here published are a small part of the fruit of that endeavor.

William L. Shirer

THE DEATH OF HITLER AND HIS BRIDE

During the afternoon of April 29 (1945) one of the last pieces of news to reach the bunker from the outside world came in. Mussolini, Hitler's fellow fascist dictator and partner in aggression, had met his end and it had been shared by his mistress, Clara Petacci.

They had been caught by Italian partisans on April 26 while trying to escape from Como into Switzerland, and executed two days later. On the Saturday night of April 28 the bodies were brought to Milan in a truck and dumped on the piazza. The next day they were strung up by the heels from lampposts and later cut down so that throughout the rest of the Sabbath day they lay in the gutter, where vengeful Italians reviled them. On May Day Benito Mussolini was buried beside his mistress in the paupers' plot in the Cimitero Maggiore in Milan. In such a macabre climax of degradation Il Duce and Fascism passed into history.

It is not known how many of the details of the Duce's shabby end were communicated to the Fuehrer. One can only speculate that if he heard many of them he was only strengthened in his resolve not to allow himself or his bride to be made a "spectacle, presented by the Jews, to divert their hysterical masses,"—as he had just written in his Testament —not their live selves or their bodies.

Shortly after receiving the news of Mussolini's death Hitler began to make the final preparations for his. He had his favorite Alsatian dog, Blondi, poisoned and two other dogs in the household shot. Then he called in his two remaining women secretaries and handed them capsules of poison to use if they wished to when the barbarian Russians broke in. He was sorry, he said, not to be able to give them a better farewell gift, and he expressed his appreciation for their long and loyal service.

Evening had now come, the last of Adolf Hitler's life. He instructed Frau Junge, one of his secretaries, to destroy the remaining papers in his files and he sent out word that no one in the bunker was to go to bed until further orders. This was interpreted by all as meaning that he judged the time had come to make his farewells. But it was not until long after midnight, at about 2:30 A.M. of April 30, as several witnesses recall, that the Fuehrer emerged from his private quarters and appeared in the general dining passage, where some twenty persons, mostly the women members of his entourage, were assembled. He walked down the line shaking hands with each and mumbling a few words that were inaudible. There was a heavy film of moisture on his eyes and, as Frau Junge remembered, "they seemed to be looking far away, beyond the walls of the bunker."

After he retired, a curious thing happened. The tension which had been building up to an almost unendurable point in the bunker broke, and several persons went to the canteen—to dance. The weird party soon became so noisy that word was sent from the Fuehrer's quarters requesting more quiet. The Russians might come in a few hours and kill them all—though most of them were already thinking of how they could escape—but in the meantime for a brief spell, now that the Fuehrer's strict control of their lives was over, they would seek pleasure where and how they could find it. The sense of relief among these people seems to have been enormous and they danced on through the night.

Not Bormann. This murky man still had work to do. His own

prospects for survival seemed to be diminishing. There might not be a long enough interval between the Fuehrer's death and the arrival of the Russians in which he could escape to Doenitz. If not, while the Fuehrer still lived and thus clothed his orders with authority, Bormann could at least exact further revenge on the "traitors." He dispatched during this last night a further message to Doenitz.

Doenitz!

Our impression grows daily stronger that the divisions in the Berlin theater have been standing idle for several days. All the reports we receive are controlled, suppressed, or distorted by Keitel . . . The Fuehrer orders you to proceed at once, and mercilessly, against all traitors.

And then, though he knew that Hitler's death was only hours away, he added a postscript, "The Fuehrer is alive, and is conducting the defense of Berlin."

But Berlin was no longer defensible. The Russians already had occupied almost all of the city. It was now merely a question of the defense of the Chancellery. It too was doomed, as Hitler and Bormann learned at the situation conference at noon on April 30, the last that was ever to take place. The Russians had reached the eastern end of the Tiergarten and broken into the Potsdamerplatz. They were just a block away. The hour for Adolf Hitler to carry out his resolve had come.

His bride apparently had no appetite for lunch that day and Hitler took his repast with his two secretaries and with his vegetarian cook, who perhaps did not realize that she had prepared his last meal. While they were finishing their lunch at about 2:30 P.M., Erich Kempka, the Fuehrer's chauffeur, who was in charge of the Chancellery garage, received an order to deliver immediately 200 liters of gasoline in jerricans to the Chancellery garden. Kempka had some difficulty in rounding up so much fuel but he managed to collect some 180 liters and with the help of three men carried it to the emergency exit of the bunker.

While the oil to provide the fire for the Viking funeral was being collected, Hitler, having done with his last meal, fetched Eva Braun for another and final farewell to his most intimate collaborators: Dr. Goebbels, Generals Krebs and Burgdorf, the secretaries and Fräulein Manzialy, the cook. Frau Goebbels did not appear. This formidable and beautiful blond woman had, like Eva Braun, found it easy to make the decision to die with her husband, but the prospect of killing her six young children, who had been playing merrily in the underground shelter these last days without an inkling of what was in store for them, unnerved her.

"My dear Hanna," she had said to Fräulein Reitsch two or three evenings before, "when the end comes you must help me if I become weak about the children . . . They belong to the Third Reich and to the Fuehrer, and if these two cease to exist there can be no further place for them. My greatest fear is that at the last moment I will be too weak." Alone in her little room she was now striving to overcome her greatest fear.*

Hitler and Eva Braun had no such problem. They had only their own lives to take. They finished their farewells and retired to their rooms. Outside in the passageway, Dr. Goebbels, Bormann and a few others waited. In a few moments a revolver shot was heard. They waited for a second one, but there was only silence. After a decent interval they quietly entered the Fuehrer's quarters. They found the body of Adolf Hitler sprawled on the sofa dripping blood. He had shot himself in the mouth. At his side lay Eva Braun. Two revolvers had tumbled to the floor, but the bride had not used hers. She had swallowed poison.

It was 3:30 P.M. on Monday, April 30, 1945, ten days after Adolf Hitler's fifty-sixth birthday, and twelve years and three months to a day since he had become Chancellor of Germany and had instituted the Third Reich. It would survive him but a week.

The Viking funeral followed. There were no words spoken; the only sound was the roar of Russian shells exploding in the garden of the Chancellery and on the shattered walls around it. Hitler's valet, S.S. Sturmbannfuehrer Heinz Linge, and an orderly carried out the Fuehrer's body, wrapped in an Army field-gray blanket, which concealed the shattered face. Kempka identified it in his own mind by the black trousers and shoes which protruded from the blanket and which the warlord always wore with his field-gray jacket. Eva Braun's death had been cleaner, there was no blood, and Bormann carried out her body just as it was to the passage, where he turned it over to Kempka.

> Frau Hitler [the chauffer later recounted] wore a dark dress . . . I could not recognize any injuries to the body.

The corpses were carried up to the garden and during a lull in the bombardment placed in a shell hole and ignited with gasoline. The mourners, headed by Goebbels and Bormann, withdrew to the shelter of the emergency exit and as the flames mounted stood at attention and raised their right hands in a farewell Nazi salute. It was a brief

* The children and their ages were: Hela, 12; Hilda, 11; Helmut, 9; Holde, 7; Hedda, 5; Heide, 3.

ceremony, for Red Army shells began to spatter the garden again and the survivors retired to the safety of the bunker, leaving the gasoline-fed flames to complete the work of eradicating the last earthly remains of Adolf Hitler and his wife.* For Bormann and Goebbels, there were still tasks to perform in the Third Reich, now bereft of its founder and dictator, though they were not the same tasks.

There had not yet been time for the messengers to reach Doenitz with the Fuehrer's testament appointing him as his successor. The Admiral would now have to be informed by radio. But even at this point, with power slipped from his hands, Bormann hesitated. It was difficult to one who had savored it to give it up so abruptly. Finally he got off a message.

Grand Admiral Doenitz:
In place of the former Reich Marshal Goering the Fuehrer appoints you as his successor. Written authority is on its way. You will immediately take all such measures as the situation requires.

There was not a word that Hitler was dead.

The Admiral, who was in command of all German forces in the north and had moved his headquarters to Ploen in Schleswig, was flabbergasted at the news. Unlike the party leaders, he had no desire to succeed Hitler; the thought had never entered his sailor's head. Two days before, believing that Himmler would inherit the succession, he had gone to the S.S. chief and offered him his support. But since it would never have occurred to him to disobey an order of the Fuehrer, he sent the following reply, in the belief that Adolf Hitler was still alive.

My Fuehrer!
My loyalty to you will be unconditional. I shall do everything possible to relieve you in Berlin. If fate nevertheless compels me to rule the Reich as your appointed successor, I shall continue this war to an end worthy of the unique, heroic struggle of the German people.

Grand Admiral Doenitz

That night Bormann and Goebbels had a fresh idea. They decided to try to negotiate with the Russians. General Krebs, the Chief of the Army General Staff, who had remained in the bunker, had once been

---

* The bones were never found, and this gave rise to rumors after the war that Hitler had survived. But the separate interrogation of several eyewitnesses by British and American intelligence officers leaves no doubt about the matter. Kempka has given a plausible explanation as to why the charred bones were never found. "The traces were wiped out," he told his interrogators, "by the uninterrupted Russian artillery fire."

the assistant military attaché in Moscow, spoke Russian, and on one famous occasion had even been embraced by Stalin at the Moscow railway station. Perhaps he could get something out of the Bolsheviks; specifically, what Goebbels and Bormann wanted was a safe-conduct for themselves so that they could take their appointed places in the new Doenitz government. In return for this they were prepared to surrender Berlin.

General Krebs set out shortly after midnight of April 30—May 1 to see General Chuikov,* the Soviet commander of the troops fighting in Berlin. One of the German officers accompanying him has recorded the opening of their conversation.

> KREBS — Today is the First of May, a great holiday for our two nations.†
> CHUIKOV — We have a great holiday today. How things are with you over there it is hard to say.

The Russian General demanded the unconditional surrender of every-one in the Fuehrer's bunker as well as of the remaining German troops in Berlin.

It took Krebs some time to carry out his mission, and when he had not returned by 11 A.M. on May 1 the impatient Bormann dispatched another radio message to Doenitz.

> The Testament is in force. I will join you as soon as possible. Till then, I recommend that publication be held up.

This was still ambiguous. Bormann simply could not be straight-forward enough to say that the Fuehrer was dead. He wanted to get out to be the first to inform Doenitz of the momentous news and thereby help to insure his favor with the new Commander in Chief. But Goebbels, who with his wife and children was about to die, had no such reason for not telling the Admiral the simple truth. At 3:15 P.M. he got off his own message to Doenitz—the last radio communication ever to leave the beleaguered bunker in Berlin.

Grand Admiral Doenitz

MOST SECRET

> The Fuehrer died yesterday at 1530 hours [3:30 P.M.]. Testament of April 29 appoints you as Reich President . . . [There follow the names of the principal cabinet appointments.]

---

* Not Marshal Zhukov, as most accounts have had it.
† May 1 was the traditional Labor Day in Europe.

By order of the Fuehrer the Testament has been sent out of Berlin to you . . . Bormann intends to go to you today and to inform you of the situation. Time and form of announcement to the press and to the troops is left to you. Confirm receipt.

Goebbels

Goebbels did not think it necessary to inform the new Leader of his own intentions. Early in the evening of May 1, he carried them out. The first act was to poison the six children. Their playing was halted and they were given lethal injections, apparently by the same physician who the day before had poisoned the Fuehrer's dogs. Then Goebbels called his adjutant, S.S. Hauptsturmfuehrer Guenther Schwaegermann, and instructed him to fetch some gasoline.

"Schwaegermann," he told him, "this is the worst treachery of all. The generals have betrayed the Fuehrer. Everything is lost. I shall die, together with my wife and family." He did not mention, even to his adjutant, that he had just had his children murdered. "You will burn our bodies. Can you do that?"

Schwaegermann assured him he could and sent two orderlies to procure the gasoline. A few minutes later, at about 8:30 P.M., just as it was getting dark outside, Dr. and Frau Goebbels walked through the bunker, bade goodbye to those who happened to be in the corridor, and mounted the stairs to the garden. There, at their request, an S.S. orderly dispatched them with two shots in the back of the head. Four cans of gasoline were poured over their bodies and set on fire, but the cremation was not well done. The survivors in the bunker were anxious to join the mass escape which was just getting under way and there was no time to waste on burning those already dead. The Russians found the charred bodies of the Propaganda Minister and his wife the next day and immediately identified them.

By 9 o'clock on the evening of May 1, the *Fuehrerbunker* had been set on fire and some five or six hundred survivors of the Fuehrer's entourage, mostly S.S. men, were milling about in the shelter of the New Chancellery—like chickens with their heads off, as one of them, the Fuehrer's tailor, later recalled—preparatory to the great breakout. The plan was to go by foot along the subway tracks from the station below the Wilhelmsplatz, opposite the Chancellery, to the Friedrich-strasse Bahnhof and there cross the River Spree and sift through the Russian lines immediately to the north of it. A good many got through; some did not, among them Martin Bormann.

When General Krebs had finally returned to the bunker that afternoon with General Chuikov's demand for unconditional surrender Hitler's party secretary had decided that his only chance for survival lay in joining the mass exodus. His group attempted to follow a German tank, but according to Kempka, who was with him, it received a direct hit from a Russian shell and Bormann was almost certainly killed. Artur Axmann, the Hitler Youth Leader, who had deserted his battalion of boys at the Pichelsdorf Bridge to save his neck, was also present and later deposed that he had seen Bormann's body lying under the bridge where the Invalidenstrasse crosses the railroad tracks. There was moonlight on his face and Axmann could see no sign of wounds. His presumption was that Bormann had swallowed his capsule of poison when he saw that his chances of getting through the Russian lines were nil.

Generals Krebs and Burgdorf did not join in the mass attempt to escape. It is believed that they shot themselves in the cellar of the New Chancellery.

THE END OF THE THIRD REICH

The Third Reich survived the death of its founder by seven days.

A little after 10 o'clock on the evening of the first of May, while the bodies of Dr. and Frau Goebbels were burning in the Chancellery garden and the inhabitants of the bunker were herding together for their escape through a subway tunnel in Berlin, the Hamburg radio interrupted the playing of a recording of Bruckner's solemn Seventh Symphony. There was a roll of military drums and then an announcer spoke.

> Our Fuehrer, Adolf Hitler, fighting to the last breath against Bolshevism, fell for Germany this afternoon in his operational headquarters in the Reich Chancellery. On April 30 the Fuehrer appointed Grand Admiral Doenitz his successor. The Grand Admiral and successor of the Fuehrer now speaks to the German people.

The Third Reich was expiring, as it had begun, with a shabby lie. Aside from the fact that Hitler had not died that afternoon but the previous one, which was not important, he had not fallen fighting "to the last breath," but the broadcasting of this falsehood was necessary if the inheritors of his mantle were to perpetuate a legend and also if they were to hold control of the troops who were still offering resistance and who would surely have felt betrayed if they had known the truth.

Doenitz himself repeated the lie when he went on the air at 10:20 P.M. and spoke of the "hero's death" of the Fuehrer. Actually at that moment he did not know how Hitler had met his end. Goebbels had radioed only that he had "died" on the previous afternoon. But this did not inhibit the Admiral either on this point or on others, for he did his best to muddy the confused minds of the German people in the hour of their disaster.

It is my first task [he said] to save Germany from destruction by the advancing Bolshevik enemy. For this aim alone the military struggle continues. As far and as long as the achievement of this aim is impeded by the British and Americans, we shall be forced to carry on our defensive fight against them as well. Under such conditions, however, the Anglo-Americans will continue the war not for their own peoples but solely for the spreading of Bolshevism in Europe.

After this silly distortion, the Admiral, who is not recorded as having protested Hitler's decision to make the Bolshevik nation Germany's ally in 1939 so that a war could be fought against England and later America, assured the German people in concluding his broadcast that "God will not forsake us after so much suffering and sacrifice."

These were empty words. Doenitz knew that German resistance was at an end. On April 29, the day before Hitler took his life, the German armies in Italy had surrendered unconditionally, an event whose news, because of the breakdown in communications, was spared the Fuehrer, which must have made his last hours more bearable than they otherwise would have been. On May 4 the German High Command surrendered to Montgomery all German forces in northwest Germany, Denmark and Holland. The next day Kesselring's Army Group G, comprising the German First and Nineteenth armies north of the Alps, capitulated.

On that day, May 5, Admiral Hans von Friedeburg, the new Commander in Chief of the German Navy, arrived at General Eisenhower's headquarters at Reims to negotiate a surrender. The German aim, as the last papers of OKW make clear, was to stall for a few days in order to have time to move as many German troops and refugees as possible from the path of the Russians so that they could surrender to the Western Allies. General Jodl arrived at Reims the next day to help his Navy colleague draw out the proceedings. But it was in vain. Eisenhower saw through the game.

> I told General Smith [he later recounted] to inform Jodl that unless they instantly ceased all pretense and delay I would close the entire Allied front and would, by force, prevent any more German refugees from entering our lines. I would brook no further delay.

At 1:30 A.M. on May 7 Doenitz, after being informed by Jodl of Eisenhower's demands, radioed the German General from his new headquarters at Flensburg on the Danish frontier full powers to sign the document of unconditional surrender. The game was up.

In a little red schoolhouse at Reims, where Eisenhower had made his headquarters, Germany surrendered unconditionally at 2:41 on the morning of May 7, 1945. The capitulation was signed for the Allies by General Walter Bedell Smith, with General Ivan Susloparov affixing his signature as witness for Russia and General François Sevez for France. Admiral Friedeburg and General Jodl signed for Germany.

Jodl asked permission to say a word and it was granted.

> With this signature the German people and the German Armed Forces are, for better or worse, delivered into the hands of the victors . . . In this hour I can only express the hope that the victor will treat them with generosity.

There was no response from the Allied side. But perhaps Jodl recalled another occasion when the roles were reversed just five years before. Then a French general, in signing France's unconditional surrender at Compiègne, had made a similar plea—in vain, as it turned out.

The guns in Europe ceased firing and the bombs ceased dropping at midnight on May 8–9, 1945, and a strange but welcome silence settled over the Continent for the first time since September 1, 1939. In the intervening five years, eight months and seven days millions of men and women had been slaughtered on a hundred battlefields and in a thousand bombed towns, and millions more done to death in the Nazi gas chambers or on the edge of S.S. Einsatzgruppen pits in Russia and Poland—as the result of Adolf Hitler's lust for German conquest. A greater part of most of Europe's ancient cities lay in ruins, and from their rubble, as the weather warmed, there was the stench of the countless unburied dead.

No more would the streets of Germany echo to the jack boot of the goose-stepping storm troopers or the lusty yells of the brown-shirted masses or the shouts of the Fuehrer blaring from the loudspeakers.

After twelve years, four months and eight days, an Age of Darkness to all but a multitude of Germans and now ending in a bleak night for them too, the Thousand-Year Reich had come to an end. It had raised, as we have seen, this great nation and this resourceful but so easily misled people to heights of power and conquest they had never before experienced and now it had dissolved with suddenness and a completeness that had few, if any, parallels in history.

In 1918, after the last defeat, the Kaiser had fled, the monarchy had tumbled, but the other traditional institutions supporting the State had remained, a government chosen by the people had continued to function, as did the nucleus of a German Army and a General Staff. But in the spring of 1945 the Third Reich simply ceased to exist. There was no longer any German authority on any level. The millions of soldiers, airmen and sailors were prisoners of war in their own land. The millions of civilians were governed, down to the villages, by the conquering enemy troops, on whom they depended not only for law and order but throughout that summer and bitter winter of 1945 for food and fuel to keep them alive. Such was the state to which the follies of Adolf Hitler—and their own folly in following him so blindly and with so much enthusiasm—had brought them, though I found little bitterness toward him when I returned to Germany that fall.

The people were there, and the land—the first dazed and bleeding and hungry, and, when winter came, shivering in their rags in the hovels which the bombings had made of their homes; the second a vast wasteland of rubble. The German people had not been destroyed, as Hitler, who had tried to destroy so many other peoples and, in the end, when the war was lost, themselves, had wished.

But the Third Reich had passed into history.

A BRIEF EPILOGUE

I went back that autumn to the once proud land, where I had spent most of the brief years of the Third Reich. It was difficult to recognize. I have described that return in another place. It remains here merely to record the fate of the remaining characters who have figured prominently in these pages.

Doenitz's rump government, which had been set up at Flensburg on the Danish border, was dissolved by the Allies on May 23, 1945, and all its members were arrested. Heinrich Himmler had been dismissed from the government on May 6, on the eve of the surrender at Reims, in a move which the Admiral calculated might win him favor with the Allies. The former S.S. chief, who had held so long the power of life and death over Europe's millions, and who had often exercised it, wandered about in the vicinity of Flensburg until May 21, when he set out with eleven S.S. officers to try to pass through the British and American lines to his native Bavaria. Himmler—it must have galled him—had shaved off his mustache, tied a black patch over his left eye and donned an Army private's uniform. The party was stopped the first day at a British control point between Hamburg and Bremerhaven. After questioning, Himmler confessed his identity to a British Army captain, who hauled him away to Second Army headquarters at Lueneburg. There he was stripped and searched and made to change into a British Army uniform to avert any possibility that he might be concealing poison in his clothes. But the search was not thorough. Himmler kept his vial of potassium cyanide concealed in a cavity of his gums. When a second British intelligence officer arrived from Montgomery's headquarters on May 23 and instructed a medical officer to examine the prisoner's mouth, Himmler bit on his vial and was dead in twelve minutes, despite frantic efforts to keep him alive by pumping his stomach and administering emetics.

The remaining intimate collaborators of Hitler lived a bit longer. I went down to Nuremberg to see them. I had often watched them in their hour of glory and power at the annual party rallies in this town. In the dock before the International Military Tribunal they looked different. There had been quite a metamorphosis. Attired in rather shabby clothes, slumped in their seats fidgeting nervously, they no longer resembled the arrogant leaders of old. They seemed to be a drab assortment of mediocrities. It seemed difficult to grasp that such men, when last you had seen them, had wielded such monstrous power, that such as they could conquer a great nation and most of Europe.

There were twenty-one of them* in the dock: Goering, eighty pounds lighter than when last I had seen him, in a faded Luftwaffe uniform without insignia and obviously pleased that he had been given the Number One place in the dock—a sort of belated recognition of his place in the Nazi hierarchy now that Hitler was dead; Rudolf Hess, who had been the Number Three man before his flight to England, his face now emaciated, his deep-set eyes staring vacantly into space, feigning amnesia but leaving no doubt that he was a broken man; Ribbentrop, at last shorn of his arrogance and his pompousness, looking pale, bent and beaten; Keitel, who had lost his jauntiness; Rosenberg, the muddled party "philosopher," whom the events which had brought him to this place appeared to have awakened to reality at last.

Julius Streicher, the Jew-baiter of Nuremberg, was there. This sadist and pornographer, whom I had once seen striding through the streets of the old town brandishing a whip, seemed to have wilted. A bald, decrepit-looking old man, he sat perspiring profusely, glaring at the judges and convincing himself—so a guard later told me—that they were all Jews. There was Fritz Sauckel, the boss of slave labor in the Third Reich, his narrow little slit eyes giving him a porcine appearance. He seemed nervous, swaying to and fro. Next to him was Baldur von Schirach, the first Hitler Youth Leader and later Gauleiter of Vienna, more American by blood than German and looking like a contrite college boy who has been kicked out of school for some folly. There was Walther Funk, the shifty-eyed nonentity who had succeeded Schacht. And there was Dr. Schacht himself, who had spent the last months of the Third Reich as a prisoner of his once revered Fuehrer in a concentration camp, fearing execution any day, and who now bristled with indignation that the Allies

---

* Dr. Robert Ley, head of the Arbeitsfront, who was to have been a defendant, had hanged himself in his cell before the trial began. He had made a noose from rags torn from a towel, which he had tied to a toilet pipe.

should try *him* as a war criminal. Franz von Papen, more responsible than any other individual in Germany for Hitler's coming to power, had been rounded up and made a defendant. He seemed much aged, but the look of the old fox, who had escaped from so many tight fixes, was still imprinted on his wizened face.

Neurath, Hitler's first Foreign Minister, a German of the old school, with few convictions and little integrity, seemed utterly broken. Not Speer, who made the most straightforward impression of all and who during the long trial spoke honestly and with no attempt to shirk his responsibility and his guilt. Seyss-Inquart, the Austrian quisling, was in the dock, as were Jodl and the two Grand Admirals, Raeder and Doenitz —the latter, the successor to the Fuehrer, looking in his store suit for all the world like a shoe clerk. There was Kaltenbrunner, the bloody successor of "Hangman Heydrich," who on the stand would deny all his crimes; and Hans Frank, the Nazi Inquisitor in Poland, who would admit some of his, having become in the end contrite and, as he said, having rediscovered God, whose forgiveness he begged; and Frick, as colorless on the brink of death as he had been in life. And finally Hans Fritzsche, who had made a career as a radio commentator because his voice resembled that of Goebbels, who had made him an official in the Propaganda Ministry. No one in the courtroom, including Fritzsche, seemed to know why he was there—he was too small a fry—unless it were as a ghost for Goebbels, and he was acquitted.

So were Schacht and Papen. All three later drew stiff prison sentences from German denazification courts though, in the end, they served very little time.

Seven defendants at Nuremberg drew prison sentences: Hess, Raeder and Funk for life, Speer and Schirach for twenty years, Neurath for fifteen, Doenitz for ten. The others were sentenced to death.

At eleven minutes past 1 A.M. on October 16, 1946, Ribbentrop mounted the gallows in the execution chamber of the Nuremberg prison, and he was followed at short intervals by Keitel, Kaltenbrunner, Rosenberg, Frank, Frick, Streicher, Seyss-Inquart, Sauckel and Jodl.

But not by Hermann Goering. He cheated the hangman. Two hours before his turn would have come he swallowed a vial of poison that had been smuggled into his cell. Like his Fuehrer, Adolf Hitler, and his rival for the succession, Heinrich Himmler, he had succeeded at the last hour in choosing the way in which he would depart this earth, on which he, like the other two, had made such a murderous impact.

Arthur M. Schlesinger, Jr.

The Beginning and End of
A THOUSAND DAYS

I offer these excerpts—the beginning and the end of *A Thousand Days*—not as representing any judgment about the "best," or even the least bad, in my writing, but as expressing the time of deepest public engagement in my life.

A Thousand Days, as the book's foreword tried to make clear, was not a comprehensive history of the Kennedy presidency. It was a personal memoir by one who had served in the White House during the Kennedy years. I had not originally meant to write even such a memoir. But, after President Kennedy's death, I felt an intense desire to indicate something of the manner and meaning of his presidency. Also, as the first historian to have the good luck to watch the making of national policy from that particular vantage point, I felt that I owed fellow historians some account of what I had seen.

When the book was published in 1965, there was criticism —not, it should be said, from other historians but from various keepers of the national conscience—over the fact that I had written the book at once instead of waiting for ten or twenty years. In retrospect, I can only say that I feel more justified than ever in having written it at once. A good deal of whatever abiding quality the book may have comes from its immersion in the distinctive mood and texture of that exciting time—something which it would have been impossible to recapture ten or twenty years later. In ten or twenty years a younger historian will write a comprehensive history of the Kennedy presidency. If he finds *A Thousand Days* helpful, it will be in great measure because it was an immediate record of an exceptional historical experience.

Emerson once said, "Every revolution was first a thought in one man's mind." Like all great leaders, Kennedy had the faculty of making others see the world as he saw it. When he became President, the United States was mired in a morass of dogmas—about the cold war, about the third world, about ourselves. If there was anything Kennedy hated, it was the flourish of stereotypes as if they were new thoughts. Clichés almost made him wince physically. He wanted to release his country from the tyranny of cant, to adjourn extinct quarrels and abolish obsolete formulations, to meet the problems of his own time on their own merits.

He did this with effortless ease. In part simply by being himself; for he was, above all, a free and contemporary man, "cool" immune to dogma, prejudice or platitude. He transformed faith in reason—in calm discussion and intelligent compromise—into a positive and liberating political force. He saw life differently and saw it so rationally, convincingly and vividly, with all the power of a disciplined intelligence, a strong will and an exhilarating personality, that he succeeded astonishingly in making others see differently and act differently. His own acuity of vision for a moment bathed the world itself in a fresh new light. The agony of grief which ran round the world after his death expressed not alone appropriate sorrow for a brilliant and fascinating young President but anguished lamentation for a lost hero who, people profoundly, mysteriously believed, might have led mankind from contemporary incoherence and despair into a decent and civilized future.

He has gone, and we survive. The question remains whether he was not, after all, an accident in American politics, an aberration in American history. Yet it may well be that he became the youngest man ever to be elected President precisely because he expressed so faithfully, lucidly and intrepidly the deepest and best impulses in American life. At least, I believe this to be so. It was in this faith that I set down my own observations of the thousand days—in the faith that the record of the Kennedy years will recall his countrymen to their highest standards and finest selves in all the years to come.

Arthur Schlesinger, Jr.

PROLOGUE: JANUARY 1961

It all began in the cold.

It had been cold all week in Washington. Then early Thursday afternoon the snow came. The winds blew in icy, stinging gusts and whipped the snow down the frigid streets. Washingtonians do not know how to drive in the snow: they slide and skid and spin their wheels and panic. By six o'clock traffic had stopped all over town. People abandoned their cars in snowdrifts and marched grimly into the gale, heads down, newspapers wrapped around necks and stuffed under coats. And still the snow fell and the winds blew.

At eight o'clock the young President-elect and his wife went to the Inaugural Concert at Constitution Hall. An hour later they left at the intermission to go on to the Inaugural Gala at the Armory. The limousine made its careful way through the blinding snow down the Mall. Bonfires had been lit along the path in a vain effort to keep the avenue clear. Great floodlights around the Washington Monument glittered through the white storm. It was a scene of eerie beauty. As stranded motorists cheered the presidential car, the President-elect told his friend William Walton, "Turn on the lights so they can see Jackie." With the light on inside the car, he settled back to read Jefferson's First Inaugural, which had been printed in the concert program. When he finished he shook his head and said wryly, "Better than mine."

By midnight the city was choked with snow. Workmen labored to clear Pennsylvania Avenue for next day's parade. Soldiers used flame throwers to melt the frozen drifts around the inaugural stand in the Capitol Plaza. At quarter to four in the morning, the President-elect returned to his house in Georgetown from a supper given him downtown by his father after the Gala. His wife, recuperating from the birth of their second child, had gone home hours earlier; but he found her awake, too excited to sleep, and they talked for a moment about the day that had passed and the day yet to come.

Toward dawn the snow began to stop. It covered houses and clung to trees and filled the windswept streets: the white city faintly shimmered in the pale sunrise. The President-elect arose at eight, read over the text of his inaugural address, pencil in hand, and then left to attend mass at a neighboring church. The crowd began to gather in the Capitol Plaza long before noon. At eleven the President-elect and his wife drank coffee with the retiring President and Vice-President and their wives in the Red Room of the White House. They talked formally and inconsequentially. In morning coats and top hats they entered limousines to drive along the snowy streets to the Capitol. The wife of the retiring President said, "Look at Ike in his top hat. He looks just like Paddy the Irishman."

The skies were now blue and cloudless, and the Plaza glistened in the sun, but the wind had not fallen and the temperature was barely twenty degrees above zero. The waiting crowd huddled and shivered. They enveloped themselves in sweaters and mufflers, blankets and sleeping bags. They stamped their feet to keep out the chill. They watched restlessly as the dignitaries slowly took their places on the platform. When the Vice President-elect entered, a man in a ten-gallon hat shouted, "All the way with L.B.J."; the Vice President-elect acknowledged the shout with a slight inclination of his head. Noon passed, and the crowd shuffled with impatience when the ceremony failed to begin. The President-elect, starting to come from the Capitol onto the platform, was instructed to wait. Then, at twenty minutes after twelve he appeared, and the spectators warmed themselves with applause.

Now they listened with stoicism as the Cardinal boomed out an interminable invocation. They looked with envy as blue smoke thinly curled up from a short circuit in the electric wires underneath the lectern: where there was fire, there must be heat. The Chief of the Secret Service watched the smoke with apprehension, fearful that the whole inaugural stand might go up in flames. Three times he started to give the order to clear the stand, and three times he paused; then the smoke stopped. The Chief mused that his Service would be in for a lively era protecting the athletic and fearless new President.*

---

* U. E. Baughman, *Secret Service Chief* (New York, 1962), 3, 12.

On the platform, the breath of the old poet congealed in the freezing air; and now, when he stepped forth to speak, the glare from the sun and snow blinded him. He read three lines from a manuscript:

Summoning artists to participate
In the august occasions of the state
Seems something artists ought to celebrate.

Then he stopped and said, "I'm not having a good light here at all. I can't see in this light." The Vice President-elect held out his hat to shield the old man's eyes; Robert Frost still could not see, could not conclude the poem:

It makes the prophet in us all presage
The glory of a next Augustan age
Of a power leading from its strength and pride,
Of young ambition eager to be tried,
Firm in our free beliefs without dismay,
In any game the nations want to play.
A golden age of poetry and power
Of which this noonday's the beginning hour.

Instead he said, "This was to have been a preface to a poem which I do not have to read," and from memory he recited "The Gift Outright" —"The land was ours before we were the land's"—changing the last line:

Such as we were we gave ourselves outright
(The deed of gift was many deeds of war)
To the land vaguely realizing westward,
But still unstoried, artless, unenhanced,
Such as she was, such as she will become.

At nine minutes before one the Chief Justice came forward to administer the oath. The President-elect, without hat or coat, the old Douay Bible of the Fitzgerald family open before him, gave his responses in firm tones. At last he began his inaugural address, his voice ringing out in the frosty air. "Let the word go forth from this time and place, to friend and foe alike, that the torch has been passed to a new generation of Americans —born in this century, tempered by war, disciplined by a hard and bitter peace, proud of our ancient heritage." And so he continued, striking notes of strength, conciliation and hope. "Let us begin anew," he said, "—remembering on both sides that civility is not a sign

of weakness, and sincerity is always subject to proof. Let us never negotiate out of fear. But let us never fear to negotiate." The prospect would
not be easy. "All this will not be finished in the first hundred days.
Nor will it be finished in the first thousand days, nor in the life of this
Administration, nor even perhaps in our lifetime on this planet. But let
us begin." The burden of the "long twilight struggle" lay on this people
and this generation. "And so, my fellow Americans: ask not what your
country can do for you—ask what you can do for your country."* (That
morning, reading over his text, he had scratched out "will" and replaced
it by "can.") He concluded: "My fellow citizens of the world: ask not
what America will do for you, but what together we can do for the
freedom of man."

The applause was strong and sustained. The President left the platform. His young wife joined him in the Capitol, whispered, "Oh, Jack,
what a day," and softly touched his face. Then the inaugural parade
marched through the freezing afternoon, and the thirty-fifth Presidentiad,
as Walt Whitman would say, began.

EPILOGUE

On Friday morning I had flown to New York with Katherine Graham,
whose husband Philip had died three months before, for a luncheon

---

* This thought had lain in Kennedy's mind for a long time. As far back as 1945
he had noted down in a looseleaf notebook a quotation from Rousseau: "As soon
as any man says of the affairs of the state, What does it matter to me? the state
may be given up as lost." In his address accepting the Democratic nomination
in 1960, he said of the New Frontier, "It sums up not what I intend to *offer*
the American people, but what I intend to *ask* of them." On September 5 at
Cadillac Square in Detroit, Kennedy departed from his prepared text to say:
"The new frontier is not what I promise I am going to do for you. The new
frontier is what I ask you to do for our country." He continued to polish the
thought in the back of his mind until he was ready to put it in final form in
the inaugural address.

Though this line was clearly Kennedy's own, like all such lines it had its
historic analogues. Gilbert Seldes cites the remarks of the mayor of Haverhill at
the funeral of John Greenleaf Whittier as quoted by Van Wyck Brooks in *New
England: Indian Summer*: "Here may we be reminded that man is most honored, not by that which a city may do for him, but by that which he has done
for the city." And James Rowe, Jr., Oliver Wendell Holmes's last law clerk,
points out the following lines from a Memorial Day address delivered by Justice
Holmes in 1884: "It is now the moment when by common consent we pause to
become conscious of our national life and to rejoice in it, to recall what our country has done for each of us, and to ask ourselves what we can do for our country
in return."

with the editors of her magazine *Newsweek*. Kenneth Galbraith had come down from Cambridge for the occasion. We were still sipping drinks before luncheon in an amiable mood of Friday-before-the-Harvard-Yale game relaxation when a young man in shirtsleeves entered the room and said, a little tentatively, "I am sorry to break in, but I think you should know that the President has been shot in the head in Texas." For a flash one thought this was some sort of ghastly office joke. Then we knew it could not be and huddled desperately around the nearest television. Everything was confused and appalling. The minutes dragged along. Incomprehensible bulletins came from the hospital. Suddenly an insane surge of conviction flowed through me: I felt that the man who had survived the Solomon Islands and so much illness and agony, who so loved life, embodied it, enhanced it, could not possibly die now. He would escape the shadow as he had before. Almost immediately we received the irrevocable word.

In a few moments Galbraith and I were on Katherine Graham's plane bound for Washington. It was the saddest journey of one's life. Bitterness, shame, anguish, disbelief, emptiness mingled inextricably in one's mind. When I stumbled, almost blindly, into the East Wing, the first person I encountered was Franklin D. Roosevelt, Jr. In a short time I went with my White House colleagues to Andrews Field to await the return of Air Force One from Texas. A small crowd was waiting in the dusk, McNamara, stunned and silent, Harriman, haggard and suddenly looking very old, desolation everywhere. We watched incredulously as the casket was carefully lifted out of the plane and taken to the Naval Hospital at Bethesda. Later I went to my house in Georgetown. My weeping daughter Christina said, "Daddy, what has happened to our country? If this is the kind of country we have, I don't want to live here any more." The older children were already on their way back from college to Washington.

Still later I went back to the White House to await the last return. Around four in the morning the casket, wrapped in a flag, was brought from the Naval Hospital and placed on a stand in the East Room. Tapers were lit around the bier, and a priest said a few words. Then Jacqueline approached the bier, knelt for a moment and buried her head in the flag. Soon she walked away. The rest of us waited for a little while in the great hall. We were beyond consolation, but we clung to the comradeship he had given us. Finally, just before daybreak, we bleakly dispersed into the mild night.

We did not grieve alone. Though in Dallas school children applauded the news* and in Peking the *Daily Worker* ran a savage cartoon entitled "Kennedy Biting the Dust" showing the dead President lying in a pool of blood, his necktie marked with dollar signs, sorrow engulfed America and the world. At Harvard Yard the bells tolled in Memorial Church, a girl wept hysterically in Widener Library, a student slammed a tree, again and again, with his fist. Negroes mourned, and A. Philip Randolph said that his "place in history will be next to Abraham Lincoln." Pablo Casals mused that he had seen many great and terrible events in his lifetime—the Dreyfus case, the assassination of Gandhi—"but in recent history—and I am thinking of my own lifetime—there has never been a tragedy that has brought so much sadness and grief to as many people as this." "For a time we felt the country was ours," said Norman Mailer. "Now it's theirs again." Many were surprised by the intensity of the loss. Alistair Cooke spoke of "this sudden discovery that he was more familiar than we knew." "Is there some principle of nature," asked Richard Hofstadter, "which requires that we never know the quality of what we have had until it is gone?" Around the land people sat desperately in front of television sets watching the bitter drama of the next four days. In Washington Daniel Patrick Moynihan, the Assistant Secretary of Labor, said, "I don't think there's any point in being Irish if you don't

---

* The children were not responsible; they expressed the atmosphere of the city. What was more shocking was that the Reverend William Holmes, who reported these incidents in a sermon on the following Sunday and said that "the spirit of assassination" had pervaded the city, received such threats that he had to take his own children out of school and go into hiding. The Dallas feeling evidently was that, whether true or false, Holmes's remarks reflected on their city and were therefore unforgivable. Subsequently a Dallas school teacher who asked in a letter to *Time* how her students could be expected to "grow up to be good citizens when the newspapers, their parents and the leaders of their own city preached dissension" was suspended. Judge Sarah T. Hughes of Dallas, who administered the presidential oath to Lyndon Johnson on the plane back to Washington, said, "It could have happened anywhere, but Dallas, I'm sorry to say, has been conditioned by many people who have hate in their hearts and who seem to want to destroy."
On May 29, 1965, the 48th anniversary of Kennedy's birth, the Texas House of Representatives defeated on a record vote of 72–52 (with Governor Connally's brother voting with the majority) a bill passed unanimously in the State Senate proposing to rename the state school for the mentally retarded at Richmond in President Kennedy's honor. One resident of Fort Bend County testified in the House hearings that changing the name of the school might cause local people to withdraw their support. When the *Texas Observer* asked the sponsor of the bill, Representative Neil Caldwell of Alvin, what reasons his colleagues had given him for their no votes, he said, "With most of them it's the politics of the man — the dead man. They think enough things have been named for him. 'Just wouldn't be popular back home.' 'Not well thought of.' 'Don't want to get hurt politically.' Some of 'em say, 'I didn't like him.'" In the debate Caldwell said that, though memorials had been raised to Kennedy around the world, there were none in Texas. See "And Finally, As to John F. Kennedy," *Texas Observer*, June 11, 1965.

know that the world is going to break your heart eventually. I guess that we thought we had a little more time. . . . Mary McGrory said to me that we'll never laugh again. And I said, 'Heavens, Mary. We'll laugh again. It's just that we'll never be young again.'"

In Ireland, "Ah, they cried the rain down that night," said a Fitzgerald of Limerick; he would not come back in the springtime. David Bruce reported from London, "Great Britain has never before mourned a foreigner as it has President Kennedy." As the news spread around London, over a thousand people assembled before the embassy in Grosvenor Square; they came in endless thousands in the next days to sign the condolence book. That Was The Week That Was on television, unwontedly serious: "the first western politician to make politics a respectable profession for thirty years—to make it once again the highest of the professions, and not just a fabric of fraud and sham. . . . We took him completely for granted." "Why was this feeling—this sorrow—at once so universal and so individual?" Harold Macmillan later asked. "Was it not because he seemed, in his own person, to embody all the hopes and aspirations of this new world that is struggling to emerge—to rise, Phoenix-like, from the ashes of the old?" In West Berlin people lighted candles in darkened windows. In Poland there was a spontaneous mass mourning by university students; church bells tolled for fifteen minutes on the night of the funeral. In Yugoslavia Tito, so overcome that he could hardly speak, phoned the American chief of mission; later he read a statement over the state radio and went in person to the embassy to sign the book. The national flag was flown at half-mast, and schools were instructed to devote one full hour to a discussion of the President's policies and significance. In Moscow Khrushchev was the first to sign the book, and the Soviet television carried the funeral, including the service in the church.

Latin America was devastated. Streets, schools, housing projects were named after him, shrines set up in his memory; his picture, torn from the newspaper, hung on the walls of workers' shacks and in the hovels of the *campesinos*. "For Latin America," said Lleras Camargo, "Kennedy's passing is a blackening, a tunnel, a gust of cloud and smoke." Castro was with Jean Daniel when the report came; he said, *"Es una mala noticia"* ("This is bad news"). In a few moments, with the final word, he stood and said, "Everything is changed. . . . I'll tell you one thing: at least Kennedy was an enemy to whom we had become accustomed." In Cambodia Prince Sihanouk ordered court mourning; "a light was put out," he later said, "which may not be re-lit for many years to come." In Indonesia flags flew at half-mast. In New Delhi people cried in the streets. In Algiers Ben Bella phoned Ambassador Porter in tears and said, "I can't believe it. Believe me, I'd rather it happen to me than to him." In Guinea Sékou Touré said, "I have lost my only true friend in the outside world." The embassy reported, "People expressed their grief without restraint, and just about everybody in Guinea seemed to have fallen under the spell of the courageous young hero of far away, the slayer of the dragons of discrimination, poverty, ignorance and war." In N'zérékoré in the back country, where one would hardly think they had heard of the United States let alone the American President, a group of natives presented a sum of money to their American pastor to buy, according to the custom of the Guerze people, a rush mat in which to bury President Kennedy. In Kampala Ugandans crowded the residence of the American Ambassador; others sat silently for hours on the lawns and hillsides waiting. In Mali, the most leftwing of African states, President Keita came to the embassy with an honor guard and delivered a eulogy. In the Sudan a grizzled old Bisharine tribesman told an American lawyer that it was terrible Kennedy's son was so young; "it will be a long time before he can be the true leader." *Transition,* the magazine of African intellectuals, said, "In this way was murdered the first real chance in this century for an intelligent and new leadership to the world. . . . More than any other person, he achieved the intellectual's ideal of a man in action. His death leaves us unprepared and in darkness."

In Washington grief was an agony. Somehow the long hours passed, as the new President took over with firmness and strength, but the roll of the drums, when we walked to St. Matthew's Cathedral on the frosty Monday, will sound forever in my ears, and the wildly twittering birds during the interment at Arlington while the statesmen of the world looked on. It was all so grotesque and so incredible. One remembered Stephen Spender's poem:

> I think continually of those who were truly great. . . .
> The names of those who in their lives fought for life,
> Who wore at their hearts the fire's center.
> Born of the sun they traveled a short while towards the sun,
> And left the vivid air signed with their honour.

It was all gone now—the life-affirming, life-enhancing zest, the brilliance, the wit, the cool commitment, the steady purpose. Richard Neustadt has suggested that two years are the period of presidential initiation. He had had so little time: it was as if Jackson had died before the nullification controversy and the Bank War, as if Lincoln had been killed six months after Gettysburg or Franklin Roosevelt at the end of 1935 or Truman before the Marshall Plan.*

Yet he had accomplished so much: the new hope for peace on earth, the elimination of nuclear testing in the atmosphere and the abolition of nuclear diplomacy, the new policies toward Latin America and the third world, the reordering of American defense, the emancipation of the American Negro, the revolution in national economic policy, the concern for poverty, the stimulus to the arts, the fight for reason against extremism and mythology. Lifting us beyond our capacities, he gave his country back to its best self, wiping away the world's impression of an old nation of old men, weary, played out, fearful of ideas, change and the future; he taught mankind that the process of rediscovering America was not over. He re-established the republic as the first generation of our leaders saw it—young, brave, civilized, rational, gay, tough, questing, exultant in the excitement and potentiality of history. He transformed the American spirit—and the response of his people to his murder, the absence of intolerance and hatred, was a monument to his memory. The energies he released, the standards he set, the purposes he inspired, the goals he established would guide the land he loved for years to come. Above all he gave the world for an imperishable moment the vision of a leader who greatly understood the terror and the hope, the diversity and the possibility, of life on this planet and who made people look beyond nation and race to the future of humanity. So the people of the world grieved as if they had terribly lost their own leader, friend, brother.

On December 22, a month after his death, fire from the flame burning at his grave in Arlington was carried at dusk to the Lincoln Memorial. It was fiercely cold. Thousands stood, candles in their hands; then, as the flame spread among us, one candle lighting the next, the crowd gently moved away, the torches flaring and flickering, into the darkness. The next day it snowed—almost as deep a snow as the inaugural blizzard. I went to the White House. It was lovely, ghostly and strange.

It all ended, as it began, in the cold.

---

* In the summer of 1964 Richard Wilson of *Look* asked congressional leaders whether Kennedy would have got his legislative programs, especially the civil rights and tax reduction bills, if he had lived. He received the following answers. Everett Dirksen: "This program was on its way before November 22, 1963. Its time had come." Carl Albert: "The pressure behind this program had become so great that it would have been adopted in essentially the same form whether Kennedy lived or died." Charles A. Halleck: "The assassination made no difference. The program was already made." Mike Mansfield: "The assassination made no real difference. Adoption of the tax bill and the civil-rights bill might have taken a little longer, but they would have been adopted." *Look*, November 17, 1964.

James Reston

THE KENNEDY LEGEND

Mr. Reston says he has a particular fondness for this piece
about John F. Kennedy and thinks any further comment on it
by himself unnecessary.

The Editor

November 15, 1964

Time seems to be trying to make amends to John Fitzgerald Kennedy. Robbed of his years, he is being rewarded and honored in death as he never was in life. Deprived of the place he sought in history, he has been given in compensation a place in legend. What was a monstrous personal and historic crime a year ago is now something even more elemental and enduring: it is a symbol of the tragedy and caprice of life, and it is likely to be remembered by the novelists and the dramatists long after the historians have gone on to other things.

Will he seem different to the historians from the way the dramatists will see him? What are they likely to say of his conduct of foreign affairs, domestic affairs, the Presidency itself? Are we already confusing myth with reality, as he was always telling us we should not do?

Probably we are, but this is only fair and maybe even natural. For there was always something vaguely legendary about him. He was a story-book President, younger and more handsome than mortal politicians, remote even from his friends, graceful, almost elegant, with poetry on his tongue and a radiant young woman at his side.

He was a sudden and surprising person. He never did things when other men were doing them. He went to Congress and the White House earlier than most. He married much later than his contemporaries. His war record, his political record, and his personal life were marked by flashes of crisis and even by a vague premonition of tragedy. He always seemed to be striding through doors into the center of some startling triumph or disaster. He never reached his meridian: we saw him only as a rising sun.

Accordingly, it is not easy to make an estimate of his 1,000 days in the White House. He didn't have a fair chance and he didn't even give himself a fair chance. He often made his decisions alone after a series of private talks with several individuals, none of whom shared the whole process of his thought. Oddly in one who had such an acute sense of history, he was disorderly about keeping records of what led up to his decisions, and though he had a great gift for conversation, he seems to have spent little time talking to his closest associates about how he had decided things in the past.

All this complicates the task of placing him in the catalogue of the Presidents. We do not have the record. We do not have the full story of the two Cuban crises, or his meeting with Khrushchev in Vienna, or the reasoning behind his gambles in Vietnam, or the communications that led up to the atomic test-ban treaty with the Soviets. We have only our clippings, memories, and impressions, and these can be uncertain guides.

Historians—and here we are in the realm of opinion—will probably rate President Kennedy's handling of foreign policy higher than his contemporaries did. It is a spotty record. He dreamed occasionally of an interdependent Atlantic world, and this has become part of the legend, but the reality is that the alliance was in poor shape during most of his Administration. He courted Latin America like a thoughtful lover, but, again, the Alliance for Progress was more dream than reality.

Even so, he had a feeling for the way the world was going. He understood the challenge of change. He was fascinated by the political revolution produced by the liberation of the colonial peoples: sometimes too fascinated with it, and too inclined to give it a higher priority than it deserved. He studied and understood the intricate problems of the atomic revolution and the scientific revolution, probably better than any of his predecessors.

Yet this keen, analytical intelligence was not always a help. It enabled him to see the problems, but it often depressed him about finding the answers. I always thought—perhaps wrongly—that his intelligence made him pessimistic. The evidence that science was transforming the world seemed so clear and overwhelming to him that he was irritated by the failure of men and institutions to adapt and keep up.

In his very first State of the Union message, ten days after he had been sworn in, he told the Congress and the nation: "Before my term has ended, we shall have to test anew whether a nation organized and governed such as ours can endure. The outcome is by no means certain. The answers are by no means clear."

His bungling of his first foreign-policy gamble, when he tried to help the Cuban refugees overthrow the Castro Government, made him all the more conscious, not only of the complexities of political decision, but of the possible consequences of failure.

The events of the Bay of Pigs contributed to his natural caution, and added to his problems with the Communists for most of the rest of his days in the White House. It is impossible to be sure about this but I was in Vienna when he met Khrushchev shortly after the fiasco of the Bay of Pigs, and saw him ten minutes after his meeting with the Soviet leader. He came into a dim room in the American Embassy, shaken and angry. He had tried, as always, to be calm and rational with Khrushchev, to get him to define what the Soviet Union could and would not do, and Khrushchev had bullied him and threatened him with war over Berlin.

We will have to know much more about that confrontation between Kennedy and Khrushchev, one now deprived of life and the other of power, before we can be sure, but Kennedy said just enough in that room in the embassy to convince me of the following: Khrushchev had studied the events of the Bay of Pigs; he would have understood if Kennedy had left Castro alone or destroyed him; but when Kennedy was rash enough to strike at Cuba but not bold enough to finish the job, Khrushchev decided he was dealing with an inexperienced young leader who could be intimidated and blackmailed. The Communist decision to put offensive missiles into Cuba was the final gamble of this assumption.

The missile crisis brought out what always seemed to me to be Kennedy's finest quality and produced the events on which Kennedy's place in history probably depends. There is a single fact that repeats itself in the Kennedy story like the major theme in the symphony: he was always at his best in the highest moment of crisis.

He could be ambiguous and even indecisive on secondary questions. He obviously trifled with the first Cuban crisis. He also temporized with the Vietnamese crisis, partly supporting those who wanted to intervene "to win," partly going along with those who reminded him that the French had suffered 175,000 casualties against the same Communist army, but never really defining his aims or reconciling his power with his objectives.

Yet always in his political life he acted decisively when faced with total defeat. He was supremely confident, almost presumptuous, in going for the Presidency in the first place against the opposition of the most powerful elements in his party. He was bold and effective when first Hubert Humphrey, then Harry Truman, and finally Lyndon Johnson challenged him publicly during the campaign for the nomination. He probably won the Presidency in the critical debates with Richard Nixon. And this same quality came out in the missile crisis in Cuba.

Then he was, as Robert Frost had urged him to be, "more Irish than Harvard" but with a dash of Harvard intelligence, too. If the first Cuban crisis was the worst example of the uses of American power and diplomacy in this generation, the second Cuban crisis was the best. And the significance of this fact can be understood only in relation to the longer perspective of war in this century.

Twice in this century, the leaders of the free world have been confronted by the menacing power of a totalitarian state. From 1912 until 1914, and again from 1935 until 1939, Germany made a series of moves that clearly threatened the peace and order of the world, and during those critical testing periods, Britain, France, and the United States failed either to raise enough military power or to show enough will power to avoid the holocaust. The resulting tragedies of the two great wars transformed the history of the world.

The Soviet decision to place long-range missiles in Cuba, capable of firing atomic rockets into almost any part of the United States, was a similar and in some ways even more ominous test. This lunge into the Western Hemisphere was clearly an effort to change the world balance of power in Moscow's favor, and Kennedy faced it at the risk of war and turned it back.

It is ironic that he went to his grave with many of his fellow countrymen condemning him for failing to get rid of all the Communists and all the defensive missiles in Cuba as well as all the offensive missiles. Yet this view has not been shared by most of the political leaders and historians of the world.

I saw Prime Minister Macmillan of Britain just before he resigned and before President Kennedy was murdered. "If Kennedy never did another thing," Macmillan remarked, "he assured his place in history by that single act. He did what we failed to do in the critical years before the two German wars."

Within a year of Kennedy's death, Khrushchev was removed from power partly as a result of his humiliating defeat in the Cuban missile crisis, but something important and maybe even historic remained: The Communist world was relieved of the illusion that the United States would not risk atomic wars to defend its vital interests. This new awareness greatly reduced the danger of miscalculating American intentions and led almost at once to the first really serious steps to bring atomic weapons under control.

Mr. Kennedy was more at ease in the larger world of diplomacy and the struggle between nations than he was in the world of Congressional politics and the struggle between contending national forces. He had more freedom of action in foreign than in domestic policy. He did not seem to mind the small talk of ceremonial meetings with heads of state or foreign students at the White House, and he had a rare combination of informality and dignity that made him very effective in this role. But blarneying with pompous Congressmen bored him and he simply would not take time to do it, as his successor, President Johnson, has with such marked success.

This was odd, in a way. He was a superb politician in planning and running a Presidential campaign, but he didn't really know the deck on Capitol Hill and he did not really like to play the political game there. Even though he spent most of his political life in the House and the Senate, he was always sort of a nonresident member of those peculiar clubs, always a back-bencher with a high truancy record and an excessive respect for the chairmen of the committees and the other elders of the Congress.

The very qualities of appearance, style, and cast of mind that won him the admiration of the intellectual and diplomatic worlds somehow marked him as an outsider in his dealings with the Congress. He had little patience for the tiresome loquacity and endless details of legislation, and he never cared much for the boisterous bantering and blackslapping of the cloakrooms.

He had a kind of gay magic as a political speaker, most of it as carefully contrived as it seemed spontaneous. He was good at the arts of Hollywood and Madison Avenue, and this delighted his fellow politicians, but he was a little too polished, ambitious, and out of the ordinary to escape the envy and criticism of the Hill.

Congress likes typical Americans and Kennedy was not one. In his mature life, he probably crossed the Atlantic more often than he crossed the Allegheny range. He never seemed at home in the West. The America he understood best was bounded by Harvard Yard, the State Department, Park Avenue, and Palm Beach. His political style and humor were not based on the exaggerated language and gymnastics of the American hustings but on the gentler models of the House of Commons.

Maybe these things had nothing to do with his troubles in getting a legislative program through the Congress; maybe it was just the old stubborn resistance of the Congress to change—"the government of the living by the dead"—but the fact remains that his domestic program was in deep trouble when he was killed, and some of us despaired that Capitol Hill would ever be his field of triumph.

Part of the Kennedy legend is connected with his introduction of the most radical legislation on behalf of Negro equality in this century. But again the reality is less romantic. He did not normally like to take on anything more than he had to tackle, no matter how worthy. Oddly for a man who wrote a book celebrating the heroes of lost causes (*Profiles in Courage*), he was always saying : "Why fight if you are not sure to win?" The Negro demonstrations in the summer of 1963, however, forced his hand, and he went along when some Republican leaders and his brother Robert urged that action was necessary.

Yet, on the home front, as in the foreign field, he did start one major innovation of transcending importance. At the urging of Walter Heller, the chairman of the Council of Economic Advisors, he broke with the traditional economic concepts of Capitol Hill and plunged for a large tax cut and a planned budget deficit. Liberal economists in Europe and in the American universities had been arguing for years that it was no longer necessary to redistribute the wealth of the rich in order to elevate the poor, but that the total production of wealth could be increased to the benefit of everybody if modern technology and fiscal measures were applied.

Kennedy was not by temper a fiscal reformer. He came to the White House as a rather timid liberal, but the longer he was in office the more he cried out against the restraining economic and fiscal traditions of the past and the more he appealed to the country to deal with the world as it is. He never saw his tax bill go through; he died before it was passed. But he was largely responsible for heading the country into the most prolonged period of peacetime prosperity since the last World War. There was a recession when he took over in 1961. Unemployment was up to almost 7 per cent of the work force. There was a balance-of-payments deficit of nearly $4 billion. The outflow of gold to other countries in 1960 totaled $1.7 billion. But by the time he died, this trend had been reversed, at least in part as a result of his initiatives.

Yet even if he turned the tide of the cold war toward the control of nuclear arms, and started the trend toward acceptance of the new economics of increased production and general prosperity, this is not the Kennedy story that is likely to be remembered. These things were only dramatic symbols of his critical mind. He was a critic of his age. He did not think we could deal with the menace of nuclear weapons unless we searched constantly for means of accommodation with the Communists. He did not think we could employ our people in the midst of a revolution in labor-saving machinery unless we changed our attitude toward Federal budgets and Federal deficits.

He did not think we could deal with the pressures of Communism, rising population, or galloping automation, or that we could contain the rising expectations of the nonwhite races and the new nations unless we moved faster to integrate the races at home and the nations of the free world abroad. In short, he did not believe we could deal effectively with a transformed world unless we transformed ourselves—our attitudes of mind and our institutions.

This was a youthful mind asking the big questions. He was not one for big plans and grand designs, though contemporary writers often professed to see such things in some of the speeches of Ted Sorensen. Incidentally, it was always difficult to tell where the soaring rhetoric of Sorensen's bolder and more liberal mind left off and the more cautious Kennedy mind picked up, but Kennedy was not a great planner.

I once asked him in a long private talk at Hyannis Port what he wanted to have achieved by the time he rode down Pennsylvania Avenue with his successor. He looked at me as if I were a dreaming child. I tried again: Did he not feel the need of some goal to help guide his day-to-day decisions and priorities? Again a ghastly pause. It was only when I turned the question to immediate, tangible problems that he seized the point and rolled off a torrent of statistics about the difficulty of organizing nations at different levels of economic development.

Yet there is a puzzle in all this. For while he wanted to transform the thought and institutions of the nation, and regarded the machinery of the Congress as almost an anachronism, he concentrated on working —not, on the whole, very successfully—with the Congress, and he never really exploited his considerable gifts as a public educator.

"Give me the right word and the right accent," said Joseph Conrad, "and I will move the world." This was Churchill's way, and nobody admired it more than Kennedy. But while he made a few glorious trial flights, something held him back, some fear of appealing to the people over the heads of the Congress, some fear of too much talk (he hated verbosity), some modesty, maybe—always so apparent in his embarrassment before applauding crowds.

The essence of the tragedy, however, is perfectly clear. What was killed in Dallas was not only the President but the promise. The death of youth and the hope of youth, of the beauty and grace and the touch of magic.

The heart of the Kennedy legend is what might have been. His intelligence made people think that the coming generation might make the world more rational. It even made it hard for the intellectuals of Europe to be anti-American. His good looks and eloquence put a brighter shine on politics, and made his world relevant and attractive to young people all over the world.

All this is apparent in the faces of the people who come to his grave daily on the Arlington hill. In the world of their dreams, Presidents would be young and heroic, with beautiful wives, and the ugly world would be transformed by their examples.

John Finley, the master of Eliot House at Harvard, sent me a letter which sums up this sense of loss better than anything else:

"No doubt like innumerable people, I felt suddenly old without Mr. and Mrs. Kennedy in the White House. On reflection, ours seems a society of older people; it takes a while to reach the top in science, law, business and most other things. Yet, paradoxically, only the young have the freshness to enjoy and not be wearied by the profusion and vitality of present American life.

"Not only by ability, but by sheer verve and joy, the Kennedys imparted their youth to everyone and put a sheen on our life that made it more youthful than it is. Mr. Johnson now seems Gary Cooper as President—'High Noon,' the poker game, the easy walk and masculine smile. But even Gary Cooper was growing older, and the companions and adversaries around the poker table reflect a less fresh, if no doubt practical and effective, mood. All will be well, I feel sure . . . but it is August, not June. . . ."

Always we come back to the same point. The tragedy of John Fitzgerald Kennedy was greater than the accomplishment, but in the end the tragedy enhances the accomplishment and revives the hope.

Thus the law of compensation operates. "The dice of God are always loaded," wrote Emerson. "For everything you have missed you have gained something else. . . . The world looks like a multiplication table, or a mathematical equation, which, turn it how you will, balances itself. . . . Every secret is told, every crime is punished, every virtue rewarded, every wrong redressed, in silence and certainty."

VIII

The Human Ordeal

VII

The Human Ordeal

Cornelia Otis Skinner

ORDEAL FOR SONS

Dear Mr. Burnett:

The reason I picked "Ordeal for Sons" for your forthcoming *This Is My Best* is not that I consider it great literature in any way, but because I think it is the common experience of most parents, when visiting their sons at boarding school, to find themselves in the awkward position of discovering that their children suffer from apprehension!

Sincerely,
Cornelia Otis Skinner

The time approaches for me to go mortify my young son by a visit to his school again, and it's a tossup as to which of us is anticipating the event with more happy apprehension. Not that I am not eager to see him; nor is there, I trust, any lack of filial warmth on his part. But in the environment of a large and pretty impressive boarding school and the atmosphere of one of those week ends when parents, teeming with tradition, run around with their offspring, doing a great many traditional things, something seems to happen which puts us both under a considerable nervous strain. My son suddenly appears to me as an amiable but utter stranger and it's obvious that I appear to him as a complete menace. In the tender bosom of home, I smugly pride myself that he looks upon me with devotion, respect and even periodic moments of admiration. In the Spartan bosom of boarding school, he regards me with tolerance, embarrassment and moments of profound shame, mingled with the sort of pitying affection one might feel for a harmless family imbecile. That he considers me anything but bright, is evinced by his letter concerning my impending visitation and containing instructions so detailed it surprises me he didn't at the same time write his father asking him to pin my ticket on me, tip the porter and ask him to put me off at the right place. He tells me to take the night train which goes, he says, at night, from Grand Central. "When you arrive at . . ." (and, just in case my memory needed jogging, he mentions the name of the town) . . . "get off the train." (Possibly he thought I might want to stay on for the ride.) ". . . and walk through the stashion. Go to the hotel and have breakfast allthough the dogwaggon has hamburgers but then you just take coffee. I have classes all morning so do what you like. You may want a bath. . . ." (A startling suggestion coming from a small boy so allergic to them.) "At 12, take a taxi to the Alumen" (his own basic English for Alumni) "House where I'll be waiting with severall peopel for lunch." These instructions were a replica of those he sent me prior to my previous visit and as such were superfluous, the events of that pilgrimage being indelibly impressed on my memory.

That night train which leaves at night, may do so from the Grand Central, but there are certain features of it which lead one to think it would feel more at home in the Smithsonian. It winds its way northward, stopping at all stations, signal towers and, it would seem, cattle crossings, and politely pulling off at all sidings to make way for slow freights. At Lowell, the train is dismembered and the car bound for the school town is violently clashed onto a series of other trains who will have none of it and who, the moment it is coupled to them, shake it loose in apparent fury. In between times, it is taken on a scenic tour of the yards behind a switch engine driven by a novice engineer who has a lot to learn. This goes on for three or four hours, at the end of which interlude, the brakes sigh shrilly and the car, attached at last to one train which will tolerate it, heads for the north. The school is situated in the frozen heart of New England in a climate called, by those who have survived it, "bracing." You start in bracing about two A.M. and ring for the porter in the naïve hope that he will hear the bell and bring another blanket. He does neither and you continue to brace under cover of a coat, the extra pillow and that suitcase they no longer allow you to set in the aisle. By morning, you are permanently braced in a manner which, when you manage to emerge from between the icy Pullman curtains, becomes a semicrouching position.

This trip, the weather will, blessedly, be not so bracing. But the other features will be the same. Early morning in the ladies' room there will be the same jam session of females in various states of dishevelment . . . myself in the worst state of the lot . . . lurching against one another and politely fighting for a chance at the tooth-brushing basin. This is a rude introduction to the sisterhood with whom one will be rubbing elbows for the next forty-eight hours. Last trip, my child had neglected to mention the fact that it was to be a gala week end and that a good many other parents were also coming, and I remember regarding these ladies with sentiments not untinged with venom, until, with remorseful chagrin, it occurred to me that they might be somebody's mothers, and

my glare of resentment melted into a weak leer of tentative friendliness
to which some responded wanly and some not at all.

This time also, I shall try to feel more charitably inclined toward whoever is in the drawing-room. Occupants of a drawing-room, unless I
am one of them, rouse in me sentiments of proletarian resentment. I fix
them with a Madame DeFarge stare and look about for a copy of *The
Daily Worker* to brandish in their faces. The injustice of this attitude
was proved by the fact that the room on this occasion was filled to
bursting point by a genial family also bound for the school—mother,
father, small brother entered for three years hence, little sister profoundly
bored by everything and a slap-happy Sealyham dog. The boy they
were visiting turned out to be a friend of my son's . . . a fact which
endeared them to me only a few degrees less than the happy moment
before dinner when the father, sensing my need for such encouragement,
poured me out a generous hooker of Scotch.

This time, too, I am going to know how to dress. The first trip,
under the impression that I was a lone mother going quietly to visit
her child at a country school, I dressed the part, as I thought, to
perfection in a tweed suit, flat shoes and an ancient coat which, after
years of exposure, is beginning to look less like beaver than cocker-
spaniel. With a rapidly increasing sense of inferiority, I watched the
disheveled ladies of the washroom emerge from the night-in-a-Pullman
chrysalis into visions of mink-coated smartness. In June, mink coats
will hardly be worn, but I'm asking a friend to lend me a sable scarf
in case of an emergency.

At the station, there will, I suppose, be the absence of a porter and the
scramble for a taxi which is eventually shared by five beaming mothers
and one lone father, anything but beaming. On the way to the hotel,
there is a good deal of strained merriment. Everybody asks everybody
else if they have enough room, and everybody assures everybody else
that they have, although nobody has any. Then everybody asks everybody
else what form their boy is in and somebody who is in the know recounts
the athletic events for the day and everybody says doesn't that sound
grand and everybody else says yes, doesn't it. The lone father says nothing
until the taxi approaches the hotel when he comes forth with the consoling
statement that he hears the school has two cases of scarlet fever.

The hotel is one of those New England hostelries that must have been
in its prime about the time of Rutherford B. Hayes. It may not be
aquiver with Statler efficiency, but I find in it a good deal of pristine
charm and it is perfectly comfortable. A morning spent there quietly

reading a book, writing a letter or even taking that suggested bath, is restful and pleasant. Then the village clock strikes the hour of noon and I take a conveyance to the school and the "Alumen House."

Previous experience has resigned me to the deflating fact that my small boy who, at home hurtles to meet me after an absence of only half a day, with demonstrations of rapture, will now, after an absence of several months, greet me with a formal "Hi" and a bare handshake. I know better than to try to kiss him. Last time, when I leaned forward to do so, he ducked in mortification and left me smacking the air. As before, he will be waiting for me outside the front door and will conduct me inside in the manner of someone at Tattersall's bringing in a horse, the behavior of which is uncertain. The weather being milder, he will be spared the humiliation of watching me, in the process of taking off my galoshes, remove my shoes at the same time and have to stand stocking-footed for some moments in the crowded hallway. I suppose the "severall peopel" will again be three or four of his classmates to whom he will be reluctant to exhibit me and concerning whom, albeit I have never before laid eyes on them, he will expect me to know every detail. The prospect of that luncheon reminds me to reserve a table. Last time, being a novice in such matters, we found the dining room looking like Saturday noon at Sardi's, with every table overflowing and a line-up at the door. A gracious and rather pretty lady asked us if we had reserved a table and I said why no, and my son said why hadn't I, and I countered why hadn't *he,* to which his reply was an exasperated "Really, Mother!" Our distress was evident and the gracious lady consoled us by setting us up a special festive board in an alcove of the library . . . which was all right by my son who, after the episode of the galoshes, thought it safest to keep me quietly out of sight. Lunch was nervous but pleasant. My child's buddies impressed me as being very nice and I thought, somewhat fatuously, that we all got along amazingly well; although at one point, my boy hissed at me that I didn't have to laugh so loud. If I did, it was due to a certain amount of strain which I imagine they too shared. There is a technique to carrying on social chit-chat with little boys which I am slow at mastering. All of them were on their best behavior, which meant that most of the time they maintained complete silence while I searched wildly about in my mind for topics of possible interest. With much too eager brightness, I asked the usual routine questions . . . where each of them came from, what colleges they were going to . . . how they liked school. I even ventured a few remarks concerning athletics, which, coming from me, was the equivalent of

Betty Grable discussing Relativity. They answered each question politely and then lapsed into polite silence. Once or twice I managed to come forth with something in the nature of a quip at which they would burst out in a chorus of deafening guffaws which ceased as abruptly as they started, and there would then ensue further stretches of that polite silence. All through the meal, my son regarded me with a look which was softened by momentary gleams of appreciation, but which for the most part indicated that he thought I might at any minute start dancing on the table.

Lunch ended with no greater mishap than that I forgot to pay for it, which made him again say, "Really, Mother!" He never calls me Mother unless he is particularly ashamed of me and that week end he never called me anything else.

Lunch safely over, he pulled off the first of a series of disappearing acts which he performed at intervals during the next twenty-four hours. The school is a large one, with many buildings and vast grounds. Emerging from some hall or dormitory, he would suddenly announce that now we would go to some place with a cryptic name like Big Upper or Down Lower and, before I'd have time to ask him what he meant, he'd be gone, leaving me to wander about like a derelict until he'd appear as suddenly as he had vanished, to ask impatiently why I hadn't come along. Having some extra studying to do, he then deposited me on a settee in a sort of parents' social hall, told me not to to move till he got back, and, seemingly, evaporated. My time, for the most part, was beguiled by another mother . . . an imposing woman who looked like a combination of Demeter and Susan B. Anthony. She was knitting a sea-boot with such zealous efficiency, she gave the impression of doing two at the same time.

"What form's your boy in?" came from her in a clarion tone, and I realized she was addressing me.

"The First," I replied, then, noticing the slight lift to her eyebrow added, vindicatingly, "He's only just thirteen."

"Same form as my youngest," she said. Then, doubtless to put me at ease, "He's eleven."

Being a lady, I inquired if he were her only child.

"Mercy no," she retorted. "I have five. All boys. All of them went here."

"How wonderful," I murmured.

"Their father went here before them," she continued and, being stuck for another reply, I came out with another "How wonderful."

She then started a dissertation on the subject of the school. Did I think Mr. So-and-So in the Whatsis Department was as good as old Mr.

Whosis had been, and, to my mind, did Dr. X preach as good a sermon as Dr. Y? I had to confess my ignorance on such matters and the horrid fact that this was my first visit to the place. If I had admitted to never having known about the Fourth of July, she could not have looked more horrified. But she proved to be a kindly sort, and after her initial shock, she launched forth in a detailed narrative history of the school and its traditions in the simple language of a missionary telling a heathen child the story of Christmas. This hour of instruction was cut short by the arrival of my son who said it was time for hockey practice and would I care to watch. Thanking the Mother of Men for her enlightening information, I set forth with my child who, the moment we got to territory totally unfamiliar to me, again disappeared. I wandered on aimlessly, passing stray professors and groups of boys who looked at me as if they wondered if my attendant knew I was loose. Some of the mink-coat mothers also passed and we bestowed on one another that sickly smile which can be taken for recognition or pure imbecility. After a time, my offspring hove in sight armed with skates and a stick and told me to follow him. Hockey was being played on a pond some hundred yards beyond us and the people I had passed were all heading for the barrier, which seemed to be the vantage place for watching the game. Once arrived at the pond, however, my son started leading me off in an oblique direction. When I shyly asked the reason, he said he didn't want me near the barrier . . . that I might get in the way, or fall down or otherwise make myself conspicuous. His method of making me inconspicuous was to station me off on a remote and windy promontory. A strange, solitary figure, silhouetted against the snow, I felt like that picture of Napoleon overlooking Moscow. I could hardly see what was going on, much less make out which of the distant swirling figures was my child, which, perhaps, was just as well as it saved me the anguish of seeing him make a goal on his own side which counted some sort of colossal penalty and made him a pariah for the remainder of the game. On my forthcoming visit I am told the sport will be boat racing and I suppose by way of making me inconspicuous, I shall be placed in a tree.

After hockey, we made a brief sojourn to his room, which isn't a room but a sort of cubicle in a long dormitory. It looked like the East Coast of Florida after a hurricane and I offered to neat it up a bit for him. But he said no, if I did, he'd never find anything in it. So, with a shuddering glance at a mud-caked shoe reposing on a pillow and a toothbrush handle jammed into a jar of peanut butter, we left.

Next morning was Chapel, a very charming and moving ceremony which takes place at eleven. My son, although he knows I am the soul of punctuality, told me it was at ten-fifteen, but that I'd better get there by ten. I did, and found the place locked and deserted. Nor was there any sign of my child. After a time of sitting like Leah the Forsaken on the chapel steps, waiting for the doors to open, he appeared, greeted me with one of those ardent "Hi's" and said "Come on, I'll take you to your place." He sings in the choir and I was hoping for a good view of him. However, he led me to the visitors' gallery where he placed me in a far corner of the back row. When I inquired why I couldn't sit in the front row he replied, "Because" . . . an irrefutable answer I myself have resorted to so often with him, I hadn't the nerve to pursue the matter further. Perhaps he was right in putting me off in a corner. Little boys in white surplices marching down the nave of a chapel, their clear young voices raised in song, make me cry quite badly and I was glad, for his sake, nobody could see me.

After Chapel, came the ordeal of interviewing certain terrifying powers that were, concerning his work. My boy is not of the stuff that Phi Beta Kappas are made of and his marks have been a source of anguish for him, his family and, I suspect, his instructors. I had forced him into making an appointment for me with the assistant headmaster who acted as sort of dean, holding jurisdiction over the students' academic welfare . . . or, in our case, ill-fare. He seldom, they said, came into direct contact with the boys but ruled their destinies from an Olympian distance. He sounded extremely awesome and I pictured him as something between Erasmus and Zeus, hurling down on the student body thunderbolts or diplomas as he saw fit. At the prospect of my impending interview, my child was in a panic which I shared with equal acuteness. I was convinced that he would expel my son and me along with him and my knees buckled as I neared his office, at the threshold of which my offspring turned tail and beat it. The cause of our panic proved to be a delightful, mild-mannered gentleman who with great courtesy asked me to be seated and plunged right into the matter at hand by remarking that my son's marks were not over-satisfactory . . . to which triumph of understatement I acquiesced with sorrow. Then and there we both dismissed the painful subject and there passed a charming half hour in which we talked about Katherine Hepburn's Rosalind. At the end of this I remembered that my scholar was quaking outside and excused myself, relieved that neither of us had as yet been expelled. My scholar met me with gloomy foreboding. It was apparent that he was afraid to hear the verdict.

"What did he say?" he finally managed to ask.

"He said for you to work harder," I answered. After that we then went off to lunch, just the two of us, in the hotel where, under the influence of steak, mashed potatoes and three helpings of ice cream, his formal manner relaxed and, there being nobody he knew around, I detected a gleam of the filial affection I had feared was dead.

Time came for my train. I dropped him in front of his dormitory, where was gathered a group of upper classmen. He tried to say good-by in the frozen style of his previous greeting, but in the language of departing there is no equivalent of "Hi," so he murmured an awkward "Be careful." Then he turned to leave, rushed back as if he'd forgotten something and, flinging his arms about me in a sudden tackle, smacked me shamelessly on the cheek.

I guess this impending trip will be quite similar. I shall ask the wrong questions, say the wrong things and generally shame him. In conversing with upper classmen, I shall again adopt that hearty tone of voice which, according to my son, sounds as if I were on a quarter-deck in a stiff gale. I shall again be deserted in unfamiliar portions of the grounds, I and the mink-coat mothers, now in summer prints, will again leer sheepishly at one another and I shall again weep profusely over Chapel. Some long-suffering master will again discuss with me my child's mental progress . . . or lack of it. And it will all be quite charming and rather awful. But I'm going to do it. And I guess the reason is, I wouldn't miss it for anything.

John Barth

ECHO

Dear Mr. Burnett:

"Echo," a story composed in 1967 for disembodied authorial voice, satisfies me as well as any of the short pieces in which I've attempted to make the form, the narrative viewpoint, and the medium itself rigorously metaphorical.

Cordially,
John Barth

State University of New York at Buffalo
College of Arts and Sciences
Department of English

One does well to speak in the third person, the seer advises, in the manner of Theban Tiresias. A cure for self-absorption is saturation: telling the story over as though it were another's until like a much-repeated word it loses sense. There's a cathartic Tiresias himself employs in the interest of objectivity and to rid himself of others' histories—Oedipus's, Echo's—which distract him fore and aft by reason of his entire knowledge.

Narcissus replies that the prescription is unpalatable, but he's too weary of himself not to attempt it. Where to begin. The prophet's cave seems a likely place, which he stumbles into one forenoon in flight from his admirers. What started as a stag-hunt has turned into yet another love-chase, led this time by a persisting nymph soon joined by her quarry's companions. It wants all the Narcissan craft, resentfully perfected, yet again to mislead the lot.

An imperfectly dark passage. Outside his ardentest suitor calls, pederast Ameinius, spurned. The nymph soft-seconds his bugger woo. Chaste Narcissus shivers, draws farther in, loses bearings, daresn't call, weeps. The life-long bother! Seized he gives shriek, is released. How come? What next? Hadn't he as well have his blossom plucked? Who says so?

Tiresias the prophet. What's he doing here? Conversing with Narcissus. How does he know—because he knows everything. Why isn't he in Thebes? For the reason that, as during a prior and a posterior extravagance of his, Thebes is enjoying an interregnum, hard on prophets. First there was the sphinx, whose elementary riddle was none of his affair; he withdrew to the Thespian cave, there acted as adviser to the blue nymph Leirope, Narcissus's mother. The current pass is sorer: Oedipus's tragedy, too awful to rehearse. The third and last, couple hundred months hence, darker yet from Tiresias's point of view.

Narcissus reflects that after years of elusion he's at the seer's mercy, rapewise. He wonders which is more ironic, seeking refuge for innocence where it mightn't be preserved or falling into the first hands he's ever seemed to leave cold. Thus rare Tiresiases.

Apostrophe.

Some are comelier than most, a few handsome; it's Narcissus's fate, through fault nor merit of his own, to be beautiful beyond enduring. The first catch eye, the second turn head; Narcissus like a fleshed theophany smites the whole sense. A philosopher argues that perceptible beauty is ipso facto less desirable than im—at glimpse of Narcissus he interrupts, forswears himself. A man doubtless of his virility admits what he'd sooner not: in one extraordinary case he's felt the catamitic itch. A woman indifferent thitherto to the world's including handsomer men than hers finds Narcissus so so she's cross with her lover. Thus the mature, who see to it that sight of the wonder doesn't linger or recur and so in most cases come to terms with memory: the philosophers resume their position, men manliness, women men—all chastened, one supposes, by an exception so exceptional it ruins their rules. Among the less disciplined and wise, astonishment yields to simple lust. Cynical, powerful, wanton, uncommitted, passionate, impulsive set out to have their will. Hosts of ordinary, too, strangers to emotion of extraordinary kind or force, are seized as by conversion. Snares are laid, gifts tendered, pitfalls dug. His very wetnurse, Leirope says, took liberties with her suckling, tutor tutee. Leirope herself—how was it? Undone by a meandering river-god she seeks the caved seer first. What counsel does he offer? Tiresias won't repeat it; enough to say it's of a kind with what he wishes he'd given Oedipus. The varieties of general good advice are few. Leirope suggests herself to Narcissus when he reaches young manhood and begs him to ignore her advice: take to the woods! Into the bimboed and bebuggered bush he flies, where ladies beckon every way and gentlemen crouch in ambuscado.

All this considered, one may wonder at Tiresias's immunity, unless indeed he's cat-and-mousing. Is he too ravished by his victim to recollect himself for rape? Floored for defloration? No no. Clairvoyance is anaphrodisiac. One recalls too: Tiresias has been without sex for a long time. What's more he's blind as a bat, otherwise he couldn't see so in the cave.

Is Narcissus piqued or relieved? Both know. He presently inquires how one in his position might best fend the world's importune. Why fend? Tiresias's story is to the point. And Echo's. Echo's? A nymph possessed so early and entirely by Pan that her subsequent affairs seem redundant. Afflicted with immortality she turns from life and learns to tell stories with such art that the Olympians implore her to repeat them. Others live for the lie of love; Echo lives for her lovely lies, loves for their livening. With her tongue-tried tales she amuses others and preserves her reason; but Zeus employs her, unawares, to beguile his wife while he makes free with the mountain-nymphs. Again again, begs the queen of heaven; another mount's climbed with each retelling. At fiction's end the facts are clear; Zeus unpunishable, Echo pays. Though her voice remains her own, she can't speak for herself thenceforth, only give back others' delight regardless of hers.

Has this to do with fair Narcissus, wise Tiresias? Whose story is it? It's a tale of shortcomings, lengthened to advantage. Echo never, as popularly held, repeats all, like gossip or mirror. She edits, heightens, mutes, turns others' words to her end. One recalls her encounter with Narcissus—no other has nymphed him caveward. A coincidence of opposites. One should, if it's worthwhile, repeat the tale.

I'll repeat the tale. Though in fact many are bewildered, Narcissus conceives himself alone and becomes the first person to speak.

I can't go on.

Go on.

Is there anyone to hear here?

Who are you?

You.

I?

Aye.

Then let me see me!

See?

A lass! Alas.

Et cetera et cetera. Overmuch presence appears to be the storyteller's problem: Tiresias's advice, in cases of excessive identity and coitus irrequitus, is to make of withdrawal a second nature. He sees the nymph efface herself until she becomes no more than her voice, still transfiguring senseless sound into plaints of love. Perhaps that's the end of her story, perhaps the narrative proper may resume. Not quite, not quite: though even sharp-sight Tiresias can't espy the unseeable, one may yet distinguish narrator from narrative, medium from message. One lesson remains to be learned; when Echo learns it none will be the wiser.

But Narcissus! What's become of contemptible, untemptable Narcissus, the drug so many have turned on on, and sung themselves on pretext of hymning him? Was Tiresias about to counsel him in obscurity? No. Except to declare that his true love awaits him in the spring at Donacon; discovering who he is will prove as fatal for Narcissus as it's proving for Oedipus. Queer advice! To see the truth is one thing, to speak it another.

Now where are we? That is to say, where are Tiresias and Narcissus. Somewhere near the Donaconan spring. Who's telling the story, and to whom? The teller's immaterial, Tiresias declares; the tale's the same, and for all one knows the speaker may be the only auditor. Considerable time has elapsed, it seems, since seer and seeker, prophet and lost, first met in the cave. But what's time when past and future are equally clear and dark? The gift of suiscience is a painful present: Narcissus thirsts for love; Tiresias sees the end of his second sight. Both speak to themselves. Thebes is falling; unknown to the northbound refugee, en route to found a new city, their seer will perish on the instant the Argives take the old. He it is now, thrashing through the woods near Thespiae, who calls to his lost companions and follows to exhaustion a mock response. Halloo halloo! Falling at length beside a chuckling spring he dreams or dies. The voice presently in his ears is the hallooer's; now it rehearses Narcissus's end, seen from the outset:

Why did Tiresias not tell Narcissus what he once told Leirope, that her son would lead a long and happy life if he never came to know himself? Because the message then had become its own medium. Needless to say he sees and saw Narcissus beat about the bush for love, oblivious to pursuers in the joy of his own pursuit. As for the nymph whose honey voice still recalls his calls, he scorns her, and hears his maledictions balmed to music. Like the masturbatory adolescent, sooner or later he finds himself. He beholds and salutes his pretty alter ego in the pool; in the pool his ego, altered, prettily salutes: Behold! In vain he reaches to embrace his contrary image; he recognizes what Tiresias couldn't warn him of. Has knowing himself turned him into a pansy? Not quite, not quite. He's resolved to do away with himself, his beloved likewise. Together now. Adored-in-vain, farewell!

Well. One supposes that's the end of the story. How is it this voice persists, whosoever it is? Needless to say, Tiresias knows. It doesn't sound nymphish; she must have lost hers. Echo says Tiresias is not to be trusted in this matter. A prophet blind or dead, a blossom, eyeless, a disengendered tale—none can tell teller from told. Narcissus would appear to be opposite from Echo: he perishes by denying all except himself: she persists by effacing herself absolutely. Yet they come to the same; it was never himself Narcissus craved, but his reflection, the Echo of his fancy; his death must be partial as his self-knowledge, the voice persists, persists.

Can it be believed? Tiresias has gone astray; a voice not impossibly his own has bewildered him. The story of Narcissus, Tiresias, Echo is being repeated. It's alleged that Narcissus has wearied of himself and yearns to love another; on Tiresias's advice he employs the third person to repeat his tale as the seer does, until it loses meaning. No use: his self objectified's the more enthralling, like his blooming image in the spring. In vain Tiresias's cautions that the numph may be nothing altruistic, but the soul of guile and sleight-of-tongue. Who knows but what her love has changed to mock? What she gives back as another's speech may be entire misrepresentation; especially ought one to beware what she chooses to repeat concerning herself. No use, no use: Narcissus grows fond; she speaks his language; Tiresias reflects that after all if one aspires to concern one's fatal self with another, one had as well commence with the nearest and readiest. Perhaps he'll do the same: be beguiled with Narcissus out of knowledge of himself; listen silent as his voice goes on.

Thus we linger forever on the autognostic verge—not you and I, but Narcissus, Tiresias, Echo. Are they still in the Thespian cave? Have they come together in the spring? Is Narcissus addressing Tiresias, Tiresias Narcissus? Have both expired?

There's no future for prophets. Blind Oedipus will never see the place where three roads meet. Narcissus desired himself defunct before his own conception; he's been rooted forever by the beloved he'll never know. Dead Tiresias still stares wide-eyed at Wisdom's nude entire. Our story's finished before it starts.

E. B. White

DEATH OF A PIG

Dear Mr. Burnett:

  "Death of a Pig" is a straight narrative, and, as I indicated in the opening sentence, I felt a peculiar compulsion to give an accounting. My involvement with suffering and death became great, but I was pursued by the shadow of the irony (or perhaps idiocy) of a man's desire to save the life of a creature he had every intention of murdering. And, of course, I was aware of the farcical notes that seem always to intrude, even in the great theme of death.

Sincerely,
E. B. White

North Brooklin, Maine

I spent several days and nights in mid-September with an ailing pig and I feel driven to account for this stretch of time, more particularly since the pig died at last, and I lived, and things might easily have gone the other way round and none left to do the accounting. Even now, so close to the event, I cannot recall the hours sharply and am not ready to say whether death came on the third night or the fourth night. This uncertainty afflicts me with a sense of personal deterioration; if I were in decent health I would know how many nights I had sat up with a pig.

The scheme of buying a spring pig in blossomtime, feeding it through summer and fall, and butchering it when the solid cold weather arrives, is a familiar scheme to me and follows an antique pattern. It is a tragedy enacted on most farms with perfect fidelity to the original script. The murder, being premeditated, is in the first degree but is quick and skillful, and the smoked bacon and ham provide a ceremonial ending whose fitness is seldom questioned.

Once in a while something slips—one of the actors goes up in his lines and the whole performance stumbles and halts. My pig simply failed to show up for a meal. The alarm spread rapidly. The classic outline of the tragedy was lost. I found myself cast suddenly in the role of pig's friend and physician—a farcical character with an enema bag for a prop. I had a presentiment, the very first afternoon, that the play would never regain its balance and that my sympathies were now wholly with the pig. This was slapstick—the sort of dramatic treatment that instantly appealed to my old dachshund, Fred, who joined the vigil, held the bag, and, when all was over, presided at the interment. When we slid the body into the grave, we both were shaken to the core. The loss we felt was not the loss of ham but the loss of pig. He had evidently become precious to me, not that he represented a distant nourishment in a hungry time, but that he had suffered in a suffering world. But I'm running ahead of my story and shall have to go back.

My pigpen is at the bottom of an old orchard below the house. The pigs I have raised have lived in a faded building that once was an icehouse. There is a pleasant yard to move about in, shaded by an apple tree that overhangs the low rail fence. A pig couldn't ask for anything better—or none has, at any rate. The sawdust in the icehouse makes a comfortable bottom in which to root, and a warm bed. This sawdust, however, came under suspicion when the pig took sick. One of my neighbors said he thought the pig would have done better on new ground—the same principle that applies in planting potatoes. He said there might be something unhealthy about that sawdust, that he never thought well of sawdust.

It was about four o'clock in the afternoon when I first noticed that there was something wrong with the pig. He failed to appear at the trough for his supper, and when a pig (or a child) refuses supper a chill wave of fear runs through any household, or ice-household. After examining my pig, who was stretched out in the sawdust inside the building, I went to the phone and cranked it four times. Mr. Dameron answered. "What's good for a sick pig?" I asked. (There is never any identification needed on a country phone; the person on the other end knows who is talking by the sound of the voice and by the character of the question.)

"I don't know, I never had a sick pig," said Mr. Dameron, "but I can find out quick enough. You hang up and I'll call Henry."

Mr. Dameron was back on the line again in five minutes. "Henry says roll him over on his back and give him two ounces of castor oil or sweet oil, and if that doesn't do the trick give him an injection of soapy water. He says he's almost sure the pig's plugged up, and even if he's wrong, it can't do any harm."

I thanked Mr. Dameron. I didn't go right down to the pig, though. I sank into a chair and sat still for a few minutes to think about my troubles, and then I got up and went to the barn, catching up on some odds and ends that needed tending to. Unconsciously I held off, for an hour, the deed by which I would officially recognize the collapse of the performance of raising a pig; I wanted no interruption in the regularity of feeding, the steadiness of growth, the even succession of days. I wanted no interruption, wanted no oil, no deviation. I just wanted to keep on raising a pig, full meal after full meal, spring into summer into fall. I didn't even know whether there were two ounces of castor oil on the place.

Shortly after five o'clock I remembered that we had been invited out to dinner that night and realized that if I were to dose a pig there was no time to lose. The dinner date seemed a familiar conflict: I move in a desultory society and often a week or two will roll by without my going to anybody's house to dinner or anyone's coming to mine, but when an occasion does arise, and I am summoned, something usually turns up (an hour or two in advance) to make all human intercourse seem vastly inappropriate. I have come to believe that there is in hostesses a special power of divination, and that they deliberately arrange dinners to coincide with pig failure or some other sort of failure. At any rate, it was after five o'clock and I knew I could put off no longer the evil hour.

When my son and I arrived at the pigyard, armed with a small bottle of castor oil and a length of clothesline, the pig had emerged from his house and was standing in the middle of his yard, listlessly. He gave us a slim greeting. I could see that he felt uncomfortable and uncertain. I had brought the clothesline thinking I'd have to tie him (the pig weighed more than a hundred pounds) but we never used it. My son reached down, grabbed both front legs, upset him quickly, and when he opened his mouth to scream I turned the oil into his throat—a pink, corrugated area I had never seen before. I had just time to read the label while the neck of the bottle was in his mouth. It said Puretest. The screams, slightly muffled by oil, were pitched in the hysterically high range of pig-sound, as though torture were being carried out, but they didn't last long: it was all over rather suddenly, and, his legs released, the pig righted himself.

In the upset position the corners of his mouth had been turned down, giving him a frowning expression. Back on his feet again, he regained the set smile that a pig wears even in sickness. He stood his ground, sucking slightly at the residue of oil; a few drops leaked out of his lips while his wicked eyes, shaded by their coy little lashes, turned on me in disgust and hatred. I scratched him gently with oily fingers and he remained quiet, as though trying to recall the satisfaction of being scratched when in health, and seeming to rehearse in his mind the indignity to which he had just been subjected. I noticed, as I stood there, four or five small dark spots on his back near the tail end, reddish brown in color, each about the size of a housefly. I could not make out what they were. They did not look troublesome but at the same time they did not look like mere surface bruises or chafe marks. Rather they seemed blemishes of internal origin. His stiff white bristles almost completely hid them and I had to part the bristles with my fingers to get a good look.

Several hours later, a few minutes before midnight, having dined well and at someone else's expense, I returned to the pighouse with a flashlight. The patient was asleep. Kneeling, I felt his ears (as you might put your hand on the forehead of a child) and they seemed cool, and then with the light made a careful examination of the yard and the house for sign that the oil had worked. I found none and went to bed.

We had been having an unseasonable spell of weather—hot, close days, with the fog shutting in every night, scaling for a few hours in midday, then creeping back again at dark, drifting in first over the trees on the point, then suddenly blowing across the fields, blotting out the world and taking possession of houses, men, and animals. Everyone kept hoping for a break, but the break failed to come. Next day was another hot one. I visited the pig before breakfast and tried to tempt him with a little milk in his trough. He just stared at it, while I made a sucking sound through my teeth to remind him of past pleasures of the feast. With very small, timid pigs, weanlings, this ruse is often quite successful and will encourage them to eat; but with a large, sick pig the ruse is senseless and the sound I made must have made him feel, if anything, more miserable. He not only did not crave food, he felt a positive revulsion to it. I found a place under the apple tree where he had vomited in the night.

At this point, although a depression had settled over me, I didn't suppose that I was going to lose my pig. From the lustiness of a healthy pig a man derives a feeling of personal lustiness; the stuff that goes into the trough and is received with such enthusiasm is an earnest of some later feast of his own, and when this suddenly comes to an end and the food lies stale and untouched, souring in the sun, the pig's imbalance becomes the man's, vicariously, and life seems insecure, displaced, transitory.

As my own spirits declined, along with the pig's, the spirits of my vile old dachshund rose. The frequency of our trips down the footpath through the orchard to the pigyard delighted him, although he suffers greatly from arthritis, moves with difficulty, and would be bedridden if he could find someone willing to serve him meals on a tray.

He never missed a chance to visit the pig with me, and he made many professional calls on his own. You could see him down there at all hours, his white face parting the grass along the fence as he wobbled and stumbled about, his stethoscope dangling—a happy quack, writing his villainous prescriptions and grinning his corrosive grin. When the enema bag appeared, and the bucket of warm suds, his happiness was complete, and he managed to squeeze his enormous body between the two lowest rails of the yard and then assumed full charge of the irrigation. Once, when I lowered the bag to check the flow, he reached in and hurriedly drank a few mouthfuls of the suds to test their potency. I have noticed that Fred will feverishly consume any substance that is associated with trouble—the bitter flavor is to his liking. When the bag was above reach, he concentrated on the pig and was everywhere at once, a tower of strength and convenience. The pig, curiously enough, stood rather quietly through this colonic carnival, and the enema, though ineffective, was not as difficult as I had anticipated.

I discovered, though, that once having given a pig an enema there is no turning back, no chance of resuming one of life's more stereotyped roles. The pig's lot and mine were inextricably bound now, as though the rubber tube were the silver cord. From then until the time of his death I held the pig steadily in the bowl of my mind; the task of trying to deliver him from his misery became a strong obsession. His suffering soon became the embodiment of all earthly wretchedness. Along toward the end of the afternoon, defeated in physicking, I phoned the veterinary twenty miles away and placed the case formally in his hands. He was full of questions, and when I casually mentioned the dark spots on the pig's back, his voice changed its tone.

"I don't want to scare you," he said, "but when there are spots, erysipelas has to be considered."

Together we considered erysipelas, with frequent interruptions from the telephone operator, who wasn't sure the connection had been established.

"If a pig has erysipelas can he give it to a person?" I asked.

"Yes, he can," replied the vet.

"Have they answered?" asked the operator.

"Yes, they have," I said. Then I addressed the vet again. "You better come over here and examine this pig right away."

"I can't come myself," said the vet, "but McFarland can come this evening if that's all right. Mac knows more about pigs than I do anyway. You needn't worry too much about the spots. To indicate erysipelas they would have to be deep hemorrhagic infarcts."

"Deep hemorrhagic what?" I asked.

"Infarcts," said the vet.

"Have they answered?" asked the operator.

"Well," I said, "I don't know what you'd call these spots, except they're about the size of a housefly. If the pig has erysipelas I guess I have it, too, by this time, because we've been very close lately."

"McFarland will be over," said the vet.

I hung up. My throat felt dry and I went to the cupboard and got a bottle of whiskey. Deep hemorrhagic infarcts—the phrase began fastening its hooks in my head. I had assumed that there could be nothing much wrong with a pig during the months it was being groomed for murder; my confidence in the essential health and endurance of pigs had been strong and deep, particularly in the health of pigs that belonged to me and that were part of my proud scheme. The awakening had been violent and I minded it all the more because I knew that what could be true of my pig could be true also of the rest of my tidy world. I tried to put this distasteful idea from me, but it kept recurring. I took a short drink of the whiskey and then, although I wanted to go down to the yard and look for fresh signs, I was scared to. I was certain I had erysipelas.

It was long after dark and the supper dishes had been put away when a car drove in and McFarland got out. He had a girl with him. I could just make her out in the darkness—she seemed young and pretty. "This is Miss Owen," he said. "We've been having a picnic supper on the shore, that's why I'm late."

McFarland stood in the driveway and stripped off his jacket, then his shirt. His stocky arms and capable hands showed up in my flashlight's gleam as I helped him find his coverall and get zipped up. The rear seat of his car contained an astonishing amount of paraphernalia, which he soon overhauled, selecting a chain, a syringe, a bottle of oil, a rubber tube, and some other things I couldn't identify. Miss Owen said she'd go along with us and see the pig. I led the way down the warm slope of the orchard, my light picking out the path for them, and we all three climbed the fence, entered the pighouse, and squatted by the pig while McFarland took a rectal reading. My flashlight picked up the glitter of an engagement ring on the girl's hand.

"No elevation," said McFarland, twisting the thermometer in the light.

"You needn't worry about erysipelas." He ran his hand slowly over the pig's stomach and at one point the pig cried out in pain.

"Poor piggledy-wiggledy!" said Miss Owen.

The treatment I had been giving the pig for two days was then repeated, somewhat more expertly, by the doctor, Miss Owen and I handing him things as he needed them—holding the chain that he had looped around the pig's upper jaw, holding the syringe, holding the bottle stopper, the end of the tube, all of us working in darkness and in comfort, working with the instinctive teamwork induced by emergency conditions, the pig unprotesting, the house shadowy, protecting, intimate. I went to bed tired but with a feeling of relief that I had turned over part of the responsibility of the case to a licensed doctor. I was beginning to think, though, that the pig was not going to live.

He died twenty-four hours later, or it might have been forty-eight— there is a blur in time here, and I may have lost or picked up a day in the telling and the pig one in the dying. At intervals during the last day I took cool fresh water down to him and at such times as he found the strength to get to his feet he would stand with head in the pail and snuffle his snout around. He drank a few sips but no more; yet it seemed to comfort him to dip his nose in water and bobble it about, sucking in and blowing out through his teeth. Much of the time, now, he lay indoors half buried in sawdust. Once, near the last, while I was attending him I saw him try to make a bed for himself but he lacked the strength, and when he set his snout into the dust he was unable to plow even the little furrow he needed to lie down in.

He came out of the house to die. When I went down, before going to bed, he lay stretched in the yard a few feet from the door. I knelt, saw that he was dead, and left him there: his face had a mild look, expressive neither of deep peace nor of deep suffering, although I think he had suffered a good deal. I went back up to the house and to bed, and cried internally—deep hemorrhagic intears. I didn't wake till nearly eight the next morning, and when I looked out the open window the grave was already being dug, down beyond the dump under a wild apple. I could hear the spade strike against the small rocks that blocked the way. Never send to know for whom the grave is dug, I said to myself, it's dug for thee. Fred, I well knew, was supervising the work of digging, so I ate breakfast slowly.

It was a Saturday morning. The thicket in which I found the grave-diggers at work was dark and warm, the sky overcast. Here, among alders and young hackmatacks, at the foot of the apple tree, Lennie had dug a beautiful hole, five feet long, three feet wide, three feet deep. He was standing in it, removing the last spadefuls of earth while Fred patrolled the brink in simple but impressive circles, disturbing the loose earth of the mound so that it trickled back in. There had been no rain in weeks and the soil, even three feet down, was dry and powdery. As I stood and stared, an enormous earthworm which had been partially exposed by the spade at the bottom dug itself deeper and made a slow withdrawal, seeking even remoter moistures at even lonelier depths. And just as Lennie stepped out and rested his spade against the tree and lit a cigarette, a small green apple separated itself from a branch overhead and fell into the hole. Everything about this last scene seemed overwritten—the dismal sky, the shabby woods, the imminence of rain, the worm (legendary bedfellow of the dead), the apple (conventional garnish of a pig).

But even so, there was a directness and dispatch about animal burial, I thought, that made it a more decent affair than human burial: there was no stopover in the undertaker's foul parlor, no wreath nor spray; and when we hitched a line to the pig's hind legs and dragged him swiftly from his yard, throwing our weight into the harness and leaving a wake of crushed grass and smoothed rubble over the dump, ours was a businesslike procession, with Fred, the dishonorable pallbearer, staggering along in the rear, his perverse bereavement showing in every seam in his face; and the post mortem performed handily and swiftly right at the edge of the grave, so that the inwards that had caused the pig's death preceded him into the ground and he lay at last resting squarely on the cause of his own undoing.

I threw in the first shovelful, and then we worked rapidly and without talk, until the job was complete. I picked up the rope, made it fast to Fred's collar (he is a notorious ghoul), and we all three filed back up the path to the house, Fred bringing up the rear and holding back every inch of the way, feigning unusual stiffness. I noticed that although he weighed far less than the pig, he was harder to drag, being possessed of the vital spark.

The news of the death of my pig travelled fast and far, and I received many expressions of sympathy from friends and neighbors, for no one took the event lightly and the premature expiration of a pig is, I soon discovered, a departure which the community marks solemnly on its calendar, a sorrow in which it feels fully involved. I have written this account in penitence and in grief, as a man who failed to raise his pig, and to explain my deviation from the classic course of so many raised pigs. The grave in the woods is unmarked, but Fred can direct the mourner to it unerringly and with immense good will, and I know he and I shall often revisit it, singly and together, in seasons of reflection and despair, on flagless memorial days of our own choosing.

Henry Miller

"WHERE AM I?
WHAT AM I DOING HERE?"

Henry Miller, who picked the following as his selection, thought
the piece contained its own comment.

The Editor

I am supposed to have done a lot of traveling in my time, and perhaps I have, though not nearly as much as I once hoped to do. Much of my traveling has taken place in the head, as is also the case with some of my books—the unpublished, unwritten ones. The places I have planned to see one day still haunt me; some of these places are more vivid in my mind than many of the places I have actually visited. I am thinking particularly of places like Lhasa, Timbuctoo, Mecca, Samarkand. When I read about these places I feel very much as if I knew them, which suggests that the written word is as effective, and sometimes more so, than the doing itself.

There are certain parts of the globe which I have now given up all thought of seeing in this lifetime: India, for example, Patagonia, Tierra del Fuego. Why the last named? Because a German writer I met some years ago told me of the rainbows to be seen there at all hours of the day —hundreds of them at a time—if I remember rightly. As for Patagonia, whoever has read W. H. Hudson's *Idle Days in Patagonia* will understand. The very name Patagonia suggests something like "far away and long ago."

My first sorties from home were made out of sheer boredom—hitchhiking excursions in any and every direction, wherever the car I hailed happened to be going. Ususally without a cent in my pocket, trusting to luck that the driver would invite me to lunch or dinner or slip me a few bucks to take a room for the night. (On occasion I would have the good fortune to meet with a sympathetic soul who would hand me a few extra dollars to see me on my way.) Thus I might wake up of a morning in some jerk-water town in Tennessee or South Carolina, remembering scarcely anything of the trip except the conversation with the driver. I mention this absence of impressions because it dawned on me one day during these excursions that I was really in a somnambulistic state most of the time. Or else I was completely preoccupied with the problems I had tried to ditch by running away from the hopeless state of things at home. That "street of early sorrows," for instance.

The first genuine attempt to leave home for good—I was then twenty-one and crazy enough to believe I might become a cowboy—brought me to California, where I worked at odd jobs near the Mexican border. It was while working on a ranch near Chula Vista, then connected with San Diego by a sort of Toonerville trolley, that I decided one day to spend my day off in National City. I knew nothing about the place—it was the name which attracted me, for what reason I no longer recall. At any rate, it was here that I experienced my first blackout, so to speak. I remember absolutely nothing about the place, only that while rambling through the streets, suddenly I no longer remembered where I was or who I was. The trauma, or whatever you wish to call it, lasted no more than a minute or two, I imagine, but it seemed like a lifetime. I was petrified with fright on coming out of it. I began to wonder if the experience was not the beginning of some mental disturbance which would recur in more drastic fashion as time passed.

When I reflect on all that I was then trying to put out of my mind, past, present and future, when I think what an absolute cipher I had become, how aimlessly and futilely I had been drifting about, I no longer find the incident so strange. Nothing more, let us say, than a sort of involuntary attempt at suicide. Had the attack been a bit stronger, more prolonged, I might well have gone into a coma which, for me at that time, would have been bliss.

How desperately I sought then to put the world from me! The only world I knew was one of frustration, hunger, misery. Fortunately it was but a short time after this incident that I stumbled upon that extraordinary woman, Emma Goldman (the anarchist), and through her, Nietzsche and the whole world of European dramatists. It was an event which changed the whole course of my life and led me eventually to try my hand at writing.

In the dark and turbulent days that followed, during which period I wrote volume after volume in my head but never once put pen to paper, I began to dream of going to France. I not only read all I could about

France but I would buttonhole everyone I knew who had been there and beg him to describe his impressions of the country. I would ask the most idiotic questions concerning the people, their customs, their idiosyncrasies, how the towns and villages looked—quite as if France were some place on the moon rather than a part of the planet Earth. So intensely did I attempt to visualize things that years later, even after almost ten years' residence in France, I remembered my imaginary picture of France as vividly as the actual one, and in my dreams I frequently took one for the other.

How well I remember getting off the boat train at the Gare Saint-Lazare in the year 1928, looking about frantically as if to take it all in with one sweep of the eyes. "So this is Paris," I kept saying to myself, scarcely believing that I was truly there. Everything about the city bewildered and delighted me—the shops, the bars, the advertisements, the roof tops, the flower stalls, everything. I was as if drunk.

As I write these lines I am once again in Paris, revisiting old haunts, seeking out unknown corners, visiting old friends—many of them still living in the same miserable quarters as of yore—rediscovering bars and restaurants where I had passed days and nights as in a dream. This time I am doing it all deliberately, in the company of a friend who has taken it upon himself to make a documentary film of my "anecdotal life," as Ossip Zadkine used to call it. This time Paris thrills me more than ever before. This time I am more keenly aware of its picturesque charm. In some ways, perhaps because of the face-lifting Malraux has given it, it is a very new Paris; in other ways it is the same old Paris, ever more worn, more dilapidated than ever, more like itself than it ever was. I keep wondering what is going on in the head of the young man with the camera as we roam the various quarters of the city from Ménilmontant to Montparnasse, from the Place du Tertre to the Flea Market, and so on. The 15th Arrondissement, in which I once lived (rue Auguste-Bartholdi), now assumes a magical aspect. I am at home again, everything so warm, so inviting, as if I had only left it yesterday. I keep prodding the young man with the camera. "Look at that! How about *that* street— let's go back there! What about that wall?" It is the young man's first visit to Paris, and though he is all agog he does not appear to be nearly as excited as I who have covered every square foot of the city and danced and wept in its streets. "If only I could lend him my eyes," I think. "If only he had a little more experience of life, what wonders he might behold in these quaint, sordid streets so full of life, so full of promise and misery!" The very names of the streets thrill me—rue du Théâtre, Place Violet, rue du Commerce, Avenue Emile-Zola, rue de la Convention, rue Lourmel which to thoroughly appreciate one must visit at night in a deep fog or as a sleepwalker. The colors, the variety of shops, the hustle and bustle, the old walls with their *"comédie humaine"* imprinted on them, all this is what I miss so much in America. Here in Paris a single street, such as the rue Mouffetard for example, gives me a more lasting thrill than all the streets of Los Angeles and San Francisco put together. Going on seventy-six, I am reliving scenes of thirty years ago and more, am still excited, still full of wonder and amazement, still clapping my hands like a child. Only the teeming, colorful streets of old China could possibly move me more, but then I shall never see that old China and probably not the new one either.

It is no longer "the third or fourth day of Spring," as I wrote so jubilantly in *Black Spring;* it is now the winter of my life. Perhaps I am taking a last look at this beloved city of my dreams. Like the god Indra, I am studded with a thousand eyes, hungry eyes, insatiable eyes. Looking down on the city from the heights of Ménilmontant all Paris is spread before my eyes, floating in an ethereal mist of nostalgic beauty. I hold the image as best I can, to preserve it for that moment when I close my eyes for the last time and, God willing, carry it with me into the beyond.

Back to the Gare Saint-Lazare, year 1928. My first taste of Europe. This time with money in the pocket. Paris, Marseilles, Munich, Vienna, Budapest, Czernowitz, Prague. All over the map, as it were. Almost a year of knocking about. Too much to absorb, too much to remember. Only spots here and there stand out, like random blots on a sheet of snow-white paper: the billiard table in a café in Vienne (Isère), exactly like the one Van Gogh painted, which thirty years later I came back to search for but could never find; Les Baux, near Arles, as crazy a setting as any Surrealist might dream up; the rue Visconti, Paris, where Balzac lost a fortune with his printing press and where I tried in vain to teach my wife to ride the bicycle; the University at Montpellier where I donned Rabelais' cloak, still in fair condition; the shoeshine man in Nice, an American Negro, who rescued us when we were starving, my wife and I. Everything kaleidoscopic, with an aura of fuzz about it. Or Ossip Zadkine in his Paris studio, surrounded and dwarfed by a forest of statues. The first artist I was to meet in Europe. Always felt like a boy in his presence, always the callow youth to whom he condescended to explain a multitude of things I should have known without asking. So much fuzz, so much overlapping, such sublime ignorance, such naïveté: I was still in the egg. But a real egg. Not like the one Dali steps out of to announce his divine origin.

Almost a year of it, as I say, but no diary notes, no notebook sketches. No nothing, I might almost say. Who was I? Where was I heading? What was the purpose of it all? I had already written thousands of words, but none of any consequence. Might just as well have written them in water. I wasn't even certain, then, that I liked France. I preferred Budapest to Paris. I will only get to appreciate Paris when I work and starve there. That's still to come—but sooner than I anticipate.

No, I am definitely not a traveler. A restless soul, an eternal vagabond maybe, but not a globe trotter. The real traveler is a professional. He knows what he wants to see, hear and taste: he goes straight for the bull's eye. Myself, I'm absent most of the time: I see and I don't see, if you know what I mean. I ruminate, like a cow. "Remember this, remember that!" I keep saying to myself, but I'm not remembering, I'm only remembering to remember. Just the same, it all gets stored below, in the palace of entrails. One day it will out, but that may be twenty or thirty years later. With me everything comes too late, or almost. "Always dragging behind like the cow's tail," is how my mother used to put it. But she was wrong, my mother. Not a cow's tail, but a peacock's tail. Because anything unearthed after twenty or thirty years is bound to reveal some of the brilliance of a cosmic snooze.

A snooze. Just an ordinary one. Of a sunny afternoon, let's say, twenty years later. Coming out of it, suddenly a little incident like searching for the men's room in Budapest becomes a vivid event. I can still see the silly grin of the Pole to whom I am desperately appealing for help. And how did I happen to light on a drunken Pole instead of a Hungarian?) After using up all my languages I begin making elaborate grimaces, fantastic gestures, to indicate my distress. Of a sudden he points to a sign over a nearby door on which is spelled out in English—"Men's Toilet." I step inside and as I lock the door I think to myself—what if I am locked in, how will I cry "Help!"

Traveling. In the midst of nowhere suddenly a blank. Once again—who am I? Where am I? Where did I come from? I am filling out the police card for the old woman in charge of an inn in some forgotten hamlet in Gascony. For months I have been moving steadily from town to town. I'm stopping here not because there's anything to see but because I'm dead tired. Just as I am about to put down where I came from the

day before my mind goes blank. I can't even recall the name of the town
in which I am registering. Seeing me hesitate, seeing the blank look on
my face, the old woman gives me a suspicious look. That serves to drive
me deeper into oblivion. I get panicky. (I'm always panicky when someone looks at me suspiciously.) To gain time I look up at her, pen in hand,
and without a moment's hesitation I begin telling her of my travels,
of my great fatigue, and of my joy in being back in France after my
long sojourn in India. *"India?"* she exclaims. "Do please tell me about
India. All my life I have longed to go there." Now I'm really off. I begin
a long spiel about my imaginary travels in that fabulous land. Effortlessly
I recall long passages from Élie Faure's *History of Art.* Towns, temples,
ashrams, saints, gurus, fakirs—I reel it all off as if I had truly been
there and with my own two eyes seen the wonders I am describing. The
woman looks at me with tears in her eyes. Perhaps she sees in me her
long lost son. I'm out of danger, that's for sure. Now I can ask her where
I am, she will understand. As she gives me the name of the village I
suddenly recall the name of the town I had started from the day before.
I remember everything, even the wart on the chin of the maid who
fixed my bed. Saved. Saved by the bell.

In bed that night I began thinking of Nostradamus, of my visits a
few weeks previous to Saint Rémy where he was born, and to Salon
where he died. That frightfully dilapidated house in Salon—were the
inhabitants of Salon trying to bury the memory of his existence? Such a
phenomenal book of prophecies, his *Centuries!* If, as Keyserling once said,
the *I Ching* is the most extraordinary book ever written, what must one
say of Nostradamus' immortal work? How come, I ask myself, that no
statue of this wonder man has been erected anywhere, not even in his
home town? (Today there is one, in Salon, I am told.) Today there is
also a street in Paris named after Élie Faure. But one has to search for it.
Easier to find the Passage des Thermopyles or the Impasse Satan.

Still abed, still in a reverie. Now I am back in Sète, in the cemetery
where Paul Valéry lies buried, to be precise. It's the Cimetière Marin
which he commemorated in the poem by that name. We are sitting at his
tomb, my publisher and I, talking about death. A very pleasant talk too,
I must say. I have just been telling him, Herr Ledig-Rowohlt, of my fruitless efforts to find the grave of Hölderlin in Tübingen. Suddenly a big
black dog comes over to me and begins licking me all over. He seems
to recognize me. And why not? He's the spitting image of the dog I left
behind me in Big Sur.

"Pup," we called him, though he was the size of a mastiff. Either this dog and mine are twins or I am hallucinating, think I to myself. To test him out by name—"Pup, *here Pup!*" He responds immediately. Now he is gazing into my eyes with that same soulful expression my dog back home showed at certain times, especially when I had left him alone for weeks on end. Loving eyes, with a blend of reproach and forgiveness in them.

Our talk shifts from death to reincarnation. Is it possible, I ask, that we sometimes come back as animals, or even as insects? The dog listens, nods his head knowingly. Maybe he has the answer. He is certainly tuned in. On leaving the cemetery I ask the old lady at the gate how and where the dog came from. I am hardly surprised when she informs me that he had been left her by an American, an American from California, no less.

Now it's Prades, the approach to which reminds me somewhat of the Big Sur country. We have come, my friend Vince and I, to see the village in which Pablo Casals has chosen to live. No thought of barging in on him, just curious to see the sort of place this great man has chosen for his home. (Just a few weeks earlier I had dragged my friend Vince to Montagnola, Switzerland, to have one quick look at Hermann Hesse's dwelling place. One long look and we are off again. One doesn't disturb men like Picasso, Hesse, Casals.)

We soon learn that Casals no longer lives in Prades, that he has re-moved to Puerto Rico. We take a stroll through the town, have a spot of lunch, and decide to take off. Passing the church the impulse seizes me to go in and say a prayer. Vince tags along, wondering no doubt what has come over me. After making the sign of the cross—for the first time in my life!—we kneel and begin praying silently. I do, at least. In a moment he is on his feet and making a bee line for the street. I finish my prayer and follow him out. No sign of Vince. I make for the toilet adjoining the church and there is Vince, in the *cabinets,* frantically peeling off his clothes. "What's up?" I ask. *"Fleas!"* he yells. It seems so incongruous, our praying so beautifully and then fleas. Was it a reminder from above that we should pray more often and more earnestly?

Worse than fleas, of course, are bedbugs. And bedbugs you can meet up with even in first class hotels, especially in Central Europe. In France it's best not to complain but simply change hotels because the French will maintain that you brought them with you.

But there are far worse things than fleas and bedbugs, and I don't mean things that crawl and sting or suck the blood out of you. I shall never forget driving through the outskirts of Lisbon in a heavy rain

and being besieged by ragged children in bare feet with hands outstretched to catch a few coppers. Such sad, woe-begone faces. So patiently
they stand and wait, soaked through and through and blue with cold.
Or the urchins in Spain who keep running beside your car, panting
like dogs, and run and run until you throw them a few coins. Yet
what are such sights compared to the condition of the poverty-stricken
masses of India? There one steps over sleeping bodies in order to enter
a nightclub. One doesn't even have to go to India to witness the depths
of despair and degradation. A brief stroll through downtown Los Angeles,
or along the Bowery, New York, or a glance at the steps of the Metro
stations in Paris after the Metro has shut down is enough. There are
millions and millions of hopeless creatures scattered throughout the
civilized world who have nothing left but their sick, worn, broken
bodies which they drag from place to place night and day waiting for
death to liberate them from their misery.

The sight of so much misery and the fear of catching a disease restrict
the travels of some to such sterilized countries as Sweden, Denmark,
Switzerland. But are they traveling, these cautious souls? Isn't the
purpose of travel to open one's eyes and more especially one's heart?
The countries which forbid begging deprive their citizens of the joy
of giving. It is not enough to donate to charitable organizations; one
has to touch the leper, suffer with him, even if only imaginatively.
Travel *is* a fool's Paradise, as Emerson said, only because people lack
imagination. One *could* stay right in one's own room and visualize all
the splendors, all the wonders, and all the horrors of the earth. But
most of us have to step outside to see and touch and feel. And even then
we are inclined to remain immune, immune to the suffering of our
fellow-man. And this not because we are hard-hearted or indifferent
but because the scope of human misery, human suffering, is too vast.

If the sight of human misery often becomes unbearable so too can
become the sight of flawless beauty in Nature. I remember a stay in
Locarno, Switzerland, which had precisely that effect upon me. Day after
day I gazed upon a setting which was Paradise itself. "This is *the* spot,"
I thought to myself after the first few days. Perfection, sheer perfection.
Whether I went for a stroll beside the lake, or flopped on a bench and
just stared, or peeked out of my hotel window, it was always the same:
a feeling of complete satisfaction, a sense of being saturated with the sheer
physical beauty of Nature. And then one day it began to pall. One day,
as must happen to all but the angels, Paradise became monotonous. I began
to search for flaws. I began to pray for bad weather. But there was no

change, no flaw, no slightest imperfection. The scene took on a glassy quality, as if viewed through a mirror. It became more and more unreal, more and more detached. Until the day I asked myself—"What am I doing here?" And what do you suppose the answer was? "Killing time!"

As I packed my bag I kept saying to myself, "You're not dead yet. Move on!" And so I moved on, feeling as I did so that if I were to glance backward just once I would turn into a pillar of salt.

Locarno I had come upon by accident. No one had warned me of the Paradise I was to find there. Toulouse is another story.

Toulouse began with a dream. I was living then in the Villa Seurat, Paris. For months I had been dreaming heavily night after night. After a time I taught myself how to wake up without destroying the thread of the dream. I would lie with eyes closed and follow the dream back to its beginning. Then I would get up slowly, go to the typewriter, and record the dream together with all the associations which it involved. It was quite a training and most rewarding in many ways.

My first dream of Toulouse was rather vague but ended with the feeling that a visit to that city was of importance. I had been to Toulouse once but had found nothing exciting there to inspire a second visit. The dream left me wondering. Had I perhaps overlooked something? Maybe I ought to give it another chance.

When the dream recurred a few nights later, just as vague but with a more peremptory command to go, I decided I would take the hint and go. I stayed about three days without anything of consequence happening. In fact I was bored, thoroughly bored.

About a month later I dreamed again of Toulouse. This time the command was more urgent. "Go or you will regret it," a voice seemed to say. I tried to dismiss the idea, but the more I fought it the more insistent came the command. Finally I gave in, boarded the train again and once more found myself in Toulouse. I registered at another hotel this time, thinking to change my luck thereby. Again I spent three days waiting for something to happen. Perhaps I shouldn't have waited. Maybe one has to help things along, *make things happen*. But again nothing happened. That nothing at all had happened was indeed strange, since wherever I go something usually happens. I began to wonder if there was another Toulouse somewhere, perhaps in North Africa, or if through some cosmic slip-up I had entered into someone's else's dream. At any rate I returned to Paris convinced that I was the victim of a celestial hoax.

When Toulouse popped up again I forgot all about my previous disillusionments and made haste to obey the third and last command. It's now or never, think I.

This time I'm so keyed up that even if a duck had given me the sign I would have caught it. I walk up one street and down another, go in and out of cafés and bistros, peer in shop windows, stand on street corners to make myself conspicuous, and so on. Come dusk I go back to the hotel for a little snooze. Nothing has happened so far. Nothing looked unusual, nothing was out of place, nobody looked at me twice.

I treat myself to a very good meal, order a good vintage wine to go with it, and round the dinner off with a beautiful Armagnac. I pick out a quiet café in which to have a coffee and plan the next move. Something tells me that this time all is not in vain. The waiter is moving about listlessly, now and then swatting a drugged fly with his dirty napkin. He reminds me somewhat of Fernandel, except that there isn't a spark of humor in him. Thinking that a bit of conversation might not be amiss I beckon to him to come over. At a loss for an opener I choose at random the name of a dead poet and ask him if he knows where the poet lived. "What was the name again?" he asks, and I repeat it. "Never heard of him," he says, and with that he goes to the telephone booth and brings me the telephone directory. "But he's dead," I say. "What's the difference?" he replies. "There are many in there who are long dead," and with a strange smile he adds: "Or who ought to be." He's not such a nitwit after all, I think to myself, and to go along with him I riffle the pages of the directory as if in search of the dead poet.

A few minutes later I'm in the street following my nose. Soon I'm in the outskirts of the town. Everything is getting more and more dismal. The overhead lights in the middle of the road are the type one usually sees in the provinces, shedding a wan, eerie glow which gives everything a phantasmal appearance. The street is absolutely deserted; not even a stray dog is to be seen. I'm beginning to feel a little creepy. I turn round now and then to see if anyone is following me silently.

Just when I think it's time to turn back and retrace my steps a sense of utter desolation comes over me and I stop dead in my tracks. There is a strange building opposite me which seems vaguely familiar. The effort to bring it into focus, to recall which building it is, where I have seen it before, exhausts me. I'm floundering. Once again that terrifying feeling of knowing nothing, neither who I am nor where I am. Suddenly, however, I do recognize the building. It is the police station just around the corner from my childhood home in Williamsburg, Brooklyn. And now I know who I am. I'm the little boy whom someone has dragged by the ear to the police station for using dirty language. Trembling from head to foot I'm standing at the sergeant's desk answering the charge against me. He bends over the desk to peer down at me, a monster of a man with a foul breath, and he says gently, so very gently: "But aren't you Henry Miller, the tailor's son?" I'm so frightened I can't open my mouth. He bends over still farther and pats my head. "That's all right," he says, in that same gentle voice. "Everybody knows you're a good little boy."

When I come to I realize that I am standing in front of the commissariat, I wipe the sweat from my brow, still trembling as of yore. I turn and walk slowly back toward the hotel. I talk to myself as I go along. "Yes, I'm Henry Miller all right, all right. Who else could I be? And I *was* a good little boy, that's correct. I've been a good little boy all my life, only nobody knows it but me. . . ."

Still walking, still talking.

"So that's why I had to come to Toulouse? No, there must be more to it than that."

I hasten my steps. Perhaps there's a message for me at the hotel?

The hotel porter is fast asleep when I arrive. I shake him gently. "Any message for me?" I ask. He shakes his sleepy head. *"Non, monsieur. Rien. Rien du tout."*

Art Buchwald

THE GOOD AND THE BAD

Dear Whit:

I chose this particular article mainly because, although it was written eight years ago, it still seems to hold up as well as any I've written.

Perhaps in fifty years it will still hold up, though then we may be talking about the Good Viet-Cong and the Bad Viet-Cong.

Cheers,
Art Buchwald

I took my son to the movies the other day. The picture was called "The Battle of the Coral Sea," and in comparison with other war pictures it was pretty bad. It had something to do with a crew of American submariners who are captured by the Japanese and are put in a prison camp. The man in charge of the prison camp is a very civilized man, by prison camp standards, and he resists torturing his charges even though he knows they know naval secrets that could change the course of the war. But the people underneath the commander are typical brutal prison guards.

There is no sense going on with the plot except to say it was no "Bridge on the River Kwai."

When we got out of the theatre we went to a sidewalk cafe to have a drink. My son was pretty quiet after the film and it had left a deep impression on him.

At the table he said to me, "The Japanese were very bad people to do those things to the Americans, weren't they?"

"Yes," I said, "but they're not bad people now."

"Why?" he wanted to know.

"Because they don't do things like that any more."

He thought about this a minute and then said, "Why did they do all those bad things then?"

"Probably they didn't know they were doing bad things. They probably thought they were doing good things."

"Why didn't someone tell them?" he wanted to know.

"We tried," I said, "but they wouldn't listen."

"Remember that war picture we saw some weeks ago? The one about the Germans and how they beat the poor people and the children in the prison camp?"

"Yes," I said.

"The Germans are bad people, aren't they?"

"No," I said. "They *were* bad people, but now they're good people."

"Are they different people?" he wanted to know.

"No, they're the same people. At least many are the same people. You see, once you fight a war you can't stay mad at the people after the war is over. You have to forget what the bad people did during the war, because if you don't, there could be another war."

"But in the movies they're still bad people," he said.

"Yes. That's to remind us they were bad people, but we're supposed to forget it."

He looked at me blankly.

"Did you kill any Russians during the war?" he wanted to know a few minutes later.

"No. Because during the war they were good people and they fought the Germans just like the British and the Americans did."

"But, if they were good people during the war and killed the bad people, why are they bad people now?"

"They're not bad people now. Most of the Russians are good people. But we don't agree with what their leaders say and want to do. And they don't agree with us. That's why we're having trouble in Germany."

"With the bad Germans?"

"No, with the good Germans. The bad Germans want to kick the good Germans out of Berlin."

"Then there are still bad Germans?"

"Yes. But there are also good Germans. You see, after the war the country was divided and the Russians occupied half of it and we occupied the other half."

"Why didn't the Russians kill the bad Germans if they were bad?"

"Well, the Russians don't think their Germans are bad. They think their Germans are good. They think our Germans are bad. We think their Germans, at least their German leaders, are bad, and our Germans are good. You understand?" He said, "No."

"Well, it doesn't make any difference if you understand it or not," I said angrily. "Everyone else does."

William Inge

I'M A STAR

It is difficult, if not impossible, for a writer to point to any single piece of his work and say, "This is my best." When asked to produce a sample of his best, all the writer can do is to look for a piece of his work that will fit into the length limitations of anthologies and still represent him fairly, if not supremely. I have written long plays that I feel represent my work more grandly; but I feel that "I'm a Star," being a whole play, represents me better than would a selection from a longer work. "I'm a Star," a conventional one-act play, expresses, I feel, my feeling for and love of tragic-comedy; for there is little that happens in life that I do not want to see both sides of, the tragic and the comic, when I write. I believe that both the women in the play are true and alive, and that what happens to them is a regrettable instance that is inherent in our lives today, not just in the theatre but in all realms of competitive endeavor. I think the story is native to our lives and that is why I felt compelled to write it.

William Inge

[*The apartment of Miss Julia Richards and her friend Bea. Julia is an actress nearing fifty who has not been employed for several years. The walls of the apartment are hung with framed handbills of the hit-plays she has been starred in, and photographs of herself and her theatre friends. She is dressed in one of the few ensembles left in her wardrobe in which she feels safe to appear publicly. She wears a hat and carries gloves and a handbag, dressed now to go out but not yet emotionally prepared. She paces the floor of the living room, talking, it seems, to herself. Her friend Bea, in old clothes, is cleaning up in the kitchen.*]

JULIA—I can't do it. I just can't do it. I just don't have the guts to walk into that office and ask them for money. I just can't do it.

[*She paces.*]

Dear God, think of all those faces that will be staring at me, whispering to each other, "There's *poor* Julia Richards. Isn't it a shame? She can't find work any more. No one will hire her."

[*She all but screams her cry of self-pity, and throws her handbag on the floor.*]

No. I can't. I can't. Dear God, I'd rather starve than make myself an object of pity.

[*Her friend Bea, mopping the kitchen floor, speaks up.*]

BEA—All right then, *starve! I* can't afford to feed you any more on what I'm getting.

JULIA—I suppose I'm an imposition.

BEA—Well, I don't put on an act because *I* have to go down and collect unemployment.

JULIA—It's different for you, Bea.

BEA—Oh, of course. I was never a *star*.

JULIA—I didn't intend to make an unflattering comparison.

BEA—No. You just couldn't help it.

JULIA—But just the same, I *was* a star. I still am. If I were to get a job tomorrow, I'd get star billing.

BEA—Meanwhile, since a job tomorrow looks pretty unlikely, if I were you, I'd go down to that office and collect my sixty-five dollars.

JULIA [*to herself*] Sixty-five dollars.

BEA—It's not much, but it's substance.

JULIA [*correcting her*] Subsistence.

BEA—*Subsistence.*

JULIA—I'm not belittling the money.

BEA—The two of us together, that'd make a hundred and thirty bucks a week. We could live on that pretty nice.

JULIA—I know, I know, I know.

> [*There is a long silence. Julia sits, looking very distressed, trying to reason herself into going. Bea continues cleaning up in the kitchen.*]

BEA—What are you doing?

JULIA—Thinking.

BEA—What about?

JULIA—Just thinking.

BEA—You can't be thinking about *nothing*.

JULIA—Then maybe I'm not thinking. Maybe I'm just enjoying memories.

BEA—Memories don't feed anything but your vanity, and that gets pretty *un*digestible after a while.

JULIA [*meekly*] . . . yes.

BEA—Memories are no good. They're no damned good for *anything*.

JULIA—I know.

BEA—Leave them at home, Baby, and go out and get your sixty-five bucks.

JULIA [*as in prayer*] Oh, Christ!

BEA—He's not gonna bring 'em back, either.

JULIA—I'm going to have to take a pill, Bea.

BEA—What good's a pill gonna do?

JULIA—I've just got to have one. That's all. I can't enter that foul-smelling bureau, reeking of all the rejects of humanity, without one. Please, Bea. Just one.

BEA—You know what the doctor said.

JULIA—To hell with the doctor. I can't face it without dulling my senses. Just a little bit. Just a bit.

BEA [*leaving her work, going to the bedroom*] Well, all right. Just one.

JULIA—I promise not to ask for more.

> [*Bea opens her dresser drawer, takes out a box to which she alone has the key, opens it, takes a pill from a small bottle, and then returns the box to the drawer and takes the pill in to Julia, trembling for it.*]

JULIA—Hurry, Bea, for God sakes! I feel as if I were going to explode into tiny pieces.

BEA—Just this one. The doctor made me promise . . .

JULIA—I know. I know.

> [*Bea hands her the pill and a glass of water. Julia downs it greedily.*]

JULIA—Thank you.

BEA—Don't mention it.

JULIA—Maybe now if I had just a tiny glass of brandy . . .

BEA [*loudly affirmative*] NO! Absolutely not.

JULIA—I . . . I just thought it might enable me to make my entrance into the bureau rather gallantly.

BEA—Why should you?

JULIA—I mean . . . as if it were all a kind of lark, you know, my going to the unemployment office to . . .

BEA [*without pity*] It's *not* a lark. You *need* that money.

JULIA [*humbled*] Yes. Yes, I know.

BEA—Besides, if you took one tiny glass of brandy now, you'd be stoned. You know you would. And word'd get around town that Julia Richards is drinking again.

JULIA—And that would never do, would it?

BEA—And why the hell should you be worrying about what kind of *entrance* you make? This is no opening night.

JULIA [*with a weak little laugh*] No. It isn't, is it?

BEA—Not by a damned sight. This is *survival*.

JULIA—Yes. Survival.

BEA—A gallant entrance, my ass!

JULIA—Please don't make fun.

BEA—Well, sometimes you force me to. Honest to God!

JULIA—I suppose my pride does make me a little ridiculous.

BEA—Pride is passé. Haven't you heard? No one can afford it any more.

[*The telephone rings. Julia almost jumps with anticipation.*]

JULIA—Oh, that may be my agent. Please answer for me, Bea. Try to sound like my secretary. Please.

BEA [*into telephone*] Miss Richards' residence.

[*At the telephone, Bea's face remains immobile for several moments, but Julia is twisting with anxiety.*]

JULIA—Who *is* it? Who *is* it?

[*Bea hangs up, an expression of sad disappointment on her face.*]

JULIA—Who *was* it, Bea? Tell me.

BEA—Well, it wasn't your agent.

JULIA—Then who . . . ?

BEA—I'm afraid it was another one of *those* calls.

[*Julia grimaces.*]

JULIA—How does he get my number? How does he get my number?

BEA—Who knows?

JULIA—Oh, those calls make me sick. It's this neighborhood we live in. It's the most sordid environment I've ever known. My God, I'm afraid even to get into the elevator.

BEA—I know. Just last week, that poor woman got raped and almost killed before help came. I guess we'll all have to start wearing hat-pins again.

JULIA—Did this one say all those . . . sordid, nasty things?

BEA—Of course. Don't make me go into details.

JULIA [*shuddering*] Ugh!

BEA—Park Avenue women get them the same as we do.

JULIA—And I thought it might possibly be a job.

BEA—Better luck next time.

JULIA [*beseechingly*] Would you go with me, Bea?

BEA—What good would I do?

JULIA—Moral support, maybe.

BEA—Moral support? Do you think someone's going to try to seduce you?

JULIA—You know what I mean.

BEA—Well, I've got an appointment to see someone at Doubleday's for a job a little later.

JULIA—I . . . I'm afraid I might faint. Honestly.

BEA—You never fainted in your life.

JULIA—But my heart is pounding so, and I feel dizzy.

BEA—Julia, you're a big girl now. I think you should be doing this on your own.

JULIA—Yes . . . I suppose I should. I just thought it might be a little easier, this first time, if I had someone to lean on.

BEA—Now look, Honey, I could walk over there with you, but I couldn't stay because, like I say, I've got to get over to Doubleday's, and those cross-town busses take forever.

JULIA—All right, Bea. I'll go alone.

BEA—You'll get along OK. You're not going to faint or have a heart attack.

JULIA—I almost wish I would.

BEA—Honestly, Julia, you're making a mountain out of a mole hill. *Every*body goes to get their unemployment. It's nothing to be ashamed of. After all, the way I figure it, it's money the government owes us. God knows, they took plenty away from us while we were makin' it, didn't they? All right then, now we're getting a little of it back.

JULIA—I don't see why they couldn't send us our checks in the mail.

BEA—Well, they decided not to, for some reason. So we have to go down and pick 'em up.

JULIA—It would save us so . . . so much humiliation.

BEA—What's so humiliating about it? Now, really, Julia! You sound as if the tumbrils were coming to take you to the guillotine.

JULIA—But it *is*. It *is* humiliating. You know it is. It's humiliating to let the whole world know that you're broke and need money. The worst humiliation in this world is to be *poor*.

BEA—Well, nothing is humiliating unless you let it be.

JULIA [*considers Bea's philosophy*] All right. I'll try. I'll try not to let it humiliate me.

[*Julia walks bravely to the door, opens it, and then loses courage and runs back to Bea's arms, sobbing.*]

JULIA—Oh Bea, I can't. I *can't*. I know it's perfectly unreasonable of me, but I simply can't do it. I can't bear the thought of all those eyes on me. I can't bear to think of the remarks they'll all whisper. I can't bear to make it look like I'm a failure.

[*Bea gives in and puts her arms around her and mothers her.*]

BEA—Now what makes you think all those eyes are going to be turned on *you*. How many people there will even *know* who you are?

JULIA [*almost insulted*] Why, Bea!

BEA—People are down there to pick up their bread. They wouldn't notice if Garbo herself walked in.

JULIA—Maybe I should have dressed more simply.

BEA—Well . . . maybe.

JULIA—I didn't know *what* to wear. After all, I've never been in this position before, but I've always believed in looking my best for any public appearance.

BEA—Of course.

JULIA—Oh, Bea, I just feel that my legs are too weak to carry me there.

BEA—All right then, what are you going to do?

JULIA [*with new hope*] I know I'll have a job next summer. I always get good jobs playing the summer circuit.

BEA—Summer's a long way off.

JULIA—I'll go see my agent again. I'll tell her I've *got* to have work on television. She'll find me something. She's bound to find me *some*thing.

BEA [*giving in*] Well . . . all right.

JULIA—Or maybe I could get some of those voice commercials to do. They pay extremely well. Really they do. Myra Stevens made a hundred thousand dollars last year doing those voice commercials. She bought herself a little home in Westport, and . . .

BEA [*dropping the subject*] OK. OK.

JULIA—Don't you believe me, Bea?

BEA [*off-hand*] Sure, I believe you.

JULIA—Unless . . . you think . . . that . . . that *no* one wants me any more.

BEA—Julia, Honey, that's not so. Now don't let yourself start thinking things like that.

JULIA—It may be true, Bea.

BEA—Now be quiet. I won't listen to talk like that.

JULIA [*semi-hysterical*] That's the feeling I have. *No* one wants me any more. No one wants me for *anything*. I've loused up my name in the entire industry.

BEA—Stop it, Julia. Stop it!

JULIA—It's true. And now I can't depend upon my agent for anything. She won't even answer my calls. She's embarrassed to see me walk into her office. She tries hard to smile at me and pretend she's glad to see me, but all the time, she's thinking to herself, Jesus Christ, what can I do for *her* now? Why doesn't she face the fact that she's through? Why doesn't she go away and quit bothering me? And I remember when everyone at the agency bowed whenever I came in.

BEA—Sure, I know.

JULIA—Now they all look embarrassed, and try to smile and make themselves be polite.

BEA—Forget it, Honey.

JULIA—I almost feel . . . as if they wonder why I just don't take an overdose of pills to keep them from being embarrassed.

BEA—You're getting morbid, Julia.

JULIA—Am I?

BEA—You know you are. You're just putting on a performance. You're just having fun, dramatizing yourself as the discarded woman.

JULIA—Have I . . . had any reason to believe that . . . that anyone wants me now? For *anything*?

BEA—Well, things are tough in the theatre now. *You* know that. All those British actors and everything, coming over here in those *avant garde* plays. They're . . . just not producing the kind of plays you and I used to do.

JULIA—It's more than that, Bea.

BEA—What is?

JULIA—People are afraid to take a chance on me now, aren't they?

BEA—Course not.

JULIA—Yes they are, Bea.

BEA—All right. If that's what you've decided to believe, how can I persuade you otherwise?

JULIA—Just because I . . . [*She can't go on*]

BEA—Because you *what*?

JULIA—*You* know.

BEA—OK. You gave a few producers a bad time. But if the right part came along now, they'd still want you.

JULIA—No. There are others now to replace me.

BEA—Not on your life.

JULIA—Yes there are, Bea. That's one thing we have to learn. There's always somebody who can replace us.

BEA—Just the same, I know perfectly well that . . .

JULIA—And sometimes it's as if life gave us fame and fortune just to show us, it can take them away.

BEA—Fame is a tricky bitch, some author said.

JULIA—And the higher we rise, the farther we fall.

BEA—Now, come off it. I'm getting depressed, too.

JULIA—Life won't let us be proud for long, will it?

BEA—I don't know.

JULIA—You fight to win a great success, and then Life shows you, very cruelly, that it was all meaningless, and all the time, you were never any better than anyone else.

BEA—"The proud shall be humbled," the Good Book says . . . somewhere.

[*Julia suddenly jumps to her feet.*]

JULIA—I'm going to have a drink.

[*She goes to a cabinet, opens the door and brings out a bottle of whiskey, Bea running to her trying to prevent her.*]

BEA—Julia, for God sakes, not on top of that pill you took. Put that down. I won't let you.

[*Bea tries unsuccessfully to get the bottle out of Julia's hands.*]

JULIA—Get away, Bea.

[*Julia drinks from the bottle.*]

BEA [*despairing*] Oh God!

JULIA [*setting the bottle down*] I feel much better.

BEA—For how long?

JULIA – Don't remind me now of the misery that's to come. Let me have these few moments to feel myself glad and free.

BEA [*returning to kitchen*] I give up.

JULIA – Stay. Be happy these few minutes with me. I want to share the happiness and relief I feel now. Come on, Bea. You have a drink, too. And let's tell funny stories about the good old days. Remember when I was having an affair with Gordon? And one night we went into some supper club together, after the show. And who should be sitting in the front booth but his old girl friend? That movie actress who was on the skids. And she yelled across the room at us. Oh, everyone there heard. She yelled at me, "Hi, you bitch! I bet my boy friend's got the biggest part *you*'ll ever play." Oh, I'll never forget. The whole room stared at us, and I . . . I turned to her very suavely and said . . . I said . . .

BEA – Don't, Julia.

JULIA [*her moment's high spirits have vanished*] The fun's all gone out of it now. It doesn't last long for me now. One drink and I've had it. One drink and I'm gone.

BEA – Do you think you can stop?

JULIA – I don't know. I've never been able to before, have I?

BEA – Do you think maybe you could make it down to the unemployment office before you drink any more?

JULIA – Of course.

BEA [*tenderly now*] All right then, Honey. Go down now, and you'll have that money coming in for future security. That'll be a big help to you. You're going to need it.

JULIA – Very well. I'll go in just a second.

> [*She goes to the cabinet and takes another drink from the bottle as Bea watches her almost as if she were watching a dear friend die.*]

BEA – I said "before you drink any more."

JULIA – Once I'm started, one more isn't going to hurt me.

BEA – Julia, if you get sick, how the hell am I going to take care of you?

JULIA – Shut up, Bea. Don't make me think about that now.

BEA – You'll have to go to a hospital, and you don't have the money.

JULIA – I'll *not* go to any hospital.

BEA – If you get sick, I can't keep you here.

JULIA—Let's cross those bridges when we come to them, please.

[*She takes her third drink, and is by now quite potted.*]

BEA—The trouble is, you never cross them. You get to the river and plunge in, and expect someone else to drag you out.

JULIA [*beginning to sound a little nasty*] Please don't concern yourself that I'm going to be any trouble to you, Bea *darling!*

BEA [*going to bedroom*] All right. I'm not going to concern myself any longer. I'm going to get dressed and go out to get a job.

JULIA—You do that, Honey. You get that job at Doubleday's and sell corny novels to all the Westchester housewives.

[*Bea begins to undress.*]

JULIA—I'm not worried any more. I'm going to tell my agent to get me one of those voice-commercial jobs and earn a hundred thousand dollars a year. *I* don't need another play. I won't ever need to act in another play again. I'll get rich.

[*Bea goes about dressing, going into the bathroom to shower, not saying a word.*]

JULIA [*with total abandon*] I'm going to be rich, rich, *rich!*

[*She becomes annoyed with Bea's silence.*]

JULIA—Did you hear me, Bea? I'm going to be rich!

BEA [*from the shower*] Yes. I heard you.

JULIA—My God, why shouldn't I be? I've got the finest voice in the theatre. They should give me a job in a minute. Of course they will. Why have I been worrying about money all this time?

[*She laughs hollowly. Then she becomes suddenly determined.*]

JULIA—By God, I'm going down town and see my agent now. Bea, you call up the office and pretend to be my secretary, and don't even bother to ask for an appointment. Just say Miss Richards is on her way. Do you hear me, Bea?

BEA [*from the shower*] Yes. I hear you.

[*Julia gets to her feet now, with some difficulty.*]

JULIA [*to herself*] Oh Jesus, my head's going 'round in circles.

[*She tries to walk but finds it difficult.*]

JULIA—Bea, where are those pills?

BEA—I put them away.

JULIA—I've got to have one more, Bea. Just one more.

BEA—Absolutely not. It's very dangerous to mix those pills with booze. You know it is.

JULIA [*commandingly*] I'm asking you for just one more pill, you bitch. Now come across and give it to me.

BEA—NO!

JULIA—All right then, I'll take it.

[*She barges into the bathroom while Bea is still in the shower.*]

JULIA—I know where you keep them, don't I? You think you've been fooling me all these weeks, but I've known where they were hid all along.

[*Now there is a struggle between the two women in the bathroom, which we may see or only hear the sounds of.*]

BEA—Get away from there.

JULIA—Shut up.

BEA—You crazy fool, you'll kill yourself. Is that what you want? To kill yourself?

JULIA—I just need one more pill to quiet me before I go down and tell my agent to get me one of those jobs. I just need one more. Now for Christ sake, I know what I'm doing.

BEA [*screaming*] DON'T! Julia, don't!

JULIA—Shut up! who ever heard of anyone making such a fuss about taking a tiny pill?

[*She comes out of the bathrom now with a new false assurance.*]

JULIA—There, I feel better already. I'll be able now to make a very gallant entrance and . . .

[*Bea bolts out of the bathroom in a robe.*]

BEA—Gallant my ass! You've peed your pants.

JULIA—I don't know what you're talking about.

[*Bea rushes to the chair where Julia was sitting.*]

BEA – Did you do it on the chair again? [*After inspection*] You did. The cushion in this chair is soaked. Oh, you pig! You pig!

JULIA – Please call my agent now and tell her I'm on my way.

BEA – Julia, you can't go out, the condition you're in.

JULIA – I assure you, I feel perfectly splendid. Remember now, pretend you're my secretary. Don't ask for an appointment. Just say, Miss Richards is on her way.

> [*She slips on her gloves and goes to the door, managing barely to walk with some dignity. Bea runs to the door and blocks Julia's exit.*]

BEA – Julia, you can't go out, the condition you're in. Please don't go out. Stay here and let me call the doctor *now* before it gets any worse.

JULIA [*with shocking ferocity*] Out of my way, please!

BEA – I'm not going to let you.

> [*With surprising force, Julia grabs Bea around the neck and hurls her out of the way, Bea falling to the floor.*]

JULIA – Out of my way, I said. Don't think you can stop me.

BEA – All right. Go on. They'll pick you up and send you to Bellevue. And frankly, I don't care.

> [*Julia opens the door and stands there for a moment.*]

JULIA – Remember, Bea. Call and say, Miss Richards is on her way.

BEA – Yes you're on your way. But where?

JULIA – I've told you. It's perfectly absurd for me to be worrying about money all this time when I could be making thousands. I'm not too proud to do those voice commercials. Of course, I'd never submit myself to be seen on them, but I see no harm at all in using my voice. I'll make thousands.

BEA [*giving in*] OK. OK.

JULIA – You'll remember to call now, won't you, Bea?

BEA – Yes. I'll call.

JULIA – And say . . . Miss Richards is on her way.

> [*Julia exits now, rather grandly. Bea remains on the floor for several reflective moments after the door has closed behind Julia.*]

BEA – Yes. Miss Richards is on her way.

Ogden Nash

A HANDFUL OF VARIED PIECES

I hope that the phrase "This Is My Best" doesn't arouse the antagonism of the reader as it does that of the writer. To me it seems to imply either defiance or apology. I have been doing verses like these for forty years now, and am quite a different person from my thirty-, forty-, or even fifty-year-old self. I feel in the position of passing judgment on another man's work. However, having committed myself to do so, I have reached into my storage bin of trivia and come up with a handful of varied pieces that are fairly representative of the lot, and trust that they may afford a moment's entertainment to the passer-by.

Ogden Nash

Baltimore, Maryland

HOW TO BE MARRIED WITHOUT A SPOUSE
or
MR. KIPLING, WHAT HAVE YOU DONE
WITH MR. HAUKSBEE?

Do any of you old fogies remember Mrs. Hauksbee? Without Mrs.
    Hauksbee, Simla and Poona
Would have been just like Altoona.
At Mrs. Hauksbee's burra khanas
Nabobs pinned tails on donkeys and viceroys bobbed for bananas.
Mrs. Hauksbee disentangled subalterns and aides-de-camp
From shopworn maids-de-camp.
Under the deodars, whatever they may be, Mrs. Hauksbee was in her
    glory,
But this is another story.
Mrs. Hauksbee was attended by a faithful old *amah,*
Which is the equivalent of in Alabama a faithful old *mamah,*
And this now *amah* was a conservative reactionary Hindu,
And she got tired of Mrs. Hauksbee all the time shifting her hemline and
    her hair-do and her skin-do,
And finally she asked Mrs. Hauksbee why she had dyed her hair again
    and she got one of the usual answers.
Mrs. Hauksbee said she was changing her style to reform young Slingsby
    of the Umpteenth Lancers,
And the *amah* (she had surreptitiously attended the Sorbonne)
Murmured, *"Plus ça change, plus c'est la memsahib,"* and wandered on.

TWEEDLEDEE AND TWEEDLEDOOM

Said the Undertaker to the Overtaker,
Thank you for the butcher and the candlestick-maker,
For the polo player and the pretzel-baker,
For the lawyer and the lover and the wife-forsaker,
Thank you for my bulging, verdant acre,
Said the Undertaker to the Overtaker.
Move in, move under, said the Overtaker.

THE PRIVATE DINING ROOM

Miss Rafferty wore taffeta,
Miss Cavendish wore lavender.
We ate pickerel and mackerel
And other lavish provender.
Miss Cavendish was Lalage,
Miss Rafferty was Barbara.
We gobbled pickled mackerel
And broke the candelabra,
Miss Cavendish in lavender,
In taffeta, Miss Rafferty,
The girls in taffeta lavender,
And we, of course, in mufti.

Miss Rafferty wore taffeta,
The taffeta was lavender,
Was lavend, lavender, lavenderest,
As the wine improved the provender.
Miss Cavendish wore lavender,
The lavender was taffeta.
We boggled mackled pickerel,
And bumpers did we quaffeta.
And Lalage wore lavender,
And lavender wore Barbara,
Rafferta taffeta Cavender lavender
Barbara abracadabra.

Miss Rafferty in taffeta
Grew definitely raffisher.
Miss Cavendish in lavender
Grew less and less stand-offisher.
With Lalage and Barbara
We grew a little pickereled,
We ordered Mumm and Roederer
Because the bubbles tickereled.
But lavender and taffeta
Were gone when we were soberer.
I haven't thought for thirty years
Of Lalage and Barbara.

THE SUNSET YEARS OF SAMUEL SHY

Master I may be,
But not of my fate.
Now come the kisses, too many too late.
Tell me, O Parcae,
For fain would I know,
Where were these kisses three decades ago?
Girls there were plenty,
Mint julep girls, beer girls,
Gay younger married and headstrong career girls,
The girls of my friends
And the wives of my friends,
Some smugly settled and some at loose ends,
Sad girls, serene girls,
Girls breathless and turbulent,
Debs cosmopolitan, matrons suburbulent,
All of them amiable,
All of them cordial,
Innocent rousers of instincts primordial,
But even though health and wealth
Hadn't yet missed me,
None of them,
Not even Jenny,
Once kissed me.

These very same girls
Who with me have grown older
Now freely relax with a head on my shoulder,
And now come the kisses,
A flood in full spate,
The meaningless kisses, too many too late.
They kiss me hello,
They kiss me goodbye,
Should I offer a light, there's a kiss for reply.
They kiss me at weddings,
They kiss me at wakes,
The drop of a hat is less than it takes.
They kiss me at cocktails,
They kiss me at bridge,
It's all automatic, like slapping a midge.
The sound of their kisses
Is loud in my ears
Like the locusts that swarm every seventeen years.

I'm arthritic, dyspeptic,
Potentially ulcery,
And weary of kisses by custom compulsory.
Should my dear ones commit me
As senile demential,
It's from kisses perfunctory, inconsequential.
Answer, O Parcae,
For fain would I know,
Where were these kisses three decades ago?

CROSSING THE BORDER

Senescence begins
And middle age ends
The day your descendants
Outnumber your friends.

A WORD TO HUSBANDS

To keep your marriage brimming,
With love in the loving cup,
Whenever you're wrong, admit it;
Whenever you're right, shut up.

THE AXOLOTL

I've never met an axolotl,
But Harvard has one in a bottle,
Perhaps—and at the thought I shiver—
The very villain from Fall River,
Where Lizzie Borden took an axolotl
And gave her mother forty whaxolotl.

THE SHRIMP

A shrimp who sought his lady shrimp
Could catch no glimpse,
Not even a glimp.
At times, translucence
Is rather a nuisance.

IF A BODER MEET A BODER,
NEED A BODER CRY? YES.

I haven't much faith in bodings; I think that all bodings are daft
    bodings.
Forebodings are bad enough, but deliver me from aftbodings.
Aftbodings are what too many of us suffer from subsequent to making
    decisions even of the most inconsequential and niggling.

Aftbodings prevent people in restaurants from enjoying their haunch of venison, because they keep wondering if they shouldn't have ordered the roast crackling suckling pigling.

Aftbodings are what women are constantly up to their midriffs amid,

Because they are always afraid that the hats or dresses they didn't buy are more becoming than the ones they did.

Aftbodings trouble the young executive who has opted for a martini instead of a bloody mary, and plague the rascally artist who too late feels that he should have forged that Gainsborough instead of this Romney.

Aftbodings are the major cause of insomny.

Consider the lines "Of all sad words . . . the saddest are these: 'It might have been!' " whittled by J. G. Whittier;

As an example of aftboding, what could be prettier?

Indeed, I deem this an example of aftboding *in excelsis,*

Because J. G. Whittier wasn't even boding after his own decision but somebody else's.

I myself am more and more inclined to agree with Omar and with Satchel Paige as I grow older:

Don't try to rewrite what the moving finger has writ, and don't ever look over your shoulder.

Joseph Heller

LIEUTENANT SCHEISSKOPF

This chapter of *Catch-22* was written in the early 1950s, when we were at war in Korea, on the brink of war with Russia, and city, state, Congressional, and Senate committees were browbeating and interrogating everybody they could about everything they could think of—really just for the hell of it. I tried very hard to capture this ludicrous and grotesque activity in a funny, frightening trial scene set in World War II. Actually, there are three interrogation scenes in the novel, each successively less humorous and more directly savage; I choose this one, "Lieutenant Scheisskopf," because it is most fully descriptive of the native dangers we faced in those days and contains my sharpest mockery of the people responsible for them. I choose it also because it warns of those same dangers today—militarism, coercion, slander, inquisition, brute force, and outright legal tyranny.

To readers who do not share my values or my alarm, I reply with the title of this chapter in its English translation. (In Germany, oddly, the title has no comic value or other meaning. They do have plenty of them there, too, but they call them by other names.)

Joseph Heller

Clevinger knew everything. Clevinger knew everything about the war except why Yossarian had to die while Corporal Snark was allowed to live, or why Corporal Snark had to die while Yossarian was allowed to live. It was a vile and muddy war, and Yossarian could have lived without it—lived forever, perhaps. Only a fraction of his countrymen would give up their lives to win it, and it was not his ambition to be among them. To die or not to die, that was the question, and Clevinger grew limp trying to answer it. History did not demand Yossarian's premature demise, justice could be satisfied without it, progress did not hinge upon it, victory did not depend on it. That men would die was a matter of necessity; *which* men would die, though, was a matter of circumstance, and Yossarian was willing to be the victim of anything but circumstance. But that was war. Just about all he could find in its favor was that it paid well and liberated children from the pernicious influence of their parents.

Clevinger knew so much because Clevinger was a genius with a pounding heart and blanching face. He was a gangling, gawky, feverish, famish-eyed brain. As a Harvard undergraduate he had won prizes in scholarship for just about everything, and the only reason he had not won prizes in scholarship for everything else was that he was too busy signing petitions, circulating petitions and challenging petitions, joining discussion groups and resigning from discussion groups, attending youth congresses, picketing other youth congresses and organizing student committees in defense of dismissed faculty members. Everyone agreed that Clevinger was certain to go far in the academic world. In short, Clevinger was one of those people with lots of intelligence and no brains, and everyone knew it except those who soon found it out.

In short, he was a dope. He often looked to Yossarian like one of those people hanging around modern museums with both eyes together on one side of a face. It was an illusion, of course, generated by Clevinger's predilection for staring fixedly at one side of a question and never seeing the other side at all. Politically, he was a humanitarian who did know right from left and was trapped uncomfortably between the two. He was constantly defending his Communist friends to his right-wing enemies and his right-wing friends to his Communist enemies, and he was thoroughly detested by both groups, who never defended him to anyone because they thought he was a dope.

He was a very serious, very earnest and very conscientious dope. It was impossible to go to a movie with him without getting involved afterward in a discussion on empathy, Aristotle, universals, messages and the obligations of the cinema as an art form in a materialistic society. Girls he took to the theater had to wait until the first intermission to find out from him whether or not they were seeing a good or bad play, and then found out at once. He was a militant idealist who crusaded against racial bigotry by growing faint in its presence. He knew everything about literature except how to enjoy it.

Yossarian tried to help him. "Don't be a dope," he had counseled Clevinger when they were both at cadet school in Santa Ana, California.

"I'm going to tell him," Clevinger insisted, as the two of them sat high in the reviewing stands looking down on the auxiliary paradeground at Lieutenant Scheisskopf raging back and forth like a beardless Lear.

"Why me?" Lieutenant Scheisskopf wailed.

"Keep still, idiot," Yossarian advised Clevinger avuncularly.

"You don't know what you're talking about," Clevinger objected.

"I know enough to keep still, idiot."

Lieutenant Scheisskopf tore his hair and gnashed his teeth. His rubbery cheeks shook with gusts of anguish. His problem was a squadron of aviation cadets with low morale who marched atrociously in the parade competition that took place every Sunday afternoon. Their morale was low because they did not want to march in parades every Sunday afternoon and because Lieutenant Scheisskopf had appointed cadet officers from their ranks instead of permitting them to elect their own.

"I *want* someone to tell me," Lieutenant Scheisskopf beseeched them all prayerfully. "If any of it is my fault, I *want* to be told."

"He *wants* someone to tell him," Clevinger said.

"He wants everyone to keep still, idiot," Yossarian answered.

"Didn't you hear him?" Clevinger argued.

"I heard him," Yossarian replied. "I heard him say very loudly and very distinctly that he wants every one of us to keep our mouths shut if we know what's good for us."

"I won't punish you," Lieutenant Scheisskopf swore.

"He says he won't punish me," said Clevinger.

"He'll castrate you," said Yossarian.

"I swear I won't punish you," said Lieutenant Scheisskopf. "I'll be grateful to the man who tells me the truth."

"He'll hate you," said Yossarian. "To his dying day he'll hate you."

Lieutenant Scheisskopf was an R.O.T.C. graduate who was rather glad that war had broken out, since it gave him an opportunity to wear an officer's uniform every day and say "Men" in a clipped, military voice to the bunches of kids who fell into his clutches every eight weeks on their way to the butcher's block. He was an ambitious and humorless Lieutenant Scheisskopf, who confronted his responsibilities soberly and smiled only when some rival officer at the Santa Ana Army Air Force Base came down with a lingering disease. He had poor eyesight and chronic sinus trouble, which made war especially exciting for him, since he was in no danger of going overseas. The best thing about him was his wife and the best thing about his wife was a girl friend named Dori Duz who did whenever she could and had a Wac uniform that Lieutenant Scheisskopf's wife put on every weekend and took off every weekend for every cadet in her husband's squadron who wanted to creep into her.

Dori Duz was a lively little tart of copper-green and gold who loved doing it best in toolsheds, phone booths, field houses and bus kiosks. There was little she hadn't tried and less she wouldn't. She was shameless, slim, nineteen and aggressive. She destroyed egos by the score and made men hate themselves in the morning for the way she found them, used them and tossed them aside. Yossarian loved her. She was a marvelous piece of ass who found him only fair. He loved the feel of springy muscle beneath her skin everywhere he touched her the only time she'd let him. Yossarian loved Dori Duz so much that he couldn't help flinging himself down passionately on top of Lieutenant Scheisskopf's wife every week to revenge himself upon Lieutenant Scheisskopf for the way Lieutenant Scheisskopf was revenging himself upon Clevinger.

Lieutenant Scheisskopf's wife was revenging herself upon Lieutenant Scheisskopf for some unforgettable crime of his she couldn't recall. She was a plump, pink, sluggish girl who read good books and kept urging Yossarian not to be so bourgeois without the *r*. She was never without a good book close by, not even when she was lying in bed with nothing on her but Yossarian and Dori Duz's dog tags. She bored Yossarian, but he was in love with her, too. She was a crazy mathematics major from the Wharton School of Business who could not count to twenty-eight each month without getting into trouble.

"Darling, we're going to have a baby again," she would say to Yossarian every month.

"You're out of your goddamn head," he would reply.

"I mean it, baby," she insisted.

"So do I."

"Darling, we're going to have a baby again," she would say to her husband.

"I haven't the time," Lieutenant Scheisskopf would grumble petulantly. "Don't you know there's a parade going on?"

Lieutenant Scheisskopf cared very deeply about winning parades and about bringing Clevinger up on charges before the Action Board for conspiring to advocate the overthrow of the cadet officers Lieutenant Scheisskopf had appointed. Clevinger was a troublemaker and a wiseguy. Lieutenant Scheisskopf knew that Clevinger might cause even more trouble if he wasn't watched. Yesterday it was the cadet officers; tomorrow it might be the world. Clevinger had a mind, and Lieutenant Scheisskopf had noticed that people with minds tended to get pretty smart at times. Such men were dangerous, and even the new cadet officers whom Clevinger had helped into office were eager to give damning testimony against him. The case against Clevinger was open and shut. The only thing missing was something to charge him with.

It could not be anything to do with parades, for Clevinger took the parades almost as seriously as Lieutenant Scheisskopf himself. The men fell out for the parades early each Sunday afternoon and groped their way into ranks of twelve outside the barracks. Groaning with hangovers, they limped in step to their station on the main paradeground, where they stood motionless in the heat for an hour or two with the men from the sixty or seventy other cadet squadrons until enough of them had collapsed to call it a day. On the edge of the field stood a row of ambulances and teams of trained stretcher bearers with walkie-talkies. On the roofs of the ambulances were spotters with binoculars. A tally clerk kept score. Supervising this entire phase of the operation was a medical officer with a flair for accounting who okayed pulses and checked the figures of the tally clerk. As soon as enough unconscious men had been collected in the ambulances, the medical officer signaled the bandmaster to strike up the band and end the parade. One behind the other, the squadrons marched up the field, executed a cumbersome turn around the reviewing stand and marched down the field and back to their barracks.

Each of the parading squadrons was graded as it marched past the reviewing stand, where a bloated colonel with a big fat mustache sat with the other officers. The best squadron in each wing won a yellow pennant on a pole that was utterly worthless. The best squadron on the base won a red pennant on a longer pole that was worth even less, since the pole was heavier and was that much more of a nuisance to lug around all week until some other squadron won it the following Sunday. To Yossarian, the idea of pennants as prizes was absurd. No money went with them, no class privileges. Like Olympic medals and tennis trophies, all they signified was that the owner had done something of no benefit to anyone more capably than everyone else.

The parades themselves seemed equally absurd. Yossarian hated a parade. Parades were so martial. He hated hearing them, hated seeing them, hated being tied up in traffic by them. He hated being made to take part in them. It was bad enough being an aviation cadet without having to act like a soldier in the blistering heat every Sunday afternoon. It was bad enough being an aviation cadet because it was obvious now that the war would not be over before he had finished his training. That was the only reason he had volunteered for cadet training in the first place. As a soldier who had qualified for aviation cadet training, he had weeks and weeks of waiting for assignment to a class, weeks and weeks more to become a bombardier-navigator, weeks and weeks more of operational training after that to prepare him for overseas duty. It seemed inconceivable then that the war could last that long, for God was on his side, he had been told, and God, he had also been told, could do whatever He wanted to. But the war was not nearly over, and his training was almost complete.

Lieutenant Scheisskopf longed desperately to win parades and sat up half the night working on it while his wife waited amorously for him in bed thumbing through Krafft-Ebing to her favorite passages. He read books on marching. He manipulated boxes of chocolate soldiers until they melted in his hands and then maneuvered in ranks of twelve a set of plastic cowboys he had bought from a mail-order house under an assumed name and kept locked away from everyone's eyes during the day. Leonardo's exercises in anatomy proved indispensable. One evening he felt the need for a live model and directed his wife to march around the room.

"Naked?" she asked hopefully.

Lieutenant Scheisskopf smacked his hands over his eyes in exasperation. It was the despair of Lieutenant Scheisskopf's life to be chained to a woman who was incapable of looking beyond her own dirty, sexual desires to the titanic struggle for the unattainable in which noble man could become heroically engaged.

"Why don't you ever whip me?" she pouted one night.

"Because I haven't the time," he snapped at her impatiently. "I haven't the time. Don't you know there's a parade going on?"

And he really did not have the time. There it was Sunday already, with only seven days left in the week to get ready for the next parade. He had no idea where the hours went. Finishing last in three successive parades had given Lieutenant Scheisskopf an unsavory reputation, and he considered every means of improvement, even nailing the twelve men in each rank to a long two-by-four beam of seasoned oak to keep them in line. The plan was not feasible, for making a ninety-degree turn would have been impossible without nickel-alloy swivels inserted in the small of every man's back, and Lieutenant Scheisskopf was not sanguine at all about obtaining that many nickel-alloy swivels from Quartermaster or enlisting the co-operation of the surgeons at the hospital.

The week after Lieutenant Scheisskopf followed Clevinger's recommendation and let the men elect their own cadet officers, the squadron won the yellow pennant. Lieutenant Scheisskopf was so elated by this unexpected achievement that he gave his wife a sharp crack over the head with the pole when she tried to drag him into bed to celebrate by showing their contempt for the sexual mores of the lower middle classes in Western civilization. The next week the squadron won the red flag, and Lieutenant Scheisskopf was beside himself with rapture. And the week after that his squadron made history by winning the red pennant two weeks in a row! Now Lieutenant Scheisskopf had confidence enough in his powers to spring his big surprise. Lieutenant Scheisskopf had discovered in his extensive research that the hands of marchers, instead of swinging freely, as was then the popular fashion, ought never to be moved more than three inches from the center of the thigh, which meant, in effect, that they were scarcely to be swung at all.

Lieutenant Scheisskopf's preparations were elaborate and clandestine. All the cadets in his squadron were sworn to secrecy and rehearsed in the dead of night on the auxiliary paradeground. They marched in darkness that was pitch and bumped into each other blindly, but they did not panic, and they were learning to march without swinging their hands. Lieutenant Scheisskopf's first thought had been to have a friend of his in the sheet metal shop sink pegs of nickel alloy into each man's thighbones and link them to the wrists by strands of copper wire with exactly three inches of play, but there wasn't time—there was never enough time—and good copper wire was hard to come by in wartime. He remembered also that the men, so hampered, would be unable to fall properly during the impressive fainting ceremony preceding the marching and that an inability to faint properly might affect the unit's rating as a whole.

And all week long he chortled with repressed delight at the officers' club. Speculation grew rampant among his closest friends.

"I wonder what that Shithead is up to," Lieutenant Engle said.

Lieutenant Scheisskopf responded with a knowing smile to the queries of his colleagues. "You'll find out Sunday," he promised. "You'll find out."

Lieutenant Scheisskopf unveiled his epochal surprise that Sunday with all the aplomb of an experienced impresario. He said nothing while the other squadrons ambled past the reviewing stand crookedly in their customary manner. He gave no sign even when the first ranks of his own squadron hove into sight with their swingless marching and the first stricken gasps of alarm were hissing from his startled fellow officers. He held back even then until the bloated colonel with the big fat mustache whirled upon him savagely with a purpling face, and then he offered the explanation that made him immortal.

"Look, Colonel," he announced. "No hands."

And to an audience stilled with awe, he distributed certified photostatic copies of the obscure regulation on which he had built his unforgettable triumph. This was Lieutenant Scheisskopf's finest hour. He won the parade, of course, hands down, obtaining permanent possession of the red pennant and ending the Sunday parades altogether, since good red pennants were as hard to come by in wartime as good copper wire. Lieutenant Scheisskopf was made First Lieutenant Scheisskopf on the spot and began his rapid rise through the ranks. There were few who did not hail him as a true military genius for his important discovery.

"That Lieutenant Scheisskopf," Lieutenant Travers remarked. "He's a military genius."

"Yes, he really is," Lieutenant Engle agreed. "It's a pity that schmuck won't whip his wife."

"I don't see what that has to do with it," Lieutenant Travers answered coolly. "Lieutenant Bemis whips Mrs. Bemis beautifully every time they have sexual intercourse, and he isn't worth a farthing at parades."

"I'm talking about flagellation," Lieutenant Engle retorted. "Who gives a damn about parades?"

Actually, no one but Lieutenant Scheisskopf really gave a damn about the parades, least of all the bloated colonel with the big fat mustache, who was chairman of the Action Board and began bellowing at Clevinger the moment Clevinger stepped gingerly into the room to plead innocent to the charges Lieutenant Scheisskopf had lodged against him. The colonel beat his fist down upon the table and hurt his hand and became so further enraged with Clevinger that he beat his fist down upon the table even harder and hurt his hand some more. Lieutenant Scheisskopf glared at Clevinger with tight lips, mortified by the poor impression Clevinger was making.

"In sixty days you'll be fighting Billy Petrolle," the colonel with the big fat mustache roared. "And you think it's a big fat joke."

"I don't think it's a joke, sir," Clevinger replied.

"Don't interrupt."

"Yes, sir."

"And say 'sir' when you do,' ordered Major Metcalf.

"Yes, sir."

"Weren't you just ordered not to interrupt?" Major Metcalf inquired coldly.

"But I didn't interrupt, sir," Clevinger protested.

"No. And you didn't say 'sir,' either. Add that to the charges against him," Major Metcalf directed the corporal who could take shorthand. "Failure to say 'sir' to superior officers when not interrupting them."

"Metcalf," said the colonel, "you're a goddamn fool. Do you know that?"

Major Metcalf swallowed with difficulty. "Yes, sir."

"Then keep your goddam mouth shut. You don't make sense."

There were three members of the Action Board, the bloated colonel with the big fat mustache, Lieutenant Scheisskopf and Major Metcalf, who was trying to develop a steely gaze. As a member of the Action Board, Lieutenant Scheisskopf was one of the judges who would weigh the merits of the case against Clevinger as presented by the prosecutor. Lieutenant Scheisskopf was also the prosecutor. Clevinger had an officer defending him. The officer defending him was Lieutenant Scheisskopf.

It was all very confusing to Clevinger, who began vibrating in terror

as the colonel surged to his feet like a gigantic belch and threatened to
rip his stinking, cowardly body apart limb from limb. One day he had
stumbled while marching to class; the next day he was formally charged
with "breaking ranks while in formation, felonious assault, indiscriminate
behavior, mopery, high treason, provoking, being a smart guy, listening
to classical music, and so on." In short, they threw the book at him,
and there he was, standing in dread before the bloated colonel, who
roared once more that in sixty days he would be fighting Billy Petrolle
and demanded to know how the hell he would like being washed out and
shipped to the Solomon Islands to bury bodies. Clevinger replied with
courtesy that he would not like it; he was a dope who would rather be
a corpse than bury one. The colonel sat down and settled back, calm
and cagey suddenly, and ingratiatingly polite.

"What did you mean," he inquired slowly, "when you said we couldn't
punish you?"

"When, sir?"

"I'm asking the questions. You're answering them."

"Yes, sir. I—"

"Did you think we brought you here to ask questions and for me
to answer them?"

"No, sir. I—"

"What did we bring you here for?"

"To answer questions."

"You're goddam right," roared the colonel. "Now suppose you start
answering some before I break your goddam head. Just what the hell
did you mean, you bastard, when you said we couldn't punish you?"

"I don't think I ever made that statement, sir."

"Will you speak up, please? I couldn't hear you."

"Yes, sir. I—"

"Will you speak up, please? He couldn't hear you."

"Yes, sir. I—"

"Metcalf."

"Sir?"

"Didn't I tell you to keep your stupid mouth shut?"

"Yes, sir."

"Then keep your stupid mouth shut when I tell you to keep your
stupid mouth shut. Do you understand? Will you speak up, please? I
couldn't hear you."

"Yes, sir. I—"

"Metcalf, is that your foot I'm stepping on?"

"No, sir. It must be Lieutenant Scheisskopf's foot."

"It isn't my foot," said Lieutenant Scheisskopf.

"Then maybe it is my foot after all," said Major Metcalf.

"Move it."

"Yes, sir. You'll have to move your foot first, colonel. It's on top of mine."

"Are you telling me to move my foot?"

"No, sir. Oh, no, sir."

"Then move your foot and keep your stupid mouth shut. Will you speak up, please? I still couldn't hear you."

"Yes, sir. I said that I didn't say that you couldn't punish me."

"Just what the hell are you talking about?"

"I'm answering your question, sir."

"What question?"

" 'Just what the hell did you mean, you bastard, when you said we couldn't punish you?' " said the corporal who could take shorthand, reading from his steno pad.

"All right," said the colonel. "Just what the hell *did* you mean?"

"I didn't say you couldn't punish me, sir."

"When?" asked the colonel.

"When what, sir?"

"Now you're asking me questions again."

"I'm sorry, sir. I'm afraid I don't understand your question."

"When didn't you say we couldn't punish you? Don't you understand my question?"

"No, sir. I don't understand."

"You've just told us that. Now suppose you answer my question."

"But how can I answer it?"

"That's another question you're asking me."

"I'm sorry, sir. But I don't know how to answer it. I never said you couldn't punish me."

"Now you're telling us when you did say it. I'm asking you to tell us when you didn't say it."

Clevinger took a deep breath. "I always didn't say you couldn't punish me, sir."

"That's much better, Mr. Clevinger, even though it is a barefaced lie. Last night in the latrine. Didn't you whisper that we couldn't punish you to that other dirty son of a bitch we don't like? What's his name?"

"Yossarian, sir," Lieutenant Scheisskopf said.

"Yes, Yossarian. That's right. Yossarian. Yossarian? Is that his name? Yossarian? What the hell kind of a name is Yossarian?"

Lieutenant Scheisskopf had the facts at his finger tips. "It's Yossarian's name, sir," he explained.

"Yes, I suppose it is. Didn't you whisper to Yossarian that we couldn't punish you?"

"Oh, no, sir. I whispered to him that you couldn't find me guilty—"

"I may be stupid," interrupted the colonel, "but the distinction escapes me. I guess I *am* pretty stupid, because the distinction escapes me."

"W—"

"You're a windy son of a bitch, aren't you? Nobody asked you for clarification and you're giving me clarification. I was making a statement, not asking for clarification. You are a windy son of a bitch, aren't you?"

"No, sir."

"No, sir? Are you calling me a goddam liar?"

"Oh, no, sir."

"Then you're a windy son of a bitch, aren't you?"

"No, sir."

"Are you trying to pick a fight with me?"

"No, sir."

"Are you a windy son of a bitch?"

"No, sir."

"Goddammit, you *are* trying to pick a fight with me. For two stinking cents I'd jump over this big fat table and rip your stinking, cowardly body apart limb from limb."

"Do it! Do it!" cried Major Metcalf.

"Metcalf, you stinking son of a bitch. Didn't I tell you to keep your stinking, cowardly, stupid mouth shut?"

"Yes, sir. I'm sorry, sir."

"Then suppose *you* do it."

"I was only trying to learn, sir. The only way a person can learn is by trying."

"Who says so?"

"Everybody says so, sir. Even Lieutenant Scheisskopf says so."

"Do you say so?"

"Yes, sir," said Lieutenant Scheisskopf. "But everybody says so."

"Well, Metcalf, suppose you try keeping that stupid mouth of yours shut, and maybe that's the way you'll learn how. Now, where were we? Read me back the last line."

"'Read me back the last line,'" read back the corporal, who could take shorthand.

"Not *my* last line, stupid!" the colonel shouted. "Somebody else's."

"'Read me back the last line,'" read back the corporal.

"That's *my* last line again!" shrieked the colonel, turning purple with anger.

"Oh, no, sir," corrected the corporal. "That's *my* last line. I read it to you just a moment ago. Don't you remember, sir? It was only a moment ago."

"Oh, my God! Read me back *his* last line, stupid. Say, what the hell's your name, anyway?"

"Popinjay, sir."

"Well, you're next, Popinjay. As soon as his trial ends, your trial begins. Get it?"

"Yes, sir. What will I be charged with?"

"What the hell difference does that make? Did you hear what he asked me? You're going to learn, Popinjay—the minute we finish with Clevinger you're going to learn. Cadet Clevinger, what did— You are Cadet Clevinger, aren't you, and not Popinjay?"

"Yes, sir."

"Good. What did—"

"I'm Popinjay, sir."

"Popinjay, is your father a millionaire, or a member of the Senate?"

"No, sir."

"Then you're up shit creek, Popinjay, without a paddle. He's not a general or a high-ranking member of the Administration, is he?"

"No, sir."

"That's good. What does your father do?"

"He's dead, sir."

"That's *very* good. You really are up the creek, Popinjay. Is Popinjay really your name? Just what the hell kind of name is Popinjay, anyway? I don't like it."

"It's Popinjay's name, sir," Lieutenant Scheisskopf explained.

"Well, I don't like it, Popinjay, and I just can't wait to rip your stinking, cowardly body apart limb from limb. Cadet Clevinger, will you repeat what the hell it was you did or didn't whisper to Yossarian late last night in the latrine?"

"Yes, sir. I said that you couldn't find me guilty—"

"We'll take it from there. Precisely what did you mean, Cadet Clevinger, when you said we couldn't find you guilty?"

"I didn't say you couldn't find me guilty, sir."

"When?"

"When what, sir?"

"Goddammit, are you going to start pumping me again?"

"No, sir. I'm sorry, sir."

"Then answer the question. When didn't you say we couldn't find you guilty?"

"Late last night in the latrine, sir."

"Is that the only time you didn't say it?"

"No, sir. I always didn't say you couldn't find me guilty, sir. What I did say to Yossarian was—"

"Nobody asked you what you did say to Yossarian. We asked you what you didn't say to him. We're not at all interested in what you did say to Yossarian. Is that clear?"

"Yes, sir."

"Then we'll go on. What did you say to Yossarian?"

"I said to him, sir, that you couldn't find me guilty of the offense with which I am charged and still be faithful to the cause of . . ."

"Of what? You're mumbling."

"Stop mumbling."

"Yes, sir."

"And mumble 'sir' when you do."

"Metcalf, you bastard!"

"Yes, sir," mumbled Clevinger. "Of justice, sir. That you couldn't find—"

"Justice?" The colonel was astounded. "What is justice?"

"Justice, sir—"

"That's not what justice is," the colonel jeered, and began pounding the table again with his big fat hand. "That's what Karl Marx is. I'll tell you what justice is. Justice is a knee in the gut from the floor on the chin at night sneaky with a knife brought up down on the magazine of a battleship sandbagged underhanded in the dark without a word of warning. Garroting. That's what justice is when we've all got to be tough enough and rough enough to fight Billy Petrolle. From the hip. Get it?"

"No, sir."

"Don't sir me!"

"Yes, sir."

"And say 'sir' when you don't," ordered Major Metcalf.

Clevinger was guilty, of course, or he would not have been accused, and since the only way to prove it was to find him guilty, it was their patriotic duty to do so. He was sentenced to walk fifty-seven punishment tours. Popinjay was locked up to be taught a lesson, and Major Metcalf was shipped to the Solomon Islands to bury bodies. A punishment tour for Clevinger was fifty minutes of a weekend hour spent pacing back and forth before the provost marshal's building with a ton of an unloaded rifle on his shoulder.

It was all very confusing to Clevinger. There were many strange things taking place, but the strangest of all, to Clevinger, was the hatred, the brutal, uncloaked, inexorable hatred of the members of the Action Board, glazing their unforgiving expressions with a hard, vindictive surface, glowing in their narrowed eyes malignantly like inextinguishable coals. Clevinger was stunned to discover it. They would have lynched him if they could. They were three grown men and he was a boy, and they hated him and wished him dead. They had hated him before he came, hated him while he was there, hated him after he left, carried their hatred for him away malignantly like some pampered treasure after they separated from each other and went to their solitude.

Yossarian had done his best to warn him the night before. "You haven't got a chance, kid," he had told him glumly. "They hate Jews."

"But I'm not Jewish," answered Clevinger.

"It will make no difference," Yossarian promised, and Yossarian was right. "They're after everybody."

Clevinger recoiled from their hatred as though from a blinding light. These three men who hated him spoke his language and wore his uniform, but he saw their loveless faces set immutably into cramped, mean lines of hostility and understood instantly that nowhere in the world, not in all the fascist tanks or planes or submarines, not in the bunkers behind the machine guns or mortars or behind the blowing flame throwers, not even among all the expert gunners of the crack Hermann Goering Anti-aircraft Division or among the grisly connivers in all the beer halls in Munich and everywhere else, were there men who hated him more.

George Plimpton

MEMBERS OF THE TEAM
from OUT OF MY LEAGUE and PAPER LION

I have always been taken by Truman Capote's analogy about literary skills—that at their best they are akin to the feat of juggling seven or a dozen balls in the air at the same time; the wonder is the ease of it all; the hands work busily but never frantically under the fine arc of balls; only the performer's eyes are slightly agog as he tends to his miracle. Every writer would wish to emulate such a display of skills when he buckles down to his day's work. So often he attempts so much—six balls in one hand, five in the other, overextending himself for certain, but hoping, somehow, that he will be able to control finally, after many false starts, what he commits to public view. As writers know, the first flurry of commitment is so often a despairing clatter, and one is left solely with the vague notion of what one wanted to do. The pieces selected here are *close,* at any rate, to what was hoped for—one a short description of a baseball game in a French meadow, the other a character study of a Detroit Lion tackle named Alex Karras. I can read back over them and sense a degree of control—for at least a page or two.

George Plimpton

I

In school, I had been a fanatic about pitching, throwing stones at tree trunks when there wasn't anyone to play catch with, but my pitching since those days had started a slow descent into decadence. At college, baseball became associated with beer tankards tilted in the grass—informal games where you forgot the score finally and played with softballs, as big as grapefruits, and as unsatisfactory to hit as pillows. And then eventually the nadir was reached in a game of softball organized in a meadow in France, the last game I played in before appearing in the Stadium. Most of the participants had never played baseball before. It had to be explained to them as we went along. We used a brightly colored beach ball which didn't travel far in the thick grass of the meadow —bordered on one side by a canal and behind us the Château of Maillebois. The only beaten-down place in the meadow was for two wicker-cased bottles of the *vin du pays* with glasses propped up around. We had two bats: one a broomstick, the other a fence post so heavy that you felt you had to begin to swing it as soon as the ball left the pitcher's hand. Out in left field was a young countess, playing in bare feet, and separated from her friend in right field—an ash-blonde girl in toreador pants—by a male center fielder, so the two girls wouldn't get to chatting with each other. The center fielder was very serious about the game: with every pitch he went forward on his toes to get a jump on the ball in case it was hit out his way. He was the one who had suggested the game at lunch in the château—had explained it gravely and organized everyone.

The Countess' husband was pitching and she watched him. Sometimes she would call warmly to him "Ah, Teddy" just to let him know she hadn't gone, and he would turn and see her there in the meadow and behind her a stand of cypress trees.

Early in the game the owner of the château came to bat. He refused to remove a blue boating blazer he was wearing; he disdained advice on the proper batting form, and arranged himself in a crouched stance in which he stood on home plate and faced the pitcher head on—like a tennis player receiving service. He picked out the first pitch thrown near him and with a convulsive sweep of his bat he smacked a towering hit out to the Countess in left field. She gave a little high cry, as faint and forlorn as a curlew's; her mouth remained open as she stared into the sky, and she threw up her arms dramatically, fingers wide, the epitome of Anguish in a Victorian mezzotint, and thus she stood rooted while the ball arched over her head and landed beyond her, rolling briefly for the cypress trees. She turned and ran for it, calling out her husband's name "Teddy! Ted-dy!" and we saw her reach the spot where the ball had dropped, fall down, and rise again with the bright ball in her hand; holding it at arm's length she began to spin as stiffly as a weathercock revolving in a capricious wind—working up speed in her turns until she let go, like a hammer thrower, and we watched the ball sail briefly against the sky, headed away from us, a toss that almost reached the distant barrier of cypress. She ran for it again. It was evident from her lack of direction, however, and from her peculiar throwing motion, her light cotton dress spinning at her knees, that the Countess might twirl the ball and then herself out of sight, beyond the grove or into the canal. Before she could reach the ball the second time, the zealous center fielder, who'd been shouting, "Peg it to second, Gabrielle!" and yelling at the second baseman to move out for the "cut-off," beat the Countess to the ball, sidestepped her headlong rush, and threw the ball mightily toward the infield.

There the château owner, the gold buttons glinting on his blazer, had watched his hit tower over the Countess' head, and then, carrying the bat with him, had charged off through the tall grass, swishing through it with great bounds toward third base, and from there, egged on by a multitude of shouts, he swooped frantically from base to base with all the hysteria of an owl trapped in a pantry—shouting Gallic oaths until the center fielder's toss was retrieved by the second baseman, who approached, knees wobbly from laughter, and tagged him out in the vicinity of the pitcher's position. The center fielder wasn't quite so serious after that. The helter-skelter routes of the play were marked by scores of tiny white butterflies flushed up by those hurried passages through the grass and they hung briefly over the meadow as luminous as fireflies.

Afterwards, much later, someone knocked the ball into the canal, where it landed with a *thonk*, bounced a few times, and floated, turning slightly, just out of reach. We coaxed it out finally, lying on our bellies above the water's edge and prodding for it with the longer of the two bats, and I remember a myriad little green frogs leaping out from under us as if our weight had squeezed them out of the canalbank. It was the end of the day, and when we walked up through the dusk there were lights burning in one of the château towers. . . .

II

At first, it was more relaxed on the bus than I had thought it was going to be—with much less tension than there had been on the bus to Pontiac. The players talked easily. Behind me, Brettschneider, one of the linebackers, was talking about an old girl friend of his who sold yoyos on the road—a particular model that lit up when it reached the bottom of the string. He was a good storyteller; in the rear of the bus the players leaned over the backs of their seats to listen to him.

But then what was in the back of everyone's mind came rapidly to the fore. As we entered the outskirts of Detroit a silence descended on the bus, quite abruptly, as if we'd suddenly been asphyxiated by the thought of what was coming—thirty men swayed by the bus's motion staring straight at the back of the seat in front of them; it was not the silence of the dumb: the tension was palpable—everyone so keyed up that finally a player could no longer contain himself and he'd bark out, "Get it up, *Detroit!*" and that would set off an explosion of feet stamping on the bus floor and a babble of exhortations, and then just as abruptly the silence would descend again, the quiet bus rocking along, so that one thought of a herd of aroused animals propelled by some nameless dread into a momentary noisy flurry of motion and milling, and then motionless again, yet still tense, the big heads watching.

The players never tired of talking about the phenomenon of tension building up on the day of a game. If a team was "up," it could perform prodigies, and each ballplayer would be swept along in the effort, playing better than he could even imagine, until everything he did seemed performed in an atmosphere of exhilaration. Before the Thanksgiving Day Green Bay game the year before, when they had won one of their great victories, the team said that the tension had built up so that they could hardly breathe—it was like a ground mist around them—and Coach George Wilson, who usually gave a little locker-room talk to build them up just before they went out on the field, knew that he could break the extraordinary tension if he fooled with it, or said too much. So he called out, "O.K., let's get 'em!" quite softly, but hard, and the team rushed out and played such an extraordinary game that the Green Bay players kept looking at them oddly, as if they suspected them of sniffing some sort of elixir.

Sensing the tension, and being part of it oneself, was not necessarily pleasurable. It was trying and difficult to get through the hours before a game, and the players adopted different habits to cope with the wait. Some preferred to go off by themselves. At the nine-o'clock breakfast one could see them eating the game-day steaks and the honey—the sauces locked away—seated almost in the bishop's section of the dining room to remain separate. I was one of them. The reason for our apartness, I think, was a fruitless attempt to keep time from passing. Involvement with others seemed to make the time go quickly, and one would look at one's watch suddenly in the middle of a conversation or a bridge game to find that a great, uncontrolled gulp of time had gone, and that the final confrontation was that much closer. One wanted time *stopped,* at least I did. It seemed to go slower for me if I kept to myself, yawning cavernously, almost caving in on the hollowness I felt in my stomach, and staring every once in a while at the sweep of the second hand on my watch in some woebegone sense that I could control time by keeping an eye on it.

As the day moved on—despite my concern—I became aware of another drift, this a slow, universal move toward the confrontation in Detroit Stadium. In their homes fans were beginning to think about the game and the officials were packing their striped shirts in kit bags; as we set out for the stadium by bus, so were the Browns stirring around in their Detroit hotel, their bus waiting for them down on the street. It was often a slow, meandering movement, like the progress of a pair of amoebas—often some element of the whole lingering behind (a player walking back across a hotel lobby to buy gum)—but it was always an inexorable motion toward confrontation. Finally the two teams would walk down a corridor and be in a locker room just a couple of *walls* away. Ultimately the confrontation was actual: like hideous magi the Browns were sprung up just a yard away across a line of scrimmage, with all their heft and skill bent on obliteration of the people opposite, who were us.

Other players craved the confrontation and they did what they could to make the time pass—they slept, or organized card games, or there was conversation.

The year after my participation I went down to Philadelphia one week-end to watch the team play the Eagles. After the game-day breakfast with them in the hotel, John Gordy took me up to his room. Alex Karras was his roommate.

Gordy said, "Alex will be telling stories, or doing some damn thing that'll keep our minds occupied. There'll be a bunch of guys up there."

"He takes the day of the game calmly?" I asked.

"Hell no," Gordy said. "He gets sick before every game—violently."

"Well," I said tentatively, "why don't we drop in on somebody else."

"Alex will be all right," Gordy said.

There were some other players sitting around the room—Terry Barr, Jim Gibbons, and Gary Lowe. Karras was lying on his bed staring up at the ceiling through his big horn-rimmed glasses. His torso was enormous. In his self-deprecatory manner he used to say that if the rest of him was in proper proportion to his torso he'd be eight feet tall. On the field he ran, his teammates said of him, like a "mad duck," but they used to swear softly thinking of his ability.

Gordy introduced me to him, and Karras stuck out a hand, remaining absolutely flat where he was on the bed.

I wished him luck that afternoon in the Eagle game. I found a chair in the corner and sat down. He raised up slowly and looked down between his feet at the television set against the wall opposite the foot of his bed. It was on. The sets were almost automatically turned on as soon as one walked into a hotel room, flicked on like pulling up a window shade, not because there was a specific program to see, but to create a second window in those airless rooms to glance at as one might glance out the real window at the walls of the air shaft opposite. "Look at that," Karras said. He was staring moodily at the image. An advertisement was showing—a young man in sharkskin trousers and a yachting jumper sitting on a boulder with the surf piling around, with a girl in close to him, and he was inhaling deeply on a cigarette. "Look at that guy," said Karras. "They always have good-looking guys puffing on cigarettes, like our quarterback, Plum. They put cigarettes in Milt Plum's mouth and snap color pictures of him for the big magazines and Milt doesn't even smoke—he hardly knows how to hold a cigarette. They had to *teach* him. What about me? I'm a long-time smoker, known how to hold a cigarette since I was eight, I inhale and all, and when the wind's down and I get a little practice, with the pressure really on me, I can put together a smoke ring, think of that. Why not me, then, instead of Plum? The reason is they only pick the good-looking guys, and the good-looking girls. They look at me, blowing away on those smoke rings, and they think, well, he's O.K. on those rings, but he's got the face of a mechanic who's got squashed working under a large touring car. There ought to be a union of us ugly cruds. I'd like to see an ad, a TV ad, in which this great mountain of a girl comes out, just horrible looking, with a name like Betty Home, and she's advertising nylons, y'see, and she draws on a pair of nylons over these enormous fat thighs. 'Sheer,' she says, working her lips up the way those thin models do."

"You're beautiful, Alex," someone said.

"Who am I kidding?" Karras said. "I know I'm not very pretty, but then the girls I talk to aren't very pretty either." He groaned. "Even with them I can't make out. I couldn't make out if I had the Hope Diamond hanging from my neck." He dropped back on the bed and stared up at the ceiling. "It wasn't always like that. In my other lives I had some grand times."

It was Karras's fantasy that he had lived a succession of different lives—stretching far back into the past. He had been, among other things, an aide-de-camp to both General Washington and Adolf Hitler.

"What about Hitler?" one of the players asked. "What was your impression?"

"Hitler was not an ordinary joe," Karras said expansively. "You knew that when you were around him as much as I was. He had this obsession to hold his breath for more than three minutes."

"No! Could he do it?"

"Nowhere near. He got red in the face very quickly, and there'd be this little popping sound when the air came rushing out. He never lasted more than eight or nine seconds—shortest-breathed man I ever saw."

"How about the others? Did you know Rommel, Hess, Goering, and all those . . . ?"

"Certainly. I knew all those cats, Rundstedt, Goering—Bavaria Fats, we called him—and Rommel. He had a terrible weak stomach, Rommel did. He used to get sick all the time. I'd come rushing up to him in the morning to fling the salute at him, and say, 'Hello, hello, heil, heil, good *morn*in', gener'l,' and he'd get sick. Hitler never trusted him for that reason. Why, he'd come striding up to Rommel at headquarters and say, 'A fine day to mount ze attack against the filthy *Schweinhund* Monty, the Britisher.' Rommel, he'd lean over and get sick into one of those tall nickel-plated upright ashtrays you find in the smoking section of railroad coaches—the kind with a button on the side of the stand you push and the trap door opens and the cigar falls down. I carried one of these things around for Rommel when he was at headquarters, ready, with my thumb on the button. Hitler was suspicious of those ashtrays. 'What is that thing?' he'd always say. I think he had an idea it was a bomb. 'It's an ashtray,' I'd say. 'It's General Rommel's ashtray.' Hitler'd take a long look, and he'd say, 'Why doesn't the general carry a smaller model around—that thing's three feet tall. What's wrong with those little *pocket* ashtrays, the kind with a hotel name on the bottom? Besides,' Hitler said, 'he doesn't smoke, Rommel, what does he need a big thing like that for if he doesn't smoke, answer me *that!*' 'Well,' I said quickly, 'the general smokes *hemp.*' 'Oh well, no wonder,' Hitler says. 'Why not say so in the beginning?'"

"What about Eva Braun? Tell us about her."

"Eva Braun was my sister."

"No!"

"She was. You may not think so, my looking the way I do, but in that life I was smart-looking, a blond cat, with boots that went up clear to the crotch, shiny as brass, and in company people was always saying, 'Who's that good-looker?' Real Aryan I was."

"Tell us more about Eva."

"She and Hitler didn't get along at all."

"No."

"My sister had this terrible laugh, a sort of cackle, and when Hitler came fooling around, pushing that mustache at her, why, she'd let out this cackle. Hitler could never figure why she was laughing. 'What's wrong?' he'd ask, looking behind him, thinking some clown back of them was making faces. Her cackling was horrible. 'You laughing at one of Bavaria Fats's jokes?' he'd ask."

Gibbons said, "History books say they were quite a pair."

"That was for appearances," Karras said. "They had to show that Hitler had normal feeling for women. So the public relations people took a bunch of pictures of the two of them together, she standing under a waterfall bare-ass, and Hitler next to her, getting his uniform wet. You ever see Hitler bare-ass? The answer is no. The fact was, and everybody around headquarters knew it, that Hitler was a woman—

my aunt, if you really want to know, Aunt Hilda, and quite a trial she turned out to be to the rest of the family."

"Did Eva know about that?"

"The fact is she *didn't*. And you know what fooled her?"

"What?"

"That mustache. You'd think it was false, Aunt Hilda being a woman and all. Well, that mustache was absolutely real. Aunt Hilda shaved five times a day. After a while Eva got over her cackle, and toward the end she fell for Aunt Hilda. No one wanted to disillusion her, so they got a marriage going there in the Berlin bunker. The Russians were turning up, so the pair committed suicide, which was maybe good for Eva. She'd have found out—"

"That Hitler was Aunt Hilda."

"Her own *mother!*" said Karras. "Aunt Hilda was Eva's mother, you see. Eva didn't know that, of course. She thought she was an orphan. And guess who Eva's *father* was?"

"Who? Bavaria Fats?" someone suggested.

"You're looking at him," said Karras comfortably from his bed.

"You! Come on," said Gary Lowe. "Eva Braun was your sister."

"Both sister *and* daughter," Karras said proudly. "Adolf Hitler was my wife."

"That's horrible," said Gordy.

We sat there reflecting on the tangled family tree of the Nazi hierarchy, the television set murmuring slightly in the background.

"Well, I hope things weren't as horrible as that in General Washington's time," Gordy finally said.

Karras stirred. "General Washington was beautiful. I was at Valley Forge, you know, real cold there, feeding on owls' heads, we were, and such things, and the general would come through the campfires and strike these poses and he'd say, 'Men, we will endure,' things like that. He was just beautiful. But they get a lot of things wrong about him. You recall the cherry-tree story?"

We nodded.

"He *had* to cut that tree down. What did it have but the Dutch Elm disease, easiest thing in the world to see, that cherry tree was top-heavy with it, and if Washington hadn't fetched an axe to it, everything around would have been infected."

"Why didn't George tell his father that?" Gordy asked. "He'd have saved himself a whipping."

"Young George had false teeth, you know, a full set, even as a young boy, and when his daddy called him in to ask him about the cherry tree, he *tried* to explain about Dutch Elm disease, but out came a lot of clacking. Washington's teeth fit badly, and when he spoke he either did this clacking, or sometimes a whistle, a high whistle." Karras demonstrated the whistle. "So when his daddy said, 'Who cut that tree down?' he was only about to understand through all that clacking and whistling that his son, George, had, but he couldn't understand the *reason*. So he took a switch to him. Beat him half-crazy."

"How could you understand him saying, 'We will endure,' and things like that at Valley Forge," someone asked, "if Washington had this speech difficulty?"

"We *couldn't* understand him," explained Karras. "But he got into all these poses, you see. He'd stand around among the campfires, and when he crossed the Delaware he struck a fine pose *that* time, with his foot up there on the bow, so you always knew what the guy had in mind. You know actually who spoke the Farewell Address?"

"Who?"

"You're looking at him," said Karras. "What happened was that I stood right behind the general up there on the platform and I spoke the words for him. He was like a wood dummy, clacking his jaw, but you couldn't tell unless you were right up close that it was me."

"How about his staff? How did they understand his orders?"

"Well, lip reading—they were all deaf mutes," Karras went blithely on. "That's not generally known, but Washington's closest people—Lafayette (French Fats, we called him), General Gates, and the rest of them—they could hear nothing; but they could *lip read*. That's why in the portraits of Washington all the generals and the staff people are standing around staring at him. You hear that's devotion they was showing. Crap. They was looking at his mouth in case Washington had it in mind to say something, so they could begin their lip reading and hop to it if there was something to be done."

There had been some other lives Karras hinted at: he had been something during the Civil War—he wasn't sure what. Something low, he thought, a camp follower perhaps.

Between lives, he told us, he would find himself on an airliner flying in heavy cloud banks, or often above them, with the sun shining. The ground was always out of sight, though he would press his forehead against the windows to look for it far down through the clouds, never succeeding, though often the clouds fell away into deep valleys that seemed to drop for miles. The flight was always very smooth and long, with pretty stewardesses coming by and leaning over to offer beef bouillon, and when the evening came their trays had tall drinks on them. He was always very tired on these flights, utterly relaxed; through half-closed eyes he would watch the stewardesses in the aisle, and when they came by he would hold out his cup for the bouillon, or the tall drink if it was in the evening. On the third day, perhaps the fourth, when he was beginning to feel more lively, a mist would suddenly settle in the cabin, increasingly thick, so that it began to take on the same consistency as the clouds outside, the walls of the cabin disappearing in it, and finally the back of the seat in front of him, so that in its thickness he felt himself in the clouds themselves, the wind beginning to sweep across his face, and as he felt himself begin to fall and turn, he knew his time was coming to be someone else and he would cross his fingers and hope to Christ he wasn't going to be a goddamn jockstrap athlete again.

"Well, what would you hope to be?" Gary Lowe asked.

"How the hell do I know?" Karras said. He seemed ill-tempered suddenly. "I tell you nothing can be worse than this—lying around in a little hotel room like a bunch of cruds. Then we get out on some field and knock some guys around for a lousy pile of pennies. What sort of a life is that? It's crud," he said. He raised up off the bed. He looked very sour.

"Let's clear out of here," he said. "I got to find me a place to puke."

When we got out in the corridor, he hurried on down in front of us and began punching at the elevator button.

"That's a mood, isn't it?" I said quietly to Lowe.

"Alex is ready," Lowe said happily. "He's right as rain. He's up for the game."

"Does he mean it when he says he's going to get sick?"

"Sure he will," said Lowe. "Just as George Wilson tells us to go out there and rock them, out in the can we'll hear Alex lose his lunch. Sure. And then in five minutes he'll be out there on the field making the poor fellow from Philadelphia opposite him pay for it."

We crowded into the elevator. No one said anything going down. Karras would sit alone in the bus.

James T. Farrell

JUMP TO CHICAGO—1955

It would be impossible for me, now, to select one work or a part of a work and call it "my best." My fiction is too inter-related. However, in selecting a story for this book, I have taken an example of one kind of story.

This is a short objective story in which the meanings are only suggested. Dialogue characterizes and creates the tone and the atmosphere of the environment—and serves the purpose of narrative.

James T. Farrell

I

The ball club won the Sunday game in St. Louis, 7–4. Both teams had played sloppily. Pat had knocked out his story, filed it, and grabbed a cab to the railroad station. The train had been held up for the ball players.

Pat Donnelly was medium sized, red-faced, and sandy-haired. The minute he got on the train, he went straight to Al Tompkins' bedroom. "Tommy" Tompkins was the Travelling Secretary for the club. He always kept a good supply of the best liquor.

Pat sat by the window. He wished that he didn't want a drink. But what the hell, that was part of the pleasure of his work. It put an edge on life, took away the dullness.

It was the custom for the ball players to eat first. This gave the writers time for a few drinks and a bull session. They were all there, in Tommy's room, waiting for the porter to bring in the ice, glasses, and soda.

"Sign the tab, boys," Tommy had said.

"Hey, Tommy," Pat called.

"What?"

"Where's the ice?"

"Call the porter. Order anything you want, boys. It's on the club."

"Where's the bourbon?" asked Pete Jones.

"Everything's there, boys. Sign the tab. It's on us tonight."

"It better be, you . . ." Pete answered jokingly; but Tommy had already left the room.

"Tommy's O.K. in my book," Pat said.

"Of course he is," Pete replied.

"It's goddamned good to be with a winner," George Farley said.

"You said it," Pete agreed.

"I suppose it is," Pat mused. "But I been travelling so long with ball clubs I don't get excited easy. Not after thirty years."

"Jesus, Pat, you covered Honus Wagner and Cy Young, didn't you?" Pete asked.

"Here's the man I'm waiting for," Pat said as the porter entered the room.

"Yes, gentlemen, Mr. Tompkins says give you anything you want," the porter told them, setting down glasses and a bucket of ice.

"Can you get us some soda?" Pat asked.

"Be a man, Pat, drink it straight," Pete said.

"I don't like it straight."

They all laughed.

"I'll be right back, gentlemen," the porter said.

"Hurry up, I need a drink," Pat told him.

"I'm going to have one straight," Pete said.

"You just want to be different," Art Dunlock accused.

"No, I just want a drink."

"Is the life of a baseball writer that hard?" George Farley asked.

"It is after thirty years," Pat said.

"What the hell are you complaining about? Would you rather be digging ditches?" Pete asked him.

"Who says I'd be digging ditches?"

"Because, you dumb sonofabitch, you don't have enough brains to do anything else."

"What did Pat ever do to you, Pete?" asked George Farley.

"He never did anything to me."

"Hell, I never did anything particular to anyone," Pat said.

"Except yourself."

"I sort of like a drink or two after a game," Pat said defensively.

He was determined not to think of his blood pressure. He was going to try not to think about it. He looked at the moving darkness outside the window. He was glad they were only going to Chicago. That meant he could sleep in a bed instead of on a train. He couldn't sleep well any place—but especially on a train. And if he couldn't sleep, he'd think about his health, his blood pressure. That would only make his condition worse.

But why worry? He felt mighty good this trip.

"Come on, Pat, pour yourself a drink," Pete said.

Sure, why not? A few drinks would be relaxing; and relaxation lowered his pressure.

He poured himself a Scotch and soda. He lit a cigar and sat back.

"Yes, it's good to be with a winner," George Farley said.

"Hell," Pat said, speaking in his loud bark, "I suppose it is. But win or lose, boys, we have to file every day. And don't none of you try to tell me that there's good copy for a story every day. I don't know what the hell I'm gonna write tomorrow."

"Write about the boys of the press playing golf," Al Oliver said.

"No kidding, boys, you know how I have to sweat for copy some days."

"Aw quit singing the blues, Donnelly," Pete shouted.

"Yeh, this isn't a funeral party. We're travelling with a pennant winner," George said.

"Say," Al Oliver said, taking a drink of plain water, "did any of you fellows talk with that guy who's making that survey about what's wrong with baseball today?"

"What did you think of him?" Pete asked.

"I think the whole idea is a lot of goddam horse manure."

"That's what I think—it's plain old horseshit," Pete said.

"Yeh," Pat added, "I don't see what the hell this guy's going to find out that we don't know already. Goin' around asking all those dumb questions like we was all dumb bastards."

"He'll find out something if he investigates you, Donnelly," Pete barked, mixing himself another drink.

"Come on, gentlemen, drink up before we eat," he said.

Pat looked at his glass. There was a little left in it. He picked it up and drank.

There, that was enough. He ought to go into the diner now and eat. He had had enough to drink.

Pat mixed himself another drink.

"You playing golf tomorrow, George?" asked Pete.

"Yessir I am," George Farley answered.

"Have you got a foursome?"

"Yes, Pete."

"Too bad. I'd like to take you boys."

"You!" Al Oliver snapped back.

"Yes, goddamn it, me. You aren't golfers."

"We're learning, boy."

"Say, this guy who's making the survey about what's wrong with baseball. What's he like?" Pat asked.

"He's a jackass."

"Then he's in good company," said Ike Cohen, sticking his head in the doorway. Ike was a short, gray-haired man.

"Come on in. Have a drink and close your trap, Ike. We're talking about golf," Pete said.

"Don't—not after the game I played on that St. Louis course," Ike said.

"Keep trying, boy. You'll break a hundred yet," Pete said.

"It's too much trouble lugging golf bags around. I never play on the road," Pat said.

"You know that's not why you don't lug golf bags around, you bastard. You're afraid it would interfere with that," Ike pointed at Pat's glass.

"I don't drink that much; just a few before I eat."

"What the hell are you talking about? You're a tank," Pete said.

"No I'm not. I'll confess I like a few every day. And I like good food. More than I should maybe with this damned blood pressure of mine."

"Pat, you ought to take care of yourself," Ike Cohen said.

"I do, Ike. I don't drink that many. Hell, just a few when we're sitting around like this. It's one of the compensations of our work."

"Are you complaining again?" asked George Farley.

"No I'm not complaining but I do think that there are easier ways for a man to make his living and support his family."

"You live like a king, travelling first class. What're you complaining about?" Pete asked.

"It is a crazy life, Pete," Ike said.

"Everything all right, boys?" asked Al Tompkins, popping into the doorway.

"Sure!"

"Eat whenever you feel like it."

"We'll be right there. Soon as we finish our drinks."

Maybe he shouldn't order a steak tonight. He ought to have something else, Pat thought. But he knew that he would order a steak. And that he would have a few more drinks before he did. He looked around at his colleagues. He felt closer to them than he did to anyone else in this man's world. Except his wife and daughter, of course. But someday, this would end. He felt sad; afraid. He took another drink.

What was the matter with him? Hell, he could go on for a long time

yet. He knew better than to worry like that. It wasn't good for him.
Pat finished his drink.

"Well, boys, I'm hungry. Let's go eat," he said.

11

The dining car was crowded; every table was filled. Most of them
were people travelling with the club. Pat was drinking a Scotch and
soda. He felt quite relaxed now. Unworried. This was all part of his
working life. It was one of the more pleasing parts of his job.

It was a life set off from the world. He couldn't quite put his finger
on the right words to describe it. But what the hell, he was only a
journeyman writer. There was plenty he couldn't describe. But he knew
what he meant. In this case, he did. He wasn't drunk.

Pat took another swallow.

All he meant, he guessed, was that they were in their own world.
That's what he meant. Take the few people here in the dining car who
weren't travelling with the club. Like that fat man at the other end of
the car. He was like a foreigner.

"How you doing, Mike?"

"Fine. Fine, Shrimp."

Shrimp was a veteran, a shortstop, and a star. He walked through
the dining car.

"He's class," George Farley said.

"Yes he is. A real class fellow," Pat agreed.

"He's hardly lost a step yet out there on the field," Pete said.

"Oh, he's slowed down a little. When we get into August, we'll
know better how he's holding his own."

Holding his own. Pat felt a doubt. He was holding his own now,
here on this train. But how long would he be able to? It was that
damned blood pressure. How long would it let him hold his own?

But what good did it do to think about it. None. None at all. He
took another drink.

III

"I don't think they were," Ike said.

"Neither do I. They make plays now as a matter of course that would have been sensational in the past," Pat said, joining in the conversation.

"They didn't have the equipment then. Hell, did you guys ever think of the difference in the gloves?" Ike asked.

"Yeh," Pat said, lifting his glass.

The waiter came with their steaks. Pat looked at his with boyish eagerness. A thick juicy steak was one of the pleasures of life. God, he enjoyed them.

"I never heard before of a man curing high blood pressure with whiskey and sirloin steak," Pete commented, cutting into his own steak.

"That isn't what hurts me, Pete," Pat explained. "I shouldn't let myself get excited. That's what I gotta watch. At home, I don't do anything but rest. My wife won't let me."

"You sure make up for it on the road," Pete said.

"How? I don't get excited the way I used to. And I don't get worked up any more, not often."

A husky young pitcher passed them.

"That kid's coming along real good," Pete said.

"Yeh, I guess he is. He looks mature out there on the mound," Pat commented, cutting into his steak.

"He might be just what the Skipper needs," George Farley said.

They were all eating now. Pat looked about. The dining car was full of healthy young men, ball players in condition who didn't seem to have a care in the world. No cares like his. Hell, he hadn't been particularly excited on this trip. In fact, he'd been doing better, lots better, since he had been in the hospital last fall.

A tall blond pitcher passed. He spoke to Pat; Pat returned the greeting.

Most of them were quiet now, eating.

He had been on trains like this, eating like this, God knows how many times, Pat thought. Thirty years of it. From the Babe down, he had seen them come and go. Coming up young and raw, developing class and manners, and then passing out of the limelight. A player's life was short, damned short.

"Waiter," he called.

A glass of beer wouldn't hurt him.

"Bring me a beer."

The Babe. He'd been super-human physically. And where was he now? There had been others, too. They were all gone. Gee, he felt rotten. Soon he would be gone. His eating and drinking. He was killing himself. But what would he do if he didn't eat and give himself a few belts of whiskey a day?

What the hell, he wasn't drunk. He was all right.

Pat went on eating his steak. The waiter brought his beer.

He took a sip. The talk was loud again and punctuated by laughter. Cups were rattling in the diner. Pat went on eating.

What else could he do? He couldn't make a decent living any other way; and in this irregular life of travelling with a ball club, how could he change his habits of eating and drinking? He couldn't. He'd just have to be careful, not get excited, take it easy.

"What are you going to do tomorrow, Pat?" asked Pete. "It's an off day."

"It's not an off day for me. I still got to find copy."

He took another bite of steak. Then he took a swig of beer.

—God, that was good.

And he was alive. He could still enjoy steak, and whiskey, and beer. Lots of things.

The train raced loudly into the night of the Illinois prairie land. The engine whistle sounded mournfully.

God, I'd hate to leave this, Pat thought.

And he took another bite of steak.

S. J. Perelman

EINE KLEINE MOTHMUSIK

Dear Mr. Burnett:

The piece that follows, from *The Rising Gorge,* in its author's opinion qualifies for inclusion here only because it deals with three major preoccupations in everyone's life—money, hostility toward dry-cleaners, and fear of moths. "I don't think that the love-hate relationship between client and cleaner has ever been properly explored," says Mr. Perelman. "I spend half my time (the other half is spent updating *Kamasutra*) in squalid, futile contention with dry-cleaners who deliberately sprinkle grease over my apparel and mislay my neckties. Years of abuse have taught me that remonstrance with these fellows is useless. They must not be coddled; they must be dealt with firmly. I generally enter their premises armed with a blacksnake whip, and the moment they begin voicing recriminations, lay about me freely." As to the identity of the characters described, Mr. Perelman admits without reserve that the cleaner was modelled on an actual person. "He subsequently asked my wife if my family had ever been dry-cleaners," reports Mr. Perelman. "I consider this praise from Sir Hubert."

S. J. Perelman

WAR ON MOTHS BEGINS

The moths are beginning to eat. Even if the weather seems cool, this is their season for gluttony. Miss Rose Finkel, manager of Keystone Cleaners at 313 West Fifty-seventh Street, urges that these precautions be taken:

All winter clothes should be dry-cleaned, even if no stains are apparent. Moths feast on soiled clothes, and if a garment has been worn several times in the last few months, it should be cleaned.

Clean clothes may be kept in the closet in a plastic bag. It is safer, however, to send all woolens to a dry cleaner to put in cold storage.

Customers should check to make sure that their clothes are really sent to a cold storage and not hung in the back of the store.

The Times.

Gay Head,
Martha's Vineyard, Mass.,
July 14

Mr. Stanley Merlin,
Busy Bee Cleaners,
161 Macdougal Street,
New York City

Dear Mr. Merlin:

I heard on the radio this morning before I went for my swim that the heat in New York is catastrophic, but you wouldn't guess it up here. There is a dandy breeze at all times, and the salt-water bathing, as you can imagine, is superlative. Miles of glorious white beach, marvelous breakers, rainbow-colored cliffs—in short, paradise. One feels so rested, so completely purified, that it seems profane to mention anything as sordid as dry cleaning. Still, that's not exactly your problem, is it? I have one that is.

Do you, by chance, remember a tan gabardine suit I sent in to be pressed three or four years ago? It's a very expensive garment, made of that changeable, shimmering material they call solari cloth. The reverse side is a reddish color, like cayenne pepper; during the British occupation of India, as you doubtless know, it was widely used for officers' dress uniforms. Anyway I'm a trifle concerned lest moths get into the closet where I left it in our apartment. The suit isn't really stained, mind you; there's just a faint smudge of lychee syrup on the right sleeve, about the size of your pinkie, that I got in a Chinese restaurant last winter. (I identify it only to help you expunge it without too much friction. I mean, it's a pretty costly garment, and the nap could be damaged if some boob started rubbing it with pumice or whatever.)

Will you, hence, arrange to have your delivery boy pick up the suit at my flat any time next Thursday morning after nine-fifteen? He'll have to show before ten-twenty, since the maid leaves on the dot and would certainly split a gusset if she had to sit around a hot apartment waiting for a delivery boy. (You know how they are, Mr. Merlin.) Tell the boy to be sure and take the right suit; it's hanging next to one made of covert cloth with diagonal flap pockets, and as the Venetian blinds are drawn, he could easily make a mistake in the dark. Flotilla, the maid, is new, so I think I'd better explain which closet to look in. It's in the hall, on his right when he stands facing the bedroom windows. If he stands facing the other way, naturally it's on his left. The main thing, tell him, is not to get rattled and look in the closet *opposite,* because there may be a gabardine suit in there, without pockets, but that isn't the one I have reference to.

Should Flotilla have gone, the visiting super will admit your boy to the flat if he arrives before eleven; otherwise, he is to press our landlord's bell (Coopersmith), in the next building, and ask them for the key. They can't very well give it to him, as they're in Amalfi, but they have a Yugoslav woman dusting for them, a highly intelligent person, to whom he can explain the situation. This woman speaks English.

After the suit is dry-cleaned—which, I repeat, is not essential if you'll only brush the stain with a little moist flannel—make certain that it goes into cold storage at once. I read a piece in the newspaper recently that upset me. It quoted a prominent lady in your profession, a Miss Rose

Finkel, to the effect that some dry cleaners have been known to hang such orders in the back of their store. You and I have had such a long, cordial relationship, Mr. Merlin, that I realize you'd never do anything so unethical, but I just thought I'd underscore it.

Incidentally, and since I know what the temperature in your shop must be these days, let me pass on a couple of hot-weather tips. Eat lots of curries—the spicier the better—and try to take at least a three-hour siesta in the midddle of the day. I learned this trick in India, where Old Sol can be a cruel taskmaster indeed. That's also the place, you'll recall, where solari cloth used to get a big play in officers' dress uniforms. Wears like iron, if you don't abuse it. With every good wish,

Yours sincerely,
S. J. Perelman

New York City,
July 22

Dear Mr. Pearlman:

I got your letter of instructions spelling everything out, and was happy to hear what a glorious vacation you are enjoying in that paradise. I only hope you will be careful to not run any fishhooks in your hand, or step in the undertow, or sunburn your body so badly you lay in the hospital. These troubles I personally don't have. I am a poor man with a wife and family to support, not like some people with stocks and bonds that they can sit in a resort all summer and look down their nose on the rest of humanity. Also my pressing machine was out of commission two days and we are shorthanded. Except for this, everything is peaches and cream.

I sent the boy over like you told me on Thursday. There was no sign of the maid, but for your information he found a note under the door saying she has quit. She says you need a bulldozer, not a servant, and the pay is so small she can do better on relief. Your landlady, by the way, is back from Amalfi, because some to the tenants, she didn't name names, are slow with the rent. She let the boy in the apartment, and while he was finding your red suit she checked over the icebox and the stove, which she claims are very greasy. (I am not criticizing your housekeeping, only reporting what she said.) She also examined the mail in the bureau drawers to see if the post office was forwarding your bills, urgent telegrams, etc.

I don't believe in telling a man his own business. Mine is dry cleaning, yours I don't know what, but you're deceiving yourself about this Indian outfit you gave us. It was one big stain from top to bottom. Maybe you leaned up against the stove or the icebox? (Just kidding.) The plant used every kind of solvent they had on it—benzine, naphtha, turpentine, even lighter fluid—and knocked out the spots, all right, but I warn you beforehand, there are a few brownish rings. The lining was shot to begin with, so that will be no surprise to you; according to the label, you had the suit since 1944. If you want us to replace same, I can supply a first-class, all-satin quarter lining for $91.50, workmanship included. Finally, buttons. Some of my beatnik customers wear the jacket open and don't need them. For a conservative man like yourself, I would advise spending another eight dollars.

As regards your worry about hiding cold-storage articles in the back of my store, I am not now nor have I ever been a chiseler, and I defy you to prove different. Every season like clockwork, I get one crackpot who expects me to be Santa Claus and haul his clothing up to the North Pole or someplace. My motto is live and let live, which it certainly is not this Rose Finkel's to go around destroying people's confidence in their dry cleaner. Who is she, anyway? I had one of these experts working for me already, in 1951, that nearly put me in the hands of the receivers. She told a good customer of ours, an artist who brought in some handpainted ties to be rainproofed, to save his money and throw them in the Harlem River. To a client that showed her a dinner dress with a smear on the waist, she recommends the woman should go buy a bib. I am surprised that you, a high-school graduate, a man that pretends to be intelligent, would listen to such poison. But in this business you meet all kinds. Regards to the Mrs.

> Yours truly,
> S. Merlin

> Gay Head, Mass.,
> July 25

Dear Mr. Merlin:

While I'm altogether sympathetic to your plight and fully aware that your shop's an inferno at the moment—I myself am wearing an imported cashmere sweater as I write—I must say you misinterpreted my letter. My only motive in relaying Miss Stricture's finkels (excuse me, the strictures of Miss Finkel) on the subject of proper cold storage was concern for a favorite garment. I was not accusing you of duplicity, and I refuse to share the opinion, widespread among persons who deal with them frequently, that most dry cleaners are crooks. It is understandably somewhat off-putting to hear that my suit arrived at your establishment in ruinous condition, and, to be devastatingly candid, I wonder whether your boy may not have collided with a soup kitchen in transit. But each of us must answer to his own conscience, Merlin, and I am ready, if less than overjoyed, to regard yours as immaculate.

Answering your question about Miss Finkel's identity, I have never laid eyes on her, needless to say, though reason dictates that if a distinguished newspaper like the *Times* publishes her counsel, she must be an authority. Furthermore, if the practice of withholding clothes from cold storage were uncommon, why would she have broached the subject at all? No, my friend, it is both useless and ungenerous of you to attempt to undermine Miss Finkel. From the way you lashed out at her, I deduce that she touched you on the raw, in a most vulnerable area of our relationship, and that brings me to the core of this communication.

Nowhere in your letter is there any direct assertion that you *did* send my valuable solari suit to storage, or, correlatively, that you are *not* hiding it in the back of the store. I treasure my peace of mind too much to sit up here gnawed by anxiety. I must therefore demand from you a categorical statement by return airmail special delivery. Is this garment in your possession or not? Unless a definite answer is forthcoming within forty-eight hours, I shall be forced to take action.

Yours truly,
S. J. Perelman

New York City,
July 27

Dear Mr. Perleman:

If all you can do with yourself in a summer place is hang indoors and write me love letters about Rose Finkel, I must say I have pity on you. Rose Finkel, Rose Finkel—why don't you marry this woman that you are so crazy about her. Then she could clean your suits at home and stick them in the icebox—after she cleans that, too. What do you want from me? Sometimes I think I am walking around in a dream.

Look, I will do anything you say. Should I parcel-post the suit to you so you can examine it under a microscope for holes? Should I board up my store, give the help a week free vacation in the mountains, and bring it to you personally in my Cadillac? I tell you once, twice, a million times—it went to cold storage. I didn't send it myself; I gave orders to my assistant, which she has been in my employ eleven years. From her I have no secrets, and you neither. She told me about some of the mail she found in your pants.

It is quite warm here today, but we are keeping busy and don't notice. My tailor collapsed last night with heat prostration, so I am handling alterations, pressing, ticketing, and hiding customer's property in the back of the store. Also looking up psychiatrists in the Yellow Pages.

> Yours truly,
> S. Merlin

> Gay Head, Mass.,
> July 29

Dear Mr. Merlin:

My gravest doubts are at last confirmed: You are unable to say unequivocally, without tergiversating, that you *saw* my suit put into cold storage. Knowing full well that the apparel was irreplaceable, now that the British Raj has been supplanted—knowing that it was the keystone of my entire wardrobe, the *sine qua non* of sartorial taste—you deliberately entrusted it to your creature, a cat's-paw who you admit rifles my pockets as a matter of routine. Your airy disavowal of your responsibility, therefore, leaves me with but one alternative. By this same post, I am delegating a close friend of mine, Irving Wiesel, to visit your place of business and ferret out the truth. You can lay your cards on the table with Wiesel or not, as you see fit. When he finishes with you, you will have neither cards nor table.

It would be plainly superfluous, at this crucial stage in our association, to hark back to such petty and characteristic vandalism as your penchant for jabbing pins into my rainwear, pressing buttons halfway through lapels, and the like. If I pass over these details now, however, do not yield to exultation. I shall expatiate at length in the proper surroundings; viz., in court. Wishing you every success in your next vocation,

> Yours truly,
> S. J. Perelman

New York City,
August 5

Dear Mr. Perlman:

I hope you received by now from my radiologist the two X-rays; he printed your name with white ink on the ulcer so you should be satisfied that you, and you alone, murdered me. I wanted him to print also "Here lies an honest man that he slaved for years like a dog, schlepped through rain and snow to put bread in his children's mouths, and see what gratitude a customer gave him," but he said there wasn't room. Are you satisfied now, you Cossack you? Even my *radiologist* is on your side.

You didn't need to tell me in advance that Wiesel was a friend of yours; it was stamped all over him the minute he walked in the store. Walked? He was staggering from the highballs you and your bohemian cronies bathe in. No how-do-you-do, explanations, nothing. Ran like a hooligan to the back and turned the whole stock upside down, pulled everything off the racks. I wouldn't mind he wrecked a filing system it cost me hundreds of dollars to install. Before I could grab the man, he makes a beeline for the dressing room. So put yourself for a second in someone else's shoes. A young, refined matron from Boston, first time in the Village, is waiting for her dress to be spot-cleaned, quietly loafing through *Harper's Bazaar*. Suddenly a roughneck, for all she knows a plainclothesman, a junkie, tears aside the curtain. Your delegate Wiesel.

I am not going to soil myself by calling you names, you are a sick man and besides on vacation, so will make you a proposition. You owe me for cleaning the suit, the destruction you caused in my racks, medical advice, and general aggravation. I owe you for the suit, which you might as well know is kaput. The cold-storage people called me this morning. It seems like all the brownish rings in the material fell out and they will not assume responsibility for a sieve. This evens up everything between us, and I trust that on your return I will have the privilege of serving you and family as in years past. All work guaranteed, invisible weaving our specialty. Please remember me to your lovely wife.

Sincerely yours,
Stanley Merlin

IX

The Colloid and the Crystal

Joseph Wood Krutch

THE COLLOID AND THE CRYSTAL

I chose "The Colloid and the Crystal"* because it seems to me the clearest statement I have ever been able to make of an assumption it is perhaps impossible to state except obliquely: namely, my quasi mystical conviction that all life is a unity. Or, as I put it to the froglet, "Don't forget that we are all in this together." As man grows more and more powerful only this conviction can restrain him from destroying himself by laying waste the earth he inhabits.

Joseph Wood Krutch

Tucson, Arizona

---

*From *The Best of Two Worlds.*

That first real snow was soon followed by a second. Over the radio the weatherman talked lengthily about cold masses and warm masses, about what was moving out to sea and what wasn't. Did Benjamin Franklin, I wondered, know what he was starting when it first occurred to him to trace by correspondence the course of storms? From my stationary position the most reasonable explanation seemed to be simply that winter had not quite liked the looks of the landscape as she first made it up. She was changing her sheets.

Another forty-eight hours brought one of those nights ideal for frosting the panes. When I came down to breakfast, two of the windows were almost opaque and the others were etched with graceful, fernlike sprays of ice which looked rather like the impressions left in rocks by some of the antediluvian plants, and they were almost as beautiful as anything which the living can achieve. Nothing else which has never lived looks so much as though it were actually informed with life.

I resisted, I am proud to say, the almost universal impulse to scratch my initials into one of the surfaces. The effect, I knew, would not be an improvement. But so, of course, do those less virtuous than I. That indeed is precisely why they scratch. The impulse to mar and to destroy is as ancient and almost as nearly universal as the impulse to create. The one is an easier way than the other of demonstrating power. Why else should anyone not hungry prefer a dead rabbit to a live one? Not even those horrible Dutch painters of bloody still—or shall we say stilled?—lifes can have really believed that their subjects were more beautiful dead.

Indoors it so happened that a Christmas cactus had chosen this moment to bloom. Its lush blossoms, fuchsia-shaped but pure red rather than magenta, hung at the drooping ends of strange, thick stems and outlined themselves in blood against the glistening background of the frosty pane—jungle flower against frostflower; the warm beauty that breathes and lives and dies competing with the cold beauty that burgeons, not because it wants to, but merely because it is obeying the laws of physics which require that crystals shall take the shape they have always taken since the world began. The effect of red flower against white tracery was almost too theatrical, not quite in good taste perhaps. My eye recoiled in shock and sought through a clear area of the glass the more normal out-of-doors.

On the snow-capped summit of my bird-feeder a chickadee pecked at the new-fallen snow and swallowed a few of the flakes which serve him in lieu of the water he sometimes sadly lacks when there is nothing except ice too solid to be picked at. A downy woodpecker was hammering at a lump of suet and at the coconut full of peanut butter. One nuthatch was dining while the mate waited his—or was it her?—turn. The woodpecker announces the fact that he is a male by the bright red spot on the back of his neck, but to me, at least, the sexes of the nuthatch are indistinguishable. I shall never know whether it is the male or the female who eats first. And that is a pity. If I knew, I could say, like the Ugly Duchess, "and the moral of that is . . ."

But I soon realized that at the moment the frosted windows were what interested me most—especially the fact that there is no other natural phenomenon in which the lifeless mocks so closely the living. One might almost think that the frostflower had got the idea from the leaf and the branch if one did not know how inconceivably more ancient the first is. No wonder that enthusiastic biologists in the nineteenth century, anxious to conclude that there was no qualitative difference between life and chemical processes, tried to believe that the crystal furnished the link, that its growth was actually the same as the growth of a living organism. But excusable though the fancy was, no one, I think, believes anything of the sort today. Protoplasm is a colloid and the colloids are fundamentally different from the crystalline substances. Instead of crystallizing they jell, and life in its simplest known form is a shapeless blob of rebellious jelly rather than a crystal eternally obeying the most ancient law.

No man ever saw a dinosaur. The last of these giant reptiles was dead eons before the most dubious half-man surveyed the world about him.

Not even the dinosaurs ever cast their dim eyes upon many of the still earlier creatures which preceded them. Life changes so rapidly that its later phases know nothing of those which preceded them. But the frost-flower is older than the dinosaur, older than the protozoan, older no doubt than the enzyme or the ferment. Yet it is precisely what it has always been. Millions of years before there were any eyes to see it, millions of years before any life existed, it grew in its own special way, crystallized along its preordained lines of cleavage, stretched out its pseudo-branches and pseudo-leaves. It was beautiful before beauty itself existed.

We find it difficult to conceive a world except in terms of purpose, of will, or of intention. At the thought of the something without beginning and presumably without end, of something which is, nevertheless, regular though blind, and organized without any end in view, the mind reels. Constituted as we are it is easier to conceive how the slime floating upon the waters might become in time Homo sapiens than it is to imagine how so complex a thing as a crystal could have always been and can always remain just what it is—complicated and perfect but without any meaning, even for itself. How can the lifeless even obey a law?

To a mathematical physicist I once confessed somewhat shamefacedly that I had never been able to understand how inanimate nature managed to follow so invariably and so promptly her own laws. If I flip a coin across a table, it will come to rest at a certain point. But before it stops at just that point, many factors must be taken into consideration. There is the question of the strength of the initial impulse, of the exact amount of resistance offered by the friction of that particular table top, and of the density of the air at the moment. It would take a physicist a long time to work out the problem and he could achieve only an approximation at that. Yet presumably the coin will stop exactly where it should. Some very rapid calculations have to be made before it can do so, and they are, presumably, always accurate.

And then, just as I was blushing at what I supposed he must regard as my folly, the mathematician came to my rescue by informing me that Laplace had been puzzled by exactly the same fact. "Nature laughs at the difficulties of integration," he remarked—and by "integration" he meant, of course, the mathematician's word for the process involved when a man solves one of the differential equations to which he has reduced the laws of motion.

When my Christmas cactus blooms so theatrically a few inches in front of the frost-covered pane, it also is obeying laws but obeying them much less rigidly and in a different way. It blooms at about Christmastime because it has got into the habit of doing so, because, one is tempted to say, it wants to. As a matter of fact it was, this year, not a Christmas cactus but a New Year's cactus, and because of this unpredictability I would like to call it "he," not "it." His flowers assume their accustomed shape and take on their accustomed color. But not as the frostflowers follow their predestined pattern. Like me, the cactus has a history which stretches back over a long past full of changes and developments. He has not always been merely obeying fixed laws. He has resisted and rebelled; he has attempted novelties, passed through many phases. Like all living things he has had a will of his own. He has made laws, not merely obeyed them.

"Life," so the platitudinarian is fond of saying, "is strange." But from our standpoint it is not really so strange as those things which have no life and yet nevertheless move in their predestined orbits and "act" though they do not "behave." At the very least one ought to say that if life is strange there is nothing about it more strange than the fact it has its being in a universe so astonishingly shared on the one hand by "things" and on the other by "creatures," that man himself is both a "thing" which obeys the laws of chemistry or physics and a "creature" who to some extent defies them. No other contrast, certainly not the contrast between the human being and the animal, or the animal and the plant, or even the spirit and the body, is so tremendous as this contrast between what lives and what does not.

To think of the lifeless as merely inert, to make the contrast merely in terms of a negative, is to miss the real strangeness. Not the shapeless stone which seems to be merely waiting to be acted upon but the snowflake or the frostflower is the true representative of the lifeless universe as opposed to ours. They represent plainly, as the stone does not, the fixed and perfect system of organization which includes the sun and its planets, includes therefore this earth itself, but against which life has set up its seemingly puny opposition. Order and obedience are the primary characteristics of that which is not alive. The snowflake eternally obeys its one and only law: "Be thou six pointed"; the planets their one and only: "Travel thou in an ellipse." The astronomer can tell where the North Star will be ten thousand years hence; the botanist cannot tell where the dandelion will bloom tomorrow.

Life is rebellious and anarchical, always testing the supposed immutability of the rules which the nonliving changelessly accepts. Because the snowflake goes on doing as it was told, its story up to the end of time was finished when it first assumed the form which it has kept ever since. But the story of every living thing is still in the telling. It may hope and it may try. Moreover, though it may succeed or fail, it will certainly change. No form of frostflower ever became extinct. Such, if you like, is its glory. But such also is the fact which makes it alien. It may melt but it cannot die.

If I wanted to contemplate what is to me the deepest of all mysteries, I should choose as my object lesson a snowflake under a lens and an amoeba under the microscope. To a detached observer—if one can possibly imagine any observer who *could* be detached when faced with such an ultimate choice—the snowflake would certainly seem the "higher" of the two. Against its intricate glistening perfection one would have to place a shapeless, slightly turbid glob, perpetually oozing out in this direction or that but not suggesting so strongly as the snowflake does, intelligence and plan. Crystal and colloid, the chemist would call them, but what an inconceivable contrast those neutral terms imply! Like the star, the snowflake seems to declare the glory of God, while the promise of the amoeba, given only perhaps to itself, seems only contemptible. But its jelly holds, nevertheless, not only its promise but ours also, while the snowflake represents some achievement which we cannot possibly share. After the passage of billions of years, one can see and be aware of the other, but the relationship can never be reciprocal. Even after these billions of years no aggregate of colloids can be as beautiful as the crystal always was, but it can know, as the crystal cannot, what beauty is.

Even to admire too much or too exclusively the alien kind of beauty is dangerous. Much as I love and am moved by the grand, inanimate forms of nature, I am always shocked and a little frightened by those of her professed lovers to whom landscape is the most important thing, and to whom landscape is merely a matter of forms and colors. If they see or are moved by an animal or flower, it is to them merely a matter of a picturesque completion and their fellow creatures are no more than decorative details. But without some continuous awareness of the two great realms of the inanimate and the animate there can be no love of nature as I understand it, and what is worse, there must be a sort of disloyalty to our cause, to us who are colloid, not crystal. The pantheist who feels the oneness of all living things, I can understand; perhaps indeed he and I are in essential agreement. But the ultimate All is not one thing, but two. And because the alien half is in its way as proud and confident and successful as our half, its fundamental difference may not be disregarded with impunity. Of us and all we stand for, the enemy is not so much death as the not-living, or rather that great system which succeeds without ever having had the need to be alive. The frostflower is not merely a wonder; it is also a threat and a warning. How admirable, it seems to say, not living can be! What triumphs mere immutable law can achieve!

Some of Charles Pierce's strange speculations about the possibility that "natural law" is not law at all but merely a set of habits fixed more firmly than any habits we know anything about in ourselves or in the animals suggest the possibility that the snowflake was not, after all, always inanimate, that it merely surrendered at some time impossibly remote the life which once achieved its perfect organization. Yet even if we can imagine such a thing to be true, it serves only to warn us all the more strongly against the possibility that what we call the living might in the end succumb also to the seduction of the immutably fixed.

No student of the anthill has ever failed to be astonished either into admiration or horror by what is sometimes call the perfection of its society. Though even the anthill can change its ways, though even ant individuals—ridiculous as the conjunction of the two words may seem —can sometimes make choices, the perfection of the techniques, the regularity of the habits almost suggest the possibility that the insect is on its way back to inanition, that, vast as the difference still is, an anthill crystallizes somewhat as a snowflake does. But not even the anthill, nothing else indeed in the whole known universe is so perfectly planned as one of these same snowflakes. Would, then, the ultimately planned society be, like the anthill, one in which no one makes plans, any more than a snowflake does? From the cradle in which it is not really born to the grave where it is only a little deader than it always was, the ant-citizen follows a plan to the making of which he no longer contributes anything.

Perhaps we men represent the ultimate to which the rebellion, begun so long ago in some amoeba-like jelly, can go. And perhaps the inanimate is beginning the slow process of subduing us again. Certainly the psychologist and the philosopher are tending more and more to think of us as creatures who obey laws rather than as creatures of will and responsibility. We are, they say, "conditioned" by this or by that. Even the greatest heroes are studied on the assumption that they can be "accounted for" by something outside themselves. They are, it is explained, "the product of forces." All the emphasis is placed, not upon that power to resist and rebel which we were once supposed to have, but upon the "influences" which "formed us." Men are made by society, not society by men. History as well as character "obeys laws." In their view, we crystallize in obedience to some dictate from without instead of moving in conformity with something within.

And so my eye goes questioningly back to the frosted pane. While I slept the graceful pseudo-fronds crept across the glass, assuming, as life itself does, an intricate organization. "Why live," they seem to say, "when we can be beautiful, complicated, and orderly without the uncertainty and effort required of a living thing? Once we were all that was. Perhaps some day we shall be all that is. Why not join us?"

Last summer no clod or no stone would have been heard if it had asked such a question. The hundreds of things which walked and sang, the millions which crawled and twined were all having their day. What was dead seemed to exist only in order that the living might live upon it. The plants were busy turning the inorganic into green life and the animals were busy turning that green into red. When we moved, we walked mostly upon grass. Our pre-eminence was unchallenged.

On this winter day nothing seems so successful as the frostflower. It thrives on the very thing which has driven some of us indoors or underground and which has been fatal to many. It is having now its hour of triumph, as we before had ours. Like the cactus flower itself, I am a hothouse plant. Even my cats gaze dreamily out of the window at a universe which is no longer theirs.

How are we to resist, if resist we can? This house into which I have withdrawn is merely an expedient and it serves only my mere physical existence. What mental or spiritual convictions, what will to maintain to my own kind of existence can I assert? For me it is not enough merely to say, I do say, that I shall resist the invitation to submerge myself into a crystalline society and to stop planning in order that I may be planned for. Neither is it enough to go further, as I do go, and to insist that the most important thing about a man is not that part of him which is "the product of forces" but that part, however small it may be, which enables him to become something other than what the most accomplished sociologist, working in conjunction with the most accomplished psychologist, could predict that he would be.

I need, so I am told, a faith, something outside myself to which I can be loyal. And with that I agree, in my own way. I am on what I call "our side," and I know, though vaguely, what I think that is. Wordsworth's God had his dwelling in the light of setting suns. But the God who dwells there seems to me most probably the God of the atom, the star, and the crystal. Mine, if I have one, reveals Himself in another class of phenomena. He makes the grass green and the blood red.

James A. Michener

FROM THE BOUNDLESS DEEP

In the years when television first exploded upon the American family and the cultural consciousness of the nation, I heard a good deal of speculation to the effect that this invention would be the death knell of reading. I doubted this, but since I did not have a television set I was not sure of my judgment. So I set aside a period of about three weeks when I did little but watch early television, at the end of which I decided that if this pablum were going to end all reading, the human race was doomed. I was certain that after a feast of violence, weak comedy and old movies the sensible man or woman would long for a book. I also concluded that if he made the jump from the nothingness of television to the substance of reading, he would want a substantial book to tie into.

Consequently, I decided as an act of conscious deduction, based upon my faith in the human intellect, that I wanted to write as massive a book as possible, one that made no concessions to contemporary standards, one that said everything I knew up to that moment. Specifically I did not want to write a small, well-constructed English novel, because that type of writing could be done better by others. I wanted a long, complex, many-faceted, intricately developed novel covering many generations and varied speculations. If this was the last book that the television-minded audience was going to read, I wanted it to be an overpowering experience that the reader would hold in his memory for a long time.

I therefore spent many months reflecting on my experiences in New England, in Japan, in China and particularly in the South

Sea islands, and when I had identified those large themes with which I wanted to deal I cast about for a form in which to put them, a frame behind which to set them, but I found none.

Nevertheless, I started work on the project and then one day I hit upon the idea of a preamble that would be so uncompromising that it would repel the casual reader, whose attention I did not want. It would be a statement of a gravity equal to the large plan I had in mind. Once this decision was made, the structure of the opening chapter came quickly to mind, and I spent about four weeks writing and rewriting the paragraphs in which no people whatever appear, in which there is no dialogue, no story, damned near nothing at all to attract the reader except the explosion of images and ideas. I wanted this to be somewhat like the magic fire with which Wotan surrounds Brunhilde: let the weak spirited keep the hell out.

The first half dozen critics who saw the manuscript for the book advised me to cut the first chapter. Literally hundreds of readers have written to me complaining that the first chapter threw them off the book, which they never finished. I am ashamed to say that when *Hawaii* was first published in paperback form, this opening chapter was printed in italic, inviting the reader to skip over it and get quickly to the main story. If ever a writer had fair warning to kill a passage, I had.

But the more I worked with the manuscript, the more I concluded that the readers I would lose were precisely those I wanted to lose and that the critics who were objecting to the opening passage were critics whose judgments I did not much appreciate at any time. So I persisted. The novel was published as I intended. And the opening chapter had exactly the effect I had wanted.

Now it is generally conceded to be the best portion of writing I ever did. From all over the world people have written to say that this chapter remains longest in their memory. It has been used in writing courses, in anthologies, and in many scientific situations where those concerned with exposition of ideas have studied it to see how abstract concepts should be unfolded for the non-scientific reader. Most appreciated have been letters like the one that arrived from South Africa: "When I was in the middle of your opening chapter I realized that you intended to tell a story of some gravity, or you would not impose such a burden upon the reader, and when the story became complicated later on, or tedious, I bore with it because I could say, 'Well, he warned me.' "

James A. Michener

Millions upon millions of years ago, when the continents were already formed and the principal features of the earth had been decided, there existed, then as now, one aspect of the world that dwarfed all others. It was a mighty ocean, resting uneasily to the east of the largest continent, a restless ever-changing, gigantic body of water that would later be described as pacific.

Over its brooding surface immense winds swept back and forth, whipping the waters into towering waves that crashed down upon the world's seacoasts, tearing away rocks and eroding the land. In its dark bosom, strange life was beginning to form, minute at first, then gradually of a structure now lost even to memory. Upon its farthest reaches birds with enormous wings came to rest, and then flew on.

Agitated by a moon stronger then than now, immense tides ripped across this tremendous ocean, keeping it in a state of torment. Since no great amounts of sand had yet been built, the waters where they reached shore were universally dark, black as night and fearful.

Scores of millions of years before man had risen from the shores of the ocean to perceive its grandeur and to venture forth upon its turbulent waves, this eternal sea existed, larger than any other of the earth's features, vaster than the sister oceans combined, wild, terrifying in its immensity and imperative in its universal role.

How utterly vast it was! How its surges modified the very balance of the earth! How completely lonely it was, hidden in the darkness of night or burning in the dazzling power of a younger sun than ours.

At recurring intervals the ocean grew cold. Ice piled up along its extremities, and so pulled vast amounts of water from the sea, so that the wandering shoreline of the continents sometimes jutted miles farther out than before. Then, for a hundred thousand years, the ceaseless ocean would tear at the exposed shelf of the continents, grinding rocks into sand and incubating new life.

Later, the fantastic accumulations of ice would melt, setting cold waters free to join the heaving ocean, and the coasts of the continents would lie submerged. Now the restless energy of the sea deposited upon the ocean bed layers of silt and skeletons and salt. For a million years the ocean would build soil, and then the ice would return; the waters would draw away; and the land would lie exposed. Winds from the north and south would howl across the empty seas and lash stupendous waves upon the shattering shore. Thus the ocean continued its alternate building and tearing down.

Master of life, guardian of the shorelines, regulator of temperatures and heaving sculptor of mountains, the great ocean existed.

Millions upon millions of years before man had risen upon earth, the central areas of this tremendous ocean were empty, and where famous islands now exist nothing rose above the rolling waves. Of course, crude forms of life sometimes moved through the deep, but for the most part the central ocean was marked only by enormous waves that arose at the command of moon and wind. Dark, dark, they swept the surface of the empty sea, falling only upon themselves terrible and puissant and lonely.

Then one day, at the bottom of the deep ocean, along a line running two thousand miles from northwest to southeast, a rupture appeared in the basalt rock that formed the ocean's bed. Some great fracture of the earth's basic structure had occurred, and from it began to ooze a white-hot, liquid rock. As it escaped from its internal prison, it came into contact with the ocean's wet and heavy body. Instantly, the rock exploded, sending aloft through the 19,000 feet of ocean that pressed down upon it columns of released steam.

Upward, upward, for nearly four miles they climbed, those agitated bubbles of air, until at last upon the surface of the sea they broke loose and formed a cloud. In that instant, the ocean signaled that a new island was building. In time it might grow to become an infinitesimal speck of land that would mark the great central void. No human beings then existed to celebrate the event. Perhaps some weird and vanished flying thing spied the escaping steam and swooped down to inspect it; more likely the roots of this future island were born in darkness and great waves and brooding nothingness.

For nearly forty million years, an extent of time so vast that it is meaningless, only the ocean knew that an island was building in its bosom, for no land had yet appeared above the surface of the sea. For nearly forty million years, from that extensive rupture in the ocean floor, small amounts of liquid rock seeped out, each forcing its way up through what had escaped before, each contributing some small portion to the accumulation that was building on the floor of the sea. Sometimes a thousand years, or ten thousand, would silently pass before any new eruption of material would take place. At other times gigantic pressures would accumulate beneath the rupture and with unimaginable violence rush through the existing apertures, throwing clouds of steam miles above the surface of the ocean. Waves would be generated which would circle the globe and crash upon themselves as they collided twelve thousand miles away. Such an explosion, indescribable in its fury, might in the end raise the height of the subocean island a foot.

But for the most part, the slow constant seepage of molten rock was not violently dramatic. Layer upon layer of the earth's vital core would creep out, hiss horribly at the cold sea water, and then slide down the sides of the little mountains that were forming. Building was most sure when the liquid rock did not explode into minute ashy fragments, but cascaded viscously down the sides of the mountains, for this bound together what had gone before, and established a base for what was to come.

How long ago this building took place, how infinitely long ago! For nearly forty million years the first island struggled in the bosom of the sea, endeavoring to be born as observable land. For nearly forty million submerged years its subterranean volcano hissed and coughed and belched and spewed forth rock, but it remained nevertheless hidden beneath the dark waters of the restless sea, to whom it was an insignificant irritation, a small climbing pretentious thing of no consequence.

And then one day, at the northwest end of the subocean rupture, an eruption of liquid rock occurred that was different from any others that had preceded. It threw forth the same kind of rock, with the same violence, and through the same vents in the earth's core. But this time what was thrown forth reached the surface of the sea. There was a tremendous explosion as the liquid rock struck water and air together. Clouds of steam rose miles into the air. Ash fell hissing upon the heaving waves.

Detonations shattered the air for a moment and then echoed away in the immensity of the empty wastes.

But rock had at last been deposited above the surface of the sea. An island—visible were there but eyes to see, tangible were there fingers to feel—had risen from the deep.

The human mind, looking back upon this event—particularly if the owner of the mind has once stepped upon that island—is likely to accord it more significance than it merits. Land was finally born, yes. The forty million years of effort were finally crowned by the emergence of a pile of rocks no larger than a man's body, that is true. But the event was actually of no lasting significance, for in the long history of the ocean many such piles had momentarily broken the surface and then subsided, forbidden and forgotten. The only thing significant about the initial appearance of this first island along the slanting crack was the fact that it held on and grew. Stubbornly, inch by painful inch, it grew. In fact, it was the uncertainty and agony of its growth that were significant.

The chance emergence of the island was nothing. Remember this. Its emergence was nothing. But its persistence and patient accumulation of stature were everything. Only by relentless effort did it establish its right to exist. For the first ten thousand years after its tentative emergence, the little pile of rock in the dead, vast center of the sea fluctuated between life and death like a thing struck by evil. Sometimes molten lava would rise through the internal channels and erupt from a vent only a few inches above the waves. Tons upon tons of material would gush forth and hiss madly as it fell back into the ocean. Some, fortunately, would cling to the newborn island, building it sturdily many feet into the air, and in that time it might seem as if the island were indeed secure.

Then from the south, where storms breed in the senseless deep, a mighty wave would form and rush across the world. Its coming would be visible from afar, and in gigantic, tumbling, whistling, screaming power it would fall upon the little accumulation of rocks and pass madly on.

For the next ten thousand years there would be no visible island, yet under the waves, always ready to spring back to life, there would rest this huge mountain tip, rising 19,000 feet from the floor of the ocean, and when a new series of volcanic thrusts tore through the vents, the mountain would patiently build itself aloft for another try. Exploding, hissing, and spewing forth ash, the great mountain would writhe in convulsions. It would pierce the waves. Its island would be born again.

This was the restless surge of the universe, the violence of birth, the cold tearing away of death; and yet how promising was this interplay of forces as an island struggled to be born, vanishing in agony, then soaring aloft in triumph. You men who will come later to inhabit these islands, remember the agony of arrival, the rising and the fall, the nothingness of the sea when storms throw down the rock, the triumph of the mountain when new rocks are lifted aloft.

For a million years the island hung in this precarious balance, a child of violence; but finally, after incredibly patient accumulation, it was established. Now each new lava flow had a solid base upon which to build, and inch by inch the debris agglutinated until the island could be seen by birds from long distances. It was indeed land, habitable had there been existing men, with shelters for boats, had there been boats, and with rocks that could have been used for building homes and temples. It was now, in the real sense of the word, an island, taking its rightful place in the center of the great ocean.

But before life could prosper on this island, soil was needed, and as yet none existed. When molten lava burst upon the air it generally exploded into ash, but sometimes it ran as a viscous fluid down the sides of mountains, constructing extensive sheets of flat rock. In either case, the action of wind and rain and cooling nights began to pulverize the newly born lava, decomposing it into soil. When enough had accumulated, the island was ready.

The first living forms to arrive were inconspicuous, indeed almost invisible, lichens and low types of moss. They were borne by the sea and by winds that howled back and forth across the oceans. With a tenacity equal to that of the island itself these fragments of life established themselves, and as they grew they broke down more rocks and built more soil.

At this time there existed, on the distant continents visited by the ocean, a well-established plant and animal society composed of trees and lumbering animals and insects. Some of these forms were already well adapted for life on the new island, but were prevented from taking residence by two thousand miles of open ocean.

Consequently, there began an appalling struggle. Life, long before man's emergence, stood poised on distant shores, pressing to make new exploratory journeys like those that had already populated the existing earth with plants and animals. But against these urgent forms stood more than two thousand miles of turbulent ocean, storm-ridden, salty, and implacable.

The first sentient animals to reach the island were of course fish, for they permeated the ocean, coming and going as they wished. But they could not be said to be a part of the island. The first nonoceanic animal to visit was a bird. It came, probably, from the north on an exploratory mission in search of food. It landed on the still-warm rocks, found nothing edible, and flew on, perhaps to perish in the southern seas.

A thousand years passed, and no other birds arrived. One day a coconut was swept ashore by a violent storm. It had been kept afloat on the bosom of the sea by its buoyant husk, traveling more than three thousand miles from the southwest, a marvel of persistence. But when it landed, it found no soil along the shore and only salt water, so it perished, but its husk and shell helped form soil for those that would come later.

The years passed. The sun swept through its majestic cycles. The moon waxed and waned, and tides rushed back and forth across the surface of the world. Ice crept down from the north, and for ten thousand years covered the islands, its weight and power breaking down rocks and forming earth.

The years passed, the empty, endless, significant years. And then one day another bird arrived on the island, also seeking food. This time it found a few dead fish along the shore. As if in gratitude, it emptied its bowels on the waiting earth and evacuated a tiny seed which it had eaten on some remote island. The seed germinated and grew. Thus, after the passage of eons of time, growing life had established itself on the rocky island.

Now the passage of time becomes incomprehensible. Between the arrival of the first, unproductive bird, and the second bearing in its bowels the vital seed, more than twenty thousand years had elapsed. In another twenty thousand years a second bit of life arrived, a female insect, fertilized on some distant island on the night before a tremendous storm. Caught up in the vast winds that howled from the south, she was borne aloft to the height of ten thousand feet and driven northward for more than two thousand miles to be dropped at last upon this new and remote island, where she gave birth. Insects had arrived.

The years passed. Other birds arrived, but they bore no seeds. Other insects were blown ashore, but they were not females, or if they were, not pregnant. But once every twenty or thirty thousand years—a period longer than that of historic man—some one bit of life would reach the island, by accident; and by accident it would establish itself. In this hit-or-miss way, over a period of time that the mind can barely digest, life populated the island.

One of the most significant days in the history of the island came when a bird staggered in from some land far to the southwest, bearing in its tangled feathers the seed of a tree. Perched upon a rock, the bird pecked at the seed until it fell away, and in the course of time a tree grew. Thirty thousand years passed, and by some accident equally absurd, another tree arrived, and after a million years of chances, after five million years of storms and birds and drifting sea-soaked logs bearing snails and borers, the island had a forest with flowers and birds and insects.

Nothing, nothing that ever existed on this island reached it easily. The rocks themselves were forced up fiery chimneys through miles of ocean. They burst in horrible agony onto the surface of the earth. The lichens that arrived came borne by storms. The birds limped in on deadened wings. Insects came only when accompanied by hurricanes, and even trees arrived in the dark belly of some wandering bird, or precariously perched upon the feathers of a thigh.

Timelessly, relentlessly, in storm and hunger and hurricane the island was given life, and this life was sustained only by constant new volcanic eruptions that spewed forth new lava that could be broken down into life-sustaining soil. In violence the island lived, and in violence a great beauty was born.

The shores of the island, weathered by the sea, were stupendous cliffs that caught the evening sun and glowed like serrated pillars of gold. The mountains were tall and jagged, their lower levels clothed in dark green trees, their upper pinnacles shod in ice, while the calm bays in which the grandeur of the mountains was reflected were deeply cut into the shore. Valleys and sweet plains, waterfalls and rivers, glades where lovers would have walked and confluences where towns could have been built, the lovely island had all these accouterments, these alluring invitations to civilization.

But no man ever saw them, and the tempting glades entertained no lovers, for the island had risen to its beauty long, long before the age of man; and at the moment of its greatest perfection it began to die. In violence it had been born; in violence it would die.

There was a sudden shudder of the earth, a slipping and a sliding, and when the readjustment was ended, covering a period of thousands of years, the island had sunk some twelve hundred feet lower into the ocean, and ice nevermore formed upon its crests. The volcanoes stopped, and no new lava poured forth to create new soil to replace that which had sunk into the sea. For a million years winds howled at the hills, the ocean gnawed away at the ramparts. Year by year the island withered and grew less. It began to shred away, to shatter and to fall back into the ocean from which it had sprung.

A million years passed, and then a million more, and the island which had grown so patiently at the northwest tip of the great crack in the ocean floor slowly, slowly vanished. The birds that had fed upon its hills went elsewhere, bearing in their bowels new seeds. From its shore fertilized insects were storm-blown to other islands, and life went on. Once every twenty or thirty thousand years some fragment of nature escaped from this island, and life went on.

But as the island subsided, a different form of life sprang into increased activity. In the warm, clear, nutritious waters that surrounded the shores, coral polyps began to flourish, and slowly they left behind them as they died their tiny calciferous skeletons, a few feet below the surface of the sea. In a thousand years they built a submerged ring around the island. In a thousand more they added to its form, and as the eons passed, these tiny coral animals built a reef.

Ice melted in the north, and the coral animals were drowned in vast weights of unexpected water. The seas changed temperature and the animals died. Torrents of rain poured down from island hills and silted up the shoreline, strangling the tiny coral. Or new ice caps formed far to the north and south, pulling water away from the dying island. Then the coral were exposed and died at once.

Always, like everything to do with this island, throughout its entire history, the coral lived precariously, poised between catastrophes. But in the breathing space available, the coral built. And so it was that this tiny animal, this child of cataclysm, built a new island to replace the old as it gradually wore itself away and sank into the sea.

How terrible this passage of life and death! How meaningless that an island that had been born of such force and violence, that had been so fair upon the bosom of the great ocean, so loved of birds, so rich in trees, so willing to entertain man, should he ever arrive . . . how wasteful it was that this island should have grown in agony and died in equal agony before ever a human eye had seen its majesty.

Across a million years, down more than ten million years it existed silently in the unknown sea and then died, leaving only a fringe of coral where sea birds rest and where gigantic seals of the changing ocean play. Ceaseless life and death, endless expenditure of beauty and capacity, tireless ebb and flow and rising and subsidence of the ocean. Night comes and the burning day, and the island waits, and no man arrives. The days perish and the nights, and the aching beauty of lush valleys and waterfalls vanishes, and no man will ever see them. All that remains is a coral reef, a calcium wreath on the surface of the great sea that had given the island life, a memorial erected by the skeletons of a billion billion billion little animals.

While this first island was rising to prominence and dying back to nothingness, other would-be islands, stretching away to the southeast, were also struggling to attain brief existence followed by certain death. Some started their cycle within the same million years as did the first. Others lagged. The latest would not puncture the surface of the sea until the first was well into its death throes, so that at any moment from the time the first island began to die, man, had he then existed, could have witnessed in this two-thousand-mile chain of islands every sequential step in the process of life and death. Like an undulating wave of the sea itself, the rocky islands rose and fell; but whereas the cycle of an ocean wave is apt to be a few minutes at the most, the cycle of the rising and falling of these islands was of the nature of sixty million years.

Each island, at any given moment of time, existed certainly and securely within that cycle; it was either rising toward birth and significance, or it was perishing. I do not mean that man, had he been able to witness the cycle, could have identified which part of the cycle a given island was in; there must have been periods of millions of years when no one could have ascertained that condition. But the impersonal, molten center of the earth knew, for it was sending that island no new supplies of lava. The waiting sea knew, for it could feel the cliffs falling into its arms a little more easily. And the coral ployps knew, because they sensed that it was now time to start erecting a memorial to this island which would soon be dead . . . that is, within twenty or thirty million years.

Endless cycle, endless birth and death, endless becoming and disappearing. Once the terrifying volcanic explosions cease, the island is already doomed. Peace and calm seas and the arrival of birds bearing seeds are pleasant to experience, but the residence of beauty is surely nominated for destruction. A song at night of insects, the gentle splash of surf against the sand, and a new ice age is beginning which will freeze out all life. Limitless cycle, endless change.

Toward the end of the master cycle, when the western islands were dying and the eastern were abuilding, a new volcano pushed its cone above the surface of the ocean, and in a series of titanic explosions erupted enough molten rock to establish securely a new island, which after eons of time would be designated by men as the capital island of the group. Its subsequent volcanic history was memorable in that its habitable land resulted from the wedding of two separate chains of volcanoes.

After the parent volcano had succeeded in establishing an island, its mighty flanks produced many subsidiary vents through which lava poured; whereupon a greater volcano, separated from the first by miles of ocean, sprang into being and erected its own majestic construction, marked by an equal chain of events.

For eons of time the two massive volcano systems stood in the sea in fiery competition, and then, inevitably, the first began to die back, its fires extinguished, while the second continued to pour millions of tons of lava down its own steep flanks. Hissing, exploding, crackling, the rocks fell into the sea in boundless accumulations, building the later volcano ever more solidly, ever more thickly at its base on the remote floor of the ocean.

In time, sinking lava from the second master builder began to creep across the feet of the first, and then to climb its sides and finally to throw itself across the exposed lava flows that had constituted the earlier island. Now the void in the sea that had separated the two was filled, and they became one. Locked in fiery arms, joined by interwining ejaculations of molten rock, the two volcanoes stood in matrimony, their union a single fruitful and growing island.

Its soil was later made from dozens of smaller volcanoes that erupted for a few hundred thousand years, then passed into death and silence. One exploded in dazzling glory and left a crater looking like a punch bowl. Another, at the very edge of the island, from where it could control the sea approaches, left as its memory a gaunt headland shaped like a diamond.

When the island was well formed—and what a heavenly, sweet, enchanting island it was—some force of nature, almost as if by subtle plan, hid in its bowels a wealth of incalculable richness. It could not be diamonds, because the island was 250,000,000 years too young to have acquired the carboniferous plant growth that produced diamonds. It could not be either oil or coal, for the same reason. It wasn't gold, for neither the age nor the conditions required for the building of that metal were present on this island. It was none of these commonly accepted treasures, but it was a greater.

The volcanic basalt from which the island was built was porous, and when the tremendous storms which swept the ocean struck the island, the waters they disgorged ran partly out to sea in surface rivers, seeped partly into the heart of the island. Billions of tons of water thus crept down into the secret reservoirs of the island.

They did not stay there, of course, for since the rock was porous, there were avenues that led back out to sea, and in time the water was lost. But if any animal—a man perhaps—could penetrate the rocks, he could intercept the water and put it to his use, for the entire island was a catchment; the entire core of the island was permeated with life-giving water.

But that was not the special treasure of this particular island, for a man could bore into almost any porous rock on any island, and catch some water. Here, on this island, there was to be an extra treasure, and the way it was deposited was something of a miracle.

When the ice came and went, causing the great ocean to rise, when the island itself sank slowly and then rebuilt with new lava—when these titanic convolutions were in progress, the south shore of the island was alternately exposed to sunlight or buried fathoms deep in ocean. When the first condition prevailed, the exposed shore was cut by mountain streams which threw their debris across the plain, depositing there claylike soils and minute fragments of lava. Sometimes the sea would wash in bits of animal calcium, or a thundering storm would rip away a cliff face and throw its remnants over the shore. Bit by bit, over a hundred thousand years at a time, the shore accumulated its debris.

Then, when next the ocean rose, it would press down heavily upon this shelving land, which would lie for ages, submerged under tons of dark, green water. But while the great brutal ocean thus pressed down hydraulically, it at the same time acted as a life-giving agent, for through its shimmering waves filtered silt and dead bodies and water-logged fragments of trees and sand. All these things, the gifts both of land and sea, the immense weight of ocean would bind together until they united to form rock.

Cataclysmically the island would rise from the sea to collect new fragments washed down from the hills, then sink beneath the waves to accumulate new deposits of life-building slime. But whenever the monstrous ocean would beat down heavily upon the shore for ten thousand years at a time, new rock was formed, an impermeable shield that sloped down from the lower foothills and extended well out to sea. It was a cap rock, imprisoning in a gigantic underground reservoir all that lay beneath it.

What lay trapped below, of course, was water. Secretly, far beneath the visible surface of the island, imprisoned by this watertight cap of rock, lay the purest, sweetest, most copious water in all the lands that bordered upon or existed in the great ocean. It lay there under vast pressure, so that it was not only available, should a man deduce its secret hiding, but it was ready to leap forth twenty or thirty or forty feet into the air, and engulf with life-giving sweetness any man who could penetrate the imprisoning rock and set it free. It waited, an almost inexhaustible supply of water to sustain life. It waited, a universe of water hidden beneath the cap rock. It waited.

The adventurous plants and insects that had reached the earliest northwest island had plenty of time in which to make their way to the newer lands as the latter rose to life. It might take a million years for a given grass to complete its journey down the chain. But there was no hurry. Slowly, with a patience that is difficult to comprehend, trees and vines and crawling things crept down the islands, while in other parts of the world a new and more powerful animal was rising and preparing himself for his invasion of the islands.

Before the two-volcanoed island with its trapped treasure of water had finished growing, man had developed in distant areas. Before the last island had assumed its dominant shape, men had erected in Egypt both mighty monuments and a stable form of government. Men could already write and record their memories.

While volcanoes still played along the chain, China developed a sophisticated system of thought and Japan codified art principles that would later enrich the world. While the islands were taking their final form, Jesus spoke in Jerusalem and Muhammad came from the blazing deserts with a new vision of heaven, but no men knew the heaven that awaited them on these islands.

For these lands were the youngest part of the earth's vast visible surface. They were new. They were raw. They were empty. They were waiting. Books which we still read today were written before these islands were known to anyone except the birds of passage. Songs which we still sing were composed and recorded while these islands remained vacant. The Bible had been compiled, and the Koran.

Raw, empty, youthful islands, sleeping in the sun and whipped by rain, they waited.

Since, when they were finally discovered, they were destined to be widely hailed as paradises, it is proper to study them carefully in their last, waiting moments, those sad, sweet, overpowering days before the first canoes reached them.

They were beautiful, that is true. Their wooded mountains were a joy. Their cool waterfalls, existing in the thousands, were spectacular. Their cliffs, where the restless ocean had eroded away the edges of great mountains, dropped thousands of feet clear into the sea, and birds nested on the vertical stones. Rivers were fruitful. The shores of the islands were white and waves that washed them were crystal-blue. At night the stars were close, great brilliant dots of fire fixing forever the location of the islands and forming majestic pathways for the moon and sun.

How beautiful these islands were! How shot through with harmony and peace! How the mind lingers on their pristine grandeur, a grandeur that nothing so far devised could permanently destroy. If paradise consists solely of beauty, then these islands were the fairest paradise that man ever invaded, for the land and sea were beautiful, and the climate was congenial.

But if the concept of paradise includes also the ability to sustain life, then these islands, as they waited in the time of Jesus and Muhammad, were far from heavenly. They contained almost no food. Of all the things that grew on their magnificent hillsides, nothing could be relied upon to sustain life adequately. There were a few pandanus trees whose spare and bitter fruits could be chewed for minimum existence. There were a few tree ferns whose cores were just barely edible, a few roots. There were fish if they could be caught and birds if they could be trapped. But there was nothing else.

Few more inhospitable major islands have ever existed than this group. Here are the things they did not have: no chickens, or pigs, or cattle, or edible dogs; no bananas, no taro, no sweet potatoes, no breadfruit; no pineapple, or sugar, or guava, or gourds, or melons, or mangoes, no fruit of any kind; no palms for making sugar; no food. The islands did not even have that one essential, that miraculous sustainer of tropical life, the coconut. Some had drifted to the shores, but in salty soil along the beaches they could not grow.

Any man who came to the islands would, if he wanted to live, have to bring with him all food. If he were wise, he would also bring most of the materials required for building a civilized society, since the islands had no bamboo for decorating a home, no candlenuts for lamps, no mulberry bark for making tapa. Nor were there any conspicuous flowers: neither frangipani, nor hibiscus, nor bright croton, nor colorful orchids. Instead of these joy-giving, life-sustaining plants there was a hidden tree, useless except that its wood when dried yielded a persistent perfume, and this was the tree of death, the sandalwood tree. Of itself, it was neither poisonous nor cruel, but the uses to which it would be put on these islands would make it a permanent blight.

The soil of the islands was not particularly good. It was not rich and black like the soil which Russian peasants were already farming, nor loamy and productive like that known to the Dakota and Iowa tribes of Indians. It was red and of a sandlike consistency, apparently rich in iron because it had been formed of decomposed basalt, but lacking in other essentials. If a farmer could add to this soil the missing minerals and supply it with adequate water, it had the capacity to produce enormously. But of itself it was not much, for the minerals were absent, and so was the water.

Tremendous quantities of rain did fall on the islands, but it fell in an unproductive manner. From the northeast, trade winds blew constantly, pushing ahead of them low clouds pregnant with sweet water. But along the northeast shores of each island high cliffs rose, and mountains, and these reached up and knocked the water out of the clouds, so that it fell in cascades where it could not be used and never reached the southwest plains where the red soil was. Of the flat lands that could be tilled, fully three fourths were in effect deserts. If one could capture the wasted water that ran useless down the steep mountainsides and back out to sea, bringing it through the mountains and onto the flat lands, then crops could be grown. Or if one could discover the secret reservoirs waiting in the kidneys of the islands, one would have ample water and more than ample food. But until this was accomplished, men who lived on these islands would never have enough water or enough food.

And so these beautiful, inhospitable islands waited for some breed of men to invade them with food and courage and determination. The best that could be said of the islands, as they waited, was that they held no poisonous snakes, no fevers, no mosquitoes, no disfiguring diseases, and no plagues.

There was one additional aspect that must be remembered. Of all the growing things that existed in these islands at the time of Jesus, ninety-five out of every hundred grew nowhere else in the world. These islands were unique, alone, apart, off the main stream of life, a secluded backwater of nature . . . or, if you prefer, an authentic natural paradise where each growing thing had its opportunity to develop in its own unique way, according to the dictates and limitations of its own abilities.

I spoke of that adventurous bird that brought the first seed in its bowels. It was a grass seed, perhaps, one whose brothers and sisters, if the term may be used of grasses, stayed behind on their original islands, where they developed as the family had always done for millions of generations. On those original islands the grass maintained its standard characteristics and threw forth to venturesome modifications; or, if such mutations were offered, the stronger normal stock quickly submerged them, and the dead average was preserved.

But on the new islands the grass, left alone in beauty and sun and rain, became a different grass, unique and adapted to these islands. When men looked at such grass, millions of years later, they would be able to discern that it was a grass, and that it had come from the original stock still existing elsewhere; but they would also see that it was nevertheless a new grass, with new qualities, new vitality, and new promise.

Did an insect from one of the huge continents reach these islands? If so, here he became a different insect, his legs longer or his nose more adapted to boring. Birds, flowers, worms, trees and snails . . . all developed unique forms and qualities in these islands.

There was then, as there is now, no place known on earth that even began to compete with these islands in their capacity to encourage natural life to develop freely and radically up to its own best potential. More than nine out of ten things that grew here, grew nowhere else on earth.

Why this should have been so remains a mystery. Perhaps a fortunate combination of rainfall, climate, sunlight and soil accounted for this miracle. Perhaps eons of time in which diverse growing things were left alone to work out their own best destinies was the explanation. Perhaps the fact that when a grass reached here it had to stand upon its own capacities and could not be refertilized by grasses of the same kind from the parent stock, perhaps that is the explanation. But whatever the reason, the fact remains: in these islands new breeds developed, and they prospered, and they grew strong, and they multiplied. For these islands were a crucible of exploration and development.

And so, with these capacities, the islands waited. Jesus died on a cross, and they waited. England was settled by mixed and powerful races, and the islands waited for their own settlers. Mighty kings ruled in India, and in China and in Japan, while the islands waited.

Inhospitable in fact, a paradise in potential, with almost no food available, but with enormous riches waiting to be developed, the islands waited. Volcanoes, still building the ramparts with fresh flows of lava, hung lanterns in the sky so that if a man and his canoe were lost on the great dark bosom of the sea, wandering fitfully this way and that, he might spot the incandescent glow of the under side of a distant cloud, and thus find a fiery star to steer by.

Large gannets and smaller terns skimmed across the waters leading to land, while frigate birds drew sharp and sure navigation lines from the turbulent ocean wastes right to the heart of the islands, where they nested. If a man in a canoe could spot a frigate bird, its cleft tail cutting the wind, he could be sure that land lay in the direction toward which the bird had flown at dusk.

These beautiful islands, waiting in the sun and storm, how much they seemed like beautiful women waiting for their men to come home at dusk, waiting with open arms and warm bodies and consolation. All that would be accomplished in these islands, as in these women, would be generated solely by the will and puissance of some man. I think the islands always knew this.

Therefore, men of Polynesia and Boston and China and Mount Fuji and the barrios of the Philippines, do not come to these islands empty-handed, or craven in spirit, or afraid to starve. There is no food here. In these islands there is no certainty. Bring your own food, your own gods, your own flowers and fruits and concepts. For if you come without resources to these islands you will perish.

But if you come with growing things, and good foods and better ideas, if you come with gods that will sustain you, and if you are willing to work until the swimming head and the aching arms can stand no more, then you can gain entrance to this miraculous crucible where the units of nature are free to develop according to their own capacities and desires.

On these harsh terms the islands waited.

John Steinbeck

EASTER SUNDAY:
SEA OF CORTEZ

John Steinbeck, whose death in December 1968 deprived America of its lone surviving male winner of the Nobel Prize for Literature, was represented in *This Is My Best* in 1942 with a short story "The Leader of the People." A reticent man and one who said that he could not make a choice of his own favorite or best writing, he had asked his lifelong editor and friend Pascal Covici to choose for him. In 1950, for the collection of 105 of the greatest living authors of the world, *The World's Best,* he made his own selection, which he said then he thought would stand for some time to come as his own choice. That selection represents him now. It is an excerpt from *Sea of Cortez, a Leisurely Journal of Travel and Research. Sea of Cortez* is a large book, part of it containing a scientific appendix of the marine animals of the Panamic Faunal Province compiled by E. F. Ricketts, the biologist whom Steinbeck joined in a unique scientific fishing expedition, the details of which constituted *Sea of Cortez.*

The Editor

The beach was hot and yellow. We swam, and then walked along on the sand and went inland along the ridge between the beach and a large mangrove-edged lagoon beyond. On the lagoon side of the ridge there were thousands of burrows, presumably of large land-crabs, but it was hopeless to dig them out. The shores of the lagoon teemed with the little clicking bubbling fiddler crabs and estuarian snails. Here we could smell the mangrove flowers without the foul root smell, and the odor was fresh and sweet, like that of new-cut grass. From where we waded there was a fine picture, still reflecting water and the fringing green mangroves against the burnt red-brown of the distant mountains, all like some fantastic Doré drawing of a pressed and em-battled heaven. The air was hot and still and the lagoon rippleless. Now and then the surface was ringed as some lagoon fish came to the air. It was a curious quiet resting-place and perhaps because of the quiet we heard in our heads the children singing in the church at La Paz. We did not collect strongly or very efficiently, but rather we half dozed through the day, thinking of old things, each one in himself. And later we discussed manners of thinking and methods of thinking, speculation which is not stylish any more. On a day like this the mind goes outward and touches in all directions. We discussed intellectual methods and approaches, and we thought that through inspection of thinking technique a kind of purity of approach might be consciously achieved—that non-teleological or "is" thinking might be substituted in part for the usual cause-effect methods.

The hazy Gulf, with its changes of light and shape, was rather like us, trying to apply our thoughts, but finding them always pushed and swayed by our bodies and our needs and our satieties. It might be well here to set down some of the discussions of non-teleological thinking.

During the depression there were, and still are, not only destitute but thriftless and uncareful families, and we have often heard it said that the country had to support them because they were shiftless and negligent. If they would only perk up and be somebody everything would be all right. Even Henry Ford in the depth of the depression gave us his solution to that problem, "Everybody ought to roll up his sleeves and get to work."

This view may be correct as far as it goes, but we wonder what would happen to those with whom the shiftless would exchange places in the large pattern—those whose jobs would be usurped, since at that time there was work for only about seventy percent of the total employable population, leaving the remainder as government wards.

This attitude has no bearing on what might be or could be if so-and-so happened. It merely considers conditions "as is." No matter what the ability or aggressiveness of the separate units of society, at that time there were, and still there are, great numbers necessarily out of work, and the fact that those numbers comprised the incompetent or maladjusted or unlucky units is in one sense beside the point. No causality is involved in that; collectively it's just "so"; collectively it's related to the fact that animals produce more offspring than the world can support. The units may be blamed as individuals, but as members of society they cannot be blamed. Any given individual very possibly may transfer from the underprivileged into the more fortunate group by better luck or by improved aggressiveness or competence, but all cannot be so benefited whatever their strivings, and the large population will be unaffected. The seventy-thirty ratio will remain, with merely a reassortment of the units. And no blame, at least no social fault, imputes to these people; they are where they are "because" natural conditions are what they are. And so far as we selfishly are concerned we can rejoice that they, rather than we, represent the low extreme, since there must be one.

So if one is very aggressive he will be able to obtain work even under the most sub-normal economic conditions, but only because there are others, less aggressive than he, who serve in his stead as potential government wards. In the same way, the sight of a half-wit should never depress us, since his extreme, and the extreme of his kind, so affects the mean standard that we, hatless, coatless, often bewhiskered, thereby will be regarded only as a little odd. And similarly, we cannot justly approve the success manuals that tell our high school graduates how to get a job —there being jobs for only half of them!

This type of thinking unfortunately annoys many people. It may especially arouse the anger of women, who regard it as cold, even brutal, although actually it would seem to be more tender and understanding, certainly more real and less illusionary and even less blaming, than the more conventional methods of consideration. And the value of it as a tool in increased understanding cannot be denied.

As a more extreme example, consider the sea-hare *Tethys,* a shell-less, flabby sea-slug, actually a marine snail, which may be seen crawling about in tidal estuaries, somewhat resembling a rabbit crouched over. A California biologist estimated the number of eggs produced by a single animal during a single breeding season to be more than 478 million. And the adults sometimes occur by the hundred! Obviously all these eggs cannot mature, all this potential cannot, *must not,* become reality, else the ocean would soon be occupied exclusively by sea-hares. There would be no kindness in that, even for the sea-hares themselves; for in a few generations they would overflow the earth; there would be nothing for the rest of us to eat, and nothing for them unless they turned cannibal. On the average, probably no more than the biblical one or two attain full maturity. Somewhere along the way all the rest will have been eaten by predators whose life cycle is postulated upon the presence of abundant larva of sea-hares and other forms as food—as all life itself is based on such a postulate. Now picture the combination mother-father sea-hare (the animals are hermaphroditic, with the usual cross-fertilization) parentally blessing its offspring with these words: "Work hard and be aggressive, so you can grow into a nice husky *Tethys* like your ten-pound parent." Imagine it, the hypocrite, the illusionist, the Pollyanna, the genial liar, saying that to its millions of eggs *en masse,* with the dice loaded at such a ratio! Inevitably, 99.999 percent are destined to fall by the wayside. No prophet could foresee which specific individuals are to survive, but the most casual student could state confidently that no more than a few are likely to do so; any given individual has *almost* no chance at all—but still there is the "almost," since the race persists. And there is even a semblance of truth in the parent sea-hare's admonition, since even here, with this almost infinitesimal differential, the race is still to the swift and/or to the lucky.

What we personally conceive by the term "teleological thinking," as exemplified by the notion about the shiftless unemployed, is most frequently associated with the evaluating of causes and effects, the purposiveness of events. This kind of thinking considers changes and cures—what "should be" in the terms of an end pattern (which is often a subjective or an anthropomorphic projection): it presumes the bettering of conditions, often, unfortunately, without achieving more than a most superficial understanding of these conditions. In their sometimes intolerant refusal to face facts as they are, teleological notions may substitute a fierce but ineffectual attempt to change conditions which are assumed to be undesirable, in place of the understanding acceptance which would pave the way for a more sensible attempt at any change which might still be indicated.

Non-teleological ideas derive through "is" thinking, associated with natural selection as Darwin seems to have understood it. They imply depth, fundamentalism, and clarity—seeing beyond traditional or personal projections. They consider events as outgrowths and expressions rather than as results; conscious acceptance as a desideratum, and certainly as an all-important prerequisite. Non-teleological thinking concerns itself primarily not with what should be, or could be, or might be, but rather with what actually "is"—attempting at most to answer the already sufficiently difficult questions *what* or *how,* instead of *why.*

An interesting parallel to these two types of thinking is afforded by the microcosm with its freedom or indeterminacy, as contrasted with the morphologically inviolable pattern of the macrocosm. Statistically, the electron is free to go where it will. But the destiny pattern of any aggregate, comprising uncountable billions of these same units, is fixed and certain, however much that inevitability may be slowed down. The eventual disintegration of a stick of wood or a piece of iron through the departure of the presumably immortal electrons is assured, even though it may be delayed by such protection against the operation of the second law of thermodynamics as is afforded by painting and rust-proofing.

Examples sometimes clarify an issue better than explanations or definitions. Here are three situations considered by the two methods.

A. *Why are some men taller than others?*

Teleological "answer": because of the underfunctioning of the growth-regulating ductless glands. This seems simple enough. But the simplicity is merely a function of inadequacy and incompleteness. The finality is only apparent. A child, being wise and direct, would ask immediately if given this answer: "Well, why do the glands underfunction?" hinting instantly towards non-teleological methods, or indicating the rapidity with which teleological thinking gets over into the stalemate of first causes.

In the non-teleological sense there can be no "answer." There can be only pictures which become larger and more significant as one's horizon increases. In this given situation, the steps might be something like this:

(1) Variation is a universal and truly primitive trait. It occurs in any group of entities—razor blades, measuring rods, rocks, trees, horses, matches, or men.

(2) In this case, the apropos variations will be towards shortness or tallness from a mean standard—the height of adult men as determined by the statistics of measurements, or by common-sense observation.

(3) In men varying towards tallness there seems to be a constant relation with an underfunctioning of the growth-regulating ductless glands, of the sort that one can be regarded as an index of the other.

(4) There are other known relations consistent with tallness, such as compensatory adjustments along the whole chain of endocrine organs. There may even be other factors, separately not important or not yet discovered, which in the aggregate may be significant, or the integration of which may be found to wash over some critical threshold.

(5) The men in question are taller "because" they fall in a group within which there are the above-mentioned relations. In other words, "they're tall because they're tall."

This is the statistical, or "is," picture to date, more complex than the teleological "answer"—which is really no answer at all—but complex only in the sense that reality is complex; actually simple, inasmuch as the simplicity of the word "is" can be comprehended.

Understandings of this sort can be reduced to this deep and significant summary: "It's so because it's so." But exactly the same words can also express the hasty or superficial attitude. There seems to be no explicit method for differentiating the deep and participating understanding, the "all-truth" which admits infinite change or expansion as added relations become apparent, from the shallow dismissal and implied lack of further interest which may be couched in the very same words.

B. *Why are some matches larger than others?*

Examine similarly a group of matches. At first they seem all to be of the same size. But to turn up differences, one needs only to measure them carefully with calipers or to weigh them with an analytical balance. Suppose the extreme comprises only a .001 percent departure from the mean (it will be actually much more); even so slight a differential we know can be highly significant, as with the sea-hares. The differences will group into plus-minus variations from a hypothetical mean to which not one single example will be found exactly to conform. Now the ridiculousness of the question becomes apparent. There is no *particular* reason. It's just so. There may be in the situation some factor or factors more important than the others: owing to the universality of variation (even in those very factors which "cause" variation), there surely *will* be, some even predominantly so. But the question as put is seen to be beside the point. The good answer is: "It's just in the nature of the beast." And this needn't imply belittlement; to have understood the "nature" of a thing is in itself a considerable achievement.

But if the size variations should be quite obvious—and especially if uniformity were to be a desideratum—then there might be a particularly dominant "causative" factor which could be searched out. Or if a person must have a stated "cause"—and many people must, in order to get an emotional understanding, a sense of relation to the situation and to give a name to the thing in order to "settle" it so it may not bother them any more—he can examine the automatic machinery which fabricates the products, and discover in it the variability which results in variation in the matches. But in doing so, he will become involved with a larger principle or pattern, the universality of variation, which has little to do with causality as we think of it.

C. *Leadership*.

The teleological notion would be that those in the forefront are leaders in a given movement and actually direct and consciously lead the masses in the sense that an army corporal orders "Forward march" and the squad marches ahead. One speaks in such a way of church leaders, of political leaders, and of leaders in scientific thought, and of course there is some limited justification for such a notion.

Non-teleological notion: that the people we call leaders are simply those who, at the given moment, are moving in the direction behind which will be found the greatest weight, and which represents a future mass movement.

For a more vivid picture of this state of affairs, consider the movements of an ameba under the microscope. Finger-like processes, the pseudopodia, extend at various places beyond the confines of the chief mass. Loco-motion takes place by means of the animal's flowing into one or into several adjacent pseudopodia. Suppose that the molecules which "hap-pened" to be situated in the forefront of the pseudopodium through which the animal is progressing, or into which it will have flowed subsequently, should be endowed with consciousness and should say to themselves and to their fellows: "We are directly leading this great procession, our leadership 'causes' all the rest of the population to move this way, the mass follows the path we blaze." This would be equivalent to the attitude with which we commonly regard leadership.

As a matter of fact there are three distinct types of thinking, two of them teleological. Physical teleology, the type we have been considering, is by far the commonest today. Spiritual teleology is rare. Formerly predominant, it now occurs metaphysically and in most religions, especially as they are popularly understood (but not, we suspect, as they were originally enunciated or as they may still be known to the truly adept). Occasionally the three types may be contrasted in a single problem. Here are a couple of examples:

(1) Van Gogh's feverish hurrying in the Arles epoch, culminating in epilepsy and suicide.

Teleological "answer": Improper care of his health during times of tremendous activity and exposure to the sun and weather brought on his epilepsy out of which discouragement and suicide resulted.

Spiritual teleology: He hurried because he innately foresaw his imminent death, and wanted first to express as much of his essentiality as possible.

Non-teleological picture: Both the above, along with a good many other symptoms and expressions (some of which could probably be inferred from his letters), were parts of his essentiality, possibly glimpsable as his "lust for life."

(2) The thyroid-neurosis syndrome.

Teleological "answer": Over-activity of the thyroid gland irritates and over-stimulates the patient to the point of nervous breakdown.

Spiritual teleology: The neurosis is causative. Something psychically wrong drives the patient on to excess mental irritation which harries and upsets the glandular balance, especially the thyroid, through shock-resonance in the autonomic system, in the sense that a purely psychic shock may spoil one's appetite, or may even result in violent illness. In this connection, note the army's acceptance of extreme homesickness as a reason for disability discharge.

Non-teleological picture: Both are discrete segments of a vicious circle, which may also include other factors as additional more or less discrete segments, symbols or maybe parts of an underlying but non-teleological pattern which comprises them and many others, the ramifications of which are *n,* and which has to do with causality only reflectedly.

Teleological thinking may even be highly fallacious, especially where it approaches the very superficial but quite common *post hoc, ergo propter hoc* pattern. Consider the situation with reference to dynamiting in a quarry. Before a charge is set off, the foreman toots warningly on a characteristic whistle. People living in the neighborhood come to associate the one with the other, since the whistle is almost invariably followed within a few seconds by the shock and sound of an explosion for which one automatically prepares oneself. Having experienced this many times without closer contact, a very naïve and unthinking person might justly conclude not only that there was a cause-effect relation, but that the whistle actually caused the explosion. A slightly wiser person would insist that the explosion caused the whistle, but would be hard put to explain the transposed time element. The normal adult would recognize that the whistle no more caused the explosion than the explosion caused the whistle, but that both were parts of a larger pattern out of which a "why" could be postulated for both, but more immediately and particularly for the whistle. Determined to chase the thing down in a cause-effect sense, an observer would have to be very wise indeed who could follow the intricacies of cause through more fundamental cause to primary cause, even in this largely man-made series about which we presumably know most of the motives, causes, and ramifications. He would eventually find himself in a welter of thoughts on production, and ownership of the means of production, and economic whys and wherefores about which there is little agreement.

The example quoted is obvious and simple. Most things are far more subtle than that, and have many of their relations and most of their origins far back in things more difficult of access than the tooting of a whistle calculated to warn bystanders away from an explosion. We know little enough even of a man-made series like this—how much less of purely natural phenomena about which also there is apt to be teleological pontificating!

Usually it seems to be true that when even the most definitely apparent cause-effect situations are examined in the light of wider knowledge, the cause-effect aspect comes to be seen as less rather than more significant, and the statistical or relational aspects acquire larger importance. It seems safe to assume that non-teleological is more "ultimate" than teleological reasoning. Hence the latter would be expected to prove to be limited and constricting except when used provisionally. But while it is true that the former is more open, for that very reason its employment necessitates greater discipline and care in order to allow for the dangers of looseness and inadequate control.

Frequently, however, a truly definitive answer seems to arise through teleological methods. Part of this is due to wish-fulfillment delusion. When a person asks "Why?" in a given situation, he usually deeply expects, and in any case receives, only a relational answer in place of the definitive "because" which he thinks he wants. But he customarily accepts the actually relational answer (it couldn't be anything else unless it comprised the whole, which is unknowable except by "living into") as a definitive "because." Wishful thinking probably fosters that error, since everyone continually searches for absolutisms (hence the value placed on diamonds, the most permanent physical things in the world) and imagines continually that he finds them. More justly, the relational picture should be regarded only as a glimpse—a challenge to consider also the rest of the relations as they are available—to envision the whole picture as well as can be done with given abilities and data. But one accepts it instead of a real "because," considers it settled, and, having named it, loses interest and goes on to something else.

Chiefly, however, we seem to arrive occasionally at definitive answers through the workings of another primitive principle: the universality of quanta. No one thing ever merges gradually into anything else; the steps are continuous, but often so very minute as to seem truly continuous. If the investigation is carried deep enough, the factor in question, instead of being graphable as a continuous process, will be seen to function by discrete quanta with gaps or synapses between, as do quanta of energy, undulations of light. The apparently definitive answer occurs when causes and effects both arise on the same large plateau which is bounded a great way off by the steep rise which announces the next plateau. If the investigation is extended sufficiently, that distant rise will, however, inevitably be encountered; the answer which formerly seemed definitive now will be seen to be at least slightly inadequate and the picture will have to be enlarged so as to include the plateau next further out. Everything impinges on everything else, often into radically different systems, although in such cases faintly. We doubt very much if there are any truly "closed systems." Those so called represent kingdoms of a great continuity bounded by the sudden discontinuity of great synapses which eventually must be bridged in any unified-field hypothesis. For instance, the ocean, with reference to waves of water, might be considered as a closed system. But anyone who has lived in Pacific Grove or Carmel during the winter storms will have felt the house tremble at the impact of waves half a mile or more away impinging on a totally different "closed" system.

But the greatest fallacy in, or rather the greatest objection to, teleological thinking is in connection with the emotional content, the belief. People get to believing and even to professing the apparent answers thus arrived at, suffering mental constrictions by emotionally closing their minds to any of the further and possibly opposite "answers" which might otherwise be unearthed by honest effort—answers which, if faced realistically, would give rise to a struggle and to a possible rebirth which might place the whole problem in a new and more significant light. Grant for a moment that among students of endocrinology a school of thought might arise, centering upon some belief as to etiology—upon the belief, for instance, that all abnormal growth is caused by glandular imbalance. Such a clique, becoming formalized and powerful, would tend, by scorn and opposition, to wither any contrary view which, if untrammeled, might discover a clue to some opposing "causative" factor of equal medical importance. That situation is most unlikely to arise in a field so lusty as endocrinology, with its relational insistence, but the principle illustrated by a poor example is thought nevertheless to be sound.

Significant in this connection is the fact that conflicts may arise between any two or more of the "answers" brought forth by either of the teleologies, or between the two teleologies themselves. But there can be no conflict between any of these and the non-teleological picture. For instance, in the condition called hyperthyroidism, the treatments advised by believers in the psychic or neurosis etiology very possibly may conflict with those arising out of a belief in the purely physical cause. Or even within the physical teleology group there may be conflicts between those who believe the condition due to a strictly thyroid upset and those who consider causation derived through a general imbalance of the ductless glands. But there can be no conflict between any or all of these factors and the non-teleological picture, because the latter includes them—evaluates them relationally or at least attempts to do so, or maybe only accepts them as time-place truths. Teleological "answers" necessarily must be included in the non-teleological method—since they are part of the picture even if only restrictedly true—and as soon as their qualities of relatedness are recognized. Even erroneous beliefs are real things, and have to be considered proportional to their spread or intensity. "All-truth" must embrace all extant apropos errors also, and know them as such by relation to the whole, and allow for their effects.

The criterion of validity in the handling of data seems to be this: that the summary shall say in substance, significantly and understandingly, "It's so because it's so." Unfortunately the very same words might equally derive through a most superficial glance, as any child could learn to repeat from memory the most abstruse of Dirac's equations. But to know a thing emergently and significantly is something else again, even though the understanding may be expressed in the self-same words that were used superficially. In the following example* note the deep significance of the emergent as contrasted with the presumably satisfactory but actually incorrect original naïve understanding. At one time an important game bird in Norway, the willow grouse, was so clearly threatened with extinction that it was thought wise to establish protective regulations and to place a bounty on its chief enemy, a hawk which was known to feed heavily on it. Quantities of the hawks were exterminated, but despite such drastic measures the grouse disappeared actually more rapidly than before. The naïvely applied customary remedies had obviously failed. But instead of becoming discouraged and quietistically letting this bird go the way of the great auk and the passenger pigeon, the authorities enlarged the scope of their investigations until the anomaly was explained. An ecological analysis into the relational aspects of the situation disclosed that a parasitic disease, coccidiosis, was endemic among the grouse. In its incipient stages, this disease so reduced the flying speed of the grouse that the mildly ill individuals became easy prey for the hawks. In living largely off the slightly ill birds, the hawks prevented them from developing the disease in its full intensity and so spreading it more widely and quickly to otherwise healthy fowl. Thus the presumed enemies of the grouse, by controlling the epidemic aspects of the disease, proved to be friends in disguise.

In summarizing the above situation, the measure of validity wouldn't be to assume that, even in the well-understood factor of coccidiosis, we have the real "cause" of any beneficial or untoward condition, but to say, rather, that in this phase we have a highly significant and possibly preponderantly important relational aspect of the picture.

However, many people are unwilling to chance the sometimes ruthless-appearing notions which may arise through non-teleological treatments. They fear even to use them in that they may be left dangling out in space, deprived of such emotional support as had been afforded them by

* *Abstracted from the article on ecology by Elton*, Encyclopaedia Britannica, *14th Edition, Vol. VII, p. 916.*

an unthinking belief in the proved value of pest control in the conservation of game birds: in the institutions of tradition; religion; science; in
the security of the home or the family; or in a comfortable bank account.
But for that matter emancipations in general are likely to be held in
terror by those who may not yet have achieved them, but whose thresh-
olds in those respects are becoming significantly low. Think of the
fascinated horror, or at best tolerance, with which little girls regard
their brothers who have dispensed with the Santa Claus belief; or the
fear of the devout young churchman for his university senior who has
grown away from depending on the security of religion.

As a matter of fact, whoever employs this type of thinking with other
than a few close friends will be referred to as detached, hardhearted,
or even cruel. Quite the opposite seems to be true. Non-teleological
methods more than any other seem capable of great tenderness, of an
all-embracingness which is rare otherwise. Consider, for instance, the fact
that, once a given situation is deeply understood, no apologies are
required. There are ample difficulties even to understanding conditions
"as is." Once that has been accomplished, the "why" of it (known now
to be simply a relation, though probably a near and important one)
seems no longer to be preponderantly important. It needn't be condoned
or extenuated, it just "is." It is seen merely as part of a more or less
dim whole picture. As an example: A woman near us in the Carmel
woods was upset when her dog was poisoned—frightened at the thought
of passing the night alone after years of companionship with the animal.
She phoned to ask if, with our windows on that side of the house
closed as they were normally, we could hear her ringing a dinner bell
as a signal during the night that marauders had cut her phone wires
preparatory to robbing her. Of course that was, in fact, an improbable
contingency to be provided against; a man would call it foolish fear,
neurotic. And so it was. But one could say kindly, "We can hear the bell
quite plainly, but if desirable we can adjust our sleeping arrangements
so as to be able to come over there instantly in case you need us,"
without even stopping to consider whether or not the fear was foolish,
or to be concerned about it if it were, correctly regarding all that
as secondary. And if the woman had said apologetically, "Oh, you must
forgive me; I know my fears are foolish, but I am so upset!" the wise
reply would have been, "Dear person, nothing to forgive. If you have
fears, they *are;* they are real things and to be considered. Whether or not
they're foolish is beside the point. *What* they are is unimportant alongside the fact *that* they are." In other words, the badness or goodness,

the teleology of the fears, was decidedly secondary. The whole notion could be conveyed by a smile or by a pleasant intonation more readily than by the words themselves. Teleological treatment which one might have been tempted to employ under the circumstances would first have stressed the fact that the fear was foolish—would say with a great show of objective justice, "Well, there's no use in *our* doing anything; the fault is that *your* fear is foolish and improbable. Get over that" (as a judge would say, "Come into court with clean hands"); "then if there's anything *sensible* we can do, we'll see," with smug blame implied in every word. Or, more kindly, it would try to reason with the woman in an attempt to help her get over it—the business of propaganda directed towards change even before the situation is fully understood (maybe as a lazy substitute for understanding). Or, still more kindly, the teleological method would try to understand the fear causally. But with the non-teleological treatment there is only the love and understanding of instant acceptance; after that fundamental has been achieved, the next step, if any should be necesssary, can be considered more sensibly.

Strictly, the term non-teleological thinking ought not to be applied to what we have in mind. Because it involves more than thinking, that term is inadequate. *Modus operandi* might be better—a method of handling data of any sort. The example cited just above concerns feeling more than thinking. The method extends beyond thinking even to living itself; in fact, by inferred definition it transcends the realm of thinking possibilities, it postulates "living into."

In the destitute-unemployed illustration, thinking, as being the evaluatory function chiefly concerned, was the point of departure, "the crust to break through." There the "blame approach" considered the situation in the limited and inadequate teleological manner. The non-teleological method included that viewpoint as correct but limited. But when it came to the feeling aspects of a human relation situation, the non-teleological method would probably ameliorate the woman's fears in a loving, truly mellow, and adequate fashion, whereas the teleological would have tended to bungle things by employing the limited and sophisticated approach.

Incidentally, there is in this connection a remarkable etiological similarity to be noted between cause in thinking and blame in feeling. One feels that one's neighbors are to be blamed for their hate or anger or fear. One thinks that poor pavements are "caused" by politics. The non-teleological picture in either case is the larger one that goes beyond blame or cause. And the non-causal or non-blaming viewpoint seems to us very often relatively to represent the "new thing," the Hegelian "Christ-child" which arises emergently from the union of two opposing viewpoints, such as those of physical and spiritual teleologies, especially if there is conflict as to causation between the two or within either. The new viewpoint very frequently sheds light over a larger picture, providing a key which may unlock levels not accessible to either of the teleological viewpoints. There are interesting parallels here: to the triangle, to the Christian ideas of trinity, to Hegel's dialectic, and to Swedenborg's metaphysic of divine love (feeling) and divine wisdom (thinking).

The factors we have been considering as "answers" seem to be merely symbols or indices, relational aspects of things—of which they are integral parts—not to be considered in terms of causes and effects. The truest reason for anything's being so is that it *is*. This is actually and truly a reason, more valid and clearer than all the other separate reasons, or than any group of them short of the whole. Anything less than the whole forms part of the picture only, and the infinite whole is unknowable except by *being* it, by living into it.

A thing may be *so* "because" of a thousand and one reasons of greater or lesser importance, such as the man oversized because of glandular insufficiency. The integration of these many reasons which are in the nature of relations rather than reasons is that he *is*. The separate reasons no matter how valid, are only fragmentary parts of the picture. And the whole necessarily includes all that it impinges on as object and subject, in ripples fading with distance or depending upon the original intensity of the vortex.

The frequent allusions to an underlying pattern have no implication of mysticism—except inasmuch as a pattern which comprises infinity in factors and symbols might be called mystic. But infinity as here used occurs also in the mathematical aspects of physiology and physics, both far away from mysticism as the term is ordinarily employed. Actually, the underlying pattern is probably nothing more than an integration of just such symbols and indices and mutual reference points as are already known, except that its power is n. Such an integration might include nothing more spectacular than we already know. But, equally, it *could* include anything, even events and entities as different from those already known as the vectors, tensors, scalars, and ideas of electrical charges in mathematical physics are different from the mechanical-model world of the Victorian scientists.

In such a pattern, causality would be merely a name for something that exists only in our partial and biased mental reconstructings. The pattern which it indexes, however, would be real, but not intellectually apperceivable because the pattern goes everywhere and is everything and cannot be encompassed by finite mind or by anything short of life—which it is.

The psychic or spiritual residua remaining after the most careful physical analyses, or the physical remnants obvious, particularly to us of the twentieth century, in the most honest and disciplined spiritual speculations of medieval philosophers, all bespeak such a pattern. Those residua, those most minute differentials, the 0.0001 percentages which suffice to maintain the races of sea animals, are seen finally to be the most important things in the world, not because of their sizes, but because they are everywhere. The differential is the true universal, the true catalyst, the cosmic solvent. Any investigation carried far enough will bring to light these residua, or rather will leave them still unassailable as Emerson remarked a hundred years ago in "The Oversoul" —will run into the brick wall of the *impossibility* of perfection while at the same time insisting on the *validity* of perfection. Anomalies especially testify to that framework; they are the commonest intellectual vehicles for breaking through; all are solvable in the sense that any *one* is understandable, but that one leads with the power *n* to still more and deeper anomalies.

This deep underlying pattern inferred by non-teleological thinking crops up everywhere—a relational thing, surely, relating opposing factors on different levels, as reality and potential are related. But it must not be considered as causative, it simply exists, it *is,* things are merely expressions of it as it is expressions of them. And they *are* it, also. As Swinburne, extolling Hertha, the earth goddess, makes her say: "Man, equal and one with me, man that is made of me, man that is I," so all things which are *that*—which is all—equally may be extolled. That pattern materializes everywhere in the sense that Eddington finds the non-integer q "number" appearing everywhere, in the background of all fundamental equations,* in the sense that the speed of light, constant despite compoundings or subtractions, seemed at one time almost to be conspiring against investigation.

The whole is necessarily everything, the whole world of fact and fancy, body and psyche, physical fact and spiritual truth, individual and collective, life and death, macrocosm and microcosm (the great-

* The Nature of the Physical World, *pp. 208–10.*

est quanta here, the greatest synapse between these two), conscious and unconscious, subject and object. The whole picture is portrayed by *is,* the deepest word of deep ultimate reality, not shallow or partial as reasons are, but deeper and participating, possibly encompassing the Oriental concept of *being.*

And all this against the hot beach on an Easter Sunday, with the passing day and the passing time. This little trip of ours was becoming a thing and a dual thing, with collecting and eating and sleeping merging with the thinking-speculating activity. Quality of sunlight, blueness and smoothness of water, boat engines, and ourselves were all parts of a larger whole and we could begin to feel its nature but not its size.

John Gunther

INSIDE NOWHERE—THE SAHARA

Dear Whit:

I picked "Inside Nowhere" for you because it seems to me, on looking back, to be a vivid and authentic recountal of a very special journalistic experience, something I will never forget for its aroma and carefully underplayed descriptive quality. (Alan Paton incidentally thought it was the best thing in all the 500,000 words of *Inside Africa,* which I still believe to be my best book.) No politics in it, unusual for me.

Best,
John Gunther

New York

I don't need to be measured for a space jacket, and I am never going to stand in line waiting for the first tickets to the moon. I have already seen the moon. That is I have seen Tamanrasset in the Sahara, the chief town of the Hoggar and home of the blue-veiled Tuareg. The Tamanrasset region is positively lunar in its bleak grandeur, its quality of moon-dipped, freezing loneliness.

Even the etiolated trees look lunar, the few that exist. They are a species of willow, greenish white, almost like bushes washed with silver paint—spiky, gnarled, and both brilliant and forbidding. As for the mountains, they are lunar to a conspicuous degree. A million or so years ago (geologists will forgive my imprecision) the fires under the Sahara vomited up a few hundred million tons of earth, and so made the macabre formation known as the Hoggar.

The lava spurted up, and then, so to speak, froze. Hence, today, separate peaks rise like scattered puffballs, solitary and individual; they do not form part of a range. They look like the mushroom clouds that shoot out of the atomic bomb. And, indeed, something like the atomic bomb—a volcanic explosion of immense magnitude—produced them when the earth of the Sahara split. But these puffballs are not clouds. They are savagely solid formations of cold red rock.

I can list several words that suggest the shape of mountains; in tamer countries they look like sugar loaves, or tents, or caterpillars. But the mountains of the Hoggar near Tamanrasset take abnormal forms. They resemble frightful miscarriages of nature, like a monkey with three heads; they look like thumbs sticking out of a cracked glove, or a woman's breast with the nipple torn out, or a collapsed snake.

During the day, the Cyclopean sun eats up all the color, but at dawn and sunset, the mountains are radiantly painted with gamboge, slate-blue, purple, coral, and above all crimson-rose. And there is no life in them whatever. At night arrive the stars. Everybody knows what desert stars are like, but not everybody knows the Hoggar stars, which hang down, just overhead, like enormous silver cherries. The Tuareg have a story about the planet Venus, saying that she was a naughty goddess who sold her father into slavery to gain beauty, and was punished by being fixed in cold space forever. We watched her blink.

One day we drove a few miles out into the desert, beyond the place where the *piste* (unimproved road) stops.

My wife said, "Look—a lake!"

The silver shimmering water lay on the horizon like a shallow flat disk of mercury. It was our first mirage.

Within a week, we had seen so many mirages—sometimes they lay glistening on three sides of the horizon at once—that we did not even pause to look at them.

I had always been told that the Sahara was notable for being flat, hot, and full of sand. Around Tamanrasset it is about as flat as Switzerland and, in winter, cold as a cadaver. As for sand, it was several days before we found any, but when we did there was plenty.

The Sahara is, of course, an area so vast and so diversified that it is impossible to generalize about it. There are oases in the Sahara with a million palms, moist as wet blotters; there are also areas so blindingly hot and arid that they have never yet been traversed. In Arabic, the word "Sahara" means "emptiness," or "nothing."

FLIGHT TO TAMANRASSET

Practically all communication in the Sahara is by way of the oases; one travels like a golf ball, hopping from green to green. Our route was Algiers-El Goléa-Adrar-Aoulef-Tamanrasset. The plane goes once a week, and is an old DC-3 operated by Air France; we are a long, long way now from the kind of commercial air service familiar in the United States or western Europe. Half the space is for cargo, strapped by thongs to the naked sides of the fuselage and carpetless metal floor. The roof is painted white, partly to deflect the sun's heat, partly because white is the easiest color to see in the desert, and sometimes even the best-run planes have forced landings. Bus and automobile tops are similarly white on vehicles devoted to Saharan travel.

This Air France route is the life line of the western Sahara. It sucks life into the desert from the north like a hose. We left Algiers at 4:45 on a winter morning bristling with wind and rain. At El Goléa, two hours away, the sun was burning a big yellow hole on the horizon but it was so cold that my hands were numb. The Saharan airports have no runways in our sense; they are nothing but primitively marked strips pared off the desert. At each the haphazard routine was the same. We would discharge cargo—a bundle of news-papers, a crate of tomatoes, a cask of butter—into waiting arms. The weekly arrival from the Mediterranean is a big event. French soldiers always stood about, to gossip with our crew. Some were Zouaves. The non-coms wore blue kepis, baggy black pantaloons, and native sandals of any color—scarlet, gold, magenta, pale blue—with their toes sticking out. Arabs always lay about in their burnouses, as inert as logs.

We arrived in Tamanrasset—almost halfway across the Sahara—late that afternoon, and felt instantly swallowed up by the Saharan void. I have never known any place so startlingly silent. If a leaf falls it sounds like a firecracker. The remoteness is immeasurable. It was a crazy touch to learn that radio reception here is best from, of all places, Monte Carlo. Our guest house was an ocher-red building made of baked mud, like an adobe structure in New Mexico, but with the color more intense. Most buildings in Tamanrasset are designed to withstand summer heat, with thick walls and small windows; they do not even have fireplaces, and in winter are ice cold. They carry latticed designs on their exterior walls, made of mud and shaped like paper patterns cut out by a child. The surfaces are faintly corrugated by long shallow scoops, made by the fingers of those who built them. Later I looked at the mountains, which have the same kind of hol-low furrows, clawed out by the wind. Hand of God, hand of man, leave the same marks in Tamanrasset.

The mud houses are apt to melt down if it rains, and vicious storms can come in the autumn, but once it did not rain in Tamanrasset for seven solid years. The altitude is 4,822 feet, and in August the shade temperature can reach 126 degrees. But while we were there it was only moderately hot by day, if freezingly cold at night. Life goes by zigzags. The thermometer can drop sixty degrees—literally—between noon and night. We wore light tweeds by day, and slept shivering in sweaters and an overcoat.

This is still part of the Southern Territories of Algeria—though the frontier of French Equatorial Africa is only 250 miles away—and Tamanrasset is capital of an administrative area called the *Annexe* of the Hoggar, this covers 375,000 square kilometers and is thus three-quarters the size of France. The town has about 2,000 people, of whom 135 are French. It has no bank, no newspaper, no plumbing, no telephones, and the electricity works for only three hours a day, from 6 to 9 P.M. I have never seen before shops so rawly primitive as the few that line Tamanrasset's single street, dark as caves, windowless, and selling padlocks, combs, and odd bits of cloth. Tamanrasset compares to Ouarzazate as Ouarzazate compares to Fez or Fez to London. Existence here has certain primitive complexities. If you have a cat you must be careful not to let it out by night. The local Negroes love to eat cats, because catmeat makes them strong (so they say) and their women fertile.

Our host was a young French military officer, Captain Lecointre, the chief administrator of the Hoggar region, and a former *Méhariste,* or member of the Camel Corps. His military duties are few, since the area has been pacified since 1916. He needs practically no troops, except Camel Corps men out on patrol. But, like the administrators in the Atlas region, he keeps quite busy—as governor, judge, and superintendent of such realms as sanitation, agriculture, engineering, maintenance of the *pistes,* the economy of the area, and public health. "Life can be very hard here," he told us. "I like it." We sat before his small, smoky fire—wood is more precious than platinum—and I stared suddenly at the ceiling. It was made of rough boughs of *ételle,* a kind of tamarisk, still clothed in bark, and set under a straw matting, the kind of matting normally used for covering a floor. It was the first time in my life I ever saw a floor used as a ceiling.

One thing that Capatin Lecointre does not have to worry about is nationalism, which is utterly unknown in these regions. The population is altogether docile and friendly, and almost everybody we passed on the silent, buff-colored streets muttered a gentle *"Bon jour."*

Tamanrasset is the principal Tuareg center, but few Tuareg are to be seen, since these nomads live in tents or mobile encampments in the surrounding desert; they have no villages or towns. The local traders are mostly M'zabites, and there is a small Arab community composed of ex-soldiers. One day a beggar stopped us; he was a Sherifian, a lineal descendant of Mohammed. He said he had had nothing to eat for four days. He was not telling the truth. The bulk of the population is Negro. This was the first predominantly Negro town, if it can be called a town, that we saw in Africa. The poorest Negroes live in their own quarter, a clayey shantyville on the outskirts; similarly do poor Negroes live in hovels where American cities fray at the edges. These Negroes were, until comparatively recent times, slaves of the Tuareg nobles, and some would like to be slaves again, because it was easier to work as a servant for nothing than break rock on the roads for wages. In fact, when the French administration freed the slaves, many refused to leave their masters. Today, the Negroes have little push or sense of responsibility. Their heritage is to understand nothing but command. Being slaves, they had no reason to learn anything. The Arabs get along with them quite well, but despise them. I sent an Arab boy on an errand, and offered him a small tip. He refused it proudly with the words, "Do you think I am a Negro?"

There are no date palms in Tamanrasset, which makes it unique among Saharan oases. Once palms were abundant, owned by the Tuareg nobles. The Tuareg shared grain with their slaves, but not dates, even though the Negroes tended the trees. In resentment the Negroes began to neglect them, and in time they died. Now, to obtain dates, the Tuareg have to travel to some neighboring oasis. Trade is largely a matter of barter; for dates, they give sheep or grain. One afternoon outside the local inn—vividly French, boiling with a robust bonhomie, and packed with bearded non-coms in billowing pantaloons— we saw Tuareg swords for sale, but we never found any shields, which are becoming very scarce; they are made of antelope skin and are taut as parchment. A few yards away is the *fondouk,* the native hostel for men and animals; here tall men in blue gowns slept beside their camels. One rose as we approached, and with calisthenic genuflexions prayed to Mecca.

There are some remarkable sights in and near Tamanrasset, deriving from local history and folklore. One is Mount Laperrine, which commands the oasis like a savage fingerless red hand. It is not particularly high, about 11,000 feet, but few people have ever climbed it except professional Alpinists; lumps of lava break off, and make any ascent treacherous. It was named for a French general who crashed in an airplane not far away, and died of thirst before he could be rescued.[1] Then we saw the *bordj* (shelter) where the celebrated Père de Foucauld lived, and where he was killed in 1916 by Senussi Arabs. About Charles de Foucauld one could write much. He is one of the substantial heroes of French Africa. He was a dissolute, worldly youth, an army officer of great promise, who retired melodramatically into the desert, embraced religion, devoted himself to mysticism, aroused much enmity as well as adulation, and founded an order based on the most extreme asceticism, called the Petits Frères du Sacré Coeur. Its membership is not large today, but it still exists. Also near Tamanrasset is Abalessa, where an ancient Tuareg queen held court, the heroine of Pierre Benoit's novel *L'Atlantide*. Below—far below—are almost mythical Saharan cities like Gao on the Niger, Agadès, and Zinder, the goal of camel caravans. Tamanrasset is the hub of a spider web of *pistes* faintly scratched on the desert that reach all the way to Kano (in Nigeria), Lake Chad, and Fort Lamy, 2,680 kilometers away.

But Tamanrasset itself provides enough romantic color for anybody not a glutton, if only because of the Tuareg in their shrouds of indigo.

THE BLUE-VEILED MEN

One reason why Tuareg[2] are so striking is that it is the men, not the women, who wear veils. These are of a magnificent deep blue, dyed by indigo. The dye is, however, not very fast, and is apt to smudge, like carbon paper, so that the very skins of the Tuareg nobles seem blue. Moreover, they use blue eye paint, ringing the lids, and the women are tattooed. The men muffle their faces even while eating and drinking, passing up food from underneath the veils. I never saw a male Tuareg face. These nobles are tall men, with a splendid bearing, and the combination of white hood and blue veil makes them resemble armored,

[1] Tamanrasset was originally named Fort Laperrine, and still appears as this on some maps.

[2] Correctly—but I don't want to be pedantic—"Tuareg" is the plural form of the word. The singular is Targui.

helmeted creatures out of science fiction. They look like blue bullets with a blunt white tip.

How did the practice arise for men, not women, to be veiled? One explanation is that the Tuareg wanted to differentiate themselves from the Arabs. Ask a Targui about this and the usual answer is that it is a matter of such ancient custom that nobody knows. Probably the old Tuareg simply sought to protect their faces from the merciless sun. Also, a proud people, they wanted to hide any wounds they might receive in battle, so as not to be humiliated before their women. Now the veil is a convenient device, if only because it makes the men virtually anonymous. Talk with a Tuareg noble is an interesting experience, in that it is impossible to read his face.

Use of the color blue is easier to explain. Tuareg *like* blue, just as American women like pink or red for fingernails. Also, blue is a good color for cutting off rays of the sun.

No one knows much about the origin of the Tuareg. They are a Hamitic people, probably descendants of the Berbers, and were headstrong warriors, camel raiders, and slave traders till the French came to the Sahara. Unlike other Berbers, they have a written language. The characters are fascinatingly rectilinear, and vowels do not exist. This is more or less the way my name looks in Tamachek, which is what the Tuareg language is called:

$$ \text{⋊I} \qquad \text{⋉I+:} $$
$$ \text{J \; N} \qquad \text{G \; N \; T \; R} $$

The Tuareg are a matriarchy. A man named Akhamouk, known as the Aménocal, is king, but rank is passed on by the women, not the men. If an Aménocal should marry a lady not of the royal line, his children could not succeed. We shall find this matriarchal system of inheritance almost universal when we reach Black Africa.

There are two distinct classes among Tuareg—nobles and vassals. The chief distinguishing mark of the noble is that he does no work. Work is solely the province of vassals, and no vassal may ever rise to become a noble. He is fixed in this status for life. But if a male vassal marries a female noble (such marriages are rare) the children are noble. Contrariwise, children of a male noble and a female vassal are not noble, strange as this may seem. There are three noble tribes, the Kel-Rela, Taïtok, and Tedjehe-Mellet.

The Tuareg marry late as a rule, and, unlike almost all other Moslems, are monogamous. Tuareg girls—nobles and vassals alike—are among the few women in the Islamic world who ever have a chance to flirt, since they do not wear veils. If a girl is a vassal, she may be deflowered before marriage with impunity; if a noble, she may not.

The Tuareg are poor, frugal, and clean. The venereal rate among Arabs in the neighborhood is 90 per cent; among Tuareg, nil. They are law-abiding, and crime is virtually unknown. They are almost never homosexual, as Arabs often are. They live on their herds of sheep, traveling by camel from pasture to pasture. (There is a fair amount of pasture in this part of the Sahara, where the mountain slopes collect rain.) When they need money, they go into the nearest town and sell a camel to the butcher. The basis of their diet is camel's milk and farina; meat is far too dear. They eat with spoons, not with their fingers as Moors do.

The schoolmaster in Tamanrasset is Claude Blanquernon, as solid and splendid a person as any I ever met, and one of the world's foremost authorities on the Tuareg. It was he who invented "nomad schools" in the Sahara. He wanted to get education out into the tribes. He could only do so by camel. So he traveled with a Tuareg tribe for the whole length of the school year, as it moved grazing its herds from camp to camp—a one-man school on camel-back for seven months, teaching as he went along. Now, three young Frenchmen have similar jobs in the Hoggar area, and this system of instruction, greeted with incredulity at first, is firmly entrenched. Blanquernon is a real pioneer.

This striking character (he and his wife are Normans) took us out to see some Tuareg. It happened, by luck, that a detachment of nobles had camped nearby; otherwise, since they are perpetually on the move, it might have been laborious to find any. (Only two Tuareg have, incidentally, *ever* left their desert homeland. One was taken to Paris as a curiosity by Père de Foucauld some forty years ago; one was flown to Constantine, Algeria, in 1951, by our friend M. Blanquernon, in order—of all things—to vote. The French wanted to have at least one Targui at the Algerian election then taking place. Blanquernon showed him a steamship in the harbor and explained what made it go. "Ah, just like a teapot!" he replied.)

We set out in an open truck. With us were two Tuareg nobles who had come into town, and who volunteered to show us the way. They sent their camels back to the camp, led by a vassal, but carefully kept their saddles with them, in our truck; these are objects of considerable beauty, with the front shaped like the hilt of a giant sword. We were the first Americans these Tuareg had ever seen. They had heard about New York, though. It was a large city like Adrar or El Goléa, but without camels and beyond the sea.

We drove over a hard, rattling crust of gravel toward the Tuareg camp. Excited children clung to the truck like flies, and had to be brushed off, until we passed out of the town. But we could not brush off small birds that followed us; these are called *boula-boula,* and the Tuareg say that they can talk to them. We left the *piste* and bumped over red granite rocks and clumps of talha, a variety of thorny mimosa. We knew we were getting somewhere when we saw a few goats; then a breath-taking line of white camels stood profiled against a rim of ruddy hill.

The ceremonial tent, where we were greeted, was made of copper-colored leather, stretched flat between poles; a red rug projected out on the ground. A fire was laboriously made, out of scraps and twigs, and we sat down, cross-legged, until water for the tea was boiling. "They ruin themselves to get tea," M. Blanquernon explained. We had brought a small gift of sugar.

In the tent were the brother-in-law of the Aménocal, by name Mustapha; his wife, the sister of the Aménocal; another lady who was the widow of the previous Aménocal; and one of the Aménocal's nephews—a regal company indeed. I happened to be wearing an old leather waistcoat, soft with use; this and its zipper were objects of amazed curiosity. One by one each nobleman made the zipper work, and kept patting the leather, as if no leather so pliable had ever been seen before.

The ladies, unveiled, in blue robes, shy, like frightened birds, sat back timidly in the tent. But soon, unable to resist their curiosity, they came forward and began to finger softly my wife's jewelry, especially a small St. Christopher's medal. M. Blanquernon explained what this was. One of the nobles at once grinned, and pointed to some good luck charms— made of leather, like tobacco pouches—that *he* wore to ward off evil. The world is, after all, one.

First we had camel's milk, which is creamy and delicious, served to all from a common bowl, to which each person puts his lips. Then came the tea, poured in a thick stream from a tiny pot held high above the glasses. It was strong and sweet, and took a long time to prepare, because the fire was so puny. Ceremoniously, we each had to drink three cups.

What did the Tuareg talk about, as M. Blanquernon interpreted? Mostly about what a farmer in Montana might talk about, or a herdsman in Northumberland—crops, prices, the weather, local gossip. A few weeks before, Blanquernon had gone out into the desert to take a tape recording of the Aménocal's voice. The Aménocal, curious about the machine, asked how much it cost, and had been horrified to learn that it was worth four camels. This anecdote was repeated with great relish. Then one of our hosts told our fortune by swiftly drawing quick, delicate designs with his finger in the sand. We offered everybody cigarettes. These the men put aside carefully because they do not smoke, eat, or take money in front of women.

When we left, we gave one of the ladies a lift to the vassals' camp a few miles away. It was the first time in her life she had ever been in an automobile.

EN ROUTE NORTH

An expedition by car across the Sahara is an interesting business. There are elaborate regulations to fulfill and precautions to be taken, even on such an easy route as the one we took.[8] Anybody crossing the desert in his own conveyance must notify the authorities of the exact route contemplated, and post a sizable bond as a deposit toward the expenses of a rescue car that will be sent out if, after twenty-four hours, the destination is not reached. You must carry shovels, wire netting, pails, and rope, as well as food and water. People have died of thirst on the brink of a well, because they could not get their pails down deep enough. Nowadays few Europeans ever get lost in this part of the desert, because of the severe precautions imposed by the Service Saharienne. Still, an Englishman died on the road from Tamanrasset to Zinder last winter. Natives die more frequently, largely because they have become somewhat careless. They think that, with the increase in travel, a car will be bound to come along sooner or later, if they are lost or waterless. Sometimes rescuers do happen to come along. And sometimes not.

The French say that in summer, without water, a man lost in this region cannot expect to live more than twelve or fourteen hours. A full day in full sun between dawn and sunset will kill him.

It may be useful to keep the following symptoms in mind, if your truck breaks down. If you become dehydrated to the extent of 1 to 5 per cent of your body weight, there will be thirst, anorexia, flushed skin, impatience, sleepiness, increased temperature, and nausea. For a loss of 6 to 10 per cent, dizziness, headache, dyspnea, decreased blood volume,

---

[8] The Sahara was never crossed by automobile until the 1920's.

cyanosis, indistinct speech, and inability to walk. For 11 to 20 per cent, delirium, spasticity, swollen tongue, inability to swallow, deafness, shriveled skin, and anuria.[4] I met a Belgian diplomat who almost died in the Nubian desert. What he remembers most is that his tongue became so swollen that he could not speak, his lips split, and for weeks after his rescue he was thirsty all the time. If you die your body will remain in good condition for some months or even longer, because of its desiccation.

French officers talk about the heat as if it were something living. One told us that, from May 15 to October 15, the average temperature inside his house at Adrar, day and night, was 95 degrees Fahrenheit. In the shade outside, it could reach 122 degrees; in the sun, 140 degrees. "It is hot," he said gravely, "but supportable." Once he ordered fifty kilograms of potatoes from Ghardaïa, a few hundred miles up the road; when they arrived, they weighed forty kilograms, and were inedible. The heat had sucked ten kilograms of water out of them in fourteen hours. While he told us this story, we were shivering with cold.

Our own trip overland from Tamanrasset had every element of picturesqueness, but no danger; this was winter, and we were lucky. We rode with two French non-coms in a type of military vehicle called a *savanne* —a tough, squat, high-bodied car that can go anywhere over sand or rocks, like a rabbit. The *pistes* were not too bad; I have known worse roads in Scotland and Vermont, but not over such extended distances. It took us a long, hard day to reach Arak (395 kilometers), another to get to In Salah (275 kilometers), and a third to reach that wonderful oasis, El Goléa (420 kilometers) where seventeen hidden springs pump water at the rate of 22,000 cubic meters per minute. Yet El Goléa sits on a thin belt of rock directly between the two most feared areas in the whole Sahara, the Great Western Emptiness (*Grand Erg Occidental*) and the Great Eastern Emptiness (*Grand Erg Oriental*).

First day, Tamanrasset to Arak. We drove eleven hours, and never saw another vehicle except one. This was a SATT bus (of the Société Africaine des Transports Tropicaux), en route to Algiers all the way from Fort Lamy, which was twelve *days* late. It had repeatedly broken down, and we rescued and took with us one of its passengers. Nearby was a cluster of blanched camel skeletons. The *piste* is a wide track, a stony belt almost indistinguishable from the desert it cuts across. We saw only one sign of habitation during the entire day, a cluster of Arab huts, and not a single gas pump in 395 kilometers. One *carrefour* pointed

[4] From *Afoot in the Desert, A Contribution to Basic Survival,* published by the Air University, Maxwell Air Force Base, Alabama, which in turn uses a chart from *Physiology of Man in the Desert,* by E. F. Adolph and Associates, New York.

the way to Gao, 1,200 kilometers away; not one town exists in all this distance. There were occasional signs to indicate wells—*eau sanitaire* —and at one point we crossed the Tropic of Cancer, neatly marked.

The mountains looked like elephants, like swollen gourds, like crushed duffel bags. If this road had signs saying "Falling Rocks" like those in New York State, there would have been a dozen in a hundred miles. Our car crawled and slid among rocks like a lizard. Our chauffeur every few minutes stopped abruptly, lifted up his carbine, and shot out of the window at gazelles. Half a dozen times we left the *piste* to chase gazelles through the dense forest of rocks, without descending from the car. We never got one. The chauffeur kept grunting. "I think I *touched* that one!" or "A near miss!"

Arak is a *bordj* deep in a crater; it is here only because the regulations provide that there must be a shelter every 250 miles. Nothing exists at Arak except this shelter, nothing else whatever. We had an extraordinarily good dinner (the two main courses were potatoes) and the host, who may see a European once every two weeks or so, told us about the rock paintings characteristic of this part of the Sahara. The trip we made this day would have taken between two and three weeks to do by camel. Until twenty-odd years ago, there was no other way to do it.

Second day, Arak to In Salah. All signs of vegetation ceased. Before this there had been isolated patches of desert scrub, enough for goats to feed on. But now we passed through a barren wilderness of nothing but stones. In the distance, slopes of white sand lay against the red mountains, and looked like flanks of snow. At noon we spread blankets out on rough black gravel and had a picnic. To my amazement a living thing appeared—a fly. Then obvious signs of civilization began to appear. The kilometer posts were neater, and were spaced five kilometers apart instead of ten. The *piste* became more controlled, and did not meander so much; we no longer had the sense of driving in an interminable dry rocky river bed. But we passed no single car all day, nor did we see a single human being, until we hit a camp of oil prospectors near the outskirts of In Salah.

In Salah has forty-three French, 5,000 *indigènes* (mostly Negro) and 80,000 palms. Mud prickles adorn the orange-colored buildings, and clay gates and walls carry the familiar cutout frieze. This oasis is much less picturesque than Tamanrasset, but nearer Europe; there is electric light till 10 P.M. The *souk* was the emptiest and most forlorn I have ever visited. Flies clung to children like lumps of licorice.

What makes an oasis, God or man? In general one will be formed wherever date palms can reach subterranean moisture, oases are usually at low points, where water creeps invisibly down through the sand and rocks. Then elaborate engineering work is necessary to make irrigation channels, tap springs, and improve their flow. There are, so to speak, three different layers or levels of vegetation in a well-tended oasis—the dates above, citrus and other fruit trees in their shade below, and vegetables and flowers on the ground. The water pumped in these groves is, only too manifestly, the lifeblood of the Sahara; each oasis is a heart. For years it has been a grandiose dream to "irrigate" parts of the Sahara, particularly in the area of the *chotts* (dried-up lakes), and scientific research to this end goes on constantly. Only about one-sixth of the Sahara as a whole is sand. When President Roosevelt visited North Africa he talked about a Saharan TVA. If you can get water to gravel, crops will grow, and the desert could burst into bloom. But the difficulties are almost insurmountable, partly because communications are so scant. For instance, in the entire vastness of the French Sahara, which is wider than the United States, there are only two north-south roads. One of these is the one we were on.

Third day, In Salah to El Goléa. For two hours we saw nothing, not even a scrap of bush. The desert here is black, not yellow; the very rocks are sunburned black. We reached the great Tademait Plateau, and climbed it almost as one would climb a flight of stairs. We saw a long camel caravan at the top, marching slowly against the sky; it looked so much like caravans in movies that it was hard to believe that it was real. We had lunch at an oil camp in Fort Miribel, and saw a signpost almost outrageously romantic—Bidon Cinq, 1,379 kilometers; Tombouctou 2,293; Fort Lamy 3,907. Here at Fort Miribel a Dutch prospecting team is working for Shell of Algiers. There have been no actual oil discoveries in this area as yet. Many who love the Sahara do not like these developments. One French officer told us, "For twenty years we have been trying to teach the natives to grow crops, to develop a satisfactory agriculture, to learn about irrigation, to live decently on the land. Now come the oil invaders, and everybody rushes off to work in their camps. Oil may enrich the Sahara. Also, it may ruin it."[5]

---

[5] In 1952 a company called BEIN (Bureau for African Industrialization) was set up with a $30,000,000 annual subsidy from the French government to make an economic survey of the Sahara and investigate such possible innovations as "solar batteries" to provide power. (*New Statesman*, August 7, 1954.) Meantime a British company, headed by the well-known forestry expert Richard St. Barbe Baker, has been formed to investigate ways to "arrest the progress" of the Sahara by an afforestation program. The Sahara at present spreads "thirty miles a year."

Then we passed onto the brittle rocky channel between the great emptinesses, the solid sandy ergs, and our car had a minor breakdown. Sand in the carburetor. There were mirages on three sides, glittering, shimmering, brighter than silver. I walked over the earth, which had the consistency of foam crushed solid, and said to my wife, "Look at the frost." Actually there had been a drop of cold rain, but my joke was poor. What we were walking on was salt.

El Goléa is one of the great, smiling, voluptuous oases. We stayed in the comfortable SATT hotel; rough palm fronds made a fire at night, and in bed we had metal bottles filled with boiling water, much more efficacious than a rubber hot-water bag. By day we waded in the dunes, which slide massively in on the oasis from each side and take on every color—puce, amber, fawn, white—as the vibrating sunlight changes; the sand is soft and fine, and you can sink in it to your knees. When the winds blow along the ridges of these formidable smooth dunes, the natives say that the sand is "smoking."

When the French came to El Goléa there were 6,000 date palms in the oasis; today, 127,000. Water spurts out of the ground all year, with no seasonal fluctuation, from a stable water table—good water, fit to drink. A good many French people buy a stand of palms in El Goléa, as an investment, the way Americans buy real estate in Florida. Few, however, come to El Goléa to live, beautiful as it is in the spring and fall. In summer it is so hot that even airplane traffic has to stop, and provisioning is done by truck and camel. The total French population is only 150, and of these 110 are oil men newly arrived; the natives number about 10,000, mostly Arabs and a variety of Berber known as Zenetes. When the slaves were freed, the French had to give them part of the oasis, where they still maintain their own community; otherwise they would have starved. One old Negro lady remembers with pride that she was bought, because of her beauty, for a record price—50 kilograms of salt.[6] Nowadays it takes about sixty trees to support a family.

The great sight of El Goléa is the slate-colored Vieux Ksar, or fort, dominating a bleak hill nearby. It has been there for nine hundred years. A Swiss engineer was asked recently if any modern architect could build such a structure, out of mud, without steel, without nails, without cement, and hope to have it last that long. Answer: "No." Here until recent times a Zenete queen held fashionable and pompous court. The highest reward one of her warriors could get, for valor on the field of battle, was a night in her company; in exceptional cases, two nights or even

---

[6] Of course this happened before the French abolished slavery.

three. The Arabs at the end captured this Ksar through treachery, and slaughtered every man, woman, and child it contained. It became French in 1891. One oil man working in El Goléa today is the son of a French officer who died taking it, and who is buried at its summit. (Père de Foucauld is also buried in El Goléa; his remains were moved here from Tamanrasset in 1929.)

We spent one afternoon with the White Fathers in El Goléa, and saw the school run by their associates, the Soeurs Blanches. Their building looks like nothing I ever saw in the realm of architecture; the roof is covered solidly by smooth white cupolas, like beehives, to break the rays of the sun. The order of White Fathers was founded by Cardinal Charles Lavigerie in 1874, with the design of Christianizing Moslems in Africa, and is justly celebrated. Its members wear immaculate white robes, and are always bearded; many are men of the most exquisite cultivation, who have done much good work for education all over Africa. In the Sahara there are practically no attempts at proselytism by the Pères Blancs any longer, because it is almost impossible—in this region—to convert a Mohammedan. Father Lusson in El Goléa told us, "The Moslems here do not *bend* either to the forces of reason or of history." This was the first time that we saw the work of the White Fathers. Later, particularly in Ruanda-Urundi and the Congo, we met them several times again.

At the El Goléa hospital the resident doctor told us that, in ten years, he has never had a case of appendicitis in a native, or seen a cancer. Elsewhere in Africa we subsequently found doctors who reported this same extraordinary thing. Tuberculosis? "None as yet in the Sahara. We may bring it in."

CAMELS

These are odd beasts—so measured, slow, and supercilious to their menial tasks. A good riding camel costs thirty to thirty-five thousand francs ($85–$100), a baggage camel around twenty thousand ($57). But most people do not buy camels; they grow them. The favored color for a smart riding camel is called *azrem*—a pale pinkish eggshell. There is little affinity between the camel and his master; few camels are named, as a dog or a horse is named, and I never came across anybody who said that a camel recognized him, even after months of being ridden by the same person. A camel is adult at seven years, and has a working life up to about the age of fifteen.

Normally, a camel can do fifteen miles a day; twenty-five is exceptional even in cool weather. In winter, a camel can go literally for months without water, *if* he has access to good pasture, and is not working; if working, he can live without water for ten or twelve days in good pasture, and five or six days in bad. In summer, no matter what the pasture is, he must have water every other day.

The *Méharistes,* officers and men of the Camel Corps, go out in a platoon of fifty or sixty men, and are in motion almost the whole year; they inspect tribes, watch the pasturage, administer justice, look at wells, and punish thieves. They carry medicine and a radio. Each officer has four camels, two of which march while the other two wait in pasture; each non-com has two. The French like camels trained by a variety of Arab nomads known as the Chaamba. Female camels are never used, and the males are castrated. In a forced march, a platoon may lose 25 per cent of its animals. The world's record for camel travel was made many years ago by a French officer who did almost five hundred miles in eleven days, without losing a single beast.

The basis of caravan traffic is, of course, trade. A caravan can consist of anything from six to two hundred camels; forty to fifty is the average. If you see a cluster of two or three camels, it is a family on the move. Arabs leading caravans find their way by an almost superhuman instinct for terrain. They will remember a basic dune pattern even if half of it has blown away.

Camels always travel by soft ground, if possible, never on the *pistes,* because hard ground splits their hoofs. But their worst enemy is mud. They are less fatiguing to ride than horses, provided they do not gallop. They are fragile beasts, and have one disconcerting characteristic; if tired or sick, they never appear to be in trouble, but die at once without warning. Generally, you can tell the state of health of a camel by the hardness of his hump. If a camel is overworked or underfed (they eat a lot) the hump diminishes; when it is put to good pasture the hump will grow again, if the beast is not too old. For every day that a camel is "forced," it needs a full week's rest.

I asked if camels would ever be replaced by the marvelous, omnipresent jeep. No. There are at least three reasons. First, gasoline costs money. Second, even a jeep cannot traverse the great ergs. Third, you cannot eat a jeep if it dies.

Margaret Mead

TOWARDS MORE VIVID UTOPIAS

Dear Mr. Burnett:

I have chosen "Towards More Vivid Utopias"* because it represents a point where science and literature meet, where the writer has to combine an appeal to the imagination with precision and to exercise scientific as well as artistic responsibility. I have chosen it also because it is concerned with the future and because I hope that as we move into the future my style will change and grow.

Margaret Mead

The American Museum of Natural History
New York

* This article is based on a Phi Beta Kappa lecture delivered before the American Association for the Advancement of Science at the New York meeting, December 1956.

When one is asked to speak to a group primarily interested in the sciences from a platform defined by the humanities, it seems important to state more specifically where one's own discipline lies within the academic fields and what contribution one may expect to make from its specific interests. Anthropology holds a unique position, formally recognized in its inclusion in the National Research Council, where it belongs as a biological science; the Social Science Research Council, among those sciences which take man's biological nature as given; and the American Council of Learned Societies, because of its concern with language, so often defined as a pure humanity, without reference to the larynx or the delicate mechanism of the human ear.

This triple membership springs partly from the tradition of anthropological field work, in which single workers, with small funds and a narrow margin of time, visited, in what was conceived as probably the only careful study which would ever be made, small primitive societies whose ancient and distinctive ways of life were disintegrating even as we tried to set them down. Not only did we work with urgency, as might a student of literature, trying to take down from dictation a new poem from the lips of a dying poet, or a student of painting, who found a painter of great gift drawing in an impermanent ink on the exposed, whitewashed walls of a public square—where the rain would wash it all away tomorrow or the next day—but we also, both by the nature of the situation in which we found ourselves and by the canons of our craft, looked at the whole people, at their bodies as well as at the social arrangements of their lives; at the music they made, or at least at the musical

instruments with which they made it; at the dances, which might be seen
as art to be appreciated as well as analyzed; at their rituals, which might
be catalogued as *rites de passage* or regarded as an artistic product of
generations of imaginative creativity, anonymous, time binding, with its
own esthetic.

The anthropologist who works in this way comes to have an equal
interest and respect for those aspects of human life which are concerned
with the perception and ordering of observed regularities in nature and
for those aspects of human life in which the "seeing eye" turns as much
inward as outward, as the mind matches proprioception with perception
in an outer world which already contains—in the shape of a roof, the line
of a dance, the flick of a wrist at a sacrifice—the patterned perpetuation
of earlier imaginative and creative acts.

Because we are also always committed to a scientific ordering of our
material, these products of human imagination cannot only be subjected
to analysis of their function in a given society but can also be related to
certain capacities of the human mind—themselves becoming better known
through the imaginative scientific inquiries of investigators like Piaget
and Inhelder, Gesell and Ilg, Erikson, and Margaret Lowenfeld. Delight
in the imaginative creation of individuals or in the intuitive—that is,
simultaneous and so unanalyzed—grasp of these as wholes by whole
societies, does not prevent analytic work, also. The two methods of
approach—that of the humanities, which focuses upon a recognition of
the unique character of a work of the imagination, and that of the
sciences, which attempt by careful observation, analysis, and finally experiment to understand the lawfulness of the behavior involved—can be used.

It is from this particular background of research that I wish to describe
the role which men's visions of a possible and more desirable future
play in the development of a culture. Utopias may be seen from many
points of view—as projections from individual experience; as projections
from individual experiences stamped by the point of view of a particular
period; as sterile blueprints, too narrow to confine the natural varieties
of the human mind for very long, as when they are lived out by small
cult groups who pare and mould the individuals born within them to a
confining and crippling mode. Or they may be seen as those visions of
future possibilities which lead the minds of men forward into the future,
giving life a meaning beyond the grave or beyond the simple domestic
perpetuation of one's own life in the lives of one's children, with an
interest in the trees planted in one's own garden but no interest in the
trees in one's neighbors' gardens. The Golden Age, a retrospective utopia

of the days when all men lived like gods, and walked and talked with gods —the days before death or work or separation came into the world—may also, of course, play a significant role in keeping a whole people caught in a dream unrelated to the requirements of the contemporary world.

Using models from primitive cultures, we may, from this point of view, look at those cultures in which life is held steady by a view of the past, of which the present is a poor copy, a vale of tears where once there was Olympian laughter, at those cultures which live a hand-to-mouth existence, wrapt in the small urgencies of the present, and at those which move, generation after generation, towards Heaven—which may be the heavenly Jerusalem "with milk and honey blest," the Jerusalem to be rebuilt and reinhabited, which informed the imagination of Jews throughout the Diaspora, or the Jerusalem to be built "in England's green and pleasant land." Against these may be placed Nirvana, with its insistent comment on the lack of value in all earthly and individualized life.

Within a culture as complex as our own, which draws on the inheritance of so many earlier and partly recorded pasts and which now has available an even larger number of incomparable and imaginatively stimulating "presents," from accounts of the peoples whose lives were part of a different stream—in Africa, in the Orient, and in the New World—it is obvious that we may live not only on different visions at different periods but also on different and incompatible visions at the same time. Part of the excitement and the difficulty of the modern world, which makes the artist feel that he has no whole context within which to create his personal, special new vision and which makes the scientist turn to the anonymous writing of science fiction nightmares, is just the way in which different sorts of utopias—one man's dream and another man's nightmare—jostle each other even within the confines of one political speech or one brief editorial, as we yearn for a past, rage at or delight in the present, or promise or threaten a future. While it always has been and will probably always be the mark of the more educated man that he lives in a longer time perspective, both into the past and into the future, than his less well educated contemporaries, where this education is underwritten by no habitual pattern of thought and speech within which such time perspectives are implicitly expressed, the presence of so many and such contrasting world views may seem fragmenting and mechanical rather than living.

Yet, from comparative materials, it seems quite clear that the utopias men live by are of vital importance in such mundane matters as whether they will struggle to preserve the identity of their society, their class, their religion, or their vocation; whether they will plant trees which take two lifetimes to mature; whether they will take thought to stop the forests from being depleted, the good soil from being washed into the sea, or the gene pool from becoming exposed to too much radiation. Men who believe that the ultimate good state will mean the abolition of identity are hardly likely to take an active interest in public health, and those who believe that the Day of Judgment is near, when the sheep will be separated from the goats and the whole world will go up in a holocaust directed by a punishing Deity, see the atom bomb as an addition to the Lord's armory of destruction.

Within any determinedly other-worldly religion, there is a perpetual conflict between the active acceptance of early death (so the little, innocent souls may go up to God at once, unstained by sin) and the need for public health measures and preventive medicine as well as for the compassionate dole to the beggar or care for the dying. The Catholic Church has fought a long battle against an otherworldliness which would have as its logic an overvaluation of death—which has occasionally been the response of literal-minded savages to enthusiastic Christian preaching about heaven. On the other hand, the modern public health movement has its problems in an overvaluation of the importance of individual life, which leads to a lowering of death rates before there is a compensating rise in the standard of living and a fall in the birth rate, with the result that famine and misery are the portion of the very individuals whose lives were to be bettered.

At the same time, all visions of heaven, in this world and in the next, have a curiously tasteless, pale blue and pink quality, whether the image is one of cherubim and seraphim "casting down their golden crowns around the glassy sea" or of a time when "ploughs in peaceful industry shall supersede the sword," when "the dictatorship of the proletariat shall be realized in ideological completeness," or when lions shall lie down with lambs, or of a world in which woman shall have been freed from all the incidental consequences of their reproductivity and will spend long vacations with their lovers of the moment, flying Chinese kites.

Beside any picture of heaven above or heaven on earth, the pictures of hell and destruction stand out in vivid and compelling intensity, each detail strong enough to grip the imagination as the horrid creations of a Wells, an Orwell, or an Aldous Huxley unroll before our horrified eyes. Where positive utopias are insipid and a detailed heaven is unbearable to think of as a permanent abode, the creators of terror, the repudiators of man's future, have no such problem. So, if utopian visions are the stuff by which men live, it would seem a legitimate subject of inquiry to ask what is the matter with them? Why is Hell always so much more vivid than Heaven? Why, as I heard a young priest say recently, are all images of heaven "while not exactly not true, not as true as they might be"?

There have been attempts to give scientific answers to this question: that the prefiguration of bliss lies in the womb, where the child has no chance to use its distance receptors, and so the feeling remains one of undifferentiated and unspecified ecstasy; that analysis destroys a vision by introducing an element of self-consciousness and detachment of part of the self. These may be adequate explanations of the way in which the individual, in terms of his life experience, seeks for or experiences visionary ecstasy, but they seem insufficient answers to the problem of why the imagination of the human race, which has produced its long procession of great creations, has never yet succeeded in building a picture of a future really unlike the present, either in this world or in the next, where anyone passionately wished to live except when it was counterpointed against a Hell, delineated with the greatest precision. Heaven and all the pallid utopias are, in fact, even like Nirvana, black white spaces—or spaces a little tinted with pastel and furnished with plastic gadgets—and are given reality only by contrast with the fear, pain, and agony of some other state.

Yet it is by visions of a better world or place or state that men make positive efforts—in contrast to fiddling while Rome burns or refraining from evil all their days in fear of hell-fire. So it would seem legitimate to ask why human imaginations are, apparently, so handicapped in the creation of such essential visions and whether there is any way in which our present scientific knowledge of human behavior and of the way in which societies function can be used to create conditions within which utopias might be created whose positive hold on men's minds would be stronger than the negative hold of the Infernos and Lost Paradises. For the last 50 years we have experimented with the compelling character of negative images, as the prophecies of the dangers of modern warfare have grown ever sharper. When warfare is upon them, men will struggle; but they sink into a kind of paralysis when there is need to fight even harder—in peacetime—to prevent a recurrence of war. We need more vivid utopias.

One answer to the question comes from an examination of the struggle that institutionalized religions, which present the other world as desirable, must go through to deal with suicide, either condemning it as a dereliction in stewardship, as Christianity does, and treating the living out of life on earth as a trust, or hedging it around with terribly difficult steps, as in parts of India, where, in order to die a holy and self-elected death, a man must give up caste and family and must become purified until, at last, dressed for the next world and in a trance, he is lowered into the earth "alive." The next world must not be so desirable that it completely competes with this one and leads a majority of believers to suicide or towards a too-willing death in war, with the promise of a warriors' heaven. A long life of preparation—as a shaven and dedicated celibate, completely cloistered or moving through the streets with a begging bowl and making a contribution to the ongoing life of the world as teacher, nurse, or supplicant—this is feasible.

Similarly, Communism has always had difficulties with those who, regarding the Soviet Union as heaven on earth, have wished to go and live there instead of remaining in their own unregenerate countries, working at dull organizational jobs in the hope of a World Revolution which they themselves might not live to see. Sometimes short trips to the Soviet Union, as circumscribed as visions of the next world to a cloistered religious, were permitted. But the tension between the vision and the present must not include any way of immediately slackening it by a self-elected entry into heaven.

In fact, through the emphasis on dedication, attention is shifted from the self to the fate of others; through prayer for the souls in purgatory, teaching the young, or preparing for the revolution from which others will benefit, the necessary distance seems to be created so that a vision can be compelling, drawing one on like a magnet, but not too fast or too far. So perhaps it may be said that it is only when the visionary or the prophet, the poet or the painter wants to involve the individual directly in the future vision that the danger of immediate response is allowed for in the interpreters and spectators by a dilution of its intensity. Then Heaven or the Perfect Socialist State may be seen as being too insipid and as tasting like sawdust. A feeling of less involvement may be achieved by concentrating the individual's effort on the relation between someone else and the desired state—where the nexus can have both the intensity of devotion to the other and devotion to the dream without the temptation to relax and try to get there oneself.

Even here the other temptation—to force history at once to disgorge a visionary paradise at no matter what cost of suffering and death—is present as soon as Heaven is too vividly conceived even for the other, who must then be saved, by the rack or by brain washing, to become a denizen of someone else's too compelling dream. The ability of any people to cultivate protective devices against other people's compelling visions—against which the best defenses seem to be either laughter or else revolt against any individual being in thrall to the will of another —must also be considered as one component in their ability to create utopian dreams which inspire but do not limit them.

But there seems also to be another explanation of the relative lack of vividness of the good vision as compared with the nightmare. In pictures of Hell, of dictatorships armed with concentration camps and thought control, the appeal is made to human beings' most shared and least differentiated responses; pain, hunger, thirst, being bound, tortured, cut off from other human beings, and battered day and night by intolerable stimuli—these are experiences which repel every human being and under which the savage and the civilized, the illiterate and the scholar ultimately break down.

Men of different temperaments will break in different ways and at different points, but the effect of Medieval images of the tortures of Hell, when conjured up by a gifted preacher, or of the tortures actually administered in Nazi and Communist prisons is, in the end, to break all but the exceptional martyr sustained by a vision (which, only in this exceptional situation, cannot be called too vivid) of another world to which he is personally totally committed. (So Jehovah's Witnesses are said to stand up well to Communist pressures, and Orthodox Jews went chanting to the gas chambers as the early Christians, in the days when the Second Coming was felt to be very near, faced the lions.)

But the utopian vision, which is vivid enough to compel men's imagination and yet not so compelling that men must resort to rack and torture to bring others into it—the vision which men want to share with others and entrust to their expanding imagination rather than the vision in which they wish to entrap and imprison others—is built not upon the universals of fear and pain, hunger and thirst, ultimate fatigue and weakness, but upon the great diversity of human propensities and gifts. It must be, in terms of modern information theory, redundant enough to catch the developed imagination of each so-different member of any society.

Reduction to fear and pain gives men a common basis of the unbearable which can be elaborated—a nightmare peopled with Sisyphus endlessly rolling his stone and Tityus in agony. But reduction to our common good human experience leaves us with images of milk and honey, which stand very little elaboration before they are disintegrated by the involvement of our specific imaginations, by the differences in our childhood images of love and trust and bliss: it was not honey but strawberry jam, not the hum of bees but the flash of dragonfly wings, not a pointed breast but a round one which gave one suck. The recitation of such particular delights of food and drink as goat's milk or palm wine, durian, or witchetty grubs only resonate in the minds of those who once drank or ate them and fall dead upon the ears of those who never knew these pleasures. A whole society can be drawn on only by a utopian vision which contains the separate experiences of different regions, different classes, and different vocations, combined with the varied notes on each theme played by men of different temperament, disciplined and shaped by the prevailing forms of the culture. So it is no wonder that utopias are hard to come by.

Yet the world today is sorely in need of a vision which will endow our lives with meaning and responsibility and will make safe the terrible powers of destruction and the almost limitless powers of construction which scientific research has put into our hands. We can specify some of the characteristics this vision must have: it must be vivid enough to compel the heart, but not so vivid that one moves too quickly, by death or emigration or the coercion of others, to attain it; it must be so conceived that it is sought for the sake of others rather than solely for the self—for other men, for the whole next generation, or for men eons ahead—with nice adjustments which make it not too immediate (just the next generation) and not too distant, lest one become lost in a world without imaginable relation to the present; and it must be complex, redundant enough to catch and hold the imaginations of men and women of many different types of temperament and experience, and stylized enough, in terms of culture and period, to carry the weight of past ages of formal esthetic moulding and polishing and to speak with cadences and lines grown powerful by long usage.

These prescriptions I am giving are of the sort which can be derived from the scientific comparison of cultures; they are prescriptions for conditions. So one may compare ages and countries in which a particular art or science has flourished with those in which they have not so flourished, dissect out what appear to be the facilitating conditions, list and describe them.

Possibly all these may be necessary but not sufficient causes. Yet it is by the specification and attempted realization of conditions within which events desired and deemed necessary may occur that the sciences that deal with man can work in the world, stating conditions within which a child can grow, an idea can take root, an institution can flourish, and a man's hand and eye can grow cunning, his mind sharp, and his imagination wide. Though we remain dependent upon the caliber of individuals for our great achievements, the contrasts between one culture and another —between peoples whose every movement is a work of art and peoples, of the same human species, who limit their artistry to a few scratches on the edge of a pot—leave little doubt that the cultural conditions for any kind of creativity are very important. And as, by the scientific comparative study of cultures, we learn more about them, we can turn from hand-wringing, viewing with alarm, and the role of Cassandra to build the world closer to our heart's desire.

What, then, may the conditions be within which we may foster more vivid utopias? Three resources which seem accessible to us with our present knowledge are these: the imaginations of little children, where each newborn child brings a unique and new potential to our perception and ordering of the world; the provision of materials from other cultures, so that in the interplay between the great achievements of the human race in the many separate, unique, but comparable cultures men have built, new combinations and forms may occur; and the creation of conditions within which those who know the possibilities for the future, which are emerging from scientific discoveries, can combine their insights with the insights of those who know the full and astounding range of what man has achieved in the past, without mutations or the hypertrophies of extrasensory perception currently invoked by the creators of our folklore of the future, the writers of science fiction.

The imaginative capacities of young children, initially part of the processes of growth and evolution, as Edith Cobb has phrased it, are then one source to which we must turn. Within the growing child, the capacity to bring order out of the perception of the outside world and the capacity to create something unique and new out of his perception of himself in the world are, initially, two parts of one process. Concentration on one at the expense of the other robs the child, and so the world, of what could have come from both.

The current experiments of Jean Piaget and Barbel Inhelder, in Geneva, provide a vivid illustration of these two approaches. Piaget and Inhelder have developed a set of experiments to test the child's growing capacity to recognize some of the principles essential to scientific thought. One of these, which Piaget calls "reversibility," is exemplified in the child's recognition that when a large, round lump of clay is thinned out to a narrow cylinder, it will still have the same weight and be the same amount of clay. When these experiments are reported only in words, with the emphasis placed upon growth, with chronological age and school training, of the ability to recognize such points, the *other* things the child does are catalogued simply as failure. But when a method of reporting is used which records the entire behavior of children at different ages—through sound film, film and tape, or the verbatim recording of words—then the whole child comes into the picture and we see something else.

Thus, in the test situation the child is presented with a laboratory apparatus by which a colored fluid can be released gradually from the upper glass chamber, through a cock, into a glass below. The child is shown how this works and is allowed to try it. Then he is given series of cards picturing the state of the apparatus before any fluid enters the glass, at various stages, and, finally, when all of it has entered the glass. The card series are presented to the child in a scrambled state, and the child is asked to arrange them. One little boy, whose achievement on the test—like that of many children of his age—would have been reported as "failure," made a response which can be described as poetic as he "rhymed" the cards instead of arranging them to represent the reality of colored water passing into a glass in an orderly way. Using the same materials, he drew on another capacity of his mind. Had this been a class in "design" or in "making pleasing patterns," his answer would have been the "right" answer, whereas when he was being tested for ability to use a kind of thinking basic to modern science, it was a "wrong" answer.

In the kind of training given in European schools of the Swiss type, the child has to learn to handle this kind of reversibility after first encountering a world in which rigid one-way sequences in behavior and among material things have been heavily emphasized. By contrast, it is the problem of how to handle rigid sequences—which cannot be reversed in fact, however they may be reversed in thought—that must be learned by the first generation of a people who encounter factory methods, people who have arranged life in their heads in poetic patterns and who have not been told that this is the "wrong" answer. Recently I saw a group of educated men and women who had been presented with some simple problems in building manifolds by means of brightly colored units; the men classified the exercise as "art" and, although they were much better in mathematics and science in college than the women, failed, while the women, who also classified the exercise as "art," at which they thought themselves good, succeeded easily. By failing to cultivate both sides of the child's ability, by opposing them and negating one or the other, we are losing not only artists but also scientists, and we are splitting our society, as well as our individual children, into incompatible parts, destructively at war with each other. A different type of education, which recognizes the early stage in which children can apprehend form through color and kinesthetic feel and the recognition of sets, is a precondition for preserving the creativity with which each generation of newborn children enters the world.

The second necessary condition, a knowledge of what men have done before, again involves the presentation of wholes—not the current split between the history of science and technology, on the one hand, and art museums and literature courses, on the other. In real life the imagination of the painter and the poet are essential to the conditions within which the scientist works, for the fearful presage of the poet reaches ahead of invention. A few years ago an attempt was made to design an exhibition which would show the effect upon painting of modern scientific invention in building design; but in looking at the materials it was discovered that in every case the painter's vision had preceded the necessary technological invention, as the myth of Icarus preceded the Wright brothers. So we need arrangements which will bring together, for the experience of the student and the adult, whole historic periods—their buildings and their ideas, their books and their economics, their painting and their technology, their mathematics and their poetry—so that out of the perceived relationships and comparisons among them new ideas may be born and the present ignorance among scientists of man's past and present greatness, surpassed only by the ignorance among most humanists and many artists of man's future, made possible by science, may be overcome.

Finally, it seems to me, in this age when the very survival of the human race and possibly of all living creatures depends upon our having a vision of the future for others which will command our deepest commitment, we need in our universities, which must change and grow with the world, not only chairs of history and comparative linguistics, of literature and art—which deal with the past and sometimes with the present —but we need also Chairs of the Future, chairs for those who will devote themselves, with all the necessary scholarship and attention, to developing science to the full extent of its possibilities for the future, and who will devote themselves as faithfully to the fine detail of what man might very well—in the light of all our knowledge—be as any classicist or medievalist devotes himself to the text of Pindar and Horace or to the thought of St. Thomas Aquinas.

Isaac Asimov

IS ANYONE THERE?

Dear Mr. Burnett:

I am best-known as a science fiction writer, though for twelve years now I have written scarcely any science fiction. Perhaps that is just, though, for even in my present incarnation as a non-fiction writer and a sober-sided expositor of "straight science," I am only truly happy when that science is science-fictional in flavor.

And it is one of the delights of the changes that have taken place over the last few decades that the touch that was once at home in a few wild-eyed magazines only, can now be introduced everywhere.

What, for instance, can be more science-fictional in atmosphere than the possibility of intelligent life elsewhere in the universe? And where, in the 1930s (when I first began writing) might one legitimately have speculated on the possibility of communicating with unseen civilizations in the sky, outside the science fiction magazines?

Well, the following article (which I consider particularly representative of my work because it is thoroughly scientific in basis, yet purely science-fictional in flavor) originally appeared in 1964 in no less an outlet than *The New York Times.**

How, in a nutshell, can one more spectacularly indicate, from the vantagepoint of the 1960s, the vast expansion of man's outlook on the universe since the 1930s?

Isaac Asimov

---

* This article appeared under the title of "Hello CTA-21—Is Anyone There?" in *The New York Times Magazine*, November 29, 1964.

> *Sit, Jessica. Look how the floor of heaven*
> *Is thick inlaid with patines of bright gold:*
> *There's not the smallest orb which thou behold'st*
> *But in his motion like an angel sings,*
> *Still quiring to the young-eyed cherubins.*
> *Such harmony is in immortal souls;*
> *But whilst this muddy vesture of decay*
> *Doth grossly close it in, we cannot hear it.*

Thus spoke Lorenzo in Shakespeare's *The Merchant of Venice,* as he yearned to hear the music of the spheres, and knew he could not.

Since Shakespeare's time, man has overcome part of the handicap of his "muddy vesture of decay" by means of new instruments: telescopes, spectroscopes, cameras, and microwave amplifiers. Now we can pick up the singing of the orbs in a very literal way, for the universe broadcasts radio waves. Translated into sound, they seem to make a coarse and rasping static, but to the ravished ears of astronomers, the crackling is angelic indeed.

From some invisible spots in the heavens come waves not quite like those in others. Two such spots were first observed in 1960 and later included in a listing of heavenly radio sources drawn up by the California Institute of Technology. From their numbers on that list, the sources in question are called CTA-21 and CTA-102. In 1963, a team of Anglo-American astronomers pointed out these sources as worthy of special study, and in October 1964, a leading Soviet astronomer, Nikolai S. Kardashev, supplied some of that study.

He came to the conclusion that the natural phenomena of the inanimate universe might not be responsible for the broadcasts from CTA-21 and CTA-102. Instead, he suggested, it was just conceivable that we might be observing radio beacons sent out by intelligent beings of high technological proficiency.

Should this be dismissed at once as fantasy? Not at all! Highly unlikely, of course (as Kardashev would himself admit), but not fantasy. Since World War II, astronomers have grown more and more convinced that somewhere out in the infinite depths of space are, indeed, other intelligences. This has come about chiefly because of changing theories concerning the origin of the solar system, and life.

There are two general kinds of theories about the origin of the solar system: catastrophic and evolutionary. According to the first, as two stars pass close to each other, huge tides of matter are pulled out of each star and these condense to form planets. According to the second, a star is formed out of a huge cloud of swirling dust and gas, and out of the material at the edges of this cloud, planets are automatically formed as a star takes shape at the center.

During the first half of the 20th century, the catastrophic theory was generally accepted. As the nature of the interior of stars came to be better understood, however, astronomers threw it out. Material pulled from the sun by an approaching star could not condense to form planets. The extruded material would be too hot.

In 1944, a German astronomer, Carl F. von Weizäcker, put forth a new version of the evolutionary theory which met with wide approval. Astronomers may argue over just how to modify it to meet various difficulties but virtually all agree, now, that some version of the evolutionary theory is the most useful way of looking at the matter.

This has an important bearing on the question of whether other intelligent creatures exist. If planets originate in catastrophes, then there can be very few of them in the universe, for stars virtually never come close to each other.

If, however, planets originate as part of the natural evolutionary changes undergone in the formation of a star, then they must be exceedingly common. Practically every star ought to have a train of planets—and this is what astronomers now believe.

How many of these planets are sufficiently like the earth, however, to qualify as possible abodes of life as we know it? Dr. Stephen H. Dole of the Rand Corporation has tried to answer that question on the basis of present knowledge.

In our own galaxy, the Milky Way, he points out, there exist an estimated 135 billion stars. Of these, however, only stars of a certain size range would make suitable suns for planets like ours. Particular planets would have to be of a certain size, a certain distance from the star, turn with a certain period of rotation, and so on, before they could be truly "earthlike."

Taking all reasonable considerations into account, Dr. Dole concludes that there are some 640 million earthlike planets scattered here and there in our own galaxy.

If these earthlike planets are distributed evenly throughout our galaxy, then the nearest would be 27 light-years away (a distance equal to 150 million million miles). Within 100 light-years of earth, in all directions, there might be as many as 50 earthlike planets.

Could these planets bear life? Right now the conclusion is: Yes, almost certainly. Recent experiments seem to show that life is no rare accident arising out of an unusual combination of chemicals, but that it would tend to originate anywhere where the conditions were similar to those on the primordial earth.

But how many of these planets would bear *intelligent* life?

Ah, there science is still stumped completely. There is no way of telling. Life on earth existed for some two or three billion years before an intelligent species developed. And might this not have been but a rare and lucky accident? Might it not be far more likely that life might have continued throughout the entire lifetime of a planet without happening to develop intelligence?

We don't know the answer to that (and Dr. Dole ventures no guesses), but even if intelligence rose only on one out of a million life-bearing planets, there might still be nearly a thousand intelligent species scattered throughout the galaxy. And if this is so, then the activities of some of them may give them away, if we listen carefully enough and subtly enough—especially if, for some reason, they are trying to make themselves heard. It is not likely that we will hear anything by listening to the universe; but it is not impossible, either.

If we wanted to send a message to some life form on a planet circling another star, or to receive a message from it, some signal that could reach across vast gulfs of space is necessary. We ourselves receive three types of such signals from outer space. They are (1) gravitational effects, (2) streams of subatomic particles, and (3) electromagnetic radiation.

Of these three, gravitational force reaches us most strongly from the sun and the moon. Our path about the sun is in response to its giant pull, and the ocean tides rise in response to the moon's.

The weaker pulls of Venus and Mars can be detected in small variations in the moon's motion.

However, gravitational force is the weakest force in nature, and it reaches us from other stars with an intensity so weak that there is no practical way of detecting it. Nor could we send out a useful gravitational beam even if it were a stronger force than it is, since we know of no practical way of turning gravity on and off in order to send out a gravitation dot-dash code, for instance.

Streams of subatomic particles (objects far smaller even than atoms) reach us in the form of protons and electrons from the sun and in the form of cosmic rays (very high energy protons and still more massive electrically charged particles) from farther out in space. We can produce streams of such particles easily enough and turn them on and off, too, but only in small quantities.

Even if we could produce them in mighty streams with a force that would squirt them from star to star, we couldn't send them outward in a smoothly aimed line. The paths of electrically charged particles would curve and veer whenever they passed through the magnetic fields that are so thickly strewn through space. Furthermore, they, together with most uncharged particles, would be absorbed and changed by the atmosphere that would undoubtedly surround an earthlike planet.

One type of subatomic particle, the neutrino, suffers from none of these disadvantages. It could be made to travel in a straight line from star to star, and would be affected by neither gravity, magnetic fields, or atmospheres. Unfortunately, this particle is nearly impossible to detect.

That leaves electromagnetic radiation, of which two types penetrate our atmosphere. One is ordinary light and the other high-frequency radio waves of a type usually termed "microwaves." Both are easy to produce, easy to detect, are not affected by magnetic fields or atmospheres, and, in short, are nearly ideal for the purpose.

Of the two, light might seem to be the first choice. You can easily imagine a huge searchlight sending out flashes in Morse code toward the stars. There are some basic difficulties to this, however.

First, there are a great many light sources in the galaxy, considering its billions of stars, so that one dim signal would be lost among them. In particular, the light originating on some far-off planet, would be bound to be blotted out by the superior light of the planet's own sun. To be sure, one could argue around this. Suppose the beacon light were that of a gigantic laser. The characteristic light of a laser could be differentiated from that of stars and, indeed, the mere existence of laser light might well be considered a sign of intelligence at the other end. An even more daring suggestion is that a sufficiently advanced civilization might learn to use the stars themselves as beacons. Thus, some of the quasars vary in light intensity with time. Could some superbeings be using them to send a kind of Morse code? Not at all likely, I hasten to emphasize, but very interesting to think about.

Another difficulty with light, however, is that it cannot penetrate great thicknesses of dust and our neighborhood of the galaxy is pretty dusty. We cannot see the glorious burst of light of the billions of stars in the core of our galaxy, for instance. Dust clouds block it off.

That leaves microwaves. These penetrate dust clouds nicely, and we can detect microwaves coming from the core of our galaxy without trouble.

The sources of microwaves in the sky ("radio sources," some of which are visible by the light they also emit, but most of which have not yet been associated with visible objects) are far fewer than are the sources of light. That makes an oddly behaving radio source far easier to spot. Furthermore, a strong radio source on a planet is not likely to be blotted out by the sun of that planet, for few stars are strong microwave emitters.

It is easy to measure the length of the individual waves of the microwave beam arriving from outer space. From most radio sources, this "wavelength" is a matter of feet and yards. However, for purposes of communication, it would be better to use shorter microwaves. It is suggested that wavelengths of 3 to 6 inches would be ideal. Such waves would be least likely to undergo distortion or interference on long voyages or to be drowned out by natural sources of microwaves.

That is why the emissions of CTA-21 and CTA-102 rouse such interest. The microwaves received from these sources are chiefly in the 4- to 20-inch range, with a peak at about 12 inches or so. This isn't quite ideal, but it is fairly close, much closer than is true for other sources. Furthermore, as best astronomers can tell, those microwaves arise from a tiny "point-source" in the heavens, as though they were originating from planets. In the case of the usual radio source, the origin is more extended, indicating the source to be a large volume of gas.

If, indeed, the microwave emissions of CTA-21 and CTA-102 are the product of intelligent life, then they must represent civilizations far more advanced than our own.

Right now, mankind on earth is producing power at the rate of 4 billion kilowatts. Even if all of this were poured into a microwave beacon and sent out into space it would not suffice. The beacon would spread out and grow dilute, even though it were made as coherent as possible, and by the time even the nearest intelligent beings had been reached, it would have grown too feeble to detect. To produce beacons strong enough to detect would require a civilization capable of wielding far more energy than we do.

Mankind's energy output is growing at the rate of 3 to 4 percent a year. If nothing happens to interfere with this, then in a matter of 3,200 years we will be producing energy at the rate of the sun and we could then announce our own existence with beams that will stretch through the length and breadth of our galaxy. And if we can detect the beams of other life forms *now,* then those life forms must be at least several thousand years ahead of us in technology.

To be sure, one ought not to take too seriously the specific cases of CTA-21 and CTA-102. They are enormously distant objects that are probably quasars, and no doubt their microwave radiation can be explained without having to assume intelligences out there.

Still, suppose some intelligence on some fairly nearby star *is* trying to reach us. Or suppose we try to reach them. What is there to say in the announcements being sent out or received? We can't really use Morse code or expect any foreign intelligence to speak English. We must find something universally understandable. We could assume, for instance, that the people of any supercivilization would understand mathematics and that whatever mathematical statements are true here are also true there.

For instance, suppose we sent out two pulses of microwaves, followed by two more and then by four. Then, after a longer pause, we send out first three, then three, then nine, then go back to the first group, and so on. We would have the following messages: 2,2,4 ... 3,3,9 ... 2,2,4 ... 3,3,9 ... and so on.

If then, from somewhere out in space, we got the message, 4,4,16, even once, we would have successfully established communication.

Or we might try the universal language of chemistry. There are a fixed number of types of stable atoms that should be the same all over the universe. Each different type is made up of a definite combination of two kinds of particles: protons and neutrons.

The simplest, hydrogen-1, is composed of a single proton, while the next, hydrogen-2, has a proton plus a neutron. We can therefore send out numbers representing the structure of the different atoms in order of increasing complexity. We could start with hydrogen-1 (1) and hydrogen-2 (1-1). We could then go on to helium-3 (2-1), helium-4 (2-2), lithium-6 (3-3) and lithium-7 (3-4).

Suppose then we repeat the number combination 1 . . . 1-1 . . . 2-1 . . . 2-2 . . . 3-3 . . . 3-4 . . . over and over again. Some alien intelligence receiving this series of number combinations might recognize it as representing the structure of the first few simple atoms and return signals for the next atoms in line: beryllium-9 (4-5) and boron-10 (5-5). If they did so, we would have established communication.

Or we might try the geometric approach. We might send out a string of rapid pulses among which there was, periodically, a pulse of a special kind. There would follow a pause, then another string, and so on. Each string would have a somewhat different pattern of special pulses.

If the strings are recorded one under the other, the special pulses might combine to form a circle or some other pattern. In this way, simple geometric theorems could be transmitted; a right triangle with squares built on each side would indicate that the square of the hypotenuse is equal to the sum of the squares of the legs.

Even simple cartoons might be sent in this way, cartoons which might indicate that human beings had four limbs and stood on two of them; that they existed as two sexes, and so on. If the answer came in similar cartoons we would *really* be in communication.

Such communication would be exceedingly slow, of course, since a planet capable of answering could be anywhere in our galaxy, up to thousands of light-years away. Suppose that the intelligence we detect is 500 light-years away, a supposition which, if anything, errs on the side of optimism.

In that case, radio waves, or any other conceivable form of information-carrying signal, must take fully 500 years to travel from here to there. Another 500 years will pass before the answer will travel from there to here.

Of what use would a dialogue be in which individual remarks take place at intervals of a thousand years?

In the first place, the mere fact that the dialogue exists at all would be of tremendous importance. Mankind will know itself *not* to be the only intelligence or even (very likely) the greatest intelligence in the universe, and this is bound to have a profound effect on religion and philosophy, and on our very approach to the world about us.

In the second place, neither we nor they need wait for an answer to continue talking. We can well vary our messages at will once we have established our communication. They will do the same and the end result will be a complex conversation consisting of comments intended for answer in the future, and answers for comments in the past.

Nor will the wait have to be useless. It can be extremely fruitful. If we send out simple cartoons, we can accompany each with the equivalent of a Morse code signal. A cartoon of a man would be accompanied by MAN. Men in different attitudes could be MAN WALK, MAN STAND, and whatever else ingenuity might suggest.

In 500 years we could send out a great many signals and if the intelligence we reach is superior to our own, there should be no trouble in their breaking our code. Given a certain vocabulary to begin with, they may even require no further pictures, but be able to deduce the meaning of words they don't understand from words they do.

When the 500 years are up and they start responding, we may well find that they have caught on quite quickly and after only a single century, perhaps, they will have switched to straight English. (Or straight Russian, perhaps?)

It is possible that even the simple forms of communciation with which intelligences must start may yet serve as cross-fertilization in the realm of ideas. If we list the proton-neutron combinations of the atoms, they may respond, eventually, with a somewhat different listing of the atoms and in puzzling out the new listing we might, conceivably, see a regularity that now escapes us.

It is not even necessary to suppose direct and specific information. The mere fact of interstellar communication may help advance our technology. The effort to send out stronger and stronger beams with greater efficiency, or to detect weaker and weaker ones, will encourage advances that may have application in fields far removed from that of interstellar communication.

Then, too, the effort to concentrate as much information into as few symbols as possible will encourage us to concentrate even more intensely on information theory. In attempting to reach the alien minds of intelligent beings many light-years away, we may better fit ourselves for communicating with dolphins here on earth. More important still, man may even learn how to communicate effectively with his fellow man. That consequence alone would justify almost any conceivable effort put into an attempt to contact aliens.

One question remains: Is it dangerous? Is it wise to draw the attention of some supercivilization to ourselves? What if chimpanzees somehow drew our attention to a fertile continent on which they were the highest form of life? Would we not take over that continent, wiping out the chimpanzees without a qualm if we felt like doing so?

Well, 500 light-years is a long distance to cross at any level of technology, for every crossing would take an absolute minimum of 500 years of earth time. Distance alone would probably save us.

Then, too, why ought we to be so certain that an alien intelligence would find nothing better to do than to destroy us? Even we ourselves, a species capable of perpetrating the Nazi horrors, have reached the point where many of us feel twinges of regret over the extinction of any form of even nonintelligent life, and would go to great lengths to prevent unnecessary interference with chimpanzees in their native habitat. Are supercivilizations to be less decent than our imperfect selves? No! I rather feel that a contact of minds across the great gaps of space could result only in good, not in evil.

X
Art and the Symbol

Mary McCarthy

SETTLING THE COLONEL'S HASH

Dear Whit Burnett:
 For me, being asked to make such a selection is like choosing
among your children. So I'm leaving the decision to the editors.*

Sincerely,
Mary McCarthy

 * This was given first as a talk at the Breadloaf School of English, in Middle-
bury, Vermont.

Some years ago, when I taught in a progressive college, I had a pretty girl student in one of my classes who wanted to be a short-story writer. She was not studying writing with me, but she knew that I sometimes wrote short stories, and one day, breathless and glowing, she came up to me in the hall, to tell me that she had just written a story that her writing teacher, a Mr. Converse, was terribly excited about. "He thinks it's wonderful," she said, "and he's going to help me fix it up for publication."

I asked what the story was about; the girl was a rather simple being who loved clothes and dates. Her answer had a deprecating tone. It was just about a girl (herself) and some sailors she had met on the train. But then her face, which had looked perturbed for a moment, gladdened.

"Mr. Converse is going over it with me and we're going to put in the symbols."

Another girl in the same college, when asked by us in her sophomore orals why she read novels (one of the pseudo-profound questions that ought never to be put) answered in a defensive flurry: "Well, of course I don't read them to find out what happens to the hero."

At the time, I thought these notions were peculiar to progressive education: it was old-fashioned or regressive to read a novel to find out what happens to the hero or to have a mere experience empty of symbolic pointers. But I now discover that this attitude is quite general, and that readers and students all over the country are in a state of apprehension, lest they read a book or story literally and miss the presence of a symbol. And like everything in America, this search for meanings has become a socially competitive enterprise; the best reader is the one who detects the most symbols in a given stretch of prose. And the benighted reader who fails to find any symbols humbly assents when they are pointed out to him; he accepts his mortification.

I had no idea how far this process had gone until last spring, when I began to get responses to a story I had published in *Harper's*. I say "story" because that was what it was called by *Harper's*. I myself would not know quite what to call it; it was a piece of reporting or a fragment of autobiography—an account of my meeting with an anti-Semitic army colonel. It began in the club car of a train going to St. Louis; I was wearing an apple-green shirtwaist and a dark-green skirt and pink earrings, we got into an argument about the Jews. The colonel was a rather dapper, flashy kind of Irish-American with a worldly blue eye; he took me, he said, for a sculptress, which made me feel, to my horror, that I looked Bohemian and therefore rather suspect. He was full of the usual profound clichés that anti-Semites air, like original epigrams, about the Jews: that he could tell a Jew, that they were different from other people, that you couldn't trust them in business, that some of his best friends were Jews, that he distinguished between a Jew and a kike, and finally that, of course, he didn't agree with Hitler: Hitler went too far; the Jews were human beings.

All the time we talked, and I defended the Jews, he was trying to get my angle, as he called it; he thought it was abnormal for anybody who wasn't Jewish not to feel as he did. As a matter of fact, I have a Jewish grandmother, but I decided to keep this news to myself: I did not want the colonel to think that I had any interested reason for speaking on behalf of the Jews, that is, that I was prejudiced. In the end, though, I got my comeuppance. Just as we were parting, the colonel asked me my married name, which is Broadwater, and the whole mystery was cleared up for him, instantly; he supposed I was married to a Jew and that the name was spelled B-r-o-d-w-a-t-e-r. I did not try to enlighten him; I let him think what he wanted; in a certain sense, he was right; he had unearthed my Jewish grandmother or her equivalent. There were a few details that I must mention to make the next part clear: in my car, there were two nuns, whom I talked to as a distraction from the colonel

and the moral problems he raised. He and I finally had lunch together in the St. Louis railroad station, where we continued the discussion. It was a very hot day. I had a sandwich; he had roast-
beef hash. We both had an old-fashioned.

The whole point of this "story" was that it really happened; it
is written in the first person; I speak of myself in my own name,
McCarthy; at the end, I mention my husband's name, Broadwater.
When I was thinking about writing the story, I decided not to treat
if fictionally; the chief interest, I felt, lay in the fact that it happened, in real life, last summer, to the writer herself, who was a
good deal at fault in the incident. I wanted to embarrass myself and,
if possible, the reader too.

Yet, strangely enough, many of my readers preferred to think of
this account as fiction. I still meet people who ask me, confidentially,
"That story of yours about the colonel—was it really true?" It seemed
to them perfectly natural that I would write a fabrication, in which
I figured under my own name, and sign it, though in my eyes this
would be like perjuring yourself in court or forging checks. Shortly
after the "story" was published, I got a kindly letter from a man
in Mexico, in which he criticized the menu from an artistic point
of view: he thought salads would be better for hot weather and it
would be more in character for the narrator-heroine to have a Martini. I did not answer the letter, though I was moved to, because
I had the sense that he would not understand the distinction between
what *ought* to have happened and what *did* happen.

Then in April I got another letter, from an English teacher in
a small college in the Middle West, that reduced me to despair. I
am going to cite it at length.

"My students in freshman English chose to analyze your story,
'Artists in Uniform,' from the March issue of *Harper's*. For a week
I heard oral discussions on it and then the students wrote critical
analyses. In so far as it is possible, I stayed out of their discussions,
encouraging them to read the story closely with your intentions as
a guide to their understanding. Although some of them insisted that
the story has no other level than the realistic one, most of them decided it has symbolic overtones.

"The question is: how closely do you want the symbols labeled?
They wrestled with the nuns, the author's two shades of green with

pink accents, with the 'materialistic godlessness' of the colonel. . . .
A surprising number wanted exact symbols; for example, they searched
for the significance of the colonel's eating hash and the author eating
a sandwich. . . . From my standpoint, the story was an entirely
satisfactory springboard for understanding the various shades of prejudice, for seeing how much of the artist goes into his painting. If
it is any satisfaction to you, our campus was alive with discussions
about 'Artists in Uniform.' We liked the story and we thought it
amazing that an author could succeed in making readers dislike the
author—for a purpose, of course!"

I probably should have answered this letter, but I did not. The gulf
seemed to me too wide. I could not applaud the backward students
who insisted that the story has no other level than the realistic one
without giving offense to their teacher, who was evidently a well-
meaning person. But I shall try now to address a reply, not to this
teacher and her unfortunate class, but to a whole school of misunderstanding. There were no symbols in this story; there was no deeper level.
The nuns were in the story because they were on the train; the contrasting
greens were the dress I happened to be wearing; the colonel had hash
because he had hash; materialistic godlessness meant just what it means
when a priest thunders it from the pulpit—the phrase, for the first time,
had meaning for me as I watched and listened to the colonel.

But to clarify the misunderstanding, one must go a little further and
try to see what a literary symbol is. Now in one sense, the colonel's
hash and my sandwich can be regarded as symbols; that is, they typify
the colonel's food tastes and mine. (The man in Mexico had different
food tastes which he wished to interpose into our reality.) The hash and
the sandwich might even be said to show something very obvious about
our characters and bringing-up, or about our sexes; I was a woman, he
was a man. And though on another day I might have ordered hash
myself, that day I did not, because the colonel and I, in our disagreement, were polarizing each other.

The hash and the sandwich, then, could be regarded as symbols of
our disagreement, almost conscious symbols. And underneath our discussion of the Jews, there was a thin sexual current running, as there
always is in such random encounters or pickups (for they have a strong
suggestion of the illicit). The fact that I ordered something conventionally
feminine and he ordered something conventionally masculine represented,

no doubt, our awareness of a sexual possibility; even though I was not attracted to the colonel, nor he to me, the circumstances of our meeting made us define ourselves as a woman and a man.

The sandwich and the hash were our provisional, *ad hoc* symbols of ourselves. But in this sense all human actions are symbolic because they represent the person who does them. If the colonel had ordered a fruit salad with whipped cream, this too would have represented him in some way; given his other traits, it would have pointed to a complexity in his character that the hash did not suggest.

In the same way, the contrasting greens of my dress were a symbol of my taste in clothes and hence representative of me—all too representative, I suddenly saw, in the club car, when I got an "artistic" image of myself flashed back at me from the men's eyes. I had no wish to stylize myself as an artist, that is, to parade about as a symbol of flamboyant un-conventionality, but apparently I had done so unwittingly when I picked those colors off a rack, under the impression that they suited me or "expressed my personality" as salesladies say.

My dress, then, was a symbol of the perplexity I found myself in with the colonel; I did not want to be categorized as a member of a peculiar minority—an artist or a Jew; but brute fate and the colonel kept resolutely cramming me into both those uncomfortable pigeonholes. I wished to be regarded as ordinary or rather as universal, to be anybody and therefore everybody (that is, in one sense, I wanted to be on the colonel's side, majestically above minorities); but every time the colonel looked at my dress and me in it with my pink earrings I shrank to minority status, and felt the dress in the heat shriveling me, like the shirt of Nessus, the centaur, that consumed Hercules.

But this is not what the students meant when they wanted the symbols "labeled." They were searching for a more recondite significance than that afforded by the trite symbolism of ordinary life, in which a dress is a social badge. They supposed that I was engaging in literary or artificial symbolism, which would lead the reader out of the confines of reality into the vast fairy tale of myth, in which the color green would have an emblematic meaning (or did the two greens signify for them what the teacher calls "shades" of prejudice), and the colonel's hash, I imagine, would be some sort of Eucharistic mincemeat.

Apparently, the presence of the nuns assured them there were over-tones of theology; it did not occur to them (a) that the nuns were there because pairs of nuns are a standardized feature of summer Pull-man travel, like crying babies, and perspiring businessmen in the club car, and (b) that if I thought the nuns worth mentioning, it was also because of something very simple and directly relevant: the nuns and the colonel and I all had something in common—we had all at one time been Catholics—and I was seeking common ground with the colonel, from which to turn and attack his position.

In any account of reality, even a televised one, which comes closest to being a literal transcript or replay, some details are left out as irrelevant (though nothing is really irrelevant). The details that are not eliminated have to stand as symbols of the whole, like stenographic signs, and of course there is an art of selection, even in a newspaper account: the writer, if he has any ability, is looking for the revealing detail that will sum up the picture for the reader in a flash of recognition. But the art of abridgment and condensation, which is familiar to any-body who tries to relate an anecdote, or give a direction—the art of natural symbolism, which is at the basis of speech and all representation —has at bottom a centripetal intention. It hovers over an object, an event, or series of events and tries to declare what it is. Analogy (that is, comparison to other objects) is inevitably one of its methods. "The weather was soupy," i.e., like soup. "He wedged his way in," i.e., he had to enter, thin edge first, as a wedge enters, and so on. All this is obvious. But these metaphorical aids to communication are a far cry from literary symbolism, as taught in the schools and practiced by certain fashionable writers. Literary symbolism is centrifugal and flees from the object, the event, into the incorporeal distance, where concepts are taken for sub-stance and floating ideas and archetypes assume a hieratic authority. In this dream-forest, symbols become arbitrary; all counters are inter-changeable; anything can stand for anything else. The colonel's hash can be a Eucharist or a cannibal feast or the banquet of Atreus, or all three, so long as the actual dish set before the actual man is disparaged. What is depressing about this insistent symbolization is the fact that while it claims to lead to the infinite, it quickly reaches very finite limits —there are only so many myths on record, and once you have got through Bulfinch, the Scandinavian, and the Indian, there is not much left. And if all stories reduce themselves to myth and symbol, qualitative differences vanish, and there is only a single, monotonous story. American fiction of the symbolist school demonstrates this mournful truth, without precisely intending to. A few years ago, when the mode was at its height, chic novels and stories fell into three classes: those which had a Greek myth for their framework, which the reader was supposed to detect, like finding the faces in the clouds in old newspaper puzzle contests; those which had symbolic modern figures, dwarfs, hermaphrodites, and cripples, illustrating maiming and loneliness; and those which contained symbolic animals, cougars, wild cats, and monkeys. One young novelist, a product of the Princeton school of symbolism, had all three elements going at once, like the ringmaster of a three-ring circus, with the freaks, the animals, and the statues.

The quest for symbolic referents had as its object, of course, the deepening of the writer's subject and the reader's awareness. But the result was paradoxical. At the very moment when American writing was penetrated by the symbolic urge, it ceased to be able to create symbols of its own. Babbitt, I suppose, was the last important symbol to be created by an American writer; he gave his name to a type that henceforth would be recognizable to everybody. He passed into the language. The same thing could be said, perhaps, though to a lesser degree, of Caldwell's Tobacco Road, Eliot's Prufrock, and possibly of Faulkner's Snopeses. The discovery of new symbols is not the only function of a writer, but the writer who cares about this must be fascinated by reality itself, as a butterfly collector is fascinated by the glimpse of a new specimen. Such a specimen was Mme. Bovary or M. Homais or M. de Charlus or Jupien; these specimens were precious to their discoverers, not because they repeated an age-old pattern but because their markings were new. Once the specimen has been described, the public instantly spots other examples of the kind, and the world seems suddenly full of Babbitts and Charlus, where none had been noted before.

A different matter was Joyce's Mr. Bloom. Mr. Bloom can be called a symbol of eternal recurrence—the wandering Jew, Ulysses the voyager— but he is a symbol thickly incarnate, fleshed out in a Dublin advertising canvasser. He is not *like* Ulysses or vaguely suggestive of Ulysses; he is Ulysses, circa 1905. Joyce evidently believed in a cyclical theory of history, in which everything repeated itself; he also subscribed in youth to the doctrine that declares that the Host, a piece of bread, is also God's body and blood. How it can be both things at the same time, transubstantially, is a mystery, and Mr. Bloom is just such a mystery: Ulysses in the visible appearance of a Dublin advertising canvasser.

Mr. Bloom is not a symbol of Ulysses, but Ulysses-Bloom together, one and indivisible, symbolize or rather demonstrate eternal recurrence. I hope I make myself clear. The point is transubstantiation: Bloom and Ulysses are transfused into each other and neither reality is diminished. Both realities are locked together, like the protons and neutrons of an atom.

Finnegans Wake is a still more ambitious attempt to create a fusion, this time a myriad fusion, and to exemplify the mystery of how a thing can be itself and at the same time be something else. The world is many and it is also one.

But the clarity and tension of Joyce's thought brought him closer in a way to the strictness of allegory than to the diffuse practices of latter-day symbolists. In Joyce, the equivalences and analogies are very sharp and distinct, as in a pun, and the real world is almost querulously audible, like the voices of the washerwomen on the Liffey that come into Earwicker's dream. But this is not true of Joyce's imitators or of the imitators of his imitators, for whom reality is only a shadowy pretext for the introduction of a whole *corps de ballet* of dancing symbols in mythic draperies and animal skins.

Let me make a distinction. There are some great writers, like Joyce or Melville, who have consciously introduced symbolic elements into their work; and there are great writers who have written fables or allegories. In both cases, the writer makes it quite clear to the reader how he is to be read; only an idiot would take *Pilgrim's Progress* for a realistic story, and even a young boy, reading *Moby Dick,* realizes that there is something more than whale-fishing here, though he may not be able to name what it is. But the great body of fiction contains only what I have called natural symbolism, in which selected events represent or typify a problem, a kind of society or psychology, a philosophical theory, in the same way that they do in real life. What happens to the hero becomes of the highest importance. This symbolism needs no abstruse interpretation, and abstruse interpretation will only lead the reader away from the reality that the writer is trying to press on his attention.

I shall give an example or two of what I mean by natural symbolism and I shall begin with a rather florid one: Henry James' *The Golden Bowl*. This is the story of a rich American girl who collects European objects. One of these objects is a husband, Prince Amerigo, who proves to be unfaithful. Early in the story, there is a visit to an antique shop in which the Prince picks out a gold bowl for his fiancée and finds, to his annoyance, that it is cracked. It is not hard to see that the cracked bowl is a symbol, both of the Prince himself, who is a valuable antique but a little flawed, morally, and also of the marriage, which represents an act of acquisition or purchase on the part of the heroine and her father. If the reader should fail to notice the analogy, James calls his attention to it in the title.

I myself would not regard this symbol as necessary to this particular history; it seems to me, rather, an ornament of the kind that was fashionable in the architecture and interior decoration of the period, like stylized sheaves of corn or palms on the façade of a house. Nevertheless, it is handsome and has an obvious appropriateness to the theme. It introduces the reader into the Gilded Age attitudes of the novel. I think there is also a scriptural echo in the title that conveys the idea of punishment. But having seen and felt the weight of meaning that James put into this symbol, one must not be tempted to press further and look at the bowl as a female sex symbol, a chalice, a Holy Grail, and so on; a book is not a pious excuse for reciting a litany of associations.

My second example is from Tolstoy's *Anna Karenina*. Toward the beginning of the novel, Anna meets the man who will be her lover, Vronsky, on the Moscow-St. Petersburg express; as they meet, there has been an accident; a workman has been killed by the train. This is the beginning of Anna's doom, which is completed when she throws herself under a train and is killed; and the last we see of Vronsky is in a train, with a toothache; he is off to the wars. The train is necessary to the plot of the novel, and I believe it is also symbolic, both of the iron forces of material progress that Tolstoy hated so and that played a part in Anna's moral destruction, and also of those iron laws of necessity and consequence that govern human action when it remains on the sensual level.

One can read the whole novel, however, without being conscious that the train is a symbol; we do not have to "interpret" to feel the import of doom and loneliness in the train's whistle—the same import we ourselves can feel when we hear a train whistle blow in the country, even today. Tolstoy was a deeper artist than James, and we cannot be sure that the train was a conscious device with him. The appropriateness to Anna's history may have been only a *felt* appropriateness; everything in Tolstoy has such a supreme naturalness that one shrinks from attributing contrivance to him, as if it were a sort of fraud. Yet he worked very hard on his novels—I forget how many times Countess Tolstoy copied out *War and Peace* by hand.

The impression one gets from his diaries is that he wrote by ear; he speaks repeatedly, even as an old man, of having to start a story over again because he has the wrong tone, and I suspect that he did not think of the train as a symbol but that it sounded "right" to him, because it was, in that day, an almost fearsome emblem of ruthless and impersonal force, not only to a writer of genius but to the poorest peasant in the fields. And in Tolstoy's case I think it would be impossible, even for the most fanciful critic, to extricate the train from the novel and try to make it say something that the novel itself does not say directly. Every detail in Tolstoy has an almost cruel and viselike meaningfulness and truth to itself that make it tautological to talk of symbolism; he was a moralist and to him the tiniest action, even the curiosities of physical appearance, Vronsky's bald spot, the small white hands of Prince Andrei, told a moral tale.

It is now considered very old-fashioned and tasteless to speak of an author's "philosophy of life" as something that can be harvested from his work. Actually, most of the great authors did have a "philosophy of life" which they were eager to communicate to the public; this was one of their motives for writing. And to disentangle a moral philosophy from a work that evidently contains one is far less damaging to the author's purpose and the integrity of his art than to violate his imagery by symbol-hunting, as though reading a novel were a sort of paper-chase.

The images of a novel or a story belong, as it were, to a family, very closely knit and inseparable from each other; the parent "idea" of a story or a novel generates events and images all bearing a strong family resemblance. And to understand a story or a novel, you must look for the parent "idea," which is usually in plain view, if you read quite carefully and literally what the author says.

I will go back, for a moment, to my own story, to show how this can be done. Clearly, it is about the Jewish question, for that is what the people are talking about. It also seems to be about artists, since the title is "Artists in Uniform." Then there must be some relation between artists and Jews. What is it? They are both minorities that other people claim to be able to recognize by their appearance. But artists and Jews do not care for this categorization; they want to be universal, that is, like everybody else. They do not want to wear their destiny as a badge, as the soldier wears his uniform. But this aim is really hopeless, for life has formed them as Jews or artists, in a way that immediately betrays them to the majority they are trying to melt into. In my conversation with the colonel, I was endeavoring to play a double game. I was trying to force him into a minority by treating anti-Semitism as an aberration, which, in fact, I believe it is. On his side, the colonel resisted this attempt and tried to show that anti-Semitism was normal, and he was normal, while I was the queer one. He declined to be categorized as anti-Semite; he regarded himself as an independent thinker, who by a happy chance thought the same as everybody else.

I imagined I had a card up my sleeve; I had guessed that the colonel was Irish (i.e., that he belonged to a minority) and presumed that he was a Catholic. I did not see how he could possibly guess that I, with my Irish name and Irish appearance, had a Jewish grandmother in the background. Therefore when I found I had not convinced him by reasoning, I played my last card; I told him that the Church, his Church, forbade anti-Semitism. I went even further; I implied that God forbad it, though I had no right to do this, since I did not believe in God, but was only using Him as a whip to crack over the colonel, to make him feel humble and inferior, a raw Irish Catholic lad under discipline. But the colonel, it turned out, did not believe in God, either, and I lost. And since, in a sense, I had been cheating all along in this game we were playing, I had to concede the colonel a sort of moral victory in the end; I let him think that my husband was Jewish and that that "explained" everything satisfactorily.

Now there are a number of morals or meanings in this little tale, starting with the simple one: don't talk to strangers on a train. The chief moral or meaning (what I learned, in other words, from this experience) was this: you cannot be a universal unless you accept the fact that you are a singular, that is, a Jew or an artist or what-have-you. What the colonel and I were discussing, and at the same time illustrating and enacting, was the definition of a human being. I was trying to be something better than a human being; I was trying to be the voice of pure reason; and pride went before a fall. The colonel, without trying, was being something worse than a human being, and somehow we found ourselves on the same plane—facing each other, like mutually repellent twins. Or, put in another way: it is dangerous to be drawn into discussions of the Jews with anti-Semites: you delude yourself that you are spreading light, but you are really sinking into muck; if you endeavor to be dispassionate, you are really claiming for yourself a privileged position, a little mountain top, from which you look down, impartially, on both the Jews and the colonel.

Anti-Semitism is a horrible disease from which nobody is immune, and it has a kind of evil fascination that makes an enlightened person draw near the source of infection, supposedly in a scientific spirit, but really to sniff the vapors and dally with the possibility. The enlightened person who lunches with the colonel in order, as she tells herself, to improve him, is cheating herself, having her cake and eating it. This attempted cheat, on my part, was related to the question of the artist and the green dress; I wanted to be an artist but not to pay the price of looking like one, just as I was willing to have Jewish blood but not willing to show it, where it would cost me something—the loss of superiority in an argument.

These meanings are all there, quite patent, to anyone who consents to look *into* the story. They were *in* the experience itself, waiting to be found and considered. I did not perceive them all at the time the experience was happening; otherwise, it would not have taken place, in all probability —I should have given the colonel a wide berth. But when I went back over the experience, in order to write it, I came upon these meanings, protruding at me, as it were, from the details of the occasion. I put in the green dress and my mortification over it because they were part of the truth, just as it had occurred, but I did not see how they were related to the general question of anti-Semitism and my grandmother until they *showed* me their relation in the course of writing.

Every short story, at least for me, is a little act of discovery. A cluster of details presents itself to my scrutiny, like a mystery that I will understand in the course of writing or sometimes not fully until afterward, when, if I have been honest and listened to these details carefully, I will find that they are connected and that there is a coherent pattern. This pattern is *in* experience itself; you do not impose it from the outside and if you try to, you will find that the story is taking the wrong tack, dribbling away from you into artificiality or inconsequence. A story that you do not learn something from while you are writing it, that does not illuminate something for you, is dead, finished before you started it. The "idea" of a story is implicit in it, on the one hand; on the other hand, it is always ahead of the writer, like a form dimly discerned in the distance; he is working *toward* the "idea."

It can sometimes happen that you begin a story thinking that you know the "idea" of it and find, when you are finished, that you have said something quite different and utterly unexpected to you. Most writers have been haunted all their lives by the "idea" of a story or a novel that they think they want to write and see very clearly: Tolstoy always wanted to write a novel about the Decembrists and instead, almost against his will, wrote *War and Peace;* Henry James thought he wanted to write a novel about Napoleon. Probably these ideas for novels were too set in their creators' minds to inspire creative discovery.

In any work that is truly creative, I believe, the writer cannot be omniscient in advance about the effects that he proposes to produce. The suspense in a novel is not only in the reader, but in the novelist himself, who is intensely curious too about what will happen to the hero. Jane

Austen may know in a general way that Emma will marry Mr. Knightley in the end (the reader knows this too, as a matter of fact); the suspense for the author lies in the how, in the twists and turns of circumstance, waiting but as yet unknown, that will bring the consummation about. Hence, I would say to the student of writing that outlines, patterns, arrangements of symbols may have a certain usefulness at the outset for some kinds of minds, but in the end they will have to be scrapped. If the story does not contradict the outline, overrun the pattern, break the symbols, like an insurrection against authority, it is surely a still birth. The natural symbolism of reality has more messages to communicate than the dry Morse code of the disengaged mind.

The tree of life, said Hegel, is greener than the tree of thought; I have quoted this before but I cannot forbear from citing it again in this context. This is not an incitement to mindlessness or an endorsement of realism in the short story (there are several kinds of reality, including interior reality); it means only that the writer must be, first of all, a listener and observer, who can pay attention to reality, like an obedient pupil, and who is willing, always, to be surprised by the messages reality is sending through to him. And if he gets the messages correctly he will not have to go back and put in the symbols; he will find that the symbols are there, staring at him significantly from the commonplace.

Thornton Wilder

THE DRUNKEN SISTERS

The tragic poets of Greece did not merely have to submit three interrelated tragedies for a single morning's performance. The rules of the festivals required that the poets furnish an afterpiece called the satyr play. It was a reflection of the Greek sense of proportion that after those hours of horror and awe this afterpiece should be written in the comic spirit and should deal with some element in the plots of the preceding trilogy. Tradition says that Aeschylus and Sophocles and Euripides were great comic poets also, though very few of these satyr plays have survived. Having written a trilogy on the subject of the life of Alkestis, I then wrote this short play to follow it. The reader is reminded that when Admetos, King of Thessaly, lay at the point of death, a message came from Apollo's temple at Delphi saying that the King need not die if a volunteer could be found to die in his stead. His wife Alkestis offered her life; she died, but was later brought back from the underworld by Herakles. This play shows us how Apollo was able to obtain from the Fates that extension of Admetos' life.

Thornton Wilder

[*Enormous, the Fates.*
   They wear the masks of hags. They rock back and forth as they
work.]

CLOTHO—What is it that goes first on four legs, then on two legs—?
Don't tell me! Don't tell me!
LACHESIS—You know it!
CLOTHO—Let me pretend that I don't know it.
ATROPOS—There are no new riddles. We know them all.
LACHESIS—How boring our life is without riddles! Clotho, make up
a riddle.
CLOTHO—Be quiet, then, and give me a moment to think . . . What is
it that . . . ? What is it that . . . ?

   [*Enter Apollo. He wears a cone-shaped straw hat with a wide
   brim to conceal his face. Three flagons are hanging from a rope
   around his neck.*]

APOLLO—I am Apollo. In the disguise of a kitchen boy.
   I hate disguises. And I hate drunkenness—but see these bottles I
have hanging around my neck?
   I hate lies and stratagems; but I've come here to do crookedly what
even Allfather Zeus could not do without guile.
   These are the great sisters—the Fates. Clotho weaves the threads of
life; Lachesis measures the length of each; Atropos cuts them short.

I have come to do a thing which has never been done before—to extend a human life; to arrest the scissors of Atropos.

Oh, to change the order of the universe.

ATROPOS—Sister! Your elbow! Do your work without striking me.

LACHESIS—This thread is s-o-o l-o-o-ong! Never have I had to reach so far.

CLOTHO—Long and gray and dirty! All those years to a slave!

LACHESIS—So it is! [*To Atropos*] Cut it, dear sister. [*Atropos cuts it—click!*] And now this one; cut this. It's a blue one—blue for bravery.

ATROPOS—*So* easy to see! [*Click.*]

LACHESIS—You almost cut that purple one, Atropos.

ATROPOS—*This* one?—purple for a king.

LACHESIS—Yes—watch what you're doing, dear. It's the life of Admetos, King of Thessaly.

APOLLO—Aïe!

LACHESIS—I've marked it clearly. He's to die at sunset.

APOLLO [*to the audience*] No! No!

LACHESIS—He's the favorite of Apollo, as was his father before him, and all that tiresome house of Thessaly. The Queen Alkestis will be a widow tonight.

APOLLO—Alkestis! Alkestis!—No.

LACHESIS—There'll be howling in Thessaly. There'll be rolling on the ground. Not now, dear, there's an hour yet.

APOLLO—To work! To work. Apollo the crooked. [*He starts the motions of running furiously while remaining in one place. He complains noisily.*] Oh, my back! Aïe, aïe. They beat me, but worst of all they've made me late. I'll be beaten again.

LACHESIS—Who's the sniveler?

APOLLO—Don't stop me now. I haven't a moment to talk. I'm late already. Besides, my errand's a terrible secret. I can't say a word.

ATROPOS—Throw your yarn around him, Clotho. What's the fool doing with a secret? It's we who have all the secrets.

[*Clotho lassos him with thick strands of yarn. Apollo, crying piteously, falls to his knees, rises and falls repeatedly.*]

APOLLO—Ladies, beautiful ladies, let me go. If I'm late all Olympus will be in an uproar. Aphrodite will be mad with fear—but, oh, already I've said too much. My orders were to come immediately, and to say nothing—especially not to women. The thing's of no interest to men. Dear ladies, let me go.

ATROPOS—Pull on your yarn, sister.

APOLLO—You're choking me. You're squeezing me to death.

CLOTHO [*forcefully*] Stop your whining and tell your secret at once.

APOLLO—I can't. I can't.

LACHESIS—Pull harder. Boy, speak or strangle.

APOLLO—Ow! Ow! Wait! I'll tell the half of it, if you let me go.

ATROPOS—Tell the whole or we'll hang you up in the air in that noose.

APOLLO—I'll tell. I'll tell. But—[*he looks about him fearfully*] promise me! Swear by the Styx that you'll not tell anyone, and swear by Lethe that you'll forget it.

LACHESIS—We have only one oath—by Acheron. And we never swear by it, least of all to a sniveling slave. Tell us what you know, or you'll be by all three rivers in a minute.

APOLLO—I tremble at what I am about to say. I . . . sh . . . I carry . . . here . . . in these bottles . . . Oh, ladies, let me go. Let me go.

LACHESIS and ATROPOS—Pull, sister.

APOLLO—No! No! I am carrying the wine for . . . for Aphrodite. Once every ten days she renews her beauty . . . by . . . drinking this.

ATROPOS—Liar! Fool! She has nectar and ambrosia, as they all have.

APOLLO [*confidentially*] But is she not the fairest? . . . It is the love-gift of Hephaestos, from the vineyards of Dionysos; from grapes ripened under the eye of Apollo—of Apollo who tells no lies.

[*The Sisters smile confidentially to one another in blissful anticipation.*]

LACHESIS—Sisters!

ATROPOS—Sisters!

CLOTHO—Sisters!

ATROPOS [*like sugar*] Pass the bottles up, dear boy.

APOLLO [*in terror*] Not that! Ladies! It is enough that I have told you the secret! Not that!

ATROPOS—Surely, Lachesis, you can find on your lap the thread of this worthless slave—a yellow one destined for a long life.

APOLLO [*falling on his knees*] Spare me!

ATROPOS—Look, that's it—the sallow one, with the tangle in it of dishonesty, and the stiffness of obstinacy, and the ravel-ravel of stupidity. Pass it over to me, dear.

APOLLO [*his forehead touching the floor*] Oh, that I had never been born.

LACHESIS—This is it. [*With a sigh*] I'd planned to give him five score.

APOLLO [*rising and extending the bottles, sobbing*] Take them! Take them! I'll be killed anyway. Aphrodite will kill me. My life's over.

ATROPOS [*strongly, as the Sisters take the bottles*] Not one more word out of you. Put your hand on your mouth. We're tired of listening to you.

[*Apollo, released of the noose, flings himself face down upon the ground, his shoulders heaving. The Sisters put the flagons to their lips. They drink and moan with pleasure.*]

LACHESIS—Sisters!

ATROPOS—Sisters!

CLOTHO—Sisters!

LACHESIS—Sister, how do I look?

ATROPOS—Oh, I could eat you—and I?

CLOTHO—Sister, how do I look?

LACHESIS—Beautiful! Beautiful—and I?

ATROPOS—And not a mirror on all the mountain, or a bit of still water, to tell us which of us is the fairest.

LACHESIS [*dreamily, passing her hand over her face*] I feel like . . . I feel as I did when Kronos followed me about, trying to catch me in a dark corner.

ATROPOS—Poseidon was beside himself—dashing across the plains trying to engulf me.

CLOTHO—My own father—who can blame him?—began to forget himself.

ATROPOS [*whispering*] This is not such a worthless fellow, after all. And he's not bad-looking. Ask him what he sees.

LACHESIS—Ask him which of us is the fairest.

CLOTHO—Boy! Boy! You bay meek. I mean, you: you may thpeak. Thpeak to him, Lakethith—I've lotht my tongue.

LACHESIS—Boy, look at us well! You may tell us: which is the fairest?

[*Each of the Sisters is drunk in a different way. Clotho becomes a little girl, Lachesis arrogant and quarrelsome, Atropos tearful.*]

CLOTHO—Of course, I'm the youngeth. I've alwayth been a darling.

Everybody saith—thimply everybody saith—Darling Clotho. Thweet
Clotho.

LACHESIS [*striking her*] Yes, youngest and silliest—and vulgarest.
I don't care who the fool says is the fairest. I wouldn't expect to find
taste in a kitchen boy. Who cares for the admiration of the market
place?

ATROPOS—No one has ever been just to me. People say that I'm cruel.
I'm not cruel. I've the tenderest heart in the world. I spend my life
doing my duty, and what do I get for it?—ingratitude!

[*They start talking simultaneously. Lachesis is the loudest.*]

LACHESIS—Go find a judge who knows beauty when he sees it. Not a
shallow prettiness, like you, Clotho, nor a bitter face like yours, Atropos,
but soul. Soul. Spirit. Majesty. Dignity. Soul.

CLOTHO—Of courth, I'm *little*. I've always been little. When I path'd
everybody thaid: mi-mi-mi-mi; come here, you little darling. Mi-mi-mi-
mi, you little darling.

ATROPOS—Hidden away on this mountain. One injustice after another.
And what do I get for it?—ingratitude. The tenderest heart in the
world—that's what I have.

LACHESIS [*silencing them*] Hold your tongues, geese, and let's put
the question to this young man. Boy, get up. Don't be afraid. Tell us:
in your opinion, which of us is the fairest?

[*Apollo has remained face downward on the ground. He now
rises and gazes at the Sisters. He is blinded: he covers and un-
covers his eyes, gazing first at one and then at another.*]

APOLLO—What have I done? This splendor. What have I done? You,
and you, and you! Kill me, if you will, but I cannot say, which one is
the fairest. [*Falling on his knees*] Oh, ladies—if so much beauty has
not made you cruel—let me now go and hide myself. Aphrodite will
hear of this. Let me escape to Crete and take up my old work.

ATROPOS—*What* was your former work, dear boy?

APOLLO—I help my father in the market place: I am a teller of stories
and riddles.

[*The Sisters are transfixed. Then almost with a scream*]

THE SISTERS—What's that? What's that you said?

APOLLO—A teller of stories and riddles. Do the beautiful ladies enjoy
riddles?

THE SISTERS [*rocking from side to side and slapping one another*] Sisters! Do we enjoy riddles!

ATROPOS—Oh, he would only know the *old* ones. Puh! The blind horse. The toe.

LACHESIS—The cloud. The eyelashes of Hera.

CLOTHO—What is it that first goes on four legs—?

ATROPOS—The porpoise. Etna.

APOLLO—*Everyone* knows *those!* I have some new ones—

THE SISTERS [*again, a scream*] New ones!

APOLLO [*slowly*] What is it that is necessary to— [*He pauses. The Sisters are riveted.*]

LACHESIS—Go on, boy, go on. What is it that is nceessary to—

APOLLO—But—I only play for forfeits. See! If I lose . . .

CLOTHO—If you looth, you mutht tell uth which one is the faireth.

APOLLO—No! No! I dare not!

LACHESIS [*sharply*] Yes.

APOLLO—And if I win—

ATROPOS—Win? Idiot! Stupid. Slave! No one has ever won from us.

APOLLO—But if I win—

LACHESIS—He doesn't know who we are!

APOLLO—But if I win—

CLOTHO—The fool talkth of winning!

APOLLO—If I win, you must grant me one wish. One wish, any wish.

LACHESIS—Yes, yes. Oh, what a tedious fellow. Go on with your riddle. What is it that is necessary to—

APOLLO—Swear by Acheron!

CLOTHO and LACHESIS—We swear! By Acheron! By Acheron!

APOLLO [*to Atropos*] You, too.

ATROPOS [*after a moment's brooding resistance, loudly*] By Acheron!

APOLLO—Then: ready?

LACHESIS—Wait! One moment. [*Leaning toward Atropos, confidentially*] The sun is near setting. Do not forget the thread of Ad—! You know, the thread of Ad—!

ATROPOS—What? What Ad? What are you whispering about, silly?

LACHESIS—Not to forget the thread of Admetos, King of Thessaly. At sundown. Have you lost your shears, Atropos?

ATROPOS—Oh, stop your buzzing and fussing and tend to your own business. Of course I haven't lost my shears. Go on with your riddle, boy.

APOLLO—So! I'll give you as much time as it takes to recite the
names of the Muses and their mother.

LACHESIS—Hm! Nine and one. Well, begin!

APOLLO—What is it that is necessary to every life—and that can save
only one?

[*The Sisters rock back and forth with closed eyes, mumbling the
words of the riddle. Suddenly Apollo starts singing.*]

APOLLO—Mnemosyne, mother of the nine;
　　　　Polyhymnia, incense of the gods—

LACHESIS [*shrieks*] Don't sing! Unfair!

CLOTHO—Stop your ears, sister.

ATROPOS—Unfair! What is that can save every life— [*They put their
fingers in their ears.*]

APOLLO—Erato, voice of love;
　　　　Euterpe, help me now.

　　　　Calliope, thief of our souls;
　　　　Urania, clothed of the stars;
　　　　Clio of the backward glances;
　　　　Euterpe, help me now.

　　　　Terpsichore of the beautiful ankles;
　　　　Thalia of long laughter;
　　　　Melpomene, dreaded and welcome;
　　　　Euterpe, help me now.

[*Then in a loud voice*] Forfeit! Forfeit!

[*Clotho and Atropos bury their faces in Lachesis' neck, moaning.*]

LACHESIS [*in a dying voice*] What is the answer?

APOLLO [*flinging away his hat, triumphantly*] Myself—Apollo the sun.

LACHESIS [*savagely*] Pah! What life can *you* save?

APOLLO—My forfeit! *One* wish! *One* life! The life of Admetos, King
of Thessaly.

[*A horrified clamor arises from the Sisters.*]

THE SISTERS—Fraud. Impossible. Not to be thought of!

APOLLO—By Acheron.

THE SISTERS—Against all law. Zeus will judge. Fraud.

APOLLO—By Acheron.

THE SISTERS—Zeus! We will go to Zeus about it.

APOLLO—Zeus swears by Acheron and keeps his oath.

[*Sudden silence.*]

ATROPOS [*decisive but ominous*] You will have your wish—the life of King Admetos—*but*—

APOLLO—I shall have the life of Admetos.

THE SISTERS—*But*—

APOLLO—I shall have the life of Admetos. What is your *but?*

ATROPOS—Someone else must die in his stead.

APOLLO [*lightly*] Oh—choose some slave. Some gray and greasy thread on your lap, divine Lachesis.

LACHESIS [*outraged*] What? You ask *me* to take a life?

ATROPOS—You ask *us* to murder?

CLOTHO—Apollo thinks that *we* are criminals?

APOLLO [*beginning to be fearful*] Then—great sisters—how is this to be done?

LACHESIS—Me—an assassin? [*She spreads her arms wide and says solemnly*] Over my left hand is Chance; over my right hand is Necessity.

APOLLO—Then—gracious sisters—how will this be done?

LACHESIS—Someone must *give* his life for Admetos. Of free choice and will. Over such deaths we have no control. Neither Chance nor Necessity rules the free offering of the will. Someone must choose to die in the place of Admetos, King of Thessaly.

APOLLO [*covering his face with his hands*] No! No! I see it all! [*With a loud cry*] Alkestis! Alkestis! [*And he runs stumbling from the scene.*]

William F. Buckley, Jr.

THE FINAL SOLUTION TO
THE LATIN MASS

I am asked why I appointed the succeeding little essay to represent me in this volume. Why I came to write the piece is therein explained, so that I need not cover that point. Instead I touch upon, for the curiosity of practitioners, "how" I wrote it; and, at the explicit instruction of the editor, "why" I selected it.

I called the editor of *Commonweal Magazine,* which is a liberal Catholic journal, on hearing the news that the following Sunday the Canon of the mass was to be spoken in the vernacular —would the editor publish something by me on the general subject, yes he would, I got the deadline and the following Saturday, after a longish dinner, I went to my study and wrote it between midnight and two A.M. I read over it the next day, made a few corrections, and sent it in. It appeared a week or two later, and drew some interesting reactions—in fact, the editor told me that it drew in more mail than anything *Commonweal* had published in quite a while. Much of it no doubt from Catholics moved less by the piece than by the liturgical change it deplores.

I select the piece (a) because it is about the right length as suggested by the editor; (b) because I consider it to be an effective polemic sustained right through to the end by a deeply-felt indignation; (c) because when I wrote it it flowed, and seemed to compose itself; (d) because the long sentences and complicated syntax are more or less, alas, typical; and (e) because it is not political, and I suppose I care that someone, somewhere, should become aware that I can write other than to call for nuclear war, the election of Senator Goldwater, or the repeal of the social security laws. Orate.

William F. Buckley, Jr.

November 10, 1967

In January of this year my sister died, age forty-nine, eldest of ten children, and mother of ten children, the lot of us catapulted into a dumb grief whence we sought relief by many means, principal among them the conviction, now reified by desire, that our separation from her is impermanent. It was the moment to recall not merely the promises of Christ, but their magical cogency; the moment to remind ourselves as forcefully as we knew how of the depths of the Christian experience, of the Christian mystery, so that when one of us communicated with her priest, we asked if he would consent to a funeral mass in the manner of the days gone by, which request he gladly granted. And so, on January 18, in the subzero weather of a little town in northwestern Connecticut, in the ugly little church we all grew up in, the priest recited the mass of the dead, and the organist accompanied the soloist who sang the Gregorian dirge in words the mourners did not clearly discern, words which had we discerned them we would not have been able exactly to translate, and yet we experienced, not only her family but her friends, not alone the Catholics among us but also the Protestants and the Jews, something akin to that synesthesia which nowadays most spiritually restless folk find it necessary to discover in drugs or from a guru in Mysterious India.

Six months later my sister's oldest daughter—the first of the grand-children—was married. With some hesitation (one must not be over-bearing) her father asked the same priest (of noble mien and great heart) whether this happy ritual might also be performed in the

Latin. He replied with understanding and grace that that would not be possible, inasmuch as he would be performing on this occasion not in a remote corner of Connecticut, but in West Hartford, practically within the earshot of the bishop. We felt very wicked at having attempted anything so audacious within the walls of the episcopacy, and so the wedding took place according to the current cant, with everybody popping up, and kneeling down, and responding, more or less, to the stream of objurgations that issued from the nervous and tone-deaf young commentator, all together now, Who Do We Appreciate? Jesus! Jesus! Jesus! Je-*zus*—it was awful. My beloved wife—to whom I have been beholden for seventeen years, and who has borne with me through countless weddings of my countless relations, who was with me and clutched my hand during the funeral a few months earlier, whom I had not invited to my church since the vulgarizations of 1964, so anxious was I that, as a member of the Anglican Communion, she should continue to remember our services as she had known them, in their inscrutable majesty—turned to me early in the ritual in utter incredulity, wondering whether something was especially awry. Hypersensitive, I rebuked her, muttering something to the effect that she had no right to be so ignorant of what had been going on for three years, and she withdrew in anger. She was right; I was utterly wrong. How could she, an innocent Protestant, begin to conceive of the liturgical disfigurations of the past few years? My own reaction was the protective reaction of the son whose father, the chronic drunkard, is first espied unsteady on his feet by someone from whom one has greatly cared to conceal the fact. Let it be objected that the essential fact of the matter is that the sacrament of matrimony was duly conferred, and what else is it that matters? My sensibilities, that's what.

They do not matter, of course, in any Benthamite reckoning of the success of the new liturgy. Concerning this point, I yield completely, or rather almost completely. It is absolutely right that the vernacular should displace the Latin if by doing so, the rituals of Catholic Christianity bring a greater satisfaction to the laity and a deeper comprehension of their religion. There oughtn't to be any argument on this point, and there certainly isn't any from me—though I cherish the bodkin Sir Arnold Lunn so deftly inserted in the soft tissues of that argument: "If it is so," he said, arguing along with Evelyn Waugh and others for one (1) Latin mass each Sunday in the larger churches, "that the Latin Mass is only for the educated few, surely Mother Church in all her charity can find a little place *even* for the educated few?"

Indeed, when a most learned and attractive young priest from my own parish asked me to serve as a lector in the new mass, I acquiesced, read all the relevant literature, and, to be sure warily, hoped that something was about to unfold before me which would vindicate the progressives.

I hung on doggedly for three years, until a month ago, when I wrote my pastor that I no longer thought it appropriate regularly to serve as lector. During those three years I observed the evolution of the new mass and the reaction to it of the congregation (the largest, by the way, in Connecticut). The church holds 1,000 people, and at first, four hymns were prescribed. They were subsequently reduced to three, even as, in the course of the experiment, the commentator absorbed the duties of the lector, or vice versa, depending on whether you are the ex-commentator or the ex-lector. At our church three years ago perhaps a dozen people out of 1,000 sang the hymn. Now perhaps three dozen out of 1,000 sing the hymn. (It is not much different with the prayers.) That is atypical, to be sure; the church is large and overawing to the uncertain group singer—*i.e.,* to most non-Protestant Americans. In other Catholic churches, I have noted, the congregations tend to join a little bit more firmly in the song. In none that I have been to is there anything like the joyous unison that the bards of the new liturgy thrummed about in the anticipatory literature, the only exception being the highly regimented school my son attends, at which the reverend headmaster has means to induce cooperation in whatever enterprise strikes his fancy. (I have noticed that my son does not join in the hymn singing when he is home, though the reason why is not necessarily indifference, is almost surely not recalcitrance, is most likely a realistic appreciation of his inability to contribute to the musical story line.)

I must, of course, judge primarily on the basis of my own experience; but it is conclusive at my own church, and I venture to say without fear of contradiction that the joint singing and prayers are a fiasco, which is all right, I suppose—the Christian martyrs endured worse exasperations and profited more from them than we endure from or are likely to benefit from the singing of the hymns at St. Mary's Church. What is troublesome is the difficulty one has in dogging one's own spiritual pursuits in the random cacophony. Really, the new liturgists should have offered training in yogi or whatever else Mother Church in her resourcefulness might baptize as a distinctively Catholic means by which we might tune off the Fascistic static of the contemporary mass, during which one is either attempting to sing, totally neglecting the prayers at the foot of the altar which suddenly we are told are irrelevant; or

attempting to read the missal at one's own syncopated pace, which we
must now do athwart the obtrusive rhythm of the priest or the commentator; or attempting to meditate on this or the other prayer or
sentiment or analysis in the ordinary or in the proper of the mass,
only to find that such meditation is sheer outlawry, which stands
in the way of the liturgical calisthenics devised by the central coach,
who apparently judges it an act of neglect if the churchgoer is permitted more than two minutes and forty-six seconds without being made
to stand if he was kneeling, or kneel if he was standing, or sit—or sing—
or chant—or *anything* if perchance he was praying, from which
anarchism he must at all costs be rescued: "LET US NOW RECITE THE
INTROIT PRAYER," says the commentator, to which exhortation I find
myself aching to reply in that "loud and clear and reverential voice"
the manual for lectors prescribes: "LET US NOT!" Must we say the introit
prayer together? I have been reading the introit prayer since I was
thirteen years old, and I continue unaware that I missed something—
e.g., at the Jesuit school in England when at daily mass we read the
introit prayers all by our little selves, beginning it perhaps as much
as five seconds before, or five seconds after, the priest, who, enjoying
the privacy granted him at Trent, pursued his prayers, in his own way,
at his own speed, ungoverned by the metronomic discipline of the
parishioners or of the commentator.

Ah, but now the parish *understands* the introit prayer! But, my beloved
friends, the parish does not understand. Neither does the commentator.
Neither does the lector. Neither, if you want the truth of the matter,
does the priest—in most cases. If clarity is the purpose of the liturgical
reform—the reason for going into English, the reason for going into
the vernacular—then the reforms of the liturgy are simply incomplete.
If clarity is the desideratum, or however you say the word in English,
then the thing to do is to jettison, just to begin with, most of St. Paul,
whose epistles are in some respects inscrutable to some of the people
some of the time and in most respects inscrutable to most of the people
most of the time. The translation of them from archaic grandeur to
John-Jane-Gyp contemporese simply doesn't do the trick, particularly
if one is expected to go in unison. Those prayers, which are not
exacting or recondite—are even they more galvanizing when spoken in
unison? LET US NOW RECITE THE INTROIT PRAYER. *Judge me, O God, and
distinguish my cause from the nation that is not holy; deliver me from
the unjust and deceitful man.* Judge-me-O-God/And-distinguish-my-cause-
from-the-nation-that-is-not-holy / Deliver-me-from-the-unjust-and-deceitful-

man/—Why? How come? Whose idea—that such words as these are better spoken, better understood, better appreciated, when rendered metrically in forced marches with the congregation? Who, thinking to read these holy and inspired words reverentially, would submit to the iron rhythm of a joint reading? It is one thing to chant together a refrain—Lord deliver us/Lord save us/Grant us peace. But the extended prayer in unison is a metallic Proscrusteanism which absolutely defies the rationale of the whole business, which is the communication of *meaning*. The rote saying of anything is the enemy of understanding. To reduce to unison prayers whose meaning is unfamiliar is virtually to guarantee that they will mean nothing to the sayer. *"Brethren: Everything that was written in times past was written for our instruction, that through the patience and encouragement afforded by the scriptures we might have hope. I say that Christ exercised his ministry to the circumsized to show God's fidelity in fulfilling his promises to the fathers, whereas the Gentiles glorify God for his mercy, as it is written: 'Therefore will I proclaim you among the nations, and I will sing praise to your name.' "* These were the words with which I first accosted my fellow parishioners from the lector's pulpit. I do not even now understand them well enough to explain them with any confidence. And yet, the instruction manual informs me, I am to communicate their meaning "clearly" and "confidently." And together the congregation will repeat such sentences in the gradual.

Our beloved Mother Church. How sadly, how innocently, how—sometimes—strangely she is sometimes directed by her devoted disciples! *Hail Mary, full of Grace, the Lord is with you* . . . The Lord is with *who! Thee to you, Buster,* I found myself thinking during the retreat when first I learned that it is a part of the current edification to strip the Lord, His Mother, and the saints of the honorific with which the simple Quakers even now address their children and their servants. And the translations! *"Happy the Humble—they shall inherit. . . ."* One cannot read on without the same sense of outrage one would feel on entering the Cathedral of Chartres and finding that the windows had been replaced with pop art figures of Christ sitting in against the slumlords of Milwaukee. One's heart is filled with such passions of resentment and odium as only Hilaire Belloc could adequately have voiced. O God O God O God, why has thou forsaken us! My faith, I note on their taking from us even the canon of the mass in that mysterious universal which soothed and inspired the low and the mighty, a part of the mass—as Evelyn Waugh recalled—"for whose restoration the Elizabethan martyrs had gone to the scaffold [in which] St. Augustine,

St. Thomas à Becket, St. Thomas More, Challoner and Newman would have been perfectly at their ease among us," is secure. I pray the sacrifice will yield a rich harvest of informed Christians. But to suppose that it will is the most difficult act of faith I have ever been called on to make, because it tears against the perceptions of all my senses. My faith is a congeries of dogmatical certitudes, one of which is that the new liturgy is the triumph, yea the resurrection, of the Philistines.

Marianne Moore

WHAT ARE YEARS?

For *This Is My Best*, 1942:
   "What Are Years?" partly written in 1931 and finished in 1939, is elegiac.
   The desperation attendant on mortal fallibility is mitigated for me by admitting that the most willed and resolute vigilance may lapse, as with the Apostle Peter's denial that he could be capable of denial; but that failure, disgrace, and even death have now and again been redeemed into inviolateness by a sufficiently transfigured courage.

Marianne Moore

Brooklyn, N.Y.
March 22, 1942

For *This Is My Best*, 1970:
Dear Whit:
Again, "What Are Years?" Again, Bach plays back Bach.

Marianne

N.Y. 1968

W hat is our innocence,
   what is our guilt? All are
   naked, none is safe. And whence
is courage: the unanswered question,
the resolute doubt,—
dumbly calling, deafly listening—that
in misfortune, even death,
      encourages others
      and in its defeat, stirs

   the soul to be strong? He
sees deep and is glad, who
   accedes to mortality
and in his imprisonment, rises
upon himself as
the sea in a chasm, struggling to be
free and unable to be,
      in its surrendering
      finds its continuing.

   So he who strongly feels,
behaves. The very bird,
   grown taller as he sings, steels
his form straight up. Though he is captive,

his mighty singing
says, satisfaction is a lowly
thing, how pure a thing is joy.
    This is mortality,
    this is eternity.

Lewis Mumford

ART AND THE SYMBOL

In what sense do I dare to call this specimen my 'best?' Certainly not in any single limited sense, such as brilliance of expression, originality of thought, or richness of pattern. Without setting myself to re-read my entire product over half a century, what I sought to pick out was a selection, coherent and complete in itself, that would represent most fully the tone and style of my whole life. Art and Technics have always been, certainly, among my major concerns; but it is because this lecture likewise shows the wide range of interests that characterizes my work, moving freely over literature, philosophy, science, and history, indeed human culture generally, that I have singled it out. Not least these pages disclose an essential facet of my thinking; and that is its constant reference, whether in dealing with the past or the future, to the contemporary situation. Though my observations on art and technics go back to the paleolithic beginnings of human culture, these pages bear the unmistakable mark of the period when they were written: the aftermath of the Second World War, amid the gross anxieties created by nuclear weapons, magnified by the day to day pressures of technological automatism, short-sighted military and political commitments, and moral disintegration. In short, while the focus is on Art and the Symbol, the field of vision persistently takes in many other relevant matters. This style of thinking, if I may venture a judgment upon my own work, may prove to be my most important contribution.

Lewis Mumford

Amenia, New York

At the beginning of a series of lectures, it is perhaps well to establish some common point of agreement between the lecturer and his audience; and to ensure this I shall begin by making a flat observation: *We live in an interesting age!* This is not quite so innocent a commonplace as you may fancy; for like the Chinese, who have lived through many periods of disorder and violence, similar to our own, I would use the word interesting in a somewhat acrid sense. We are told that when traditionally a Chinese scholar wished to utter a withering curse upon his enemy, he merely said, May you live in an interesting age! The Chinese knew that few of the good things of life could come to consummation in the midst of moral landslides and political earthquakes.

What makes our age so interesting, of course, is the number of shocking contradictions and tragic paradoxes that confront us at every turn, creating problems that tax our human capacities for understanding, releasing forces we lack the confidence to control. We have seen starvation in the midst of plenty, as millions of desolate people in India still see it: we have seen the heartfelt renunciation of war, which followed the First World War, leading to the enthronement of military dictatorships: we are even now seeing the hatred of totalitarianism producing, in our own constitutional republic, many of the most repulsive features of totalitarianism, including the hysterical worship of a military leader. And so it has been with many other *apparent blessings.* Certainly Art and Technics, the subject of the present lectures, have not escaped these contradictions.

Three and a half centuries ago Francis Bacon hailed the advancement of scientific learning and mechanical invention as the surest means of relieving man's estate: with a few expiatory gestures of piety, he turned his back upon religion and philosophy and art and pinned every hope for human improvement on the development of mechanical invention. He met his death, indeed, not after writing a series of final aphorisms about the conduct of life, but after exposing himself to the elements in one of the first experiments in the use of ice for preserving food. Neither Bacon nor his eager followers in science and technics, the Newtons and Faradays, the Watts and the Whitneys, had any anticipation of the fact that all our hard-won mastery of the physical world might, in the twentieth century, threaten the very existence of the human race. If by some clairvoyance Bacon could have followed to their ultimate conclusions the developments he forecast with such unqualified optimism, he might easily have decided, instead of continuing his speculations in science, to write Shakespeare's plays, as at least a more innocent occupation. Bacon did not foresee that the humanization of the machine might have the paradoxical effect of mechanizing humanity; and that at this fatal moment the other arts, once so nourishing to man's humanity and spirituality, would become equally arid, and so incapable of acting as a counterpoise to this one-sided technical development.

None of these tendencies, we must be thankful, has yet been carried to its ultimate conclusion: this is still 1951, not yet "1984." But in a recent book, which should have been more widely discussed and pondered than it actually was, Mr. Roderick Seidenberg made a canvass of the tendencies toward mechanical organization and automatism that have been displacing man from the center of the stage, and reducing him to a mere shadow of the machine he had created; and it is very plain from his analysis that if the present forces are not controlled and redirected, the end is in sight, and a new creature, called by Mr. Seidenberg "Post-Historic Man"—this is the title, too, of his book—will occupy the stage, or rather, will merge himself with the props and backdrops and lighting fixtures, indistinguishable, so to speak, from the scenery.

If that fate were the only one open to us, the human race, in a final effort at its own self-preservation, might have to take to heart Samuel Butler's suggestion, in *Erewhon,* and not merely destroy all our old machines, but severely penalize any effort to make new ones. Neither of these alternatives, plainly, should be accepted until we have at least made a bold effort to bring together the mechanical and the personal, the objective and the subjective sides of our life, in order to establish them once more in an organic working relationship. But before we shall have the energy to make such an effort, we must show a better understanding than most of us have yet shown of the nature of our present predicament.

During the last two centuries there has been a vast expansion of the material means of living throughout the world. But instead of our thus producing a state of widely distributed leisure, favorable to the cultivation of the inner life and the production and enjoyments of the arts, we find ourselves more absorbed than ever in the process of mechanization. Even a large part of our fantasies are no longer self-begotten: they have no reality, no viability, until they are harnessed to the machine, and without the aid of the radio and television they would hardly have the energy to maintain their existence. Compare our present situation with that which accompanied the relatively technical primitive era of the seventeenth century. In that time a good London burgher, like Samuel Pepys, a practical man, a hard-working administrator, would select the servants in his household partly on the basis of their having a good voice, so that they might sit down with the family in the evening to take part in domestic singing. Such people not merely listened passively to music, but could produce it, or at least reproduce it, in their own right. Today, in contrast, we often see people wandering around with a portable radio set on Riverside Drive, listening to a radio musical program, with no thought that they might sing a song freely in the open air without invoking any mechanical aid.

Even worse, the very growth of mechanical facilities has given people a false ideal of technical perfectionism, so that unless they can compete with the products of the machine or with those whose professional training qualifies them for such a public appearance, they are all too ready to take a back seat. And, to complete this process, not in the least to offset it, in those special realms of art, above all painting, that once recorded the greatest freedom and creativeness, we find that the symbols that most deeply express the emotions and feelings of our age are a succession of dehumanized nightmares, transposing into esthetic form either the horror and violence or the vacuity and despair of our time. Undoubtedly one of the great paintings of our day is Picasso's Guernica mural, just as he himself is one of the great artists of our time, with a capacity for beautiful rhythmic expression like that of a dancer; a gift that the stroboscopic camera has recently revealed. But the fresh symbols that come forth from his masterly hand reveal chiefly the wounds and scars of our time, with not even the faintest hint of a new integration. At times, as in the preliminary sketches for the Guernica mural, the emotion is so lacerating that the next step beyond would be either insanity or suicide.

Violence and nihilism: the death of the human personality. This is the message that modern art brings to us in its freest and purest moments; and that, obviously, is no counterpoise to the dehumanization wrought by technics.

Most of the great artists of the last two centuries—and this has been equally true, I think, in music and poetry and painting, even in some degree in architecture—have been in revolt against the machine and have proclaimed the autonomy of the human spirit: its autonomy, its spontaneity, its inexhaustible creativeness. Actually, the religious impulse, suppressed by the institutionalism of the Churches, manifested itself during this period chiefly in the arts, so that the great saints of the last century were as often as not artists, like Van Gogh or Ryder or Tolstoy. This strong reaction against a too-singleminded commitment to mechanical invention and practical effort helped produce great works of music and painting, perhaps as great as any other age could show. In the great symphonic music of the nineteenth century the human spirit utilized its characteristic division of labor, its specialization of functions, and its intricate organization of time and rhythm to express the tragic yearnings and joyful triumphs of this new epoch. Because of the traditional separation of art and technics we have yet sufficiently to realize that the symphony orchestra is a triumph of engineering, and that its products, such as the music of Mozart and Beethoven, etherealized into symbols, will probably outlast all our steel bridges and automatic machines.

But that protest was possible, those triumphs could be expressed, only so long as a belief in the human person, and particularly in the inner life, the creative moment, remained dominant, carried over from the older cultures that had nourished the human spirit. By the end of the nineteenth century, this evocative protest began to die away. In a mood of submission and self-abnegation, sensitively recorded by Henry Adams, people began to worship the machine and its masters. If anyone was *un*real, Adams wrote, it was the poet, not the businessman. We had created a topsyturvy world in which machines had become autonomous and men had become servile and mechanical: that is, thing-conditioned, externalized, de-humanized—disconnected from their historic values and purposes. And so it has come about that one whole part of man's life, springing from his innermost nature, his deepest desires and impulses, his ability to enjoy and bestow love, to give life to and receive life from his fellow men, has been suppressed. Those deep organic impulses for which art is both the surrogate in immediate action and the ultimate expression of that action as transferred to the life of other men—all this part of man's nature has become progressively empty and meaningless. The maimed fantasies, the organized frustrations, that we see in every comprehensive exhibition of modern painting today are so many symptoms of this deep personal abdication. Pattern and purpose have progressively disappeared, along with the person who once, in his own right, embodied them. Man has become an exile in this mechanical world: or rather, even worse, he has become a Displaced Person.

On one hand, through the advance of technics, we have produced a new kind of environment and a highly organized routine of life, which satisfies, to a fabulous degree, man's need to live in an orderly and predictable world. There is something noble, as Emerson recognized long ago, in the fact that our railroads, our ocean steamships, our planes, run on a time-schedule almost as regular as the movement of the heavenly bodies. Uniformity, regularity, mechanical accuracy and reliability all have been advanced to a singular degree of perfection. And just as the autonomic nervous system and the reflexes in the human body free the mind for its higher functions, so this new kind of mechanical order should bring about a similar freedom, a similar release of energy for the creative processes. Because of our achievement of mechanical order throughout the planet, the dream of Isaiah might in fact come true: the dream of a universal society in which men shall be weaned from habits of hostility and war. Originally these aggressions were perhaps the natural outcome of anxiety for the future, in periods when there was never enough food or goods to go round: periods when only the powerful could arrogate to themselves all the resources men needed to be fully human.

But the good fairy who presided over the development of technics did not succeed in forestalling the curse that accompanied this genuine gift: a curse that came from this very overcommitment to the external, the quantitative, the measurable, the external. For our inner life has become impoverished: as in our factories, so throughout our society, the automatic machine tends to replace the person and to make all his decisions—while, for its smoother working, it anesthetizes every part of the personality that will not easily conform to its mechanical needs.

All these are the veriest commonplaces of our "interesting age"; I remind you only of what you already know. On one side, the highest degree of scientific and technical refinement, as in the atomic bomb; on the other side, moral depravity, as in the use of that bomb not to conquer armies, but to exterminate defenseless people at random. On one side, intellectual maturity, as in the cooperative activities of science; on the other, crass emotional immaturity—the kind painfully exhibited by the traitorous physicist Fuchs. External order: internal chaos. External progress: internal regression. External rationalism: internal irrationality. In this impersonal and overdisciplined machine civilization, so proud of its objectivity, spontaneity too often takes the form of criminal acts, and creativeness finds its main open outlet in destruction. If this seems like an exaggeration, that is due only to the illusion of security. Open your eyes and look around you!

Now I put these paradoxes and contradictions before you at the beginning, dismaying though they may be, because I believe that the relations between art and technics give us a significant clue to every other type of activity, and may even provide an understanding of the way to integration. The great problem of our time is to restore modern man's balance and wholeness: to give him the capacity to command the machines he has created instead of becoming their helpless accomplice and passive victim; to bring back, into the very heart of our culture, that respect for the essential attributes of personality, its creativity and autonomy, which Western man lost at the moment he displaced his own life in order to concentrate on the improvement of the machine. In short, the problem of our time is how to prevent ourselves from committing suicide, precisely at the height and climax of our one-sided mechanical triumphs.

There are doubtless many other excellent reasons for studying the relation of art and technics; and in a happier period of history I might have been tempted to dwell on them more extensively than I propose to do in the present lectures. By now, however, every intelligent observer knows—as Mr. Arnold Toynbee, among others, has impressively demonstrated—that our civilization cannot go on indefinitely in the present fashion. Like a drunken locomotive engineer on a streamlined train, plunging through the darkness at a hundred miles an hour, we have been going past the danger signals without realizing that our speed, which springs from our mechanical facility, only increases our danger and will make more fatal the crash. If we are to find a different destination for our civilization, every part of our life must be re-examined and overhauled, every activity must undergo criticism and revaluation; every institution must seek its own renovation and renewal. Precisely in those areas where modern man has seemed most prosperous and secure, most efficient in action, most adept in thought, we begin to realize that something has been left out of his regimen, something essential to his organic balance and development.

What is that missing element? That missing element, I suggest, is the human person. Our power and knowledge, our scientific discoveries and our technical achievements, have all been running wild because Western man turned his back upon the very core and center of his own life. He has not merely lost confidence in himself: he has made his proper life insignificant, and so he finds the rest of the world equally empty of values, equally insignificant. More and more, from the sixteenth century on, modern man patterned himself upon the machine. Despite sentimental compunctions of various sorts, compunctions expressed in the romantic movement, in nationalism, in the reactivation of Christian theology, Western man has sought to live in a nonhistoric and impersonal world of matter and motion, a world with no values except the value of quantities; a world of causal sequences, not human purposes. Even when he has added depth to his life by his exploration of the human soul, as Sigmund Freud and his followers undoubtedly have done in psychology, he has used his new-found knowledge to a large degree only to continue the general process of self-devaluation.

In such a world, man's spiritual life is limited to that part of it which directly or indirectly serves science and technics: all other interests and activities of the person are suppressed as "non-objective," emotional, and therefore unreal. This decision in effect banished art, because art is one of the essential spheres of man's autonomous and creative activities. Art as the domain of symbol and form, of pattern and significance became the blighted area of modern life, within whose dilapidated mansions a few pious caretakers and family servants fought a hopeless battle against neglect and the final abandonment of the deserted homes themselves. That is why, with all our boasted efficiency of machines, with all our superabundance of energy, food, materials, products, there has been no commensurate improvement in the quality of our daily existence; why the great mass of comfortable well-fed people in our civilization live lives of emotional apathy and mental torpor, of dull passivity and enfeebled desire—lives that belie the real potentialities of modern culture. *Art degraded, imagination denied, war governed the nations.* Thus spoke William Blake; and we have lived to understand the truth of that aphorism.

My special purpose in these lectures, then, springs out of our common responsibility to restore order and value and purpose, on the widest

scale, to human life. This means two things. We must find out how
to make our subjective life more disciplined and resolute, endowed with
more of the qualities that we have poured into the machine, so that
we shall not equate our subjectivity with the trivial and the idle, the
disorderly and the irrational, as if the only road to free creativity lay
through a complete withdrawal from the effort to communicate and
cooperate with other men. When society is healthy, the artist reinforces
its health; but when it is ailing, he likewise reinforces its ailments. This
is probably the reason that the artists and the poets are looked upon
with suspicion by moralists like Plato or Tolstoy, who write in a time
of decay. Though the esthetic movements of our time—post-impres-
sionism, futurism, cubism, primitivism, surrealism—have taught us much
about the actual nature of our civilization, they themselves, from this
point of view, are so conditioned by the very disintegration they draw
upon for nourishment that they are incapable, without themselves undergoing a profound spiritual change, of bringing a new balance and
security into our life.

Fortunately, here and there, one still finds truly integrated artists.
Surviviors of a better past, precursors of a better future can in fact
be found: people like Naum Gabo in sculpture and Frank Lloyd Wright
in architecture; artists whose work begins once more to have fresh
meaning for the younger generation. But if our life as a whole is to take
on the qualities foreshadowed in the work of these artists, the world
of technics itself must be transformed: salvation lies, not in the pragmatic
adaptation of the human personality to the machine, but in the re-
adaptation of the machine, itself a product of life's needs for order
and organization, to the human personality. A human pattern, a human
measure, a human tempo, above all, a human goal must transform
the activities and processes of technics, curbing them, when they become dangerous to a man's development, even cutting them off for
a while—as a more prudent world statesmanship would have cut off
our present developments of atomic energy—until the appropriate political instruments and social institutions had been created for directing
technics into the channels of human development. If our civilization
is not to go further in the disintegration now manifested in the
state of art and technics, we must salvage and redeem the Displaced
Person; and that means that we must pour once more into the arts
some of the vitality and energy now almost wholly drained off by a
depersonalized technics.

Already, by my use of the terms art and technics, I have partly

defined them; but now let me make their definition a little more precise.
Technics is a word that has only lately come into use in English; people
still sometimes try to Frenchify it into "techniques" and thereby give it a
quite different meaning. We ordinarily use the word technology to
describe both the field of the practical arts and the systematic study
of their operations and products. For the sake of clarity, I prefer to use
technics alone to describe the field itself, that part of human activity
wherein, by an energetic organization of the process of work, man controls and directs the forces of nature for his own purposes.

Technics began when man first used his fingers for pincers or a stone
for a projectile: like art itself, it is rooted in man's use of his own
body. But man has gone on developing his technical facilities, slowly,
fitfully, only rarely in such rapid spurts as we have seen during the
last century; so that by now he has extended the range and power of many
of his organic aptitudes: he can kill at a distance of five thousand yards
and converse at a distance of five thousand miles; and in certain
complicated mathematical calculations he can, by the aid of an electronic
brain, perform in a few seconds operations that might otherwise take
a lifetime of strenuous effort. All these magnified human powers are the
result of human desires, human contrivances, human efforts. However
formidably automatic the machine may look, there is always a man
lurking in the background, adjusting it, correcting it, nursing it; and
the machine itself is half slave, half god. You might in fact call the
machine modern man's totem animal.

Art, in the only sense in which one can separate art from technics,
is primarily the domain of the person; and the purpose of art, apart
from various incidental technical functions that may be associated with
it, is to widen the province of personality, so that feelings, emotions,
attitudes, and values, in the special individualized form in which they
happen in one particular person, in one particular culture, can be transmitted with all their force and meaning to other persons or to other
cultures. Sympathy and empathy are the characteristic ways of art: a
feeling with, a feeling into, the innermost experiences of other men.
The work of art is the visible, potable spring from which men share
the deep underground sources of their experience. Art arises out of
man's need to create for himself, beyond any requirement for mere
animal survival, a meaningful and valuable world: his need to dwell
on, to intensify, and to project in more permanent forms those precious
parts of his experience that would otherwise slip too quickly out of
his grasp, or sink too deeply into his unconscious to be retrieved.

Because of their origin and purpose, the meanings of art are of a different order from the operational meanings of science and technics: they relate, not to external means and consequences, but to internal transformations, and unless it produce these internal transformations the work of art is either perfunctory or dead. Man's technical contrivances have their parallel in organic activities exhibited by other living creatures: bees build hives on engineering principles, the electric eel can produce electric shocks at high voltage, the bat developed its own form of radar for night flight long before man. But the arts represent a specifically human need, and they rest on a trait quite unique in man: the capacity for symbolism. Unlike animals, man not merely can respond to visible or audible signals; he is also able to abstract and re-present parts of his environment, parts of his experience, parts of himself, in the detachable and durable form of symbols. With the sounds that come forth from his mouth in childish babble, with the images that haunt him, detached from the visible world, both by night and by day, eventually with many other different kinds of sounds and images and forms and structures, man found the means of internalizing the external world and of externalizing his internal world. Long before man had achieved any degree of casual insight or rational order, long before he had conceived of the operation of impersonal forces, he had developed in the arts a special means of perpetuating, of recalling, of sharing with others his own essential experience of life. Even today it is not without significance, perhaps, that an infant develops recognizable gestures and achieved any degree of causal insight or rational order, long before he begins to crawl or walk: the function of communication precedes the function of work, and is of immensely greater significance for the development of human society.

The greatest of man's symbolic functions is of course speech; but speech, as the Danish philologist Otto Jespersen pointed out, was probably a source of emotional communion long before it became a useful instrument of practical communication. By tone and rhythm, by poetic and musical qualities, words became a special bond between mother and child, or between lovers who needed an extra outlet for their enchantment and ecstasy. Whatever primitive man may have been, he surely was not a logical positivist. Essentially the symbolic functions begin as expressions of inner states, as an externalization and projection of attitudes and desires, sometimes in response to inner promptings, sometimes in response to the external world and its inhabitants. By the feat of symbolic representation, man freed himself from the pressing suggestions of his immediate environment, from a limited here and now. He not merely found a way of creating circuitous responses which enabled him to enlist other aspects of his life than those aroused by the immediate situation. He not merely found a way to recombine past experiences in a single symbolic representation, but what is perhaps even more characteristically human, he was able to project new potentialities for life, new experiences, which as yet had no objective existence. Art at its best discloses heretofore hidden meanings. It tells more than the eye sees or the ear hears or the mind knows. With the aid of the symbol man not merely united time past with time present, but time present with ideal possibilities still to emerge in the future. With the aid of the symbol, man not merely remembered the vanished past: he took in the emergent or the potential future. Beginning in dream, word, gesture, man attempts to establish a personal relationship, an I-and-thou relationship with every other dimension of his experience. This "saying" is as important for man's spiritual development as "doing" is for his physical subsistence. Without the symbols of art, in all their many manifestations—painting and music, costume and architecture, poetry and sculpture—man would live culturally in a world of the deaf, the dumb, and the blind. It is only at a very late stage of history that the symbol becomes useful as a device of abstract thought, in the service of science and eventually of technics. The mythic and poetic functions of the symbol, as Vico long ago correctly pointed out, antedated its rational and practical uses.

Do not misunderstand me here. Not all symbolism, of course, is art. Once man had given an independent form to sounds and images, using them not merely for intimate communion but for specific factual communication, he was too intelligent not to grasp their immense practical importance in every transaction of daily life. By means of symbols, man was able to escape from the clumsy concreteness, the overwhelming multiplicity, of the immediate world. The human mind functions symbolically, as the philosopher Alfred North Whitehead put it, "when some components of its experience elicit consciousness, beliefs, emotions, and usages respecting other components of its experience." That is an admirable definition of the symbolic function in general; and I would qualify it only by adding that the components that perform these functions are necessarily logical abstractions or esthetic condensations of the immediate experience. Otherwise every symbol would have to be as large as life and therefore indistinguishable from the original experience.

In other words, mere substitution without abstraction would be as boring as the habit of total recall in telling a story—and more futile.

Art, it follows, in all but its most trivial and imitative forms, is not a substitute for life or an escape from life: it is a manifestation of significant impulses and values that can come forth in no other way. Even in the oldest paleolithic cave painting, the artist reveals more to us than the fact that he had observed the bison carefully, or that he venerated it as a totem animal: he also reveals, in the very quality of his line—in its selectivity, its sureness, its expressive rhythm—something even more essential about the nature of his own experience and culture. And if a dozen anthropologists had been observing and recording his life, they could not tell us more: indeed, in certain ways—the artist's "secret"—they could not tell us half as much. Or suppose we look at three nudes by Cranach, Rubens, and Manet: the virginal wife of the Middle Ages, the lusty bed fellow and willing mother of the Renascence, the cold, almost boyish courtesan of the nineteenth century. We find, in these condensed esthetic forms, three different ways of looking at the world, three different kinds of personality, three different philosophies: three cultures, not just three women. Art uses a minimum of concrete material to express a maximum of meaning. And if what we read into a Rorschach ink blot reveals our innermost nature, what do we not find and disclose about ourselves in the complex and deliberately evocative symbols of art?

We might say further, then, to differentiate between art and technics, that art is that part of technics which bears the fullest imprint of the human personality; technics is that manifestation of art from which a large part of the human personality has been excluded, in order to further the mechanical process. No matter how abstract art is—and even in the most realistic convention every work of art is an abstraction—it can never be entirely impersonal or entirely meaningless. When art seems to be empty of meaning, as no doubt some of the abstract painting of our own day actually does seem, what the painting says, indeed what the artist is shrieking at the top of his voice, is that life has become empty of all rational content or coherence. And that, in times like these, is far from a meaningless statement.

Though the world we live in is constantly modified by our use of symbols, it has taken us a long time to notice the way in which symbols mediate all experiences above the level of our animal reflexes. Since the time of David Hume we have tended to take for granted that our sense-data, rather than our symbols, form the solid groundwork of

experience. But the brilliant researches of Adelbert Ames have experimentally established the fact that sensations are no more primary than
any other element in experience: that they do not impinge upon us
directly, but are always being linked up with the meanings and values
and purposes of the organism, as established either in the general plan
of life of the species, or in man's particular interests and needs, conditioned as they are by his history and culture. Once we recognize the
part played generally by the symbol, in subjectifying and personalizing
the world, we can understand the limitations of science and technics,
since they are by intention an expression of that part of the personality
from which emotion and feeling and desire and sympathy—the stuff
of both life and art—have been eliminated.

Strangely, it is only in our own day that the work of George
Mead, Ernst Cassirer, W. M. Urban, and Suzanne Langer in philosophy
has drawn attention to the constant part played by man's propensity
to symbolize his experience; and in particular to the dynamic role of
the esthetic symbol, in revealing man's nature and further modifying
it. Our long neglect of the symbol, like our complete withdrawal of
interest from the dream, was due perhaps to a cultural change that
took place in the eighteenth century, through the naive rationalism and
practical enthusiasm of the *philosophes,* led by Diderot. In his biography
of Diderot, indeed, John Morley suggested that our devaluation of
symbols was perhaps part of a more general shift in the intellectual
climate: a turning away from an interest in words to an interest in
things, from matters of value to matters of fact. This movement both
resulted from the advances of technics and gave further encouragement
to those advances; but, though it was hailed as a great emancipation of
the spirit, we can now see that it actually involved a displacement of
the rest of the personality, and a disparagement of a good half of human life—that which has its source, not in external conditions and
forces, but in the inner nature and historic values of man. In correcting
this one-sided development we must not make the mistake of attempting
to repress the impersonal, the practical, the technical; we should rather
seek to bring these activities into working unity with other parts of
the personality. They have an important contribution to make, once they
cease to exercise a one-sided dominion.

Now, one does not have to be a follower of Benedetto Croce to see
that all art is fundamentally expression: not expression in general,
but expression by means of esthetic symbols. Art stands as visible
sign of an indwelling state of grace and harmony, of exquisite percep-

tion and heightened feeling, focused and intensified by the very form into which the artist translates his inner state. This kind of expression is fundamental to man's own sense of himself: it is both self-knowledge and self-realization. Historically, art comes into existence not as an after-thought, in the way that the industrial magnates of an older generation imported art into their communities after they had built their factories and steel mills and made their pile. Just the contrary, art arises at the very beginning of man's specifically human, his superanimal, develop-ment. Though this is only a speculation, supported by analogy, the most elemental form of art is probably body decoration, an art that remains today the most universally practiced of all the arts. By this means, primitive man probably sought to lift himself out of his generic animal state, if only by smearing yellow or red clay over his face: he thus attempted to identify himself and his group, to externalize himself in a new form, to visualize himself in a fashion that set him off from his animal condition.

We derive the very word person from the Latin word for mask, and body decoration was the first of man's efforts to mask his animal propensities and to achieve, and make visible, a different self. That earliest expression was perhaps more communal than personal. But as man developed both in self-confidence and in skill, he sought to dif-ferentiate himself and to project himself in other forms than his own body. With the development of language in general, that marvelous structure for communion and communication added immensely both to the domain of the symbol and the province of the self; so that in time everything man touched—not merely his body, but his tools and utensils, his clothes and gear, his houses and his temples and his cities—was wrought in some degree in his own image, and passed on to other men his feelings and thoughts, about himself, about nature, about the cosmic processes. The development of technics itself aided this expression. Did it not take a hundred thousand slaves and immense technical skill to make visible, in the Pyramids, the Egyptian notion of eternity? But for long the technical instrument lagged behind the symbol in its development.

In the course of history, art has taken many forms and said many things. But in contrast to technics, which is mainly concerned with the enlarge-ments of human power, art is essentially an expression of love, in all its many forms from the erotic to the social. Do not think that I purpose to bore you by once more tracing art back to its most infantile oral and anal manifestations; though there is no reason why we should reject whatever measure of truth there may be in this Freudian analysis.

I would begin rather with the simpler facts of common experience, which psychological analysis has only confirmed for us: namely, that the development of art historically has its parallel in the development of the individual, and that human infants exhibit, without embarrassment, many characteristics we find most marked in the artist—above all a certain innocent self-love, which makes him regard his own productions as precious and worthy of attention. Without that fundamental vanity, man might never have had sufficient respect for the materials of symbolism to transform them into works of art—works taking stable form under an exacting discipline, and so capable of influencing the feelings and conduct of other men.

There are, as I see it, three stages in the development of art. Let us pause to examine them a little more closely. I should call them first, the self-enclosed or infantile stage, the stage of self-identification; second, the social or adolescent stage, when exhibitionism passes into communication, with an effort not merely to attract attention but to create something worthy of approval; and finally, a personal or mature stage, when art, transcending the immediate needs of the person or the community, becomes capable of begetting fresh forms of life: when the work of art becomes itself an independent force, directly energizing and renewing those who come into contact with it, even though they may be separated by time and space from the original culture, now vanished, or the original person, now dead. At this final stage, the highest degree of individuation produces the widest range of universality.

Let us follow these stages of maturation. Every person, to begin with, is an object of naive interest to himself: at first, in infancy, he lives almost wholly immersed in his own world, gurgling and babbling, moving and gesturing, full of wonder at all the potentialities for expression he finds in his own organs. This self-preoccupation, I repeat, is a fundamental ingredient in art; and the sense of self-importance that goes with it expresses itself very early in one of the child's earliest commands: *Look at me!* Presently a child finds that he has a better chance of being obeyed if he can, by some grimace or posture, by some cuteness or sweetness, persuade his elders to enter into the game: even bears, monkeys and seals at the zoo advance so far on the road to art. The more lovable a child is or the more beautiful he is in his own person, the easier he finds it to gain attention without simply making a nuisance of himself; and that early lesson in form is underlined by social experience. With the growth of consciousness the demand, "Look at me!" becomes more complicated: in time it means, Look at what is peculiar in me, what is precious in me, what makes me different from every other creature in the world. The individuated, the personal, the nonrepeatable, these are essential characteristics of the esthetic symbol. Perhaps this explains, incidentally, why a perfect forgery in art does not, once we have found the fraud out, please us as much as a relatively poor original.

The second stage of art goes beyond this primitive expressionism and self-identification, indeed self-glorification. After "Look at me!" comes an invitation: *I have something to show you!* Now it is not enough to shout or grimace or shock in order to gain attention; and the artist is no longer content just to satisfy his own vanity. Even Narcissus needs a mirror: and the best mirror, better than any pool or looking glass, however objective its reflection, is another pair of responsive human eyes. Beginning with the artist's self-love, the work of art now becomes a special bond of union. At some very early stage in his development as artist, man discovers the fact that works of art must have attributes of form and proportion and organization similar to—though surely not identical with—those that attract him in natural forms. To gain more than passing attention, the work of art must take on such character.

Here again there is a parallel in childhood. A very little child, after he has gained your attention, will sometimes show you a stone or a dead fly, in an effort to hold your interest; but if he shows you a scrawl on paper he has a better chance of keeping your interest; and, if his drawing shows even a hint of good rhythm or color, he will bring forth even more positive enthusiasm. This brings us to the second characteristic of works of art: they do not hold one long if they are merely insistent or merely shocking; they must also be captivating, and, in some not too blatant way, significant. And yet that significance must not be too obvious and definite, like a numerical sign, which says precisely what it means. On the contrary, it must be a little ambiguous, a little mysterious; it must leave play for an answering response, of an equally indeterminable kind, in the spectator or listener, who thus participates in the creative act.

Not the least peculiarity of art is that it must be capable of stirring hidden depths in the beholder, making him conscious, through his reading of the artist's secret, or a similar secret in his own bosom, just as the virgin, awakened by the first approaches of a lover, becomes conscious of hidden longings and ardors that had hitherto been locked up —or had been attached to cold instructions on the topography and geology of the sexual organs, in dull books entitled "How to be Happy though Adolescent." This second stage in art involves more than self-disclosure: it involves courtship. And at that stage, the artist's gift, his very development, depends upon the existence of a responsive audience, of people not too busy to listen, not so preoccupied with getting and spending that they treat as contemptible or negligible what the artist has to give, above all, not too tired or bored to make the effort of understanding him. Though the true artist paints or writes or composes what he must, and only secondarily to please his contemporaries, he is furthered in that effort by their interest, their pleasure, their intuitive response—and may lose the very incentive to creation for lack of this response. What my friend Matthew Nowicki used to say about architecture—that a great client was essential in the production of a great building—holds for every other form of art; though there have been times when the artist has had to create in fantasy those who would at some later day understand him. This second stage marks the passage from exhibitionism to communication, from the sensational to the emotionally significant and sharable.

But there is a third stage in the development of art: this is the transition from self-love and exhibitionism, from technical virtuosity and courtship, to mature love, capable of giving and taking, of capturing and surrendering, of forming a union that will bring forth a new life. In the third stage, the artist says, through his symbols: Whatever I have shall be yours; whatever life has given me I shall put at your feet, not for any ulterior reward, but because I love you and wish to serve you. I have nothing to hide: you shall know the worst as well as the best, and through art bless both sides of life. Let us share this gift together; and with your help, it will live and grow. This is the stage of full maturity, the stage that only great art reaches, for in both the artist and his community it demands a certain dedication, indeed a certain sacrifice, that sets it off from the more decorative and pleasurable phases of art. At this stage, the esthetic symbol becomes detached from the immediate life of the artist; after draining to the utmost his vitality, it starts, as it were, on an independent career of its own; or perhaps it would be truer to say that the artist's self dissolves into the work of art and transcends the limitations of his personality and culture. When art rises to this stage, the artist feels himself the instrument and agent of a higher force: the final triumph of the person is to lose himself in this act. That is the moment of mature and fruitful love, when with his whole person the artist embraces life as a whole and embodies it in symbols that reconcile its tragic contradictions and release its fullest potentialities.

As you have doubtless noticed, these three stages are a sort of paradigm of sexual love itself; and like sexual love, this development likewise brings with it the same danger of premature arrest or fixation at one of its infantile or adolescent phases, the same difficulty of making the passage from untroubled spontaneity and reckless delight to the full responsibility of a durable sexual union, with all the duties involved in begetting and nurturing offspring. Our society, because it has recklessly overdeveloped both the technics of power and the power of technics, shows many signs of these arrests and these rejections; and the result has been damaging to the arts. Because the very division of labor, with its magnification of the specialist, is hostile to the needs of the whole personality, our society makes life difficult for those who would in any way alter its routine to further such development: so it turns aside, with a disdainful smile, from the artist's secret. Thus, by our own preoccupations with the practical, we condemn the artist, if he seeks to gain attention, to sheer exhibitionism, or at worst, to committing a nuisance, just to attract some small modicum of attention. The Salvador Dalis and the Ezra Pounds are obvious examples of artists who use infantile means to recapture the normal status of the artist in a balanced society. And just because our world is now unwilling to meet the artist half way, it either forces him to make his secret more impenetrable, causing him to invent a private language, even a private mythology, like that of William Blake or James Joyce, to hide his lack of auditors; or its rejection has the effect of turning his love into hate. In that mood, the artist spoils the possibility of union by committing, symbolically, acts of sadistic violence, defying his fellows to have anything to do with him: deforming and dismembering the very body of love, in revenge for his rejection. At this point even the artist's original narcissism becomes negative: instead of self-love there is self-rejection and what is worse, self-hatred. What the esthetic symbols then say, more plainly than downright words, is: "I hate myself; I hate the world; I hate you. *Drop dead!*" Or in the still more significant curse of current slang, the artist now says something even more sadistic and more sinister: *Don't die: suffer!* When life has driven the artist to that point of desperation, such value as the work of art possesses is but a medicinal one for the artist; beyond that there lies only manic violence or blank self-destruction.

You will forgive me, I hope, for dwelling so often on these negative aspects of modern art; but it is sometimes only by understanding the nature of morbid phenomena that one can define the more obvious aspects of health, sanity, balance. As I have sought to interpret it here, art is one of the primary ways in which man has cultivated his own humanness: in which he has developed his sensitiveness, in which he has established rich emotional ties, by means of symbols, with his fellow men, in which he has revealed his constant need for love, first in falling in love with himself and his own organs of expression, and then, through a long process of maturation, reaching the stage of deep communion and unreserved communication, that state which widens into a unity and self-surrender similar to that of erotic love. If art has this essential function in life, it is no accident perhaps that an age that has disregarded art and cast the artist aside, having no use for him except as a vehicle of advertisement or propaganda, it is no accident that this age has also descended close to the level of barbarism in other departments. Nor is it strange that the artist has been driven, almost in self-defense, to cultivate his *in*humanity, or to ally himself with that part of our life, the practical and the technical, which has come to serve as a sterile substitute for the more vital processes and relations. These results follow from our bias.

Let me sum up. Art and technics both represent formative aspects of the human organism. Art stands for the inner and subjective side of man; all its symbolic structures are so many efforts to invent a vocabulary and a language by which man became able to externalize and project his inner states, and most particularly, give a concrete and public form to his emotions, his feelings, his intuitions of the meanings and values of life. Technics, on the contrary, develop mainly out of the necessity to meet and master the external conditions of life, to control the forces of nature and to expand the power and mechanical efficiency of man's own natural organs, on their practical and operational side. Though technics and art have at various periods been in a state of effective unity—so that the fifth century Greeks, for example, used the word technics to apply both to fine art and utilitarian practice, to sculpture and stonecutting—today these two sides of culture have split wide apart. Technics is steadily becoming more automatic, more impersonal, more "objective"; while art, in reaction, shows signs of becoming more neurotic and self-destructive, regressing into primitive or infantile symbolism, to babble and mud pies and formless scrawls. My purpose in these lectures is to bring once more these two sides of life into working relationship.

Allen Tate

SEASONS OF THE SOUL

Dear Whit:

   I am told that it is not an "easy" poem. I have chosen it because it seems to have greater precision of diction than any other
poem of mine; and I like the formal symmetry of the external
features: the ten-line stanza, the refrain of each section, six
stanzas to each section; and then that seasonal progression from
Summer through a Spring which is not completed by a second
Summer. I like it too because an English critic called it "one of
the great longish short poems of this century."

                                                        Allen Tate

To the memory of John Peale Bishop, 1892–1944

Allor porsi la mano un poco avante,
e colsi un ramicel da un gran pruno;
e il tronco suo gridò: Perchè mi schiante?

I. SUMMER

Summer, this is our flesh,
The body you let mature;
If now while the body is fresh
You take it, shall we give
The heart, lest heart endure
The mind's tattering
Blow of greedy claws?
Shall mind itself still live
If like a hunting king
It falls to the lion's jaws?

Under the summer's blast
The soul cannot endure
Unless by sleight or fast
It seize or deny its day
To make the eye secure.
Brothers-in-arms, remember
The hot wind dries and draws
With circular delay
The flesh, ash from the ember,
Into the summer's jaws.

It was a gentle sun
When, at the June solstice
Green France was overrun

With caterpillar feet.
No head knows where its rest is
Or may lie down with reason
When war's usurping claws
Shall take the heart escheat—
Green field in burning season
To stain the weevil's jaws.

The southern summer dies
Evenly in the fall:
We raise our tired eyes
Into a sky of glass,
Blue, empty, and tall
Without tail or head
Where burn the equal laws
For Balaam and his ass
Above the invalid dead,
Who cannot lift their jaws.

When was it that the summer
(Daylong a liquid light)
And a child, the new-comer,
Bathed in the same green spray,
Could neither guess the night?
The summer had no reason;
Then, like a primal cause
It had its timeless day
Before it kept the season
Of time's engaging jaws.

Two men of our summer world
Descended winding hell
And when their shadows curled
They fearfully confounded
The vast concluding shell:
Stopping, they saw in the narrow
Light a centaur pause
And gaze, then his astounded
Beard, with a notched arrow,
Part back upon his jaws.

II. AUTUMN

It had an autumn smell
And that was how I knew
That I was down a well:
I was no longer young;
My lips were numb and blue,
The air was like fine sand
In a butcher's stall
Or pumice to the tongue:
And when I raised my hand
I stood in the empty hall.

The round ceiling was high
And the gray light like shale
Thin, crumbling, and dry:
No rug on the bare floor
Nor any carved detail
To which the eye could glide;
I counted along the wall
Door after closed door
Through which a shade might slide
To the cold and empty hall.

I will leave this house, I said,
There is the autumn weather—
Here, nor living nor dead;
The lights burn in the town
Where men fear together.
Then on the bare floor,
But tiptoe lest I fall,
I walked years down
Towards the front door
At the end of the empty hall.

The door was false—no key
Or lock, and I was caught
In the house; yet I could see
I had been born to it
For miles of running brought
Me back where I began.
I saw now in the wall
A door open a slit
And a fat grizzled man
Come out into the hall:

As in a moonlit street
Men meeting are too shy
To check their hurried feet
But raise their eyes and squint
As through a needle's eye
Into the faceless gloom,—
My father in a gray shawl
Gave me an unseeing glint
And entered another room!
I stood in the empty hall

And watched them come and go
From one room to another,
Old men, old women—slow,
Familiar; girls, boys;
I saw my downcast mother
Clad in her street-clothes,
Her blue eyes long and small,
Who had no look or voice
For him whose vision froze
Him in the empty hall.

III. WINTER

Goddess sea-born and bright,
Return into the sea
Where eddying twilight
Gathers upon your people—
Cold goddess, hear our plea!
Leave the burnt earth, Venus,
For the drying God above,
Hanged in his windy steeple,
No longer bears for us
The living wound of love.

All the sea-gods are dead.
You, Venus, come home
To your salt maidenhead,
The tossed anonymous sea
Under shuddering foam—
Shade for lovers, where
A shark swift as your dive
Shall pace our company
All night to nudge and tear
The livid wound of love.

And now the winter sea:
Within her hollow rind
What sleek facility
Of sea-conceited scop
To plumb the nether mind!
Eternal winters blow
Shivering flakes, and shove
Bodies that wheel and drop—
Cold soot upon the snow
Their livid wound of love.

Beyond the undertow
The gray sea-foliage
Transpires a phosphor glow
Into the circular miles:
In the centre of his cage
The pacing animal
Surveys the jungle cove
And slicks his slithering wiles
To turn the venereal awl
In the livid wound of love.

Beyond the undertow
The rigid madrepore
Resists the winter's flow—
Headless, unageing oak
That gives the leaf no more.
Wilfully as I stood
Within the thickest grove
I seized a branch, which broke;
I heard the speaking blood
(From the livid wound of love)

Drip down upon my toe:
"We are the men who died
Of self-inflicted woe,
Lovers whose stratagem
Led to their suicide."
I touched my sanguine hair
And felt it drip above
Their brother who, like them,
Was maimed and did not bear
The living wound of love.

IV. SPRING

Irritable spring, infuse
Into the burning breast
Your combustible juice
That as a liquid soul
Shall be the body's guest
Who lights, but cannot stay
To comfort this unease
Which, like a dying coal,
Hastens the cooler day
Of the mother of silences.

Back in my native prime
I saw the Orient corn
All space but no time,
Reaching for the sun
Of the land where I was born:
It was a pleasant land
Where even death could please
Us with an ancient pun—
All dying for the hand
Of the mother of silences.

In time of bloody war
Who will know the time?
Is it a new spring star
Within the timing chill,
Talking, or just a mime,
That rises in the blood—
Thin Jack-and-Jilling seas
Without the human will?
Its light is at the flood,
Mother of silences!

It burns us each alone
Whose burning arrogance
Burns up the rolling stone,
This earth—Platonic cave
Of vertiginous chance!
Come, tired Sisyphus,
Cover the cave's egress
Where light reveals the slave,
Who rests when sleeps with us
The mother of silences.

Come, old woman, save
Your sons who have gone down
Into the burning cave:
Come, mother, and lean
At the window with your son
And gaze through its light frame
These fifteen centuries
Upon the shirking scene
Where men, blind, go lame:
Then, mother of silences,

Speak, that we may hear;
Listen, while we confess
That we conceal our fear;
Regard us, while the eye
Discerns by sight or guess
Whether, as sheep foregather
Upon their crooked knees,
We have begun to die;
Whether your kindness, mother,
Is mother of silences.

Erich Fromm

HOPE, FAITH, FORTITUDE

In order to explain why I selected the following pages as being representative of my work, a few words may suffice. In my practice as a psychoanalyst it became clear to me that one can neither understand nor help a person unless one pays the same attention to hope, faith, love, integrity, identity, which has usually been given to doubt, hate, anxiety and fear. Usually the former attitudes are considered as belonging to ethics and philosophy, rather than to psychoanalysis. But clinical experience can show that the lack of hope or faith, the absence of integrity and a sense of identity, can lead to psychic disturbances no less severe than any of the more conventional "complexes" considered in psychopathology. At the same time these "philosophical" concepts, taken by themselves and dealt with without reference to their affective roots remain abstract thought concepts, words conducive only to other words.

The psychoanalytic study of ethical concepts and values is, however, representative only of one part of my work. Most of the book from which these pages are taken deals with another part: the understanding of the interaction between psychic and socio-economic forces. Man can neither be understood without considering his values, nor can he be understood isolated from the society in which he lives. His character is molded by the structure and needs of his society, while in turn man's desires and passions mold society. Man is nothing when considered outside of society; on the other hand society is an abstraction when one forgets that it is made up of living individuals with their given psychic equipment. All this amounts to saying that psychology, philosophy and sociology must be integrated if we want to arrive at a valid "science of man."

Erich Fromm

I. WHAT HOPE IS NOT

Hope is a decisive element in any attempt to bring about social change in the direction of greater aliveness, awareness, and reason. But the nature of hope is often misunderstood and confused with attitudes that have nothing to do with hope and in fact are the very opposite.

What is it to hope?

Is it, as many think, to have desires and wishes? If this were so, those who desire more and better cars, houses, and gadgets would be people of hope. But they are not; they are people lusty for more consumption and not people of hope.

Is it to hope if hope's object is not a thing but a fuller life, a state of greater aliveness, a liberation from eternal boredom; or, to use a theological term, for salvation; or, a political term, for revolution? Indeed, this kind of expectation could be hope; but it is non-hope if it has the quality of passiveness, and "waiting for"—until the hope becomes, in fact, a cover for resignation, a mere ideology.

Kafka has beautifully described this kind of resigned and passive hope in a story in *The Trial*. A man comes to the door leading into heaven (the Law) and begs admittance from the doorkeeper. The doorkeeper says he cannot admit the man at the moment. Although the door leading into the Law stands open, the man decides that he had better wait until he gets permission to enter. So he sits down and waits for days and years. He repeatedly asks to be allowed in, but is always told that he cannot be allowed to enter yet. During all these long years the man studies the doorkeeper almost incessantly and learns to know even the fleas in his fur collar. Eventually, he is old and near death. For the first time, he asks the question, "How does it come about that in all these years no one has come seeking admittance but me?" The doorkeeper answers, "No one but you could gain admittance through this door, since this door was intended for you. I am now going to shut it."

The old man was too old to understand, and maybe he would not have understood if he had been younger. The bureaucrats have the last word; if they say no, he cannot enter. If he had had more than this passive, waiting hope, he would have entered and his courage to disregard the bureaucrats would have been the liberating act which would have carried him to the shining palace. Many people are like Kafka's old man. They hope, but it is not given to them to act upon their heart's impulse, and as long as the bureaucrats do not give the green light they wait and wait.[1]

This kind of passive hope is closely related to a generalized form of hope, which might be described as hoping for *time*. Time and the future become the central category of this kind of hope. Nothing is expected to happen in the *now* but only in the next moment, the next day, the next year, and in another world if it is too absurd to believe that hope can be realized in this world. Behind this belief is the idolatry of "Future," "History," and "Posterity," which began in the French Revolution with men like Robespierre, who worshiped the future as a goddess: I do nothing; I remain passive, because I am nothing and impotent; but the future, the projection of time, will bring about what I cannot achieve. This worship of the future, which is a different aspect of the worship of "progress" in modern bourgeois thought, is precisely the alienation of hope. Instead of something I do or I become, the idols, future and posterity, bring about something without my doing anything.[2]

While passive waiting is a disguised form of hopelessness and impotence, there is another form of hopelessness and despair which takes exactly the opposite disguise—the disguise of phrase making and ad-

---

[1] The Spanish word *esperar* means at the same time waiting and hoping, and quite clearly it refers to that particular kind of passive hope that I am trying to describe here.

[2] The Stalinist concept that history decides what is right and wrong and good and evil is a direct continuation of Robespierre's idolatry of posterity. It is the extreme opposite to the position of Marx, who said, "History is nothing and does nothing. It is man who is and does." Or, in the Theses on Feuerbach, "The materialist doctrine that men are products of circumstances and upbringing, and that, therefore, changed men are products of other circumstances and changed upbringing, forgets that it is men that change circumstances and that the educator himself needs educating."

venturism, of disregard for reality, and of forcing what cannot be forced. This was the attitude of the false Messiahs and of the *Putsch* leaders, who had contempt for those who did not under all circumstances prefer death to defeat. In these days, this pseudo-radical disguise of hopelessness and nihilism is not rare among some of the most dedicated members of the young generation. They are appealing in their boldness and dedication but they become unconvincing by their lack of realism, sense of strategy, and, in some, by lack of love for life.[3]

2. THE PARADOX AND NATURE OF HOPE

Hope is *paradoxical*. It is neither passive waiting nor is it unrealistic forcing of circumstances that cannot occur. It is like the crouched tiger, which will jump only when the moment for jumping has come. Neither tired reformism nor pseudo-radical adventurism is an expression of hope. To hope means to be ready at every moment for that which is not yet born, and yet not become desperate if there is no birth in our lifetime. There is no sense in hoping for that which already exists or for that which cannot be. Those whose hope is weak settle down for comfort or for violence; those whose hope is strong see and

[3] Such hopelessness shines through Herbert Marcuse's *Eros and Civilization* (Boston: Beacon Press, 1955) and *One-Dimensional Man* (Beacon Press, 1964). All traditional values, like love, tenderness, concern, and responsibility, are supposed to have had meaning only in a pretechnological society. In the new technological society—one without repression and exploitation—a new man will arrive who will not have to be afraid of anything, including death, who will develop yet-unspecified needs, and who will have a chance to satisfy his "polymorphous sexuality" (I refer the reader to Freud's *Three Contributions to the Theory of Sex*); briefly, the final progress of man is seen in the regression to infantile life, the return to the happiness of the satiated baby. No wonder that Marcuse ends up in hopelessness: "The critical theory of society possesses no concepts which could bridge the gap between the present and its future; holding no promise and showing no success, it remains negative. Thus it wants to remain loyal to those who, without hope, have given and give their life to the Great Refusal" (*One-Dimensional Man*, p. 257).

These quotations show how wrong those are who attack or admire Marcuse as a revolutionary leader; for revolution was never based on hopelessness, nor can it ever be. But Marcuse is not even concerned with politics; for if one is not concerned with steps between the present and the future, one does not deal with politics, radical or otherwise. Marcuse is essentially an example of an alienated intellectual, who presents his personal despair as a theory of radicalism. Unfortunately, his lack of understanding and, to some extent, knowledge of Freud builds a bridge over which he travels to synthesize Freudianism, bourgeois materialism, and sophisticated Hegelianism into what to him and other like-minded "radicals" seems to be the most progressive theoretical construct. This is not the place to show in detail that it is a naïve, cerebral daydream, essentially irrational, unrealistic, and lacking love of life.

cherish all signs of new life and are ready every moment to help the birth of that which is ready to be born.

Among the confusions about hope one of the major ones is the failure to distinguish between conscious and unconscious hope. This is an error of course, which occurs with regard to many other emotional experiences, such as happiness, anxiety, depression, boredom, and hate. It is amazing that in spite of the popularity of Freud's theories his concept of the unconscious has been so little applied to such emotional phenomena. There are perhaps two main reasons for this fact. One is that in the writings of some psychoanalysts and some "philosophers of psychoanalysis" the whole phenomenon of the unconscious—that is, of repression—refers to sexual desires, and they use repression—wrongly—as synonymous with *suppression* of sexual wishes and activities. In doing so they deprive Freud's discoveries of some of their most important consequences. The second reason lies probably in the fact that it is far less disturbing for the post-Victorian generations to become aware of repressed sexual desires than of those experiences like alienation, hopelessness, and greed. To use only one of the most obvious examples: most people do not admit to themselves feelings of fear, boredom, loneliness, hopelessness—that is to say, they are *unconscious*[4] of these feelings. This is so for a simple reason. Our social pattern is such that the successful man is not supposed to be afraid or bored or lonely. He must find this world the best of all worlds in order to have the best chance for promotion; he must repress fear as well as doubt, depression, boredom, or hopelessness.

There are many who feel consciously hopeful and unconsciously hopeless, and there are a few for whom it is the other way around. What matters in the examination of hope and hopelessness is not primarily what people *think* about their feelings, but what they truly feel. This can be recognized least from their words and phrases, but can be detected from their facial expressions, their way of walking, their capacity to react with interest to something in front of their eyes, and their lack of fanaticism, which is shown in their ability to listen to reasonable argument.

The dynamic viewpoint applied in this book to social-psychological phenomena is fundamentally different from the descriptive behaviorist approach in most social-science research. From the dynamic standpoint,

[4] I want to stress that speaking of "the unconscious" is another form of alienated thinking and speaking. There is no such thing as "the unconscious" as if it were an organ or a thing in space. One can be "conscious of" or "unconscious of" outer or inner events; that is, we deal with a psychic *function,* not with a localized *organ.*

we are not primarily interested in knowing what a person thinks or says or how he behaves *now*. We are interested in his character structure—that is in the semipermanent structure of his energies, in the directions in which they are channeled, and in the intensity with which they flow. If we know the driving forces motivating behavior, not only do we understand present behavior but we can also make reasonable assumptions about how a person is likely to act under changed circumstances. In the dynamic view, surprising "changes" in a person's thought or behavior are changes which mostly could have been foreseen, given the knowledge of his character structure.

More could be said about what hope is *not,* but let us press forward and ask what hope is. Can it be described at all in words or can it only be communicated in a poem, in a song, in a gesture, in a facial expression, or in a deed?

As with every other human experience, words are insufficient to describe the experience. In fact, most of the time words do the opposite: they obscure it, dissect it, and kill it. Too often, in the process of talking about love or hate or hope, one loses contact with what one was supposed to be talking about. Poetry, music, and other forms of art are by far the best-suited media for describing human experience because they are precise and avoid the abstraction and vagueness of worn-out coins which are taken for adequate representations of human experience.

Yet, taking these qualifications seriously, it is not impossible to touch upon feeling experience in words which are not those of poetry. This would not be possible if people did not share the experience one talks about, at least to some degree. To describe it means to point out the various aspects of the experience and thus to establish a communication in which the writer and the reader know that they are referring to the same thing. In making this attempt, I must ask the reader to work with me and not expect me to give him an answer to the question of what hope is. I must ask him to mobilize his own experiences in order to make our dialogue possible.

To hope is a state of being. It is an inner readiness, that of intense but not-yet-spent activeness.[5] The concept of "activity" rests upon one

[5] I owe the term "activeness" (instead of the usual term "activity") to a personal communication from Michael Maccoby; correspondingly I use the term passiveness instead of passivity, when activeness or passiveness refers to an attitude or state of mind.

I have discussed the problem of activity and passivity, especially in connection with the productive orientation, in several books. I want to call the reader's attention to the excellent and profound discussion of activity and passivity in *Metamorphosis* by Ernest Schachtel (New York: Basic Books, 1959).

of the most widespread of man's illusions in modern industrial society. Our whole culture is geared to activity—activity in the sense of being busy, and being busy in the sense of busyness (the busyness necessary for business). In fact, most people are so "active" that they cannot stand doing nothing; they even transform their so-called leisure time into another form of activity. If you are not active making money, you are active driving around, playing golf, or just chatting about nothing. What is dreaded is the moment in which you have really nothing "to do." Whether one calls this kind of behavior activity is a terminological question. The trouble is that most people who think they are very active are not aware of the fact that they are intensely passive in spite of their "busyness." They constantly need the stimulus from the outside, be it other people's chatter, or the sight of the movies, or travel and other forms of more thrilling consumption excitements, even if it is only a new man or woman as a sexual partner. They need to be prompted, to be "turned on," tempted, seduced. They always run and never stand. They always "fall for" and never get up. And they imagine themselves to be immensely active while they are driven by the obsession to do something in order to escape the anxiety that is aroused when they are confronted with themselves.

Hope is a psychic concomitant to life and growth. If a tree which does not get sun bends its trunk to where the sun comes from, we cannot say that the tree "hopes" in the same way in which a man hopes, since hope in man is connected with feelings and awareness that the tree may not have. And yet it would not be wrong to say that the tree hopes for the sunlight and expresses this hope by twisting its trunk toward the sun. Is it different with the child that is born? He may have no awareness, yet his activity expresses his hope to be born and to breathe independently. Does the suckling not hope for his mother's breasts? Does the infant not hope to stand erect and to walk? Does the sick man not hope to be well, the prisoner to be free, the hungry to eat? Do we not hope to wake up to another day when we fall asleep? Does love making not imply a man's hope in his potency, in his capacity to arouse his partner, and the woman's hope to respond and to arouse him?

3. FAITH

When hope has gone life has ended, actually or potentially. Hope is an intrinsic element of the structure of life, of the dynamic of man's spirit. It is closely linked with another element of the structure of life: *faith*. Faith is not a weak form of belief or knowledge; it is not faith in this or that; faith is the conviction about the not yet proven, the knowledge of the real possibility, the awareness of pregnancy. Faith is rational when it refers to the knowledge of the real yet unborn; it is based on the faculty of knowledge and comprehension, which penetrates the surface and sees the kernel. Faith, like hope, is not prediction of the *future;* it is the vision of the *present* in a state of pregnancy.

The statement that faith is certainty needs a qualification. It is certainty about the reality of the possibility—but it is not certainty in the sense of unquestionable predictability. The child may be stillborn prematurely; it may die in the act of birth; it may die in the first two weeks of life. That is the paradox of faith: *it is the certainty of the uncertain.* It is certainty in terms of man's vision and comprehension; it is not certainty in terms of the final outcome of reality. We need no faith in that which is scientifically predictable, nor can there be faith in that which is impossible. Faith is based on our experience of living of transforming ourselves. Faith that others can change is the outcome of the experience that I can change.

There is an important distinction between rational and irrational faith. While rational faith is the result of one's own inner activeness in thought or feeling, irrational faith is submission to something given, which one accepts as true regardless of whether it is or not. The essential element of all irrational faith is its passive character, be its object an idol, a leader, or an ideology. Even the scientist needs to be free from irrational faith in traditional ideas in order to have rational faith in the power of his creative thought. Once his discovery is "proved," he needs no more faith, except in the next step he is contemplating. In the sphere of human relations, "having faith" in another person means to be certain of his *core*—that is, of the reliability and unchangeability of his fundamental attitudes. In the same sense we can have faith in ourselves—not in the constancy of our opinions but in our basic orientation to life, the matrix of our character structure. Such faith is conditioned by the experience of self, by our capacity to say "I" legitimately, by the sense of our identity.

Hope is the mood that accompanies faith. Faith could not be sustained without the mood of hope. Hope can have no base except in faith.

4. FORTITUDE

There is still another element linked with hope and faith in the structure of life: courage, or, as Spinoza called it, fortitude. Fortitude is perhaps the less ambiguous expression, because today courage is more often used to demonstrate the courage to die rather than the courage to live. Fortitude is the capacity to resist the temptation to compromise hope and faith by transforming them—and thus destroying them—into empty optimism or into irrational faith. Fortitude is the capacity to say "no" when the world wants to hear "yes."

But fortitude is not fully understood unless we mention another aspect of it: fearlessness. The fearless person is not afraid of threats, not even of death. But, as so often, the word "fearless" covers several entirely different attitudes. I mention only the three most important ones: First, a person can be fearless because he does not care to live; life is not worth much to him, hence he is fearless when it comes to the danger of dying; but while he is not afraid of death, he may be afraid of life. His fearlessness is based on lack of love of life; he is usually not fearless at all when he is not in the situation of risking his life. In fact, he frequently looks for dangerous situations, in order to avoid his fear of life, of himself, and of people.

A second kind of fearlessness is that of the person who lives in symbiotic submission to an idol, be it a person, an institution, or an idea; the commands of the idol are sacred; they are far more compelling than even the survival commands of his body. If he could disobey or doubt these commands of the idol, he would face the danger of losing his identity with the idol; this means he would be running the risk of finding himself utterly isolated, and thus at the verge of insanity. He is willing to die because he is afraid of exposing himself to this danger.

The third kind of fearlessness is to be found in the fully developed person, who rests within himself and loves life. The person who has overcome greed does not cling to any idol or any thing and hence has nothing to lose: he is rich because he is empty, he is strong because he is not the slave of his desires. He can let go of idols, irrational desires, and fantasies, because he is in full touch with reality, inside and outside himself. If such a person has reached full "enlightenment," he is completely fearless. If he has moved toward this goal without having arrived, his fearlessness will also not be complete. But anyone who tries to move toward the state of being fully himself knows that whenever a new step toward fearlessness is made, a sense of strength and joy is awakened that is unmistakable. He feels as if a new phase of life had begun. He can feel the truth of Goethe's lines: "I have put my house on nothing, that's why the whole world is mine." (*Ich hab mein Haus auf nichts gestellt, deshalb gehoert mir die ganze Welt.*)

Hope and faith, being essential qualities of *life,* are by their very nature moving in the direction of transcending the *status quo,* individually and socially. It is one of the qualities of all life that it is in a constant process of change and never remains the same at any given moment. Life that stagnates tends to die; if the stagnation is complete, death has occurred. It follows that life in its moving quality tends to break out of and to overcome the *status quo.* We grow either stronger or weaker, wiser or more foolish, more courageous or more cowardly. Every second is a moment of decision, for the better or the worse. We feed our sloth, greed, or hate, or we starve it. The more we feed it, the stronger it grows; the more we starve it, the weaker it becomes.

What holds true for the individual holds true for a society. It is never static; if it does not grow, it decays; if it does not transcend the *status quo* for the better, it changes for the worse. Often we, the individual or the people who make up a society, have the illusion we could stand still and not alter the given situation in the one or the other direction. This is one of the most dangerous illusions. The moment we stand still, we begin to decay.

Edward Albee

BOX

I have decided to let my brief play, *Box*, represent me in the present edition of *This Is My Best* for several reasons. For one, I would rather be represented by a complete work than an excerpt from a long piece, and while it is true that *Box* is, in a sense, attached in performance to another shortish play, *Quotations from Chairman Mao Tse-Tung*, it does stand by itself as (to my mind) a complete dramatic experience. Also, *Box* is among my newest works and in that sense makes, I suppose, a pertinent if not necessarily coherent statement of my present dramatic intentions. And finally, I'm quite attached to this particular play.

Edward Albee

Curtain *rises in darkness. Lights go up slowly to reveal the interior of a large cube. The cube should take up almost all of a small stage opening. The side facing the audience is open, but we should see the other five sides clearly, therefore the interior of the cube should be distorted, smaller at the backstage side, for example; also, none of the sides should be exactly square in shape, but the angles of distortion should not be very great— not so great as to call attention to themselves and destroy the feeling of a cube. The twelve joins, including those at the open side, should be painted with a thin line of either black or dark red. The interior of the cube itself should be a greyish white with a faint blue cast. When the lights are fully up on the cube —quite bright light which stays constant until the final dimout —there should be five seconds silence.*

VOICE—[*The* VOICE *should not come from the stage, but should seem to be coming from nearby the spectator—from the back or the sides of the theatre. The* VOICE *of a woman; not young, but not ancient, either; fiftyish. Neither a sharp, crone's voice, but not refined. A middle-western farm woman's voice would be best.*

Matter-of-fact; announcement of a subject] Box. [*Five second silence*] Box. [*Three second silence*] Nicely done. Well put . . . [*Pause*] . . . together. Box [*Three second silence. More conversational now*] Room inside for a sedia d'ondalo, which, in English—for that is

BOX 957

Italian—would be, is, rocking chair. Room to rock. *And* room to move about in . . . some. Enough. [*Three second silence*] Carpentry is among the arts going out . . . or crafts, if you're of a nonclassical disposition. There are others: other arts which have gone down to craft and which are going further . . . walls, brick walls, music . . . [*Pause*] . . . the making of good bread if you won't laugh; living. Many arts: all craft now . . . and going further. But *this* is solid, perfect joins . . . good work. Knock and there's no give—no give of sound, I mean. A thud; no hollow. Oh, very good work; fine timber, and so fastidious, like when they shined the bottoms of the shoes . . . *and* the instep. Not only where you might *expect* they'd shine the bottoms if they *did* . . . but even the instep. [*Two second silence. Grudging, but not very*] *And* other crafts have come up . . . if not to replace, then . . . occupy. [*Tiny laugh*] Nature abhors, among so many, so much else . . . amongst so much, us, itself, they say, vacuum. [*Five second silence. A listening*] System as conclusion, in the sense of method as an end, the dice so big you can hardly throw them any more. [*Some awe, some sadness*] Seven hundred million babies dead in the time it takes, took, to knead the dough to make a proper loaf. Well, little wonder so many . . . went . . . cut off, said no instead of hanging on. [*Three second silence*] Apathy, I think. [*Five second silence*] Inevitability. And progress is merely a direction, movement. [*Earnest*] When it was *simple* . . . [*Light, self-mocking laugh*] Ah, well, yes, when it was simple. [*Three second silence. Wistful*] Beautiful, beautiful box. [*Three second silence*] *And* room enough to walk around in, take a turn. [*Tiny pause*] If only they had *told* us! Clearly! When it was clear that we were not only corrupt—for there is nothing that is not, or little— but corrupt to the selfishness, to the corruption that we should die to keep it . . . go under rather than . . . [*Three second silence. Sigh*] Oh, my. [*Five second silence*] Or was it the milk? *That* may have been the moment: spilling and spilling and killing all those children to make a point. A penny or two, and a symbol at that, and I suppose the children were symbolic, too, though they died, and couldn't stop. Once it starts—gets to a certain point—the momentum is too much. But spilling milk! [*Two second silence. Firmly felt*] Oh, shame! [*A little schoolmarmish*] The *Pope* warned us; *he* said so. There are no possessions, he said; so long as there are some with nothing we have no right to anything [*Two second silence*] It's the *little* things, the *small* cracks. Oh, for every pound of milk they spill you can send a check to someone, but that does not unspill. That it *can* be *done* is the crack. And if you go back to a partita . . . ahhhhh, what when it makes you cry!? Not from the beauty of it, but from solely that you cry from loss . . . so precious. When art begins to hurt . . . when art begins to hurt it's time to look around. Yes it is. [*Three second silence*] Yes it is. [*Three second silence*] No longer just great beauty which takes you more to everything, but a reminder! And not of what *can* . . . but what *has*. Yes, when art hurts . . . [*Three second silence*] Box. [*Two second silence*] And room enough to move around, except like a fly. That would be *very* good! [*Rue*] Yes, but so would so much. [*Two second silence. Schoolmarmish*] Here is the thing about tension and the tonic—the important thing. [*Pause*] The release of tension is the return to consonance; no matter how far travelled, one comes back, not circular, not to the starting point, but a . . . setting down again, and the beauty of art is order —not what is familiar, necessarily, but order . . . on its own terms. [*Two second silence. Sigh*] So much . . . flies. A billion birds at once, black net skimming the ocean, or the monarchs that time, that island, blown by the wind, but going straight . . . in a direction. Order! [*Two second silence*] And six sides to bounce it all off of. [*Three second silence. Brave start again*] When the beauty of it reminds us of *loss*. Instead of the attainable. When it tells us what we cannot have . . . well, then . . . it no longer relates . . . *does* it. That is the thing about music. That is why we cannot listen any more. [*Pause*] Because we cry. And *if* he says, or *she* . . . why are you doing that?, and, and your only honest response is: art hurts . . . [*Little laugh*] Well. [*Five second silence*] Look! More birds! Another . . . sky of them. [*Five second silence*] It is not a matter of garden, or straight lines, or even . . . morality. It's only when you can't come back; when you get in some distant key; that when you say, the tonic! the tonic! and they say, what is *that*? It's *then*. [*Three second silence*] There! More! A thousand, and one below them, moving fast in the opposite way! [*Two second silence.*] What was it used to frighten me? Bell buoys and sea gulls; the *sound* of them, at night, in a fog, when I was very young. [*A little laugh.*] Before I had ever seen them, before I had heard them. [*Some wonder.*] But I knew what they *were* . . . a thousand miles from the sea. Land-locked, never been, and yet the sea sounds . . . [*Three second silence. Very matter-of-fact*] Well, we can exist with *anything*; without. There's little that we need to have to go on . . . evolving. Goodness; we

BOX   959

all died when we were thirty once. Now, much younger. Much. [*Suddenly aware of something*] But it *couldn't* have been fog, not the sea-fog. Not way back *there*. It was the memory of it, to be seen and proved later. And more! and more! they're all moving! The memory of what we have not known. And so it is with the fog, which I had never seen, yet knew it. And the resolution of a chord; no difference. [*Three second silence*] And even that can happen here, I guess. But unprovable. Ahhhhh. That makes the difference, does it *not*. Nothing can seep here except the memory of what I'll not prove. [*Two second silence. Sigh*] Well, we give up something for something. [*Three second silence. Listening again; pleased*] Sturdy, light . . . interesting . . . in its way. Room enough for a sedia d'ondalo, which is the Italian of . . . or for . . . of, I prefer . . . The Italian of rocking chair. [*Three second silence*] When art hurts. That is what to remember. [*Two second silence*] What to look for. Then the corruption . . . [*Three second silence*] Then the corruption is complete. [*Five second silence. The sound of bell buoys and sea gulls begins, faintly, growing, but never very loud*] Nothing belongs. [*Three second silence. Great sadness*] Look; more of them; a black net . . . skimming. [*Pause*] And just one . . . moving beneath . . . in the opposite way. [*Three second silence. Very sad, supplicating*] Milk. [*Three second silence*] Milk. [*Five second silence. Wistful*] Box.

Silence, except for the sound of bell buoys and sea gulls. Very slow fading of lights to black, sound of bell buoys and sea gulls fading with the light.

Pearl S. Buck

Last Pages from
A BRIDGE FOR PASSING

Dear Mr. Burnett:

   Your letter catches me as I am about to catch a plane for
Korea . . .

   I enclose a few pages from the last of my book, *A Bridge for
Passing*.

Sincerely yours,
Pearl S. Buck

I say New York, although of course New York is only on the way to
my farmhouse home in Pennsylvania. But I have a stopping place in
New York, that city of wonders and grief. He and I always kept a place
there. He needed it for his work and for his spirit, and I have continued
our tradition. It is not the same place we shared for so many years.
Within the confines of our old apartment I could not escape the torture
of memory. Whether I would have stayed I do not know, but the sky-
scrapers of steel and glass had pushed their way up our avenue, and the
building in which we had made a city home was to be torn down. I
found a place farther uptown in a new building, where there were no
memories except the ones I carry hidden wherever I am.

And here I tell a story that has nothing to do with the picture, except
that it provides a closing scene for myself. When I was looking for the
new apartment a daughter helped me by sorting out the impossibles
and bringing me at last to see the two or three possibles. It was night,
I remember, when I looked at these places. I was in haste and it did not
seem to matter much where I lived. We entered bare unpainted rooms.
I saw a wide window and through the darkness I discerned dimly a
building whose roof faced my window, a school, my daughter said, and
fortunate for me, for there would be no high building to cut off the view.
I did not care very much about that, either, for when do I have time
in New York to look at a view? Besides, I have plenty of view in my
Pennsylvania home. So I decided upon impulse.

"I'll take it."

The choice was haphazard, I would have said, a chancy thing. But I am beginning to believe that there is no such thing as pure chance in this world. For here is the preliminary to this closing story:

When I was a child and often reluctant to do my duty, my father used to say to me firmly but gently,

"If you will not do it because it is right, then do it for the greater glory of God."

For the greater glory of God then, and for my father's sake, though still reluctant, I did do what had to be done, at least as often as possible.

Now to return to the apartment. I did not once see it while it was being decorated. When all was finished I opened the door and went straight to the big window. It was a bright day, I remember, one of New York's best, the air fresh from the sea and the sky blue. And facing me, across the building, under the eaves and along the roof, I saw these words carved in huge stone letters:

AD MAIOREM DEI GLORIAM

They face me now as I write. To the greater glory of God! What does it mean, this voice from the grave, my father's grave? He lies buried on a mountaintop in the very heart of a China lost to me. I am here and alive and thousands of miles away. Are we in communication, he and I, through my father? It is not possible.

How dare I say it is not?

Some day we shall know. What day? That day, perhaps, when saints and scientists unite to make a total search for truth. It is the saints, the believers, who should have the courage to urge the scientists to help them discover whether the spirit continues its life of energy when the mass we call body ceases to be the container. Faith supplies the hypothesis, but only science can provide the computer for verification. The unbeliever will never pursue the search. He is already static, a pillar of salt, forever looking backward.

There are no miracles, of that I am sure. If one walks on water and heals the sick and raises the dead to life again, it is not a matter of magic but a matter of knowing how to do it. There is no supernatural; there is only the supremely natural, the purely scientific. Science and religion, religion and science, put it as I may, they are two sides of the same glass, through which we see darkly until these two, focusing together, reveal the truth.

On the day when the message comes through from over the far horizon where dwells "that great majority," the dead, the proof will reach us, not as a host of angels in the sky but as a wave length recorded in a laboratory, a wave length as indisputable and personal as the fingerprint belonging to someone whose body is dust. Then the scientist, recognizing the wave length, will exclaim, "But that's someone I know! I took his wave length before he died." And he will compare his record with the wave length just recorded and will know that at last a device, a machine, is able to receive a message dreamed of for centuries, the message of the continuing individual existence, which we call the immortality of the soul.

Or perhaps it will not be a scientist who receives, but a woman, waiting at a window open to the sky.

Perkasie, Pennsylvania

Conrad Aiken

THEE

I think poetry is now facing, as it has always had to face,
whenever man's mind, as it develops, runs too fast and far in so
short a time—as in the great period of Greek poetry, or that of
the Elizabethans—an extraordinary challenge. Those of us who
came to consciousness sixty or seventy years ago—Robinson,
Eliot, Frost, Stevens, Williams, Pound and myself—faced a new
world. And not the world the pretty history books had been
laying out before us. Henry Adams was its prophet: in his
astonishing book, *The Degradation of the Dogma,* he had predicted that the second decade of this century would initiate a
new phase of history, with revolutions, social, intellectual,
scientific and moral, which would change our world forever.
Sure enough, Freud, on the one hand, and Einstein, on the
other, were prompt to take their cues, with the Russian revolution, as it were, for orchestra. Impossible, challenged by these,
and the shadows of Nietzsche and Darwin behind them, ever
again to accept the neat little religious or philosophical systems
we had inherited in a universe that now looked rather alarmingly like pure mathematics. And this is where the poet comes
in, where he *must* come in. He is vis-à-vis with a revelation
the like of which man has never seen before, in its complexity
and order and beauty. It is he who can articulate this magnificent vision for us, and give us its meaning, and, with it, *our*
meaning. The vacuum left by lost beliefs and myths must be
filled. And it will be filled, I feel no doubt about that, by the
poets. How to go about it—? That's the question for each of us
to answer. Relativity will have a place in the answer, and all

the new knowledges now at our disposal. We must become
explorers again, and worshipers too again, but in a new sense.
As for my own choice for this anthology, I was torn between
two poems, "Thee," and "The Crystal," the former because it
deals with the problem of worship, and of what, the latter
because it makes a mathematical and Pythagorean approach to
somewhat the same thing. "Thee" was chosen finally because
it was the more recent. And also because, though it describes
the search for the Absolute, it exists as a poem in its own right,
and with the ambiguities which that implies.

                                                    Conrad Aiken

How to condemn THEE
yet also hymn THEE
how to praise THEE
yet also paraphrase THEE
how to proclaim THEE
yet also shame THEE

Wind blows
and mind blows with it
water flows
and mind flows with it
where shall I abide
cries the spirit
mind changes
and body changes with it
body changes
and mind changes with it
where shall I abide

cries the spirit
but also
says the spirit
north
south
east
west
at every compass point
I am still
I am at rest
I had and have no name
without it came
perhaps the wet
and still-by-night-dew-tightly-twisted
morning-glory

tiger at evening drinking
by moonlit water
and the all-thinking
skin of the earth
in which we move
and are a part
are single and same
all one hate
all one love.

Wind blows
but over what shall it blow
dead men encased in ice
men dying in snow
children lying in stretchers
their faces under the rain
the wounded animal
seeking out a hole
in which to lick his pain
and the bird
that symbol of the soul
coasting on the wind
for the last time
under the balsam

to hide his
death.
Cry death cry death
we come into the world
kicking and screaming
we go out of the world
kicking and screaming
and all between
is but
scheming
and
dreaming
and
seeming.

The spirit says
I am I
The spirit says
somewhere my cry
inarticulate and ignorant
though it be
may be heard
by the ultimate
unimaginable
THEE.
Who is that pitiless THEE
whom only in ourselves we see
or in the lightning-stroke
and stricken oak
and our young darlings doomed too soon to bed
without sin
and from within
by THEE and THINE?

Who is that hateful THEE
who makes a music of the sea
and of the clouds a harmony
or spreads a meadow broad and bright
with colors of delight
or brings the young with joy together

as birds of a feather
makes all the visible world a wedding feast
with love in every eye
and every breast
so that we think too long
that life is only song?
Unfaithful THEE
for suddenly the sea
rises and breaks the ship
blues every lip
cry death cry death
and we
and all the world we brought with us
thanks to THEE
go out of the world
or back to the world
to rejoin
unwillingly
and unconsciously
THEE.

Who is that splendid THEE
who makes a symphony
of the one word
be
admitting us to see
all things but THEE?
In the microcosm
in the macrocosm
it is THEE that we seek out
seeking to find
the workings of our mind
and THINE.
Wild columbine
admits THEE
wild rose
permits THEE
the seasons obey
THY reasons
yet further in our explorations do we go

the less we know.
Visible to the child
as butterfly
as lion
as mother
as father
moving under the microscope
or telescope
as smallest item or utmost star
yet THEE is still invisible
still indivisible.
How explain the morning that we wake to
the opening of the eye
the toothbrush
the toilet
the basket for soiled clothes
the fly's wing so designed
that it might be
a cathedral window
meant
for THEE?
Unkind THEE
did THEE have the fly in mind
and in THY warp and woof enwind
him and all his kind
to live his glorious dunghill day
then swept like snot away?

Who is that glorious THEE
sleeping and waking
the slow hushed life of tree
barely knowing
THINE own growing
then breaking and weeping
from THINE own sleeping?
We break and bud with THEE
put arms out like THY tree
and sing
inaudibly
in spring

as cold bark buds and breaks
and THEE awakes
and south wind shakes
the leaves that are THINE eyes
also THY breath
and
when THY calendar names it
death.

Nameless and shameless we
take THINE identity
to be
then
not to be
sharing with THEE
and daring
and O caring
for what is delicious
and what precious
learning how slowly what to choose
and what refuse
what use
and what abuse.
Laboriously the spirit learns
THY shadow upon us like the cloud's
shadow upon the meadow
as if perhaps in our slow growing
and the beginnings of our knowing
as if perhaps
O could this be
that we
be
THEE?
THEE still learning
or first learning
through us
to be
THY THEE?

Self-praise were then our praise of THEE
unless we say divinity
cries in us both as we draw breath
cry death cry death
and all our hate
we must abate
and THEE must with us meet and mate
give birth give suck be sick and die
and close the All-God-Giving-Eye
for the last time to sky.

Weather changes
and the spirit changes with it
climate changes
and the spirit changes with it
where shall I abide
cries the spirit
north
south
east
west
yet at no compass-point
is final rest
what fatal quest
is this
that we and THEE
in every THING
and every breast
must still pursue
and do?

Magnificent THEE
the syllables I speak
and which are THINE
and mine
still cannot equal THEE
who art becoming and have yet to be
and learn to speak
as we
with THEE.

Biographies and Bibliographies

The following biographies and bibliographies have been carefully compiled from the best available sources, and have been checked personally by each author. While every effort has been taken to make them complete in every detail, some authors have requested that some early books be excluded from the bibliographies as juvenilia and others have requested the exclusion of pamphlets, textbooks, etc.

An asterisk before a title indicates the author has selected from that book material printed in *This Is My Best*. Unless otherwise specified most publishing houses mentioned are located in New York City.

The Editor

CONRAD (POTTER) AIKEN was born in Savannah, Georgia, August 5, 1889, and graduated from Harvard in 1911, contemporary with Walter Lippmann, John Reed, and T. S. Eliot. His first book appeared in 1914, followed to date by more than forty books of poetry, short stories, novels, criticism, drama and autobiography, besides several anthologies.

Mr. Aiken held the Chair of Poetry at the Library of Congress from 1950 to 1952. From 1933 to 1936 he was London correspondent of *The New Yorker*, from 1917 to 1919 contributing editor of *The Dial*. He has been married three times and now lives in Savannah, and at Brewster, Massachusetts.

He has won the following honors: Pulitzer Prize for poetry, 1929; Bryher Award, 1952; National Book Award for *Collected Poems*, 1954; Fellow in American Letters, 1947; Bollingen Prize for poetry, 1956, Gold medal for poetry, National Institute of Arts and Letters, 1958; Huntington Hartford Foundation Award in Literature, 1961; St. Botolph Award, 1964; Brandeis Medal for poetry, 1967. In 1969 he received the National Book Committee's Medal for Literature. He is a member of the American Academy of Arts and Letters.

*"Thee," the metaphysical work published by George Braziller, 1967, represents Mr. Aiken in *This Is My Best*.

Earth Triumphant, and Other Tales, Macmillan, 1914

Turns and Movies (poetry), Houghton, 1916

The Jig of Forslin (poetry), Four Seas, 1916

Nocturne of Remembered Spring (poetry), Four Seas, 1917

The Charnel Rose (poetry), Four Seas, 1918

Scepticisms—Notes on Contemporary Poetry, Knopf, 1919

The House of Dust (poetry), Four Seas, 1920

Punch, the Immortal Liar (poetry), Knopf, 1921

Priapus and the Pool (poetry), Dunster House, 1922

Modern American Poets (anthology), Secker, 1922

The Pilgrimage of Festus (poetry), Knopf, 1923

Selected Poems of Emily Dickenson (editor), Jonathan Cape, London, 1924

Priapus and the Pool, and Other Poems, Liveright, 1925

Bring! Bring!, and Other Stories, Liveright, 1925

Blue Voyage (novel), Scribners, 1927

Costumes by Eros (short stories), Scribners, 1928

Prelude (poetry), Equinox Cooperative Press, 1929

Selected Poems, Scribners, 1929

American Poetry, 1671–1928 (anthology), Modern Library, 1929

John Deth, and Other Poems, Scribners, 1930

Gehenna (short story), Random, 1930

The Coming Forth by Day of Osiris Jones (poetry), Scribners, 1931

Preludes for Memnon (poetry), Scribners, 1931

Great Circle (novel), Scribners, 1933

And in the Hanging Gardens (poetry), privately printed, 1933

Among the Lost People (short stories), Scribners, 1934

Landscape West of Eden (poetry), Scribners, 1935

King Coffin (novel), Scribners, 1935

Time in the Rock (poetry), Scribners, 1936

A Heart for the Gods of Mexico (novel), Secker, London, 1939

The Conversation (novel), Duell, 1940

And in the Human Heart (poetry), Duell, 1940

Brownstone Eclogues (poems), Duell, 1942

The Soldier (poem), New Directions, 1949

Skylight One (poems), Oxford, 1949

The Short Stories of Conrad Aiken, Duell, 1950

Ushant (autobiography), Duell, 1952

Collected Poems, Oxford, 1953

A Letter From Li Po (poems), Oxford, 1956

Mr. Arcularis, Harvard Univ. Press, 1957

Sheepfold Hill (poems), Sagamore Press, 1957

A Reviewer's ABC (criticism), *Meridian Books,* 1958

The Collected Short Stories of Conrad Aiken, World, 1960

Selected Poems, Oxford, 1961

20th Century American Poetry, (editor), Modern Library, 1963

The Morning Song of Lord Zero (poems), Oxford, 1963

The Collected Novels of Conrad Aiken, Holt, 1964

A Seizure of Limericks (poems), Holt, 1964

Cats and Bats and Things with Wings (poems), Atheneum, 1965

Tom, Sue and the Clock (poem), Collier, 1966

Preludes (poems), Oxford, 1966

EDWARD ALBEE was born March 12, 1928, in Washington, D.C., adoptive son of Reed A. and Frances (Cotter) Albee. He attended Lawrenceville School, Valley Forge Military Academy and graduated Choate School. He also attended Trinity College, Hartford, Connecticut, for a year and a half and, before settling down to being a writer, in 1958, he had worked at various jobs including that of record salesman, luncheonette counterman, music program writer for WNYC, New York, and messenger for Western Union. In 1953 Thornton Wilder suggested he try writing plays, and *The Zoo Story* was his first professional production in 1959. At twelve, however, he had already tried his hand at a play, a three-act sex farce.

In 1960 Mr. Albee received the Vernon Rice Memorial Award for *The Zoo Story,* and the Lola D'Annuzio Award in 1961; *Who's Afraid of Virginia Woolf* received the New York Drama Critics Award, the American National Theatre and Academy Award, Foreign Press Association Award, five Tony Awards and three Outer Circle Critics Awards. For *A Delicate Balance* he received the Pulitzer Prize in 1966–1967.

Mr. Albee lives in New York City and Montauk, Long Island.

The Zoo Story, produced in Berlin, 1959; New York, 1960; New American Lib., 1961

The Death of Bessie Smith, Coward, 1959

The Sandbox, Coward, 1960

The Sandbox, Dramatists Play Service, 1960

The American Dream, Coward, 1961

Who's Afraid of Virginia Woolf? Atheneum, 1962

Ballad of the Sad Cafe (adaptation), 1963; Atheneum-Houghton, 1963

Tiny Alice, produced 1964; Atheneum, 1965

Malcolm, (adaptation), Atheneum, 1965

A Delicate Balance, Atheneum, 1966

Everything in the Garden (adaptation), produced 1967; Atheneum, 1968

*Box, and *Quotations from Chairman Mao Tse-tung*, Atheneum, 1968

ISAAC ASIMOV, who writes also under the name of Paul French, was born January 2, 1920, in the Union of Soviet Socialist Republics, son of Judah and Anna Rachel (Berman) Asimov, and was brought to the United States at three, becoming an American citizen five years later. He was educated at Columbia University, B.S. in 1939, M.A., in 1941, and PhD. in 1948. He is married, has a son and daughter and lives in Massachusetts. Since 1955, he has been associate professor of biochemistry at Boston University School of Medicine.

Dr. Asimov, who says he has "ceased to list" his books* is one of the most prolific writers in his adopted country, having produced more than one hundred volumes since 1950, many of them science fiction novels and others in many fields of science, from *The Search for the Elements*, *The Human Body* and *Inside the Atom*, to *Satellites in Outer Space*, and *Asimov's Biographical Encyclopedia of Science and Technology*. He has also edited anthologies of science fiction.

"Is Anyone There?" may be found among the essays on science and its possibilities in a volume of the same title, Doubleday, 1967. Doubleday is only one of his numerous publishers. In the autumn of 1969 Dr. Asimov published selections from his varied writings as his hundredth book. It appeared under the title *Opus One Hundred* and he prefaced each selection with a short comment. It was published by Houghton Mifflin Co., Boston.

Dr. Asimov's *Fantastic Voyage*, Houghton Mifflin, 1966, was made from the science fiction motion picture.

LOUIS (STANTON) AUCHINCLOSS, born September 27, 1917, in Lawrence, Long Island, New York, is a descendant of a Scottish merchant family which settled in New York City at the beginning of the last century. Author of eighteen books, most of them novels written while practicing law with a Wall Street firm, Mr. Auchincloss, a member of the National Institute of Arts and Letters, finds time to serve as President of the Museum of the City of New York. He is married, has three children and lives with his family in Manhattan, the scene of many of his books.

Mr. Auchincloss spent six years at Groton School and three at Yale. He quit Yale "in a fit of immature discouragement over a publisher's rejection of my first novel." He graduated law school at the University of Virginia in 1941 when he joined the Navy, serving in the Canal Zone, and both the Atlantic and Pacific. He was Executive Officer of an LST in the landings in Normandy and in command of one in the Pacific.

The Indifferent Children (pseudonym, ANDREW LEE) Prentice-Hall, 1947

The Injustice Collectors (stories) Houghton, 1950

Sybil, Houghton, 1952

A Law for the Lion, Houghton, 1953

The Romantic Egoists, Houghton, 1954

*A listing of the Asimov books appears as an appendix in his *Opus One Hundred*.

The Great World and Timothy Colt,
Houghton, 1956
Venus in Sparta, Houghton, 1958
Pursuit of the Prodigal, Houghton, 1959
The House of Five Talents, Houghton,
1960
Reflections of a Jacobite, Houghton, 1961
Portrait in Brownstone, Houghton, 1962
Powers of Attorney, Houghton, 1963
*The Rector of Justin, Houghton, 1964
Pioneers and Caretakers (nine American
Women Novelists) Univ. of Minnesota,
Press, 1965
The Embezzler, Houghton, 1966
Tales of Manhattan, Houghton, 1967
A World of Profit, Houghton, 1968
Motiveless Malignity (on Shakespeare),
Houghton, 1969

W. H. (WYSTAN HUGH) AUDEN was born
February 21, 1907, in York, England, but
came to the United States in 1939 where
he became a citizen in 1946. Educated at
Oxford, he was a schoolmaster near Mal-
vern, England, from 1930 to 1935; took
part in the founding of the Group Theatre in 1932; worked with a film unit of
the General Post Office in 1935 (*Night
Mail* and *Coal-Face*); traveled to Iceland
in 1936, was a stretcher bearer for the
Loyalists in Spain in 1937, and traveled in
China with Christopher Isherwood in
1938.

Mr. Auden began teaching in America
in 1939 at St. Mark's School, Massachusetts, New School for Social Research
in 1940, University of Michigan, 1941,
Swarthmore, 1942–45, Bryn Mawr College, 1943–1945, Bennington College,
1946, Barnard College, 1947, Smith, 1953.
He was professor of poetry at Oxford
from 1956 to 1961. He has been editor
of the *Yale Series of Younger Poets* since
1947. He was founder with Lionel Trilling
and Jacques Barzun of the Reader's Subscription Book Club serving from 1951
to 1959 when they established the Mid-
Century Book Society.

He has been a member of the Ameri-
can Academy of Arts and Letters since
1954, and has received the following
awards: King's Gold Medal for poetry,
1937; Guggenheim fellowships, 1942,
1945; Award of Merit Medal, American
Academy of Arts and Letters, 1945; Pulitzer Prize in Poetry, 1948, for *The Age of
Anxiety;* Bollingen Prize in Poetry, 1954;
National Book Award, 1956, for *The
Shield of Achilles;* Feltrinelli Prize
(Rome), 1957; Alexander Droutzkoy
Memorial Award, 1959; shared Guiness
Poetry Award (Ireland) with Robert
Lowell and Edith Sitwell, 1959; honored
on Chicago Poetry Day, 1960; Honorary
Student (Fellow), Christ College, Oxford,
1962; National Medal for Literature,
1967; National Arts Club gold medal for
poetry, 1969.

Poems, hand printed by Stephen Spender,
Oxford, 1928; Faber, 1930; second ed.,
1933; Random, 1934; revised, Faber,
1960
The Orators, An English Study (poems
and prose), Faber, 1932
Look, Stranger, Faber, 1936; in America
as *On This Island,* Random, 1937
Spain, Faber, 1937
Letters from Iceland, Random, 1937
Selected Poems, Faber, 1938
Journey to War (with CHRISTOPHER ISHER-
WOOD), Random, 1939
Another Time, Random, 1940
Some Poems, Faber, 1940
Three Songs for St. Cecilia's Day, pri-
vately printed, 1941
The Double Man, Random, 1941; in Eng-
land as *New Year Letter,* Faber, 1941
For the Time Being, Random, 1944
The Collected Poems of W. H. Auden,
Random, 1945
The Age of Anxiety: A Baroque Eclogue,
Random, 1947
Collected Shorter Poems, 1930–1944, Fa-
ber, 1950
Nones, Random, 1951
Mountains, Faber, 1954
The Shield of Achilles, Random, 1955
The Old Man's Road, Voyage Press, 1956
Selected Poetry, Modern Library, 1959
Homage to Clio, Random, 1960
*About the House, fourth printing, Ran-
dom, 1965
Collected Shorter Poems, 1927–1957,
Random, 1967

Orators, Random, 1967

Collected Longer Poems, Random, 1969

The Dance of Death, Faber, 1933; second printing, 1935

The Dog Beneath the Skin, or *Where Is Francis* (with ISHERWOOD), Faber, 1935

A Tragedy in Two Acts: The Ascent of F6 (with ISHERWOOD), Faber, 1936, (published as *The Ascent of F6,* Random, 1937, second ed., 1956

On the Frontier, a Melodrama in Three Acts (with ISHERWOOD), Random, 1938, (previous two plays appeared in one volume, *The Ascent of F6* and *On the Frontier,* Faber, 1958)

Two Great Plays (The Dog Beneath the Skin and *The Ascent of F6;* with ISHERWOOD), Random, 1959

City Without Walls (poems) Random, 1970

Mr. Auden has written a number of volumes of critical works including *The Dyer's Hand,* Random, 1962, and has edited many volumes of verse and prose including a *Portable Greek Reader, Elizabethan and Jacobean Poets, Mediaeval and Renaissance Poets,* and translations. He has also written librettos and lyrics to music by Benjamin Britten, Igor Stravinsky and others.

JAMES (ARTHUR) BALDWIN was born in Harlem, New York City, Aug. 2, 1924, the first of nine children the father of whom was a minister. He graduated from De Witt Clinton High School in New York in 1942 and six years later, after a series of temporary jobs, he went to Europe to live and write for the next ten years.

A novelist and the author of three plays, Mr. Baldwin is also an essayist in the field of black and white relationship and is ranked high in the contemporary literary world as an outspoken champion of the American Negro and a rejector of "white American myths."

He is a member of the Congress of Racial Equality, the National Committee for a Sane Nuclear Policy, Actors' Studio, Authors League, Dramatists Guild, Inter-

national P.E.N., and has received the following literary honors: Eugene F. Saxton Fellowship, 1945; Rosenwald Fellowship, 1948; Guggenheim Fellowship, 1954; grant in literature from the National Institute of Arts and Letters, 1956; the *Partisan Review* Fellowship, 1956; Ford Foundation grant-in-aid, 1959; National Conference of Christians and Jews Award, 1961. He lives in New York City.

Go Tell It on the Mountain (novel), Knopf, 1953

Notes of a Native Son (essays), Beacon, 1955; Dial, 1963

The Amen Corner (play) produced 1955, 1964, 1965, State Dept. world tour, 1965

Giovanni's Room (novel), Dial, 1956

Giovanni's Room (play) produced by Actors Studio Workshop, 1958

*Nobody Knows My Name (essays), Dial, 1961

Another Country (novel), Dial, 1962

The Fire Next Time (essays), Dial, 1963

Blues for Mister Charlie (play), Dial, 1964, produced, 1964

Nothing Personal (photographs by Richard Avedon), Atheneum, 1964

Going to Meet the Man (stories), Dial, 1965

Tell Me How Long the Train's Been Gone (novel), Dial, 1968

JOHN (SIMMONS) BARTH, born May 27, 1930, in Cambridge, Maryland, is the author of four novels and one volume of "fiction for print, tape and live voice." He attended the Julliard School of Music, in New York, and the Johns Hopkins University, receiving his M.A. in 1951. He lives in Buffalo, New York, where he is professor of English at the State University of New York. He is married and has a daughter and two sons.

Mr. Barth's admirers, who include many outstanding critics (and Katherine Anne Porter who thought his Rabelaisian satirizing historical novel of the seventeenth century in Maryland and England was "a gorgeous burst of humor in our best tradition"), have accorded him a unique place in contemporary writing as an "existential humorist and novelist of ideas."

The Floating Opera, Appleton, 1956; revised edition, 1967
The End of the Road, Doubleday, 1958; revised, 1967
The Sot-Weed Factor, Doubleday, 1960; revised, 1967
Giles Goat-Boy, Doubleday, 1966
*Lost in the Funhouse, Doubleday, 1968

SAUL BELLOW, born June 10, 1915, in Lachine, Quebec, Canada, son of Abraham and Liza (Gordon) Bellow, grew up in Chicago, where he attended the University of Chicago from 1933 to 1935. He received his B.S. from Northwestern University in 1937 and Litt. D., in 1962. He has taught at the Pestalozzi Froebel Teachers College, Chicago, University of Minnesota, Bradford College at Yale, Bard College, and Princeton and is now a professor on the Committee on Social Thought at the University of Chicago.

Mr. Bellow's long works in fiction have repeatedly won him honors, *The Adventures of Augie March*, winning the 1953 National Book Award and *Herzog* winning the 1965 Award as well as the International Literary Prize and the James L. Dow Award. He won the National Institute of Arts and Letters Award in 1952, and the Friends of Literature Fiction Award in 1960. He is a member of the National Institute of Arts and Letters, the Authors League and Yaddo Corporation.

Mr. Bellow has three sons and lives in Chicago.

Dangling Man, Vanguard, 1944
The Victim, Vanguard, 1947
The Adventures of Augie March, Viking, 1953
Seize the Day (short stories; one-act play), Viking, 1957
Henderson the Rain King, Viking, 1959
Herzog, Viking, 1964
Last Analysis (play), 1964
Under the Weather (short plays), 1964

*Mosby's Memoirs (short stories), Viking, 1968.
Mr. Sammler's Planet (novel), Viking, 1970

JOHN BERRYMAN, born Oct. 25, 1914, in McAlester, Oklahoma, was educated at Columbia College, taking his A.B. in 1936, and at Clare College, Cambridge, where he was Kellett fellow 1936–38, and Oldham Shakespeare Scholar in 1937. He took his B.A. in 1938, later his M.A., and now is professor of humanities at the University of Minnesota, Minneapolis, where he has lived since 1954.

Mr. Berryman has taught at Wayne (now Wayne State) University, Detroit; Harvard University, Princeton and the University of Cincinnati. He was awarded a Rockefeller Fellowship in 1944–46, a *Kenyon Review* Doubleday short story award in 1949, the Levinson Prize in poetry in 1950, a National Institute of Arts and Letters grant in literature in 1950, two Guggenheim Fellowships, 1952–53, 1966–67; a *Partisan Review* Fellowship in 1957.

In 1969, with the publication of *His Toy, His Dream, His Rest*, Mr. Berryman won the National Book Award in Poetry. The book was a continuation of 77 *Dream Songs*, published in 1964 and awarded the Pulitzer Prize for poetry that year. In January 1969 he was awarded the Bollingen Prize for poetry. In 1966 he was named Fellow of the Academy of American Poets and awarded $5000 for poetic achievement. He has also won the 1963 prize of *Ramparts*, the Loines Award for Poetry in 1964, the Shelley Memorial Award of 1948, the Harriet Monroe Award for poetry in 1957, and the Brandeis University Creative Arts Award, 1959–60.

Mr. Berryman told the National Book Award audience, "I set up *The Dream Songs* as hostile to every visible tendency in both American and English poetry . . . The aim was the reproduction or invention of the motions of a human personality, free and determined."

Of the *Dream Songs*, Robert Lowell

has said: "It is one of the glories of the age, the single most heroic work in English poetry since the War, since Ezra Pound's *Pisan Cantos* . . ."

Poems, New Direction, 1942
The Dispossessed (poetry) Sloane, 1948
Stephen Crane (biography), Sloane, 1950
Homage to Mistress Bradstreet and Other Poems, Farrar, 1956; Faber, 1959
His Thought Made Pockets and the Plane Buckt (poetry) C. Fredericks, 1958
Thomas Nash, Unfortunate Traveller (editor), or *The Life of Jack Wilton,* Putnam, 1960
77 Dream Songs (poetry), Farrar, 1964
Short Poems, Farrar, 1967
The Monk by MATTHEW GREGORY LEWIS (introduction), Grove Press, 1952
Berryman's Sonnets, Farrar, 1967
*His Toy, His Dream, His Rest (poetry) Farrar, 1968
The Job of Reading (literary criticism; with RALPH ROGG and ALLEN TATE), 1960

KAY BOYLE, author of thirteen novels, seven books of short stories, and three volumes of her collected poems, was born February 19, 1903, in St. Paul, Minnesota, she studied the violin at the Cincinnati Conservatory of Music and architecture at the Ohio Mechanics Institute. She has lived in England, Austria and France for nearly twenty years prior to 1941 and in Germany and France following World War II.

Kay Boyle has had three marriages: to Richard Brault in 1923, Laurence Vail in 1931, both ending in divorce. Her third husband, Baron Joseph von Franckenstein, died in 1963. She has six children and she has been a member of the English faculty of San Francisco State College since 1963.

She is a member of the National Institute of Arts and Letters, has been awarded two Guggenheim Fellowships, and has twice won Awards for the best short stories in the O. Henry Memorial Award collections. She has been a fellow at the Wesleyan Center for Advanced study and the Radcliffe Institute for Independent Studies.

Miss Boyle's contribution to *This Is My Best* first appeared in *The Saturday Evening Post.*

Wedding Day and Other Stories, Cape & Smith, 1930
Plagued by the Nightingale (novel), Cape & Smith, 1931
Year Before Last (novel), Smith, 1932
Gentlemen, I Address You Privately (novel), Smith, 1933
The First Lover, and Other Stories, Random, 1933
My Next Bride (novel), Harcourt, 1936
365 Days (editor; with LAURENCE VAIL, NINA CONARAIN, and others; story collection) 1936
Death of a Man (novel), Harcourt, 1936
The White Horses of Vienna (stories), Harcourt, 1936
Monday Night (novel), Harcourt, 1938
A Glad Day (poems), New Directions, 1938
The Youngest Camel (juvenile), Little, Brown, 1939
The Crazy Hunter (three short novels), Harcourt, 1940
Primer for Combat (novel), Simon & Schuster, 1942
Avalanche (novel), Simon & Schuster, 1944
American Citizen (poem), Simon & Schuster, 1944
A Frenchman Must Die (novel), Simon & Schuster, 1946
Thirty Stories, Simon & Schuster, 1946
1939 (novel), Simon & Schuster, 1948
His Human Majesty (novel), Whittlesey House, 1949
The Smoking Mountain (story collection), McGraw, 1951
The Seagull on the Step (novel), Knopf, 1955
Generation Without Farewell (novel), Knopf, 1960
Collected Poems, Knopf, 1962
Nothing Ever Breaks Except the Heart (stories), Doubleday, 1966
The Autobiography of Emanuel Carnevali (compiled and edited), Horizon, 1967

Being Geniuses Together (revised and supplemented) Doubleday, 1968

GWENDOLYN BROOKS, a black American, whose name, next to Ezra Pound, was the most often written in by reader-balloters in the nation-wide poll for inclusions in this book, was born in Topeka, Kansas, June 7, 1917, but from her first month has lived mostly in Chicago. She is married to Henry Blakely and they have a son, Henry, and a daughter, Nora. She graduated from Englewood High School and Wilson Junior College and was cited for creative writing by the American Academy of Arts and Letters in 1946 and received two Guggenheim Fellowships for creative writing in 1946 and 1947. She received the Pulitzer Prize for Poetry in 1950 for *Annie Allen,* a ballad of Chicago Negro life, and in 1968 she was named Poet Laureate for the State of Illinois, succeeding the late Carl Sandburg.

Miss Brooks has taught creative writing and black literature at Northeastern Illinois State College and Columbia College in Chicago, Elmhurst College in Elmhurst, Illinois, and the University of Wisconsin, at Madison.

A Street in Bronzeville (poems; out of print), Harper, 1945
Annie Allen (poems; out of print), Harper, 1949
Maud Martha (novel), Harper, 1953
Bronzeville Boys and Girls (poems; juvenile), Harper, 1956
The Bean Eaters (poems; out of print), Harper, 1960
*Selected Poems, Harper, 1962
*In the Mecca (poems), Harper, 1968

ART BUCHWALD was born October 20, 1925, in Mount Vernon, New York, son of Joseph, a curtain manufacturer, and Helen (Kleinberger) Buchwald. He quit high school to join the Marines and left the University of Southern California in 1948 without a degree to live in Paris. After a short stint as correspondent for

Variety, he became a columnist for the New York *Herald Tribune* in Paris, a column which fourteen years later he transferred to Washington and national syndication to 450 newspapers. He is married and has three children and lives and writes in the national capital. He was awarded the Grand Prix de la Humor in France in 1959.

Art Buchwald's Paris, Little, Brown, 1953
The Brave Coward, Harper, 1955
More Caviar, Harper, 1957
A Gift from the Boys, Harper, 1958
Don't Forget to Write, World, 1960
*How Much Is That in Dollars? World, 1961
Is It Safe to Drink the Water? World, 1962
I Chose Capitol Punishment, World, 1963
Son of the Great Society, Putnam, 1966
Have I Ever Lied to You? Putnam, 1968
The Establishment is Alive & Well in Washington, Putnam, 1969
Sheep on the Runway, play, 1970

PEARL BUCK (Pearl Comfort Sydenstricker) winner of both the Nobel and the Pulitzer Prize for literature, was born in Hillsboro, West Virginia, June 26, 1892, but when only a few months old was taken to China where her parents were Southern Presbyterian missionaries. She remained in China until she entered Randolph-Macon College and after graduating in 1914 she returned to China. She was in America again in 1925 for one year to take her master's degree at Cornell. She taught English at Southeastern University and Chung Yang University, both of Nanking.

The Good Earth, her second book, published in 1931, won the Pulitzer Prize that year and in 1938 she received the Nobel Prize for the entire body of her work, the first American woman to be so honored.

Pearl Buck has also written more than a dozen books for children, many with Oriental backgrounds. She learned to speak Chinese before English, but her first writings in English appeared in the English-language newspaper *Shanghai Mercury*'s weekly edition section for children. The first novel she wrote was lost in March 1927 in a Communist raid on her home in Chinkiang.

Since 1934, as Mrs. Richard J. Walsh (her husband until his death in 1960 was president of John Day, publishers) she has made her home in rural Pennsylvania. She is the mother of a daughter by her first husband, John L. Buck (divorced in 1915), and four adopted sons and one adopted daughter, and in 1949 she founded Welcome House, Inc., an adoption agency for Asian-American children, and in 1964 she set up the Pearl S. Buck Foundation devoted to the health, education and welfare of children born in Asia of American fathers and Asian mothers and who must remain in the lands of their birth. For this work she received the highest award of honor from the Government of the Republic of South Korea.

She is member of the National Institute of Arts and Letters, American Academy of Arts and Letters, Phi Beta Kappa, and has received honorary degrees from thirteen American universities and colleges.

East Wind: West Wind (novel), Day, 1930
The Good Earth (novel), Day, 1931
Sons (novel), Day, 1932
Is There a Case for Foreign Missions? (pamphlet), Day, 1932
The Young Revolutionist (juvenile), Day, 1932
The First Wife and Other Stories, Day, 1933
All Men Are Brothers (*Shui Hu Chuan*; translator), Day, 1933
The Mother (novel), Day, 1934
A House Divided (novel), Day, 1935
House of Earth (trilogy including *The Good Earth*, revised, *Sons* and *A House Divided*), Day, 1935
The Exile, Day, 1936
Fighting Angel, Day, 1936
This Proud Heart, (novel), Day, 1938
The Patriot (novel), Day, 1939
The Chinese Novel, Day, 1939

Stories for Little Children (juvenile), Day, 1940
Other Gods (novel), Day, 1941
Today and Forever (novel), Day, 1941
Of Men and Women, Day, 1941
Dragon (novel), Day, 1942
American Unity and Asia, Day, 1942
The Chinese Children Next Door (juvenile), Day, 1942
The Promise (novel), Day 1943
What America Means to Me, Day, 1943
The Water-Buffalo Children (juvenile), Day, 1943
The Spirit and the Flesh (combining *The Exile* and *Fighting Angel*), Day, 1944
The Dragon Fish (juvenile), Day, 1944
Portrait of a Marriage (novel), Day, 1945
The Townsaan (novel; pseudonym, JOHN SEDGES), Day, 1945
Tell the People, Day, 1945
Talk About Russia (with MASHA SCOTT); Day, 1945
Yu Lan: Flying Boy of China (juvenile), Day, 1945
Pavilion of Women (novel), Day, 1946
Far and Near: Stories of Japan, China, and America, Day, 1947
The Angry Wife (novel), Day, 1947
How It Happens: Talk about the German People, 1914–1933 (with ERNA VON PUSTAU), Day, 1947
Peony (novel), Day, 1948
The Big Wave (juvenile), Day, 1948
Kinfolk (novel), Day, 1949
The Long Love (novel; pseudonym, JOHN SEDGES), Day, 1949
American Argument (with ASLANDA GOODE ROBESON), Day, 1949
The Child Who Never Grew, Day, 1950
One Bright Day (juvenile), Day, 1950
God's Men (novel), Day, 1951
Bright Procession (novel; pseudonym, JOHN SEDGES), Day, 1952
The Hidden Flower (novel), Day, 1952
Voices in the House (novel; pseudonym, JOHN SEDGES), Day, 1953
Come, My Beloved (novel), Day, 1953
The Man Who Changed China, Random, 1953
My Several Worlds, Day, 1954
Johnny Jack and His Beginnings (juvenile), Day, 1954
The Beech Tree (juvenile), Day, 1955

Imperial Woman (novel), Day, 1956
Letter from Peking (novel), Day, 1957
My Several Worlds (abridged for younger readers), Day, 1957
Christmas Miniature (juvenile), Day, 1957
Friend to Friend (with CARLOS P. ROMULO), Day, 1958
Command the Morning (novel), Day, 1959
The Delights of Learning, U. of Pittsburgh Press, 1960
The Christmas Ghost (juvenile), Day, 1960
Fourteen Stories, Day, 1961
*A Bridge for Passing (novel; pseudonym, JOHN SEDGES), Day, 1962
The Living Reed (novel), Day, 1963
The Joy of Children, Day, 1964
Welcome Child (juvenile), Day, 1964
Death in the Castle (novel), Day, 1965
The Gifts They Bring (with GWENETH T. ZARFOSS), Day, 1965
Children for Adoption, Random, 1965
Fairy Tales of the Orient (juvenile; editor), Simon & Schuster, 1965
The Big Fight (juvenile), Day, 1965
Little Fox in the Middle (juvenile), Macmillan, 1965
For Spacious Skies: Journey in Dialogue (with THEODORE F. HARRIS), Day, 1966
People of Japan, Simon & Schuster, 1966
The Time Is Noon (novel), Day, 1967
To My Daughters, With Love, Day, 1967
Matthew, Mark, Luke and John (juvenile), Day, 1967
The New Year (novel), Day, 1968
The Good Deed (novel), Day, 1969
The Three Daughters of Liang (novel), Day, 1969

WILLIAM F. BUCKLEY, JR., born November 24, 1925, in New York City, is the sixth of ten children of William Frank, a lawyer and oilman, and Aloise (Steiner) Buckley. He was schooled in France, England, and Mexico. He is a graduate of the Millbrook School, 1943, and Yale University, 1950, where he taught Spanish, edited the *Yale Daily News,* debated on the varsity team, and earned academic honors. After graduating, he married Patricia Taylor of Vancouver, and their son, Christopher, was born in 1952. Mr. Buckley worked briefly for the *American Mercury* and then, in 1955, founded the *National Review.* In 1965 he ran for mayor of New York on the Conservative ticket.

A controversial figure in his magazine writings, Mr. Buckley has been frequently seen on television in debates on political and cultural issues.

God and Man at Yale, Regnery, 1951
McCarthy and His Enemies (with BRENT BOZELL), Regnery, 1954
Up From Liberalism, Obolensky, 1959
The Story of Ocean Racing, Van Nostrand, 1959
The Committee and Its Critics (editor and contributor), Putnam, 1962
Rumbles Left and Right, Putnam, 1963
What is Conservatism? edited by F. S. MEYER (contributor), Holt, 1964
The Unmaking of a Mayor, Viking, 1966
*The Jeweler's Eye, Putnam, 1968

ERSKINE CALDWELL, born in White Oak, Coweta County, Georgia, December 17, 1903, the son of Ira Sylvester, a minister, and Caroline Preston (Bell) a high school Latin teacher, attended Erskine College, South Carolina, the University of Virginia and the University of Pennsylvania, and began his writing career as a newspaperman, but has been, in his early days, a cotton picker, stage hand, professional football player, book reviewer, lecturer, editor (for fifteen years) of *American Folkways,* screen writer, correspondent in Mexico, Spain, Czechoslovakia, China, Mongolia and Turkestan, war correspondent in Russia for *Life,* the newspaper *PM,* and Columbia Broadcasting Company. At all times he has been a fiction writer, in both novels and hundreds of short stories.

One of Mr. Caldwell's earliest books was *Tobacco Road,* which was dramatized and filmed, depicting the life of poor whites in the Deep South, and *God's Little Acre,* which brought its author into court to defend an obscenity charge. These two books and others of Mr. Caldwell's which have gone into paper back editions have made him one of the biggest sellers in recent publishing history. Fifty of his books have been published in the United States, fifty-three of them also in Great Britain, thirty-seven have been translated into Japanese and others into thirty-six other languages, including thirty-three into Italian, twenty-nine into French and Portuguese, twelve into Russian and one into Vietnamese. *God's Little Acre* has a publishing history of 8,340,815 copies printed in the United States and 1,360,713 copies printed in various languages abroad, for a total of 9,701,528 copies; *Tobacco Road*, a total of 6,181,828 copies here and abroad; and *Journeyman*, a total of 4,273,288 American and foreign copies.

Mr. Caldwell has been married four times. One of his wives, Margaret Bourke-White, whom he married in 1939, was his collaborator as a photographer on several of his books of reportage. His present wife is the former Virginia Moffett Fletcher.

The Bastard, 1929
Poor Fool, 1930
American Earth, 1931
Tobacco Road, 1932
God's Little Acre, 1933
We Are the Living, 1933
Journeyman, 1935
Kneel to the Rising Sun, 1935
Some American People, 1935
You Have Seen Their Faces (with MARGARET BOURKE-WHITE), 1937
Southways, 1938
North of the Danube (with MARGARET BOURKE-WHITE), 1939
Trouble in July, 1940
Jackpot (collection of stories), 1949
Sayl Is This the U.S.A? (with MARGARET BOURKE-WHITE), 1941
All-Out on the Road to Smolensk, 1942
Moscow Under Fire, 1942
All Night Long, 1942
Georgia Boy, 1943
Stories, 1944
Tragic Ground, 1944
A House in the Uplands, 1946
The Sure Hand of God, 1947

This Very Earth, 1948
Place Called Esthersville, 1949
Episode in Palmetto, 1950
Call It Experience (autobiography), 1951
The Courting of Susie Brown, 1952
A Lamp for Nightfall, 1952
The Complete Stories of Erskine Caldwell, 1953
Love and Money, 1954
Gretta, 1955
Erskine Caldwell's Gulf Coast Stories, 1956
Certain Women, 1957
Molly Cottontail, 1958
The Sacrilege of Alan Kent, 1958
Claudelle Inglish, 1959
When You Think of Me, 1959
Jenny by Nature, 1961
Close to Home, 1962
The Last Night of Summer, 1963
Around About America, 1964
In Search of Bisco, 1965
The Deer at Our House, 1966
In the Shadow of the Steeple, 1966
Writing in America, 1966
Miss Mamma Aimee, 1967
Deep South, 1968
Summertime Island, 1968
The Weather Shelter, 1969

Mr. Caldwell lists his current publishers of hard cover books as Farrar, Straus and Giroux, Inc., New York; Little, Brown & Co., Boston, and World Publishing Co., New York; his reprint editions have been made available through Fawcett Publications, Inc., New American Library, Modern Library, and Pocket Books, all of New York.

TRUMAN CAPOTE was born in New Orleans, Louisiana, September 30, 1924, son of Joseph G. and Nina (Faulk) Capote. He attended Trinity School and St. John's Academy in New York City and public schools in Greenwich, Connecticut. When he is not in Russia, Capri, or someplace else in Europe, he lives in New York City.

Except for a brief time in the art department of *The New Yorker*, Truman Capote has been an independent writer of short stories, novels, plays, "observations," and nonfictional sketches and reportage, many of which have appeared in *The New Yorker*, including parts of his account of a trip to Moscow and sections of *In Cold Blood*, his best-selling account of a Kansas smalltown murder case.

He has twice won an O. Henry Memorial short story prize and in 1959 he received an award from the National Institute of Arts and Letters.

Other Voices, Other Rooms (novel), Random, 1948
A Tree of Night and Other Stories, Random, 1949
Local Color (sketches), Random, 1950
The Grass Harp (novel), Random, 1951
The Grass Harp (play), Random, 1952
*The Grass Harp, A Tree of Night and Other Stories, New American Lib., 1956
The Muses Are Heard, an Account, Random, 1958
Breakfast at Tiffany's, a Short Novel and Three Stories, Random, 1958, New American Lib., 1959
Observations (with RICHARD AVEDON; commentary), Simon & Schuster, 1959
Selected Writings, Random, 1963
A Christmas Memory (story), Random, 1966
The Thanksgiving Visitor, Random, 1968
Beat the Devil (film script), 1953
House of Flowers (Broadway play script), 1954

BRUCE CATTON, born October 9, 1899, in Petoskey, Michigan, son of George R. (a Congregational minister) and Adella (Patten) Catton. After leaving Oberlin College, he became a reporter on Boston and Cleveland newspapers, serving between 1920 and 1962 when he moved to Washington, D.C., to be correspondent there for the Newspaper Enterprise Association. In 1941 he was named associate director, later director, of information for the War Production Board. He later held the same position with the Department of Commerce. He became special assistant to the Secretary of Commerce, but resigned in 1947 to devote full time to writing. Since 1954 he has been senior editor of the magazine *American Heritage*.

Mr. Catton won the Pulitzer prize for history and the National Book Award in 1954 for his book *A Stillness at Appomattox* and between 1955 and 1956 he was awarded the honorary degree of doctor of letters by thirteen universities and colleges. He served in the U. S. Navy in World War I, is married and has one son.

*War Lords of Washington, Harcourt, 1948
Mr. Lincoln's Army, Doubleday, 1951
Glory Road, Doubleday, 1952
A Stillness at Appomattox, Doubleday, 1953
U. S. Grant and the American Military Tradition, Little, Brown, 1954
Banners at Shenandoah, Doubleday, 1955
American Heritage Reader (editor), Dell, 1956
This Hallowed Ground, Doubleday, 1956
America Goes to War, Wesleyan Univ. Press, 1958
The Battle of Gettysburg by FRANKLIN HASKELL (editor), Houghton, 1958
American Heritage Picture History of the Civil War (editor), American Heritage Pub. Co., 1960
Grant Moves South, Little, 1960
The Coming Fury, Doubleday, 1961
The Army of the Potomac (consolidation of *Mr. Lincoln's Army* and *A Stillness at Appomattox*), Doubleday, 1962
This Hallowed Ground (juvenile), Doubleday, 1962
American Heritage Short Story of the Civil War, Dell, 1963
Two Roads to Sumter (with WILLIAM BRUCE CATTON), McGraw, 1963
The Terrible Swift Sword, Doubleday, 1963
Grant Takes Command, Vol. 3, Little, 1969

JOHN CIARDI was born June 24, 1916, in Boston. Married Judith Hostetter, July 1946. Has two sons and a daughter and lives in Metuchen, New Jersey, commuting at times to New York City where since 1956 he has been poetry editor of the *Saturday Review*. He is also director of the Bread Loaf Writers' Conference, in Vermont, and makes frequent lecture appearances.

Mr. Ciardi attended Bates College, took his A.B. in 1938 at Tufts, and his M.A., at the University of Michigan in 1939 where he won an Avery Hopwood Award. He taught English at Kansas City University from 1940–42, served in the Army Air Forces from 1942 to 1945 as a gunner on a B-29 and was awarded an Air Medal with oak leaf cluster. He is a Fellow of the American Academy of Arts and Sciences, and member of the National Institute of Arts and Letters, and Phi Beta Kappa. He taught at Harvard from 1946 to 1953, and Rutgers from 1953 to 1961 when he resigned to write and edit.

He received the Oscar Blumenthal prize in 1943, Eunice Tietjens award, 1945; Levinson prize, 1946; Golden Rose trophy, of New England Poetry Club, 1948; Harriet Monroe Memorial prize, 1955; Fellowship in Literature at the American Academy in Rome, 1956; Boys Clubs of America Junior Book Award, 1962, for a juvenile, *The Man Who Sang the Sillies;* and honorary degrees from Tufts College in 1960 and Wayne State University in 1963, Ursinus, and Kalamazoo college in '64.

Mr. Ciardi's poem in this book first appeared in *Saturday Review*.

Homeward to America (poetry), Holt, 1940
Other Skies (poetry), Atlantic Monthly Press, 1947
Live Another Day (poetry), Twayne, 1949
Mid-Century American Poets (editor), Twayne, 1950
From Time to Time (poetry), Twayne, 1951
The Inferno by DANTE (verse; translator), Rutgers, 1954
As If (poetry), Rutgers, 1955

I Marry You, A Sheaf of Love Poems, Rutgers, 1958
Thirty-Nine Poems, Rutgers, 1959
How Does a Poem Mean? (prose), Houghton, 1960
In the Stoneworks (poetry), Rutgers, 1961
The Purgatorio by DANTE (verse; translator), New American Library, 1961
In Fact (poetry), Rutgers, 1962
Dialogue With an Audience (prose), Lippincott, 1963
Person to Person (poetry), Rutgers, 1964
An Alphabestiary (poetry), Lippincott, 1965
This Strangest Everything (poetry), Rutgers, 1966
The Reason for the Pelican (juvenile), Lippincott, 1959
Scrappy, the Pup, Lippincott, 1960
The Man Who Sang the Sillies, Lippincott, 1961
I Met a Man, Houghton, 1961
You Read to Me, I'll Read to You, Lippincott, 1962
The Wish-Tree, Crowell-Collier, 1962
John J. Plenty and Fiddler Dan, Lippincott, 1961
The King Who Saved Himself, Lippincott, 1964
The Monster Den, Lippincott, 1967

HENRY STEELE COMMAGER, long-time professor of history at Columbia University and professor of history at Amherst College since 1956, since 1942 one of the American historians lecturing in more universities abroad than almost any other, was born in Pittsburgh, Pennsylvania, October 25, 1902, the son of James Williams and Anna Elizabeth (Dan) Commager. His early education was in Toledo and Chicago. He obtained his Ph.B. and M.A. in philosophy in 1923 and 1924, studied a year at the University of Copenhagen where he wrote his thesis on Danish history and returned to Chicago for his doctorate.

Since his first book, *The Growth of the American Republic* (1930), which was written in collaboration with Samuel Eliot Morison, Professor Commager has been preoccupied with subjects of contemporary and historical import, and in recognition of his works he has received honorary degrees in literature, education, or civil law from fifteen universities and colleges in the United States and Europe.

Professor Commager has long been active in public affairs, and he is a trustee of the American-Scandinavian Federation, the American Friends of Cambridge University, and vice president of the Committee for an Effective Congress.

In the summer of 1943 Professor Commager was sent to Britain for the War Department and the Office of War Information, and in 1964 to Britain, France and Belgium. He was lecturer in American History at Cambridge University, England, 1942–43, Bacon lecturer, Boston University, 1943, Richards lecturer, University of Virginia, 1944, Pitt professor of American history at Cambridge University, England, 1947–48, Harmsworth professor, Oxford, 1952–53, Gottesman lecturer, Uppsala University, 1953, visiting professor University of Copenhagen, 1956; lecturer for the Department of State at German universities, 1954, Israel and Italy, 1955, Trinidad, 1959, Italy, spring of 1960, Chilean universities, 1963, Ziskind professor at Brandeis University, 1955; Aix-en-Provence at Nice, 1957; University of Jerusalem, 1958. He was made honorary professor at the University of Santiago de Chile, decorated as Knight of the Order of Dannebrog, and was a Guggenheim Fellow in 1960–61.

In 1928 Professor Commager married Evan Carroll, author of four well-known children's books. They have three children. He lives in Amherst and in Linton, England.

The Growth of the American Republic (with S. E. MORISON) 1931, 1942, 1969
Theodore Parker, Little, Brown, 1936
The Heritage of America (with A. NEVINS), Little, Brown, 1939 et seq.
Our Nation (with E. C. BARKER), Row Peterson, 1941
America: the Story of a Free People (with A. NEVINS), Clarendon, 1942 et seq.

Majority Rule and Minority Rights, Oxford, 1943
The Blue and the Gray (2 vols.) Bobbs, 1950
The American Mind, Yale Univ. Press, 1951
Living Ideas in America, Harper, 1952, et seq.
Freedom, Loyalty, Dissent, Oxford, 1954
Europe and America since 1492 (with G. BRUUN), Heath, 1954
The Great Declaration, Bobbs, 1958
The Spirit of Seventy-Six (2 vols.; with R. B. MORRIS), Harper-Row, 1958
The Era of Reform, Van Nostrand, 1960
The Great Proclamation, Bobbs, 1960
Theodore Parker (an anthology), Beacon, 1960
Crusaders for Freedom, Doubleday, 1962
Lester Ward and the Welfare State, Bobbs, 1965
Nature and Problems of History, Bobbs, 1965
Documents of American History (editor), Appleton, 1934, 1940, 1950 et seq.
Tocqueville's Democracy in America (editor), 1946
A St. Nicholas Anthology (editor), Random, 1948
The Second St. Nicholas Anthology (editor), Random, 1950
America in Perspective (editor), New American Lib., 1947
The Rise of the American Nation (50 vols.; in process; editor),
Selected Writings of William Dean Howells (editor), Random
Atlas of the Civil War (editor), Yoseloff, 1958
Immigration in American History (editor), U. of Minnesota Press, 1961
Conscience of a Liberal by CHESTER BOWLES (editor), Harper, 1962
The Defeat of the Confederacy (editor), Van Nostrand, 1964
History of the English Speaking People by WINSTON CHURCHILL (editor),

NORMAN COUSINS was born June 24, 1915, in Union Hill, New Jersey. Within four years after completing his work at Teachers College, Columbia University, he began his career with the *Saturday Review*, as executive editor and, from 1942 to date, as editor-in-chief. Mr. Cousins has been an active force in publishing, education, government work and crusading for civic and international causes; this has earned him honorary degrees from twenty-two universities and colleges and the title of First Honorary Citizen Hiroshima, Japan, for his rehabilitation work in that city after the atomic bombing of 1945. During World War II he was editor of *U.S.A.* He has represented the United States at educational or cultural functions and on projects in India, Pakistan, Japan, the Philippines, West Germany, Soviet Union, and Ethiopia. He was Presidential representative at the inauguration of President Marcos of the Philippines in 1966. He is now President of the World Association of World Federalists, Chairman of the Planning Committee of the Kettering Foundation, Member of the Board of Directors of National Educational Television. He was appointed by President Johnson to be Chairman of the Cultural Committee for International Cooperation Year, 1967.

The Good Inheritance: The Democratic Chance, Coward, 1942
Editor: *A Treasury of Democracy*, Coward, 1942
*Modern Man Is Obsolete, Viking, 1945
An Anthology of the Poetry of Liberty (editor; with WILLIAM ROSE BENÉT), Modern Library, 1945
Writing for Love or Money: Thirty-five Essays from the Saturday Review of Literature (editor), Longmans, 1949
Years of the Modern edited by JOHN W. CHASE (contributor), Longmans, 1949
Talks With Nehru (with JAWAHARLAL NEHRU), Day, 1951
Who Speaks for Man? Macmillan, 1953
Amy Loveman, 1881–1955: a Eulogy (pamphlet), Overbrook Press, 1956, 1958
In God We Trust: The Religious Beliefs of the Founding Fathers, Harper, 1958
Francis March, Thesaurus Dictionary (editor), Doubleday, 1958

The Rejection of Nothingness (pamphlet), Pacific School of Religion, 1959
Dr. Schweitzer of Lambaréné, Harper, 1960
In Place of Folly, Harper, 1961; revised ed., Washington Square Press, 1962
Can Cultures Co-Exist? (symposium), Ministry of Scientific Research and Cultural Affairs (New Delhi), 1963
"*. . . Therefore Choose Life, That Thou Mayest Live, Thou and Thy Seed*," (with others), Center for the Study of Democratic Institutions, 1965
Present Tense, McGraw-Hill, 1967
Encyclopaedia Britannica (member of the board of editors)

MALCOLM COWLEY was born August 24, 1898, in Belsano, Pa., son of William and Josephine (Hutmacher) Cowley. He took his A.B. from Harvard in 1920 and studied at the University of Montpellier, France, in 1921–22. He has received honorary degrees from Franklin and Marshall College, 1961, and Colby College, 1962. He is married to the former Muriel Maurer, has one son, and lives in Sherman, Connecticut.

Beginning as a free-lance writer and translator, Mr. Cowley became associate editor of *The New Republic*, 1929–44, and has been literary advisor to the Viking Press since 1948. He has been visiting professor at many universities, including Stanford, Michigan, California, Washington and Cornell. He is past president of the National Institute and chancellor of the American Academy of Arts and Letters.

Mr. Cowley's essay in *This Is My Best* first appeared in *The Atlantic*.

Blue Juniata, Cape and Smith, 1929
Exile's Return, Norton, 1934; revised, Viking, 1951
After the Genteel Tradition (with others), Norton, 1937; revised, Southern Illinois, 1964
The Literary Situation, Viking, 1954
Black Cargoes (with DANIEL P. MANNIX), Viking, 1962
The Faulkner-Cowley File, Viking, 1966

Think Back on Us, Southern Illinois, 1967

Blue Juniata: Collected Poems, Viking, 1968

A Many-Windowed House, Southern Illinois, 1970

Variety by PAUL VALÉRY (translator, from the French), Harcourt, 1927

The Sacred Hill by MAURICE BARRES (translator), Macaulay, 1929

Imaginary Interviews by ANDRÉ GIDE (translator), Knopf, 1944

Adventures of an African Slaver by CAPTAIN CANOT (editor), A. and C. Boni, 1927

Books That Changed Our Minds (editor), Doubleday, 1939

The Portable Hemingway (editor), Viking, 1944

The Portable Faulkner (editor), Viking, 1946

The Portable Hawthorne (editor), Viking, 1948

The Complete Whitman (editor), Pellegrini and Cudahy, 1948

The Stories of F. Scott Fitzgerald (editor), Scribner's, 1950

Writers at Work (editor), Viking, 1958

Leaves of Grass: The First Edition (with Robert Cowley), Viking, 1959

Fitzgerald and the Jazz Age (editor), Scribner's, 1966

JAMES (LAFAYETTE) DICKEY was born February 2, 1923 in Atlanta, Georgia, attended Clemson College briefly, took his B.A. (*magna cum laude*) from Vanderbilt University in 1949 and his M.A. in 1960. He has taught in the English departments of Rice University and the University of Florida, and been writer in residence at Reed College, San Fernando Valley State College, the University of Wisconsin, and the University of South Carolina. He has given many public readings of his work, and has recorded his poetry for the Library of Congress and for Spoken Arts. He received a creative writing fellowship from the *Sewanee Review,* another from the Guggenheim Foundation, and a grant from the National Institute of Arts and Letters. In 1958 he was awarded *Poetry*

magazine's Union League Civic and Arts Foundation prize, and in 1959 its Vachel Lindsay Award. From 1966 to 1968 he served two successive terms as Consultant in Poetry to the Library of Congress. His *Buckdancer's Choice* won the National Book Award for poetry in 1965.

Married, with two sons, Mr. Dickey lives in Columbia, South Carolina. He was a flyer with the U. S. Air Force during World War II and the Korean War. He is a member of Phi Beta Kappa.

Mr. Dickey's poem in *This Is My Best* first appeared in *The Atlantic.*

Into the Stone, and Other Poems, Scribner's, 1960

Drowning With Others (poems), Wesleyan Univ. Press, 1962

Two Poems of the Air, Centicore Press, 1964

Helmets (poems), Wesleyan, 1964

Buckdancer's Choice, Wesleyan, 1965

*Poems 1957–1967, Wesleyan, 1967

The Eye-Beaters, Blood, Victory, Madness, Buckhead and Mercy, Doubleday, 1970

The Suspect in Poetry (prose), Sixties Press, 1964

Babel to Byzantium (criticism), Farrar, 1968

Deliverance (novel), Houghton Mifflin, 1970

JOHN DOS PASSOS, grandson of a Portuguese immigrant, was born in Chicago, January 14, 1896. After graduating *cum laude* from Harvard, he went to Spain to study architecture, but, instead, served in the French ambulance service in World War I and in the U. S. Medical Corps.

Dos Passos' first book *One Man's Initiation,* 1917, records his ambulance days and *Three Soldiers,* in 1921, was regarded as a powerful indictment of war in a novel of that period. In 1925, *Manhattan Transfer* marked the beginning of the "Dos Passos style" flowering five years later in *The 42nd Parallel,* included in the *U. S. A. Trilogy* containing *1919* and *The Big Money.*

After his war service, Dos Passos returned to the United States and married

Katherine Smith who died in an automobile accident in 1947. He married again in 1950 and has one daughter. He lives in Virginia.

Dos Passos, one of the founders of the leftish magazine *New Masses* in 1926, was arrested for demonstrating in behalf of Sacco and Vanzetti, reported labor disputes in Kentucky, protested Party actions in an open letter to the Communist Party in 1934, and was war correspondent in the Pacific for *Life* in 1945, in South America in 1948.

He is a member of the American Academy of Arts and Letters, Academy of Arts and Sciences, and Authors League. He was awarded Guggenheim Fellowships in 1939, 1940 and 1942, the National Institute of Arts and Letters Gold Medal Award for fiction in 1957, and the Feltrinelli prize for narrative prose awarded in 1967 by the Accademia Nazionale dei Sincei in Rome.

One Man's Initiation—1917 (novel), Allen & Unwin, London, 1920
Three Soldiers (novel), Doran, 1921
A Pushcart at the Curb (poetry), Doran, 1922
Rosinante to the Road Again (essays), Doran, 1922
Streets of Night (novel), Doran, 1923
Manhattan Transfer (novel), Harper, 1925
The Garbage Man (play), Harper, 1926
Orient Express (travel diary), Harper, 1927
Airways, Inc. (play), Macaulay, 1928
The 42nd Parallel (novel), Harper, 1930
1919 (novel), Harcourt, 1932
In All Countries (travel), Harcourt, 1934
Three Plays, Harcourt, 1934
The Big Money (novel), Harcourt, 1936
U.S.A. (trilogy), Harcourt, 1937
Journeys Between Wars (travel and current history), Harcourt, 1938
Adventures of a Young Man (novel), Harcourt, 1939
The Living Thoughts of Tom Paine (selections, with essay), Longmans, Green, 1940
The Ground We Stand On (political essays), Harcourt, 1941

Number One (novel), Houghton, 1943
State of the Nation (essays), Houghton, 1944
First Encounter (reprint of *One Man's Initiation*), Philosophers Lib., 1945
Tour of Duty (war correspondence), Houghton, 1946
The Grand Design (novel), Houghton, 1949
The Prospect Before Us (essays on current history), Houghton, 1950
Life's Picture History of World War II, Time Inc., 1950
Chosen Country, Houghton, 1951
The Head and Heart of Thomas Jefferson, Doubleday, 1954
Most Likely to Succeed, Prentice-Hall, 1954
The Theme Is Freedom, Dodd, 1956
The Men Who Made the Nation, Doubleday, 1957
Essays on Individuality (contributor), Pennsylvania Press, 1958
The Great Days (novel), Sagamore, 1958
Prospects of a Golden Age, Prentice, 1959
Midcentury: A Contemporary Chronicle, Houghton, 1961
Mr. Wilson's War, Doubleday, 1962
Brazil on the Move (travel), Doubleday, 1963
Occasions and Protests 1936–1964 (essays), Regnery, 1964
Shackles of Power, 1801–1826, Doubleday, 1966
The World in a Glass: A View of Our Century (from the novels of JDP), Houghton, 1966
The Best Times (reminiscences), New American Lib., 1966
The 42nd Parallel (trilogies), Harcourt, 1930
1919, Harcourt, 1932
The Big Money, Harcourt, 1936; (trilogy published as *U.S.A.*), Harcourt, 1937
Adventures of a Young Man, Houghton, 1939
Number One, Houghton, 1945
The Grand Design, Houghton, 1949 (trilogy published as *District of Columbia*), Houghton, 1952

The Garbage Man (play), (produced 1926), Harper, 1926

Airways, Inc. (play), Macaulay, 1928

Three Plays (*The Garbage Man, Airways, Inc.,* and *Fortune Heights*), produced in U.S.S.R. 1933; Harcourt, 1934

The Great Days (reissue), Houghton, 1967

Manhattan Transfer (reissue), Houghton, 1967

WILL (WILLIAM JAMES) DURANT who was born November 5, 1885, in North Adams, Massachusetts, son of a superintendent of a Du Pont company branch and Marie (Allors) Durant, married (Ida) Ariel Kaufman, October 31, 1913, and the two have collaborated on one of the most ambitious works of this generation, *The Story of Civilization* in ten oversized volumes from *Our Oriental Heritage* to *Rousseau and Revolution,* with a summary volume *The Lessons of History,* for good measure, appearing in 1969.

Dr. Durant took his Ph.D. at Columbia University in 1917 after having worked as a reporter on the *New York Evening Journal* in 1908, taught Latin and French at Seton Hall, South Orange, New Jersey, until 1911, and served as the only teacher in one New York school between 1911 and 1913. He served as director of the Labor Temple School, New York City, from 1914 to 1927, and he has said that his extensive work in popularizing history began as a lecture series in New York City in 1914 before working people who he says "demanded complete clarity."

Dr. Durant was professor of philosophy at the University of California at Los Angeles in 1935 when he resigned to take up full time writing. He is a member of the National Institute of Arts and Letters and has an honorary doctorate from Syracuse University.

Philosophy and the Social Problem, Macmillan, 1917

The Story of Philosophy, Simon & Schuster, 1926

Transition: A Sentimental Story of One Mind and One Era (novel), Simon & Schuster, 1927

Mansions of Philosophy: A Survey of Human Life and Destiny, Simon & Schuster, 1929

Case for India, Simon & Schuster, 1930

Adventures in Genius (essays and articles), Simon & Schuster, 1931

Program for Americans, Simon & Schuster, 1931

On the Meaning of Life (correspondence) R. R. Smith, 1932

Tragedy of Russia: Impressions from a Brief Visit, Simon & Schuster, 1933

The Story of Civilization, Simon & Schuster

Vol. 1, *Our Oriental Heritage,* 1935

Vol. 2, *The Life of Greece,* 1939

Vol. 3, *Caesar and Christ,* 1944

Vol. 4, *The Age of Faith,* 1950

Vol. 5, *The Renaissance,* 1953

Vol. 6, *The Reformation,* 1957

Vol. 7, *The Age of Reason Begins* (with Ariel Durant), 1961

Vol. 8, *The Age of Louis XIV,* (with Ariel Durant), 1963

Vol. 9, *The Age of Voltaire* (with Ariel Durant), 1965

Vol. 10, *Rousseau and the Revolution* (with Ariel Durant), 1968

The Lessons of History (with ARIEL DURANT), Simon & Schuster, 1968

RICHARD EBERHART, poet, teacher, 1966 Pulitzer Prize winner, and former Consultant in Poetry at the Library of Congress, was born in Austin, Minnesota, April 5, 1904. He took his A.B. degree at Dartmouth College in 1926 and at Cambridge University, St. John's College, in 1929. He received his master's degree also at Cambridge, in 1933, and studied at the Harvard Graduate School of Arts and Sciences in 1932–33.

In World War II, Mr. Eberhart served as a naval aircraft gunnery instructor in the U. S. Naval Reserve, leaving in 1946 with the rank of lieutenant commander, and for the next six years in civilian life he entered business as assistant manager of the Butcher Polish Co., in Boston. In 1952 and thereafter he was Poet in Residence, professor or lecturer at the Universities of Washington, Connecticut, Wheaton College (Massachusetts), and Princeton. In 1956 he was named Professor of English and Poet in Residence at Dartmouth where, since 1968, he has held the Class of 1925 Professorship.

Besides winning the Pulitzer Prize for poetry in 1966, Mr. Eberhart has been honored by the Harriet Monroe Memorial Prize, the Harriet Monroe Memorial Award (University of Chicago), the Shelley Memorial Prize, and in 1969 he was awarded a $5000 fellowship by The Academy of American Poets "for distinguished poetic achievement." He also received a grant from the National Institute of Arts and Letters and was a co-winner in 1962 of the Bollingen Prize from Yale University Library. Mr. Eberhart was a founder and first president of the Poets' Theatre at Cambridge, Massachusetts, in 1950. From 1959 to 1961, he was Consultant in Poetry at the Library of Congress, and served as Honorary Consultant from 1963 to 1969.

He is a member of the National Institute of Arts and Letters, The American Academy of Arts and Sciences, and holds honorary Doctor of Letters degrees from Dartmouth, 1954, Skidmore, 1966, and Wooster, 1969.

He married Helen Elizabeth Butcher of Cambridge, Massachusetts, in 1941. They have two children, Rick and Gretchen, and live in Hanover, New Hampshire.

A Bravery of Earth, Cape, London, Cape-Smith, N.Y., 1930

Reading the Spirit, Chatto & Windus, London, 1936; Oxford University Press, N.Y. 1937

Song and Idea, Chatto, London, 1940; Oxford, N.Y., 1942

Poems New and Selected, New Directions, 1944

Burr Oaks, Chatto, London, 1947; Oxford, N.Y., 1947

Selected Poems, Chatto, London, 1951; Oxford, N.Y., 1951

Undercliff, Poems 1946–1953, Chatto, London, 1954; Oxford, N.Y., 1954

Great Praises, Chatto, London, 1957; Oxford, N.Y., 1957

Collected Poems, 1930–1960, Chatto, 1960; Oxford, 1960

Collected Verse Plays, University of North Carolina Press, 1962

The Quarry, Chatto, London, 1964; Oxford, N.Y., 1964

Selected Poems, 1930–1965, New Directions, 1965 (paperback)

Lope de Vega's *Justice Without Revenge,* retitled *The Bride from Mantua,* produced at Dartmouth in verse adaptation, 1964

Thirty One Sonnets, The Eakins Press, N.Y., 1967

*Shifts of Being, Chatto, London, 1968; Oxford, N.Y., 1968

A biography by Joel Roache, Oxford, is scheduled for late 1970, and a critical study of his poetry by Bernard Engle is scheduled from Twayne.

*John Ledyard appeared in the London *Times Literary Supplement,* May 22, 1969, and *Will* in the *Saturday Review,* New York, March 28, 1970.

RALPH (WALDO) ELLISON, born March 1, 1914, in Oklahoma City, was trained as a musician at Tuskegee Institute from 1933 to 1936, when a visit to New York and a meeting with Richard Wright led to his first attempts at fiction. He won a Rosenwald Fellowship and, following the publication of his first novel, *Invisible Man,* he was awarded the National Book Award and the Russwurm Award. From 1955 to 1957 he was a fellow of the American Academy in Rome.

On his return from Europe he taught at Bard College and in 1961 served as an Alexander White Visiting Professor at the University of Chicago. From 1962 to 1964 he was Visiting Professor of Writing at Rutgers University. He is a charter member of the National Council on the Arts and Humanities and a trustee of the John F. Kennedy Center for the Performing Arts. He was appointed to the American Institute of Arts and Letters in 1964, and was recently named a Chevalier in the Order of Arts and Letters by the French government.

Mr. Ellison is married to Fanny McConnell, formerly an executive administrator who now assists her husband full-time. They live in New York City and in Plainfield, Massachusetts.

Invisible Man (novel), Random, 1952
Shadow and Act (essays), Random, 1964
Cross Section edited by E. SEAVER (contributor), Fischer, 1944
Best Short Stories of World War II edited by CHARLES A. FENTON (contributor), Viking, 1957
I Have Seen War edited by DOROTHY STERLING (contributor), Hill & Wang, 1960
The Living Novel edited by GRANVILLE HICKS (contributor), Macmillan, 1957
A New Southern Harvest edited by ROBERT PENN WARREN and ALBERT ERSKINE (contributor), Bantam, 1957
The Angry Black edited by JOHN A. WILLIAMS (contributor), Lancer, 1962
Soon One Morning edited by HERBERT HILL (contributor), Knopf, 1963

JAMES (THOMAS) FARRELL, who began writing in 1927 and two years later was at work on his famous young man of Chicago, *Studs Lonigan,* was born in Chicago, February 27, 1904. His earliest jobs there were for the American Railway Express, clerking in a cigar store, serving as a filling station attendant and acting as a part time newspaper reporter from the University of Chicago, which he attended for about three years.

In his sixty-fifth year, James Farrell is the author now of forty-seven books, forty-five of them published since 1932 and two of his latest already written and contracted for. He has, he says, put on paper more than five million words, and although much of his literary output grew out of his background on Chicago's South Side, he has treated various environments both American and European. The critical remark sometimes made of his writing that he is "in a naturalistic tradition" he takes exception to. "A writer has his own way of seeing life and creates his world

parallel to a real world. When it is said I am a naturalist, it needs to be defined. I am also very impressionistic in the way I write and order my novels. What I did has lead to what I am doing, and it is full of surprises."

In 1937 Mr. Farrell was awarded a Book-of-the-Month Club Prize of $2500 for *Studs Lonigan,* which in its trilogy form had appeared the year before. The prize was awarded that year to four authors who had not had big sales. The others included Katherine Anne Porter and Robinson Jeffers. In 1936 he was called in by the Guggenheim Foundation (after the appearance of *Studs*) and asked to accept a Guggenheim Fellowship, his application for one on three previous occasions having been turned down.

In 1931 James Farrell married Dorothy Patricia Butler, the marriage ending in divorce. He married Hortense Alden, they were divorced in 1955 and he remarried Dorothy Butler Farrell in the same year. He has one son, Kevin, by his second wife, and he makes his home in New York City.

He is a member of the National Institute of Arts and Letters and was awarded an honorary degree of doctor of letters in 1968 by Miami University in Oxford, Ohio.

Young Lonigan, Vanguard, 1932, World, 1943
Gas-House McGinty, Vanguard, 1933
The Young Manhood of Studs Lonigan, Vanguard, 1934, World, 1944
Calico Shoes (short stories), Vanguard, 1934
Judgment Day, Vanguard, 1935, World, 1945
*Guillotine Party and Other Stories, Vanguard, 1935
Studs Lonigan, a Trilogy, Vanguard, 1935, Modern Library, 1938
A Note on Literary Criticism (essay), Vanguard, 1936
A World I Never Made, Vanguard, 1936
Can All This Grandeur Perish? and Other Stories, Vanguard, 1937

The Short Stories of James Thomas Farrell, Vanguard, 1937
Fellow Countrymen (collected stories), Constable, London, 1937
No Star Is Lost, Vanguard, 1938
Tommy Gallagher's Crusade, Vanguard, 1939
Father and Son, Vanguard, 1940, World, 1947
Ellen Rogers, Vanguard, 1941
$1000 a Week (stories), Vanguard, 1942
My Days of Anger, Vanguard, 1943, World, 1947
Short Stories, Sun Dial Press, 1943
Fifteen Selected Stories, Avon, 1943
To Whom It May Concern and Other Stories, Vanguard, 1944
Twelve Great Stories, Avon, 1945
The League of Frightened Philistines and Other Papers, Vanguard, 1945
When Boyhood Dreams Come True, Vanguard, 1946, Sun Dial, 1948
More Stories, Sun Dial, 1946
More Fellow Countrymen, Routledge & Kegan Paul, 1946
Bernard Clare, Vanguard, 1946, New American Lib., 1952
The Fate of Writing in America, New Directions, 1946
The Life Adventurous and Other Stories, Vanguard, 1947
Literature and Morality, Vanguard, 1947
A Hell of a Good Time and Other Stories, Avon, 1948
The Road Between, Vanguard, 1949
A Misunderstanding, House of Books, 1949
An American Dream Girl, Vanguard, 1950
The Name Is Fogarty: Private Papers on Public Matters (pseudonym, JONATHAN TITULESCU FOGARTY), Vanguard, 1950
This Man and This Woman, Vanguard, 1951
Poet of the People (contributor; with HORACE GREGORY and JEANETTE NOLAN), Indiana Univ. Press, 1954
Yet Other Waters, Vanguard, 1952
The Face of Time, Vanguard, 1953
Reflections at Fifty and Other Essays, Vanguard, 1954
French Girls Are Vicious and Other Stories, Vanguard, 1955

Best Short Stories by THEODORE DREISER (introduction), World, 1956
An Omnibus of Short Stories, Vanguard, 1956
My Baseball Diary, A. S. Barnes, 1957
A Dangerous Woman and Other Stories, Vanguard, 1957
Saturday Night and Other Stories, Hamilton, 1958
It Has Come to Pass, T. Herzl Press, 1958
Prejudices by H. L. Mencken (editor), Vintage, 1958
Dialogue on John Dewey (participating with CORLISS LAMONT and others), Horizon, 1959
The Short Stories of James Thomas Farrell (3 vols.), Grosset, 1962
The Silence of History (Vol. 1 of 3), Doubleday, 1963
A Dreiser Reader (with introduction), Dell, 1963
What Time Collects, Doubleday, 1964
The Collected Poems of James T. Farrell, Fleet, 1965
Lonely for the Future, Doubleday, 1966
When Time Was Born (prose poem), The Smith, N.Y., Horizon Press distributor, 1966
New Year's Eve: 1929 (novel), Horizon, 1966
*Childhood Is Not Forever (stories), Doubleday, 1969

ERICH FROMM, who was born March 23 1900, in Frankfurt-am-Main, Germany, but who has made his home in the United States since 1934, is adjunct professor of psychology at New York University and his work for the last quarter of a century has centered around the development of psychoanalytic theory, both in its clinical aspects and in relation to social, cultural and philosophical problems.

He took his doctorate in philosophy at Heidelberg in 1922 and was graduated from the Berlin Institute of Psychoanalysis in 1931. He has been guest lecturer at Columbia University, Terry lecturer at Yale University, lecturer at the New School for Social Research, and is diplomate of the American Psychological Association. He has been a member of the faculty of Bennington College, professor at Michigan State University, and was head of the department of psychoanalysis of the Medical School of the National University of Mexico, 1955 to 1966.

Escape From Freedom, Holt, 1941
Man For Himself, Holt, 1947
Psychoanalysis and Religion, Yale Univ. Press, 1950
The Forgotten Language, Holt, 1951
The Sane Society, Holt, 1955
The Art of Loving, Harper, 1956
Zen Buddhism and Psychoanalysis (with SUZUKI and DE MARTINO), Harper, 1960
Sigmund Freud's Mission, Harper, 1959
Marx's Concept of Man, Ungar, 1961
May Man Prevail? Doubleday, 1961
Beyond the Chains of Illusion, Simon & Schuster, 1962
The Dogma of Christ and Other Essays, Holt, 1963
The Heart of Man, Harper, 1964
You Shall Be as Gods, Holt, 1966
*The Revolution of Hope, Harper, 1968
The Crisis of Psychoanalysis, Essays on Freud, Marx and Social Psychology, Holt, Rinehart and Winston, Inc., 1970

JOHN KENNETH GALBRAITH, the economist, was born in Ontario, Canada, October 15, 1908. He took his B.S. at the University of Toronto, 1931, and his Masters at the University of California in 1933, his Ph.D. there in 1934. He studied at Cambridge University, England, in 1937–38.

Professor of Economics at Harvard University since 1949 and Paul M. Warburg Professor since 1959, he had earlier (1939–42) been Assistant Professor of economics at Princeton, and for five prior years instructor and tutor at Harvard.

Professor Galbraith first became active with government in 1940 when he became economic adviser to the National Defense Advisory Commission, later assistant administrator in charge of Price Division. He was deputy administrator in the Office of Price Administration from

1942 to 1943. He was a member of the board of editors of *Fortune* from 1943 to 1948, American Ambassador to India from 1961 to 1963. In 1945 he was director of the U. S. Strategic Bombing Survey, and director of the Office of Economic Security Policy, for the State Department, in 1946, a year in which he was awarded the Medal of Freedom.

In 1937 he married Catherine Atwater and they have three sons. He is a member of the National Institute of Arts and Letters.

American Capitalism, Houghton, 1952
A Theory of Price Control, Houghton, 1952
The Great Crash, Houghton, 1955
The Affluent Society, Houghton, 1958
The Liberal Hour, Houghton, 1960
Economic Development, Houghton, 1963
The Scotch, Houghton, 1964
The New Industrial State, 1967
Indian Painting (with RANDHAWA), Houghton, 1968
Ambassador's Journal: A Personal Account of the Kennedy Years, Houghton, 1969

ALLEN GINSBERG, born June 3, 1926, in Newark, New Jersey, is the son of Louis and Naomi (Levy) Ginsberg. His father is a poet with whom Allen Ginsberg sometimes appears in poetry readings. His mother is an emigré from Russia. He received his B.A. at Columbia University in 1949.

Since the publication in 1956 of *Howl, and Other Poems*, by the San Francisco publisher City Lights, Allen Ginsberg has been a leading gnostic poet of this generation, advocating a high element of personal awareness and permissiveness as a "space age anarchist" in politics and in religion a "Hindu-Buddhist-Jewish-Muslim-Xtian." Between 1945, when he was a welder in the Brooklyn Navy Yard, and 1962 when he was a motion picture actor in such non-commercial productions as "Pull My Daisy" and "Chappaqua," he had worked at various jobs including that of dishwasher, night porter, literary agent, copy boy on the old New York *World Telegram,* reporter in New Jersey, book reviewer (for *Newsweek* in 1950), and a market research consultant in New York and San Francisco. He is a member of the P.E.N., and the New York Eternal Committee for Conservation of Freedom in the Arts, Committee on Poetry, and he received a Guggenheim Fellowship in 1965–66. He was elected King of May, 1965, at the Prague Student Festival.

Howl, and Other Poems, City Lights, 1956
Kaddish Poems 1958–1960, City Lights, 1961
Empty Mirror, Corinth-Jargon, 1962
Reality Sandwiches (poems 1953–1960), City Lights, 1963
The Yage Letters (with WILLIAM BURROUGHS), City Lights, 1964
*Planet News, 1961–1967, City Lights, 1968
Indian Journals, DAVE HASELWOOD, City Lights, 1969

JOHN GUNTHER, journalist-historian, was born in Chicago, August 30, 1901, and took his degree of Ph.B. at the University of Chicago in 1922, hoping to be a chemist, but in 1924 he joined the *Chicago Daily News* and has been a writer of either facts, opinion or fiction ever since. He is author of more than thirty volumes, six of which are novels, the remainder biographies or political reporting which, in the past and current generation, has covered most of the inhabited globe. His "Inside" books—which bridge the gap between history and contemporary politics on five of the seven continents (Australia and Antarctica excepted) won him the appellation of a British critic as "Surveyor-General of the Universe." His work has been translated into 33 different languages and fourteen of his books have been distributed by the major book clubs, a record for any one author.

Mr. Gunther's work for the *Chicago Daily News* as foreign correspondent located him in London, various capitals of Europe and the Near East, India, China, and Japan between 1924 and 1939, when he became roving correspondent in Europe for the National Broadcasting Company. He covered the outbreak of war in London, invasion of Sicily, and in 1944–1945 was correspondent in Europe for *Look* and the New York *Herald Tribune.* He circled the globe in 1950, covered the Summit Conference in Paris in 1960, and at one time or another has met and interviewed practically all contemporary world leaders, such as Gandhi, Nehru, Khrushchev, Trotsky, Churchill, Roosevelt, Eisenhower, Chiang Kai-shek, Chou En Lai, Haile Selassie, De Gaulle, Tito, and many others.

Mr. Gunther lives in New York City when he is not on the wing somewhere. He is married to Jane Perry Vandercook who accompanies him on all his travels. His first wife, deceased, was Frances Gunther, whom he married in 1927. Their son John, who died of a brain tumor at 17 in 1947, was the subject of one of John Gunther's finest books, *Death Be Not Proud,* proceeds of which he devoted to cancer research.

The Red Pavilion, Harper, 1926
Peter Lancelot: An Amusement, M. Secker, 1927
Eden for One: An Amusement, Harper, 1927
The Golden Fleece, Harper, 1929
The Bright Nemesis, Bobbs, 1932
Inside Europe, Harper, 1936; fifth edition, 1942
The High Cost of Hitler, Hamish Hamilton, 1939
Inside Asia, Harper, 1939; school ed., 1942
Inside Latin America, Harper, 1941
D Day, Harper, 1944
The Troubled Midnight (novel), Harper, 1945
Inside U.S.A., Harper, 1947, revised, 1956
Behind the Curtain, Harper, 1949; in England *Behind Europe's Curtain,* Hamilton, 1949
Death Be Not Proud, a Memoir, Harper, 1949
Roosevelt in Retrospect, Harper, 1950; in

England, *Roosevelt: A Profile in History*
The Riddle of MacArthur: Japan, Korea and the Far East, Harper, 1951
Eisenhower, Harper, 1952
The Story of TVA, Harper, 1953
Alexander the Great, Random, 1953
Inside Africa, Harper, 1955
Days to Remember (with BERNARD QUINT), Harper, 1956
Meet North Africa (with SAM and BERYL EPSTEIN), Harper, 1957
Inside Russia Today, Harper, 1958; revised 1962; second revision, Penguin, 1964
Meet South Africa (with SAM and BERYL EPSTEIN), Harper, 1958; in England, *Meet Southern Africa*
Meet the Congo and Its Neighbors, Harper, 1959; in England, *Meet Central Africa*
Julius Caesar, Random, 1959
Taken at the Flood: The Story of Albert D. Lasker, Harper, 1960
Inside Europe Today, Harper, 1961; revised ed., 1962
Meet Soviet Russia, Harper, 1962
A Fragment of Autobiography; The Fun of Writing the Inside Books, Harper, 1962; in England, *The Story of the Inside Books*
The Lost City (novel), Harper, 1964
Procession, Harper, 1965
Twelve Cities, Harper, 1969
Mainstream of Modern World History Series (editor), Doubleday
The Indian Sign (novel), Harper, 1970

JOSEPH HELLER, who was born May 1, 1923, in Brooklyn, New York, was educated at New York University, B.A., 1948, Columbia University, M.A., 1949, and Oxford University, Fulbright scholar, 1949–1950. From 1950 to 1952 he was instructor in English at the Pennsylvania State University, an advertising writer for *Time* from 1952 to 1956, and presentations manager from 1958 to 1961 for McCall's.

Mr. Heller's military service was with the United States Army Air Forces during World War II. He became a lieutenant and his experiences were background for his famous anti-war novel *Catch-22, published by Simon & Schuster in 1961. His play, *We Bombed in New Haven*, was produced at Yale University in 1967 and on Broadway the following year. The play was published by Knopf in 1968.

The author lives in New York, is married and has two children. He is a Phi Beta Kappa and was made a member of the National Institute of Arts and Letters, with a grant in literature, in 1963.

JOHN HERSEY, son of Grace (Baird) and Roscoe Monroe Hersey, for twenty-five years a YMCA secretary in China, was born in Tientsin, June 17, 1914, and spent the first ten years of his life in China. He was bi-lingual as a child. In 1925 he was brought to the United States and became a student at the Hotchkiss School, Connecticut, and was graduated from Yale in 1936. He was a year at Cambridge University, England, and in the summer of 1937 he was private secretary to the author Sinclair Lewis.

Mr. Hersey was a war correspondent in the Pacific in 1942, the Mediterranean in 1943, Russia in 1944 and 1945, and China and Japan both before World War II and in 1945 and 1946.

Since 1965, Mr. Hersey has been master at Pierson College, Yale University, and since 1962 a trustee of the National Committee for the Support of Public Schools.

He was awarded the Pulitzer Prize for his novel *A Bell for Adano* in 1945, and his reportage on the atom bombing, *Hiroshima*, which first appeared in *The New Yorker*, later in book form, and *The Wall*, his notable novel on Poland under the Nazis, attracted world-wide attention.

Mr. Hersey has been twice married and has four children by his first wife and a daughter in his second marriage. He lives in Connecticut.

The Marmot Drive, Alfred A. Knopf, 1953
A Single Pebble, Knopf, 1956
The War Lover, Knopf, 1959

The Child Buyer, Knopf, 1960
Here to Stay, Knopf, 1963
White Lotus, Knopf, 1965
Too Far to Walk, Knopf, 1966
Under the Eye of the Storm, Knopf,
   1967
The Algiers Motel Incident, Knopf, 1968

WILLIAM INGE, winner of a Pulitzer Prize for a play and an Academy Award for a screenplay, was born in Independence, Kansas, May 3, 1913, and after graduation from the University of Kansas and a year of graduate work at Peabody Teachers College, he taught at Stephens College for Women in Columbia, Missouri, and after a three-year stint as drama and music critic for the St. Louis *Star-Times*, returned to teaching at Washington University there. It was during his newspaper life that he wrote his first play, *Farther off from Heaven*, which the late Margo Jones produced in her Dallas Theatre the summer of 1947. Mr. Inge lives in Los Angeles.

Mr. Inge's contribution to *This Is My Best* has not been previously published anywhere.

Come Back, Little Sheba, produced 1950
Picnic, Pulitzer Prize, Drama Critic's
   Prize, Donaldson Award, 1953
Bus Stop, produced 1955
The Dark at the Top of the Stairs, pro-
   duced 1957
A Loss of Roses, produced 1959
Natural Affection, produced 1963
Where's Daddy? produced 1966
Splendor in the Grass, screen play winner
   of the Academy Award for best original
   script

JAMES JONES, son of Ramon and Ada (Blessing) Jones, was born in Robinson, Illinois, November 6, 1921. He was a student at the University of Hawaii in 1942 and at New York University in 1945. From his service in the United States Army, between 1939 and 1944, when he was invalided out, came the experiences and background which went into his first novel, *From Here to Eternity*, which was a sales and critical success and won him the National Book Award in 1951. His war services were honored by a Purple Heart and a bronze star medal, and his first book was considered by at least one critic as "the best pictures of Army life ever written by an American."

Mr. Jones married Gloria Mosolino in 1957, and has two children, a daughter, Kaylie, and a son, Jamie. Since some of his books, including his first one, have sold to the moving pictures, he has long since abandoned living in a trailer and moving around the country, and has a home of his own on the Île Saint Louis in the heart of Paris.

From Here to Eternity, Scribner, 1951
Some Came Running, Scribner, 1957
The Pistol, Scribner, 1959
The Thin Red Line, Scribner, 1962
*Go to the Widow-Maker, Delacorte,
   1967; Dell, 1968
*The Ice Cream Headache and Other Sto-
   ries*, Delacorte, 1968

MACKINLAY KANTOR was born in Webster City, Iowa, February 4, 1904. He was graduated from the local high school, but never attended college. In 1921 he became a reporter on the Webster City *Daily News*; later he wrote for newspapers in Chicago, Cedar Rapids and Des Moines; and eventually was a popular short story writer whose work appeared in major magazines. As of 1969 he had published thirty-nine books—novels, collections of stories, juvenile histories, verse, and memoirs. In 1956 his novel *Andersonville* won the Pulitzer prize.

MacKinlay Kantor has been a writer for major studios and independent producers in the motion picture industry, and spent a year and a half as an associate producer. At one time he worked for nearly two years with the uniformed division of the New York City Police Department to gain accurate information for his novel, *Signal Thirty-two*.

His honorary degrees include Doctor

of Literature from Grinnell College, 1957; Doctor of Letters, Drake University, 1958; Doctor of Literature, Lincoln College (Illinois), 1959; Doctor of Letters, Ripon College (Wisconsin), 1961; and Doctor of Laws, Iowa Wesleyan College, 1961. He serves on the National Council of the Boy Scouts of America, and is an Honorary Trustee of Lincoln College.

He married Irene Layne, an artist, in 1926. They have two children and six grandchildren. Their home is on Siesta Key, near Sarasota, Florida.

During World War II, MacKinlay Kantor flew in combat as a war correspondent with the Royal Air Force. Although a civilian, he graduated from the gunnery school at Bovingdon, England, and flew many missions with the Eighth and Ninth Air Forces of the United States Army. During the Korean war he flew the 92nd Bomb Wing, USAF. Mr. Kantor served as technical consultant to the United States Air Force Chief of Staff, 1951–53; and made a special study of personnel, equipment, training and operations at Mediterranean bases of the Italian and Royal Hellenic (Greek) Air Forces, in 1963.

On November 26, 1947, by order of President Truman, he was decorated with the Medal of Freedom by General Carl A. Spaatz.

Diversey, Coward (their first book), 1928
El Goes South, Coward, 1930
The Jaybird, Coward, 1932
Long Remember, Coward, 1934
Turkey in the Straw (verse), Coward, 1935
The Voice of Bugle Ann, Coward, 1935
Arouse and Beware, Coward, 1936
The Romance of Rosy Ridge, Coward, 1937
The Noise of Their Wings, Coward, 1938
Here Lies Holly Springs, Colophon Press (Pynson Printers), 1938
Valedictory, Coward, 1939
Cuba Libre, Coward, 1940
Gentle Annie, Coward, 1942
Angleworms on Toast (juvenile), Coward, 1942
Happy Land, Coward, 1943

Author's Choice (stories), Coward, 1944
Glory for Me (basis for the motion picture *The Best Years of Our Lives*), Coward, 1945
But Look, the Morn (personalia), Coward, 1947
Midnight Lace, Random, 1948
Wicked Water, Random, 1949
The Good Family, Coward, 1949
One Wild Oat, Gold Medal Books, (Fawcett), 1950
Lee and Grant at Appomattox (juvenile), Random, 1950
Signal Thirty-two, Random, 1950
Don't Touch Me, Random, 1951
Gettysburg (juvenile), Random, 1952
Warwhoop, Random, 1952
The Daughter of Bugle Ann, Random, 1953
God and My Country, World, 1954
Andersonville, Pulitzer prize novel, World, 1955
Lobo (personalia), World, 1957
The Work of Saint Francis, World, 1958
If the South Had Won the Civil War, Bantam Books, 1961
*Spirit Lake, World, 1961
Mission with LeMay (personalia), Doubleday, 1965
Story Teller (stories), Doubleday, 1967
The Day I Met a Lion (personalia), Doubleday, 1968
Beauty Beast, Putnam, 1968
Missouri Bittersweet (personalia), Doubleday, 1969

ALFRED KAZIN, who was born June 5, 1915, in Brownsville, then largely a Polish-Russian-Jewish section of Brooklyn, New York, began his literary career book reviewing for magazines and newspapers while attending the College of the City of New York during the Depression of the Thirties. He attained the acclaim of his contemporaries in 1942 with his first book, *On Native Grounds,* which evaluated American literature in successive stages of development from 1880 to 1940.

Mr. Kazin took his M.A. at Columbia University in 1938, taught at City College, was for a time literary editor of

The New Republic, a reporter on *Fortune,* and a teacher at Black Mountain College in North Carolina. Since 1963 he has been Distinguished Professor of English at the State University of New York at Stony Brook. He was lecturer at the Salzburg Seminar of American Studies, 1947; Harvard, 1953; William Allan Neilson Research professor, Smith College, 1954–1955, Berg Professor of literature, New York University, 1957, professor of American Studies, Amherst, 1955–1958 and Beckman professor, University of California in 1963. He was awarded Guggenheim Fellowships in 1940 and in 1947, and a Rockefeller Fellowship for the study of educational movements in Great Britain in 1945. He is a member of the National Institute of Arts and Letters, and the American Academy of Arts and Sciences.

He has been twice married and has a son by his first wife and a daughter by his second, the novelist Ann Birstein.

On Native Grounds, Harcourt, 1942
A Walker in the City, Harcourt, 1951
Contemporaries, Little, Brown, 1962
The Inmost Leaf (essays; editor), Harcourt, 1955
Starting Out in the Thirties, (autobiography), Atlantic-Little Brown, 1965
The Works of Anne Frank (co-author with ANN BIRSTEIN), Doubleday, 1959
The Portable William Blake (editor), Viking, 1946
F. Scott Fitzgerald, The Man and His Work, World, 1951
Moby-Dick, Houghton, 1956
Selected Stories of Sholem Aleichem (with introduction), 1956
The Open Form: Essays for Our Time, Harcourt, 1961, 1965
Selected Short Stories of Nathaniel Hawthorne (introduction), Fawcett, 1966
The Stature of Theodore Dreiser (co-editor) Indiana Univ. Press, 1955
Ralph Waldo Emerson: A Modern Anthology (with DANIEL AARON), Houghton, 1958

Mr. Kazin has also done introductions to the works of Dostoevsky, D. H. Lawrence and others.

JOSEPH WOOD KRUTCH, essayist, teacher and critic, was born in Knoxville, Tenn., November 25, 1893. He received his B.A. from the University of Tennessee in 1915, and his M.A. at Columbia in 1916 and his Ph.D. in 1923.

Mr. Krutch became Brander Matthews professor of dramatic literature at Columbia University in 1943, but retired from teaching in 1952, gave up his position as drama critic of *The Nation,* which he had held since 1924, and moved to Arizona where he wrote *The Desert Year.* His book *The Measure of Man* won the National Book Award for non-fiction in 1955.

In World War I, Mr. Krutch served in the United States Army Psychological Corps. He is a trustee of the Arizona-Sonora Desert Museum, at Tucson, and since 1967 has been Consultant on American Culture to the Library of Congress, prior to his retirement, he taught at the Polytechnic Institute of Brooklyn, Vassar College, School of Journalism of Columbia University, and the New School for Social Research, New York. He received a Guggenheim Fellowship in 1930, the Richard Prentice Ettinger medal in 1964, the Emerson-Thoreau medal of the American Academy of Arts and Sciences, in 1967, of which he is a fellow. He is a member of the American Philosophical Society, and a member of the board of editors of the *American Men of Letters Series,* a post he has held since 1947.

In 1923 Mr. Krutch married Marcelle Leguia and he lives in Tucson.

Comedy and Conscience after the Restoration, Columbia University Press, 1924, 1961
Edgar Allen Poe: A Study in Genius, Knopf, 1926
The Modern Temper: A Study and a Confession, Harcourt, 1929, 1956
Five Masters: A Study in the Mutations of th. Novel, Smith & Haas, 1930
Experience and Art: Some Aspects of the Aesthetics of Literature, Smith & Haas, 1932, Collier Books, 1962
Was Europe a Success?, Farrar, 1934
The American Drama Since 1918, Random 1939, Braziller, 1957

Samuel Johnson, Sloane, 1944
Henry David Thoreau, Sloane, 1948
The Twelve Seasons, Sloane, 1949, 1961
Great American Nature Writing (editor),
1950
The Desert Year, Sloane, 1952
*The Best of Two Worlds, Sloane, 1953
Modernism in American Drama, Cornell
Univ. Press, 1953
The Measure of Man, Bobbs, 1954, 1962
Is the Common Man Too Common?
(with others), U. of Oklahoma Press,
1954
The Voice of the Desert, Sloane, 1955
The Great Chain of Life, Houghton, 1957
Grand Canyon: Today and All Its Yes-
terdays, Sloane, 1958
Human Nature and the Human Condi-
tion, Random, 1959
The Gardener's World, Putnam, 1958
The Forgotten Peninsula, Sloane, 1951
The World of Animals, Simon & Schuster,
1961
More Lives Than One (autobiography),
Sloane, 1962
The Plays of William Congreve (editor),
Farrar, 1927
Nine Plays by Eugene O'Neill (editor),
Farrar, 1932
Remembrance of Things Past by MAR-
CELL PROUST (editor), Farrar, 1934
Representative American Dramas (editor),
Farrar, 1941
Select Letters of Thomas Gray (with in-
troduction; editor), Farrar, Straus, 1952
Our Changing Morals (editor; with
others), Hill & Wang, 1925
Living Philosophies (editor), Hill & Wang,
1931
America Now (editor), Hill & Wang,
1931
A Treasury Of Bird Lore (editor; with
PAUL S. ERIKSON), Hill & Wang, 1969
If You Don't Mind My Saying So (es-
says), Sloane, 1964
And Even If You Do—, Morrow, 1967
The Most Wonderful Animals That Never
Were (juvenile), Houghton, 1969
The Best Nature Writing of Joseph Wood
Krutch, Morrow, 1969

ROBERT (TRAILL SPENCE) LOWELL, JR.,
was born in Boston, March 1, 1917, son

of a naval officer. He attended St. Mark's
School and Harvard College. He was
graduated, in 1940, *summa cum laude,*
from Kenyon College, in Ohio, where he
studied poetry with John Crowe Ransom, and majored in classics. During
World War II he was a conscientious ob-
jector and served a jail sentence.

Following the publication of his second
volume of poetry, *Lord Weary's Castle,*
Mr. Lowell was appointed (1947–48)
Consultant in Poetry at the Library of
Congress. He has received a Guggenheim
Fellowship and a grant from the Institute
of Arts and Letters, and has lectured at
many colleges including the State Univer-
sity of Iowa, the Kenyon School of
English and the Salzburg Seminar in
American Studies in Austria.

Mr. Lowell is a great-grandnephew of
James Russell Lowell and a distant cousin
of Amy Lowell. He has been twice married, his first wife the novelist Jean Stafford, and his present wife the critic
and editor, Elizabeth Hardwick, who is
identified with the *New York Review of*
Books.

In 1947 Mr. Lowell was awarded the
Pulitzer prize for poetry, and in 1959
the Guinness Poetry Award and the National Book Award (for *Life Studies*).
He is a member of Phi Beta Kappa and
of the American Academy of Arts and
Letters. He lives in New York City, but
in the fall of 1969 was spending part of
each week teaching at Harvard University.

Land of Unlikeness (out of print), Cum-
mington Press, 1944
Lord Weary's Castle, Harcourt, 1946
The Mills of the Kavanaughs, Harcourt,
1951
Life Studies (National Book Award), Far-
rar, 1959, 1967
Phaedra and Figaro, Farrar, Straus &
Cudahy, 1961
Imitations (Bollingen translation prize),
Farrar, 1961
For the Union Dead, Farrar, 1964
Prometheus Bound (adaptation as pre-
sented at the Yale School of Drama in
1967), Noonday, 1967

Old Glory, Farrar, 1968
Notebook 1967–68, Farrar, 1969

ARCHIBALD MACLEISH, who has won the Pulitzer Prize three times, twice for poetry and once for drama, was born May 7, 1892, in Glencoe, Illinois. He was graduated from Yale in 1915 and received his LL.B. from Harvard in 1919. He served in World War I, entering the army as a private and leaving it a captain. He practiced law for three years, then, between 1923 and 1928, lived in France, to devote more time to his writing.

Mr. MacLeish's epic of the conquest of Mexico, *Conquistador,* won the 1932 Pulitzer prize for poetry, his *Collected Poems* won it in 1953, and *J.B.,* a verse play, won the prize for drama in 1959. He was also awarded the Bollingen prize for poetry in 1953 and the National Book Award for poetry the same year, and the Antoinette Perry award in drama in 1959. Honorary degrees have been conferred upon him by Yale, Tufts, Wesleyan, Colby College, the University of Pennsylvania, University of Illinois, Dartmouth, Johns Hopkins, University of California, Queens University in Ontario, Carleton College, Amherst, Rockford College, Harvard, the University of Pittsburgh, Union College, the University of Puerto Rico, Princeton University, and Williams College.

A man, and poet, concerned with social and intellectual currents of his time and the backgrounds of American thought and culture, Mr. MacLeish has been an active participant in the issues and politics of the last two generations. He was one of the editors of *Fortune* from its 1938 beginning, set up the Nieman Fellowships in Journalism at Harvard, served as Librarian of Congress from 1939 to 1944, directed the United States Office of Facts and Figures, and was assistant director of the Office of War Information from June 1942 to February 1943. He was American delegate to the Conference of Allied Ministers of Education, London, 1944. From 1944 to 1945 he was an assistant Secretary of State, in 1945 he was chairman of the American delegation to the London Conference to draw up the constitution for UNESCO, and he was chairman of the first American delegation to the first general conference, and the first American member of the executive council. He is a Commander of the Legion of Honor (France) and Encomienda Order del Sol de Peru.

Mr. MacLeish married Ada Hitchcock in 1916 and is the father of three children. Mr. and Mrs. MacLeish live on a 200-acre farm in Conway, Massachusetts, to which he retired when he left his post six years ago as Boylston Professor of Rhetoric and Oratory at Harvard. They spend their winters in Antigua in the Caribbean.

Songs for a Summer Day, Yale Univ. Press, 1915
Tower of Ivory, Yale, 1917
The Happy Marriage, Houghton, 1924
The Pot of Earth, Houghton, 1925
Nobodaddy (drama), Dunster House, Boston, 1926
Streets in the Moon, Houghton, 1926
The Hamlet of A. MacLeish, Houghton, 1928
Einstein, Black Sun, Paris, 1929
New Found Land, Black Sun, 1930
Before March, Knopf, 1932
Conquistador, Houghton, 1932
Frescoes for Mr. Rockefeller's City, Day, 1933
Selected Poems of Archibald MacLeish 1924–1933, Houghton, 1933
Panic (drama), Houghton, 1935
Public Speech, Farrar & Rinehart, 1936
The Fall of the City (verse play for radio), Farrar, 1937
Land of the Free, Harcourt, 1938
Air Raid (verse play for radio), Harcourt, 1938
America Was Promises, Duell, Sloan, & Pearce, 1939
The Irresponsibles, Duell, 1940
The States Talking (pamphlet), Free Company, 1941
The American Cause (essay), Duell, 1941

Prophets of Doom (lecture), University of Pennsylvania Press, 1941

A Time to Speak (selected prose), Houghton, 1941

American Opinion and the War (lecture), Macmillan, 1942

A Time to Act (selected addresses), Houghton, 1943

American Story (broadcasts), Duell, 1944

Act Five (poems), Random, 1948

Poetry and Opinion, (prose), U. of Illinois, 1950

Freedom Is the Right to Choose, Beacon Press, 1951

Collected Poems, 1917–52, Houghton, 1963

Songs for Eve, Houghton, 1954

J.B. (verse play), Houghton, 1958

Poetry and Experience (prose), Houghton, 1961

Eleanor Roosevelt Story (book), Houghton, 1965

1965 (motion picture; Academy Award), 1965

Herakles (verse play), Houghton, 1967

An Evening's Journey to Conway, Massachusetts (play), 1967

Continuing Journey, Houghton, 1968

**"The Wild Old Wicked Man" and Other Poems,* Houghton, 1968

NORMAN MAILER, who was born in Long Branch, New Jersey, January 31, 1923, son of Isaac Barnett and Fanny (Schneider) Mailer, was graduated from Harvard in 1943 and did graduate study at the Sorbonne. At Harvard he had planned a career in science—he envisaged being an aeronautical engineer—but a literary prize (*Story* Magazine) changed his mind and he gave up engineering for literature. His first book, based on his experiences as an infantryman in the United States Army in the Pacific, 1944–46, was *The Naked and the Dead,* which enjoyed a huge success and was generally considered one of the most impressive novels to come out of World War II. It was praised, among other things, for its "reportorial sense," a quality Mailer was later to bring to bear on national politics and mores in

his reports on the Miami and Chicago national political conventions of 1968.

A controversial literary figure, Mr. Mailer has identified himself with the rebels of his and a later generation, participated in various protests and national "marches," has pilloried the Establishment and in 1969 he ran, with a fellow columnist and newspaperman, James Breslin, for public office in New York City, Mailer for the mayoralty and Breslin for Comptroller. They lost.

Mr. Mailer has four daughters and two sons in four marriages. He lives with his present wife, the former Beverly Bentley, in Provincetown, Massachusetts, and Brooklyn, New York.

Much of Mr. Mailer's writing has first appeared in newspapers or magazines. He has written regular columns for *Esquire,* for *Dissent,* 1954–55–56, for *The Village Voice,* of which he was co-founder, the *Partisan Review, Harpers, Life, Commentary,* and others. He was an editor of *Dissent* from 1953 to 1963.

Mr. Mailer was given a grant in literature in 1960 by the National Institute of Arts and Letters, and his reportage of the anti-Vietnam demonstrations in Washington in October, 1967, *The Armies of the Night,* was awarded the Pulitzer Prize for non-fiction and the 1969 National Book Award for arts and letters. He has recently written, produced and acted in three experimental films.

The Naked and the Dead, Rinehart, 1948

Barbary Shore, Rinehart, 1951

The Dear Park, dramatized 1967; Putnam, 1955

Advertisements for Myself, Putnam, 1958

The White Negro, City Lights Books, 1959

Deaths for the Ladies, and Other Disasters (poems), Putnam, 1962

The Presidential Papers (essays), Putnam, 1962

**An American Dream,* Dial, 1964

Cannibals and Christians, Dial, 1966

Why Are We in Vietnam (novel), Putnam, 1967

The Armies of the Night, New American Lib., 1968

Miami and the Siege of Chicago, World, New American Lib., 1968

BERNARD MALAMUD was born in Brooklyn, New York, April 26, 1914, the son of Max and Bertha Malamud, and at eighteen his experiences as a grocery clerk incorporated into a short story entitled "Life—From Behind a Counter" won him first prize in the Scholastic Magazine's Writing Awards. The experiences later he developed into the novel *The Assistant.*

He took his B.A. at the College of the City of New York in 1936 and his M.A. at Columbia University in 1942 and was a teacher of English in the evening high school system of New York City from 1940 to 1949. He was associate professor of English at the Oregon State University, where he taught from 1949 to 1961. Since then he has been a member of the language and literature division of Bennington College in Vermont. He was visiting lecturer at Harvard University in 1966 and 1967.

Mr. Malamud's novel *The Fixer* won the National Book Awards for fiction in 1967 and the Pulitzer Prize the same year. His writing has been credited with displaying unique gifts of insight and expressive power. Philip Rahv has characterized one of his stories, *The Magic Barrel,* as "perhaps the best story produced by an American in recent decades."

The author was awarded a *Partisan Review* Fellowship in fiction in 1956–1957, the Rosenthal award of the National Institute of Art and Letters, 1958, the Daroff Memorial Award, 1958, the National Book Award for fiction in 1959 for *The Magic Barrel* and a Ford Fellowship in the Humanities and Arts Program, 1959–1961. He is a member of the National Institute of Arts and Letters and the American Academy of Arts and Letters.

Mr. Malamud married Ann de Chiara in 1945: they have a son and a daughter and live in Vermont.

The Natural (novel), Harcourt, 1952
The Assistant (novel), Farrar, 1957
*The Magic Barrel (stories), Farrar, 1958
A New Life (novel), Farrar, 1961
Idiots First (stories), Farrar, 1963
The Fixer (novel), Farrar, 1966
Pictures of Fidelman (novel), Farrar, 1969

MARY (THERESE) MCCARTHY was born June 21, 1912, in Seattle, Washington. She took her A.B. at Vassar in 1933 and her literary life has been spent in editing, teaching, novel writing, traveling, and criticizing—either drama, books, manners or politics.

Miss McCarthy was an editor with the publishing firm of Covici-Friede, between 1936 and 1937 and drama critic for *Partisan Review* between 1937 and 1956. She taught at Bard College from 1945 to 1946 and at Sarah Lawrence College in 1948. She is a Phi Beta Kappa and a member of the National Institute of Arts and Letters and has won several distinguished literary awards including a Guggenheim Fellowship, 1949–50, the *Horizon* prize of 1949, and a National Institute grant in literature in 1957. Her novel, *The Group,* was a nomination of 1964 for the National Book Award.

She is married to James West, an American diplomat, and lives in Paris. Her present marriage is her fourth. One of her husbands was the critic Edmund Wilson from whom she was divorced. She has one son, Reuel Wilson.

The Company She Keeps, Simon & Schuster, 1942; Weidenfeld & Nicolson, 1957
The Oasis, Random, 1949; as *Source of Embarrassment,* Heinemann, 1950
Cast a Cold Eye, Harcourt, 1950
The Groves of Academe, Harcourt, 1952
A Charmed Life, Harcourt, 1955
Sights and Spectacles, 1937–56, Farrar, 1956
Venice Observed, Reynal, 1956; Heinemann, 1961
Memories of a Catholic Girlhood, Harcourt, 1957

Sights and Spectacles, 1937–56, Meridian, 1957

The Stones of Florence, Harcourt, 1959, 1963

**On the Contrary,* Farrar, 1961

Mary McCarthy's Theatre Chronicles 1937–62, Farrar, 1963

The Group, Harcourt, 1963

Vietnam, Harcourt, 1967

Hanoi, Harcourt, 1967

PHYLLIS MCGINLEY, who was born March 21, 1905, in Ontario, Oregon, is a graduate of the University of Utah and attended the University of California. Before her marriage to an executive of the New York Telephone Company in 1937 she taught school in Utah, served as a copy writer for a New York advertising agency, and was staff writer for *Town and Country.*

Her first book of verse appeared in 1934, followed by many since as well as seventeen or eighteen books for children. She also wrote the lyrics for a Broadway review and the narration for a film. She is a member of the National Institute of Arts and Letters, received the Pulitzer Prize for poetry in 1961 for her volume, *Times Three,* and for other books of verse was honored by the Christopher Book Award in 1955, Catholic Writers Guild Award in 1955, Edna St. Vincent Millay Memorial Award, 1955, St. Catherine of Sienna medal in 1956, Catholic Institute of the Press Award, 1960, Gold Book Award, and the National Association of Independent Schools Award, 1961, the Spirit gold medal of the Catholic Poetry Society of America in 1962, the Notre Dame Lastare medal, 1964, and the Campion Award, 1967.

The author, who is Mrs. Charles L. Hayden in private life has two daughters who have often figured in her writings, and the family lives in Larchmont, New York.

Miss McGinley has been given honorary degrees by Wheaton College (Massachusetts), St. Mary's College, Notre Dame, Marquette University, Dartmouth, Boston College, Smith, Wilson College, and St. John's University.

In addition to her books, Miss McGinley wrote the lyrics for *Small Wonder,* a Broadway revue, in 1948, and the narration for the film, *The Emperor's Nightingale,* in 1951.

On the Contrary (verse), Doubleday, 1934

One More Manhattan, Harcourt, 1937

A Pocketful of Wry, Duell, 1940; Grosset, 1959

Husbands Are Difficult or *The Book of Oliver Ames,* Duell, 1941

Stones from a Glass House, Viking, 1946

A Short Walk from the Station, Viking, 1951

The Love Letters of Phyllis McGinley, Viking, 1954

Merry Christmas, Happy New Year, Viking, 1958

**Times Three,* Viking, 1960

The Horse Who Lived Upstairs (juvenile), Lippincott, 1944

The Plain Princess (juvenile), Lippincott, 1945

All Around the Town (juvenile), Lippincott, 1948

A Name for Kitty (juvenile), Simon & Schuster, 1948

The Most Wonderful Doll in the World (juvenile), Lippincott, 1950

The Horse Who Had His Picture in the Paper (juvenile), Lippincott, 1951

Blunderbus (juvenile), Lippincott, 1951

The Make-Believe Twins (juvenile), Lippincott, 1953

The Year Without a Santa Claus (juvenile), Lippincott, 1957

Lucy McLockett (juvenile), Lippincott, 1959

Sugar and Spice: The ABC of Being a Girl (juvenile), Watts, 1960

Mince Pie and Mistletoe (juvenile), Lippincott, 1961

The B Book (juvenile), Crowell-Collier, 1962

Boys Are Awful (juvenile), Watts, 1962

How Mrs. Santa Claus Saved Christmas (juvenile), Lippincott, 1963

A Girl and Her Room (juvenile), Watts, 1963

The Province of the Heart (essays), Viking, 1959

Sixpence in Her Shoe (Essays), Macmillan, 1964

Wonderful Time (essays), Lippincott, 1966

A Wreath of Christmas Legends (essays), Macmillan, 1967

Saint Watching (essays), Viking, 1969

MARGARET MEAD, Curator Emeritus of Ethnology since 1969 at the American Museum of Natural History, New York City, and adjunct professor of anthropology at Columbia University since 1954, was born December 16, 1901, in Philadelphia. She took her Ph.D. in 1929 at Columbia University and has been given honorary degrees from seventeen universities and colleges in the past twenty-eight years.

Dr. Mead, an authority on primitive cultures, has held lectureships from coast to coast and in Great Britain, France, Austria, and Australia. She was named Outstanding Woman of the Year in the Field of Science by the Associated Press in 1949, and Viking Medalist in General Anthropology, awarded by the Wenner-Gren Foundation for Anthropological Research in 1957–58, and voted One of the Outstanding Women of the Twentieth Century by Nationwide Women Editors in 1965. She is a fellow of a dozen learned societies and has been awarded numerous medals and citations for distinguished service in the social sciences.

Her expeditions, beginning in Samoa, in 1925 have carried her to New Guinea, among American Indian tribes, Bali, and the Admiralty Islands. They have involved her living with various South Seas peoples, learning and using their languages, and writing books on the relationships between character structure and social forms, family life, and cultural building and change.

When not on an expedition or lecture tour, Dr. Mead may be found at her office in the American Museum of Natural History, off Central Park, in New York City.

Out of a background of cultural experiences with primitive and highly educated peoples, and explaining one to the other, Miss Mead commented recently on the crisis of "faith and hope, a crisis in which most parents are too uncertain to assert old dogmatisms—as they look at the children whom they never were—and most children are unable to learn at all from the parents and elders they will never be." But she is not pessimistic about the world or its youth. "Once the fact of a deep, new, unprecedented, worldwide generation gap is firmly established, in the minds of both the young and the old," she believes, "communication can be established again."

Dr. Mead has been twice married and has one daughter, Mary Catherine Bateson Kassarjian, by her second husband, Mr. Bateson.

Coming of Age in Samoa, Morrow, 1928, 1949 and 1968; New American Library, 1953; Modern Library, 1962; Dell, 1953

Growing Up in New Guinea, Morrow, 1930, 1953, 1962; New American Library, 1953

The Changing Culture of an Indian Tribe, Columbia Univ. Press, 1932; Capricorn Books, 1966

Sex and Temperament in Three Primitive Societies, Morrow, 1935, 1963; NAL, 1950; Dell, 1968

From the South Seas, Morrow, 1939

And Keep Your Powder Dry, Morrow, 1942, 1965

Male and Female, Morrow, 1949, 1967; NAL, 1955

The School in American Culture, Harvard Univ. Press, 1951, 1964

Soviet Attitudes Toward Authority, McGraw-Hill, 1951; Schocken, 1966

New Lives for Old, Cultural Transformation—Manus (tribe), 1928–1953; Morrow, 1956, 1961, 1966; NAL, 1961

An Anthropologist at Work, Writings of Ruth Benedict, Houghton Mifflin, 1959; Atherton Press, 1966

People and Places, World, 1959; Bantam, 1963

Continuities in Cultural Evolution, Yale Univ. Press, 1964, 1966
Anthropology: A Human Science, Van Nostrand, 1964
Anthropologists and What They Do, Watts, 1965
Culture and Commitment, Doubleday, 1970
A Way of Seeing (with Rhoda Metraux) McCall, 1970

Dr. Mead is also co-author of many monographs, technical papers, and books on primitive people, the family, cultures, etc., in collaboration with Gregory Bateson, Francis C. MacGregor, Kenneth Heyman, Muriel Brown, Rhoda Metraux, and others. She also worked on six films on primitive cultures with Mr. Bateson, and on others with the Canadian Film Board and National Educational Television.

JAMES MICHENER was U.S. naval historian in the South Pacific from 1944–46, but fiction rather than history brought him the Pulitzer Prize in 1948 for his *Tales of the South Pacific,* which later became the widely popular Broadway musical *South Pacific,* by Rodgers and Hammerstein.

He was born February 3, 1907, in New York City, graduated in 1929, *summa cum laude,* from Swarthmore College, took his M.A. at Colorado State College of Education in 1937 and did research study at the Universities of Pennyslvania, Virginia, Ohio State, Harvard and later in Scotland and Italy.

Although Mr. Michener is best known as a novelist, he has done a number of social studies. Most of his works are concerned with Asia and the Pacific. Motion pictures have made use of his material not only in *South Pacific,* but in *Return to Paradise, Sayonara* and *The Bridges at Toko-Ri.*

Mr. Michener campaigned for John F. Kennedy, Lyndon B. Johnson, and Hubert Humphrey and for himself as a Democrat running for Congress in one of Pennsylvania's Republican strongholds. In the winter of 1967–68 he served as secretary of Pennsylvania's Constitutional Convention and contributed to the resulting overhaul of his state's governmental structure. More recently he was the president of the Electoral College of Pennsylvania and later he served as co-chairman of a commission to modernize the Pennsylvania legislature.

He has had two divorces. His present wife, whom he married in 1955, is the former Mari Yoriko Sabusawa. He lives in Pennsylvania.

Tales of the South Pacific, Macmillan, 1948
The Fires of Spring, Random, 1949
Voice of Asia, Random, 1951
Return to Paradise, Random, 1951
The Bridges at Toko-Ri, Random, 1953
Sayonara, Random, 1954
The Floating World, Random, 1954
Selected Writings, Modern Library, 1957
Rascals in Paradise (with A. GROVE DAY), Random, 1957
The Bridge at Andau, Random, 1957
Hokusai Sketchbooks by HOKUSAI TUTTLE (editor), 1958
*Hawaii, Random, 1959
Japanese Prints, Tuttle, 1959
Report of the County Chairman, Random, 1961
Caravans, Random, 1963
The Source, Random, 1965
Iberia, Random, 1968
Presidential Lottery, the Reckless Gamble in Our Electoral System, Random, 1969

ARTHUR MILLER, who was born October 17, 1915, in the Harlem section of New York City, son of Isidore and Augusta (Barnett) Miller—his father was a manufacturer and his mother a teacher—took his A.B. at the University of Michigan in 1938. Before attending college, he worked for a couple of years in a warehouse, and at other times in a box factory and at the Brooklyn Navy Yard. At Michigan he won an Avery Hopwood Award in 1936 for his writing and again in 1937. In 1938 he won the first award of the Theatre Guild national playwriting contest and was for a time connected with the Federal Theatre Project.

Mr. Miller won the New York Drama Circle Award in 1947 for *All My Sons*, the Pulitzer Prize for *Death of a Salesman* in 1949, the Antoinette Perry Award in 1954 for *The Crucible*, and the Gold Medal for drama from the National Institute of Arts and Letters for *A View from the Bridge* in 1959. The University of Michigan awarded him an honorary doctorate of letters in 1956, and he was made international president of P.E.N. (Poets, Editors and Novelists) in 1965 and presided at its International Congress in 1969 in Menton, France.

Mr. Miller has had three marriages and has two daughters and a son. His second marriage was to the actress Marilyn Monroe. His present wife is Inge Morath, internationally known photographer.

The Man Who Had All the Luck, produced on Broadway, 1944

Situation Normal (reportage on Army), Reynal, 1944

Focus (novel), Reynal, 1945

All My Sons, produced 1947; Reynal, 1947

Death of a Salesman, produced 1949; Viking, 1949

Henrik Ibsen, Enemy of the People (adaptor), produced 1950; Viking, 1950, Viking, 1951

The Crucible, produced 1953; Viking, 1953

A View from the Bridge, produced 1955; one-act version with *A Memory of Two Mondays*, Viking, 1955; two-act version, Cresset, 1957

Collected Plays, Viking, 1957

The Misfits (novelized film script), Viking, 1961

Jane's Blanket, (juvenile), Collier, 1963

After the Fall, produced 1964; Viking, 1964

I Don't Need You Anymore (short stories), Viking, 1967

Incident at Vichy, produced 1965; Viking, 1965

The Price, produced 1968; Viking, 1968

HENRY MILLER, who came into literary prominence (and controversy) in the 1930s with books written in Paris (1930 to 1939), was born in the Yorkville section of New York City, December 26, 1891. In 1909, for a few weeks, he attended The College of the City of New York, leaving to take various odd jobs, in the Atlas Portland Cement Co., New York, in his father's tailor shop, as employment manager of the messenger department for Western Union, in the Bureau of Economic Research, and many other places. In 1925 he peddled prose poems from door to door and in 1927 he ran a speakeasy in Greenwich Village.

Mr. Miller visited Europe in 1928, went to London in 1930 for a few weeks, and then to Paris. In 1932 he was hired as a proofreader for the Paris Edition of the Chicago *Tribune* and began the kind of frank, semi-confessional fiction writing that made him famous and has been revived with widespread acceptance after years of having been censored and banned, both in the United States and in France.

In 1932, Mr. Miller taught English for a few weeks at the Lycée Carnot, Dijon, France. With Lawrence Durrell and Alfred Perles, Mr. Miller was co-editor of a Paris magazine, *The Booster*, and in 1936 he was contributing editor of the French review *Volontés*.

From 1942 to 1962, Mr. Miller lived in Big Sur, California. His present wife, the former Hoki Tokuda, is his fifth. He has two daughters and one son.

He has had more than a dozen exhibitions of his paintings in various parts of the world, the last two in Japan and Paris.

Many of Mr. Miller's works, once banned from the United States because of their frankness in treating sex, have been republished in the last decade, many in paper backs, enjoying extraordinary sales. In 1961 he was cited by the Formentor Prize Committee, which met in Majorca, as "one of the most important literary figures of the twentieth century." He is a member of the National Institute of Arts and Letters and now lives in Pacific Palisades, California.

Tropic of Cancer, Obelisk Press, 1934, 1939; Grove, 1961

Aller Retour-New York, Obelisk, 1935; American ed. privately printed, 1945

Black Spring, Obelisk, 1936; Grove, 1963

Scenario, Obelisk, 1937

Un Etre Etoilique, privately printed, 1937

Money and How It Gets That Way, Paris, 1938; Bern Porter, 1945

What Are You Going to Do About Alf? privately printed, 1938; Bern Porter, 1944

Max and the White Phagocytes, Obelisk, 1938

Tropic of Capricorn, Obelisk, 1939; Grove, 1962

The Cosmological Eye, New Directions, 1939, 1944

Hamlet, Vol. 1 (correspondence with MICHAEL FRAENKEL), Carrefour, 1939, 1943

The World of Sex, privately printed, 1940; revised, Olympia Press, 1957

Hamlet Vol. 2 (correspondence with MICHAEL FRAENKEL), Carrefour, 1941

The Wisdom of the Heart, New Directions, 1941

The Colossus of Maroussi, Colt Press, 1941

The Angel Is My Water-Mark, Holve-Barrows, 1944

Sunday After the War (stories and essays), New Directions, 1944

The Plight of the Creative Artist in the United States of America, Bern Porter, 1944

Murder the Murderer, Bern Porter, 1944

Semblance of a Devoted Past, Bern Porter, 1945

Henry Miller Miscellanea, Bern Porter, 1945

The Air-Conditioned Nightmare, New Directions, 1945

Obscenity and the Law of Reflection, Alicat Book Shop, 1945

The Rosy Crucifixion (Book 1: *Sexus*), Obelisk, 1945

Maurizius Forever, Colt Press, 1946

Patchen: Man of Anger and Light, Padell, 1946

Into the Night Life (with BEZALEL SCHATZ, taken from *Black Spring*), Berkeley, 1947

Of, By and About Henry Miller (a collection of pieces by Miller and others), Alicat Bookshop, 1947

Portrait of General Grant, London, 1947

Remember to Remember (Vol. 2 of *The Air-Conditioned Nightmare*), New Directions, 1947

Varda: The Master Builder, Berkeley, 1947

The Smile at the Foot of the Ladder, Duell, 1948

The Rosy Crucifixion (Book I: *Sexus;* Book II, *Plexus*), Obelisk, 1949

The Waters Reglitterized, John Kides, 1950

The Books in My Life, New Directions, 1952

A Devil in Paradise, New American Lib., 1954

Nights of Love and Laughter, NAL, 1955

Argument About Astrology, Manas Publishing Co., 1956

Big Sur and the Oranges of Hieronymus Bosch, New Directions, 1956

Quiet Days in Clichy, Olympia, 1956

Rimbaud or The Time of the Assassins, New Directions, 1956; in England, Neville Spearman, 1956

The Red Notebook (contains Miller's horoscope), Jargon, 1958

Art and Outrage (with LAWRENCE DURRELL and ALFRED PEARLES) McClelland, 1959

The Henry Miller Reader edited by LAWRENCE DURRELL, New Directions, 1959; in England as *The Best of Henry Miller,* Heinemann, 1960

The Intimate Henry Miller (collection of stories, essays, autobiographical sketches), NAL, 1959

Nexus (Vol. 1), Olympia, 1959

To Paint Is to Love Again, Cambria Books, 1960

A Letter (with H. HILER), Wittenborn, 1962

Stand Still Like the Hummingbird, New Directions, 1962

Watercolors, Drawings, and The Angel Is My Watermark (essay), Thames, 1962

Just Wild About Harry (a Melo-Melo in 7 Scenes), New Directions, 1963

Lawrence Durrell and Henry Miller, a Private Correspondence edited by GEORGE WICKES, Dutton, 1963
Greece, Viking, 1964
Henry Miller on Writing, New Directions, 1964

MARIANNE MOORE, who passed her 81st birthday amidst hosannas of critical praises and the glitter of gold medals for her poetic achievements, was born November 15, 1886, in St. Louis, Missouri, the home town, incidentally, also of T. S. Eliot who wrote an introduction to her first book of selected poems in 1935.

For many years of her writing life, Miss Moore lived in Brooklyn and lives now on Ninth Street in Manhattan. When she accepted the Gold Medal for Distinguished Achievement from the Poetry Society of America at its 57th Annual dinner in 1967 she was hailed by Mayor John Lindsay as "truly the poet laureate of New York City." She is probably the only American poet, male or female, who ever received the three major American poetry prizes—the National Book Award for Poetry, the Bollingen Prize in poetry and the Pulitzer Prize for poetry—all in one year (1952). She is also the only poet who is such an avowed baseball fan that she not only has rooted for teams as far back as the Dodgers, but has written poetry about them.

Miss Moore graduated from Bryn Mawr in 1909, and after a year of study at a commercial college, she taught commercial subjects for four years at the Carlisle Industrial School for Indians. From 1921 to 1925 she was an assistant in the New York Public Library. Following publication of her first two books of poetry, she received the *Dial* Award of 1924 and from 1925 to 1929 she was acting editor of the magazine.

She received the Shelley Memorial Award in 1941, the Harriet Monroe Poetry Award in 1944, a Guggenheim Fellowship in 1945, a grant from the Na-

tional Institute of Arts and Letters in 1946, the National Institute of Arts and Letters Gold Medal and the M. Carey Thomas Award in 1953, the Brandeis Award for poetry in 1963, the $5,000 fellowship of the Academy of American Poets for distinguished poetic achievement over a period of more than four decades, and the National Medal for Literature, with its $5,000 prize, from the National Book Committee in 1968.

Miss Moore is a member of the National Institute of Arts and Letters, and the American Academy of Arts and Letters.

Nevertheless (poems), Macmillan, 1944
*Collected Poems, Macmillan, 1951
Like a Bulwark, Viking, 1956
O to be a Dragon, Viking, 1959
A Marianne Moore Reader, Viking, 1961
Rock Crystal, (co-translator), Pantheon, 1945
Selected Fables of La Fontaine (translator), Faber, 1955
Predilections (essays), Viking, 1955
Letters From and to the Ford Motor Company, Pierpont Morgan Library, 1957
Riverside Poetry Three (an anthology; with others), Twayne, 1958
Idiosyncrasy & Technique (lectures), Univ. of California Press, 1958
The Absentee (a comedy in four acts based on the Maria Edgeworth novel), House of Books, 1962
Three Fairy Tales (based on the French of Charles Perrault), Macmillan, 1963
The Arctic Ox, Fable, 1964
Tell Me, Tell Me (poetry and prose), Viking, 1966

LEWIS MUMFORD was born in Flushing, Long Island, October 19, 1895, and was educated in the public schools of New York City, the City College of New York, Columbia University, and the New School for Social Research. He was a radio electrician in the U. S. Navy in 1918–19.

Mr. Mumford was associate editor of the fortnightly *Dial* in 1919, acting editor of the *Sociological Review,* London, in 1920, and co-editor of the *American Caravan,* 1927–35. He is the author of twenty-four books, the first of which was *The Story of Utopias,* 1922. Seventeen of his books are still in print, including the first seven.

From 1930 on he was visiting professor at intervals at Dartmouth College, University of Pennsylvania, Massachusetts Institute of Technology, and the University of California at Berkeley. He was also professor of humanities at Stanford University, 1942 to 1944.

He is an honorary fellow, Stanford University, 1941, Hon. Ll.D. of Edinburgh University, 1965, and Hon. Dr. Arch., Rome, 1967. His honors include Royal Gold Medal of the Royal Institute of British Architects; Gold Medal of the Town Planning Institute; Emerson and Thoreau Medal of the American Academy of Arts and Sciences. He is a member of the American Philosophical Society, Fellow of the American Academy of Arts and Letters, and one of its past presidents. He is currently writing the sequel to *The Myth of the Machine,* which was published in 1967.

The Story of Utopias, Boni & Liveright, 1922
Sticks and Stones, Boni & Liveright, 1924
The Golden Day, Boni & Liveright, 1926
Herman Melville, Harcourt, 1929; revised 1963
The Brown Decades, Harcourt, 1931
Technics and Civilization, Harcourt, 1934
The Culture of Cities, Harcourt, 1938
Men Must Act, Harcourt, 1939
Faith for Living, Harcourt, 1940
The South in Architecture, Harcourt, 1941
The Condition of Man, Harcourt, 1944
City Development, Harcourt, 1945
Values for Survival, Harcourt, 1946
Green Memories: The Story of Geddes, Harcourt, 1947
The Conduct of Life, Harcourt, 1951
*Art and Technics, Columbia Univ. Press, 1952
In the Name of Sanity, Harcourt, 1954
The Human Prospect, Beacon Press, 1955
From the Ground Up, Harcourt, 1956

The Transformations of Man, Harper, 1956
The City in History (National Book Award), Harcourt, 1961
The Highway and the City, Harcourt, 1963
The Myth of the Machine, Harcourt, 1967
The Urban Prospect, Harcourt, 1968

VLADIMIR (VLADIMIROVICH) NABOKOV, Russian-born novelist, playwright, translator, and an authority on lepidoptera, is a descendant of an old Russian family in which a maternal great-grandfather was the first president of the Russian Imperial Academy of Medicine, and a paternal grandfather was state minister of justice. He was educated at St. Petersburg and Trinity College, Cambridge, England, where he took his B.A. in 1922.

Vladimir's father was a member of the liberal Constitutionalist Democratic Party, was imprisoned in 1906 by the Czar's forces, participated in the Revolution of 1917 and was assassinated at a Berlin lecture in 1922 by a rightist hoodlum. From a household with scores of servants and an estate of two thousand acres, the Nabokov family fled Russia in 1919 and from 1922 to 1937 Vladimir Nabokov lived in Berlin, writing and teaching English, and tennis. From 1937 to 1940 he lived, and wrote, in Paris.

In 1940 the writer came to the United States and in 1941 he was teaching Russian literature and creative writing at Stanford University, Palo Alto, Calif. He became an American citizen in 1945. Under the name of V. Sirin he wrote and published a number of works in Berlin and Paris, from 1926 on, books which after four decades are coming to light again in translations into English.

The author was born April 23, 1899, in St. Petersburg, son of Vladimir Dmitrievich Nabokov, a jurist and statesman and Elena Ivanovna (Rukavishnikov) Nabokov, whom he has described in his autobiography, *Speak, Memory.* The book which brought him the most renown in the United States was *Lolita,* the love of a middle-aged European exile, Humbert

Humbert, for a twelve-year-old "nymphet," a term Nabokov seems to have coined.

Mr. Nabokov has taught at Wellesley, Harvard, Cornell, and was awarded Guggenheim Fellowships for creative writing in 1943 and again in 1952, a grant in literature from the National Institute of Arts and Letters in 1951, a medal and a grant from Brandeis University in 1964, and the medal of merit from the American Academy of Arts and Letters in 1969. He married Vera (Evseevna) Slonim in 1925, they have one son and are now living in Switzerland.

Laughter in the Dark, Bobbs, 1938
The Real Life of Sebastian Knight, New
  Directions, 1941
Bend Sinister, Holt, 1947
Pnin, Doubleday, 1957
Lolita, Putnam, 1958 (earlier publication,
  2 vols.), Olympia Press, Paris, 1955
Invitation to a Beheading, Putnam, 1959
Pale Fire, Putnam, 1962
The Gift, Putnam, 1963
Nine Stories, New Directions, 1947
Nabokov's Dozen, a Collection of
  Thirteen Stories, Doubleday, 1958; as
  Spring in Fialta, Popular Library, 1959
Poems, Doubleday, 1959
Nikolai Gogol (criticism), New Directions, 1944
*Speak, Memory, revised ed., Putnam,
  1967
Three Russian Poets: Selections from
  Pushkin, Lermontov and Tyutchev,
  New Directions, 1945
Hero of Our Time by Mikhail Lermontov
  (introduction and notes), Doubleday,
  1958
The Song of Igor's Campaign (translation
  from Old Russian), Vintage, 1950
Eugene Onegin, by ALEXANDER PUSHKIN
  (4 vols.; translation and commentary),
  Pantheon, 1964
The Waltz Invention (a play in three
  acts), 1938
The Defense, Putnam, 1964
The Eye, Phaedra, 1965
Despair, Putnam, 1966
The Waltz Invention, Phaedra, 1966
Nabokov's Quartet, Phaedra, 1966

King, Queen, Knave, McGraw-Hill, 1968
Ada or Ardor: A Family Chronicle,
  McGraw-Hill 1969

OGDEN NASH, probably America's most popular contemporary versifier, was born August 19, 1902 in Rye, New York, son of Edmund Strudwick and Mattie (Chenault) Nash. He attended St. George's School at Newport, Rhode Island, from 1917 to 1920 and from 1920 to 1921 was at Harvard. In New York, he was briefly in the bond business and worked in editorial and publicity at Doubleday, Doran & Co., and in the copy department of an advertising agency.

His first book was a juvenile—and he has written several juveniles in his later years—and his next a book of sketches with Christopher Morley and Cleon Throckmorton. Then followed numerous books of wit and satire in the original light verse form which has made him so well known. A frequent contributor to the New Yorker, of which he has been an editorial staff member, Mr. Nash also wrote the lyrics for a Broadway musical, One Touch of Venus, with Kurt Weill and S. J. Perelman. He is a member of the National Institute of Arts and Letters and the American Academy of Arts and Sciences.

The Cricket of Carador (juvenile; with
  JOSEPH ALGER), Doubleday, Page, 1925
Born in a Beer Garden (sketches; with
  others), Rudge, 1930
Free Wheeling, Simon & Schuster, 1931
Hard Lines, Simon & Schuster, 1931
Happy Days, Simon & Schuster, 1933
Four Prominent So and So's (song;)
  Simon & Schuster, 1934
The Primrose Path, Simon & Schuster,
  1935
The Bad Parents' Garden of Verse, Simon
  & Schuster, 1936
Boy Voyage (folder), Doubleday Doran
  Book Shops, 1936
I'm a Stranger Here Myself, Little,
  Brown, 1938
The Face Is Familiar (selected poems),
  Little, Brown, 1940

The Selected Works of Ogden Nash,
Little, 1940
Good Intentions, Little, 1942
The Ogden Nash Pocket Book, Blakiston,
1944
Many Long Years Ago, Little, 1945
The Selected Verse of Ogden Nash, Modern
Library, 1946
Ogden Nash's Musical Zoo, Little, 1947
Versus, Little, 1949
Family Reunion, Little, 1950
Parents Keep Out, Little, 1951
*The Private Dining Room, Little, 1953
The Moon Is Shining Bright as Day
(An Anthology), Lippincott, 1953
The Pocket Book of Ogden Nash, Pocket
Books, 1954
*You Can't Get There From Here, Little,
1957
The Boy Who Laughed at Santa Claus,
Little, 1957
The Christmas That Almost Wasn't, Little,
1957
I Couldn't Help Laughing (stories selected
and introduced), Lippincott,
1957
Verses from 1929 On, Little, 1959; in
England, *Collected Verses,* Dent, 1961
Custard, the Dragon, Little, 1959
A Boy Is a Boy, Watts, 1960
Everybody Ought to Know (verses selected
and introduced by), Lippincott,
1961
The New Nutcracker Suite, Little, 1962
Girls Are Silly, Watts, 1962
*Everyone But Thee and Me, Little, 1962
A Boy and His Room, Watts, 1963
The Adventures of Isabel, Little, 1963
The Untold Adventures of Santa Claus,
Little, 1964
Marriage Lines—Notes of a Student Husband,
Little, 1964
*There's Always Another Windmill, Little,
1968

ALLAN NEVINS, who lists himself in
Who's Who as a "researcher and author,"
has twice won the Pulitzer Prize for
biography, in 1933 for his study of
Grover Cleveland and in 1937 for *Hamilton
Fish—The Inner History of the Grant
Administration.* He was born in Camp

Point, Illinois, May 20, 1890, took his
A.B. at the University of Illinois in 1912,
his masters in 1913, and for ten years he
was connected with newspapers, much of
the time concurrently with university
teaching.

From 1913 to 1923, Allan Nevins was
an editorial writer for the New York
Evening Post, for *The Nation* from 1913
to 1918, literary editor of the *New York
Sun* from 1924 to 1925 and on the editorial
staff of the New York *World* until
it ceased publication in 1931.

Dr. Nevins was professor of American
history at Cornell from 1927 to 1928,
associate in history at Columbia University,
1928 to 1931, and professor of
American history at Columbia from 1931
to 1958. Since 1958 he has been senior
research associate at the Huntington Library,
and now makes his home there
in San Marino, California.

His various teaching posts have included
the Sir George Watson Chair of
American History in Great Britain, 1934
to 1935, visiting professor at the California
Institute of Technology, 1937 to
1938, visiting scholar at the Huntington
Library, 1937, Harmsworth professor at
Oxford University 1940 to 1941 and
from 1964 to 1965. He was special representative
of the Office of War Information
in Australia and New Zealand,
1943–44, and chief public affairs officer,
American embassy, London, 1945 to
1946. He was visiting professor at the
Hebrew University of Jerusalem in 1952,
and Distinguished Professor of American
History at Claremont Graduate College,
1968–69.

Member of many learned societies, Dr.
Nevins has served as president of the
American Academy of Arts and Letters,
president of the American Historical Association
and the Society of American
Historians. He is an honorary fellow
of the New York State Historical Association.

Dr. Nevins received the Scribner Centenary
prize and the Bancroft prize in
1947, the Gold Medal for history and
biography from the National Institute
of Arts and Letters in 1957, and gold

medals from the New York Historical Society in 1958, the Commonwealth Club of California in 1960 and from Rice University in 1962. Honorary degrees have been conferred upon him by twenty-eight universities and colleges.

Dr. Nevins married in 1916 and has two married daughters and six grandchildren.

The Life of Robert Rogers, Caxton Club, Chicago, 1914

Illinois, Oxford University Press, 1917

The Evening Post—A Century of Journalism, Boni & Liveright, 1922

American Social History Recorded by British Travelers, Holt, 1923

The American States During and After the Revolution, Macmillan, 1924

The Emergence of Modern America, Macmillan, 1927

Frémont, the West's Greatest Adventurer, Harpers, 1927

American Press Opinion, Washington to Coolidge (anthology), Heath, 1928

Henry White—Thirty Years of American Diplomacy, Harper, 1930

Grover Cleveland—A Study in Courage, Dodd, Mead, 1932

Abram S. Hewitt, with Some Account of Peter Cooper, Harper, 1935

Hamilton Fish—The Inner History of the Grant Administration, Dodd, Mead, 1936

The Gateway to History (historiography), Appleton-Century, 1938

Frémont, Pathmarker of the West (revision and enlargement of Frémont, the West's Greatest Adventurer), Appleton-Century, 1939

John D. Rockefeller: the Heroic Age of American Enterprise, two volumes, Scribners, 1940

This Is England Today, Scribners, 1941

America in World Affairs, Oxford, 1942

America, The Story of a Free People (with HENRY STEELE COMMAGER), Little, 1942; revised, 1956

A Brief History of the United States, Clarendon Press, 1942

A Select Bibliography of the History of the United States, Wyman, 1942

The Making of Modern Britain (with J. B. BREBNER), Norton, 1943

A Century of Political Cartoons (with FRANK WEITENKAMPF), Scribner's, 1944

A Short History of the United States (with H. S. COMMAGER) Mod. Lib., 1945; revised, 1956

Old American in a Young World, Newcomen Society, 1945

Sail On: The Story of the American Merchant Marine, U. S. Lines, 1946

Ordeal of the Union, Scribner's, 1947

The Emergence of Lincoln, Scribner's, 1950; 2 vols., 1952

The New Deal and World Affairs, 1933–1945, Yale Univ., Press, 1950

The United States in a Chaotic World, 1918–1933, Yale, 1950

The World of Eli Whitney, (with JEANNETTE MIRSKY), Macmillan, 1952

Study in Power: John D. Rockefeller, Scribner's, 1953; abridged ed., 1959

The Statesmanship of the Civil War, Macmillan, 1953; revised, Collier, 1962

Ford: The Times, The Man, The Company (with FRANK E. HILL), Scribner's, 1954

Ford: Expansion and Challenge, 1915–1933, Scribner's, 1957

The War for the Union (2 vols.), Scribner's, 1959, 1961

Ford: Decline and Rebirth, Scribner's, 1963

Herbert H. Lehman and His Era, Scribner's, 1963

Dr. Nevins has been the editor of numerous books from 1927 on. He is the general editor of the American Political Leader series, the Yale Press Chronicles of America series and D. C. Heath's College and University History series. He has also edited the published diaries of John Quincy Adams, the Letters of Grover Cleveland and the Letters and Journal of Brand Whitlock, the Interpretations of Walter Lippman, the Diary of George Templeton Strong in four volumes, Diary of Battle: Personal Journals of Col. Charles S. Wainwright, 1861–1865; The Burden and the Glory: Speeches of John F. Kennedy; Timber and Men: The

Weyerhaeuser Story (with R. HIDY and F. HILL), and many other readers and histories.

S. J. PERELMAN, whose humor has been bound in numerous books of light, ironic and satiric sketches, but who has also written for the stage and did the screen play for *Around the World in Eighty Days*, was born in Brooklyn, February 1, 1904. He graduated from Brown University in 1925 and began his writing career as an artist and writer for the magazine *Judge* and later *College Humor*.

For some years he has lived in Bucks County, Pennsylvania. In 1929 he married Laura West, with whom he wrote two plays. He contributes frequently to *The New Yorker*. He is the father of two children. At last reports he was engaged in writing his autobiography and staying out of New York City as much as possible.

Preparing for the ordeal of encountering Manhattan, he said to a New York *Times* reporter, "I confined myself for tw o days to a closet without any air holes and I turned on the radio full blast; I got into as many claustrophic situations as I could around the house."

Dawn Ginsbergh's Revenge (essays), Liveright, 1929
Parlor, Bedlam, and Bath (with QUENTIN REYNOLDS), Liveright, 1930
Strictly From Hunger (essays), Random, 1937
Look Who's Talking! (essays), Random, 1940
The Dream Department, Random, 1943
Crazy Like a Fox, Random, 1944
Keep It Crisp, Random, 1946
Acres and Pains, Reynal, 1947
The Best of S. J. Perelman, Modern Lib., 1947
Westward Ha! Simon & Schuster, 1948
Listen to the Mocking Bird, Simon & Schuster, 1949
The Swiss Family Perelman, Simon & Schuster, 1950
The Ill-Tempered Clavichord, Simon & Schuster, 1952

Perelman's Home Companion, Simon & Schuster, 1955
The Road to Miltown, Simon & Schuster, 1957
The Most of S. J. Perelman, Simon & Schuster, 1958, 1962
*The Rising Gorge, Simon & Schuster, 1961
The Beauty Part, Simon & Schuster, 1963
Chicken Inspector No. Twenty-Three, Simon & Schuster, 1966
The Third Little Show (sketches)
Walk a Little Faster (sketches)
Plays:
All Good Americans (with LAURA WEST PERELMAN), 1934
The Night Before Christmas (with LWP), 1941
One Touch of Venus (with OGDEN NASH), 1943
Sweet Bye and Bye (with AL HIRSCHFELD and OGDEN NASH), 1947
Monkey Business (Marx Brothers, film script)
Horsefeathers (Marx Brothers, film script)
Around the World in Eighty Days (film script), Academy Award, N. Y. Film Critics Award

GEORGE (AMES) PLIMPTON was born March 18, 1927, in New York, N.Y., son of Francis T. R. (former Ambassador to the United Nations) and Pauline Ames Plimpton. He graduated from Phillips Exeter Academy, took his A.B. at Harvard University in 1948 and his M.A. at Cambridge University, England, in 1950. He was a tank driver in the infantry in World War II.

In 1953 Mr. Plimpton joined a group of writers in Paris and founded the literary quarterly *The Paris Review*. He remains its editor-in-chief.

His three books to date deal largely with his forays as an amateur into the world of professional sport, major league baseball in one, playing quarterback with the Detroit Lions while researching pieces for *Sports Illustrated* in another, and the world of professional golfers in *The Bogey Man*.

Mr. Plimpton served in the U. S. Army

as a second lieutenant from 1945 to 1948. He was an instructor at Barnard College from 1956 to 1958, associate editor of *Horizon* magazine from 1959 to 1961, and an associate fellow of Trumbull College, Yale, in 1967.

He was recipient of the Distinguished Achievement Award of the University of Southern California in 1967 for his contribution to American letters. He married Freddy Espy in 1968 and lives in New York City where he is the co-editor of the *American Literary Anthology*, an annual volume sponsored by the National Foundation of the Arts and Humanities.

The Rabbit's Umbrella (juvenile), Viking Press, 1956
Out of My League, Harper-Row, 1961
Paper Lion, Harper-Row, 1966
The Bogey Man, Harper-Row, 1969
Editor: *Writers at Work, Interviews from The Paris Review*, Viking, 1959
Writers at Work, 2nd Series, Viking, 1963
Writers at Work, 3rd Series, Viking, 1967
The American Literary Anthology (with PETER ARDERY) Farrar, Straus & Giroux, 1968
The American Literary Anthology (with PETER ARDERY) Random House, 1969
The American Literary Anthology (with PETER ARDERY) Viking, 1970

KATHERINE ANNE PORTER was born May 15, 1890, at Indian Creek, Texas, daughter of Harrison Boone and Mary Alice (Jones) Porter. She was educated at home and in Southern girls' schools. Except for her novel, *Ship of Fools*, her work has mainly been in the short story form, and for *The Collected Stories of Katherine Anne Porter* she was awarded both the Pulitzer Prize of 1966 and the National Book Award.

Miss Porter was the first woman faculty member in the history of Washington and Lee University, Lexington, Va., in 1959 and has appeared as teacher or lecturer at more than 200 universities and colleges in the United States and Europe. She was also a member of Presi-dent Johnson's Committee on Presidential Scholars, a fellow of the Library of Congress in regional American literature (1944), and one of six representatives of American Literature at the International Exposition of the Arts in Paris in 1952, and Fulbright lecturer in English literature at the University of Liege, Belgium, 1954–1955.

She received a Guggenheim Fellowship for literature in 1931, renewed in 1938, the first annual gold medal of the Society of the Libraries of New York University for *Pale Horse, Pale Rider* in 1940, a Ford Foundation grant in 1959–1961, a State Department grant in International Exchange of Persons to Mexico, 1960, 1964, the O. Henry Memorial Award first prize for the short story "Holiday" in 1962, the Emerson-Thoreau Bronze Medal for Literature from the American Academy of Arts and Letters in 1962 and the gold medal of the National Institute of Arts and Letters in 1967. She has been given honorary degrees by six universities.

A distant cousin of William Sidney Porter (O. Henry) ("I am as unlike O. Henry as any writer could be"), Miss Porter published her first story at the age of thirty, her long novel of a voyage from Vera Cruz to Bremerhaven at seventy-two, a piece of writing based on an experience in 1931 which she began as a novel in 1940. It had high critical approval and a very wide distribution.

In 1966 the University of Maryland gave her a library, named for her, and she plans to leave her furniture, books and literary papers to the library. She is an honorary Phi Beta Kappa, University of Maryland, was vice president of the National Institute of Arts and Letters from 1950 to 1952 and is a member of the American Academy of Arts and Letters.

Katherine Anne Porter has been married three times, her first marriage at sixteen. She lives at present in College Park, Maryland.

Outline of Mexican Popular Arts and Crafts, Young & McCallister, 1922

Flowering Judas (stories), Harcourt, 1930, 1935
Katherine Anne Porter's French Songbook (translator), Harrison, 1933
Hacienda, Harrison, 1934
Noon Wine, Schuman, 1937
Pale Horse, Pale Rider (three short novels), Harcourt, 1939
Fernandez de Lizardi: The Itching Parrot (translator), Doubleday, 1942
Fiesta in November by FLORES and POORE (preface), Houghton, 1942
The Leaning Tower and Other Stories, Harcourt, 1944
The Days Before (essays), Harcourt, 1952
A Defense of Circe, Harcourt, 1954
Ship of Fools (novel), Little, Brown, 1962
The Collected Stories of Katherine Anne Porter, Harcourt, 1965
The Collected Essays and Occasional Writings of Katherine Anne Porter, Delacorte Press, 1970

EZRA (LOOMIS) POUND, poet, critic, polemicist, and sometimes called the founder and moving spirit of modern poetry in English, was born in Hailey, Idaho, October 30, 1884, son of Homer Loomis and Isabel (Weston) Pound. He took his Ph.B. at Hamilton College in 1905 and his master's degree at the University of Pennsylvania in 1906. After a year as an instructor at Wabash College he went to Europe, traveling in Spain, Italy, and Provence, and published his first volume of poetry in Venice in 1908.

From 1908 until 1919 Mr. Pound was foreign correspondent for *Poetry* Magazine, living in London, where in 1914 he married Dorothy Shakespear and, with Wyndham Lewis, founded the magazine *Blast*. He was London editor of *The Little Review* from 1917 to 1919 and Paris correspondent for *The Dial* in 1922. In 1927 he founded the short-lived magazine, *The Exile*.

In 1941, Mr. Pound, who had long been living in Italy, began broadcasting over the Italian radio to the United States. His purpose, he said later, was to "save the American constitution." His broadcasts were part literary criticism, part his own interpretation of history, the New Deal, Franklin Delano Roosevelt, the war and other topics. Rigorously criticized, he gave himself up to the American Army in 1945 and for a time he was held in the Army's Disciplinary Training Center at Pisa. In the several months of his confinement, much of it in a cage, he began the poems later collected as the *Pisan Cantos*. Returned by the Army to the United States to be tried for treason, he was declared psychologically unfit to stand trial and was committed to a hospital in Washington, D.C. As the result of a long campaign by fellow poets and other literary and publishing figures, he was released in 1958 and allowed to return to Italy.

While still in St. Elizabeth's Hospital, Mr. Pound was awarded the newly created $1000 Bollingen-Library of Congress award for poetry for his *Pisan Cantos*, the fifth section of an epic poem in which he is said to hope to make a poetic synthesis of world cultural history. The controversy over the Award to Mr. Pound by the judges (T. S. Eliot, W. H. Auden, Allen Tate, Robert Penn Warren, Katherine Anne Porter and others) caused the Library of Congress to discontinue its practice of judging the Bollingen prizes, the function being transferred to Yale University.

In 1928 Mr. Pound was the recipient of an award from *The Dial* for distinguished service to American letters. He received an honorary degree from Hamilton College in 1939 and in 1969 he made a brief visit to his alma mater to attend the awarding of an honorary degree to his publisher, James Laughlin, of New Directions.

Mr. Pound, who is the father of Omar Shakespear Pound and Mary (Princess) de Rachewiltz, makes his home in Venice, with occasional stays in another Italian city of his choice in the past, Rapallo.

A Quinzaine for This Yule, Pollock, 1908
POETRY: *A Lume Spento*, Venice, 1908;

A Lume Spento and Other Early Poems, New Directions, 1965

Personae, Mathews, 1909, Boni & Liveright, 1921; Personae and Collected Shorter Poems, New Directions, 1950; Faber, 1952

Exultations, Mathews, 1909

Provença, Small, Maynard, 1910

Canzoni of Ezra Pound, Mathews, 1911

Ripostes of Ezra Pound, Swift, 1912

Canzoni and Ripostes of Ezra Pound, Mathews, 1913

Lustra of Ezra Pound, privately printed, 1916; Knopf, 1917

Quia Pauper Amavi, The Egoist, 1919

Hugh Selwyn Mauberley, Ovid Press, 1920

Umbra, Mathews, 1920

Poems 1918–21, Boni & Liveright, 1921

Selected Poems, edited with an introduction by T. S. Eliot, Faber & Gwyer, 1928

A Draft of the Cantos, 17–27, of Ezra Pound, (London), 1928

A Draft of XXX Cantos, Hours Press, 1930

Homage to Sextus Propertius, Faber, 1934

Eleven New Cantos, XXXI–XLI, Farrar & Rinehart, 1934, (under pseudonym), Alfred Venison's Poems, Nott, 1935

The Fifth Decad of Cantos, Farrar, 1937

Cantos LII–LXXI, New Directions, 1940

A Selection of Poems, Faber, 1940

The Cantos of Ezra Pound, New Directions, 1949

The Pisan Cantos, ND, 1948

Section, Rock-Drill, 85–95 de los Cantares, Pesce d'Oro, (Milan), 1955; New Directions, 1956

Thrones, 96–109 de los Cantares, ND, 1959

* Selections from the Cantos, Faber (London) 1967

Drafts and Fragments of Cantos CX–CXVII, new passages, completed in recent years, New Directions, 1969

PROSE: The Spirit of Romance, Dent, 1910, Dutton, 1910

Graudier-Brzeska, John Lane, 1916

Noh, or Accomplishment, a Study of the Classical Stage of Japan, (with Ernest Fenollosa) Knopf, 1917, (appeared as The Classic Noh Theatre of Japan, New Directions, 1959)

Pavannes and Divisions, Knopf, 1918; New Directions, 1958

Instigations of Ezra Pound, Boni & Liveright, 1920

Indiscretions, Three Mountains Press, (Paris), 1923

Antheil and the Treatise on Harmony, Three Mountains, 1924; P. Covici, 1927

Imaginary Letters, Black Sun Press, (Paris), 1930

How to Read, Harmsworth, 1931

A B C of Economics, Faber, 1933; New Directions, 1939; 2nd edition, Russell, 1953

A B C of Reading, Yale Univ. Press, 1934

Make It New, Faber, 1934, Yale, 1935

Jefferson and/or Mussolini, Nott, 1935, Liveright, 1936

Social Credit An Impact (pamphlets), Nott, 1935

Polite Essays, Faber, 1937, ND, 1940

Culture, ND, 1938 (later edition, Guide to Kulchur, ND, 1952)

What Is Money for? Greater Britain Publications, 1939

Introduction alla Natura Economica degh S. U. A., (Venice), 1944 (appeared as An Introduction to the Economic Nature of the United States, translated by Carmine Amore, Russell, (London), 1958)

If This Be Treason, (four original drafts of Rome broadcasts), privately printed, 1948

Letters, 1907–1941, edited by D. D. Paige, Harcourt, 1950

Patria Mia, R. F. Seymour, 1950

Gold and Work, translated from Italian by Peter Russell, (London), 1951

Literary Essays, edited with introduction by T. S. Eliot, ND, 1954

Brancusi, (Milan), 1957

Impact: Essays on Ignorance and the Decline of American Civilization, edited with an introduction by Noel Stock, Regnery, 1960

TRANSLATIONS: Sonnets and Ballate of Guido Cavalcanti, Small, Maynard, 1912

Cathay (from the Chinese of Li T'ai Po, from the notes of Fenollosa and the decipherings of Mori and Ariga), Mathews, 1915

Twelve Dialogues of Fontenelle, 1917

Ta Hio, The Great Learning, (*Confucius*, University of Washington Bookstore, 1928

Digest of Analects (*Confucius*), G. Scheiwiller, 1937

Confucius, The Unwobbling Pivot and the Great Digest (Chung Yung and Ta Hsueh), New Direction series, 1947, (New York), 1951

The Confucian Odes (*Shih Ching*), Harvard Univ. Press, 1954; New Directions, 1959

Pensieri Sull'Amore, by Richard of St. Victor, (Milan), 1956

Moscardino, by Enrico Pea, (Milan), 1956

Women of Trachis (*Sophocles*), Spearman, 1956, ND, 1957

The Confucian Analects, P. Owen, 1956, Square $ Series, 1957

Rimbaud, (Milan), 1957

The Natural Philosophy of Love (*Remy de Gourmont*), Spearman, 1957

Love Poems of Ancient Egypt, (with Noel Stock and Boris de Rachewiltz) ND, 1962

The Translations of Ezra Pound, introduction by Hugh Kenner, ND, 1963

Des Imagistes (anthology), A. and C. Boni, 1914

Passages from the Letters of John Butler Yeats, Cuala Press, 1917

Profile (anthology) (Milan), 1932

Active Anthology, Faber, 1933

The Chinese Written Character as a Medium for Poetry, by Fenollosa, Square $ Series, 1935, Kasper & Horton, 1956; City Lights Books, 1968

Confucius to Cummings (anthology), New Directions, 1964

JAMES (BARRETT) RESTON, who was born in Clydebank, Scotland, November 3, 1903, and brought to the United States in 1910, was a student at the Vale of Leven Academy in Alexandria, Scotland, from 1914 to 1920, but took his

Bachelor of Science degree from the University of Illinois in 1932 and his doctorate in literature from Colgate University in 1951. He has been awarded other degrees from Oberlin and Rutgers Universities and honorary degrees from Dartmouth, New York, University of Illinois, Boston College, Brandeis University, Kenyon College, Columbia and Michigan. He married in 1935 and has three sons.

Beginning in newspaper work on the Springfield (Ohio) *Daily News,* in 1932, Mr. Reston did publicity for Ohio State University in 1933 and for the Cincinnati baseball club in 1934. From 1934 to 1937 he was a reporter for the Associated Press in New York, and from 1939 to 1941 he was with the London Bureau of the *New York Times.* He joined that paper's Washington bureau in 1941 and was chief Washington correspondent from 1953 to 1964 when he was made associate editor of the *New York Times.* He was appointed executive editor in 1968 and vice-president in 1969.

He was awarded the Pulitzer Prize for national correspondence in 1945, and again in 1957 for national reporting, the Overseas Press Club award for interpretation of international news in 1949, 1951 and 1955; the George Polk Memorial Award for National Reporting, 1953; University of Missouri Medal, 1961, J. P. Zenger Award, 1964, and has been recipient of the Legion of Honor, France, Order of St. Olav, Norway, and the Order of Merit, Chile.

Artillery of the Press, Harper, 1967

* *Sketches in the Sand,* Knopf, 1967. (Mr. Reston's selection appeared first in the *New York Times,* November 15, 1964, under the title *What Was Killed Was Not Only the President But the Promise*

PHILIP (MILTON) ROTH was born March 19, 1933, in Newark, New Jersey, son of Herman and Bess (Finkel) Roth. He was educated in the public schools and high school of Newark, attended Rutgers University there from 1950 to 1951, took his A.B. in 1954 from Bucknell University, and his M.A. from the University of Chicago in 1955.

Both in the short story and the novel Mr. Roth has had wide critical approval for his fictional treatment of contemporary middle-class Jewish life. He won a first prize in 1958 in the *Paris Review* short story contest (the Aga Khan prize for fiction) the National Book Award, a Houghton, Mifflin Literary Fellowship, and the Daroff Award of the Jewish Book Council of America in 1960 for *Goodbye, Columbus,* and an O. Henry Memorial Award second prize the same year for a short story.

He has received a Ford Foundation grant in playwrighting, and grants from the National Institute of Arts and Letters, the Guggenheim Foundation, and the Rockefeller Foundation.

His novel of a Jewish family in Newark, *Portnoy's Complaint,* was the *succès de scandale* of 1969, receiving more praise and abuse than any book of its kind that year.

Mr. Roth was an instructor at the University of Chicago from 1956 to 1958, a visiting lecturer at the University of Iowa from 1960 to 1962 and writer in residence at Princeton University from 1962 to 1964, and at the University of Pennsylvania in 1965. He was in the United States Army in 1955 and 1956. He is a member of Phi Beta Kappa.

Goodbye, Columbus (novella and stories), Houghton, 1959
Letting Go (novel), Random, 1962
When She Was Good (novel), Random, 1967
*Portnoy's Complaint (novel), Random, 1969

HARRISON E. SALISBURY, assistant managing editor of the *New York Times* since 1964 and frequent winner of international awards for reporting in foreign fields including the Pulitzer Prize for international correspondence in 1955 and the George Polk Memorial Award for foreign reporting in 1957, was born in Minneapolis, Minnesota, November 14, 1908,

and began his newspaper career as a reporter on the Minneapolis *Journal.*

Son of Percy Pritchard and Georgiana (Evans) Salisbury, Harrison Salisbury took his A.B. at the University of Minnesota in 1930, when he left the *Journal* for the United Press, working for the wire service in Chicago, Washington and New York, becoming manager of the London bureau in 1943, the Moscow bureau in 1944 and foreign news editor between 1944 and 1948. In 1949 he became Moscow correspondent for the *New York Times,* serving there until 1954 when he joined the New York staff and he has been on home office or roving assignments since.

He received the Distinguished Achievement medal of the University of Minnesota in 1955 and the Sigma Delta Chi Award for foreign correspondence in 1958, the *Asia Magazine* Award of the Overseas Press Club of America for the best report on Asia, 1967.

Mr. Salisbury is married, has two sons, and lives in New York City.

Russia on the Way, Macmillan, 1946
American in Russia, Harpers, 1955
The Shook Up Generation, Harpers, 1958
To Moscow and Beyond, Harpers, 1960
Moscow Journal, Chicago Press, 1961
The Northern Palmyra Affair, Harpers, 1962
Key to Moscow (juvenile), Lippincott, 1963
A New Russia, Harpers, 1962
Russia, Atheneum, 1965
Behind the Lines: Hanoi, Harper-Row, 1965
Orbit of China, Harper-Row, 1967
Soviet Union: The Fifty Years (editor: *New York Times* Book), Harcourt, 1967
The Nine Hundred Days: The Siege of Leningrad, Harper-Row, 1969
War Between Russia and China, Norton, 1969

WILLIAM SAROYAN, who brought youth, ebullience and personality into the short story in America in the proletarian-tract-ridden days of the 1930s was born August 31, 1908, in Fresno, California, son of Armenak, a Presbyterian minister and writer, and Takoohi (Saroyan) Saroyan, natives of Bitlis, Armenia. His formal education ended in high school at fifteen. Grocery clerk, vineyard worker, telegraph messenger, and telegraph company office manager before he was twenty, Saroyan quit all his odd jobs to become a writer after his first story, *The Daring Young Man on the Flying Trapeze,* appeared in *Story* Magazine in 1934. His subsequent book collection of stories launched him soon afterward into the literary world in which he has been a colorful figure ever since.

His play, *The Time of Your Life,* for which he refused the Pulitzer Prize in 1940, was revived in the winter of 1969 at Lincoln Center in New York to perhaps even more rave reviews than when it first opened thirty years before. Although he turned down the Pulitzer, he accepted the Award of the Drama Critics Circle.

He has produced and directed a number of his own plays and directed the motion picture *The Good Job,* in 1942, and in the same year opened his own theatre, the Saroyan Theatre, in New York City. He is also creator of *The Great American Goof,* produced by the Ballet Theatre in New York in 1940 and 1941.

These days Saroyan maintains a home in Paris, "travels every year, drives a big car, rides a bicycle, writes something funny every month, refuses the services of lawyer, agent, accountant, manager, and similar fish, in his determination not to become a millionaire."

The Daring Young Man on the Flying Trapeze (short stories), Random House, 1934
A Christmas Psalm, 1935 (poetry), Crelber, Lilienthal, San Francisco, 1935
Inhale and Exhale (short stories), Random House, 1936
Three Times Three (short stories), Conference Press, Los Angeles, 1936
Those Who Write Them and Those Who Collect Them (pamphlet), Black Archer Press, Chicago, 1936
Little Children (short stories), Harcourt, Brace, 1937
The Gay and Melancholy Flux (short stories), Faber & Faber, London, 1937
Love, Here Is My Hat (short stories), Modern Age, 1938
A Native American (short story), Fields, San Francisco, 1938
The Trouble with Tigers (short stories), Harcourt, Brace, 1938
My Heart's in the Highlands (play), Harcourt, Brace, 1939
Peace, It's Wonderful (short stories), Modern Age, 1939
The Hungerers (play), French, 1939
The Time of Your Life (play and essays), Harcourt, Brace, 1939
The Dogs, and Two Other Plays, Phaedra, 1939
My Name Is Aram (short stories), Harcourt, Brace, 1940
The State of the Nation (essays; with others), Little Man Press, Cincinnati, 1940
The Ping-Pong Game (play), French, 1940
Subway Circus (play), French, 1940
Three Plays, Harcourt, Brace, 1940
A Special Announcement (radio sketch), House of Books, 1940
Saroyan's Fables, Harcourt, Brace, 1941
Insurance Salesman, and Other Stories, Faber & Faber, London, 1941
Love's Old Sweet Song (play), French, 1941
Curtain Preface (pamphlet), Community Playhouse, Pasadena, Cal., 1941
The People with Light Coming Out of Them (pamphlet), Free Company, 1941
48 Saroyan Stories, Avon, 1942
The Human Comedy (novel), Harcourt, 1943, World, 1945
Thirty-one Selected Stories, Avon, 1943
Fragment, Albert M. Bender, 1943
Get Away Old Man (play: produced, 1943), Harcourt, 1944
Some Day I'll Be a Millionaire Myself, Avon, 1944
Dear Baby (stories), Harcourt, 1944

The Adventures of Wesley Jackson (novel), Harcourt, 1946
Jim Dandy (play), Harcourt, 1947
The Saroyan Special, Harcourt, 1948
The Fiscal Hoboes, Press of Valenti Angelo, 1949
Don't Go Away Mad and Two Other Plays, Harcourt, 1949
Hello Out There, S. French, 1949
A Decent Birth, A Happy Funeral, S. French, 1949
Sam Ego's House, S. French, 1949
The Assyrian, and Other Stories, Harcourt, 1950
The Twin Adventures, Harcourt, 1950
Rock Wagram, Doubleday, 1951
Tracy's Tiger, Doubleday, 1951
The Bicycle Rider in Beverly Hills, (autobiography), Scribner, 1952
The Laughing Matter, Doubleday, 1953
Mama I Love You, (novel), Atlantic-Little, 1956
The Whole Voyald, (stories), Atlantic-Little, 1956
Papa You're Crazy, Atlantic-Little, 1957
The Cave Dwellers, Putnam, 1958
The William Saroyan Reader, Braziller, 1958
The Slaughter of the Innocents, S. French, 1958
Once Around the Block, S. French, 1959
Sam the Highest Jumper of Them All, or *The London Comedy*, Faber, 1961
Here Comes, There Goes, You Know Who, (autobiography), Trident Press, 1962
Boys and Girls Together, Harcourt, 1963
Me, (juvenile), Crowell-Collier, 1963
Not Dying, (autobiography), Harcourt, 1963
One Day in the Afternoon of the World, Harcourt, 1964
After Thirty Years: The Daring Young Man on the Flying Trapeze, Harcourt, 1964
Human Comedy, rev. ed., Dell, 1966
My Kind of Crazy, Wonderful People, Harcourt, 1966
Short Drive, Sweet Chariot, Phaedra, 1967
Look at Us (with Arthur Rothstein), Cowles, 1967

*Letters From 74 rue Taitbout, World Publishing Co., 1969
Days of Life and Death and Escape to the Moon, Dial, 1970

ARTHUR M. SCHLESINGER, JR., was born in Columbus, Ohio, in 1917 and graduated from Harvard University in 1938. His senior honors essay, *Orestes A. Brownson: A Pilgrim's Progress*, was published in 1939. After a year at Cambridge University, England, and a term in the Society of Fellows at Harvard, Mr. Schlesinger in 1942 joined the Office of War Information in Washington. He later served in the Office of Strategic Services and the United States Army in London, Paris and Germany. *The Age of Jackson*, written in 1940–42 and published in 1945, won the Pulitzer Prize for History in 1946.

Mr. Schlesinger, who became Special Assistant to President Kennedy in 1961 and continued for a time in that role for President Johnson, resigned in 1965 to write *A Thousand Days: John F. Kennedy in the White House*, which was published in November, 1965 and subsequently won the National Book Award for History and Biography as well as the Pulitzer Prize for Biography.

In January 1966, Mr. Schlesinger became a visiting fellow at the Institute for Advanced Study in Princeton. In the fall of 1966 he moved to the City University of New York as Albert Schweitzer Professor of the Humanities.

Mr. Schlesinger received a Guggenheim Fellowship in 1946 and a grant from the American Academy of Arts and Letters the same year. He received the Francis Parkman Prize for history in 1957 and the Bancroft prize a year later. In 1967 he was awarded the National Institute of Arts and Letters gold medal for history and biography. He is a member of the Massachusetts Historical Society, Colonial Society, American Historical Association, the National Institute of Arts and Letters, the National Society of Film Critics, and is vice chairman of Americans for Democratic Action.

He is the father of four children and lives in New York City.

Orestes A. Brownson: A Pilgrim's Progress, 1939
The Age of Jackson, Little, Brown, 1945
The Vital Center, Houghton Mifflin, 1949
The General and the President (with R. H. ROVERE), Houghton, 1951
The Crisis of the Old Order, Houghton, 1957
The Coming of the New Deal, Houghton, 1958
The Politics of Upheaval, Houghton, 1960
Kennedy or Nixon, Houghton, 1960
The Politics of Hope, Houghton, 1963
A Thousand Days: John F. Kennedy in the White House, Houghton, 1965
The Bitter Heritage: Vietnam and American Democracy, Houghton, 1966
The Crisis of Confidence: Ideas, Power and Violence in America, Houghton, 1969
CO-EDITOR: Harvard Guide to American History (co-editor), 1954
Guide to Politics—1954, 1954
Paths of American Thought (with MORTON WHITE), Houghton, 1963

KARL (JAY) SHAPIRO was born November 10, 1913, in Baltimore, son of Joseph and Sarah (Omansky) Shapiro. He studied at the University of Virginia, 1932–33, Johns Hopkins University, 1937–39, and the Enoch Pratt Library School in 1940.

Mr. Shapiro was consultant in poetry at the Library of Congress from 1947 to 1948, associate professor at Johns Hopkins University from 1948 to 1950, visiting professor Loyola University, Chicago, 1951–52, and has been professor at the University of Nebraska since 1956. From 1953 until 1955 he was editor of the *Newberry Library Bulletin*, and from 1956 to 1963 editor of *Prairie Schooner*, in Lincoln, Nebraska.

He lectured through India in 1955 for the U. S. Department of State and has been visiting professor at the University of California at Berkeley and Davis and the University of Indiana, and lecturer at the Salzburg Seminar in American Studies.

Mr. Shapiro won the Jeanette Davis Prize and Levinson Prize for Poetry in 1942, Contemporary Poetry Prize in 1943, an American Academy of Arts and Letters grant in 1944, the Pulitzer Prize in Poetry for *V-Letters and Other Poems* in 1945, the Shelley Memorial Prize in 1948, and Guggenheim Foundation Fellowships in 1944 and 1953. In 1969 he won the Bollingen Prize for poetry.

He is a member of the American Academy of Arts and Sciences, as of 1969, and earlier was made a member of the National Institute of Arts and Letters. He is also a Phi Beta Kappa.

Mr. Shapiro married Evalyn Katz in 1945 and he is the father of a son and two daughters. The couple divorced in 1967 and he is now married to the former Teri Kovach and lives in Davis, California, where Mr. Shapiro is professor of English at the University of California.

He served in the United States Army from 1941 to 1945.

Poems, privately printed, Waverly Press, 1935
Person, Place and Thing, Reynal, 1942
The Place of Love, Comment Press, 1942
V-Letter and Other Poems, Reynald, 1944
Essay on Rime, Secker & Warburg, 1945
Trial of a Poet, Reynal, 1947
English Prosody and Modern Poetry, Johns Hopkins Press, 1947
Bibliography of Modern Prosody, Johns Hopkins, 1948
Poets at Work (contributor) Harcourt, 1948
Poems, 1940–1953, Random, 1953
Beyond Criticism, Univ. of Nebraska Press, 1953
Modern Amer. and Modern British Poetry, (with Untermeyer and Wilbur, Harcourt, 1955
The Tenor (libretto to opera) Westminster Recording, 1956
Poems of a Jew, Random, 1958

In Defense of Ignorance (essays), Random, 1960
American Poetry, anthology (editor), Crowell, 1960
Start With the Sun, (with Slote and Miller), Univ. Nebraska Press, 1960
The Bourgeois Poet, Random, 1964
Prosody Handbook (with Robert Beum), Harper, 1965
A Primer for Poets, Univ. Nebraska Press, 1965
Selected Poems, Random House, 1968
To Abolish Children, Quadrangle, 1968
White-Haired Lover, Random, 1968

WILLIAM (LAWRENCE) SHIRER, who in two massive books recorded the decline of two great European nations, *The Rise and Fall of the Third Reich,* and *The Collapse of the Third Republic,* is a native of America's Midwest. He was born Feb. 23, 1904 in Chicago, son of Seward Smith, a lawyer, and Josephine (Tanner) Shirer. He took his B.A. at Coe College, Iowa, in 1925 and from 1925 to 1927 he studied European history at the College de France in Paris.

As a reporter for the *Chicago Tribune* in Paris, 1925–1929, Mr. Shirer began to interest himself in the political life of Europe, and from Paris he went to Vienna where he was chief of the Central European bureau from 1929 to 1932, with the *New York Herald,* Paris edition, in 1934, with Universal News Service, 1935 to 1937, and Columbia Broadcasting correspondent from 1939 to 1945 and as commentator from 1945 to 1947. He was with Mutual Network as a commentator from 1947 to 1949 and has been a full-time book writer since 1950.

Mr. Shirer's *Berlin Diary* recorded his day-to-day experiences as a correspondent in Germany from 1934 to 1941. It was widely distributed, and his later book on Hitler's Germany headed the bestseller list, the first time a book of its price, $10, had ever done so.

Mr. Shirer lives in Lenox, Mass., and New York when he is not traveling or researching. He is a member of the Council on Foreign Relations, former president of the Authors Guild, a Phi Beta Kappa, member of the P.E.N. and Tau Kappa, Epsilon. He is an honorary doctor of letters, Coe College and the University of Hartford, a Chevalier of the Legion d'Honneur, winner of the George Foster Peabody Award, 1947, Wendell Willkie One World Award, 1947, and the National Book Award, 1961, (for *The Rise and Fall of the Third Reich*).

Berlin Diary (journal, 1934–1941) Knopf, 1941
End of a Berlin Diary, Knopf, 1947
The Traitor (novel), Farrar, Straus, 1950
Midcentury Journey, Farrar, 1952
Stranger Come Home (novel), Little, Brown, 1954
The Challenge of Scandinavia, Little, 1955
The Counsul's wife (novel), Little, 1956
The Rise and Fall of the Third Reich, Simon & Schuster, 1960
The Rise and Fall of Adolf Hitler, Random, 1961
The Sinking of the Bismarck, Random, 1962
The Collapse of the Third Republic, Simon & Schuster, 1969

CORNELIA OTIS SKINNER was born in Chicago, May 30, 1901, daughter of a theatrical family, her father Otis Skinner, a famous actor, and Maud (Durbin) Skinner, an actress.

She attended the Baldwin School, Bryn Mawr and the Sorbonne and studied for the stage with the *Societaires de Comedie Française* and the School of Jacques Copeau. She made her debut on the American stage in 1921 in Blasco Ibañez's *Blood and Sand,* and has divided her time since then as an actress, a monologist and as a writer.

As a writer of humorous essays, she is more or less alone among her sex, and the short character sketches of her own authorship are known through her personal presentation tours from one coast to the other. She is an honorary Phi Beta Kappa, a member of the Actors' Equity Association, a second vice-president in 1941, and won the Barter Theatre Award in 1952 for outstanding acting on the Broadway stage. She was made an officer of the Academie Française in 1954.

In 1928 she married Alden S. Blodget and their son is named for his actor grandfather Otis.

Miss Skinner has been awarded a D.F.A., Clark University, L.H.D., University of Pennsylvania and Doctor of Humanities degrees from St. Lawrence University, New York University, the University of Rochester, and Temple University, and other degrees from Mills College, Hofstra University, and Tufts College.

She has appeared in many Broadway productions and in several films, and *Our Hearts Were Young and Gay* was dramatized by Jean Kerr in 1946 and *Family Circle* by Anne Martens in 1950.

Tiny Garments, Farrar, 1932
Excuse It, Please!, Dodd, 1936
Dithers and Jitters, Dodd, 1938
Soap Behind the Ears, Dodd, 1941
Our Hearts Were Young and Gay (with EMILY KIMBROUGH), Dodd, 1942
Popcorn, Constable, 1943
Family Circle (autobiography), Houghton, 1948; in England, *Happy Family*, Constable, 1950
That's Me All Over (selected from four earlier books), Dodd, 1948
Nuts in May, Dodd, 1950
Bottoms Up! Dodd, 1955
The Ape in Me, Houghton, 1959
Elegant Wits and Grand Horizontals, Houghton, 1962
Madame Sarah, (biography of Sarah Bernhardt), Houghton, 1967

JEAN STAFFORD was born July 1, 1915, in Covina, California, daughter of a writer of Western fictions, John Richard, and Mary (McKillop) Stafford, and spent her early years in the West. She attended the University of Colorado, getting her B.A. and M.A. in 1936. She also spent from 1936 to 1937 as a student at the University of Heidelberg.

Miss Stafford was married to the poet Robert Lowell in 1940. They were divorced in 1948 and she married Oliver Jensen, now a writer, in 1950. The marriage ended in divorce in 1953 and she was married to A. J. Liebling, the writer, 1959 until his death in 1963.

For a time Miss Stafford taught at Stephens College, Columbia, Missouri, and later was a fellow at the Wesleyan University Center for Advanced Studies. She was also associated with the *Southern Review* of Louisiana.

In 1955 her story "In the Zoo" won the O. Henry Memorial Award for the best short story. In 1944 she won the Merit Award from *Mademoiselle* and a grant in literature from the National Institute of Arts and Letters in 1945. She was awarded Guggenheim Fellowships in fiction in 1945 and 1948.

In 1970 Miss Stafford's *Collected Stories* won the Pulitzer Prize for fiction.

She lives on Long Island.

Boston Adventure, Harcourt, 1944
The Mountain Lion, Farrar, 1947; Random, 1966
The Catherine Wheel, Random, 1952
Children Are Bored on Sunday, Farrar, 1953
New Short Novels (with others), Ballantine, 1954
Stories (with others), Farrar, 1956
Elephi, The Cat With the High I.Q. (juvenile), Farrar, 1962
The Lion and the Carpenter (juvenile), Macmillan 1962
Bad Characters (stories), Farrar, 1964
A Mother in History, Farrar, 1966
*The Collected Stories of Jean Stafford, Farrar, 1969

JOHN (ERNST) STEINBECK was born February 27, 1902, in Salinas, California, the son of John Ernst Steinbeck, a pioneer of the valley and a county treasurer, and Olive, a schoolteacher, whose maiden name was Hamilton. He was graduated from Salinas High School and was a special student at Stanford University from

1919 to 1925, his attendance broken by jobs as ranch hand, fruitpicker, painter, hod-carrier and construction worker. He was a reporter for the New York *American,* served as a special writer for the U. S. Army Air Forces during World War II and was a correspondent in Europe for the New York *Herald Tribune* (1943).

For the body of his work, John Steinbeck was awarded the Nobel Prize for literature in 1962. He won the Pulitzer Prize for the novel, *The Grapes of Wrath* in 1940, perhaps his most famous work, a novel of an Okie farm family during the Depression of the Thirties. While living in California, where he did most of his writing, he was three times the winner of the Commonwealth Club of California general literature gold medal for work by a California author. The books so honored were *Tortilla Flat, In Dubious Battle* and *The Grapes of Wrath.* He also was awarded the New York Drama Critics Circle silver plaque in 1938 for his play, *Of Mice and Men.* He was a lifelong friend and champion of the underprivileged, the migrant, and the farm worker, and his attitutde was reflected in his writings.

John Steinbeck died in December 1968, at his home in New York City, at the age of sixty-six. His son, Thom, on leave from Saigon, attended the funeral services. His other son, John, in the Army in Vietnam was unable to be at the services, which brought together three hundred of his friends from the literary world.

Steinbeck was a member of the American Center of the P.E.N., and a delegate at the P.E.N. International Congress in Tokyo in 1957.

He married three times, Carrol Henning in 1930, Gwyn Conger in 1943, and Elaine Scott in 1950.

Cup of Gold (fictionalized biography), McBride, 1929
The Pastures of Heaven (short stories), Brewer, Warren, & Putnam, 1932
To a God Unknown (novel), Ballou, 1933

Tortilla Flat (novel), Covici-Friede, 1935
In Dubious Battle (novel), Covici-Friede, 1936
Nothing So Monstrous (story), privately printed, 1936
Saint Katy the Virgin (short story), Covici-Friede, 1936
The Red Pony (story), Covici-Friede, 1937
Of Mice and Men (novel), Covici-Friede, 1937
Of Mice and Men (play), Covici-Friede, 1937
The Long Valley (short stories), Viking, 1938
Their Blood Is Strong (pamphlet), Simon J. Lubin Society of California, San Francisco, 1938
The Grapes of Wrath (novel), Viking, 1939
Steinbeck Replies (pamphlet), Friends of Democracy, 1940
The Forgotten Village (documentary narrative), Viking, 1941
*Sea of Cortez (non-fiction; with E. F. RICKETTS), Viking, 1941
The Moon is Down (novel), Viking, 1942
The Moon is Down (play), Viking, 1942
Bombs Away: The Story of a Bomber Team (photographs by JOHN SWOPE), Viking, 1942
The Portable Steinbeck (selected by PASCAL COVICI with an introduction by LEWIS GANNETT), Viking, 1943
Cannery Row (novel), 1945
The Wayward Bus (novel), Viking, 1947
The Pearl (fiction), Viking, 1947
A Russian Journal (personal narrative, illustrated with 70 photographs by ROBERT CAPA), Viking, 1948
Burning Bright (play in story form), Viking, 1950
East of Eden, Viking, 1952
Sweet Thursday, Viking, 1954
The Short Reign of Pippin IV, A Fabrication, Viking, 1957
Once There Was a War, Viking, 1958
The Winter of Our Discontent, Viking, 1961
Travels With Charley in Search of America, Viking, 1962
The Short Novels of John Steinbeck, Viking, 1963

America and Americans, Viking, 1966 Syndicated columns written during stay in Vietnam, 1966–67

Of Mice and Men (play in three acts), Covici-Friede, 1937

The Forgotten Village (film), Viking, 1941

The Moon Is Down (play in two parts), Viking, 1943

A Medal for Benny edited by JOHN GASS-NER and DUDLEY NICHOLS (in Best Film Plays—1945), 1946

Burning Bright (acting edition), Dramatists Play Service, 1951

Viva Zapata (film), abridged in *Argosy,* February, 1952

Journey of a Novel, The East of Eden Letters, Viking, 1969

IRVING STONE, who has described himself as a "bio-historian" for his fictionalized biographies of notable figures, was born July 14, 1903, in San Francisco. He took his B.A. at the University of California in 1923, his Master's at the University of Southern California in 1924, and became a candidate for the Ph.D. at Berkeley, 1924–26.

After three years as an instructor in economics at the University of Southern California and the University of California, Mr. Stone settled down to research and authorship, principally in the field of biography.

In his chosen field he has won the Christopher Award and the Silver Spur Award of the Western Writers of America for *Men to Match My Mountains.* For *The Agony and the Ecstasy* he has won the Rupert Hughes Award, the Gold Medal of the Commonwealth Club, the Golden Lily of Florence, the Gold Medal, Council of American Artists; and has been made a Commendator, Knight Commander of the Republic of Italy. *Those Who Love* was the first work of fiction to win the American Revolution Round Table award; and was one of thirty fictio.. titles selected over a four year period for presentation to the White House library. Mr. Stone has an Hon. Doc. of Letters from U.S.C., an Hon.

Doc. of Literature from Coe College, Iowa, and an Hon. Doc. of Laws from U. C., Berkeley.

Mr. Stone has spent as much as two and a half years in research before beginning to write a book, as in the case of his novel about Michelangelo, *The Agony and the Ecstasy.* Some of his manuscripts, he says, have run to half a million words before he turns them over to his wife for "severe editing."

Mr. Stone married Jean Factor (his editor since 1933) on February 11, 1934, and they have two children, Paula Stone Hubbell and Kenneth Stone. He lives in Beverly Hills, Calif. Three of his biographical novels, *Lust for Life, The President's Lady,* and *The Agony and the Ecstasy* have been filmed.

Pageant of Youth, A. H. King, 1933

Lust for Life (about Van Gogh), Longmans, 1934

Dear Theo (editor of letters of Van Gogh, with JEAN STONE), Houghton, 1937

Sailor on Horseback (about Jack London), Houghton, 1938

False Witness, Doubleday, 1940

Clarence Darrow for the Defense, Doubleday, 1941

They Also Ran (about defeated presidential candidates), Doubleday, 1943

Immortal Wife (about Jessie B. Fremont), Doubleday, 1944

Adversary in the House (about Eugene V. Debs), Doubleday, 1947

Earl Warren, Doubleday, 1948

The Passionate Journey (about John Noble), Doubleday, 1949

We Speak for Ourselves, Doubleday, 1950

The President's Lady (about Rachel Jackson), Doubleday, 1951

Love Is Eternal (about Mary Todd Lincoln), Doubleday, 1954

Men to Match My Mountains, Doubleday, 1956

*The Agony and the Ecstasy, Doubleday, 1961

I, Michelangelo, Sculptor (editor of letters; with JEAN STONE), Doubleday, 1962

Lincoln, A Contemporary Portrait, (edi-

tor with ALLAN NEVINS), Doubleday, 1962
The Irving Stone Reader, Doubleday, 1963
The Story of Michelangelo's Pietà, Doubleday, 1964
The Great Adventure of Michelangelo (juvenile edition of *Agony*), Doubleday, 1965
Those Who Love (about Abigail Adams), Doubleday, 1965
There Was Light, Autobiography of a University, Berkeley, 1868–1968 (editor and contributor), Doubleday, 1970
The Dark Mirror, (play), 1928
The White Life (on Spinoza; play), 1929
Truly Valiant (play), 1936
Magnificent Doll (screenplay), 1946

JESSE STUART, farmer, poet, tale-teller, biographer, poet laureate of Kentucky and probably one of the best-known writers and school teachers of the South, was born in W-Hollow, near Greenup, Kentucky, August 8, 1907. He received his A.B. in 1929 from Lincoln Memorial University and attended Vanderbilt University in 1931 and 1932.

From his first published book, containing 700 sonnets, some of which, the story goes, were written with a whittled stick on smooth broad poplar leaves while tending sheep on his father's farm, he has made the Kentucky hills his own in many books. He was the second in a family of seven born to Mitchell and Martha Hylton Stuart, a father who was a coal miner, tenant farmer and railroad section laborer, who could not read or write, and a mother who had gone to only the second grade. He entered high school after twenty-two months of elementary schooling, passing eleven subjects, four of which he had never studied in school, and, encouraged by a teacher who gave him a book of Robert Burns' poetry, he began writing.

His first poems appeared in *Man With a Bull-Tongue Plow* and his first story in *Story* magazine. He married Naomi Deane Norris, October 14, 1939, and they have one daughter, Jessica Jane (now Mrs. Julian Juergensmeyer) also a writer and a teacher (of Greek and Latin) at the University of Indiana where she took her Doctorate in Italian.

Jesse Stuart's farm, under his care, has grown to 1000 acres. He has traveled around the world, professionally, but lives in the same valley in which he was born in a one-room log cabin. He is active in conservation work, health and education.

He has lectured in nearly every state. He taught at the American University in Cairo, Egypt, in 1958, and in 1962 the State Department sent him on a world tour to lecture in Europe, the Near East, Middle East, and the Orient. He was American representative that year to the Asian writers' Conference.

Awarded honorary degrees by eleven universities, Jesse Stuart also received (in 1937) a Guggenheim fellowship for foreign travel, a $500 prize, in 1941, from the Academy of Arts and Letters for *Men of the Mountains,* the Thomas Jefferson Memorial Award of $2500 for *Taps for Private Tussie,* the National Education Association Award of 1949 for the best book of the year, *The Thread That Runs So True,* the Berea College Centennial Award for Literature in 1955, and the $5000 Award of the Academy of American Poets in 1961 for distinguished service to American poetry. He was made poet laureate of Kentucky in 1954.

Aside from writing, farming and teaching, Mr. Stuart has chaired the Kentucky Heart Drive, and served in a group for revising the Kentucky State Constitution. In World War II he was a lieutenant commander in the United States Navy.

Harvest of Youth, Scroll Press, 1930
Man With a Bull-Tongue Plow (poetry), Dutton, 1934; revised, 1959
Head o' W-Hollow (stories), Dutton, 1936
Beyond Dark Hills, (autobiography), Dutton, 1938
Trees of Heaven (novel), Dutton, 1940
Men of the Mountains (stories), Dutton, 1941
Taps for Private Tussie (novel), Dutton, 1943

Album of Destiny (poetry), Dutton, 1943

Mongrel Mettle; The Autobiography of a Dog, Dutton, 1944

Foretaste of Glory (novel), Dutton, 1946

Tales From the Plum Grove Hills, Dutton, 1946

The Thread That Runs So True, (autobiographical teaching experiences), Scribner's, 1949

Clearing in the Sky and *Other Stories*, McGraw, 1950

Hie to the Hunters (novel), Whittlesey House, 1950

Kentucky Is My Land (poetry), Dutton, 1952

The Beatinest Boy (juvenile), Whittlesey House, 1953

The Good Spirit of Laurel Ridge (novel), McGraw, 1953

A Penny's Worth of Character (juvenile), Whittlesey House, 1954

Red Mule (juvenile), Whittlesey House, 1955

The Year of My Rebirth (journal), McGraw, 1956

Plowshare in Heaven (stories), McGraw, 1960

God's Oddling (biography of author's father), McGraw, 1960

The Rightful Owner (juvenile), Whittlesey House, 1960

Huey, the Engineer, (short story), James Beard, 1960

Andy Finds a Way (juvenile), McGraw, 1961

Hold April (verse), McGraw, 1962

A Jesse Stuart Reader, McGraw, 1963

Outlooks Through Literature (textbook), Scott, Foresman, 1964

Save Every Lamb, McGraw, 1964

A Jesse Stuart Harvest (stories), Dell, 1964

Short Stories for Discussion (co-editor), Scribner's, 1965

Daughter of the Legend (novel), McGraw, 1965

My Land Has a Voice (stories), McGraw, 1966

A Ride With Huey, the Engineer, (juvenile), McGraw, 1966

Mr. Gallion's School (educational novel), McGraw, 1967

*Come Gentle Spring (stories), McGraw, 1969

To Teach, To Love (autobiography), McGraw, 1969

Old Ben (junior book), McGraw, 1970

WILLIAM STYRON was born June 11, 1925, in Newport News, Virginia, son of William Clark, a shipyard engineer, and Pauline (Abraham) Styron. He graduated from Duke University, B.A., in 1947.

Lie Down in Darkness, his first novel, won the American Academy of Arts and Letters Prix de Rome in 1952. His interest in the pre-Civil War South, from 1800 to 1860, led to Styron's longest and most impressive work, *The Confessions of Nat Turner*, concerning the leader of a slave insurrection in Virginia in 1831. The book had a wide public acceptance and won the Pulitzer Prize in 1968. After its appearance, Styron was invited to be the sole American observer at the 10th African-Asian Writers' Conference in Tashkent, where he protested the jailing of writers in the Soviet Union.

Mr. Styron spent three and a half years in the U. S. Marine Corps, leaving the service, after Korea, as a first lieutenant. For a time after that he was an editor with McGraw-Hill and has been an advisory editor of the magazine *Paris Review* since 1953. He was made a fellow of Silliman College, Yale, in 1964, and is a member of the National Institute of Arts and Letters, and a fellow, American Academy of Arts and Letters.

In 1953 Mr. Styron married Rose Burgunder and the Styrons have three daughters and a son and live in Connecticut, where, since 1963, the author has been a member of the Roxbury Library board.

Lie Down in Darkness, Bobbs, 1951

The Long March, Compass Books, 1957

Set This House on Fire, Random, 1960

*The Confessions of Nat Turner, Random, 1960

Best Stories from the Paris Review, (editor), Random, 1959

ALLEN TATE was born at Winchester, Kentucky, November 19, 1899. He was educated at home until nine, and at private schools in Louisville and Washington, D.C. He took his B.A. degree at Vanderbilt University in 1922, *magna cum laude,* Phi Beta Kappa, and his M.A. (*honoris causa*) at Oxford University, England, in 1958.

Mr. Tate was one of the founders and editors of *The Fugitive,* at Nashville, Tenn., from 1922 to 1925; he freelanced in New York between 1924 and 1928. He received a Guggenheim Fellowship for Poetry and spent 1928 to 1930 in France and England.

He was poet in residence at Princeton University from 1939 to 1942 and held the chair of poetry at the Library of Congress in 1943–1944. From 1944 to 1946 he was editor of the *Sewanee Review.* He has held many teaching posts, which include his being Fulbright lecturer at the University of Oxford in 1953, University of Rome, 1953 to 1954, and Universities of Oxford and Leeds, 1958 to 1959. He is Regents' Professor of English Emeritus, University of Minnesota.

Mr. Tate has been occasional lecturer at more than 100 American colleges and universities and lecturer for the American Specialists Program, Department of State, at the Universities of Liège and Louvain in 1954, the Universities of Delhi, Bombay, the Sorbonne, and Nottingham in 1956 and Urbino and Florence, Italy, in 1961.

He was elected to the National Institute of Arts and Letters in 1949, to the American Academy of Arts and Letters in 1964, the American Academy of Arts and Sciences in 1965, and elected president of the National Institute of Arts and Letters in 1968. He has received the National Institute's $1000 grant in poetry, (1948) the Bollingen Prize for Poetry, Yale University, 1956, the Brandeis Medal Award in 1961, the Medaglia d'Oro di Societa Italiana di Dante Alighieri, Florence, Italy, 1962, and the $5,000 Fellowship award of the Academy of American Poets, 1963.

In 1924 Allen Tate married the writer Caroline Gordon and they have a married daughter. They were divorced and Mr. Tate married again, in 1959, to Isabella Gardner, and now with his third wife, the former Helen Heinz, whom he married in 1966, lives in Sewanee, Tenn.

Mr. Pope and Other Poems, Minton, Balch & Co., 1928
Stonewall Jackson: The Good Soldier, Minton, 1928
Jefferson Davis: His Rise and Fall, Minton, 1929
Poems: 1928–1931, Scribner's, 1932
Reactionary Essays on Poetry and Ideas, Scribner's, 1936
The Mediterranean and Other Poems, Alcestis Press, 1936
Selected Poems, Scribner's, 1937
The Fathers (a novel), Putnam's, 1938; Eyre & Spottiswood, 1939; Swallow, 1960, 1968
Reason in Madness (essays), Putnam's, 1941
The Language of Poetry, Princeton Univ. Press, 1942
The Vigil of Venus (translation of *Pervigilium Veneris*), Cummington Press, 1943
The Winter Sea (poems), Cummington Press, 1944
On the Limits of Poetry (essays), Swallow-Morrow, 1948
The Hovering Fly (essays), Cummington Press, 1949
Poems: 1922–1947, Scribner's, 1948
The Forlorn Demon (essays), Henry Regnery, 1953
The Man of Letters in the Modern World (essays), Meridian, 1955
Saggi (selected essays translated from Italian, *Edizioni di Storia e Letteritura*), 1957
Collected Essays, Swallow, 1959
Poems, Scribner's, 1960
Essays of Four Decades, revised ed., Swallow, 1969
Fugitives: An Anthology of Verse (with others), Harcourt, 1927
I'll Take My Stand, by Twelve Southerners, Harper, 1930

A Southern Vanguard, John Peale Bishop Memorial Anthology (editor), Prentice-Hall, 1945
American Harvest (with JOHN PEALE BISHOP), Fisher, 1944
The House of Fiction (with CAROLINE GORDON), Scribner's, 1950, 1960
Modern Verse in English: 1900–1950 (with LORD DAVID CECIL), Macmillan, 1958, 1959
Man and His Work (about T. S. Eliot), Delacorte, 1966

LIONEL TRILLING was born July 4, 1905, in New York City, son of David W., a businessman, and Fannie Cohen Trilling. He took his B.A. in 1925 from Columbia University, his M.A. at the same university in 1926 and his Ph.D. degree in 1938. In June 1929 he married Diana Rubin, who writes under her married name. They have one son.

Dr. Trilling has taught at the University of Wisconsin and Hunter College, and since 1932 at Columbia University where he is now the George Edward Woodberry Professor of Literature and Criticism. With John Crowe Ransom and F. O. Mathiessen he organized the Kenyon School of Letters at Kenyon College in 1948 and has since served as a Senior Fellow of the school, which is now the Indiana University School of Letters. He was the George Eastman Visiting Professor at Oxford University in 1964–65 and the Charles Eliot Norton Visiting Professor of Poetry at Harvard University in 1969–1970, and he holds honorary degrees from Trinity College (Hartford, Connecticut), Harvard University, and Northwestern University.

He is a member of the National Institute of Arts and Letters, and the National Academy of Arts and Letters.

Matthew Arnold, Norton, 1939; Columbia Univ. Press, 1949
E. M. Forster, New Directions, 1943
The Middle of the Journey (novel), Viking, 1947
The Liberal Imagination, Viking, 1950
The Opposing Self, Viking, 1955

Freud and the Crisis of Our Culture, Beacon, 1955
A Gathering of Fugitives, Beacon, 1956
Beyond Culture, Viking, 1965
The Portable Matthew Arnold (editor), Viking, 1949
The Letters of John Keats, 1950
Selected Short Stories of John O'Hara, Modern Library, 1956
The Life and Works of Sigmund Freud (with ERNEST JONES), Basic Books, 1961
Introduction: The Adventures of Huckleberry Finn by MARK TWAIN (introduction), Rinehart, 1948
Literary Criticism: An Introductory Reader, Holt, Rinehart and Winston, Inc., 1970

BARBARA W. (WERTHEIM) TUCHMAN was born in New York City, January 30, 1912, daughter of Maurice and Alma (Morgenthau) Wertheim. She took her B.A. degree at Radcliffe College in 1933 and became a research assistant at the Institute for Pacific Relations in New York City the following year. She spent 1935 in Tokyo on the staff of the IPR and was an editorial assistant on *The Nation* in 1936. She was a staff writer in Spain during part of 1937. In 1939 she was American correspondent for the *New Statesman and Nation*, London, and with the Far East news desk of the Office of War Information in New York, N.Y., 1943 to 1945. In June 1967 she reported the immediate aftermath of the six-day Arab-Israeli war for the *Atlantic Monthly*.

For her book *The Guns of August*, Barbara Tuchman retraced the route of the German armies in 1914 in their march from Liège through Belgium and France. The book won her the Pulitzer Prize for non-fiction in 1963.

She has been a trustee of Radcliffe College since 1960, member of the Committee for the Humanities, Yale University Council, from 1966 to 1967, and is a member of the Council of the Authors' League, the Council of the Society of American Historians, and a member of the National Institute of Arts and Letters.

She received honorary doctor of letters degrees from Bates College, 1963, the University of Massachusetts, 1966, Columbia University, Yale University, and the New School for Social Research, in 1967, and the Hebrew Union College in 1968.

She married Lester R. Tuchman in 1940 and has three daughters. The Tuchmans live in New York City.

The Lost British Policy, United editorial, 1938
Bible and Sword, New York Univ. Press, 1956
The Zimmerman Telegram, Viking, 1958
The Guns of August (Book-of-the-Month), Macmillan, 1962
*The Proud Tower (Book-of-the-Month), Macmillan, 1966

JOHN UPDIKE, born March 18, 1932, in Shillington, Pennsylvania, son of a school teacher father and a mother who was an author (Linda Grace Hoyer), took his A.B. at Harvard, *summa cum laude,* in 1954. He attended the Ruskin School of Drawing and Fine Arts in Oxford, England, the following year, and in 1955 and for two years he wrote in the Talk of the Town department of *The New Yorker.*

Mr. Updike is the author of five novels, three collections of stories, three volumes of verse, a book of essays, and four juveniles.

Subject of much favorable critical attention for the felicity of his style if not always for the generally middle-class people in his books, Mr. Updike, one of the youngest of this generation's writers to reach a wide audience, has told a *Life* interviewer, "As aristocracies have faded so have heroes. You cared about Oedipus and Hamlet because they were noble and you were a groundling. Now either nobody is a hero or everyone is. I vote for everyone."

He is a member of the National Institute of Arts and Letters; he received a Guggenheim Fellowship in poetry in 1959, a National Institute Award for *The Poorhouse Fair* in 1960, a National Book Award for *The Centaur* in 1963 and the *Prix de Meilleur Livre Etranger,* 1966, for the same novel. He lives in Ipswich, Mass., with his wife, the former Mary Entwistle Pennington, and their four young children.

The Carpentered Hen (poems), Harper, 1958; Gollancz, 1959
The Poorhouse Fair (novel), Knopf, 1959
The Same Door (stories), Knopf, 1959
Rabbit, Run (novel) Knopf, 1960
**Pigeon Feathers and Other Stories,* Knopf, 1962
The Centaur (novel), Knopf, 1963
Telephone Poles and Other Poems, Knopf, 1963
Assorted Prose (parodies, reminiscence, journalism, reviews), Knopf, 1965
Of the Farm (novel), Knopf, 1965
The Music School (stories), Knopf, 1966
Couples (novel), Knopf, 1968
Midpoint and Other Poems, Knopf
The Magic Flute (juvenile; adoption of opera plot), Knopf, 1962
The Ring (juvenile; adoption of opera plot), Knopf, 1964
Bottom's Dream (juvenile; a version of *Midsummer Night's Dream*), Knopf, 1965
Child's Calendar (juvenile), Knopf, 1965

MARK VAN DOREN, born June 13, 1894, in Hope, Illinois, the son of a physician, is a poet, short story writer, essayist, playwright, one-time literary and motion picture editor of *The Nation,* and one of the most influential and best-remembered teachers at Columbia University. He taught there from 1920 until his retirement in 1959.

Best known for his poetry, which he began writing at 26, he saw his latest collection, *That Shining Place* (Hill & Wang) published in June 1969 on his seventy-fifth birthday, when, in looking back, he admitted the world "is in bad shape, but no matter how bad things get, somehow I 'bounce off.' Most people are really like that . . . Anyone who wants to go on living had better try to be happy."

Mark Van Doren received both his B.A. and M.A. degrees in 1915 from the University of Illinois. His thesis was on Henry Thoreau and it was published by Houghton Mifflin the following year. He served two years in the U. S. Army in World War I. In 1920, he joined the English faculty at Columbia after concluding work on his doctorate, a dissertation on the poet Dryden.

In 1922 he married Dorothy Graffe, herself a writer and editor, and the couple have two children, Charles and John. Mr. Van Doren's family tree dates from Pieter Van Doorn, who landed in New Jersey, from Holland, in 1699. The Van Dorens are long-time residents of Cornwall, Connecticut.

Mr. Van Doren is a member of the National Institute of Arts and Letters and the American Academy of Arts and Letters. His awards and honors include: The Pulitzer Prize for Poetry, 1940, for *Collected Poems;* the 1962 Creativity Award of the Huntington Hartford Foundation, the Emerson-Thoreau Award of the American Academy of Arts and Sciences, 1963, and the $5000 Prize of the Academy of American Poets, in 1967. He has received honorary doctor of letters degrees from Bowdoin College, 1944, University of Illinois in 1958, Columbia University in 1960, Knox College in 1957, Mount Mary College in 1965, St. John's College fellowship in 1959, an honorary degree in medicine from Connecticut State Medical Society in 1966, the Alexander Hamilton Medal from Columbia College in 1959, and the Sarah Joseph Hale Award of the Richards Free Library of Newport, N.H., and the Brotherhood Award of the National Conference of Christians and Jews, both in 1960.

Henry David Thoreau—A Critical Study,
  Houghton, 1916
The Poetry of John Dryden, Harcourt,
  1920, Holt, 1946
Spring Thunder, and Other Poems, Seltzer, 1924

American and British Literature Since 1890 (with CARL VAN DOREN), Century, 1925, revised 1939)
7 p.m., and Other Poems, Boni, 1926
Edwin Arlington Robinson, Literary Guild, 1927
An American Bookshelf (anthology), five volumes, Macy & Masius, 1927–1928
Now the Sky, and Other Poems, Boni & Liveright, 1928
An Anthology of World Poetry, Boni & Liveright, 1928 (revised, Reynal & Hitchcock, 1936)
An Autobiography of America (compilation of American autobiographical documents), Boni & Liveright, 1929
Correspondence of Aaron Burr and His Daughter Theodosia (compilation of letters, with preface), Covici-Friede, 1929
Dick and Tom (juvenile), Macmillan, 1931
Jonathan Gentry (narrative poem), Boni & Liveright, 1931
Dick and Tom in Town (juvenile), Macmillan, 1932
American Poets, 1630–1930 (anthology), Little, Brown, 1932
The Oxford Book of American Prose (anthology), Oxford Univ. Press, 1932
The Transients (novel), Morrow, 1935
A Winter Diary, and Other Poems, Macmillan, 1935, Holt, 1938
The Last Look, and Other Poems, Holt, 1937
Studies in Metaphysical Poetry (essay and bibliography; with THEODORE SPENCER), Columbia Univ. Press, 1939
Collected Poems, 1922–1938, Holt, 1939
Shakespeare, Holt, 1939
Windless Cabins (novel), Holt, 1940
The Transparent Tree (juvenile), Holt, 1940
Invitation to Learning (transcripts of radio broadcasts; with others), Random, 1941
The Mayfield Deer (narrative poem), Holt, 1941
The Private Reader (critical essays and reviews), Holt, 1942
Our Lady Peace and Other War Poems, New Directions, 1942
The New Invitation to Learning (tran-

scripts of radio broadcasts; with others), Random, 1942

The Seven Sleepers and Other Poems, Holt, 1944

Liberal Education, Holt, 1943; Beacon, 1959

Tilda, Holt, 1943

The Country Year (poems), 1946

The Noble Voice: A Study of Ten Great Poems, Holt, 1946; Collier Books, 1962

The Careless Clock (poems), Sloane, 1947

New Poems, Sloane, 1948

Nathaniel Hawthorne, Sloane, 1949

Humanity Unlimited, College of William and Mary Press, 1950

The Witch of Ramoth and Other Tales, Maple Press, 1950

The Short Stories of Mark Van Doren, Abelard, 1950

In That Far Land, Prairie Press, 1951

Introduction to Poetry, Sloane, 1951

Mortal Summer, Prairie Press, 1953

Spring Birth and Other poems, Holt, 1953

Nobody Say a Word and Other Stories, Holt, 1953

Man's Right to Knowledge, Columbia Univ. Press, 1954

Selected Poems, Holt, 1954

Home With Hazel and Other Stories, Harcourt, 1957

The Autobiography of Mark Van Doren, Harcourt, 1958

Don Quixote's Profession, Columbia Univ. Press, 1958

The Last Days of Lincoln (play), Hill & Wang, 1959

Morning Worship and Other Poems, Harcourt, 1960

The Happy Critic, Hill & Wang, 1961

Collected Stories, Hill & Wang, 1962

Collected and New Poems, Hill & Wang, 1963

The Narrative Poems of Mark Van Doren, Hill & Wang, 1964

Collected Stories, Vol. II, Hill & Wang, 1965

Somebody Came (juvenile), Harlan Quist, 1966

Three Plays, Hill & Wang, 1966

Mark Van Doren: 100 Poems, Hill & Wang, 1967

Introduction to Poetry, Hill & Wang, 1968

Collected Stories, Vol. III, Hill & Wang, 1968

That Shining Place (poems), Hill & Wang, 1969

GORE VIDAL was born at West Point, October 3, 1925, son of an Army instructor in aeronautics. He is a grandson of the late blind Senator T. P. Gore of Oklahoma. A month after graduation from Phillips Exeter Academy in New Hampshire, he enlisted in the Army, serving from 1943 to 1946. He was first mate of an Army F.S. ship in the Aleutians where at the age of nineteen he wrote his first novel, *Williwaw,* published in 1946.

After his discharge from the Army, Vidal settled in upstate New York where he entered politics. As Democratic-Liberal candidate for Congress from New York's 29th Congressional District in 1969, he lost by a narrow margin. From 1961 to 1963 he served on President Kennedy's Advisory Council of the Arts.

Mr. Vidal has written poetry, essays, criticism, television and film scripts, and plays. He has often been seen as a commentator on television, sometimes opposite William F. Buckley, Jr. He now lives in Klosters, Switzerland.

Williwaw (novel), Dutton, 1946

In a Yellow Wood (novel), Dutton, 1947

The City and the Pillar (novel), Dutton, 1948

The Season of Comfort (novel), Dutton, 1949

A Search for the King (novel), Dutton, 1950

Dark Green, Bright Red (novel), Dutton, 1950

The Judgment of Paris (novel), Dutton, 1952

Messiah (novel), Dutton, 1954

A Thirsty Evil (short stories), Zero Press, 1956

Visit to a Small Planet, Little, Brown, 1957

The Best Man, Little, Brown, 1960

Romulus (adapted from F. DUERREN-MATT), Dramatists Play Service, 1962

Rocking the Boat (essays), Little, Brown, 1962

Julian (novel), Little, Brown, 1964

*Washington, D.C. (novel), Little, Brown, 1967

Myra Breckinridge (novel), Little, Brown, 1968

Reflections Upon a Sinking Ship, Little, 1969

About Gore Vidal: *Gore Vidal* by RAY LEWIS WHITE, Twayne, 1968

ROBERT PENN WARREN, poet, novelist, essayist, short story writer, critic, and teacher, was born April 24, 1905, in Guthrie, Kentucky, son of Robert Franklin, a businessman, and Anna Ruth (Penn) Warren. He took his B.A. (*summa cum laude*) at Vanderbilt University in 1925 where he had been a student of the poet John Crowe Ransom, Donald Davidson, and where one of his roommates was Allen Tate. Under such influences he opted out of chemistry and into literature.

Mr. Warren received his M.A. at the University of California, Berkeley, in 1927, did graduate study at Yale, 1927–28, and was a Rhodes Scholar at Oxford, B. Litt., 1928–30.

He was a member of the Fugitive Group of Poets in Nashville from 1923 to 1925 and from 1930 to 1950 he held teaching posts in various Southern and Middlewestern universities. In 1950 he became professor of playwrighting at Yale, resigning in 1956; from 1961 to the present, he has been professor of English.

Mr. Warren was a founding editor (with Cleanth Brooks) of *The Southern Review*, 1935 to 1942, and an advisory editor of *Kenyon Review*, 1938–1961. He won the Caroline Sinkler Award in poetry in 1936, in 1937 and in 1938, the Levinson Prize (*Poetry* Magazine) in 1936, a Houghton Mifflin literary fellowship in 1929 for *Night Rider*, a Guggenheim Fellowship in 1939 and 1947, the Shelley Memorial Award in 1943, the Pulitzer Prize for fiction in 1947 for *All The King's Men*, the Southern Prize in 1947, Robert Meltzer Award of the Screen Writers Guild in 1949, the Union League Civic and Arts Foundation Prize (*Poetry* Magazine) in 1953, the Sidney Hillman Prize, 1957, for *Segregation*, Edna St. Vincent Millay Memorial Award, American Poetry Society, 1958, for *Promises*, the National Book Award of 1958 for *Promises*, the Pulitzer Prize in poetry, 1958, for *Promises*, and the *Herald Tribune* Van Doren award of 1965 for *Who Speaks for the Negro?* In 1967 he received the Bollingen Prize for Poetry, for *Selected Poems: New and Old*. He has honorary degrees from seven universities and colleges.

With Cleanth Brooks and others he has edited a number of collections of writing, short stories, poetry, Southern regional writings, and books on rhetoric, fiction, the understanding of poetry and approaches to literature.

In 1930 he married Emma Brescia, the marriage ending in divorce in 1950. In 1952 he married Eleanor Clark, the writer; they have two children, Rosanna Phelps and Gabriel Penn, and live in Fairfield, Conn.

John Brown: The Making of a Martyr, Payson & Clarke, 1929

I'll Take My Stand (contributor), Harper, 1930

Thirty-Six Poems, Alcestis, 1936

Who Owns America?, edited by HERBERT AGAR and ALLEN TATE (contributor), Houghton, 1936

Night Rider (novel), Houghton, 1939

Eleven Poems on the Same Theme, New Directions, 1942

At Heaven's Gate (novel), Harcourt, 1943

Selected Poems, Harcourt, 1944

*All the King's Men (novel), Harcourt, 1946

Blackberry Winter, Cummington Press, 1946

The Circus in the Attic, and Other Stories, Harcourt, 1948

World Enough and Time (novel), Random, 1950

Brother to Dragons (poem), Random, 1953

Band of Angels (novel), Random, 1955

Segregation: The Inner Conflict in the South, Random, 1956

Promises: Poems 1954–1956, Random, 1957

Selected Essays, Random, 1958

The Cave (novel), Random, 1959

All the King's Men (play), Random, 1960

You, Emperors and Others: Poems 1957–1960, Random, 1960

The Legacy of the Civil War, Random, 1961

Wilderness: A Tale of the Civil War (novel), Random, 1961

Flood: A Romance of Our Time (novel), Random, 1964

Who Speaks for the Negro?, Random, 1965

Selected Poems New and Old, 1923–1966, Random, 1966

Incarnations: Poems 1966–1967, Random, 1968

Audubon: A Vision (poem), Random, 1969

EUDORA WELTY was born in Jackson, Mississippi, the daughter of the president of an insurance company, Christian Webb, and Chestina (Andrews) Welty. She attended the Mississippi State College for Women, took her B.A. at the University of Wisconsin, and studied for a year at the Columbia University School of Business. She returned to live in Mississippi, which is a region she has made her own in many short stories and a number of novels.

Miss Welty's first book of short stories was introduced by Katherine Anne Porter in 1941.

She received a Guggenheim Fellowship in 1942 which was renewed in 1949, and a National Institute of Arts and Letters Grant in literature in 1944. She was given the Lucy Donnelly Fellowship Award from Bryn Mawr College, the Ingram Memorial Foundation Award in Literature, the William Dean Howells Gold Medal for Fiction from the Ameri-

can Academy of Arts and Letters, the Brandeis Medal for Literature, and the Hollins Medal. She has been honorary consultant for the Library of Congress, Neilson Professor at Smith College, and is a member of the National Institute of Arts and Letters. She won first prize in the O. Henry Short Story collections in the years 1942, 1943, and 1968.

**A Curtain of Green* (stories), Doubleday, 1941

The Robber Bridegroom (novella), Doubleday, 1942

The Wide Net, and Other Stories, Harcourt, 1943

Delta Wedding (novel), Harcourt, 1946

The Golden Apples (collected stories), Harcourt, 1949

Selected Stories, Modern Library, 1953

The Ponder Heart (novel), Harcourt, 1954

The Bride of the Innisfallen (stories), Harcourt, 1955

Thirteen Stories (paperback), Harcourt, 1965

The Shoe Bird (juvenile), Harcourt, 1964

Losing Battles, Random House, 1970

E. B. (ELWYN BROOKS) WHITE was born in Mount Vernon, New York, July 11, 1899, attended the public schools there and graduated from Cornell, after a college year had been interrupted by Army service, in 1921. He worked for the United Press, was a reporter for the Seattle *Times*, messboy aboard a ship, and worked for an advertising agency before he joined the staff of *The New Yorker* in 1925, where he remained for more than forty years famous for his "Talk of the Town" contributions, "Notes and Comment," his verse and satirical sketches. From 1938 to 1943 he also wrote a column, "One Man's Meat" for *Harper's* Magazine.

President Kennedy named Mr. White one of the thirty-one Americans to receive the Presidential Medal of Freedom, and he has also been honored with the Gold Medal for Essays and Criticism given by the National Institute of Arts and Letters (1960), and the New York Newspaper Guild Page One Award in 1954 for his book *The Second Tree from the Corner*. He has been awarded honorary degrees from seven colleges and universities.

Mr. White married Katharine S. White, a *New Yorker* editor, in 1929, and they live on a farm in Maine.

The Lady Is Cold (verse), Harper, 1929
Is Sex Necessary? (satire with JAMES THURBER), Harper, 1929
Ho Hum, Farrar, 1931
Another Ho Hum, Farrar, 1932
Every Day Is Saturday (editorials), Harper, 1934
Farewell to Model T (essay), Putnam, 1936
The Fox of Peapack (verse), Harper, 1938
Quo Vadimus? (essays), Harper, 1939
One Man's Meat (essays), Harper, 1944; Torchbook, 1964; Perennial Library, 1966
Stuart Little (juvenile), Harper, 1945
The Wild Flag (editorials), Houghton, 1946
Here Is New York (essay), Harper, 1949
Charlotte's Web, (juvenile), Harper, 1952
The Second Tree From the Corner (miscellany), Harper, 1954
The Points of My Compass (essays), Harper, 1962
A Subtreasury of American Humor (with KATHARINE S. WHITE), Coward, 1941
The Elements of Style (with WILLIAM STRUNK, JR.), Macmillan, 1959
An E. B. White Reader (edited by WILL WATT AND ROBERT BRADFORD), Harper, 1966

THEODORE (HAROLD) WHITE was born in Boston, May 6, 1915, son of David and Mary (Winkeller) White. He attended Boston Latin School and was graduated *summa cum laude* from Harvard University in 1938. Given a Sheldon traveling fellowship, he went to China and from 1939 to 1945 he was correspondent and, eventually, bureau chief for *Time* in China, covering the China war front, Indian uprising, the Honan famine and the surrender of the Japanese. Out of his China experiences came his first book (with Annalee Jacoby), *Thunder Out of China*, in 1946.

Mr. White returned to the United States, where he served as an editor of *The New Republic*, and edited *The Stilwell Papers* before going to Europe where he became correspondent for *The Reporter*. He was the magazine's chief European correspondent from 1950 to 1953, national correspondent from 1954 to 1955. He was also a free-lance writer, and a consultant for Columbia Broadcasting System from 1961 to 1968 and has been consultant to Atheneum Publishers since 1962.

Mr. White's interest in the American political scene led to his three books about recent presidential campaigns, the first one, *The Making of the President—1960*, winning him the Pulitzer Prize for non-fiction in 1962.

He is a Phi Beta Kappa and the recipient of the U. S. Air Medal (1944).

He received the Sidney Hillman Foundation Award of 1954 and the National Association of Independent Schools Award for *The Mountain Road, Fire in the Ashes*, and *The Making of the President—1960*. He won the Emmy Award of the National Academy of Television Arts and Sciences for the best television film of 1964, and another Emmy in 1967 for his documentary, *China—The Roots of Madness*. His first, third, fourth and sixth books were Book-of-the-Month Club selections and *The View From the Fortieth Floor*, his second novel, was distributed by The Literary Guild. He has been honored by awards from the U. S. Department of Defense, the Newspaper Guild, Sigma Delta Chi and the Overseas Press Club.

Mr. White is a member of the Committee on Foreign Relations and a member of the board of overseers of Harvard College. He lives in New York City with his wife, the former Nancy Ariana Van Der Heyden Bean, and their two children, Heyden and David.

Thunder Out of China (with Annalee Jacoby), Sloane, 1946
The Stilwell Papers (editor), Sloane, 1948
Fire in the Ashes, Sloane, 1953
The Mountain Road (novel), Sloane, 1958
The View From the Fortieth Floor (novel), Sloane, 1960
The Making of the President—1960, Atheneum, 1961
The Making of the President—1964, Atheneum, 1965
*Caesar at the Rubicon (play), Atheneum, 1968
The Making of the President—1968, Atheneum, 1969

RICHARD (PURDY) WILBUR, poet and educator, was born in New York City March 1, 1921, son of the artist Lawrence Wilbur and Helen (Purdy) Wilbur, daughter of an editor of the Baltimore *Sun*. He took his A.B. at Amherst College in 1942, his A.M. in 1952, and his D.Litt., in 1967. He also took a master's degree at Harvard in 1947 and an L.H.D. at Lawrence College in 1960.

Mr. Wilbur spent his early years in semi-rural New Jersey, edited the college newspaper at Amherst and, he says, toured most of the forty-eight states, in the summers, by freight car. In World War II he was in the United States Army at Cassino, Anzio and the Siegfried Line, a period when he "began to versify in earnest."

From 1950 to 1954, Mr. Wilbur was assistant professor of English at Harvard, from 1955 to 1957 associate professor at Wellesley College and since 1957 professor of English at Wesleyan University in Connecticut.

He was the recipient of the Harriet Monroe prize of *Poetry* Magazine in 1948, the Oscar Blumenthal prize in 1950, the Edna St. Vincent Millay Memorial Award of 1957 and the National Book Award and the Pulitzer Prize in 1957. He also received Guggenheim Fellowships in 1952 and in 1963, the Prix de Rome, American Academy of Arts and Letters, 1954, and a Ford Fellowship in 1960–61. He is a member of the American Academy of Arts and Letters and the National Institute of Arts and Letters.

In 1942, Mr. Wilbur married Mary Charlotte Hayes Ward. They have four children—Ellen Dickinson, Christopher Hayes, Nathan and Aaron—and live in Middletown, Connecticut.

Mr. Wilbur's translations of Molière have been played in repertory in New York to high critical praise. His translation of *Tartuffe* (1963) was co-recipient of the Bolligen Prize for translation.

The Beautiful Changes and Other Poems, Reynal, 1947; Harcourt, 1954
Ceremony and Other Poems, Harcourt, 1950
A Bestiary, Pantheon, 1955
Molière's *Misanthrope* (translation), Harcourt, 1955
Things of This World, Harcourt, 1956
Poems 1943–56, Faber (London) 1957
Candide (comic opera, with Lillian Hellman), Random House, 1957
Advice to a Prophet, and Other Poems, Harcourt 1961
Poems of Richard Wilbur, Harcourt, 1963
*Walking to Sleep (poetry), Harcourt, 1969
Tartuffe (translation from Molière), Harcourt, 1963
Editor: *Complete Poems of Poe*, Dell, 1959
Poems of Shakespeare, Penguin, 1966
Loudmouse, Crowell-Collier, 1963

THORNTON WILDER, who has won the Pulitzer Prize twice for plays and once for a novel, was born in Madison, Wisconsin, April 17, 1897. The son of a newspaper editor, he was taken by his father to China when he was nine years old, when his father was American consul-general at Hong Kong and Shanghai. His education began at the usual age of five or six, at Madison, and at nine he attended a German school in Hong Kong for six months. Returning to the United States, still nine, he went to the public schools in Berkeley, California. Back in China for another year and a half he attended another German school in Shanghai, an English boarding school in Chefoo for a year, then the Thacher School in Ojai, Calif., for a year, and graduated from the Berkeley High School in 1915. He attended Oberlin College from 1915 to 1917, and took his A.B. at Yale University in 1920. He studied at the American Academy in Rome 1920–21 and taught at the Lawrenceville (N.J.) School from 1921 to 1928, taking out two years to get an M.A. at Princeton in 1926 and write *The Bridge of San Luis Rey,* his Pulitzer Prize novel.

Mr. Wilder became a member of the faculty of the University of Chicago in 1930 and remained there until 1936. He was Charles E. Norton professor of poetry at Harvard from 1950 to 1951.

Entering the U. S. Air Corps Intelligence in June, 1942, as a captain, he ended his military career as a lieutenant colonel in 1945. He has been awarded the Legion of Merit, the Bronze Star, the Military Order of the British Empire, the Legion d'Honneur, the Order of Merit of West Germany, and the Peace Prize, Frankfurt-am-Main, 1957.

Among his other honors are the Gold Medal for Fiction awarded by the American Academy of Arts and Letters, 1952; the Medal of Honor, Science and Art, Austria, 1959; Edward MacDowell Medal for Contribution to Letters, 1959; the Presidential Award, 1963; National Book Award, 1965, Medal for Literature, National Book Committee, 1965; National Book Award for *The Eighth Day,* 1968.

Mr. Wilder has been given honorary degrees from ten universities including Goethe University, Frankfurt, Germany, and the University of Zurich, Switzerland. He is a member of the American Academy of Arts and Letters, and lives in Connecticut.

NOVELS

The Cabala, A. & C. Boni, 1926
The Bridge of San Luis Rey (Pulitzer Prize), A. & C. Boni, 1927
The Woman of Andros, A. & C. Boni, 1930

Heaven's My Destination, Harper & Brothers, 1935
The Ides of March, Harper, 1948
The Eighth Day (National Book Award) Harper & Row, 1967

PLAYS

The Trumpet Shall Sound, play in four acts, published while an undergraduate in the *Yale Literary Magazine,* 1919–20, produced by The American Laboratory Theatre, New York, 1926
The Angel That Troubled The Water, and Other Plays, Subtitled *Three Minute Plays for Three People,* Coward-McCann, Inc., 1928
The Long Christmas Dinner and Other Plays in One Act, collection of six plays, Yale University Press and Coward-McCann, Inc., 1931
Lucrece, translated and adapted from the French of *Le Viol de Lucrèce* by André Obey for Katharine Cornell, opened in New York 1932, published by Houghton-Mifflin Company, 1933
A Doll's House, translated and adapted from Henrik Ibsen for Ruth Gordon, opened at the Drama Festival in Central City, Colorado, summer of 1937 and brought to New York that same year. Not published.
OUR TOWN, play in Three Acts played in Princeton and Boston before opening in New York 1938. Published by Harper & Brothers (Pulitzer Prize).
The Merchant of Yonkers: A Farce in Four Acts, played in Boston before opening in New York, 1938. Published by Harper & Brothers, 1939
The Skin of Our Teeth, play in three acts, played in New Haven, Baltimore, Philadelphia and Washington before opening in New York in 1942. Published by Harper and Brothers (Pulitzer Prize)
The Victors, translated and adapted from the French of J. P. Sartre's *Morts Sans Sepulcres,* produced off-Broadway, 1949. Not published in this translation.
The Matchmaker, a slightly altered version of *The Merchant of Yonkers* written for Ruth Gordon, presented at the Edinburg Festival, 1954, played

in London a year and opened in New York autumn of 1955. Published by Harper & Row in the volume *Three Plays* with *Our Town* and *The Skin of Our Teeth* with a preface by the author, 1957

A Life in the Sun, play in three acts presented under that title at the Edinburgh Festival, 1955. (Real title *The Alcestiad*). German translation *Die Alkestiade* opened in Zurich, Switzerland, 1957, published by S. Fischer Verlag, Frankfurt.

The Long Christmas Dinner, opera in one-act, libretto by T.W. made from the play of that name in the volume *The Long Christmas Dinner and Other Plays,* with music by Paul Hindemith. World opening at Mannheim, Germany, 1961

Die Alkestiade, opera in three acts, libretto made by T.W. from his play of that name, music by Louise Talma, world opening Frankfurt, Germany, 1962

Plays for Bleecker Street, three one act plays, produced at the Circle in the Square, Bleecker Street, New York, 1962

Hello, Dolly!, Musical comedy based on his play *The Matchmaker,* New York, 1964

TENNESSEE (THOMAS LANIER) WILLIAMS, who received more votes than any other on the ballots which nominated authors for inclusion in *This Is My Best,* has twice received the Pulitzer Prize for drama—in 1947 for *A Streetcar Named Desire* and in 1955 for *Cat on a Hot Tin Roof.* Since he began writing in the late Thirties, he has written not only one-act and full-length plays, but he is the author of books of poetry, short stories, a novel, and screen plays, and ten of his works have been made into motion pictures.

Mr. Williams was born March 26, 1912, in Columbus, Miss., the son of Cornelius Coffin Williams, a traveling salesman and descendant of Tennessee pioneers. His mother was from New England Quaker

stock. Part of his childhood was spent at the home of his grandfather, an Episcopal clergyman in the town of his birth. He changed his name from Thomas Lanier Williams, under which he had written considerable youthful poetry, when he began to try to sell his short stories which he wrote as a college student. His education at the University of Missouri, 1931–33, was interrupted for financial reasons. He took his B.A. degree in 1938 from the University of Louisiana.

Although a published poet when very young, and although his first short story was published in *Story* Magazine in 1939, Mr. Williams feels that his major recognition came in 1940 when he received a Rockefeller Fellowship and his first play, *Battle of Angels,* was produced in Boston by the Theatre Guild. His first financial break, which enabled him to give full attention to his writing, came with an offer from Metro-Goldwyn-Mayer, taking him from a $17 a week ushering job to a screen-writing job at $250 a week, out of which he saved enough to write *The Glass Menagerie,* which won the Drama Critics Circle Award in 1944.

Besides the Pulitzer Prizes, Tennessee Williams won the Drama Critics Circle Award for *Streetcar,* in 1947, and the same group's award for *Cat on a Hot Tin Roof,* in 1954, and for *The Night of the Iguana,* 1962. He was the recipient of the Brandeis University Creative Arts Medal in Theatre in 1965. In 1969 he won the highest honor, the Gold Medal for Drama, bestowed by the National Academy of Arts and Letters.

Battle of Angels (play), New Directions, 1945 (produced in Boston, 1940)

The Glass Menagerie, Random, 1945 (produced in New York, 1944)

Twenty Seven Wagons Full of Cotton (produced, 1955) *and Other One-Act Plays,* New Directions, 1946, 1953

You Touched Me! (three-act comedy) with Donald Windham, S. French, 1947 (produced, 1946)

A Streetcar Named Desire (play) ND,

1947, revised edition, Dramatists Play Service, 1953

American Blue (four one-act plays), Dramatists Play Service, 1948

Summer and Smoke (play), ND, 1948

One Arm and Other Stories, ND, 1948

The Roman Spring of Mrs. Stone (novel), ND, 1950

I Rise in Flame Cried the Phoenix (play), J. Laughlin, 1951 (produced, 1959)

The Rose Tattoo (play), ND, 1951 (produced, 1950)

*Camino Real (play), ND, 1953

Hard Candy (short stories), ND, 1954, 1967

Cat on a Hot Tin Roof (play), ND, 1955

Baby Doll (film script), ND, 1956

In the Winter of Cities (poems), ND, 1956

Four Plays, Secker & Warburg, 1956

Orpheus Descending (rewriting of *Battle of Angels*), ND, 1958 revised acting ed. Dramatists Play Service, 1959 (produced, 1957)

Suddenly Last Summer (play), ND, 1958 (produced, 1957)

The Rose Tattoo and *Camino Real,* Penguin, 1958

A Perfect Analysis Given by a Parrot (play), Dramatists Play Service, 1958 (not produced)

Sweet Bird of Youth (play), ND, 1959, revised ed., 1962

A Streetcar Named Desire and *The Glass Menagerie,* Penguin, 1959

Garden District (consisting of *Something Unspoken* and *Suddenly Last Summer*), Secker & Warburg, 1959 (produced, 1957)

Period of Adjustment (play), ND, 1960 (produced in Miami, 1959, co-directed by Williams, produced in New York, 1960)

Three Players of a Summer Game and Other Stories, Secker & Warburg, 1960

The Night of the Iguana (play), ND, 1961

Orpheus Descending, Something Unspoken, Suddenly Last Summer, Penguin, 1961

Five Plays, Secker & Warburg, 1962

The Milk Train Doesn't Stop Here Anymore, ND, 1964 (produced, 1963, revised text produced, 1964)

The Eccentricities of a Nightingale and *Summer and Smoke,* ND, 1965

The Knightly Quest, a novella and four short stories, ND, 1967

The Two Character Play, produced in England, 1967, limited edition, ND, 1969

The Dragon Country, containing eight plays: *The Slapstick Tragedies (The Mutilated* and *The Gnädige Fraulein*), *In the Bar of a Tokyo Hotel, Confessional, I Rise in Flame Cried the Phoenix, I Cannot Imagine Tomorrow, A Perfect Analysis Given by a Parrot,* and *The Frosted Glass Coffin,* New Directions, 1970

Short plays include "The Lady of Larkspur Lotion," "The Purification," (later a ballet), "This Property is Condemned," (produced off-Broadway, 1956), and "Portrait of a Madonna," (produced, 1959). Wrote libretto for Raffaello de Banfield's *Lord Byron's Love Letter,* Ricordi, 1955

Films based on his works: "The Glass Menagerie," "A Streetcar Named Desire," "Summer and Smoke," "The Roman Spring of Mrs. Stone," "The Rose Tattoo," "Cat on a Hot Tin Roof," "Suddenly Last Summer," "The Fugitive Kind," (based on *Orpheus Descending*), "Sweet Bird of Youth," "Period of Adjustment," and "The Night of the Iguana," "Boom," (based on *The Milk Train Doesn't Stop Here Anymore*).

TOM (THOMAS KENNERLY, JR.) WOLFE was born in Richmond, Virginia, March 2, 1931, son of a scientist and business executive, Thomas Kennerly and Helen (Hughes) Wolfe. He was educated at Washington and Lee University, B.A., 1951, and at Yale University, where he took his doctorate in American Studies in 1957.

Beginning as a reporter with Springfield *Union,* Springfield, Massachusetts, where he remained from 1956 to 1959, he went to work next for the Washington

Post, until 1962. He was a writer for the New York *Herald Tribune* until its collapse. He has contributed frequently to *New York Magazine.*

In his feature work, Mr. Wolfe has initiated a new style in contemporary journalistic writing and although he has published few books, his influence has been felt through his magazine and hardcover works. He is also an illustrator. He received Front Page Awards for humor and foreign news reporting (Washington Newspaper Guild) in 1961.

The Kandy-Kolored Tangerine-Flake Streamline Baby (essays), Farrar, 1965
The Pump-House Gang (essays) Farrar, 1968
*The Electric Kool-Aid Acid Test (chronicle) Farrar, 1968

HERMAN WOUK, whose novel *The Caine Mutiny* was one of the most widely read books coming out of World War II and won the Pulitzer Prize for fiction in 1952, was born in New York City, May 27, 1915. He graduated from Columbia University in 1934 and spent the next six years in radio work, much of it as a writer for the comedian Fred Allen. In World War II he served as a naval officer of the line, his last post second in command of the U.S.S. *Southard.* He was awarded four campaign stars, and a minesweeper on which he served received a unit commendation for its service in the Solomons campaign.

Five of Mr. Wouk's works have been made into motion pictures. *The Caine Mutiny,* one part of which the author dramatized himself, was at one time running on Broadway at the same time it was being shown in a film version.

Mr. Wouk in 1941 served as a dollar-a-year presidential consulting expert to the United States Treasury. He taught writing as visiting professor at Yeshiva University in New York from 1953 to 1957. He was awarded the Columbia University medal for excellence in 1952 and has received honorary degrees from Yeshiva and Clark Universities.

He married Betty Sarah Brown in 1945; they have two sons and they live in Washington, D.C. He is a member of the board of directors of the Orthodox Jewish Council of Congregations, the Reserve Officers Naval Services, and the Authors' Guild.

He married Betty Sarah Brown in 1945; they have two sons and they live in Washington, D.C. The author is a member of several clubs there, and active in community affairs. Over the years he has been a founder and trustee of several synagogues. He is a council member of the Authors' Guild.

Aurora Dawn (novel), Simon & Schuster, 1947; Doubleday, 1956
The City Boy (novel) Simon & Schuster, 1948; Doubleday, 1952
The Traitor (drama), Samuel French, 1949
The Caine Mutiny (novel), 1951. (This and all following published by Doubleday):
The Caine Mutiny Court-Martial (drama), 1953
Marjorie Morningstar (novel), 1955
Nature's Way (comedy), 1957
This Is My God (non-fiction), 1959
*Youngblood Hawke (novel), 1962
Don't Stop the Carnival (novel), 1965
The City Boy (anniversary ed.), 1969

Lists of Ballot Signers

The 50 authors receiving the highest number of votes in the nationwide balloting:

1	Tennessee Williams	26	Robert Penn Warren
2	John Steinbeck	27	Will and Ariel Durant
3	W. H. Auden	28	Arthur Schlesinger, Jr.
4	J. D. Salinger*	29	James Reston
5	Edward Albee	30	Ogden Nash
6	Thornton Wilder	31	James Michener
7	Arthur Miller	32	Margaret Mead
8	Vladimir Nabokov	33	William L. Shirer
9	Walter Lippmann*	34	John Cheever*
10	Archibald MacLeish	35	Art Buchwald
11	John Kenneth Galbraith	36	Eudora Welty
12	Truman Capote	37	John O'Hara*
13	John Updike	38	Theodore H. White
14	Katharine Anne Porter	39	Bruce Catton
15	Marianne Moore	40	Pearl Buck
16	Robert Lowell	41	William Styron
17	Norman Mailer	42	John Gunther
18	John Dos Passos	43	Mary McCarthy
19	Edmund Wilson*	44	Lillian Hellman*
20	Saul Bellow	45	Erich Fromm
21	William Saroyan	46	Henry Steele Commager
22	James Baldwin	47	Lewis Mumford
23	John Hersey	48	Joseph Wood Krutch
24	Bernard Malamud	49	Barbara W. Tuchman
25	E. B. White	50	Mark Van Doren

The alphabetical listing of the others in the book:

Conrad Aiken	Erskine Caldwell
Isaac Asimov	John Ciardi
Louis Auchincloss	Norman Cousins
John Barth	Malcolm Cowley
John Berryman	James Dickey
Kay Boyle	Richard Eberhart
Gwendolyn Brooks	Ralph Ellison
William F. Buckley, Jr.	James T. Farrell

* Unable to choose their best.

Allen Ginsberg
Joseph Heller
William Inge
James Jones
MacKinlay Kantor
Alfred Kazin
Phyllis McGinley
Henry Miller
Allan Nevins
S. J. Perelman
George Plimpton
Ezra Pound
Philip Roth

Harrison E. Salisbury
Karl Shapiro
Cornelia Otis Skinner
Jean Stafford
Irving Stone
Jesse Stuart
Allen Tate
Lionel Trilling
Gore Vidal
Richard Wilbur
Tom Wolfe
Herman Wouk

THE MOST VOTED-UPON AUTHORS IN AMERICA

The following tables show how authors ranked with more than 900 of their fellow authors, critics, librarians, trade personnel and general readers in thirteen categories of nominators who filled out their ballots: (1) authors listed on the ballot itself, (2) special advisors to the editor, (3) members of the American Center of the P.E.N. Club, (4) critics and reviewers, (5) members of the Poetry Society of America, (6) librarians, (7) bookstore personnel, (8) publishers' representatives, and a nationwide cross section of the subscribers of (9) *The Atlantic,* (10) *Harper's Magazine,* (11) the *New York Review of Books,* (12) *Saturday Review,* and (13) a few scattered miscellaneous voters not accounted for in other lists.

BALLOT GROUP NO. I

110 *Authors whose names were on the Ballot . . .* And since this is a book of authors, by authors and voted upon by authors themselves, we are revealing the names of the first fifty authors most heavily voted upon for *This Is My Best.* Ties appeared in the tenth most voted upon authors, and continued thereafter, requiring forty-nine authors to fill the first thirty positions.

1 W. H. Auden
2 Tennessee Williams
3 Thornton Wilder
4 Vladimir Nabokov
5 Edmund Wilson
6 Robert Lowell
7 J. D. Salinger
8 Marianne Moore
9 Arthur Miller
10 John Kenneth Galbraith, Walter Lippmann

11 John Dos Passos, Norman Mailer
12 John Steinbeck
13 Edward Albee, Bernard Malamud
14 John Hersey, Archibald MacLeish, E. B. White
15 Katherine Anne Porter
16 Saul Bellow
17 Truman Capote, Lillian Hellman, Robert Penn Warren
18 William Saroyan, William L. Shirer
19 John Updike, Eudora Welty
20 Arthur M. Schlesinger, Jr., Mark Van Doren
21 Ralph Ellison
22 Ogden Nash
23 Henry Steele Commager, William Styron
24 Conrad Aiken, Mary McCarthy, John O'Hara
25 Bruce Catton, John Cheever, Margaret Mead, James Reston
26 James Baldwin, Lewis Mumford, Barbara W. Tuchman
27 Brooks Atkinson
28 Will Durant
29 Catherine Drinker Bowen, James Michener
30 John Berryman

BALLOT GROUP NO. 2

13 Advisors* in the early formulation of the ballot placed the following 46 authors in the first six positions:

1 John Dos Passos
2 Norman Mailer, Robert Penn Warren
3 John Kenneth Galbraith, Archibald MacLeish, Bernard Malamud, Arthur Miller, Vladimir Nabokov, William L. Shirer, John Steinbeck
4 Edward Albee, Truman Capote, George F. Kennan, Walter Lippmann, Katherine Anne Porter, J. D. Salinger, Arthur M. Schlesinger, Jr., Barbara W. Tuchman, John Updike, E. B. White, Thornton Wilder, Tennessee Williams, Edmund Wilson
5 Conrad Aiken, Jacques Barzun, Saul Bellow, Bruce Catton, John Cheever, James Gould Cozzens, Will and Ariel Durant, Ralph Ellison, John Hersey, James Jones, Marianne Moore, William Styron
6 W. H. Auden, James Baldwin, Malcolm Cowley, Paul Horgan, Alfred Kazin, Joseph Wood Krutch, S. J. Perelman, James Reston, Lionel Trilling, Mark Van Doren, Eudora Welty

(Dos Passos received 10 of the 13 votes, those in sixth position, 5 votes. Twenty-three other authors on the ballot received 4 votes. Twenty-seven received 3 votes. Sixty received 2 votes. One hundred thirty-six of the 517 authors on the ballot received one vote each. Two hundred eight authors on the ballot received no votes.)

* (Editor's note: The individuals whose advice is gratefully acknowledged and whose individual ballots are, of course, confidential, are listed in Group 2, *The Signers of the Ballots*).

BALLOT GROUP NO. 3

94 *Members of the American Center of the P.E.N.* (Poets, Editors, Novelists) *Club* voted their first ten choices:

1 W. H. Auden
2 Tennessee Williams
3 Vladimir Nabokov
4 Edmund Wilson
5 Robert Lowell
6 Marianne Moore
7 Thornton Wilder
8 Katherine Anne Porter
9 Edward Albee
10 Arthur Miller

BALLOT GROUP NO. 4

46 *Critics and Reviewers* in various cities throughout the country picked nineteen authors (many authors tied) for the "first ten" positions:

1 Tennessee Williams
2 Thornton Wilder
3 Vladimir Nabokov, John Updike
4 Edward Albee
5 Truman Capote, J. D. Salinger
6 Arthur Miller
7 W. H. Auden, Robert Lowell, John Steinbeck
8 Norman Mailer, Marianne Moore, Katherine Anne Porter
9 William Styron, Edmund Wilson
10 Ogden Nash, James Reston, Robert Penn Warren

BALLOT GROUP NO. 5

147 *Members of the Poetry Society of America* nominated the following authors in this order as their first ten choices:

1 W. H. Auden
2 Tennessee Williams
3 Arthur Miller
4 Archibald MacLeish
5 John Steinbeck
6 J. D. Salinger
7 Robert Lowell
8 Katherine Anne Porter
10 Walter Lippmann

BALLOT GROUP NO. 6

34 *Librarians,* and their first ten choices:

1 John Dos Passos, John Steinbeck
2 James Michener
3 Pearl Buck, Truman Capote, Katherine Anne Porter, Thornton Wilder
4 Bruce Catton, Will Durant, Paul Gallico, John Hersey, Arthur Miller, William Saroyan, John Updike, Tennessee Williams
5 MacKinlay Kantor, Vladimir Nabokov, Irving Stone
6 Isaac Asimov, Marianne Moore, Ogden Nash, J. D. Salinger
7 Conrad Aiken, Brooks Atkinson, James Baldwin, John O'Hara, Herman Wouk
8 Henry Steele Commager, Norman Cousins, Walter Lippmann
9 Louis Auchincloss, W. H. Auden, John Kenneth Galbraith, John Gunther, Bernard Malamud, Henry Miller, Arthur M. Schlesinger, Jr., Leon Uris, Gore Vidal
10 Edward Albee, John Ciardi, Lillian Hellman, Joseph Wood Krutch, William L. Shirer

BALLOT GROUP NO. 7

50 *Bookstore Personnel,* and their nominations in the first ten positions:

1 Tennessee Williams
2 John Steinbeck
3 Bruce Catton, John Kenneth Galbraith, James Michener, J. D. Salinger
4 John Cheever, E. B. White
5 Edward Albee, Will Durant
6 Catherine Drinker Bowen, John Updike
7 Louis Auchincloss, John Ciardi, John Gunther, Joseph Wood Krutch, John O'Hara, William L. Shirer
8 Saul Bellow, John Hersey, Phyllis McGinley, Arthur Miller, Irving Stone
9 Ayn Rand, Leon Uris
10 William F. Buckley, Jr., James Gould Cozzens, Bernard Malamud, Marianne Moore, Ogden Nash

BALLOT GROUP NO. 8

45 *Publishers' Representatives,* and their first ten positions:

1 J. D. Salinger
2 Truman Capote, Bruce Catton, James Michener
3 Edward Albee, John K. Galbraith, John Steinbeck, Tennessee Williams
4 Arthur M. Schlesinger, Jr.
5 John Updike
6 Allen Drury, Arthur Hailey

1046

7 Art Buchwald, John O'Hara
8 John Barth, Theodore H. White, Thornton Wilder, Herman Wouk
9 William F. Buckley, Jr., Paddy Chayefsky, John Dos Passos, MacKinlay Kantor, Arthur Miller, William L. Shirer, Irving Stone
10 Will Durant, Walter Lippmann, William Saroyan, Upton Sinclair

BALLOT GROUP NO. 9

97 *Subscribers to* The Atlantic, and their authors in the first ten positions:

1 Walter Lippmann
2 John Steinbeck
3 Tennessee Williams
4 John Kenneth Galbraith
5 Arthur Miller
6 Truman Capote, J. D. Salinger
7 Art Buchwald, Arthur M. Schlesinger, Jr.
8 William L. Shirer
9 Will Durant
10 John Gunther, Margaret Mead

BALLOT GROUP NO. 10

85 *Subscribers to* Harper's *Magazine,* and their choices in the first ten positions:

1 John Steinbeck
2 John Kenneth Galbraith, James Michener
3 Tennessee Williams
4 Arthur Miller, Thornton Wilder
5 Bruce Catton, J. D. Salinger
6 Edward Albee
7 Archibald MacLeish, John Updike
8 Art Buchwald
9 Pearl Buck, Will Durant, John Hersey, Walter Lippmann, Ogden Nash
10 Truman Capote, John Gunther, Arthur M. Schlesinger, Jr.

BALLOT GROUP NO. 11

70 *Subscribers to the* New York Review of Books, and their first ten choices:

1 Edward Albee
2 Tennessee Williams
3 James Baldwin, Vladimir Nabokov, J. D. Salinger
4 Archibald MacLeish, John Updike
5 Saul Bellow

6 Norman Mailer
7 W. H. Auden
8 Robert Lowell, John Steinbeck
9 Bernard Malamud
10 Erich Fromm, Edmund Wilson

BALLOT GROUP NO. 12

96 *Subscribers to* The Saturday Review, and their first ten choices:

1 John Steinbeck
2 Tennessee Williams
3 Arthur Miller
4 Edward Albee, J. D. Salinger
5 Archibald MacLeish
6 Thornton Wilder
7 William L. Shirer
8 Truman Capote, John Kenneth Galbraith
9 Art Buchwald, James Michener
10 Pearl Buck, John Ciardi, William Saroyan

BALLOT GROUP NO. 13

12 *Miscellaneous Public Figures.* (Ties produced 50 authors in the first four places)

1 W. H. Auden
2 Pearl Buck, Walter Lippmann, Archibald MacLeish
3 Bruce Catton, Norman Cousins, Will Durant, John Kenneth Galbraith, John Gunther, William Inge, Phyllis McGinley, Margaret Mead, James A. Michener, Arthur Miller, Marianne Moore, Ogden Nash, J. D. Salinger, William Saroyan, Theodore Sorensen, John Steinbeck, Thornton Wilder, Tennessee Williams, Herman Wouk
4 Edward Albee, Robert Anderson, Brooks Atkinson, Louis Auchincloss, Art Buchwald, Truman Capote, John Ciardi, John Dos Passos, Clifton Fadiman, Paul Gallico, Lillian Hellman, John Hersey, Gilbert Highet, James Jones, Jean Kerr, Walter Kerr, Harper Lee, Norman Mailer, Lewis Mumford, John O'Hara, James Reston, William L. Shirer, Cornelia Otis Skinner, Barbara W. Tuchman, Mark Van Doren, Gore Vidal, E. B. White

THE SIGNERS OF THE BALLOTS

The Editor wishes to thank the individuals who took the time to study a list of 517 authors and to sign their names to the ballots on which they recorded their choices of those authors they thought most suitable for inclusion in this book. And thanks are due, too, to those who filled out the ballots but did not wish, as a member of one group or another, to sign them.

AUTHORS WHOSE NAMES WERE ON THE BALLOTS

BALLOT GROUP NO. I

Leonie Adams, New Milford, Conn.; Conrad Aiken, Brewster, Mass.; Daisy Aldan, New York, N.Y.; Sidney Alexander, Florence, Italy; William Alfred, Cambridge, Mass.; Brother Antoninus, Oakland, Calif.; Isaac Asimov, West Newton, Mass.; John Bakeless, Seymour, Conn.; Melanie Gordon Barber, Taconic, Conn.; Donald Barthelme, New York, N.Y.; Robert Bly, Madison, Minn.; Arna Bontemps, Nashville, Tenn.; Hal Borland, Salisbury, Conn.; Ray Bradbury, Los Angeles, Calif.; Frederick Buechner, Saratoga, Calif.; Hallie Burnett, Wilton, Conn.; Erskine Caldwell, Dunedin, Fla.; Taylor Caldwell, Buffalo, N.Y.; Melville Cane, New York, N.Y.; Tristram Coffin, Chevy Chase, Md.; Margaret L. Coit, Rutherford, N.J.; Marc Connelly, New York, N.Y.; Frank Conroy, Brooklyn, N.Y.; Malcolm Cowley, Sherman, Conn.; Babette Deutsch, New York, N.Y.; Borden Deal, Sarasota, Fla.; Richard Eberhart, Hanover, N.H.; Richard Ellman, New Haven, Conn.; Richard M. Elmann, New York, N.Y.; James T. Flexner, New York, N.Y.; Thomas Gallagher, New York, N.Y.; William H. Gass, West Lafayette, Ind.; Peter Gay, New York, N.Y.; Maxwell Geismar, Harrison, N.Y.; Martha Gellhorn, London, England; K. B. Gilden, Bridgeport, Conn.; Allen Ginsberg, New York, N.Y.; Harry Golden, Charlotte, N.C.; William Goyen, New York, N.Y.; Gerald Green, Stamford, Conn.; Nancy Hale, Charlottesville, Va.; Donald Hall, Ann Arbor, Mich.; Roger Hilsman, New York, N.Y.; Daniel Hoffman, Swarthmore, Pa.; Edgar Johnson, New York, N.Y.; Gerald W. Johnson, Baltimore, Md.; Stanley Kaufman, New York, N.Y.; Justin Kaplan, Cambridge, Mass.; Alexander Klein, New York, N.Y.; Fletcher Knebel, Princeton, N.J.; Joseph Wood Krutch, Tucson, Ariz.; Jeremy Larner, New York, N.Y.; Mary Lavin, Bective, Ireland; Victoria Lincoln, Baltimore, Md.; Louis P. Lochner, Fair Haven, N.J.; Stefan Lorant, Lenox, Mass.; Ross MacDonald, Santa Barbara, Calif.; Ashley Montagu, Princeton, N.J.; Willie Morris, Old Greenwich, Conn.; Anais Nin, New York, N.Y.; Elder Olson, Chicago, Ill.; Bentz Plagemann, Palisades, N.Y.; Richard Poirier, New Brunswick, N.J.; Katherine Anne Porter, Washington, D.C.; Chaim Potok, Philadelphia, Pa.; Roger Price, New York, N.Y.; Vermont Royster, New York, N.Y.; Harrison E. Salisbury, New York, N.Y.; Winthrop Sargeant, New York, N.Y.; Richard Schickel, New York, N.Y.; Mark Schorer, Berkeley, Calif.; Frank G. Slaughter, Jacksonville, Fla.; William Stafford, Lake Oswego, Oreg.; Elizabeth Spencer, Quebec, Canada; John Steinbeck, New York, N.Y.; Jesse Stuart, Greenup, Ky.; Frank Sullivan, Saratoga Springs, N.Y.; May Swenson, Sea Cliff, N.Y.; Richard Tregaskis, Honolulu, Hawaii; John Toland, Danbury, Conn.; Diana Trilling, New York, N.Y.; Agnes Sligh Turnbull, Maplewood, N.J.; Joseph Tusiani, New York, N.Y.; Jean Starr Untermeyer, New York, N.Y.; Mark Van Doren, Falls Village, Conn.; Kurt Vonnegut, Jr., West Barnstable, Mass.; Diana Wakoski, New York, N.Y.; Aileen Ward, Cambridge, Mass.; Gerald Weales, Philadelphia, Pa.; George Weller, Rome; Evelyn Wells, Seattle,

Wash.; John Hall Wheelock, New York, N.Y.; William H. Whyte, New York, N.Y.; Tom Wolfe, New York, N.Y.; Frank G. Yerby, New York, N.Y.; Marguerite Young, New York, N.Y.;

ADVISORS PRIOR TO BALLOTING

BALLOT GROUP NO. 2

John Barkham, critic and reviewer of the *Saturday Review* Syndicate; Norman Cousins, author, editor *Saturday Review;* John Gunther, journalist-historian, novelist; Loyd Haberly, poet, former president of the Poetry Society of America, dean of arts and sciences, Fairleigh Dickinson University, Rutherford, N.J.; Robert Halsband, author, associate professor of English, Columbia University, and President, American Center of the P.E.N. Club, New York; Harry Hansen, author, editor, critic; Hiram Haydn, author, publisher, editor *The American Scholar,* Washington, D.C.; Robert Lowell, poet, New York; Allan Nevins, historian, San Marino, California; a National Book Award judge who asked his name be withheld; William Peden, Professor of English, University of Missouri, author and short story analyst; Harry Scherman, founder and chairman Book-of-the-Month Club, and Hallie Burnett, novelist, teacher, and for many years co-editor of the magazine *STORY*.

MEMBERS OF THE AMERICAN CENTER OF THE P.E.N. (Poets, Editors, Novelists) CLUB

BALLOT GROUP NO. 3

Aaron Asher, Viking Press, N.Y.; Beril Becker, New York City; Harry Behn, Greenwich, Conn.; Robert Bendiner, Huntington, N.Y.; Ann Birstein, New York City; Warren Bower, New York City; Millen Brand, New York City; Herma Briffault, New York City; Faubion Bowers, New York City; Peg Bracker, Bolinas, Calif.; Abraham S. Burack, Editor, *The Writer,* Boston; Margaret Freeman Cabell (Mrs. James Branch) Richmond, Va.; William Cole, New York City; J. V. Cunningham, Sudbury, Mass.; Mrs. Anita Daniel, New York City; Christopher Davis, Philadelphia, Pa.; Peter Davison, Little-Brown, Boston; Roger B. Dooley, New York City; Edward Ellsberg, Southwest Harbor, Me.; John Farrar, New York City; Feike Feikema, Luverne, Minn.; K. v. Fraunhofer, New York City; Anne Fremantle, New York City; Eleanor Friede, New York City; Walker Gibson, Amherst, Mass.; Eleanor Gilchrist, Sharon, Conn.; M. A. Goldzieher, New York City; Henry F. Graff, Scarsdale, N.Y.; Allen Grauer, New York City; Josh Greenfeld, Croton on Hudson, New York; Nicholas Halvor, New York

City; Worth Tuttle Hedden, Westport, Conn.; Diana Chang Herrmann, New York City; Cecilia Holland, Woodbridge, Conn.; Riley Hughes, Georgetown University, Washington, D.C.; Calvin Kentfield, Stinson Beach, Calif.; Ruth Adams Knight, South Pasadena, Calif.; Ferenc Kormendi, Washington, D.C.; Helen La Pente, New York City; Harding LeMay, New York City; Emil Lengyel, New York City; Leonard C. Lewin, Taconic, Conn.; Alison Lurie, Ithaca, New York; Richard Lyons, Fargo, N.D.; Frank MacShane, Columbia University; Tom Mahoney, New York City; James McCague, Sarasota, Fla.; David McDowell, New York City; Larry McMurty, Houston, Tex.; Frederick Morgan, *The Hudson Review,* New York City; Howard Moss, New York City; Cyril Peyers, New York City; Arnold A. Rogow, Nyack, N.Y.; Ralph Ross, Claremont, Calif.; H. B. Rouse, Fayetteville, Ark.; Mrs. Joan A. Sanders, Logan, Utah; Nina Schneider, New York City; Webster Schott, Kansas City, Mo.; Sigrid Schultz, Westport, Conn.; Mrs. Samuel Shellabarger, Princeton, N.J.; James A. Silberman, Random House, New York; Lore Segal, New York City; Joseph T. Shipley, New York City; William Sloane, Rutgers University Press, New Brunswick, N.J.; T. O'Conor Sloane III, Westport, Conn.; Donald G. Stanford, Baton Rouge, La.; Mark Strand, New York City; Richard Taplinger, New York City; John Tebbel, New York City; Martin Tucker, Brooklyn, N.Y.; H. W. Varself, New York City; Gordon Weber, New York City; Lael Tucker Wertenbaker, Marlborough, N.H.; Victor Weybright, New York City; Thaddeus A. Wittlin, Washington, D.C.; Louis Zara, Philadelphia, Pa.

CRITICS, REVIEWERS

BALLOT GROUP NO. 4

Phoebe-Lou Adams, Boston; Holmes Alexander, Tampa, Fla.; L. T. Anderson, *Charleston* (W. Va.) *Gazette;* Gerald Ashford, *Express and News,* San Antonio, Tex.; Malcolm Bauer, *The Oregonian,* Portland, Ore.; Van Allen Bradley, *Chicago Daily News;* J. Adger Brown, the *State Newspaper,* Columbia, S.C.; Ernest Cady, *The Columbus Dispatch,* Columbus, O.; Harriet Doar, *Charlotte,* (N.C.) *Observer;* John Dorsey, *Sunday Sun,* Baltimore; William M. Dwyer, *Trenton* (N.J.) *Times;* Norman Fournier, *Maine Sunday Telegram,* Portland, Me.; Philip C. Fastwater, Sacramento, Calif.; James Garrett, *The Cleveland Press;* Cody Hall, *Anniston Star,* Alabama; Victor P. Hass, *Omaha World-Herald;* Joseph G. Herzberg, *New York Times;* Ralph Hickock, *The Standard-Times,* New Bedford, Mass.; Vernice Hillier, Odessa, Tex.; Ed Hirshberg, *St. Petersburg Times,* Fla.; Diana Hobby, *The Houston Post;* William Hogan, *San Francisco Chronicle;* Theodore L. Holden, *The Hartford Times,* Conn.; Elizabeth North Hoyt, Cedar Rapids; Herbert H. Hyde, *The Lincoln Journal,* Nebraska; Norman Julian, *Dominion News Panorama,* Morgantown, W. Va.; Herbert A. Kenny. *Boston Globe;* C. W. Johnson, *News and Leader,* Springfield, Mo.; Duane LaFleche, *The Knickerbocker News,* Albany, N.Y.; James R. McAdory, Jr., *The Birmingham News,* Ala.; Thorpe Menn, *Kansas City Star,* Mo.; William R. Melton, Jr., La Habra, Calif.; Mrs. Ann Lloyd Merrionan, *The News Leader,* Richmond, Va.; Virginia Pasley, *News Day,* Long Island City, N.Y.; Peter S. Prescott, *Look,* New York, N.Y.; John Raymond, *The Atlanta Journal-Constitution,* Ga.; James S. Richmond, Savannah, Ga.; Leonard Sanders, Fort Worth, Texas; Fred Shaw, South Miami, Fla.; Donald Stanley, Lagunitas,

Calif.; Edwin Tribble, *Washington Star,* D.C.; Daisy S. Quaker, *Ledger-Enquirer,* Columbus, Ga.; Ben Wasson, *Delta Democrat-Times,* Greenvilla, Miss.; Geoffrey A. Wolff, Washington, D.C.; Robert Woessner, *Press-Gazette,* Green Bay, Wis.

MEMBERS OF THE POETRY SOCIETY OF AMERICA

BALLOT GROUP NO. 5

Bernice Ames, Los Angeles; Mrs. Helen Fraser Aronson, Washington, D.C.; John Williams Andrews, Westport, Conn.; Marguerite Enlow Barze, Daytona Beach, Fla.; Lynne Belaiel, New York, N.Y.; Madeline Benedict, New York, N.Y.; Sue Abbott Boyd, Ft. Smith, Ark.; Kate Brackett, Pigeon Cove, Mass.; Bruce Bennett Brown, Zebulon-on-Coon, Ky.; Marel Bronen, Atlanta, Ga.; Hugh F. Burgess, McDonogh, Md.; Donald J. Calby, San Jose, Calif.; Madison Cawlin, Denville, N.J.; Eleanor Alletta Chaffee, Ridgewood, N.J.; Margaret Brewster Chard, Brunswick, Me.; David R. Clark, Amherst, Mass.; Joseph Cohen, Boston, Mass.; E. R. Cole, Yakima, Wash.; Mary Ann Coleman, Athens, Ga.; Francis Colvin, Burbank, Calif.; Marion Collins, Albany, N.Y.; Hasye Cooperman, N.Y.C.; Howard McKinley Corning, Portland, Oreg.; Elizabeth E. P. Dabrey, Norfolk, Va.; Clarence Decker, New York, N.Y.; Harriet L. Delafield, Saranac Lake, N.Y.; Albert DePietro, Garden City, N.Y.; Dr. Alfred Dorn, Long Island City, N.Y.; Cornelia P. Draves, New Hyde Park, N.Y.; Prof. Fraser Drew, Kenmore, N.Y.; Evelyn Eaton, Lone Pine, Calif.; Richard Esler, Tarentum, Pa.; Thelma Finefrock, Palmer Lake, Colo.; Paris Flammonde, New York, N.Y.; Ruby Fogel, Miami Beach, Fla.; Jean Robert Foster, Schenectady, N.Y.; Nelchen Foster, Tenafly, N.J.; Isabella Gardner, New York, N.Y.; Roberta B. Goldstein, Burlington, Vt.; Guanetta Gordon, Annandale, Va.; Darcy Gottlieb, Jackson Heights, N.Y.; Arthur Gregor, New York, N.Y.; Mary Gregory, Pelham, N.Y.; Amanda Benjamin Hall, New London, Conn.; Barbara Harr, New York, N.Y.; Hyacinthe Hill, New York, N.Y.; Aletha Humphreys, Toledo, Iowa; Lyris Hyatt, Bryn Athyn, Pa.; Clara Hyde, Winter Park, Fla.; Colette Inez, New York, N.Y.; Roderick Jellena, Adelphi, Md.; Ann Jonas, Louisville, Ky.; Hannah Kahn, Miami, Fla.; Martha Keller, Drexel Hill, Pa.; James H. Koch, New York, N.Y.; Ann Kregal, New York, N.Y.; Fania Kruger, Austin, Tex.; Clifford J. Laube, Ozone Park, N.Y.; Jacques Le Clercq, New York, N.Y.; Cornel Adam Legyel, Georgetown, Calif.; Theodore Lavington, Staten Island, N.Y.; Florence Becker Lennon, Boulder, Colo.; Dominick J. Lepore, Enfield, Conn.; Cecil Robert Lloyd, Santa Fe, N. Mex.; Will Luman, The American University, Washington, D.C.; E. Louise Mally, New York, N.Y.; Margery Mansfield, Monterey, Mass.; Harry M. Meacham, Richmond, Va.; J. Wm. Myers, Pittsburgh, Pa.; Starr Nelson, New Britain, Conn.; Mrs. H. J. Nicolais, Laguna Niguel, Calif.; Mary Oliver, Provincetown, Mass.; William Packard, New York, N.Y.; Winthrop Palmer, Oyster Bay, N.Y.; Grace Perry, N.S.W., Australia; Frank Peters, Glendale Calif.; Alvin Reiss, Jacksonville, Oreg.; Dorothy Lee Richardson, Cambridge, Mass.; Elisavietta Ritchee, Washington, D.C.; Liboria Romano, New York, N.Y.; Elizabeth Rose, South Egremont, Mass.; Larry Rubin, Emory University, Atlanta, Ga.; Maude Rubin, Santa Ana, Calif.; Victoria Rudd, Mamaroneck, N.Y.; Maria M. Rushing, Fayetteville, Ark.; F. H. Savage, Scarsdale, N.Y.; Aaron Schmuller, Brooklyn, N.Y.;

Myra Scovel, Stony Point, N.Y.; Ralph W. Seager, Penn Yan, N.Y.; Prof. William W. Seward, Jr., Norfolk, Va.; Knute Skinner, County Clare, Ireland; Hiram Lyday Sloanaker, Belmont, Mass.; Woodridge Spears, Georgetown, Ky.; Margaret Stavely, Chestertown, Md.; J. Stern, Florida State U., Tallahassee, Fla.; Bernice A. Stevens, Gatlinburg, Tenn.; Norma Mclain Stoop, Greenwich, Conn.; Adrian Stoutenburg, Lagunitas, Calif.; Nancy Sullivan, Peace Dale, R.I.; Thomas Burnett Swann, Boca Raton, Fla.; Mary G. Swope, Weston, Mass.; Richard Snyder, Ashland, Ohio; Alice Mackenzie Swaim, Dillsburg, Penn.; Janice Thaddeus, New York, N.Y.; John Thornton, New York, N.Y.; Forence N. Trefethen, Lexington, Mass.; Harvey Tucker, Brooklyn, N.Y.; William S. Wabnitz, Cincinnati; Iram Wassall, Wichita, Kans.; Mary Ball Westerlind, Nancy Willard, Poughkeepsie, N.Y.; Edward A. Williams, Buffalo, N.Y.; Loring Williams, South Berwick, Me.; Wallace Winchell, Broad Brook, Conn.; Katherine Walcott, Red Bank, N.J.; Celeste T. Wright, Davis, Calif.; Roscoe C. Wright, Jamaica, N.Y.; Jane Yolen, Conway, Mass.

LIBRARIANS

BALLOT GROUP NO. 6

Mrs. Benjamin Ackley, H. W. Smith Jr. High School, Syracuse, N.Y.; Miss Catherine Beal, Supervisor Extension Services, Omaha Public Library, Omaha, Neb.; Kay E. Beighle, Jackson-Wilson H. S. Library, Jackson, Wyo.; Mrs. H. H. Bennett, Dover, Del.; Juliana Brown, New York, N. Y.; Marva C. Brown, Washington County Librarian, St. George, Utah; Marian R. Capozzi, Baltimore, Md.; Joan E. Clark, Elsmere, N.Y.; Mrs. Edgar Detjer, Kiel Public Lib., Kiel, Wis.; Miami Beach Public Library, Miami, Fla.; Mrs. Agnes Farris, Roaring Fork High School, Carbondale, Colo.; Mrs. Lyn Hart, Enoch Pratt Free Library, Baltimore; Helen Hartup, High School Librarian, Wapako- neta, Ohio; Sister Helen, librarian, Sacred Heart College, Wichita, Kans.; Carol Ann Henka, Kewaskum, Wis.; Ida Hoaglund, Grand Valley High School, Grand Valley, Colo.; John D. Horgan, Carson City High School, Carson City, Nev.; Lenore R. Imandi, Greystone Elementary School, North Providence, R.I.; E. A. Johnson, Library Association of Portland, Portland, Oreg.; J. E. Kramer, Port Washington High School, Port Washington, Wis.; Laramie County Library System, Cheyenne, Wyo.; Gene Martin, Daniel Boone Regional Library, Columbia, Mo.; Nina Martin, Montgomery, Ala.; Sam Molad, West Hartford, Conn.; Eric Moon, *Library Journal*, New York, N.Y.; India A. Newton, Shasta College, Redding, Calif.; Brantley H. Parsley, Campbellsville College Library, Campbellsville, Ky.; Jean H. Porter, Director—WNY Regional Library Center, Medina, N.Y.; Augusta R. Richardson, Director—Northeast Regional Library, Corinth, Miss.; Emily Sheftall, Augusta Prep. School, Augusta, Ga.; Mary C. Shemorry, Williston, N. Dak.; Anna Hall Terry, Hillsborough High School, Tampa, Fla.; Richard Uhler, Monkton, Md.; Faye Wade, Northside High School, Fort Smith, Ark.; A. M. Wilson, Highline College, Midway, Wash.

BOOKSTORE PERSONNEL

BALLOT GROUP NO. 7

Elizabeth Agee, bookseller, Birmingham, Ala.; Nancy Brown, Des Moines, Iowa; Alice Carlson, Minneapolis, Minn.; Jerry Charlier, Kankakee, Ill.; Clapp & Tuttle, Woodbury, Conn.; Harlan Davidson, Northfield, Ill.; Henry L. Daignault, Jr., Hartford, Conn.; Mrs. E. W. DeMotte, Corner Bookstore, Ithaca, N.Y.; Dan Everett, Columbus, Ohio; Rosemary V. Forester, Houston, Texas; Georgia Glynn, Cincinnati, Ohio; Robert Harwood, Norwich, Conn.; H. Joseph Houlihan, Lexington, Ky.; Philip A. Hubert, Jr., The Sou'wester Bookshop, Bellport, N.Y.; Trumbull Huntington, Hartford, Conn.; William J. Johnston, Little Silver Book Shop, Little Silver, N.J.; Mary C. Kennedy, Oxford, Conn.; Phoebe C. Kline, Westport, Conn.; Jules Kronish, Hamden, Conn.; Agnes Krarup, Pittsburgh, Pa.; W. H. Kuralt, The Intimate Bookshop, Chapel Hill, N.C.; Norbert A. Kustka, Manitowoc, Wis.; Nancy Herman, Horizon Book Store, Traverse City, Mich.; Raymond F. Male, Princeton, N.J.; Sylvia Mathew, Ratcliffe Book Store, Lawton, Okla.; M. Maytag, Unicorn Book Shop, Goleta, Calif.; M. Muse and P. Schober, Elk Grove Village, Ill.; Evilyn Nantz, Greensboro, N.C.; Lucile B. Oliver, Olivers' Book Shop, Tulsa, Okla.; Pat Robinson, Hanover N.H.; Mary Read Rogers, Wyoming State Library, coordinator of Publications and Public Relations, Cheyenne Wyo.; Ishbel Ross, New York, N.Y.; Rachel Shute, Columbus, Miss.; Margaret W. Smith, Columbus, Ohio; Leroy Soper, University Book Store, Seattle, Wash.; Ethel Woodward Stanton, Seattle, Wash.; Mrs. Charles Stough, Lawrence, Kan.; Robert Sutherlin, Iowa City, Iowa; R. J. Tappert, Greenport, N.Y.; Fay Taylor, Oklahoma City, Okla.; James H. Tibbetts, Altadena, Calif.; Damon L. Webb, Dallas, Tex.; Thomas G. Young, Brown's Book Shop, Madison, Wis.

PUBLISHERS REPRESENTATIVES

BALLOT GROUP NO. 8

Richard A. Adams, Skaneateles, N.Y.; S. Tremaine Arkley, Jr., Seattle, Wash.; William E. Bartels, District Manager, San Bruno, Calif.; Bob Breinholt, Fresno, Calif., Jule Brousseau-Roth, Stamford, Conn.; Harold M. Brown, Venice, Fla.; Richard Butcher, Sharonville, Ohio; Jim Charlton, Doubleday Sales Dept.; Bruce A. DeGarmo, Walnut Creek, Calif.; Charles de Grasse, Philadelphia, Pa.; R. R. Dugan, Madison, Fla.; Roger H. Fowler-Dixon, Park Forest, Ill.; Dexter Hamilton, Wauwatosa, Wis.; John F. Kinny, Reading, Mass.; Wayne King, Regional Sales Manager of Doubleday & Co., Prairie Village, Kans.; A. Scott Lepine, Carmichael, Calif.; Richard Lewis, Clinton, Conn.;

Chuck Morrell; George M. Logan, Atlanta, Ga.; Frank J. McCullaugh, Ohio; John E. Moore, Plainwell, Mich.; Carl Oberg, Jr.; Sparta, N.J.; Thomas O'Donohue, Indianapolis, Ind.; J. Daniel Otell, Kittanning, Pa.; Ray Philley, Dallas, Tex.; Aaron Priest, Dallas, Tex.; Waldo W. Ransom, Chicago, Ill.; P. W. Ribble, Longmeadow, Mass.; Ronald B. Robbins, Chagrin Falls, Ohio; Joseph A. Rosock, Silver Spring, Md.; Fred Schmalz-Reidt, Tempe, Ariz.; Bob Shaeffer, Harrisburg, Pa.; Evans Sibert; Ed Springer, Wexford, Pa.; John Thorne, Newport Beach, Calif.; Jane Van Cleve, Lake Oswego, Oreg.; Gerald Wasserman, Columbus, Ohio; Gordon J. Weel, Miami Beach, Fla.; Earl Wilson, San Francisco, Calif.; John D. White, Baltimore, Md.

SUBSCRIBERS TO *THE ATLANTIC*

BALLOT GROUP NO. 9

James W. Alcox, San Carlos, Calif.; Joseph J. Anderson, Carson City, Nev.; Mrs. David Barber, Fort Stanton, N. Mex.; Charles N. Barnum, Beaufort, S.C.; Mrs. Warner W. Bayley, Beaufort, S.C.; James L. Becker, St. Louis, Mo.; S. T. Bendos, St. Louis, Mo.; Ervin Biggs, Morocco, Ind.; Mary Bobev, Highland Park, N.J.; Mrs. Myrtle B. Bond, Charleston, Ark.; Elizabeth Bowen, Craig, Colo.; Esther M. Boyce, San Carlos, Calif.; Lela M. Bush, Wichita, Kans.; Mrs. Champlin Butterfield, Waverly, Tenn.; Clare F. Cabeal, San Carlos, Calif.; Geoffrey N. Carter, St. Louis, Mo.; David Laurence Chamberlain, Sandusky, Ohio; Herbert Cohn, San Carlos, Calif.; Tony Cowan, Nashville, Tenn.; Michael B. Coyle, Elizabethtown, Ky.; J. H. Cunningham, Denver, Colo.; Christie Currie, New Haven, Conn.; David A. Dix, Smyrna, Tenn.; Mrs. Ann C. Driver, Saginaw, Mich.; John O. Emerson, New Haven, Conn.; Curt Frankenstein, Chicago, Ill.; Thomas Garrick, Chicago, Ill.; Mrs. Richard F. Giles, Columbia, S.C.; Hazel Goff, Glenside, Pa.; Joy Gotter, Chicago; Mrs. Leonard W. Hay, Rock Springs, Wyo.; George Henry, Eastman, Ga.; Richard A. Hodges, Palermo, N. Dak.; Pat Houlahan, San Antonio, Tex.; Mrs. George J. Kandzic, Orange Park, Fla.; Paul E. Kelly, Rensselaer, Ind.; Mrs. Pearl Kline, Williston, N. Dak.; Mrs. Philip S Kline, San Antonio, Tex.; Anne Lebkicher, Rollins, Mont.; J. L. Linder, Wichita, Kans.; Virginia Linton, Hilton Head Island, S.C.; Mrs. W. A. Litzenberger, Elizabethtown, Ky.; William Lytle, Saginaw, Mich.; Mrs. Douglas Matz, Hartland, Wis.; Mrs. W. P McClelland, Wichita, Kans.; Mrs. Bertha Milliken, Hundred, W. Va.; Randyll Miseph, Taunton, Mass.; Will W. Moody, M.D., Vaughnsville, Ohio; Edna Muldrow, Holloman A.F.B., N. Mex.; Mrs. Mary Ann Mushel, Big Horn, Mont.; Dale E. Narsten, chairman, English Dept., Foley High School, Foley, Minn.; Kalo Neidert, College of Business Adm., Reno, Nev.; Kraig Noble, Delaware, Ohio; James K. Peterschick, Spokane, Wash.; Miss Jane Peterson, Benton City, Wash.; Marion M. Plunkett, Fort Smith, Ark.; Lyle W. Porter, Moscow, Idaho; Claude H. Powell, Mintorn, Colo.; Rod Radford, Florida State University, Tallahassee Fla.; Sandra Robinette, N. Tazewell, Va.; Edward W. Roberts, Highland Park, N.J.; B. Rothfeld, Perry Point, Md.; Laurence J. Sasso, Jr., Esmond, R.I.; John R. Schell, Minneapolis, Minn; Mrs. Mona Smith, Wichita, Kans.; Mrs. Donald L. Snider, Monticello, Ind.; Henry L. Strangmeyer, Highland Park, N.J.; H. C. Steffan, Asheville, N.C.; Professor Carrie W. Taylor, Union, Oreg.; William H. Tenney, Moscow, Idaho; Doris Todd, White House, Tenn.; Deward E. Walker, Jr.,

Dept. of Social Anthropology, University of Idaho, Moscow, Idaho; Judy Zumwalt, Green River, Wyo.

SUBSCRIBERS TO *HARPER'S MAGAZINE*

BALLOT GROUP NO. 10

Carol Barnum, Atlanta, Ga.; Conaly Bedell, Fort Smith, Ark.; Mrs. William Berger, Englewood, Colo.; John K. Bettersworth, State College, Miss; Prentice Bloedel II, Seattle, Wash.; A. Tom Challis, Cedar City, Utah; Evelyn M. Conger, Hot Springs, S. Dak.; Mrs. Louise C. Daniels, Sanibel Island, Fla.; E. A. Denson, Beltsville, Md.; Robert E. Douglas, St. Joseph, Miss.; Eugene England, S.C.; Irene P. Ertman, St. Joseph, Miss.; Karen Featherman, Elmira, N.Y.; R. G. Geiser, Honolulu, Hawaii; Barbara L. Glasson, Basking Ridge, N.J.; Joclyn Hake, East Providence, R.I.; Lynn L. Hagan, Elmira, N.Y.; Mrs. Joseph Handros, Scottsdale, Ariz.; Ardis Hitelcock, Portland, Oreg.; Lourea J. Holland, Portland, Oreg.; Shirley P. Horning, Wallace, Idaho; Glee Hume, Burkesville, Ky.; Leigh Hunt, Jr., Portland, Oreg.; Leigh Y. Inouye, Honolulu, Hawaii; A. M. Johnston, Fort Meade, S. Dak.; Mary Jean Jones, Murphysboro, Ill.; Mrs. E. S. Juda, St. Joseph, Mo.; Caroline Klock, Wallingford, Vermont; Mrs. Jerry Leake, Lancaster, S.C.; Robert E. Liedquist, Bowie, Md.; Paul S. Koyatch, St. Paul, Minn.; Ray Kirschbaum, Davenport, Iowa; Julie Kisielewski, Beltsville, Md.; Hazel C. Marshall, Grand Blanc, Mich.; Donald W. Marystone, Minneapolis, Minn.; Malcolm R. McDonald, Yakima, Wash.; Betty J. McGillis, Mt. Edgecumbe, Alaska; Ruth McGrail, Hanover, N.H.; Mrs. Dean R. Morgan, Ketchikan, Alaska; Alex Morley, Jackson Hole, Wyo.; Bruce T. Mott, Miles City, Mont.; Mary W. Murphy, Ketchikan, Alaska; Lyle E. Nelson, Starkville, Miss.; Samuel A. North, Atlanta, Ga.; Muriel O'Rorke, Washington, D.C.; Dennis Orwin, W. Lebanon, Ind.; Verna Perry, Sr., Laurel, Del.; Mrs. Donald Peterson, Sitka, Alaska; Robert Poage, Wash.; Hester H. Robinson, St. Joseph, Mo.; Norman Rosenberg, Albuquerque, N. Mex.; Nancy Sasser, Moscow, Idaho; Verda Schlichting, Deadwood, S. Dak.; Howard C. Shepp, Bowie, Md.; T. Suzuki, Honolulu, Hawaii; Myrna Sweeney, Elko, Nev.; Jean Tasaka, Honolulu, Hawaii; Phyllis Rose Thompson, Honolulu, Hawaii; Michael J. Toomey, New Haven, Conn.; Brad Uhlenhake, Rensselaer, Ind.; Sidney Smith, Yakima, Wash.; Nola Talbott, Albany, Ky.; Lucretia J. Talbott, Coalton, W. Va.; Mrs. Bradford Van Ness, Scottsdale, Ariz.; Irving Ward-Steinman, Alexandria, La.; Mrs. T. P. Warrick, Honolulu, Hawaii; Mrs. D. E. Waters, Aiken, S.C.; Patty Watkins, St. Joseph, Miss.; Ruth L. Williams, Fremont, Nebr.

SUBSCRIBERS TO THE
NEW YORK REVIEW OF BOOKS

BALLOT GROUP NO. II

Brent T. Adams, Las Vegas, Nev.; Paul R. Ash, Phoenix, Ariz.; Patricia Barber, Amherst, Mass.; Paul John Barguinero, Phoenix, Ariz.; Alice Barter, Arlington Heights, Ill.; Dr. E. M. Beekman, English Dept., University of Massachusetts, Amherst, Mass.; J. L. Benson, Dept. of Art, University of Massachusetts; Erich R. Brandt, Phoenix, Ariz.; John S. Brown, Phoenix, Ariz.; Jane H. Callura, Bowie, Md.; Roland Commons, Sherman, Texas; Marion W. Copeland, Amherst, Mass.; Prof. Louise S. Cowan, Irving, Texas; Lois W. Davis, Brooklyn, New York; Robert M. Dunbar, Detroit, Mich.; Jack Ewing, Oakdale, Pa.; William H. Feierabend, West Caldwell, N.J.; Harold L. Fletemeyer, Omaha, Neb.; Patricia M. Gertrup, Bancroft, Neb.; George H. Glover, Jr., Birmingham, Mich.; Marilyn Gras, Champaign, Ill.; Bobby L. Gregory, Garland, Texas; Harold Grubin, Bloomfield, Conn.; Jack Hamilton, Edgewater, Fla.; Walter L. Harrison, Ann Arbor, Mich.; Edward L. Hoffman, Gambier, Ohio; K. Don Jacobusse, Birmingham, Mich.; Mrs. H. Phillips Jesup, Bristol, Conn.; Sharon S. Johnson, Barrington, Ill.; Irwin T. Holtzman, Birmingham, Mich.; Dr. R. Allan Killen, Ballwin, Mo.; Edward LaChapelle, Kirkland, Wash.; Dr. James F. Mason, Ormond Beach, Fla.; John Mazurek, Palatine, Ill.; Hugh A. Martin, Delaware, Ohio; William E. McCulloh, Gambier, Ohio; John McKinsey, Cary, Ill.; George L. Meshke, Bellevue, Wash.; Lucy Miller, Littleton, Colo.; Walter E. Mitchell, Jr., Delaware, Ohio; B. E. Moodey, Jr., Phoenix, Ariz.; J. C. Morison, Hubbard, Ohio; Mrs. Charles T. Neilson, Mesquite, Texas; Michael Newman, Las Vegas, Nev.; Richard H. Oatberg, Englewood, Colo.; Charlotte B. Pfaff, Irving, Tex.; Robert L. Polley, Brookfield, Wis.; Norman M. Robinson, Palatka, Fla.; J. V. Rodricks, Bladensburg, Md.; Howard Rogers, The Dalles, Oreg.; Clarence R. Salmeier, Gresham, Ore.; Donald E. Schwalke, Florissant, Mo.; Oscar Shefler, Gibsonia, Pa.; Sidney Speiglman, Omaha, Nebr.; Stanley R. Stefancic, Birmingham, Mich.; Floyd E. Sykes, Aurora, Colo.; Alan Swenson, Bloomfield, N.J.; Evelyn Tullos, Crescent City, Fla.; Harry H. Weil, Cheswick, Pa.; Travis L. Williams, Crandall, Tex.; Mrs. Robert P. T. Young, Ponte Vedra, Fla.

SUBSCRIBERS TO *THE SATURDAY REVIEW*

BALLOT GROUP NO. 12

K. J. Balthaser, Fort Wayne, Ind.; Donald A. Bass, Houston, Texas; James H. Bamir, Anderson, Calif.; Mrs. Peter D. Branton, Westfield, New Jersey; Maxine S. Brinson, Phoenix, Ariz.; Helen M. Brown, New York, N.Y.; Mrs. K. J. Burnett, Hubbard, Ohio; Robert H. Busch, Garden City, N.Y.; Catherine A. Butler, Seattle, Wash.; Mrs. Emil C. Carpenter, Rockport, Wash.; Jimi Carter, Bloomington, Ind.; Martin S. Cole, New York, N.Y.; Joseph T. Conaway, Bridgeville, Del.; D. N. Consigny, Park Ridge, Ill.; Kenneth F. Cooney, Redding, Calif.; Mrs. C. H. Daniels, Redding, Calif.; Mrs. Daniel L. Davidson; Joseph R. Del Papa, New Orleans, La; John Eskilson, Kearny, N.J.: Mrs. Keener W. Eutsler, Shepherdstown, W. Va.; S. M. Fast, New Haven, Conn.; Edith P. Ferguson, Athens, Ohio; G. R. Fleischman, McCormick Hall, Cambridge, Mass.; Loraine Wayne Freeman, Cheyenne, Wyo.; Carol Frese, Harrisburg, Pa.; Kay Gerlach, Ridgewood, N.J.: S. Giffa, Redding, Calif.; Donald L. Guimary, Redding, Calif.; Ruth Guyton, Springfield, Ohio; W. M. Hagist, Saunderstown, R.I.; Pamela Hall, Winchester, Mass.; June Hanson, Escanaba, Mich.; Hilary Helmrich, Pattenburg, N.J.; Mr. and Mrs. Roger Hill, San Francisco, Calif.; Gay J. Howell, Minneapolis, Minn.; Clark F. Hull, Redding, Calif.; W. Mason James, Seattle, Wash.; Arthur Kapteyn, Redding, Calif.; Wm. Katzenberg, Long Beach, N.Y.; Mrs. Malcolm F. Kent, Round Hill, Va.; Barbara Lampen, Holland, Mich.; Hylan Lewis, New York, N.Y.; Elsie M. Lindblam, Portland, Maine; Aaron Lockley, Jacksonville, Fla.; Ruth Long, New York, N.Y.; Kathryn A. Lowe, Tempe, Ariz.; Sam Marra, Wickliffe, Ohio; Max Marshall, Omaha, Nebr.; John T. Mathison, Evanston, Ill.; Philip R. McElroy, New Brunswick, N.J. Anna L. McNeel, Anderson, Calif.; Ila Meadows, Chinle, Ariz.; Glenn M. Miller, Buffalo, Miss.; Edward Moritz, Jr., Los Angeles, Calif.; Mr. and Mrs. Alfred W. Morse, Kennett Square, Pa.; Carol Dumrich, San Gabriel, Calif.; William W. Oliver, Redding, Calif.; Louis Parley, Washington, D.C.; Frederic W. Payne, Hyannis, Mass.; Anello V. Pepe, Bridgeport, Conn.; J. K. Pickering, J.D., Redding, Calif.; Peter Pinchera, Eau Gallie, Fla.; Lee Root, St. Charles Minn.; Rosemary Ruiz, Los Angeles, Calif.; Mrs. Robert Schlicher, Rickford, Ill.; Laurence Segall, Nanuet, N.Y.; Nancy Sheaff, Red Bluff, Calif.; Mrs. William E. Shepherd, Columbus, N.C.; Diann M. Sherwin, Arlington, Va.; Edward Steiner, Whittier, Calif.; Luther E. Timmons, Jr.; Chattanooga, Tenn.; Belle L. Trash, Redding, Calif.; Marie A. Turner, New Haven, Conn.; Mrs. Norbert J. Walser, Glassboro, N.J.; Donald B. Webster, Red Bluff, Calif.; Mrs. Milton Weinberg, Orange, Calif.; Robert S. Williams, Hempstead, N.Y.; Pamela Witthoft, New York, N.Y.; Philip Wong, San Francisco, Calif.; Bill M. Woods, East Northport, N.Y.; E. Ann Wooten, Newark, Del.; Mrs. Daniel A. Yates, Schenectady, N.Y.; Barry Zalma, Los Angeles, Calif.; Louis J. Zapata, New York, N.Y.

MISCELLANEOUS VOTERS

BALLOT GROUP NO. 13

Ellis Amburn, senior editor, Coward-McCann, Inc., New York; Lydia J. Billings, New Canaan, Conn.; Richard J. Hurley, Fairfax, Va.; Miss Paulin Layton, Atlanta, Ga.; Dean McLaughlin, Ann Arbor, Mich.; John A. Morgan, New Canaan, Conn.; Mrs. Elsa Vaught, Fayetteville, Ark.

Index by Authors